10/2012

BOWEN ISLAND LIBRARY

3 0947 0004 3348 8

D0977388

THE ROUGH GUIDE TO

Malaysia, Singapore and Brunei

written and researched by

David Leffman and Richard Lim

with additional contributions by

John Oates

BOWEN ISLAND PUBLIC LIBRARY

ROUGH
GUIDES

roughguides.com

Contents

Introduction to
Malaysia, Singapore and Brunei

Populated by a blend of Malays, Chinese, Indians and indigenous groups, Malaysia, Singapore and Brunei boast a rich cultural heritage, from a huge variety of annual festivals and wonderful cuisines, to traditional architecture and rural crafts. There's astonishing natural beauty to take in too, including gorgeous beaches and some of the world's oldest tropical rainforest, much of which is surprisingly accessible. Malaysia's national parks are superb for trekking and wildlife-watching, and sometimes for cave exploration and river rafting.

As part of the Malay archipelago, which stretches from Indonesia to the Philippines, Malaysia, Singapore and Brunei share not only similarities in their ethnic make-up but also part of their **history**. Each became an important port of call on the trade route between India and China, the two great markets of the early world, and later became important entrepôts for the Portuguese, Dutch and British empires. Malaysia has only existed in its present form since 1963, when the federation of the eleven Peninsula states was joined by Singapore and the two Bornean territories of Sarawak and Sabah. Singapore left the union to become an independent country in 1965; Brunei, preferring to remain outside the federation in Borneo, only lost its British colonial status in 1984.

Since then, Malaysia, Singapore and Brunei have been united in their **economic predominance** among Southeast Asian nations. While Brunei is locked into a paternalistic regime, using its considerable oil wealth to guarantee its citizens a respectable standard of living, the city-state of Singapore has become a giant in commerce, having transformed itself from a strategic port. Malaysia, always competitive with its southern neighbour, is pursuing a similarly ambitious goal, to

ABOVE FROM LEFT PETRONAS TOWERS; PULAU PERHENTIAN; MOUNT KINABALU **OPPOSITE** THAI TEMPLE IN PENANG which end the country is investing heavily in new infrastructure, from highways to ports and factories.

Today, the dominant cultural force in the region is undoubtedly **Islam**, adopted by the Malays in the fourteenth century, though in Chinese-dominated Singapore, **Buddhism** and **Taoism** together hold sway among half the population. But it's the religious plurality – there are also sizeable Christian and Hindu minorities – that is so attractive, often providing surprising juxtapositions of mosques, temples and churches. Add the colour and verve of Chinese temples and street fairs, Indian festival days and everyday life in Malay kampungs (villages), and the indigenous traditions of Borneo, and it's easy to see why visitors are drawn into this celebration of ethnic diversity; indeed, despite some issues, both Malaysia and Singapore have something to teach the rest of the world when it comes to building successful multicultural societies.

Where to go

Malaysia's capital, **Kuala Lumpur** (usually referred to as KL), is the social and economic driving force of a nation eager to better itself, a fact reflected in the relentless proliferation of air-conditioned shopping malls, designer bars and restaurants in the city, and in the continuing sprawl of suburbia and industry around it. But KL is also firmly rooted in tradition, where the same Malay executives who

FACT FILE

With 28 million inhabitants, Malaysia is divided into two distinct regions. **Peninsular Malaysia**, where the capital, Kuala Lumpur, is situated, is separated by more than 600km of the South China Sea from East Malaysia, comprising the states of **Sabah** and **Sarawak** on the island of Borneo.

• At just 700 square kilometres in size, **Singapore** is a crowded nation of nearly 5 million people. Alongside hard drugs, the import, sale or possession of **chewing gum** is banned.

• Made up of two enclaves in eastern Sarawak, **Brunei** is nearly ten times the size of Singapore, but holds less than one tenth of the population.

• Both Malaysia and Singapore are British-style **parliamentary democracies**, the former with a ceremonial head of state known as the Yang di-Pertuan Agung (the post rotates among the sultans from each state of the federation). Brunei is ruled by its **sultan**.

• The world's largest flower, **Rafflesia**, is a Malaysian rainforest plant measuring a metre across and smelling of rotten meat. It's named after the naturalist and founder of Singapore, Sir Stamford Raffles.

• Malaysia's **economy**, historically dominated by agriculture and mining, now features a healthy manufacturing sector, as does Singapore, where shipping and financial services are also key industries. Brunei profits handsomely from its reserves of oil and gas.

wear suits to work dress in traditional clothes at festival times, and markets and food stalls are crowded in among high-rise hotels and bank towers, especially in older areas such as Chinatown and Little India.

Just a couple of hours' drive south of the capital lies the birthplace of Malay civilization, **Melaka**, its historical architecture and mellow atmosphere making it a must on anybody's itinerary. Much further up the **west coast**, the island of **Penang** was the site of the first British settlement in Malaysia. Its capital, **Georgetown**, still features beautifully restored colonial buildings and a vibrant Chinatown district, and is, together with Melaka, recognized for its cultural and architectural diversity as a UNESCO World Heritage Site. For a taste of Old England, head for the hill stations of **Fraser's Hill** and the **Cameron Highlands**, where cooler temperatures and lush countryside provide ample opportunities for walks, birdwatching, rounds of golf and cream teas. North of Penang, Malay, rather than Chinese, traditions hold sway at **Alor Star**, the last major town before the Thai border. This far north, the premier tourist destination is **Pulau Langkawi**, an island with international-style resorts and picture-postcard beaches.

The Peninsula's **east coast** is much more rural and relaxing, peppered with rustic villages and stunning islands such as **Pulau Perhentian** and **Pulau Tioman**, busy with backpackers and package tourists alike. The state capitals of **Kota Bharu**, near the northeastern Thai border, and **Kuala Terengganu**, further south, showcase the best of Malay traditions, craft production and performing arts.

Crossing the Peninsula's mountainous **interior** by road or rail allows you to venture into the majestic tropical rainforests of **Taman Negara**. The national park's four thousand square kilometres hold enough to keep you occupied for days: trails, salt-lick hides for animal-watching, aerial forest-canopy walkways, limestone caves and waterfalls. Here you may well also come across the **Orang Asli**,

SHOPHOUSES

A standard feature of local townscapes is rows of **shophouses** – two- or three-storey buildings traditionally containing a shop at street level, with residential quarters behind and above. For visitors, their most striking feature is that at ground level the front wall is usually set back from the street. This creates a so-called "**five-foot way**" overhung by the upper part of the house, which shelters pedestrians from the sun and pelting rain.

Shophouses were fusion architecture: facades have **Western** features such as shuttered windows and gables, while inside there might be an area open to the sky, in the manner of **Chinese** courtyard houses. Some, especially from the early part of the last century, are bedecked with columns, floral plaster motifs and beautiful tilework, while later properties feature simpler Art Deco touches. Sadly, shophouses ceased to be built after the 1960s and many have been demolished to make way for modern complexes, though some have won a new lease of life as swanky restaurants and boutiques.

the Peninsula's indigenous peoples, a few of whom cling to a semi-nomadic lifestyle within the park.

Across the sea from the Peninsula lie the east Malaysian states of Sarawak and Sabah. For most travellers, their first taste of **Sarawak** comes at **Kuching**, the old colonial capital, and then the Iban **longhouses** of the Batang Ai river system. **Sibu**, much further north on the Rajang River, is the starting point for trips to less touristed Iban, Kayan and Kenyah longhouses. In the north, **Gunung Mulu National Park** is the principal destination; many come here to climb up to view its extraordinary razor-sharp limestone Pinnacles, though spectacular caves also burrow into the park's mountains. More remote still are the **Kelabit Highlands**, further east, where the mountain air is refreshingly cool and there are ample opportunities for extended treks.

The main reason for a trip to **Sabah** is to conquer the 4095m granite peak of **Mount Kinabalu**, set in its own national park, though the lively modern capital **Kota Kinabalu** and its idyllic offshore islands, Gaya and Manukan, have their appeal, too. Beyond this, Sabah is worth a visit for its **wildlife**: turtles, orang-utans, proboscis monkeys and hornbills are just a few of the exotic residents of the jungle and plentiful islands. Marine attractions feature in the far east at **Pulau Sipadan**, pointing out towards the southern Philippines, which has a host of sharks, other fish and turtles, while neighbouring **Pulau Mabul** contains hip, but often pricey, diving resorts.

An easy entry-point for first-time visitors to Southeast Asia, **Singapore** is exceptionally safe, organized and accessible, thanks to its small size, excellent modern infrastructure, and Western standards of hygiene – and despite prices that are likewise at Western levels. The island has fascinating Chinese and Indian quarters, excellent historical museums and a smattering of colonial architecture as well as great shopping, all of which will keep you occupied for several days. Singapore also rightly holds a reputation as one of Asia's **gastronomic capitals**, where you can just as readily savour fantastic snacks at simple hawker stalls or an exquisite Chinese banquet in a swanky restaurant.

For those who venture into the tiny kingdom of **Brunei**, enveloped by Sarawak's two most northerly divisions, the capital **Bandar Seri Begawan** holds the entrancing

OPEN-AIR FOOD STALL

Author picks

Our authors traversed every corner of Malaysia, Singapore and Brunei, from KL's shopping malls and Sarawak's longhouses to the jungles of Taman Negara and the summit of Mount Kinabalu. Here are some of their favourite experiences.

Wildlife-spotting See elephants and tapir at Taman Negara (p.191); orang-utan at Kinabatangan (p.439); and proboscis monkeys near Bandar Seri Begawan (p.464).

Tastiest laksa Compare famous variations of the region's signature seafood soup in Penang (p.159), Singapore (p.552) and Kuching (p.331).

Shadow puppets Experience the magical Malay tradition of *wayang kulit* at Kota Bharu's Cultural Centre (p.225).

Eccentric desserts Satisfy your sweet tooth with ABC – a shaved ice drenched in condensed milk and luridly coloured fruit syrups (p.42).

Turtle beaches Stay up late to catch marine turtles digging nests and laying eggs at Cherating (p.256) and Penang National Park (p.167).

Glittering cityscapes Admire the night lights from atop Menara KL (p.80) and *Marina Bay Sands'* Sky Park in Singapore (p.512).

Rowdiest festival You can't beat the crowds and slightly gory celebrations surrounding the Hindu festival of Thaipusam at KL's Batu Caves (p.110).

Our author recommendations don't end here. We've flagged up our favourite places – a perfectly sited hotel, an atmospheric café, a special restaurant – throughout the Guide, highlighted with the ★ symbol.

Kampung Ayer, a sprawling stilt village built out over the Brunei River, plus a handful of interesting museums and mosques. In the sparsely populated Temburong district, you can visit unspoiled rainforest at the **Ulu Temburong National Park**, where abundant wildlife roams and the rivers are clear.

When to go

Temperatures vary little in Malaysia, Singapore and Brunei, hovering constantly at or just above 30°C by day, while humidity is high year-round (for a climate chart, see p.53). Showers occur year-round too, often in the mid-afternoon, though these short, sheeting downpours clear up as quickly as they arrive. The major distinction in the seasons is marked by the arrival of the northeast monsoon (ushering in what is locally called the **rainy season**). This particularly affects the east coast of Peninsular Malaysia and the

WILDLIFE

Peninsular Malaysia, Borneo and Singapore are a paradise for wildlife-spotters, harbouring over 600 types of birds and 200 mammal species – including Asian elephants, sun bears, tigers, tapirs, barking deer, gibbons, hornbills and pythons. Borneo's speciality is the **proboscis monkey**, so-called because of its bulbous, drooping nose. The island is also one of only two natural habitats (with Sumatra) for **orang-utans** – indeed, the name is Malay for "man of the forest". **Marine life** is equally diverse: divers can swim with white-tip sharks, clown fish and barracuda, not to mention green and hawksbill **turtles**, which drag themselves ashore in season to lay their eggs by night. Even cosmopolitan Singapore maintains a pocket of primary rainforest that's home to long-tailed macaques and snakes.

western end of Sarawak, with late November to mid-February seeing the heaviest rainfall. On the Peninsula's west coast and in Sabah, September and October are the wettest months. Monsoonal downpours can be heavy and prolonged, sometimes lasting two or three hours and prohibiting more or less all activity for the duration; boats to most islands in affected areas won't attempt the sea swell at the height of the rainy season. In mountainous areas like the Cameron Highlands, the Kelabit Highlands and in the hill stations and upland national parks, you may experience more frequent rain as the high peaks gather clouds more or less permanently.

The **ideal time** to visit most of the region is between March and early October, when you will avoid the worst of the rains and there's less humidity, though both ends of this period can be characterized by a stifling lack of breezes. Despite the rains, the months of January and February are rewarding, and see a number of significant **festivals**, notably Chinese New Year and the Hindu celebration of Thaipusam. Visiting just after the rainy season can afford the best of all worlds, with verdant countryside and bountiful waterfalls, though there's still a clammy quality to the air. Arrive in Sabah a little later, in May, and you'll be able to take in the Sabah Fest, a week-long celebration of Sabahan culture, while in Sarawak, June's Gawai Festival is well worth attending, when longhouse doors are flung open for several days of rice-harvest merry-making, with dancing, eating, drinking and music.

OPPOSITE ASIAN ELEPHANTS **ABOVE** KELABIT HIGHLANDS

23

things not to miss

It's not possible to see everything that Malaysia, Singapore and Brunei have to offer in one trip – and we don't suggest you try. What follows is a selective taste, in no particular order, of the countries' highlights: natural wonders, stunning buildings and a colourful heritage. Each entry has a page reference to take you straight into the Guide, where you can find out more.

1

1 LANGKAWI
Page 176

Luxurious resorts on sublime beaches pretty much sums up these west-coast islands, close to the border with Thailand.

2 GEORGETOWN
Page 149

A bustling Chinese-dominated haven with elaborate temples, colonial-era mansions and beaches galore.

3 MOUNT KINABALU
Page 422

Watch dawn over Borneo from the summit of Southeast Asia's highest mountain.

7

4 TAMAN NEGARA
Page 191

Malaysia's premier national park, Taman Negara, is one of the world's oldest rainforests, with hides for wildlife-spotting, treetop walkways and treks lasting from an hour to a whole week.

5 KAMPUNG AYER
Page 461

Take a boat ride around this wooden village in the middle of the Brunei River.

6 ADVENTURE TOURISM
Page 48

Whitewater rafting, caving and paragliding are among activities widely available in Malaysia.

7 SINGAPORE'S ARTS SCENE
Page 555

As befits the largest city in the region, Singapore offers a dynamic range of artistic activity – catch anything from Chinese street opera to indie rock gigs.

8 KELABIT HIGHLANDS
Page 381

These remote uplands offer excellent walks and hikes, plus encounters with friendly tribal communities along the way.

8

10

13 CAMERON HIGHLANDS
Page 121

Misty tea plantations, afternoon tea and jungle trails in cool mountain air.

14 SUNGAI KINABATANGAN
Page 439

Cruise through pristine jungle along this spectacular river, spotting proboscis monkeys and, occasionally, orang-utans.

15 SHOPPING IN KL
Page 104

Malaysia's capital boasts a host of excellent malls, as well as vibrant street markets where bargaining is de rigueur.

16 THE PETRONAS TOWERS
Page 77

KL's iconic towers not only hold your gaze from all angles but also house one of the city's best shopping malls.

17 LITTLE INDIA, SINGAPORE
Page 495

On Serangoon Road you can almost believe you're in downtown Chennai – the area has all the sights, sounds and smells of the Indian subcontinent.

18 TRADITIONAL CRAFTS
Page 51

Malaysia boasts a wide range of crafts, from batik and *songket* (brocade) to rattan baskets and *labu*, gourd-shaped ceramic jugs.

13

14

19

20

21

22

19 LONGHOUSES IN SARAWAK
Page 346
Large communal dwellings, home to members of indigenous tribes, are found along rivers and in remote mountain locations.

20 RAINFOREST MUSIC FESTIVAL
Page 338
Held annually near Kuching, this world-music festival is an opportunity to see indigenous performers alongside musicians from across the globe.

21 PROBOSCIS MONKEYS, BAKO
Page 340
These odd-looking creatures roam *kerangas* forest and mangrove swamps in the national park, not far from Kuching.

22 ULU TEMBURONG PARK
Page 471
A beautiful approach by longboat brings you to Brunei's only national park; treks and a canopy walkway will keep you busy during your stay.

23 DIVING AT PULAU SIPADAN
Page 446
The spectacular islands off Sabah offer the thrill of swimming with sharks and turtles.

Itineraries

Malaysia, Singapore and Brunei cover such a spread-out area that it would be impossible to see everything, but each of the following routes makes a great way to spend two or three weeks in the region. While the Peninsula Circuit is the most varied, head east to Borneo if you prefer an outdoor-focused option. Singapore is obviously more of a long-weekend destination, but a stay here could easily be tacked on to a wider trip north up into Peninsular Malaysia.

PENINSULA CIRCUIT

For a straightforward taster of everything the region has to offer, try this three-week circuit.

❶ Kuala Lumpur Malaysia's capital offers shiny malls, showcase architecture and a mix of Muslim, Chinese and Hindu districts, with some of the best street food in the country. **See p.62**

PENINSULA CIRCUIT
SINGAPORE AND MELAKA

THAILAND

PENINSULAR MALAYSIA

INDONESIA

SINGAPORE

❷ Cameron Highlands This former retreat for colonial administrators is now a rural idyll of tea plantations and forest walks. **See p.121**

❸ Pulau Pangkor Kick back at this low-key resort island that's a favourite with Malaysian families. **See p.134**

❹ Penang Packed with historic guildhalls and streets, eccentric temples and surprisingly wild gardens and national parks. **See p.145**

❺ Kota Bharu One of the last places in this Muslim country that allows shadow-puppet performances of the Hindu epics. **See p.221**

❻ Perhentian islands Superb tropical hangouts with gorgeous beaches and splendid snorkelling and scuba diving. **See p.233**

❼ Jungle railway This slow-moving commuter train chugs past languid towns, tiny kampungs and market gardens along the way. **See p.206**

❽ Taman Negara One of the world's oldest rainforests features superlative wildlife-spotting and jungle treks lasting up to a week or more. **See p.191**

SINGAPORE AND MELAKA

You can pack this round-up of great food and a centuries-old history into a week.

❶ Little India, Singapore Charismatic area of temples and shops selling gold and sarees with the liveliest market in Singapore. **See p.495**

❷ Chinatown, Singapore Amid the modern shophouses, restaurants and markets, don't miss the Buddha Tooth Relic temple, full of dynamic statuary and the tooth itself. **See p.501**

❸ Night Safari, Singapore The highlight of what is already a superbly displayed collection of native wildlife, the night safari lets you see nocturnal creatures such as tigers, leopards, elephants and rhinos. **See p.519**

❹ Bukit Timah, Singapore The last patch of real rainforest left in Singapore offers an easy, leech-free introduction to jungle trails and colourful birdlife. **See p.518**

❺ Eating, Singapore Indulge in one of the world's gastronomic capitals, with varied menus of Indian, Chinese and Malay dishes. **See p.541**

❻ Istana, Melaka An exquisite Malay palace, built without nails and founded during the fifteenth century. **See p.277**

❼ Baba-Nonya Heritage Museum, Melaka An elegant row of traditional houses decorated in tiling, lanterns and woodcarvings of the Chinese-Malay Peranakan culture, now – aside from its cuisine – virtually extinct. **See p.279**

❽ Bukit China, Melaka Hilltop covered in many crescent-shaped Chinese graves, some dating to the seventeenth century. **See p.281**

SARAWAK AND MT KINABALU

Allow at least three weeks for this adventurous trip into Malaysia's least-developed corners.

❶ Kuching Find your bearings at Sarawak's small, likeable capital: the museum's ethnological collection is worth a browse, and the Semenggoh orang-utan sanctuary makes a rewarding day-trip. **See p.321**

❷ Bako Sarawak's oldest national park, this small patch of well-preserved coastal forest is home to waterfalls, proboscis monkeys and bizarre pitcher plants. **See p.339**

❸ Batang Ai Take a boat through spectacular riverine forest in this often overlooked national park, and visit traditional longhouse communities such as Nanga Sumpa. **See p.344**

❹ Gunung Mulu National Park Spectacular jungle scenery, particularly the three-day trek out to a "forest" of limestone towers, and a network of rugged caverns. **See p.374**

❺ Miri A stepping stone to the remoter corners of Sarawak – not to mention Sabah. Don't miss the caves at Niah National Park, inhabited by humans over 40,000 years ago. **See p.363**

❻ Bario Set out on some demanding multi-day trekking via remote Kelabit longhouses or up Mount Murud. **See p.383**

❼ Kota Kinabalu Sabah's capital has lively markets, a district of traditional houses built over the water on piles, and an interesting indigenous museum. **See p.396**

❽ Kinabulu National Park This small reserve surrounds wind-seared Mount Kinabulu, one of the toughest hikes in Malaysia. **See p.422**

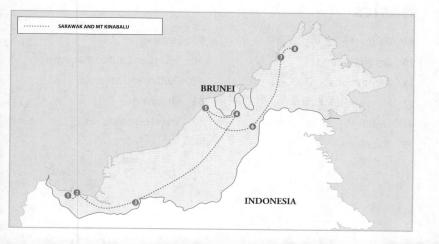

SARAWAK AND MT KINABALU

BRUNEI

INDONESIA

WAYANG KULIT (SHADOW PUPPETRY)

Basics

Getting there

Located at the heart of Southeast Asia, on the busy aviation corridor between Europe and Australasia, Malaysia and Singapore enjoy excellent international air links. Singapore is served by many more flights than Kuala Lumpur (KL), but can also be slightly more expensive to fly into. Of Malaysia's regional airports, those in Kota Kinabalu, Kuching and Penang have the most useful international connections, albeit chiefly with other cities in East Asia. If you're flying long-haul to east Malaysia or, for that matter, Brunei, you may well have to transit in Kuala Lumpur or Singapore.

During the **peak seasons** for travel to Southeast Asia – the Christmas New Year period, typically from mid-December until early January, and July and August – fares can be up to twice the price at other times of year, though you can often avoid the steepest fares by booking well in advance. Fares also rise at weekends and around major local festivals, such as Islamic holidays and the Chinese New Year. Sample fares given here include taxes and current fuel surcharges.

From the UK and Ireland

London Heathrow has daily **nonstop** flights to KL (with Malaysia Airlines) and to Singapore (British Airways, Qantas and Singapore Airlines); both take around thirteen hours. Flying with any other airline involves a change of plane in Europe or the Middle East, and possibly an additional stopover elsewhere. If you're flying from UK regional airports or from **Ireland**, you'll have to change planes at London or a hub elsewhere in Europe. The very best **fares** to KL or Singapore are around £500/€450 outside high season – though it's not uncommon to pay twenty percent more.

From the US and Canada

In most cases the trip from North America, including a stopover, will take at least twenty hours if you fly the **transatlantic** route from the eastern seaboard, or nineteen hours minimum if you cross the Pacific from the west coast. If you're in a rush, you could take advantage of Singapore Airlines' **nonstop flights** from Los Angeles (17hr) and New York Newark (18hr) to Singapore – the longest scheduled passenger services in the world.

The quickest route isn't always the cheapest: it can sometimes be cheaper to fly westwards from the east coast, stopping off in Northeast Asia en route. **Fares** start at around US$1100 or Can$1200 for flights from a major US or Canadian airport on either coast.

Plenty of airlines operate to East Asia from major North American cities. If your target is Borneo, it's worth investigating the possibility of connecting with one of the east Asian airlines – Kota Kinabalu, for example, has flights from Hong Kong operated by Malaysia Airlines and at least one other carrier.

From Australia and New Zealand

There's a particularly good range of flights from Australia and New Zealand into Malaysia, Singapore and Brunei, including a useful link between Melbourne and **Borneo** with Royal Brunei Airlines, plus **budget flights** from Australia and New Zealand to KL with AirAsia X and to Singapore with Tiger Airways and Jetstar.

If you're flying from, say, Perth to Singapore or KL, **fares** start at Aus$550 return in low season, while Melbourne to KL will set you back at least Aus$750. Christchurch to KL generally starts at NZ$1300 return on AirAsia X.

From South Africa

The quickest way to reach Malaysia or Singapore from South Africa is to fly with **Singapore Airlines**, which offers nonstop flights to Singapore from

---

A BETTER KIND OF TRAVEL

At Rough Guides we are passionately committed to travel. We feel that travelling is the best way to understand the world we live in and the people we share it with – plus tourism has brought a great deal of benefit to developing economies around the world over the last few decades. But the growth in tourism has also damaged some places irreparably, and climate change is exacerbated by most forms of transport, especially flying. All Rough Guides' trips are carbon-offset, and every year we donate money to a variety of charities devoted to combating the effects of climate change.

Johannesburg, with connections from Cape Town; reckon on around ten hours' flying time. That said, it's often cheaper to book a ticket that involves changing planes en route, usually in the Middle East. If you're lucky you may land a fare of around ZAR6000 return, including taxes, though it's not uncommon to have to pay ZAR1000–2000 more.

From elsewhere in Southeast Asia

Budget airlines make it easy to explore Malaysia, Singapore and Brunei as part of a wider trip through Southeast Asia. The most useful no-frills carriers for the three countries covered in this book are Malaysia's **AirAsia** (Ⓦwww.airasia.com) and **Firefly** (Ⓦwww .fireflyz.com.my), and Singapore's **Jetstar Asia** (Ⓦwww.jetstar.com) and **Tiger Airways** (Ⓦwww .tigerairways.com). Though fuel surcharges and taxes do take some of the shine off the fares, prices can still be keen, especially if you book well in advance.

You can, of course, reach Malaysia or Singapore from their immediate neighbours by means other than flying. There are **road** connections from Thailand and from Kalimantan (Indonesian Borneo), **ferries** from the Indonesian island of Sumatra and from the southern Philippines, and **trains** from Thailand. Below is a round-up of the most popular routes.

From Thailand

There are two daily express **rail** services between Thailand and Malaysia – one between the southern Thai city of **Hat Yai** and **KL**, run by the Malaysian rail company KTM (Ⓦwww.ktmb.com.my), and the other between **Bangkok** and the Malaysian west-coast city of **Butterworth** (close to Penang island), run by State Railway of Thailand (Ⓦwww.railway.co.th). The

KTM service leaves Hat Yai at 4pm, taking twelve hours to reach KL; the Bangkok train leaves Hualamphong Station at 2.45pm, calling en route at (among others) Hua Hin, Surat Thani, Hat Yai and Alor Star in Kedah, and arriving in Butterworth 24 hours later. Also useful is the Thai rail service from Hat Yai across to **Sungai Golok** on the east coast of the Kra isthmus, close to the Malaysian border crossing at Rantau Panjang, from where buses run to Kota Bharu. Hat Yai–KL **fares** start at RM46 in an ordinary seat, rising to RM58 in a lower-berth sleeper.

As regards **flights**, plenty of services connect Bangkok, Chiang Mai and Thai resort destinations with Malaysian airports and Singapore. Some are run by the low-cost airlines, while others are provided by Bangkok Airways (Ⓦwww.bangkokair .com) and Singapore Airlines subsidiary SilkAir (Ⓦwww.silkair.com).

A few scheduled **ferry** services sail from the most southwesterly Thai town of Satun to the Malaysian west-coast town of Kuala Perlis (30min) and to Pulau Langkawi (1hr 30min). Departing from Thailand by sea for Malaysia, ensure your passport is stamped at the immigration office at the pier to avoid problems with the Malaysian immigration officials when you arrive. Another option is the ferry from the southern Thai town of Ban Taba to the Malaysian town of Pengkalan Kubor, where frequent buses run to Kota Bharu, 20km away. Buses connect Ban Taba with the provincial capital, Narathiwat (1hr 30min).

The easiest road access from Thailand is via Hat Yai, from where **buses** and shared taxis run regularly to Butterworth (4hr) and nearby Georgetown on Penang island. From the interior Thai town of Betong, there's a road across the border to the Malaysian town of **Keroh**, from where Route 67 leads west to meet Route 1 at Sungai Petani; shared

---

THE EASTERN & ORIENTAL EXPRESS

Unlike some luxury trains in other parts of the world, the **Eastern & Oriental Express** isn't a recreation of a classic colonial-era rail journey, but a sort of fantasy realization of how such a service might have looked had it existed in the Far East. Employing 1970s Japanese rolling stock, given an elegant old-world cladding with wooden inlay work and featuring Thai and Malay motifs, the train departs from Bangkok on certain Sundays bound for Singapore, returning on Thursdays, with one to three departures a month. En route there are extended stops at Kanchanaburi for a visit to the infamous bridge over the **River Kwai**, and at Butterworth, where there's time for a half-day tour of **Georgetown**. An observation deck at the rear of the train makes the most of the passing scenery.

The trip takes four days and three nights (three days if done from Singapore) and costs around £1400/US$2250 per person in swish, en-suite Pullman accommodation, including meals of Eurasian fusion food, though alcohol costs extra. On the southbound leg it can be worth leaving the train in KL, saving 15 percent on the full fare. For **bookings** contacts in various countries and more details of the trip, see Ⓦwww.orient-express.com.

taxis serve the route. You can also get a taxi from Ban Taba for the few kilometres south to Kota Bharu.

From Indonesia

Plenty of flights, including many operated by the low-cost airlines, connect major airports in Java and Sumatra, plus Bali and Lombok, with Malaysia and Singapore There's also a service between Manado in Sulawesi and Singapore with Singapore Airlines subsidiary SilkAir. As for Kalimantan, AirAsia operates between Balikpapan and KL, and by the time you read this Malaysia Airlines' subsidiary MASwings (ⓦmaswings.com.my) should be operating between Pontianak and Kuching, and also between Tarakan and Tawau in southeastern Sabah."

It's possible to reach Sarawak from Kalimantan on just one road route, through the western border town of Entikong and onwards to Kuching. The bus trip from the western city of Pontianak to Entikong takes seven hours, crossing to the Sarawak border town of Tebedu; stay on the same bus for another three hours to reach Kuching.

As for **ferries**, a service operates from Medan in northern Sumatra to Penang (4hr), while Dumai, further south, has a daily service to Melaka (2hr), with more sailings from Dumai and Tanjong Balai to Port Klang near KL (3hr). There are also a few services from Bintan and Batam islands in the Riau archipelago (accessible by plane or boat from Sumatra or Jakarta) to Johor Bahru (30min) or Singapore (30min); and a minor ferry crossing from Tanjung Balai to Kukup (45min), just southwest of Johor Bahru. Over in Borneo, daily ferries connect Nunakan in Kalimantan with Tawau in Sabah (1hr).

From the Philippines

Despite the proximity of Sabah to the southern Philippines, few transport links connect the two, though a ferry service operates between Zamboanga and Sandakan. As for **flights**, there are low-cost options from Clark to KL and Kota Kinabalu (both AirAsia), and from Cebu and Davao to Singapore (Tiger Airways) and Manila. Other connections are provided by full-cost airlines as well as some Philippine budget operators, including Manila to Bandar Seri Begawan (Royal Brunei Airlines).

TRAVEL AGENTS AND TOUR OPERATORS

Adventure Center US ☎ 1800 228 8747, ⓦ www.adventurecenter .com. A good range of packages, mainly focused on east Malaysia.

Adventure World Australia ☎ 1300 295 049, ⓦ www .adventureworld.com.au; New Zealand ☎ 0800 238368, ⓦ www .adventureworld.co.nz. Short Malaysia tours, covering cities and some wildlife areas.

Allways Dive Expedition Australia ☎ 1800 338 239, ⓦ www .allwaysdive.com.au. Dive holidays to the prime dive sites of Sabah.

Asia Classic Tours US ☎ 1800 717 7752, ⓦ www.asiaclassictours .com. Malaysia tours, lasting ten days or more, taking in various parts of the country and sometimes Singapore, too.

Asian Pacific Adventures US ☎ 1800 825 1680, ⓦ www .asianpacificadventures.com. A handful of Malaysia packages, dominated by Borneo.

Bestway Tours US & Canada ☎ 1800 663 0844, ⓦ www.bestway .com. A handful of cultural tours featuring Malaysia and Singapore.

Borneo Tour Specialists Australia ☎ 07 3221 5777, ⓦ www .borneo.com.au. Small-group, customizable tours of all of Borneo, covering wildlife, trekking and tribal culture.

Deep Discoveries US & Canada ☎ 1800 667 5362, ⓦ www .deepdiscoveries.com. Sabah dive packages with optional extensions to wildlife sites on land.

Dive Adventures Australia ☎ 1800 222234, ⓦ www .diveadventures.com.au. Sabah and Labuan dive packages.

Eastravel UK ☎ 01473 214305, ⓦ www.eastravel.co.uk. A small range of Malaysia and Singapore trips.

eMalaysiaTravel.com US ☎ 618 529 8033, ⓦ www .emalaysiatravel.com. Various Malaysia offerings – KL city breaks, diving off Sabah, Taman Negara trips and so forth.

Emerald Global UK ☎ 0207 312 1708, ⓦ www.etours-online.com. A good range of Malaysia packages based in cities or resorts; Singapore too.

Explore Worldwide UK ☎ 0845 508 3212, ⓦ www.explore .co.uk. Adventure trips to Malaysia, plus Singapore.

Explorient US ☎ 1800 785 1233, ⓦ www.explorient.com. Short tours, focused on major cities and with a cultural emphasis, which can be combined with one another.

Golden Days in Malaysia UK ☎ 0208 893 1781, ⓦ www .goldendays.co.uk. A good range of Malaysia itineraries emphasizing Borneo and the main cities of the Peninsula, with some Singapore and Brunei add-ons.

Intrepid Travel US ☎ 1800 970 7299; Canada ☎ 1866 360 1151; UK ☎ 0203 147 7777; Australia ☎ 1300 364 512; New Zealand ☎ 0800 600 610, ⓦ www.intrepidtravel.com. Several Malaysia offerings, mainly focused on Borneo or taking in Thailand and Singapore as well.

Jade Tours US ☎ 212 349 1350; Canada ☎ 905 787 2588, ⓦ www.jadetours.com. Borneo and Peninsular Malaysia trips.

Kumuka US & Canada ☎ 1800 517 0867; UK ☎ 0800 068 8855; Ireland ☎ 1800 946843; Australia ☎ 1300 667277; New Zealand ☎ 0800 440499; South Africa ☎ 0800 991 503, ⓦ www.kumuka .com. East Malaysia tours geared to families.

Lee Travel Ireland ☎ 021 427 7111, ⓦ www.leetravel.ie. Flights worldwide.

Lee's Travel UK ☎ 0800 811 9888, ⓦ www.leestravel.com. Far Eastern flight deals, including discounted Malaysia and Singapore Airlines tickets.

LTI Tours US & Canada ☎ 1888 962 6111, ⓦ www.ltitours.com. A good range of Malaysia and Singapore packages.

Pandaw Cruises US ☎ 1800 798 4223, ⓦ www.pandaw.com. Multi-day trips along the Rejang River in Sarawak, in their own luxury boat.

Pentravel South Africa ☎ 0860 106264, ⓦ www.pentravel.co.za. Flights deals plus KL, Langkawi, Penang and Singapore-based holidays.

Peregrine Adventures UK ☎ 0845 004 0673; Australia ☎ 03 8601 4444, ⓦ www.peregrineadventures.com. Experienced operator with a handful of east Malaysia packages.

Premier Holidays UK ☎ 0844 493 7531, ⓦ www.premierholidays .co.uk. Tours of east Malaysia and Brunei, plus resort-centred holidays in Peninsular Malaysia and Singapore.

Ramblers Worldwide Holidays UK ☎ 01707 331133, ⓦ www .ramblersholidays.co.uk. Walking holidays in Malaysia.

Reef & Rainforest US ☎ 1800 794 9767, ⓦ www.reefrainforest .com. Sabah dive packages based in resorts or a liveaboard.

Rex Air UK ☎ 020 7439 1898, ⓦ www.rexair.co.uk. Specialist in discounted flights to the Far East, with a few package tours to boot.

Sayang Holidays US ☎ 415 986 1293, ⓦ www.sayangholidays .com. City-based Peninsular Malaysia and Singapore tours, plus Borneo.

STA Travel US ☎ 1800 781 4040, ⓦ www.statravel.com; UK ☎ 0871 230 0040, ⓦ www.statravel.co.uk; Australia ☎ 134 782, ⓦ www.statravel.com.au; New Zealand ☎ 0800 474 400, ⓦ www .statravel.co.nz; South Africa ☎ 0861 781 781, ⓦ www.statravel .co.za. Worldwide specialists in low-cost flights for students and under-26s; other customers also welcome.

Symbiosis US ☎ 1866 7237903; UK ☎ 0845 123 2844, ⓦ www .symbiosis-travel.com. Diving, trekking and longhouse stays in various Malaysian locations.

Tour East Canada ☎ 1 877 578 8888, ⓦ www.toureast.com. Packages combining Singapore with another Southeast Asian attraction, plus a couple of extended Malaysia excursions.

Trailfinders UK ☎ 020 7368 1200, ⓦ www.trailfinders.com; Ireland ☎ 01 677 7888, ⓦ www.trailfinders.ie. Efficient agent selling flights and a few Malaysia adventure tours.

Travel Masters US ☎ 512 323 6961, ⓦ www.travel-masters.net. Dive packages at Sipadan and Mabul.

USIT Ireland ☎ 01 602 1906, ⓦ www.usit.ie. Student and youth travel.

Getting around

Public transport in Malaysia, Singapore and Brunei is reliable and inexpensive. Much of your travelling, particularly in Peninsular Malaysia, will be by bus, minivan or, less often, long-distance taxi. Budget flights are a great option for hopping around the region, especially given that no ferries connect Peninsular and east Malaysia. Although the Peninsula's rail system (there's also a small stretch in Sabah), has to some extent been superseded by highways and faster buses, it still has its uses, particularly in the interior and on the express run north from Butterworth to Bangkok.

Sabah and **Sarawak** have their own travel peculiarities – in Sarawak, for instance, you're reliant on boats, and occasionally planes, for some long-distance travel. **Brunei**'s bus service, covering routes through the main towns, is supplemented by boats in remote areas like the Temburong district. The chapters on Sarawak, Sabah, Brunei and Singapore contain detailed information on their respective transport systems; the emphasis in the rest of this section is largely on Peninsular Malaysia.

The transport system is subject to heavy pressure during any nationwide **public holiday** – particularly Muslim festivals, the Chinese New Year, Deepavali, Christmas and New Year. A day or two before each festival, whole communities embark upon what's called **balik kampung**, which literally means returning to their home villages (and towns) to be with family. Make bus, train or flight reservations at least **one week in advance** to travel at these times; if you're driving, steel yourself for more than the usual number of jams.

And finally, bear in mind that **chartering** transport – longboats, or cars with drivers – to reach some off-the-beaten-track national park or island, is always an expensive business.

By bus

Malaysia's national **bus network** is comprehensive and easy to use, with regular **express** coaches between all major cities and towns, and much slower local services within, usually, a 100-km radius.

Peninsular Malaysia

Buying a **ticket** at any sizeable Malaysian bus station is like wandering into a street market: routes can be served by dozens of companies, each with their own ticket booths and staff vying for your attention. The atmosphere is never aggressive, however – touts won't grab your bags as hostage or hustle you into the wrong bus – and in practice things work reasonably well. The plethora of bus companies also means departures are pretty **frequent** (in practice, hourly or every other hour during daylight hours). Much of the time you can just turn up and buy a ticket for the next bus, though you might want to do this a day in advance on popular routes, such as those involving the Cameron Highlands. While comprehensive timetables are never available, bus station staff (and even staff for competing bus companies) can fill you in about schedules and connections.

BUS COMPANIES

A handful of well-established bus companies give reliable service in Peninsular-Malaysia. The largest is **Transnasional** (W transnasional.com.my), whose services have the entire Peninsula pretty well covered. Alternatives include **Plusliner** (W plusliner.com.my) and **Konsortium Bas Ekspres** (W kbes.com.my).

Most intercity buses are comfortable, with **air conditioning** and curtains to screen out the blazing tropical sun, though seats can be tightly packed together. Buses rarely have toilets, but longer journeys feature a rest stop every couple of hours or so, with a half-hour meal stopover if needed. On a few plum routes, notably KL–Singapore and KL–Penang, additional **luxury** or "executive" coaches charge double the regular fares and offer greater legroom plus on-board TVs and toilets.

Fares are cheap (see box, p.33), but note that if you want to leave the bus at a small town en route, you may be charged the full fare or the fare until the next major town. Local buses, where available, are more cost-effective for such journeys, but take much longer.

Express and local buses usually operate from separate stations; the local bus station is often fairly central, the express-bus station a little further out. In some towns, buses may call at both stations before terminating.

Sabah and Sarawak

In Sabah and **Sarawak**, modern air-conditioned buses ply the various long-distance routes, including Sarawak's trans-state coastal road between Kuching and the Brunei border, serving Sibu, Bintulu and Miri en route. In addition, local buses serve satellite towns and villages; these are particularly useful when exploring southwestern Sarawak and for the cross-border trip to Pontianak in Indonesian Kalimantan. Details of routes are given in the Guide.

By train

The Peninsula's intercity train service is operated by **KTM** (short for "Keretapi Tanah Melayu" or Malay Land Trains; W www.ktmb.com.my). The network is shaped roughly like a Y, with the southern end anchored at Singapore and the intersection north inside Malaysia at the small town of Gemas. The northwest branch travels into Thailand via KL, Ipoh and Butterworth, crossing the border at Padang Besar; the northeast branch cuts up through the interior along a stretch known as the Jungle Railway (see p.206), to terminate at Tumpat, outside the port of Kota Bharu.

There are two main classes of train. **Express** services call mostly at major stations and are generally modern, fully air-conditioned and well maintained; **local** trains, often not air-conditioned and of variable quality, operate on various segments between Singapore and Tumpat, and call at every town, village and hamlet en route.

Unfortunately, not even the express trains can keep up with buses where modern highways exist alongside. The 370km journey from KL to Johor Bahru, for example, takes the train five and a half hours; on a good day, buses are roughly an hour quicker. Until the rail tracks themselves are modernized, you're unlikely to rely heavily on trains for journeys along the west coast and in the south.

The rail system does, however, retain a couple of advantages. **Sleeper services** – between KL and Singapore, KL and Hat Yai in Thailand, and Singapore and Tumpat, not to mention the international service from Butterworth to Bangkok – can save on a night's accommodation. Express trains also remain the quickest way to reach some parts of the forested **interior**, while local trains through the interior can also be handy for reaching small settlements. Moreover, there's still a certain thrill in arriving at some of the splendidly solid colonial stations, built when the train was the prime means of transport.

Seats and berths

Seats on the trains divide into **economy**, **superior** and **premier** class, though not all are available on

KERETA SAPU

Especially in Sabah and Sarawak – though also in Peninsular Malaysia – private cars, vans and (on rough roads) four-wheel-drives known as **kereta sapu** (sometimes informally called "taxis") operate like buses or taxis along certain routes, usually from the main bus stations. They've pretty well replaced buses into Thailand from Penang, for example, and are also useful crossing from Miri in Sarawak to Brunei's Bandar Seri Begawan.

Elsewhere, if a bus doesn't seem to exist for your route, check with accommodation or the local tourist office if they know of a *kereta sapu* service.

THE MALAYSIAN RAIL NETWORK

BANGKOK (International Express)

Hat Yai (Thailand)

Padang Besar

Arau

Alor Setar

Gurun

Sungai Petani

Bukit Mertajam

Butterworth

Nibong Tebal

Parit Buntar

Bagan Serai

Taiping

Kuala Kangsar

Sungai Siput

Ipoh

Batu Gajah

Kampar

Tapah Road

Sungkai

Slim River

Tanjung Malim

Rawang

Sungai Buloh

KL SENTRAL

Kajang

Seremban

Rembau

Tampin

Batang Melaka

Tumpat (Kelantan coast)

Wakaf Bharu (for Kota Bharu)

Pasir Mas

Tanah Merah

Kuala Krai

Dabong

Gua Musang

Kuala Lipis

Jerantut

Kuala Krau

Mentakab

Triang

Bahau

Gemas

Segamat

Labis

Paloh

Kluang

Kulai

Kempas Bahru

Johor Bahru

SINGAPORE (Woodlands)

Malaysian long-distance rail services

Express
Kuala Lumpur–Butterworth
Kuala Lumpur–Ipoh (weekends)
Kuala Lumpur–Tumpat
Kuala Lumpur–Hat Yai (Thailand)
Butterworth–Bangkok (International Express)
Singapore–Butterworth
Singapore–Tumpat

Local
Gemas–Kuala Lipis
Kuala Lipis–Tumpat
Gua Musang–Tumpat
Singapore–Kluang (Tebrau Express)

Local trains call at virtually every station on the network.
This map shows only stations served by most express trains.

all services – local trains on interior routes tend to be economy only. In reality there's very little difference between them anyway, besides slight increases in padding, seat size and legroom.

Some night services also offer **sleeper berths**, which come in **superior, deluxe and 2plus**. Superior are two tiers of twenty bunks in an open carriage, with a curtain for privacy on each tier, while deluxe and 2plus are private cabins – only deluxe has its own washroom.

Buying tickets

While tickets can be **bought up to 30 days in advance** for any train, you can only book seat and berth reservations on express services – and you'll need to for these popular trains. Make bookings at major stations, by phone on ☎1300 885 862, or online at ⓦktmintercity.com.my. **Timetables and fare tables** are available online, and at major train stations.

Long-distance taxis

Most towns in Malaysia have a **long-distance taxi** rank, usually at or around the express bus station. Taxis run between cities and towns throughout the country, and can be a lot quicker than buses. The snag is that they operate on a **shared** basis, so you have to wait for enough people to show up to fill the four passenger seats in the vehicle. In most major towns this shouldn't take too long, especially early in the day; afternoon journeys can involve a bit of thumb-twiddling. **Fares** usually work out at two to three times the corresponding fare in an express bus. Note that long-distance taxi fares, in particular, may jump when fuel prices are rising rapidly.

For visitors travelling in small groups, the real advantage of these taxis is that you can **charter** one for your journey, paying for the vehicle rather than per person. Not only does this mean you'll set off immediately, but it also allows you to reach destinations that may not be served directly by buses, or even by normal shared taxis. There's little danger of being ripped off: charter prices to a large number of destinations, both popular and obscure, are set by the authorities, and usually chalked up on a board in the taxi office or listed on a laminated tariff card (*senarai tambang*), which you can ask to see.

Some taxi operators assume any tourist who shows up will want to charter a taxi; if you want to use the taxi on a shared basis, say "*nak kongsi dengan orang lain*".

Ferries and boats

Ferries sail to Langkawi, Penang, the Perhentians, Tioman and Pangkor islands off Peninsular Malaysia. Vessels are either modern speedboats or, occasionally, converted *penambang*, compact motorized fishing craft. You generally buy your ticket in advance from booths at the jetty, though you can sometimes pay on the boat.

Within **Sarawak**, the only scheduled boat services you're likely to use are those between Kuching and Sibu and on up the Rejang River to Belaga. To head up smaller tributaries, it's often necessary to charter a longboat.

Sabah has no express-boat river services, though regular ferries connect Pulau Labuan with Kota Kinabalu, Sipitang and Menumbok, all on the west coast.

In **Brunei**, useful boat services include the speedboat service from Bandar Seri Begawan to Bangar for Temburong Park, and the regular boats from Muara, near Bandar, to Lawas in Sarawak and Labuan Island off the coast of Sabah.

Details for all ferries and boats are given in the text.

By air

Thanks to some low-cost carriers, flying around the region is fairly inexpensive. Malaysian domestic flights are operated by Malaysia Airlines (**MAS**) and the budget carriers **AirAsia** and **Firefly**. From Singapore, **Singapore Airlines** and the budget companies **Tiger Airways** and **Jetstar** offer connections to the major Peninsular and east Malaysian cities, while **Royal Brunei Airlines** flies from Bandar Seri Begawan to Kuching, Kota Kinabalu and KL.

If you're flying within Malaysia, note that many connections between regional airports require a change of plane in KL, making flying less of a time-saver than it might seem. Note also that flights between Malaysia and Singapore or Brunei are more expensive than the distances involved suggest, as these count as international services.

Airfares throughout this section are for one-way tickets (return fares usually cost double) and include taxes and any fuel surcharges. Check all fares online with competing airline websites; huge discounts are sometimes available.

MAS, MASwings and Firefly

MAS (Malaysia ☎ 1300 883 000, Ⓦ malaysiaairlines .com) flies from KL to most state capitals, as well as Langkawi, Labuan, Singapore and Brunei. Its subsidiary **MASwings** (Ⓦ maswings.com.my) operates flights within East Malaysia, some services using propeller-driven Twin Otter planes that are something of a lifeline for rural communities.

MAS's budget arm, **Firefly** (Ⓦ fireflyz.com.my), mostly serves smaller destinations around the Peninsula, but has recently added services to Kota Kinabalu and Sandakan in Sabah, and Sebu and Kuching in Sarawak.

Short hops within the Peninsula start at around RM150 on MAS; going with Firefly can halve fares if they operate on the same route. As for Borneo flights, MASwings' fare for Kuching to Kinabalu is around RM100 if booked early. Note that many Malaysian cities no longer have a downtown MAS office; book online.

AirAsia

The no-frills carrier **AirAsia** (Ⓦ airasia.com) offers a network of internal flights rivalling those of MAS, though flights are prone to short delays. Most of its services originate at KL airport's low-cost-carrier terminal, though conveniently it also flies between Senai airport near **Johor Bahru** and Penang, Kuching, Miri, Sibu and Kota Kinabalu.

AirAsia's fares for short hops within the Peninsula are as low as RM40, while the very longest domestic route offered, from KL to Kota Kinabalu in eastern Sabah (2hr 30min), weighs in at around RM133 one-way if booked early enough. Note, however, that hefty surcharges apply if your checked-in baggage weighs more than 15kg, and that the lowest fares are hard to come by for travel on or close to public holidays, and during the school holidays.

AVERAGE FARE COMPARISONS

Journey	By bus	By shared taxi	By train (seat only)	By plane
KL–Johor Bahru	RM38; 4hr 30min	RM90; 4hr	RM27; 6hr 15min	RM150; 40min
KL–Penang	RM38; 5hr 30min	RM120; 4hr 30min	RM26; 6hr	RM150; 45min
KL–Kota Bharu	RM43; 8hr 30min	RM115; 8hr	RM34; 12hr	RM150; 50min
Johor Bahru–Kota Bharu	RM64; 12hr	–	RM31; 13hr	–

Other airlines

Singapore Airlines (Singapore ☎6223 8888, Malaysia ☎03 2692 3122, Brunei ☎224 4902; ⓦsingaporeair.com) and its subsidiary **SilkAir** (Singapore ☎6223 8888, ⓦsilkair.com) between them fly from Singapore to several key Malaysian destinations, including KL, Kota Kinabalu, Kuching, Langkawi and Penang, plus Brunei. Expect to pay around S\$220 to Kuala Lumpur, S\$250 to Penang, S\$270 to Kuching, and S\$370 to Kota Kinabalu. **Royal Brunei Airways** (Brunei ☎221 2222, Malaysia ☎03 2070 7166, Singapore ☎6235 4672; ⓦbruneiair.com) flies from Bandar Seri Begawan to KL (S\$200), Singapore (S\$460) and Kota Kinabalu (S\$100). Much cheaper are **Jetstar** (Singapore ☎800 616 1977, ⓦwww.jetstar.com) and **Tiger Airways** (Singapore ☎6538 4437, ⓦwww.tigerairways.com), on which it's sometimes possible to find Singapore–Penang tickets for as little as S\$65.

Two Malaysian resort islands, **Redang** and **Tioman**, are served by **Berjaya Air** (Malaysia ☎03 7845 8382, Singapore ☎6227 3688; ⓦberjaya-air.com); both host resorts owned by the conglomerate Berjaya Corporation. Flights originate in KL and Singapore; reckon on S\$110–180 each way.

Driving and vehicle rental

The **roads** in **Peninsular Malaysia** are good, making driving a viable prospect for tourists – though the cavalier local attitude to road rules takes some getting used to. It's mostly the same story in **Sarawak** and **Brunei**, though in **Sabah** a sizeable minority of roads are rough, unpaved and susceptible to flash flooding. **Singapore** is in another league altogether, boasting modern highways and a built-in road-use charging system that talks to a black-box gizmo fitted in every car.

All three countries **drive on the left**, and wearing seat belts is compulsory in the front of the vehicle (and in the back too, in Singapore). To **rent a vehicle**, you must be 23 or over and need to show a clean driving licence.

Because of Singapore's unique road-pricing technology, and the fact that some car rental outlets don't allow their cars to be driven between Malaysia and Singapore, the rest of this section concentrates on Malaysia. For information on driving in Singapore and Brunei, see the respective chapters.

Malaysian roads

Malaysian highways – called **expressways** and usually referred to by a number prefixed "E" – are a pleasure to drive; they're wide and well maintained, and feature convenient **rest stops** with toilets, shops and small food courts. In contrast, the streets of major cities can be a pain, regularly traffic-snarled, with patchy signposting and confusing one-way systems. Most cities and towns boast plenty of **car parks**, and even where you can't find one, there's usually no problem with parking in a lane or side street.

Speed limits are 110kph on expressways, 90kph on the narrower trunk and state roads, and 50kph in built-up areas. For intercity journeys, expressways are almost always quicker than using a trunk road, even if the latter passes through the town where

---

MALAY VOCABULARY FOR DRIVERS

The following list should help decipher road signage in Peninsular Malaysia and parts of Brunei, much of which is in Malay.

Utara	North	**Jalan sehala**	One-way street
Selatan	South	**Kawasan rehat**	Highway rest stop
Barat	West	**Kurangkan laju**	Reduce speed
Timur	East	**Lebuhraya**	Expressway/ highway
Di belakang	Behind		
Di hadapan	Ahead	**Lencongan**	Detour
Awas	Caution	**Pembinaan di hadapan**	Road works ahead
Berhenti	Stop		
Beri laluan	Give way	**Pusat bandar/ bandaraya**	Town/city centre
Dilarang meletak kereta	No parking		
		Simpang ke...	Junction/turning for...
Dilarang memotong	No overtaking		
Had laju/jam	Speed limit/per hour	**Zon had laju**	Zone where speed limit applies
Ikut kiri/kanan	Keep left/right		

you're starting out while the expressway is a little way away. Whatever road you're on, stick religiously to the speed limit; speed traps are commonplace and fines hefty. If you are pulled up for a traffic offence, note that it's not unknown for Malaysian police to ask for a bribe, which will set you back less than the fine. Never offer to bribe a police officer and think carefully before you give in to an invitation to do so.

All expressways are built and run by private concessions and as such attract **tolls**, generally around RM20 per 100km, though on some roads a flat fee is levied. At toll points (signed "Tol Plaza"), you can pay in cash (cashiers can dispense change) or by waving a stored-value **Touch 'n Go** card in front of a sensor (⒲ touchngo.com.my; see p.88). Get in the appropriate lane as you approach the toll points: some lanes are for certain types of vehicle only.

Once out on the roads, you'll rapidly become aware of the behaviour of quite a few Malaysian motorists, which their compatriots might term *gila* (Malay for "insane"). Swerving from lane to lane in the thick of the traffic, overtaking close to blind corners and careering down hill roads are not uncommon, as are tragic press accounts of pile-ups and road fatalities. Not for nothing does the exhortation *"pandu cermat"* (drive safely) appear on numerous highway signboards, though the message still isn't getting through.

If you're new to driving in Malaysia, the best approach is to take all of this with equanimity and drive conservatively; concede the right of way if you're not sure of the intentions of others. One confusing local habit is that some drivers flash their headlights to claim the right of way rather than concede it.

Car and bike rental

Car rental rates begin at around RM120 per day for weekly rental of a basic 1.5-litre Proton, including unlimited mileage and collision damage waiver insurance. The excess can be RM1500 or more, but can be reduced or set to zero by paying a surcharge of up to ten percent on the daily rental rate. Fuel is subsidized: at the time of writing, petrol cost RM1.9 per litre, diesel was RM1.8 per litre and gas about RM48 per tank.

Motorbike rental tends to be informal, usually offered by Malaysian guesthouses and shops in more touristy areas. Officially, you must be over 21 and have an appropriate driving licence, though it's unlikely you'll have to show the latter; you'll probably need to leave your passport as a deposit. Wearing helmets is compulsory. Rental costs

around RM20 per day, while **bicycles**, useful in rural areas, can be rented for a few ringgit a day.

CAR RENTAL AGENCIES

Avis ☎ 1800 881 054, ⒲ avis.com.my. Offices in KL, KL airport, Johor Bahru, Kuantan and Penang.

Hawk ☎ 03 5631 6488, ⒲ hawkrentacar.com.my. KL, KL airport, Johor Bahru, Melaka, Kota Bharu, Kuantan, Subang and Penang.

Hertz ☎ 03 2148 6433, ⒲ hertz.com. Locations include KL, Alor Star, Johor Bahru, Kuantan, Kuching, Kota Kinabalu and Penang.

Mayflower ☎ 1800 881 688, ⒲ mayflowercarrental.com. KL, Johor Bahru, Kota Kinabalu, Penang and Kuching.

City and local transport

Local bus networks in most Malaysian cities and towns serve both urban areas and hinterland; details are given in the text. Fares are always low (typically under RM2), though schedules – particularly in KL – can be unfathomable to visitors (and to some locals). KL also has efficient commuter rail, light rail and monorail systems.

Taxis are metered in KL, Singapore and some other large cities, though Malaysian drivers often prefer to turn off the meter illegally, and negotiate a fare. If you encounter this, simply get straight out of the cab and flag down another. At a few taxi ranks you can pay a sensible fixed fare at a booth before your trip.

Outside the largest cities, taxis neither use meters nor ply the streets looking for custom. In these places, whether you want to make a standard journey within town or charter a cab for a specific itinerary, you should head to a taxi rank and will probably have to bargain if you're doing an unusual route. Your accommodation might be able to charter a vehicle for you, or at least provide an idea of likely prices; reckon on at least RM30 per hour.

Trishaws (bicycle rickshaws), seating two people, are seen less and less these days, but they're still very much part of the tourist scene in places like Melaka, Penang and Singapore. You're paying for an experience here, not transport as such; see city accounts for prices.

Accommodation

Accommodation in Malaysia is good value: basic double rooms start at around RM45 (£9/US$14), while mid-range en-suite rooms can go for as little as RM100 (£20/US$32), including breakfast. With a little shopping around, you may well turn up a plush, four-star

hotel room for RM250 (£50/US$80). This section focuses mainly on accommodation across Malaysia; you'll find fuller details elsewhere for Singapore (see p.536), where prices are significantly higher.

The cheapest form of accommodation is a **dormitory** at a hostel, guesthouse or lodge. These generally exist in well-touristed spots, such as Kuala Lumpur, Georgetown, Kota Bharu, Cherating, Kuching, Miri, Kota Kinabalu and Sandakan. At the other end of the scale, luxury hotels offer a level of comfort and style to rank with any in the world. Many mid-range and top-bracket hotels also offer **promotional discounts** that slash twenty percent or more off the rack rate; either check online or simply ask if you turn up without a reservation. Discounted long-term rates – anything over two weeks – are also often available.

Advance reservations are essential to be sure of securing a budget or mid-range room during major festivals such as Chinese New Year, Hari Raya and Deepavali (see p.46), or school holidays (see p.58). **Rates** remain relatively stable throughout the year, rising slightly during these popular periods.

At the budget end of the market you'll have to **share a bathroom**, which in most cases will feature a shower and Western-style toilet. **Air conditioning** is standard in hotels, and is increasingly common at the budget end of the market. Note that a single room may contain a double bed, while a double can have a double bed, two single beds or even two double beds; a triple will usually have three doubles or a combination of doubles and singles. Baby cots are usually available only in more expensive places.

Guesthouses, hostels and chalets

The mainstay of the travellers' scene in Malaysia and Singapore are **guesthouses** (also sometimes called hostels, B&Bs or **backpackers**). Located in popular tourist areas, these can range from simple affairs in renovated shophouses to modern multistorey buildings complete with satellite TV, DVD players and internet. Their advantage for travellers on a tight budget is that almost all offer **dorm beds**, costing anywhere between RM10 and RM30. Basic double rooms are usually available, too, with a fan and possibly a mosquito net at the cheaper end of the market, from RM35 upwards.

In national parks, islands and in resort-style compounds you'll find accommodation in so-called **chalets**, ranging from simple A-frame huts to luxury affairs with a veranda, sitting area, TV, minibar, etc. While the cheapest chalets cost the same as a basic double in a guesthouse, at the top end you could pay over RM1000 for a two-night package at the dive resorts off Sabah's east coast.

Hotels

Malaysia's **cheapest hotels** tend to cater for a local clientele and seldom need to be booked in advance: just go to the next place around the corner if your first choice is full. Rooms are usually divided from one another by thin partitions and contain a washbasin, table and ceiling fan, though never a mosquito net. In the better places you may be treated to polished wooden floors and antique furniture. That said, showers and toilets are often shared and can be pretty basic. Another consideration is the **noise** level, which as most places are on main streets can be considerable. Note that some of the hotels at the cheaper end of the scale also function as brothels, especially those described using the Malay term *rumah persinggahan* or *rumah tumpangan*, or those that allow rooms to be paid for by the hour.

Mid-range hotels, often the only alternative in smaller towns, are rarely better value than a well-kept budget place. The big difference is in the comfort of the mattress – nearly always sprung – and getting your own Western-style, but cramped, bathroom. Prices start at around RM60, for which you can expect air conditioning, en-suite facilities and relatively decent furnishings, as well, sometimes, as a telephone and refrigerator. In these places, too, a genuine distinction is made between single rooms and doubles.

High-end hotels are as comfortable as you might expect, and many have state-of-the-art facilities, including a swimming pool, spa and gym. Some may add a touch of class by incorporating kampung-style architecture, such as saddle-shaped roofs with woodcarving. While rates can be as low as RM200 per night, in popular destinations such as Penang and Kota Kinabalu they can rocket above the RM300 mark, though this is obviously still great value compared to equivalent hotels in Western cities. Many five-star hotels adjust their rates on a daily basis depending on their occupancy level; check websites for the latest rates.

Camping

Despite the rural nature of much of Malaysia, there are few official opportunities for camping, perhaps because guesthouses and hotels are so reasonable, and because the heat and humidity, not to mention the generous supply of insects, make camping something only strange foreigners would willingly do. Where there are **campsites**, typically in nature parks, they are either free to use or charge around RM10 per person per night; facilities are basic and may not be well maintained. A few lodges and camps (at Taman Negara, for example) have sturdy A-frame tents and other equipment for rent, but you generally need to bring all your own gear (see p.49).

If you go trekking in more remote regions, for example through central Taman Negara National Park in Peninsular Malaysia and parts of the Kelabit Highlands in Sabah, camping is about your only option. Often, visitors find it easier to go on package trips organized by specialist tour operators who will provide tents and equipment, if necessary.

Longhouses

A stay in a **longhouse**, de rigueur for many travellers visiting Sarawak, offers the chance to experience tribal community life, do a little trekking and try activities such as weaving and using a blowpipe. It used to be that visitors could simply turn up at a longhouse, ask to see the tuai rumah (headman), and be granted a place to stay, paying only for meals and offering some gifts as an additional token of thanks for the community's hospitality. While some tourists still try to work things like this, for example at longhouses along the Rejang River, these days most longhouse visits are invariably arranged through a **tour operator**.

More expensive packages put visitors up in their own section of the longhouse, equipped with proper beds and modern washing facilities; meals will be prepared separately rather than shared with the rest of the community. More basic trips generally have you sleeping on mats rather than beds, either in a large communal room or on the veranda, and the main washing facilities may well be the nearest river. For meals the party will be divided up into smaller groups, each of which will eat with a different family.

It can be fantastic to visit a longhouse during the annual **Gawai Dayak** festival at the start of June and witness traditional celebrations, though don't expect to get much sleep: the merry-making, generally fuelled by copious consumption of tuak (rice wine), will continue long into the night, and the place may be so crowded that people end up sleeping sardine-fashion in the communal areas.

Homestays

In certain areas **homestay programmes** are available, whereby you stay with a Malaysian family, paying for your bed and board. Though facilities are likely to be modest, homestays can be a good way to sample home cooking and culture. Tourist offices can usually furnish a list of local homestays if requested; the main things to ask about are whether a special programme will be laid on for you – not necessarily a good thing if you simply want to be left to relax – and whether your hosts are able to speak English, without which you may find yourself somewhat cut off from them and the community.

Food and drink

One of the best reasons to come to Malaysia and Singapore (even Brunei, to a lesser extent) is the food, comprising two of the world's most venerated cuisines – Chinese and Indian – and one of the most underrated – Malay. Even if you think you know two out of the three pretty well, be prepared to be surprised: Chinese food here boasts a lot of the provincial diversity that you just don't find in the West's Cantonese-dominated Chinese restaurants, while Indian fare is predominantly southern Indian, lighter and spicier than northern food.

Furthermore, each of the three cuisines has acquired more than a few tricks from the other two – the Chinese here cook curries, for example – giving rise to some distinctive fusion food. Add to this cross-fertilization a host of regional variations and specialities, plus excellent seafood and unusual tropical produce, and the result is – if you dare to order enterprisingly – a dazzling gastronomic experience.

None of this need come at great expense. From the ubiquitous food stalls and cheap street diners called **kedai kopis**, the standard of cooking is high and food everywhere is remarkably good value. Basic noodle- or rice-based one-plate meals at a stall or kedai kopi rarely cost more than a few ringgit or Singapore dollars. Even a full meal with drinks in a fancy restaurant seldom runs to more than RM50 a head in Malaysia, though expect to pay Western prices at quite a few places in Singapore. The most renowned culinary centres are Singapore, George-town, KL, Melaka and Kota Bharu, although other towns have their own distinctive dishes too.

Places to eat

One myth to bust immediately is the notion that you will get food poisoning eating at street stalls and cheap diners. Standards of hygiene are usually good, and as most food is cooked to order (or, in the case of rice-with-toppings spreads, only on display for a few hours), it's generally pretty safe. Note also that **tipping** is not expected in restaurants where bills include a service charge (as they usually do) – and is never the practice in *kedai kopis* or food courts.

Food stalls and food courts

Some of the cheapest and most delicious food available in Malaysia and Singapore comes from **stalls**, traditionally wooden pushcarts on the roadside, surrounded by a few wobbly tables with stools to sit at. Most stalls serve one or a few standard **noodle** and **rice dishes** or specialize in certain delicacies, from oyster omelettes to squid curry.

For many visitors, however, there is a psychological barrier to having a meal by the roadside. To ease yourself into the *modus operandi* of stalls, take advantage of the fact that nowadays many are assembled into user-friendly **medan selera** (literally "appetite square") or **food courts**, also known as **hawker centres** in Singapore. Usually taking up a floor of an office building or shopping mall, or housed in open-sided market buildings, food courts feature stall lots with menus displayed and fixed tables, plus toilets. You generally don't have to sit close to the stall you're patronizing: find a free table, and the vendor will track you down when your food is ready (some Singapore food centres have tables with numbers that must be quoted when ordering). You generally pay when your food is delivered, though payment is sometimes requested when you order.

Stalls open at various times from morning to evening, with most closing well before midnight except in the big cities. During the Muslim fasting month of **Ramadan**, however, Muslim-run stalls don't open until mid-afternoon, though this is also when you can take advantage of the **pasar Ramadan**, afternoon food markets at which stalls sell masses of savouries and sweet treats to take away; tourist offices can tell you where one is taking place. Ramadan is also the time to stuff yourself at the massive fast-breaking buffets laid on by most major hotels throughout the month.

The kedai kopi

Few downtown streets lack a **kedai kopi**, sometimes known as a *kopitiam* in Hokkien Chinese. Although both terms literally mean "coffee shop", a *kedai kopi* is actually an inexpensive diner rather than a café. Most serve noodle and rice dishes all day, often with a *campur*-style spread (see opposite) at lunchtime, sometimes in the evening too. Some *kedai kopis* function as miniature food markets, housing a handful of vendors – perhaps one offering curries and griddle breads, another doing a particular Chinese noodle dish, and so on.

Most *kedai kopis* open at 8am to serve breakfast, and don't shut until the early evening; a few stay open as late as 10pm. Culinary standards are seldom spectacular but are satisfying all the same, and you're unlikely to spend more than small change for a filling one-plate meal. It's worth noting that in some Malaysian towns, particularly on the east coast, the Chinese-run *kedai kopis* are often the only places where you'll be able to get **alcohol**.

Restaurants, cafés and bakeries

Sophisticated **restaurants** only exist in the big cities. Don't expect a stiffly formal ambience in these places, however – while some places can be sedate, the Chinese, in particular, prefer restaurants to be noisy, sociable affairs. Where the pricier restaurants come into their own is for **international food** – anything from Vietnamese to Tex-Mex. KL, Singapore and Georgetown all have dynamic restaurant scenes, and the five-star hotels usually boast a top-flight restaurant of their own. The chief letdown is that the service can be amateurish, reflecting how novel this sort of dining experience is for many of the staff.

EATING ETIQUETTE

Malays and Indians often eat with the **right hand**, using the palm as a scoop and the thumb to help push food into the mouth. **Chopsticks** are, of course, used for Chinese food, though note that a spoon is always used to help with rice, gravies and slippery fare such as mushrooms or tofu, and that you don't attempt to pick up rice with chopsticks (unless you've a rice bowl, in which case you lift the bowl to your mouth and use the chopsticks as a sort of shovel). If you can't face either local style of eating, note that **cutlery** is universally available – for local fare, always a fork and spoon, the fork serving to push food onto the spoon.

Most large Malaysian towns feature a few attempts at Western **cafés**, serving passable fries, sandwiches, burgers, shakes and so forth. It's also easy to find **bakeries**, which can represent a welcome change from the local rice-based diet – though don't be surprised to find chilli sardine buns and other Asian Western hybrids, or cakes with decidedly artificial fillings and colourings. For anything really decent in the café or bakery line, you'll need to be in a big city.

Cuisines

A convenient and inexpensive way to get acquainted with a variety of local dishes is to sample the food spreads available at many of the *kedai kopis*, particularly at lunchtime. The concept is pretty much summed up by the Malay name for such spreads, **nasi campur** ("mixed rice"), though Chinese and Indian *kedai kopis*, too, offer these arrays of stir fries, curries and other savouries, set out in metal trays or plates. As in a cafeteria, you simply tell the person behind the counter which items you want, and a helping of each will be piled atop a largish serving of rice. If the plainness of the rice soon palls, ask for it to be doused with a scoopful of gravy (*kuah* in Malay) from any stew or stir fry on display.

Campur food is not haute cuisine – and that's precisely the attraction. Whether you have, say, *ikan kembong* (mackerel) deep-fried and served whole, or chicken pieces braised in soy sauce, or bean sprouts stir-fried with salted fish or shrimp, any *campur* spread is much closer to **home cooking** than anything served in formal restaurants.

Nasi campur and noodle dishes are meals in themselves, but otherwise eating is generally a **shared** experience – stir fries and other dishes arrive in quick succession and everyone present helps themselves to several servings of each, eaten with rice, as the meal progresses.

Breakfast can present a conundrum in small towns, where the rice and noodle dishes that locals enjoy at all times of day may be all that's easily available. If you can't get used to the likes of rice porridge at dawn, try to find a stall or *kedai kopi* offering *roti bakar*, toast served with butter and **kaya**. The latter is a scrumptious sweet spread, either orange or green, not unlike English lemon curd in that it's made with eggs, though coconut is the magic ingredient that accounts for most of the flavour.

Malay food

In its influences, Malay cuisine looks to the north and east, most obviously to China in the use of noodles and soy sauce, but also to neighbouring Thailand, with which it shares an affinity for such ingredients as lemon grass, the ginger-like galingale and fermented fish sauce (the Malay version, *budu*, is made from anchovies). But Malay fare also draws on Indian and Middle East cooking in the use of spices, and in dishes such as *biriyani* rice. The resulting cuisine is characterized by being both spicy and a little sweet. Naturally there's a particular emphasis on **local ingredients**: *santan* (coconut milk) lends a sweet, creamy undertone to many stews and curries, while *belacan*, a pungent fermented prawn paste (something of an acquired taste), is found in chilli condiments and sauces. Unusual **herbs**, including curry and kaffir-lime leaves, also play a prominent role.

The cuisine of the southern part of the Peninsula tends to be more *lemak* (rich) than further north, where the Thai influence is strongest and where you'll thus find many a *tom yam* stew – spicy and sour (the latter by dint of lemon grass) – on offer. The most famous Malay dish is arguably **satay** (see p.40), though this can be hard to find outside the big cities; another classic, and this time ubiquitous, is *nasi lemak* (see p.40), standard breakfast fare. Also quintessentially Malay, **rendang** is a dryish curry made by slow-cooking meat (usually beef) in coconut milk flavoured with galingale and a variety of herbs and spices.

For many visitors, one of the most striking things about Malay food is the bewildering array of **kuih-muih** (or just *kuih*), or sweetmeats, on display at markets and street stalls. Often featuring coconut and sometimes *gula melaka* (palm-sugar molasses), *kuih* come in all shapes and sizes, and in as many colours (often artificial nowadays) as you find in a paints catalogue – rainbow-hued layer cakes of rice flour are about the most extreme example.

Chinese food

The range of Chinese cooking available in Malaysia and Singapore represents a mouthwatering sweep through China's southeastern seaboard, reflecting the historical pattern of emigration from **Fujian**, **Guangzhou** and **Hainan Island** provinces. This diversity is evident in popular dishes served at any collection of stalls or *kopitiams*. Cantonese *char siew* (roast pork, given a reddish honey-based marinade) is frequently served over plain rice as a meal in itself, or as a garnish in noodle dishes such as *wonton mee* (*wonton* being Cantonese pork dumplings); also very common is Hainanese chicken rice, comprising steamed chicken accompanied by savoury rice cooked in chicken stock. Fujian province contributes

SIX OF THE BEST

The culinary highlights listed below are mostly fairly easy to find, and many of these foods cut across racial boundaries as well, with each ethnic group modifying the dish slightly to suit its own cooking style.

Nasi lemak Rice fragrantly cooked in coconut milk and served with fried peanuts, tiny fried anchovies, cucumber, boiled egg and spicy *sambal*.

Roti canai Called *roti prata* in Singapore, this Indian-inspired griddle bread comes with a thin curry sauce. The most ubiquitous of a long list of rotis, it's served by Malay and Indian *kedai kopis* and stalls.

Nasi goreng Literally, fried rice, though not as in Chinese restaurants; Malay and Indian versions feature a little spice and chilli, along with the usual mix of vegetables plus shrimp, chicken and/or egg bits.

Char kuay teow A Hokkien Chinese dish of fried tagliatelle-style rice noodles rendered dark by soy sauce and garnished with egg, pork and prawns. The Singapore

version is decidedly sweet. Malay *kuay teow goreng* is also available and tends to be plainer, though also spicier.

Satay A Malay dish of chicken, mutton or beef kebabs on bamboo sticks, marinaded and barbecued. The meat is accompanied by cucumber, raw onion and *ketupat*, which is sticky-rice cubes steamed in a wrap of woven leaves. All are meant to be dipped in a spicy peanut sauce. Chinese satay featuring pork also exists.

Laksa A spicy seafood noodle soup, Nonya in origin. Singapore *laksa*, served with fishcake dumplings and beansprouts, is rich and a little sweet thanks to copious use of coconut milk, while Penang's *asam laksa* features flaked fish and a sour flavour from tamarind.

---

dishes such as *hae mee*, yellow noodles in a rich prawn broth; *yong tau foo*, from the Hakka ethnic group on the border with Guangzhou, and comprising bean curd, fishball dumplings and assorted vegetables, poached and served with broth and sweet dipping sauces; and *mee pok*, a Teochew (Chaozhou) dish featuring ribbon-like noodles with fishball dumplings and a spicy dressing.

Restaurant dining tends to be dominated by **Cantonese** food. Menus can be predictable – including standbys such as sweet-and-sour pork, lemon chicken, steamed sea bass, claypot rice (rice cooked in an earthenware pot with sweet *lap cheong* pork sausage) and so forth – but the quality of cooking is usually very high.

Many Cantonese places offer great **dim sum** lunches, at which small servings of numerous savouries such as *siu mai* dumplings (of pork and prawn), crispy yam puffs and *chee cheong fun* (rice-flour rolls stuffed with pork and dredged in sweet sauce) are consumed. Traditionally, all are served in bamboo steamers and ordered off trolleys wheeled by waitresses, though these days you might well simply order off a menu.

Where available, take the opportunity to try **specialities** such as steamboat, a sort of fondue that involves dunking raw vegetables, meat and seafood into boiling stock to cook (the stock itself is drunk as part of the meal), or chilli crab (served at some seafood places), in which crab pieces are served in a

spicy tomato sauce. It's also worth sampling humdrum but very commonplace stomach-fillers such as **rice porridge** – either plain, with salted fish and omelette strips added for flavour, or already flavoured by being cooked with chicken or fish – and **pow**, steamed buns containing a savoury filling of *char siew* or chicken, or sometimes a sweet filling of red bean paste. Both porridge and *pow* are widely available as breakfast fare, while *pow* is sold throughout the day as a snack.

Nonya food

Named after the word used to describe womenfolk of the Peranakan communities (see p.280), Nonya food is to Penang, Melaka and Singapore as Creole food is to Louisiana, a product of the melding of cultures. Here the blend is of Chinese and Malay (and also Indonesian) cuisines, and can seem more Malay than Chinese thanks to its use of spices – except that pork is widely used.

Nonya **popiah** (spring rolls) is a standard dish: rather than being fried, the rolls are assembled by coating a steamed wrap with a sweet sauce made of palm sugar, then stuffed mainly with stir-fried *bangkwang*, a crunchy turnip-like vegetable. Another classic is **laksa**, noodles in a spicy soup flavoured in part by *daun kesom* – a herb fittingly referred to in English as *laksa* leaf. Other well-known Nonya dishes include **asam fish**, a spicy, tangy fish stew featuring tamarind (the *asam* of the name);

and **otak-otak**, fish mashed with coconut milk and chilli paste, then put in a narrow banana-leaf envelope and steamed or barbecued.

Indian food

The classic **southern Indian** dish is the *dosai* or *thosai*, a thin rice-flour pancake, often stuffed with a vegetable mixture. It's usually served accompanied by *sambar*, a basic vegetable and lentil curry, *rasam*, a tamarind broth; and perhaps a few small helpings of vegetable or dhal curries. Also very common are roti griddle breads, plus the more substantial *murtabak*, thicker than a roti and stuffed with egg, onion and minced meat, with sweet banana versions sometimes available. At lunchtime many South Indian cafés turn to serving *daun pisang* (literally, banana leaf), a meal comprising rice heaped on a banana-leaf "platter" and small, replenishable heaps of various curries placed alongside. In some restaurants you'll find more substantial dishes such as the popular fish-head curry (don't be put off by the idea – the "cheeks" between the mouth and gills are packed with tasty flesh).

A notable aspect of the eating scene in Malaysia is the "**mamak**" *kedai kopi*, run by Muslims of South Indian descent (and easily distinguished from Hindu Tamil places by the framed Arabic inscriptions on the walls). *Mamak* establishments have become de facto meeting places for all creeds, being halal and open late. Foodwise, they're very similar to other south Indian places, though perhaps with more emphasis on meat in *mamak* joints and some attempt at northern Indian dishes as well. There are also a few Indian Muslim *kedai kopis* in Singapore, too, particularly in Little India and around Arab Street, but the term *mamak* is little used there.

The food served in **northern Indian** restaurants (only found in big cities), is richer, less fiery and more reliant on mutton and chicken. The most famous style of **North Indian** cooking is tandoori – named after the clay oven in which the food is cooked; you'll commonly come across tandoori chicken marinated in yoghurt and spices and then baked. Breads such as nan also tend to feature rather than rice, though just about every restaurant has a version of *biriyani*.

SPECIAL DIETS

Malay food is, unfortunately, a tough nut to crack for **vegetarians**, as meat and seafood are well integrated into the cuisine. Among the standard savoury dishes, veggies can only really handle *sayur lodeh* (a rich mixed-vegetable curry made with coconut milk), *tauhu goreng* (deep-fried tofu with a peanut dressing similar to satay sauce), and *acar* (pickles). Eating places run by the **Chinese** and **Indian** communities are the best bets, as these groups have some familiarity with vegetarianism thanks to the cultural influence of Buddhism and Hinduism. Chinese restaurants can always whip up veg stir fries to order, and many places now feature **Chinese vegetarian** cuisine, using textured veg protein and gluten mock meats – often uncannily like the real thing, and delicious when done right.

Strict vegetarians will want to avoid **seafood derivatives** commonly used in cooking. This means eschewing dishes like *rojak* (containing fermented prawn paste) and the chilli dip called *sambal belacan* (containing *belacan*, the Malay answer to prawn paste) – though for some visitors, vegetarian or not, the pungency of prawn paste is enough of a deterrent. Oyster sauce, used in Chinese stir fries, is omitted for vegetarian purposes in favour of soy sauce or just salt. Note also that the delicious gravy that accompanies **roti canai** generally comes from a meat curry, though some places offer a lentil version, too.

If you need to **explain in Malay** that you're vegetarian, try *saya hanya makan sayuran* ("I only eat vegetables"). Even if the person taking your order speaks English, it can be useful to list the things you don't eat; in Malay you'd say, for example, *saya tak mahu ayam dan ikan dan udang* for "I don't want chicken or fish or prawn". Expect a few misunderstandings; the cook may leave out one thing on your proscribed list, only to substitute another.

HALAL FOOD

Halal fare doesn't just feature at Malay and *mamak* restaurants and stalls. The catering at mid-range and top-tier Malaysian hotels is in fact mostly halal, or at least "**pork-free**", and even the Chinese dishes served at top hotel restaurants have their pork content replaced with something else. Of course, the pork-free billing doesn't equate to being halal, but many local Muslims are prepared to overlook this grey area, or get round it by ordering seafood.

In **Singapore**, most hawker centres have a row or two of Muslim stalls, and in areas where the great majority of the population is Muslim, such as **Kelantan** and **Terengganu**, halal or pork-free food is the norm, even at Chinese and Indian restaurants.

Borneo cuisine

The diet of the indigenous groups living in settled communities in **east Malaysia** tends to revolve around standard Malay and Chinese dishes. In remoter regions, however, or at festival times, you may have an opportunity to sample indigenous cuisine. Villagers in **Sabah**'s Klias Peninsula and in **Brunei** still produce *ambuyat*, a gluey, sago-starch porridge; then there's the Lun Bawang speciality of *jaruk* – raw wild boar, fermented in a bamboo tube and definitely an acquired taste. Sabah's most famous dishes include *hinava*, raw fish pickled in lime juice. In **Sarawak**, Iban and Kelabit communities sometimes serve wild boar, cooked on a spit or stewed, and served with rice (perhaps *lemang* – glutinous rice cooked in bamboo) and jungle ferns. River fish is a longhouse basic; the most easily available, tilapia, is usually grilled with pepper and herbs, or steamed in bamboo cylinders.

Tropical fruit

Markets feature a delightful range of locally grown **fruit**, though modern agricultural practices are leading to a decline in some varieties. Below are some of the more unusual fruits to watch out for.

Bananas (pisang) Look out for the delicious *pisang mas*, small, straight, thin-skinned and aromatically sweet; *pisang rastali*, slightly bigger, with dark blotches on the skin and not quite so sweet; plus green- and even red-skinned varieties.

Cempedak This smaller version of the *nangka* (see jackfruit below) is normally deep-fried, enabling the seed, not unlike a new potato, to be eaten too.

Ciku Looks like an apple; varies from yellow to pinkish brown when ripe, with a soft, pulpy flesh.

Durian One of Southeast Asia's most popular fruits, durians are also, for many visitors, the most repugnant thanks to their unpleasant smell. In season (March–Aug & Nov–Feb), they're the size of soccer balls and have a thick green skin covered with sharp spikes. Inside, rows of large seeds are coated with squidgy yellow-white flesh, whose flavour has been likened to vomit-flavoured custard.

Jackfruit Like some kind of giant grenade, the jackfruit (*nangka*) grows up to 40cm long and has a coarse greenish-yellow exterior, enclosing large seeds whose sweet flesh has a powerful odour, vaguely like overripe pineapple. The unripe fruit is sometimes served as a savoury stir fry that's a bit like bamboo shoots.

Langsat Together with its sister fruit, the *duku*, this looks like a small, round potato, with juicy, segmented white flesh containing small, bitter seeds.

Longan Not unlike the lychee, this stone fruit has sweet, juicy translucent flesh inside a thin brown skin.

Mangosteen Available June–Aug & Nov–Jan, mangosteens have a segmented white flesh with a sweet, slightly tart flavour. Be warned: the thick purple rind contains juice that stains clothes indelibly.

Pomelo Much grown around Ipoh, this pale green citrus fruit is slightly smaller than a soccer ball and, at its best, is juicier and sweeter than grapefruit. Slice away the rind with a knife, then separate and peel the giant segments with your hands.

Rambutan The shape and size of hen's eggs, rambutans have a soft, spiny exterior that gives them their name – *rambut* means "hair" in Malay. To get at the sweet translucent white flesh coating the stone inside, simply make a small tear in the peel with your nails and twist open.

Salak Teardrop-shaped, the *salak* has a skin rather like a snake's and a bitter taste.

Soursop Inside the bumpy, muddy-green skin of this fruit, the smooth white flesh is like blancmange. Margaret Brooke, wife of Sarawak's second rajah, Charles, described it as "tasting like cotton wool dipped in vinegar and sugar".

Star fruit This waxy, pale green fruit, star-shaped in cross section, is said to be good for high blood pressure. The yellower the fruit, the sweeter its flesh – though it can be rather insipid.

Desserts

Appropriately, given the steamy climate, stalls offer a range of desserts that often revolve around **ice** milled down to something resembling slush. More jarringly, desserts often include ingredients such as **pulses**, **sticky rice** or even **yam** and **sweet potato**, all of which can be turned into a sweet stew or porridge.

At their best, local desserts are certainly a lot more interesting than most ice-cream sundaes ever get. Easy to find and worth trying is **eis kacang** (also known as *air batu campur* – "mixed ice" – or ABC), comprising a small helping of aduki beans, sweetcorn and bits of jelly, covered with a snowy mound doused in colourful syrups. Even better, though high in cholesterol, is **cendol**, luscious coconut milk sweetened with *gula melaka* and mixed with green fragments of mung-bean-flour jelly. You'll even find delicious red-bean ice cream on sale, its flavour dominated by coconut milk rather than the beans.

Drinks

While **tap water** is generally safe to drink, **bottled water** is widely available at around RM2 a litre. Among freshly squeezed **juices**, watermelon, orange and carrot are pretty common, as is the faintly sappy but invigorating sugar cane, extracted by pressing the canes through mangles. Some street stalls also offer cordial-based drinks, nowhere near as good. Rather better are lychee and *longan* drinks, made with diluted tinned juices and served with some of the fruit at the bottom. The usual fizzy **soft drinks** are available everywhere for around RM1.50 a can or carton, with the F&N and Yeo companies providing more unusual flavours. Sweetened soya milk in cartons or – much tastier – freshly made at stalls is another popular local choice, as is the refreshing, sweet *chin chow*, which looks like cola but is in fact made from a seaweed and comes with strands of seaweed jelly.

Tea (*teh*) and **coffee** (*kopi*) are as much national drinks as they are in the West. If ordered with milk, they'll come with a generous amount of the sweetened condensed variety or sometimes evaporated milk (only large hotels and smarter Western-style cafés have regular milk). If you don't have a sweet tooth, either ask for your drink *kurang manis* (literally "lacking in sweetness"), in which case less condensed milk will be added, or have it black (use the suffix "o", eg *kopi o* for black coffee); see our separate section for more on the intricacies of ordering drinks (see p.610).

Locals adore their tea or coffee **tarik**, literally "pulled", which in practice means frothing the drink by repeatedly pouring it out of a container in one hand to another container in the other hand, and back. Occasionally this can be quite an entertaining feat, the drink being poured from head height with scarcely a drop being spilled.

Alcohol

Alcohol is not generally hard to find in **Malaysia** and **Singapore**. Most big cities have a bar scene, though in Malaysian towns drinking is limited to non-Muslim eating places, drinks stalls at food courts (which usually have beer and perhaps stout) and Chinese-run bars – sometimes little more than tarted-up *kedai kopis*, the walls perhaps plastered with posters of Hong Kong showbiz poppets. However, in strongly Muslim areas, particularly Kelantan and Terengganu, only a small number of establishments, usually Chinese *kedai kopis* and stalls, will have alcohol. **Brunei** is officially dry (for more, see p.457).

Anchor and Tiger **beer** (lager) are locally produced and easily available, though you can also get Western and Thai beers as well as the Chinese Tsingtao and various **stouts**, including Guinness and the Singaporean ABC. Local **whisky** and **rum**

are cheap enough, too, though they're pretty rough and benefit from being mixed with coke. More upmarket restaurants and bars serve beer on draught, cocktails and (generally pricey) imported **wine**. In the longhouses of Sabah and Sarawak, you will probably be invited to sample *tuak*, a rice wine that can be as sickly as sweet sherry; it's about the same strength as beer.

Where bars exist in numbers, fierce competition ensures **happy hours** are a regular feature, bringing the beer price down to around RM10 a glass, though spirits still remain pricey. While some bars open from lunchtime till late, most tend to open from early evening until the small hours.

Health

No inoculations are required for visiting Malaysia, Singapore or Brunei, although the immigration authorities may require a yellow-fever vaccination certificate if you have transited an endemic area, normally Africa or South America, within the preceding six days.

It's a wise precaution to visit your doctor no less than two months before you leave to check that you are up to date with your polio, typhoid, tetanus and hepatitis inoculations. **Tap water** is drinkable throughout Malaysia, Singapore and Brunei, although in rural areas it's best to buy bottled water, which is widely available.

MEDICAL RESOURCES FOR TRAVELLERS

US AND CANADA

CDC Ⓦ www.cdc.gov travel. Official US government travel health site.

Canadian Society for International Health Ⓦ www.csih .org. Extensive list of travel health centres.

International Society for Travel Medicine Ⓦ www.istm .org. Includes a directory of travel health clinics, not just in North America.

AUSTRALIA, NEW ZEALAND AND SOUTH AFRICA

Travellers' Medical and Vaccination Centre Australia ☎ 1300 658 844, Ⓦ www.tmvc.com.au. Travel clinics in Australia, New Zealand and South Africa.

UK AND IRELAND

MASTA (Medical Advisory Service for Travellers Abroad) Ⓦ www.masta.org. MASTA has some fifty clinics around the UK and posts useful factsheets online.

Tropical Medical Bureau Ireland ☎ 1850 487 674, Ⓦ www .tmb.ie. A dozen or so clinics across Ireland.

Medical problems

Levels of hygiene and medical care in Malaysia, Singapore and Brunei are higher than in much of Southeast Asia; with any luck, the most serious thing you'll go down with is an upset stomach.

Heat problems

Travellers unused to tropical climates may suffer from sunburn and **dehydration**. The easiest way to avoid this is to restrict your exposure to the midday sun, use high-factor sun screens, wear sunglasses and a hat. You should also drink plenty of water and, if you do become dehydrated, keep up a regular intake of fluids. Rehydration preparations such as Dioralyte are handy; the DIY version is a handful of sugar with a good pinch of salt added to a litre of bottled water, which creates roughly the right mineral balance. **Heat stroke** is more serious and can require hospitalization: its onset is indicated by a high temperature, dry red skin and a fast pulse.

Stomach problems

The most common complaint is a stomach problem, which can range from a mild dose of diarrhoea to full-blown dysentery. The majority of stomach bugs may be unpleasant, but are unthreatening; however, if you notice blood or mucus in your stools, then you may have amoebic or bacillary dysentery, in which case you should seek medical help.

Stomach bugs are usually transmitted by contaminated food and water, so steer clear of raw vegetables and shellfish, always wash unpeeled fruit, and stick to freshly cooked foods, avoiding anything reheated. However careful you are, food that's spicy or just different can sometimes upset your system, in which case, try to stick to relatively bland dishes and avoid fried food.

Dengue fever and malaria

The main mosquito-borne disease to be aware of – and the chief reason to take measures to avoid mosquito bites (see below) – is **dengue fever**. The disease is caused by a virus spread by the *Aedes aegypti* mosquito (which has distinctive white marks on its legs) and there are periodic outbreaks, not just in rural areas but also in the major cities. Symptoms include severe headaches, pain in the bones (especially of the back), fever and often a fine, red rash over the body. There's no specific treatment, just plenty of rest, an adequate fluid intake and painkillers when required.

Although the risk of catching **malaria** is extremely low, consider protection against it if you think you might be staying in remote parts of Borneo for some time. Most doctors will advise taking antimalarial tablets which, though not completely effective in protecting against the disease, do considerably lessen the risk and can help reduce the symptoms should you develop the disease. Bear in mind you have to start taking the tablets before you arrive in a malaria zone, and continue taking them after you return – ask your doctor for the latest advice.

Altitude sickness

Altitude sickness (or acute mountain sickness) is a potentially life-threatening illness affecting people who ascend above around 3500m. Symptoms include dizziness, headache, shortness of breath, nausea; in severe cases it can lead to a swelling of the brain and lungs that can prove fatal. In Malaysia it's only likely to be relevant to those climbing **Mount Kinabalu** (4095m), and most people report only mild symptoms at this altitude. If you're affected, there's little you can do apart from descending to lower altitude, although certain prescription drugs may temporarily control the symptoms.

Cuts, bites and stings

Wearing protective clothing when swimming, snorkelling or diving can help avoid sunburn and protect against any sea stings. **Sea lice**, minute creatures that cause painful though harmless bites are the most common hazard; more dangerous are **jellyfish**, whose stings must be doused with vinegar to deactivate the poison before you seek medical help.

Coral can also cause nasty cuts and grazes; any wounds should be cleaned and kept as dry as possible until properly healed. The only way to avoid well-camouflaged sea urchins and stone fish is by not stepping on the seabed: even thick-soled shoes don't provide total protection against their long, sharp spines, which can be removed by softening the skin by holding it over a steaming pan of water.

As for **mosquitoes**, you can best avoid being bitten by covering up as much as is practical, and applying repellent to exposed flesh. Note that most repellents sold locally are based on **citronella**; if you want a repellent containing **DEET**, which some say is more effective, it's best to buy it at home. Rural or beachside accommodation often features **mosquito nets**, and some places also provide slow-burning **mosquito coils** which generate a little smoke that apparently deters the insects.

For many people, the ubiquitous **leech** – whose bite is not actually harmful or painful – is the most irritating aspect to jungle trekking. Whenever there's been rainfall, you can rely upon the leeches to come out. Always tuck your trousers into your socks and tie your bootlaces tight. The best anti-leech socks are made from calico and available in specialist stores. If you find the leeches are getting through, soak the outside of your socks and your boots in insect repellent (see also p.48).

Venomous **snakes** are not that common, and any that you might encounter will usually slink away. If you are unlucky enough to be bitten then remain still and call for an ambulance or get someone else to summon help. If it's one of your limbs that has been bitten, ideally a pressure bandage should also be applied to slow the spread of any venom present.

Pharmacies, clinics and hospitals

Medical services in Malaysia, Singapore and Brunei are excellent; staff almost everywhere speak English and use up-to-date treatments. Details of pharmacies and hospitals are in the "Directory" sections of the Guide for cities and major towns.

Pharmacies stock a wide range of medicines and health-related items, from contraceptives to contact lens solution; opening hours are the same as for other shops. Pharmacists can recommend products for skin complaints or simple stomach problems, though it always pays to get a proper diagnosis.

Private **clinics** can be found even in small towns – your hotel or the local tourist office will be able to recommend a doctor. In Malaysia a consultation costs around RM30, not including the cost of any prescribed medication; keep the receipts for insurance-claim purposes. Finally, the emergency department of each town's general hospital will see foreigners for a small fee, though obviously costs rise rapidly if continued treatment or overnight stays are necessary.

The media

Both Malaysia and Singapore boast plenty of newspapers, TV channels and radio stations serving up lively reportage of events, sports and entertainment, though don't expect to come across hard-hitting or healthily sceptical coverage of domestic politics. The major media organizations in each country are
at least partly owned by the government in question; in Singapore, most newspapers have actually been herded into a conglomerate in which the state has a major stake.

Furthermore, the media are kept on their toes by a legal requirement that they must periodically renew their licence to publish. Thus the *Sarawak Tribune* was suspended indefinitely in 2006 after it reproduced the controversial Danish cartoons of the Prophet Muhammad; only in 2010 did it resume publication as the *New Sarawak Tribune*.

Given these circumstances, it's no surprise that in the 2011/12 Press Freedom Index, issued by the pressure group Reporters Without Borders, Malaysia and Singapore were far down the rankings at no. 122 and no. 135 respectively – below much poorer nations not exactly noted for being exemplars of free speech, such as Mongolia and Lesotho. Brunei, which was at no. 142, has a much less well-developed media sector than Malaysia or Singapore, and its newspapers are packed with anodyne stories about the latest deeds of the sultan and other royals.

Foreign newspapers and magazines are sold in the main cities, and international TV channels are available via satellite and cable. That said, issues of foreign magazines containing pieces that displease the authorities have occasionally been banned, while Singapore's leaders have a long history of winning defamation suits against foreign publications in the island's courts.

If this all seems an unremittingly bleak picture, it should be said that coverage of Malaysia's opposition parties has increased since they took power in several states in the 2008 general election. Furthermore, the advent of **independent news websites** and **blogs** has been a breath of fresh air in both Malaysia and Singapore. Elsewhere in cyberspace, it's possible to turn up various **YouTube** clips of discussion forums and interviews with activists, offering an alternative take on local issues.

Newspapers, magazines and online news

Both Malaysia and Singapore have English, Malay, Chinese and Tamil newspapers, while Brunei's papers appear in English and Malay. Though Malaysia's national dailies are available in towns in east Malaysia, locally published English-language papers such as the *Borneo Post* in Sarawak (Ⓦtheborneopost.com) and the *Daily Express* in Sabah (Ⓦdailyexpress .com.my) are more popular there.

MALAYSIA

Aliran Monthly Ⓦ www.aliran.com. Campaigning magazine with an avowed pro-human-rights stance.

Malaysia Insider Ⓦ www.themalaysiainsider.com. Considered more moderate than some of its online counterparts, the *Insider* provides intelligent news and commentary in English and Malay.

Malaysia Today Ⓦ www.malaysia-today.net. This news website and blog was thrust into the international spotlight after the man behind it, Raja Petra Kamarudin, was interned under Malaysia's Internal Security Act for two months in 2008.

Malaysiakini Ⓦ www.malaysiakini.com. Invigorating reportage and opinion with an anti-establishment slant.

New Straits Times Ⓦ www.nst.com.my. Closely linked to the UMNO party, this offshoot of Singapore's *Straits Times* was created after the island separated from the Federation. A tabloid, it offers a broad range of news, sports and arts coverage.

Sarawak Report Ⓦ www.sarawakreport.org. Not a Malaysian site – it's run out of London – but worth a look for its hard-hitting coverage of issues such as logging, native peoples' rights and the probity of Sarawak's government.

The Star Ⓦ www.thestar.com.my. Founded by the MCA party, *The Star* is Malaysia's best-selling English daily and has a separate Sarawak edition. Ironically, its Insight Down South column is more probing of Singapore affairs than most stuff in the island state's own papers.

SINGAPORE

The Online Citizen Ⓦ theonlinecitizen.com. An alternative and rather less sanguine view of Singapore affairs than you find in the island's mainstream media.

Straits Times Ⓦ www.straitstimes.com. This venerable broadsheet was founded in 1845, though sadly its pedigree isn't matched by the candour of its journalism; not bad on foreign news, however.

Today Ⓦ www.todayonline.com. A free paper from the state-owned broadcaster Mediacorp, *Today* is generally less bland than the *Straits Times* and carries worthwhile arts reviews at the weekend.

TR Emeritus Ⓦ tremeritus.com. The *Temasek Review*, as was, pioneered independent reporting of the island's affairs

BRUNEI

Brunei Times Ⓦ www.bt.com.bn. Pleasant enough but hardly the most challenging of reads.

Television and radio

TV and radio in Malaysia, Singapore and Brunei are dominated by the state-owned broadcasters **RTM**, **Mediacorp** and **RTB** respectively, putting out programmes in several languages. Terrestrial **television** features an unexceptional mix of news, documentaries and dramas made locally and abroad, cookery and talk shows, Islamic discussions and so forth; **radio** is even less original and tends to be dominated by pop music and talk shows. Various foreign TV channels, including CNN, BBC World,

National Geographic, ESPN Sports and Al Jazeera (which has its East Asian base in KL), are available on cable and satellite in Malaysia, and on cable in Singapore (where ownership of satellite dishes is banned). Note that Malaysian broadcasts are easily picked up in Singapore, and Singapore broadcasts in southern Johor.

MALAYSIA

Cats FM Ⓦ www.catsfm.my. Kuching-based FM station offering music plus Sarawakian news; see the website for frequencies around the state.

RTM1 & RTM2 Ⓦ www.rtm.gov.my. Malaysia's staple state-owned TV channels, with some programming in English, Chinese and Tamil. News in English is broadcast on RTM2 at 8pm daily.

Traxxfm Ⓦ www.traxxfm.net. Established RTM station with a mix of news and music in English, available on various frequencies around the Peninsula.

TV3 Ⓦ www.tv3.com.my. English and Malay news, drama and documentaries, plus some Chinese programmes. Along with the youth-oriented channels NTV7, 8TV and TV9, it's part of the same conglomerate as the *New Straits Times*.

XFresh Ⓦ www.xfresh.com. A good station for home-grown pop and rock music in Malay and English, though the patter is in Malay only. Audible in cities nationwide.

SINGAPORE

BBC World Service Ⓦ www.bbcworldservice.com. 88.9FM, 24hr.

Channel News Asia Ⓦ www.channelnewsasia.com. Mediacorp's CNN-like diet of rolling TV news, via cable.

Channel 5 Ⓦ 5.mediacorptv.sg. The main terrestrial channel for English programming, with plenty of imported shows.

Mediacorp Radio Ⓦ www.mediacorpradio.sg. Several English-language radio stations, including the speech-based 938 Live (93.8FM) and Symphony (92.4FM) for classical music.

BRUNEI

Radio and Television Brunei (RTB) Ⓦ www.rtb.gov.bn. Locally made dramas, religious programmes and news, interspersed with dramas and soaps from as far afield as Korea and Venezuela.

Festivals

With so many ethnic groups and religions represented in Malaysia, Singapore and Brunei, you'll be unlucky if your trip doesn't coincide with some sort of festival. Religious celebrations range from exuberant family-oriented pageants to blood-curdlingly gory displays of devotion. Chinese religious festivals are the best times to catch free performances of Chinese opera, or wayang, featuring

crashing cymbals, clanging gongs and stylized singing. Secular events might comprise a parade with a cast of thousands, or just a local market with a few cultural demonstrations laid on.

Bear in mind that the major festival periods may play havoc with even the best-planned travel itineraries, and that some festivals are also public holidays (see p.58).

A festival and events calendar

The dates of many festivals change annually according to the lunar calendar. The Islamic calendar in particular shifts forward relative to the Gregorian calendar by about ten days each year, so that, for example, a Muslim festival that happens in mid-April one year will be nearer the start of April the next. We've listed rough timings; actual dates can vary by a day or two in practice depending on the sighting of the new moon.

JANUARY & FEBRUARY

Ponggal (mid-Jan) A Tamil harvest and New Year festival held at the start of the Tamil month of Thai. Ponggal translates as "overflow", and the festival is celebrated by boiling sugar, rice and milk together in a new claypot over a wood fire till the mixture spills over, symbolizing plenty.

Thaipusam (late Jan/early Feb) Entranced Hindu penitents carry elaborate steel arches (*kavadi*), attached to their skin by hooks and skewers, to honour Lord Subramaniam. The biggest processions are at Kuala Lumpur's Batu Caves and from Singapore's Sri Srinivasa Perumal Temple to the Chettiar Hindu Temple.

Chinese New Year (late Jan/early to mid-Feb) At which Chinese communities settle debts, visit friends and relatives and give children red envelopes (*hong bao/ang pao*) containing money; Chinese operas and lion- and dragon-dance troupes perform in the streets, while markets sell sausages and waxed ducks, pussy willow, chrysanthemums and mandarin oranges. Singapore and the major towns of west-coast Malaysia see Chingay parades, featuring stilt-walkers, lion dancers and floats.

Chap Goh Mei (Feb) The fifteenth and climactic night of the Chinese New Year period (known as Guan Hsiao Chieh in Sarawak), and a time for more feasting and firecrackers; women who throw an orange into the sea at this time are supposed to be granted a good husband.

Brunei National Day (Feb 23) The sultan and tens of thousands of Bruneians watch parades and fireworks at the Sultan Hassanal Bolkiah National Stadium, just outside Bandar Seri Begawan.

MARCH–MAY

Easter (March/April) Candlelit processions are held on Good Friday at churches such as St Peter's in Melaka and St Joseph's in Singapore.

Qing Ming (April) Ancestral graves are cleaned and restored, and offerings made by Chinese families at the beginning of the third lunar month, signifying the start of spring and a new farming year.

Vesak Day (May) Saffron-robed monks chant prayers at packed Buddhist temples, and devotees release caged birds to commemorate the Buddha's birth, enlightenment and attainment of Nirvana.

Sabah Fest (late May) A week of events in Kota Kinabalu, offering a chance to experience Sabah's food, handicrafts, dance and music; right at the end comes Rumah Terbuka Malaysia Tadau Kaamatan, a harvest festival in Kota Kinabalu.

JUNE–AUGUST

Yang di-Pertuan Agong's Birthday (June) Festivities in KL to celebrate the birthday of Malaysia's king, elected every five years by the country's nine sultans or rajahs from among their number.

Gawai Dayak (June) Sarawak's people, especially the Iban and Bidayuh celebrate the end of rice harvesting with extravagant longhouse feasts. Aim to be in a longhouse on the Rejang or Batang Ai rivers, or around Bau.

Feast of St Peter (June 24) Melaka's Eurasian community decorate their boats to honour the patron saint of fishermen.

Dragon Boat Festival (June/July) Rowing boats, bearing a dragon's head and tail, race in Penang, Melaka, Singapore and Kota Kinabalu, to commemorate a Chinese scholar who drowned himself in protest against political corruption.

Sultan of Brunei's Birthday (July 15) Starting with a speech by the sultan on the padang, celebrations continue for two weeks with parades, lantern processions, traditional sports competitions and fireworks.

Sarawak Extravaganza (Aug) Kuching hosts a month of arts and crafts shows, street parades, food fairs and traditional games, all celebrating the culture of Sarawak.

Singapore National Day (Aug 9) Singapore celebrates its independence with a huge show featuring military parades and fireworks.

Festival of the Hungry Ghosts (late Aug) Held to appease the souls of the dead released from purgatory during the seventh lunar month. Chinese street operas are staged, and joss sticks, red candles and paper money are burnt outside Chinese homes.

Ramadan (starts second week of July in 2013) Muslims spend the ninth month of the Islamic calendar fasting in the daytime, and breaking their fasts nightly with delicious Malay sweetmeats served at stalls outside mosques.

Hari Raya Puasa/Aidilfitri (falls in July or August) Muslims celebrate the end of Ramadan by feasting, and visiting family and friends; this is the only time the region's royal palaces are open to the public.

Malaysia National Day (Aug 31) Parades in KL's Merdeka Square and other cities mark the formation of the state of Malaysia.

SEPTEMBER–DECEMBER

Moon Cake Festival (Sept) Also known as the Mid-Autumn Festival, this is when Chinese people eat and exchange moon cakes, made from sesame and lotus seeds and sometimes stuffed with a duck egg. Essentially a harvest festival.

Navarathri (Sept–Oct) Hindu temples devote nine nights to classical dance and music in honour of the consorts of the Hindu gods, Shiva, Vishnu and Brahman.

Thimithi (Oct/Nov) Hindu firewalking ceremony in which devotees prove the strength of their faith by running across a pit of hot coals; best seen at the Sri Mariamman Temple in Singapore.

Deepavali (Oct/Nov) Also known as Diwali, this Hindu festival celebrates the victory of Light over Dark: oil lamps are lit outside homes to attract Lakshmi, the goddess of prosperity, and prayers are offered at all temples.

Hari Raya Haji/Aidiladha (late Oct) Muslims gather at mosques to honour those who have completed the hajj, or pilgrimage to Mecca; goats are sacrificed and their meat given to the needy.

Christmas (Dec 25) Shopping centres in major cities compete to create the most spectacular Christmas decorations.

Sports and outdoor activities

With some of the world's oldest tropical rainforest and countless beaches and islands, trekking, snorkelling and scuba diving are common pursuits in Malaysia. The more established resorts on the islands of Penang, Langkawi and Tioman also offer jet skiing and paragliding, while the exposed, windy bay at Cherating, the budget travellers' centre on the east coast, is a hot spot for windsurfers.

If you intend to take up any of the pursuits below, check that they are covered by your insurance policy.

Snorkelling, diving and windsurfing

The crystal-clear waters and abundant tropical fish and coral of Malaysia make snorkelling and diving a must for any underwater enthusiast. This is particularly true of Sabah's **Sipidan Island Marine Reserve** and the Peninsula's east coast, with islands like the **Perhentians**, **Redang**, **Kapas** and **Tioman**.

Dive shops, for example in Sabah's Kota Kinabalu and Sarawak's Miri, offer all-inclusive, internationally recognized certification courses, ranging from a beginner's open-water course (around RM1300), right through to the dive-master certificate (RM2200). If you're already qualified, expect to pay RM180 per day for dive trips including gear rental.

Most beachside guesthouses rent **snorkelling** equipment for around RM20 per day. Some popular **snorkelling** areas mark out lanes for motorboats with buoy lines – stay on the correct side of the line to avoid a nasty accident. If you're not sure where it's safe to swim or snorkel, always seek local advice. Never touch or walk on coral as this will cause irreparable damage – besides which, you risk treading on the armour-piercing spines of sea urchins, or a painful encounter with fire coral.

Windsurfing has yet to take off in all but the most expensive resorts in Malaysia, with the notable exception of Cherating. Its large, open bay and shallow waters provide near-perfect conditions during the northeast monsoon season.

Whitewater rafting

Whitewater rafting has become a popular activity on Sabah's **Sungai Padas**, a grade 3 river which, at its northern end, runs through the spectacular Padas Gorge (see p.400). Opportunities for rafting in **Peninsular Malaysia** tend to be in out-of-the-way spots in the interior; it's best to go with an operator such as Nomad Adventure (Ⓦ nomadadventure .com) or Khersonese Expedition (Ⓦ thepaddlerz .com). Expect a day's rafting to cost around RM250, including equipment.

Trekking

The majority of treks in Malaysia require forethought and preparation. As well as the fierce

---

COMBATING LEECHES

Leeches are gruesome but pretty harmless creatures that almost all hikers will encounter. A tiny, muscular tube with teeth at one end, they lie dormant in rainforest leaf litter until, activated by your footfalls and body heat, they latch onto your boot, then climb until they find a way through socks and trousers and onto your skin. Their bites (about the size of a pinhead) are completely painless, but they bleed a lot and sometimes itch as they heal.

Keeping leeches off isn't easy; they can get through all but the closest-mesh fabrics. Tights work (but get very hot), though some guides recommend simply wearing open shoes and shorts, so that you can see them – an approach that requires an advanced jungle mentality.

The quickest way to **remove** a leech is to repeatedly flick its head end with your fingernail. Otherwise salt, tiger balm or tobacco juice, rubbed onto the leech, will cause them to let go rapidly.

CHECKLIST OF CAMPING AND TREKKING EQUIPMENT

As camping and trekking are not especially popular with Malaysians, you need to bring your own gear if possible – especially core items like tents and sleeping bags – or buy the locally made version available at markets and general product stores. These might not look good or even last long, but at least won't cost a fortune.

Hiking boots are especially hard to find, though one-piece rubber slip-on shoes (*kasut gatah*) costing just RM10 are sold everywhere (up to around size 40). Many national park guides use them as they dry out instantly and give good grip on forest floors, but they're not suitable for multi-day trekking in difficult terrain.

There are small (and very expensive) "proper" outdoor gear stores in KL, Kota Bharu and elsewhere; you might also be able to rent some of what you'll need on site, especially at Taman Negara, or have it supplied as part of a hiking package.

ESSENTIALS

Backpack
Sleeping bag
Tent (if sleeping out)
Mosquito net
Water bottle
Water purification tablets
Toiletries and toilet paper
Torch (and/or head torch)
Sewing kit
Pocket knife
Sunglasses (UV protective)
Sun block and lip balm

Insect repellent
Compass
Breathable shirts/T-shirts
Lightweight, quick-drying trousers
Rainproof coat or poncho
Cotton hat with brim
Fleece jacket
Trekking boots
Sandals (for wading through streams)
Cotton and woollen socks
Basic first-aid kit

OTHER USEFUL ITEMS

Heavy-duty refuse bag (to rainproof your pack)
Emergency snack food
Spare bootlaces

Small towel
Insulation mat
Binoculars
Leech socks

---

sun, the tropical climate can unleash torrential rain without warning, which rapidly affects the condition of trails or the height of a river – what started out as a ten-hour trip can end up taking twice as long. That said, the time of year is not a hugely significant factor when planning a trek. Although in the rainy season (Nov–Feb) trails can be slow going (or even closed for safety reasons), conditions are less humid then, and the parks and adventure tours are not oversubscribed.

Treks in national parks almost always require that you go in a group with a **guide**; solo travellers can usually join a group once there. Costs and conditions vary between parks; each park account in the Guide contains details, while tour operators in Kuala Lumpur, Kuching, Miri and Kota Kinabalu (listed throughout) can also furnish information on conditions and options in the parks.

For inexperienced trekkers, **Taman Negara** is probably the best place to start, boasting the greatest range of walks, many of which can be done without a guide, while **Bako National Park** in

southwest Sarawak offers fairly easy, day-long hikes. For the more experienced, other parks in Sarawak, especially **Gunung Mulu**, should offer sufficient challenges for most tastes, while Sabah's **Maliau Basin** is at the very demanding end of the scale. The largely inaccessible Endau-Rompin Park in the south of Peninsular Malaysia is for serious expeditions only. **Mount Kinabalu Park** in Sabah is in a class of its own, the hike to the top of the mountain a demanding but highly rewarding combination of trekking and climbing.

Culture and etiquette

Despite the obvious openness to influences from around the globe, and the urbanity of Kuala Lumpur, Singapore, Penang and Kuching, society in Malaysia, Singapore and Brunei remains fairly

conservative and conformist. Behaviour that departs from established cultural and behavioural norms – basically, anything that draws attention to the individuals concerned – is avoided.

Though allowances are made for foreigners, until you acquire some familiarity with where the limits lie, it's best to err on the side of caution. Get the balance right and you'll find locals helpful and welcoming, while respectful of your need for some privacy.

Dress

For both men and women, exposing lots of bare flesh is generally a no-no, and the degree to which you should **cover up** can seem surprisingly prim. Islamic tradition suffuses the dress code for locals, Muslim or otherwise, and dictates that both men and women should keep torsos covered; shirt sleeves, if short, should come down to the elbow (for women, long-sleeved tops are preferable), while shorts or skirts should extend down to the knee (long trousers are ideal). Figure-hugging clothes are often frowned upon, particularly for women.

Dress codes are more liberal in most cities (Singapore and Kota Kinabalu in particular), on the beach, and when pursuing sporting activities, but it's surprising how often the minimum standards mentioned above are complied with. Also, remember that in Muslim tradition, the soles of shoes are considered unclean, having been in contact with the dirt of the street. Thus before entering any home (Muslim or otherwise), it's almost universal practice to remove footwear at the threshold or before stepping onto any carpeted or matted area.

Discretion and body language

Two things to avoid in this moderately conservative, Muslim region are public shows of affection (holding hands is OK, kissing is not) and drinking alcohol outside designated bars or clubs – even in resort areas frequented by foreigners. In a situation where you need to make a **complaint**, the most effective approach is not to raise your voice but to go out of your way to be reasonable while stating your case.

As for body language, note that **touching someone's head**, be they Muslim or otherwise, must be avoided, as the head is considered sacred in Eastern culture. Handshakes are fairly commonplace when meeting someone; Muslims often follow this by touching the palm of the right hand to their own chest. Some Muslims may be reluctant to shake hands with the opposite sex; however, in this case a smile, nod and that same right-hand-palm gesture will suffice. Muslims and Indians also avoid using their left hand for human contact or eating, while polite Chinese wait staff or shop owners might hand over your change with both hands.

Visiting places of worship

It's common to see various temples and mosques happily existing side by side, each providing a social as well as a religious focal point for the corresponding community. Architectural traditions mean that the Chinese and Indian temples, built out of brick, have long outlasted the timber Malay mosque, and some are among the oldest structures you're likely to see in the region. Many such buildings are worth a look around, though only at the largest temples might you get a little tour, courtesy of the caretaker.

When **visiting mosques**, men should wear long trousers and a shirt or top with sleeves coming down to the elbows (long sleeves are even better); women will also have to don a long cloak and headdress, which is provided by most mosques. You'll be required to remove your shoes

---

THE STATUS OF MALAY WOMEN

Malay women are among the most emancipated in the Islamic world. They often attain prominent roles in business, academia and other areas of public life, and lack neither confidence nor social skills, as a visit to any Malay-run shop, hotel or market stall will attest. Malay women are also very much the lynchpin of the family, and husbands often give way to their wives in domestic matters.

Although the more conservative tide running through the Islamic world has had relatively little impact on this situation, many Malay women now wear a *tudung* (**headscarf**). Sometimes this merely indicates an acceptance of the trappings of the religion or the desire to please parents – it's not unusual to see Malay women at a club partying away in the unlikely combination of headscarf, skimpy T-shirt and tight jeans.

before entering. No non-Muslim is allowed to enter a mosque during prayer time or go into the prayer hall at any time, although it's possible to stand just outside and look in.

Most Chinese and Hindu temples are open from early morning to early evening; devotees go in when they like, to make offerings or to pray. Hindu temples also expect visitors to remove shoes.

Women travellers

Women who respect local customs and exercise common sense should have few problems travelling alone or with other women.

Some Western women have been known to find the atmosphere in largely Muslim areas, such as Kelantan or Terengganu, off-putting. Arriving there from Thailand or from a more cosmopolitan part of Malaysia, some women still find themselves being stared at or subjected to wolf-whistles or lewd gestures, despite observing local dress codes. This is all the more annoying if you spot local Chinese women wandering around in skimpy tops with no one batting an eyelid. Though it's no consolation, it's worth noting that the ground rules are different for locals; the Malay, Chinese and Indian communities, having lived together for generations, have an unspoken understanding as to how the respective communities can behave in public.

Shopping

Southeast Asia can offer bargain shopping, with electrical equipment, cameras and fabrics all selling at competitive prices. What's more, the region's ethnic diversity means you'll be spoiled for choice when it comes to souvenirs and handicrafts.

One point to be aware of is that a lot of the crafts on sale in Malaysia are in fact made elsewhere in the region, particularly in Indonesia. Worthwhile buys, especially domestically made ones, are highlighted throughout the Guide. Also be aware that prices in small outlets such as family-run shops tend to be negotiable, and bargaining is expected. Asking for the "best price" is always a good opening gambit; from there, it's a question of technique, though be realistic – shopkeepers will soon lose interest if you offer an unreasonably low price. If you buy any electrical goods, it can be worth ensuring you get an international guarantee, endorsed by the shop.

Fabrics

The art of producing **batik** cloth originated in Indonesia, but today batik is available across Southeast Asia and supports a thriving industry in Malaysia. It's made by applying hot wax to a piece of cloth with either a pen or a copper stamp; when the cloth is dyed, the wax resists the dye and a pattern appears, a process that can be repeated many times to build up colours. Note that some vendors try to pass off printed cloth as batik. Make sure the brightness of the pattern is equal on both sides – if it's obviously lighter on one side, it is likely the cloth is printed.

Batik is used to create shirts, skirts, bags and hats, as well as traditional **sarongs**. The exquisite gold-threaded brocade known as **songket**, used to make sarongs, headscarves and the like, is a big step up in price from batik; RM200 for a sarong-length of cloth is not uncommon, and prices soar for the finest pieces.

Unique to Sarawak is **pua kumbu** (in Iban, "blanket"), a textile whose complex designs are created using the *ikat* method of weaving (see p.327). The cloth is sold in longhouses as well as in some souvenir outlets.

Woodcarving

Woodcarving skills, once employed to decorate the palaces and public buildings of the early sultans, are today used to make less exotic articles such as mirror frames. However, it's still possible to see statues and masks created by the Orang Asli. As animists, Orang Asli artists draw upon the natural world – animals, trees, fish, as well as more abstract elements like fire and water – for their imagery. Of particular interest are the carvings of the Mah Meri of Selangor, which are improvisations on the theme of *moyang*, literally "ancestor", the generic name for all spirit images. In Borneo, look out for tribal face masks and rectangular shields adorned with intricate motifs. It's also possible to buy hardwood blowpipes, though these are drilled rather than carved.

Metalwork

Of the wealth of metalwork on offer, **silverware** from Kelantan is among the finest and most intricately designed; it's commonly used to make earrings, brooches and pendants, as well as more substantial pieces. Selangor is known for its **pewter** – a blend of tin, antimony and copper, which can result in some elegant vases, tankards and ornaments.

DUTY-FREE GOODS

Malaysia has no duty on cameras, watches, cosmetics, perfumes or cigarettes. Labuan, Langkawi and Tioman are duty-free islands, which in practice means that goods there (including alcohol) can be a third cheaper than on the Malaysian mainland, though it's not as though a particularly impressive range of products is on sale. Duty-free products in Singapore include electronic and electrical goods, cosmetics, cameras, clocks, watches, jewellery, precious stones and metals.

Other souvenirs

Rattan, cane, bamboo and *mengkuang* (pandanus) are traditionally used to make baskets, bird cages, mats, hats and shoulder bags. The best items make surprisingly impressive accessories, and in Borneo it's possible to find baskets and bags bearing traditional motifs, too. Another unusual raw material is breadfruit bark; in Sarawak it's pressed to produce a "cloth" that makes excellent hats and jackets, as well as a canvas for paintings.

Malay pastimes throw up some interesting purchases: leather *wayang kulit* (shadow play) puppets, portraying characters from Hindu legend, are attractive and light to carry; equally colourful but impractical if you have to carry them around are Malay kites, which can be a couple of metres long.

Pottery, though sometimes mass-produced, can be a worthwhile decorative acquisition. Examples include the Malay *labu*, a gourd-like slender-necked water jug (it's made in, among other places, Perak) and Sarawak pots and jars bearing tribal motifs. Finally, it's possible to buy some fine examples of beadwork – from pricey Peranakan beaded slippers to Kelabit jackets from the northern highlands of Sarawak.

Travel essentials

Climate

The climate in Malaysia, Singapore and Brunei remains remarkably consistent throughout the year (see box opposite), with typical daytime temperatures of around 30°. However, the northeast monsoon brings torrential rains and heavy seas between September and February, concentrating its attentions on the west coast of the Peninsula in September and October, and on the east coast after that.

Costs

Anyone entering Malaysia from Thailand will find that costs are slightly higher – both food and accommodation are more expensive – whereas travellers arriving from Indonesia will find prices a little lower overall. Travelling in a group naturally helps keep costs down. The region affords some savings for senior citizens, and an ISIC student card might occasionally pay dividends.

Note that **bargaining** is routine throughout Malaysia and Singapore when buying stuff in markets or small shops, though you don't haggle for meals or accommodation.

Malaysia

In **Peninsular Malaysia** you can scrape by on £12/US$20/RM60 per day staying in dorms, eating at hawker stalls and getting around by bus. Double that and you'll be able to exist in relative comfort without thinking too hard about occasionally treating yourself. Over in **east Malaysia**, where accommodation and tours tend to cost a little more, the minimum daily outlay is more like £16/US$25/RM80.

Singapore and Brunei

Costs in **Singapore** are much steeper than in Malaysia, with a minimum budget of around £25/US$40/S$50 per day. Upgrading your lodgings to a private room in a guesthouse, eating one daily meal in a cheap restaurant, and having a beer or two could require £40/US$62/S$80 per day.

Costs in **Brunei** are on a par with Singapore if you manage to take advantage of the capital's limited budget accommodation, or stay in one of the cheaper mid-range hotels and don't do a lot of sight-seeing. Otherwise, costs can spiral as you'll have to rely on taxis or package trips to reach outlying places of interest, notably the Ulu Temburong National Park.

Crime and personal safety

If you lose something in Malaysia, Singapore or Brunei, you're more likely to have someone run after you with it than run away. Nevertheless, don't become complacent: pickpockets and **snatch-thieves** frequent Malaysia's more touristed cities, and theft from dormitories by other tourists is fairly common. If you have to report a crime, be sure to get a copy of the police report for insurance purposes.

AVERAGE DAILY TEMPERATURES AND RAINFALL

CAMERON HIGHLANDS

	Jan	Feb	Mar	Apr	May	Jun	Jul	Aug	Sep	Oct	Nov	Dec
Max/min °C	21/14	22/14	23/14	23/15	23/15	23/15	22/14	22/15	22/15	22/15	22/15	21/15
Rain (mm)	120	111	198	277	273	137	165	172	241	334	305	202

KOTA BHARU

	Jan	Feb	Mar	Apr	May	Jun	Jul	Aug	Sep	Oct	Nov	Dec
Max/min °C	29/22	30/23	31/23	32/24	33/24	32/24	32/23	32/23	32/23	31/23	29/23	29/23
Rain (mm)	163	60	99	81	114	132	157	168	195	286	651	603

KOTA KINABALU

	Jan	Feb	Mar	Apr	May	Jun	Jul	Aug	Sep	Oct	Nov	Dec
Max/min °C	30/23	30/23	31/23	32/24	32/24	31/24	31/24	31/24	31/23	31/23	31/23	31/23
Rain (mm)	153	63	71	124	218	311	277	256	314	334	296	241

KUALA LUMPUR

	Jan	Feb	Mar	Apr	May	Jun	Jul	Aug	Sep	Oct	Nov	Dec
Max/min °C	32/22	33/22	33/23	33/23	33/23	32/23	32/23	32/23	32/23	32/23	31/23	31/23
Rain (mm)	159	154	223	276	182	119	120	133	173	258	263	223

KUCHING

	Jan	Feb	Mar	Apr	May	Jun	Jul	Aug	Sep	Oct	Nov	Dec
Max/min °C	30/23	30/23	31/23	32/23	33/23	33/23	32/23	33/23	32/23	32/23	31/23	31/23
Rain (mm)	683	522	339	286	253	199	199	211	271	326	343	465

PENANG

	Jan	Feb	Mar	Apr	May	Jun	Jul	Aug	Sep	Oct	Nov	Dec
Max/min °C	32/23	32/23	32/24	32/24	31/24	31/24	31/23	31/23	31/23	31/23	31/23	31/23
Rain (mm)	70	93	141	214	240	170	208	235	341	380	246	107

SINGAPORE

	Jan	Feb	Mar	Apr	May	Jun	Jul	Aug	Sep	Oct	Nov	Dec
Max/min °C	32/23	32/23	32/24	32/24	31/24	31/24	31/23	31/23	31/23	31/23	31/23	31/23
Rain (mm)	70	93	141	214	240	170	208	235	341	380	246	107

Sensible **precautions** include carrying your passport and other valuables in a concealed money belt, and using the safety deposit box provided by many guesthouses and hotels. Take a photocopy of the relevant pages of your passport, too, in case it's lost or stolen. If you use travellers' cheques, keep a separate record of the serial numbers, together with a note of which ones you've cashed.

It's worth repeating here that it's very unwise to have anything to do with illegal drugs of any description in Malaysia, Singapore and Brunei (see p.54).

Malaysia

To report a crime in Malaysia, head for the nearest police station, where someone will invariably speak English. In many major tourist spots, specific tourist police stations are geared up to problems faced by foreign travellers.

Restrictions on contact between people of the opposite sex (such as the offence of *khalwat*, or "close proximity") and eating in public during daylight hours in the Ramadan month apply to Muslims only.

Singapore

Singapore is known locally as a "fine city". Substantial **fines** punish misdemeanours like littering, jaywalking – defined as crossing a main road within 50m of a designated pedestrian crossing – and so forth, though these penalties are seldom enforced as the populace has become compliant over the years. Bear in mind that **chewing gum** is outlawed in Singapore, on the grounds that used gum can foul the streets.

EMERGENCY NUMBERS

MALAYSIA
Police/Ambulance ☎ 999
Fire Brigade ☎ 994

SINGAPORE
Police ☎ 999
Fire Brigade/Ambulance ☎ 995

BRUNEI
Police ☎ 993
Ambulance ☎ 991
Fire Brigade ☎ 995

Singapore's police, who wear dark-blue uniforms, keep a fairly low profile, but are polite and helpful when approached (see p.561).

Electricity

Mains voltage in Malaysia, Singapore and Brunei is **230 volts**, so any equipment using 110 volts will need a converter. The plugs in all three countries have three square prongs like British ones.

Entry requirements

Nationals of the UK, Ireland, US, Canada, Australia, New Zealand and South Africa do not need **visas** in advance to stay in Malaysia, Singapore or Brunei, and it's easy to extend your permission to stay. That said, check with the relevant embassy or consulate, as the rules on visas are complex and subject to change. Ensure that your passport is valid for at least six months from the date of your trip, and has several blank pages for entry stamps.

Malaysia

Upon arrival in Malaysia, citizens of Australia, Canada, the UK, Ireland, US, New Zealand and South Africa receive a passport stamp entitling them to a **90-day stay**. Visitors who enter via Sarawak, however, receive a 30-day stamp. Visa requirements for various nationalities are listed on ⓦ malaysia.visahq.com.

It's straightforward to extend your permit through the Immigration Department, who have offices (listed in the Guide) in Kuala Lumpur and major towns. Visitors from the above countries can also cross into Singapore or Thailand and back to be granted a fresh Malaysia entry stamp.

Tourists travelling from the Peninsula to east Malaysia (Sarawak and Sabah) must be cleared again by immigration; visitors to Sabah can remain as long as their original entry stamp is valid, but arriving in Sarawak from whichever territory generates a new 30-day stamp, which can be easily renewed.

When you arrive, you will normally be given a lengthy landing card to complete; hang onto the small **departure portion** of the card for when you leave Malaysia.

EMBASSIES AND CONSULATES

Australia 7 Perth Ave, Yarralumla, Canberra, ACT 6000 ☎ 02 6120 0600, ⓦ malaysia.org.au.
Brunei No. 61, Simpang 336, Kg Sungai Akar, Jalan Kebangsaan, P.O. Box 2826, Bandar Seri Begawan ☎ 02 381095.
Canada 60 Boteler St, Ottawa, ON K1N 8Y7 ☎ 613 241 5182.
Indonesia Jalan H.R. Rasuna Said, Kav. X/6, No. 1–3 Kuningan, Jakarta Selatan 12950 ☎ 021 5224947.
Ireland Shelbourne House, Level 3A–5A, Ballsbridge, Dublin 4 ☎ 01 667 7280.
New Zealand 10 Washington Ave, Brooklyn, Wellington ☎ 04 385 2439.
Singapore 301 Jervois Rd ☎ 6325 0111.
South Africa 1007 Schoeman St, Arcadia, Pretoria 0083 ☎ 012 342 5990.
Thailand 35 South Sathorn Rd, Bangkok 10120 ☎ 02 629 6800.
UK 45 Belgrave Square, London SW1X 8QT ☎ 020 7235 8033, ⓦ malaysia.embassyhomepage.com.
US 3516 International Court, NW Washington, DC 20008 ☎ 202 572 9700.

Singapore

Upon arrival in Singapore, citizens of the UK, Ireland and the US get a 90-day stamp, while those of Canada, Australia, New Zealand and South Africa are

DRUGS: A WARNING

In Malaysia, Singapore and Brunei, the possession of **illegal drugs** – hard or soft – carries a hefty prison sentence or even the death penalty. If you are arrested for drugs offences you can expect no mercy from the authorities and little help from your consular representatives. The simple advice, therefore, is not to have anything to do with drugs in any of these countries. Never agree to carry anything through customs for a third party.

given 30 days; details can be found at Ⓦ singapore .visahq.com. To extend your stay beyond these limits, take a bus up to Johor Bahru just inside Malaysia, then return to Singapore, whereupon you're given a new entry stamp.

EMBASSIES AND CONSULATES

Australia 17 Forster Crescent, Yarralumla, Canberra, ACT 2600 Ⓣ 02 6271 0700, Ⓦ mfa.gov.sg/canberra.

Indonesia Block X/4 Kav No. 2, Jalan H.R. Rasuna Said, Kuningan, Jakarta Ⓣ 021 2995 0400, Ⓦ mfa.gov.sg/jkt.

Ireland 2 Ely Place Upper, Dublin 2 Ⓣ 01 669 1700.

Malaysia 209 Jalan Tun Razak, Kuala Lumpur 50400 Ⓣ 03 2161 6277, Ⓦ mfa.gov.sg/kl.

New Zealand Level 7, Revera House, 48–54 Mulgrave St, Wellington Ⓣ 04 470 0850, Ⓦ mfa.gov.sg/wellington.

South Africa 980 Schoeman St, Arcadia, Pretoria 0083 Ⓣ 012 430 6035, Ⓦ mfa.gov.sg/pretoria.

Thailand 129 South Sathorn Rd, Bangkok 10120 Ⓣ 02 286 2111, Ⓦ mfa.gov.sg/bangkok.

UK 9 Wilton Crescent, Belgravia, London SW1X 8SP Ⓣ 020 7235 8315, Ⓦ singapore.embassyhomepage.com.

US 3501 International Place NW, Washington, DC 20008 Ⓣ 202 537 3100.

Brunei

US nationals are allowed to stay in Brunei for up to 90 days on arrival; British, Australian and New Zealand passport holders are granted 30 days; and Canadians get 14 days. South African citizens need to apply for a visa in advance; the closest embassy is in Egypt (see below) but you can also apply in Singapore – the process takes around three working days. Once in Brunei, extending your permission to stay is usually a formality; apply at the Immigration Department in Bandar Seri Begawan.

EMBASSIES AND CONSULATES

Australia 10 Beale Crescent, Deakin, ACT 2600 Canberra Ⓣ 02 6285 4500, Ⓦ brunei.org.au.

Canada 395 Laurier Ave, Ottawa, ON, KIN 6R4 Ⓣ 613 234 5656.

Indonesia Jalan Tanjung Karang 7, Jakarta 10230 Ⓣ 021 3190 6080.

Malaysia No. 19-10, 19th floor, Menara Tan & Tan, Jalan Tun Razak, Kuala Lumpur 50400 Ⓣ 03 2161 2800.

Singapore 325 Tanglin Rd Ⓣ 6733 9055.

South Africa see the embassy in Singapore, or contact the embassy in Egypt: 24 Hassan Assem St, Zamalek, Cairo Ⓣ 20 2341 6365.

Thailand 12, Ekamai 2, 63 Sukhumvit Rd, Bangkok 10110 Ⓣ 02 714 7395.

UK 19/20 Belgrave Square, London SW1X 8PG Ⓣ 020 7581 0521, Ⓦ brunei.embassyhomepage.com.

US 3520 International Court NW, Washington, DC 20008 Ⓣ 202 237 1838, Ⓦ bruneiembassy.org

Customs allowances

Malaysia's duty-free allowances are 200 cigarettes or 225g of tobacco, and 1 litre of wine, spirits or liquor. There's no customs clearance for passengers travelling from Singapore or Peninsular Malaysia to East Malaysia, nor for people passing between Sabah and Sarawak.

Entering **Singapore** from anywhere other than Malaysia (with which there are no duty-free restrictions), you can bring in 1 litre each of spirits, wine and beer duty-free; duty is payable on all tobacco.

Visitors to **Brunei** may bring in 200 cigarettes, 50 cigars or 250g of tobacco, and 60ml of perfume; non-Muslims over 17 can also import two bottles of liquor and twelve cans of beer for personal consumption (any alcohol brought into the country must be declared upon arrival).

Gay and lesbian travellers

Though Malaysia's largest cities, plus Singapore, have long had a discreet gay scene, the public profile of gays and lesbians was until recently still summed up by the old "don't ask, don't tell" maxim. However, cyberspace has helped galvanize gay people in both countries, providing a virtual refuge within which to socialize and campaign. Hitherto strait-laced **Singapore** is now home to a gay news and lifestyle website (Ⓦ www.fridae.asia), permits exploration of gay themes in the arts, and for a time even played host to outdoor gay rave parties, which drew major international participation. While the environment in **Malaysia** is always going to be more conservative – illustrated by the fact that *Brokeback Mountain* failed to be screened there, and by occasional raids on gay saunas – the Malaysian government has no obvious appetite, Islamically inspired or otherwise, to clamp down on the existing, limited gay nightlife.

For all the general loosening up over the years, it's very much a case of two steps forward and one step back. In 2007, following an extraordinary parliamentary debate, Singapore MPs finally agreed to repeal **colonial-era laws** criminalizing anal and oral sex, though they retained the injunction on such activity between men. Speaking in the debate, Prime Minister Lee Hsien Loong noted that public opinion on gay matters was divided, though he reiterated that government would continue not to enforce the law against gay sex and had no intention of compelling gay venues to "go underground". The same colonial legislation remains on the statute book in Malaysia, and what gay-related campaigning exists tends to be channelled into the relatively uncontentious issue of HIV AIDS. Meanwhile, Singapore has consistently declined to give official recognition to its **gay lobby** group, People Like Us (ⓦwww.plu.sg). Needless to say, all this makes legal recognition of gay partnerships a distant prospect in either country.

This mixed picture shouldn't deter gay visitors from getting to know and enjoy the local scene, such as it is. A small number of gay establishments are reviewed in this guide, and more listings are available on ⓦwww.fridae.asia and the Bangkok-based ⓦwww.utopia-asia.com.

Insurance

A typical travel insurance policy usually provides cover for the loss of bags, tickets and – up to a certain limit – cash or cheques, as well as cancellation or curtailment of your journey. Some policy premiums include dangerous sports; in Malaysia, for example, this can mean scuba diving, whitewater rafting or trekking (notably in the Maliau Basin of Sabah). Always ascertain whether medical coverage will be paid out as treatment proceeds or only after return home, and whether there's a 24-hour medical emergency number. When securing baggage cover, make sure that the per-article limit will cover your most valuable possession. If you need to make a claim, you should keep receipts for medicines and medical treatment, and in the event you have anything stolen, you must obtain an official statement from the police.

Internet

Internet cafés and shops can be found in all Malaysian cities and large towns, often in malls or in upstairs premises along central streets, and most backpacker guesthouses have free wi-fi connections. While many serve the odd coffee or coke, the emphasis often isn't on beverages or even getting online, but on networked gaming, the terminals swamped by kids playing noisy shoot-em-ups late into the night. Periodic crackdowns temporarily compel the internet cafés to keep sensible hours and, it's hoped, the youths in their beds. At least the cafés do provide reliable internet access, costing RM3–6 per hour in practically all cases.

Likewise, it's not hard to get online in Brunei or Singapore; for details, see the respective chapters.

Laundry

Most Malaysian towns have laundries (*dobi*) where you can have clothes washed cheaply and quickly, according to weight (typically RM3 a kilo), picking them up later in the day or early the next day. Some hostels and guesthouses have washing machines that guests can use for a small charge. Dry-cleaning services are less common, though any hotel of a decent standard will be able to oblige.

Living in Malaysia and Singapore

Opportunities for non-residents to find short-term **employment** in Malaysia and Singapore are few and far between. On an unofficial basis, helpers are often required in guesthouses; the wages for such tasks are low, but board and lodging are often included. On a more formal level, both Singapore and KL in particular hold large communities of skilled expats with work permits, secured by their employer. In Malaysia expats can still expect elevated salaries, but this perk is increasingly rare in Singapore, where living standards are high enough as it is.

English-language-teaching qualifications are in demand by language schools in both countries, while qualified diving instructors can also find work in Malaysia. There are also a few volunteer schemes, mainly focusing on nature conservation fieldwork, though they're seldom cheap to join.

ROUGH GUIDES TRAVEL INSURANCE

Rough Guides has teamed up with WorldNomads.com to offer great travel insurance deals. Policies are available to residents of over 150 countries, with cover for a wide range of adventure sports, 24hr emergency assistance, high levels of medical and evacuation cover and a stream of travel safety information. Roughguides.com users can take advantage of their policies online 24/7, from anywhere in the world – even if you're already travelling. And since plans often change when you're on the road, you can extend your policy and even claim online. Roughguides.com users who buy travel insurance with WorldNomads.com can also leave a positive footprint and donate to a community development project. For more information go to ⓦroughguides.com/shop.

STUDY AND WORK PROGRAMMES

AFS Intercultural Programs Ⓦ afs.org. Community service schemes in Malaysia.

Earthwatch Institute Ⓦ earthwatch.org. A range of nature-conservation projects; past projects include bat conservation and climate-change studies in Malaysia.

Fulbright Program Ⓦ fulbrightacademy.org. Regular opportunities for US citizens to spend several months teaching English in rural Malaysia, without requiring teaching experience.

Wild Asia Ⓦ wildasia.org. Conservation group working to protect natural areas and promote responsible tourism and resource use across the region; offers internships.

W-O-X Ⓦ orangutanproject.com. Orang-utan conservation in Malaysia, mostly at rehabilitation centres or upriver locations in Borneo.

Mail

Malaysia has a well-organized postal service operated by Pos Malaysia (☎ 1300 300 300, Ⓦ www.pos.com.my), whose website details postage rates, express mail and courier ("PosLaju") services and so forth. Expect airmail delivery to take one to two weeks depending on the destination.

In **Brunei**, post offices are open Monday to Thursday and Saturday between 8am and 4.30pm, while some may open part of Friday as well. Postal services in **Singapore** are detailed on p.561.

Maps

The best commercially available maps of Malaysia are the city and regional maps published by the Johor Bahru-based World Express Mapping, sold in many local bookshops. Online mapping offered by the usual internet giants tends to be littered with inaccuracies, especially with regard to Malaysian road names. Most Malaysian tourist offices have their own free maps of the local area, though these are of decidedly variable quality and offer little that the maps in this book don't already include. Whichever maps you use, be aware that the high rate of highway construction and road alterations in rural and urban areas alike means that inaccuracies plague most maps almost as soon as they appear. Singapore maps are covered on p.536).

Money

Malaysia's currency is the **ringgit** (pronounced *ring-git* and abbreviated to "RM"), divided into 100 sen. Notes come in RM1, RM5, RM10, RM20, RM50 and RM100 denominations. Coins are currently minted in 5 sen, 10 sen, 20 sen and 50 sen denominations, with 1 sen coins still in circulation. You sometimes hear the word "dollar" used informally to refer to the ringgit.

At the time of writing, the **exchange rate** was around RM3 to US$1 and RM5 to £1. Rates are posted daily in banks and exchange kiosks, and published in the press.

Singapore's currency is the **Singapore dollar**, written simply as $ (or S$ in this book to distinguish it from other dollars) and divided into 100 cents. Notes are issued in denominations of $2, $5, $10, $20, $50 and $100, with a couple of larger notes, rarely seen; coins come in denominations of 1, 5, 10, 20 and 50 cents, and $1. At the time of writing, the **exchange rate** was around S$1.2 to US$1, S$2 to £1.

Brunei's currency, the **Brunei dollar**, is divided into 100 cents; you'll see it written as B$, or simply as $. The Brunei dollar has parity with the Singapore dollar and both are accepted by banks and larger businesses in either country. Notes come in $1, $5, $10, $50, $100, $500 and $1000 denominations; coins come in denominations of 1, 5, 10, 20 and 50 cents.

Banks

Major banks in **Malaysia** include Maybank, HSBC, Citibank, Standard Chartered, RHB Bank and CIMB Bank. Banking hours are generally Monday to Friday 9.30am to 4pm and Saturday 9.30 to 11.30am (closed on every first and third Sat of the month), though in the largely Muslim states of Kedah, Kelantan and Terengganu, Friday is a holiday and Sunday a working day. Banks in all sizeable towns and most tourist areas have ATMs; details are given through the Guide.

Licensed **moneychangers'** kiosks, found in bigger towns all over the country, tend to open later, until around 6pm; some open at weekends and until 9pm, too. Some hotels will exchange money at all hours. Exchange rates tend to be more generous at moneychangers, though they don't generally exchange travellers' cheques.

You're only likely to be really stuck for accessing money in remote rural areas; if, for example, you're travelling upriver through the interior of Sabah or Sarawak, it's a wise idea to carry a fair amount of cash, in smallish denominations.

For details of Singapore banks, see p.561. Brunei **banking hours** are Monday to Friday 9am to 3pm and Saturday 9 to 11am. Banks represented in Brunei include the International Bank of Brunei, Citibank, Standard Chartered Bank and the Overseas Union Bank.

Plastic

Credit and debit cards have limited uses in the region, except to pay for goods and services in upmarket locations – you won't, for example, be able to use your Visa card at a local *kedai kopi*, though a café chain in Kuala Lumpur or Singapore will likely accept it, as indeed might a guesthouse in either place. Watch out too for an ongoing spate of credit card fraud in Malaysia, involving data swiped in genuine transactions being extracted and used to create a duplicate of your card.

Opening hours and public holidays

In **Malaysia**, shops are open daily from around 9.30am to 7pm, though outlets in shopping centres and malls are typically open daily from 10am to 10pm. Government offices tend to work Monday to Friday from 8am to 4.15pm or 9am to 5pm, with an hour off for lunch, except on Friday when the break lasts from 12.15 to 2.45pm to allow Muslims to attend prayers. Note that in the states of Kedah, Kelantan and Terengganu, the working week runs from Sunday to Thursday, with Friday and Saturday as days off.

In **Singapore**, shopping centres open daily 10am to 10pm. Offices generally work Monday to Friday 8.30am to 5pm and sometimes on Saturday mornings.

Opening hours for temples and mosques are given in the text where they keep to a formal schedule (often not the case).

Public and school holidays

As a guide, public holiday dates for 2012 are given below (the relevant government websites issue new lists for each year a few months in advance). Note that Muslim holidays (marked with an asterisk) move earlier by ten or eleven days each year, and that precise dates depend on the sighting of the new moon, which determines when each month of the Muslim calendar begins. Note also that each Malaysian state has its own additional holidays, which could be to do with its sultan's birthday or an Islamic (in states with a largely Muslim population) or tribal event, such as Gawai in June in Sarawak. Some of the holidays below are marked by special festivities (see p.46).

It pays to be aware of not just public holidays but also local **school holidays**, as Malaysian accommodation can be hard to come by during these periods. In Malaysia, schools get a week off in mid-March and late August, and two weeks off at the start of June, with a long break from mid-November to the end of the year. Singapore school breaks are almost identical, except that the June holiday lasts the whole month, and kids get a week off in early September rather than late August.

MALAYSIAN PUBLIC HOLIDAYS (2012)

January 1 New Year's Day
January 23 Chinese New Year
February 5 Birthday of the Prophet Muhammad*
May 1 Labour Day
May 5 Vesak Day
June 2 Yang Dipertuan Agong's Birthday
August 19 & 20 Hari Raya Puasa*
August 31 National Day
September 16 Malaysia Day
October 26 Hari Raya Haji (or Korban)*
November 13 Deepavali
Novmber 15 Maal Hijrah (the Muslim New Year)*
December 25 Christmas Day

SINGAPOREAN PUBLIC HOLIDAYS

Note that Singapore has designated dates for Islamic festivals and does not adjust them to fit sightings of the new moon.
January 1 New Year's Day
January 23 & 24 Chinese New Year
April 6 Good Friday
May 1 Labour Day
May 5 Vesak Day
August 9 National Day
August 19 Hari Raya Puasa*
October 26 Hari Raya Haji*
November 13 Deepavali
December 25 Christmas Day

BRUNEI PUBLIC HOLIDAYS

January 1 New Year's Day
January 23 Chinese New Year
February 6 Birthday of the Prophet Muhammad*
February 23 National Day
May 31 Armed Forces' Day
June 18 Israk Mikraj (the night when the Prophet ascended to heaven)*
July 16 Sultan's Birthday
July 21 First day of Ramadan*
August 6 Anniversary of Revelation of the Koran*
August 20 Hari Raya Aidilfitri*
October 27 Hari Raya Aidiladha*
November 15 Maal Hijrah (the Muslim New Year)*
December 25 Christmas Day

Phones

Malaysia, Singapore and Brunei all have a comprehensive mobile network. If your phone is unlocked and GSM compatible (likely unless you're from the US), you can buy a local SIM card from corner shops and 7–11 stores, which will of course give you a new number. Top up value at the same outlets; you either get a receipt with a pin number on it for you to dial and activate the recharge, or the shop staff will do this for you. If you need to buy a mobile (known locally as "hand phones"), outlets specializing in them are easily found, even in small towns.

Malaysia

There are public phones in most Malaysian towns. Local calls are very cheap at just 10 sen for three minutes, but for long-distance calls, it can be more convenient to buy a **phonecard**, from service stations, 7–Eleven outlets and newsagents. Your best bet is to use a card such as iTalk (W tm.com.my; from RM10), which enables you to make discounted calls from the line in your hotel room as well as from payphones.

The two big players in the **mobile phone** market are Hotlink/Maxis (W hotlink.com.my) and Celcom (W celcom.com.my), with the smaller DiGi (W digi .com.my) bringing up the rear. On the Peninsula you'll usually get a signal on both coasts, along highways and major roads, and on touristy islands. In the forested interior, as a rule your phone will work in any town large enough to be served by express trains (as well as at the Taman Negara headquarters). Sabah and Sarawak coverage is much patchier, focusing on cities and the populated river valleys, though even in the Kelabit Highlands mobile calls are possible.

Mobile tariffs can be complex, though you can expect calls made to other Malaysian numbers to cost no more than RM0.50 per minute.

Singapore

Payphones are not too hard to find in Singapore, though many take **phonecards** rather than coins; the cards (S$5/10) are available from post offices, 7–Elevens and retail outlets of the phone company, Singtel (W singtel.com). Both Singtel and its rival Starhub (W starhub.com) also offer phonecards that are geared to international calls (from S$10), with their own international access codes; details of these cards, sold by the same outlets as regular phonecards, are available from both companys' websites. The same two firms dominate the mobile phone market in Singapore; their **SIM cards** (from S$10) are available from post offices and 7–Eleven stores, though note that your passport will be scanned as a form of registration of any SIM purchase.

Local calls cost 10¢ for three minutes if made from a payphone, or 10¢ per minute from a mobile. The island has no area codes – the only time you'll punch more than eight digits for a local number is if you're dialling a toll-free (☎ 1800) or special-rate (eg ☎ 1900) number. For directory enquiries, call ☎ 100 (☎ 104 for international enquiries).

Brunei

International calls can be made from cardphones. To call collect, substitute ☎ 01 for the usual ☎ 00 international code, then dial the number as though making an ordinary international call; this brings the number up on the operator's system. **Phonecards** start at $10 and can be bought from post offices. **SIM cards** can be obtained from outlets of the mobile provider DST Communications (W dst-group.com).

Time

For administrative convenience, Malaysia, Singapore and Brunei are all eight hours ahead of Universal Time (GMT), all year. This close to the

---

INTERNATIONAL CALLS

To make international calls to any of the countries below, dial your international access code (☎ 00 in Malaysia and Brunei, usually ☎ 001 in Singapore) then the relevant country code from the list, then the number (including any area code, but excluding any initial zero). From Singapore, you can call Malaysia by dialling ☎ 020, then the area code (omitting the initial zero), then the number.

IDD COUNTRY CODES

Australia ☎ 61	Malaysia ☎ 60	South Africa ☎ 27
Brunei ☎ 673	New Zealand ☎ 64	UK ☎ 44
Ireland ☎ 353	Singapore ☎ 65	US & Canada ☎ 1

OPERATOR AND DIRECTORY SERVICES

MALAYSIA

Local directory enquiries: ☎103
Operator-assisted calls (including international collect/reverse charge): ☎101
Business number online searches: ⓦyellowpages.com.my

SINGAPORE

Local directory enquiries: ☎100
Operator-assisted international calls: ☎104
Business number online searches: ⓦyellowpages.com.sg

BRUNEI

Local directory enquiries: ☎113

equator, you can rely on dawn being around 6.30am in the Peninsula and Singapore, dusk at around 7.30pm; in Borneo both happen roughly an hour earlier. Not taking into account daylight saving time elsewhere, the three countries are two hours behind Sydney, thirteen hours ahead of US Eastern Standard Time and sixteen hours ahead of US Pacific Standard Time.

Tipping

Tipping is seldom necessary in Malaysia, Singapore and Brunei. When eating out at a proper restaurant, it's customary to tip if a service charge isn't included, though note that you are never required to tip in *kedai kopis* or *kopitiams*. It's not necessary to tip taxi drivers either, unless they have gone out of their way to be helpful. Otherwise you might want to offer a modest tip to a hotel porter or hairdresser, or a tour guide who has been exceptional.

Tourist information

Tourism Malaysia (ⓦtourism.gov.my) has offices in most state capitals. These are complemented by tourist offices, sometimes called **Tourism Information Centres**, run by state governments and again found in most state capitals. Such offices are generally helpful, if not widely knowledgeable: they have plenty of glossy brochures to hand out, but information here (and on websites) is often patchy, if not downright inaccurate. For out-of-the-way attractions you're better off contacting local accommodation or tour operators – phone is best, as emails often elicit slow responses.

Singapore is another proposition altogether. A huge amount of generally reliable information on everything from bus times to museum exhibitions is available in print and online. Tourist information is

put out by the **Singapore Tourism Board** (ⓦyoursingapore.com), which has an incredibly thorough website and operates several downtown **Visitor Centres** (see p.536). Brunei's official tourism website is ⓦbruneitourism.travel.

MALAYSIAN STATE TOURISM CONTACTS

Johor ☎07 223 4935, ⓦtourismjohor.com.
Kelantan ☎09 748 5534, ⓦtic.kelantan.gov.my
Labuan ☎087 422622, ⓦlabuantourism.com.my.
Melaka ☎06 281 4803, ⓦwww.melaka.gov.my.
Pahang ☎09 516 1007, ⓦpahangtourism.com.my.
Penang ☎04 262 0202, ⓦtourismpenang.gov.my.
Sabah ☎088 212 121, ⓦsabahtourism.com.
Sarawak ☎082 423 600, ⓦsarawaktourism.com.
Selangor ☎03 5511 1122, ⓦtourismselangor.my.
Terengganu ☎09 622 1553, ⓦterengganutourism.com.

OTHER TOURIST INFORMATION SOURCES

ⓦ**allmalaysia.info** Excellent tourism compendium put together by *The Star* newspaper, featuring travel-related news stories, state-by-state accounts of sights and background articles on culture and events.

ⓦ**journeymalaysia.com** Comprehensive, if patchy, coverage of just about everywhere and everything for tourists to see and do in Malaysia. Especially strong on outdoor activities.

ⓦ**www.malaysiasite.nl** Run by an enthusiastic expat, this site provides thumbnail sketches of popular destinations around Malaysia, including some out-of-the-way locations. Practical info isn't always current, but it's a useful resource with plenty of photos.

ⓦ**virtualmalaysia.com** The tourism portal of Malaysia's Ministry of Tourism, with coverage of sights, tourism-related directories and assorted packages on sale.

ⓦ**wildasia.org** Dedicated to sustainable and responsible tourism, this Malaysia-based site features numerous articles on Southeast Asia with plenty on Malaysia itself, of course, including descriptions of forest reserves and dive sites, plus a list of the more environmentally aware resorts.

Travellers with disabilities

Of the three countries covered in this book, **Singapore** is the most accessible to travellers with disabilities; tax incentives are provided for developers who include disabled access features into new buildings. In contrast, Malaysia and Brunei make few provisions.

Across the region, life is made a lot easier if you can afford the more upmarket hotels, which usually have disabled provision, and to shell out for taxis and the odd domestic flight. Similarly, the more expensive international airlines tend to be better equipped to get you there in the first place: MAS, British Airways, KLM, Singapore and Qantas all carry aisle wheelchairs and have at least one toilet adapted for disabled passengers. However, few tour operators in the region accommodate the needs of those with disabilities.

Singapore is certainly making a concerted effort to improve disabled provision: the **MRT** metro system has lifts on most, if not all, of its stations, and some ninety bus routes have wheelchair-accessible vehicles, though these operate only at certain times of day (see ⓦ www.sbstransit.com.sg for details). Most major **taxi** companies have accessible vehicles available to book, too.

In Malaysia, wheelchair users will have a hard time negotiating the uneven pavements in most towns and cities, and find it difficult to board buses, trains, ferries and the LRT metro system in Kuala Lumpur, none of which has been adapted for wheelchairs. The situation is similar if not worse in east Malaysia and Brunei, with little provision for disabled travellers.

CONTACTS FOR TRAVELLERS WITH DISABILITIES

Malaysian Confederation of the Disabled ☎ 03 7956 2300, 🖂 mcd_dpimalaysia@yahoo.com. A member of Disabled Peoples International, working for equal opportunities for disabled people in Malaysia.

Disabled People's Association Singapore ☎ 6899 1220, ⓦ www.dpa.org.sg. Nonprofit organization whose website has information on accessible taxis and local buildings.

Travelling with children

Malaysia, Singapore and Brunei are very child-friendly countries in which to travel. Disposable nappies and powdered milk are easy to find (fresh milk is sold in supermarkets), and bland Chinese soups and rice dishes, or bakery fare, are ideal for systems unaccustomed to spicy food. Many restaurants and the slicker *kedai kopis* have high chairs, though only upmarket hotels provide baby cots or a baby-sitting service. However, rooms in the cheaper hotels can usually be booked with an extra bed for little extra cost. Children under 12 get into many attractions for half-price and enjoy discounts on buses and trains.

BOWEN ISLAND PUBLIC LIBRARY

Kuala Lumpur and around

KL SKYLINE

1

Kuala Lumpur and around

Founded at the head of the Klang Valley in the mid-nineteenth century, Kuala Lumpur – widely known as KL – has never had a coherent style. The earliest grand buildings around Merdeka Square, dating from the 1890s, are eccentric fusings of influences from across the British Empire, now overshadowed by soaring modern landmarks (notably the Petronas Towers) that wouldn't be out of place in Hong Kong or New York. This melange extends to the people too; attractions aside, you could spend a visit simply soaking up KL's excitingly diverse Malay, Chinese and Indian cultures: the conversations heard on the street, the huge range of food, and the profusion of mosques, Buddhist temples and Hindu shrines.

Although KL is also a noticeably sociable and safe place, many Malaysians have mixed feelings about their capital. Though the city is second only to Singapore in regional economic clout, the former prime minister, Abdullah Badawi, hit the mark when describing KL's first-class infrastructure as betrayed by a third-world mentality, and demonstrating a poor grasp of planning, maintenance and service. Untrammelled development over the last decade has bequeathed the city many featureless buildings, follies and terrible traffic snarl-ups, which some locals tolerate only because KL offers them good money and experience before they retire to a cherished provincial village. Conversely, others feel that it has been their salvation, the one city in the country that's big and broad-minded enough to allow them to explore their true artistic or spiritual identity.

Travellers who visit both KL and Singapore often conclude that if only KL could acquire some of Singapore's ability to organize systematically and transparently, while Singapore had some of KL's pleasingly organic qualities and didn't take itself quite so seriously, then both cities would benefit. As things stand, they remain **rivals**, competing in their own way for investment and recognition while grudgingly admiring each other.

A stay of a few days is enough to appreciate the best of KL's **attractions**, including the colonial core around **Merdeka Square** and the adjacent enclaves of **Chinatown** and **Little India**, plus, to the east, the restaurants, shops and nightlife of the so-called **Golden Triangle**, the modern heart of downtown KL. It can be equally rewarding just to take in KL's street life, in particular its boisterous **markets**, ranging from fish and produce markets stuffed into alleyways, to stalls selling cooked food of every shape and description, or inexpensive clothes and accessories.

KL's hinterland is hardly devoid of worthwhile sights either, among them the rugged limestone **Batu Caves**, which contain the country's most sacred Hindu shrine; **FRIM**, or the **Forest Research Institute of Malaysia**, with a treetop canopy walkway for a quick taste of the rainforest; **Kuala Selangor** and its magical fireflies; and the hard-to-reach birding hotspot of **Fraser's Hill**.

JALAN ALOR

Highlights

❶ **Petronas Towers** Come to gawp at these surprisingly serene twin structures, then browse in one of KL's best shopping malls, right beneath. **See p.77**

❷ **Menara KL** Forget the Petronas Towers' Skybridge – this is the place to come for bird's-eye views of KL in all its messy glory. See p.80

❸ **Islamic Arts Museum** One of the most sophisticated museums in the capital, documenting Muslim cultures through arts and crafts. **See p.82**

❹ **Eating** KL has excellent restaurants offering cuisine from around the world, but it's the street food, notably at Jalan Alor, that's often the most memorable dining experience. **See p.96**

❺ **Clubbing** KL is definitely Malaysia's party capital, home to some exceptional clubs that draw big-name DJs. **See p.102**

❻ **Shopping** Whether you prefer the bright lights of the state-of-the-art malls or the bustle of the city's endless street markets and bazaars, KL is a city made for shopping. **See p.104**

❼ **Batu Caves** A blend of religion and theme park, these limestone caves on the very edge of KL house a Hindu temple complex and offer adventure caving explorations in a side cavern. **See p.108**

HIGHLIGHTS ARE MARKED ON THE MAP ON P.66

KUALA LUMPUR & AROUND

HIGHLIGHTS
1. Petronas Towers
2. Menara KL
3. Islamic Arts Museum
4. Eating
5. Clubbing
6. Shopping
7. Batu Caves

KTM Railway

0   10
kilometres

N

Brief history

KL was founded in 1857 when the ruler of Selangor State, Rajah Abdullah, sent a party of Chinese to prospect for **tin** deposits around the junction of the Gombak and Klang rivers. The pioneers duly discovered rich deposits 6km from the confluence near **Ampang** (east of the present-day city centre), which grew into a staging post for Chinese mine labourers. Unusually, the settlement acquired the name Kuala Lumpur ("muddy confluence") rather than, as convention dictated, being named after the lesser of the two rivers – KL should, by rights, have been called "Kuala Gombak".

At first, KL was little more than a wooden shantytown; small steamers could approach within 30km along Sungai Klang, but the rest of the trip was either by shallow boat or through the jungle. Yet settlers poured in, seeking to tap the wealth of this unexplored region: British investors, Malay farmers, Chinese *towkays* (merchants) and labourers. The Chinese *also* formed two **secret societies**, the fierce rivalry between which restrained the township's growth until the influential former miner **Yap Ah Loy** was appointed as Kapitan Cina, or Chinese headman, in 1869. Ah Loy brought law and order to the frontier town by ruthlessly making an example of criminals, parading them through the streets on a first offence and executing them if they re-offended twice. He led the rebuilding of KL after it was razed during the **Selangor Civil War** (1867–73) and personally bore much of the cost of a second rebuilding after a devastating fire in 1881.

The British Resident of Selangor State, **Frank Swettenham**, had most of KL's remaining wooden huts demolished in the 1880s and imported **British architects** from India to design solid, grand edifices suitable for a new capital. By 1887 the city had five hundred brick buildings, and eight times that number in the early 1900s, by which time KL had also become capital of the **Federated Malay States**.

The early twentieth century

Development continued steadily in the first quarter of the twentieth century, during which time Indians from Tamil Nadu swelled the population. Catastrophic floods in 1926 inspired a major engineering project that straightened the course of Sungai Klang, confining it within reinforced, raised banks. By the time the **Japanese invaded** the Peninsula in December 1941, the commercial zone around Chinatown had grown to eclipse the original colonial area, and the *towkays*, enriched by the rubber boom, were already installed in opulent townhouses along today's Jalan Tuanku Abdul Rahman and Jalan Ampang. While the city suffered little physical damage during World War II, the Japanese inflicted terrible brutality on their historic enemies, the Chinese (at least five thousand of whom were killed in the first few weeks of the occupation alone), and sent thousands of Indians to Burma to build the infamous railway, of whom very few survived. At the same time, the Japanese ingratiated themselves with certain Malays by suggesting that loyalty to the occupiers would be rewarded with independence after the war.

Following the **Japanese surrender** in September 1945, the British found that nationalist demands had replaced the Malays' former acceptance of the colonizers, while many Chinese felt alienated by talk that a future Malay government would deny them full citizenship. The ensuing Communist-inspired **Emergency** (see p.573) left KL relatively unscathed, but the atmosphere in the city was tense. These issues finally came to a head in KL's May 1969 **race riots**, in which at least two hundred people lost their lives, though things calmed down rapidly after the imposition of a state of emergency.

Recent times

In 1974 KL was plucked from the bosom of Selangor State and designated **Wilayah Persekutuan** (Federal Territory), an administrative zone in its own right; **Shah Alam**, west along the Klang Valley, replaced it as Selangor's capital. After a period of consolidation, KL and the rest of the Klang Valley, including KL's satellite new town of **Petaling Jaya**,

1

became a thriving conurbation in the 1990s. That decade, and the early part of the new millennium, saw the realization of several huge infrastructural ventures that are part and parcel of local life today – KL's international **airport** and the **Formula One racetrack**, both at Sepang in the far south of Selangor; the **Petronas Towers** and the attendant **KLCC** shopping development; the various urban **rail systems** across the city; and **Putrajaya**, the government's administrative hub off to the south (though KL remains the legislative centre and seat of parliament). The transformation of swathes of KL and much of Selangor is less dramatic today, but still proceeds apace – not least in the ongoing construction of the **Klang Valley MRT rail network** – and concerns are being voiced over the potential strain on water resources and other environmental repercussions.

Kuala Lumpur

Rather than a discernible city centre, Kuala Lumpur has several hubs of activity. Close to the rivers' original "muddy confluence", the former **colonial district** and its distinctive architecture surrounds **Merdeka Square** – don't miss the informative new **Textile Museum** here – with the busy tourist hub of **Chinatown** just southeast. In between the two lie the city's attractive old **Jamek Mosque** and the craft cornucopia that is **Central Market**. Worthwhile forays can be made north to **Little India's** more locals-oriented shops and altogether grittier **Chow Kit Market**.

Some 2km east, the **Golden Triangle** presents the city's modern face, lively **Bukit Bintang** packed with upmarket hotels, restaurants and designer shopping malls. Overlooking it to the north is the tall, strikingly modernist **Petronas Towers**; visitors flock to the skybridge here, though in fact the westerly **Menara KL Tower**, poking out of wooded Bukit Nanas, has better views.

Southwest of the centre – and tricky to reach across one of KL's many pedestrian-unfriendly traffic flows – a clutch of worthwhile sights surround the green and airy **Lake Gardens**, notably **Masjid Negara**, one of the country's largest mosques, and excellent **Islamic Arts Museum**. Below here, the **National Museum** is not as good as it could be, while **Brickfields** is another strongly Indian district, worth a peek for its day-to-day residential streetlife.

The colonial district

Pasar Seni or Masjid Jemak LRT; Kuala Lumpur KTM

The small **colonial district** (see map, p.73), which developed around the confluence of the Gombak and Klang rivers in the 1880s, is the area of KL that best retains its historic character. At its heart on the west bank of the Klang, the beautifully tended open padang (field) of **Merdeka Square** is where on August 31, 1957, Malaysia's first prime minister, Tunku Abdul Rahman, hauled down the British flag and declared *merdeka*, or independence. The 95m-high **flagpole** to the south is supposedly the tallest in the world, and the tiled square below is a popular spot for people to gather in the evenings.

East across Jalan Raja, the superbly florid 1897 **Sultan Abdul Samad Building** is a fine example of **Anthony Norman**'s Moorish-style architecture. Its elegant two-storey grey-and-red-brick colonnade frontage, pierced by arches and windows, supports a facade topped by a 41m-high clock tower and copper cupolas. Formerly the headquarters of the colonial administration, then law courts, it currently houses the Information, Communication and Culture Department; come here at night to see it outlined in fairy lights.

The Royal Selangor Club

On the western side of Merdeka Square, the **Royal Selangor Club,** founded in 1884, was the British elite's favourite watering hole, popularly known as the "Spotted Dog" after a

KUALA LUMPUR'S MOORISH STYLE

KL's colonial "look" originated with **Charles Edwin Spooner**, the state engineer, and architect **Anthony Norman**, who in the 1890s fused a Neoclassical Renaissance style – then the standard for government buildings throughout the British Empire – with "Eastern" motifs, which were felt to be more appropriate for an Islamic country. This **Moorish style**, however, characterized by onion domes, cupolas, colonnades, arched windows and wedding-cake plasterwork, owed more to Indian Moghul architecture than wooden Malay structures. Buildings by Norman in this mould include the Sultan Abdul Samad Building, the old Post Office next door, and the Textile Museum further south. Norman was succeded in 1903 by **A.B. Hubbock**, who had actually lived in India and so smoothly continued the Moorish theme in the Jamek Mosque, old Kuala Lumpur train station and elsewhere.

former Dalmatian mascot. It was here on 30 November, 1938 that **Albert Gispert** and some fellow drinkers at the club's *Hash House* bar organized a weekly cross-country run; thus the now international **Hash House Harriers** were born. The original KL group, respectfully regarded as the mother of all hashing groups, is still in existence (ⓦmotherhash.com). Closed to non-members, the club's history outweighs its facade, an oversized 1970s mock-Tudor affair that replaced a 1910 structure built by A.B. Hubbock, after the original burned down.

To the north, the Anglican **St Mary's Cathedral** (1894), usually open in the daytime, welcomed the city's European inhabitants every Sunday before they repaired to the club.

The National Textile Museum
Jalan Raja • Daily 9am–6pm • Free • ⓦ jmm.gov.my/en/museum/national-textiles-museum

Housed in a striped and frilly Moorish building dating to 1896, KL's **National Textile Museum** highlights Malaysia's diversity by focusing on the widespread importance of dress in local cultures. With **four galleries** on two floors, it takes an hour to do the fairly dense collection justice – though the highlights can be skimmed over in far less time.

Downstairs, the **Pohon Budi Gallery** focuses more on history than actual examples, though it holds some fine block-printed batiks, a technique introduced from India in the eighteenth century. Look too for a small but superb silk nyonya embroidery of peonies, birds and butterflies in characteristic pink and green; *pua kumba* blankets from Sarawak's Ibn, decorated in dream-inspired patterns of crocodiles and hornbills; and a couple of tree-bark cloth jackets, also from Sarawak, which look as if they're made from coarse brown paper. The adjacent **Pelangi Gallery** displays tools and machinery for producing different types of cloth – looms, mallets to pound tree bark into fibres, brushes for applying gold foil onto *kelingkan* cloth.

Upstairs, the **Teluk Beranti Gallery** is dedicated to Malay textiles, especially iridescent *songket* and *limar* cloth, which incorporates fine gold thread into its almost tartan-like patterns, influenced in part by traditional Bugis sarongs from Sulawesi, Indonesia. There's also a splendid *bereyat*, or scripted jacket, with "The wearer is in good health" woven optimistically into the design in Arabic. The final **Ratna Sari Gallery** departs into ceremonial metalwork, including finely chased filigree tobacco boxes, golden anklets worn by Malay women in the early twentieth century, and a small case of flame-bladed *kris* daggers and Ibn head-hunting *madau* machettes from Sarawak.

Jamek Mosque (Masjid Jamek)
Entrance on Jalan Tun Perak • Sat–Thurs 8.30am–12.30pm & 2.30–4pm, Friday 3–4pm • Free

East over the river from Merdeka Square, Lebuh Pasar Besar connects the colonial quarter with the more frenetic life of the old commercial district. Just north of the river bridge is the **Jamek Mosque**, on a promontory at the confluence of the Klang and

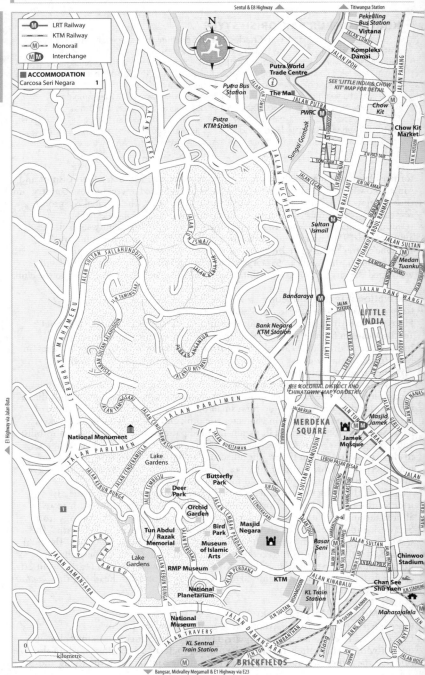

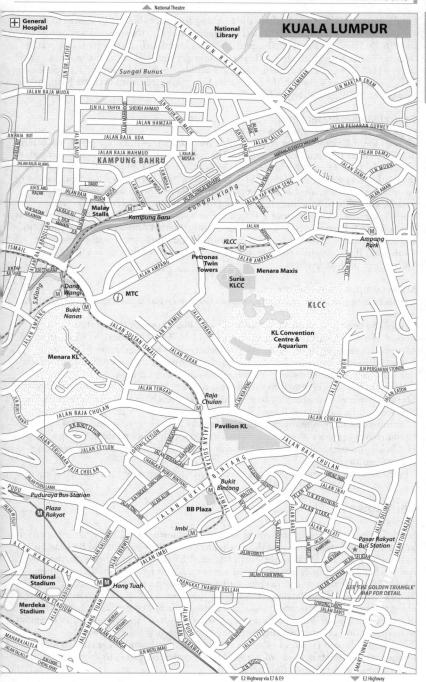

1

Gombak rivers, pretty much where the first tin prospectors built their shacks in the 1850s. Part of the second great period of expansion in KL, the mosque was completed in 1909 by Hubbock, its attractive pink brick walls and arched colonnades topped by oval cupolas and squat minarets. There's an intimacy here lacking at the modern, much larger Masjid Negara to the south, and the grounds, bordered by palms, are a pleasant place to sit and rest – though the best view of the mosque is from over the Klang at the base of the HSBC building on Jalan Benteng.

Central Market (Pasar Seni)

Backing onto the Klang River, south off Lebuh Pasar Besar • Daily 9am–10pm

The Art Deco **Central Market** is housed in a blue and white brick hangar that was built in the 1920s as the capital's wet market. The butchers and fishmongers have long since left for places like Chow Kit and the back alleys of nearby Chinatown, however, and the market was converted in the mid-1980s into what's known as Pasar Seni, meaning "art market". In fact, most of the shops within now sell souvenirs: Royal Selangor pewter, specialist antique shops, Malay regional crafts, carvings and batiks, plus clothes, sarongs, silverware and T-shirts; there's also a decent food court upstairs. Most artists, in fact, have moved into the newer **Central Market Annexe** immediately north, and the pavement in between is clogged with their enthusiastic – if unmemorable – canvases. If it's blatantly touristy, the market is also enjoyable, with a lively atmosphere in the evenings.

Kuala Lumpur train station

Best reached south from Central Market along Jalan Tun Sambanthan, over the river and past the post office, then via the footbridge to the station

One of the city's best-known colonial buildings, **Kuala Lumpur train station** – now a stop on the KTM lines – was completed in 1911 by A.B. Hubbock. As with his Jamek Mosque, its meshing spires, minarets and arches reflect his inspiration from North Indian Islamic architecture. Inside, the main platforms sit under an airy, light vault of fine ironwork, recalling those of Victorian-era stations in London.

Although the station is architecturally linked to similar-vintage buildings around Merdeka Square, feverish traffic makes it difficult to reach on foot from there. For the best view of the facade, you'll need to get across to the western side of Jalan Sultan Hishamuddin. Conveniently, a pedestrian subway links the station with **KTM's headquarters** opposite – yet another attractive Moorish structure designed by Hubbock, finished around the same time as the station and actually more imposing than its counterpart.

From here, it's a few minutes' walk to either Masjid Negara or the National Museum.

Chinatown

Pasar Seni LRT

Spreading out southeast from Central Market, **Chinatown** was KL's original commercial kernel, dating from the arrival of the first traders in the 1860s. Bordered by Jalan Sultan to the east, Jalan Tun Perak to the north and Jalan Maharajalela to the south, the area had reached its current extent by the late nineteenth century, with southern Chinese shophouses, coffee shops and temples springing up along narrow streets such as Jalan Tun H.S. Lee and **Jalan Petaling**. Though the shophouses today are fairly workaday, it is encouraging that many period buildings are being refurbished despite recurrent threats of redevelopment; in 2011, public outcry saved a row of old shophouses on **Jalan Sultan** from demolition during construction of the ongoing Klang Valley railway.

Although Chinatown scores more on atmosphere than essential sights, it's a hub for **budget accommodation**, and holds a wealth of inexpensive places to shop and eat, so you'll probably spend some time here.

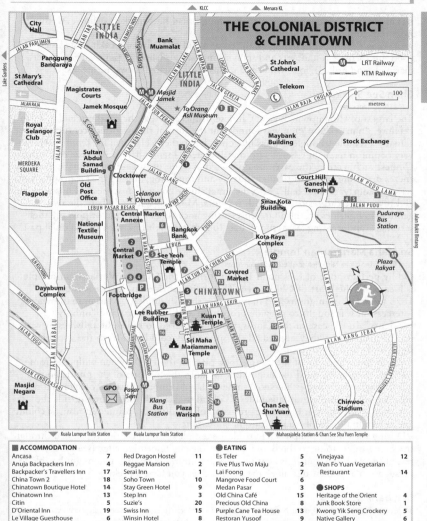

THE COLONIAL DISTRICT & CHINATOWN

■ ACCOMMODATION				● EATING			
Ancasa	7	Red Dragon Hostel	11	Es Teler	5	Vinejayaa	12
Anuja Backpackers Inn	4	Reggae Mansion	2	Five Plus Two Maju	2	Wan Fo Yuan Vegetarian	
Backpacker's Travellers Inn	17	Serai Inn	1	Lai Foong	7	Restaurant	14
China Town 2	18	Soho Town	10	Mangrove Food Court	6		
Chinatown Boutique Hotel	14	Stay Green Hotel	9	Medan Pasar	3	● SHOPS	
Chinatown Inn	13	Step Inn	3	Old China Café	15	Heritage of the Orient	4
Citin	5	Suzie's	20	Precious Old China	8	Junk Book Store	1
D'Oriental Inn	19	Swiss Inn	15	Purple Cane Tea House	13	Kwong Yik Seng Crockery	5
Le Village Guesthouse	6	Winsin Hotel	8	Restoran Yusoof	9	Native Gallery	6
Mandarin Pacific	21			Santa	1	Peter Hoe	8
Matahari Lodge	16	■ DRINKING & NIGHTLIFE		Seng Kee	11	Popular Bookshop	7
Oasis Guesthouse	22	Reggae Bar	2	Sri Ganesa	4	Professor	3
Orange Hotel	12	Speakeasy	1	Tang City Food Court	10	Sri Malaya	2

Jalan Petaling

For locals and visitors alike, pedestrianized **Jalan Petaling** (still often called **Petaling Street**) is very much Chinatown's main draw. Home to brothels and gambling dens in KL's early years, these days it's a gauntlet of closely packed market stalls doing a roaring trade in selling tourists clothing, watches and fake designer handbags from late morning until well into the evening. Check goods thoroughly for workmanship – stitching especially – and bargain hard; in truth, you might find better deals in ordinary shops nearby. The narrow lanes parallel and either side of Petaling host grittier

1

wet markets too, and a popular early morning bric-a-brac market, selling everything from old clothes to mobile phones.

Crossing Petaling at right angles, the eastern end of **Jalan Hang Lekir** hosts a slew of good, inexpensive restaurants and stalls selling *ba kwa* (slices of pork, given a sweet marinade and grilled), local fruits and molasses-like herbal brews in tureens.

Chan See Shu Yuen

Daily 8.30am–5pm • Free

The largest of Chinatown's several Chinese shrines, sited at the southern end of Jalan Petaling, **Chan See Shu Yuen** was founded at the turn of the twentieth century. It's not actually a temple (though it looks like one), but rather a clan hall for families with the very common name of Chan – also transliterated Chen and Tan. A classic of southern Chinese architecture, the eaves are decorated in a riot of three-dimensional ceramic friezes depicting events in Chinese history and mythology; inside the green walls are a series of courtyards and halls, with the inner shrine covered in scenes of lions, dragons and mythical creatures battling with warriors. Most engaging of all are the two gentleman figurines on the altar, representing ancestors of the clan or possibly their servants – and wearing Western top hats to indicate their link with the colonial past.

Sri Maha Mariamman Temple

Jalan Tun H.S. Lee • Open 24hr • Free, small donation appreciated

Oddly perhaps, one of KL's main Hindu shrines, the **Sri Maha Mariamman Temple**, is located in the heart of Chinatown. The earliest shrine on the site was built in 1873 by Tamil immigrants and named after the Hindu deity, Mariamman, whose intercession was sought to provide protection against sickness and "unholy incidents". In the case of the Tamils, who had arrived to build the railways or work on the plantations, they needed all the solace they could find from the appalling rigours of their working life.

Significant rebuilding of the temple took place in the 1960s, when sculptors from India were commissioned to design idols to adorn the five tiers of the multicoloured, 22.9m-high gate tower – these now shine with gold embellishments, precious stones and exquisite Spanish and Italian tiles. Garland-makers sell their wares outside the entrance, while above it is a hectic profusion of Hindu gods, painted in realistic colours and frozen in dozens of scenes from the *Ramayana*.

During the Hindu **Thaipusam** festival, the temple's golden chariot is paraded through the streets on its route to the Batu Caves, on the city's northern edge (see p.108). The rest of the year, the chariot is kept in a large room in the temple; you might be able to persuade an attendant to unlock the door and let you have a peek.

Maybank Building

On Chinatown's northeastern edge, where Jalan Tun Perak and Jalan Tun Tan Cheng Lock converge at the Puduraya intersection

Designed in the late 1980s by Hijjas Kasturi, the **Maybank Building** is typical of the new KL, with a tall white facade designed with Islamic principles of purity in mind.

On the lobby floor, the small, unusually interesting **Numismatic Museum** (daily 10am–6pm; free) kicks off with tin ingots, gold dust and bars of silver or, for what the caption describes as "ordinary people", cowrie shells, rice and beads – all formerly used for transactions in the region. Coins were introduced with the arrival of the colonizing powers; early sixteenth-century Portuguese examples are delicately engraved with miniatures of the Malay Peninsula and tiny kites billowing in the air. The first mass-produced coins, issued by the British East India Company, bore the company's coat of arms – a practice echoed later by timber and rubber companies, who until the late eighteenth century minted tokens to pay their expanding labour pool. During the Japanese invasion, the occupying administration produced its own bank notes which, after the Japanese surrender, the British diligently collected and stamped "not legal tender".

1

Court Hill Ganesh Temple

9 Jalan Pudu Lama • Daily 4.30–9.30am & 4–8.30pm • Free

East of the Maybank Building and hidden up a small lane, **Court Hill Ganesh Temple** is KL's second most important Hindu shrine, dating to 1897 and reputedly founded by a gardener – which may explain why there's a **tree** growing beside the building. Being dedicated to the elephant-headed Lord Ganesh, who specializes in the removal of all obstacles to prosperity, peace and success, the temple was understandably popular with visitors on their way to KL's original law courts, once sited nearby. Now small and crowded, with stalls outside selling garlands, incense, sweetmeats and charms, the temple was undergoing major reconstruction at the time of writing.

Jalan TAR

On foot from Chinatown, it takes around 1hr to reach Chow Kit via Little India along Jalan TAR; the LRT, Monorail and buses also traverse the area

Running north from Chinatown, Jalan Tuanku Abdul Rahman – universally abbreviated to **Jalan TAR** – brings you within reach of a series of small-scale, local neighbourhoods, somewhat unexpected in such a large city. First is **Little India**, a bustling commercial district renowned for fabrics, especially saris and *songket*s, as well as jewellery. The clothing theme persists immediately west, where Gulati's Silk House and the SOGO department store stock everything from saris to brand-name outdoor gear. There are also some fine 1920s Neoclassical and Art Deco buildings, including the dove-grey **Coliseum Cinema**, screening Indian releases, and the adjacent **Coliseum Hotel** (at no. 98). Once a favourite watering hole with British rubber plantation owners, its interior can't have been decorated since independence, and the clientele look of similar vintage. Drop in for the atmosphere and a cold beer rather than the food, which is very ordinary.

Beyond here, **Chow Kit Market** is somewhere to find bargain clothing and local produce, while **Kampung Bahru**, off to the east of Jalan TAR, is a low-key enclave of Malay housing. There are no major sights, but a visit adds depth to KL's character, and all three have excellent eating opportunities.

Little India

Masjid Jamek or Bandaraya LRT

East off the lower end of Jalan TAR, **Little India** is a commercial centre for KL's Indian community, though these days it is being eclipsed by Brickfields (see p.85). Only a few steps north from the Masjid Jamek LRT station, **Jalan Melayu** holds Indian stores, some selling excellent *burfi* and other sweet confections; its name derives from the former Malay community here. Approaching **Jalan Masjid India**, you encounter a popular covered market, smaller but otherwise similar to Chinatown's Jalan Petaling. Further up is **Masjid India** itself, an Indian-influenced affair dating from the 1960s and tiled in cream and brown.

A few minutes further along the street, you come to a little square, to the right (east) of which you'll find plenty of *kedai kopi*s and, come evening, street vendors selling food; turn off to the left to reach Lorong Tuanku Abdul Rahman, whose northern end is dominated by a **night market**, busiest at weekends. Mainly Malay-run, the stalls sell both food and eclectic bits and pieces, from T-shirts to trinkets. Just past here, Madras and Semua are two huge haberdasheries, packed to their roofs with **Indian textiles**.

Chow Kit

Chow Kit Monorail; bus #16, #41, #43, #50 from Lebuh Pudu by Central Market, or almost any bus from Jalan Raja Laut, west of Little India

Chow Kit district, 1.5km north of Little India, is mostly known for the sprawling, busy **Chow Kit Market**, which fills the lanes east off Jalan TAR. One of KL's busiest, in-your-face produce markets, it's a tight, overcrowded grid of alleyways under low-slung awnings. Stalls sell everything fit to put in your mouth: bulk tropical fruits at bargain

1

LITTLE INDIA & CHOW KIT

Map legend:
- M LRT Railway
- KTM Railway
- M Monorail

Map labels:
JALAN IPOH, JALAN PAHANG, JALAN RAJA MUDA ABDUL AZIZ, Chow Kit (M), JLN CHOW KIT, Hawker Stalls, Kamdar Building, Chow Kit Market, JALAN RAJA BOT, JALAN RAJA ALANG, JALAN HAJI TAIB, Market, JALAN RAJA ALANG, JALAN DEWAN SULTAN SULAIMAN, JALAN SRI AMAR, LORONG TIONG NAM LIMA, JLN TIONG NAM, LORONG TIONG NAM TIGA, JLN RAJA LAUT, JALAN TUANKU ABDUL RAHMAN (JALAN TAR), JLN HAJI HUSSEIN, Putra Bus Station & Putra World Trade Centre, Kampung Bahru, Kampung Bahru, JALAN SULTAN ISMAIL, JALAN BELLA, Sultan Ismail (M), Maju Junction, Medan Tuanku (M), Imperial Court, Sheraton Hotel, Asian Heritage Row, Mara Building, JALAN MEDAN TUANKU, JLN SEMARANG, Pertama Shopping Complex, Campbell Shopping Centre, DANG WANGI, JALAN, Sogo Department Store, Munshi Abdullah Complex, Bandaraya, JALAN ISFAHAN, JLN BUNUS 6, Night Market, Bank Negara Station, LORONG GOMBAK, Coliseum Cinema, JALAN BUNUS, LITTLE INDIA, JLN BUNUS, JALAN MUNSHI ABDULLAH, Sungai Gombak, JLN KUCHING, City Hall, Masjid India, Market, JALAN PARLIMEN, JLN MELAYU, S. Klang, JALAN AMPANG, Masjid Jamek, KLCC

● SHOPS
Madras — 2
Semua — 1

0 ... 200 metres

---

prices, live and dismembered fish and poultry, hunks and haunches of various animals, and piles of fresh or dried vegetables and fungi. Hawkers around the edge sell freshly cooked snacks too, many with a definite Indonesian slant.

Chow Kit is also a good place to buy **secondhand clothes** (sometimes called "*baju* bundle"). The best deals are west of Jalan TAR along Jalan Haji Taib, where you may chance upon items like Levi's 501s in reasonable condition and at prices that are almost too reasonable to be true – starting from RM20 a pair. The market operates much of the day and into the evening, but note that some locals prefer to give Chow Kit a wide berth after dark, as it's also something of a red-light area.

Kampung Bahru

Kampung Baru LRT

If you've time on your hands and enjoy a wander, head 1km east from Chow Kit (along either Jalan Raja Bot or Jalan Raja Alang) into **Kampung Bahru**, one of the Peninsula's several designated Malay reserve areas – land that only people whose ID defines them as ethnic Malays can own, and indeed with its own status in law, not under the direct control of the KL city council. Though the Petronas Towers are visible off to the south, Kampung Bahru's quiet lanes and painted wooden bungalows with gardens – not to mention chickens wandering the pavements – lend it a distinct village feel. Sadly, plans to "redevelop" the district may well involve wholesale demolitions.

Despite its proximity, you can't walk southeast to KLCC from here, owing to the riverside expressway.

The Golden Triangle

The heart of modern KL, the **Golden Triangle** is a sprawling area bounded to its north by **Jalan Ampang**, and to the west by Chinatown and Sungai Klang. Many visitors make a beeline

---

● EATING
Capital Café	2
Jai Hind	4
Saravanaa Bhavan	3
Sithique Nasi Kandar	1

■ DRINKING & NIGHTLIFE
@space	2
Coliseum Hotel	1
Heritage Live	1

■ ACCOMMODATION
Coliseum Hotel	4
Garden City Hotel	6
Grand Orchard	5
Hostel Cosmopolitan	1
Maytower Hotel	3
Palace	7
Tune Hotel	2

1

for **KLCC** (Kuala Lumpur City Centre; ⊕klcc.com.my), a group of huge developments surrounding the bland KLCC Park, on a site once home to the Selangor Turf Club. The chief attractions here are the **Petronas Towers**, soaring above one of KL's best malls, **Suria KLCC**, and the city's glossy **aquarium**.

Further south, the Golden Triangle's other magnet is **Bukit Bintang** ("Star Hill"), home to upmarket and workaday malls, many of KL's best hotels and restaurants, and some engaging street life. East, **Kompleks Budaya Kraf** is the city's largest handicrafts gallery, while northwest lies **Bukit Nanas**, a forested hill where the **Menara KL** communications tower affords great views of the city.

The Petronas Towers

Tues–Sun 9am–7pm, Fri closed 1–2.30pm; 1000 passes per day issued at the base of tower 2 from 8.30am onwards, usually sold out by 10am • Skybridge RM10; Skybridge plus Observation Deck RM40; Premium Package (Skybridge, Observation Deck and meal at *Malaysian Petroleum Club* on Level 43) RM200–350 • ⊕ petronastwintowers.com.my

Very much the symbol of modern Malaysia, the twin columns of the **Petronas Towers** rise 451.9m above KL's downtown, completely dwarfing the enormous **Suria KLCC Mall** at their base. When they were completed in 1998, as the headquarters of the state-owned oil company Petronas, many questioned whether the US$1.6 billion price tag was an unwarranted drain on the Malaysian economy, but the tapering steel-clad structures (designed by the Argentinean architect Cesar Pelli) are a stunning piece of architecture. Despite a definite Art Deco feel, the unusual eight-pointed cross-sectional profile obviously draws on Islamic art, while the profusion of squares and circles on the interior walls symbolize harmony and strength. The project is also permeated by Chinese numerology in that the towers have 88 floors and the postcode 59088 – eight being a very auspicious number for the Chinese.

One tower was built by a Japanese team, the other by rivals from Korea; while the Japanese topped out first, the Koreans had the honour of engineering the **skybridge**, which joins the towers at both the forty-first and forty-second floors. The **views** from the skybridge of KL's sprawl are pretty spectacular, thanks not least to the blue, glassy towers soaring either side of you – though not as good as from the **Observation Deck** on Level 86.

The aquarium

Jalan Pinang; can also be accessed by a long pedestrian underpass from Suria KLCC • Mon–Fri 11am–8pm, Sat & Sun 10.30am–8pm, last tickets sold at 7pm; feeding times on website, book shark scuba dives via website • RM45 • ⊕ klaquaria.com

KL's **aquarium** is housed within the sizeable **KL Convention Centre**, which sits on the southern edge of KLCC. It's expensive, and labelling is occasionally lost in the muted lighting, but some sections are wonderful. Prime examples include the well-lit **Living Reef** tank, packed with multicoloured, multiform anemones and corals, which will help you make sense of the riches on view at the Perhentians and elsewhere, and the **Flooded Forest** tank, with its pair of hefty, 2m-long Amazonian arapaima freshwater fish. It also holds electric eels, otters and even piranhas, but the *pièce de résistance* is the vast **Living Ocean** tank, traversed on a moving walkway through a transparent tunnel, replete with sand tiger sharks, octopus and huge rays.

Bukit Bintang

Bukit Bintang Monorail

For tourists and locals alike, **Bukit Bintang** – the broad corridor either side of **Jalan Bukit Bintang** – is one of the best spots in town for a wander. There's a **mall** here to suit everyone: the gigantic, massively modern Pavilion KL and Berjaya Times Square, both packed with international chains and designer outlets; posh Starhill Gallery, with an exclusive, snazzy Art Deco feel; the more casually modest Lot 10 Mall and BB Plaza, and surprisingly bland Farenheit 88; and the glib, claustrophobic and slightly shifty Imbi Plaza. The southwestern end of Jalan Bukit Bintang is lined with royal palms and

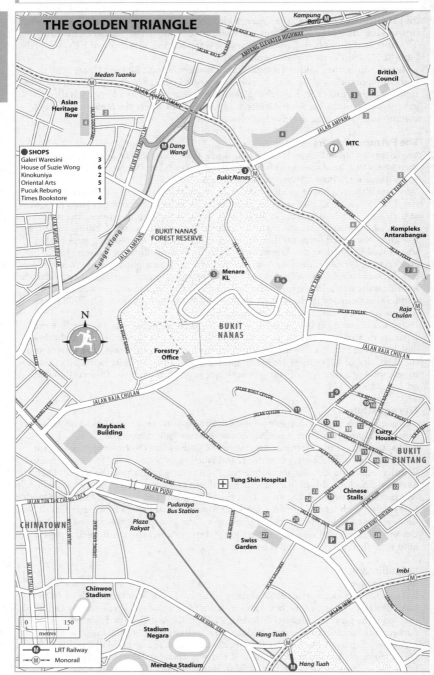

THE GOLDEN TRIANGLE

● SHOPS
Galeri Waresini	3
House of Suzie Wong	6
Kinokuniya	2
Oriental Arts	5
Pucuk Rebung	1
Times Bookstore	4

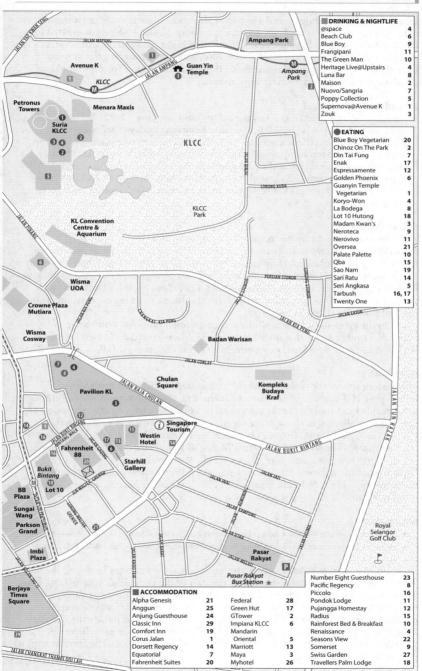

■ DRINKING & NIGHTLIFE

@space	4
Beach Club	6
Blue Boy	9
Frangipani	11
The Green Man	10
Heritage Live@Upstairs	4
Luna Bar	8
Maison	2
Nuovo/Sangria	7
Poppy Collection	5
Supernova@Avenue K	1
Zouk	3

● EATING

Blue Boy Vegetarian	20
Chinoz On The Park	2
Din Tai Fung	7
Enak	17
Espressamente	12
Golden Phoenix	6
Guanyin Temple Vegetarian	1
Koryo-Won	4
La Bodega	8
Lot 10 Hutong	18
Madam Kwan's	3
Neroteca	9
Nerovivo	11
Oversea	21
Palate Palette	10
Qba	15
Sao Nam	19
Sari Ratu	14
Seri Angkasa	5
Tarbush	16, 17
Twenty One	13

■ ACCOMMODATION

Alpha Genesis	21	Federal	28
Anggun	25	Green Hut	17
Anjung Guesthouse	24	GTower	2
Classic Inn	29	Impiana KLCC	6
Comfort Inn	19	Mandarin	
Corus Jalan	1	Oriental	5
Dorsett Regency	14	Marriott	13
Equatorial	7	Maya	3
Fahrenheit Suites	20	Myhotel	26

Number Eight Guesthouse	23
Pacific Regency	8
Piccolo	16
Pondok Lodge	11
Pujangga Homestay	12
Radius	15
Rainforest Bed & Breakfast	10
Renaissance	4
Seasons View	22
Somerset	9
Swiss Garden	27
Travellers Palm Lodge	18

1

inexpensive clothing shops – and a few too many touts hissing "massage, woman, sexy massage" at passers-by – while the pavement around the Lot 10 Mall has evolved into **Bintang Walk**, home to a parade of smart cafés. By night the centre of attention, at least as regards dining, switches to nearby **Jalan Alor**, which boasts some great alfresco Chinese eating. Close by, Changkat Bukit Bintang and Tengkat Tong Shin hold more excellent restaurants, serving differing cuisines.

Kompleks Budaya Kraf

Jalan Conlay, just south of KLCC • Daily 9am–6pm • Free • ☎ 03 2162 7459, ⓦ kraftangan.gov.my

The sprawl of Malay-style buildings housing **Kompleks Budaya Kraf** is a good opportunity to see excellent examples of Malaysia's crafts in one place – including pewter, carved wooden boxes, modern textiles, woven baskets, gaudy ceramics and Orang Asli woodcarvings – and to do some serious souvenir shopping. Their small, well-presented **museum** (RM3) is also worth a half-hour browse to explore the intricacies of the weaving, tie-dyeing and batik processes, *keris* casting, and Malay kite construction.

Badan Warisan

2 Jalan Stonor • Mon–Sat 10am–5.30pm • Free • ☎ 03 2144 9273, ⓦ badanwarisan.org.my

Badan Warisan, Malaysia's architecture conservation trust, campaigns to preserve the rich heritage of shophouses, temples and colonial buildings that developers and many municipal authorities seem intent on destroying. It's housed close to Komplex Budaya Kraf in a 1925 colonial mansion that contains a gift shop, good for books on local architecture, and hosts occasional temporary exhibitions, focusing on anything from colonial furniture to restoration work.

Also in the grounds is the beautifully restored **Rumah Penghulu Abu Seman**, a traditional timber house that once belonged to a Malay chieftain. Moved here from Kedah, it can only be visited on a guided tour (11am & 3pm; RM10).

Bukit Nanas

The western side of the Golden Triangle is dominated by forested **Bukit Nanas** ("Pineapple Hill"), above which rises the **Menara KL** communications tower. Although most people head straight for the tower and its brilliant views, you can also follow an easy 40min **walking trail** through the forest from the **Forestry Office** on Jalan Raja Chulan (daily 9am–6pm; free map available; see Menara KL for free guided walks) to Jalan Ampang, close to the Bukit Nanas Monorail station; there are big trees, subdued gloom, bird's nest ferns, stands of bamboo and a few monkeys.

Just west of the hill, on Jalan Bukit Nanas, the fine collection of **colonial school buildings** include the St John's Institution (1904) and Bukit Nanas Convent School – still rated among KL's top schools.

Menara KL

Access via Jalan Ramlee and Jalan Puncak; free shuttles every 15min from Jalan Puncak, or a 15min walk uphill • Daily 9am–10pm, last tickets 9.30pm; free guided forest walks from the base of the tower at 10am, 12pm, 2.30pm & 4.30pm • RM45 • ☎ 03 2020 5444, ⓦ menarakl.com.my

At 421m, the **Menara KL tower** offers vistas east across the Petronas Towers to the blue peaks of the Titiwangsa range that marks the start of the Peninsula's interior, and west along the unmitigated urban sprawl of the Klang Valley. Dusk is an especially worthwhile time to come, as the city lights up, as does the tower itself on special occasions – green for Muslim festivals, purple for Deepavali and red for the Chinese New Year. Though free audio guides describe what can be seen in each direction, it's probably best to hold off visiting until you know KL well enough to be familiar with its general layout.

CLOCKWISE FROM TOP MERDEKA SQUARE (P.68); JAMEK MOSQUE (P.69); BATU CAVES (P.108) >

1

The **observation deck** sits inside in the bulbous portion of the tower, which was designed in the shape of a *gasing*, the Malay spinning top. Fixed binoculars (free) allow you to espy city life in minute detail, even picking out pedestrians narrowly avoiding being run over as they scurry across the streets of Chinatown. You can also combine a visit with tea or a meal at the revolving *Seri Angkasa* restaurant one floor higher (see p.99).

The Lake Gardens and around

Kuala Lumpur train station KTM

West of the colonial quarter, the **Lake Gardens** offer a pleasant escape from KL's more frenetic streets amid a humid, hilly spread of green. Behind the sizeable modern **Masjid Negara**, which fronts the area on Jalan Sultan Hishamuddin, a cool white building contains the superb **Islamic Arts Museum**. Uphill lie the gardens themselves, complete with close-cropped lawns, water and a host of children-friendly attractions – including a Butterfly Park, a Bird Park and the National Planetarium – while Malaysia's **National Museum** is just south. Although you could easily spend half a day strolling around, focus on the two museums if you're pushed for time.

The easiest **access** on foot is via Kuala Lumpur train station and the underpass to the KTM building (see p.72), from where you can edge around to the mosque – otherwise you have to risk crossing the usual furious traffic flows. As smaller roads run through the gardens, however, it's perhaps easiest to get here by taxi.

Masjid Negara

Jalan Sultan Hishamuddin • Sat–Wed 9am–6pm, Fri 2.45–6pm

Opened in 1965, **Masjid Negara** (National Mosque) is starting to look rather dated, but does impress with the scale of its paved courtyards and colonnades, all rectangles of white marble bisected by pools of water. The prayer hall can hold up to ten thousand worshippers, though size gives way to decorative prowess in its finely detailed stone archways, the dome adorned with eighteen points signifying the five pillars of Islam and the thirteen states of Malaysia. To enter as a visitor (between prayers only), you must be properly dressed: robes can be borrowed (free) at the mosque entrance.

Islamic Arts Museum

Just up Jalan Lembah Perdana from Masjid Negara • Daily 10am–6pm • RM12, RM15 during temporary exhibitions • ☎ 03 2274 2020, ⓦ iamm.org.my

The ultramodern **Islamic Arts Museum** is housed in an elegant open-plan building with gleaming marble floors. This well-documented collection is a real standout; allow around ninety minutes to do it justice, and bear in mind that there's an excellent on-site Middle Eastern **restaurant** (open during museum hours, daily except Mon). If you're arriving by taxi, you may find that the driver will know only the museum's Malay name, Muzium Kesenian Islam – if that doesn't work, just ask for the Masjid Negara.

Level 1 begins with a rather bland collection of dioramas of Muslim holy places, though that of the Great Mosque of Xi'an in central China draws attention to the neglected subject of Islam in the Far East, a theme continued elsewhere on this level. In the India gallery, devoted to the Moghuls, look for an intricately carved wooden locking mechanism, designed to cloister the harem away from the rest of the world, while the China gallery features porcelain and scroll paintings bearing Arabic calligraphy. Best of all is an impressive 3m-high archway in the Malay gallery, once part of a house belonging to an Indonesian notable, with black, red and gold lacquering and a trelliswork of leaves as its main motif. An equally fine trunk below it was used as a travelling box by Terengganu royalty. Built of the much-prized *cengal* hardwood, it's decorated in red and gold and bears the names of Islam's revered first four caliphs.

Level 2

On **level 2**, richly embroidered textiles and marquetry back up unusual examples of Western European ceramic crockery, influenced by the Islamic world in their design – and sometimes produced for that market. Most interesting here is the terrace containing the museum's main **dome**, a blue-and-white affair with floral ornamentation. Built by Iranian craftsmen, it's the only one of several similar examples in the building that's intended to illustrate the exterior of a grand mosque. Finally, look out for the bizarre reversed dome ceiling, bulging downwards from above – it's the last thing you see as you make your way back to the foyer from the area containing the excellent **gift shop**.

The RMP Museum

Jalan Perdana, beyond the Islamic Arts Museum • Tues–Thurs, Sat & Sun 10am–6pm, Fri 10am–noon & 3–6pm • Free

The **RMP Museum** covers the vivid history of the **Royal Malaysian Police** force. Fascinating photographs on show include a shot of British officers and their local charges on patrol on buffaloes, around 1900. The museum also displays weapons confiscated from the Communists during the Emergency, including a vicious assortment of *parangs* and a curved, bladed implement known as a Sarawak or Iban axe. Once you've had a look around, you can, if you're feeling energetic, continue up Jalan Perdana into the Lake Gardens (see p.83) or head up the flight of steps opposite the museum to the hill where the National Planetarium is located (see p.84).

The Lake Gardens (Taman Tasik Perdana)

KL's **Lake Gardens** were originally laid out in the 1890s by the British state treasurer to Malaya, Alfred Venning, though much of the landscaping has been carried out in the last 25 years. Not quite parkland or gardens in the sense of somewhere you can stroll at leisure between formal arrangements of flower beds and trees, they're probably best seen as a pleasant setting for various attractions, all connected by paths and sealed roads.

If you're out this way in the afternoon, consider dropping into KL's most exclusive hotel, the **Carcosa Seri Negara** (see p.96), off to the west. Their oh-so-English **cream tea** is a fitting reward for a hot day's wander around the Lake Gardens – as long as you don't mind dressing smartly and paying RM80 a head for the privilege.

The Butterfly Park

Off Jalan Tugu, north of Masjid Negara, Lake Gardens • Daily 9am–6pm • RM18 • ☎ 03 2693 4799

The beautiful **Butterfly Park** is an unexpected delight. Enclosed in invisibly fine netting, this garden of tropical vines, shrubs and ferns nurtures 120 species of gorgeous butterflies – some with fifteen-centimetre wingspans – flitting about between the undergrowth and feed stations baited with pineapple and banana. There are also tranquil ponds full of giant koi carp, and a small but informative insect museum.

The Bird Park

Lake Gardens • Daily 9am–6pm • RM45 • ⓦ klbirdpark.com

Billed as the world's largest, KL's popular **Bird Park** features a well-designed network of ponds and streams underneath a huge mesh tent, all linked together by a looped walkway. There are free-flying egrets, storks, African starlings, nutmeg pigeons and parrots all over the place, a flock of flamingoes lives in one of the ponds, and cages of indigenous species that you might well encounter in Malaysia's wilder corners – hornbills, birds of prey such as the Brahminy kite, and the sizeable argus pheasant. Give yourself an hour to look around; the only real downside is the park's outrageous cost, relative to any other attraction in town.

1

The Orchid and Hibiscus Gardens

Lake Gardens • Daily 9am–6pm • Mon–Fri free, Sat & Sun RM1

If you're into tropical plants, you'll love the **Orchid** and **Hibiscus Gardens**. They claim to have over 800 Malaysian orchids alone, all lining paved walkways in brightly coloured, formal arrangements. The hibiscus collection is laid out in terraces and includes Malaysia's national flower, the bright red Bunga Raya. There are also groves of South American **heliconias** in the gardens, looking a bit like a ginger plant but with brightly coloured, strikingly shaped flowers. The garden **shop** sells orchid cuttings in sterile gel, suitable to take home.

Tun Abdul Razak Memorial

Lake Gardens

The main road through the Lake Gardens weaves south past a field of deer to the **Tun Abdul Razak Memorial**, a house built for the second Malaysian prime minister. He's commemorated by assorted memorabilia inside, while his motorboat and golf trolley are ceremonially positioned outside. Behind here is the **lake** itself, which takes nearly an hour to walk around.

The National Planetarium

Lake Gardens • Tues–Sun 9.30am–4.30pm • RM1, Space Theatre RM3 • ☎ 03 2273 4301, ⓦ angkasa.gov.my/planetarium

Set on a forested hill east of the lake, the **National Planetarium** is reachable on foot using the steps opposite the RMP Museum (see p.83). Its blue dome and geometrically latticed walls make this an unlikely example of the city's Islamic-influenced architecture. The interior is, frankly, dull, albeit often full of happy, screaming children on school trips; there's a cutaway space capsule, a Viking rocket engine and spacesuits in glass cases, all lit by lavish blue lighting. The **Space Theatre** also shows an hourly film on various topics, not necessarily about space.

A **pedestrian bridge** runs south from the planetarium to the National Museum.

The National Museum

Jalan Travers • Daily 9am–6pm, free guided tours Mon–Thurs & Sat 10am • RM5 • ☎ 03 2282 1111, ⓦ muziumnegara.gov.my • KL Train Station; walking, use the underpass to the KTM building as there are no other crossings on Jalan Sultan Hishamuddin

Built in 1963, the **National Museum** (Muzium Negara) has a sweeping roof characteristic of northern Malay architecture, and **four galleries** that focus perhaps too much on the Malay side of things, giving relatively little space to the Orang Asli, Indians, Chinese and Europeans who have also left their mark on the nation's history and culture. Despite this, the museum is definitely worth an hour's study, especially if you've seen the Textile Museum's complementary exhibits.

On the first floor, **Gallery A** offers a dry stroll through prehistory, though human skeletal remains from Kelantan prove that settlers were present on the Peninsula around 6000 BC. **Gallery B** covers early Malay kingdoms, in particular the Melaka Sultanate, with a particularly good collection of finely chased *kris* daggers and items recovered from sunken Chinese trading vessels. The pace accelerates upstairs, where **Gallery C** covers the colonial era, from reconstructions of Melaka's Portuguese fortifications to a fine seventeenth-century German Bellarmine jug depicting a bearded face – characteristic of such jugs – on the neck of the vessel. There's also ungenerous coverage of the British "interference" in the Malay States, including a diorama of the signing of the Pangkor treaty (see p.134). Tin, the metal that opened up Malaysia to development, dominates the final part of the gallery; mining equipment sits alongside ridiculous animal-shaped coinage – including a thirty-centimetre crocodile – once used in Selangor and Perak.

Gallery D parcels Modern Malaysia into a triumphant photo parade of the nation's founding fathers, of various races, whose names you see on street signs in downtown – though there's only cursory coverage of broader history, such as the Emergency during the 1950s (see p.573).

Finally, don't miss the open-air courtyard out the back, featuring an excellent rundown of the Peninsula's **indigenous groups**, alongside fantastic totem-pole-like objects and grotesque face masks such as the one-fanged *moyang melor*, which were used in rites of ancestor worship.

Brickfields and KL Sentral

KL Sentral LRT, KTM and Monorail

The laidback residential neighbourhood of **Brickfields**, 2km south of the city centre near **KL Sentral** station, was first settled by Tamils employed to build the railways, and named after the brickworks that lined the rail tracks. Even today, the area retains a strong South Indian presence along **Jalan Tun Sambanthan** – the main thoroughfare – especially the western stretch beyond the huge pink fountain marking the intersection with Jalan Travers; the road has flowers painted on it, buildings are pastel-hued, and Indian pop tunes blare out of sari shops and grocers. This is another corner of town to visit for local ambience rather than monumental sights, though it does hold some good places to eat (see p.99).

Kandaswamy Temple

Jalan Scott, at the eastern edge of Brickfields

The Hindu **Kandaswamy Temple** was founded by the Sri Lankan Tamil community in the 1900s, though the present structure was consecrated in 1997. Its facade a riot of brightly coloured statues reminiscent of Chinatown's Sri Maha Mariamman Temple, it's all the more appealing for being little visited by tourists; just don't expect to find anyone who can explain the layout, which includes, in the far right corner of the entrance wall, a collection of nine garlanded deities representing the planets.

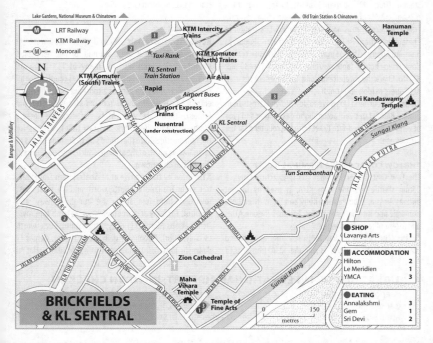

1

ARRIVAL AND DEPARTURE
KUALA LUMPUR

BY PLANE

KL's three airports are some way out of the city, but linked to it by an efficient transit system. Between them they cover all major destinations and hubs across Malaysia, plus Singapore, Bandar Seri Begawan and many Southeast Asian and international airports.

KUALA LUMPUR INTERNATIONAL AIRPORT (KLIA)

Always abbreviated to KLIA, Kuala Lumpur International Airport (ⓦ klia.com.my) is 55km south of KL, and handles most domestic and international traffic.

Facilities The arrivals hall contains a Tourism Malaysia Visitor Centre (open 24hr; ☎ 03 8776 5651) and 24-hour bureau de change, with ATMs and other exchange facilities dotted around. Assorted desks represent the main car rental outlets and KL's pricier hotels.

Trains Two fast, convenient rail links (ⓦ kliaekspres.com) connect the airport with downtown KL Sentral station: KLIA transit (from KL Sentral 4.30am–midnight, from KLIA 5.30am–1am; every 30min; 35min; RM35) stops three times along the way; and the nonstop KLIA ekspres (from KL Sentral 5am–12.30am, from KLIA 6am–1am; every 15–30min; 28min; RM35). Though using the same track, they have different entrances at KLIA.

Airport buses Buses between KLIA and KL are much cheaper, if slower, than the trains. Airport Coach (ⓦ airportcoach.com.my) depart hourly for KL Sentral station (from KL Sentral 5am–10.30pm, from KLIA 6.30am–12.30am; 1hr; RM10); while Star Shuttle (ⓦ starwira.com) runs hourly to Puduraya bus station in Chinatown (from KLIA 6am–2am, from Puduraya 5am–10.30pm; 1hr 15min; RM12), and to certain downtown hotels (approx 7am–12.30am; 1hr 30min; RM18). Check their website for long-distance services from KLIA direct to Ipoh and Lumut.

Taxis The hour-long taxi drive to downtown KL costs from around RM60; fares vary according to destination and type of vehicle. Buy a fixed-fare ticket from the counter near the arrivals exit.

THE LOW COST CARRIER TERMINAL (LCCT)

The Low Cost Carrier Terminal (LCCT; ⓦ lcct.com.my), a 15min shuttle-bus ride from KLIA, is used by budget airlines AirAsia, Cebu Pacific, Firefly and Tiger, flying both domestic and international routes. Facilities include ATMs and a 24hr bureau de change.

Trains The quickest way between the airport and downtown Kuala Lumpur is via the KLIA transit LCCT (ⓦ kliaekspres.com), which uses a shuttle bus between LCCT and Salak Tinggi station to the east, where you pick up the KLIA transit train to KL Sentral station (from LCCT 7.25am–12.35am, from KL Sentral 4.30am–midnight; every 30min; 50min; RM12.50).

Buses Bus services to KL include Skybus to KL Sentral every 30min–1hr (LCCT–KL Sentral 7am–4.30am, KL Sentral–LCCT 3am–10pm; 1hr 15min; RM9; ⓦ skybus .com.my) and Starshuttle's service to Puduraya bus station (at least hourly 6am–2am; RM12; ⓦ starwira.com).

Taxis A taxi ride to KL will cost from RM80, depending on type of vehicle; buy a ticket from the taxi counter.

SUBANG SKYPARK (SULTAN ABDUL AZIZ SHAH (SAAS) AIRPORT)

KL's small third airport, Subang Skypark, 25km west of the city, hosts only Firefly and Berjaya airlines at present, covering a few domestic destinations plus Singapore and Koh Samui in Thailand.

Trains The quickest way into town is to catch a taxi from the airport to Kelana Jaya LRT train station, and then the LRT to KL Sentral or Pasar Seni (around RM32 in total).

Buses Much cheaper, RapidKL bus #U81 travels from Skypark to Pasar Seni (Central Market) in Chinatown via KL Sentral (6am–midnight; every 30min; 40min; RM2; ⓦ myrapid.com.my); while bus #9 terminates at Klang bus station in Chinatown (see p.88).

BY TRAIN

KL Sentral station Located just southwest of downtown KL, this is the main hub for the Peninsula's intercity trains, and also for many of KL's local rail services. Inside, you'll find separate ticket counters for all train services, plus the various airport buses. By the north entrance near where the *Hilton* and *Meridien* hotels are located, there are also ATMs, left-luggage lockers (8am–10.30pm; RM5/day), and taxi ticket counters for the rank outside. Note that there's no pedestrian access to Jalan Travers north of the station, which rules out walking the 2km to Chinatown.

KTM Intercity trains arrive at KL Sentral from Singapore, Hat Yai in Thailand via Butterworth and the west coast towns, or from Tumpat via the "Jungle Railway" and Jerantut. For fares and timetables, see ⓦ ktmb.com.my.

Destinations Alor Star (1 daily; 11hr 45min); Butterworth (3 daily; 10hr); Dabong (1 daily; 10hr 30min); Gemas (1 daily; 3hr 15min); Gua Musang (1 daily; 9hr 30min); Hat Yai

---

KUALA LUMPUR INTERNATIONAL AIRPORT: IN-TOWN CHECK-IN

Passengers departing from KLIA can check bags in up to 2hr before departure time at the KLIA Express ticket desks at KL Sentral station. It's a useful option if you have a late flight and don't want to lug your bags around all day after you check out of your accommodation.

TRAVEL AGENTS AND TOUR OPERATORS

For advice on local tours, Perhentian trips, or packages to Taman Negara, either ask at your hotel or hostel, or visit the **MTC** (see p.91).

Specific **Taman Negara operators** include **NKS** (ⓦ taman-negara-nks.com) and **Han Travel** (ⓦ taman-negara.com), who both charge upwards of RM200 per person for a three-day trip (see p.196).

Recommended agents for domestic and international travel:

Discovery Overland 66 Jalan Metro Pudu 2, Fraser Business Park, off Jalan Yew (near the Pudu LRT station, ☏ 03 9222 8113, ⓦ discoveryoverland.com).

Jet Asia 2-01-02, D'Alamanda, 2 Jalan Pudu Impian

(☏ 03 203505989, ⓦ jetasiatravel.com).

MSL Youth specialist, just east of PWTC train station, next to the *Hotel Grand Central* (☏ 03 4042 4722, ⓦ msltravel.com).

(Thailand; 1 daily; 12hr); Ipoh (4 daily; 3hr 30min); Jerantut (1 daily; 7hr); Johor Bahru (3 daily; 6hr 30min); Kuala Kangsar (4 daily; 6hr 30min); Kuala Lipis (1 daily; 8hr); Singapore (3 daily; 7hr); Sungai Petani (1 daily; 9hr); Taiping (4 daily; 5hr); Wakaf Bharu (for Kota Bharu; 1 daily; 12hr 50min).

KTM Komuter Connects KL Sentral with Pelabuhan Klang, where ferries from Indonesia dock (frequent; 1hr 15min).

Getting into town Pasar Seni station in Chinatown is just one stop from KL Sentral on the Kelana Jaya–Gombak LRT line (ⓦ myrapid.com.my). For Bukit Bintang, you need the Monorail which, in a minor planning lapse, is 200m away on Jalan Tun Sambanthan – descend to street level on the southeast side of KL Sentral and follow a signed walkway around what's currently a vast building site.

BY BUS

Buses depart from KL for major destinations around the Peninsula, typically hourly or every 2hr throughout the day, with additional night-time services on the longest routes. Frequencies are given below only where there are significant departures from this pattern. To buy tickets, you need to turn up and speak to the various bus companies directly. There are no central enquiry numbers for the bus stations, but a few of the larger companies can be contacted by phone (see p.90).

PUDURAYA

KL's largest long-distance bus station, Puduraya, occupies a block-sized, multistorey complex on Jalan Pudu, just east of Chinatown. It deals with northbound traffic, with dozens of bus companies ensuring regular departures to most places through the day. On the main passenger level are ATMs and food stalls, with a bank upstairs.

Arriving at Puduraya Exit the west side of the building for the short walk to Chinatown, or access to an alley leading east to Plaza Rakyat LRT station. A useful

pedestrian bridge crosses Jalan Pudu from the north side, from where Bukit Bintang's hostels are a 15min walk. Alternatively, reach Bukit Bintang aboard RapidKL buses #U27, #U31, #U32, #U44, #U45, #U46, #U47 or #U48, which all head east along Jalan Pudu and Jalan Imbi, then north up Jalan Sultan Ismail to the Lot 10 Mall.

Departing from Puduraya Walk into the ticket hall and you'll be beckoned over to a score of booths all eager for your custom. Aside from seat number and departure time, your ticket will be marked with the departure bay in the basement; each of the 23 bays is reached by a separate numbered staircase.

Destinations Alor Star (6hr); Butterworth (4hr 30min); Cameron Highlands (4hr 30min); Genting Highlands (1hr); Georgetown (4hr); Hat Yai (Thailand; 9hr); Ipoh (3hr 30min); Kangar (8hr); Kuala Kangsar (3hr); Kuala Perlis (7hr 30min); Lumut (3hr 30min); Penang (4hr 30min); Taiping (4hr 30min).

PUTRA

Housed in a tunnel-like building 3km northwest of central KL, reached down an access ramp off a busy intersection, Putra bus station mostly handles traffic from the east coast, including Kuantan, Kuala Terengganu (via the Perhentian islands' jetty at Kuala Besut) and Kota Bharu (via Kuala Lipis and Gua Musang). Ticket offices are in a line down one side of the station, but there are no ATMs or much else on site.

Arriving at Putra Putra KTM station is 200m from the bus station, while PWTC station and the LRT line are 500m away, past the well-signed *Legend Hotel* in The Mall shopping centre.

Destinations Gua Musang (several daily; 5hr); Kota Bharu (9hr); Kuala Besut (for the Perhentians; 1–2 daily; 8hr); Kuala Terengganu (several daily; 7hr); Kuantan (3 daily; 3hr 30min); Tasik Kenyir (2 daily; 8hr).

PEKELILING

Pekeliling bus station is an open-air affair 3km northwest

1

of central KL on Jalan Tun Razak, and used mainly by buses from the interior and Kuantan, along with some services from Sungai Petani via Ipoh and Butterworth. Conveniently, the separate Titiwangsa stations on the Monorail and the LRT are just to the north.

Destinations Butterworth (4 daily; 6hr); Ipoh (4hr); Jerantut (4 daily; 3hr 30min); Kuala Lipis (6 daily; 4hr 30min); Kuala Terengganu (several daily; 7hr); Kuantan (3hr 30min); Sungai Petani (2 daily; 8hr); Temerloh (2hr 30min); Triang (several daily; 4hr).

BERSEPADU SELATAN (TBS)

KL's newest bus station, Bandar Tasik Selatan – south of the centre towards the airport, and accessible on the LRT line – serves most southern destinations, which can also be reached from Kuala Lumpur train station, downtown.

Destinations Johor (4hr); Melacca (2hr); Singapore (6hr).

OTHER BUS STATIONS

KL train station Luxury buses from the old Kuala Lumpur train station (see p.87) serve destinations including: Johor (4hr); Melacca (2hr); Singapore (6hr).

Klang bus station Located in Chinatown, at the south end of Jalan Sultan Mohammed, the Klang bus station serves Port Klang (2hr), but it's far quicker to make this journey aboard the KTM Komuter train to Pelabuhan Klang station.

Jalan Imbi Transtar (⌨transtar.com.sg) luxury buses to and from Singapore (several daily; 6hr) arrive and leave here, at a spot opposite the *Oversea* restaurant. It's convenient as it's practically in the heart of Bukit Bintang.

BY LONG-DISTANCE TAXI

Long-distance taxis As well as the car parks on the upper floors of Puduraya bus station, a few long-distance taxis can be found at Putra and Pekeliling stations. Typical fares per vehicle: around RM260 to Cameron Highlands, RM380 to Kuala Tahan (the main Taman Negara entrance) and RM460 to Kota Bharu or Kuala Terengganu.

BY CAR

Leaving KL by car onto the Peninsula's main highways is hampered by confusing road signage, one-way systems and countless express bypasses.

E1 The North–South Expressway, northbound, is signed from Jalan Duta, which branches off Middle Ring Road I west of the Lake Gardens.

E2 The North–South Expressway, southbound, starts at Sungai Besi 2km south of Chinatown, and is most quickly reached using the long underground SMART tunnel on the eastern section of Jalan Tun Razak.

E8 To reach the E8, which is linked to the East Coast Highway to Kuantan, and Route 8 into the interior, get onto Jalan Tun Razak (or Jalan Raja Laut if starting from Chinatown) and head northwest to Jalan Ipoh; proceed up this for a short distance, then turn right onto Jalan Sentul and follow signs for the highway.

BY FERRY

Ferries The only ferries from the vicinity of KL are those from Port Klang to Dumai (Sumatra; 1 daily; 3hr 30min); check current schedules on ☎ 03 3167 7186. The port is on the KTM Komuter line to KL Sentral and Kuala Lumpur train stations.

GETTING AROUND

Downtown KL isn't that large, so it's tempting to do a lot of your exploring **on foot**, but many pedestrians soon find themselves wilting thanks to the combined effects of humidity and traffic fumes from the vehicle-choked roads. Thankfully, the light rail transit (**LRT**) lines and the **Monorail**, along with **KTM Komuter** train services and **taxis**, are efficient and inexpensive. However, having been created piecemeal, the services don't always coordinate well – ticketing isn't unified and interchanges may involve inconvenient walks. The main governing body is **RapidKL** (⌨myrapid.com.my), which runs the LRT and Monorail lines, plus many of the city's buses; its website includes network maps and details of monthly transport passes.

TOUCH 'N GO CARDS

Though KL's dreams of a properly integrated transport system remain just that, the **Touch 'n Go card** (⌨touchngo.com.my) is a useful **stored-value card** that you simply brush across the sensors at KTM Kommuter, LRT and Monorail stations, plus as you board RapidKL buses. You can also use it to pay Expressway tolls on the Peninsula, and in various car parks and fast-food joints around KL. Cards cost RM10 from many stations (look for the logo); ticket office staff at the same places can recharge them (RM10–500 at a time; cash only), as can 7–11 stores and highway toll stations. As the cards save time queuing, rather than money, they're of most use if you'll be in the city a good deal or plan to drive yourself around the Peninsula.

KUALA LUMPUR TRANSPORT SYSTEM

- **A** Sentul–Port Klang (KTM Komuter)
- **B** Rawang–Seremban (KTM Komuter)
- **C** Ampang–Sentul Timur (LRT)
- **D** Sri Petaling–Sentul Timur (LRT)
- **E** Kelana Jaya–Terminal Putra (LRT)
- **F** KL Sentral–Titiwangsa (Monorail)
- **G** Kuala Kubu Bharu–Rawang (KTM)

Klia Ekspres
Klia Transit
Interchange station
Interchange station (within walking distance)
★ For long-distance trains to Butterworth & Hat Yai
★★ For long-distance trains to Singapore & Tumpat

THE LRT

The Light Rail Transit (every 5–10min 6am–midnight; RM0.70–2.50; ⓦmyrapid.com.my) is a metro network comprising two, mostly elevated, lines, with a convenient central interchange at Masjid Jamek near Little India.

Kelana Jaya Line The more useful of the two LRT lines passes through KL Sentral, Chinatown and the old colonial district (Pasar Seni/Masjid Jamek stations) and KLCC.

Ampang and Sri Petaling The two branches of this LRT line join at Chan Sow Lin station and continue to Sentul Timur in the north of the city. For visitors, it's mainly of use for travel between Chinatown (Plaza Rakyat station) and Little India (Masjid Jamek or

1

Bandaraya stations) and Chow Kit Market (Sultan Ismail station).

THE MONORAIL

Monorail Trains on this elevated rail system (every 5–10min 6am–midnight; RM1.20–2.50; ⓦ myrapid.com .my) have a noticeable tilt as they camber around bends. From its KL Sentral terminus (200m from the KL Sentral rail hub), the line at first heads east, through Brickfields and the southern edge of Chinatown, then swings north and west through Bukit Bintang and along Jalan Sultan Ismail, nearly reaching Jalan TAR before heading north through Chow Kit to terminate at Titiwangsa station on Jalan Tun Razak. There are interchanges with the LRT at Bukit Nanas (requiring a 5min walk to Dang Wangi station) and at Hang Tuah.

KTM KOMUTER TRAINS

KTM Komuter Trains Run by national rail operator KTM (ⓦ ktmkomuter.com.my), trains travel on two lines: one from Sungai Gadut, out past the airport, northwest to Tanjung Malim; the other from coastal Pelabuhan Klang, off to the southwest, up to the northern suburb of Batu Caves. Both connect downtown at four stations: Putra, near the Putra World Trade Centre; Bank Negara, near Little India; the Kuala Lumpur train station, in the colonial district; and KL Sentral. Trains run every 15–20min during the day, but only every 30min after 8pm. Tickets (RM1–9) can be purchased from the stations and automatic machines at the stops; return tickets cost double the one-way fare. Weekly and monthly passes for designated journeys are also available. Note that Komuter trains all have a central women-only carriage.

BUSES

KL has a comprehensive city bus network, with Metrobus and RapidKL as the two main operators, but the lack of clearly marked terminuses and bus stops can make it baffling for outsiders to use. Services start up around 6am and begin winding down from 10pm onwards. Given KL's frequent traffic snarl-ups, do allow plenty of time for your journey. The small grid of streets around Puduraya and Central Market is a

hub of sorts; buildings with key stops close by, including the Sinarkota Building, the Kotaraya Building and the Bangkok Bank, appear on the Chinatown map on p.72.

RapidKL Bus numbers on RapidKL (ⓦ myrapid.com.my). are prefixed B (downtown), E (express buses), T (local services) and U (for travel into and out of the centre). On RapidKL's unusual day-pass system, any ticket entitles you to make additional journeys on the same route the rest of the day; fares are RM2, RM5, RM1 and RM2 for B, E, T and U services respectively.

Metrobus Buses operated by Metrobus (☏ 03 5635 7897) have regular numbers, and use a zonal fare system, starting at under RM1 downtown and rising to RM2.50 for journeys to the city limits. On some buses you pay the conductor; on others you pay the driver or drop the money into a machine close to the driver (in which case change isn't given).

TAXIS

KL taxis are cheap and convenient, though drivers are notorious for trying to negotiate an inflated price for journeys, rather than use the meter. There are two ways to deal with this: ask if they use the meter before getting in, failing which simply flag down another cab; or buy a prepaid coupon for your journey from booths attached to designated cab ranks. Some drivers don't speak much English, so you may want to have the address of your destination written down in Malay, or mention a well-known landmark nearby.

Metered fares Generally low: in regular taxis the flagfall is RM2, and the tariff is 10 sen for every 150m travelled. This translates into just RM4–5 for a typical journey between Bukit Bintang and Chinatown, or RM6–7 for Bukit Bintang to KL Sentral, or Chinatown to KLCC. Expect to pay a few ringgit more for downtown journeys in the smarter taxis; luggage in the boot is charged at RM1/bag.

Taxi ranks There are numerous taxi ranks around the city, usually close to bus stops and outside shopping malls.

Phone numbers To book a taxi, which costs an extra couple of ringgit, call: Public Cabs (☏ 03 6259 2020, ⓦ publiccab.com), Sunlight Radio Taxis (☏ 03 9057 5757, ⓦ sunlighttaxi.com), Comfort Taxi (☏ 03 8024 2727), Supercab (☏ 03 2095 3399) and SW Taxis (☏ 03 2693 6211).

BUS COMPANY PHONE NUMBERS

KL Sentral Transnasional ☏ 03 2273 6473.

Jalan Imbi Transtar ☏ 03 2141 1771 (luxury buses to Singapore).

Pekeliling Plusliner ☏ 03 4042 1256.

Puduraya Konsortium Bas Ekspress ☏ 03 2070 9410 (Penang/Kedah), ☏ 03 2070 1321 (JB/Singapore); Plusliner ☏ 03 2070 2617; Transnasional ☏ 03 2070 3300; Utama Ekspres ☏ 03 2070 3940.

Putra Ekspres Mutiara ☏ 03 4045 2122; Transnasional ☏ 03 4042 9530; Triton ☏ 03 4044 6591; Utama Ekspres ☏ 03 4045 2122.

Old Railway Station Plusliner/Nice ☏ 03 2272 1586 (luxury buses to Penang & Singapore).

HOP-ON, HOP-OFF BUSES

KL's **hop-on, hop-off buses** loop around a set circuit via a string of tourist sights (daily 8.30am–8.30pm; every 15–30min; unlimited use day ticket RM38, two days RM65). Buses are open-top double deckers, with running commentaries in a handful of languages, but it is all rather expensive and prone to getting delayed in the sludge-like traffic.

INFORMATION

Bear in mind that, given the chaotic nature of KL city planning, maps and listings tend to go out of date fairly quickly; don't be surprised if roads, venues and buildings have sprung into existence or ceased to be.

Tourism Malaysia The national tourist board has branches across the city (✆tourism.gov.my), handing out brochures and general advice; staff are helpful if not especially clued up. You can also book accommodation, local tours and packages to Taman Negara and the like through in-house travel agents. The main office is at MTC, 109 Jalan Ampang, not far from the Bukit Nanas Monorail stop (daily 8am–10pm; ☎03 9235 4900); bus #B105 also runs here from Central Market in Chinatown. Other branches: KL Sentral Station, Level 1 (daily 9am–6pm; ☎03 2272 5823); Putra World Trade Centre, Level 2 (Mon–Fri 9am–6pm; ☎03 2615 8540); KLIA international arrivals hall (24hr; ☎03 8776 5647).

Listings To keep an ear to the ground on happenings around town, check out the monthly listings magazines *Klue* (✆klue.com.my) and *Time Out KL* (✆timeoutkl.com). Also worth a look is ✆visionkl.com, a handy repository of sights, restaurants, clubs and events.

Maps *Road Map & Highway Guide of Kuala Lumpur* (RM10), published by World Express Mapping and available in most city bookstores, is a handy two-sided foldaway sheet covering the city and the surrounding Klang Valley, surprisingly detailed given the scale. Drivers might need *The Big Atlas of Klang Valley and Beyond* (RM37), a hefty street atlas for the same area.

ACCOMMODATION

While **Chinatown** has traditionally been the favourite location for budget travellers, with its surfeit of inexpensive places to sleep, eat, drink and shop, it faces growing competition from **Bukit Bintang**, a 15min walk east. Here, close to the abundant fancy hotels and malls, not to mention the celebrated Chinese food stalls of Jalan Alor, you'll find plenty of excellent guesthouses on and around Tengkat Tong Shin. Even though they're more expensive than Chinatown, these are often better value – less cramped and noisy, with slicker facilities and self-service breakfasts included in the rate. Slightly further afield, more upscale hotels can be found along **Jalan Sultan Ismail** and **Jalan Ampang**, which, together with Bukit Bintang, form part of KL's **Golden Triangle**. All other parts of KL pale as regards accommodation, though **Little India** and nearby **Chow Kit**, linked by the fiendishly busy **Jalan Tuanku Abdul Rahman**, feature several mid-range options.

Rates Thanks to an over-supply of rooms for much of the year, rates remain competitive – a bed in a dorm can be had for RM12, and it's seldom hard to find a simple double in a guesthouse with shared facilities for RM50/night, or RM80 if you need en-suite facilities and air conditioning. A good mid-range hotel room costs around RM150, while anything above RM250/night will be pretty luxurious. Check online or ask when booking about promotional rates or weekday hotel discounts; the prices below refer to weekend rates.

Bookings Although it's almost inconceivable that you'd be unable to find somewhere to stay in your price range, it always makes sense to book ahead, especially during busy periods – July, August, November and December, plus school and public holidays. As well as individual accommodation websites, try ✆hostelworld.com or ✆hostelbookers.com for hostels and guesthouses, or the many dedicated KL hotel-booking websites.

Wi-fi Almost everywhere has wi-fi, or at least computer terminals, usually free for guests.

CHINATOWN AND AROUND

Chinatown's wealth of backpacker-oriented guesthouses are mostly concentrated either side of Jalan Petaling, alongside increasing numbers of budget hotels offering backpacker-sized rooms but with better facilities. Both are increasingly modern and efficiently run, though furnishings are minimal and the cheapest rooms are unlikely to have windows. Older, more mundane establishments are clustered north of

Puduraya bus station. Only upmarket options feature frills like in-house swimming pools, though there is an ageing public pool nearby at the Chinwoo Stadium (see p.107).

HOTELS

Ancasa Jalan Tun Tan Cheng Lock ☎03 2026 6060, ✆ancasa-hotel.com; map p.73. Slick hotel with small, smart rooms featuring big-screen TVs and very comfy beds.

1

There's also a pricey spa for massages, aromatherapy and other treatments, plus a decent restaurant and bar, though breakfast isn't included in the rate. RM380

China Town 2 70–72 Jalan Petaling ☎ 03 2072 9933, ⊛ hotelchinatown2.com; map p.73. Identical in concept and feel to the *Chinatown Inn* below (the owners are brothers), though with slightly smarter rooms, including some singles, crammed deep into a building that runs all the way to Jalan Sultan. RM99

★ **Chinatown Boutique Hotel** 34–36 Jalan Hang Lekir, off Jalan Sultan ☎ 03 2072 3388, ⊛ chinatown boutiquehotel.com; map p.73. Exactly what it says on the label: stylish budget hotel with spacious, Chinese-themed rooms (Longevity Room, Shaolin Kungfu Room etc) all sporting windows, chic glass-walled bathrooms and a/c. Front desk can be abruptly business-like, and furnishings are a little superficial, but otherwise great for the price. The entrance is hidden behind stalls, but it's clearly signed. RM100

Chinatown Inn 52–54 Jalan Petaling ☎ 03 2070 4008, ⊛ chinatowninn.com; map p.73. Reached by an unobtrusive doorway behind the market stalls, this is a little haven in the heart of Chinatown. The rooms are bland but spacious enough; all have TV and attached bathroom, and most have a/c – which is just as well, as many are windowless. Internet access and wi-fi in the lobby. RM99

Citin 38 Jalan Pudu ☎ 03 2031 7777, ⊛ citinhotels .com; map p.73. A cheerful, modern hotel, albeit nowhere near as smart as the lobby suggests. Their small, bright twins have flat-screen TV and sparkling bathrooms, and rates include breakfast. RM150

D'Oriental Inn 82 & 84 Jalan Petaling ☎ 03 2026 8181, ⊛ dorientalinn.com; map p.73. Nicely located in the thick of the market, the bland modern rooms have en-suite facilities and TVs; rooms with/without windows are the same price. RM99

Mandarin Pacific 2–8 Jalan Sultan ☎ 03 2070 3000, ⊛ mandpac.com.my; map p.73. The rough brick exterior looks unappealingly downmarket, but this is a decent hotel for the price, with reasonably sized en-suite rooms and breakfast included. RM150

Orange Hotel 16 Jalan Petaling ☎ 03 2070 2208, ⊛ stayorange.com; map p.73. Kitted out in the colour scheme of a big-name European budget airline, and likewise featuring ridiculously cheap prices if you book way ahead. Rooms are en suite but cramped, despite containing a minimum of furniture; there are also boxy rooms with bunks that share facilities. Bunks RM65, doubles RM95

Soho Town 113 Jalan Sultan ☎ 03 2031 8133, ⊛ sohotownhotel.com; map p.73. One of a new crop of budget hotels in the area, with spotless tiled floors, neat modern furnishings, TV, a/c and en suite, but almost no extra space at all. Larger, pricier rooms have windows. RM90

Swiss Inn 62 Jalan Sultan ☎ 03 2072 3333, ⊛ swissgarden.com; map p.73. This much-liked modern hotel has a wide range of rooms – some windowless, others larger with an extra sofa bed – offering stylish minimalist decor. The coffee house affords a good view of the Petaling Street market. Rates include breakfast. RM290

Winsin Hotel 1–3 Jalan Petaling ☎ 03 2031 5011, ⊛ winsinchinatownhotel.com.my; map p.73. Older building with small modern rooms, all en suite and with a/c, a few of which are windowless. Well placed for Central Market. RM88

HOSTELS AND GUESTHOUSES

Anuja Backpackers Inn 28 Jalan Pudu ☎ 03 2026 6479, ✉ anujainn@sgsmc.com; map p.73. Boxy and slightly scruffy rooms, some with a/c. The shared bathrooms are in good order; there's also a tiny lounge with a TV, and the price is right. Dorms RM12, doubles with fan RM35, a/c doubles RM48

Backpacker's Travellers Inn 60b Jalan Sultan ☎ 03 2078 2473, ⊛ backpackerskl.com; map p.73. Well-established place where the narrow corridors are lined with louvred windows belonging to rather plain rooms. Some rooms and the dorms have a/c; a few are also en suite. The chief attractions are the cool rooftop bar with affordable beers, and the travel agency offering assorted trips. Breakfast available for a few ringgit extra. Dorms RM11, doubles with fan RM38, doubles a/c RM56

Le Village Guesthouse 99a Jalan Tun H.S. Lee ☎ 03 2026 6737, ✉ dwahashim@yahoo.com; map p.73. The abstract paintings in the entrance stairway set the tone at this shabby, chilled-out place, in a building that was among the grandest shophouses in KL when it was built in the 1910s. It's a little worse for wear now; inside are simple rooms and three-bed dorms with sliding doors, all with fans (the windowless ones can still be stuffy, though) and shared facilities. Dorms RM12, doubles RM28

★ **Matahari Lodge** 58–1 Jalan Hang Kasturi ☎ 03 2070 5570, ⊛ mataharilodge.com; map p.73. Immaculate guesthouse with gleaming white corridors and spotless showers and toilets. There's a/c in the common areas, and the cool air is sucked into the rooms – sparsely kitted out, with floral bed linen and the odd fancy lamp – by extractor fans in the walls. Shared bathrooms, complimentary self-service breakfast, satellite TV and very helpful staff. Not the place if you want a funky vibe, but ever so relaxed. Dorms RM30, doubles RM76

Oasis Guesthouse 125 Jalan Petaling ☎ 03 2031 0188, ✉ oasiskl@yahoo.com; map p.73. Amiable, mildly shabby hostel, with tidy rooms in pastel colour schemes, some with en suite and a/c. Dorms RM15, doubles RM55

Red Dragon Hostel 80 Jalan Sultan ☎03 2078 9366, ✉hostelrd@yahoo.com; map p.73. A labyrinthine, threadbare affair on several levels, past its prime but reasonably run. Some rooms have a/c, and there's an enormous TV lounge and a café open to the hubbub of Jalan Sultan. Dorms RM18, doubles RM45

Reggae Mansion 49–59 Jalan Tun H.S Lee ⓦreggaemansionkl.com; map p.73. Warehouse-sized colonial-era block, recently converted to house a hostel, restaurant and club/bar. It's a bit of a tourist-trail factory – despite the excellent level of furnishings, there isn't much atmosphere – and everything seems geared towards ensuring that you plan your entire time in Malaysia through the hostel's services. Dorms RM30, doubles RM80

Serai Inn Second floor, 62 Jalan Hang Lekiu ☎03 2070 4728, ⓦseraiinn.com; map p.73. Entered via an alley off Jalan Hang Lekiu, this spotless and secure backpackers' place offers dorms and a range of rooms, all with a/c and shared bathrooms, plus simple breakfasts. Dorms RM25, doubles RM75

Stay Green Hotel 9–11 Jalan Petaling ☎03 2031 5268, ⓦstaygreeninn.blogspot.com; map p.73. Immaculately modernized old shophouse, with polished wooden floors, large and comfy common area and generous quantities of green paint inside and out. Dorms are open-plan, each tier of bunks screened by curtains; doubles are fair value if small. The whole place is kept absolutely spotless by attentive staff. Dorms RM30, doubles RM75

Step Inn 35–37 Jalan Pudu Lama ☎03 2070 7770, ✉stepinn.kualalumpur@gmail.com; map p.73. Pleasant, unpretentious Indian-run guesthouse with shared facilities, where all the spacious rooms have windows; a few doubles come with a/c too. There's also a small terrace to sit out on, with cane furniture. Dorms RM15, doubles RM60, doubles a/c RM120

★ **Suzie's** 179 Jalan Tun H.S. Lee ☎03 2032 2821, ✉suzies_guesthouse@yahoo.com; map p.73. Facilities are all shared, and just one room has a window; otherwise the cheerful colour schemes, tidy rooms and spotless common area with TV make this secure, well-managed modern hostel stand out from the crowd. Dorms RM20, doubles RM40

THE GOLDEN TRIANGLE, INCLUDING BUKIT BINTANG

Many of the Bukit Bintang guesthouses occupy nicely restored old shophouses, with small, comfortable rooms separated from one another using simple partitions of plywood or other material. It's hard to go wrong with any of these, just as it's difficult to be badly disappointed with any of the Golden Triangle's upmarket hotels. The area also boasts excellent serviced apartments offering a lot more space than you'd get in a similarly priced hotel room.

HOTELS

Alpha Genesis 45 Tengkat Tong Shin ☎03 2141 2000, ⓦalphagenesishotel.com; map pp.78–79. Modern business-oriented hotel that has the distinction of being a little cosier than many others in the same price bracket. Rates include breakfast. RM199

★ **Anggun** 7 & 9 Tengkat Tong Shin ☎03 2145 8003, ⓦanggunkl.com; map pp.78–79. Splendidly stylish boutique hotel, in a restored Chinese building on three floors around a central atrium, decorated with Chinese-Malay furnishings. Rooms feature wooden floors, four-poster beds and shuttered windows, plus modern en-suite facilities, a/c and TV. The top-floor dining room is open-plan, under a thatched roof. RM280

Comfort Inn 65 Changkat Bukit Bintang ☎03 2141 3636, ⓦhotelcomfort.biz. Behind the ugly concrete exterior is a tiny hotel – the cheapest in the area – offering smallish, plain a/c rooms, each with TV and a boxy attached bathroom. RM90

Corus Jalan Ampang ☎03 2161 8888, ⓦcorushotelkl.com; map pp.78–79. Tried-and-tested 1980s hotel that's maturing well despite an ill-advised exterior makeover involving pale orange paint. Thankfully, decor in the plush rooms is suitably muted. Amenities include Chinese and Japanese restaurants, swimming pool and sauna. RM640

Dorsett Regency 172 Jalan Imbi ☎03 2716 1000, ⓦdorsettregency.com; map pp.78–79. Great-value mid-range hotel, even if the brown tower-block design lacks style: it's central, modern and some rooms have superb views of the Petronas Towers. RM200

Equatorial Jalan Sultan Ismail ☎03 2161 7777, ⓦequatorial.com; map pp.78–79. Vast five-star hotel with tastefully decorated, Chinese-themed rooms, a swimming pool and some good restaurants and cafés. RM500

★ **Federal** 35 Jalan Bukit Bintang ☎03 2148 9166, ⓦfhihotels.com; map pp.78–79. This venerable hotel, dating from the 1950s, has been nicely updated over the decades. Its current incarnation sports a marbled lobby, while facilities include a pool, bowling alley and the revolving *Bintang* restaurant which, like some of the rooms, offers views over the concrete jungle of malls that dominate Bukit Bintang. RM290

GTower 199 Jalan Tun Razak ☎03 2168 1919, ⓦgtowerhotel.com; map pp.78–79. Upmarket executive-class hotel, whose smart rooms, sleek with dark tiling and spotlights, are just a sideshow for the conference facilities, outdoor pool, gym and rooftop bar, where you can admire the night-time cityscape while cradling a cool drink. RM450

Impiana KLCC 13 Jalan Pinang ☎03 2147 1111, ⓦimpiana.com; map pp.78–79. This tastefully decorated hotel offers subdued but stylish rooms with slick bathroom fittings. Ideally placed for both Bintang Walk and KLCC, it also features a swimming pool and spa, and keener rates than other hotels in its class. RM520

1

Mandarin Oriental Kuala Lumpur City Centre ☎03 2380 8888, ⓦ mandarinoriental.com; map pp.78–79. Enormous hotel – it only looks small by virtue of being conveniently next to the Twin Towers – that's as sumptuous as they come, with its own luxury spa, swimming pools, tennis courts and some tiptop restaurants. RM600

Marriott 183 Jalan Bukit Bintang ☎03 2715 9000, ⓦ marriott.com; map pp.78–79. Among the crème de la crème of KL hotels, with top-notch rooms and facilities including the obligatory pool, spa and gym, plus several good restaurants. RM450

★ **Maya** 138 Jalan Ampang ☎03 2711 8866, ⓦ hotelmaya.com.my; map pp.78–79. This stunning boutique hotel has two hundred rooms arranged around a vast, futuristic central atrium, and is distinguished by chic designer furnishings throughout. Each grade of room has its own design quirks, such as bathrooms with glass walls (and privacy curtains) so you can watch the big-screen TV while soaking. The hotel also boasts a range of spa treatments and restaurants, and offers free airport transfers. RM700

Myhotel 120 Jalan Pudu ☎03 2143 5000, ⓦ myhotels .com.my; map pp.78–79. Budget business hotel, offering the usual value-concious, low-frills rooms: trim modern furnishings, en-suite bathrooms and a/c, with little space for anything else. RM20 extra gets you a window. RM108

Piccolo 101 Jalan Bukit Bintang ☎03 2146 5000, ⓦ piccolohotel.com.my; map pp.78–79. They brag that they're a "hip boutique hotel" and indeed sport modish designer touches everywhere, plus an Italian restaurant and a Japanese-style spa. Good rates for the location. RM337

Radius 51a Changkat Bukit Bintang ☎03 2715 3888, ⓦ radius-international.com; map pp.78–79. Substantial, bustling hotel with reasonable rooms, a restaurant and café, and a terrace swimming pool with views of Menara KL and the Maybank Tower. RM250

Renaissance Junction of Jalan Sultan Ismail and Jalan Ampang ☎03 2162 2233, ⓦ marriott.com; map pp.78–79. Part of the Marriott group, and featuring an excellent outdoor swimming pool, gym and restaurants. The older east wing is around twenty percent cheaper. Rates exclude breakfast. RM350

Seasons View 61 Jalan Alor ☎03 2145 7577, ⓦ seasonsview.com; map pp.78–79. A mundane, smallish hotel that's competently run, has tidy en-suite rooms, a good location amid the culinary splendour of Jalan Alor, and great rates (which include breakfast). RM110

Swiss Garden 117 Jalan Pudu ☎03 2141 3333, ⓦ swissgarden.com; map pp.78–79. This substantial modern hotel, which also features good-value serviced apartments, is conveniently located at the edge of Bukit Bintang and halfway to Chinatown. Facilities include satellite TV, a couple of restaurants plus a pool, gym and spa. RM250, serviced apartments RM330

GUESTHOUSES

★ **Anjung Guesthouse** 4 Tengkat Tong Shin ☎03 2148 6812, ⓦ anjungkl.com; map pp.78–79. Friendly place offering a range of rooms plus an eight-bed dorm, all with nice tiled floors, a/c and shared facilities. Doubles rooms have queen-sized beds. You can relax watching satellite TV in the lounge or sit at tables out front. There's a book exchange too. Rates include breakfast. Dorms RM40, doubles RM70

Classic Inn 52 Lorong 1/77a, Changkat Thambi Dollah ☎03 2148 8648, ⓦ classicinn.com.my; map pp.78–79. Don't be put off by the anonymous backstreet location; once onto the patio, decked in plants, this is a modern, quiet, friendly guesthouse. Rooms are en suite and have a/c and TV; there's also a lounge kitted out with stylish wooden furniture and featuring satellite TV. A Western breakfast is included in the rate, or you can order local favourites like *roti canai* if you prefer. RM128

★ **Green Hut** 48 Tengkat Tong Shin ☎03 2142 3339, ⓦ thegreenhut.com; map pp.78–79. Easily spotted thanks to its lime-green exterior, with further bright multicoloured walls and a suitably romantic jungle mural within, *Green Hut* is a relaxed place boasting simple a/c rooms that share spotless facilities, plus a few en-suite rooms. The cosy lounge has internet terminals and satellite TV. Rates includes breakfast. RM60

Number Eight Guesthouse 8–10 Tengkat Tong Shin ☎03 2144 2050, ⓦ numbereight.com.my; map pp.78–79. A guesthouse infusing designer chic into shophouse surroundings, evident in the stylish furnishings in the two lounges and permeating every room. All rooms have a/c and marble-topped sinks, though only a few rooms are en suite. Rates include a self-service breakfast of toast, fruit and coffee/tea. Dorms RM85, en suite RM135

Pondok Lodge 20–1b Jalan Changkat Bukit Bintang ☎03 2142 8449, ⓦ pondoklodge.com; map pp.78–79. There's something genteel about this spacious, long-established guesthouse, with its simply furnished, somewhat boxy rooms, plus a four-bed dorm; front rooms, looking out over nightclubs, can be noisy though. All have a/c but share bathrooms. Satellite TV and internet in the lounge. Dorms RM25, doubles RM65

Pujangga Homestay 21 Jalan Berangan ☎032141 4243, ⓦ pujangga-homestay.com; map pp.78–79. A couple of adjacent 1970s terraced houses, combined to produce a sprawling guesthouse with single and double rooms and dorms. There are also a couple of lounges with satellite TV, plus a kitchen. Rates include breakfast. Dorms RM25, doubles RM75

Rainforest Bed & Breakfast 27 Jalan Mesui ☎032145 3525, ⓦ rainforestbnbhotel.com; map pp.78–79. Cute place with a strong antique Chinese flavour, despite claustrophobic corridors decked in a bright red pebbledash finish. Rooms are all en suite with

TV and a/c, and there's wi-fi in the lobby. Really, it's more of a budget hotel than a B&B, though breakfast is indeed included. RM140

★ **Travellers Palm Lodge** 10 Jalan Rembia ☎03 2145 4745, ⓦtravellerspalm-kl.com; map pp.78–79. Delightful guesthouse, down a lane off Tengkat Tong Shin and fronted by two travellers' palms in the tiny front garden. Inside, the spacious lounge is dotted with old furniture; there's a range of rooms plus an eight-bed dorm, all with a/c and shared facilities. Snug and secure – only guests have a front gate key – and rates include breakfast. Dorms RM25, doubles RM70

SERVICED APARTMENTS

See also *Swiss Garden* (p.94) and *Maytower Hotel* (below).

Fahrenheit Suites Floor 5, Fahrenheit 88 Mall, 179 Jalan Bukit Bintang ☎03 2148 2686, ⓦfahrenheit suites.com; map pp.78–79. Modern serviced apartments, including some that sleep up to six, with their own pleasant lounge, kitchenette, plus use of swimming pool. Parking available. Online rates sometimes vastly reduced. RM800

Pacific Regency Menara Panglobal, Jalan Puncak, off Jalan P. Ramlee ☎03 2332 7777, ⓦpacific-regency .com; map pp.78–79. Luxury apartments complete with kitchenette, huge bathroom, satellite TV, free wireless internet access and, on the roof, a swimming pool and the excellent *Luna* bar (see p.101). Ample parking too. RM370

Somerset 8 Lorong Ceylon ☎03 2055 8877, ⓦsomerset.com; map pp.78–79. Popular with executive types, these immaculate one- and two-bed apartments in a modern tower block are equipped with swish furnishings, satellite TV/DVD systems and internet. On the fourth floor are a sauna, gym, a swimming pool with good views and a poolside café, open only for breakfast (included in the rate). RM310

LITTLE INDIA AND CHOW KIT

Coliseum Hotel 98–100 Jalan TAR ☎03 2692 6270; map p.76. End-of-the-road atmosphere at this famous 1920s survivor, though the moderately atmospheric lobby and bar don't make up for the plain, frayed rooms (with fan – there's no a/c), ancient furniture and shared bathrooms. RM40

Garden City Hotel 214 Jalan Bunus, off Jalan Masjid India ☎03 2711 7777, ⓦgarden-city-hotel.com; map p.76. An unmistakable, dark green Art Deco exterior bizarrely festooned with window boxes packed with plastic tulips. It's kitsch, but at least there's some character to the place, with serviceable, modern en-suite rooms. Rates include breakfast. RM125

Grand Orchard 141 Jalan Bunus, off Jalan Masjid India ☎03 2698 6333, ✉grand_orchard@yahoo.com; map p.76. Budget hotel with recently redecorated rooms – all

with a/c and en suite, the pricier ones with windows – set around a central well. RM120

Hostel Cosmopolitan fourth floor, 73 & 75 Jalan Haji Hussein ☎03 2691 5686, ⓦhostelcosmopolitan .blogspot.com; map p.76. The management here runs a tight ship and this secure hostel does just fine, despite a location at the rougher end of Chow Kit market. There are four double rooms plus a fourteen-bed women's dorm and an eighteen-bed mixed dorm, all with bright bed linen and shared facilities, including a kitchen. It could use more showers and toilets, though. Dorms RM20, doubles RM60

Maytower Hotel 7 Jalan Munshi Abdullah ☎03 2692 9298, ⓦmaytower.com.my; map p.76. International-standard hotel, with choice of smart modern rooms or apartments. Rooms are much better value, stylishly appointed in earthy tones and equipped with flat-screen TV and safe. Cityscape views are good too. Ask about monthly rates. Rooms RM350, apartments RM530.

Palace 46–1 Jalan Masjid India ☎03 2698 6122, ⓦpalacehotel.com.my; map p.76. 1970s-style red-flock carpets and hangings make this large hotel a little gloomy and dated, though all rooms have a/c and it's in a lively location. RM145

Tune Hotel 316 Jalan TAR ☎03 7962 5888, ⓦtunehotels.com; map p.76. AirAsia-supported no-frills hotel, very cheap if you book very early. The cookie-cutter en-suite rooms are small and functional in the extreme, with fans; you pay extra for a/c, towels, TV, wi-fi etc if you want them, which can add RM40 to the basic rate. Lobby facilities amount to a couple of fast-food outlets and a convenience store. Best deals online; the rate here is for walk-ins. RM104

BRICKFIELDS AND KL SENTRAL

Hilton 3 Jalan Stesen Sentral ☎03 2264 2264, ⓦkuala -lumpur.hilton.com; map p.85. Lavish hotel whose lobby wouldn't look out of place fronting a modern art museum, while the rooms could be straight out of a style magazine. RM600

Le Meridien 2 Jalan Stesen Sentral ☎03 2263 7888, ⓦkualalumpur.lemeridien.com; map p.85. Not quite as opulent as the *Hilton* next door, but grand by anyone else's standards, with a pool and spa, and a fancy Lebanese restaurant. RM400

YMCA 95 Jalan Padang Belia ☎03 2274 1439, ⓦymcakl.com; map p.85. Well-maintained if institutional and sterile place, open to male and female guests. Rooms, all with a/c, en suite and TV, range from singles to quads. Facilities include a café, laundry, barber and tennis courts (you'll need your own gear, though). Good value, particularly as breakfast is included. RM120

1

FURTHER OUT

Carcosa Seri Negara Taman Tasik Perdana ☎ 03 2295 0888, ⊕ shr.my; map pp.70–71. Set in their own grounds just west of the Lake Gardens, these two elegant, whitewashed colonial mansions, containing thirteen suites, date to 1904. Without a doubt the most exclusive place to stay in KL – the management can truthfully boast "Queen Elizabeth slept here". If a night here is out of the question, consider donning smart-casual clothes and dropping in for their English cream tea (RM80). RM1000

EATING

Food is without doubt a highlight of any visit to KL. There are simply more opportunities to enjoy high-calibre cooking here, in assorted local and international styles, than anywhere else in the country, and whether you dine in a chic bistro-style restaurant or at a humble roadside stall, prices are almost always very reasonable. Despite plenty of scope for cosmopolitan, upmarket dining, eating for many locals is still fundamentally about Malay, Chinese and Indian **street food**. Stalls, whether on the street or collected into **food courts** (found in or close to major office blocks and shopping malls), are your best bets for inexpensive, satisfying meals, as are **kedai kopis**, though these are a little scarce in the Golden Triangle. The best-known food stalls are held in the same kind of reverence as a top-flight restaurant might be in a Western city, and people will travel across KL just to seek out a stall whose take on a particular dish is said to be better than anyone else's; if you find customers lining up to partake of some stall's spring rolls or *laksa*, it's a sure-fire indicator of quality. Ranging from small affairs in beautifully refurbished shophouses to banqueting halls in five-star hotels, KL's **restaurants** are an equally vital part of the food experience. Be aware, however, that price and decor are not a watertight indicator of consistency or quality, and that service can be hesitant even in big hotels.

CHINATOWN AND AROUND

Superb food stalls in Chinatown serve up everything from rich yet subtle *bak kut teh* (pork-rib consommé) to cooling sweet treats like *cendol*. Foreign visitors can find it hard to get to grips with the stalls, especially as some are signed only in Chinese or not at all. Still, for an excellent taster of how they operate, and of street food in general, try the *Tang City Food Court* (see opposite). Otherwise, the area has plenty of *kedai kopis* and a few cheap or mid-priced restaurants, with some touristy places at the eastern end of Jalan Hang Lekir. You're not limited to Chinese food; since the fringes of Chinatown, especially north of Jalan Hang Lekir and around the Central Market, feature plenty of Indian and *mamak* places.

Es Teler 77 Jalan Hang Kasturi and Lebuh Pudu; map p.73. Indonesian fast food, with colour photos of available dishes at the counter – *nasi goreng*, *mie ayam* and *otak-otak*. It's the sweet desserts that stand out. Try the house special, *es teler* (a sort of chilled fruit cocktail in coconut milk) or *cendol*. RM6. Daily 10am–8pm.

Five Plus Two Maju Jalan Hang Lekiu; map p.73. The unusual name (*maju* means "progress") apparently came during a moment of prayer to someone associated with this Indian *kedai kopi*. Reliable *nasi campur* and *rojak*, and some days there's also fish-head curry and South Indian *apam* pancakes. Noodles can be fried to order. Mon–Sat 8am–5pm.

Lai Foong Corner of Jalan Tun Tan Cheng Lock and Jalan Tun H S Lee; map p.73. Locals flock to this extremely popular, rapid-turnover *kedai kopi* for its noodle and rice dishes – in particular the Hainanese beef noodle, flavoured with herbs and served with not just beef slices but also tripe. Possibly the slowest service in all Malaysia though. Mon–Sat 7.30am–5pm.

Mangrove Food Court Central Market; map p.73. The outlets here, specializing in food from different corners of the Peninsula, can be indifferent, but the Rasa Kelantan stall is outstanding, serving east-coast specialities like *nasi kerabu* and *nasi dagang*, plus a range of curries and unusual stir fries such as *pucuk paku* (edible fern). For dessert, the *Thai Corner* stall is as good a place as any to try to get to grips with Malay sweets (*kuih*, *bubur pulut hitam*, and so forth). Daily 10am–evening.

Medan Pasar Jalan Benteng; map p.73. As well as the usual run of Malay-Chinese fried rice, noodles and eggs, what this clean and busy canteen does best is tandoori chicken and naan, served straight out of the streetside oven. Round things off with Three-Layer Tea – tea, palm syrup and condensed milk, each poured slowly into the glass so they don't mix. Fill up for RM12. Daily 10am–9pm.

★ **Old China Café** 11 Jalan Balai Polis ☎ 03 2072 5915, ⊕ oldchina.com.my; map p.73. Nonya restaurant atmospherically housed in a 1920s shophouse that was once home to KL's laundry guild; much of the decor, including the saloon-style swing doors at the entrance, is original and lovingly preserved. Must-trys include classic dishes such as *pie tee*, fried shredded vegetables served in crispy pastry cups; *itek tim*, duck soup; *babi pong teh*, soy pork cooked with preserved soybeans; *chap chye*, the classic Nonya veg stir fry; and desserts such as *bubur cha cha* or sago with *gula melaka*. Not expensive either – RM65 is ample to feed two. Daily 11.30am–11pm.

Precious Old China upstairs in the southwestern corner of Central Market ☎ 03 2273 7372, ⊕ oldchina .com.my; map p.73. A posher version of *Old China Café*, run by the same management and packed with more antique furniture, though not as atmospheric as the original. The menu is slightly more comprehensive, though no pork is served. Daily 11.30am–9.30pm.

Purple Cane Tea House Third floor, 6 Jalan Panggong ☎ 03 2072 1349; map p.73. Calm retreat from Chinatown's hubbub, accessible only by elevator, and serving a range of speciality Chinese teas, from finely scented green to heavy *pu'er*, reddish-brown like some of Malaysia's jungle rivers and imbued with a strong smoky flavour. Staff show you how to brew a cup properly; they also serve light snacks. RM5–25 depending on tea type. Daily 11am–7pm.

Restoran Yusoof Jalan Kasturi, right outside Central Market; map p.73. Clean and friendly Muslim Indian-Malay diner, featuring excellent *murtabak*, roti, fried rice and *rojak*, plus reasonable tandoori chicken, with a meal costing RM10 or less. Portions are generous and, inside, the piped Islamic music doesn't intrude as much as you'd think from the street. Daily 7.30am–5pm.

Santa 7 Jalan Tun H.S. Lee; map p.73. Maintain a healthy dietary fibre intake at this otherwise unremarkable Indian *kedai kopi* that, unusually, offers freshly made chapatis and chickpea curry, plus other more commonly found curries and rice dishes. RM10 for a full meal. Daily 8am–3pm.

★ **Seng Kee** 50 Jalan Sultan; map p.73. Unassuming but frenetically busy, quintessentially Chinese restaurant serving up great Cantonese fare – everything from standards like beef with *kai lan* to river-fish dishes. The house speciality, however, is *loh shee fun*, which unappetizingly translates as "mouse noodles" but is actually fantastic: stubby lengths of noodle fried with soy sauce, served in a claypot and topped with pork crackling and a raw egg. Daily 10.30am–late.

Sri Ganesa next to the Court Hill Ganesh Temple; map p.73. You can't site an Indian restaurant next to a major Hindu shrine without it thriving. This one is indeed frequently packed and boasts as many as two dozen offerings in its vast *nasi campur* spread, including fried spicy cauliflower, green egg curry and other meaty and veggie options. Daily 8am–4pm.

Tang City Food Court Jalan Hang Lekir; map p.73. A collection of fairly priced, tourist-friendly stalls, all recommended. This is a great place to try prawn *mee* (available from the Lim Kee stall) or *yong tau foo* (available at a couple of other stalls – scan the signs). For afters, try the whimsically named Summer Shala'la stall at the front on the left, which does souped-up versions of local desserts, such as *batu campur* augmented with various fruit toppings. Daily 10am–11pm.

Vinejayaa Jalan Sultan Mohammed, behind the Sri Maha Mariamma Temple; map p.73. South Indian canteen with blisteringly hot curries from about RM5/ portion, and a spectacular range of Indian sweets that you can buy to take away. Daily until late.

Wan Fo Yuan Vegetarian Restaurant Jalan Panggong; map p.73. Extremely plain a/c establishment,

lurking behind unprepossessing dark glass doors, but serving inversely tasty food. The picture menu features catfish, fried goose rice and other "meaty" treats, all made with soya-, gluten- or yam-based substitutes and exhibiting miraculous depths of flavour considering the vegetarian ingredients. Servings are generous, and most dishes cost around RM12 (rice or noodle one-plate meals RM6). Daily 10am–10pm.

THE GOLDEN TRIANGLE AND KAMPUNG BAHRU

Besides numerous restaurants, the Golden Triangle also boasts one of KL's best alfresco experiences in **Jalan Alor**. The street actually has a double layer of food outlets: the open-fronted restaurants that line the street, and the food stalls arranged in front of them. Food is predominantly Chinese, with a strong seafood bias – and some of the city's tastiest Hokkien noodles, comprising egg noodles fried in lard, seasoned with dark soy sauce and garnished with prawn, pork and fishcake slices, and greens – but there are plenty of Thai and Malaysian options too, plus fresh fruit and drink vendors. It all fires up from 6pm, and the stalls stay open into the small hours. Some menus omit prices, so fix them when ordering to avoid nasty surprises when the bill arrives. Dishes cost RM5–25; you can usually order small, medium or large portions.

Blue Boy Vegetarian unnamed lane off Jalan Tong Shin ☎ 03 2144 9011; map pp.78–79. This collection of stalls, occupying the ground floor of an apartment block, serve veggie versions of street food – everything from chicken rice to *asam laksa*. Daily 7.30am–9.30pm.

★ **Chinoz On The Park** G47, Suria KLCC ☎ 03 2166 8277; map pp.78–79. Smart, convivial café-restaurant with generally Mediterranean-slanted food, from Lebanese lamb wraps to various pizzas (some of the best in town, from RM25), plus a good range of cocktails. The icing on the cake is the great location facing KLCC's kitsch musical fountains. Daily 8am–midnight.

Din Tai Fung Level 6, Pavilion KL mall, next to Times bookstore ☎ 03 2148 8292, ⓦ dintaifungmalaysia .com; map pp.78–79. Michelin-starred Taiwanese light-meal chain, specializing in Shanghainese *xiaolong bao* – little pork dumplings served in a bamboo steamer, eaten dipped in ginger vinegar. Also good are the substantial bowls of spicy *dan dan* noodle soup, though other dishes often lack character. The ambience is "smart café", and it gets very busy at lunchtime. Expect RM25 a head. Daily 11am–10pm.

Enak Lower Ground Floor, Starhill Gallery ☎ 03 2141 8973, ⓦ enakkl.com; map pp.78–79. One of the best Malay restaurants in KL, though toning down the starchy red-and-white decor would provide a more relaxed experience. Food is excellent: try the *penbuku selera* (grilled prawns in tamarind juice), chicken with ginger flowers, the fragrant *otak-otak* steamed fish parcels, plus an array of *sambal* relishes. Round things off with *sago gula melaka* (coconut milk and palm sugar) and black coffee. Reservations essential. Mains around RM30. Daily 9am–midnight.

Espressamente Outside at the Pavilion KL, facing Starhill Gallery; map pp.78–79. Small Italian-style café featuring chrome furniture, pavement tables and strong imported brews, all for a price: an espresso will set you back a steep RM9.30. Daily 8am–5pm.

Golden Phoenix *Hotel Equatorial*, Jalan Sultan Ismail ☎ 03 2161 7777, ⓦ equatorial.com; map pp.78–79. Smart Cantonese restaurant, which includes a few Beijing, Sichuan and even Thai items. Excellent seafood, with a broad vegetarian choice too; the weekend dim sum breakfasts and seasonal crispy soft-shell crab are the business. Mains around RM40 except for seafood, dim sum Sat & Sun 10am–3pm. Reservations advisable. Daily noon–2.30pm & 6.30–10.30pm.

★ **Guanyin Temple Vegetarian** Jalan Ampung; map pp.78–79. Behind the main hall of this shrine to the multi-armed, multi-eyed Chinese goddess of mercy is a sea of plastic chairs and communal tables, packed to bursting at lunchtime with office workers making the most of the inexpensive self-serve selection of Chinese vegetarian dishes. RM5 or so, depending on how full your plate is. Mon–Fri noon–2pm.

Koryo-Won Starhill Gallery ☎ 03 2143 2189; map pp.78–79. Upmarket Korean restaurant specializing in Korean "smoke barbecues", done to a turn at your table; also fine ginseng chicken and *kimchi jigae*, a fiery home-style stew. RM65 per person, excluding rice. Daily noon–1am.

La Bodega Lot C3.06.00, Level 3, in the side Connection block at Pavilion KL mall ☎ 03 2148 8018, ⓦ bodega .com.my; map pp.78–79. Well-regarded local chain serving up tapas plus deli food (including all-day breakfasts and great sandwiches and cakes) and modern European fare. Daily 10am–2am.

Lot 10 Hutong Basement, Lot 10 Mall, Jalan Bukit Bintang; map pp.78–79. Chinese hawker and *kopitiam* stalls, some claiming to date back to the 1930s, in modern, hygenic conditions. Despite very few local faces and elevated prices, the food isn't bad, from Hainan chicken and bbq duck to beef noodle soups, dim sum dumplings and desserts like ABC or *cendol*. RM10–12. Daily 11am–10pm.

Madam Kwan's Lot 420/421, Level 4, Suria KLCC mall ☎ 03 2026 2297; map pp.78–79. When street stalls and *kedai kopis* don't appeal, come here to try elaborate takes on classic local fare in a smart-casual restaurant environment. Mains such as *nasi lemak*, chicken rice and *rendang* around RM25. Daily 11am–10.30pm.

Neroteca Ground floor, Somerset Apartments, 8 Lorong Ceylon ☎ 03 2070 0530, ⓦ neroteca.com; map

pp.78–79. More relaxed sister restaurant to *Nerovivo* just up the hill, and cheaper too, serving deli food, including sandwiches and (unlike its pork-free sibling) parma ham. Mon & Wed–Sun 9.30am–midnight, Tues 6.30pm–midnight.

Nerovivo 3a Jalan Ceylon ☎ 03 2070 3120, ⓦ nerovivo .com; map pp.78–79. Among the best Italian places in KL, with upmarket, chic modern decor and an extensive menu including plenty of excellent meat and seafood options. Busy rather than intimate ambience, and not cheap – pizzas and pasta dishes start at RM35, while main courses cost RM60 and up. Booking essential. Mon–Fri noon–3pm & 5.45–11.30pm, Sat 5.45–11.30pm, Sun 5.45–11pm.

★ **Oversea** 84–88 Jalan Imbi ☎ 03 2148 7567, ⓦ oversea.com.my; map pp.78–79. Much-loved, if rather "old-style" Cantonese restaurant, well known for excellent roast meats such as *char siew*, plus dim sum at lunchtime and great seafood, including its trademark (non-Cantonese) *asam* fish head. Mains from RM25. Daily 11.30am–2.30pm & 5.30–10.30pm.

Palate Palette 21 Jalan Mesui ☎ 03 2142 2148, ⓦ palatepalette.com; map pp.78–79. Friendly, arty atmosphere, with the emphasis on style – snazzy, colourful decor and rather minimalist fusion food, such as Thai roast beef sandwiches and lamb chops with black bean sauce. Mains from RM30, with cheaper sandwiches, soups and salads available, and a vast range of cocktails; portions tend to be small. Tues–Sun noon–late.

Qba *Westin Hotel*, 199 Jalan Bukit Bintang ☎ 03 2731 8333, ⓦ westin.com/kualalumpur; map pp.78–79. Latin American-themed restaurant with generous portions and a cosy ambience, though on the pricey side – plenty on the menu is around the RM60 mark. Put together your own grill platters featuring steak, chicken or seafood (charged by weight) or go for lighter tapas or other options. Daily 5pm–late.

★ **Sao Nam** 21 Tengkat Tong Shin ☎ 03 2144 1225, ⓦ saonam.com.my; map pp.78–79. Unpretentious but stylish and consistently excellent Vietnamese restaurant, with top-notch service and food. Beneath wall posters extolling the collectivist life, definitive beef *pho* noodles are served up, alongside delightful mangosteen salad – a house speciality – and, to wash it down afterwards, Vietnamese drip-style coffee. Good-value set lunches Tues–Fri (RM30); otherwise expect RM75 a head with drinks. Tues–Sun 12.30–2.30pm & 7–10.30pm.

Sari Ratu 42–4 Jalan Sultan Ismail ☎ 03 2141 1811; map pp.78–79. Basically a smart canteen, with Indonesian food from around the archipelago laid out in trays; you get a plate of rice and then pay per dollop of curry you put on it, at around RM6 each. A couple is plenty – try the *rendang*, and curried jackfruit. Daily 11am–11pm.

Seri Angkasa Revolving atop Menara KL ☎03 2020 5055, ⓦserimalayu.com; map pp.78–79. The buffets, which are what most customers go for, aren't that spectacular – but the views of downtown KL certainly are. Smart-casual dress required: no shorts, sleeveless tops or sandals. On weekdays, lunch costs RM70, tea RM40, and dinner 7–11pm; at the weekend, brunch is RM80 and high tea RM50. Mon–Fri noon–2.30pm, 3.30–5.30pm & 7–11pm; Sat & Sun 11.30am–3pm & 3.30–5.30pm.

Tarbush LG16, Starhill Gallery ☎03 2144 6393, ⓦtarbush.com.my; map pp.78–79. A classy Lebanese *par excellence*, with plenty for carnivores, including classic *shish tawook* (grilled chicken breast) plus a best-of-everything mixed grill at around RM35, as well as loads for veggies if you order up meze (selections, all at around RM12, include hummus, stuffed vine leaves and tabbouleh). The fruity milkshakes are as luscious as anything sold on the streets of Beirut. The same owners have another outlet at 138 Jalan Bukit Bintang. Daily 11am–late.

★ **Twenty One** 20–21 Changkat Bukit Bintang ☎03 2142 0021, ⓦdrbar.asia; map pp.78–79. This trendy restaurant specializes in clever fusion cuisine – almond-crusted rack of lamb, for example – with more straightforward risottos, salads and plenty of cakes for dessert. Quality varies but is reliable by and large; mains from RM40. Reserve at weekends. Daily noon–late.

LITTLE INDIA, CHOW KIT AND BEYOND

Little India is a good area for both Indian and Malay food – inexpensive Indian restaurants and sweetmeat shops are ranged along Jalan Melayu, while in and around Lorong TAR's *pasar malam* are quite a few Malay food stalls and Indian *kedai kopis*, and a useful food court opposite the *Palace Hotel* stays open late. A few truly venerable *kedai kopis*, some housed in equally venerable shophouses, can be found along hectic Jalan TAR, while there are more stalls, Malay and even Indonesian, around Chow Kit Market.

★ **Capital Café** 213 Jalan TAR; map p.76. Housed in a Neoclassical block, this endearing *kedai kopi* is something of a period piece itself, looking as though little has been altered since it first opened in the 1950s. The halal food caters to all tastes, with meals from about RM10: there's *nasi lemak* in the morning, *rojak* and *nasi padang* during the day and excellent satay in the evenings, plus Chinese rice and noodle dishes cooked to order throughout. Mon–Sat 10am–8pm.

Jai Hind 11–15 Jalan Melayu; map p.76. Friendly Sikh-run *kedai kopi* which, besides an impressively wide-ranging *campur*-type spread of curries and stir fries, also has an extensive menu of North Indian savouries and sweets, as good as you'll get in much posher restaurants but at half the price. RM15 should see you full. Mon–Sat 8am–9pm, Sun 10am–7pm.

Saravanaa Bhavan Jalan Masjid India ☎03 2287 1228, ⓦsaravanabhavan.com; map p.76. Member of a slightly eccentric Madras-based chain of vegetarian restaurants that's spread its tentacles as far afield as London and New York. Concentrate on the South Indian dishes – *dosai*, *idli*, *uthapam*, and so forth – and be warned that spicing can be incendiary. Inexpensive, with main courses under RM10. Daily 8am–10pm.

Sithique Nasi Kandar 233 Jalan TAR; map p.76. One of a handful of popular *kedai kopis* on Jalan TAR serving Penang-style variations on *mamak* fare, with an impressive range of fiery curries, including fish-head as well as cuttlefish. One-plate meals about RM8. Daily 7.30am–7.30pm.

BRICKFIELDS

Naturally enough, Indian food dominates the Brickfields eating scene.

★ **Annalakshmi** Temple of Fine Arts, 114–116 Jalan Berhala ☎03 2274 0799, ⓦannalakshmi.com.sg; map p.85. Community-run South Indian vegetarian restaurant with a stupendous eat-all-you-want buffet, featuring terrific home cooking. You pay what you feel the meal is worth to you, and the profits go to support various projects. Smart-casual dress; no shorts, sports clothes or open shoes. Tues–Sun 11.30am–3pm & 6.30–10pm.

Gem 124 Jalan Tun Sambanthan, Brickfields ☎03 2260 1373; map p.85. Reliable, moderately smart restaurant serving South Indian chicken, mutton and seafood curries. The vegetarian *thali* platters cost around RM11.50 for a lot of food. Conveniently close to the Monorail station. Daily 11.30am–3pm & 6–11pm.

Sri Devi Jalan Travers ☎03 2274 4173; map p.85. Widely reckoned to sell some of Brickfields' best Indian food, this little place does excellent banana-leaf curries from midday onwards and wonderful *dosai* all day. The *masala dosai* (RM6) is particularly fine. Daily 8am–4pm.

BANGSAR

The small grid of streets known as Bangsar Baru, 4km southwest of Chinatown, is one of several satellite suburbs known for smart restaurants and bars, here catering to expats as well as well-heeled professionals. Bus #U87 travels to Bangsar from the Sultan Mohamed terminal in Chinatown, via KL Sentral. Bangsar LRT station isn't convenient for Bangsar Baru, being some way downhill with busy highways to cross in between. A taxi from Chinatown shouldn't cost more than RM8.

Alexis Bistro 29 Jalan Telawi 3 ☎03 2284 2880, ⓦalexis.com.my; map p.100. The de facto clubhouse of Kuala Lumpur's movers and shakers – you'll see newspaper editors, academics, film-makers and politicos chewing the fat and putting Malaysia to rights here. Both local and Western fare is served, so don't be surprised that slick noodle and pasta dishes feature on the menu. There's also a formidable gateau counter. Main courses from around RM20. Daily 9am–late.

1

EATING
Alexis Bistro	5
Brux Ale	2
Chawan	8
Daily Grind	9
Delicious	6
House Frankfurt	1
La Bodega	3
Nature's Vegetarian	4
Sri Nirwana Maju	7

DRINKING
Ronnie Q's	1

SHOPS
Outdoors	1
Rock Corner	3
Yellow Stone	2

Brux Ale 4 Jalan Telawi 2 ☎ 03 2287 2628; map above. Not just a mighty range of Belgian beer, but also Belgian cuisine served up in smart-casual bistro setting. Distinctive takes on bangers and mash, seafood-vegetable soup and even African chicken – not to mention chocolate ice cream – from the country that brought you Tintin, the saxophone and Audrey Hepburn. Set lunches RM40. Mon 5pm–late, Tues–Sun noon–midnight.

★ **Chawan** Jalan Telawi 3 ☎ 03 2287 5507; map above. Popular open-sided coffee house in chic concrete and steel, which doesn't detract from the cheerfully noisy ambience. Specializing in regional coffee blends from around Malaysia, it also serves *kopitiam*-style one-dish meals, from roti and *nasi lemak* to *asam laksa* and *soto ayam*. An espresso or americano is RM3.80, with all meals under RM15. Daily 8am–1am.

Daily Grind Lower ground level, Bangsar Village mall ☎ 03 2287 6708, ⓦ thedailygrind.com.my; map above. Gourmet burger joint with not just beef patties but also burgers of salmon, crab, chicken and lamb, plus a great array of side orders and their own range of relishes. Not cheap though – most burgers cost RM25–40. Daily 11am–11pm.

★ **Delicious** Ground floor, Bangsar Village II mall ☎ 03 2288 1554, ⓦ thedeliciousgroup.com; map above. Originally a store selling clothes for the larger woman that has branched out into health-conscious catering, resulting in this superb café-restaurant. The food's not actually starved of fat, sugar and salt, but is expertly prepared and reasonably priced – sandwiches, quiches, pastas and salads start at RM20. The luscious cakes, which probably boost their clothing sales, are recommended. Breakfasts available until 6pm at weekends. Mon–Fri 11am–1am, Sat & Sun 9am–1am.

House Frankfurt 12 Jalan Telawi 5 ☎ 03 2284 1624, ⓦ housefrankfurt.com; map above. If the pork-free nature of a lot of KL dining is getting you down, come to this agreeable bar-restaurant to enjoy *schweinfleisch* – as grilled pork knuckle, *wurst* or schnitzel. They also do classic southern German *spätzle*, little pasta bits with cheese and bacon. A great place for a drink too (see below). Mains RM32 and up. Daily noon–midnight.

La Bodega 16 Jalan Telawi 2 ☎03 2287 8318, ⓦbodega.com.my; map opposite. Tapas bar augmented by a bistro and deli. There's also a lounge with cosy armchairs, cocktails and yet more tapas. Deli daily 8am–10pm; rest of the place Mon–Fri noon–late, Sat & Sun 10am–late.

Nature's Vegetarian 24 Jalan Telawi 3 ☎03 2283 5523; map opposite. Antique-style Chinese teahouse serving vegetarian light meals, best visited for dim sum, which is served daily until 6pm. The barbecue "spare ribs"

and steamed spring rolls are great, the "prawn" dumplings a bit gloopy. Portions RM5 or so. Mon–Fri 9am–10pm, Sat & Sun 8am–10pm.

Sri Nirwana Maju 43 Jalan Telawi 3 ☎03 2287 8445; map opposite. Bright, heavily popular banana-leaf curry house with canteen decor – proving that not every Bangsar establishment is upmarket. About the most you can pay is RM15 for the lamb *biryani*. Expect to wait a few minutes for a table.

The Social 57–59 Jalan Telawi 3 ☎03 2282 2260; map opposite. Convivial bar-restaurant with a mix of Asian and Western fare, plus football matches on satellite TV, and terrace tables. Set lunches at RM25 are good value. Daily noon–2am.

DRINKING, NIGHTLIFE AND ENTERTAINMENT

KL's most fashionable **bars** and **clubs** are concentrated in the Golden Triangle, while Bangsar also plays host to a few slick bars. If the drinking scene seems to tick over healthily enough, KL's **clubbing** scene appears surprisingly buoyant for its size. Only during Ramadan are both the bars and clubs distinctly quiet. The modest local **performing arts** scene is split between KL and its satellite town Petaling Jaya, which, with its complex system of numbered roads that even residents don't understand, is best accessed by taxi. **Theatre** is probably the strongest suit, with concerts, musicals and so forth throughout the year, by local as well as international performers and troupes. There's also a dedicated community of people working in the **visual arts**.

Events listings Check the national press and also the monthly magazines *Klue* (ⓦklue.com.my) and *Time Out* (ⓦtimeoutkl.com). In a similar spirit, ⓦkakiseni.com is worth consulting not only for listings but also for an intelligent look at how the performing arts can find a balance with the multicultural Asian and Muslim values that hold sway in Malaysia.

Club listings and entry To keep up with happenings, including which big-name DJs might be in town, check out the Friday club listings in the *Star* newspaper, *Juice* magazine (ⓦjuiceonline.com) or the clubs' own websites. Most clubs open Wednesday to Sunday 9pm to 3am or so; the typical cover charge of RM20–40 rises if well-known DJs are playing.

BARS AND PUBS

Bar hours vary from one venue to the next, but most places are open from mid-afternoon until midnight, at least. Beer in KL costs around RM12 a pint (when available on draught; bottles and cans are more common), a couple of ringgit less during the happy hours that most places offer.

Coliseum Hotel 98 Jalan TAR ☎03 2692 6270 map p.76. Endearingly antiquated – or creakingly ancient – the bar here has a rich history and relaxed atmosphere, though some of the cocktails are a bit iffy. Sip a chilled beer and imagine the planters and colonial administrators of yesteryear gathering to quench their thirst. Daily 10am–10pm.

Frangipani 25 Changkat Bukit Bintang, ☎03 2144 3001, ⓦfrangipani.com.my; map pp.78–79. Behind the impressive Art Deco-style facade lies a bar with sleek minimalist decor, excellent cocktails, pumping house sounds and a beautiful straight and gay clientele, almost as pretty as the downstairs restaurant's pricey nouvelle cuisine, served 7.30–10.30pm only. Tues–Sun 6pm–late.

The Green Man 40 Changkat Bukit Bintang ☎03 2141 9924, ⓦgreenman.com.my; map pp.78–79. Small, likeable pub serving reasonably priced local and imported beer and bacon and cheese toasties. Particularly busy when there's football or rugby on TV (there's also a pool table). Mon–Thurs 4pm–late, Fri–Sun noon–late.

House Frankfurt 12 Jalan Telawi 5, Bangsar ☎03 2284 1624, ⓦhousefrankfurt.com; map opposite. Relaxed venue with amicable management and walls lined with vintage photos of German movie stars. They offer a terrific range of Pilseners and German dark beers and *weissbier*, plus *schnapps* and German wines. Daily noon–midnight.

Luna Bar Level 34, Pacific Regency Hotel Apartments, Menara Panglobal, Jalan Puncak ☎03 2332 7777, ⓦluna.my; map pp.78–79. If you've only time to take in one bar while in KL, you could do far worse than head for this gorgeous rooftop poolside venue, with loungey sounds and breathtaking views of KL's skyline. Daily 5pm–late.

Reggae Bar 158 Jalan Tun H.S. Lee, Chinatown ☎03 2041 8163, ⓦreggaebarkl.com; map p.73. No-frills bar

1

that's very popular with backpackers, though a few locals drop by too. The walls are plastered with Bob Marley memorabilia, though the DJs do recognize that other reggae artistes are available. Daily 11am–3am.

Ronnie Q's 32 Jalan Telawi 2, Bangsar ☎ 03 2282 0722, ⓦ ronnieq.com; map p.100. Plenty of bars feature football matches on satellite TV, but at *Ronnie Q's* the focus is very much on sport – not just soccer but also cricket and rugby. The closest thing KL has to a Western sports bar. Daily 5pm–late.

Speakeasy 9 Jalan Ampang ☎ 03 2078 8830; map p.73. A rare example of its species in the Chinatown area, this bar-restaurant serves Tiger on draught plus Heineken, as well as a menu of light meals and snacks. Pool tables available. Mon–Fri 10am–11pm.

CLUBS AND LIVE MUSIC

KL's clubland largely focuses around the junction of Jalan Sultan Ismail and Jalan P. Ramlee in the Golden Triangle, although venues are also springing up around Asian Heritage Row on Jalan Doraisamy, near Medan Tuanku Monorail station. The music policy at each venue tends to change with alarming frequency, but as a rule weekends feature more serious dance sounds, while during the week retro hits and fairly accessible R&B take over. Unfortunately, **live music** in KL isn't much to write home about. With Malaysia a centre for music piracy, most international bands won't show up, and it doesn't help that religious conservatives have kicked up a huge stink when the likes of Avril Lavigne and Gwen Stefani have performed here. Consequently most concerts are safe big-name pop, soul or country artists, plus occasional indie bands. That said, KL has a few small venues where local English-language singer-songwriters and bands get to strut their stuff, and shows by Malay pop stars and old-school rockers are occasionally publicized in the press.

CLUBS AND LIVE VENUES

@space Asian Heritage Row ☎ 03 2698 3328, ⓦ asianheritagerow.com; map p.76. Yes, they've taken the name seriously and gone for a mild sci-fi theme here (well, overdone neon and coloured lighting on the dance-floor anyway); the sounds are DJ-driven House, Electronica and R&B. Wed–Sat 9pm–3am, Sun 10pm–3am.

Beach Club 97 Jalan P. Ramlee, Golden Triangle ☎ 03 2166 9919, ⓦ trendmatrixenterprises.com; map pp.78–79. Established venue with a somewhat clichéd thatched-tropical-hut theme; definitely something of a meat market. Still, the mix of commercial chart and house sounds does pull in the punters, and it audaciously claims to have been voted Asia's best bar (presumably by the owner). Wed–Sun 5pm–late.

Blue Boy 50 Jalan Sultan Ismail (actually in a small lane off the main drag) ☎ 03 2142 1067; map pp.78–79. Kuala Lumpur's chief gay venue is a bit of a dive but still attracts a large local and foreign crowd to its bar and dance area, though beware the odd hustler. Daily 8pm–3am.

Heritage Live@Upstairs Asian Heritage Row ⓦ asianheritagerow.com; map p.76. A mixture of house, R&B and retro sounds at this sleek and surprisingly spacious venue. Wed, Thurs & Sat 9pm–4am, Fri 9pm–3am.

Maison Jalan Yap Ah Shak, behind the Sheraton and very close to Asian Heritage Row ☎ 03 2694 3341, ⓦ maison .com.my; map pp.78–79. An impressive conversion of colonial-era property, retaining the period facade but all minimalist decor within. Nightly except Mon.

Nuovo/Sangria 16 Jalan Sultan Ismail ☎ 03 2170 6666; map pp.78–79. A mix of locals and tourists head downstairs to *Sangria* for the bar and small outdoor dance-floor, or upstairs to swanky *Nuovo* for hip-hop and indie sounds. Expect to queue on Saturdays. Wed–Sat, 9pm–late, Sun, 10pm–3am.

Poppy Collection 18–1 Jalan P. Ramlee ⓦ trendmatrixenterprises.com; map pp.78–79. Swanky designer venue, spinning soul and R&B downstairs in the Poppy Garden, with largely unadulterated house sounds above in the Passion Living Room and varied sounds in their Mandalay Lounge and Havanita Cigar Room. No cover charge except during special events. Wed–Sat 9pm–3am, Sun 10pm–3am.

Supernova@Avenue K 156 Jalan Ampang; map pp.78–79. Recently renovated live band and star DJ venue, hoping to attract international and local talent.

Zouk 113 Jalan Ampang, Golden Triangle ☎ 03 2171 1997, ⓦ zoukclub.com.my; map pp.78–79. Set inside a distinctive, organically curvy building, this offshoot of one of Singapore's top clubs has become a mainstay of the KL scene. The half-dozen venues here – zouk, barsonic, phuture, velvet underground, Aristo and the Relish terrace

---

GAY KL

KL's gay community is fairly discreet, though the smart cafés of fashionable **Bintang Walk** – the stretch of Jalan Bukit Bintang just east of Jalan Sultan Ismail – attract a noticeably gay clientele at weekends. Friday is gay night at *Frangipani* (see p.101), *Nuovo* (above) hosts a GLBT night the last Sunday of the month, and if you see other clubs advertising "boys' nights", you'll know you can head there too. There's also *Blue Boy* (see above). For more on gay venues and social events in the city, try ⓦ utopia-asia.com or ⓦ gaygetter.com.

bar – spin an eclectic range of music, including a smidgeon of indie. Tues–Sat nights.

THEATRE AND CLASSICAL MUSIC

Aside from the Actors Studio, other drama companies worth making time for include the Five Arts Centre (ⓦ fiveartscentre.org) and the satirical Instant Café (ⓦ instantcafetheatre.com). There are two home-grown orchestras to choose from, namely the Malaysian Philharmonic Orchestra (ⓦ mpo.com.my) and the Dama Orchestra (ⓦ damaorchestra.com), the latter specializing in Chinese classical music and musicals. Watch the press for news of international recitals.

THEATRES, PERFORMANCE SPACES AND CONCERT HALLS

Besides the venues listed here, there are occasional concerts at the KL Convention Centre and also at out-of-town resorts such as Genting Highlands; check the press for details.

Actors Studio Roof Top, Level 8, Lot 10 Shopping Centre, 50 Jalan Sultan Ismail ⓣ 03 2142 2009, ⓦ theactorsstudio.com.my. Most prominent of KL's **theatre** companies, the studio mounts several productions each year, ranging from Malaysianized versions of foreign classics to work by local playwrights, and has been instrumental in the creation and running of one of the city's more impressive independent arts centres, KLPac (see below).

Dewan Filharmonik Petronas Twin Towers, KLCC, box office ⓣ 03 2051 7007, ⓦ mpo.com.my. The home of the Malaysian Philharmonic, it also hosts concerts by other performers, not just in the classical domain. Box office is on the ground floor, Tower 2. Box office Mon–Sat 10am–6pm.

Istana Budaya (National Theatre) Jalan Tun Razak, east of the junction with Jalan Pahang and south of Titiwangsa Gardens ⓣ 03 4026 5555, ⓦ istanabudaya .gov.my. Besides providing a spacious modern home for the National Theatre Company and the National Symphony Orchestra, this venue sees performances by visiting international orchestras as well as staging pop concerts, plays and ballets. Just over 1km from Titiwangsa (LRT/Monorail) or Chow Kit (Monorail) stations.

KLPac Jalan Strachan, off Jalan Ipoh ⓣ 03 4047 9000, ⓦ klpac.com. A joint project of the stalwart Actors Studio company and the construction conglomerate that's redeveloping the area, the KL Performing Arts Centre is housed in a former rail depot revamped to look like something Frank Lloyd Wright could have doodled. It hosts jazz, indie and dance events plus, of course, plays by various companies. The location couldn't be more awkward, in the depths of the old Sentul Raya Golf Club and cut off from the nearby Sentul Komuter station by the rail line, which you can't cross safely without a big detour. Get here by taxi; just pray that the driver is a culture vulture or

remembers the golf course. As for heading back, be prepared for a trudge out to Jalan Ipoh, where you can pick up a taxi.

Panggung Bandaraya Corner of Jalan Sultan Hishamuddin and Jalan Tun Perak, Sultan Abdul Sumad building, colonial district ⓣ 03 2617 6307; map p.73. Occasional performances of Malay drama (*bangsawan*) take place in this historic theatre with a Moorish facade.

FILM

Cinema Both the two main cinema chains charge RM12–50/seat, depending on the time and film. Golden Screen Cinemas (ⓦ gsc.com.my) are at Pavilion KL and Berjaya Times Square in Bukit Bintang; their Mid Valley Megamall screen is your best bet for occasional foreign art-house films. TGV (ⓦ tgv.com.my) has a conveniently located multiplex at Suria KLCC, Bukit Bintang. As a total contrast, the Coliseum Cinema, in Little India on Jalan TAR (see p.75), is perhaps worth a trip for its 1930s Art Deco character, even if its Bollywood and Chinese kung fu films aren't your thing.

CULTURAL SHOWS

Traditional dance can be seen at the cultural shows put on by the Malaysian Tourism Centre and by a couple of restaurant theatres, though what's on offer is inevitably touristy. Indian dance is better catered for, thanks to the Temple of Fine Arts.

Malaysia Tourism Centre (MTC) 109 Jalan Ampang ⓣ 03 2164 3929, ⓦ tourism.gov.my. Half-hour dance shows, featuring performers from Borneo as well as the Peninsula, are held on Mondays and Tuesdays from 3pm. More interesting are occasional music sessions featuring *dikir barat*, improvised Malay folk music with shades of rap from the east coast; check the website for details.

Saloma Next to MTC, Jalan Ampang ⓣ 03 2161 0122, ⓦ saloma.com.my. Similar in concept to the better-established *Seri Melayu*, this offers "tiffin set lunch" (RM38 per person, minimum 2), and an evening buffet (RM70) with a performance of traditional dance, supposedly focusing on different states of the Federation each night. Daily 11am–10.30pm.

Seri Melayu Jalan Conlay ⓣ 03 2145 1811, ⓦ serimelayu.com. Touristy but fun Malay buffets served in a traditional wooden house, with "Culture Show Performance" of Malay dancing at 8.30–9.15pm. Smartish dress required – no shorts or sleeveless tops. Expect to pay RM46 at lunchtime, RM72 in the evening. Mon–Fri noon–3pm & 6.30–11pm, Sat 6.30–11pm.

Temple of Fine Arts 114–116 Jalan Berhala, Brickfields ⓣ 03 2274 3709, ⓦ tfa.org.my. Community-run cultural centre set up to preserve Tamil culture by promoting dance, theatre, folk, classical music and craft-making. Probably the best place in KL to see traditional Indian dance. Check website for event schedules.

1

SHOPPING

There's no city in Malaysia where consumerism is as widespread and in-your-face as KL. The malls of the Golden Triangle are big haunts for youths and yuppies alike, while **street markets** remain a draw for everyone, offering a gregarious atmosphere and goods of all sorts. Jalan Petaling in Chinatown (see p.73) is where to find fake watches and leather goods; some of these have started to creep into the covered market on Jalan Masjid India and the nearby Lorong Tuanku Abdul Rahman *pasar malam* (see p.75), but their mainstays remain clothes and fabrics, plus a few eccentricities such as herbal tonics and various charms alleged to improve male vigour. Chow Kit Market (see p.75) has some clothing bargains but little else of interest. A great just-out-of-town market for knick-knacks and general bric-a-brac happens every weekend inside the **Amcorp Mall** in Petaling Jaya, close to Taman Jaya station on the LRT. If no specific **business hours** are given in the shop listings that follow, then the establishment keeps the usual Malaysian shopping hours, opening by mid-morning and shutting at 8pm (an hour or two later in the case of outlets within malls), six or seven days a week.

ANTIQUES

Antiques are extremely expensive in Southeast Asia, and often fake; dealers listed below are sound but even experts can be fooled, so don't fork out unless you know what you're doing. The biggest market is for Chinese and Peranakan (Nonya) porcelain, woodcarvings and artefacts, though there are also some Malaysian and Asian specialists in town.

Heritage of the Orient Ground Floor, Central Market, Chinatown ☎01220 82685, ⓦheritageoftheorient .com; map p.73. Select range of genuine antiques from Tibet, China and Central Asia, plus a few pieces from Sarawak. Pricey. Daily 10am–8pm.

House of Suzie Wong Lot 10 Mall, Bukit Bintang ☎03 2143 3220; map pp.78–79. Interesting, ecclectic range of antiques and collectibles from mainland China and Tibet, including furniture and carpets; high quality but reasonable prices. Daily 10am–6pm.

Madame Butterfly Floor 2, Mid Valley Mall ☎03 2282 8088. Antiques and antique-style arts and crafts, best for Burmese jade jewellery and Nonya porcelain. Daily 10am–6pm.

Oriental Arts Level 6, Pavilion KL, ☎03 2148 8992 ⓦorientalartskl.blogspot.com; map pp.78–79. Chinese ceramics at relatively reasonable prices (RM500 for an antique rice bowl). Daily 10am–6pm.

Pucuk Rebung Level 3, Ampang Mall, Suria KLCC ☎03 2382 0769; map pp.78–79. Excellent range of Malaysian modern art and museum-quality antiques, from Chinese shipwreck porcelain to Malay betel-nut scissors and tobacco boxes. The manager is a mine of information about the history of Chinese culture in Malaysia. Daily 10am–6pm.

Sri Malaya Ground Floor, Central Market, Chinatown; map p.73. High-quality collection of porcelain, antique woodwork and the like, at relatively moderate prices. Daily 10am–6pm.

BOOKS AND CDS

The larger KL bookshops are pretty impressive, split into Chinese, English and Malay language sections, and carrying a range of publications comparable to what you'll find at a good bookshop in the West. They tend to be strong in literature about Malaysia and the rest of Southeast Asia – everything from historical monographs and classics-in-translation, to manga, cookbooks and coffee-table tomes on architecture and garden design. Unfortunately, in this country of rampant piracy, music shops are nothing to write home about.

Junk Book Store 78 Jalan T.S. Lee, Chinatown; map p.73. Ancient establishment, jammed to its dusty rafters with secondhand books, most in English, covering every conceivable topic, from pulp fiction to gardening. Daily 10am–10pm.

Kinokuniya Level 4, Suria KLCC ☎03 2164 8133, ⓦkinokuniya.com; map pp.78–79. Huge and efficient Japanese chain, with the broadest selection of books in KL. A pleasure to use. Daily 10am–6pm.

MPH Unit JA1, ground floor, Mid Valley Megamall ⓦmphonline.com. This veteran survivor of the local book trade is resting on its laurels somewhat, though it still carries a decent mix of novels and nonfiction titles. They also have smaller outlets on the ground floor at BB Plaza, Bukit Bintang; level 1, KL Sentral; and in Bangsar Baru at the Bangsar Village mall. Daily 10am–10pm.

Popular Bookshop Lee Rubber Building, Jalan T.S. Lee, Chinatown ☎03 2078 1953, ⓦpopular.com.my; map p.73. Stationer-style bookshop, worth checking for maps, paperbacks and cookbooks before heading further afield. Daily 10am–8.30pm.

Rock Corner First floor, Bangsar Village mall ☎03 2284 6062; map p.100. Bravely independent music retailer, good for hard-to-find rock and indie CDs. Daily 10am–7pm.

Times Bookstore Level 6, Pavilion KL mall ☎03 2148 8813, ⓦtimesbookstores.com.my; map pp.78–79. Large, well-organized member of the Singapore-based chain. Daily 10am–10pm.

HANDICRAFTS

KL is a good place to bone up on handicrafts, though they tend to be available a little more cheaply in the provincial areas where they originate, and some here might even have been imported from overseas. For a broad range – everything from Royal Selangor pewter models of the Petronas Towers, to bright batik, tribal textiles and original paintings or sculptures – visit Chinatown's Central Market (p.72) and Komplek Budaya Kraf (p.80).

Galeri Waresini Jalan Ampang, Bukit Nanas; map pp.78–79. Downstairs there's a small range of batik and paintings by local artists; upstairs you'll find beautiful, hand-carved furniture and wooden screens at premium prices.

Kwong Yik Seng Crockery 144 Jalan Tun H.S. Lee, Chinatown ☎03 2078 3620; map p.73. Hand-carved wooden Chinese cake moulds, Nonya *pie tee* moulds, and stacks of modern pink-and-green Nonya porcelain (at almost antique prices, however). They'll generally bargain a little. Mon–Sat 10am–6pm.

Lavanya Arts Temple of Fine Arts, 114–116 Jalan Berhala, Brickfields ⓦtfa.org.my; map p.85. If you've an interest in Indian handicrafts, this small outlet is the place to come. Tues–Sat 10am–8pm, Sun 10am–2pm.

Native Gallery 6 Jalan Hang Lekir ☎03 2070 4567; map p.73. Huge stock of mostly wooden crafts and carvings from Malaysia and Southeast Asia, with a little cache of *pua kumbu* weaving from Sarawak hidden away in one corner. Daily 10am–6pm.

Peter Hoe Second floor, Lee Rubber Building, corner of Jalan Tun H.S. Lee ☎03 2026 0711; map p.73. Reached by the side entrance of the Lee Rubber Building, this large shop sells a range of arty-crafty soft furnishings, knick-knacks, textile bags and so forth, with a Southeast Asian flavour. A smaller outlet at 2 Jalan Hang Lekir specializes in batik, made in Indonesia to their own designs and in less garish colours than usual. Daily 10am–7pm.

Royal Selangor Pewter Factory 4 Jalan Usahawan Lima, Setapak Industrial Area ☎03 4145 6000, ⓦroyalselangor.com. Pewter – an alloy of tin – is something of a souvenir cliché in Malaysia, though platters, mugs and other objects can be elegant. This factory, 5km northeast of Chow Kit, is most easily reached by taxi from the Wangsa Maju LRT stop, 2km east, and offers free guided tours as well as the opportunity to buy their products. They also have stores in Central Market and malls around town. Daily 9am–5pm.

MALLS

Locals and visitors alike come to KL's shopping malls to seek refuge from the heat as much as to shop; for local young people, the malls are also important places to socialize. Mostly located outside the old centre, particularly in the Golden Triangle, the malls divide into two categories – gargantuan affairs in the manner of Western malls and featuring international chains and designer names, and smaller, denser Southeast Asian-style complexes, basically indoor bazaars

with row upon row of tiny independent retailers. The simpler malls tend to be much more popular than their more sophisticated, pricier counterparts, and can be atmospheric places to wander. Many malls, of whatever type, house a **supermarket** or department store of one sort or another.

BUKIT BINTANG

BB Plaza Jalan Bukit Bintang, just west of Jalan Sultan Ismail. Teeming local-style mall with good deals on cameras and electronic equipment.

Berjaya Times Square Jalan Imbi, right opposite the Monorail's Imbi stop ⓦtimessquarekl.com. Enormous mall with indoor theme park rides, though not as buzzing as it really ought to be considering its size and living somewhat in the shadow of Pavilion KL and Suria KLCC.

IMBI Plaza Jalan Imbi. Warren of several dozen stalls on two crowded floors selling electronics, computer accessories and components, plus some suspiciously cheap software. Check everything thoroughly and don't expect refunds for faulty goods.

Pavilion KL Between Jalan Bukit Bintang and Jalan Raja Chulan ⓦpavilion-kl.com. One of the very largest malls in the city – and that's saying something – with a parade of big-name designer outlets on Jalan Bukit Bintang and branches of Singapore's Tangs department store and Malaysia's Parkson chain, present here in an especially upmarket version. There's also a Times bookshop, GSC cinema and a plethora of eating and nightlife outlets.

Lot 10 Shopping Centre Bintang Walk ⓦlot10 .com.my. Specializes in designer clothes and accessories.

Starhill Gallery next to the Marriott, Bintang Walk ⓦstarhillgallery.com. More designer names than is healthy, orbiting a suitably grand atrium. Just as noteworthy is the maze of top-notch restaurants at the base of the building.

Sungei Wang Plaza Jalan Sultan Ismail ⓦsungeiwang .com. Joined onto BB Plaza and just as popular as its neighbour, KL's first mall offers everything from clothes to consumer electronics. Generally keenly priced.

KLCC

Avenue K 156 Jalan Ampang, just across from the Petronas Twin Towers and over KLCC LRT station. Worth a look if you're into designer outlets, but a bit staid.

Suria KLCC At the base of the Petronas Twin Towers ⓦsuriaklcc.com.my. A mall so large it's subdivided into sub-malls for ease of reference, Suria KLCC's oval atriums are home to UK department store Marks & Spencer, Isetan and Cold Storage supermarkets, plus numerous restaurants and a TGV multiplex cinema.

BANGSAR AND MID VALLEY

Bangsar Shopping Centre 285 Jalan Maarof, Bangsar ⓦbsc.com.my. Upmarket affair, a good place to have a suit

1

made, buy gifts or just find some food from home that you miss. Plenty of restaurants and coffee shops to boot.

Bangsar Village and Village II Bangsar Baru ⓦbangsarvillage.com. The boutiques tend to play second fiddle to the restaurants in these two malls, joined by a bridge above street level. Shopping highlights include an MPH bookshop and the Country Farm Organics supermarket, selling organic produce and even eco-friendly detergent – the likes of which you'll hardly see on sale anywhere else in the country.

Mid Valley Megamall/Gardens Mall Off Jalan Syed Putra, 2km south of Brickfields ⓦmidvalley.com.my. The sprawling Mid Valley mall certainly gives Suria KLCC a run for its money; come here for the Carrefour hypermarket, the Jusco and Metrojaya department stores, the MPH bookshop, the GSC cinema and the usual plethora of outlets selling everything from cosmetics to computers. The newer, adjacent Gardens Mall has sprung up alongside, joined by a bridge from Level 2, home to designer labels and the Singapore-based department store Robinsons. Both malls are easy to reach as the KTM Mid Valley Komuter station is close by.

OUTDOOR GEAR

Outdoors 26 Jalan Telawi 5, Bangsar Baru ☎03 2282 5721; map p.100. Good for small, low-tech essentials – seam sealer, plastic water bottles, small nylon bags – plus sleeping bags and even basic tents. Some decent snorkelling gear too.

Professor Top floor at Central Market, Chinatown; map p.73. Scouts outfitters, which means they stock useful knives, hexamine stoves, compasses, aluminium cooking pots and flashlights. Daily 10am–7pm.

Yellow Stone 16 Jalan Telawi, Bangsar Baru ☎03 2287 1118; map p.100. Small but serious outdoor shop with stock of hiking boots, waterproofs, sleeping bags, water purifiers, camping stoves, packs, water bottles and accessories.

DIRECTORY

Banks and exchange Banks with ATMs are located throughout KL; Maybank is usually your best bet for foreign exchange. You may get better rates from official moneychangers, which can be found in shopping malls and in and around transport hubs.

Casino KL has long had a casino at Genting Highlands (ⓦrwgenting.com), which also attracts vacationing locals as it features several fairly pricey resorts, a theme park, shopping malls and so forth. It's 30km out of town, best reached via the Karak Highway (E8); express buses head there from Puduraya and Pekeliling bus stations, and there are also share taxis from Puduraya.

Cultural centres Alliance Française, 15 Lorong Gurney ☎03 2694 7880, ⓦkl.alliancefrancaise.org.my; British Council, West Block, Wisma Selangor Dredging, Jalan Ampang (next to the *Maya* hotel) ☎03 2723 7900, ⓦbritishcouncil.org/malaysia.htm; Goethe-Institut, sixth floor, 374 Jalan Tun Razak ☎03 2164 2011, ⓦgoethe.de.

Embassies and consulates Australia, 6 Jalan Yap Kwan Seng ☎03 2146 5555, ⓦmalaysia.embassy.gov.au; Brunei, Menara Tan & Tan, 207 Jalan Tun Razak ☎03 2161 2800; Cambodia, 46 Jalan U Thant ☎03 4257 1150; Canada, Menara Tan & Tan, 207 Jalan Tun Razak ☎03 2718 3333, ⓦcanadainternational.gc.ca; China, Plaza OSK, 25 Jalan Ampang ☎03 2163 6814, ⓦmy.china-embassy.org; India, 2 Jalan Taman Duta ☎03 2093 3510, ⓦindianhighcommission.com.my; Indonesia, 233 Jalan Tun Razak ☎03 2116 4000, ⓦkbrikualalumpur.org; Ireland, The Amp Walk, 218 Jalan Ampang ☎03 2161 2963, ⓦembassyofireland.ru; Japan, 11 Persiaran Stonor ☎03 2143 1739, ⓦmy.emb-japan.go.jp; Laos, 12 A Persiaran Madge ☎03 4251 1118; Netherlands, The Amp Walk, 218 Jalan Ampang ☎03 2168 6200, ⓦnetherlands .org.my; New Zealand, Menara IMC, Jalan Sultan Ismail ☎03 2078 2533, ⓦnzembassy.com/malaysia; Philippines, 1 Changkat Kia Peng ☎03 2148 9989, ⓦphilembassykl .org.my; Singapore, 209 Jalan Tun Razak ☎03 2161 6277, ⓦmfa.gov.sg/kl; South Africa, 3 Jalan Kia Peng ☎03 2170 2412; South Korea, Jalan Nipah ☎03 4251 2336; Thailand, 206 Jalan Ampang ☎03 2143 2107, ⓦmfa.go.th; UK, 185 Jalan Ampang ☎03 2170 2200, ⓦukinmalaysia.fco.gov .uk; US, 376 Jalan Tun Razak ☎03 2168 5000, ⓦmalaysia .usembassy.gov; Vietnam, 4 Persiaran Stonor ☎03 2148 4534, ⓦvietnam-embassy.org.

Emergencies Police and ambulance ☎999, fire and rescue ☎994.

Hospitals and clinics General Hospital, Jalan Pahang ☎03 2615 5555; Gleneagles Hospital, Jalan Ampang ☎03 4257 1300; Pantai Medical Centre, Jalan Bukit Pantai, not far from Kerinchi LRT station ☎03 2282 5077; Tung Shin Hospital, Jalan Pudu ☎03 2072 1655.

Internet access Accommodation aside, many cafés and malls have free wi-fi, and there are a few netbars scattered through downtown (RM3–6/hr) – check maps for locations.

Left luggage Luggage can be stored for a few ringgit per day at KL Sentral station and Puduraya bus station (look out for a couple of counters at the back of the passenger level). At KLIA, the service costs RM10–30/day depending on the size of the bags.

Police KL has its own Tourist Police station, where you can report stolen property for insurance claims. Useful locations include at MTC, 109 Jalan Ampang (☎03 2163 3657), and at Puduraya bus station.

Post office The General Post Office is just south of the Dayabumi Complex (Mon–Fri 8am–4pm, Sat 8am–2pm);

poste restante/general delivery mail comes here. A post office with extended hours can be found at Suria KLCC (daily 10am–6pm).

Racing The Sepang F1 International Circuit, 50km south of KL (ⓦmalaysiangp.com.my), hosts the Formula 1 Grand Prix in April, the Malaysia Merdeka Endurance Race in September, and the Motorcycle Grand Prix in October. Trains make commuting from downtown KL fairly quick.

Rock Climbing Vertical Adventure, (ⓣ016 332 0122, ⓦvertical-adventure.com) run excursions for novices or experienced climbers to sites around Batu Caves. Trips cost RM88–150 per person, min 3 people; guides, hotel pick-ups and all equipment supplied.

Sports facilities Public sports facilities in downtown KL are limited. The most convenient pool is at Chinwoo Stadium, uphill south off Jalan Hang Jabat (Mon–Fri 2–8pm; Sat & Sun 9am–8pm; RM4). The pool is well maintained but the showers and changing faciltiies

are basic, and they have an odd rule that baggy swimwear is not allowed (they'll sell you appropriate swimming trunks if required). Private health clubs, with gyms and other facilities, include Fitness First (ⓦfitnessfirst.com .my), with central locations at Avenue K mall, Jalan Ampang, next to the KLCC LRT station; and at 22 Jalan Ismail, near the Raja Chulan Monorail station. For a round of golf, the KL Golf and Country Club is at Bukit Kiara, 8km west of the centre by taxi (ⓣ03 2093 1111, ⓦklgcc.com); non-members should contact them about access.

Visa extensions The Immigration Office is at Block 1, Pusat Bandar Damansara (ⓣ03 2095 5077), just beyond the Bangsar Shopping Centre; Mon–Fri 7.30am–1pm and 2–5.30pm. Metrobus #6 from Chinatown or RapidKL bus #U82 from KL Sentral will get you there.

Walking tours Malaysian Tourist Guides Council (ⓦmtgc .my) runs three-hour guided walks; they typically start from Merdeka Square and cost RM200 for up to ten people.

Around Kuala Lumpur

With the reckless urbanization of the Klang Valley proceeding apace, worthwhile excursions from KL are becoming increasingly rare. The most obvious attraction is 13km north, where limestone peaks rise up from the forest at the Hindu shrine of **Batu Caves**, one of Malaysia's main tourist attractions. Nearby, the **Forest Research Institute of Malaysia** (FRIM) encompasses a small but surprisingly thick portion of primary rainforest, where you can see birds and a few animals within an hour of downtown KL.

Further northwest of KL, the quiet town of **Kuala Selangor** offers the chance to observe the nightly dance of **fireflies**, while northeast, **Fraser's Hill** is one of Malaysia's many hill stations, set up in colonial times to allow government officials an escape from lowland heat. The most surreal day-trip you can make from KL is to the very Chinese fishing village on **Pulau Ketam**, off the coast near southwesterly Pelabuhan Klang, which hardly feels like Malaysia at all.

Batu Caves and Pulau Ketam are easy to reach on **public transport**, but you'll need a car or taxi to reach FRIM. About the only package trip widely offered by KL's accommodation and tour agents goes to see the fireflies; you can do this on public transport, but it's a bit of a slog and requires an overnight stay at Kuala Selangor.

FRIM

16km northwest of KL • Daily 7am–7pm, canopy walk Tues–Thurs, Sat & Sun 9am–1.30pm • RM5, canopy walk RM10 • ⓦfrim.gov.my • KMT Komuter train to Kepong station (20min, RM1), then taxi final 5km (10min; RM7)

The **Forest Research Institute of Malaysia** sits amid a fifteen-square-kilometre reserve of rainforest and parkland, threaded with sealed roads and walking trails. A popular spot for weekend picnics, appealing to birdwatchers, joggers and anyone after some greenery and fresh air, it has the added attraction of a short **canopy walk** between the treetops, providing views of KL's skyline. It also makes a good warm-up for wilder affairs at Taman Negara (see p.191). A couple of hours here is plenty of time for a walk around; for a full day out you could always continue to the Batu Caves and Orang Asli Museum (see p.110).

Taxis deliver to the gates; pick up a **map** and follow the main road 1km into the park, past open woodland and lawns, to the **One Stop Centre**, where you can book the canopy walk and seek general advice. A small **museum** nearby, strongly biased towards the timber industry, gives thumbnail sketches of the different types of tropical forests and the commercial uses of various woods.

For a good walk, follow the clear "Rover" walking track past the mosque and uphill into the forest; there are some huge trees, birds and butterflies here, and a rougher side-track to the canopy walk, a single-plank suspension bridge across a deep gully. You may see monkeys too, and can join up with a couple of other tracks that bring you back to the One Stop Centre in about 90min.

Batu Caves

13km north of KL on Jalan Batu Caves, roughly midway between the junctions with Jalan Ipoh and the E8 • Free • KTM Komuter train to Batu Caves (30min; RM1.80)

The **Batu Caves** sit right on the northern edge of Greater KL, where forested limestone thumbs poke out of a ridge of hills in the suburb of Gombak. In 1891, ten years after the caves were noticed by American explorer William Hornaby, local Indian dignitaries convinced the British administration that the caves were ideal places in which to worship (probably because their geography was reminiscent of the sacred Himalayas). Soon ever-increasing numbers of devotees were visiting the caves to pray at the shrine established here to Lord Murugan, also known as **Lord Subramaniam**; later the temple complex was expanded to include a shrine to the elephant-headed deity **Ganesh**. Although the caves are always packed with visitors, to be honest they're a little underwhelming – unless, of course, you join the thousands upon thousands of devotees who descend during the annual three-day **Thaipusam festival** in late January or early February.

Arriving at the site, you're immediately struck by the immense staircase leading up into the limestone crags, with a gigantic golden statue of **Lord Murugan**, the Hindu god of war, to one side; it's claimed to be the tallest such statue in the world. A number of minor temples stand at ground level, but most visitors head straight up the 272 steps to the caves, pausing only to catch their breath or take photos of the marauding macaques who make their presence all too obvious.

Dark Caves

Batu Caves • Tues–Sun 9.30am–5pm • RM35 for 30min education tour, RM80 for 3–4hr adventure tour, in group of five or more

Three quarters of the way up the steps – at step 204, to be precise – a turning on the left leads to a vast side cavern known as the **Dark Caves**, which can only be visited on a guided tour. Here a 2km-long passageway opens into five chambers populated by a large range of insects and at least three types of **bats**, which can be distinguished by their faces and calls. The caves also house interesting limestone formations, including several towering **flow stones**, so called because a continuous sheet of water runs down them.

Subramaniam Swamy Temple

Batu Caves • Daily 8am–7pm

At the top of the main staircase in the Batu Caves, there's a clear view through to the **Subramaniam Swamy Temple**, devoted to Lord Subramaniam and another deity, Rama.

THE FRIM–BATU CAVES–ORANG ASLI MUSEUM CIRCUIT

The proximity of FRIM, the Orang Asli Museum and the Batu Caves to Middle Ring Road II (also known as Jalan Batu Caves) makes it feasible for drivers to visit all three in a circuit. From KL, either take the E8 highway, which intersects Jalan Batu Caves, or use Jalan Ipoh, which starts at Chow Kit and meets Jalan Batu Caves 4km west of the E8. FRIM is west of Jalan Ipoh, the Orang Asli Museum close to the E8, and the caves are in between the two.

Unfortunately, no buses connect the three, but you could use taxis to reach FRIM and the Orang Asli Museum from Batu Caves.

OPPOSITE GOLDEN STATUE OF LORD MURUGAN, BATU CAVES >

1

THAIPUSAM AT THE BATU CAVES

The most important festival in the Malaysian Hindu calendar (along with Deepavali), **Thaipusam** honours the Hindu deity Lord Subramaniam. It's held during full moon in the month of "Thai" (which in the Gregorian calendar always falls between mid-Jan and mid-Feb), when huge crowds arrive at the Batu Caves. Originally intended to be a day of penance for past sins, it has now become a major tourist attraction, attracting Malaysians and foreigners alike each year.

The start of Thaipusam is marked by the departure at dawn, from KL's Sri Maha Mariamman Temple, of a golden chariot bearing a statue of Subramaniam. Thousands of devotees follow on foot as it makes its seven-hour procession to the caves. As part of their penance – and in a trance-like state – devotees carry numerous types of **kavadi** ("burdens" in Tamil), the most popular being milk jugs decorated with peacock feathers placed on top of the head, which are connected to the penitents' flesh by hooks. Others wear wooden frames with sharp protruding spikes, which are carried on the back and hooked into the skin; trident-shaped skewers are placed through some devotees' tongues and cheeks. This rather grisly procession has its origins in India, where most of Lord Subramaniam's temples were sited on high ridges that pilgrims would walk up, carrying heavy pitchers or pots. At Batu Caves, the 272-step climb up to the main chamber expresses the idea that you cannot reach God without expending effort.

Once at the caves, the Subramaniam statue is placed in a tent before being carried up to the temple cave, where devotees participate in ceremonies and rituals to Subramaniam and Ganesh. Things climax with a celebration for Rama, when milk from the *kavadi* vessel can be spilt as an offering; incense and camphor are burned as the bearers unload their devotional burdens.

Extra buses run to the caves during Thaipusam. Get there early (say 7am) for a good view. Numerous vendors sell food and drink, but it's a good idea to take water and snacks with you, as the size of the crowd is horrendous.

It's set deep in a cave around 100m high and 80m long, the walls of which are lined with idols representing the six lives of Lord Subramaniam. Illuminated via the huge void in the cave ceiling beyond another set of steps far inside the caves, the temple has an entrance guarded by two statues, their index fingers pointing upwards towards the light. A dome inside is densely sculpted with more scenes from the scriptures. In a chamber at the back, a statue of Rama, adorned with silver jewellery and a silk sarong, watches over the wellbeing of all immigrants. If you want to look closely at this inner sanctum, the temple staff will mark a small red dot on your forehead, giving you a spiritual right to enter.

Orang Asli Museum

20km north of KL • Sat–Thurs 9am–5pm • Free • Bus #174 (signed "Gombak Batu 12"; RM3) from Lebuh Ampang in Chinatown (ask where to get out, it's not obvious) – leaving the bus, cross to the east side of the road and head 50m further up, where a steep side road leads to the museum; driving, turn east off E8 onto Jalan Batu Caves to reach Jalan Gombak after 1km, turn left (north) there and continue another 2km to reach the site

Run by the government's Department for Orang Asli Affairs, the **Orang Asli Museum** aims to present a portrait of the various groups of Orang Asli, former nomadic hunter-gatherers in the jungle who are now largely resident in rural settlements.

A large map of the Peninsula in the foyer makes it clear that the Orang Asli can be found, in varying numbers, in just about every state. That surprises some visitors, who see little sign of them during their travels. Besides collections of the fishing nets, guns and blowpipes the Orang Asli use to eke out their traditional existence, the museum also has photographs of Orang Asli press-ganged by the Malay and British military to fight communist guerrillas in the 1950s (see p.573). Other displays describe the changes forced more recently on the Orang Asli – some positive, like the development of health and school networks, others less encouraging, like the erosion of the family system as young men drift off to look for seasonal work.

The head carvings

Hidden in an annexe to the rear of the building, examples of traditional handicrafts include the **head carvings** made by the Mah Meri tribe from the swampy region on the borders of Selangor and Negeri Sembilan, and the Jah Hut from the slopes of Gunung Benom in central Pehang. Around 50cm high, the carvings show stylized, fierce facial expressions, and are fashioned from a strong, heavy hardwood. They still have religious significance – the most common image used, the *moyang*, represents the spirit of the ancestors.

Kuala Selangor

Coastal **KUALA SELANGOR** lies 70km northwest of KL, close to the junction of routes 5 and 54 on the banks of Sungai Selangor. A former royal town, today it's a small, sleepy affair; the chief reason visitors continue to come here is to see the river's **fireflies**, which glow spectacularly in the early evening. This natural spectacle appeared at one stage to be in terminal decline: the fireflies' mangrove habitat was rapidly being cleared, and the river becoming polluted. Government intervention seems to have stabilized things, and you stand a reasonable chance of enjoying a decent light show, **weather** permitting – the flies don't perform in rain. It's easiest to see Selangor's highlights on an evening firefly **package tour** from KL, though you can visit independently if you're prepared to stay overnight.

Fort Altingberg

Daily 9am–4.30pm • Free

All that remains of Kuala Selangor's glorious past are the remnants of two forts overlooking the town. The largest, **Fort Altingberg**, recalls an era when this part of the country changed hands, bloodily, on several occasions. Originally called Fort Melawati, Altingberg was built by local people during the reign of Sultan Ibrahim of Selangor in the eighteenth century, and later captured by the Dutch (who renamed it) as part of an attempt to wrestle the tin trade from the sultans. The fortress was partly destroyed during local skirmishes in the Selangor Civil War (1867–73). Within its grounds is a cannon, reputed to be from the Dutch era, and a rock used for executions. **Bukit Melawati**, the hill on which the fort is based, also holds a **lighthouse** and a British colonial resthouse.

FIREFLY TRIPS

Kuala Selangor's **fireflies**, known as *kelip-kelip* in Malay, are actually six-millimetre-long beetles of a kind found between India to Papua New Guinea. During the day, the fireflies rest on blades of grass or in palm trees behind the river's mangrove swamps. After sunset they move to the mangroves themselves, the males attracting mates with **synchronized flashes** of light at a rate of three per second. Females flash back at males to indicate interest and initiate mating. The most successful males are apparently those that flash brightest and fly fastest.

Boats leave on 30min firefly-spotting trips from two locations several kilometres from town: **Bukit Belimbing** (run by Firefly Park Resort, see p.112) on the north bank across the river bridge; and at **Kampung Kuantan**, on the south bank (daily 7.45–10pm; RM15 per person). There are no buses to either of the jetties, so taxis from Kuala Selangor get away with pretty steep prices – expect the ride to cost at least RM15. It's important to remain quiet when watching the firefly display and not to take flash photographs, as such behaviour scares the insects away.

It's also possible to take firefly tours all the way **from KL** with Han Travel, ⓦ taman-negara .com (RM180 per person including return transport, all fees and seafood dinner).

Kuala Selangor Nature Park

Directly below Fort Altingberg • Daily 9am–5.30pm

The **Kuala Selangor Nature Park**, which encompasses mud flats, mangroves and a small patch of forest, is host to around 150 species of birds, with thirty more migratory species passing through, as well as silverleaf monkeys, which live in the forest, and crabs and fish in the mangroves. Clearly marked trails take between 30min and 1hr 30min to walk.

The park is a 500m walk from Bukit Melawati (follow signs for "Taman Alam"). You can also get here on the **buses** that run up Route 5 from Klang; ask to be let off at the park, and you'll be dropped at a petrol station, from where the park is 200m up Jalan Klinik.

ARRIVAL AND DEPARTURE	KUALA SELANGOR

By bus Selangor Omnibus buses to Kuala Selangor leave from KL's Puduraya station (2hr; last bus back 8pm; RM5.50)

ACCOMMODATION AND EATING	KUALA SELANGOR

Your best bet for **eating** in the Kuala Selangor area, is the row of waterside restaurants, serving mainly Chinese seafood, in Pasir Penambang, on the north bank of the Selangor River 5km from Kuala Selangor. Make your way across the river bridge, turn left and it's signed down a turning on the left; it's a very romantic spot at night.

Firefly Park Resort Kampung Bukit Belimbing ☏ 03 3260 1208, ⌨ fireflypark.com. The slickest accommodation in the area, where simple modern chalets, sleeping four, have a/c and en-suite facilities. There's a barbecue area, and a Chinese seafood restaurant, with breakfast available at weekends only. Rates drop by RM50 Mon–Thurs. RM180

Kuala Selangor ☏ 03 3289 2709. The only hotel in town itself, on the central square. A simple, homely place, it has a range of rooms, including some with a/c and en-suite facilities. RM80

Nature Park Chalets Kuala Selangor Nature Park ☏ 03 3289 2294, ✉ ksnaturepark@gmail.com. A mix of basic chalet and hostel accommodation; chalet guests get free use of the kitchen, while others pay RM5/day. Book in advance as school groups can fill the place up. There's nowhere to eat nearby, so bring all provisions. Chalets RM45, hostel dorms RM25

Pulau Ketam

The moment you set foot aboard ferries to **PULAU KETAM** (Crab Island) you're in a kind of parallel universe: this is Chinese day-tripper land, with videos of Chinese karaoke clips or soap operas blaring from the on-board screens. Ketam's five thousand inhabitants are Teochew and Hokkien Chinese, who traditionally live almost entirely by fishing from their low, flat, mangrove-encrusted island. Every house is built on pilings above the sand, and practically every street is a concrete walkway or boardwalk raised in the same fashion. Aside from the chance to eat tasty, inexpensive seafood, you'd visit mainly for a slightly surreal break from KL's pace, with a couple of places to stay if you like the quiet.

From the jetty, walk past the mosque and into the village main street, lined with grocers, general stores, and stalls and **restaurants** selling seafood – including, of course, crab. Beyond a shop selling Buddhist paraphernalia is a sort of central square where you'll find the **Hock Leng Temple**, as well as a small grotto containing a representation of Kwan Yin, the Goddess of Mercy, looking decidedly Madonna-like with a halo of red electric lights. On from here, you come to a residential area of concrete and wooden houses, nearly all with their front doors left wide open. There's plenty of refuse littering the mud flats beneath, unfortunately, but more appealingly you'll also see shrines outside many homes and occasional collections of pans made of netting containing seafood products being left out to dry.

ARRIVAL AND DEPARTURE	PULAU KETAM

By train and ferry Take the KTM Komuter train 25km southwest of KL to Pelabuhan Klang (Klang Port; 1hr 20min; RM4.40); the ferry terminal is opposite the train station. Ferries depart daily 8.30am–6.30pm (Mon–Fri hourly, Sat & Sun every 45min; 45min; RM7).

GETTING AROUND

Tours Not far from the jetty, Greenway (🌐greenway2u .com) offers walking tours and boat rides to a floating fish farm (RM60 for 4 people). You can also rent bicycles here for RM5.

ACCOMMODATION AND EATING

Hotel Sea Lion Near the jetty, in a distinctive yellow and white building ☎03 3110 4121, 🌐hotelsealion .ec-enabler.com.my. Simple, clean and tidy establishment, with a nice deck overlooking the water; cheapest rooms are windowless with a fan, while others have a/c and a bit of space. You can book good-value packages here, including accommodation, food and a fishing trip. <u>RM70</u>

Pulau Ketam Inn Just past the mosque ☎03 3110 5206, 🌐pulauketam.com. Simple hotel, three minutes' walk from the jetty, featuring plain, neat, tiled rooms with en-suite facilities. <u>RM60</u>

Restoran Seng Huat On the main street. Typical of many similar friendly places to eat nearby, but just a bit livelier; excellent seafood omlettes, prawns, crab, noodles soups and generic stir fries. RM15 should leave you bloated.

Fraser's Hill (Bukit Fraser)

Set 1500m up in the forested Titiwangsa mountains, 75km northeast of KL, the collection of colonial bungalows comprising **FRASER'S HILL** was established after World War I as one of Malaysia's earliest **hill stations**, a retreat for administrators seeking relief from the torrid lowland climate. Though less visited than the much larger Cameron Highlands to the north, Fraser's Hill boasts excellent **nature trails** and superb **birdwatching**; some 250 species have been recorded here, and the **Fraser's Hill International Bird Race** each June (🌐pkbf.org.my) sees teams competing to clock up as many as possible within a day. Even if you don't have the slightest insterest in twitching, the hill remains a good getaway from the heat and hubbub of KL, and at weekends (when accommodation prices shoot up) it draws families from as far away as Singapore. Bear in mind that **no public transport** comes all the way up here.

The hill station

Sprawling amid a handful of wooded slopes, the **hill station** focuses on a T-intersection at the south end of a **golf course**. The *Quest Resort* and *Puncak Inn* are located here, along with a distinctive **clock tower**, post office and bank, while roads and trails head off in all directions to clusters of hidden bungalows and cabins.

The easiest targets for a **stroll** are **Allan's Water**, a small lake less than 1km from the clock tower, and **Jeriau Waterfall**, 4km north via *Ye Olde Smokehouse*, where the convincing English country decor and **cream teas** (daily 3.30–6pm) are a strong inducement to pause for a breather. Another good walk involves taking Jalan Lady Guillemard east to the loop road, Jalan Girdle; this leads to the most remote section of the hill station, bordering **Ulu Tramin Forest Reserve**, though completing the entire circle only takes around ninety minutes.

COMMUNISTS ON THE HILL

During the Emergency in the 1950s (see p.573), the mountainous jungle at Fraser's Hill provided perfect cover for some of the communist guerrillas' secret camps, from where they launched strikes on British-owned plantations and neighbouring towns.

If you approach Fraser's Hill via Kuala Kubu Bharu, due north of KL, roughly halfway up you'll see a sign, "Emergency Historical Site", marking the spot where **Sir Henry Gurney**, the British High Commissioner for Malaya at the height of the communist insurgency in 1951, was ambushed and killed. The guerrillas hadn't known how important their quarry was: their aim had been only to steal guns, ammunition and food, but when Gurney strode towards them demanding that they put down their weapons, they opened fire.

1

Longer trails

Most of the **longer trails** can be covered in less than two hours; indeed it would only take a couple of days to cover them all. Signage, however, can be spotty – don't be paranoid about losing your way, but talk to the tourist office about your route before you set out, and consider hiring a guide. The trails can get slippery in wet weather, so be sure to wear proper footgear; leeches can sometimes be a problem.

The **Abu Suradi trail** begins on Jalan Genting close to the mosque, and takes about twenty minutes to reach its southern end, also on Jalan Genting, near the clinic. Also starting near the mosque, the **Hemmant trail** snakes along the edge of the golf course just within the jungle. At its far end, you can turn left and either walk on to Jalan Lady Maxwell, or continue as far as the Bishop's House, where you can pick up the **Bishop's trail**. After about 45 minutes, this route joins the **Maxwell trail**, at which point you can either leave the trail by turning right up the hill and returning to town via Jalan Lady Maxwell, or continue another hour on the Maxwell trail until it reaches Jalan Quarry. Here there's a course for **woodball** – a hybrid of croquet and golf, played with long mallets – with equipment to rent.

ARRIVAL AND DEPARTURE   FRASER'S HILL

By car Fraser's Hill is reached by a single-lane road that branches off Route 55, which connects Kuala Kubu Bharu (KKB, on Route 1), and Raub (Route 8) at a spot called the Gap. In theory, this road takes summit-bound traffic only, while downhill traffic uses a road that joins the KKB–Raub road 1km northeast. When either is closed by landslips, however, traffic alternates hourly in each direction on the

other. The entire journey to or from KL typically takes 2hr or so. There is no fuel station at Fraser's Hill.
By public transport Catch a Komuter train from KL to Rawang (3 hourly), then change for a KKB train (2 hourly). If you time it right, the journey should take just over 1hr 30min (RM5.50). From KKB, you have to catch a taxi to Fraser's Hill (RM80–100).

INFORMATION

Tourist office In the colonial building alongside the vine-covered clock tower at the centre of the hill station (Mon–Fri 8am–5pm, Sat & Sun 8am–10pm; ☎ 09 517 1623, ⓦ pkbf.org.my); they can book accommodation, provide maps, advise on current trail conditions and put you in

touch with local guides.
Useful website ⓦ fraserhill.info.
Banks There are no ATMs at Fraser's Hill, but you can change money at a small branch of Maybank outside the *Shahzan Inn*.

ACCOMMODATION

Accommodation in Fraser's Hill is mostly motel-like and geared to families and groups, though some **bungalows** – here either detached single-storey houses or small apartment blocks – are also available. Always book in advance, and expect rates given below to rise by half at weekends and during holidays.

Fraser's Pine Resort Jalan Peach Batu ☎ 09 362 2122, ⓦ thepines.com.my. One of the largest developments in the area, unobtrusively positioned in a valley between two hills. On offer are modern one- to three-bedroom apartments with basic kitchen facilities. Breakfast is included. **RM300**
Highland Rest House Holding ☎ 03 2693 6996, ⓦ hrhbungalows.com. Six slick, mock-Tudor, family-sized bungalows, with multiple en-suite bedrooms, stone fireplaces, private gardens and parking – plus a caretaker. Most have to be rented entire; only Pekan has individual rooms available. Bungalows **RM1000–2000**, rooms **RM200**
Jelai Highlands Resort Jalan Ampang, near Allan's Water ☎ 09 362 2600. Spacious but minimally maintained en-suite rooms with green carpets and a small amount of cane furniture. The rates include breakfast, which,

unusually, is a cooked Western one (rice or noodles are an option on weekends only). **RM100**
★ **Puncak Inn** Jalan Genting ☎ 09 362 2195, ⓦ pkbf .org.my. This tourist-office-run budget hotel wins no prizes for its institutional atmosphere, but the rooms are clean, modern and come with heating and en-suite facilities – both welcome given the local climate. There's an on-site canteen too. **RM80**
Shahzan Inn Jalan Lady Guillemard ☎ 09 362 2300. Located next to the golf course, this bland modern hotel consists of tiers of rooms ascending a terraced hillside. It's characterless but everything's in good shape; rooms have en-suite facilities and satellite TV. Breakfast is included. **RM200**
Silverpark Apartments ☎ 09 362 2888. Hilltop residential block with unconvincing mock-Tudor flourishes

and a range of 2- to 6-person units for let, all with cooking facilities and plenty of elbow room. There's also a café and indoor games room. RM180

★ **Ye Olde Smokehouse** Jalan Semantan ☎ 09 362 2226, ⓦ thesmokehouse.com.my. Founded in 1924 as a resort for British servicemen who fought in World War I, this stereotypical English country inn offers fireside chairs and spacious rooms with four-poster beds, guaranteed to make the cool nights pass all the more blissfully. The restaurant serves some of the most delightful (non-spicy) food you might have in Malaysia. Rates (it doesn't hurt to ask about discounts) include a full English breakfast. RM450

EATING AND DRINKING

Fraser's Hill doesn't offer much choice for eating: aside from hotel restaurants – of which only that at the *Smokehouse* is worth specifically seeking out – there's a central **food court**, offering a mix of Malay, Indian and Chinese staples.

Ye Olde Smokehouse Jalan Semantan ☎ 09 362 2226, ⓦ thesmokehouse.com.my. Well worth the expense for a slap-up meal in a nostalgic setting. Their Thai food is decent, but go for the convincing English dishes – beef Wellington, grilled rainbow trout, sherry trifle and the like – while the service is suitably reserved and unhurried. They also do cream teas (daily 3.30–6pm), as well as a good range of beers and whiskies, plus shandy, all of which go down especially well in the country-pub-style lounge. Things are fairly informal during the day, but don't turn up in a T-shirt and shorts in the evening. RM75–100 per head for a three-course meal. Daily noon–3pm & 6–11pm.

The west coast

PULAU LANGKAWI

The west coast

Peninsular Malaysia's densely populated west coast, from Kuala Lumpur north to the open border with Thailand, is rich in cultural diversions and natural attractions. Nowhere showcases Malaysia's rural delights better than the Cameron Highlands, a former hill station offering fresh air, forest treks and British-style cream teas. Between here and the coast, Perak state (*perak* meaning "silver") once boasted the world's richest tin field, which during the nineteenth century spearheaded Malaysia's phenomenal economic rise. Perak's major towns – Ipoh and Taiping echo those days in extensive quarters of Chinese shophouses, with a more Malay experience available at unassuming Kuala Kangsar. Offshore, Pulau Pangkor is known for its pleasant, low-key beaches, a popular weekend break for families from KL.

North up the coast, **Penang Island** – or rather its capital, **Georgetown** – is a major destination. Centuries of trade and interaction with India, Britain, Indonesia, Thailand and China have left a melting-pot of cultures (not to mention architecture and food). Penang's drab beaches, however, are probably best skipped in favour of exploring the island's smaller settlements and forested corners.

After Penang, most visitors aim straight for the Thai border, though the intervening states of **Kedah and Perlis** hold some interest. These are Malaysia's historical *jelapang padi*, or "rice bowl", a sprawl of rippling, emerald-green paddy fields; there's a strong Thai influence too, though the state capitals, **Alor Star** and **Kangar**, are visually very Malay, sporting prominent mosques and royal buildings. The biggest regional attraction is **Pulau Langkawi**, an upper-end resort island with a couple of fine beaches, clearly targeting international, rather than domestic tourists. Harder to reach and far inland on the Kedah–Thai border, **Ulu Muda Eco Park** offers adventurous nature trekking, though access can be tricky.

GETTING AROUND

Thanks to its economic importance, the west coast has a well-developed transport infrastructure. Both road and rail routes pass through all the major towns: Ipoh, Taiping, Butterworth (for Penang Island) and Alor Star.

By car The wide North–South Expressway (also referred to as "NSE", and here as the E1), generally free of heavy traffic, runs from Malaysia's northern border at Bukit Kayu Hitam all the way to Singapore.

By train Running more or less parallel to the highway, the rail line from Singapore, via Sentral Station in KL,

crosses into southern Thailand and terminates at Hat Yai.

By bus Express buses provide the fastest and most frequent way to travel between the cities, while local buses serve the hills and the coast.

PULAU PANGKOR

Highlights

❶ Cameron Highlands Cool down amid the tea plantations and jungle trails of this former colonial hill station. **See p.121**

❷ Ipoh Lively, workaday city surrounded by intriguing attractions, including the romantic – and very bizarre – Kellie's Castle. **See p.129**

❸ Pulau Pangkor Laidback tropical island with some of the best beaches on the west coast. See p.134

❹ Taiping Traditional town with tranquil gardens and a mini hill station; Malaysia's largest Mangrove Reserve lies nearby. **See p.141**

❺ Georgetown Animated street life, rows of old shophouses and elaborate temples characterize Penang Island's Chinese-dominated capital. **See p.149**

❻ Ulu Muda Eco Park West Malaysia's unexplored nature reserve with over 500 square kilometres of preserved rainforest. See p.175

❼ Langkawi Upmarket resort island on the Thai border, featuring white-sand beaches and a cable car over the forested interior. See p.176

HIGHLIGHTS ARE MARKED ON THE MAP ON P.120

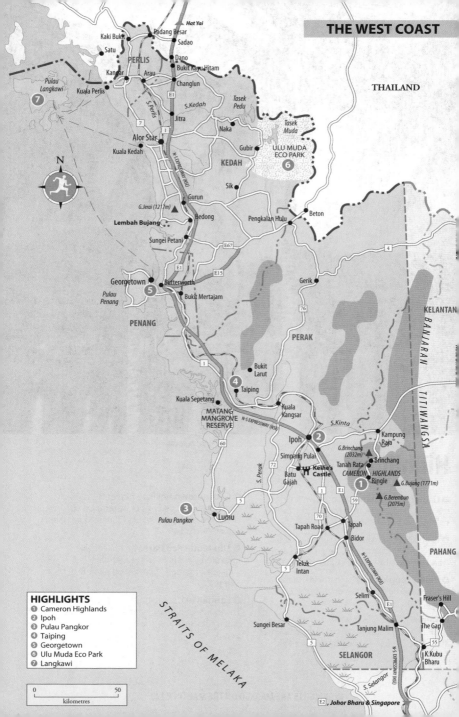

The Cameron Highlands

Around 200km north of KL, surrounded by the dark blue, forested peaks of **Banjaran Titiwangsa**, the Peninsula's main mountain range, the **CAMERON HIGHLANDS** form Malaysia's most extensive hill station. The place took its name from William Cameron, a government surveyor who stumbled across the area in 1885, though not until forty years later did civil servant Sir George Maxwell propose developing a hill station here. Indian tea planters, Chinese vegetable farmers and wealthy landowners in search of a weekend retreat flocked in, establishing **tea plantations** and leaving a swathe of mock-Tudor buildings in their wake. Though it gets packed out at times – especially during the March to May hot-season school holidays – it offers excellent **nature walks**, a pleasantly cool climate, plenty of fresh air, and the chance to sample locally grown strawberries or relax with tea and scones.

The Highlands cover around 700 square kilometres, cut by the twisting **Route 59**, which links the three main townships. Southerly **Ringlet** is a busy little marketplace surrounded by modern housing estates, close to a couple of attractions but otherwise forgettable. Some 15km northeast, **Tanah Rata** is the Highlands' main town and favoured base, at the core of walking trails and flush with places to stay and eat; 5km further north, scruffier **Brinchang** offers more of the same, plus several nearby fruit and vegetable farms.

With hills in every direction, the **weather** in the Cameron Highlands is unpredictable, and you can expect rainstorms even in the dry season. It makes sense to avoid the area during the monsoon itself (Nov–Jan), and at major holiday times if you want to avoid the crowds. Given the 1000m-plus altitude, temperatures drop dramatically at night – whatever the season – so you'll need warm clothes, as well as waterproofs.

Tanah Rata

The tidy town of **TANAH RATA**, the Highlands' most developed settlement, is a bustling place festooned with hotels, white-balustraded buildings, flowers and parks. It comprises little more than one 500m-long street (officially called **Jalan Besar**, but

---

TEA AND TOURS

Tea is such a feature of the Cameron Highlands that it would be perverse not to visit a plantation during your stay, where you can investigate the growing process and enjoy a local cuppa. Despite the romantic imagery used on packaging, **handpicking** is now far too labour-intensive to be economical; instead, the small, green leaves are picked with shears. Once in the factory, the leaves are withered by alternate blasts of hot and cold air for sixteen to eighteen hours; this removes around fifty percent of their moisture. They are then rolled by ancient, bulky machines that break up the leaves and release more moisture for the all-important process of **fermentation**. Following ninety minutes' grinding, the soggy mass is fired at 90°C to halt the fermentation, and the leaves turn black. After being sorted into grades, the tea matures for three to six months before being packaged and transported to market.

PLANTATIONS

The following plantations are open to the public, and offer varying attractions:

Boh 8km northeast of Ringlet via Habu (wboh.com.my). Free tour Tues–Sun 11am–3pm. See the whole production process – from picking to packing of the tea – at Malaysia's largest tea producer. Some areas of the tour are extremely dusty, so take a handkerchief to cover your mouth and nose. There's also a pleasant café on the premises.

Bharat between Ringlet and Tanah Rata (wbharattea.com.my). No tours, but the café serves a range of local teas along with scones and other snacks, and enjoys views out over the tea terraces.

Sungai Palas 6km north of Brinchang (wboh.com.my). The northern Highlands' branch of the Boh estates, though tea drinking, not tours, is offered here.

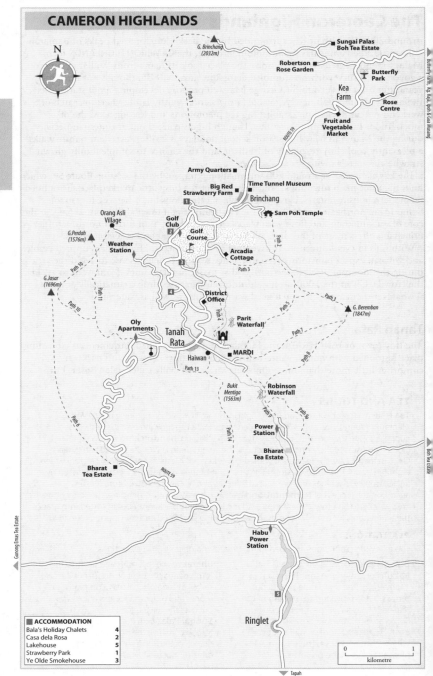

CAMERON HIGHLANDS

N

Sungai Palas
Boh Tea Estate

Robertson
Rose Garden

Butterfly
Park

Kea
Farm

Rose
Centre

G. Brinchang
(2032m)

Path 1

ROUTE 59

Fruit and
Vegetable
Market

Army Quarters

Big Red
Strawberry Farm

Time Tunnel Museum

Brinchang

Sam Poh Temple

Orang Asli
Village

Golf
Club

Golf
Course

Path 2

G. Perdah
(1576m)

Weather
Station

Arcadia
Cottage

Path 3

G. Jasar
(1696m)

Path 10

Path 11

District
Office

Path 5

Path 3

G. Beremban
(1847m)

Path 10

Path 4

Parit
Waterfall

Path 7

Oly
Apartments

Tanah
Rata

MARDI

Path 8

Haiwan

Path 13

Bukit
Mentiga
(1563m)

Robinson
Waterfall

Path 6

Path 14

Path 9

Path 9a

Power
Station

Bharat
Tea Estate

Bharat
Tea Estate

ROUTE 59

Habu
Power
Station

Ringlet

Butterfly Farm, Ag. Raja, Ipoh & Gua Musang

Boh Tea Estate

Gunong Emas Tea Estate

■ ACCOMMODATION	
Bala's Holiday Chalets	4
Casa dela Rosa	2
Lakehouse	5
Strawberry Park	1
Ye Olde Smokehouse	3

0 | 1
kilometre

Tapah

usually just known as "Main Road"), full of stores, services and restaurants; most of the accommodation lies off down the handful of side lanes. Since the street also serves as the main thoroughfare into the rest of the Highlands, it suffers from daytime traffic noise, but at night becomes the centre of the Cameron Highlands' social life, with restaurant tables spilling out onto the pavement.

Tanah Rata is an ideal base to explore the Cameron Highlands, with many **walks** starting nearby, a couple of waterfalls, and three reasonably high mountain peaks all within hiking distance.

Brinchang

Some 5km north of Tanah Rata, **BRINCHANG** is a more compact, built-up, busier and less attractive township; with additional places to stay and eat, it makes a decent alternative to Tanah Rata if the latter is full, and a lively **night market** takes place uphill from the centre on Fridays and Saturdays. Brinchang also sits at one end of the walking trail up to the summit of **Gunung Brinchang** (see p.124).

Sights on Brinchang's outskirts include the modern **Sam Poh Temple**, 1km southeast, a Buddhist affair whose gaudy red concrete halls and terraces offer views over the area. Just north past the night market, the quirky **Time Tunnel Memorabilia Museum** (daily 9am–6pm; RM5) is a private collection of photos, toys, shop signs and bric-a-brac dating back to the 1950s. Five minutes' walk west lands you at the **Big Red Strawberry Farm** (daily 8.30am–6pm; ⓦbigredstrawberryfarm.com), where you can pick your own strawberries and tomatoes, or drop in for tea and scones at the café.

North of Brinchang

All over the Cameron Highlands – but especially north of Brinchang – you'll pass small sheds or greenhouses by the roadside, selling cabbages, leeks, cauliflowers, mushrooms and strawberries. These are the produce of the area's various fruit and vegetable **farms**, where narrow plots are cut out of the sheer hillsides to increase the surface area for planting, forming giant steps all the way up the slopes; over forty percent of the produce is for export to Singapore, Brunei and Hong Kong. **Sungai Palas tea plantation** (see p.121) is out this way too, along with the vehicle road up Gunung Brinchang.

Kea Farm

Butterfly Farm Daily 8am–6pm • RM5 • **Rose Centre** Daily 8am–5pm • RM3 • Kampung Raja bus from Tanah Rata via Brinchang; taxi from Tanah Rata about RM15

About 5km north of Brinchang, **Kea Farm** hosts some fun attractions. The **Butterfly Farm** sports hundreds of butterflies of various species flitting among the flowers and ponds. Flower-lovers are well served by the **Rose Centre**, 5km east, which has a spectacular view of the surrounding valleys from its summit, crowned in surreal fashion by a colourful Mother-Hubbard-like boot. The sculptures here, of which the boot is one, were created by Burmese craftsmen and do a lot to liven up a potentially dull attraction. Besides roses, other temperate-climate flowers – rare and expensive in tropical Southeast Asia – are also cultivated here.

ARRIVAL AND DEPARTURE
CAMERON HIGHLANDS

By train The nearest train station to the Highlands is at Tapah, a crossroads town down below on the E1 expressway.

Destinations Alor Star (daily; 9hr); Butterworth (2 daily; 6hr 45min); Ipoh (5 daily; 1hr 30min); Kuala Kangsar (2 daily; 3hr); Kuala Lumpur (5 daily; 4hr); Sungai Petani (daily; 8hr); Taiping (2 daily; 4hr). Catch a bus from Tapah station (5 daily; 1hr 20min) for the final 50km run to Tanah Rata.

By bus The Highlands' main bus station is at the north end of Tanah Rata, though some express buses pause in

2

WALKING IN THE CAMERON HIGHLANDS

A network of **walking trails** makes the Cameron Highlands' forests uniquely accessible, with prolific **flora** against a tremendous canopy of trees – ferns, pitcher plants, bird's nest ferns, orchids and thick moss – through which you can sometimes glimpse spectacular views of misty mountain peaks. Some of the walks are no more than casual strolls through secondary growth woodland, while others are romps through what seems like the wild unknown, giving a sense of real isolation. Despite the presence of large mammals in the deep forest, such as honey bears and monkeys, you're unlikely to see more than insects and the odd wild pig or squirrel.

Unfortunately, the trails are often badly signposted and poorly maintained, though despite their apparent vagueness, the various sketch **maps** sold in Tanah Rata (RM3–4) and at many of the hotels do make some sort of sense on the ground. The *Cameronian Inn* and *Father's Guest House* (see p.127) in Tanah Rata are good contacts for current trail information and hiring guides.

The **official trails**, detailed below, are varied enough for most tastes and energies. The timings given are for one-way walks for people with an average level of fitness. You should always inform someone, preferably at your hotel, where you are going and what time you expect to be back. On longer hikes, take warm clothing, water, a torch and a cigarette lighter or matches for basic survival should you get lost. If someone doesn't return from a hike and you suspect they may be in **trouble**, inform the District Office immediately. It's not a fanciful notion that hiking can have its dangers – mudslides after rain, for example, are not uncommon.

TRAILS

The following paths are numbered according to the **local area map**. Check before you set off; several paths may be closed or out of use.

Path 1 (2hr) Ascending **Gunung Brinchang**, the 2000m-high apex of the Highlands, is a tiring proposition, though you could always cheat by taking a taxi to the top from Brinchang (RM15) and walking down. This is the highest road in Peninsular Malaysia and there's a terrific view of the Highlands from the summit, plus a boardwalk through the ethereal **Mossy Forest**, where the trees are covered in a spongy, soft mat of green.

To walk up, start just north of Brinchang, on a rarely used and unmaintained track near the army quarters. Look for the white stone marker 1/48 that marks the beginning of the trail. From

the south of town near the information office, so you might not have to lug your bags down to the bus station – ask when buying tickets.

Destinations Butterworth (5 daily; 4hr); Ipoh (6 daily; 2hr); Kuala Lumpur (9 daily; 4hr); Melaka (1 daily; 5hr 30min); Penang (2 daily; 5hr); Singapore (1 daily; 10hr); Tapah (for the train; 5 daily; 1hr 20min).

By minibus Tour agents in Tanah Rata operate minivans to popular destinations; they might need minimum numbers to run.

Destinations Gua Musang (2 daily; 2hr); Kota Bahru (1 daily; 6hr 30min); Kuala Besut (2 daily; 5hr); Taman Negara (Kuala Tahan; 3 daily; 4hr); Penang (3 daily; 5hr); Perhentians (2 daily; 6hr).

By car The Cameron Highlands can be reached off Highway E1 via Tapah, a service town 100km north of KL; from there, the highly scenic Route 59 twists northeast into the hills, passes through the Highlands via Ringlet, Tanah Rata and Brinchang, and joins the Gua Musang–Simpang Pulai road at the hamlet of Kampung Raja. Alternatively, from Simpang Pulai, on Highway E1 just outside Ipoh, the road climbs swiftly to Kampung Raja, from where you turn south down along Route 59.

GETTING AROUND

By bus Local services from Tanah Rata's bus station run north along Route 59 to Kampung Raja (on Gua Musang–Ipoh road), and south to Tapa (on E1 expressway).

Destinations Bharat Tea Plantation (hourly, 7.30am–6.30pm); Brinchang (hourly, 7.30am–6.30pm; RM1.50); Kampung Raja (hourly, 7.30am–6.30pm); Kea (hourly, 7.30am–6.30pm); Ringlet (5 daily, 8am–5pm); Tapah (5 daily, 8am–5pm).

By taxi The main taxi rank is next to Tanah Rata's bus station (☎05 491 2355); in Brinchang, ask at accommodation. A taxi between Tanah Rata and Brinchang costs around RM8.

the summit, you can either return the way you came or walk east along the sealed access road back to the main road, passing an access road to the Sungai Palas Tea Estate en route.

Path 2 (1hr 30min) Starting just before the Sam Poh Temple below Brinchang, it's not clearly marked, and often a bit of a scramble, so you'll need to be reasonably fit and well prepared. The route undulates severely and eventually merges with Path 3.

Path 3 (2hr 30min) Starts at *Arcadia Cottage* southeast of the golf course, crossing streams and climbing quite steeply to reach the peak of Gunung Beremban (1841m). Once at the top, you can retrace your steps, or head down Path 5, 7 or 8.

Path 4 (20min) Paved in stretches, this walk starts south of the golf course and goes past Parit Waterfall, leading on to a watchtower with good views over Brinchang. From the last stop, the Forest Department HQ, a sealed path leads back to the main road.

Path 5 (1hr) Branches off from Path 3 and ends up at the Malaysian Agriculture Research and Development Institute (MARDI). It's an easy walk through peaceful woodland, after which you can cut back up the road to Tanah Rata.

Path 7 (2hr) Starts near MARDI and climbs steeply to Gunung Beremban; an arduous and very overgrown hike best recommended as a descent route from Path 3.

Path 8 (3hr) Another route to Gunung Beremban, a tough approach from Robinson Waterfall; even more taxing than Path 7.

Path 9 and **9A** (1hr) The descent from Robinson Waterfall to the power station is steep and strenuous; the station caretaker will let you through to the road to Boh. Path 9A, an easier downhill grade than Path 9, branches off from the main route and emerges in a vegetable farm on the Boh road.

Path 10 (2hr 30min) Starts just behind the *Oly Apartments* and involves a fairly strenuous climb to Gunung Jasar (1696m). It then drops down to the Orang Asli village, where you join a small road leading back to the main road.

Paths 11 & 12 (2hr) Takes you up to Gunung Perdah (1576m), a slightly shorter and less challenging route than Path 10. Again, you come out at the Orang Asli village and take the small road back into town.

Path 13 (1hr) An alternate access to Path 14, starting a half-hour's walk southwest of the *Cameronian Holiday Inn* in Tanah Rata.

Path 14 (3hr) A tricky and initially steep route via Bukit Mentiga (1563m), with great views. It begins at Haiwan (a veterinary centre) and continues south, becoming very hard to make out until it joins the road 8km from Tanah Rata. Best not to do this one alone.

INFORMATION AND TOUR AGENTS

Tourist information The Cameron Tourist Information Centre in Tanah Rata (Mon–Fri 9am–5pm, ☎05 491 1452) is friendly but generally clueless. You're probably better off making enquiries at your accommodation or private agents (see below), though obviously they will promote their own tours. For general information on the Highlands – including road conditions, accommodation listings and eating recommendations – visit ⓦ cameronhighlands.com.

TOUR AGENTS

The following can arrange accommodation and day-trips around the Highlands, plus express coach tickets, flights, and minivan transfers to Taman Negara and elsewhere.

Cameron Secrets *Father's Guesthouse*, Tanah Rata (see p.127), ⓦ cameronsecrets.com.

CS Travel & Tours 47 Jalan Besar, Tanah Rata ☎05 491 1200, ⓦ cstravel.com.my.

Titiwangsa Tours & Travel 36 Jalan Besar, Brinchang ☎05 491 1452, ⓦ titiwangsatours.com.

ACCOMMODATION

Tanah Rata and Brinchang host the bulk of the highlands' **accommodation** – Tanah Rata is especially good for budget establishments – with some ritzier, self-contained places on the road in between. It's also possible to rent **apartments** or cottages in the locality, advertised in shop windows. Prices everywhere rise by up to thirty percent at weekends, and double at peak holiday times (Christmas, Easter, Hari Raya and Deepavali). Always book ahead to ensure a place.

RINGLET

Lakehouse Ringlet ☎05 495 6152, ⓦ lakehouse -cameron.com; map p.122. The one deluxe option in Ringlet, which otherwise makes a rather isolated base. This elegant Tudor-style mansion offers a real slice of the old days. Its stone fireplaces, heavy wooden furniture and

2

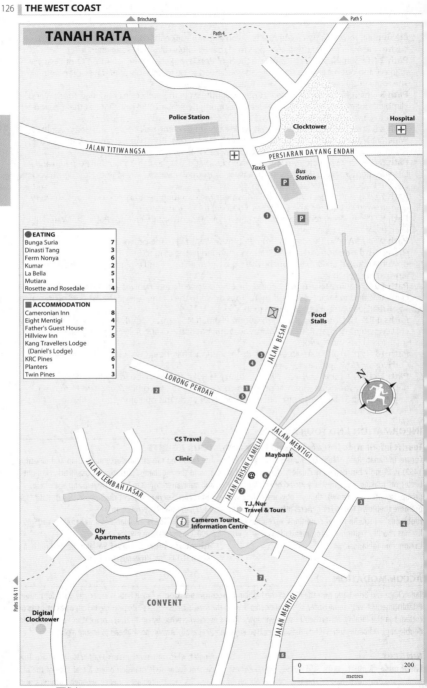

TANAH RATA

Brinchang
Path 5
Path 4

Police Station

Clocktower

Hospital

JALAN TITIWANGSA

PERSIARAN DAYANG ENDAH

Taxis

Bus Station

P

❶

P

❷

EATING

Bunga Suria	7
Dinasti Tang	3
Ferm Nonya	6
Kumar	2
La Bella	5
Mutiara	1
Rosette and Rosedale	4

ACCOMMODATION

Cameronian Inn	8
Eight Mentigi	4
Father's Guest House	7
Hillview Inn	5
Kang Travellers Lodge (Daniel's Lodge)	2
KRC Pines	6
Planters	1
Twin Pines	3

Food Stalls

JALAN BESAR

❸

❹

❷

LORONG PERDAH

❶

❺

JALAN MENTIGI

CS Travel

Clinic

Maybank

JALAN LEMBAH JASAR

JALAN PERISAN CAMELIA

@

❻

❼

T.J. Nur Travel & Tours

❸

Oly Apartments

i Cameron Tourist Information Centre

❹

❼

N

CONVENT

JALAN MENTIGI

Paths 10 & 11

Digital Clocktower

❽

0   200
metres

Ringlet

2

HIGHLANDS TOURS

Tours of the whole region, which take around three hours, can be arranged by any hotel or hostel, and depart from your place of accommodation at 9.30am or 2.30pm daily (typical RM25). Though somewhat whistle-stop, they do at least cover a tea plantation, butterfly farm, strawberry farm and Sam Poh Temple in one swoop.

More adventurous options are offered by agents around town: sunrise views from the Highlands' apex at Gunung Brinchang; visits to thatched wooden Orang Asli villages, with the chance to try out blow-pipes; guided forest treks by day and night; and, in season (June–July and Dec–Jan) hikes to find rare and extraordinary *Rafflesia* flowers (see p.596). These typically cost RM70–120; contact agents below for further information.

exposed beams conceal the fact that it's also a modern, efficiently run place, which also holds a suitably pub-like restaurant and bar, and a reading lounge. RM600

TANAH RATA

Cameronian Inn 16 Jalan Mentigi ☎ 05 491 1327, ⓦ thecameronianinn.com; map opposite. Plain but airy dorms and doubles (some with en-suite facilities) inside a spotless old house, surrounded by a bougainvillea trellis and small garden, all pretty quiet. There's also wi-fi, and breakfast can be ordered. The manager is a mine of information about local walks. Dorms RM15, doubles RM45

Eight Mentigi 18a Jalan Mentigi ☎ 05 491 5988, ⓦ eightmentigi.com; map opposite. A low-set, bright and sparklingly clean tiled house with large, well-appointed rooms and a front patio to sit out on. A good deal for the price. Dorms RM15, doubles RM50, en-suite doubles RM80

★ **Father's Guest House** Off Jalan Gereja ☎ 05 491 2888, ⓦ fathers.cameronhighlands.com; map opposite. The best budget accommodation in the Highlands, set on a quiet, wooded hill. Doubles in a stone house with French doors opening onto a secluded garden, plus dorm beds in aluminium huts. They also have a large library, internet terminals, wi-fi and very friendly staff who go out of their way to ensure you enjoy yourself. A nice little café serves local and Western dishes. Dorms RM15, doubles RM60, en-suite doubles RM90

Hillview Inn 17 Jalan Mentigi ☎ 05 491 2915, ⓦ hillview-inn.com; map opposite. Delightful, modern mock-Tudor buildings with small front garden; inside all the spacious rooms have en-suite bathrooms and balconies, and there are large common areas on each floor. Amenities include a laundry, a simple restaurant and internet access. Good value, though staff are unhelpful. RM140

Kang Travellers Lodge (Daniel's Lodge) 9 Lorong Perdah ☎ 05 491 5823, ⓦ daniels.cameronhighlands .com; map opposite. This laidback place has one huge attic dorm and doubles with fans and shared or private toilets. There's a communal sitting area and café – *The Jungle Bar* – with a pool table, movie library and a

bonfire (weather permitting), but some of the furniture could do with a good scrub. Dorms RM12, doubles RM30, en-suite doubles RM50

KRC Pines 7 Jalan Mentigi ☎ 05 491 2169, ⓦ twinpines .cameronhighlands.com; map opposite. Pale pink apartments on three storeys; spartan modern rooms are characterless but there's plenty of space, plus a kitchen and surrounding garden. Doubles with bathroom RM60, family rooms RM110

Planters 44A Jalan Besar ☎ 05 490 1001, ⓦ plantershotel.com.my; map opposite. Rather smart and trim boutique hotel, trading on the Highlands' old days with careful use of period furniture and decorations amid plainer modern fittings. The large, bright rooms are fair value midweek. RM150

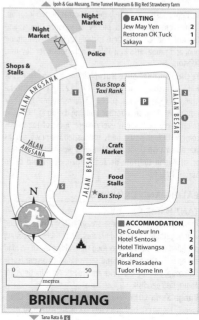

▲ Ipoh & Gua Musang, Time Tunnel Museum & Big Red Strawberry farm

● EATING
Jew May Yen	2
Restoran OK Tuck	1
Sakaya	3

■ ACCOMMODATION
De Couleur Inn	1
Hotel Sentosa	2
Hotel Titiwangsa	6
Parkland	4
Rosa Passadena	5
Tudor Home Inn	3

Night Market
Night Market
Police
Shops & Stalls
JALAN ANGSANA
Bus Stop & Taxi Rank
P
JALAN BESAR
JALAN ANGSANA
Craft Market
JALAN BESAR
Food Stalls
N
Bus Stop

0 — 50
metres

BRINCHANG

▼ Tana Rata & 6

2

Twin Pines 2 Jalan Mentigi ☎ 05 491 2169, ⓦtwinpines.cameronhighlands.com; map p.126. Set back from the road with a blue roof, this laidback place is popular with travellers and has well-informed and friendly staff, though it can be noisy due to the thin-walled rooms. There's an attractive patio garden, a café and online facilities. Dorms RM15, doubles RM35, doubles with shower RM70

ON THE ROAD TO BRINCHANG

Bala's Holiday Chalets Tanah Rata–Brinchang road ☎ 05 491 1660, ⓦbalaschalet.com; map p.122. Huge rambling mansion, covered in vegetation and dating from the 1950s or earlier. A bit of a let-down at present, the rooms are gradually being renovated and are certainly worth checking out, as the place has real old-world panache. There's also a lounge, dining rooms and a log fire plus beautiful gardens, which are a great spot for afternoon tea. RM180

Casa dela Rosa 1.5km south of Brinchang ☎ 05 491 1333, ⓦhotelcasadelarosa.com.my; map p.122. Huge, modern pile, on the Tanah Rata–Brinchang bus route, surrounded by lawns and facing the Sultan Ahmed Shah Golf Course. The rooms are comfortable, large and echo a mock-Tudor theme with wooden furniture and four-poster beds, but lack the panache of the Highlands' older establishments. RM320

Strawberry Park Tanah Rata–Brinchang road ☎ 05 491 1166, ⓦstrawberryparkresorts.com; map p.122. A modern apartment-style hotel in a great hilltop location. Rooms are smart, with plenty of wooden floors and furniture; added attractions include an indoor swimming pool and sauna, also available to non-guests for day-use. RM600

Ye Olde Smokehouse Hotel Midway along the Tanah Rata–Brinchang road ☎ 05 491 1215, ⓦthesmoke house.com.my; map p.122. Twelve suites inside a ridiculously English suburban building dating to 1937. The colonial-era pedigree is everywhere: most of the rooms come with four-poster beds and leaded windows, and as you down a whisky in the stone-and-wood-beam lounge, or sit out in the rose-decked garden, you could be in Surrey. RM600

BRINCHANG

Most hotels in Brinchang line the east and west sides of the central square, and are relatively overpriced, with few budget options.

★ **De Couleur Inn** 12 Jalan Besar ☎ 05 491 5125, ⓦdecouleurinn.com; map p.127. Look for the entrance to the side of a bright orange building. A cheerful budget hotel with simple, clean rooms, shared facilities and small central atrium with goldfish pond and tables. RM60

Flora De Cottage 18 Jalan Angsana ☎ 05 491 1700, ⓔflora.enquiry@gmail.com; map p.127. Approached via a cute, flowery entrance opposite the new row of stalls in the west side of town, this is ideal for visiting the night market, and has clean rooms with TVs and hot showers. RM68

Hotel Sentosa 38 Jalan Besar ☎ 05 491 5492; map p.127. With wooden floors throughout, this is a good-value option, though their cheapest rooms are windowless. RM68

Hotel Titiwangsa 187–188 Jalan Besar ☎ 05 490 1188, ⓦhoteltitiwangsa.com; map p.127. A modern, long block of a hotel with perfectly clean, decent en-suite rooms – just absolutely no character. Management are friendly, and there's wi-fi in the lobby. RM120

Parkland 45 Jalan Besar ☎ 05 491 1299; map p.127. In a five-storey shophouse with the obligatory mock-Tudor gables, the *Parkland* has clean, decent-sized rooms, but you'd expect lifts and newer furnishings for the price. They also offer apartments further up the hill. RM130

Rosa Passadena 1 Bandar Baru Brinchang ☎ 05 491 2288, ⓦcameronpremierhotels.com.my; map p.127. Large, modern, professionally run hotel, though the climate has prematurely mildewed the exterior and the en-suite rooms, complete with TVs and safes, are looking tired. Extremely busy nonetheless, and one of the few mid-range hotels in the Highlands, with a slew of attached Chinese restaurants. RM200

★ **Tudor Home Inn** 10a Jalan Angsana ☎ 05 490 1353, ⓔronny@tudorhomeinn.com.my; map p.127. An unmissable exterior, painted bright yellow and pink, with mock-Tudor patterns. Inside, rooms are basic, clean and come with en-suite facilities and wi-fi, making this friendly family-run hotel great value. RM60

EATING AND DRINKING

TANAH RATA

The local speciality, Chinese steamboat, involves cooking your vegetables, meat and prawns at the table in a boiling pot filled with stock. Malay food stalls along the main road are open in the evening and serve satay, *tom yam* (spicy Thai soup) and the usual rice and noodle combinations, for about RM5 per dish.

Bunga Suria Jalan Perisan Camelia; map p.126. Clean, friendly Indian establishment set back off the main road, good

for *thosais*, self-serve curries and surprisingly sound banana-chocolate cake, omelettes, lamb chops and chips. Main courses typically cost around RM8. Daily 8am–10pm.

Dinasti Tang Jalan Besar; map p.126. Cute place serving Chinese-Malay desserts, great on a hot day: ABC (shaved ice) with strawberries; *tong yuan* (sesame paste rice balls in sweet soup); plus herbal, fruit and "beautifying" drinks. There's a balcony for people-watching. Around RM8 a serve. Daily 11am–8pm.

★ **Ferm Nonya** Jalan Perisan Camelia; map p.126. Excellent Nonya-style home cooking; try the *kerabu* (spicy salad of shredded vegetables with lime juice and chillies) and seasonal steamed fish. One of many popular Chinese restaurants in this block. Mains RM10 and up. Daily noon–10pm.

Kumar Jalan Besar; map p.126. Spicy Southern Indian food, thalis, and Chinese claypot chicken, plus tandoori chicken and naan bread hot from the oven. Decent portions, and almost impossible to spend more than RM12. Daily 8am–8pm.

La Bella Jalan Besar; map p.126. Restaurant-café whose awful coffee is compensated for by magnificent Deveonshire cream teas, featuring home-made scones and as much cream, butter and strawberry jam as you can handle for RM14.50. Daily 8am–9pm.

Mutiara Jalan Besar; map p.126. An appetizing range of dishes from both India and China, with a *nasi kandar* selection; also good for a roti and black coffee breakfast. Daily 8am–5pm.

Rosette and Rosedale, Jalan Besar; map p.126. Restaurant and café, both offering eclectic menus featuring tasty herbal duck soup, *tom yam*, satay and spaghetti bolognese. Extras include full cooked breakfasts and wi-fi. Mains around RM10. Daily 11am–9pm.

BRINCHANG

As well as the Malay food stalls in the central square, the following places are worth a try.

Jew May Yen Jalan Besar, west side of square; map p.127. Good busy Chinese restaurant, which is popular with the locals. Steamboat and tasty soups. Daily 11am–9pm.

Restoran OK Tuck Jalan Besar; map p.127. Huge, busy Chinese place specializing in steamboat, with excellent black vinegar spareribs, fried prawns and *blechan* asparagus beans. Fix prices when ordering because they're not on the menu. Mains around RM12. Daily 11am–9pm.

Sakaya Jalan Besar; map p.127. This inexpensive Chinese eating house does buffet lunches, costing from RM5 for three dishes, including rice. Daily 11am–9pm.

DIRECTORY

TANAH RATA

Banks Several banks with ATMs along Jalan Besar, and in the block beside Jalan Perisan Camelia.

District office 39007 Tanah Rata ☎ 05 491 1066, ✆ 491 1843 (Mon–Thurs 8am–1pm & 2–4.30pm, Fri 8am–12.15pm & 2.45–4.30pm, Sat 8am–12.15pm). Contact them immediately if you suspect someone has got lost on a walk.

Hospital Jalan Besar, opposite the park ☎ 05 491 1966. There's also a clinic at 48 Main Rd (8.30am–12.30pm, 2–5.30pm & 8–10pm). Ring doorbell after clinic hours in emergencies.

Police station Jalan Besar, opposite the *New Garden Inn* ☎ 05 491 1222.

Post office Jalan Besar. Incredibly slow service; you also need to buy envelopes, boxes and tape for packing from nearby stores. Mon–Sat 8am–4.30pm.

Service station There are service stations in both Tanah Rata and Brinchang.

Sport Cameron Highlands Golf Club (ⓦ cameron highlandsresort.com) has an 18-hole course; check the website for day rates, caddy fees and equipment rental. The dress code bans collarless shirts, shorts and flip-flops.

Perak

Most visitors whisk through **Perak State**, which occupies most of the area between KL and Penang, and is crossed by the rail line and fast expressway. Between the sixteenth century and the 1960s, **tin** kept Perak wealthy, causing fisticuffs at various times between Dutch, British, Thai and Malay factions, funding a royal seat outside modern **Kuala Kangsar** and leaving the cities of **Taiping** and **Ipoh** awash with solid colonial and Chinese architecture. These, along with the Cameron Highlands (see p.121) remain interesting places to step off the tourist trail for a day or two and take in ordinary life in modern Malaysia, though Perak's most popular attraction is the laidback resort island of **Pulau Pangkor**, accessed from Ipoh via the port of **Lumut**.

Ipoh

IPOH, around halfway between KL and the Thai border, is named after the *upas* tree which once thrived in the area, whose sap was used by the Orang Asli for blowpipe-dart poison. But like the rest of Perak, Ipoh's wealth – and position as Malaysia's third largest city – comes from **tin mining**. With the discovery of a major field here in 1880, Ipoh became a prime destination for pioneers, merchants and fortune-seekers

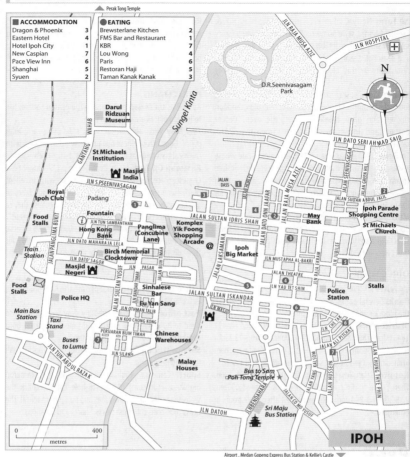

▲ Perak Tong Temple

■ ACCOMMODATION		● EATING	
Dragon & Phoenix	3	Brewsterlane Kitchen	2
Eastern Hotel	4	FMS Bar and Restaurant	1
Hotel Ipoh City	1	KBR	7
New Caspian	7	Lou Wong	4
Pace View Inn	6	Paris	6
Shanghai	5	Restoran Haji	5
Syuen	2	Taman Kanak Kanak	3

IPOH

Airport , Medan Gopeng Express Bus Station & Kellie's Castle ▼

from all over the world. To accommodate the rapidly increasing population, the city expanded across the muddy and lethargic **Sungai Kinta** into a "new town" area, its economic good fortune reflected in a multitude of **colonial buildings** and Chinese shophouses. Now the Perak **state capital** and home to half a million people, Ipoh's low-key, likeable historic streets make for an appealing day's stopover, with the bonus of the outlying Chinese cave temple of **Perak Tong**, and the anachronistic ruin of **Kellie's Castle**.

The colonial district

Downtown Ipoh's northwest side sports some prominent **colonial architecture**, the most striking of which is the **train station**, completed in 1917 at the height of the tin boom. A brilliant white wedding-cake of a building, it's fronted by a 200m-long veranda and topped in Moorish turrets and domes. Just east, the **Birch Memorial Clocktower** commemorates the first British Resident of Perak, who was murdered after his abruptness offended the local sultan. South of here, the modern **Masjid Negeri** on Jalan Sultan Iskandar is all tacky 1960s cladding, with a minaret that rises 40m above its mosaic-tiled domes.

2

STREET NAMES IN IPOH

The **layout** of central Ipoh is reasonably straightforward, since the roads more or less form a grid system. What makes things confusing is that some of the old colonial **street names** have been changed in favour of more Islamic alternatives, but the street signs haven't always caught up; hence, Jalan C.M. Yusuf instead of Jalan Chamberlain, Jalan Mustapha Al-Bakri for Jalan Clare and Jalan Bandar Timar for Jalan Leech. In practice, locals recognize either name.

Darul Ridzuan Museum

Sat–Thurs 9.30am–5pm, Fri 9.30am–12.15pm & 2.45–5pm • Free

The **Darul Ridzuan Museum**, a short walk north from the station along Jalan Panglima Bukit Gantang Wahab, is housed in an elegant former tin-miner's mansion. Covering two floors, the museum holds evocative photos of Ipoh's glory days during the tin boom.

Chinatown and Malay houses

Much of the centre of Ipoh could be classed as a Chinatown, but for an interesting walk past rows of pastel-coloured, mildewed **shophouses** (some still with their original names moulded in Chinese characters on their facades), first head west of the river to **Jalan Bijih Timah**. Look for narrow **Panglima Lane**, formerly known as Concubine Lane, where wealthy Chinese merchants once kept their mistresses; it's a real time capsule, lined with decaying terrace homes, their doorways shuttered by traditional wooden barred gates.

Back on Bijih Timah, you pass Indian rug shops and an ancient **Sinhalese bar** with saloon-style swing doors, before crossing busy Jalan Sultan Iskandar. South on Jalan Bandar Timar, **Eu Yan Sang** is a traditional Chinese pharmacy, originally founded near Ipoh in 1879 to nurse immigrant miners and now an international chain, listed on the Singapore Stock Exchange. One block west, the lower end of Bijih Timah is lined with old Chinese **warehouses**, overflowing onto the streets with fruit, dried foods and household goods waiting to be picked up by cruising trucks.

Continue south, cross a footbridge, and then turn north along the riverside path. A handful of rickety old wooden **Malay houses** lurk here under towering fig trees, recalling a time when this must have all been fields. The walk winds up at attractive Panglima Kinta mosque, the first in Ipoh, with unusual Moorish-style arches.

ARRIVAL AND DEPARTURE   **IPOH**

Both the North–South Expressway and Route 1 pass through Ipoh, which is also a major stop for express buses and trains between Butterworth and KL.

BY PLANE

Sultan Azlan Shah airport is 15km from the city (☎ 05 312 2460, ⊛ ipoh.airport-authority.com), served by Firefly and Malaysia Air. Flights to Singapore (2 daily; 2hr). A taxi into the centre costs RM25.

BY TRAIN

Train station The train station (☎ 05 254 0481) is on Jalan Panglima Bukit Gantang Wahab (more simply Jalan Panglima), west of the old town.

Destinations Alor Star (1 daily; 7hr); Butterworth (3 daily; 4hr 30min); Hat Yai (Thailand; 1 daily; 9hr); Kuala Kangsar (4 daily; 1hr 30min); Kuala Lumpur (6 daily; 3hr 30min); Sungai Petani (1 daily; 5hr 30min); Singapore (1 daily; 9hr); Taiping (4 daily; 1hr 30min).

BY BUS

Main bus station South of the train station, where Jalan Tun Abdul Razak meets Jalan Panglima, and also known as "steysen bas Medan Kidd". It deals in local destinations, and also the Cameron Highlands. Note that buses to Kuala Kangsar are marked "Perak". Arriving, either walk into town, or catch city bus marked "Ipoh Garden Jaya Jusco".

Destinations Gopeng (5 daily); Kuala Kangsar (1hr); Taiping (1hr 30min); Tanah Rata (Cameron Highlands; 4 daily; 2hr).

Lumut Bus Station Buses to Lumut, the port for Pulau Pangkor (see p.135), depart from an open-air depot next to the Shell Garage on Jalan Tun Abdul Razak. Buses to Lumut (hourly 6am–7pm; 2hr).

2

EXPRESS BUS STATIONS

Express bus stations Two express bus stations serve much the same destinations: a huge affair near the roundabout on Jalan Bendahara run by the Sri Maju bus company (ⓦsrimaju.com); and Medan Gopeng, Ipoh's official long-distance station, inconveniently located 4km out of town on Jalan Gopeng.

Destinations Alor Star (4 daily; 4hr); Butterworth (3 daily; 3hr); Cameron Highlands (4 daily; 2hr); Johor Bahru (2 daily; 7hr 30min); Kangar (3 daily; 4hr); KLIA and LCCT Airports (11 daily; 3hr); Kota Bahru (2 daily; 8hr); Kuala Kangsar (every 45min; 1hr); Kuala Lumpur (hourly; 3hr 30min); Kuala Perlis (1 daily; 5hr); Kuala Terengganu (2 daily; 11hr); Kuantan (1 daily; 8hr); Melaka (1 daily; 6hr); Penang (hourly; 2hr 30min); Seremban (2 daily; 5hr); Singapore (6 daily; 9hr).

GETTING AROUND

By taxi There's a taxi stand opposite Ipoh's main bus station (Teksi Ipoh; ☏ 05 253 4188 or ☏ 05 241 1388).

INFORMATION

Tourist office Jalan Tun Sambanthan, Ipoh ☏ 05 241 2959. Mon–Fri 8am–5pm. Good crop of brochures; staff are pleasant and helpful but not very knowledgeable about the area.

ACCOMMODATION

Most places to stay in Ipoh are east of the river, in the "new" town, which is the better option for night markets and late-night restaurants, as the old town practically closes down when the sun sets.

Dragon & Phoenix 23–25 Jalan Toh Puan Chah ☏ 05 253 4661. A relatively quiet and friendly older hotel, nicely maintained and welcoming; rooms are plain but decent. RM62

Eastern Hotel 118 Jalan Sultan Idries Shah ☏ 05 254 3936. Modern budget business hotel with slightly too much brown colouring the otherwise smart furnishings; rooms have en-suite bathrooms with powerful showers. RM88

Hotel Ipoh City 18 Jalan Dass ☏ 05 241 8282. Bright orange and aquamarine block, with wi-fi, a/c, fridge, hairdryer and tea- and coffee-making facilities in all rooms. Staff are a bit offhand. RM160

New Caspian Hotel 6–10 Jalan Jubilee ☏ 05 242 3327. 1950s budget hotel that's holding up well; en-suite rooms are neatly tiled and come with a/c, while the furniture is elderly but serviceable. RM72.

★ **Pace View Inn** 3–9 Jalan Ali Pitchay ☏ 05 241 3644, ⓦpaceview.blogspot.com. Efficiently run with windows, a/c, TV and clean bathrooms in all rooms; good value for this price bracket. RM66

★ **Shanghai** 85 Jalan Mustapha Al-Bakri ☏ 05 241 2070. This 1960s guesthouse wouldn't have been cutting edge even when new, but it's well looked after and the owner is friendly. Some rooms are fan only, but most come with a/c and all have en-suite bathrooms; there's charm too in the dated ply-and-laminex furniture. Close to night market. RM40

Syuen 88 Jalan Sultan Abdul Jalil ☏ 05 253 8889, ⓦsyuenhotel.com.my. Beyond the swish Neoclassical lobby with its frilly balconies and gold trim, the rooms are – inevitably – a slight let-down; spacious, well appointed and with huge beds, but otherwise ordinary. Buffet breakfast included. RM350

EATING AND DRINKING

Ipoh's best food – mostly Chinese – is served at the night markets and various hawker centres around town, though there are some good restaurants too. For the best variety – stir fries, soups, rice noodles, ABC and fruit dishes, plus a dash of karaoke – head one block east of the *Shanghai* guesthouse to Jalan Greenhill, where nearly a hundred stalls fire up from 7pm until late.

Brewsterlane Kitchen 140 Jalan Sultan Idris Shah. This almost European-looking place, decked out in elegant wooden furniture, does good tempura and claypot dishes alongside steak and salmon. Mains around RM15. Friendly service. Daily 11am–3pm & 5–10pm.

FMS Bar and Restaurant At the far end of the padang. Being restored at the time of writing, this colonial-style building is said to house Malaysia's oldest bar, founded by Chinese immigrants from Hainan Island in 1906.

KBR Main street, Little India. Vegetarian southern Indian food on the main street in Ipoh's unremarkable "Little India". Inexpensive and tasty food, with a one-plate *thali* for just RM6. Daily 11am–9pm.

★ **Lou Wong** On the corner of Jalan Yau Tet Shin and Jalan Raja Musa Aziz. This busy, open-sided place specializes in juicy salt chicken, sliced and served with soy-sesame oil dressing for around RM8, eaten with a side order of crispy beansprouts and noodle soup. At night they set up tables in the road too. Daily 10am–9pm.

Paris Jalan Sultan Iskandar. Set inside a classic blue-and-white shophouse, this brusque Hakka Chinese *kedai kopi* serves superb "dry" noodles in a meat sauce, for around RM6, as well as fishball soup. Daily 7am–4pm.

Restoran Haji On the corner of Dato Jafnar and Yau Te Shin. Open-sided place with a canvas roof; a good choice for an RM8 Malay breakfast – roti, *nasi lemak*, *nasi kerabu*, fried chicken – with strong coffee. Daily, mornings only.

Taman Kanak Kanak East off Jalan Raja Musa Aziz. Covered food stalls with a definite Malay (rather than Chinese) flavour, surrounding a small children's play area. Stall 18, Popiah SS Ali, is locally famous for *popiah*, a vegetable-filled spring roll served with a gloopy hot-sweet sauce. Shop around and fill up for RM5. Daily 7pm–late.

DIRECTORY

Banks Maybank and Bank Bumiputra are on Jalan Sultan Idris Shah.

Books Popular Bookstore, upstairs at the Ipoh Parade mall, is one place to find works by local cartoonist Lat aka Mohammad Nor Khalid (see p.599); something of a national institution, he's been gently highlighting the absurdity of Malay life and politics since the 1970s.

Cinemas Fourth floor of the Ipoh Parade shopping complex, Jalan Sultan Abdul Jalil, just east of the *Syuen Hotel*.

Hospital On Jalan Hospital ☎ 05 253 3333.

Internet access Several places around the Kompleks Yik Foong shopping arcade on Jalan Laksamana.

Police On Jalan Panglima between the bus and train stations ☎ 05 245 1500.

Post office The GPO is practically next door to the train station, on Jalan Panglima.

Travel agents Keris Travel 15–19 Jalan Ali Pitchay ☎ 05 255 2666, ⓦ keristravel.net. Efficient and reliable agent, part of a national chain.

Visa extensions The Immigration Office is over halfway to Kuala Kangsar on Jalan Bandar Meru Raya (☎ 05 501 7100).

Around Ipoh

Ipoh's sprawling suburbs and noisy outer roads are overlooked by craggy **limestone peaks**, some riddled with caves where Chinese workers established popular **shrines** that are now especially busy during Chinese New Year. The **Perak Tong Temple** is the pick of these, but if there's one sight really worth your time outside Ipoh it's **Kellie's Castle**, an eccentric footnote to the colonial era whose absurdity makes up for the hassle of reaching it.

Perak Tong Temple

Kuala Kangsar • Daily 8am–5pm • Free • Bus #141 from Ipoh's main bus station (20min)

Located in dramatic surroundings 6km north of Ipoh, the **Perak Tong Temple** doubles as a centre for Chinese art. Its gaudy exterior – bright red-and-yellow pavilions flanked by feathery willows and lotus ponds – gives no hint of the eerie atmosphere inside, where darkened cavern upon cavern honeycombs up into the rock formation. The huge first chamber is dominated by a 15m-high golden statue of the Buddha flanked by two startled-looking companions dancing and playing instruments. From time to time, a massive bell fills the chamber with booming echoes; it's rung by visiting devotees to draw attention to the donation they've just offered. In the next chamber, the walls are decorated with complex calligraphy and delicate flower paintings. Towards the back of this musty hollow, a steep flight of 385 crudely fashioned steps climbs up and out of the cave to a sort of balcony, with views of great limestone outcrops and ugly factory buildings.

Kellie's Castle

Kinta Kelas Rubber Estate, 12km south of Ipoh • Taxi from Ipoh about RM50 return including a wait while you look around; alternatively, take bus #36 or #37 from Ipoh's main bus station to Batu Gajah (departures every 1hr 30min; 30min), from where you can either walk the remaining 4km on the clearly signposted A8 road or take a taxi (around RM5)

Kellie's Castle symbolizes the prosperity achieved by many enterprising foreigners in the rubber and tin industries in the early 1900s. One of these was **William Kellie**

Smith, a Scot who celebrated his financial success – and the birth of a long-desired son – by designing this extraordinary mansion. A 1920 influenza epidemic killed many of the Tamil workers; when work resumed, Smith left on a trip to England in 1925, but fell ill and died in Portugal and Kellie's Castle was never completed.

Far from being a ruin, however, the castle is a spectacular memorial to Kellie's vision, a sort of tropical Italianate-Hindu palace in apricot-coloured bricks, with a rectangular, off-centre tower. It incorporates a lift (the first in Malaysia), underground tunnels only rediscovered in 2003, and rows of beautiful arched colonnades in Moorish style. Heavily influenced by Indian culture, Smith imported many of the bricks from Madras and even constructed an adjacent **Hindu temple** in thanks for the birth of his son. Amid the rooftop deities you can see a figure dressed in a white suit and pith helmet, presumably Smith himself.

Pulau Pangkor

With some of the best beaches on this side of the Malay Peninsula, the laidback island of **PULAU PANGKOR**, though barely 10km long, makes a thoroughly pleasant place to spend a weekend, and an increasingly popular retreat with Malaysian families up for an easy break from KL. Its mountainous centre remains thickly forested and largely inaccessible, so there's little distraction from enjoying beach life. There are a couple of fishing towns on the east coast, developing tourist enclaves across the island at **Pasir Bogak** and hornbill-infested **Teluk Nipah**, and not really that much in between. Surprisingly then, Pulau Pangkor played an important part in Malaysian history when the **Pangkor Treaty** was signed here in 1874, which led to the creation of the Resident System.

THE RESIDENT SYSTEM

In 1873, Rajah Abdullah of Perak invited the new Governor of the Straits Settlements, Andrew Clarke, to appoint a **Resident** (colonial officer) to Perak, in exchange for recognizing Abdullah as the Sultan of Perak instead of his rival. This held some appeal for the British, whose involvement in Malay affairs had hitherto been unofficial, so on January 20, 1874, the two men signed the **Pangkor**. The idea was that the Resident – each state would have its own – would play an advisory role in Malay affairs in return for taking a sympathetic attitude to Malay customs and rituals.

The interpretation of the newly created post was in the hands of **Hugh Low**, whose jurisdiction of Perak (1877–89) was based in Kuala Kangsar. The personable Low lived modestly by British standards and his linguistic skills won him favour with local chiefs. Having spent nearly thirty years in Borneo, Low was great friends with Charles and James Brooke (see p.319), and sought to emulate their relatively benign system of government.

The approval of the Malay nobility, vital to the success of the Residency scheme, was secured by compensating them for the income lost from taxes and property. This suited the sultans; they obtained financial security through healthy stipends, and also got political protection from rivals. As time went on, lesser figures were given positions within the bureaucracy, thus weaving the Malays into the fabric of the administration, of which the cornerstone was the **State Council**. Although the sultan was its ceremonial head, the Resident chose the constituent members and set the political agenda, in consultation with his deputies – the district officers – and the governor.

It is doubtful that the Malays understood the treaty's long-term consequences, as initially the decision-making process was collective, much like the Malays' own courts. As the power of central government increased, however, fewer meetings of the council were held, and the British involvement became less advisory and more reformatory. Sultan Abdullah, bent on acquiring local power and status, thereby inadvertently allowed the British a foot in the door, which ultimately led to their full political intervention in the Peninsula.

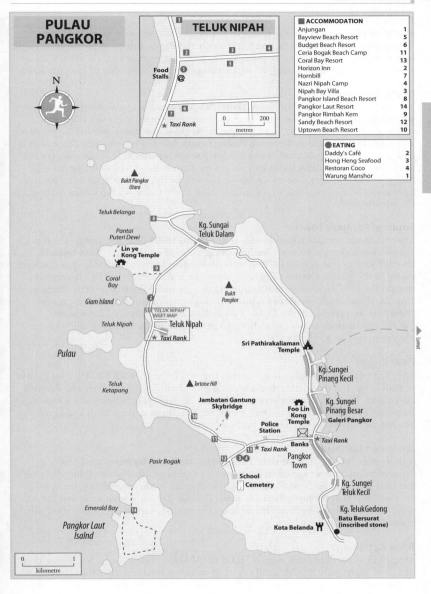

PULAU PANGKOR

TELUK NIPAH

Food Stalls

★ Taxi Rank

0   200
metres

ACCOMMODATION

Anjungan	1
Bayview Beach Resort	5
Budget Beach Resort	6
Ceria Bogak Beach Camp	11
Coral Bay Resort	13
Horizon Inn	2
Hornbill	7
Nazri Nipah Camp	4
Nipah Bay Villa	3
Pangkor Island Beach Resort	8
Pangkor Laut Resort	14
Pangkor Rimbah Kem	9
Sandy Beach Resort	12
Uptown Beach Resort	10

EATING

Daddy's Café	2
Hong Heng Seafood	3
Restoran Coco	4
Warung Manshor	1

Bukit Pangkor Utara

Teluk Belanga

Pantai Puteri Dewi

Lin ye Kong Temple

Coral Bay

Giam Island

Teluk Nipah

Pulau

Teluk Ketapang

Kg. Sungai Teluk Dalam

Bukit Pangkor

SEE 'TELUK NIPAH' INSET MAP

Teluk Nipah

★ Taxi Rank

Tortoise Hill

Jambatan Gantung Skybridge

Sri Pathirakaliaman Temple

Kg. Sungei Pinang Kecil

Kg. Sungei Pinang Besar

Galeri Pangkor

Foo Lin Kong Temple

Police Station

Banks

★ Taxi Rank

Pangkor Town

Pasir Bogak

★ Taxi Rank

School

Cemetery

Kg. Sungei Teluk Kecil

Emerald Bay

Pangkor Laut Isalnd

Kg. Teluk Gedong

Batu Bersurat (inscribed stone)

Kota Belanda

Lumut

0   1
kilometre

Pangkor is an easy ferry ride from mainland **LUMUT**, a small port and Malaysian Navy base 80km southwest of Ipoh. The only time things get really busy on the island is during school holidays and the Hindu festival of **Thaipusam** (see p.47), celebrated on the full moon in mid-February or early March. The unmissably gruesome spectacle lasts two days; processions start out on the beach at Pasir Bogak, and end at the Sri Pathirakaliaman Temple on the east coast.

2

Pangkor Town

PANGKOR TOWN is the island's principal settlement, where ferries from Lumut dock. There's a covered market area, and a few shops and banks, but most people get straight on a minibus taxi to west-coast resort areas. After you've settled in, vary beach life by returning to check out a couple of sights along the coast either side of Pangkor Town.

North of Pangkor Town

Just up the hill from Pangkor Town, **Galeri Pangkor** (free) is a small museum with nineteenth-century photos of the Pangkor Treaty signatories, a few fish traps, and pieces of Chinese porcelain. From the terrace outside, look down over fishing trawlers and cargo ships docked at **Kampung Pinang Besar**'s wooden wharfs, then descend to the village and take a signed road 1km inland to **Foo Lin Temple**. This Taoist complex is a riot of red and gold decorations and sculptures of animals – real and imaginary – in bright primary colours. There's a semi-wild garden behind, with a fishpond inhabited by enormous arapaima, and a miniature version of the Great Wall of China snaking up the hillside above.

South of Pangkor Town

The traditional wooden stilted houses at **KAMPUNG TELUK GEDONG** stand 1.5km south of town along the coastal road. Set back from the road on the right, **Kota Belanda**, or Dutch fort, was founded in 1670 to store tin supplies from Perak and keep a check on piracy in the Straits. Destroyed twenty years later, it was rebuilt in 1743 but finally abandoned in 1748; the half-built structure you see today is a recent reconstruction.

About 100m south, the **Batu Bersurat** is a huge granite boulder under a canopy. Look here for carvings of the Dutch East India Company logo, an intertwined "VOC", and a **tiger** – a warning after a Dutch child was carted off by one while playing nearby in 1743.

Pasir Bogak

The 2km road from Pangkor town reaches the west coast at **PASIR BOGAK**, a long curve of sand fringed in shade trees, looking out over a placid bay to much smaller **Pangkor Laut island**. Bogak is Pangkor's main resort area, with hotel complexes and a knot of shops and services at the south end; there's some high-rise development and better beaches further north, but it's still pretty relaxed.

Jambatan Gantung

A short walk inland, 1km north of Pasir Bogak, **Jambatan Gantung** is a 75m-long suspension bridge over a gully in the forest; it's nothing earth-shattering but there are a few large trees and vines, a chance to glimpse Pangkor's otherwise almost inaccessible interior. Note that **hiking trails** north across the island's centre from here, marked on some local maps, are absolutely invisible on the ground – ask at your hotel about hiring essential guides.

Teluk Ketapang

Around 2km north of Pasir Bogak, **TELUK KETAPANG** ("Turtle Bay"), is a 500m-long stretch of slightly gritty, wide sand edged by palm trees, named after the leatherback turtles that once nested here. Aside from an old, decaying jetty and a lookout tower, there are no facilities, but it's an attractive spot to come for a picnic and a splash in the water.

Teluk Nipah

First impressions of **TELUK NIPAH** are of a crowded strip of road lined in food and beachware stalls, edged with trees and with a lovely strip of white sand fringing the water. Views over the bay are beautiful at suset, with **hornbills** gliding over the rooftops and hunchbacked **Pulau Mentagor** rising darkly against the dusk. In keeping with the rest of the island, Nipah is busy but not intrusive, despite the abundant budget accommodation, the bay echoing to the delighted squeals of people splashing about in the shallows and being towed behind speedboats on "banana" rides. If this is your first Malaysian resort beach, you'll notice that locals go in the water modestly wrapped in shirts and sarongs, which effectively precludes swimming.

Coral Bay

Just north of Teluk Nipah, **Coral Bay** is a perfect cove with a 500m strip of smooth, white sand, backed by dense jungle climbing steeply to **Bukit Pangkor**, one of the island's three peaks. It's a casually developed spot with a couple of places to stay and the **Lin Ye Kong Temple**, a small tin-roofed shrine amid a jumble of boulders and concrete statues – including giant toadstools, a voulptuous mermaid, a Taoist crane and "Mickey Rat". Cross the bridge behind the temple and follow the path at the edge of the forest to reach a very small, secluded beach, hidden among large boulders.

| **ARRIVAL AND DEPARTURE** | **PULAU PANGKOR** |

By ferry Ferries (2 hourly; 45min; RM10 return) run Lumut–Pangkor Town daily 7am–8.30pm, and Pangkor Town–Lumut daily 6.30am–8.30pm. Two companies operate the route, and tickets are only valid for the correct vessels. The Lumut ferry terminal is 100m from Lumut bus station, surrounded by snack stalls and shops selling kitsch beachware. Arriving at Pangkor Town, you exit the terminal into the arms of motorbike rental touts and minibus taxi drivers. A ride to Teluk Nipah in the latter is RM15.

By bus Lumut's bus station, 100m from the ferry port, within sight of the sea, has services to: Butterworth (3 daily; 3hr); Ipoh (hourly; 1hr 45min); Johor Bahru (3 daily; 8hr 30min); KLIA (9 daily; 5hr); Kuala Kangsar (2 daily; 1hr 30min); Kuala Lumpur (hourly; 4hr); Taiping (4 daily; 1hr 10min); Singapore (3 daily; 10hr).

By taxi Lumut's taxi rank is outside the bus station. A cab to Ipoh costs RM120 (1hr 30min).

GETTING AROUND

There is **no public transport** on Pulau Pangkor. A sealed **road** of varying quality loops around much of the island's circumference, avoiding the mountainous interior and cutting inland only between Pangkor Town, where the ferry docks, and the tourist developments at Pasir Bogak, 2km away on the west coast.

By motorbike Renting a motorbike in Pangkor Town or via your hotel costs RM30–40/day. As there's only about 18km of road on the island, you shouldn't need it for more than one day.

By minibus taxi Bright pink, shared minibus taxis charge RM8 from Pangkor Town to Pasir Bogak, RM15 to Teluk Nipah and RM80 for a 2hr, round-island trip. There are ranks at the ferry port, outside the Coral Bay Resort at Pasir Bogak, and by the road just south of Teluk Nipah.

PULAU PANGKOR WATER ACTIVITIES

If you fancy time out on the water, your hotel or beach-side operators at Teluk Nipah and Pasir Bogak can book you on the following. The best **snorkelling** – though don't expect too much – is off little Giam Island (RM15); you can also do an island hop by **speedboat** to Giam and larger Mentangor (RM15), while Pangkor Laut costs RM30 (or do all three for RM50). A **banana boat** ride – being towed behind a speedboat on a float – costs RM15; and you can also rent **kayaks** (RM20/hour) or **jet skis** (RM100/30min).

There's also **Sea Park** at Coral Bay (RM5), a giant inflatable obstacle course moored offshore, great for children of all ages.

For serious **fishing** or **diving** excursions out to Nine Islands, well west of Pangkor, you need to rent a boat for the day, costing perhaps RM1000.

ACCOMMODATION

Most of Pangkor's resorts are around Pasir Bogak. Prices seesaw between low (weekdays), high (weekends) and peak (holidays), with peak prices around fifty percent higher than in low season. Prices listed below are for double rooms during low season. Hotels can also organize bus tickets, laundry, motorbike and bicycle rental, massage, jet-ski rental, snorkelling and fishing trips.

PASIR BOGAK

Ceria Bogak Beach Camp Pasir Bogak ☎05 685 4942, ⓦceriabogakbeachcampangkor.blogspot.com. A block of no-frills chalets, but they do all have a/c, it's right on the beach and the attached restaurant features evening barbecues. RM80

Coral Bay Resort Pasir Bogak ☎05 685 5111, ⓦpangkorcoralbay.com.my. Huge high-rise resort complex, providing everything you'll need — shops, restaurants, pool and gym — while insulating you from Pangkor's attractive, laidback ambience. Breakfast included. RM160, apartments RM250

★ **Sandy Beach Resort** Pasir Bogak ☎05 685 3027, ⓦpangkorsandybeach.com. Low-key, low-rise and unpretentious modern affair, built in a crescent facing the sea over a small pool (though only upstairs rooms have views). Avoid the older and smaller chalets. RM185

Uptown Beach Resort Pasir Bogak ☎05 685 4510, ⓦuptownbeachresort.com. Large hotel complex perched on the hillside, whose nice chalets with sea-view balconies easily out-compete the very ordinary doubles — though some of the latter are huge. Doubles RM100, chalets RM140

TELUK NIPAH

Teluk Nipah concentrates on the budget end of the market. Most places are small and family-run, offering chalets and double rooms with much the same facilities.

★ **Anjungan** Teluk Nipah ☎05 685 1500, ⓦanjungan resortpangkor.com. The only mid-range resort here, comprising four-storey apartment-style buildings surrounding a pool and lawn. It's relaxed but professional and welcoming; the en-suite rooms all feature terracotta tiling, a/c, TV and wi-fi, with large beds. RM170

Bayview Beach Resort Teluk Nipah ☎05 685 3540, ⓦpangkorbayview.com. No views of the bay at all, but this large, family-friendly chalet resort does feature a pool and a restaurant. All rooms have a/c, and full-board packages for groups are available. RM105

Budget Beach Resort Teluk Nipah ☎05 685 3529, ⓦbudgetbeachresort.com. A bright place with the usual run of chalets and doubles lined up in a block, but cheaper

and much tidier than most, with cheerful staff. RM75

Horizon Inn Teluk Nipah ☎05 685 3398. This two-storey building sits at the north end of the coast road and has spacious en-suite rooms above a souvenir shop; front rooms have large balconies facing the sea, but those at the rear are quieter. RM90

Hornbill Teluk Nipah ☎05 685 2005, ⓦpangkor hornbillresort.com. All the rooms in this two-storey building boast wooden floors, a/c, showers, balconies and a view of the beach. Breakfast included. RM120

★ **Nazri Nipah Camp** Teluk Nipah ☎05 685 2014. Very popular with travellers and well laid out with chalets and simple A-frames around a pleasant communal garden area, perfect for chilled-out socializing. A little café serves breakfast and coffees. Dorms RM20, doubles RM40, chalets RM80

Nipah Bay Villa Teluk Nipah ☎05 685 2198, ⓦpulaupangkornipahbayvilla.blogspot.com. A long block packed with cabins and a shaded restaurant at the front. All chalets and rooms have a/c, satellite TV and hot water in good, clean bathrooms. Wi-fi area at the front. Doubles RM100, chalets RM180

ELSEWHERE

Pangkor Island Beach Resort Teluk Belanga, north of Coral Bay ☎05 685 1091, ⓦpangkorislandbeach .com. Unimaginative but well-furnished resort complex situated in secluded Teluk Belanga, with its own golf course and private beach. RM600

★ **Pangkor Laut Resort** Pangkor Laut Island ⓦpangkorlautresort.com. In a completely different league to any other place on the entire west coast of Malaysia, this exclusive, immaculate and very expensive retreat features wooden chalets built on stilts over the sea. RM800

Pangkor Rimbah Kem Coral Bay ☎0135/109384, ⓔpangkorrimbahkem@yahoo.com. A row of unassuming chalets lined up beneath the shade of huge trees, and set in between the beach and road; an older bunkhouse is now a dorm and they'll let you camp here too (assuming you have a tent) and use the shared bathrooms. The management is fairly stern and seems to make up prices on the day according to demand. Dorms RM20, chalets RM70

EATING AND DRINKING

PASIR BOGAK

Hong Heng Seafood Pasir Bogak. A good all-rounder, serving up stir fries, Penang-style sour *laksa*, similar *tom*

yam campur, whole grilled fish, steamboats and cold desserts. Nothing much over RM15. Daily 11am–after dark.

Restoran Coco 100m inland from the main road in Pasir Bogak. Alfresco dining under trees; the decor is flashing lights, concrete tables and plastic chairs, but you're here for the cold beers and Chinese-Malay seafood. Can get quite noisy and sociable at times, with karaoke often firing up. RM20 a head. Daily, evenings only.

TELUK NIPAH

Beachside stalls just south of the village serve all the usual suspects plus great fresh grilled seafood. A couple of places also specialize in *lempeng pisang*, a thick and sticky pancake batter spread on a banana leaf, sprinkled with shredded coconut and then grilled.

★ **Daddy's Café** Five minutes' walk up the road from Teluk Nipah. This beachside restaurant-bar has tables on the sand overlooking the bay, a nice setting for a romantic candlelit dinner. The menu covers a range of Western dishes, including steak and fish and chips, but the jumbo grilled prawns are spectacular. Beer is frosty-cold, prices high but good value and service laidback, to say the least. Mains RM30. Daily 11am–11pm.

Warung Manshor Teluk Nipah. One of several simple Malay restaurants opening early for coffee, roti, scambled eggs on toast and tuna sandwiches. Daily 7am–afternoon.

DIRECTORY

Banks Turn left from the ferry at Pangkor Town to find a small Maybank with ATM under the covered market street. Otherwise, the closest banks and moneychangers are at Lumut jetty.

Internet Some accommodation has wi-fi; netbars at Pasir Gombak and Teluk Nipah.

Kuala Kangsar

While Ipoh is the administrative capital of Perak, **KUALA KANGSAR**, 50km northwest, is its **royal town**, home to the sultans of Perak since the fifteenth century and later the seat of Perak's first Resident, Hugh Low. Built at a grandiose sweep of Sungai Perak, it's a small, workaday town, with a colonial monument in the **Malay College** on Jalan Tun Razak, its elegant columns and porticoes visible as you approach the centre from the train station. Founded in 1905 as an "Eton of the East", it was a training ground for the sons of Malay nobility, with its discipline and traditions more English than in England, even if the schoolboys were required to wear formal Malay dress, as they still do today.

Along the river

Around 3km downstream from town, **Masjid Ubudiah** sports a splendid array of golden, onion-shaped domes soaring skywards from between four elegantly striped minarets; non-Muslims should ask permission before entering. A five-minute walk up the same road lands you outside the imposing white marble **Istana Iskandariah**, the sultan's official palace, whose Art Deco lines date to 1933. It's closed to the public, though a stroll to the left of the huge gates gives a good view down the river.

Royal Museum of Perak

Just south of Istana Iskandariah • Fri–Wed 9am–5pm, Thurs 9am–12.45pm • Free

Now the **Royal Museum of Perak**, the sultan's former palace, the traditional stilted wooden **Istana Kenangan**, lies south of his current one. Some 40m long, it was built as a temporary residence while the Istana Iskandariah was under construction in the 1920s, and decorated with intricate friezes and geometric-patterned wall panels. Inside it houses a collection of royal medals, costumes and so on, although the building itself, and photographs of past and present royalty in Perak, are of more interest.

ARRIVAL   **KUALA KANGSAR**

By train Kuala Kangsar's train station is on the main west-coast train line ; it's on the northwestern outskirts of town,

a 20min walk from the central clock tower.
Destinations Alor Star (1 daily; 5hr); Butterworth (3 daily;

2

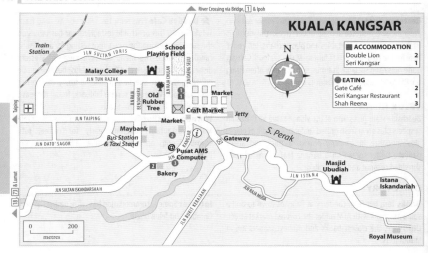

Train Station
JLN SULTAN IDRIS
Malay College
JLN TUN RAZAK
School
Playing Field
JLN RAJA CHULAN
JLN DAENG SELILI
Old Rubber Tree
Market
JLN BAIL BENDAHARA
Craft Market
JLN TAIPING
Market
Jetty
Maybank
Bus Station & Taxi Stand
JLN DATO' SAGOR
Bakery
Pusat AMS Computer
JLN SULTAN ISKANDAR SHA H
Gateway
S. Perak
JLN BUKIT KERAJAAN
JLN RAJA MUDA
JLN ISTANA
Masjid Ubudiah
Istana Iskandariah
Royal Museum

0   200
metres

Taiping
18 73 & Lumut

River Crossing via Bridge, 1 & Ipoh

KUALA KANGSAR

N

■ **ACCOMMODATION**
Double Lion — 2
Seri Kangsar — 1

● **EATING**
Gate Café — 2
Seri Kangsar Restaurant — 1
Shah Reena — 3

3hr); Ipoh (4 daily; 1hr); Kuala Lumpur (4 daily; 4hr 20min); Sungai Petani (1 daily; 4hr); Taiping (4 daily; 40min).

By bus The bus station is at the bottom of Jalan Raja Bendahara, a few minutes' walk from town. Direct services to Lumut are posted, but weren't running at the time of writing. Destinations Butterworth (3hr); Ipoh (1hr 30min); Kuala Lumpur (4hr); Taiping (1hr).

INFORMATION

Tourist information By the clock tower (☎ 05 777 7717; daily 9am–1pm & 2–6pm, but often unattended).

Internet Pusat AMS Computer, second floor, 86 Jalan Kangsar.

ACCOMMODATION

Double Lion 74 Jalan Kangsar ☎ 05 776 1010. Basic but large doubles in an airy old building, just south of the bus station, above an open-sided *kedai kopi*. Some rooms have fans, others a/c; most come with attached bathrooms. Fan RM45, a/c RM65

Seri Kangsar 33 Jalan Daeng Selili ☎ 05 777 7301, ⓦ kangsar-hotel.com. Bright green affair in the centre of town; very clean and well run, with a/c, TV and a *mandi* or shower in all rooms. The lobby has wi-fi. RM70

EATING

Snack stalls set up near the jetty in the late afternoon, selling doughnuts, fried bananas, cold drinks, fresh coconut milk and *rojak*; the *kuih apam*, a small, spongy cake made using fermented rice, is locally famous. There's also the "Agro Bazaar" fruit market here, selling seasonal produce at low prices.

The Gate Café In the market area behind Jalan Kangsar. Cheerful, modern Malay café with ice-cold fruit drinks and snacks for RM6 or so; there's also wi-fi and they show Malay films on a pull-down screen in the evenings. Daily 11am–after dark.

Seri Kangsar Restaurant 33 Jalan Daeng Selili ☎ 05 777 7301, ⓦ kangsar-hotel.com. Inexpensive restaurant at street level, serving one-plate noodle and rice dishes for around RM10, plus fruit juices. Daily 8am–8pm.

Shah Reena 53 Jalan Kangsar. Bright and busy *mamak* restaurant serving a raft of dhals, noodle and rice dishes, typically priced at RM5; their *roti sardin* makes a good breakfast. Daily 8am–late afternoon.

SHOPPING

The undercover **craft market**, on the left as you walk down towards the jetty, sells wickerwork, farm tools, bamboo birdcages, fishing nets, knives, miracle oils and even locally forged *keris* (starting at RM2700). There are also **labu** pots, gourd-shaped vessels designed to keep liquids cool even in the blazing midday sun, made at nearby **Sayong** village.

Taiping

Set against the backdrop of the mist-laden Bintang Hills, **TAIPING** – like so many places in Perak – owes its existence to the discovery of **tin** in the first decades of the nineteenth century. The name is Chinese; it could mean either "Great Plain" or "Great Peace", though the latter is unlikely given the numerous violent **clan wars** here between rival Cantonese and Hakka factions during the 1860s. Despite this, mining wealth helped fund many Malaysian **firsts** at a time when Kuala Lumpur was barely on the map: the first English-language school in 1878; the first hospital in 1880, established by the Chinese; the first rail line in 1882, built to facilitate tin exports; and the first museum in 1883. As Perak state's capital until 1937, and with the nearby hill station of **Bukit Larut** (formerly Maxwell Hill) serving as a retreat for its administrators, Taiping was at the forefront of the colonial development of the Federated Malay States.

Nowadays, bypassed by the North–South Expressway and replaced in administrative importance by Ipoh, Taiping is declining gracefully, its streets lined with tattered architectural mementos of its glory days. Even so, it's a pleasant place to spend a few hours at leisure, exploring the small, walkable centre and green **Lake Gardens**, though you'll need a full day to ascend Bukit Larut or take in the nearby **mangrove reserve**.

The town centre

As you'd expect from its Chinese heritage, most of central Taiping comprises mildewed shophouses with their colonnaded "five step" arcades, worth a look if you haven't seen them before. The **central market** is more unusual, housed inside two huge, century-old, tin-roofed wooden sheds occupying entire blocks, with a similarly scaled **hawker centre** nearby (see p.143). Both are busiest in the mornings, though the hawker centre stays open until late. Incidentally, the faint, high-pitched shrieking heard throughout downtown Taiping is recorded **swiftlet calls**, played to encourage the birds, whose edible nests are so esteemed by the Chinese, to lay in specially built coops.

First Galleria

Jalan Stesen • Mon–Thurs & Sat 9.30am–5.30pm, Fri 9.30am–12.30pm, Sun 12.30–5.30pm • RM5

Housed inside an immaculately restored colonial-Malay hybrid building, with a solid stone ground floor and graceful timber upper, this newly established museum houses a scanty collection of artefacts detailing Taiping's early years. A mandatory **guided tour** adds some depth; period photos prove that many landmarks – the church, prison, Residents' House – were already established by the 1880s.

All Saints' Church

Jalan Taming Sari

All Saints' Church is the oldest in Malaysia, founded in 1887 and built in a lightweight English Gothic style – though look closely and you'll see the roof is tiled in very Malaysian wooden shingles, and the pink and grey walls are built of tin sheeting. The tiny adjacent churchyard contains the graves of the earliest British and Australian settlers, many of whom died young. Others, after many years of service to the Malay States, failed to obtain a pension to allow them to return home.

The Perak Museum and prison

Jalan Taming Sari • Museum Sat–Thurs 9.30am–5pm, Fri 9.30am–noon & 2.30–5pm • Free

Housed in a spacious, purpose-built colonial building, the **Perak Museum** boasted thirteen thousand exhibits when it opened in 1883. It holds three collections, portraying Malaysia's anthropology, zoology and local history with displays of stuffed local fauna, as well as an extensive collection of ancient weapons and Orang Asli implements and ornaments.

2

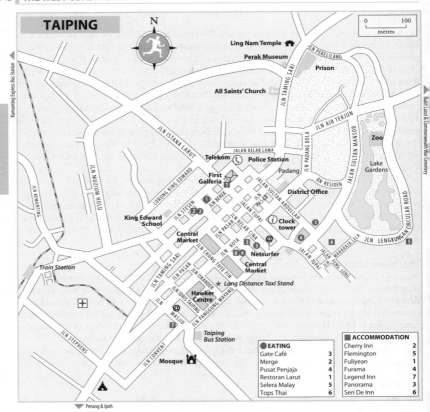

The grim grey wall opposite the museum is Taiping's **prison**, built in 1879 and subsequently used by the Japanese during World War II – today it's where some executions of Malaysia's drug offenders are carried out.

Lake Gardens (Taman Tasik)

Zoo daily 8.30am–6pm, night tours 8–11pm · RM12, night tours RM16 · ⓦ zootaiping.gov.my

Taiping's extensive **Lake Gardens**, northeast of the centre, were created in 1880 when the Resident decided that the unsightly mess left by two tin mines should be landscaped and turned into a park. There are clumps of bamboo, large old trees covered in moss and ferns, neatly trimmed lawns, little pavilions and even a giant fountain; it's a good spot for a picnic. On the east side, the small **zoo** stretches to tigers, hornbills, orang-utan, gibbons, civets, elephant and even some African fauna (hippos, for example); the **night safari** is fun too.

The Commonwealth War Cemetery

Bukit Larut road, 1km northeast of the Lake Gardens

A serene memorial to the casualties of World War II, the **Commonwealth War Cemetery** contains the graves of 866 men, many of whom could not be identified. Split in two by the road, it's divided between Hindu and Muslim Indians on one side and Christian British and Australians on the other.

ARRIVAL AND DEPARTURE

BY TRAIN

Train station On Jalan Stesen, just over a kilometre west of the centre of Taiping.

Destinations Alor Star (1 daily; 4hr 20min); Butterworth (3 daily; 3hr 15min); Hat Yai (1 daily; 6hr 30min); Ipoh (4 daily; 2hr); Kuala Kangsar (4 daily; 40min); Kuala Lumpur (4 daily; 5hr); Sungai Petani (1 daily; 3hr 10min).

BY BUS

Taiping Bus Station Jalan Panggung Wayang.
Destinations Ipoh (1hr 30min); Kuala Kangsar (1hr).

Kamunting Express Bus Station About 7km north of the centre. Local bus #8 (40min; RM2) runs to Taiping Bus Station; a taxi costs RM10 (15min).

Destinations Butterworth (1hr 20min); Johor (5 daily; 8hr 30min); Kuala Lumpur (3hr 30min); Pinang (1 daily; 1hr 30min); Singapore (1 daily; 9hr).

INFORMATION

Visitor information centre Inside the old clock tower on Jalan Tupai (Mon–Fri 8.30am–5.30pm, Sat 8.30am–3pm; often closed for an hour from noon). Helpful with heaps of brochures, maps (RM2) and practical information about Taiping and its surroundings. They can also arrange bicycle rental (RM5/day).

ACCOMMODATION

For a town of its size, Taiping has a remarkable number of **hotels**, which is just as well because in high season it often has to cater for the overspill from Bukit Larut. It's worth noting that the florid Peranakan-style *Peace Hotel* on Jalan Panggung Wayang is actually a brothel, as has been reported about the *Peking Hotel* on Jalan Idris. Note that though addresses are given in the text, Taiping has frustratingly few street signs, and the grid layout makes it easy to get disoriented.

Cherry Inn 17 Jalan Stesen ☎05 805 2223. Neat and tidy modern bedrooms, off a central sitting room covered in Chinese mementoes, this well-run place offers small a/c rooms with TV and shared or en-suite facilities. There is also a family wing with two rooms and a sitting area. RM60, en suite RM75

Flemington Jalan Samanea Saman ☎05 820 7777, ⓦflemingtonhotel.com.my. Newly renovated executive hotel in slate and glass, with great views out over the Lake Gardens – fully exploited with their rooftop pool. Rooms are smart rather than opulent, with en-suite facilities, wi-fi and soft, decent-sized beds. RM150

★ **Fuliyean** 14 Jalan Berek ☎05 806 8648. This place has spotless rooms with TVs and en-suite bathrooms; much the same as *Cherry Inn*, but a mite cheaper for what you get. RM60

★ **Furama** 30 Jalan Peng Long ☎05 807 1077, ⓦhotelfurama.com.my. A clean, bright older hotel, well managed and with helpful staff. The a/c, en-suite rooms come with kettle and wi-fi. Laundry service available. RM80

Legend Inn 2 Jalan Long Jaafar ☎05 806 0000, ⓦlegendinn.com. Mid-range hotel, the most comfortable in the city centre, conveniently near the bus station and with its own coffee house. RM100

Panorama 61–79 Jalan Kota ☎05 8084111, ⓦpanoramataiping.com. Absolutely central, rooms in this functional, comfortable 1990s block come with a/c, bathrooms, wi-fi, big beds and little character. RM95

Seri De Inn 14 Jalan Boo Bee ☎05 808 3977. Old and plain but spotless establishment, where rooms come with a bed, bathroom, TV and the choice of fan or a/c. RM45

EATING AND DRINKING

Taiping's most atmospheric meals in town are at numerous **hawker centres**, on almost every street. The largest is just up from the bus station on Jalan Panggung Wayang, full of excellent Chinese food: try the *char kway teow*, fried in a smoking-hot wok; *char siu* barbecue pork on rice; and cold drinks.

Gate Café Cnr Sultan Mansor and Sultan Abdullah, near the gardens. The closest thing to a European café between KL and Penang, with chrome furniture spilling out onto the street, a choice of lattes, espressos and americanos, and over-generous slices of chocolate-rich cakes. The wi-fi, TV and light pop rounds everything off. Daily 11am–10pm.

Merge Jalan behind the *Cherry Inn*. Small cold juice bar, an a/c refuge on a hot day, where you can work through the list of shaved ice and fruit desserts, fresh juices and coffee, typically priced around RM6. Daily 11am–7pm.

Pusat Penjaja Up near the gardens on Jalan Tupai. One of Taiping's many hawker centres, known for stalls specializing in satay, fried chicken and *yong tau foo* stew which, despite the "tofu" label, includes a stack of meat, seafood and vegetables at around RM5. Daily, dawn until evening.

Restoran Larut On the corner of Jalan Berek and Cross St 5. Like many similar places in town, this open-sided restaurant seems stuck in a 1960s laminex-and-chrome timewarp, but it's definitely worth trying their tasty, RM8 *ayam kapitan*, a rich home-style chicken curry. Daily 8am–6pm.

Selera Malay Jalan Kelab Cina. The busiest Malay establishment in town, with RM8 fiery prawn noodles,

plus tamer fried chicken chop on rice. Daily 8am–5pm.

Tops Thai Below the *Seri De Inn*, 14 Jalan Boo Bee. Popular place dishing up fast food with Penang overtones, heavy on pungent spices, for around RM8: *kuay teow*, fishball soup with *tang hoon* (glass noodles), *nasi nenas* (with pineapple and prawns) and *tom yam*. Daily, morning until early evening.

Bukit Larut (Maxwell Hill)

Up in the hills 13km northeast of Taiping, **BUKIT LARUT** – known in colonial times as **Maxwell Hill** – is Malaysia's smallest and oldest hill station. The climate is wonderfully cool, and on a clear day there are spectacular views down to the west coast. This is the wettest place in Malaysia, however, so the top is often atmospherically shrouded in cloud. A scattering of elderly bungalows offer **accommodation**, but for many visitors the stiff **walk** up here through the forests, with the chance to do some birdwatching, is the main draw; you'll need a full day for this, even if you manage to catch the limited **Land Rover service** up to the top and then walk back to town.

Walking to the summit

The marked **walking trail** to the summit starts at **Kaki Bukit**, 1.5km past Taiping's Lake Gardens via Jalan Air Terjun, where you'll also find a **Ranger Station** here and the Land Rover terminus (see below).

About 5km along, the Tea Garden House, once part of an extensive tea estate but now little more than a shelter, makes an ideal rest stop. The view is superb, with the town of Taiping and the mirror-like waters of the gardens visible below. The main **hill station area**, home to the remaining bungalows, is around 10km from town at 1036m, a few minor trails and circuits in the vicinity. Ambitious walkers continue to **The Cottage** – a stone bungalow built in the 1880s for British officialdom – and then a further 3km through groves of evergreens along an overgrown trail to the 1250m-high summit of **Gunung Hijau**. Protect yourself against leeches, which can be a problem in the forest (particularly just after rainfall), by wearing long trousers, and socks and shoes, not sandals. There are long-term plans to build a cable car to the summit, much against locals' wishes; ask around in town to see if any progress has been made.

ARRIVAL AND INFORMATION
BUKIT LARUT

By Land Rover Departures from the Kaki Bukit Ranger Station hourly (daily 8am–3pm; 35min; RM7 return trip); seats are on a first-come, first-served basis. The road up twists and turns round some 72 terrifying bends; private vehicles are prohibited. The last vehicle down is at 4pm; be sure to be there at least 15min before.

On foot Allow at least 3hr up and 2hr down; most people start well before 9am.

Ranger Station For current transport schedules, to book accommodation or hire guides for birdwatching; ☎ 05 807 7241 or ☎ 807 7243.

ACCOMMODATION

Bukit Larut's choice of **accommodation** rests between **resthouses** and **bungalows**, all basic, shabby places offering hot water, kitchen facilities and spacious rooms. **Food** is available at resthouses, while bungalows are self-catering – buy provisions in Taiping. Bungalow prices are for the whole building, while resthouses rent out individual rooms. Most places are within a twenty-minute walk of the upper Land Rover terminus, though drivers can also deliver to the door. **Book in advance**, as the place can be busy at weekends and during holidays; if you don't, get up here early enough to walk back to Taiping if no rooms are available.

Ankasa Around the 10km mark near the Land Rover terminus ☎05 807 7241 or ☎807 7243. Government-run bungalow sleeping 10–12 people; the same number also handles reservations for the similar *Beringin* and *Permai View*. RM150

Cendana Near the Land Rover terminus ☎05 806 1777. Resthouse and café with tulip-growing business; a popular spot for day-trippers to call into, so can get noisy through the day. Doubles RM80

Matang Mangrove Forest Reserve

16km west of Taiping, near Kuala Sepetang • Daily 9am–5pm • Free • ☎05 858 1762 • Bus #77 from Taiping Bus Station (daily 6am–7pm; hourly) to Kuala Sepetang, or taxi 2km from Kuala Sepetang to reserve

The **Matang Mangrove Forest Reserve** is Peninsular Malaysia's largest surviving spread of mangrove forest, most of which has been extensively cleared for development, or in more manageable quantities for **charcoal production** (still practised nearby). However, since the 2004 tsunami off Sumatra killed over 200,000 people across Southeast Asia, there's been a lot of interest in preserving mangroves; the trees' mesh of aerial support roots form a natural breakwater, absorbing some of the force of tsunamis and thus protecting coastlines from inundation. They're also rich breeding grounds for small marine creatures from jellyfish to fiddler crabs, mudskippers and archer fish (and, sadly for visitors, sandflies and mosquitoes), meaning plenty of food for larger animals – including rare marine otters and river dolphins.

Over a century old, Matang Mangrove Reserve is reckoned to be a model of environmental protection. Extensive **boardwalks** lead above the black mud through a forest of tall, thin trunks and mangrove ferns; keep eyes peeled for monkeys, wild pigs and swimming snakes. You can also **stay** here in basic, self-catering cabins – contact the reserve for details.

Penang

Way up the west coast, 370km from KL and 170km from the Thai border, **PENANG** is a confusing amalgam of state and island. Mainland roads and the rail line converge at unattractive **Butterworth**, jumping-off point for the brief ferry ride over to **Pulau Pinang**, Britain's first toehold on the Malay Peninsula. The island's lively "capital", **Georgetown**, sports a fascinating blend of colonial, Indian, Malay and – especially – immigrant Chinese culture. Along with Melaka and Singapore, Georgetown is also considered a centre for **Peranakan** heritage, the Chinese-Malay melange frequently known as "Straits Chinese" or "Baba-Nyonya" (see p.280), though – aside from some food and a splendid mansion – there's little evidence of this. What does survive, however, are spectacular **Chinese temples and guildhalls**, built by merchants and clan societies to display their wealth, alongside a whole central quarter of **shophouses**, many being thoughtfully restored after they helped the city become a UNESCO World Heritage site in 2008.

Georgetown is likely to be your base on Pulau Pinang, and three days would be enough to cover its main sights. A day or two extra spent touring the rest of the island – all 285 square kilometres of it – will turn up minor beach resorts, a coastal national park where you might see **nesting turtles**, a couple of unusual temples, plus plenty of renowned **food stalls**.

If you're headed towards Thailand, you can catch direct ferries from Pulau Pinang to **Langkawi**, and change there for cross-border boats to **Satun** (see p.181).

Brief history

Pulau Pinang was ruled by the **sultans of Kedah** until the late eighteenth century. But increasing harassment by Thai and Burmese raiding parties encouraged the sultan to seek military protection from **Francis Light**, a plausible British adventurer

2

FESTIVE PENANG

Pulau Pinang is the focus of several important **festivals** and events throughout the year, starting with the riotous Hindu celebration **Thaipusam** (see p.47). Perhaps the best known of the rest is the November **Penang Bridge Run** (ⓦpenangmarathon.gov.my), when thousands of competitors run a pre-dawn marathon via the bridge to Butterworth. June sees the **International Dragonboat Race** (ⓦpenangdragonboat.gov.my), a nominally Chinese event commemorating the death of a patriotic poet in 278 BC, while the July **Cultural Festival** (ⓦgeorgetownfestival.com) provides a showcase for Penang's ethnic groups, with a three-day food festival, art events and traditional Chinese opera performances at the temples. In November or December, Batu Ferrenghi also hosts the **Penang Jazz Festival** (ⓦpenangjazz .com), attracting local and international performers.

---

searching for a regional trading base to counter the Dutch presence in Sumatra. After a decade of wrangling, a deal was struck: Light would provide military aid through the **British East India Company** and the sultan would receive 30,000 Spanish dollars a year. There was one snag – the East India Company's Governor-General, **Charles Cornwallis**, refused to be party to the plans. Concealing the facts from both parties, Light went ahead anyway and took **possession** of Penang on August 11, 1786, then spent five years assuring the sultan that the matter of protection was being referred to authorities in London. The sultan finally caught on but failed to evict the British, ending up with an annuity of 6000 Spanish dollars and no role in the island's government.

Penang thus became the **first British settlement** in the Malay Peninsula. Within two years, four hundred acres were under cultivation and the population – many of them Chinese traders quick to grasp the island's strategic position in the busy Straits of Melaka – had reached ten thousand. Francis Light was made superintendent and declared the island a **free port**, renaming it "Prince of Wales Island" after the British heir apparent. Georgetown took its name from the British king, George III, and retained its colonial label even after the island's name reverted to Penang.

For a time, all looked rosy for Penang, with Georgetown proclaimed as capital of the **Straits Settlements** (incorporating Melaka and Singapore) in 1826. But the **founding of Singapore** in 1819 was the beginning of the end for Georgetown, as the new colony overtook its predecessor in every respect. This had one beneficial result: with Georgetown stuck in the economic doldrums well into the twentieth century, no significant development took place within the city, and consequently many of its colonial and early Chinese buildings survive to this day.

Butterworth

Sitting 94km north of Taiping, the dusty, industrial port of **BUTTERWORTH** looks over a narrow strait to a far more attractive Pulau Pinang from an intricate concrete mesh of flyovers, highways and rail lines. With **ferries** crossing to the island every few minutes from early morning until late into the evening, the only reason to spend any time here is in transit. The **bus station**, **ferry pier**, long-distance-**taxi stand** and **train station** are all next door to each other, so this shouldn't take long – just follow the signed **pedestrian overpasses** to whichever you need.

ARRIVAL AND DEPARTURE   **BUTTERWORTH**

Aside from buying tickets at Butterworth's bus and train stations, there are agents at Georgetown's KOMTAR building (see p.156). Note that through trains to Bangkok originate in Butterworth. Ferries run between Butterworth and Georgetown's Terminal Weld (see p.156).

OPPOSITE FROM TOP KHOO KONGSI TEMPLE, GEORGETOWN (P.155); CHEONG FATT TZE MANSION, GEORGETOWN (P.151) >

2

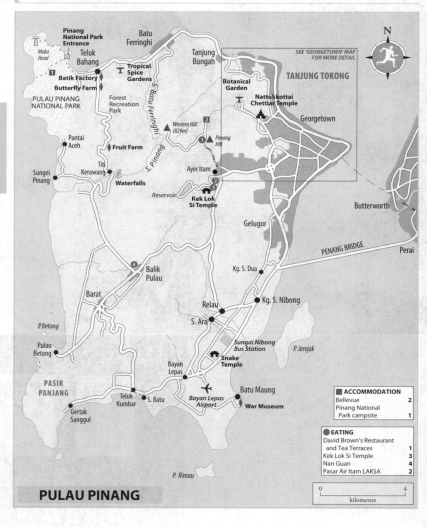

PULAU PINANG

■ ACCOMMODATION	
Bellevue	2
Pinang National	
Park campsite	1

● EATING	
David Brown's Restaurant	
and Tea Terraces	1
Kek Lok Si Temple	3
Nan Guan	4
Pasar Air Itam LAKSA	2

0   4
kilometres

By train Alor Star (1 daily; 2hr 45min); Bangkok (Thailand; 1 daily; 22hr); Hat Yai (Thailand; 1 daily; 4hr 45min); Ipoh (3 daily; 3hr 45min); Kuala Kangsar (3 daily; 2hr 45min); Kuala Lumpur (3 daily; 7hr); Singapore (1 daily; 12hr 30min); Sungai Petani (daily; 1hr 40min); Taiping (3 daily; 2hr).

By bus Alor Star (every 30min; 1hr 30min); Cameron Highlands (3 daily; 4hr); Hat Yai (Thailand; 4 daily; 3hr); Ipoh (9 daily; 2hr 30min); Johor Bahru (10 daily; 10hr); Kangar (hourly; 2hr 15min); Kota Bharu (4 daily; 6hr);

Kuala Kangsar (2 daily; 2hr 45min); Kuala Lumpur (hourly 8am–12.30am; 5hr); Kuala Terengganu (1 daily; 8hr); Kuantan (2 daily; 9hr); Lumut (7 daily; 3hr); Melaka (2 daily; 8hr); Seremban (9 daily; 6hr); Singapore (at least 2 daily; 10hr); Sungai Petani (every 45min; 40min); Taiping (hourly; 2hr 15min).

By ferry Butterworth to Georgetown (every 20min–1hr, 6am–12.30am; 20min; RM1.20); Georgetown to Butterworth (every 20min–1hr, 5.45am–12.30am; 20min; free).

Georgetown

Visiting **GEORGETOWN** in 1879, stalwart Victorian traveller **Isabella Bird** called it "a brilliant place under a brilliant sky", a simple statement on which it's hard to improve – though the confusion of buses, lorries and scooters make Georgetown's modern downtown unnervingly frenetic and polluted. Filling a triangular projection at Pulau Pinang's northeastern corner, Georgetown's heart lies between the decaying remains of **Fort Cornwallis**, which guarded the city in its earliest years, and the towering modern bulk of the **KOMTAR centre**, overlooking everything 1.5km to the south. In between is **Chinatown**, a maze of lanes liberally sprinkled with grand **clan association halls** and two-storey **shophouses** in various stages of decay and restoration, which itself encloses the smaller ethnic enclave of **Little India** and a vaguely identifiable **Muslim quarter**.

Certainly no sleepy backwater (most of the island's one-million-strong population lives here), Georgetown's historic lanes and street life make it an appealing place to explore, and a hangout for budget travellers seeking to renew Thai visas. The city's main arteries are traffic-clogged **Lebuh Chulia** (named after the Tamil word for "merchant"), which cuts east–west through central Georgetown, and slightly less busy **Jalan Masjid Kapitan Kling** (or Lebuh Pitt), which crosses it at right angles. Almost everything of interest – shops, museums, temples, restaurants and accommodation – lies within a short walk of these roads, while the rest of the island can be reached on **buses** from KOMTAR or **Terminal Weld**, on the seafront where ferries from Butterworth dock.

Fort Cornwallis

Daily 9am–7pm • RM2

Occupying the northeastern tip of Pulau Pinang, **Fort Cornwallis** marks the spot where Francis Light landed to take possession of the island on July 16, 1786. The current defences, named after Lord Charles Cornwallis, Governor-General of India, date from twenty years later. Square in shape with redoubts at each corner, it's all a bit forlorn nowadays, the mildewed, lightly vegetated brickwork conveying little sense of history. The **statue** of Francis Light by the entrance was cast in 1936 for the 150th anniversary of the founding of Penang, his features copied from a portrait of his son, Colonel William Light, founder of Adelaide in Australia. Inside the walls, look for the early nineteenth-century church, powder magazine and much-revered bronze **Sri Rambai cannon**, sited in the northwest corner – locals belief that barren women can conceive by laying flowers on its barrel.

Padang Kota Lama

The large expanse of green that borders the fort, the **Padang Kota Lama**, was once the favourite promenade of the island's colonial administrators and thronged with rickshaws and carriages. On the south side, opposite the grand sweep of the

---

STREET NAMES IN GEORGETOWN

Georgetown's original **street names** reflected the city's colonial past. The current trend, however, is either to **rename** streets after indigenous worthies – as in Jalan Sultan Ahmad Shah – or to **translate** the existing name, such as Lebuh Gereja for Church Street. This would be straightforward enough, except that the new names have not always been popularly accepted – Lorong Cinta, for example, is almost universally known as Love Lane – and even official maps might use either name. The most awkward of the new names is Jalan Masjid Kapitan Kling for Pitt Street, which more often than not is referred to simply as Lebuh Pitt. Several names are also used repeatedly, so watch out for Lorong Chulia (Chulia Lane) and Lebuh Chulia (Chulia Street), Lorong Penang and Lebuh Penang, and so on. Finally, don't confuse Lorong Cinta with Lebuh Cintra.

2

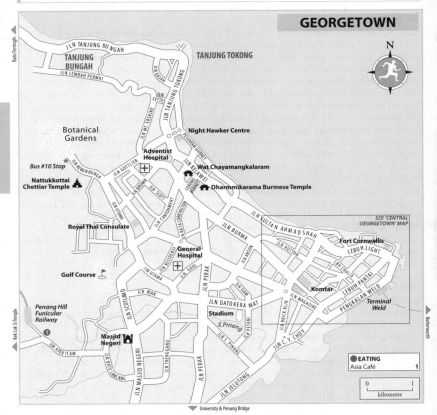

GEORGETOWN

N

JLN TANJUNG BU NGAH

TANJUNG BUNGAH

TANJUNG TOKONG

JLN LEMBAH PERMAI

Batu Ferringhi

Botanical Gardens

Bus #10 Stop

Nattukkottai Chettiar Temple

Night Hawker Centre

Adventist Hospital

Wat Chayamangkalaram

Dharmmikarama Burmese Temple

Royal Thai Consulate

General Hospital

Golf Course

Penang Hill Funicular Railway

SEE 'CENTRAL GEORGETOWN' MAP

Fort Cornwallis

LEBUH LIGHT

JLN SULTAN AHMAD SHAH

JLN BURMA

Komtar

Terminal Weld

Masjid Negeri

Stadium

Kek Lok Si Temple

Butterworth

● EATING
Asia Café   1

0   1
kilometre

▼ University & Penang Bridge

Esplanade, now used for sports and other public events, the padang is bordered by the superb Anglo-Victorian architecture of the **Dewan Undangan Negeri** (State Legislative Building) and **Dewan Seri Pinang** (town hall), with their weighty porticos and ornate gables.

At the southeast corner, the junction of Lebuh Light and Lebuh Pantai is graced by a four-storey Moorish-style **clock tower**, with onion-dome roof, scalloped Arabesque windows, and incongruously European clock face. Presented in 1897 to mark Queen Victoria's Diamond Jubilee, it's 60ft (20m) high, a foot for each year of her reign. Japanese bombing during World War II caused the tower to tilt slightly.

The Eastern & Oriental Hotel (E&O)

Lebuh Farquhar • ⓦ eohotels.com

Facing the sea, and built in 1885 by the Armenian Sarkies brothers (who also ran Singapore's *Raffles Hotel*), the legendary **Eastern & Oriental Hotel** is colonial elegance personified, from the smart staff dressed in starched linen, to the potted palms, Neoclassical facade and airy, dark timber and plasterwork interior. Rudyard Kipling and Somerset Maugham both stayed here, taking tiffin on the terrace and enjoying the cooling sea breeze; if you can't afford to stay, at least stroll through the grand lobby with its cool marble floors and high dome, or drop in for **afternoon tea** (see p.159).

Now sadly neglected, the **grave of Francis Light** is 150m west, beneath the gloom of a frangipani grove at the end of Lebuh Farquhar, across Jalan Sultan Ahmad Shah.

Cheong Fatt Tze Mansion

14 Lebuh Leith • Entry on guided tour only daily 11am, 1.30pm & 3pm • RM12 • ☎ 04 262 0006, ⓦ cheongfatttzemansion.com

Hidden behind a purple-blue exterior, the **Cheong Fatt Tze Mansion** is a splendid example of Penang's eclectic nineteenth-century house design, built by Thio Thiaw Siat, a Cantonese businessman. It's broadly southern Chinese in form, with projecting fire-baffle eaves, good-luck motifs and complex decorative mouldings along the tiled roof, though its **arches** and **shutters** are definitely European touches, as are the Art Nouveau stained glass and the sweeping interior staircase, even if the delicate iron tracery and balconies might owe a nod to wooden Malay verandas. The beautifully proportioned interiors are again furnished with a pleasant cross-cultural mix of screens, dining tables and stone-flagged light wells decorated with potted plants. Note that the mansion is also a **hotel** (see p.159).

Hainan Temple

Lebuh Muntri • Daily 8am–5pm • Free

Although Georgetown is awash with small Chinese shrines and guildhalls, the **Hainan Temple** is more relevant than most, being founded by sailors from an island-province off southern China. The entrance gate and facade are minutely carved with dragons, tigers and heroic battle scenes, though the interior is rather plain and calm. Given the nautical connection, it's little surprise to find the temple mainly dedicated to **Mazu**, also known as **Tian Hou**, patron goddess of seafarers; shrines to her are common in Chinese coastal communities across Southeast Asia.

Penang Museum

Lebuh Farquhar • Daily 9am–5pm • RM1 • ⓦ penangmuseum.gov.my

Penang Museum is housed in a fine colonial building, built as a free school between 1896 and 1906. It holds an excellent collection of memorabilia: rickshaws, Peranakan furniture, clothing and ceramics, faded black-and-white photographs of early Penang's Chinese millionaires, and a panoramic photograph of Georgetown taken in the 1870s (note just how many buildings still survive). Focused downstairs on the people and cultures living in Penang, and upstairs on its political past, it makes an interesting introduction to life on the island.

St George's Church

Jalan Masjid Kapitan Kling • Daily 9am–5pm • Free

One of Penang's oldest buildings, the Anglican **St George's Church** is as simple and unpretentious as anything built in the Greek style in Asia can be. It was constructed in 1817–19 by the East India Company using convict labour; its cool, pastel-blue interior must have been a welcome retreat from the heat for the new congregation. In 1886, on the centenary of the founding of Penang, a memorial to Francis Light was built in front of the church in the form of a Greek temple.

Kuan Yin Teng

Halfway up Jalan Masjid Kapitan Kling • Daily 8am–6pm • Free

The oldest and liveliest of Georgetown's Chinese temples, **Kuan Yin Teng** (Kuan Yin Pavilion) is a down-to-earth granite hall dating to 1801, whose dragon-carved pillars and wooden roof beams are blackened by incense smoke. Kuan Yin being the Goddess of Mercy, the temple is perpetually jammed with devotees, mostly beggars down on their luck and women praying for children, grandchildren and safe childbirth. The

2

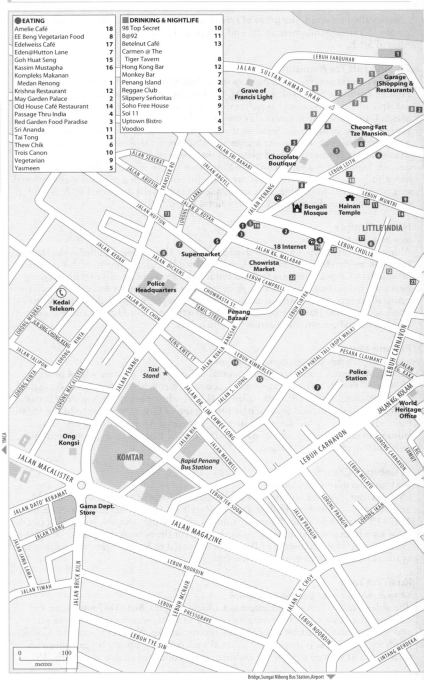

EATING	
Amelie Café	18
EE Beng Vegetarian Food	8
Edelweiss Café	17
Eden@Hutton Lane	7
Goh Huat Seng	15
Kassim Mustapha	16
Kompleks Makanan Medan Renong	1
Krishna Restaurant	12
May Garden Palace	2
Old House Café Restaurant	14
Passage Thru India	4
Red Garden Food Paradise	3
Sri Ananda	11
Tai Tong	13
Thew Chik	6
Trois Canon	10
Vegetarian	9
Yasmeen	5

DRINKING & NIGHTLIFE	
98 Top Secret	10
B@92	11
Betelnut Café	13
Carmen @ The Tiger Tavern	8
Hong Kong Bar	12
Monkey Bar	7
Penang Island	2
Reggae Club	6
Slippery Señoritas	3
Soho Free House	9
Soi 11	1
Uptown Bistro	4
Voodoo	5

Bridge, Sungai Nibong Bus Station, Airport ▼

2

CENTRAL GEORGETOWN

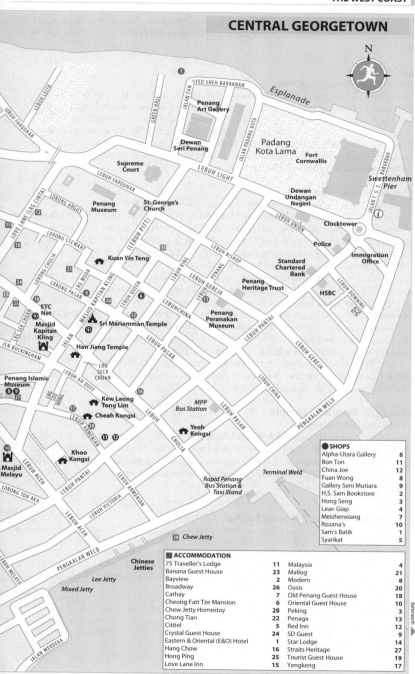

SHOPS

Alpha-Utara Gallery	6
Bon Ton	11
China Joe	12
Fuan Wong	8
Gallery Seni Mutiara	9
H.S. Sam Bookstore	2
Hong Seng	3
Lean Giap	4
Meizhenxiang	7
Rozana's	10
Sam's Batik	1
Syarikat	5

ACCOMMODATION

75 Traveller's Lodge	11	Malaysia	4
Banana Guest House	23	Mallog	21
Bayview	2	Modern	8
Broadway	26	Oasis	20
Cathay	7	Old Penang Guest House	18
Cheong Fatt Tze Mansion	6	Oriental Guest House	10
Chew Jetty Homestay	28	Peking	3
Chong Tian	22	Penaga	13
Cititel	5	Red Inn	12
Crystal Guest House	24	SD Guest	9
Eastern & Oriental (E&O) Hotel	1	Star Lodge	14
Hang Chow	16	Straits Heritage	27
Hong Ping	25	Tourist Guest House	19
Love Lane Inn	15	Yengkeng	17

Butterworth

huge bronze bell in the first hall is rung by those who have made a donation, while the flagstoned forecourt features performances of **Chinese opera** during festivals, laid on by travelling troupes.

Little India

North of Lebuh Chulia between Pitt and Penang

Georgetown's compact **Little India** exudes a real sense of identity, with Bollywood soundtracks blasting into the streets, strings of bright yellow flowers hanging up outside businesses, jewellers, sari shops, restaurants and the all-pervading smell of incense. That said, there's little to see beyond the towering **Sri Mariamman Temple** on Lebuh Queen (daily 8am–noon & 4–9pm), founded in 1833. Its pale green and red entrance tower is a riot of sculpted deities, among which four **swans** represent incarnations of the goddess Mariamman.

The Peranakan Mansion

29 Lebuh Gereja (Church St) • Daily 9.30am–5pm • RM10 • ⓦ pinangperanakanmansion.com.my

The brilliantly flamboyant **Peranakan Mansion** was built in the 1890s for Kapitan Cina Chung Keng Kwee, a Penang personality and "secret society" leader. It's a solid, square-sided edifice, painted pastel green with white piping and balconies outside. Visitors step through into a light and airy central atrium floored in patterned tiles, whose upper storey is supported by ornate iron balustrades. Chinese wooden doors, heavy inlaid furniture and carved screens are everywhere, alongside more European touches, like the florid glass light fittings and full-length mirrors on the stairs. Check out the **display cases** full of trinkets: green-and-pink Nyonya porcelain painted with phoenixes and peonies, made in China for the local market; snuffboxes, anklets and necklaces in precious metals; embroideries and shoes. Upstairs, a **bedroom** complete with four-poster bed and wedding canopy has been left as last used. A small **gift shop** sells souvenirs, books and a few antiques (see p.162).

Sadly, Peranakan culture is on the wane in Penang; rather than Malay, people now speak Chinese dialects, and the present generation don't necessarily see themselves as "Baba-Nyonya" at all, rather just "Chinese" (see p.585).

Han Jiang Ancestral Temple

127 Lebuh Chulia • Daily 9am–6pm • Free

The newly restored **Han Jiang Ancestral Temple** is worth a quick look for its typical southern Chinese tiled roof, alive with brightly coloured dragons, its deeply carved granite columns, and unusually informative, English-language accounts of the history and heritage of Penang's **Teochew** (Chaozhou) community, who originate from the Han River in southern China.

KONGSI AND CLAN MANSIONS

In modern Chinese, **kongsi** simply means "a company", but in former times each was more like a clan or regional association providing help and protection for nineteenth-century immigrants, who naturally tended to band together according to the district in China from which they came. Formerly a focus for community rivalry, the *kongsi*s have now reverted to their supportive role, helping with the education of members' children, settling disputes between clan members, or advancing loans.

Many of the *kongsi* buildings in Penang are excellent examples of traditional southern Chinese architecture: there is generally a spacious courtyard in front of the clan house, opposite which is a stage for theatrical performances, and two halls in the main building itself, one for the shrine of the clan deity, the other for the display of the ancestral tablets (the equivalent of gravestones).

Muslim Quarter

There's a definite Islamic theme off the southern end of **Jalan Masjid Kapitan Kling**, though calling this a "Muslim Quarter" is a slight overstatement. The street takes its name from **Masjid Kapitan Kling** (Sat–Mon 1–5pm, Fri 3–5pm; free), the elegant mosque at the corner of Lebuh Chulia, which was founded in 1801 by Indian Muslim settlers (originally East India Company troops). A few minutes' walk south at 128 Lebuh Armenian, the **Penang Islamic Museum** (Wed–Mon 9am–5.30pm; RM3) sits inside the elegant colonial **Syed Alatas Mansion**, named after the Achenese merchant and arms dealer who lived here in the 1870s; the interior has been beautifully restored to its nineteenth-century appearance. Finally, south again at Jalan Canon's southern intersection with Lebuh Aceh, **Masjid Melayu**, built in 1808, is unusual for its hexagonal, two-tier minaret. The hole halfway up was supposedly made by a cannonball fired from Khoo Kongsi during the Penang riots (see below).

Cheah Kongsi

Lebuh Armenian • Daily 9am–5pm • Free

Tucked away off the street in a large courtyard, **Cheah Kongsi** is a Chinese **clan mansion** founded in 1820 by a family that's now one of the largest landowners in Georgetown. Dating from the 1870s, the present building comprises a frankly ugly, russet-coloured block out of which an ornate theatre stage projects over the main entrance; note the incongruous European-style plaster **lion** heads on the support posts.

Khoo Kongsi

18 Canon Square • Daily 9am–5pm • RM10 • ⓦ khookongsi.com.my

Any doubts about the vast fortunes that were made when Penang was a hub of regional trade will disappear the moment you enter **Khoo Kongsi**. An overpoweringly gaudy complex of ancestral halls, shrines and administrative buildings, its bowed main hall looks ready to collapse under the weight of the multicoloured ceramic sculptures, wood-carvings and shining gold leaf adorning its roof. Finished in 1894, this is actually a lesser version of an even more extravagant original that had just burned down – some say destroyed by jealous deities, angered by its ostentation.

Guarded by unlikely statues of Sikh and Sepoy soldiers, every inch of the main hall's portico is superbly carved, featuring the obligatory dragon pillars alongside scenes of Confucian moral tales – even the bars on the windows are carved to resemble bamboo. The interior sports more of the same, plus plain murals of Taoist guardian figures

---

THE PENANG RIOTS

Chinese immigrants to Penang brought their traditions with them, including **secret societies**, which provided mutual aid and protection for the Chinese community – bolstered in Georgetown by alliances with similar Malay religious groups.

As the societies grew in wealth and power, gang warfare and extortion rackets became commonplace. Matters came to a head in the **Penang Riots** of 1867: for nine days Georgetown was shaken by fighting between the Tua Peh Kong society, supported by the Malay Red Flag, and the Ghee Hin, allied with the Malay White Flag. Police intervention resulted in a temporary truce, but on August 1, 1867, the headman of the Tua Peh Kong falsely charged the Ghee Hin and White Flag societies with stealing cloth belonging to Tua Peh Kong dyers. All hell broke loose, and fighting raged around Lebuhs Armenian Church and Chulia. Barricades were erected around the Khoo Kongsi, where some of the fiercest skirmishes occurred – you can still find bullet holes in the surrounding shops and houses.

The fighting was eventually quelled by **sepoys** (Indian troops) brought in from Singapore by the Governor-General, but by then hundreds had been killed and scores of houses burned. A penalty of RM5000 was levied on each of the secret societies, some of which was later used to finance the building of four police stations to deal with any future trouble.

astride mostly mythical beasts. The hall on the left is a richly decorated shrine to **Tua Peh Kong**, the god of prosperity; the right-hand hall contains the gilded ancestral tablets. Out the back, a further mural represents the blessing of "100 sons, 1000 grandsons" – a traditional Chinese theme appropriate for an ancestral temple.

The Chinese Jetties

Pengkalan Weld (Weld Quay) seafront, south of Lebuh Armenian • Donation requested

Before Georgetown was properly established, Chinese immigrants set themselves up in communities of stilt houses built over the water, connected by wooden boardwalks. These **Chinese Jetties** are still inhabited by their descendants, one jetty to each clan: they're not exactly tourist sights, though nobody seems to mind your wandering the wooden "streets". There are even a couple of places to stay and some lean-to teahouses on Pengkalan Weld where most residents seem to spend their days. **Chew Jetty** is the largest community, whose 250m-long boardwalk terminates at a little temple looking out to sea over a scattering of fishing nets, crab pots and motorboats; adjacent **Lee Jetty** is smaller, its corrugated tin clan temple painted yellow and red, with two rows of neat houses facing each other. Moving south, there's a **Mixed Jetty** of no actual clan affiliations, built as late as 1960. The jetties look finest hung with red lanterns at Chinese New Year (late Jan or Feb).

KOMTAR

Georgetown's most prominent landmark, if not its most aesthetically pleasing, is the Komplex Tun Abdul Razak (or **KOMTAR**), a 65-storey, 232m-high cylinder towering over the western corner of the city centre. Its main purpose is to house the Penang State Government, but – alongside a surprisingly despondent shopping mall – it's of more interest to visitors for its basement **bus station**, where you can catch services to all parts of the island (see opposite).

ARRIVAL AND DEPARTURE   GEORGETOWN

Tickets for all journeys can be bought at the relevant departure point or via local agents (see p.163).

BY PLANE

Penang International Airport At Bayan Lepas, 16km south of Georgetown on the southeastern tip of the island. Rapid Penang buses #401, #401E and #401A (hourly 6am–9pm; 45 min; RM2.7) travel from the airport via the KOMTAR building to Terminal Weld. A taxi into the city costs RM35 – buy a coupon from inside the airport building.

Airlines AirAsia, 332 Lebuh Chulia ☏ 04 250 0020; Cathay Pacific, Block 39, Jalan Sultan Ahmed Shah ☏ 04 226 0411; China Airlines Block 39, Jalan Sultan Ahmad Shah ☏ 04 228 9227; China Southern, Block 51, Jalan Sultan Ahmad Shah, ☏ 04 227 8878; Firefly, KOMTAR building, Jalan Penang ☏ 04 261 1000; Malaysia Airlines, KOMTAR building, Jalan Penang ☏ 04 250 2000; Silk Air, Plaza MWE, 8 Lebuh Farquhar ☏ 04 263 3201; Tiger Airways ⓦ tigerairways .com; Thai International, level 3, Burmah Place, Burmah Rd ☏ 04 226 6000.

International destinations China, Hong Kong, Indonesia (Medan, Surabaya and Jakarta), Thailand (Bangkok and Phuket) & Singapore.

Domestic destinations Johor Bahru (2 daily; 1hr); Kota Bharu (daily; 1hr); Kota Kinabalu (daily; 2hr); Kuala Lumpur (at least 13 daily; 45min); Kuantan (daily; 1hr 15min); Kuching (daily; 2hr); Langkawi (2 daily; 45min).

BY TRAIN

Train station The nearest train station to Pulau Pinang is opposite on the mainland at Butterworth. Arriving at Butterworth train station (see p.146), either catch a cab to Georgetown (20min; RM20) or follow the signed footbridge to the ferry. There is also a booking office at Terminal Weld.

BY BUS

Long-distance bus station Pulau Pinang's long-distance station, 8km southwest of Georgetown at Sungai Nibong, handles the same destinations as Butterworth's (see p.146). Book tickets for either station via accommodation, or with agents on Jalan Chulia or on the ground floor of the KOMTAR building; transfers to Sungai Nibong station are sometimes included. Arriving at Sungai Nibong, catch bus #401A to Sungai Tiram, then a #401 or #401E to KOMTAR; a taxi costs about RM25.

BY FERRY

From Butterworth Ferries from Butterworth arrive at Terminal Weld, on busy Pengkalan Weld. Butterworth to Georgetown (every 20min–1hr, 6am–12.30am; 20min; RM1.20); Georgetown to Butterworth (every 20min–1hr, 5.45am–12.30am; 20min; free). You exit into a sea of taxis and Rapid Penang buses: #101 is the most useful, travelling along Jalan Chulia (get off at the 7–11 store for Love Lane/Lorong Cinta and many of Georgetown's hostels), then turning south down Jalan Penang and KOMTAR. If you want to walk to town, there's a pedestrian bridge outside over Pengkalan Weld.

From Langkawi Ferries from Langkawi (2 daily; 2hr 30min; RM60; ⓦ langkawi-ferry.com) use Swettenham Pier, just east of Fort Cornwallis; catch a cab into town from here, or to walk. Tickets are sold by the handful of agencies near the clock tower, which open around 8am; book at least a day in advance.

BY CAR

Driving to Georgetown The 13.5km-long Penang Bridge crosses from 1.5km south of Butterworth – turn west off Highway E1 for the bridge – to the east coast of Pulau Pinang, 8km south of Georgetown (RM7 toll, payable only on the journey from the mainland). Catching a taxi over, check whether the toll is included in the fare. Arriving on the island, bear right (north) up the coast along the Jelutong Expressway to Georgetown. Driving into the city is unnerving – expect narrow streets, pedestrians, random obstructions and heavy traffic – though the major routes are well signposted. There's a useful car park in the KOMTAR building on Jalan Penang, within walking distance of the hotel area (mid-range and above hotels usually have private car parks).

TO THAILAND

Make all arrangements for Thai travel through your accommodation, or travel agents in Penang.

Entry requirements Check visa requirements at ⓦ thaiembassy.com, as regulations change frequently. At present, visas are available on arrival; 15 days at land borders, and 30 days if arriving by air. You can also get sixty-day, single-entry tourist visas through Penang's Thai Consulate (Mon–Fri 9am–11am, closed during Thai and Malay holidays; RM130); download and fill in the application form (ⓦ mfa.go.th) and take it to the consulate along with your passport, fee and two passport photos. Same-day processing is normal, but note that double entry visas are not currently available in Penang. Agents can do all this for you.

By plane Direct flights connect Penang with Phuket (from RM200; ⓦ fireflyz.com.my) and Bangkok (from RM200; ⓦ airasia.com).

By train The train from Butterworth to Bangkok (1 daily; 24hr; RM112; ⓦ ktmb.com.my) travels via the border, Hat Yai and Surat Thani.

By bus and minibus Buses to Hat Yai depart both Butterworth and Sungai Nibong (3 daily; 3hr 30min; RM25). Private minibuses, usually picking up from accommodation, run daily – via a change at the border – to many destinations, including: Bangkok (18hr; RM125); Hat Yai (4hr; RM30); Phuket (12hr; RM76); Surat Thani (9hr; RM60).

GETTING AROUND

Central Georgetown is small and best explored on foot; short-cutting through alleys and back lanes is half the fun of being here. One drawback, especially along frenetic Lebuh Chulia, is that few of the old streets have **pavements** and you have to jaywalk; in theory, you should be able to use the shophouses' "**five-foot way**", the colonnaded walkway between the building and the road, but people park their mopeds here, set up stalls, use them as office space or simply block them off. Alternative modes of transport – essential if you plan to explore out of town – range from local buses to renting a bicycle.

By bus Rapid Penang buses (ⓦ rapidpg.com.my) cover Georgetown and the entire island. Services originate at open-air Terminal Weld and travel via KOMTAR, where the latest schedules are displayed. Fares are RM1–2.7; pay on board with exact change. Bus stops are easily missed; they're often just a pole with a faded pink "Rapid Penang" logo, though out of town there are usually bus shelters too. Operating hours are about 5.30am–midnight, with services running from anywhere between every 5min to once every 2hr.

By taxi Stands at Terminal Weld and on Jalan Dr Lim Chwee Long, off Jalan Penang. Drivers don't use their meters, so agree the fare in advance – a trip to the Thai Embassy costs about RM20, while a ride out to the airport or Batu Ferringhi costs RM30–40. To book a taxi in advance, call the 24hr Taxis Services Centre (☎ 04 262 5721 or ☎ 262 9842).

By rickshaw A traditional, touristy way to see the city is by tricycle-rickshaw. Drivers wait outside hotels and along Lebuh Chulia. An hour's pedal around the old town costs RM30; anything else has to be by negotiation. Drivers will try to exact a commission from your chosen accommodation if you take one to look for a room.

By bike For bicycle rental and tours of Georgetown, contact EGC Bike Tour, 261 Jalan Green Hall, off Jalan Tun Syed Sheh Barakbah ☎ 04 262 3821, ⓦ egcbiketour .com. Some guesthouses all rent them at around RM20/day.

By motorcycle Motorbikes (RM30/day) can be hired from agents such as Banana Travel & Tours at 84 Jalan Penang, or Sam Bookstore at 473 Lebuh Chulia.

By car Local operators rent cars from about RM80/day, slightly discounted by the week. International firms charge more. Avis, at the airport ☎ 04 643 9633; Hertz, 38 Lebuh Farquhar ☎ 04 263 5914; Kereta Sewa ⓦ keretasewapenang .blogspot.com.

INFORMATION

Tourism Malaysia 10 Jalan Tun Syed Shah Barakbah ☎04 262 0066. An extremely helpful bunch who can provide you with bus schedules, shopping advice, restaurant recommendations and information about sights. Mon–Fri 8am–5pm.

Penang Heritage Trust 26 Lebuh Gereja across from the Peranakan Mansion ☎04 264 2631, ⒲pht.org.my.

Staffed by knowledgeable volunteers who can provide you with free heritage trail maps, organize heritage tours and sell you books. Mon–Fri 9am–5pm, Sat 9am–1pm.

World Heritage Office 116–118 Lebuh Aceh ☎04 261 6606. Inside a suitable venerable, pale blue colonial-era building, and a mine of current information about the state of Penang's preservation. Mon–Fri 9am–5pm.

ACCOMMODATION

Georgetown has a profusion of hotels and guesthouses, with plenty of budget choices. Many are inside converted mansions and shophouses, often featuring courtyards and period fittings; some are ramshackle, others splendidly restored, though facades and lobbies often outperform rooms. Most places can also arrange bike or car rental, and organize onwards travel – including Thai visas and transport. The core of the budget trade is along Lebuh Chulia, Lebuh Muntri and Lorong Cinta (Love Lane), where new businesses seem to spring up each month. Almost everywhere offers free internet and wi-fi.

LEBUH CHULIA

Banana Guest House 355 Lebuh Chulia ☎04 262 6171, ⒲bananapenang.com. Established backpacker hangout with cheap, basic rooms; the downstairs café-bar has a pool table and can get rowdy. Their newer branch across the road is quieter, with the same rates. Dorms RM18, doubles RM60

Crystal Guest House 294 Lebuh Chulia ☎04 263 8068, ⒲crystalguesthouse.blogspot.com. One long corridor with clean doubles off either side; few have windows but all are a/c, either with or without bathrooms. Owners are brusque but friendly enough, and there's a café at the front. RM55

Hang Chow 511 Lebuh Chulia ☎04 261 0810. Clean and tidy fan rooms. A few ringgit more will get you your own shower (all are hot); and a few more buy a/c. A nice *kopitiam* restaurant downstairs serves local and continental food, including pizza. RM45

Hong Ping 273 Lebuh Chulia ☎04 262 5243. Another faded, forgettable hotel in good order; it's clean and well run and all rooms have a/c, TVs and hot showers. RM60

Oasis 431 Lebuh Chulia ☎04 262 2345. Good-value, clean and functional hostel with sturdier walls than most. It's set back from the road (the sign above the entrance reads *Swiss Hotel*), with parking as well as an airy café with wi-fi. RM50

Tourist Guest House 425 Lebuh Chulia ☎04 261 4427. Good sturdy doors and either shared or private bathrooms and fans or a/c make this place great value. RM45

Yengkeng 362 Lebuh Chulia ☎012 262 2177, ⒲yengkenghotel.com. Lively old Chinese mansion with florid roof ridges on the outside, though the blandly comfortable interior is a missed opportunity: nice touches include Indian rugs, wooden-shuttered windows, period furniture and large beds. There's also a mini-pool and small garden terrace. RM380

LORONG CINTA (LOVE LANE)

Love Lane Inn 54 Lorong Cinta ☎016 419 8409. The rooms are spartan and clean, but rather sterile; the more

expensive en-suite and a/c rooms are by far the best. Very knowledgeable Indonesian staff, and free tea and coffee are a nice touch. Dorms RM13, doubles RM45

★ **Old Penang Guest House** 53 Lorong Cinta ☎04 263 8805, ⒲oldpenang.com. Wonderfully restored house with twelve rooms, wooden floors and a dorm. The sheets are crisp and clean, and a plasma screen shows movies in the beautiful common room. Light breakfast included. Dorms RM23, doubles RM65

Red Inn 55 Lorong Cinta ☎04 262 0991, ⒲redinnheritage.com. Converted-shophouse treasure: large, high-ceilinged lounge with huge central TV and free tea/coffee, polished wooden floors, free internet and wi-fi. Rooms are ordinary though – paper-thin walls, a bed, a clothes hook – with shared facilities. A generous Malay breakfast is included. RM70

LEBUH MUNTRI

75 Traveller's Lodge 75 Lebuh Muntri ☎04 262 3378. An old favourite with travellers who like things cheap and cheerful, though the rooms are the standard cubicles. A good common area for socializing, and very helpful staff. Fan and shared shower RM25, otherwise RM45

Modern 179c Lebuh Muntri ☎04 263 5424. "Modern" here means c1930, with many original features (though a few coats of paint since then have kept it cheerful). You've a choice of basic rooms with fans or a/c, all sharing toilets and showers; the nicest rooms have private balconies. RM45

Oriental Guest House 81 Lebuh Muntri ☎04 261 3378. With a great downstairs communal area, these cubicle rooms have high ceilings and the ones downstairs have original tile floors. All fan rooms with shared facilities. RM25

SD Guest House 28 Lebuh Muntri ☎04 261 6102, ⒲penangnet.com/sdmotel. With a sister hotel on Lorong Cinta, this relatively new place is very clean, though spartan, with dorms and fan or a/c doubles. Dorms RM15, doubles RM28

Star Lodge 39 Lebuh Muntri ☎04 262 6378. Run by the same management as the *75 Traveller's Lodge* a few doors away, the rooms come with either fan, a/c and shared or private facilities with new bathrooms. Can be very noisy. RM25

JALAN PENANG

Cititel 66 Jalan Penang ☎04 370 1183, ⓦcititelpenang.com. Large and stylish business hotel with modern, well-appointed but smallish rooms. There's a jacuzzi and three restaurants: Japanese, Chinese and a 24-hour café. Rate includes breakfast. RM185

Malaysia 7 Jalan Penang ☎04 263 3311, ⓦhotelmalaysia.com.my. Dated but busy 1970s urban hotel with functional en-suite rooms and wi-fi; not bad for the price. RM170

Peking 50a Jalan Penang ☎04 263 6191. Budget hotel from the 1950s featuring large, clean rooms with nice tile floors – though the walls could use a lick of paint. All rooms are en suite, with a/c and TV, and the management are helpful. RM60

LEBUH FARQUHAR & LEBUH LEITH

Bayview 25a Lebuh Farquhar ☎04 263 3161, ⓦbayviewhotels.com. Modern luxury high-rise close to the sea, with its own pool, Thai-style spa and fantastic views over the bay from the revolving rooftop restaurant. No character, but net one of their frequent discount packages and you've got a good deal. RM550

Cathay 15 Lebuh Leith ☎04 262 6271, ⓔcathayhbh @gmail.com. Everything about this 1920s Chinese hotel is stylish – the white-shuttered Neoclassical facade, cool atrium interior, the floor tiling, the wrought ironwork and staircases – until you reach the rooms, which are spacious but in desperate need of renovation. RM75

★ **Cheong Fatt Tze Mansion** 14 Lebuh Leith ☎04 262 0006, ⓦcheongfatttzemansion.com. This huge, century-old Chinese mansion with fifteen stylish suites offers guests a reading and TV room, a games room with ping-pong table, and a stunning atrium open to the sky, where you can while away the day sipping beer and admiring the intricately carved Chinese scrollwork. If you're lucky you'll be in the courtyard during a cloudburst and experience the house being naturally cooled by the rain as the architects intended. Rate includes breakfast. Book ahead. RM380

★ **Eastern & Oriental (E&O) Hotel** 10 Lebuh Farquhar ☎04 222 2000, ⓦeohotels.com. Penang's historic colonial hotel has been a city landmark since 1885; see p.150 for more about the building. Drop in for afternoon tea, served 2–5pm, at RM48 per person; dress is smart-elegant, with definitely no beachwear or sportswear. Rates vary enormously, but are consistently high. RM750

ELSEWHERE

Broadway 35f Jalan Masjid Kapitan Kling ☎04 262 8550, ⓦbroadwaybudgethotel.com. In a modern building, this friendly hostel has small and very basic but tidy fan rooms with thin walls and a/c rooms with two double beds. All rooms have shared facilities. RM60

Chew Jetty Homestay 59a Chew Jetty, ☎012/410 7736, ⓦmychewjetty.com. For something completely different, stay out at the old Chinese Jetties off Pengkalan Weld (see p.156) – you get a private twin room in a family house, with breakfast included. RM168

Chong Tian 38–42 Jalan Pintal Tali, ☎04 263 1881, ⓦ1881chongtian.com. Not quite open at the time of writing, this ancient hotel was being splendidly restored and furnished by an art collector, and expects to charge premium rates. RM700

Mallog 5 Lorong Muda ☎012/497 2681 ⓔmallog budgethotel@yahoo.com. Pink, newly converted budget hotel; rooms are small and extremely simple – literally just a bed – but it's spotless and well run, with a tiny terrace. Doubles with fan and shared bathroom RM35, with a/c and shower RM50

★ **Penaga** Cnr of Hutton and Clarke ☎04 261 1891 ⓦhotelpenaga.com. Old building renovated to a high standard, in a heritage-modern fusion that works well: antique tiles, coloured-glass panel doors, period furniture, polished teak floors, Chinese four-poster beds in each room. Add jacuzzi en suites, a/c and TV in the rooms, plus a spa and sauna, and it's a winner. RM470

★ **Straits Heritage** 92 Lebuh Armenian ☎04 263 8128 ⓦstraitsheritage.com. Quirky boutique hotel in a lovingly restored Chinese terrace shophouse, featuring exposed beams, polished wooden floors, large double beds and antique furnishings. Each of the two options – a double room plus a slightly stuffy attic, or a double on the top floor – gives you an entire floor of the building, though that isn't as roomy as it sounds. Private bathroom and toilet either way. RM300

EATING

There's good eating to be had in Georgetown, especially from **hawker stalls**; people come from as far as Singapore to chase down their favourite versions of humble **asam laksa** and other local snacks. Keep your eyes open too for **nutmeg juice**, *jus pala*, made not from the familiar soapy nut (poisonous in large quantities) but the apricot-like fruit; it's aromatic and salty, not to everyone's taste. Sadly, it's hard to find distinctive **Nyonya** places, though plenty of southern Chinese fare is served up in typically featureless, bustling canteens, from Cantonese dim sum to Hokkien and Teowchow oyster omelettes. Make sure you try Malay **nasi kandar** – a plate of rice served with tasters of various curries around the edge – which though found

2

across Malaysia originated in Penang. Little India is, unsurprisingly, where to head for **Indian** meals, but **Western food** is poorly represented – just a few European-style cafés, and foreign-friendly bars serving pub grub.

HAWKER STALLS

Chinatown Lebuh Chulia, opposite Lorong Cinta. Open late into the night, stalls prepare every sort of noodle and rice dish, typically costing RM5. The location – right in the road – can be a bit unnerving given the amount of traffic. Daily 7–11pm or later.

Kompleks Makanan Medan Renong Jalan Tun Syed Shah Barakah. Just above the sea, with the surf breaking in the background, this is a low-key, casual affair, popular with locals with children. Mostly Malay stalls, especially seafood – including cockles – plus *laksa*. Prices average RM3. Daily 7–11pm or later.

★ **Pesiaran Gurney (Gurney Drive)** 3km northwest along the coast. One of the most popular hawker stall areas in all Penang; with scores setting up on paving above the seafront; catch bus #10, #101 or #304 from KOMTAR and look out for the Sunrise Building at a broad intersection. Try the *char kway teow*, fried oyster omelettes (actually more like clam omelettes) and *asam laksa* at about RM3 a serve, or load a plate with fried crab, prawns, spring rolls, tofu and squid, and pay accordingly. Daily 6–10pm.

Red Garden Food Paradise Lebuh Leith. Probably the most popular hawker market with foreign visitors, though the food has become fairly tame from catering to their perceived tastes. A wider range of cuisines than normal, stretching to Japanese and *Filipino* as well as the usual Malay and Chinese, but more expensive too. The bar is run separately and rather pushy waiters will come to your table. Daily 6–11pm.

CAFÉS

★ **Amelie Café** Lebuh Armenian, right by the entrance to Chea Kongsi. Minute and charming Italian café seating about ten people, run by a young Chinese couple; the furniture is home-made and tumblers are jam-jars, but the freshly brewed coffee is first-rate; they also serve a small range of cakes, pasta, pizza and salads. Mains RM15. Thurs–Tues 9am–6pm.

Trois Canon Lebuh Chulia. Chinese-run café serving all-day breakfasts of scrambled egg, grilled ham, sausage and toast – plus a coffee – for RM6. Daily 8am–6pm.

RESTAURANTS

EE Beng Vegetarian Food Lebuh Dickens. Opposite the police HQ, two-thirds down the road. The excellent Chinese vegetarian buffet is cheap and delicious with many fake meat dishes and vegetable curries. Daily 6am–9.30pm.

Edelweiss Café 38 Lebuh Armenian. Swiss restaurant located inside an attractively restored shophouse. A B-52

– a large pork sausage, chips, salad and rosti – and the cheese fondue are the most traditional dishes; pork ribs are good too. Mains upwards of RM35. Tues–Fri 11am–3pm & 6.30–10pm, Sat noon–10pm, Sun noon–7pm.

Eden@Hutton Lane Jalan Hutton ☎ 04 263 9262. A pub-like institution dating back to 1964, specializing in tasty pasta dishes, seafood chowder, chicken chops, lobster thermidor and grilled steak. Portions are on the large side, their drinks are good, and there's even a lounge to indulge in a port and cigar. Mains around RM25. Daily noon–3pm & 6–10pm.

★ **Goh Huat Seng 59** Lebuh Kimberley. This completely decor-free Teowchow Chinese restaurant is locally famed for its excellent steamboat, where you cook a pile of meat, vegetables, seafood and noodles in a pot of stock at the table. Best in a group; come prepared to wait for space. About RM10/head. Daily 11.30am–2pm & 6–10pm.

★ **Kassim Mustapha** Cnr Lebuh Chulia and Lebuh Penang. Filling half a block with green and yellow frontage, *Kassim*'s is the most famous *nasi kandar* joint in Penang, having evolved from a humble roadside stall in 1980. Most dishes cost around RM8. Open 24hr.

Krishna Restaurant 75 Lebuh Pasar. Excellent banana-leaf curry house with rock-bottom prices. Try their *dosai*. Daily 7am–9.30pm; closed one Wed each month.

May Garden Palace 70 Jalan Penang ☎ 04 261 6435. Plush Cantonese restaurant with excellent food; go for the artery-clogging crisp-skinned suckling pig, poached tiger prawns or the village festival dish "poon choi", a selection of duck, pork and seafood gently poached together in broth. Popular with tourists from the nearby high-rise hotels. Mains RM25 and up. Daily 11.30am–2pm & 6–10pm.

★ **Old House Café Restaurant** 145–153 Lebuh Kimberley ☎ 04 262 2113. Smart Teowchow establishment with antique touches, though the atmosphere is informal. Braised duck and rice, plus a side dish of stewed mushrooms or spring rolls will only set you back RM20; they also do excellent fried crab or prawn balls (RM18 each) and a set banquet for four involving a lot of seafood (RM38/head). Daily 11.30am–2pm & 6–10pm.

Passage Thru India 11a Lebuh Leith, opposite the Cheong Fatt Tze Mansion. Varied dishes from around the subcontinent – tandoori, *biriyani*, Kashmiri and rarer Hyderabad cuisine. It's comfy inside, with abundant hangings and an eclectic range of light fittings; service is good and portions large. Mains RM15. Daily 11.30am–2pm & 6–10pm.

Sri Ananda Lebuh Penang, Little India. Excellent South and North Indian veggie food at cheap prices – RM5–7 for tasty lunchtime *thalis*, an array of spicy dishes with crispy pancakes. Daily noon–10pm.

Tai Tong Lebuh Cintra. A perfectly normal cheap Chinese restaurant, whose dim sum sessions from 7am every Saturday morning turn it into an obstacle course of plastic chairs, trolleyfuls of delicacies and noisy diners navigating between the two. Find a space, order a pot of tea and wait your turn. Around RM3 per serve. Daily, opens early, closed by 3pm.

Thew Chik 336 Lebuh Chulia. Rapid-turnover Chinese joint full of lunchtime crowds clamouring for their renowned Hainan chicken rice. Closes by mid-afternoon, or whenever they sell out. RM5. Daily 11am–4pm.

Vegetarian Cnr of Jalan Masjid Kapitan Kling and Lorong Pasar. Simple Chinese *kedai kopi* serving stir fry vegetable and mock-meat dishes, usually busy with supplicants from the nearby Kuan Yin Teng. You get a plate of rice and pay per portion of toppings; it's hard to spend more than RM6. Daily 11am–6pm.

Yasmeen Jalan Penang. Delicious and cheap halal Indian food, including lots of spicy, cumin-coloured vegetables and curries to dip your roti into, priced around RM8. The tandoori chicken is good too. Daily 11.30am–2pm & 6–10pm.

DRINKING AND NIGHTLIFE

Most of Georgetown's **bars and clubs** are up at the northern end of town, particularly around the pedestrianized top 100m of **Jalan Penang**, which is lined with competing businesses. Clubs fire up nightly around 7pm and fizzle out by 3pm; expect a cover charge of RM50, various happy hour deals, and for live bands or DJs churning out light rock and pop from 10pm onwards. Relatively uninhibited for conservative Malaysia, there's little real sleaze – anyone after that sort of thing heads up to Thailand for the weekend – though the periodic arrival of the Malaysian navy can turn even the tamest joint into a meat market. If you just want to hang out with a beer, try bars at backpacker hostels like *Banana* on Lebuh Chulia (see p.158), or the couple of Western-oriented places elsewhere – *Reggae Club* and *B@92* are the best.

BARS

98 Top Secret 98 Lebuh Muntri. Small bar with pub-style menu of RM15 dishes – chicken curry, chilli con carne – but also much better Sri Lankan seafood grill. Daily 5pm–late.

★ **B@92** 92 Lebuh Gereja. Small bar in former shophouse with original tiled floor and shutters, long mirrors and dark wooden furniture. Bit of a barfly hangout and best for beer and conversation, plus pub staples – sandwiches and pasta – at around RM15. Occasional live bands. Daily, afternoon–late.

Betelnut Café 360 Lebuh Chulia. Very popular with travellers, with tables spilling onto the pavement. Limited choice of spirits on offer as well as beer and a snack menu. Daily 5pm–late.

Hong Kong Bar Lebuh Chulia. A classic liberty-port dive with command plaques and photos of warships adorning the walls – if you happen to be here when the Australian fleet is in port, give this place a wide berth. Daily 5pm–late.

Monkey Bar Jalan Penang. Pop Art pictures of simians dot the walls at this small and crowded place, popular with Georgetown's trendy youth. Easy-going atmosphere, events nights and somewhere for a drink before heading to the clubs opposite. Daily 5pm–late.

Reggae Club Jalan Penang. Bistro with piped Caribbean ambience, good for either a few chilled beers and a chat, or a relaxed meal. Daily 5pm–late.

Soho Free House Jalan Penang. Pub-style place with a livid purple exterior and, it claims, more types of beer on offer than anywhere else in Malaysia. There's a sports bar with big TV upstairs too, a pool table and a menu including the likes of shepherd's pie. Daily 5pm–late.

CLUBS

Carmen @ The Tiger Tavern Basement, City Bayview Hotel, 25a Lebuh Farquhar. Open until late, every night except Sunday, with live bands and DJs from 9.30pm. Mon–Sat 9.30pm–3am.

Penang Island Bar Jalan Penang. Classy decor in a renovated colonial building. Something for everyone with live pop music nightly (except Sun), sports on TV, a well-stocked bar and a small menu. Daily 9pm–late.

Slippery Señoritas Jalan Penang. Popular with foreign tourists, this is the island's liveliest pick-up joint, a Latin-themed disco of the kind that has popped up all over Asia in the last half-decade. Except for half-hearted tapas, there's really nothing Latin about it, but they have got a seriously overpowered sound system. Daily 9pm–late.

Soi 11 Jalan Penang. Nicely set up, this is a good alternative to the bigger clubs, if you want to be able to have a relatively audible conversation as well as a dance over a cocktail or beer. Daily 9pm–late.

Uptown Bistro 20 Jalan Sultan Ahmad Shah. This stand-alone building is hard to miss. There's a nightly live band (Chinese pop) indoors as well as a beer garden in the courtyard. Daily 7pm–late.

Voodoo Jalan Penang. Pub and bistro with a huge outdoor terrace and bar, hosting the Fame Dance Club – popular with local college students – and regular DJ competitions. Daily 9pm–3am.

2

ENTERTAINMENT

CINEMAS

GSC Cinema Gurney Plaza on Persiaran Gurney, 2km to the west; ⓦgsc.com.my; catch bus #101. The place to head to for current Malay, Chinese and Western blockbusters.

Odeon Jalan Penang. Ancient, but a fun place to be blasted by Bollywood spectaculars – there are no subtitles but you hardly need them. Films shown noon to midnight (RM10).

SHOPPING

Georgetown is good for **curios** and Chinese and Peranakan **porcelain** – decent reproductions if not actual antiques – though much of the fun is in browsing through piles of unlikely junk, rather than buying. Cheap and cheery **clothing** is well represented too, though if you're after a contemporary souvenir with a little panache, head to the emerging clutch of **art and craft galleries** along Lebuh Armenian and ajacent lanes. Georgetown's liveliest **market** is Chowrista Market, on Jalan Penang, full of all sorts of fruit, meat and vegetables; stalls at the entrance sell candied nutmeg, salak, papaya and others.

Alpha-Utara Gallery 83 Lebuh Cina. Showcases paintings and sculpture by contemporary Penang artists in a converted old shophouse. Tues–Sun 10am–6pm.

Bon Ton/China Joe's 86 Lebuh Armenian. Home furnishings, modern batiks, art books and stylish sarongs in bright colours. Daily 10am–7pm.

Fuan Wong 88 Lebuh Armenian, ⓦfuanwong.com. The top-floor gallery parades local photographic talent, with handmade fused-glass sculptures and silver jewellery on the lower two floors. Daily 10am–6pm.

Galery Seni Mutiara Lebuh Armenian. Fine art by local artists, though the collection is almost upstaged by the superbly restored shophouse that contains the gallery. Daily 10am–6pm.

Hong Seng 86 Jalan Penang. Crammed to the roof with decorative, mostly modern china. Daily 10am–6pm.

H.S. Sam Bookstore 473 Lebuh Chulia. The best of several secondhand bookshops at this end of the road; the enterprising owner also rents bikes, books tickets, handles Thai visas and stores luggage. Daily 9.30am–1.30pm & 3–9.30pm.

Lean Giap Lebuh Chulia. Two branches, one dealing in old-style crockery, the other in a fascinating mix of general curios (old fob watches, tobacco tins, cameras, trinkets, amulets and woodcarvings). Daily 10am–6pm.

Meizhenxiang 191 Lebuh Kimberley. Only signed in Chinese, but you can't miss this long pink warehouse,

fronted by incense burners and giant granite statues of gods and heroes. Inside is overflowing with every imaginable type of temple accessory, plus crockery, furniture and cooking utensils. Daily 10am–6pm.

Peranakan Mansion 29 Lebuh Gereja. The small gift shop here is the only place in town likely to have genuine antique porcelain, though the selection of bowls, cups and dishes changes continually according to supply (see p.154). Daily 9.30am–5pm.

Popular Books Floor 2, KOMTAR. The usual mix of English-language cookbooks, novels, guides and maps. Daily 10am–6pm.

Rozana's Lebuh Aceh. Small, family-run store specializing in handmade batik on cotton or silk cloth; you can buy clothes off the peg, purchase raw fabric (RM180/2.5m), or have clothing tailor-made (shirts cost RM35–75). Daily 10am–6pm.

Sam's Batik Jalan Penang ⓦsamsbatikhouse.com. A warehouse full of of silk, batik and saris, plus shirts, skirts, sarongs and dresses galore; there's more of this a few doors south at Penang Bazaar. Daily 10am–6pm.

Syarikat Jalan Penang. Prominently signed (though the name simply means "Company"), this place is packed with porcelain, plus Javanese sarongs, shadow puppets, silk embroideries, old photos, *keris* knives, betel-nut choppers, snuffboxes, woodcarvings from Sarawak and even a few pieces of shipwreck porcelain. Daily 10am–6pm.

DIRECTORY

Banks and exchange The major banks along Lebuh Pantai, such as Standard Chartered and HSBC Bank (all Mon–Fri 9.30am–3pm, Sat 9.30–11.30am), charge hefty commissions, so the licensed moneychangers on Lebuh Pantai, Lebuh Chulia and Jalan Masjid Kapitan Kling (daily 8.30am–6pm), which charge no commission and often offer better rates, are preferable.

Consulates Australia, 1c Lorong Hutton ☎04 263 5285; Indonesia, 467 Jalan Burma ☎04 227 4686; Thailand, 1 Jalan Tunku Abdul Rahman ☎04 262 8029; UK,

Northam Tower, 57 Jalan Sultan Ahmad Shah ☎04 227 5336.

Hospitals Adventist Hospital, Jalan Burma (☎04 226 1133; Rapid Penang bus #101 or #102); General Hospital, Jalan Utama (☎04 229 3333).

Pharmacy Several along Jalan Penang (Daily 10am–6pm).

Police The police headquarters is on Jalan Penang; emergencies ☎999.

Post office General Post Office is on Lebuh Downing

(Mon–Fri 8.30am–5pm, Sat 8.30am–4pm). The efficient poste restante/general delivery office is here; book and stationery shops on Lebuh Chulia offer parcel-wrapping service.

Travel agents For travel bookings, Thai visas, vehicle rental and transfers to Thailand, Langkawi, Taman Negara, the Tioman Islands and Cameron Highlands, try either your accommodation; Banana Travel & Tours, 84 Jalan Penang

(☎ 04 262 1171, ⓦ bananaguesthouse.com); or AM Sinar, 397 Lebuh Chulia (☎ 04 263 4851).

Visa extensions Pejabat Imigresen, cnr Lebuh Pantai and Lebuh Light (Mon–Fri 7.30am–1pm & 2–5.30pm for same-day visa extensions; ☎ 04 250 3410). Bring two passport photos, fill in the form, take a number for the queue and settle in for a long wait.

Temples and gardens near Georgetown

A short bus ride from KOMTAR through Georgetown's western suburbs passes three interesting **temples** and winds up at the island's attractive – and surprisingly wild – **Botanic Gardens**. You could spend a morning out this way, or simply stop off en route to Batu Ferringhi and points west (see p.166). Rapid Penang **bus #10** comes within range of all the sights and terminates at the gardens, though you might need to ask the driver where to get off elsewhere.

Wat Chayamangkalaram Temple

Lorong Burma (off Jalan Burma) • Daily 7am–6pm • Free • Rapid Penang bus #10, #101 or #103

Wat Chayamangkalaram is a Thai Buddhist temple dating to the 1900s, very different in design from Chinese equivalents elsewhere in Penang with its bright colours, flame-edged eaves and huge gilded pagoda, all soft curves, to one side. The main hall's entrance is flanked by nagas, fierce snake-like creatures painted gold and bright green, and guarded by two hefty demons holding swords. The aircraft-hangar-like interior is a stark contrast, filled by a 33m-long **Reclining Buddha** statue, looking rather feminine and draped in a gold sarong with his aura flaming about him. Murals depict episodes from Buddha's life.

Dharmmikarama Temple

Lorong Burma (off Jalan Burma) • Daily 7am–6pm • Free • Rapid Penang bus #10, #101 or #103

While the Burmese **Dharmmikarama Temple** is similar to the Wat Chayamangkalaram Temple opposite, its guardians are two snarling white and gold lions, with scales, claws and fiery trim. The Buddha here is standing, smiling mysteriously into the gloom and with oversized white hands, one pointing upwards and one down. The temple grounds are a bit nicer than those over the road, with more greenery and less concrete, and a few naturalistically painted statues dotted about.

Nattukottai Chettiar Temple

Jalan Kebun Bunga (Waterfall Road) • Daily 7am–6pm • Free • Rapid Penang bus #10

Penang's **Nattukottai Chettiar Temple** is the focus of the riotous three-day Hindu **Thaipusam** festival, in honour of Lord Subramanian (Jan or Feb). One of the crowning moments is the arrival of a silver chariot and statue of Lord Murugan, which have been carried from the sister temple in Georgetown. At other times of year, you're free to concentrate on the temple itself, in which an unusual wooden colonnaded walkway with exquisite pictorial tiles leads up to the inner sanctum, where a life-sized solid-silver peacock – the birds crop up throughout the temple – bows its head to the deity, Lord Subramanian.

The Botanic Gardens

Jalan Kebun Bunga (Waterfall Road), 6km west of central Georgetown • Daily 5am–9pm • Free • Rapid Penang bus #10, 45min

Dating to 1884, Georgetown's **Botanic Gardens** were designed to beautify an old quarry. You wouldn't know that now: there are lawns, a stream flowing through, paved walking tracks, groves of bamboos and ornamental trees, an orchid house, ferns and cactus, and surrounding forested hills. Saturday and Sunday mornings it's packed with family groups of exercising Chinese, who storm around the circuit trail in about thirty minutes; take it slower and it's good for an hour's stroll. Picnics tend to be torpedoed by invading **monkeys**, but there are gentler creatures too, not least **flying lizards**, which coast between trees on the forest edge.

You can **walk to Penang Hill** from here in around three hours, but it's a tough uphill hike – better to come down this way.

Ayer Itam

6km southwest of Georgetown on the Balik Pulau road • Rapid Penang bus #204 or #502; the latter continues to Balik Pulau

The suburb of **Ayer Itam** (also written "Air Hitam") amounts to little more than a 100m-long bottleneck, where the traffic squeezed between shops and the canvas awnings of a busy wet market. There are two reasons to visit: the colonial-era retreat of **Penang Hill**, slightly north, which is rich in refreshingly cool air and greenery, and **Kek Lok Si**, a ludicrously over-built hilltop Buddhist complex.

Penang Hill (Bukit Bendera)

Jalan Bukit Bendera • **Hill** Dawn–dusk • Free • **Funicular** Sun–Fri 6.30am–9.30pm, Sat 6.30am–11.15pm • RM30 return, exact money only • Rapid Penang bus #204

At 821m high, **Penang Hill** makes a nice escape from Georgetown's pollution and humidity: there are walking trails, flowers and bungalows (now hotels) dating from colonial times, when this hill station was a retreat for the British administrators. Nowadays, it's a popular local excursion; avoid weekends and holidays if possible.

The bus delivers to the foot of the hill on Jalan Bukit Bandera; signs a short way north point to the "bat cave temple", **Tua Pek Kong**. "Bat" in Chinese sounds like the word for "good fortune", so the tiny shrine – named after a colony of bats out the back – is naturally dedicated to the god of luck.

From the top of Jalan Bukit Bandera, a **funicular railway** whisks visitors to the top of the near-vertical hillside in a few minutes – a fun ride, were it not for the extortionate fee. Views from the top terraces stretch beyond Georgetown and over the straits to Butterworth; gentle, badly marked walks lead out to Tiger Hill and Western Hill, while a sealed road at the back descends steeply to the Botanic Gardens in around two hours. **Cream teas** are offered by a few establishments, and you can also **stay** up here (see p.166).

Kek Lok Si

Daily morning to late evening • Free; climbing the 193 steps to the top costs RM4

Supposedly the largest Buddhist temple in Malaysia, **Kek Lok Si** was founded by the abbot of Georgetown's Kuan Yin Teng in 1885, and originally modelled on Fok San Monastery in Foochow, China. It certainly doesn't resemble any normal temple complex nowadays: the hill sprouts all sorts of fantastic shrines and pagodas, linked by hundreds of steps, and bedecked with flags, lanterns and statues. The two most prominent features are the white, seven-tier wedding-cake assemblage that is the **Ten Thousand Buddhas Pagoda**, capped by a golden Burmese stupa; and a 30m-high bronze statue of the goddess of mercy, **Kuan Yin**, sheltered from the elements by an open-sided pavilion, its pillars wreathed in carved dragons.

For such an obvious landmark, the route up here is hard to find. From the Balik Pulau road, follow the market street up towards Kek Lok Si; just before the road bends uphill, look for a row of shops to the left concealing a gauntlet of trinket stalls, their awnings forming a tunnel. Steps ascend to the temple forecourt, past a pond for turtles, which represent eternity. A **vegetarian restaurant** at the top is open throughout the day (see p.166).

OPPOSITE FUNICULAR RAILWAY, PENANG HILL >

2

Bellevue Penang Hill ☏ 04 829 9500. Founded as the sheriff's house in 1780, but totally rebuilt since as a quiet retreat, with large rooms and a terrace affording superb views over Georgetown. There's a decent restaurant too – especially good at sunset when the city's lights flicker in the distance – and an aviary full of colourful local species. RM180

EATING

Asia Café Downhill from the Penang Hill entrance, at the junction with the Georgetown–Ayer Itam road. A comfortable hawker centre open around the clock; the food is nothing spectacular but is better value than anywhere on Penang Hill, with decent dim sum breakfasts, oyster omelettes and *char kway teow*. Main dishes RM8. Open 24hr.

David Brown's Restaurant and Tea Terraces 100m from the upper funicular terminus, Penang Hill ☏ 04 828 8337, ⊕ penanghillco.com.my. Sandwiches, afternoon tea, roasts for dinner and an excellent wine list, all served in a smart country-kitchen environment (though in good weather there are outdoor tables too). A pot of tea, two scones and jam plus cream costs RM20; full afternoon tea with petit fours is RM70; main courses start at RM56. Daily 9am–9pm.

Kek Lok Si Temple Ayer Itam. The vegetarian restaurant at the top of the steps serves meatless versions of Chinese "spiced duck", "crispy eel", "kung pao chicken", plus Malay staples like *laksa, bak kut teh, nasi lemak* and "fish-head" curry. Set lunch for one costs RM8, up to RM145 for a seven-course banquet with soup. Daily 10am–7pm.

★ **Pasar Air Itam LAKSA** On the side road leading up to Kek Lok Si Temple, Ayer Itam. Look for a small stall with a big red sign behind, with the name written in Malay and Chinese characters, and you'll find what many rate as the best *asam laksa* in Penang, costing just RM3. The sauce is salty, sour and thick with *heh koh* prawn paste, all topped off with rice noodles, shredded vegetables, pounded fish and a handful of fresh herbs. Daily, morning until mid-afternoon.

The northwest

A 15km-long road runs along the coast northwest of Georgetown, squeezed for much of its journey between the sea and dense forests inland. Despite tourist-industry hype, the main settlement out this way, the ugly resort strip of **Batu Ferringhi**, lacks both character and, more importantly, a decent beach. Beyond, the area's attractions are better presented at the **Tropical Spice Garden**, before the road runs out beyond quiet **Teluk Bahang** at **Pulau Penang National Park**, where you can make easy hikes through coastal forest to undeveloped beaches, or even **camp**. If you've time to wait for the infrequent buses – or your own vehicle – you can visit a small clutch of rural sights along the road south of Teluk Bahang, en route to Balik Pulau (see opposite).

Batu Ferringhi

Rapid Penang bus #101

A twenty-minute bus ride from Georgetown, **BATU FERRINGHI** is a 2km strip of road lined with low-rise shops and high-rise hotels, all seeking to capitalize on a long stretch of gritty sand and dirty grey sea which brochures would have you believe is one of Malaysia's best beaches. If your main interest is swimming or snorkelling, or you simply want to kick back in attractive surrounds and work on your tan, you'll be sorely disappointed. During the day most businesses are shut too, though an evening meal here makes a break from Georgetown, and when the sun goes down the road comes alive with brightly lit stalls selling batik, T-shirts and fake designer watches.

The Tropical Spice Garden

Daily 9am–5.30pm • RM14, or RM22 including guided tour • ⊕ tropicalspicegarden.com • Rapid Penang bus #101

Between Batu Ferringhi and Teluk Bahang, the delightful **Tropical Spice Garden** has turned an abandoned rubber plantation into a cornucopia of herbs, spices and decorative flora, all set in a stylishly landscaped, eight-acre gully and shaded by former plantation trees. Three short, easy circuit trails loop between waterfalls and streams and introduce you to the different types of plants and their commercial, culinary and traditional uses; it's worth taking a tour for the insights (as opposed to plain facts) offered by the guides. There's an excellent **café** too, and **cookery courses** daily except Monday.

Teluk Bahang

Rapid Penang bus #101

Set at the intersection of the coastal road and the route south to Balik Pulau, **TELUK BAHANG** is a somnambulant, unfocused settlement of fishing kampung, mildewed residential blocks and roadside food stalls. It's around an hour from Georgetown; buses set down at the intersection, beyond which the settlement strings out for 1.5km along the shadeless road to the gates of Pulau Pinang National Park.

Pulau Pinang National Park (Taman Negara Pulau Pinang)

Daily 7.30am–6pm; park office Sat–Mon 9am–6pm, Fri 9am–noon & 3–6pm; canopy walkway Sat–Mon 10am–1pm & 2.30–4pm • Free; boat transfers to beaches RM200, split between passengers • ☏ 04 881 3530, ⊕ wildlife.gov.my • Some Rapid Penang #101 buses terminate at the park gates

The coastal road winds up at the gates of **Pulau Pinang National Park**, a compact, hilly chunk of old-growth coastal forest, pandanus and mangroves. Walking trails lead through it all to a handful of secluded, undeveloped **beaches**, nesting grounds for rare marine **turtles**, which visit through the year. With your own gear, you can also **camp** (see p.168).

Register at the National Park office, and pick up a free **map**, before setting off; trails are easy to follow and well used, though steep and badly eroded in places. The 5km-long north-coast track passes attractive **Monkey Beach** (3.5km), one of the best for camping, sand and swimming, before terminating at **Muka Head Lighthouse**, where you might see sea eagles cruising the headland. The other main trail cuts southwest over the forested hills, via a short **canopy walkway**, to **Pantai Kerachut** (3.5km), another scenic camping beach where you just might encounter turtles.

The Balik Pulau road

Rapid Penang bus #501 operates only between Teluk Bahang and Balik Pulau; check with staff at KOMTAR or Terminal Weld that it's running before you set out

A string of small local industries line the first stretch of the 15km road south from Teluk Bahang to **Balik Pulau**, best toured in your own vehicle as buses are unreliable.

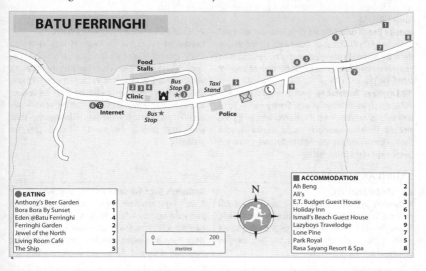

BATU FERRINGHI

Food Stalls

Bus Stop

Taxi Stand

Clinic

Internet

Bus Stop

Police

N

0   200
metres

● EATING

Anthony's Beer Garden	6
Bora Bora By Sunset	1
Eden @Batu Ferringhi	4
Ferringhi Garden	2
Jewel of the North	7
Living Room Café	3
The Ship	5

■ ACCOMMODATION

Ah Beng	2
Ali's	4
E.T. Budget Guest House	3
Holiday Inn	6
Ismail's Beach Guest House	1
Lazyboys Travelodge	9
Lone Pine	7
Park Royal	5
Rasa Sayang Resort & Spa	8

2

At a **Batik Factory**, 1km along (daily 9am–6pm; free; ⊛penangbatik.com.my), you can watch the waxing and dyeing process, and buy the finished product. The same distance again brings you to Penang's **Butterfly Farm** (daily 9am–6pm; RM27; ⊛butterfly-insect.com), also home to all manner of frogs, snakes, stick insects and scorpions; and then the **Forest Recreation Park** (Tues–Sun 9am–5pm; free or RM28 for a guided tour), a semi-wild patch of jungle with small waterfalls, marked trails and a children's playground. Finally, 4km south, the **Tropical Fruit Farm** (daily 9am–6pm; RM28; ⊛tropicalfruits.com.my) produces over 200 varieties of tropical and subtropical fruits – you get to try a range of them on their tour.

ACCOMMODATION

BATU FERRINGHI

If planning to stay in Batu Ferringhi, check for deals online and book in advance – it can get packed out at weekends and during holidays. Rates are higher for what you get than in Georgetown; pricier places have pools and run free shuttle buses into Georgetown through the day.

Ah Beng Batu Ferringhi ☎04 881 1036. Serene, family-run place with polished wood floors, a communal balcony overlooking the sea and a washing machine. **RM70**

Ali's Batu Ferringhi ☎04 881 1316. Friendly Muslim place – no alcohol allowed – with relaxing open-air café and garden, and a pleasant wooden veranda. Fan rooms have either shared or private bathrooms. **RM70**, family room sleeping five **RM150**

E.T. Budget Guest House Batu Ferringhi ☎04 881 1553. One of the better budget options at Batu Ferringhi, spotlessly clean and with helpful staff, shared facilities and functional doubles, some with a/c. **RM70**

Holiday Inn Batu Ferringhi ☎04 881 1601, ⊛penang .holiday-inn.com. In two separate blocks connected by a bridge spanning the road; there are pleasant lawns and a small pool, while rooms are well appointed, some with parquet flooring. A kids' club makes this a good option for families. **RM350**

Ismail's Beach Guest House Batu Ferringhi ☎04 881 2569. Tastefully furnished, all rooms with a/c and fridges, this is the best mid-range place to stay in town. The most expensive room is right on the beach, but the others are not far off. **RM180**

★ **Lazyboys Travelodge** Batu Ferringhi ☎04 881 2486, ⊛lazyboystravelodge.net. Small rooms – some with en-suite facilities – but it's all very clean, bright and well run. There are hammocks on the veranda, wooden floors, a kitchen and bar, and the friendly owners make you feel like part of the family. **RM80**

THE NORTHWEST

Lone Pine Batu Ferringhi ☎04 881 1511, ⊛lonepinehotel.com. Founded in 1948 but completely renovated and expanded since then, this boutique hotel is managed by Georgetown's *Eastern & Oriental*. The main building echoes the original colonial bungalow, though inside there's a strangely Nordic feel to the use of space and designer furniture. Staff are fairly slack. **RM800**

Park Royal Batu Ferringhi ☎04 881 1133, ⊛parkroyalhotels.com. Huge block of a resort complex, sprawling along the beachfront, with most of the rooms facing seawards. There's a gym, tennis court, obligatory pool and a massage spa; service is good all round. **RM400**

Rasa Sayang Resort & Spa Batu Ferringhi ☎04 881 1811, ⊛shangri-la.com. This stylish low-rise hotel boasts traditional Malay architecture with its Minangkabau-style roofs; there's a landscaped pool and good attention to detail. **RM400**

Shalini's Guest House Batu Ferringhi ☎04 881 1859, ⊛shalinisguesthouse.blogspot.com. Somewhat eccentric family residence (the entrance is through their living room) and guesthouse which also rents out apartments. A range of rooms, from fans with shared bathrooms, through to a/c en suites. **RM100**

PULAU PINANG NATIONAL PARK

Campsites Pulau Pinang National Park ☎04 881 3530, ⊛wildlife.gov.my. The national park has free campsites at Sungai Teluk Tukun (1km from the entrance), Monkey Beach (3.5km) and Pantai Kerachut (3.5km). Book in advance as spaces are limited. There are showers and toilets at Pantai Kerachut, but otherwise only benches; you need to bring all gear, including tents, food, water and cooking equipment – wood fires are prohibited.

EATING AND DRINKING

BATU FERRINGHI

Restaurants in Batu Ferringhi tend to be good but overpriced, catering for the overspill from the large hotels. There's cheaper food at hawker centres and cafés, mostly down by the beach, along with a few bars charging upwards of RM12 a beer.

Anthony's Beer Garden Batu Ferringhi. Popular, very friendly expat-run place, set back a little from the main road at the western end of town. There's cold beer, pleasant company, a TV but no food. Daily noon–10pm.

Bora Bora By Sunset Batu Ferringhi. Tucked off the main drag at the end of a row of anonymous businesses, this place tries hard to capture the beachside theme, with palm thatching, tables on decking above the sand and a well-stocked bar. Food ranges from vegetarian pizza through to Mexican and Malaysian staples, typically costing RM10; it's not cuisine but the sunset compensates. Daily 5pm–late.

Eden @Batu Ferringhi Batu Ferringhi. The boast at this huge beachfront place with 36 tanks full of live seafood is "Anything that swims, we cook it". A cultural show accompanies the evening meal. Around RM30 a dish. Daily 3.30–11pm.

★ **Ferringhi Garden** Batu Ferringhi ☎ 04 881 1193. Well-appointed place set in a garden – with palms and shrubs nicely lit at night – with a charcoal BBQ, steaks, seafood and a resident dessert chef. Indoors is stylishly finished in wood – tables, chairs, even screens and panelling – and the high thatched roof is very Malay-tropical. Mains upwards of RM30. Daily 4pm–midnight.

Jewel of the North Batu Ferringhi. A range of dishes, including Thai and Malay, but best by far for their native North Indian food, with tandoori a speciality – served in far cleaner (if less atmospheric) surrounds than places in Georgetown. Around RM45 a head. Daily 7am–11pm.

Living Room Café Batu Ferringhi. Good-value, eclectic menu – chicken salad, pork ribs, Thai chicken, burgers – furnishings made from driftwood, comfortable lounge area and friendly atmosphere make this a pleasant place to relax over a meal. Mains RM20. Thurs–Tues 10am–3pm & 6.45–10.30pm.

The Ship Batu Ferringhi. It's a ship that's a restaurant, so fairly hard to miss. The staff wear nautical clothes and the mainstay is seafood served in Thai or Chinese style, though they also do a decent steak. Good food and it's fun, though very touristy. Count on RM35 a head in a group. Daily noon–1am.

The south of the island

Of the various esoteric sights in the south of the island, none comes stranger than Penang's **Snake Temple**, out near the airport, which is infested with live reptiles. The nearby **War Museum** dwells on events through the 1940s, but the tiny crossroads town of **Balik Pulau** makes a more interesting spot to soak up past times.

The Snake Temple

Sungai Kluang, 12km south of Georgetown • Daily 6am–7pm • Free • Rapid Transit bus #401

Founded in memory of Chor Soo King, a thirteenth-century Chinese monk who gained local fame as a healer, Penang's **Snake Temple** is a bright Buddhist affair, its modern concrete-and-tile forecourt cluttered with souvenir and food stalls and guarded by two stone lions. Inside, the front altar – like strategically placed shrubs in other halls – is draped in handfuls of bull-headed, poisonous **green pit vipers** which, legend has it, mysteriously appeared upon completion of the temple in 1850. Pit vipers are naturally lethargic creatures – they hunt by staying still and ambushing their prey – but even so it's hard to account for the way the ones here completely ignore visitors, though you'd best not poke them to see if they're real, as some people do. There's also a large – but non-venomous – Burmese python on hand for photo ops.

Penang War Museum

Daily 9am–6pm • RM35 • Rapid Penang bus #302 or #307

The **Penang War Museum** stands on the site of a 1930s British military fortress. You climb the hill to an area of bunkers, forts, underground tunnels and an observation tower, all sensibly designed to defend the position from a naval attack; unfortunately for the British, the Japanese stormed it from inland. The fort became a prison, abandoned after the war partly because it was believed to be haunted by those tortured to death here. Recovered from undergrowth and opened as a museum during the 1980s, it's full of artefacts and photos from the war.

Balik Pulau

Rapid Transit bus #401 via Snake Temple, #502 via Ayer Itam, or #501 from Teluk Bahang (if running)

Balik Pulau (literally "The Back of the Island") is a small, self-contained town, set on a plain between Penang's west coast and the steep hills that run down the centre of the island. The town is famed for a mid-year glut of fruit – it hosts a **Durian Festival** all through June – and its own version of *asam laksa*, which includes pineapple. The 250m-long main street is lined in old buildings, though only **Fong Silversmith**, on the corner near the roundabout, is especially compelling; its charming owner has been turning out simple, attractive jewellery for decades. At the other end of town there's a nineteenth-century convent and the **Sacred Heart Church**, a pale grey and cream tin-sided structure dating to 1854.

EATING	BALIK PULAU
Nan Guan Balik Pulau main street. Just a shopful of seats with a cart out front cooking up *asam laksa*, but people gather an hour before they start serving around	11am to make sure they get a RM3 bowl. If you enjoyed eating it at Ayer Itam (p.164), then you need to come here and decide which is best. Daily 11am–late afternoon.

Kedah and Perlis

The northernmost third of the west coast is filled by the states of **Kedah** and **Perlis**, the latter being Malaysia's smallest state at just 800 square km. These are the country's **agricultural heartlands**, the landscape dominated by lustrous, bright green paddy fields stretching off in all directions. That wealth has seen the region (ruled by Malay sultans since the fifteenth century) invaded over the centuries by the Thais, the British, the Thais again, and the Japanese in World War II. Indeed, Kedah only reluctantly joined the Federated Malay States in 1948.

Neither state's capitals– Kedah's **Alor Star**, or **Kangar** in Perlis – demands a trip in its own right, but the major resort island of **Pulau Langkawi**, with its fine beaches and forested interior, makes an attractive (if expensive) place to pull up for a few days, perhaps en route to the **Thai border** – which you can cross by boat from the island, or by road and rail through Perlis. Less visited local sights include **Ulu Muda Eco Reserve**, and the important **archeological remains** outside tiny **Sungai Petani**.

Sungai Petani

SUNGAI PETANI, 35km north of Butterworth, is the jumping-off point for the archeological site of **Bujang Valley**, and **Gunung Jerai**, the state's highest peak. Both lie northwest from town, on separate roads; without your own vehicle, you can't visit both in a single day. The town itself has nothing to detain you beyond its transport terminals and handful of places to stay. A **clock tower** dominates Jalan Ibrahim, the main north–south road through town; from here, a side road directly to the east leads to the **train station**. One block south of the clock tower, another side road branching east, Jalan Kuala Ketil, crosses over the tracks and leads to the **express bus stop** – little more than an open yard and some food stalls. A further block south and west is Jalan Petri, which continues west past the **local bus** station, taxi stand and some budget **hotels**.

Bujang Valley (Lembah Bujang)

From Sungai Petani's local bus station, catch a Merbok bus (hourly; 45min; RM3), then follow signposts for the museum for 2km through fruit orchards

Around 10km northwest of Sungai Petani, outside the one-street town of **MERBOK** on the banks of the Sungai Bujang, **Lembah Bujang** is Malaysia's most important archeological site, highlighting the remains of a significant Hindu-Buddhist kingdom that flourished here between the fourth and fourteenth centuries. That said, there's not a huge amount to see beyond a small **museum** and some reconstructed temple foundations, built before the rise of Islam saw the culture fade and the buildings reclaimed by jungle.

The archeological museum

Mon–Sun 9am–5pm • Free

The on-site **archeological museum** gives a thumbnail history of the Lembah Bujang kingdom, from the visit of the Chinese pilgrim I-Ching in 671 through to its absorption by the Sumatran Srivijaya Empire, successful resistance to the Indian Chola attack in 1025, and its gradual decline as a trading centre over the following centuries. There are photographs of finds being excavated, as well as a number of carved stone pillars, pots and jewels. Behind the museum, the neat stone bases of eight tomb temples (including the large Candi Bukit Batu Pahat) have been reconstructed using original materials. There's a snack shop on the premises, and accommodation nearby.

Gunung Jerai (Kedah Peak)

From Sungai Petani, local bus #2 (every 45min; 30min) runs to the bottom of the mountain; either walk up to the summit (a gentle 2hr climb) or catch a minibus (daily, every 45min 8.30am–5pm; RM5 return)

The massive 1200m limestone outcrop of **Gunung Jerai**, the highest peak in Kedah, dominates the otherwise flat landscape northwest of Sungai Petani near the highway town of **GURUN**. On clear days, it offers panoramic views over the rolling rice fields stretching up the coastline from Penang to Langkawi. The mountain is replete with legend; tales abound of the infamous **Rajah Bersiong** who held court over the ancient kingdom of Langkasuka, and archeological digs have revealed a water temple (Candi Telaga Sembilan) believed to be his private pool. Today there's a **resort** on the mountain (see below) and the **Sungai Teroi Forest Recreation Park** halfway up, with rare orchids; you might also encounter lesser mouse deer and the long-tailed macaque.

ARRIVAL AND DEPARTURE — SUNGAI PETANI

By train Alor Star (2 daily; 1hr 10min); Bangkok (Thailand; 1 daily; 21hr); Butterworth (1 daily; 1hr 20min); Hat Yai (Thailand; 2 daily; 3hr 30min); Ipoh (1 daily; 5hr); Kuala Kangsar (1 daily; 4hr); Kuala Lumpur (1 daily; 8hr 30min); Surat Thani (Thailand; 1 daily; 9hr); Taiping (3hr 30min).

By bus Alor Star (1hr 40min); Butterworth (45min); and Sik (2hr), en route to Ulu Muda (see p.175).

ACCOMMODATION

SUNGAI PETANI

Duta 7 Jalan Petri, Sungai Petani ⓣ 04 421 2040. Just west of the local bus station (look for the large "Hotel" sign on the side), with large, colourful and comfortable en-suite doubles. Fans RM45, a/c RM55.

Sungai Petani Inn 427 Jalan Kolam Air, Sungai Petani ⓣ 04 421 3411, ⓦ hotelspinn.blogspot.com. A nice pool and comfortable rooms at this recently refurbished urban hotel, though at the time of writing it strangely lacked wi-fi. RM150

LEMBAH BUJANG

Damai Park Resort Signposted off the road from Merbok, Lembah Bujang ⓣ 04 457 3340. Simple, motel-like en-suite chalets dotted around a shady park planted with fruit trees, with a large clean dorm up the hill; kitchen facilities are available. A quiet retreat during the week – all you hear are the sounds of the nearby stream – it's often booked out at weekends. Dorms RM15, chalet RM100

GUNUNG JERAI

★ **Regency Jerai Hill Resort** Gunung Jerai ⓣ 04 466 7777, ⓦ theregency.com.my. Surprisingly exclusive and well-run hotel in open woodland, with rooms in a range of smart, modern, colonial-style bungalows and units. All meals available. RM300

Alor Star (Alor Setar)

The tidy state capital of Kedah, **Alor Star** is a thoroughly Malay city, very conservative in feel for the west coast, with a prominent mosque and former **sultan's palace** right in the centre. This traditionalism is doubtless partly a reaction to the proximity of the Thai border, just 45km north; the town has been through a century of Thai rule since its foundation as a royal capital in 1735. A compact place that can be easily seen in a day, Alor Star holds enough architectural and cultural interest to make a worthwhile pause on your way to or from Thailand, Ulu Muda Eco Park (see p.175) or the ferry to Langkawi. Be sure to dress appropriately, given its largely Muslim population.

Menara Alor Setar
North of the centre on Jalan Kanchut • Daily 10am–10pm • RM10

Menara Alor Setar is a mini-version of KL's similar Menara Tower, a 165m-tall Telecom tower with views from the halfway observation platform of pancake-flat paddy fields pierced by distant limestone outcrops. It's a good place to get your bearings for the mostly low-rise, ugly town below: the padang, a concrete modern centre, and a knot of tin-roofed houses along the dirty grey Sungai Kedah that might mark an earlier incarnation of the settlement.

The padang

Alor Star's open **padang** fills a good few acres just west of the business centre, dotted with buildings from Kedah's past. At the north is the low, Neoclassical facade of the former **High Court**, and the **Balai Nobat**, a curious octagonal tower housing the sacred instruments of the royal orchestra, played only during royal ceremonies. Across Jalan Pekan Malayu, the cream-and-black **Masjid Zahir** is beautifully proportioned, with a slender minaret and delicately scalloped arches on its colonnades. The south end of the padang is taken up by the long white-stucco **Balai Seni Negeri** (Mon–Sat 9am–5pm, Sun 8am–3pm; free), a former courthouse and now a gallery showcasing local artists.

Istana Balai Besar
West side of the padang

The history of the padang's most important building, the elegant **Istana Balai Besar** (Royal Audience Hall), mirrors that of the city. Founded in 1735, it was badly damaged in 1770 by the Bugis (seafaring raiders from Sulawesi in Indonesia), and

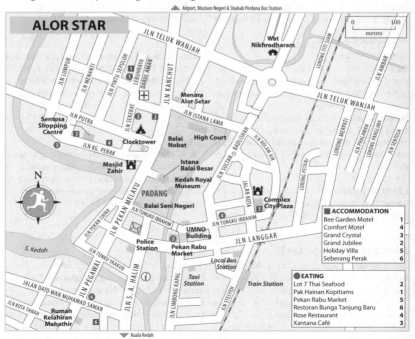

later by Thai armies in 1821. Rebuilt at the end of the nineteenth century, the current version has a Malay multilayered shingle roof, supported by colonial-style iron columns and eave decorations, alongside a very European-influenced flowing staircase. One of its first functions was to host the **marriages** of Sultan Abdul Hamid's five eldest children in 1904: the celebrations lasted three months, and the three million ringgit cost bankrupted Kedah – forty buffaloes had to be slaughtered to feed the crowds each day.

Kedah Royal Museum (Muzium Di Raja)

Behind the Balai Besar, west side of the padang • Sat–Mon 9am–5pm, Fri 9am–12.30pm & 2.30–5pm • Free

Guarded by a motley collection of bronze cannon (some stamped with the "VOC" of the Dutch East India Company), Alor Star's old royal palace now houses the **Kedah Royal Museum**. The sprawling wooden building, dating to 1930, must have made a fairly modest palace, and though the cases of ceremonial *keris* daggers, silver dinner services, gold anklets and brass betel-nut sets hint at a comfortable wealth, there's no feel of splendid indulgence – indeed, some exhibits (including a pair of binoculars used by one sultan on safari in Africa) are decidedly mundane. Note that no cameras are allowed in the museum, and visitors must remove their shoes.

Rumah Kelahiran Mahathir

18 Lorong Kilang Ais, south of the padang across the terminally polluted Sungai Kedah • Tues–Thurs, Sat & Sun 10am–5pm, Fri 10am–noon & 3–5pm • Free

The birthplace and family home of Dr Mahathir Mohamad, **Rumah Kelahiran Mahathir**, is now a museum, documenting the life of the local doctor who became the most powerful Malaysian prime minister of modern times. Even if you're not interested in Mahathir himself, it's worth taking a glimpse inside his former house to get an idea of what traditional middle-class Malay houses looked like in the 1950s.

Pekan Rabu Market

Jalan Tunku Ibrahim

Pekan Rabu Market is one of the busiest in the city, three floors of preserved and fresh food, clothes, handicrafts and household necessities, plus local farm produce. Look for stalls selling **dodol durian**, a sort of black, gooey jam made from the fruit; and "durian cake" a plain mix of pulp and palm sugar.

Wat Nikhrodharam

East of Manara Alor Setar on Jalan Teluk Wanjah

The flamboyant gold gates and painted statuary at **Wat Nikhrodharam** are testimony to the continuing influence of Thai culture in Alor Star, though this modern Buddhist temple seems to attract mainly local Chinese. The big annual event here is **Vesakha** (Buddha's Birthday) in April or May, celebrated by Buddhists of all denominations with a night procession from here through the town.

Muzium Negeri

Jalan Lebuhraya Darulaman, 2km north of the centre • Tues–Thurs, Sat & Sun 10am–6pm, Fri 10am–noon & 3–6pm • Free • any bus north from Jalan Pekan Melayu

Alor Star's **Muzium Negeri** (State Museum) fills in on Kedah's history, including background to the archeological finds at Lembah Bujang (see p.170). A delicate silver tree near the entrance is known as the *bunga mas dan perak* ("the gold and silver flowers"). The name refers to a practice, established in the seventeenth century, of honouring the ruling government of Thailand by a triennial presentation of two small trees of gold and silver, a metre tall, and meticulously detailed down to the birds nesting in their branches

2

ARRIVAL AND DEPARTURE   ALOR STAR

Located close to the E1 and the main west-coast train line, Alor Star is something of a transport hub, with connections to Thailand, KL and Langkawi, as well as most cities on the Peninsula.

BY PLANE
Sultan Abdul Halim Airport is 11km north of town, accessible by the hourly Kepala Batas bus from Shahab Perdana, or by taxi (around RM25). The following have desks at the airport: AirAsia (ⓦ airasia.com), Firefly (ⓦ fireflyz.com.my), Malaysia Airlines (ⓦ malaysiaairlines .com).
Destinations Kuala Lumpur KLIA (3 daily; 1hr); Kuala Lumpur Sultan Abdul Aziz Shah (2 daily; 1hr).

BY TRAIN
Train station A short walk southeast of the centre on Jalan Stesyen.
Destinations Arau (1 daily; 40min); Bangkok (Thailand; 1 daily; 20hr); Butterworth (1 daily; 2hr 45min); Hat Yai (Thailand; daily; 2hr); Ipoh (daily; 8hr); Kuala Kangsar (daily; 6hr); Kuala Lumpur (daily; 12hr); Sungai Petani (daily; 1hr); Taiping (daily; 5hr 20min).

BY BUS
Shahab Perdana Alor Star's main Shahab Perdana express bus station is 5km northwest of the centre, connected to town by city buses (RM1.20) and taxis (RM10). Some buses pass through town first, setting passengers down at the local bus stop (see below).
Destinations Butterworth (2hr); Ipoh (4 daily; 4hr); Johor Bahru (3 daily; 12hr); Kangar (1hr 15min);

Kota Bharu (2 daily; 8hr); Kuala Kedah (15min); Kuala Lumpur (8hr); Kuala Terengganu (2 daily; 9hr); Kuantan (2 daily; 9hr); Melaka (2 daily; 9hr); Seremban (3 daily; 7hr); Singapore (3 daily; 13hr); Sungai Petani (1hr 15min).
Local bus stop Jalan Tunku Ibrahim, opposite the Pekan Rabu market. Some long-distance buses to/from Shahab Perdana also set down or pick up here. It's just an open-air affair with an awning and benches, but no staff, ticket office or timetables – you just wait for buses to appear.
Destinations Kuala Kedah (every 15min; 15min); Naka (for the Ulu Muda Eco Park; hourly; 2hr); Sungai Petani (every 30min; 1hr 15min).

BY FERRY
Kuala Kedah Langkawi ferries (ⓦ langkawi-ferry.com) dock at Kuala Kedah, 12km west of town. Buses shuttle between the port and Shahab Perdana bus station via the local bus stop; a taxi costs around RM20.
Destinations Langkawi (Kuah; 10 daily, 7am–7pm; 1hr 45min; RM23).

BY TAXI
Taxis From the long-distance taxi station south of the Pekan Rabu market, a ride to the main Thai border crossing at Padang Besar costs RM50 per person (2hr).

INFORMATION

Tourist office Inside the 1930s Lower Courthouse, Jalan S.A. Halim (Daily 9am–5pm, varying lunchtime closures; ☎ 04 730 1322). Fairly helpful office, though not amazingly knowledgeable, with plenty of local brochures.

ACCOMMODATION

Bee Garden Motel Lebuhraya Darul Aman, opposite the hospital ☎ 04 733 5355. Institutional in feeling, with multiple floors of identically bare, tiled corridors, but the modern rooms are tidy, clean and a/c, with rock-hard beds and TVs. Wi-fi in lobby. Shared bathroom RM45, en suite RM60
★ **Comfort Motel** 2c Jalan Kampung Perak ☎ 04 734 4866. Clean, cheap, Malay-style wooden house, whose basic doubles come with a/c, TV and bathroom. RM45
Grand Crystal 40 Jalan Kampung Perak ☎ 04 731 3333, ⓦ ghihotels.com.my. 1970s business block wearing its age well, though in a slightly scruffy corner of town given the price. All rooms have a/c, shower and bathtub, there's wi-fi, and breakfast is included. RM115

Grand Jubilee 429 Lebuhan Darulman ☎ 04 733 0055. Friendly, if slightly threadbare, hotel with simple en-suite a/c rooms; a good deal for the price as long as you're not looking for luxury. RM56
Holiday Villa Complex City Plaza, Jalan Tunku Ibrahim ☎ 04 734 9999, ⓦ holidayvillahotelalorstar.com. This spiffy business hotel is by far the most luxurious in town, with views from the upper floors, a gym, spa, satellite TV and several restaurants. RM300
Seberang Perak Lorong Kilang Ais, Jalan Muhamad Saman ☎ 04 772 2288, ✉ ibsoew@yahoo.com. Right behind the Ruhmah Kelahiran Mahathir, this quiet and friendly family-run hotel has small, pink-painted, basic but clean rooms with a/c and attached (Asian) toilets and shower. RM55

EATING

Lot 7 Thai Seafood Jalan Sekerat. Busiest of several open-air food courts in the street; not just Thai stir fries and curries, but also a good amount of Malay and Chinese chow. Fill to bursting for RM10. Daily dawn–9pm.

Pak Hainan Kopitiams Right next to the Bee Garden Motel. This modern coffee house has noodle and rice dishes along with teas, coffees and cakes. Daily 10am–8pm.

Pekan Rabu Market Ground-floor. Daytime food court, known for its fried snacks and kueh, Malay cakes. Daily 8am–late afternoon.

Restoran Bunga Tanjung Baru On the corner of Jalan Pegawai and Jalan Dato Wan Muhamad Saman. Near the Rumah Kelahiran Mahathir, you'll find this restaurant offering South Indian fare. Daily 10am–6pm.

Rose Restaurant Jalan Sultan Badlishah. This South Indian place is best for *nasi lemak* and breakfasts of coffee and *murtabak*, which they make in huge trays and then carve up. They also do a few Chinese dishes, typically costing around RM8. Daily 8am–late afternoon.

Xantana Café Opposite the Grand Crystal, Jalan Kampung Perak. Bar and café with a friendly owner, and a good lunch selection of Chinese and Thai food as well as a popular BBQ outside at night. Daily 11am–3pm & 6–9pm.

Ulu Muda Eco Park

Hidden away in Kedah's northeastern corner, up against a remote section of the Thai border, **Ulu Muda Eco Park** is thick with salt licks, old-growth rainforest and wildlife. As well as birds and reptiles galore, it offers a reasonable chance of encountering elephants and tapir, though sightings of the resident tigers and sun bears are far less likely. The park also encloses a man-made **lake**, Tasik Muda, and the only way in is by boat from **Gubir**, not much more than a jetty and resort 75km east of Alor Star; a two-hour sampan ride from here lands you deep inside the park at the **Earth Lodge Field Research Centre**. Hiking tracks link the lodge to limestone caves, hot springs (which many animals visit early in the morning or at night, when the temperatures drop), and wildlife hides.

Despite the threat of **logging** that hangs over the area, Ulu Muda remains genuinely remote, so getting here is both time-consuming and expensive. The only practical way to see the park is on a **tour**, but if you want to experience less touristed jungle than that at Taman Negara, this might be the place to come. Note that August to December can see heavy **rainfall**, but the park is still accessible; in the dry season, you might have to push your boat over a few sandbanks to reach the lodge.

ARRIVAL AND DEPARTURE
ULU MUDA ECO PARK

By bus and taxi The closest you can get to Gubir by public bus is either Sik, 30km southwest (buses from Sungai Petani), or Naka, 25km northwest (buses from Alor Star). From either of these, you'll need to find a taxi (most likely, just a local with a car) and expect to pay RM50.

By car From Alor Star, take Route K8 through Naka to Gubir – about an hour and a half drive. From Butterworth, take the North–South Expressway and exit at Gurun, taking route K10 to Sik, where you turn onto Route K8 to Gubir.

INFORMATION AND TOURS

Packages As a trip to Ulu Muda requires a bit of planning – you need permits, as well as boats and somewhere to stay – an all-inclusive package organized through one of the following makes everything much simpler. Expect to pay upwards of RM400 per person for a 3-day, 2-night package; you might need a group of four, though solo travellers can always ask about rates.

Earth Lodge Tours ☎ 04 959 4772, ⊛ earthlodgemalaysia .webs.com. As the only accommodation based inside the park, these are probably the best people to contact about organizing a trip.

Ron's Adventures ☎ 04 977 7578 or 019 45 6578, ⊛ ronsadventures@hotmail.com. Ron has been organizing excellent tailor-made trips into Ula Muda for several years, though he can be slow at responding to emails and text messages – or fail completely.

ACCOMMODATION

Earth Lodge ☎ 04 959 4772, ⓦ earthlodgemalaysia .webs.com. Newly renovated and modernized cabins inside the park; you can also camp by arrangement (tents might be available on site). 3-day, 2-night package, per person RM400

Mada Resort ☎ 04 752 1779, ⓦ mada.gov.my. Good, sturdy a/c chalets and one large open dormitory; there's a pool and meals are by prior arrangement. Dorms RM10, doubles RM70

Pulau Langkawi

Situated 30km off the coast, just south of the Thai border, **Pulau Langkawi** is at 500 square kilometres the largest of an archipelago of mostly uninhabited islands. Its white-sand **beaches** are easily the best along the entire west coast of Peninsular Malaysia, and Langkawi's charms consist largely of lazing around on the sand, perhaps taking time off for a **mangrove cruise** after sea eagles, to snorkel or scuba dive south at **Pulau Payar Marine Park**, or to ride the **Langkawi Cable Car** over the interior forests to the top of **Gunung Mat Cincang**.

Once a haven for pirates, Langkawi has in recent years been converted into an upmarket **resort** destination aimed at Saudis and Europeans, complete with its own airport and some of the country's priciest hotels. That said, there's relatively little high-density development, and a growing sprinkle of budget-end accommodation means that the island is fairly affordable for a couple of days, even if your funds are limited. It's also popular with Western **yachties**, as a cheaper place to hang out than Phuket in Thailand – and Langkawi's special **duty-free status** means a case of beer costs only RM25.

There's no reason to stay longer in Langkawi's main port, **Kuah**, than it takes to arrange transport west to the beaches and mid-range developments at **Pantai Tengah** and **Pantai Cenang**, or the exclusive, self-contained resorts scattered around the island's northwest. Well-formed **roads** circuit Langkawi, though with no bus service, exploring further than walking distance from your hotel can be costly. If you are on a budget, don't come anywhere near Langkawi during national or school holidays, when room rates can double.

Kuah

Lining a large sweep of bay in the southeastern corner of the island, **KUAH**, with a population of thirteen thousand, is Langkawi's de facto capital. Down at the south, **Kuah Jetty** is a large complex of cafés, banks and duty-free shops where vessels from the mainland and Thailand dock; beside the ferry terminal **Dataran Lang** – Eagle Square; Langkawi means "red eagle" – is graced by an enormous sculpture of a sea eagle. **Jalan Persiaran Putra** runs north from here for 3km or so – the grey, concrete town on one side, the sea on the other – before heading off around the rest of the island.

Makam Mahsuri

Kampung Mawat • Daily 8am–6pm • RM10

On the highway west out of Kuah, about 10km from town, signs point inland to **Makam Mahsuri**, a flat black tombstone set in pleasant gardens, where the local nineteenth-century heroine Mahsuri was buried after having been falsely accused of adultery and executed. Dying, she is said to have cursed the island, and the next decades were blighted by famine, fires and invasions from Thailand. The story is taken fairly seriously by locals and – for Malays at any rate – the tomb is one of the most famous sights on the island.

Pantai Cenang

Around 18km west from Kuah, **PANTAI CENANG** is Langkawi's main beach, where most of the island's mid-range and budget accommodation options, along with a slew of services and places to eat and shop, are strung along a scruffy 2km stretch of road. Even so, the tourist industry here isn't as in-your-face as you might expect, with generally low-rise development and a fairly relaxed vibe.

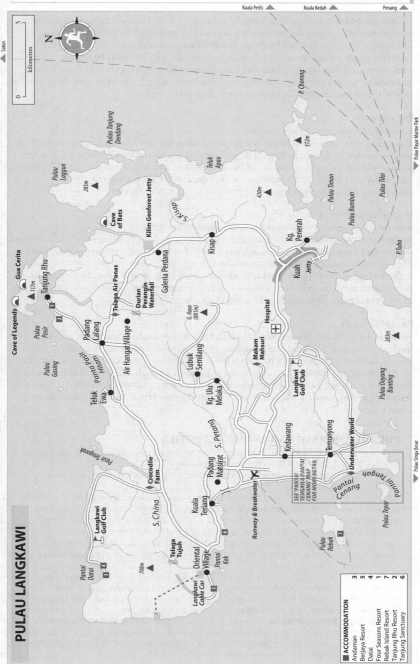

PULAU LANGKAWI

Kuala Perlis ▲   Kuala Kedah ▲   Penang ▲

Satun ▲

N

0   5
kilometres

2

▶ Pulau Payar Marine Park

P. Chorong

372m ▲

Pulau Timon

Pulau Bumbun

Pulau Tiloi

P.Tuba

Pulau Tanjung Dendang

Teluk Apau

420m ▲

S. Kisap

Pulau Laggun

285m ▲

Cave of Bats ◗

Kilim Geoforest Jetty

Kisap ●

Kg. Penerah ●

Kuah

Jetty

283m ▲

Gua Cerita ◗

Cave of Legends ◗

117m ▲

Tanjung Rhu
1

Galeria Perdana ●

Telaga Air Panas

Durian Perangin Waterfall

G. Raya (881m) ▲

Hospital ✚

Pulau Pasir

Pulau Gasing

Padang Lalang

2

Pantai Pasir Hitam

Teluk Ewa ●

Air Hangat Village ●

Lubuk Semilang ●

Kg. Ulu Melaka ●

S. Petang

Makam Mahsuri ▲

Langkawi Golf Club ▲

Kedawang ●

Temonyong ▲

Pulau Dayang Bunting

Pasir Tengkorak

S. China

Crocodile Farm ●

Langkawi Golf Club ▲

Padang Matsirat ●

Kuala Teriang

6

Runway & Breakwater

Underworld ◗

Pantai Cenang

Pantai Tengah

SEE 'PANTAI TENGAH & PANTAI CENANG' MAP FOR MORE DETAIL

▶ Pulau Singa Besar

Pulau Tepor

Pulau Rebak

7

708m ▲

Pantai Datai
3 **4**

Telaga Tujuh

Oriental Village

Pantai Kok

Langkawi Cable Car

5

■ ACCOMMODATION	
Andaman	3
Berjaya Resort	5
Datai	4
Four Seasons Resort	1
Rebak Island Resort	7
Tanjung Rhu Resort	2
Tanjung Sanctuary	6

Cenang's **beach** is beautiful, a long, broad strip of fine white sand, busy all day with people strolling, sitting out, swimming and arranging paragliding or jet-ski rides. Offshore, the view is framed by **Pulau Rebak Besar**, a decent-sized island with an exclusive resort tucked away on its south side (see p.182). At dusk, beachside restaurants and bars set up tables and turn on their fairy lights and sound systems, somewhere to enjoy the sunset over a cold drink and a feed. Just note that there may be **jellyfish** in the water, so take local advice before you swim.

Rice museum

Northern end of Pantai Cenang • Daily 10am–6pm • Free

The rather deserted **rice museum** is a good idea that nobody knows what to do with. A small complex housing a herb garden, gallery and restaurant looks over acres of green paddy fields, populated by ducks, buffalo scarecrows and mud; you may be able to get a personal tour which provides a hands-on experience with traditional planting equipment and even gives you the opportunity to get your feet wet.

Underwater World

On the low headland that separates Pantai Cenang from Pantai Tengah • Daily 10am–6pm • RM38

Underwater World claims to be the largest aquarium in Asia, housing over five thousand marine and freshwater fish. Although the attached duty-free shopping complex seems like the main reason for the operation, the fish are well presented, the highlight being a walk-through tunnel where sharks, turtles and hundreds of other sea creatures swim around and above boggle-eyed visitors in a transparent tunnel. There's also a touch pool where you can get feely with starfish, sea slugs and sea cucumbers.

Pantai Tengah

South of Underwater World, **PANTAI TENGAH** is a quieter, less developed and less focused version of Cenang; the 2km-long beach here isn't quite as nice either, with coarser sand and occasionally **rough surf** – in September and October the waves can get as high as 4m, though usually the sea is tranquil enough. All this means, of course, that there are fewer people about, which can be a bonus. **Island cruises** leave from a couple of **jetties** about 1.5km south of Tengah; operators will tell you where to go when you book.

PULAU LANGKAWI TOURS AND ACTIVITIES

Operators based at Panati Cenang and elsewhere offer a wide range of tours around Langkawi; the price for non-beach activities often includes pick-up.

On the beach, a couple of **watersport operators** charge about RM60 for paragliding, or RM120 for 30min on a jet ski.

Accommodation and main road agencies can book you on **mangrove cruises** (5hr; RM60 per person; see p.180); and **island-hopping boat trips** (4hr; RM25 per person) to forested Pregnant Maiden Island (Pulau Dayang Bunting), whose crater lake is good for swimming, Singa Besar for eagle feeding, and Beras Basah for beach and clear water.

For a **sunset cruise** or fishing trip contact Crystal Yacht (Ⓦ crystalyacht.com); they're upmarket but you get superb treatment, with all drinks and a generous barbecue seafood meal included.

If it's **wildlife** you're after, the very professional Dev's Adventure Tours (Ⓦ langkawi-nature .com; RM120–220) offer guided cycling trips, birding, mangrove tours (by boat or kayak), and evening jungle treks after the bizarre *colugo*, a sort of cross between a fruitbat and a squirrel. Minimum numbers are required, but they often tag solo travellers onto existing trips if running.

Pulau Payar Marine Reserve is the place to head for **snorkelling and scuba diving**; south of Langkawi, halfway to Penang, it features seasonally clear water and colourful fish life including giant potato cod. The best operator is East Marine (Ⓦ eastmarine.com.my; RM350), though agents in Pantai Cenang offer cheaper deals.

Northwest Langkawi

Up the coast from Pantai Cenang, past the **airport**, Langkawi's northwestern corner holds the island's two major attractions – the **Langkawi Cable Car** and cascades at **Telaga Tujuh**. Unless you're staying nearby (the island's best hotels are up here), don't bother with the local **beaches**, however – the Cenang – Tengah stretch is far superior.

Langkawi Cable Car

Oriental Village Shopping Complex · Daily 9.30am–7pm · RM30 return; Segway RM30 per hour

Much of Langkawi's northwest is untouched rainforest, with **Gunung Mat Cinang** rising a modest 710m above the treetops. At its base, the tourist-trap Oriental Village Shopping Complex is worth a stop for two things: to hire a **Segway** stand-up scooter with chunky tyres and zip through the rainforest on a special track; and to ride the magnificent **Langkawi Cable Car** up the mountain. With a 42-degree incline, this is not only the steepest such ride in the world, it also boasts the longest free span for a mono-cable car; a thrilling 950m long, great for eagle spotting. At the end, a superb **canopy walkway** overlooks the forest treetops with a spectacular view over the Andaman Sea; on a clear day you can see several Thai islands in the distance.

Incidentally, do **not** follow hiking tracks down the mountain from the cable car's upper station; the trails are unmaintained and people have become permanently lost attempting them.

Telaga Tujuh

Parking RM2

A couple of kilometres past the Langkawi Cable Car turning, the main road terminates at the entrance to **Telaga Tujuh** (literally, "Seven Pools"), a cascading freshwater stream that has pounded large recesses into the rock, forming several pools down a slope. During the rainy season, the slipperiness of the moss covering the rock in between the pools helps you slide from one pool to another, before

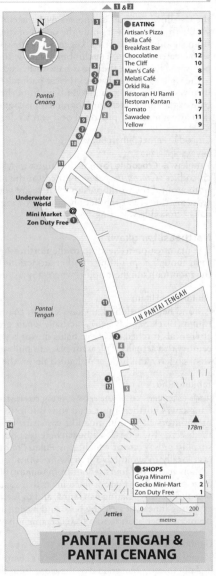

● EATING

Artisan's Pizza	3
Bella Café	4
Breakfast Bar	5
Chocolatine	12
The Cliff	10
Man's Café	8
Melati Café	6
Orkid Ria	2
Restoran HJ Ramli	1
Restoran Kantan	13
Tomato	7
Sawadee	11
Yellow	9

● SHOPS

Gaya Minami	3
Gecko Mini-Mart	2
Zon Duty Free	1

PANTAI TENGAH & PANTAI CENANG

■ ACCOMMODATION

AB Motel	9	Sandy Beach Resort	8
Beach Garden Resort	5	Sweet Inn	6
Bon Ton	1	Temple Tree	2
Casa del Mar	4	Zackry Guest House	13
Delta Motel	11		
Frangipani	12	**■ DRINKING & NIGHTLIFE**	
Langkapuri Inn	10	Babylon Mat Lounge	1
Meritus Pelangi Beach	3	Chillout Bar	4
Rainbow Lodge	7	Debbie's Irish Pub	2, 3
Rebak Island Resort	14	Sunba Retro Bar	5

the fast-flowing water disappears over the cliff to form the 90m-high **waterfall** that's visible from below – it's only the depth of the water in the last pool that prevents you from shooting off the end. Legends say the spot is the playground of mountain fairies, who created the *sintuk* (a climbing plant with enormous pods) that grows around these pools; the locals use them as a hair wash, said to rinse away bad luck.

The walk to the pools from the car park takes about 45 minutes, the last stage of which involves a steep 200m-high climb up from the inevitable cluster of souvenir stalls at the base of the hill. Watch for long-tailed **macaques** on the trail; they are playful, but can display aggression if provoked or if you are (or look like you are) carrying food.

Crocodile Farm (Taman Buaya)

Daily 9am–6pm • RM20

Langkawi's **Crocodile Farm** is the largest in Malaysia, with around 1500 saltwater crocodiles (*Crocodilus porosus*) raised for the handbag trade, and various other species from around the world on show. There are youngsters, some enormous adults (saltwater crocs are the largest reptiles on earth, growing to over 5m in length), feeding shows and daily "crocodile wrestling".

Northeast Langkawi

The main reason to head up to the northeast part of Langkawi is to take a **mangrove tour**, though a sprinkling of other attractions include craft galleries and **Gunung Raya**, the mountain's highest point, where a road runs to the summit.

Pantai Pasir Hitam

Around halfway along Langkawi's north coast, the colour of the beach at **Pantai Pasir Hitam** (Black Sand Beach) – actually a pale grey – is said to have been caused by ash, after locals torched their rice fields during a war with the Thais in the eighteenth century. It's actually a pleasant place to pull up for a few minutes, with a traditional wooden jetty and little craft hauled up on the gently sloping shoreline.

Tanjung Rhu

Mangrove tour charters RM250–500 per eight-seater boat, depending on itinerary, cash only

Langkawi's northernmost road runs out to the tip of **Tanjung Rhu**, a 4km-long promontory fringed in pine-like casuarina trees, which make a gentle sighing noise in the breeze. The west-coast **beach** here is good, well sheltered and overlooking several small islands – one of which, tiny **Pulau Chabang**, can be reached on foot at low tide (ask locally to avoid having to swim 500m back to shore if the tide comes in).

Many **mangrove tours** set out from **Tanjung Rhu Jetty** at the road's end to explore the maze of muddy, mangrove-lined inlets that sprawl east. Tours inevitably include stops at one of the many floating **fish farms**, and to **feed fish eagles**; add-ons also spend time exploring limestone caves by boat, and having a swim. You can organize a tour on the spot; payment is per boat, so solo travellers might have to join an existing tour.

Gunung Raya

Reached off the road through Langkawi's centre, **Gunung Raya** (881m) is topped by a **lookout tower**. On a good day, the views from the island's apex, down over jungle to the coast, rival those seen from the cable car (see p.179). Note that the twisting 7km access track is too steep for some rental vehicles – check with the agent if you plan to drive up here.

Galeria Perdana

Gallery daily 8.30am–5.30pm • RM10

Galeria Perdana contains over ten thousand state gifts and awards presented to former PM Mahathir – an eclectic collection ranging from African woodcarvings to Japanese ceramics. It sits close to the short access road northeast to **Kilim Geoforest jetty**, another departure point for **mangrove tours** with the same features as those available at Tanjung Rhu.

ARRIVAL AND DEPARTURE   PULAU LANGKAWI

Agents at Kuah's ferry terminal and along the main road at Pantai Cenang, and also most hotels, can make travel bookings, including combined ferry-bus transfers to a dozen destinations in Thailand. The nearest consulate where you can get a Thai visa is in Penang (see p.162).

BY PLANE

Airport Langkawi Airport is halfway up the west coast, 5km north of Pantai Cenang and 20km by road from Kuah. A taxi to Cenang or Tengah costs RM20; ask hotels elsewhere what fare to expect. AirAsia, Firefly and Malaysia Airlines have desks at the airport.
Destinations Kuala Lumpur (3 daily; 1hr); Penang (1 daily; 45min); Singapore (1 daily; 1hr 30min).

BY FERRY

Ferry terminal Langkawi's ferry terminal (ⓦ langkawi-ferry.com) is at Kuah Jetty, on the island's southeastern tip. A taxi to Cenang or Tengah costs RM25.
Destinations Kuala Kedah (10 daily; 1hr 30min; RM23); Kuala Perlis (18 daily; 1hr; RM18); Penang (2 daily; 2hr 30min; RM60); Satun in Thailand (3 daily; 1hr 30min; RM30). Book Penang tickets a day in advance; the others are only available on day of departure.

GETTING AROUND

There's a circuit road around Langkawi, with various branches up to the northwest and through the centre. Almost all are sealed, and there's a veritable expressway between Kuah and Pantai Cenang. As Langkawi is barely 25km across at its widest point, even a comprehensive tour of the island is likely to be under 100km. With no public bus service, however, to get around you'll need a taxi, or to rent a vehicle.

By taxi Taxis run on set fares; for example, Kuah Jetty to Pantai Cenang costs RM25, while a four-hour taxi tour of the island runs to around RM100 per vehicle. There are stands at Kuah Jetty ferry terminal and Pantai Cenang.
Vehicle rental Rental agents at arrival points and – for better rates – at Pantai Cenang. The very cheapest car

– tiny-engined, slightly battered automatics – will set you back RM60 a day; include insurance and manual transmission and you're looking at RM80; something able to tackle the Gunung Raya road will cost upwards of RM100. Scooters, motorbikes or bicycles all cost around RM18 a day.

INFORMATION

Langkawi tourist office Jalan Persiaran Putera, near the mosque in downtown Kuah, has helpful staff who can advise about all activities (daily 9am–5pm; ☎ 04 966

7789). There are also less useful desks at the airport and Kuah Jetty (daily 8am–6pm); all hand out maps of the island.

ACCOMMODATION

Pulau Langkawi being one of Malaysia's major resort areas, it's always advisable to book accommodation in advance, especially at the cheaper end of things. The bulk of the island's accommodation – including all its budget options – is spread along the 4km stretch between Pantai Cenang and Pantai Tengah, with the highest concentration at northerly Cenang.

PANTAI CENANG AND PANTAI TENGAH

★ **AB Motel** Pantai Cenang ☎ 04 955 1300, ⊚ abmotel@hotmail.com. Rooms in beachside motel or cheaper, a/c, self-contained cabins inland across the road. It's all a bit plain, what with concrete and tiling everywhere, but very clean and a good deal for Langkawi. Beachside RM120, otherwise RM80
Beach Garden Resort Pantai Cenang ☎ 04 955 1363, ⓦ beachgardenresort.com. Rustic, comfortable chalets tightly grouped inside an attractive tropical garden of palms, gingers and bamboo. There's a

small swimming pool and a restaurant on the beach. RM250
★ **Bon Ton/Temple Tree** On the shore road 2km north of Pantai Cenang, ☎ 04 955 3643, ⓦ bontonresort .com.my, or ⓦ templetree.com.my. Adjacent sections of the same resort. The *Bon Ton* comprises traditional kampung-style Malay wooden housing, with a small pool and large, open-sided lounge and dining area in a similar style; *Temple Tree* features modern, colonial-style villas. Service and food are impeccable. It all overlooks a lily-fringed lagoon, rich in birdlife. *Bon Ton* RM590, *Temple Tree* RM990

2

★ **Casa del Mar** ☎ 04 955 2388, ⊛ casadelmar-langkawi.com. Intimate, comfortably scaled boutique resort, with terracotta tiling, wooden furnishings, pool, spa and gardens. It's popular with couples; packages offer meals, spa treatment, massage and drinks. RM800

Delta Motel Pantai Cenang ☎ 04 955 1307. Closely spaced, two-person wooden chalets with fans, a/c and TV, in a shady garden right by the beach. Larger motel-style rooms have a/c and sea views. The restaurant serves local food (no alcohol allowed). Chalets RM60, rooms RM120

Frangipani Langkawi Resort and Spa Pantai Tengah ☎ 04 952 0000, ⊛ frangipanilangkawi.com. Pleasant, kampung-style resort in a garden setting. The accommodation is in well-designed, two-storey chalets with all the trimmings. There's a pool and a seaside restaurant. RM400

Langkapuri Inn Pantai Cenang ☎ 04 955 1202. Concrete motel chalets with tiled interiors and tiny verandas, all with a/c, satellite TV and hot showers; there's an on-site spa and restaurant. Not many frills, but you are literally on the beach. RM140

Meritus Pelangi Beach Pantai Cenang ☎ 04 952 8888, ⊛ meritushotels.com. Two-storey timber chalets, echoing traditional Malay architecture, among beachside flower and palm gardens; there's a pool, spa, mini-golf course and a beachside grill restaurant. All rooms have views, though not necessarily by the beach. RM1000

★ **Rainbow Lodge** Pantai Cenang ☎ 04 955 5991, ⊛ rainbowlangkawi.com. Set beside a paddy field, 5min walk from the beach, this peaceful and friendly place offers basic but pleasant dorms, plus doubles with fans and bathrooms. There is a little café with a bar for socializing. Long-term rates available. Dorms RM20, doubles RM35

Rebak Island Resort Pulau Rebak Besar, offshore from Pantai Cenang ☎ 04 966 5566, ⊛ tajhotels.com. Reached from Langasuka Port, 5km north of Pantai Cenang near the airport, this upmarket hotel offers Malay-style villas and suites (all with garden or sea views), with plenty of polished wooden floors. The attached marina is one of the busiest yacht harbours in Langkawi. Online deals slash rates. RM600

★ **Sandy Beach Resort** Pantai Cenang ☎ 04 955 1308, ⊛ langkawisandybeachresort.com. Skip the cheaper cabins over the road and go for the beachside A-frames, tin-roofed chalets with a/c, TV and showers, where a hearty breakfast is included. It's nothing lavish, but a very good deal for the price and staff are welcoming. Chalets RM160

Sweet Inn Pantai Cenang ☎ 04 955 8864. This 22-room complex about 200m inland is run by a hospitable Muslim family with a liking for cats. The spotless rooms are tiled and come with bathrooms, TV and a/c, and there's a

communal patio downstairs. Breakfast is included, meals available at the café through the day. RM80

Zackry Guest House Pantai Tengah ⊜ zackryghouse @gmail.com. Quiet backpacker place with well-maintained cabins surrounded by rainforest shrubs and bamboo; the atmosphere is laidback but it's well organized and managed, with helpful staff (and three dogs). Bookings by email only. Dorms RM20, fan doubles with shared bathroom RM45, a/c en suite RM65

NORTHWEST

Andaman Teluk Datai at Langkawi's extreme northwest corner ☎ 04 959 1088, ⊛ theandaman.com. The "downmarket" wing of the adjacent *Datai*, this is a large, comfortable, self-contained resort, set in thick rainforest above the beach. Facilities include a spa and handful of restaurants. Most rooms come with balconies, and suites feature sea views. RM1000

Berjaya Langkawi Beach and Spa Resort At the end of the road past the cable car ☎ 04 959 1888, ⊛ berjayaresorts.com.my. Attractive wood-frame pole cabins set amid rainforest, and an ugly batch of red-roofed concrete lookalikes out over the sea. Facilities are good in both, with smart furnishings, balconies, a/c and en-suite bathrooms. Package deals include meals. RM900

★ **The Datai** Teluk Datai, at Langkawi's extreme northwest corner ☎ 04 959 2500, ⊛ thedatai.com.my. The quintessential luxury retreat, built of timber and volcanic rock and surrounded by rainforest. The views across the bay to Thailand are stunning, as is the price. The restaurant is open to non-guests, but the rest of the facilities are not. RM1500

Tanjung Sanctuary Langkawi Jalan Pantai Kok ☎ 04 955 2977, ⊛ tanjungsanctuary.com.my. Set on a forested rocky headland with its own private beach, plus a swimming pool and a restaurant built on stilts over the water. Non-guests aren't allowed near the place, so solitude is guaranteed. RM850

TANJUNG RHU

Four Seasons Resort Langkawi Tanjung Rhu ☎ 04 950 8888, ⊛ fourseasons.com/langkawi. Superbly stylish retreat, with a mix of cabins and villas surrounded by gardens, just moments from the beach. There's a pool, spa, gym and countless activities to keep children entertained. RM2000

Tanjung Rhu Resort Tanjung Rhu ☎ 04 959 1033, ⊛ tanjungrhu.com.my. Extremely well-designed rooms set this resort apart; though none is small, all seem larger than they actually are. Plenty of wooden floors, teak furnishings and balconies; the pricier end of things includes sea views. There is, of course, a spa as well as two pools, one including a bar. RM1500

EATING

Food on Langkawi is varied – you can find Malay, Middle Eastern, Indian, Chinese and Western – and generally expensive; expect to pay at least RM30 for a restaurant meal, more at a resort. Beach bars also serve meals, usually Malay and Chinese fast food, Western-style burgers and the like.

Artisan's Pizza Pantai Cenang. Popular shack with a couple of tables only, as they concentrate on takeaway (or free local delivery). Aside from 11" pizzas (RM30), they also turn out great cheeseburgers (RM13.50) and fish and chips (RM20). Daily 10am–2am.

Bella Café Pantai Cenang. One of the cheapest options in town, with tin roof and unmarked except for a "roti canai" sign outside in the mornings. Straightforward Malay breakfasts and sandwiches; you can get a portion of *nasi ayam* for just RM3.50. Daily 9am–6pm.

Breakfast Bar Pantai Cenang. Friendly place with some outdoor seating serving sandwiches, pancakes, baguettes and Western breakfasts. RM15 for a one-plate meal plus coffee. Daily 8am–10pm.

★ **Chocolatine** Pantai Tengah. Gem of a French patisserie and bistro, where just having a coffee is an experience, thanks to their pain au chocolat, amadine and chocolate eclairs, all baked on the premises. The goat's cheese salad with walnuts and raisins is pretty special too. Coffee and cake about RM25. Daily 10am–6pm.

★ **The Cliff** At the end of the lane beside the aquarium ☎ 04 953 3228, ⓦ thecliflangkawi.com. Nice modern Malay-fusion restaurant with ocean views, built out on piles over the water, with the surf crashing beneath. Lobster served various ways (RM60), house specials such as *ayam tok janggui* (chicken and prawns in a spicy sauce, RM48) or plain steak (RM80). Atmospheric place just for a coffee and strudel too (RM35). Bookings advisable. Daily 11am–11pm.

Man's Café Pantai Tengah. Bright and friendly restaurant serving inexpensive Thai dishes, including excellent prawn *tom yam* (RM15), plus plenty of fried fish, prawn and squid options. A full meal here shouldn't cost more than RM25. Daily noon–2pm & 5.30–10pm.

Melati Café Pantai Cenang. Opens around 7am for mugs of good strong coffee, and RM15 breakfasts of eggs, toast and fruit salad. Daily 7am–mid-afternoon.

★ **Orkid Ria** Pantai Cenang. Chinese place serving fresh seafood grilled, steamed, fried or however you want it, dished up among noisy, cheerful crowds in an alfresco environment. Huge tiger prawns (RM16/100g), lobster (RM18/100g) and whole crab (RM7/100g) are some of the best you'll find in town. Daily 11am–3pm & 6–11pm.

Tomato Pantai Cenang. Indian-run *nasi kandar* restaurant, best for their tasty RM15 tandoori chicken and naan; service is offhand though, and little details – the relish and sliced onions – which would normally be included are missing. Daily 10am–9pm.

Restoran HJ Ramli Pantai Cenang. An open-sided barn with minimum fixtures and relatively low prices; they do reliable staples (*nasi campur*, *nasi ayam* etc) and decent steamboats and grilled fish, for around RM35. Daily 8am–late afternoon.

★ **Restoran Kantan** Pantai Tengah. In a wooden Malay-style building, raised off the ground on stilts, this smart place is unusual for serving good-quality Malay food at reasonable prices: rendang, *ayam percik*, hot-and-sour Nonya fish, seafood and even some street snacks like *ikan bilis* and *cendol*. Mains around RM24. Daily 11.30am–3pm & 6–10pm.

Sawadee Pantai Tengah. Pleasant Thai place, decked in painted rattan matting and specializing in seafood, though the menu stretches to duck, chicken and even deer. Mains RM15–40. Daily noon–2pm & 5.30–10pm.

Yellow Pantai Cenang. Beach bar-café, good for a sundowner and swing in the hammocks, with smarter adjacent restaurant serving expensive "surf and turf" meals featuring imported Australian steak (RM70). Daily 10am–10pm.

DRINKING AND NIGHTLIFE

The staple soundtracks at Cenang's handful of beach bars are from the Eagles, Beatles, Eric Clapton and Bob Marley back catalogue, either CDs or covered by competent live bands. The cheapest place for a drink is your room, given that a duty-free bottle of beer cost RM1.40, and a litre of spirits RM40. Don't consume your own alcohol in public – Langkawi is laidback, but this is still a Muslim country.

Babylon Mat Lounge Pantai Cenang. A popular beachfront bar and café, serving snacks, burgers and cocktails with downbeat music. Daily 6pm–late.

Chillout Sports Bar Pantai Cenang. Dark open-fronted place set back off the road, with pool table, dartboard and huge TV screen. Happy hour, with half-priced drinks, daily 8–11pm. Daily 6pm–late.

Debbie's Irish Pub Pantai Cenang. Lively little nooks in two locations, both with Guinness, Gaymers cider and TV screens for watching soccer matches. They also serve Irish stew, pasta and chips. Daily 6pm–late.

Sunba Retro Bar Pantai Tengah. Currently the only real club on the Canang–Tengah strip, a moderately intimate place where DJs generally play easy listening or dance music, and there's sometimes a live reggae band. Daily 7pm–2am.

DIRECTORY

KUAH

Money There are ATMs at the Kuah Jetty ferry terminal, and banks in Kuah town – the only place you'll find either on the island. Pantai Cenang's main street is thick with moneychangers.

Post office Main road; Sat–Mon 9am–5pm.

Shopping The Kuah Jetty ferry terminal is one big duty-free mall, mostly dealing in trinkets.

PANTAI TENGAH AND PANTAI CENANG

Books A couple of secondhand bookshops towards the north end of Cenang sell a well-thumbed collection of airport-bought stock from RM15, perfect for the beach.

Internet Most mini-markets also provide internet terminals.

Shopping Stores line the Pantai Cenang road, selling batik beachware, sunglasses and colourful rattan baskets; for more upmarket souvenirs, try Galla Minami at Pantai Tengah, a Japanese-run store with home furnishings, batik sarongs, *songket* cloth, woodware and Dyak earrings. The Zon duty-free barn next to the aquarium is stocked with more clothes, scent, booze and souvenirs. The best of the many family-run supermarkets selling snacks, basic supplies, toiletries and power adapters is Gecko Mini Mart down towards Pantai Tengah, which also has a small cache of imported butter and cheese.

Kuala Perlis

Despite being the second largest settlement in Perlis, the little coastal town of **KUALA PERLIS**, 45km northwest of Alor Star, has only two streets. The **bus station** is on one and the other winds up 100m away at the **ferry port**, with connections to Langkawi. Try not to overnight here – you shouldn't need to, as ferries run until 7pm – as there are no banks and not much in the way of food, entertainment or accommodation.

ARRIVAL AND DEPARTURE   KUALA PERLIS

By bus Six daily buses run to Kuala Lumpur (10hr); there are better long-distance connections from Kangar, just 15km west (30min).

By ferry Arriving from Langkawi (16 daily, 7am–7pm; no advance bookings; 1hr 15min; RM18; ⓦ langkawi-ferry .com), exit the ferry terminal and the bus station is directly ahead, though you have to walk around the buildings in between.

ACCOMMODATION AND EATING

In case you get stuck, there are a few places to stay around the port, though the cheaper options are grotty. Food stalls set up along here at dusk.

T Hotel 45 Persiaran Putra Timur, 200m heading left from the ferry port ⓞ 04 985 3888, ⓦ thotel.com.my. Neatly tiled, cell-like rooms in a purpose-built block with cable TV, wi-fi, a/c and en-suite facilities. **RM90**

Kangar and Around

KANGAR, the Perlis state capital, is an unremarkable town whose compact city centre, a shabby mix of old shophouses and concrete box architecture focused around the **Kangar Square D'Mara shopping complex**, sits immediately north of the little **Sungai Perlis**. It's really only somewhere to change buses, most likely if you're heading between the Thai border and Langkawi. About 10km east, **ARAU** is the least interesting of all Malaysia's royal towns – the Royal Palace on the main road is closed to the public and looks like little more than a comfortable mansion – but it's the nearest **train station** to Kangar.

ARRIVAL AND DEPARTURE   KANGAR AND AROUND

BY TRAIN

Train station The nearest station to Kangar is 10km east in Arau.

Destinations Alor Star (2 daily; 40min); Bangkok (1 daily; 19hr); Butterworth (1 daily; 3hr 10min); Hat Yai (Thailand; 2 daily; 2hr 30min); Ipoh (1 daily; 7hr); Kuala Kangsar (1 daily; 5hr 40min); Kuala Lumpur (1 daily; 21hr 30min); Padang Besar (2 daily; 40min); Sungai Petani (2 daily; 2hr); Taiping (1 daily; 5hr).

BY BUS

Express station Express services to and from Kangar stop just south of the river and the city centre.

Destinations Alor Star (1hr 15min); Butterworth (2hr 30min); Ipoh (3 daily; 6hr); Kota Bahru (2 daily; 8hr); Kuala Lumpur (6 daily; 8hr); Kuala Perlis (every 45min; 30min); Melaka (2 daily; 9hr); Padang Besar (2hr).

Local station Kangar's local bus station is 1km north of the express station, under the multistorey Perlis Bowl building.

Destinations Alor Star (hourly 9.15am–2.30pm; 1hr 15min); Kaki Bukit (4 daily; 2hr); Kuala Perlis (7 daily; 30min).

TO THAILAND

The border crossings at Padang Besar, 30km northeast of Kangar, where the rail line enters Thailand and there's also a road crossing, and Bukit Kayu Hitam, 20km southeast in Kedah on Route E1, which runs up the west coast all the way from Kuala Lumpur, are both open 6am–10pm.

By train At Padang Besar, a very long platform connects the Malaysian service with its Thai counterpart. Though you don't change trains, you must get off and go through customs. One service runs daily in each direction between Butterworth and Bangkok, and another between KL and Hat Yai – see ⓦ ktmb.com.my.

By bus Regular buses from both border crossings go to Hat Yai, southern Thailand's transport hub, 60km away. Travelling by bus or taxi via Padang Besar, you have to get off before the border and cross the 2km of no-man's-land on foot or by taxi (RM30–50 each way).

ACCOMMODATION

Ban Cheong 79 Jalan Kangar (street labelled Jalan Penjara) ⓣ04 976 1184. The usual elderly but well-maintained rooms in this family-run hotel; a/c en suites as well as cheaper doubles with fan and shared bathroom. Doubles with fan <u>RM38</u>, en suite <u>RM60</u>

Kangar 16 Jalan Penjara, above KFC ⓣ04 976 7225. Family-run, low-frills guesthouse featuring a range of rooms with fans, a/c and shared bathrooms. <u>RM60</u>

The interior

THE JUNGLE RAILWAY

The interior

Peninsula Malaysia's interior comprises a vast swathe of territory, stretching northeast of Kuala Lumpur all the way up to Kota Bharu on the east coast. Until recent times this was a remote region of steep, sandstone peaks with knife-edge ridges and luxuriant valleys inhabited by Orang Asli groups. Colonial administrator Hugh Clifford described the terrain in the 1880s as "smothered in deep, damp forest, threaded across a network of streams and rivers." Indeed, rivers were the sole means of transportation until prospectors, investors and planters opened the interior up through the twentieth century; companies built the earliest roads and a railway arrived in the 1920s, helping to establish the townships of Temerloh, Gua Musang and Kuala Lipis.

3

Much of the interior has now been logged, settled and tamed, though Clifford's deep, damp forests survive in the dense chunk of undeveloped jungle that is **Taman Negara** (literally "National Park"). Gazetted as Malaysia's **first national park** in 1925 and covering 4343 square kilometres, Taman Negara forms by far the largest tract of rainforest in Peninsular Malaysia; it contains some of the **oldest rainforest** in the world, which has evolved over 130 million years as a home for a fabulous array of wildlife. Some of the Peninsula's one thousand **Batek** Orang Asli live here too, many as hunter-gatherers; the park authorities generally turn a blind eye to their hunting game.

Reached via the transport nexus of **Jerantut**, Taman Negara's main entry point, the riverside township **Kuala Tahan**, is the trailhead for jungle hikes lasting from anywhere between a few minutes and two weeks. With so much to see here, it's easy to overlook the rest of the region, but outside the park you can ride the "**Jungle Railway**" north through the interior, touching on lesser known sections of wilds – caves and waterfalls at **Kenong Rimba State Park**; remoter areas of Taman Negara at **Merapoh** and **Kuala Koh**; and more forest, waterfalls and views at **Stong State Park**.

GETTING AROUND

By bus Buses along Route 8 and the East Coast Highway can get you within range of all the main sights, but remoter corners require the help of your own vehicle, taxis or local tour operators.

By car Route 8, the interior's main artery, runs for 500km from Bentong near KL to Kota Bharu. It's a relatively old road, not a multi-lane highway, so expect to be periodically slowed behind ponderous lorries. The quickest way to reach Route 8 from KL is the E8 (the Karak Highway), a roller coaster of a road that careers through the foothills of the Genting Highlands northeast of KL. Expect a few thrilling, cambered descents – and be warned that there are often nasty accidents, too. The E8 also connects onto the East Coast Highway, crossing the interior from KL to Kuantan.

THE SUNGAI TAHAN

Highlights

❶ Taman Negara via Kuala Tahan The Peninsula's largest and oldest nature reserve offers river trips, hikes and wildlife spotting amid a vast tract of ancient rainforest, best visited via the park headquarters at Kuala Tahan. **See p.191**

❷ The jungle railway Ride the train across the interior past country villages, fruit and oil plantations, and – between Kuala Lipis and Gua Musang – patches of rainforest. **See p.206**

❸ Kenong Rimba A barely developed reserve adjoining Taman Negara, offering its own trekking and wildlife spotting opportunities. **See p.207**

❹ Taman Negara via Kuala Koh Though isolated, Kuala Koh is worth the effort of reaching: this is Kuala Tahan in miniature, rewarding visitors with trails, river excursions and a canopy walkway. **See p.213**

❺ Stong State Park In the interior of Kelantan State, Stong boasts a picturesque waterfall, good trekking up a mountainside and a marvellous jungle camp. **See p.214**

HIGHLIGHTS ARE MARKED ON THE MAP ON P.190

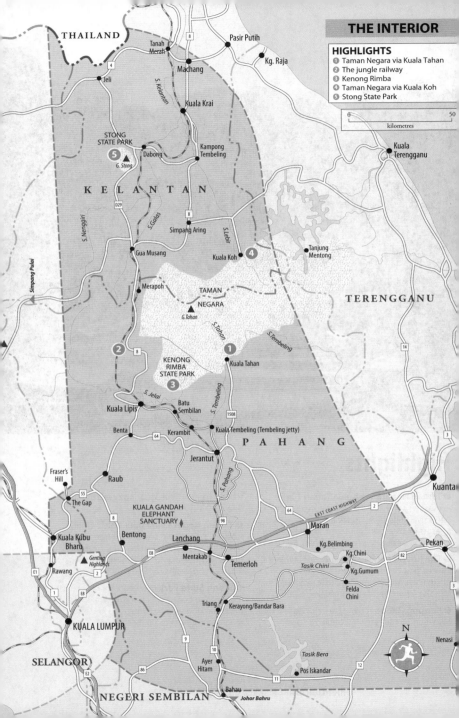

THE ORANG ASLI

The twentieth-century spread of the timber, rubber and palm-oil industries through the interior had a huge impact upon the region's **Orang Asli**, who were traditionally nomadic peoples living by hunting and slash-and-burn agriculture. These days many have been forced to settle down, existing at the fringes of the cash economy (a transition steered in large part by the government's Department of Orang Asli Affairs). The mountain-dwelling **Temiar**, for instance, trade in forest products such as herbal medicines and, increasingly, **timber** (though their logging activities are minimal compared with those of the State Forestry Department). Some **Batek** do still live fairly traditional lives at Taman Negara, where you might meet shy groups walking in single file along forest trails, or come across their temporary vine-and-forest-brush shelters in jungle clearings.

However, three-quarters of Orang Asli peoples (including many local Batek, **Senoi** and **Semang**) live below the poverty line, compared to less than a tenth of the population as a whole. That fact makes it all the harder for them to confront the many forces, from planning agencies to Christian and Muslim groups, who seek to influence their destiny. The issue of **land rights** is among their gravest problems, for while the country's Aboriginal People's Act has led to the creation of Orang Asli reserves, at the same time many Asli traditional areas have been gazetted as state land, rendering the inhabitants there, at best, tolerated guests of the government.

Taman Negara: Kuala Tahan

The main gateway to Taman Negara, the township of **Kuala Tahan**, 250km northeast of KL, is the location of the **national park headquarters** and the pick of its visitor facilities. It's also where to get your bearings and seek advice before crossing the Tembeling River and heading into the forest: well-marked **trails** include relatively easy strolls along boardwalks to hilltops and a treetop canopy walk; tougher day-treks out to caves and hides overlooking salt licks in the jungle; or a ten-day return ascent of **Gunung Tahan**, Peninsular Malaysia's highest peak, involving steep climbs, river crossings and camping rough. If you've never been inside tropical rainforest before, just listening to the bird, insect and animal sounds, marvelling at the sheer size of the trees and peering into a tangled understorey of palms, flowering lianas, luminous fungi and giant bamboo is a memorable experience. You don't have to go far to encounter **wildlife** either; monkeys, elephant, tapir, mouse deer, seladang (wild oxen) and a host of smaller creatures can be found – with a dash of luck – within minutes of Kuala Tahan's ranger station. If you're not a hard-core hiker or wildlife spotter, you could also take advantage of opportunities for a river swim, low-key rafting or even angling.

Kuala Tahan is reached via the service town of **Jerantut**, somewhere to shop for supplies and change transport. Note that you can also enter Taman Negara further north at **Merapoh** (see p.211) and **Kuala Koh** (p.213) – or even hike to either from Kuala Tahan in a ten-day traverse of the park. Both require more effort to reach and have fewer facilities, but they're also less crowded than Kuala Tahan – though not necessarily easier places to see wildlife.

Jerantut

In bustling **JERANTUT**, 50km south of Kuala Tahan, road, rail and river converge in a small grid of streets. Activity revolves around the central, open-air **bus station**, set among market stalls close to most of the businesses, with the **train station** 500m west and **Tembeling Jetty**, for traffic upriver to Kuala Tahan, a short taxi ride north. And that's about it; the town is just somewhere to find last-minute supplies, top up with **cash** (there are no banks at Kuala Tahan), and have a feed before heading out.

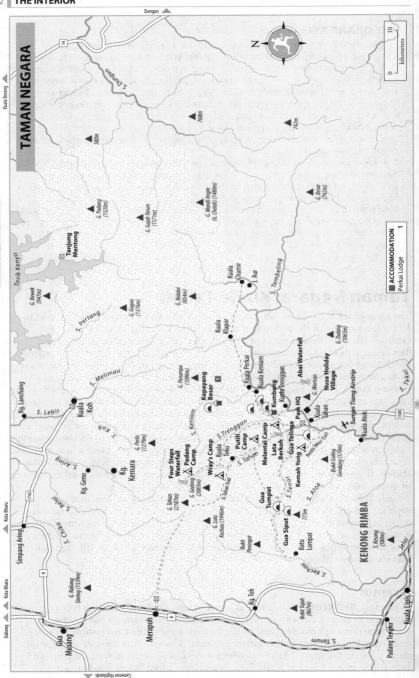

TAMAN NEGARA

Dungun

N

0 ——— 10 kilometres

S. Dungun

Kuala Berang

14

580m

768m

742m

G. Padang
(1320m)

G. Gagah Terum
(1517m)

G. Mandi Angin
(G. Chedoh) (1480m)

Tanjung
Mentong

Tasik Kenyir

G. Benek
(947m)

S. Pertang

G. Gagau
(1376m)

G. Belatai
(854m)

Kuala
Chamir

S. Tembeling

Kuala
Klapor

G. Dulang
(1065m)

S. Melimau

G. Penumpu
(1095m)

Kepayang
Besar

1

Kuala Perkai

Kuala Keniam

Abai Waterfall

G. Warisan

Nusa Holiday
Village

Kg. Landchang

S. Lebir

Kuala
Koh

S. Koh

G. Perlis
(1279m)

S. Kenlam

Kumbang

Kuala Trenggan

Park HQ

Sungei Tiang Airstrip

Kuala
Tahan

Kuala Atok

1598

S. Tekai

Kg. Geno

S. Aring

S. Redai

Kg.
Kemara

Four Steps
Waterfall

Padang
Camp

Wray's Camp

S. Trenggan

Kuala
Teku

S. Tahan

Putih
Camp

Melantai Camp

Lata
Berkoh

Gua Telinga

Kemah Yong

Rentis Tenor Trail

Bukit Guling
Gerdang) (570m)

Simpang Aring

S. Chiku

G. Tahan
(2187m)

G. Gedong
(2065m)

G. Tahan Trail

Gua
Tumpat

S. Tenor

S. Atok

Kota Bharu

8

Kota Bharu

G. Lulu
Kechau (1946m)

Bukit
Perangat

Gua Siput

Batu
Lompat

773m

S. Kechau

KENONG RIMBA

S. Kesong
(580m)

S. Jelai

Dabong

Gua
Musang

G. Rabong
Sinting (1539m)

Merapoh

8

Kg. Toh

Bukit Tioph
(867m)

S. Tanum

Kuala Lipis

Cameron Highlands

Padang Tengku

ACCOMMODATION

■ Perkai Lodge 1

PLANNING A VISIT TO TAMAN NEGARA

Given that tropical rainforest is always sodden, the **driest** time of year is between February and mid-October, with the **peak tourist season** roughly from May to August – make sure you book ahead. Mid-November to mid-January is extremely **wet**, and movement within the park can be restricted as paths go under water and rivers become impassable. Usually, however, most of the park's **trails** require no more than an average level of fitness, though of course longer trails require some stamina. Some essential **camping and trekking gear** (see p.48) is available to buy at Jerantut, or to rent at Kuala Tahan, but take your own if possible.

To **budget** for your trip, remember that for any trek involving overnighting in the forest (other than in a hide close to a park office or accessible by boat), you must hire a guide. The charge may seem steep, and boat excursions can also prove costly, but these are the only substantial outlays you'll face, as inexpensive accommodation, eating and transport options are easy to find. Many visitors never do any serious trekking and stay for just two or three nights, which is enough to get a reasonable flavour of the park.

FEES AND CHARGES

The following fees apply to all sections of Taman Negara:

Park entry	RM1 per person	**Use of hides or**	RM5 per person
Camping permit	RM1 per person per night	**fishing lodges** **Guide hire**	Around RM150 per day, plus RM100 for overnighting
Camera licence	RM5		
Fishing licence	RM10 per rod		

GETTING AROUND THE PARK

If you simply need to **cross the river** from Kuala Tahan, small on-demand wooden boats (daily dawn–9pm; RM1) cross from Kuala Tahan's floating restaurants to the jetty below the resort and national park headquarters. Put your fare in the tin by the ferryman.

Aside from trekking, **wooden longboats** seating four to ten people are the only way to get around Taman Negara from Kuala Tahan; you can use them like a taxi service to reach distant trekking trails, or speed your return journey after a long hike. Boats might wait for you or, more likely, return at an agreed time; don't expect them to hang around indefinitely if you are late. Book through the national park office; prices are the same for single or return trips.

Destination	Cost	Destination	Cost
Blau/Yong hides	RM80	Kuala Trenggan	RM120
Canopy walkway	RM60	Lata Berkoh	RM160
Gua Telinga	RM60	Lubok Lesong	RM100
Kuala Keniam	RM300	Nusa Camp	RM90
Kuala Keniam Kecil	RM650	Tabing/Cegar Anjing hides	RM60
Kuala Perkai (for Perkai Lodge)	RM480		

ARRIVAL AND DEPARTURE   JERANTUT

From Jerantut, you can reach Kuala Tahan by bus (1hr 45min) or by boat (3hr 30min); if your Taman Negara plans include another river trip, you probably won't need to do this one too.

By train Jerantut is on the Singapore–Kota Bharu line; there is one roundabout, midnight service a day to KL, but it's much faster and more convenient to take the bus. For Merapoh, change at Kuala Lipis.
Destinations Dabong (3 daily; 4hr); Gua Musang (3 daily; 3hr); Johor Bahru (2 daily; 7hr 30min); Kota Bharu (Wakaf Bharu station; 3 daily; 6hr); Kuala Lipis (4 daily; 1hr); Kuala Lumpur (1 daily; 7hr 40min); Singapore (2 daily; 8hr).
By bus There are two separate bus bays, with separate ticket windows, though helpful bilingual staff will quickly

point you to the right service. For Kuala Tahan, turn up 30min before departure and pay on the bus.
Destinations Kota Bharu (1 daily; 8hr); Kuala Lipis (hourly; 1hr 30min); Kuala Lumpur (hourly 7am–8pm; 3hr 30min); Kuala Tahan (5.30am, 8am, 1pm & 4.45pm; 1hr 45min; RM7); Kuantan (3 daily; 3hr); Tembeling Jetty (3 daily; 40min; RM2); Temerloh (12 daily; 1hr).
By taxi Taxis from the bus station run to Tembeling Jetty (RM25), Kuala Tahan (RM80) and various east-coast destinations – expect to pay at least RM250 to Kuantan, much more for Kota Bharu.

3

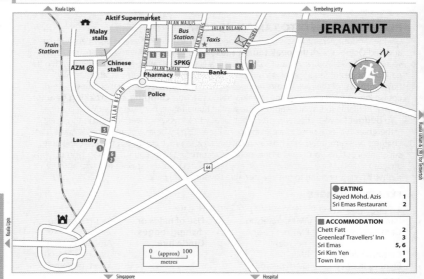

By boat Boating up to Kuala Tahan on the muddy Tembeling River takes in age-old rainforest lining both banks and the ride, in motorized ten-seater sampans, is an essential part of the Taman Negara experience – though you may prefer to save this lengthy trip for the faster return trip downstream. Ferries to Kuala Tahan (daily 9am & 2pm except Fri 9am & 2.30pm; 3hr; RM35 one-way, RM70 return) depart some way north of Jerantut from Tembeling Jetty; catch a local bus (RM2) or share taxi (RM25). A booth at the bus station sells boat tickets, though staff advise proceeding straight to the jetty and buying them there; you can also get them at NKS or Han Travel in Jerantut.

ACCOMMODATION

Chett Fatt Jalan Diwangsa ☎ 09 266 5805. A choice of double rooms, some with a/c but not en suite, or larger rooms (sleeping up to four), some with attached bathroom. All rooms have TV. <u>RM60</u>

Greenleaf Travellers' Inn Jalan Diwangsa ☎ 09 267 2131, ⓦ tamannegara.my. Green is the dominant colour at this homely if unexciting backpackers' place, with dorm beds and a variety of rooms. Some rooms have a/c and TV, though none is en suite. They also run package tours into the park. Dorms <u>RM10</u>, doubles <u>RM60</u>

Sri Emas 21–22 Jalan Besar ☎ 09 260 1770, ⓦ taman -negara-nks.com. Part of the NKS Travel juggernaut, shipping backpackers to and from Taman Negara every day as though on a conveyor belt. Besides dorms, there's a wide range of rooms, for two to four people, with fan or a/c, and with or without en-suite facilities and TV. Everything's well run; there's also a laundry service and fast internet. They also offer bus transfers to the Perhentian Islands and Cameron Highlands. Dorms <u>RM8</u>, en-suite doubles <u>RM48</u>

Sri Kim Yen Jalan Diwangsa ☎ 09 266 2168. Well-kept, simply furnished rooms above a jeweller's, with the choice of fan, a/c and shared bathrooms. <u>RM45</u>

Town Inn Jalan Tahan ☎ 09 266 6811, ⓦ towninn -hotel.com. A friendly mid-range hotel in a big block of a building. The comfortable, boxy rooms come with a/c, bathroom and TV. There's also free internet access. <u>RM48</u>

EATING

For inexpensive Malay and Chinese dishes – noodle soups, stir fries and *nasi campur*, plus Thai-style *tom yam* – head to the open-air **food courts**, just west of the centre and either side of the train station access road. Hours vary, but you should find something open 8am–8pm.

Sayed Mohd. Azis Jalan Besar. Good *murtabak*, decent curries and mediocre *biriyani*, all for under RM10. Daily 8am–8pm.

Sri Emas Restaurant Jalan Besar. This backpacker hotel has a large café serving Western and local fare for around RM10, and is open till late. Daily 8am–10pm, though staff thin out through the afternoon.

THE KUALA GANDAH ELEPHANT SANCTUARY

One attraction in the southern part of the interior is worth making a diversion for, the **Kuala Gandah Elephant Conservation Centre** (daily roughly 9am–1pm & 2–5pm except Fri closed from 12.30–2.45pm; donations appreciated; ☎ 09 279 0391, ⓦ myelephants.org), run by the government's Wildlife Department. Here they care for elephants being relocated to reserves from areas of habitat destruction, or which had to be subdued while *mengamuk* – a Malay term that would be untranslatable were it not the source of the English word "amok". The best time to turn up is 2pm (2.45pm on Fri), when for a couple of hours visitors have the chance to get hands-on with the elephants, riding, feeding or even bathing with them (bring a change of clothes).

Driving Route E8 east from KL, turn north at **Lanchang**, about 70km along, for the 20-min drive to the sanctuary. Without your own transport, **tours** are offered **from Kuala Lumpur** by NKS (ⓦ taman-negara-nks.com) and Han Travel (ⓦ taman-negara.com), usually as an add-on to a Taman Negara package; and **from Jerantut** from RM160 per person with Green Park Adventures (ⓦ my-greenpark.blogspot.com) and Greenleaf Holidays (ⓦ tamannegara.my).

3

DIRECTORY

Banks There are banks with ATMs along Jalan Tahan.
Camping and hiking gear Numerous stores opposite the bus station along Jalan Diwangsa sell day packs, rubber shoes, canvas track shoes and flashlights; check the quality before buying, especially stitching and straps on packs.
Laundry 200m southwest of centre on Jalan Besar.

Pharmacy Jalan Tahan holds two well-stocked pharmacies.
Supermarkets Aktif supermarket, 100m west of the bus bays, is the place to stock up for the park, though supplies of fresh fruit and veg are a bit patchy.

Kuala Tahan

Around 50km north of Jerantut, **KUALA TAHAN** is a grassy township of guesthouses and floating restaurants, facing a solid green wall of jungle across the turbid, 50m-wide **Tembeling River**. As a base, Kuala Tahan has many virtues: it boasts reasonable transport connections, plenty of accommodation, a few stores selling (and renting) basics you might have forgotten to bring with you, and even mobile coverage, though **no banks** or ATMs. Most importantly, current information about Taman Negara is on hand at the **national park headquarters** – where all visitors also need to register and pay park fees – just a quick ferry ride over the river at the start of the park's **hiking trails**. Take a torch with you to wander around the village in the evening, as the **electricity** can be flaky.

ARRIVAL AND DEPARTURE

KUALA TAHAN

By bus Buses drop at a roadside shelter on the edge of Kuala Tahan, a 5min walk from the river. Services to Jerantut (7.30am, 10am, 3pm & 7pm; 1hr 45min; RM7); the 7.30am bus usually arrives in Jerantut just after the 9.08am train south towards Singapore pulls out; if so, catch a taxi from Jerantut south to Temerloh (aka Merloh; RM60–80), and then the 11am Singapore bus from there.
By boat Arriving boats deposit passengers either at the park jetty, where steps lead up to the sprawling *Mutiara Taman Negara Resort* and park headquarters, or among the floating restaurants on the shingle beach opposite, with Kuala Tahan village on the bank above. If you don't already have a return ticket, reserve your ticket downstream to the Tembeling Jetty (for Jerantut; Sat–Thurs 9am & 2pm, Fri 9am & 2.30pm; RM35) the day

before your journey, at Han/SPKG (*Mama Chop* floating restaurant) or NKS jetties. In low season, afternoon departures may be curtailed; to avoid any nasty surprises, double-check with the boat operator the day before. Once at Tembeling, catch a bus (RM2) or a taxi (RM20 per person) to Jerantut.
By taxi Book taxis to Jerantut (RM80) through your accommodation.
By car The only road to Kuala Tahan, Route 1508, branches north off Route 64 10km east of Jerantut. From KL, leave the East Coast Highway at Temerloh, heading up Route 98 for Jerantut, then pick up Route 64 eastwards for the Kuala Tahan road. Starting from Kuantan, pick up Route 64 at Maran.

TRANSFERS AND PACKAGES TO KUALA TAHAN

Though it's easy enough to travel to Kuala Tahan and explore Taman Negara independently – the most inexpensive and flexible way to arrange things – many visitors book themselves on a convenient **package trip**. These typically comprise two or three nights at Kuala Tahan with a range of accommodation and meal options, and possibly activities such as walks and boat excursions as well; expect to pay upwards of RM160 per person.

The most established operators, **NKS** (ⓦ taman-negara-nks.com) and **Han Travel/SPKG** (ⓦ taman-negara.com), have offices in KL and Jerantut; Han also run the Tembeling Jetty–Kuala Tahan boats and have dedicated restaurants and accommodation at Kuala Tahan. Jerantut-based agents include **Green Park Adventure** (ⓦ my-greenpark.blogspot.com), who also offer packages to Kenong Rimba State Park (see p.207); and **Greenleaf Holidays** (ⓦ tamannegara.my).

The same companies usually offer straight **transfers** to Kuala Tahan from as far afield as Singapore, Kuala Lumpur, Kuala Besut and Tanah Rata in the Cameron Highlands, which cost more than public transport but undoubtedly save time. Despite what you may be told, there's no need in these cases to book park accommodation through the same company; simply shop around once you've arrived or call ahead.

INFORMATION

National Park Headquarters An essential first port of call to pay the nominal entry fee, pick up a map and check the latest trail conditions (Sat–Thurs 8am–6pm, Fri 8am–noon & 3–6pm; ☎ 09 266 1122, ⓦ wildlife.gov.my). You can also book hides and activity packages, charter boats and hire guides. Make sure you check the log book where sightings of interesting creatures are listed; for the record, there are about 50 tigers in Taman Negara, with some three or four sightings per year, usually deep in the forest (many national park staff have never seen one). If you have a specialist interest, call the headquarters a week in advance to see if a guide with matching knowledge can be arranged. Being trained by the Wildlife Department, the guides are generally better on fauna than flora, though many are experts on neither. As the most important component of their training is knowledge of the trails, they may fall short when it comes to more general skills, such as offering support in the event of a mishap.

ACCOMMODATION

Almost all local accommodation is located at Kuala Tahan, with the exception of the *Mutiara* on the opposite bank, and a couple of places upriver. Book in advance, especially during the May–August peak season. There's no **campsite**, though some accommodation have facilities. Aside from a bed in Kuala Tahan, you can also overnight **inside the forest**. The best option is to use one of **five hides** (see p.201); these sleep up to twelve people in bare wooden bunks (bring your own bedding), with tank water and toilets available. The closest, Tambing, is about an hour's hike away, while the Kumbang hide takes 5hr to reach. **Campsites** are scattered through the park; they have absolutely no facilities at all, though most are close to rivers where you can wash. There's a small **fee** for hides and campsites (see p.193), payable at the national park office; you need to reserve bunks in hides too, as they are fairly popular – and are periodically closed for renovations.

★ **Abot Guesthouse** At the top of the hill from the bus stop ☎ 017 916 9616. New, low-set house with sparklingly clean motel-style en-suite rooms. Fan RM40, a/c RM90

Agoh Chalet Up the river road from the bus stop ☎ 09 266 9570, ⓦ agoh.com.my/v3. An initially unpromising ramshackle, shaded lawn ringed by concrete chalets textured to look like wood; but rooms are clean and tidy and all come with a/c and attached shower. Good value for the price, with friendly management. RM80

★ **Durian Chalet** A 10min walk past Teresek View, down a steep hill and through a small stand of rubber trees ☎ 09 266 8940. Rustic, slightly scruffy chalets of woven bamboo with shack-like bathrooms attached, clustered around a pretty garden with a teeming fishpond. There's also a separate brick "family house", which can be rented out as a four-person dorm, and a campsite. A great place to get away from it all. Camping RM2, dorms RM25, doubles RM40

Dakili Walk to the top of the riverbank from the bus stop, then follow signed paths downstream ☎ 014 292 7069, ⓦ dakilihouse.blogspot.com. Basic concrete dorms and doubles with rudimentary shared bathrooms in a quiet kampung area above the river, 10min walk from town; you can camp here too with your own gear. A tiny store nearby sells essentials at low prices. Camping RM5, dorms RM13, doubles RM40

Mat Leon Reception at a floating store at Kuala Tahan; accommodation in a forest clearing above the river, 2km upstream past *Tahan Guesthouse* ☎ 013 998 9517, ⓦ matleon.com. Metal-roofed bamboo chalets with simple furnishings, fan, cell-like bathrooms and breakfast, plus a small canteen It's nice out here, but a bit isolated when occupancy is low. Dorm beds RM15, chalets RM60

★ **Mutiara Taman Negara Resort** In front of the national park headquarters, over the river from Kuala Tahan ☏09 266 3500, ⊛mutiarahotels.com. Busy three-star resort occupying a strip of land between the river and forest, mostly comprising a/c chalets, suites and bungalows with spacious bathrooms, woven bamboo walls, cane furniture and jungle or river views. There's also an expensive, institutional dorm with bunk beds. Transfers to and from the park can be arranged for an additional premium. Dorms RM80, chalets RM490

Nusa Holiday Village Around 15min upstream by boat ☏09 266 2369, ⊛tamannegara-nusaholiday .com.my. This Han/SPKG-run resort, atop the riverbank, has quite a collection of accommodation. Cheapest are the six- or eight-bed dorms, with facilities in a separate block, and slightly threadbare, en-suite A-frame chalets. The "Malay-style" houses, with cane furniture, mosquito nets, a/c and tiled bathrooms, are better value. There's a simple restaurant, and you'll need to budget a few ringgit extra per day to shuttle to and from the park HQ on SPKG's boats. If you want to hike outside the park from here, you could walk to the Abai Waterfall in about

1hr, or up to the peak of Gunung Warisan, 2hr away. Dorms RM15, rooms RM140

★ **Tahan Guesthouse** Walk uphill from the bus stop, turn left at the top and right 50m further on, and it's two minutes along on the right ☏09 266 7752. Well kept two-storey affair, painted in bright colours and featuring wildlife murals. Accommodation comprises four-bed dorms and en-suite rooms, all with fan; beds have mosquito nets and toilets are squat-style. The amicable female proprietor speaks excellent English; the only downside is the proximity of the mosque at 5.30am. RM50

Tembeling Riverview Hostel & Chalets From the bus stop, take the road to the river, turn left and it's just downhill ☏09 266 6766. Simple and shabby en-suite timber chalets with thatched roofs and a slight mildew problem, plus some four- and eight-bed dorms. It's well located though, not far from the water in a shady compound. Dorms RM12, chalets RM40

Teresek View Resort Up the hill from the bus stop, on the left ☏09 266 9744. A large pale-pink motel-like place with comfy en-suite rooms (pricier ones have a/c) on two floors, plus a café below. It's well run too; you won't envy staff trying to keep the place free of muddy footprints. RM70

Woodland Resort Just south of Kuala Tahan ☏09 266 1111, ⊛woodland.com.my. One of a handful of

3

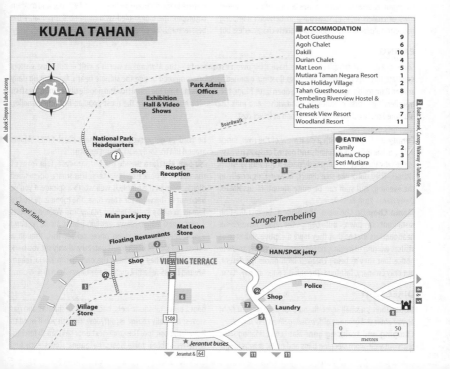

KUALA TAHAN

N

Lubok Simpon & Lubok Lesong

Bukit Teresek, Canopy Walkway & Tahan Hide

Park Admin Offices

Exhibition Hall & Video Shows

Boardwalk

National Park Headquarters
ⓘ

MutiaraTaman Negara

Shop

Resort Reception

❶

Sungei Tahan

Main park jetty

Mat Leon Store

Floating Restaurants ❷

Sungei Tembeling

Shop

VIEWING TERRACE P

❸ **HAN/SPGK jetty**

@

❸

Police

@

Shop

❻

Laundry

Village Store

❼

❾

❽

❿

1508

0   50
metres

★ **Jerantut buses**

▼ Jerantut & 64   ▼ ❶❶   ▼ ❶❶

■ ACCOMMODATION	
Abot Guesthouse	9
Agoh Chalet	6
Dakili	10
Durian Chalet	4
Mat Leon	5
Mutiara Taman Negara Resort	1
Nusa Holiday Village	2
Tahan Guesthouse	8
Tembeling Riverview Hostel & Chalets	3
Teresek View Resort	7
Woodland Resort	11

● EATING	
Family	2
Mama Chop	3
Seri Mutiara	1

KUALA TAHAN ACTIVITIES

Most people in the park for just a few days sign up for various **activity packages** offered through the park office and Kuala Tahan accommodation.

Night jungle walks (1hr–1hr 30min; RM25; bring your own torch) are easy and, despite being crowded and held along the park's most heavily used paths, can turn up everything from tapirs to scorpions, and the sharp-eyed guides invariably spot camouflaged creatures you'd otherwise miss.

Night safaris (2hr; RM40) actually take place outside the park; you're driven around a plantation in a 4WD, and may get to see leopard cats, wild pigs, civets and the occasional snake. **Orang Asli village visit** (2hr; RM60) shows you how to use a blowpipe and fire-making using sticks at a semi-permanent Batek encampment; very touristy, but interesting too.

On the river, fairly tame **rapids shooting** trips (1hr; RM60) take place a few kilometres upstream, designed to appeal to families rather than hard-core rafters; you'll ride this stretch anyway if you catch a boat back from Kuala Trenggan (see p.202). The **night river safari** (2hr; RM200) uses a tamer stretch of water, where you often see larger animals along the riverside.

Longer trips include **guided forest walks**, the best of which have you staying **overnight at a hide** (Bumbun Kumbang is a favourite; see p.202) or even a **cave**; you usually make your way down to the river on the second day and catch a boat back to Kuala Tahan. This far into the forest you really might see anything – or nothing at all. Price depends on numbers, duration and destination, but expect RM280 per person for an all-inclusive two-day, one-night trip from Kuala Tahan.

The most popular area for **fishing** is the Sungai Keniam, northeast of Kuala Tahan, where you can hope to catch catfish or snakehead; all fish must be returned. The very basic *Perkai Fishing Lodge*, around 2hr upstream from Kuala Tahan, is a popular base; a boat there costs RM480.

incongruous developments in this area, with regimented rows of chalets looking something in between kampung house and alpine hut. The rooms are utterly characterless but do pack in the creature comforts – a/c, TV, fridge and modern bathroom. The indigo-tiled swimming pool is probably the best feature. Rates include breakfast. **RM160**

EATING

Some of Kuala Tahan's places to stay have their own **restaurants** – the *Mutiara's* is worth a visit – but most visitors gravitate towards the row of ten or so floating, glorified *kedai kopis* moored beside the shingle beach. Opening up daily around 8am for breakfast and staying open until 11pm, the restaurants offer the usual rice and noodle dishes, plus Western travellers' fare such as pancakes, sandwiches and milk shakes. The ones below are the most popular, but other smaller, unnamed places often serve better food at lower cost.

Family On the river. With a clear view of the river, fancy lighting, bamboo roll-up blinds and potted orchids, it's easy to see why this place is constantly packed out with Western visitors. They don't like solo diners, however, especially in the evening, and staff can be quite abrupt. Mains RM10. Daily 8am–2pm & 6–9pm.

Mama Chop On the river. The biggest, busiest floating restaurant in town, but being the Han Travel/SPGK headquarters means that they have a captive audience of visitors waiting to begin guided tours – who don't seem to notice that they're being charged high prices for decent, but only ordinary, fast food. Though it's open all day, it can be hard to get served outside main meal times. Mains around RM10. Daily 8am–9pm or later.

★ **Seri Mutiara** Beside the Mutiara resort, in front of the national park headquarters. This smart, open-sided dining room in the jungle is well worth a splurge if you've been out in the wilds for a few days. The menu is geared to Taman Negara's better-heeled Malay and Western guests – pizza, *nasi lemak*, prawn *sambal*, T-bone steak, *rendang* – and the relatively steep prices reflect this, though a coffee and slice of black forest gateau will only set you back RM20 or so. They also have the only bar in Kuala Tahan. Around RM85 for a full meal. Daily 8am–2pm & 6–9pm.

DIRECTORY

Books There's a small secondhand bookstore on your right as you enter the grounds of *Tembeling Riverview Hostel*.
Camping and trekking gear Mat Leon's floating store rents out well-worn sleeping bags and mats, canvas jungle boots, tents, mosquito nets, backpacks, flashlights and gas stoves; the daily charge is fairly low, though you'll need to leave a deposit too. The store next door sells small torches, batteries, rubber ankle boots, hexamine stoves with fuel

and day packs. Nowhere seems to stock waterproof bags or sheets though.

Internet There's a netbar across from *Teresek View* (RM6/hr) and another over the river at the Mutiara (RM10/30min).

Supplies Several mini-marts at Kuala Tahan, open roughly 8am–10pm, sell water, biscuits and snacks, rubber ankle boots, tinned sardines and *rendang*, soft drinks, ice creams, batteries, a raft of insect repellents, antiseptic wipes and toothpaste. The most expensive is attached to the *Mutiara*; that opposite the *Teresek View* is good for snacks and general necessities; while the one on the river has the best range of canned and dried food and camping essentials.

Day treks

Cross the river and turn right at the national park headquarters, and you're at the start of most of the **hiking trails** that spread into the park. Popular and easy places to visit close to the park headquarters include **Bukit Teresek**; the **canopy walkway**, where you might be able to observe treetop jungle life close up; the large limestone cavern of **Gua Telinga**; and the waterfall at **Lata Berkoh** (the first part of the trail there is a good way to kill a couple of spare hours). You could feasibly tackle two, perhaps three, of these in a day.

3

Bukit Teresek

3.5km return from the national park office, 2hr

Although it's the most heavily used trail in the park, the route to the summit of **Bukit Teresek** (342m) is an excellent starter trek, taking about an hour in each direction. Heading northeast away from the river, the trail passes an impressive stand of **giant bamboo** before ascending Bukit Teresek itself via a steeply rising series of fibreglass **steps**; if somehow you haven't already noticed the sauna-like conditions, you will now, and it would be self-flagellating not to pause at least once to catch your breath. The clanking of your shoes against the steps is enough to scare off most wildlife, so content yourself with the promise of views – though the clearing at the top of the steps is largely screened by trees. Continue along the top for another 15min to reach the so-called **second view**, where on clear days you can get marvellous vistas north over the valley to **Gunung Tahan** (2187m; see p.204) and smaller Gunung Perlis. Back at

---

HIKING AT KUALA TAHAN

The shortest hiking trails from Kuala Tahan are clearly signposted and easy to follow, but go any distance and trails deteriorate into slippery tangles of roots and leaf litter, and you'll be relying on small, reflective **markers** attached to convenient trees, and the photocopied **trail maps** handed out by the national park headquarters. On treks ranging more than about 10km from base, it's strongly recommended that you **hire a guide**. The Kumbang hide is the furthest you're meant to go without one, and they're absolutely essential for any of the longer trails. If you're moderately fit, the hiking **time estimates** given out by the park authorities (and in the text) are pretty reliable; expect to average 2km per hour.

Except on the very simplest day hikes, you should **inform** park staff of your plans so they know where to look if you get into difficulty. You won't be able to phone for help, as the mobile phone signal dies out just a little way from Kuala Tahan. Perhaps the most important advice is to **know your limitations** and not run out of time. Slipping and sliding along in the dark is no fun and can be dangerous – it's easy to fall and impossible to spot snakes or other forest-floor creatures that might be on the path. If you do get **lost** and night is about to close in, it's best to make your way down to either the Tahan or Tembeling rivers (assuming you're near them); there is boat traffic on both into the evening, and if you are unlucky enough not to be spotted, you may be able to find a dry section of bank where you can spend the night.

Don't be paranoid about encountering large **wildlife** on the trails – in fact, count yourself lucky if you do, as most animals don't hang around after they hear you coming. There's almost no way you can avoid getting bitten by a few **leeches**, however, and their numbers increase dramatically after rain; see p.45 for general tips on keeping them at bay.

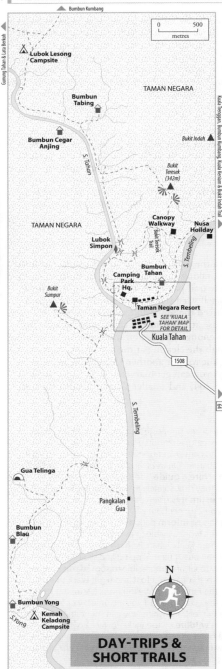

the base of the hill, the canopy walkway is just 300m to the south along a clearly marked path.

Canopy walkway

Sat–Thurs 9.30am–3.30pm, Fri 9am–noon; limited numbers allowed at any one time, so waits possible • RM6

About thirty minutes' walk from the national park office, along the riverside Bukit Indah trail (see below), the **canopy walkway** is one of Taman Negara's highlights – though it's better for views down over the canopy to the Tembeling River, rather than wildlife spotting. You climb a sturdy wooden tower and step out, 30m above the forest floor, onto a 500m-long swaying aluminium bridge, anchored to some suitably placed, 250-year-old *tualang* trees. Animals you may well see include the grey-banded leaf monkey, with a call that sounds like a rattling tin can, and the white-eyed dusky leaf monkey, with its deep, nasal "ha-haw" cry; both lope about in groups of six to eight. At the end, you return to terra firma by another wooden stairwell.

Bukit Indah

6.5km return from the national park office, 3hr 30min

The track to **Bukit Indah** heads upstream via the early stages of the Kumbang hide trail; you can also reach it from the canopy walkway. Despite its proximity to Kuala Tahan, early in the day you're likely to see monkeys, plenty of birdlife, squirrels, shrews, a multitude of insects and – with some luck – perhaps tapir or *seladang* (wild ox). After about 3km you'll see a signposted path heading uphill to the top of Bukit Indah itself, which offers views over the Tembeling.

Gua Telinga and Kemah Keladong

A popular area, 5km downriver from Kuala Tahan on the far side of Sungai Tembeling, takes in limestone **caves** at Gua Telinga, the Blau and Yong **hides**, and a **campsite** at Kemah Keladong. You can tackle this either by catching a boat to drop-off points for the cave or hides (15–20min; see p.194 for fares); or by crossing by sampan to a trailhead just up the Sungai Tahan from Kuala Tahan (ask national park staff about this) and hiking – in which case, allow a full day for the return trip.

Gua Telinga

5.5km return from the national park office, 3hr 30min

Gua Telinga looks small and unassuming, but this cavern is deceptively deep – something you only discover when you slide through it. Although in theory it's possible to follow a guide rope through the 80m-deep cave, in practice only small adults or children will be able to tug themselves through the narrow cavities – most people have to crawl along dark narrow passages in places and negotiate areas of deep, squishy guano. Thousands of tiny **roundleaf bats** roost here, named after the "leaves" of skin around their nostrils, which help direct the sound signals each bat transmits.

Kemah Keladong

From Gua Telinga, it's another 2km through beautiful tall forest, via the **Yong** and **Blau hides**, to where the trail divides. North is the track to Kemah Rentis (see p.205), while southeast, it's just 500m to the tranquil **Kemah Keladong campsite** on the terraced bank of Sungai Yong. With an early start, it's quite possible to reach this point, have a swim in the river and get back to the resort before dusk. If you stay the night, you might want to make the short ascent of nearby **Bukit Pecah Piring** the following morning, though the 308m-high summit is cloaked in forest.

Lata Berkoh

17km, 7hr return on foot from the national park office; ask about river levels before setting out • Return trip by boat RM160

Most visitors catch a boat (at least in one direction) to the "roaring rapids" of **Lata Berkoh**, around 8.5km up the Sungai Tahan; the return trip is a long way to walk in a day, and if water levels are high you may face a swim across the river near the end.

The **trail** from the national park headquarters leads gently downhill, past the turning for the **Tabing hide** to the east. After around 3km you reach the campsite at **Lubok Simpon**, to the left of which a broad, pebbled beach leads down to a deep **pool** in the Sungai Tahan, a popular place for a dip. The route to the waterfall veers west from the main trail, crossing gullies and steep ridges before reaching the river, which must be forded. The final part of the trail runs up along the west side of the Sungai Tahan, passing the simple **Berkoh Lodge**, a small shelter in a clearing, and a **campsite** before reaching the falls.

The **waterfall** itself drops into a deep pool with surprisingly clear water for swimming (tread carefully around the large rocks on the river bed). You can picnic here too, overlooking the swirling water. Keep eyes peeled for kingfishers with their yellow-and-red wings and white beaks; large grey-and-green fish eagles; and, on the rocks, camouflaged monitor lizards.

KUALA TAHAN HIDES

Spending a night in one of the park's **hides** (known as **bumbuns**) doesn't guarantee sightings of large mammals, especially in the dry season when the **salt licks** – where plant-eating animals come to supplement their mineral intake – are often so waterless that there's little reason for deer, tapir, elephant, leopard or seladang to visit, but it's an experience you're unlikely to forget. It's best to go in a group and take turns keeping watch, listening hard and occasionally shining a **torch** at the salt lick – if an animal is present its eyes will reflect brightly in the beam.

Kuala Tahan's five hides are covered in the hiking trail accounts, but at the time of writing, only those at Lata Berkoh (above) and Kumbang (p.202) were open – the others were closed indefinitely. For details of costs and time-saving boat rides to/from the hides, see p.193.

Overnight trips

The 28km-long, two- to three-day trail northeast of Kuala Tahan to **Kuala Perkai** involves overnighting in the jungle, either at **Kumbang hide** or one of several **caves**, with the chance of seeing large animals, after which you could organize a **boat** back to base, rather than having to retrace your steps. If you're pushed for time or simply not so dedicated, hiking as far as Kumbang hide (12km), staying the night there, then taking the alternative return trail – or again, catching a boat – is an excellent compromise. Note that you need to arrange any **boat transfers** before you head out, and that **guides** are recommended beyond the Kumbang hide.

Trails to the Kumbang hide

10–12km from the national park office, 5–7hr hike, depending on route • Boat direct from Kuala Tahan takes 45min (RM120).

Both the **two trails** to Kumbang are fairly damp and muddy. The longer, flatter, easier route initially follows the Lata Berkoh trail (see p.201), then arcs northeast to the narrow **Sungai Trenggan** – which has to be waded across, and may be impassable after heavy rain – beyond which you're about 1km from the hide.

The more direct, but tougher, route follows the Sungai Tembeling upstream past the Bukit Indah turn-off (see p.200), crossing numerous **creeks**, each involving a steep, slippery scramble and clamber up the far side. Eventually things settle down, and you might see signs of **Batek** people – abandoned shacks and camps – before crossing the small Sungai Tembeling **bridge**. The path seems to peter out on the far side, but keep going and you soon come to a definite junction. Turn left and Kumbang hide is a 30min walk; right, and it's 1km to **Kuala Trenggan**, where some broken-down wooden cabins overlook the confluence of the Tembeling and Trenggan rivers.

Kumbang hide

Book bunks through the national park office

Raised high off the ground on concrete posts, **Kumbang hide** sits at the edge of a clearing, about 200m from a natural **salt lick** that attracts animals at wetter times of the year. As always, seeing anything is down to luck, though scan the muddy trails nearby and you'll often find tapir prints. Given the distance between the hide and the salt lick, however, you'll need binoculars and a powerful torch if you're hoping for more than a glimpse of vague grey shapes.

Kumbang to Kuala Keniam

13km one-way, 7hr

The superb hike between Kumbang and Kuala Keniam combines the real possibility of seeing **elephants** with visits to three **caves**, one of which is big enough for an army to camp in. The trail is slow going, even in drier conditions, with innumerable streams to wade through, hills to circumvent and trees blocking the path; some people take two days, overnighting in a cave or on a stretch of clear ground near a stream.

Limestone caves

From Kumbang, it takes around three hours on a boggy trail before you enter limestone-cave country, first reaching **Kepayang Kecil**. A line of fig trees here drops a curtain of roots down the rock, behind which lies a small chamber, with a slightly larger one to the right, containing stalactites and stalagmites. A short way on is much larger **Kepayang Besar**, where the huge chamber at the eastern side of the outcrop makes an excellent place to spend the night (especially as you don't need to use a tent). Despite its popularity with trekkers, civets and leopard cats are often seen here after dark. Fifteen minutes north – keep an eye on the indistinct path – are **Gua Luas** and more impressive **Gua Daun Menari** ("Cave of the Dancing Leaves"), a breezy chamber inhabited by thousands of roundleaf bats.

Kuala Keniam

Once beyond the limestone band, the rest of the route to Kuala Keniam passes through *meranti* forest of tall, straight trees with distinctive reddish-brown bark, much prized as timber. Finally, you reach the river at **Kuala Keniam**, where there's a **campsite** and **jetty** for transport back to Kuala Tahan (RM300).

Kuala Keniam to Kuala Perkai

3km, 2hr • Book Perkai Lodge through the national park office

From Kuala Keniam, you can hike northwest beside the Sungai Keniam to **Kuala Perkai**, where the grandly named **Perkai Lodge** – actually a basic shelter with beds but no mattresses – is a popular base for fishing groups, who cruise up directly from Kuala Tahan (there's a **campsite** too). This far from civilization, the region is rich in **wildlife**, including banded and dusky leaf monkeys, long-tailed macaques and white-handed gibbons, all of which are relatively easy to spot, especially with binoculars. As for big mammals, elephants certainly roam in these parts; smaller animals like tapirs, civets and deer are best seen at night or early in the morning.

Longer trails

For the two major **long-distance hiking trails** at Taman Negara, you'll need to hire guides and bring full camping and trekking gear, including cooking equipment and water-purifying tablets, plus food. The five-day **Gunung Tahan trail**, undoubtedly the toughest in the park, culminates in the ascent of one of Malaysia's highest peaks, after which you have to hike out again (perhaps via the alternative, shorter trail to Merapoh; see p.211); you'll definitely need sleeping bags for a couple of nights spent at altitude. The other option is the three- to four-day **Tenor trail**, a lasso-shaped trek leading west from Kuala Tahan to Gua Telinga, then northwest to the campsite on the Sungai Tenor. Either way, expect to see plenty of jungle, and to get soaked during river crossings and rain; allow a day extra either side of the trek to sort out arrangements.

Gunung Tahan trail

55km one-way, 7-day return from Kuala Tahan • Book one month in advance

To the Batek Orang Asli, **Gunung Tahan** – Peninsular Malaysia's highest peak at 2187m – is the Forbidden Mountain, its summit the home of a vast monkey, who stands guard over magic stones. Though the Batek rarely venture beyond the foothills, ascending Gunung Tahan is the highlight of any adventurous visitor's stay in Taman Negara. Although hundreds complete the trail every year, the sense of individual achievement after tackling the innumerable river crossings, steep hills and nights camping in the jungle – let alone the arduous ascent – is supreme.

Day 1–2

The first day involves an easy six-hour walk from Kuala Tahan to **Melantai**, the campsite on the east bank of Sungai Tahan, across the river from Lata Berkoh. On the second day more ground is covered, the route taking eight hours and crossing 27 hills, including a long trudge up Bukit Malang ("Unlucky Hill"). This section culminates at **Gunung Rajah** (576m), before descending to Sungai Puteh, a tiny tributary of the Tahan. Before the campsite at **Kuala Teku** you'll ford the Tahan half a dozen times – if the river's high, extra time and energy is spent following paths along the edge of the river, crossing at shallower spots.

If you're really enjoying the hike, consider a two-day detour from Kuala Teku to **Four-Steps Waterfall**, east of Gunung Tahan. The trail up to it spends eight hours following the course of the Sungai Tahan right to the foot of the 30m-high falls; it's a gorgeous forest setting, and flat stones by the path are a good point to rest, listen to the sound of the water and look out for birds and monkeys.

Day 3

The third day on the trail to Gunung Tahan sees you climb from 168m to 1100m in seven hours of steady, unrelenting legwork, leaving you on a ridge. Prominent among the large trees here is *seraya*, with a reddish-brown trunk, though as the ridge runs west these are replaced by montane oak forest, where **elephant tracks** are common – though less dense than lower down the forest is still rich enough in foliage to provide the elephants with food. The night is spent at the Gunung Tahan base camp, **Wray's Camp**, named after the leader of the team that first conquered the mountain in 1905.

Day 4: to the summit

Day four involves six hours of hard climbing along steep gullies, ending up at **Padang Camp**, on the Tangga Lima Belas Ridge, sited on a plateau sheltered by tall trees. The summit is now only two and a half hours away, through open, hilly ground with knee-high plants, exposed rocks and peaty streams, which support thick shrubs and small trees – look for pitcher plants and orchids. The trail follows a ridge and soon reaches **Gunung Tahan's summit**; provided it's clear, there's a stupendous view, around 50km in all directions. Weather conditions up here can't be relied upon, however: **moss forest**, which dominates above 1500m, is often shrouded in cloud.

On from the summit

Most hikers make a straight return trip, spending the fifth night back at the padang, the sixth at Sungai Puteh, and reaching Kuala Tahan late on day seven.

If you don't fancy retracing your steps, it's also possible to continue westwards from the mountain for a further five days, exiting Taman Negara at **Merapoh** (see p.211) after completing a **traverse** of the park. For more information about the route, contact the park offices at Kuala Tahan and Merapoh.

Tenor trail
30km circuit from Kuala Tahan, 3-4 days

Shorter and not as tough as the hike to Gunung Tahan, the mostly low-lying **Tenor trail** is more likely to be flooded out during extra-wet conditions, but is otherwise an extremely satisfying trek, with a few easy ascents to viewpoints along the way.

Day 1

Initially, the **Tenor trail** follows the track southwest from Kuala Tahan to Gua Telinga and the Yong hide (see p.201), before bearing northwest along the small **Sungai Yong** and reaching the campsite at **Kemah Yong**, around 10km from the start.

A side trail from here ascends **Bukit Guling Gendang** (570m), a steep ninety-minute climb best undertaken in the morning, after a good night's rest. Towards the summit the terrain changes from lowland tropical to montane forest, where tall conifer trees allow light to penetrate to the forest floor and **squirrels** predominate, with the black giant and cream giant the main species. Both are as big as a domestic cat, their call varying from a grunt to a machine-gun burst of small squeaks. From the top, views reach north to Gunung Tahan, west to Gua Siput and beyond that to Bukit Penyengat (713m), the highest limestone outcrop in Peninsular Malaysia.

Day 2

From Kemah Yong campsite, the main trail continues into the upper catchment of Sungai Yong, then over a low saddle into the catchment of **Sungai Rentis**. The path narrows through thick forest alongside the river, crossing it several times, until it joins **Sungai Tenor** three hours later, marked by a remote and beautiful riverside clearing, **Kemah Rentis**, where you camp. You're about halfway around the trail here.

Day 3

You can make it back to Kuala Tahan in one day from Kemah Rentis, though many people take it easy and rest up in one of the campsites along the way. Following the river downstream through undulating terrain brings you first to rapids at **Lata Keitiah**, beyond which there's a campsite at **Kemah Lameh**. You're now in lowland open forest where walking is fairly easy; after four hours the trail leads to the **Cegar Anjing hide** (another possible overnight stop) from where it's a final 3km to Kuala Tahan.

North through the interior

North from Jerantut, Route 8 and the parallel **Jungle Railway** run around 200km to Kota Bharu, up on the east coast. Head this way if you want to spend time among the region's abundant forests and limestone hills at **Kenong Rimba State Park**, or reach the alternative entrances to Taman Negara at **Merapoh** and **Kuala Koh**, or the forested waterfall trails at **Gunung Stong State Park**. Settlements along the way – including relatively substantial **Gua Musang** and **Kuala Lipis** – are more jumping-off points for nearby sections of wilds, rather than destinations in their own right.

THE JUNGLE RAILWAY

It took indentured Tamil labourers eight years to build the 500km-long **jungle railway** from **Gemas**, southeast of KL, to **Tumpat**, on the northeast coast near Kota Bharu. The first section from Gemas to Kuala Lipis opened in 1920, with the full extent of the line following in 1931. Initially it was used exclusively for freight – tin and rubber, and later oil palm – until a passenger service, originally known as the "Golden Blowpipe", opened in 1938. Today the route is mostly served by trains from **Singapore**, with just one daily service from KL.

By dint of its very existence, the line doesn't pass through virgin jungle; instead much of the route **south of Gua Musang** is flanked by regrowth forest and belukar-type woodland, and the line often dips through cuttings below ferny embankments, or skirts the backs of kampung gardens, within eyeshot of bougainvillea and fruiting rambutan and mango trees. On the final section, the mountainous, river-gashed terrain is replaced by plantations of rubber, pepper and oil palm, which – given their sprawl of uninterrupted vegetation – actually look more jungly than the real forest. None of this is to detract from the fact that as a way to encounter **rural life**, a ride on the jungle train can't be beaten, giving you the chance to take in backwater scenery in the company of cheroot-smoking old men in sarongs, and fast-talking women hauling kids, poultry and vegetables to and from the nearest market. For the unadulterated jungle railway experience, you need to be on one of the slow **local trains**, which call at just about every obscure hamlet on the route, some with Orang Asli names.

Rolling stock is worn and fairly ordinary, dating to the 1980s; the only advantages of the so-called "first class" carriages seem to be air conditioning and slightly larger seats. Buy **tickets** at the station if possible (you shouldn't need to book in advance except on express services during school holidays), though you can also pay the conductor on board – indeed, you often have to, as rural station offices keep erratic hours.

The Jungle Railway's official name is the less romantic "Sektor Timur & Selatan" (East and South Route), managed by KTM. **Timetables** (🌐 ktmb.com.my) are to be taken with a pinch of salt, as delays aren't uncommon – cattle grazing along the track sidings cause constant problems for train drivers. It's not unknown for trains to show up early either; be at the station fifteen minutes ahead of the scheduled departure. Occasionally you may find the time on the ticket doesn't match the timetable, in which case ask station staff for clarification. Even if everything appears to be going to schedule, note that there's only one set of tracks on long stretches of the route: delays elsewhere may mean your train being held at a siding or even reversing for an extended period to let an oncoming train pass.

ESSENTIALS

Climate Weather considerations are damp through the year, though driest April–September; you'll need to check in advance about access if heading here during the November–January wet season.

Banks The only regional **banks** with ATMs are at Kuala Lipis and Gua Musang.

Kenong Rimba State Park

Entry fee RM12

Covering 128 square kilometres and backing onto the remote southwestern corner of Taman Negara, **Kenong Rimba State Park** offers jungle trails, riverside camping, mammal-spotting and excellent birdwatching, plus the likelihood of crossing paths with the nomadic **Batek** people. You can see the main sights within **five days**, using a 50km-long **loop trail** through the park that passes a string of caves, the **Lata Kenong waterfall** and several limestone outcrops with **rock-climbing** potential. If you've only time for a brief visit, head straight for the waterfall and camp there for a night, leaving along the same route the next day. There's some accommodation at the park, otherwise bring all you'll need with you (see p.48), or organize a **tour** from Kuala Lipis (see below).

ARRIVAL AND DEPARTURE
KENONG RIMBA STATE PARK

Kenong Rimba lies about 20km east of Kuala Lipis, back towards Jerantut; the nearest train station is **Batu Sembilan**, about 2km from the park gates via **Tanjung Kiara jetty**, where boats to the park arrive.

By train From Batu Sembihan to: Jerantut (1 daily; 40min); Kuala Lipis (1 daily; 15min); Singapore (1 daily; 9hr).

By bus The *Kenong Lodge* (see below) runs a private bus twice daily from Kuala Lipis bus station, and can also pick up from Jerantut (RM80 per person each way).

By boat Boats are all by arrangement only, through agents in Jerantut or Kuala Lipis. From Tanjung Kiara Jetty to: Jerantut (1hr 30min; RM400); Kuala Lipis (1hr; RM300).

TOUR AGENTS AND INFORMATION

Though it's possible to make your own way to Kenong Rimba, it's much easier to organize a package through an agent; these are all-inclusive with meals and accommodation (in cabins or tents) as part of the deal. If you're planning any serious trekking here, you'll need a guide, which these agents can also arrange.

Appu At Appu's Guesthouse, 63 Jalan Besar, Kuala Lipis ☎09 312 3142, ✉jungleappu@yahoo.com. Appu has been exploring Kenong Rimba since the 1990s, and sets up tailor-made budget packages based around hiking and camping out in the park. Die-hards can make a five-day circuit with him , on which the trekking can be quite tough, though distances are not so long. The general rate is RM80 per person per day (minimum group size four) including food, plus RM150 return per group to cover transport.

Kiara Holidays Level 4 of the Centrepoint Complex in Kuala Lipis ☎09 312 2777, ⊛kiaraholidays.com. Don't be put off by their threadbare office or the shabby building; they offer a range of packages from RM250 per person that include transfers, meals and accommodation in chalets, dorms or tents. Rock climbing and rafting also available.

Green Park Travel Jerantut ☎019 9657 8388, ⊛my -greenpark.blogspot.com. Transfers by boat or 4WD from Jerantut to Tanjung Kiara, plus they manage the *Kenong Lodge* (see below).

ACCOMMODATION AND EATING

Camping in the park costs RM5 per person per night; the most established campsite is at **Gunung Kesong**, about 1hr in from the entrance, with the popular **Kenong campsite** another 5hr north of here at **Lata Kenong waterfall**.

Kenong Lodge About 30min from the Gunung Kesong campsite ⊛kenong-lodge.blogspot.com. Dorm and private rooms inside well-maintained pole-frame huts in the jungle; the only alternative to camping in the park. Meals available by arrangement (RM8–15 per person per meal). Dorms RM15, doubles RM50

3

3

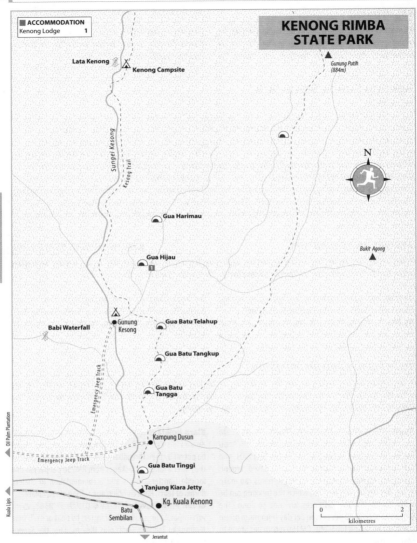

ACCOMMODATION
Kenong Lodge — 1

KENONG RIMBA STATE PARK

Gunung Putih
(884m)

Lata Kenong — **Kenong Campsite**

Sungei Kesong

Kesong Trail

Gua Harimau

Gua Hijau
1

Bukit Agong

N

Babi Waterfall

Gunung
Kesong

Gua Batu Telahup

Gua Batu Tangkup

**Gua Batu
Tangga**

Emergency Jeep Track

Kampung Dusun

Oil Palm Plantation

Emergency Jeep Track

Gua Batu Tinggi

Tanjung Kiara Jetty

Kuala Lipis

Batu
Sembilan

● **Kg. Kuala Kenong**

Jerantut

0   2
kilometres

Kuala Lipis

It's hard to believe that **KUALA LIPIS**, 50km northwest of Jerantut, was the state capital of **Pahang state** from 1898 to 1955. Today, it's a sleepy, inconsequential place, situated at the confluence of Sungai Lipis and Sungai Jelai (a tributary of the Pahang), dwarfed by steep hills and surrounded by plantations. There are a few mementoes from colonial days – many associated with the veteran administrator, **Sir Hugh Clifford** (the Pahang Resident 1896–1905), plus plenty of shops and places to eat, but Kuala Lipis' biggest draw is access to the relatively unvisited rainforest trails at nearby **Kenong Rimba State Park**.

The old town

Kuala Lipis started life as a **trading centre** for *gaharu* (a fragrant aloe wood used to make joss sticks) and other jungle products, collected by the Semiar and traded with Chinese *towkays*. Those times survive in the town's old centre, a busy grid of 1920s **shophouses** squeezed between the train station and the Jelai River, where the former jetty and steps can still be seen, even if goods no longer arrive and depart by river. Overlooking the river to the west, the small, tin-roofed **Mesjid Negeri**, dating from 1888, was reputedly founded by a trader from Yemen.

Pahang Club

Jalan Club • Daily from 6pm

Incongruously hidden behind the huge, brand new **hospital**, the old **Pahang Club** dates to 1867. It's an archetypal tropical colonial building, a sprawling structure of whitewashed timber with black trim and wraparound veranda, raised slightly off the ground on stumps as protection against damp and termites – which, given the lean on the building, hasn't been entirely successful. It's technically open to members only, but there's usually no trouble dropping in for a quick drink and look around.

3

Lipis District Office

Kuala Lipis was chosen as a headquarters for the colonial government despite the town's relative isolation – the trip upriver from Singapore took over two weeks, and there was no road out until the 1890s – though small **tin deposits** brought short-lived prosperity. These boom days are showcased at the former **Lipis District Office**, which overlooks Kuala Lipis from a small hilltop 1km southeast of town: a solid, two-storey crimson-and-white Edwardian edifice, it now serves as the local law court.

Clifford School

Below the District Office, at the back of green playing fields, **Clifford School** was built in 1913 and part-funded by Hugh Clifford; the original buildings are at the far end of the compound. The school is still one of a select group where the country's leaders and royalty are educated – though these days it's perhaps equally known for having been attended by Malaysia's biggest-selling pop songstress, Siti Nurhaliza.

Bukit Residen

A small rise just south of town is crowned by **Bukit Residen**, a graceful two-storey house built in the 1890s as Hugh Clifford's residence. Clifford arrived in Malaysia in 1883, aged 17, and worked his way up through the colonial administration, serving in Malaysia, Sri Lanka and West Africa before ending his career as the Malaya High Commissioner in 1930. The house's associations are more interesting than the building itself (now the *Government Rest House*), though there's a mini-ethnographic **museum** downstairs.

ARRIVAL AND DEPARTURE
KUALA LIPIS

By train Kuala Lipis' train station is right in the old town (ticket office daily 9.30am–2.30pm & 3.30–4.30pm). Walk straight ahead up the lane and you'll be on Jalan Besar, within a short walk of most of the accommodation.

Destinations Batu Sembilan (1 daily; 15min); Dabong (5 daily; 3hr); Gua Musang (5 daily; 2hr); Jerantut (4 daily; 1hr); Kuala Lumpur (1 daily; 8hr); Merapoh (2 daily; 1hr 20min); Singapore (3 daily; 9hr); Wakaf Baru (for Kota Bharu; 5 daily; 7hr).

By bus The main bus station is about 1km north of the centre; cross the bridge, head up the hill and turn right into the small, brand-new cluster of shops, where you'll see the open-sided barn of a station. Some buses also travel via the old bus station, now just a small shelter west of the train station.

Destinations Gua Musang (2 daily; 2hr); Jerantut (3 daily; 1hr); Kuala Lumpur (10 daily; 4hr); Kuantan (4 daily; 6hr); Merapoh (2 daily; 1hr 30min).

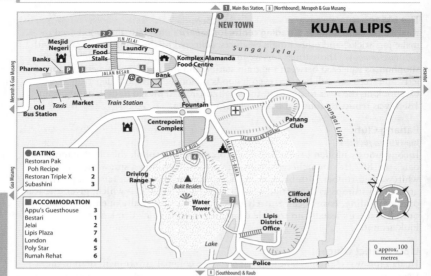

ACCOMMODATION

Appu's Guesthouse 63 Jalan Besar ☎ 09 312 3142, ✉ jungleappu@yahoo.com. A bedrock, no-frills hostel geared to foreign backpackers; a range of basic rooms share facilities. Owner Appu has been leading trips to Kenong Rimba State Park for decades (see p.207). Dorms **RM10**.

Bestari 42–43 Lorong BBKL, just north of town ☎ 09 312 6626. This modern, motel-like affair, about 5min walk from the bus station on the opposite side of the road, is popular with travelling business folk; they take credit cards and rooms come with wi-fi, DVD library, a/c and en-suite facilities. **RM73**

★ **Jelai** 44 Jalan Jelai ☎ 09 312 1192, ✉ hjelai @streamyx.com. First impressions here are of receptionists barricaded behind glass like bank tellers, and bare, tiled corridors. However, it's well run, secure and spotless; rooms have a/c, bathroom and TV, and some overlook the river. Book ahead; they're often full. Their second branch, south of the railway tracks on Jalan Bukit Bius, is not as good. **RM48**

Lipis Plaza Komplek Taipan, Jalan Benta–Lipis ☎ 09 312 5588, ⊛ lipisplaza.com. Spacious but rather plain rooms in a modern complex at the base of Bukit Residen. Rates include breakfast; there's wi-fi too. **RM80**

London Jalan Besar, across from the Subashini restaurant ☎ 09 312 1618. Brusque management, and the rooms are sweatboxes with just enough floor space for the bed and your bag; it's clean though, and you can't argue about the price. All share bathrooms. **RM18**

Poly Star 5 Jalan Bukit Bius ☎ 09 312 3225. Your best bet if the *Jelai* is full. Rooms here are newer and of a similar clean standard – tiled, with basic furnishings and attached bathroom and a/c – but much smaller. **RM48**

Rumah Rehat (Government Rest House) Bukit Residen ☎ 09 312 2784. Clifford's former home has been jazzed up with a coat of scarlet paint; the rooms – all with a/c and TV – are well kept, and the attached bathrooms are large, dwarfing rooms in many cheap hotels. The café isn't open for breakfast. A taxi from town will cost around RM6. **RM78**

EATING AND DRINKING

The market area south of the mosque holds a few despondent Malay stalls, but most fast food is Chinese, with kedai kopis in the covered arcade between Jalan Besar and Jalan Jelai. There's also a **night market** with plenty of food from 3pm every Friday in the purpose-built Kompleks Melati next to the bus station, a 15min walk from the old town.

Restoran Pak Poh Recipe Overlooking town from the north bank of the river, near the Bestari hotel. Great setting, and nice "jungle" theme with rattan decor and potted palms and ferns. The food – including staples such as noodle soups and chicken chop 'n' chips, through to deer stew with medicinal herbs – isn't as good as it should be for the price,

though you could just come for a cold beer and game of pool. Mains RM10–25. Daily 6pm–late.

★ **Restoran Triple X** 44 Jalan Jelai, below the Jelai hotel. A bright, bustling, barely furnished room opening onto the street, serving the tastiest Chinese food in town; people actually dress up to eat here. Try the boneless "Thai-style" chicken, served in a hot and sour sauce; this and a plate of vegetables, plus a large cold drink, costs RM20. Daily noon–3pm & 6pm until customers leave.

Subashini Jalan Besar. A terrific, friendly Tamil curry house with the usual spread of fiery fare for around RM10, as well as *nasi lemak* and *mee goreng* at breakfast; get there early if you want dinner, as it shuts early. Daily 8am–7pm.

DIRECTORY

Bank There's a Maybank with ATM on Jalan Besar.

Internet The Lipis Internet bar on Jalan Besar is marked in English, a few doors along from the *Subashini* restaurant.

Laundry A same-day service is available at a laundry on Jalan Jelai; make sure you fix the price in advance, as the manageress likes to charge foreigners extra.

Supplies If you can't find what you need along Jalan Besar in the old town, head south of the tracks to the Aktif supermarket on the ground floor of the Centrepoint Complex – intended to be a grand shopping development, but in reality a shoddy, mildewed block, with largely untenanted offices.

Merapoh (Sungai Relau)

The small market township of **MERAPOH**, served by road and rail 80km north of Kuala Lipis, marks a 7km-long access road east to **Taman Negara's western entrance**, officially known as **Sungai Relau**. This is the only part of Taman Negara where a proper vehicle road runs deep into the park, providing access to the trails – most famously, that to **Gunung Tahan** (see p.204). Although there's accommodation and the local park headquarters at the entrance, even with your own car there's not much point in turning up here unless you're prepared to arrange for a guide and transport, as the 14km-long park road is closed to private vehicles. What might make it worth the cost is the above-average chance of seeing elephants and even tigers (though don't get your hopes up), plus leopard cat, civets, otters, huge monitor lizards and even packs of dog-like **dhole**.

Into the park

Beyond the park headquarters, accommodation and picnic ground, you cross the little Sungai Relau via a small **bridge** and find yourself on the narrow surfaced road that undulates through the jungle. Several trails lead off the initial few kilometres, including the **Rentis Gajah** ("elephant trail"), leading to Gua Gajah ("elephant cave"); allow 5hr for the return hike from the road, plus an hour exploring. A few kilometres on, a short trail north off the road leads down in a matter of minutes to the park's **hide**, Bumbun Rimau (where you can stay overnight and spotlight for wildlife), close to a salt lick. Drive another few kilometres on to reach the red Menara Bukit Seraya, an **observation tower** with views of forested ridges and valleys to the north, and, on a clear day, east to Gunung Tahan.

The road ends at **Kuala Juram**, a picturesque spot where trees overhang the limpid Juram River, a stretch of which teems with *kelah* (mahseer) fish. If you came to Merapoh to take on the challenge of Gunung Tahan, the suspension bridge over the river here is the gateway to your exertions on the mountain trail.

ARRIVAL AND DEPARTURE — MERAPOH

Merapoh is tiny, with the train station on one side of Route 8, facing a few shops and the junction of the 7km road to the park entrance. There's no bus station, but passing traffic can drop you off; the Relau Agency (see below) can also deliver/collect from Gua Musang, just 30min north.

By train Southbound trains from Merapoh terminate at Kuala Lipis. No transport is available between Merapoh train station and the park; it takes 1hr 30min to walk if you can't hitch a ride.

Destinations Dabong (2 daily; 2hr); Gua Musang (2 daily; 25min); Kuala Lipis (2 daily; 1hr 30min); Wakaf Baru (for Kota Bharu; 2 daily; 6hr).

TOURS AND GUIDES

Relau Agency ☏ 017 915 3034. Tours and transport into the park. Fees include RM20 between the park gates and

Merapoh; RM150 for a day-trip to Gua Gaja; and RM150 for a night safari (compared with RM40 at Kuala Tahan). Their drivers tend to speak little English, but park staff should be able to smooth communication once you've arrived.

Guide service Organizing a guide (either through the Relau Agency or at the park headquarters) for day hikes costs RM100, with fixed rates for trails deeper into the park:

a return 4-day hike from Merapoh to Gunung Tahan (see p.204) costs RM900; a week-long traverse of the park between Merapoh and Kuala Tahan costs RM1200; while the little-used Merapoh–Gunung Tahan–Kuala Koh route takes 10 days (RM1500).

ACCOMMODATION

Park Headquarters 📞09 912 4894, ✉tnsgrelau @wildlife.gov.my. A set of huts here offer tatty dorms or doubles with fans, shower and squat toilets; floors are poured concrete and the tiling is ad hoc. There's also a

spacious campsite with toilets and showers. Everything gets booked solid at weekends and during school holidays. Dorms RM15, doubles RM60

EATING

The canteen at the park headquarters only opens during busy periods; otherwise you'll need to bring all your own food and cooking gear, or use the clutch of *kedai kopis* 7km away in Merapoh, where there's also a busy evening **market**. The nearest places to buy supplies are in Kuala Lipis or Gua Musang.

Gua Musang

GUA MUSANG (Civet Cave), 30km from Merapoh, is a former logging town strung thinly along a stretch of Route 8. A 100m-wide knot of scruffy old buildings, shops and services surrounds the **train station**, while a **new satellite town** coalesces 3km south. With Kota Bharu just a couple of hours away, the Malay accent here displays a distinctive Kelantanese twang, and alcohol is practically unavailable (for more on Kelantan society and politics, see chapter 4).

Gua Musang is fairly close to **Taman Negara entrances** at Merapoh (see p.211) and Kuala Koh (see opposite); time spent between connections can be filled exploring the **caves** that riddle a mass of limestone above the train station.

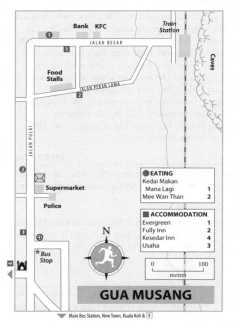

Main Bus Station, New Town, Kuala Koh & [8]

The caves

Local guides around RM10 • Trail difficult after rain, strong shoes and torch necessary

To reach the caves, cross the rail track at the station and walk through the small kampung in the shadow of the rock behind the station. Once you've scrambled up the 20m-high rock face, along a loose path, you'll see a narrow ledge; turn left and edge carefully along until you see a long slit in the rock that leads into a cave – you'll need to be fairly thin to negotiate it. The interior is enormous, 60m long and 30m high in places, and well lit by sunlight from holes above. The main cave leads to lesser ones, where rock formations jut from the walls and ceilings. The only way out is by the same route, which you'll need to take very carefully, especially the near-vertical descent off the ledge and back down to the kampung.

ARRIVAL AND DEPARTURE

By train The train station is in the northern, older part of town.

Destinations Dabong (6 daily; 1hr 15min); Jerantut (4 daily; 3hr 15min); Kuala Lipis (6 daily; 2hr); Kuala Lumpur (1 daily; 9hr 30min); Merapoh (2 daily; 35min); Singapore (2 daily; 10hr); Wakaf Baru (for Kota Bharu; 6 daily; 4hr).

By bus Gua Musang's main bus station is 3km south of the train station in the new town; taxis between the two cost RM5. Some services set down or collect at a stop 1km south of the train station

Destinations Kota Bharu (4hr); Kuala Lipis (2 daily; 2hr 30min); Kuala Lumpur (4 daily; 6hr).

ACCOMMODATION

Evergreen 57 Jalan Besar, near the train station ☎ 09 912 2273. Very plain and slightly mildewed rooms with dismissive staff, a/c, TV and attached bathroom. Good value for money, at least for one night. RM40

Fully Inn 75 Jalan Pekan Lama, near the train station ☎ 09 912 3311. This Chinese-run hotel must have been quite smart when new; now slightly scuffed, with faded carpets and wallpaper starting to peel, it's still a fair deal. Rooms are large and comfortable, with satellite TV, a/c and bathroom, though wi-fi only works in the lobby. Rates include breakfast. RM80

Kesedar Inn About 1km from the station ☎ 09 912 1229, Malay-only site ⓦ kesedar.gov.my. Modern motel complex with doubles and self-contained chalets, at the end of a 400m-long kampung lane lined with wooden stilt houses and fruit trees. Doubles RM70, chalets RM150

Usaha 187 Jalan Besar, across from midway bus stop ☎ 09 912 4003, ✉ ssaliati@yahoo.com. A friendly Malay-run hotel with a popular restaurant below. Not quite as well kept as it should be, but the simple rooms, en suite with TV and a/c, are more than acceptable. RM55

EATING

Kedai Makan Mana Lagi Jalan Besar. Open-air Malay food court that's festooned with coloured lights in the evening. Food has a Thai twist, as is often the case in Kelantan; even the humble fried *kangkung* with squid has a lemongrass kick to it. A good range of *tom yam* and *kerabu*-style dishes for around RM10, plus seafood, including house specialities *ikan tiga rasa* – though none of the staff

can explain what the three flavours of the name derive from. Daily 5pm–late.

Mee Wan Than Jalan Besar. Chinese *kedai kopi* that's about the only place near the station serving food through the day; they do decent roast pork and noodle soup, and chicken on rice for RM10. Daily 8am–late afternoon.

DIRECTORY

Banks There are several banks, including a Maybank with ATM, near the station.

Supplies Stores along Jalan Besar sell everything from food to batteries and umbrellas.

Kuala Koh

Entry RM1, camera permit RM5 • ⓦ wildlife.gov.my

Kuala Koh, Taman Negara's northern entrance 85km east of Gua Musang, offers a similar experience to Kuala Tahan, but within a much smaller area and – unless you happen to encounter a tour party – nowhere near as crowded. **Wildlife** isn't obviously more abundant, though it certainly includes wild boar (whose wallows you see everywhere), tapir, mouse deer and occasionally elephant. Get here at the right time of year – park staff say February – and you might strike lucky and encounter the bizarre stinky blooms of **Rafflesia** (see p.596). Although trails at Kuala Koh are relatively short, it's also possible to **trek** right through to other park entrances at Kuala Tahan (p.191) or Merapoh (p.211) – these routes are seldom used and require advance preparation. There's good-value **accommodation and food** at Kuala Koh, but transport here can be expensive.

Canopy walkway

Sat–Thurs 9.30am–12.30pm & 2.30–4.30pm, Fri 9.30am–noon & 3.30–4.30pm; closed during rain or if lightning is likely • RM5

A **suspension bridge** from the park reception area leads over the Lebir River into the forest; turn left on the far side and it's 500m to the circular **canopy walkway**. This narrow, swaying aerial pathway looks down from 20m over partially cleared forest, at bamboo and the barbed trailers of rattan palms reaching skywards; it's anchored halfway along by an enormous, stout *tualang* tree, with whitish bark. Look for birds, insects and the occasional troop of monkeys.

Forest trails

Beyond the canopy walkway, several kilometres of **trails** weave through the forest and along the river. During the day, **listen** for wildlife – the zithering of cicadas, whooshing of hornbill wings, outsized crashing of monkeys and staccato rustle of lizards amid the leaf litter. Pick of the routes are the **Rentis Ara** (Fig Trail), an easy 3km circuit, and the 3km-long **Rentis Bumbun**, ending at a pole-frame **hide** overlooking a salt lick – somewhere to sit still for an hour and see what turns up, or even sleep overnight.

On the river

Book boats and water activities with the park office (see below)

A pleasant **river trip** heads up the Lebir for half an hour to **Kuala Pertang**, passing a few sandy banks where you can camp, swim or fish; the river is home to *ikan kelah* and other freshwater denizens. The ride takes you under the overhanging boughs of leaning neram trees, some hung with the leafy tresses of **tiger orchids**, among the world's largest orchid species. You can also go **tubing** along the river, being carried downstream inside or on an inflated rubber ring, or arrange a trip to a semi-permanent **Batek camp** 2hr upstream.

ARRIVAL AND DEPARTURE   KUALA KOH

By car Driving, turn off Route 8 at Simpang Aring (half an hour north of Gua Musang) and follow signs along a sealed but extremely rough and winding road through the Felda Aring oil-palm plantation (look out for plantation and mining vehicles), to reach the entrance after 1hr 30min. The road ends at the park reception building above the confluence of the Lebir and Koh rivers; the jetty for boat

trips is at the base of the hill, while next door to the park offices is a restaurant.

By taxi Taxis from Gua Musang charge a negotiable RM120 each way; alternatively, the resort management (see below) make a run into town most days, and might be able to give you a ride for RM70 each way.

INFORMATION AND ACTIVITIES

Park headquarters Inside the reception building at the end of the road ✉ tnkelantan@wildlife.gov.my. They can give you a photocopied schematic map of Kuala Koh, and accept payment of the nominal entry and

photography fees. Book guides and all river activities here too: inner tubes for the river cost RM25 each (minimum of four people), while an hour-long guided night walk, when you might see slow loris and civets, is RM30.

ACCOMMODATION AND EATING

Bumbun (forest hide). Book through the park office and take food, water, sleeping bag and a strong flashlight to watch for animals using the accompanying salt lick. There's no toilet at the hide. RM5

Taman Negara Kuala Koh Resort At the park entrance ☎ 012/965 4788, 🌐 taman-negara-koh .blogspot.com. The reception is at the restaurant, next to the park office desk, with cabins and bunkhouse-style hostel on the lawn behind; you can also camp. The VIP

cabins come with mosquito netting, a/c and en-suite facilities; the dorms and basic cabins with fans and shared bathrooms. Book in advance; given the lack of transport, you're stuck if they don't have any room. The restaurant serves decent *kedai kopi* fare, including fried rice, *sotong*, *tom yam*, grilled fish, *char kway teow* and cold drinks, at only slightly inflated prices – around RM6 a dish. Camping RM1, dorms RM12, cabins RM50–120. Restaurant daily 8am–10pm.

Stong State Park (Taman Jelawang)

RM12 · 🌐 gunung-stong.blogspot.com

Around 55km north of Gua Musang, **Stong State Park** is an off-the-beaten-track gem based around 1400m-high **Gunung Stong**, a prominent, forested granite mountain

7km outside the small rail township of **DABONG**. Current train schedules make it a great day stop, with a tough but short hike up through lush forest to a series of **waterfalls** and plunge pools, where you can have a swim and catch a late afternoon train out. That said, it's also worth staying **overnight** on the mountainside, for the magical sunrise views.

Lata Jelawang

The access road from Dabong ends at the foot of the mountain, where you register with the park authorities and pay fees. From here you follow a path through the resort (see below), over a small bridge and into the forest, where the paving immediately gives out to a muddy path, tangled with tree roots but perfectly clear. This is extremely steep – actually vertical in a few short sections – with chains to help you up the worst bits, but the gritty soil gives a decent grip. It takes around 1hr 30min to reach **Lata Jelawang** (also known as Air Terjun Stong), Peninsular Malaysia's **highest waterfall**, which cascades 540m down a bald granite rock face. There's a pool that's great for a **swim**; *Baha's Camp* is here too, where you'll want to be up at dawn to watch the **sunrise** over a sea of cotton-wool clouds blanketing the plains.

Mountain trails

Baha's Camp is the trailhead for the **Elephant trek**, which follows the main path up the mountain for two hours to the top of Gunung Stong, before winding along the ridge and crossing over onto neighbouring Gunung Ayam. Although it's possible to return *to Baha's* the same day, it's preferable to camp for the night at a clearing along the trail, near a small stream – you'll need some warm clothing and a sleeping bag. Elephants are sometimes seen here, and there's a chance of encountering **tapir** and **deer** in the early morning or early evening.

ARRIVAL AND DEPARTURE
STONG STATE PARK

By train Trains in either direction stop in Dabong before 10am, with the last train out at 5pm or later (check schedules at ⓦ ktmb.com.my) – giving you enough time to visit the falls and have a swim.

Destinations Gua Musang (6 daily; 1hr 15min); Jerantut (3 daily; 4hr); Kuala Lipis (5 daily; 2hr 45min); Kuala Lumpur (1 daily; 10hr 30min); Merapoh (2 daily; 2hr 20min); Singapore (2 daily; 12hr); Wakaf Baru (for Kota Bharu; 6 daily; 2hr 45min). Ask diners or staff at Dabong station's small *kedai kopi* for a lift to the park; they're

happy with RM20. When you leave the park, staff there should be able to give you a ride back to the station by motorbike (RM5).

By car Dabong is just off Route D29, 55km north of Gua Musang; from the parallel Route 8, it's 20km west of Kampung Tembeling. Once at Dabong, cross the river by the train station and head north for 7km, before taking a dirt track towards the mountain that ends at the park gates; on a clear day, the mountain's bald flank and waterfall are unmissable.

ACCOMMODATION AND EATING

Meals in the park are by arrangement only, and the nearest places to eat outside are at the simple *kedai kopis* next to Dabong train station. The closest places to buy supplies are Gua Musang or Kota Bharu.

Baha's Camp Inside the forest, 1hr 30min from the park gates, right by Lata Jelawang ☏ 019 959 1020. A superb – if extremely basic – place to stay, with ageing rattan and bamboo cabins roofed in tarpaulins. There's no electricity or toilets – though you can bathe in the adjacent pools – and you might find yourself contesting the bed with some of the smaller forest creatures who wander in through the night. If you can't contact the camp in advance (they're sometimes out of range), bring all your own food – and a tent, just in case they're full – and they should be able to cook it for you. The camp also organize

essential guides for treks higher up the mountain. **RM10**

Gunung Stong State Park Resort Just inside the park gates ☏ 09 936 2000, ✉ gsspresort@gmail.com. A group of attractive timber cabins on stilts, laid out among open forest either side of a small stream. The interiors are simple and comfortable, with bathrooms, plus TV and wi-fi (though don't expect too much from either). There's a restaurant too, but it's only open if they know you're coming, so – as always in remote locations – book in advance. Dorms **RM10**, doubles **RM110**, family (2 doubles and a single) **RM150**

The east coast

KITE MAKER NEAR KOTA BHARU

The east coast

The 400km-long stretch from the northeastern corner of the Peninsula to Kuantan, roughly halfway down the east coast, draws visitors for two major reasons: the beaches and islands, and traditional Malay culture. Islands such as Pulau Perhentian, Pulau Redang and Pulau Kapas offer great opportunities for diving and snorkelling; further south, the backpackers' coastal enclave of Cherating is a deservedly popular place simply to kick back for a few days. Among the cities, vibrant Kota Bharu, close to the Thai border, stands out for its opportunities to access Malay crafts and performing arts.

The east coast displays a different cultural legacy to the more populous, commercial western seaboard, from which it is separated by the mountainous, jungled interior. For hundreds of years, the Malay rulers of the northern states of **Kelantan** and **Terengganu** were vassals of the Thai kingdom of **Ayuthaya**, suffering repeated invasions as well as the unruly squabbles of their own princes. Nevertheless, the Malays enjoyed a great deal of autonomy, and both states remained free of British control until 1909. Only in 1931 did the rail line arrive in Kelantan; previously, the journey from KL involved thirteen river crossings. In 1941 Kelantan saw the landing of the first Japanese troops, facilitated by the Thai government – who were rewarded by being given control over Kelantan once more from 1943 until 1945.

While immigrants poured into the tin and rubber towns of the west during the twentieth century, the east remained rural. As a result, Kelantan and Terengganu remain very much **Malay heartland** states. There's a rustic feel to the area, the economy being largely based on agriculture and fishing, with the obvious exception of Terengganu's petroleum industry.

The country's religious opposition party, **PAS**, which was born in Kelantan in the middle of the last century, has governed its home state since 1990. For foreign visitors, the political backdrop distils down to the simple truth that the **social climate** of Kelantan and Terengganu is more obviously **conservative: alcohol** is harder to obtain than in other states; most restaurants, whatever cuisine they serve, are **halal**; and **dress** – for both men and women – needs to be circumspect, except at well-touristed beaches. You will also find that **English** is less understood in Kelantan and Terengganu than in most other parts of the Peninsula.

GETTING AROUND

While **flights** to Kota Bharu or Kuala Terengganu can be useful time-savers, **road** access to the east coast has really opened up with the development of the **East Coast Expressway** (E8). The only **rail** service is the atmospheric "jungle railway" through the interior (see p.206) to Tumpat, near Kota Bharu.

GREEN TURTLE OFF PULAU PERHENTIAN

Highlights

❶ **Kota Bharu** One of the Peninsula's most appealing cities, home to Malay crafts, traditional art forms and a popular night food market, with Thai temples within easy reach. **See p.221**

❷ **Pulau Perhentian** Two of the most enticing islands the Peninsula has to offer, with excellent snorkelling and accommodation ranging from backpacker chalets to slick resorts. **See p.233**

❸ **Pulau Kapas** A delightful little island with decent sands and opportunities for snorkelling

and kayaking – perfect for a couple of days' relaxation. **See p.251**

❹ **Cherating** Chill by the beach, watch fireflies or just enjoy the amiable, low-key nightlife in this long-established travellers' hangout. **See p.255**

❺ **Pekan** An appealingly quiet royal town, with a scattering of palaces, impeccable kampung houses and a newly renovated museum housed in a colonial building. **See p.263**

HIGHLIGHTS ARE MARKED ON THE MAP ON P.220

By car The E8 arrives on the coast just north of Kuantan, reducing the drive from KL to a 3hr whizz, then runs north as far as Kuala Terengganu. The next phase is planned to link up with Kota Bharu. Meanwhile, the region's old backbone roads remain intact: the coast road (called Route 3 between Kuala Terengganu and Kuantan) and its shadow, running 10 to 20km inland (Route 14 south of Kuala Terengganu, Route 3 to the north). Not surprisingly, the coastal road, connecting a string of laidback small towns and fishing kampungs, is the most interesting if you have time.

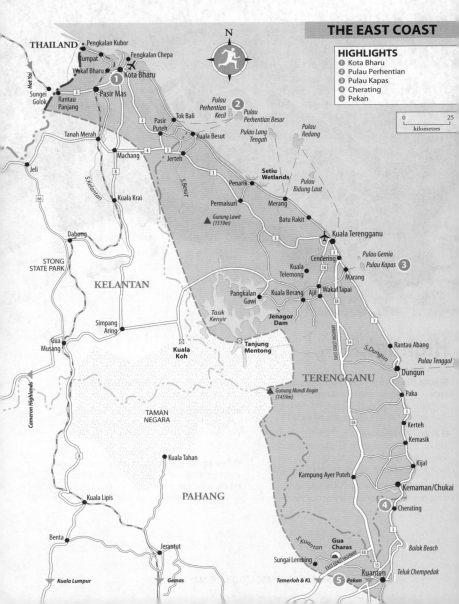

THE EAST COAST

HIGHLIGHTS
1. Kota Bharu
2. Pulau Perhentian
3. Pulau Kapas
4. Cherating
5. Pekan

Kota Bharu

The capital of Kelantan, **KOTA BHARU,** sits at the very northeastern corner of the Peninsula, on the east bank of the broad, muddy Sungai Kelantan. Many visitors arrive across the nearby Thai border, and for most of them the city is simply a half-decent place to rest up and get their Malaysian bearings. To breeze through Kota Bharu and the rest of Kelantan, however, would be to gloss over one of the most culturally fascinating states in the country.

Kelantan has historically been a crucible for **Malay culture**, fostering art forms that drew on influences from around Southeast Asia and as far away as India. Kota Bharu is the ideal place to witness the region's distinctive heritage, on show at its **Cultural Centre** and at the various **cottage industries** that thrive in its hinterland – among them kite-making, batik printing and woodcarving. The city also boasts its share of historical buildings, now largely **museums**, plus some excellent **markets,** as well as numerous **Buddhist temples** in the surrounding countryside.

The city centre is compact and easily negotiated on foot. Useful **reference points** include the rocket-like clock tower that marks the junction of the town's three major roads, Jalan Hospital, Jalan Sultan Ibrahim and Jalan Temenggong; the towering radio mast off Jalan Doktor, which is illuminated at night; and, in the south, the gleaming Pacific KB Mall complex. Most of the **markets** and many of the **banks** and the biggest stores lie between Jalan Hospital and Jalan Pintu Pong, a few blocks north.

Around Padang Merdeka

West of the main markets, close to the river, the quiet oasis of **Padang Merdeka** marks Kota Bharu's historical centre. It was here that the British displayed the body of the defeated Tok Janggut (Father Beard), a peasant spiritual leader who spearheaded a revolt against the colonial system of land taxes and tenancy regulations in 1915. Today the main attractions are a handful of old buildings, several of which have been converted into museums.

One of the most obvious landmarks is the **Sultan Ismail Petra Arch**, beyond which is the **Istana Balai Besar** – a mid-nineteenth-century palace, closed to the public but still used for ceremonial functions – and the squat former **State Treasury Bank**.

Istana Jahar

North of Sultan Ismail Petra Arch, Jalan Hilir Kota • Sat–Thurs 8.30am–4.45pm • RM3 • ☎ 09 748 2266

The impressive traditional building known as **Istana Jahar** was built in 1887 with a timber portico and polished decorative panels adorning the exterior. In 1911 Sultan Mohammed IV added an Italian marble floor and two wrought-iron spiral staircases.

THE EAST COAST IN THE OFF-SEASON

Many visitors give the east coast a wide berth during the especially wet **northeast monsoon**, which sets in during late October and continues until February. It's true that heavy rains and sea swells put paid to most boat services to the east-coast islands at this time, and most beach accommodation, whether on the mainland or offshore, is shut anyway. The rains will, however, usually be interspersed with good sunny spells, just as the so-called dry season can bring its share of torrential downpours. With luck, and a flexible schedule, you will find boats heading sporadically to and from the islands during the northeast monsoon; some island accommodation opens year-round, although you should contact places to be sure. While diving and snorkelling aren't great at this time of year thanks to reduced visibility, the east coast comes into its own for **surfing** and **windsurfing**, with Cherating the prime destination. Away from the beaches, there's always reasonable sightseeing in Kota Bharu and Kuala Terengganu – just be prepared to take lengthy refuge in cafés or malls when yet another thunderstorm breaks.

KOTA BHARU

0 — 400 metres

PCB & Tokong Mek

Clock Tower
Istana Jahar
Padang Merdeka
Central Market
Jetty
JLN TENGKU BESAR
JLN HULU
JLN PADANG GAR ONG
JLN TOK HAKIM
JLN T. P. SEMERAK
JLN CHE SU
JLN POST OFFICE
JLN TEMENGGONG
JLN DATO PATI
JLN DOKTOR

Bird Singing Contests
JLN KEBUN SULTAN
JALAN SRI CEMERLANG
JLN PINTU PONG
JLN PENGKALAN CHEPA

Thai Consulate

S. Kelantan

Clock Tower
JLN GAJAH MATI
State Museum
SEE 'CENTRAL KOTA BHARU' INSET FOR DETAIL

General Hospital
JLN HOSPITAL
JLN SULTAN ZAINAB
JLN DUSUN MUDA

Immigration Office

Istana Kota Lama
JLN ZAINAL A BIDIN
JLN SULTANAN ZAINAB
Police
Gelanggang Seni (Cultural Centre)
Stadium
JLN BAYAM
JLN-SULTAN-IBRAHIM
JLN BAYAM

N

Masjid Langgar

■ ACCOMMODATION
Pasir Belanda — 1
Renaissance — 4
Tune — 3
Zeck's Travellers' Inn — 2

K B Permai
Pacific KB Mall
JLN HAMZAH
JLN KUALA KERAI
JLN PASIR PUTIH

● EATING
Four Seasons — 2
Warisan Nasi Kukus — 1

Tesco Bus Station

Wakaf Bharu & Tumpat

4

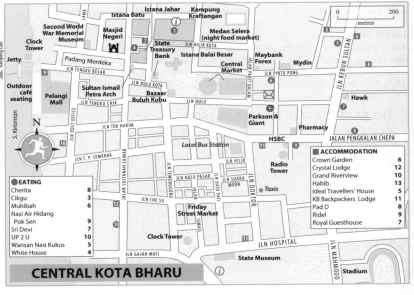

Kampung Laut

Istana Jahar
Kampung Kraftangan
Second World War Memorial Museum
Istana Batu
Masjid Negeri
State Treasury Bank
Medan Selera (night food market)
Istana Balai Besar
Central Market
Maybank Forex
Mydin

Clock Tower
Jetty
Padang Merdeka
JLN TENGKU BESAR
LAMA
JLN HILIR KOTA
JALAN PARIT DALAM
JLN PINTU PONG
JLN KEBUN SULTAN

Outdoor café seating
Pelangi Mall
Sultan Ismail Petra Arch
Bazaar Buluh Kubu
JLN HULU KOTA
JLN HULU
Hawk

S. Kelantan

JLN POST OFFICE
JLN TENGKU CHIK
JLN TOK HAKIM
Parkson & Giant
Pharmacy
JALAN PENGKALAN CHEPA

N

JLN T. P. SEMERAK
Local Bus Station
JLN SULTANAN ZAINAB
JLN TEMENGGONG
JLN HULU PASAR
JLN SUARA MUDA
JLN HILIR
JLN DATO PATI
JLN DOKTOR
HSBC
Radio Tower
★ Taxis

● EATING
Cherita — 8
Cikgu — 3
Muhibah — 6
Nasi Air Hidang Pok Sen — 9
Sri Devi — 7
UP 2 U — 10
Warisan Nasi Kukus — 5
White House — 4

JLN CHE SU
Friday Street Market
ISMAIL
Clock Tower
JLN GAJAH MATI
State Museum
JLN HOSPITAL
JLN MAHMOOD
Stadium

■ ACCOMMODATION
Crown Garden — 6
Crystal Lodge — 12
Grand Riverview — 10
Habib — 13
Ideal Travellers' House — 5
KB Backpackers Lodge — 11
Pad D — 8
Ridel — 9
Royal Guesthouse — 7

CENTRAL KOTA BHARU

ISLAM IN KELANTAN

Unlike elsewhere in the country, Kelantan's legal system traditionally operated according to **Islamic law** – an important factor in the maintenance of national pride under Thai overlordship. This wholehearted embrace of Islam was encouraged by trading contacts with the Arab world, enabling a free flow of new ideas from as early as the 1600s. One of Kota Bharu's most famous sons is **To' Kenali**, a religious teacher who, after years of study in Cairo, returned at the start of the twentieth century to establish *sekolah pondok* – huts functioning as religious schools.

Kelantan retains its distinctive identity today, to the extent that it's even difficult for anyone from outside the state to buy property here. It's also the scene for an intense, ongoing political rivalry that has, for example, seen the national government blocking the state government's attempts to introduce *hudud* (punishments including flogging, amputation, stoning and execution, meted out for specific types of crime).

This rivalry is producing dramatic changes in Kota Bharu. After years of stagnation under PAS and a refusal by UMNO to release funds from federal coffers, both parties have decided that development is the avenue to political glory. As a result, the city now boasts a major shopping mall and a sprinkling of fancy riverside apartments – all of which would have been unthinkable until relatively recently. While some foreign visitors find Kelantan's conservatism apparent, especially if they've arrived from Thailand, by and large Kota Bharu comes across as a bustling, pragmatic sort of place.

The palace now houses an exhibition on **royal ceremonies**, which can be seen in an hour (although you may want to linger on the breezy veranda above the entrance). Rites illustrated include *istiadat pijak tanaha*, a ceremony that marked the point when young royals – aged between 5 and 7 years – were allowed to set foot on soil for the first time.

The **weapons gallery**, in a separate building to the right of the palace (included in the ticket price), features an exhibit devoted to the *kris*, a dagger which has important symbolic value to Malays (see p.245).

Istana Batu

Just north of Istana Jahar, Jalan Hilir Kota • Sat–Thurs 8.30am–4.45pm • RM2 • ☎ 09 748 7737

The yellow **Istana Batu**, an incongruous 1930s villa built as the sultan's residence, is now hidden from the main road by a new apartment building. One of the first concrete constructions in the state (its name means "stone palace"), it functions as the **Kelantan Royal Museum**.

Several rooms remain decorated as they were when the royal family moved out, and a brief wander through is worthwhile if only to survey the tat that royals the world over seem to accumulate. Here it includes stacks of crystal glassware (including items such as a glass revolver) and English crockery.

Kampung Kraftangan

Opposite Istana Batu, Jalan Hilir Kota • Sat–Thurs 8.30am–4.45pm • Free • ☎ 09 744 3949

In the **Kampung Kraftangan** (Handicraft Village), a collection of gift shops sell everything from tacky souvenirs to silverware, rattan baskets and other local products. You can try your hand at batik-making at Zecsman Design (classes starting at RM50), and the complex is also home to the excellent *Cikgu* restaurant (see p.230).

Handicraft Museum

Kampung Kraftangan, Jalan Hilir Kota • Sat–Thurs 8.30am–4.45pm • RM2 • ☎ 09 744 3949

This single-room museum within the Handicraft Village is worth a few minutes of your time, displaying traditional craft items including silverware, woven *pandan*, bamboo and rattan objects, woodcarving and *songket* (textiles woven with gold thread).

THE MARKETS OF KOTA BHARU

Kota Bharu has a fine array of **markets**, reflecting its role both as the state capital and as a centre for Malay culture and handicrafts. In addition to those listed here, see p.230 for details of the night food market.

Central market Just east of the historical centre. Kota Bharu's humming central market (aka Pasar Besar Siti Khadijah) is a focal point of the city. The main building, an octagonal hall, has a perspex roof casting a soft light over the multicoloured patchwork of the main trading floor – a mass of fruit, vegetables and textiles. The whole scene is worth contemplating at length from the upper floors. Trading continues east of here in an extension to the original market, with yet more stalls spilling out onto the surrounding pavements. Daily 8am–6pm.

Bazaar Buluh Kubu A couple of minutes' walk west of the central market. Though lacking in atmosphere, this market does have a good range of batik, *songket* and other crafts on sale. Daily 8am–6pm.

Friday market Jalan Ismail south of Jalan Hulu Pasar. A visit to the informal, morning-only Friday market is recommended as a way to witness the rustic heart of Kelantan laid bare, as traders and shoppers pour in from the surrounding kampungs on their weekend day out in the city. Fri 8am–noon.

Masjid Negeri

Jalan Sultan • Permission required from International Islamic Information Centre, Taman Hijau (daily 10am–6pm; ☎ 09 747 9376) • Free

The white **Masjid Negeri**, on the northern side of the padang, was completed in 1925. Once you have permission and are inside the mosque, note the enormous drum (*bedok*) that was formerly used to summon the faithful to prayer.

Second World War Memorial Museum

Adjacent to Masjid Negeri, Jalan Sultan • Sat–Thurs 8.30am–4.45pm • RM2

Housed in a squat, pale yellow building that was formerly the Mercantile Bank of India, the **Second World War Memorial Museum** commemorates the fact that Japanese troops first set foot in Malaya on Kelantan's beaches. They captured all of the state in December 1941, and Singapore fell just two months later. During the occupation, the bank was the local base for the Japanese secret police.

While the war artefacts are largely desultory (bits of old ordnance, ration pouches and the like), the accompanying text gives insight into the swiftness of the Japanese advance – aided by their use of bicycles – and the British collapse. The downstairs exhibition goes on to cover the years leading up to independence, while upstairs there's material on the 1960s onwards.

State Museum

Corner of Jalan Hospital and Jalan Sultan Ibrahim • Sat–Thurs 8.30am–4.45pm • RM2

Much of the ground floor of the **State Museum** is taken up with display panels detailing the history of Kelantan, although it also includes the "time tunnel", in which old photographs of locations in the city are paired with contemporary images taken from the same spots. It's fascinating to see what has – and hasn't – changed. The upper floor focuses on traditional local pastimes, with displays of kites, spinning tops and various musical instruments.

Cultural Centre

Jalan Mahmood • Feb–Oct Mon 3.30pm, Wed 3.30pm & 9pm, Sat 3.30pm & 9pm; closed during Ramadan

A high point of any visit to Kota Bharu, the excellent **Cultural Centre** (Gelanggang Seni) puts on demonstrations of Kelantan's cultural and recreational activities. Each day's session is different, so check with the state tourist office if you have a particular interest. Together they include *gasing* (spinning tops), *pencak silat* (martial arts), *rebana ubi* (giant drums), *kertok* (smaller drums formed from coconuts) and *congkak* (a game involving the strategic movement of seeds around the holes on a wooden board). Best of all, Wednesday evenings see *wayang kulit* (shadow puppetry) performances from 9–11pm.

Craft workshops

Most of Kota Bharu's **craft workshops** lie on the road to **PCB**, the uninspiring beach 11km north of the city. As they are quite spread out, the best way to see a variety of workshops (including kite-making, batik and more) is on a tour, arranged either via a guesthouse or through the state tourist office. Half-day tours cost around RM90 per person, with a minimum of two people. The workshops listed here are not on the way to PCB, and are relatively easy to visit independently.

K.B. Permai (silverware)
Jalan Sultanah Zainab, close to intersection with Jalan Hamzah

Kelantanese **silverware** is well known throughout the Peninsula. At the workshop of **K.B. Permai**, you can watch artisans shaping silver wire into fine filigree, as well as producing items such as embossed gongs and jewellery. You can buy pieces here, or at their retail outlet in the Kampung Kraftangan (see p.223), at much keener prices than in Kuala Lumpur.

4

THE PERFORMING ARTS IN KELANTAN

Kelantan has a rich artistic tradition, boasting two costumed dance/drama forms, **mak yong** and the Thai-influenced **menora**. Even more striking is **wayang kulit**, shadow puppetry, traditionally staged on a dais screened from the audience by a large cloth sheet and illuminated from behind. The cast consists of a set of stencils made of hide and formed into the shapes of the various characters, which are manipulated against the screen by a sole puppeteer, who also improvises all the dialogue. Reflecting the long history of Indian influence in the region, the tales are taken from the Hindu epic, the *Ramayana*; in the past, *wayang kulit* functioned as a sort of kampung soap opera, serializing *Ramayana* instalments nightly during the months after the rice harvest. Performances are gripping affairs, with a hypnotic soundtrack provided by an ensemble of drums, gongs and the oboe-like *serunai*, whose players are seated behind the puppeteer.

Sadly, all three of the above traditional art forms have been **banned** in Kelantan by the PAS-led state government since the 1990s. PAS has cited issues of public morality – which could mean they object to the fact that both *mak yong* and *menora* can involve an element of cross-dressing. PAS also objects to the non-Islamic nature of these performances, since they involve folk tales or Hindu mythology. Finally, the party also has a problem with the **spiritualism** permeating these arts. A *wayang kulit* performance always begins with a *buka panggung* ceremony, in which the puppeteer readies the stage by reciting mantras and making offerings of food to the spirits, while *mak yong* can be staged for an individual as part of a folk-healing tradition called *main puteri*, in which the performers enter a trance to remove a spirit believed to be affecting that person.

Whatever the reasons for the ban, the effect has been akin to cultural hara-kiri, depriving a generation of Kelantanese of their own traditions. Dozens of *wayang kulit* troupes have been reduced to a mere handful, performing largely outside Kelantan or, thanks to one **concession** from PAS, for the benefit of the mainly tourist audience at Kota Bharu's Cultural Centre. On a brighter note, all three forms mentioned here are being passed on to a new generation, and sometimes staged, at the National Academy of Arts, Culture and Heritage in KL (🔅aswara.edu.my).

AROUND KOTA BHARU

Pak Yusoff (puppets)

Kampung Laut • Boat (RM1) from the jetty close to the Ridel hotel • ☎ 012 340 6498

A *wayang kulit* **puppeteer** who also makes the tools of his trade, Pak Yusoff can be visited in **Kampung Laut**. His workshop, to the right of the pier as you get off the boat, holds examples of his distinctively translucent puppets. Call ahead as he is not always around.

Buddhist temples

The area north of Kota Bharu is dotted with **Buddhist temples**, which can be visited using buses bound for the stretch of beach called **Pantai Seri Tujuh**. Getting from one to the next can take a while by public transport, though, so it's quicker and easier to take a tour, arranged through the state tourist office or individual guesthouses. It's often possible to combine the temples with visits to handicraft workshops. They're especially worth visiting during **Wesak**, the festival (usually in May) celebrating the Buddha's birthday.

Wat Pracacinaram

Kampung Kulim, just outside Wakaf Bharu, on the road to Cabang Empat • Bus #19 or #27

The highly conspicuous main building of **Wat Pracacinaram** has an elaborate triple-layered roof decorated in gold, sapphire and red. The temple offers a herbal steam bath – with separate facilities for men and women – for RM5.

Wat Phothivihan
15km west of Kota Bharu in Kampung Jambu • Bus #19 or #27; get off at Cabang Empat then walk 3.5km or take a taxi

The 40m-long reclining Buddha at **Wat Phothivihan** is said to be the largest in Southeast Asia (although this is not a unique claim). The colossal, if rather bland, plaster statue was made by the monks themselves and contains ashes of the deceased who have been laid to rest here.

Wat Machimmaram
Kampung Jubakar, 2km south of Tumpat • Bus #27

Topped by a 30m-high statue of Buddha, the temple of **Wat Machimmaram** contains bas-reliefs that depict the graphic punishments of hell – the corrupt are, for example, doomed to have molten tin poured into their mouths. Meat eaters are shown being punished for their harm to animals; thus eaters of pork will be reincarnated as pigs and then carved up.

Wat Mai Suwankiri
Near Kampung Bukit Tanah • Bus #27 to Tumpat then change to bus #43

The main attraction in the **Wat Mai Suwankiri** complex is the temple built in the shape of a dragon boat, surrounded by a moat to give the impression that it is afloat. The use of small mirrors in the detailing enhances the fairground feel.

Pulau Suri
Taxi to Kuala Besar (20–30min; RM10) then boat (15–20min; RM2); alternatively #43 bus to Jeti Kok Majid (45min) then boat (40min; RM50 return for whole boat)

One of many small riverine islands north of Kota Bharu, **Pulau Suri** is home to around 500 people. Getting there is half the fun, requiring a trip down the wide tea-coloured Kelantan River in a motorized sampan, but the island itself has some pleasant paths for walking and a well-developed **homestay** programme (see p.230).

There are two ways to reach Pulau Suri from Kota Bharu. The quickest and cheapest is via **Kuala Besar**, which is not to be confused with Kuala Besut (the access point for Pulau Perhentian). While the second route, via **Jeti Kok Majid**, is considerably more scenic, it's also more expensive as you will probably need to charter a boat. If you're staying on the island, contact the homestay organizer in advance to arrange a boat.

Arriving at Pulau Suri, you'll spot a boatyard next to the jetty where they mend traditional wooden boats. There's also a simple **café** or two for refreshments. From here you can head inland along a path lined with coconut trees.

ARRIVAL AND DEPARTURE   KOTA BHARU

BY PLANE
Sultan Ismail Petra Airport 9km northeast of the centre. Official airport taxi into town RM27; cheaper taxis ply the main road outside, as does the #9 bus (until 7pm). A taxi straight to the Perhentians jetty at Kuala Besut should cost RM78. MAS (☎09 771 4700) and AirAsia (☎09 774 1421) have flights between Kota Bharu and KL, while Firefly (☎09 774 1377) links the city to KL and Penang.

BY TRAIN
Train station The nearest station is 7km west at Wakaf Bharu, a 20min ride on bus #19 (daytime only) from the local bus station – watch for the late-afternoon rush

hour – or a RM20 taxi journey. The express train to KL leaves Wakaf Bharu (☎09 719 6986, ⊕www.ktmb .com.my) in the early evening, with the Singapore-bound express several hours later.
Destinations Dabong (6 daily; 2hr 15min); Gua Musang (6 daily; 3hr 30min); Jerantut (4 daily; 6hr 30min); Johor Bahru (2 daily; 13hr 45min); Kuala Lipis (5 daily; 5hr 15min); Kuala Lumpur (1 daily; 13hr); Merapoh (2 daily; 4hr); Seremban (1 daily; 12hr); Singapore (2 daily; 14hr 45min).

BY BUS
Long-distance bus station (aka Tesco bus station) Close to the eponymous supermarket, near the Kelantan

river bridge on the southern edge of Kota Bharu, this replaced the Langgar and Jalan Hamzah bus stations, still shown on some maps. A taxi to the town centre costs RM15.

Destinations Alor Star (2 daily; 7hr); Butterworth (2 daily; 7hr); Gua Musang (3 daily; 4hr); Ipoh (2 daily; 7hr); Johor Bahru (2 daily; 12hr); Kuala Kangsar (2 daily; 5hr); Kuala Lumpur (at least 12 daily; 9hr); Kuala Terengganu (12 daily; 3hr); Kuantan (10 daily; 7hr); Melaka (1 daily; 10hr); Mersing (1 daily; 12hr); Pekan (1 daily; 7hr); Penang (2 daily; 8hr); Seremban (2 daily; 10hr); Singapore (1 daily; 11hr). For details of buses into Thailand, see below.

Local bus station Off Jalan Padang Garong in town centre. Used by SKMK buses which run by day to places within or just outside Kelantan – notably Wakaf Bharu (for trains), Rantau Panjang (to cross into Thailand) and Kuala Besut (bus #639, for the Perhentians; 4 daily; 2hr; RM5). Many arriving long-distance services also call here, but few do so as they leave. Tickets for long-distance buses are nonetheless sold here.

BY TAXI OR MINIVAN

Long-distance taxis park in a yard on Jalan Doktor, south of the local bus station. A taxi to Kuala Besut (1hr; for the Perhentian Islands) costs RM50–60. Kuala Terengganu should cost RM120.

Minivans Several guesthouses arrange trips to destinations including the Cameron Highlands (5hr 30min;

RM65), Taman Negara (8hr; RM85), and Kuala Besut (1hr; RM10) for the Perhentians.

TO THAILAND

There are two designated road crossings into Thailand – and none by rail – on the east coast. The closest large Thai town to either is **Narathiwat**, served by buses to other parts of southern Thailand and flights to Bangkok. Note that Thailand is one hour behind Malaysia. Although the **security situation** in southern Thailand has improved in recent years, it's worth checking on the current situation. **Visas** for Thailand can be obtained from the consulate in Kota Bharu (see p.231) if required.

Rantau Panjang The recommended crossing is at Rantau Panjang (daily 8am–9pm), 40km southwest of Kota Bharu and reached by local bus #29 (hourly, 6.45am–6.30pm; 45min) or share taxi (RM10). From Sungai Golok, a short walk across the border on the Thai side, trains run to Bangkok, via Hat Yai and Surat Thani (11.30am & 2.20pm; 20–22hr; ⓦrailway.co.th), and frequent buses head to Hat Yai (4hr).

Pengkalan Kubor The other crossing – slower to get through and with worse transport links – is at Pengkalan Kubor (daily around 8am–7pm), 25km northwest of Kota Bharu; take local bus #19, #27 or #43 (30min), or a share taxi (RM5) then a car ferry. The small town of Tak Bai stands on the Thai side.

GETTING AROUND

By bus SKMK's red Cityliner buses serve most parts of the city and its environs from dawn to dusk.

By taxi Local taxis operate from the same area as long-distance taxis, and don't use meters. Negotiate a price in advance – typical journeys within the centre cost RM10.

By trishaw A few trishaws can be found around the central market; agree fares, typically RM5–10, in advance.

Car rental Hawk (☎09 773 3824, ⓦhawkrentacar .com.my), Ping Anchorage (see 'Information') or – at the airport – J&W (☎012 988 8766, ⓦjwcarental.com).

INFORMATION

Tourist information The state tourist office (Sun–Wed 8am–5pm, Thurs 8am–3.30pm, Fri 8am–12.30pm & 2–3.30pm; ☎09 748 5534, ☻tic@kelantan.gov.my), near the clock tower on Jalan Sultan Ibrahim, can tell you about annual cultural festivals and also give you a detailed timetable of events at the Cultural Centre. The Tourism Malaysia office (Sun–Wed 8am–5pm, Thurs 8am–3.30pm; ☎09 747 7554) is at the Kampung Kraftangan, northwest of the central market.

Tours Ping Anchorage, Jalan Padang Garong (☎09 774 2020, ⓦpinganchorage.com.my); Doremi Travel & Tours (☎09 774 7458); or KB Backpackers, Jalan Sultan

Ibrahim (☎013 744 2125, ⓦkb-backpackers.com.my). Roselan Hanafiah, based at the state tourist office, can arrange craft workshop tours and homestays (see opposite). Suzilan Mohammed Salleh (☎019 9424 033, ☻ogcana@yahoo.com) runs regular hiking, rafting, climbing and kayak trips to Gunung Stong, the Gua Musang district and beyond.

Internet access There are quite a few small internet cafés, usually in upstairs premises, on the lanes between Jalan Pintu Pong and Jalan Padang Garong. There is also wi-fi at *McDonald's* on Jalan Parit Dalam, open 24 hours a day.

ACCOMMODATION

Kota Bharu has an excellent range of accommodation. Budget travellers will appreciate the good-value if sometimes a bit scruffy **guesthouses**, many of which can arrange tickets for onward travel and offer packages to Taman Negara via Kuala Koh (see p.213) and sometimes to Stong State Park (aka Jelawang; see p.214).

HOTELS

Crown Garden 302 & 303 Jalan Kebun Sultan ☎09 743 2228, ✉sales_dept@crowngardenhotel.com, ⊕crown gardenhotel.com. Opened in 2011 and at the upper end of the city's accommodation options, this 88-room hotel has laminated floors and modern decor plus a seventh-floor bar. RM220

Crystal Lodge 124 Jalan Che Su ☎09 747 0888, ⊕crystallodge.com.my. Sleek mid-range hotel, with a café-restaurant, parking, satellite TV and in-house movies. Good-value single (RM89) and superior (RM149) rooms, though the standard rooms are a bit disappointing. Breakfast included. RM119

Grand Riverview Jalan Post Office Lama ☎09 743 9988, ⊕grh.com.my. The river views are nothing special, though the sunsets can be spectacular, but this substantial hotel is modern and comfortable with spacious rooms. The jacuzzi suite even has a semi-outdoors spa bath. Rack rates, shown here, are poor value; look for discounts. Rooms RM235, jacuzzi suite RM577

Habib Lot 1159–1162, Seksyen 11, Jalan Maju ☎09 747 4788, ⊕habibhotel.com.my. Solid mid-range choice where the comfortable rooms, with flat-screen TVs, are not as stylish as the reception area might suggest. Breakfast included. RM150

Renaissance Jalan Sultan Yahya Petra ☎09 746 2233, ⊕marriott.com. The 298 rooms in Kota Bharu's only five-star hotel were refurbished in 2011, and some have great views over the city. Facilities include two restaurants, a gorgeous semi-outdoor pool, a spa and a 24-hour gym. No alcohol is served, but you can bring your own. RM325

Ridel Northern end of Pelangi mall ☎09 747 7000, ⊕ridelhotel.com.my. Minimalist decor, enlivened by fish paintings on the walls of every room. Standard rooms have twin beds; pay RM10 extra for a superior if you want a double. Breakfast included, in the *Shark Lounge* restaurant. RM97

Royal Guesthouse Jalan Hilir Kota ☎09 743 0008, ✉royalgh@streamyx.com. Despite its far-from-regal exterior, this conveniently central 45-room hotel is comparatively stylish inside. It also offers a multi-cuisine restaurant plus room service, and free wi-fi in some rooms. The proximity to the mosque may not suit light sleepers. Breakfast included. RM109

Tune Jalan Hamzah ☎03 7962 5888, ⊕tunehotels .com. This out-of-town hotel, beside KB Pacific Mall in a building that also holds a branch of *Hayaki* café, is part of the low-cost AirAsia group. Book well in advance for the best rates, and expect charges for all extras – even towels. One room offers disabled accessible features. RM60

GUESTHOUSES

Ideal Travellers' House 3954f & g Jalan Kebun Sultan ☎09 744 2246, ⊕ugoideal.com. The oldest guesthouse in town, somewhat worn but great value; most rooms have a fan and shared bathroom. Friendly owner Kang offers temple tours (3hr; RM60 per person, min two) and sells transport tickets. There's wi-fi and internet terminals. Doubles RM20, a/c doubles RM50

KB Backpackers Lodge First floor, 1872d Jalan Padang Garong ☎09 748 8841, ✉backpackerslodge2 @yahoo.co.uk. Friendly travellers' haunt with private rooms, a bare-bones dorm, lounge, roof garden and internet access. Helpful and knowledgeable staff can arrange transfers, excursions and city tours (RM80). Do not confuse it with the run-down *KB Backpacker Inn* across the road. Dorms RM10, doubles RM20, a/c doubles RM35, en-suite a/c doubles RM55

★ **Pad D** 4320-Q2 Jalan Sri Cemerlang ☎09 748 6299, ⊕paddbackpack.blogspot.com. Good backpacker option, with appealing common areas and small but decent bedrooms. At quieter times it can be hard to find the staff – look for them in the co-owned internet café across the street. Dorms RM13, a/c dorms RM18, doubles RM25, a/c doubles RM35

★ **Pasir Belanda** Jalan PCB, Banggol district, 4km north of the city ☎09 747 7046, ⊕pasirbelanda. com. This rural Dutch-run establishment consists of several traditionally styled chalets, set in a pleasant leafy compound alongside a creek. It offers batik painting (RM30) and Malay cookery lessons (RM50), plus tours and kayak and bike rental. Catch #10 bus to Banggol mosque, then follow signs 1500m east, or take a RM15 taxi. RM160

Zeck's Travellers' Inn On a lane off Jalan Sri Cemerlang ☎09 743 1613, ✉zecktravellers@yahoo.com. Friendly Malay guesthouse in a quiet residential area. Dorms and a large selection of simple rooms with fan or a/c, some with shared bathrooms. They arrange ticket reservations and Perhentians transfers, plus city tours. On Fri and Sat mornings, bird singing contests are held just opposite. Wi-fi in reception. Dorms RM10, doubles RM25, a/c doubles RM45

HOMESTAYS

KB homestay programme Various locations. Roselan Hanafiah, at the state tourist office, can arrange for visitors to stay with a local family whose members are expert in a particular craft. The price given here is per night, based on a standard two-night package for two people including all meals and craft materials. RM490

Pantai Suri homestay programme Pulau Suri ☎013 900 8820, ⊕homestaypantaisuri.blogspot .com. Contact Fadhila Hanim, the programme

4

coordinator, to stay in one of the 20 participating homes though conditions can be fairly basic. You can pay per night (including all meals) or for a two-night package that also includes activities such as fishing, crab catching and *kuih sepit* (wafer snack) making. Prices listed here are per night, for two people. **RM160**, package **RM300**

EATING AND DRINKING

Kota Bharu has a good number of **restaurants** dotted around the centre, plus an excellent outdoor *Medan Selera* (night food market). The Chinese places on Jalan Kebun Sultan are among the few restaurants that aren't halal, and are also your best bet for **alcohol**, along with some budget guesthouses and a few discreet Chinese bars. To combine eating with shopping, head to the **Pacific KB Mall**: aside from a couple of Western cafés, it has a handy food court. Another popular spot, especially with young locals, is the row of cafés on the **waterfront** close to the Pelangi Mall.

Cherita Jalan Pengkalan Chepa ⓦ cherita.com.my. Located on a quiet side road, this open-sided restaurant is best known for its excellent *nasi ayam* (chicken rice) although it also serves a *nasi campur* buffet. Daily 8am–midnight.

★ **Cikgu** Kampung Kraftangan. Busy self-service lunch place, offering the classic Malay meal *nasi ulam*. Dishes like fried chicken, vegetable curry and *asam pedas ikan patin* (catfish in spicy sauce) are laid out alongside rice and *ulam*, a salad of blanched vegetables and herbs – some of them incredibly bitter. If you're feeling brave, have the dip made of *tempoyak* (fermented durian) and *budu* (fermented fish sauce). Cheap and best enjoyed with a group. Daily except Fri 11.30am–4.30pm.

Four Seasons Jalan Sri Cemerlang ☎ 09 743 6666, ⓦ fourseasonsrestaurant.com.my. Modern Chinese restaurant where the seafood-strong menu includes reliable winners like steamed fish in soy sauce, oyster pancake and steamboat. Set menu RM60; main dishes, big enough for two, RM12. Packed at weekends. Daily noon–2.30pm & 6–10pm.

★ **Medan Selera (night food market)** Off Jalan Pintu Pong. The few dozen stalls here offer a great range of *murtabaks* (savoury stuffed pancakes) as well as Kelantanese specialities such as *nasi kerabu* (rice tinted blue, traditionally using flower petals, and typically served with fish curry). Wash your meal down with *sup ekor* (oxtail soup) or *sup tulang* (made from beef bones), or round it off by sampling the colourful *kuih* (sweets). Daily 6pm–midnight.

Muhibah Jalan Pintu Pong. Excellent, inexpensive vegetarian establishment. Downstairs a bakery and café serve local and Western pastries and ice-blended shakes; upstairs a small restaurant has a great spread of stir fries and set meals (RM5), combining noodles or rice with fish or mock meat. Daily 10am–9.30pm.

Nasi Air Hidang Pok Sen Jalan Padang Garong. Kota Bharu isn't exactly buzzing late at night, so this 24-hour Malay food court can come in handy; the *nasi air* of the name is rice porridge, but a wide range of dishes are available. There's nothing sophisticated about the food, but there's wi-fi and, usually, a good atmosphere. Daily 24hr.

Sri Devi Jalan Kebun Sultan. Top-notch South Indian *kedai kopi*, popular with locals but usually with a scattering of foreigners, serving excellent banana-leaf curries and tasty mango lassi. Daily 7.30am–8.30pm.

UP 2 U Jalan Sultanah Zainab. Small "dessert station" that's a refreshing stop on a hot day, with a wide range of milk shakes, floats and shaved ice treats. Savoury snacks also available. Mon–Sat 3pm–midnight.

Warisan Nasi Kukus Jalan Kebun Sultan. In a small row of Malay stalls, this humble pushcart operation is renowned for fresh *sambal* fish, okra curry, *ikan bakar* (grilled fish) and the like. Your preferred toppings will be poured over steamed rice (*nasi kukus*), on a banana leaf that's folded into a pyramid shape and wrapped for you to take away. Daily 6pm–late.

White House Jalan Sultanah Zainab. No grand mansion, but a tiny bungalow housing a mundane-looking *kedai kopi* that's a city institution. The trademark dish is humble *telur setengah masak* – soft-boiled eggs cracked into a saucer, seasoned with soy sauce and white pepper, and delicious scooped up with buttered toast. Washed down with *teh* or *kopi tarik*, it's great for breakfast or a late snack. Daily roughly 8am–1pm & 9pm–1am.

SHOPPING

Kota Bharu is famous for its Malay **handicrafts**, with most of the workshops located outside of town (see p.225). For general shopping, try the Pacific KB Mall, which houses the huge Pacific supermarket and plenty of other shops. More centrally, there's a Parkson department store with Giant supermarket on Jalan Padang Garong and a Mydin supermarket on Jalan Pintu Pong. Recent additions include Bazar Tok Guru on Jalan Sultan Ibrahim and Bazar Tuan Padang on Jalan Dato Pati. Finally, the night market on Jalan Parit Dalam, beside the central market and spreading east onto Jalan Pintu Pong, is worth a browse.

Books The Pacific KB mall has a branch of the Popular bookstore, while there is also a handful of small book/stationery shops in the centre.

Outdoor equipment For camping and hiking kit try the small SR Outdoor Gear Centre in Kompleks Mara.

DIRECTORY

Banks and exchange There are several banks around the rectangle bounded by Jalan Pintu Pong, Jalan Padang Garong and Jalan Kebun Sultan. Better rates for foreign exchange from Azam (next to *KB Backpackers Lodge* on Jalan Padang Garong, Sat–Thurs 9.30am–9.30pm).

Hospital Jalan Hospital ☎ 09 745 2000.

Left luggage At the local bus station (8am–8pm, RM1–2/day).

Pharmacies Central pharmacies include a Guardian pharmacy on Jalan Padang Garong and another Guardian, plus a Watsons, in the Pacific KB Mall.

Police Headquarters on Jalan Bayam (☎ 09 745 5622).

Post office GPO on Jalan Sultan Ibrahim; there's a convenient branch post office on Jalan Parit Dalam, just south of Jalan Pintu Pong.

Thai visas Many nationalities can get a visa at the border. Otherwise, visas can be obtained in advance from the Thai Consulate, 4426 Jalan Pengkalan Chepa (Sun–Thurs 9am–noon & 2–3.30pm; ☎ 09 743 0640); they have been known to refuse entry to people in shorts, so dress smartly.

Visa extensions At the Pejabat Imigresen (Immigration Department), second floor, Wisma Persekutuan, Jalan Bayam (Sun–Thurs 8am–5pm; ☎ 09 748 2120). Take bus #11 or #639; taxi RM10.

From Kota Bharu to Kuala Terengganu

Few travellers linger long on the coast south of Kota Bharu; most are simply waiting for a boat from **Kuala Besut** (for Pulau Perhentian) or **Merang** (to Pulau Redang or Pulau Lang Tengah; not to be confused with Marang further south). Get money before you set out; there are **no ATMs** on any of the mentioned islands (or in Kuala Besut), though some accommodation may accept cards, and you may be able to get cash advances at punitive rates. If you do have time to stop, then there are a few good resorts on the coast plus some interesting villages and wildlife in the **Setiu Wetlands**.

4

Kuala Besut

The only reason to visit the mainland village of **KUALA BESUT** is to catch a boat to the Perhentian Islands. It's practically a one-street affair, the street in question running past the **boat terminal** and terminating just beyond the **bus and taxi station**. You'll find **agents** selling boat tickets and Perhentians packages in the lanes along this street or in the boat terminal; all offer similar services at similar prices.

ARRIVAL AND DEPARTURE   KUALA BESUT

By bus Buses to KL at 9am and 9pm. From the closest transport hub, Jerteh, buses run to destinations as far afield as Singapore and Penang.

Destinations Jerteh (14 daily); Kota Bharu (4 daily; 2hr); Kuala Terengganu (8 daily; 3hr); Kuala Lumpur (2 daily; 8hr); Merang (6 daily; 1hr).

By taxi The taxi stand is next to the bus station.

Destinations Jerteh (RM20); Kota Bharu (RM50; RM78 to airport); Kuala Terengganu (RM78).

By minibus Several travel agents arrange minibuses to Kota Bharu and Kuala Terengganu; prices are typically a little higher than for buses.

Destinations Cameron Highlands (RM45); Penang (RM65);

Taman Negara (RM55).

By boat Boats sail to the Perhentians several times a day (40min; RM35 one-way). All will drop you at the bay of your choice, though at bays without a jetty – notably Long Beach – you have to transfer to a smaller boat (RM2) to get ashore. Return tickets cost double the one-way price and you don't need to know when or from where you're going to come back; the day before your departure, staff at your accommodation will arrange for you to be picked up (boats typically leave the islands at 8am, noon, and if there's demand 4pm). Boat service is regular only between March and October; at other times sailings are much reduced.

ACCOMMODATION

Nan Hotel Down a lane opposite the boat terminal ☎ 09 697 4892. Decent rooms, a few of which have a/c and TV. The most expensive (RM120) even has hot water. Fan RM35, a/c RM65

Samudera Jalan Pantai ☎ 09 697 9326, ⓦ kekal -samudera.com. The 26 a/c rooms here represent fine value for money and are good enough for a night, plus there's a handy seafront complex with places to eat just behind the hotel. RM55

EATING AND DRINKING

Restoran Seafood Lucky Kuala Besut. This place beside the bus station offers dishes such as chicken rice, but it's the seafood that attracts most people. Three computers offer a chance to go online before catching a Perhentians boat. Daily 5am–10pm.

The Setiu wetlands

As a breeding ground for the painted terrapin and green turtle, the **Setiu wetlands**, between Kuala Besut and Merang, have been a focus for WWF projects since the early 1990s, but even now they attract only a trickle of tourists.

Both the main settlements hereabouts, namely **Penarik**, on the main coastal road, and **Mangkok**, 6km inland, are small villages, so the easiest way to explore is on a tour organized by an operator in Kuala Terengganu.

Pewanis

Pink House, Kampung Mangkok • Sun–Thurs 8.30am–5pm • ☎ 013 702 6458

This community project improves the financial position of local women, while working with the WWF on environmental projects. With advance notice, visitors can learn how to make banana chip snacks, help plant mangrove trees or take part in kite-making sessions. Staff can usually arrange bicycle rental and organize trips to the nearby hatchery or to the "blue house" which has displays on ecology.

ARRIVAL AND DEPARTURE   SETIU WETLANDS

Tours Public transport is limited so it's better to rent a car or take a taxi; better still, come on an organized tour. Ping Anchorage, for example, can arrange a trip including a visit to Pewanis, a turtle hatchery and a man raising *ayam*

serama (chickens bred for competition, which sell for up to a staggering RM8000 each). Otherwise buses can drop you at the turning for Mangkok, and you can walk from there.

ACCOMMODATION

The women of Pewanis plan to start a homestay scheme, but in the meantime the area holds a handful of places to stay, including a stunning resort.

Pandan Laut Pantai Rhu Sepuluh ☎ 013 681 2495, ⓦ pandanlaut.com. Set in a leafy site, the rooms here range from a run-down A-frame to decent concrete rooms and wooden family cabins. Island day-trips cost RM600 for a boat (up to six people), while turtle watching is free since WWF personnel stay here. A-frame RM50, rooms RM80, cabins RM130

Penarik Inn Kampung Baru Penarik ☎ 012 626 7947, ⓦ penarikinn.blogspot.com. The most pleasant surprise at this isolated spot is not the very average rooms but the *Caribbean Coffee Shop*, where you can laze in a hammock

while listening to well-chosen music. Bicycles and snorkelling equipment are available for rent, and island day-trips can be arranged. RM80

★ **Terrapuri Heritage Village** Kampung Mangkok ☎ 09 624 5020, ⓦ terrapuri.com. A labour of love for the owner of Ping Anchorage travel agency, this site features old palace buildings that have been saved from neglect elsewhere – over the space of two decades – then reconstructed without using any nails. Staff can arrange day-trips or you can simply relax by the pool or beach; there's also a spa. RM499

EATING AND DRINKING

There are few notable places to eat other than at accommodation, although the stalls on Penarik Beach have decent seafood – look out for local speciality *ikan celup tebung* (battered fish).

Merang

Most travellers who make it to **MERANG**, along the coastal road just south of the Sungai Merang creek, only glimpse the back of the village on their way to the jetty. The beach, accessible along a couple of side roads, is not exceptional, but if you have time to kill there's reasonable swimming and memorable views of the islands offshore – from left to right, the Perhentians, Lang Tengah, Redang and finally Bidung Laut, now uninhabited but once the site of a refugee camp for Vietnamese boat people.

ARRIVAL AND DEPARTURE   MERANG

By bus S.P. Bumi's eight daily buses between Kuala Besut and Kuala Terengganu stop close to Merang's school.
By taxi A taxi to Merang costs around RM60 from Kuala Besut, RM50 from Kuala Terengganu.

By boat Jetties for the resorts on Redang and Lang Tengah line the riverside, ten minutes' walk from the bus stop. Most packages include transfers, but tickets (RM50 to either island) are also available from booths or the boatmen.

ACCOMMODATION

The Merang area has a limited amount of beachfront **accommodation**. There are also a couple of well-appointed options at Kampung Rhu Tapai, ten minutes south of Merang jetty.

Aryani Jalan Rhu Tapai ☏ 09 653 2111, ⓦ thearyani .com An attractive and peaceful Malay-styled spa resort, great for getting away from it all. Most of the accommodation is in rooms or suites with traditional design features, although the newer "terrace" rooms are more modern. Top of the range is the Heritage Suite, a century-old Malay stilt house that once belonged to a Terengganu sultan. Rooms RM415, Heritage Suite RM897
Kembara Resort 474 Pantai Peranginan ☏ 09 653 1770, ⓦ kembararesort.tripod.com. A little run-down

but still the best budget place close to Merang, set in a large well-shaded garden; follow a side road from the bus stop on the southbound side of the road then turn right. A range of rooms, some with a/c, plus two single-sex dorms. Free wi-fi. Dorms RM10, room RM30
Merang Suria Kampung Rhu Tapai ☏ 09 653 1600, ⓦ suriaresorts.com/merang. The 70 rooms at this good mid-range beach resort tend to fill up at weekends; there are attractive promotional rates for advance bookings. RM138

EATING AND DRINKING

The simple places close to the jetty are handy if you arrive early and need some breakfast.

Huge Crab Seafood Restaurant Jalan Penarik. With a name like that, how can you resist? This Chinese place is 1km off the main road – take a left just before the Shell

station if you're heading north from Kuala Terengganu – and serves up the day's catch (although sadly the crabs are the usual size). Daily lunch and dinner.

Pulau Perhentian

The name **Pulau Perhentian** actually covers two islands, **Perhentian Besar** and **Perhentian Kecil** (which mean large and small stopping places, respectively; Big Island and Small Island are sometimes used instead). Both are textbook tropical paradises, which retain considerable appeal despite having been developed for tourism. The essentials of any idyllic island holiday – fantastic sandy beaches, and great **snorkelling** and **diving** – are all in place. Both islands have jungly hills in their interior, with paths for **walking** and opportunities to spot flying foxes, monkeys and monitor lizards. All this is capped by a refreshingly laidback atmosphere that can make it difficult to tear yourself away.

For many years, large-scale development on the Perhentians was kept to a minimum. This was just as well, given that both islands are home to several **turtle nesting** sites, active from April to early August – the only organized viewing is through the *Bubbles* resort (see p.240) – and that the impact of the existing resorts on the environment is far from negligible. Shortages of **water**, for example, can be a hassle during the tourist peak.

The state government's attitude towards development has loosened up in recent years, however, and a few larger resorts have been constructed. **Alcohol** is also sold openly

4

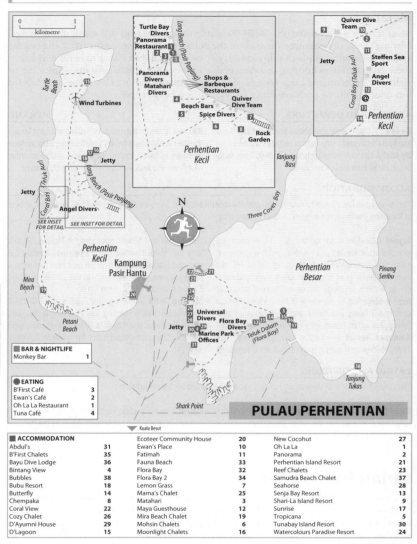

PULAU PERHENTIAN

■ **BAR & NIGHTLIFE**

Monkey Bar	1

● **EATING**

B'First Café	3
Ewan's Café	2
Oh La La Restaurant	1
Tuna Café	4

▼ Kuala Besut

■ **ACCOMMODATION**

Abdul's	31	Ecoteer Community House	20	New Cocohut	27
B'First Chalets	35	Ewan's Place	10	Oh La La	1
Bayu Dive Lodge	36	Fatimah	11	Panorama	2
Bintang View	4	Fauna Beach	33	Perhentian Island Resort	21
Bubbles	38	Flora Bay	32	Reef Chalets	23
Bubu Resort	18	Flora Bay 2	34	Samudra Beach Chalet	37
Butterfly	14	Lemon Grass	7	Seahorse	28
Chempaka	8	Mama's Chalet	25	Senja Bay Resort	13
Coral View	22	Matahari	3	Shari-La Island Resort	9
Cozy Chalet	26	Maya Guesthouse	12	Sunrise	17
D'Ayumni House	29	Mira Beach Chalet	19	Tropicana	5
D'Lagoon	15	Mohsin Chalets	6	Tunabay Island Resort	30
		Moonlight Chalets	16	Watercolours Paradise Resort	24

these days at a handful of restaurants and bars, although it seems that it is not strictly legal: the police periodically confiscate booze from businesses on the island but it isn't long before things are back in full swing.

ESSENTIALS

Accommodation As Perhentian Kecil caters largely to the backpacker scene, much of its accommodation consists of low-priced chalets and resorts, many with electricity only 7pm–7am. Perhentian Besar, on the other hand, holds most of the mid-range accommodation and is popular with families, package tourists and better-heeled independent travellers. Increasing development on Kecil, though – including some mid-range resorts – has somewhat eroded this distinction. Book in advance for the peak season, at least for the first night or two, or you may arrive to find that all the most affordable chalets are full. Most mid-range places offer their own full-board packages, typically for three days and two nights, and include boat transfers and some snorkelling or diving. Unless you're on one of the more remote beaches, though, there's no shortage of places to eat if you choose a B&B deal.

Climate Outside peak season – roughly June until the end of August – rates fall by at least a quarter. Many resorts begin closing in late October, sometimes earlier, and don't open again until February or March, but for a truly isolated island experience a few places stay open during the northeast monsoon.

GETTING AROUND

By water taxi Small speedboats operate a so-called water taxi service around the Perhentians. Fares start at a few ringgit per person for a journey between adjacent bays – rocky obstructions often preclude walking – rising to RM25 to travel from one side of Besar to the other, or one island to the other. The accommodation or restaurant where you happen to be will usually be able to rustle up a boatman within a few minutes. The exception to this is after dark, when water taxis can become scarce and you may have to pay double the usual fare. If you simply need to get across either island, you may be able to use a footpath instead (after dark a torch is essential).

Perhentian Kecil

The small island of **Perhentian Kecil** has something to please most people. If you're looking for a laidback backpacker scene with the odd beach party, you've come to the right place, but several mid-range resorts cater for those who need a comfortable bed after a day snorkelling. The most popular beaches, **Coral Bay** and **Long Beach**, are only ten minutes' walk apart, via a footpath through the woods.

Long Beach

For many visitors, east-facing **Long Beach**, boasting a wide stretch of glistening-white, deep, soft sand, is the prime attraction of Perhentian Kecil. It lacks a view of the sunset, but somehow that really doesn't matter: the light gently fades away, leaving the illumination from the beach restaurants (and their CDs of Bob Marley or dance music) to dominate the senses. There's a genuinely infectious buzz; in peak season, pop-up bars host fairly frequent **beach parties**.

Coral Bay and the west coast

While west-facing **Coral Bay** has become significantly more developed since the building of its huge and ugly jetty, it remains quieter than Long Beach. It also has sheltered waters, which make it a better bet than its eastern rival during the northeast monsoon, plus good snorkelling and sunset views if you can ignore the jetty.

A couple of quieter and more secluded beaches lie south of Coral Bay. The first, **Mira Beach**, has just one backpacker hangout, while the next, **Petani Beach**, was in an

---

PERHENTIANS DOS AND DON'TS

• Do bring more than enough **cash** – there are no banks or ATMs. Only some mid-range places accept plastic for accommodation and food, with a small surcharge. You may also be able to get a cash advance for a significant fee.

• Do bring mosquito repellent.

• Don't leave **valuables**, even clothes, on the beach – whether crowded or deserted – while you swim or snorkel. Thieves can appear seemingly from nowhere on snatch-and-grab raids.

• Do **swim with care**: look out for **boat lanes**, marked by strings of buoys, and stay on the correct side to avoid being wiped out by a speedboat. Note also that Long Beach can have a significant **undertow** from February to April and in October; a few people get swept out every year and have to be rescued.

• Do be mindful of sharp-pronged boat **anchors** sticking out of the sand as you walk along the beach at night – particularly if you're looking up at the stars.

• As always, don't touch the **coral** or disturb **marine life** when you snorkel or dive.

SNORKELLING AND DIVING AROUND THE PERHENTIANS

Outside the monsoon, the waters around the Perhentians are superb: currents are gentle, and visibility is up to 20m (although sea lice can sometimes be an irritant, inflicting unpleasant but harmless stings). A **snorkelling** foray around the rocks at the ends of most bays turns up an astonishing array of brightly coloured fish, including black-tip reef sharks, and an occasional turtle. The seas around the islands are part of a national park so the coral is protected, although as elsewhere in the region it suffered bleaching due to high sea temperatures in 2010. It remains to be seen whether that was an isolated incident.

If you just want to explore around the main beaches, then snorkels, masks and fins can be rented from accommodation, dive shops or shacks on the main beaches. **Snorkelling trips** to undeveloped coves can be arranged at beach stalls (particularly on Long Beach), or most accommodation, for around RM35 per person. Many travellers recommend the trips operated by *Maya Guesthouse* (☎019 222 9257) on Coral Beach; like most operators, though, they often take very large groups. Typical itineraries include Turtle Point (between the islands), Shark Point, Romantic Beach and the lighthouse; lunch, normally in the village on Perhentian Kecil, costs extra.

Some very good **dive sites** lie just a short boat ride offshore, including the Pinnacle (aka Temple of the Sea), T3 and Sugar Wreck (a boat that sank while carrying a cargo of sugar). In addition to fun dives (RM70–80), the islands' numerous dive shops also offer **courses**, including Open Water (around RM900), Advanced Open Water (around RM850) and the introductory Discover Scuba Diving (around RM160); a handful also offer specialist facilities such as Nitrox. Most places teach **PADI courses**, although Alu Alu (Perhentian Besar; ☎09 691 1650, ✇alualudivers.com) uses SSI certification.

With so many dive shops, it makes sense to shop around – not just on price but (more importantly) to find somewhere you feel comfortable and safe. Recommended dive shops include Turtle Bay Divers (Long Beach and the west shore of Perhentian Besar; ✇turtlebaydivers.com), Steffen Sea Sports (Coral Bay; ☎016 231 0933, ✇steffen-sea-sports.com), and Flora Bay Divers (Flora Bay; ☎09 691 1661, ✇florabaydivers.com). Steffen is the only shop to organize night dives on the Vietnamese Wreck (RM135, requires Advanced Open Water qualification); Turtle Bay is one of several that offers trips to the generally superior dive sites around Pulau Redang (RM280 for a two-dive trip). Alu Alu has three-dive trips to Redang and is the only outfit to visit Pulau Bidong.

uncertain state at the time of research. The previously recommended *Petani Beach House* was about to close, while the only other resort, the *Impiani*, was being renovated by new owners to squeeze more guests into the same amount of space.

ACCOMMODATION PERHENTIAN KECIL

The prices quoted here are for peak season, generally around June–August; there are often discounts at other times.

LONG BEACH

★ **Bintang View** Long Beach ☎09 691 1249. Run by a friendly Malay-Irish couple, a very short walk uphill away from the beach. Not the fanciest of chalets but well kept and very homely, with toilets and showers in two separate blocks; the one downside is that the chalets lack power sockets. A restaurant serves some of the island's best food – try the mango salad. **RM50**

Bubu Resort Long Beach ☎03 2142 6688 or ☎09 697 8888, ✇buburesort.com.my. Catering mainly for package holidaymakers, this motel-like complex of en-suite a/c rooms has two restaurants and offers massages on the beach. All perfectly decent, but it jars a little on Long Beach and it's hard to justify the high prices. The restaurants are worth considering as a treat. **RM370**

Chempaka Long Beach ☎013 946 6791. Tucked away at

the end of the beach, this place has a mishmash of somewhat run-down A-frames, and rather better en-suite chalets in a longhouse-type block. Electricity 7pm–7am. A-frames **RM35**, chalets **RM70**

Lemon Grass Long Beach ☎019 938 3893. Simple, sound chalets with fan and mosquito net; toilets and showers in a separate shack. Good views from the restaurant go some way to compensate for the less-than-wonderful facilities; room #14 has a sea view through one side window. Electricity 10am–2pm & 7pm–7am. **RM60**

Matahari Long Beach ☎019 914 2883, ✇mataharichalet.com. A jumble of wooden chalets and A-frames with faded blue roofs, plus some newer a/c chalets, set a little way back from the beach. They're a little rough around the edges, but pretty good value and popular, and almost all en suite. There's also a dive shop. Electricity

6.30pm–8.30am. Fan rooms RM60, a/c rooms RM120

Mohsin Chalets Long Beach ☎09 691 1363, ⓦmohsinchalet.my. Four tiers of longhouse-style wooden buildings on a hillside behind Long Beach. The rooms are en suite and many have a/c, while a mixed-sex a/c dorm sleeps 24 people. The elevated restaurant has beach views, free wi-fi and nightly movie showings. Dorms RM40, fan rooms RM130, a/c rooms RM160

Moonlight Chalets Long Beach ☎09 691 1777. A wide range of accommodation with 24-hour electricity at the northern end of the beach, including a fan-cooled, seven-bed dorm, cheap A-frames and a/c chalets. Beach-view restaurant. Dorms RM15, fan rooms RM50, a/c rooms RM65

Oh La La Long Beach, ☎019 331 9624, ⓦohlala perhentian.com. Simple, clean, good-value rooms, sharing bathrooms. Above one bar and beside another, so it's quite noisy at night. The large, pleasant communal balcony holds a hammock as well as a few chairs and tables; RM35 massages available downstairs noon–9pm. Electricity off only 8–11.30am. RM40

Panorama Long Beach ☎09 691 1590 or ☎019 960 8630, ⓦpanoramaperhentianisland.com. Chalets with fans, some en suite, plus pricey a/c rooms all set back from the beach in the jungle. There's a popular restaurant plus a dive shop; they offer all-inclusive diving packages. In high season, room rates include dinner for one person. Electricity 11am–4.30pm & 6.30pm–8am. Fan chalets RM35, a/c rooms RM125

Sunrise Long Beach ☎017 930 9053. Relatively quiet, as it's a little set back from the front. Decent private rooms plus two a/c dorms, one sleeping ten people and the other just four. RM20 wi-fi for your whole stay. Dorms RM30, fan rooms RM70, a/c rooms RM120

Tropicana Long Beach ☎016 266 1333. Ambitious new development a little back from Long Beach, initially holding 40 en-suite rooms but expected to reach 120. The site may end up feeling crowded, but for the moment the rooms are very good value (though prices soar on public holidays). Dorms RM15, fan rooms RM40, a/c rooms RM100

CORAL BAY

Butterfly Coral Bay ☎013 956 3082. Quiet, simple and good-value chalets, tucked away at the end of Coral Bay, and popular with long-term guests like divemasters. The further you get from reception, the better the sea views tend to be. Electricity 7pm–7am. RM45

★ **Ewan's Place** Just behind Coral Bay ☎014 817 8303. A great choice if you don't mind being a couple of minutes back from the beach, with clean and tidy rooms that are significantly better than you might expect at this price. Friendly owner Ewan also runs the on-site café. RM50

Fatimah Coral Bay ☎09 691 1562 or ☎019 923 2730. En-suite rooms, mostly two to a chalet and hardly sophisticated, with fan and plasticky floor lining. They're good value, though, and have mosquito nets if little else. Wi-fi RM10/day, computers RM10/hour. RM50

Maya Guesthouse Coral Bay ☎09 690 2230 or ☎012 449 6540, ⓔmayaguesthouse@yahoo.com.my. En-suite fan chalets around a garden compound, with a popular beach café. Their snorkelling trips are among the most popular on the island. RM60

Senja Bay Resort Coral Bay ☎09 691 1799, ⓦsenjabay.com. This complex of en-suite chalets, built on a hillside and connected by decking, contains quite spacious and well-maintained rooms. There's also a restaurant and dive shop; snorkelling and diving packages are available. Rates include breakfast, and there's 24-hour electricity. Fan rooms RM100, a/c rooms RM150

Shari-La Island Resort Coral Bay ☎09 691 1500 or ☎09 697 7500, ⓦshari-la.com. Dozens of chalets shoehorned in at the northern end of the bay. The a/c rooms are overpriced but comfortable; there are also a/c dorms and "budget" rooms, the former arguably the best on the island. Dorms RM20, budget rooms RM90, a/c rooms RM230

THE REST OF THE ISLAND

D'Lagoon Teluk Kerma ☎019 985 7089. Nestling in an isolated cove at the island's northeastern tip, this laidback place has its own dive shop. Accommodation includes a 12-bed dorm, a longhouse with fan rooms, and a treehouse. It's a long and exposed walk to the cove, but a water taxi costs just RM10 per person from Long Beach. Dorms RM15, fan rooms RM30, a/c rooms RM100

★ **Ecoteer Community House** Kampung Pasir Hantu ⓦecoteerresponsibletravel.com. Staying in the islands' sole village gives a very different experience, helping with turtle conservation and other projects while getting to know the community. Note that there is a RM260 membership fee if you stay a week or more. The dorm price includes the boat transfer; all packages include meals. Dorms, per person per week RM664, twin rooms/night RM440

Mira Beach Chalet Mira Beach ☎016 647 6406. Charmingly rustic – or, less charitably, run-down – chalets clustered on their own secluded cove, a 20-min walk south of Coral Bay. Friendly staff make the place a backpacker favourite; snorkelling trips RM40–55. Electricity noon–3pm & 7pm–7am. RM50

EATING AND DRINKING

Many places to **eat** are connected to accommodation; they're fine but rarely very exciting. Evening beach **barbecues** – such as at the restaurants around Long Beach's Lazy Buoy shop – are popular and often tasty, but can wear thin after a few days. As for **nightlife**, only one of Long Beach's handful of bars – the *Monkey Bar* – is any more than a simple shack. Coral Bay currently has no bars, though one is rumoured to be on its way; beers sold from the cooler box on the beach can be taken into most restaurants.

LONG BEACH

Monkey Bar Long Beach. As the only permanent bar on Long Beach, this place gets consistently busy; you can sit by the bar or lounge around in the two-storey wooden building. Beers go for RM9 while a small bottle of "monkey juice" (20% alcohol) costs RM20. Live music every night. Daily 4pm–around 3am.

Oh La La Long Beach. Very popular for its early-evening movie screenings, after which most people decamp to the *Monkey Bar* next door. It's worth trying the food, though,

with the tandoori chicken particularly recommended. Daily lunch until late.

CORAL BAY

Ewan's Café Between Coral Bay and Long Beach. Super-friendly owner Ewan ("Ee-wan") serves up great Malay dishes. Pick a main ingredient – chicken (RM12), veg (RM7.50), or prawn (RM18) – then select a cooking style and/or sauce. Daily 7.30am–10pm.

Perhentian Besar

The larger of the two islands, **Perhentian Besar**, has a more grown-up atmosphere. Although it holds a few relatively cheap options in addition to the mid-range resorts, it doesn't have the backpacker scene or nightlife of its neighbour. On the other hand, the beaches remain relaxed despite some nearly continuous strings of development.

Western shore

The string of attractive beaches on the shore facing Perhentian Kecil are separated by rocks – at high tide you'll need a boat taxi to get from one to another. It's packed with resorts, but in a pleasingly organic way; it also has a good vibe after dark when the restaurants get busy. At the northern end, reached by a concrete walkway, the *Perhentian Island Resort* is alone on one of the best stretches of sand, Teluk Pauh.

Teluk Dalam and the south coast

Also known as Flora Bay, **Teluk Dalam** is less cramped than the western shore but also tends to feel slightly institutional, and holds several of the larger resorts. Further east, the Bubbles resort sits on its own beach, only accessible by boat.

From the western shore, a steep **trail** (45min) to Flora Bay begins just past the second jetty south of *Abdul's*, behind some villas intended for visiting politicians. Another trail links Teluk Dalam with the *Perhentian Island Resort* (30min), passing the island's waterworks close to the bay.

Three Coves Bay

For the finest beaches on Besar, take a water taxi to **Three Coves Bay** (Teluk Tiga Ruang) on the north of the island, a stunning conglomeration of three beaches separated from the western shore by rocky outcrops. This area also provides a secluded haven for green and hawksbill turtles to lay their eggs.

ACCOMMODATION   PERHENTIAN BESAR

WESTERN SHORE

Abdul's Southern main beach ☎019 912 7303, ⓦabdulchalet.com. Sturdy en-suite chalets in semi-detached pairs. Most of the better and roomier ones, fronting the beach, are significantly more expensive than the garden-facing options, although a couple of "standard sea view" chalets cost RM180. Fan rooms **RM90**, a/c rooms **RM170**

Coral View Northern main beach ☎09 691 1700, ⓦcoralviewislandresort.com. A range of modern rooms, mainly in smart, steep-roofed chalets with small attached bathrooms. They're connected by walkways through a pleasant garden, and the standard rooms in particular are

good value. There's a restaurant, mini-mart, batik shop, dive shop and foreign currency exchange. Fan rooms **RM140**, a/c rooms **RM190**

★ **D'Ayumni House** Southern main beach ☎09 691 1680 or ☎019 436 4463, ⓦd-ayumnihouse.blogspot .com. Set back from the beach, this friendly and well-run place has single-sex a/c dorms, semi-detached a/c chalets, internet terminals and a chilled-out café, all set around a small garden. Free wi-fi access; electricity noon–2pm and 6pm–8am. Dorms **RM45**, rooms **RM160**

Mama's Chalet Northern main beach ☎09 690 4600 or ☎019 985 3359, ⓦmamaschalet.com.my. Prim, very

OPPOSITE MIRA BEACH CHALET, PULAU PERHENTIAN KECIL (P.237) >

decent chalets, including a few sea-facing ones with multicoloured fanlights. All rooms have private facilities, and there's a popular restaurant. Wi-fi RM10/hr, computers RM18/hr. Fan rooms RM65, a/c rooms RM160

New Cocohut Southern main beach ✆09 691 1811 or ✆697 4982, ⊚perhentianislandcocohut.com. Chinese-run establishment with reasonable en-suite a/c chalets; the same management also runs the slightly more expensive, and slightly nicer, *Cozy Chalet* resort next door. All chalets have TVs and fridges; the more expensive ones have sea views, and there's a popular restaurant. Rates include breakfast and wi-fi. RM180

Perhentian Island Resort Teluk Pauh ✆09 691 1112 or ✆03 2144 8350, ⊚perhentianislandresort .net. Set on a very appealing stretch of beach, this resort – known as PIR – has a veritable campus of bungalows and chalets, all spacious and boasting modern furnishings and verandas. Internet costs a ridiculous RM4 for 10min; forget the outside world and join a yoga class instead. RM385

Reef Chalets Northern main beach ✆09 691 1762 or ✆013 981 6762. A semicircle of a/c chalets with hints of traditional Malay architecture and largish bathrooms. The interiors have rather plain decor but the garden setting is undeniably lush. Overall, good value. Fan rooms RM100, a/c rooms RM160

Seahorse Southern main beach ✆09 691 1691. Connected with a dive shop, and a slightly better budget choice than *Suhaila Palace Chalet* next door. Acceptable for the price, the rooms have lino floors, wooden walls and firm beds. Fan rooms RM80, a/c rooms RM150

★ **Tunabay Island Resort** Southern main beach ✆09 690 2902, ⊚tunabay.com.my. This well-managed collection of chalets gets it just right, combining the comforts of a mid-range city hotel with a cool informality that's perfect for a laidback beach holiday. The bar and restaurant are deservedly popular, and breakfast is included. Wi-fi RM10/half-hour. RM250

Watercolours Paradise Resort Northern main beach ✆019 981 1852, ⊚watercoloursworld.com. En-suite chalet rooms with fan and a small veranda; those with a sea view and a/c also boast more interesting furnishings. Has a well-run dive shop and a busy restaurant

(7.30am–10pm) with free wi-fi for guests. Fan rooms RM90, a/c rooms RM120

TELUK DALAM AND THE SOUTH COAST
B'First Chalets Teluk Dalam ✆013 295 5138. This row of eight concrete buildings is nothing special but the fan rooms at least are good value for money. There's a typical beach café at the front, and all-day electricity. Fan rooms RM60, a/c rooms RM150.

Bayu Dive Lodge Teluk Dalam ✆09 691 1650, ⊚alualudivers.com. You don't have to be a diver to stay in this slick accommodation linked to the Alu-Alu dive shop. There's a large range of options set in a neat garden, including sea-view cottages, chalets and longhouse rooms. Depending on the room category, decor may include sparkling white-tiled floors, swish modern lighting and designer bathroom fittings. Fan rooms RM90, a/c rooms RM140

Bubbles Tanjung Tukas ✆012 983 8038, ⊚bubblesdsc .com. A short RM10 boat ride from Teluk Dalam, this friendly resort has a beach to itself, and combines isolation with good facilities including a dive shop. It's also the only resort arranging regular turtle watching. Free wi-fi, 24hr electricity. A/c rooms cost RM60 extra at weekends. Fan rooms RM80, a/c rooms RM120

Fauna Beach Teluk Dalam ✆09 691 1607. Most of these 27 pleasant, unremarkable chalets are fan-cooled; a few have a/c, but are shabby and a little over-priced. Fan rooms RM55, a/c rooms RM145

Flora Bay & Flora Bay 2 Teluk Dalam ✆09 691 1666, ✉florabayresort@gmail.com. En-suite accommodation ranging from inexpensive fan rooms to beachfront chalets, including some overpriced a/c units. *Flora Bay*, with its garden of frangipanis and oleanders, is marginally preferable; its counterpart features institutional two-storey blocks. There's a good dive shop and internet café. Fan rooms RM60, a/c rooms RM120

Samudra Beach Chalet Teluk Dalam ✆09 691 1677, ⊚samudrabeachchalet.com. Fairly standard fan-cooled chalets, set in pleasant garden surroundings, with two or three rooms to a unit, plus cheaper A-frames. Not bad at all; new beds offset a little fraying at the edges. Full-board packages available. RM40

EATING AND DRINKING
Almost all Besar's places to **eat** are affiliated with resorts; most of the best options are on the western shore: you can't go far wrong at *New Cocohut* for Chinese fare, *Mama's Chalet* for Malay food or *Watercolours* for pizzas. The food on Flora Bay is generally less interesting, with a few open-air restaurants serving up Western and Asian standards plus the odd barbecue. As for **drinking**, there are a couple of stand-alone places but again it's largely a matter of choosing a resort bar.

B'First Café Teluk Dalam. A good choice if you want somewhere with less of a resort feel, offering tasty versions of the usual Malay dishes. Daily breakfast, lunch and dinner.

Tuna Cafe Tunabay Island Resort, southern main beach. One of the most adventurous kitchens on either island, serving pasta, salads and seafood, plus evening barbecues. Daily breakfast, lunch and dinner.

Pulau Redang

The beautiful island of **Pulau Redang** is geared up primarily for visitors on resort-based package trips. Don't expect a quiet island getaway: during weekends and school holidays, bars along the main beach have music or karaoke until midnight.

A kampung has been built inland for the two-thousand-strong fishing community who formerly lived in a traditional floating village, which was removed to make way for a jetty and other tourist developments. The highlight of the social calendar, April's **candat sotong** festival, celebrates a pastime popular all along the east coast of the Peninsula, catching squid using small hand-held lures with hooks on one end.

Snorkelling and diving

For most visitors, the chief attraction of Redang is the abundant marine life. The **reefs** have endured a lot over recent decades, including a mid-1970s attack by the crown-of-thorns starfish, and silt deposition caused by development. More recently the coral has suffered from bleaching due to high water temperatures. Thankfully, coral reefs have remarkable properties of self-renewal, and Redang's marine environment appears to have stabilized in a reasonable state.

Conservation has certainly been helped by the designation of the Redang archipelago as one of Malaysia's **marine parks**, and by the regulation of activities such as spear-fishing, trawling and watersports. The best **snorkelling** is off the southern coast around the islets of Pulau Pinang and Pulau Ekor Tibu; the larger resorts take endless boats stuffed with tourists to the main sites, so find a smaller group if you can. **Diving** is also excellent, with most sites off Redang's eastern shore. Almost every resort has its own dive shop, and divers also come here on day-trips from the Perhentians.

ARRIVAL AND DEPARTURE

PULAU REDANG

Regular transport to Redang only runs between March and October, when the resorts are open. A **conservation fee** of RM5 covers three days' stay.

By air Berjaya Air (⌾ berjaya-air.com) flies to Redang's airstrip from KL (☎ 03 7845 8382; 2 daily) and Singapore (☎ 06 481 6302; daily). Boats carry arrivals from the airstrip to the various resorts.

By boat Most packages include a boat ticket to Redang. Departures are from Merang (see p.233), except for boats to the *Taaras Beach*, *Coral Redang* and *Redang Beach* resorts which use Kuala Terengganu's Shahbandar jetty; if in doubt, check with your accommodation. If you're on a room-only deal, expect to pay RM100 for the return trip. There are public ferries from Shahbandar, or you may be able to get onto one of the resort boats – most leave early in the morning.

ACCOMMODATION

Most of Redang's **accommodation** is on the island's eastern shore, on **Pasir Panjang** (Long Beach), the adjacent Shark Bay or, just to the south, **Teluk Kalong**. Pasir Panjang features a particularly gorgeous stretch of fine white sand; Teluk Kalung's beach is narrower and pebbly in places, but is inviting nonetheless. Unless otherwise noted, the resorts have en-suite, air-conditioned rooms and their own **restaurants**. Many also have dive shops and offer inclusive packages.

Rates Given that packages tend to be the cheapest way to visit, reviews here include the price per night of a basic two-night full-board package for two people, which typically include meals, snorkelling (but not equipment rental) and transfers from Merang. Rates shown do not include typical weekend surcharges of RM30–70 per person, and apply to the high season (July & Aug); look for discounts at the start or end of the season.

PASIR PANJANG/SHARK BAY

Coral Redang Pasir Panjang ☎ 09 630 7110 or ☎ 09 623 6200, ⌾ coralredang.com.my. All but the cheapest rooms here were being renovated at the time of research; check out the new accommodation, as this place has much more character than most others on Redang. Rooms and restaurant abound in natural materials, and there's a small swimming pool with a poolside bar. B&B RM310, full board RM555

Laguna Redang Shark Bay ☎ 09 630 7888 or ☎ 09 631 0888, ⊛ lagunaredang.com.my. Large and luxurious establishment, with over two hundred rooms and a large free-form pool, and famous within Asia as the location of the Hong Kong comedy *Summer Holiday* (1999). A wide range of packages and rooms, all very comfortable and well equipped. Activities include snorkelling, canoe rental, archery and massage. Paid wi-fi in the lobby. Full board RM448

Redang Beach Resort Shark Bay ☎ 09 623 8188, ⊛ redang.com.my. This is a sizeable collection of blocks with comfortable, modern rooms. The ring-shaped building at the front includes an internet room (RM10/hr) and souvenir shop. Full board RM459

Redang Lagoon Chalet Pasir Panjang ☎ 09 666 5020, ⊛ redanglagoon.com. While the chalets – arranged in two long rows – are nothing special, this is still good value, with free wi-fi in the canteen area. Popular with Malay families. Full board RM300

Redang Pelangi Pasir Panjang ☎ 09 624 2158, ⊛ redangpelangi.com. Standard rooms plus chalets that are marginally better and more expensive. All are pretty functional; it's cheap for Redang, but you'd pay a fraction of

the rate on the Perhentians. There's also a popular bar. Full board RM380

Redang Reef Shark Bay ☎ 09 630 2181 or ☎ 09 622 6181, ⊛ redangreefresort.com.my. Perched on the headland at the southern end of Shark Bay, and reached by a long wooden walkway, this has simply furnished rooms and a bar overlooking the sea. Good value for money. Full board RM360

TELUK KALONG

Redang Kalong Teluk Kalong (KL) ☎ 03 7960 7163, ⊛ redangkalong.com. Set on its own peaceful beach, albeit not as lovely as Long Beach, this single-storey resort is popular with overseas visitors. Many of the 39 rather sparsely furnished a/c rooms offer sea views, and there's a five-star IDC dive centre. Wi-fi RM20/day, computer RM20/hr. Full board RM400

TELUK DALAM

The Taaras Beach & Spa Resort Teluk Dalam ☎ 09 630 8888 or ☎ 03 2149 1788, ⊛ thetaaras.com. Formerly known as the *Berjaya*, this luxury resort was due to reopen under a new name; the price and facilities may well change. In its former guise it was a cut above the rest, with well-appointed rooms, a spa, two restaurants, a dive shop, a swimming pool and tennis facilities. Full board RM880

Pulau Lang Tengah

Although **Pulau Lang Tengah** is largely a package destination, it holds just a handful of spread-out places to stay and therefore offers a lower-key experience than its larger near-neighbour Pulau Redang. As well as attractive and quiet beaches, there's some good **snorkelling**, including a patch of blue coral (*Heliopora coerulea*) offshore from the *Sari Pacifica*. Both *Redang Lang* and *D'Coconut Lagoon* have **dive shops**.

Turtles lay their eggs on certain beaches; staff at *D'Coconut Lagoon* wake guests if any are spotted during the night on the nearby Turtle Beach.

ARRIVAL AND DEPARTURE	PULAU LANG TENGAH

By boat Most people visit on packages, which usually include boat transfers from Merang. Otherwise *Lang Sari* and *Redang Lang* charge RM80 return, and other resorts a little more. Most boats leave early in the morning although you can charter one if you need an afternoon transfer (contact resorts for details). There's a RM5 conservation charge.

ACCOMMODATION

Lang Tengah holds only four resorts. As *Lang Sari* and *Redang Lang* cater particularly to Malaysian and Singaporean tourists, they get very busy at weekends and public holidays (when prices rise). The full-board prices listed below are per night, based on two people sharing on a two-night package (which includes boat transfers but not snorkelling).

D'Coconut Lagoon Pulau Lang Tengah ☎ 03 4252 6686, ⊛ dcoconutlagoon.com. Split into two wings a couple of minutes' walk apart. All rooms have a/c and hot showers; the deluxe rooms in the West Wing overlook the pool and spa. The resort gives out a very handy sketch map of the island. B&B RM485, full board RM660

Lang Sari Resort Pulau Lang Tengah ☎ 03 2166 1380, ⊛ langsari.com. This down-to-earth – and slightly down-at-heel – resort has some sea-view rooms pretty much on the beach. Full board RM359

Redang Lang Island Resort Pulau Lang Tengah ☎ 09 623 9911, ⊛ redanglangresort.com.my. Packages at this resort, with accommodation either in wooden "longhouses" or concrete blocks, include meals as well as snorkelling and jungle trekking. The site also has the only mini-mart on the island. Full board <u>RM380</u>

Sari Pacifica ☎ 09/669 0100, ⓦ saripacifica.com. The Chinoiserie and bling may or may not delight, but the jacuzzi in each room is likely to do so. B&B <u>RM374</u>, full board <u>RM468</u>

Kuala Terengganu

After a long spell as an important port trading with the Chinese, **KUALA TERENGGANU** (the capital of Terengganu state) had by the late nineteenth century been eclipsed by the rise of Singapore and other new ports in the Melaka Straits. Following the transfer of Terengganu from Siamese to British control in the early twentieth century, the state became the last in the Peninsula to take a British Adviser, in 1919. It continued to languish as a rural state with, unusually, most of its settlements at river mouths rather than on the lower reaches of rivers, as elsewhere in Peninsular Malaysia.

The discovery of oil in the 1980s transformed its fortunes; modern Kuala Terengganu is even more of a hotchpotch than most Malaysian cities, sprinkled with oil-funded showpieces of varying degrees of success. There is, nevertheless, a certain **austerity** about Terengganu state that's noticeable in Kuala Terengganu. It lacks the commercial buzz of Kuantan or even Kota Bharu, partly because oil revenues have barely trickled down to ordinary people but also because in some respects the state is more conservative and inward-looking than neighbouring Kelantan.

Many visitors use the city simply as a transit point for Terengganu's best-known attractions – the pleasant **beaches** that line most of the coastline, and glorious **islands** including the Perhentians, Pulau Redang, Pulau Lang Tengah and Pulau Kapas. Using the city as a base, you can also venture inland to **Tasik Kenyir** lake. Kuala Terengganu itself does, however, hold enough to reward a day or two's sightseeing, in particular the **old town** with its lively **Central Market** and the adjacent old **Chinatown** quarter; the **State Museum**, among the best of such complexes in Malaysia; and **Pulau Duyong**, where the city's maritime heritage just about survives.

The old town

Kuala Terengganu's compact centre is built on a semicircular parcel of land that bulges north into the mouth of the Terengganu River, which flows past the western half of the city. The eastern half of the city is flanked by the South China Sea.

Bukit Puteri
Daily except Fri 9am–5pm • RM1

A lovely little park with mature trees and chirruping cicadas, the steep hillock of **Bukit Puteri** ("Princess Hill") is crowned by a white tower that still serves as a lighthouse. You can head up via the long flight of steps starting near the state tourist office or, more easily, the escalators at the Bazaar Warisan (Heritage Bazaar) next door.

Wide-ranging views take in the Terengganu River and the bell-shaped roofs of the blindingly white **Masjid Zainal Abidin** just to the south. Relics of the hill's time as a stronghold during the early nineteenth century include a fort, supposedly built using honey to bind the bricks, and several cannons imported from Spain and Portugal.

Central Market
Daily 6am–6pm

Close to the lacklustre Bazaar Warisan with its assorted batik shops and jewellers, the ground floor of the much more rewarding **Central Market** (aka Pasar Payang) is taken up by a thriving wet market. Look out for stalls selling Malay confections in just about every conceivable hue. The upper floors comprise a maze of food stalls and outlets where you can seek out batik, *songkets* and brassware.

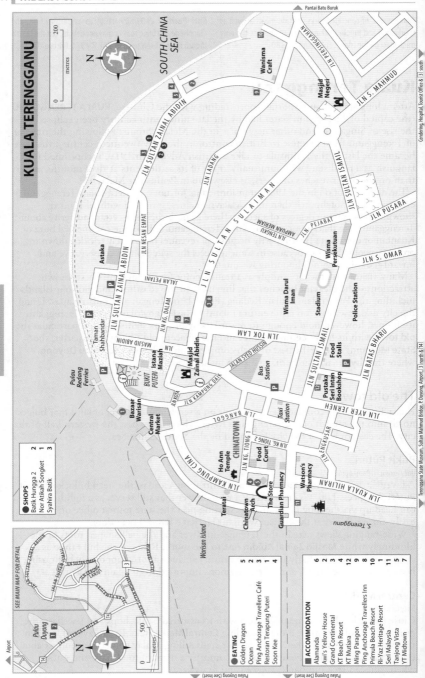

KUALA TERENGGANU

SOUTH CHINA SEA

Pantai Batu Buruk

Wanisma Craft

Masjid Negeri

Astaka

Taman Shahbandar

Pulau Redang Ferries

Bazaar Warisan

Central Market

Warisan Island

BUKIT PUTERI

Masjid Zainal Abidin

Istana Maziah

Bus Station

Taxi Station

Teratai

Chinatown Arch

The Store

Guardian Pharmacy

Ho Ann Temple

Food Court

Watson's Pharmacy

CHINATOWN

S. Terengganu

Wisma Darul Iman

Stadium

Police Station

Food Stalls

Pustaka Seri Intan Bookshop

Wisma Persekutuan

● SHOPS

Batik Hungga 2	2
Nor Atikah Songket	1
Syahira Batik	3

● EATING

Golden Dragon	5
Ocean	2
Ping Anchorage Travellers Café	3
Restoran Terapung Puteri	1
Soon Kee	4

■ ACCOMMODATION

Alamanda	6
Awi's Yellow House	2
Grand Continental	3
KT Beach Resort	4
KT Mutiara	12
Ming Paragon	9
Ping Anchorage Travellers Inn	8
Primula Beach Resort	10
Ri-Yaz Heritage Resort	1
Seri Malaysia	11
Tanjong Vista	5
YT Midtown	7

0 — 200 metres

N

SEE MAIN MAP FOR DETAIL

Pulau Duyong

Airport

0 — 500 metres

N

Cendering, Hospital, Tourist Office & 3 south

Terengganu State Museum, Sultan Mahmud Bridge, P. Duyong, Airport, 3 north & 14

Pulau Duyong (See Inset)

Pulau Duyong (See Inset)

Chinatown

Reached via Jalan Kampung Cina (aka Jalan Bandar), south of the central market, **Chinatown** was established way back in the eighteenth century, when the trading links between Terengganu and China drew in Chinese settlers. Besides good places to eat, it also holds the photogenic **Ho Ann Temple**.

Terengganu State Museum

5km west of town centre • Daily 9am–5pm, closed Fri noon–3pm • RM15 • ☎ 09 622 1444, ⓦ museum.terengganu.gov.my • *Bas bandar* service (45min) from city centre or RM20 taxi ride (one-way)

Arriving at the **Terengganu State Museum**, you might think you've strayed into *Alice in Wonderland*. Visitors are confronted by a series of buildings modelled on the archetypal Terengganu village house, but absolutely gargantuan in scale. Somehow the dislocation in size is fitting though for, although it lacks the interactive exhibits of more modern establishments, the museum far outstrips most of its provincial counterparts.

The ground floor of the **main building** holds exquisite **fabrics** from around Southeast Asia, while the next floor up displays various **crafts**. The top floor details the **history** of Terengganu. The **Petronas Oil Gallery**, in the building to the left, is sporadically interesting but predictably skewed. Behind it, the old-fashioned **Islamic Gallery** displays fine examples of Koranic calligraphy.

Allow time to see the rest of the site. Beside the river are two examples of the **sailing boats** for which Kuala Terengganu is famed – unique blends of European ships and Chinese junks. The small **Seafaring Gallery** and larger **Fisheries and Marine Park Gallery** are close by, as is a collection of smaller, beautifully decorated fishing boats. Five old timber buildings have been disassembled and reconstructed within the grounds. Among them, the **Istana Tengku Long** was originally built in 1888 entirely without nails, which to Malays signify death because of their use in coffins.

Pulau Duyong

Sporadic boats from moorings next to the Central Market, or jetty behind the *Seri Malaysia* hotel; better to take the *bas bandar* service or taxi (RM20)

The proud home of a venerable **boat-building** tradition, **Pulau Duyong** ("Mermaid Island") was once two islets in the Terengannu River but they were joined by reclamation to form what you see today. Although the northern section of Duyong was levelled to build a prestigious **yacht club** for the annual Monsoon Cup race

---

THE KRIS

The **kris** (or *keris*) occupies a treasured position in Malay culture, a symbol of manhood and honour believed to harbour protective spirits. Traditionally, all young men crossing the barrier of puberty receive one which remains with them for the rest of their lives, tucked into the folds of a sarong; for an enemy to relieve someone of a *kris* is tantamount to stripping him of his virility. In the past some weapons were reputed to have magical powers, able to fly from their owners' hand to seek out and kill an enemy.

The *kris* itself is intended to deliver a horizontal thrust rather than the more usual downward stab. When a sultan executed a treacherous subject, he did so by sliding a long *kris* through his windpipe, just above the collar bone, thereby inflicting a swift – though bloody – death. The distinguishing feature of the dagger is the hilt, shaped like the butt of a gun to facilitate a sure grip. The hilt can also be used to inflict a damaging blow to the head in combat, especially if there isn't time to unsheathe the weapon.

The daggers can be highly decorative: the iron blade is often embellished with fingerprint patterns or the body of a snake, while the hilt can be made from ivory, wood or metal. Designs are usually based on the theme of a bird's head.

BOAT-BUILDING ON PULAU DUYONG

The shipwrights of Pulau Duyong work mostly from memory rather than set plans. For hulls, their preferred material is **cengal**, a wood whose toughness and imperviousness to termite attack make it prized not only for boats but also the best kampung houses. After the hull planking is fastened with strong hardwood pegs, a special sealant – derived from swampland trees, and resistant to rot – is applied. Unusually, the frame is fitted afterwards, giving the whole structure strength and flexibility. As construction takes place in **dry docks**, the finished boats have to be manoeuvred on rollers into the water, an effort that often requires local villagers to pitch in.

Historically, the boatyards produced **schooners** that ranged from humble fishing craft to the hulking *perahu besar*, up to 30m in length. These days however, motorized, modern alternatives to the old-fashioned wooden boats, the increasing cost of timber, plus the lure of other careers, have all contributed to a steep decline in local boat-building. Today fewer than five boatyards are still engaged in the business. With the fall in local demand for traditional working boats, any salvation for Duyong's boat-building looks to lie in clients from around the world, who have been placing orders for all manner of bespoke craft.

(wmonsooncup.com.my), the rest of the island still features a rustic kampung that's a great place for an hour's stroll.

If you want to visit one of the handful of surviving **boatyards**, ask around for directions or enquire at long-standing backpacker favourite *Awi's Yellow House* (see opposite). One boatyard is owned by Awi, while another is close to the Sultan Mahmud bridge.

ARRIVAL AND DEPARTURE

KUALA TERENGGANU

By air The airport is 8km north of the city; a taxi into the centre costs around RM20. MAS (t09 662 6600) and AirAsia (t09 667 1017), both with offices at the airport, fly to KL, as does Firefly (t09 667 5377), which also serves Penang.

By bus The spacious, modern bus station, smack in the centre on Jalan Masjid Abidin, is used by intercity and local buses.

Destinations Alor Star (daily; 9hr 30min); Batu Pahat (5 daily); Bidor (daily); Butterworth (6 daily; 12hr); Cherating (8 daily; 3hr 30min); Ipoh (7 daily; 10hr); Johor Bahru (9 daily; 9hr); Kangar (daily); Kemaman/Chukai (6 daily; 3hr); Kota Bharu (6 daily; 3–4hr); Kuala Besut (8 daily; 2hr 30min); Kuala Lumpur (13 daily; 8hr 30min); Kuantan (8 daily; 4–5hr); Lumut (3 daily); Marang (several daily; 30min); Melaka (3 daily; 9hr); Merang (8 daily; 1hr–1hr 30min); Mersing (8 daily; 7hr); Muar (5 daily; 9hr); Pekan (2 daily); Penang (6 daily; Perlis (daily); Rantau Abang (several daily; 1hr 30min); Segamat (3 daily); Seremban (3 daily); Singapore (2 daily; 10hr 30min); Sungai Petani (2 daily); Taiping (5 daily); Tapah (daily).

By taxi Long-distance taxis park just south of the bus station for destinations across the Peninsula, including Kota Bharu and Kuantan (either one for RM290 charter, or around RM75 per person).

By boat The Shahbandar jetty on the seafront is used by a few resort boats to Pulau Redang (see p.241).

GETTING AROUND

By bus Besides the city's standard bus services, an hourly "heritage bus" (*bas bandar*) service, clad in wooden Malay motifs, runs a hop-on, hop-off route to the main attractions. There are three different routes each starting at the Taman Shahbandar park, and stops include Pulau Duyong, Noor Arfa (see "Shopping") and the State Museum; enquire at tourist offices for schedules and fares.

By taxi Taxis are easily found near the bus station or around the Central Market; you'd be lucky to flag one down in the street.

By trishaw Trishaws can be found near the Central Market, charging around RM30/hour.

By car Car rental is available through Ping Anchorage (see below).

INFORMATION

Tourist information The state tourist office is next to the post office on Jalan Sultan Zainal Abidin (Sat–Thurs 8.30am–4.30pm; t09 622 1553, wtourism.terengganu .gov.my). The Tourism Malaysia office is a little way south on Jalan Kampung Daik (Sun–Wed 8am–5pm, Thurs 8am–3.30pm; t09 630 9433). Ask at either about homestays in the city and its surroundings.

Travel agents Ping Anchorage Travel and Tours, 77a Jalan

Sultan Sulaiman (☎ 09 626 2020, ⓦ www.pinganchorage .com.my), is efficient and well organized, and offers numerous packages throughout the east coast and the interior. They also run the *Ping Anchorage Travellers Inn*, in the same building, and *Terrapuri Heritage Village* north of the city (see p.232).

ACCOMMODATION

Kuala Terengganu has a reasonable range of places to stay, including a few hotels overlooking the South China Sea east of the centre. On **Pulau Duyong**, the contrast could not be greater between a friendly-but-shoestring backpacker hangout and a huge (but often half-empty) resort development. With your own transport, and a taste for pricey, traditionally styled accommodation, you could base yourself out of town at the *Aryani* in **Merang** (see p.233) or at *Terrapuri Heritage Village* in **Penarik** (see p.232).

CITY CENTRE AND BEACH

Alamanda 28 & 28a Jalan Tok Lam ☎ 09 622 8888, ⓔ alamandakt@gmail.com. The tacky waterfall feature in the tiny lobby sets the tone at this budget hotel, but it's well located near the bus station. All rooms are a/c and en suite, though the cheapest are windowless and gloomy; superior-class rooms cost RM20 extra, while single rooms are also available. RM60

Grand Continental Jalan Sultan Zainal Abidin ☎ 09 625 1888, ⓦ www.ghihotels.com. The biggest and best place in town when it opened in 1997, this chain hotel is showing its age but is still worth considering if you can get a discount. Rooms have marbled bathrooms and satellite TV, plus there's a swimming pool and a coffee house. RM220

KT Beach Resort 548e Jalan Sultan Zainal Abidin ☎ 09 631 5555. Set on a miserable stretch of public beach, with huge TVs in the distinctly average rooms. They also manage some surprisingly appealing, fully furnished apartments nearby in the residential block across from the *Tian Kee* restaurant. Room RM95, apartments RM160

KT Mutiara 67 Jalan Sultan Ismail ☎ 09 622 2655. While some fittings, such as the built-in cupboards, look pretty dated, these are comfortable rooms for a decent price. Some have no windows, though at least they're quieter. RM75

Ming Paragon 219-e Jalan Sultan Zainal Abidin ☎ 09 623 9966, ⓦ mingstarhotel.com. A newer sister hotel to *Ming Star* a few doors down, with a spa (1–11.30pm). The executive room (RM212) provides a computer as well as a free minibar (minus alcohol). Even the cheaper rooms have flat-screen TV, hairdryer, iron and kettle; small windows reduce street noise. Rates include breakfast. RM116

Ping Anchorage Travellers Inn 77a Jalan Sultan Sulaiman ☎ 09 626 2020, ⓦ pinganchorage.com.my. The most backpacker-focused place in town, with rooms above a helpful travel agency. The rooms are basic and sparsely furnished, mostly with fan, cement flooring and shared facilities, though some have en-suite bathrooms and/or a/c. Rooftop café and use of a washing machine. Fan rooms RM25, a/c rooms RM50

Primula Beach Resort Jalan Persinggahan ☎ 09 622 2100, ⓦ primulahotels.com. Behind the ugly ochre and peach facade is a well-kept 246-room hotel complete with pool, spa, gym and two restaurants. Spacious rooms with wi-fi and a/c; the superior ground-floor rooms have patio doors leading to the beach (where an undertow sometimes prevents swimming). Ample parking, and free shuttle into the centre. Rates include breakfast. RM210

Seri Malaysia Jalan Hiliran, on the riverside ☎ 09 623 6454, ⓦ serimalaysia.com.my. Unexciting but sound chain hotel with views of Pulau Duyong from some rooms, including certain standard rooms (ask when you book). Rates include breakfast, but rise a little at weekends. RM120

Tanjong Vista Lot 4708 Jalan Sultan Zainal Abidin ☎ 09 631 9988, ⓦ hoteltanjongvista.com.my. The logo and uniforms may be bright pink but the rooms in this business hotel are tastefully furnished and offer good value. The small semi-outdoor swimming pool on the fourth floor has views of the beach and sea; there's also a small gym. Rates include breakfast. RM155

YT Midtown 30 Jalan Tok Lam ☎ 09 622 3088, ⓔ ythotel@streamyx.com. All rooms in this central hotel have functional modern fittings and decor, plus TV and bathroom, although they could do with an overhaul – some carpets are stained, for example. A fine choice for the price; rates include breakfast and wi-fi. RM102

PULAU DUYONG

Awi's Yellow House Pulau Duyong ☎ 017 984 0337. A delightful no-frills timber complex on stilts over the water. Accommodation is in thatched-roof huts with a solitary ceiling light, mosquito net and no locks on the doors. The toilet is a square hole in the floor, but on the plus side there's a kitchen and kayaks (RM10/day) available to rent. You can visit Awi's small boatyard, plus he has opened up rooms in his house as a homestay (meals included). Dorms RM10, hut RM30, homestay RM50–100

Ri-Yaz Heritage Resort and Spa Pulau Duyong ☎ 09 627 7888, ⓦ ri-yazheritage.com. It isn't clear where "heritage" comes into this sprawling development, but the wooden chalets are comfortable and well outfitted. The pool is a bonus, as is the restaurant with a terrace overlooking the river. The resort can arrange transfers by taxi (RM20) or boat (RM3) given notice. Look out for promotional rates. RM265

4

EATING AND DRINKING

Terengganu's signature rice dish, **nasi dagang**, consists of slightly sticky rice, steamed with a little coconut milk and chopped shallots, and often served with fish curry for breakfast. Other key dishes include **laksam** (rolled rice noodles in a thick fish and coconut milk gravy) and **keropok** – dried fish paste, served *lekor* (long and chewy), *losong* (steamed) or *keping* (crispy). There are a few decent **Malay restaurants**, and the Malay stalls at the Central Market, as well as just south of the junction of Jalan Sultan Ismail and Jalan Tok Lam, are worth trying. Chinatown is the obvious focus for **Chinese food**, with a hawker centre along Jalan Kampung Tiong 1 and several excellent restaurants on the main street. The Chinese restaurants also tend to be your best bets for **alcohol** in this largely dry city.

Golden Dragon Jalan Kampung Cina ☏09 622 3034. One of the best-established restaurants in Chinatown, with reliable seafood (try the steamed fish) and other Cantonese dishes. Daily noon–2.30pm & 6–10pm.

Ocean Jalan Sultan Zainal Abidin. Well-regarded Chinese restaurant specializing in seafood, with steamboat another popular choice; it also serves alcohol. It's a shame that this stretch of beach can smell a little unsavoury. Daily 11.30am–2.30pm & 5.30–10.45pm.

Ping Anchorage Roof Top Café Top of *Ping Anchorage Travellers Inn*, 77a Jalan Sultan Sulaiman ☏09 626 2020, ☏pinganchorage.com.my. A magnet for backpackers, serving Western café food with some

local dishes thrown in. Beer is also available. Daily 7am–10pm.

Restoran Terapung Puteri Jalan Sultan Zainal Abidin. Built on stilts over the waterfront, this smartly turned-out *kedai kopi* is popular with Malay families. While the food's not spectacular, there's plenty of choice, from *ayam bakar* (grilled chicken) to tangy mango *kerabu* – unripe mango shreds laced with dried shrimp and green chilli. Daily except Wed noon–midnight.

Soon Kee Jalan Kampung Cina. This Chinatown staple has been serving superlative *bah kut teh* for decades. If you don't like the herbal pork broth then look elsewhere, as it's the only thing on the menu. Daily 7–10am & 6–9.30pm.

SHOPPING

Astaka Jalan Sultan Zainal Abidin. Small shopping complex good for everyday purchases. Like the Store in Chinatown, this is more of a general emporium and supermarket. Mon–Thurs & Sun 10am–10.30pm, Fri & Sat 9am–10.30pm.

Noor Arfa Cendering Industrial Area, 7km south of the city. ☏09 617 9700, ☏noor-arfa.com.my. Large showroom with a more extensive choice of batik than the shops on Jalan Sultan Zainal Abidin; take the *bas bandar*

service to Cendering. Sat–Thurs 9am–7pm.

Pustaka Seri Intan On the south side of Jalan Sultan Ismail (opposite the Maybank). Only has a limited range of English novels but carries a good selection of magazines.

Teratai 151 Jalan Kampung Cina ☏09 625 2157. The longest-established of several boutiques and souvenir shops taking root on Jalan Kampung Cina. Daily except Fri 10am–5pm.

ARTS AND CRAFTS WORKSHOPS

Like neighbouring Kelantan, Terengganu is renowned for its **handicrafts**. At several places in and around the city, visitors can watch craftspeople at work and buy their products.

Abu Bakar bin Mohammed Amin 500m west of Jalan Panji Alam, 1406 Lorong Saga in Pasir Panjang ☏09 622 7968. Watch the making of the *kris*, a two-edged dagger (see box, p.245), and its decorated wooden sheath. On S.P. Bumi local bus route; get off at Sekolah Kebangsaan Pasir Panjang. Visits by appointment only.

Ky Enterprises Jalan Panji Alam, 3km south of centre ☏09 622 1063. Specializes in *mengkuang* (pandanus), fashioning the long, slender leaves into delicate but functional items like bags and floor mats. Catch S.P. Bumi local bus towards Pasir Panjang; get off on Jalan Panji Alam. Visits Sat–Thurs 9am–4.30pm.

Wanisma Craft East of the centre, near junction of Jalan Sultan Zainal Abidin and Kampung Ladang Sekolah ☏09 622 3311. Local artisans have long been known for their brassware, working in a "white brass" alloy unique to the state. Containing at least forty percent zinc, with added nickel to make it less yellow, white brass is used for decorative items such as candlesticks. At Wanisma Craft, visitors can watch craftsmen using the traditional "lost wax" technique to make brass objects, see cloth being handprinted in the batik workshop, and buy both types of product in the shop. Sat–Thurs 9am–6pm, workshops until 4pm.

DIRECTORY

Banks and exchange All the major banks have offices on Jalan Sultan Ismail, west of the junction with Jalan

Tok Lam; the Maybank is your best bet for changing money.

Hospitals and clinics The Hospital Sultanah Nur Zahirah, 1km southeast of the centre on Jalan Sultan Mahmud (☎09 621 2121). There are plenty of privately run walk-in clinics and the odd dentist's surgery along Jalan Tok Lam, some staying open well into the evening.

Left luggage At the bus station (daily 8am–10pm; ☎019 920 9679).

Pharmacy There's a branch of Watson's on Jalan Sultan Ismail.

Police The main police station is on Jalan Sultan Ismail (☎09 624 6222).

Post office The GPO on Jalan Sultan Zainal Abidin has poste restante.

Visa extensions The Immigration Department is in Wisma Persekutuan on Jalan Sultan Ismail (Sun–Wed 7.30am–5pm, Thurs 7.30am–4pm; ☎09 622 1424).

Tasik Kenyir

More than three hundred square kilometres in area, **Tasik Kenyir** (Lake Kenyir) was created in the 1980s by the building of the Kenyir hydroelectric dam across Sungai Terengganu. Much touted locally as a back-to-nature experience, the lake offers scope for **fishing**, waterborne excursions and wildlife-spotting – **elephants** are even glimpsed on the shore from time to time. It's possible to swim in many of the **waterfalls** on the periphery, while in the hills to the south you can visit the limestone **Bewah and Taat caves**. The lake is also Terengganu's gateway to Taman Negara, thanks to the park entrance at **Tanjung Mentong** at its southern end though this is so little used as to be practically moribund.

Sadly Tasik Kenyir remains a bit of a half-baked proposition thanks to poor transport connections, aggravated by the fact that the attractions are so scattered. Adding to the difficulties is the lack of accommodation; several places have closed in recent years. Unless you plan to stay at the upmarket, easily accessible *Lake Kenyir Resort*, your best bet is to book your visit through a travel agent in Kuala Terengganu. If you do arrive independently then you can book trips on a per-person basis from the resort, while the packages from the main jetty are aimed at groups so – for example – a trip to **Kelah fish sanctuary** costs RM450 for the whole boat.

ARRIVAL AND DEPARTURE

TASIK KENYIR

The jetty in the northeast of the lake, **Pangkalan Gawi**, can be reached by road and thus serves as the focal point for arrivals; a handful of tour operators have desks at the jetty and can arrange day-trips.

By bus No buses run to the lake from Kuala Terengganu, even though there's a service all the way from KL: the Tasik Kenyir Express (☎03 4044 4276; RM44) leaves from Putra bus station (daily 9am & 2pm; 8hr).

By taxi A taxi to the jetty costs around RM80 from Kuala Terengganu or RM100 from the airport.

By car Drive to the lake using Route 3 west of Kuala Terengganu; alternatively, on Route 14, turn off 30km from

Kuala Terengganu at Ajil, head west along Route 106 for Kuala Berang, then northwest. It is also possible to reach the jetty from the interior, by turning off Route 8 at Chiku Aring onto Route 1742, which serves the Taman Negara entrance at Kuala Koh; stay on the main road and you will eventually skirt around the northern edge of the lake. The drive from Gua Musang to the jetty will take around two hours, and it's a rough road in places.

INFORMATION

Tourist office At the Gawi jetty (daily 8am–5pm; ☎09 631 0063). Staff can hand out leaflets and advice, but cannot book you onto any tours – for that, speak to the companies with desks at the jetty or go to *Lake Kenyir Resort*.

Tours Packages available from companies including Ping Anchorage (see p.246) or Kenyir Naturally Holidays (☎09 681 1641).

ACCOMMODATION

A few **chalets** and **rafthouses** around the lake offer modest comforts at modest rates. However, they're presently only accessible by boat from the Gawi jetty – and chartering a standard six-seater vessel can cost several hundred ringgit a day. A houseboat sleeping 12–18 people costs RM800–1500.

Lake Kenyir Resort Near Gawi Jetty ☎ 09 666 8888 or ☎ 03 2052 7766, ⓦ lakekenyir.com. This elegant collection of buildings, with Terengganu-style pitched roofs, is the swankiest accommodation at Tasik Kenyir. It's also the easiest to arrange and the most expensive, although you should be able to get discounts (such as the price indicated here) on the published rate. Numerous tours and activities are available. **RM288**

Marang

The coastal village of **MARANG**, 17km south of Kuala Terengganu and not to be confused with Merang further north, is only visited by tourists as the departure point for the delightful **Pulau Kapas** and **Pulau Gemia**, just 6km offshore. Those islands have no banks or ATMs, so this is your last chance to withdraw money – there are branches of BSN and AmBank around 500m away from the waterfront area.

ARRIVAL AND DEPARTURE

By bus Local buses head roughly hourly between Kuala Terengganu and Marang in the daytime. It's also possible to reach Marang on the long-distance Kuantan–Kuala Terengganu buses that travel the coast road. To move on from Marang you can flag down a local bus, although southbound services go no further than Dungun or Kemaman (see p.254). You can instead take an express bus but there's no ticket office, so you'll need to have bought a ticket already in Kuala Terengganu.

By taxi Chartering a taxi between Kuala Terengganu and Marang costs around RM30.

By boat Boat operators for Pulau Kapas, including the helpful Suria Link (☎ 09 618 3754 or ☎ 019 983 9454, ✉ surialink@hotmail.com), have their offices side by side at Marang's jetty. All offer the same deal of RM20 one-way or RM40 return, and can book accommodation. Boats usually run from 9am, leaving when full, though services are rare during the northeast monsoon. Check whether your boat will stop at your desired beach; you may have to choose between wading ashore close to your resort, or getting off at the sole jetty then walking a short distance.

MARANG

■ ACCOMMODATION
Kamal Guest House	1
Marang Guest House	2
Marang Waterfront Resort	3

● RESTAURANT
| Mak Su Yam | 1 |

ACCOMMODATION

Kamal Guest House B283 Kampung Paya ☎ 09 618 2181. Rooms at this colourful motel-style place, just below *Marang Guest House*, are pricier than its neighbour's, but they're also more comfortable and spacious. Staff can arrange cuttlefish catching, river trips and day-trips to Pulau Kapas. **RM80**

Marang Guest House Bukit Batu Merah, 1367 & 1368 Kampung Paya ☎ 09 618 1976. At the top of the hill, the 23 rooms here are careworn but are a good choice if you're on a tight budget. Also known as the *Travellers' Checkpoint*. Fan rooms **RM40**, a/c rooms **RM60**

Marang Waterfront Resort Jalan Bukit Batu Merah ☎ 09 618 3999, ✉ sha_kic@yahoo.com.my. This purple and white building couldn't be handier for the jetty. The standard rooms are a bit gloomy, so go for the deluxe (RM150) or sea view (RM180) if possible. Rates include breakfast. **RM120**

EATING AND DRINKING

Mak Su Yam Marang. Convenient for the jetty, at the top of a short flight of steps, this is a simple place with an inexpensive *nasi campur* spread. Fine if you just want to fill up while waiting for transport. Daily 7am–6pm.

Pulau Kapas

Diminutive **Pulau Kapas**, less than half an hour from Marang by speedboat, boasts arcs of sandy beach the colour of pale brown sugar, and aquamarine waters that visibly teem with fish. It's a very appealing little island with a laidback charm, emphasized by the friendly approach of the best of the resorts. Just offshore, the even smaller **Pulau Gemia** is the site of just one resort. In theory it's possible to visit Kapas as a day-trip, by catching an early boat out and returning late in the afternoon, but this means making the most of the midday heat – and besides, it's really worth staying for at least a night or two.

The only season when things are not quite so idyllic is from June to August, particularly at the weekends, when the island can get pretty busy. The rest of the time it's a great place to do very little for a few days; the one notable highlight in the slim social calendar is the annual Kapas–Marang **swimathon** in April. During the northeast monsoon almost all the resorts close down.

A couple of marked trails make it possible to **hike** to the undeveloped eastern side of Kapas, ending up at the pebbly (and sadly far from litter-free) Berakit Beach where you can take a dip. The longer but more interesting route starts close to *Kapas Turtle Valley*, the shorter from behind *Kapas Island Resort*, running alongside a stream for almost all the way. You can combine them to take a circular route; both include steep sections close to the beach. Bring plenty of water and use insect repellent, particularly if you'll be in the forest after 5pm when the mosquitoes come out in force. The paths can be very slippery after rain.

ACCOMMODATION (map legend)

Pulau Kapas	
Captain's Longhouse	8
Gem Island Resort and Spa	1
Harmony Campsite	2
Kapas Beach Chalet	5
Kapas Island Resort	7
Kapas Turtle Valley	9
Mak Cik Gemuk Beach Resort	4
Pak Ya Sea View Chalet	6
Qimi Chalet	3

PULAU KAPAS

4

ARRIVAL AND DEPARTURE

PULAU KAPAS

By boat See Marang (see opposite) for information on boats to Pulau Kapas. As Kapas is a designated marine park, a conservation fee of RM5 applies for a stay of up to three days, though there isn't always an official present to collect it.

ACCOMMODATION

For such a tiny island, Kapas has a surprising range of **accommodation**. All face the mainland from the western shore, and have 24-hour electricity plus their own **restaurants**. Some mid-range places levy **surcharges** of twenty percent or more at weekends and during holidays, and most close down from November until January or February.

SNORKELLING AND DIVING AROUND PULAU KAPAS

Snorkelling is of course a draw on Kapas; most places to stay can rent out gear (from RM15), or arrange a boat trip out to a choice site (from RM30). Visibility is best between May and August, but jellyfish can be a nuisance in June and July. Some of the most popular snorkelling spots are around rocky **Pulau Gemia**. If you're just renting equipment then try the rocks at the edges of the beaches beyond *Qimi Chalet* and the campsite.

Diving isn't generally considered to be as good as on the Perhentians or Redang, but there are opportunities, particularly on the eastern side of the island. Popular sites include Berakit Reef, Octopus Reef and Coral Garden. Blacktip reef sharks are sometimes seen, and you can find turtles at Coral Garden. There's only one **dive shop**, Aqua-Sport (☏019 983 5879, ⓦdivekapas.com), which offers PADI courses as well as regular dives (RM95).

PULAU KAPAS

Captain's Longhouse Pulau Kapas ☏012 377 0214. Sometimes known by its old name, *Lighthouse*, this is a rustic elevated longhouse of dark timber with eight decent fan rooms and a large, very open dorm. All have mosquito nets and shared facilities. The driftwood beach-hut bar gives the impression that someone was shipwrecked here but made the best of it. Dorms RM30, rooms RM60

Harmony Pulau Kapas. This campsite is used mainly by locals and (despite the name) can be noisy. It's aimed at large groups and when none are booked in, you are unlikely to find any staff. Camping per person RM10, tent rental RM15

★ **Kapas Beach Chalet (KBC)** Pulau Kapas ☏012 288 2008. This Malay/Dutch-run establishment has decent A-frame chalets (RM60), plus small dorms and more basic rooms in a long bungalow; all are en suite. The restaurant is good and the *Lazy Islander Lounge* is, along with the *Captain's Longhouse*, the best backpacker hangout on Kapas. Snorkelling equipment is free for guests, as are occasional snorkelling trips further afield. Dorms RM15, rooms RM40

Kapas Island Resort Pulau Kapas ☏09 631 6468, ⓦkapasislandresort.com. Neat Malay-style a/c bungalows, all en suite and with more character than most, set in a large garden with a swimming pool. Western and Malay food is served in an airy restaurant – where wi-fi costs RM10/hr – and squid catching and snorkelling can be arranged. Rates include breakfast. RM130

★ **Kapas Turtle Valley** Pulau Kapas ☏013 354 3650, ⓦkapasturtlevalley.com. Marvellously low-key resort, run by a Dutch couple and set on a secluded cove which is a short but steep walk over the headland from the western shore – Suria Link (see p.250) can drop you off here. It has a handful of chalets, including two for families, featuring four-poster beds and swish bathrooms; the menu in the restaurant is sophisticated if not cheap. Rate includes breakfast; minimum stay two nights, credit cards accepted. RM160

Mak Cik Gemuk Beach Resort Pulau Kapas ☏09 624 5120. A cluster of en-suite chalets with the option of a/c, plus much cheaper rooms in a low "longhouse" block with shared bathrooms. Institutional but popular with student groups in particular. They do meal packages (RM40/day), plus kayaks (RM20/hr) and snorkelling equipment (RM25/day) are available. Fan rooms RM40, a/c rooms RM120

Pak Ya Sea View Chalet Pulau Kapas ☏019 960 3130. A collection of seven A-frames behind a low protective wall on the beach, some with twin beds and some with doubles. All have wall-mounted fans, lino floors and small but clean bathrooms. The café is also on the beach and serves typical Malay rice dishes. RM70

Qimi Chalet Pulau Kapas ☏019 648 1714. Comfortable chalets, the most expensive (RM300, lower for subsequent nights) with sea-facing balcony and open-air bathroom; the cheaper ones are pretty basic. The beachfront restaurant is housed in a simple pavilion – it can take a while for food to arrive, but it's worth the wait. Open all year. RM80

PULA GEMIA

Gem Island Resort and Spa Pulau Gemia ☏03 6205 5555, ⓦgem-travel.com.my/gemisland. The only resort on Pulau Gemia, with chalets on stilts; the cheapest are in a long block, with better views away from the restaurant. Turtles land to lay eggs and the resort is involved in their conservation; facilities include a spa and small swimming pool, plus yoga and meditation classes can be arranged. Ask about discounts. RM290

Southern Terengganu

The stretch of Terengganu between Marang and the Pahang border offers fairly slim pickings for travellers. Pleasant **beaches** are the main draw, any of which make a good break during a drive along the coast road, though facilities at most amount to a mere straggle of food stalls.

Rantau Abang

Little more than a handful of guesthouses strung out along a dusty road 40km south of Marang, **RANTAU ABANG** used to reap a rich reward as one of a handful of places in the world where the giant **leatherback turtle** came to lay its eggs. No longer, thanks to overfishing, pollution and poaching (see p.258). In the meantime Rantau Abang has drifted into relative obscurity. It's still a pleasant enough way station though, offering a beach with fine sand and, being on a straight stretch of coast, superb 180-degree views of blue-green sea.

Turtle Information Centre

Rantau Abang · Sun–Wed 8am–5pm, Thurs 8am–3.30pm, Sat 8am–4pm · Free · 📞 09 844 4169

The small **Turtle Information Centre** holds informative if dry displays on turtle biology and conservation. If you want to spot nesting turtles, your best bets are elsewhere in Malaysia (see p.258).

ARRIVAL AND DEPARTURE   RANTAU ABANG

By bus Buses stop on the main road close to *Jalinan Kasih* restaurant, a short walk from the Turtle Information Centre and the accommodation. Local services from Kuala Terengganu and Marang run hourly during daylight hours

to Rantau Abang.
By taxi Ask at your accommodation about long-distance taxis to Kuala Terengganu (RM40) or Dungun (RM20).

ACCOMMODATION

The decline in tourism means that most places are now geared up for student groups, seminars and team-building sessions. The exception is the luxurious *Tanjong Jara Resort*, just south of Rantau Abang.

Awang's Close to information centre, Rantau Abang 📞 09 844 3500. Friendly and long-established resort, on a stretch of golden sand. Simple en-suite rooms, with a few nice touches such as tinted glass. Food is only served to groups, so you'll have to eat elsewhere. Fan rooms <u>RM50</u>, a/c rooms <u>RM80</u>

Dahimah's Guesthouse 1km south of information centre, Rantau Abang 📞 09 845 2843, ✉ dahimahs @hotmail.com. Run by Dahimah – originally from the UK – and her Malay husband. Accommodation ranges from simple fan doubles to family rooms with TV, a/c and hot water. Meals not normally served, although they'll make breakfast if they have time. Fan rooms <u>RM35</u>, a/c rooms <u>RM60</u>, family rooms <u>RM120</u>

D'Pengkalan 200m north of information centre,

Rantau Abang 📞 09 845 7995, 🌐 angulliaresort.com /dpengkalan.htm. This establishment has 14 rooms in a leafy riverside setting; for larger groups the fan rooms, sleeping five people, are a real bargain. To reach the sea, you need to take a very short ferry journey across the river. Fan rooms <u>RM50</u>, a/c rooms <u>RM80</u>

Tanjong Jara Resort 4km south of Rantau Abang 📞 09 845 1100 or 📞 03 2783 1000, 🌐 tanjongjararesort .com. One of the priciest east-coast resorts, a complex of timber pavilions and houses almost fit for a sultan. Traditional treatments are on offer in the spa, and there's a diving and watersports centre. Activities range from waterfall treks to demonstrations of traditional Malay pastimes. <u>US$400</u>

EATING

Few accommodation options in Rantau Abang serve food other than for groups, but a handful of simple places to eat lie within walking distance.

C.B. Wee Main highway, 4km south of Rantau Abang near Tanjong Jara Resort 📞 016 933 7993. This halal Chinese restaurant is the best place to eat on this stretch of coast. As well as seafood, including great butter

prawns, they serve dishes such as shredded beef. Whatever you order, it'll be freshly prepared. Daily 9am–3pm & 6–10pm.

4

Dungun to the Pahang border

Driving south from Dungun takes you through the heartland of Terengganu's oil industry. Most of the towns have little to detain tourists, but there are a few upmarket resorts along the coast.

Dungun

The backwater town of **Dungun**, 8km south of Tanjong Jara, is predominantly Chinese, with a handful of shophouses and a night market each Thursday. The only reason to spend time here is because it's a hub for bus services.

Paulu Tenggol

Further from the mainland than the popular islands further north, **Pulau Tenggol** (reached by boat from Dungun) is correspondingly less developed. While the few tourists who stay out here have to make do with rather run-down accommodation, there's beautiful, unspoiled scenery and arguably the best **diving** and snorkelling on the east coast. It's possible to arrange a diving trip from the mainland through *Tanjong Jara* resort (see p.253).

Ma'Daerah Turtle Sanctuary

March–Sept daily 9am–5pm • ☎ 09 844 4169, ⓦ madaerah.org

A quiet beach near **Kerteh**, on the highway south of Paka, is home to the **Ma'Daerah Turtle Sanctuary** where (in season) can pay to get involved in turtle conservation. The scheme has been dormant lately but may soon relaunch.

Kemaman/Chukai

The southernmost settlement of significance in Terengganu is the fusion of **Kemaman** and neighbouring **Chukai**. It's useful mainly as a transport hub, but it also has the closest **banks** to Cherating.

ARRIVAL AND DEPARTURE	DUNGUN TO THE PAHANG BORDER
By plane Firefly has services between Kuala Lumpur and the nondescript town of Kerteh (2 daily; 1hr). **By bus** You may need to change at Dungun or Kemaman/Chukai if you are using local buses to travel the coast.	**By boat** Speedboats from Dungun to Pulau Tenggol (45 min); transfers are normally included in accommodation packages.

ACCOMMODATION

The resorts along the coast are largely aimed at business travellers so look for discounts at the weekends. The resort on Tenggol is open only from February to November, and only when there are guests, so it is essential to book ahead.

DUNGUN

Sri Gate K201 Jalan Sura Gate ☎ 09 848 1648. Three-storey Chinese hotel, set above a hair salon, with clean rooms which are fine for a night. Avoid the lowest floor; people tend to hang out around reception watching TV. Fan rooms <u>RM55</u>, a/c rooms <u>RM65</u>

TENGGOL

Tenggol Island Resort Pulau Tenggol ☎ 09 848 4862, ⓦ pulautenggol.com. Extremely basic bungalows, plus tents if you want to keep costs down. The nightly rates given are for two people sharing a two-night all-inclusive snorkelling package; the diving equivalent, including six dives, costs around 75 percent extra. Bungalows <u>RM480</u>, tents <u>RM330</u>

PAKA

Residence Resort South of Paka ☎ 09 827 3366, ⓦ residenceresortpaka.com. A luxurious development close to the beach, with appealing rooms, spa and swimming pool. Most customers are here on business; look out for promotional weekend rates. <u>RM258</u>

KEMASIK

Awana Kijal Kemasik ☎ 09 864 1188, ⓦ awana .com.my. The tall atrium certainly makes an impression, and facilities include a spa, golf course and huge swimming pool, but the rooms – while comfortable and well appointed – don't really justify the prices, and there's a penny-pinching RM25 daily charge for internet. Worth a look if they have a good promotion. <u>RM330</u>

Cherating

At first it can be hard to discern the enduring appeal of **CHERATING**, a laidback village of sorts 45km north of Kuantan. Its heyday as a tourist destination is clearly over; for proof you only need to see the abandoned tourist office at one end of **Cherating Lama** (the old town), and the closed cultural centre at the other end. Many locals have long since moved out, to the new settlement of **Cherating Baru** a little way south. What's more the beach is pleasant but pebbly in places, and hardly the best on the coast.

Nevertheless, at its best, Cherating Lama is still an appealing little travellers' community, chilled out yet warm-spirited, a place to share quality time with old companions and – chances are – to end up with a whole bunch of new acquaintances too. Local entrepreneurs have also devised an array of activities to keep tourists coming, and it's well worth giving it a few days to work its magic on you. Further down the coast in Cherating Baru, the mid-range resorts draw in families looking for a comfortable seaside break.

The beach

No trip to Cherating would be complete without time spent on the **beach**. While the sands are off-white at best, the shelter of the bay ensures calm waters; it's best to avoid swimming at low tide, when the sea recedes 100m or more. The headland obliterates any sunrise views, but in good weather it's still worth taking a dawn stroll on the beach, when only a few fishing boats disturb the stillness.

Handicrafts centre

Daily 9am–5pm, sometimes closed Sun • ☎ 09 581 9290

The two hexagonal buildings of the **handicrafts centre** sell bags (RM45–75) and other items showcasing the art of *mengkuang* (pandanus) weaving. Most items are made at home by local women, but the centre itself stages demonstrations.

Dwi D Spa

Daily 10am–10pm or 11pm • ☎ 012 986 2869

It may be located on the noisy highway, but the treatments at Dwi D Spa are good enough that (with the help of a little music) it's still possible to get seriously

---

ACTIVITIES IN CHERATING

During the northeast monsoon – and especially mid-December to January, when the waves are good and the rain not too bad – **surfing** is the big attraction in Cherating. **Windsurfing** is possible throughout the year, weather allowing, while there's also a wide range of **activities** away from the beach.

Canting Art Cherating Lama ☎ 017 930 1090. Batik classes, in which you learn how to get your own designs onto fabric or T-shirts and perhaps mix the dyes yourself. Daily 9am–10pm.

★ **Hafiz Cherating River Activities** Lot 1156, Cherating Lama ☎ 017 978 9256 or ☎ 013 939 9256, ✉ kohafiz@gmail.com. A friendly self-taught expert on fireflies, Hafiz has developed a method of attracting the insects. The effect, as seen on his evening excursions, is little short of magical. Hafiz also arranges snorkelling, river and sea fishing, kayak rental, daytime mangrove cruises and more.

Satu Suku Surf Cherating Lama ☎ 014 323 2952, ⓦ satusuku.com. Surfing lessons (3–4 hr; RM120) plus sales and rental for both surfboards and windsurfers (RM100 for two hours' rental including an hour of instruction). They can also advise on the best surf spots, and run a Billabong boutique. Oct–March daily 8am–8pm.

4

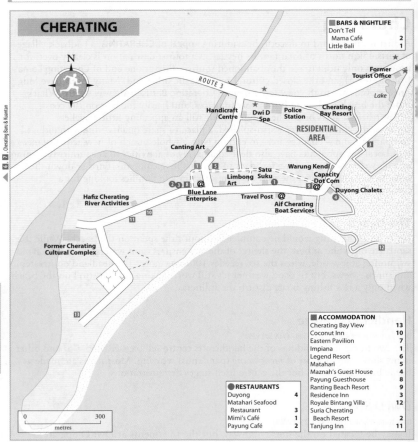

CHERATING

N

ROUTE 3

BARS & NIGHTLIFE
Don't Tell
  Mama Café   2
Little Bali   1

Former
Tourist Office

Lake

Handicraft
Centre

Dwi D
Spa

Police
Station

Cherating
Bay Resort

RESIDENTIAL
AREA

Canting Art

Satu
Suku

Warung Kendi

Capacity
Dot Com

Limbong
Art

Blue Lane
Enterprise

Travel Post

Aif Cherating
Boat Services

Duyong Chalets

Hafiz Cherating
River Activities

Former Cherating
Cultural Complex

Cherating Baru & Kuantan

RESTAURANTS
Duyong   4
Matahari Seafood
  Restaurant   3
Mimi's Café   1
Payung Café   2

ACCOMMODATION
Cherating Bay View   13
Coconut Inn   10
Eastern Pavilion   7
Impiana   1
Legend Resort   6
Matahari   5
Maznah's Guest House   4
Payung Guesthouse   8
Ranting Beach Resort   9
Residence Inn   3
Royale Bintang Villa   12
Suria Cherating
  Beach Resort   2
Tanjung Inn   11

0   300
metres

relaxed. The friendly owner draws on over twenty years' experience, combining traditional Malay massage (primarily carried out by midwives) with Western techniques for the signature Malay Ancient Heritage Relaxation Massage (1hr 30min; RM145).

Turtle sanctuary

2km east of Cherating village • Centre daily 9am–5pm, turtle watching April–Sept daily 9pm–6am • Donation • ☎ 09 581 9078

Around the rocky headland at the eastern end of the bay, near the exclusive Club Med development, Cherating has its own **turtle sanctuary**. The information centre has a few displays about the creatures, plus a few holding tanks at the back, but the real appeal comes after hours during the laying season. Arrive late at night and seek out the ranger on duty – try the hatchery on the right-hand side – to join them as they check for arriving green and (occasionally) hawksbill turtles. When there are hatchlings to release, they do so at 10.30pm. If you don't fancy just turning up on your own, arrange a visit with Hafiz (see box, p.255) or your accommodation.

ARRIVAL AND DEPARTURE

By express bus Express buses on the coast road between Kuala Terengganu and Kuantan drop passengers on request at both Cherating Lama and Cherating Baru. However, they won't stop to pick up passengers, so reserve ahead when you want to leave.

Destinations Jerteh (for Kuala Besut; 9 daily); Johor Bahru (2 daily); Kota Bharu (9 daily); Kuala Lumpur (7 daily);

Kuala Terengganu (8 daily); Marang (8 daily); Melaka (2 daily); Mersing (2 daily); Rantau Abang (8 daily); Singapore (2 daily); Tapah (2 daily); Thai border (1 daily).

By local bus If you don't have a reservation on an express bus, you can wait for one of the sporadic local services.

By taxi It's possible to catch a taxi from Kuantan to Cherating (45 min; RM70).

TOUR AGENTS

A few agencies on the main drag offer bus-ticket bookings and other travel arrangements, such as transfers to Taman Negara or islands off the east coast, while Hafiz (see p.255) comes recommended if you're booking activities.

Travel Post Lot 1006, Cherating Lama ☏012/955 3344. As well as internet access and bike rental, they sell tickets for river trips (RM20), firefly watching (RM15), turtle watching (RM50), snorkelling at Snake Island (from RM48), and day-trips to Lake Chini (from RM148).

Yahya *Payung Guesthouse* ☏014 210 2973, ✉travel planner_yahya@yahoo.com. Based in the office at the front of the guesthouse, Yahya offers good advice plus marked-up maps. As well as booking tours, he also sorts out bus tickets for a small commission.

ACCOMMODATION

Prices can rise by twenty percent or more during weekends and holidays year-round, though discounts are available during the northeast monsoon.

CHERATING LAMA

Cherating Bay View Cherating Lama ☏09 581 9248, ✉cheratingbayview@yahoo.com. At the quieter end of the bay, this complex has a range of a/c chalets – the cheapest of them around a swimming pool. While the standard seafront chalets lack the modern fixtures and fittings of the deluxe options, they actually have better sea views. Free wi-fi in reception. Poolside chalets RM135, seafront chalets RM150

Coconut Inn Cherating Lama ☏012/922 2248. A real survivor on the Cherating scene, open since 1981 and still popular with budget travellers. All chalets are fan-cooled, while larger rooms, arranged around a sandy area with plenty of trees and plants, cost more money. Wi-fi generally available. RM40

Matahari Cherating Lama ☏09 581 9835 or ☏019 935 9420. A mishmash of units, from spartan A-frames to slightly larger chalets, all arranged around a pleasant grassy area. Toilets and showers are in a separate block, although a few rooms have their own facilities and two also have a/c. There's a communal kitchen. Fan rooms RM20, en-suite rooms RM40, a/c rooms RM70

Maznah's Guest House Cherating Lama ☏09 581 9359. The basic A-frames share facilities, but you can hardly complain for the price. The spotless en-suite chalets are also good value, but the sole a/c chalet is overpriced. A-frames RM25, en-suite chalets RM60, a/c chalet RM150

Payung Guesthouse Cherating Lama ☏019 917 1934. A deservedly popular collection of ten no-frills chalets set in a small, very tidy garden. All are en suite, with fan and mosquito net; most have a double bed. The one drawback

(as with its neighbours) is night-time noise from the nearby bars. RM50

Ranting Beach Resort Cherating Lama ☏09 581 9068. Spacious, well-kept garden rooms, plus much pricier beach chalets, with nice tiled bathrooms and good views – some have patio doors leading to verandas. All options are en suite, some have a/c and TV. Rooms RM80, chalets RM180

Residence Inn Cherating Lama ☏09 581 9333. If you prefer resort-style accommodation but want to stay in Cherating Lama, then this complex of 73 tidy en suite rooms is the place to come. They have a couple of small swimming pools and can arrange snorkelling, river or deep sea fishing, and other activities. Rate includes breakfast. RM195

Royale Bintang Villa Cherating Lama ☏03 2166 3601, ⊛royalebintangcherating.com.my. Just the place to get away from it all – this four-bedroom luxury villa is far enough uphill to deter casual visitors, and you can even rent the whole place if you like. Rooms RM500, entire house RM2500

★ **Tanjung Inn (aka Villa de Fedelia)** Cherating Lama ☏09 581 9081 or ☏010 256 5667. Timber-built en-suite accommodation, ranging from simple chalets with fans to rooms in brilliant traditionally styled kampung houses, each boasting a/c, four-poster beds and a slate-tiled bathroom with hot water. All are set around two large ponds in a peaceful and pretty garden. Fan chalet RM70, a/c room RM150

NORTH OF CHERATING LAMA

Impiana North of Cherating Lama ☏09 581 9000, ⊛impianacherating.com. Large four-star beach resort

4

MARINE TURTLES

While four types of marine turtle lay their eggs on Malaysia's east coast, for years the sight of the largest – the giant, critically endangered **leatherback turtle** – was the star attraction, drawing visitors to Rantau Abang in Terengganu. In fact all other kinds of marine turtle – **green** (Malaysian nesting sites include the Perhentians, Pulau Redang, Cherating, Penarik, and the Turtle Islands National Park in Sabah), **hawksbill** (Pulau Redang, Turtle Islands National Park, Pulau Tioman and Padang Kemunting near Melaka), **olive ridley** (rarely seen), and **Kemp's ridley** and **loggerhead** (neither of which nest in Malaysia) – are also at risk.

Harmful fishing methods, such as the use of **trawl nets**, kill thousands of marine turtles each year, and help explain the dramatic reduction in leatherbacks nesting on the Terengganu coast. In 1956, more than ten thousand were recorded; in 2000, just three; in 2002, there were no sightings of leatherbacks in Rantau Abang for the first time since records began; by 2005, leatherback, hawksbill and olive ridley's statistics in Terengganu were all at zero, and green turtle figures were significantly down. On the rare occasions when a leatherback turns up – there was a lone turtle in 2010 – their eggs often fail to hatch. This is probably because of the increasing rarity of male–female turtle encounters.

With a very meagre survival rate among hatchlings under ordinary conditions, any human pressure on turtle populations has drastic consequences for their survival. For the Chinese in Malaysia and Singapore, turtle soup is a classic delicacy, and while Malays eschew turtle meat, they do consume **turtle eggs**, which look like ping-pong balls and are sold at markets throughout the east coast. Their collection is licensed at certain sites, but there's no guarantee that anything on sale was collected legally. There appears to be no political will to outlaw this traditional food, a sad irony given Malaysia's general turtle conservation efforts: in many places, hatcheries pay licensed collectors for eggs rather than see them go to markets. At least the deliberate slaughter of turtles for their shells, once fashioned into bowls and earrings, has been banned since 1992.

TURTLE SPOTTING AND CONSERVATION

Nowadays, humans are excluded from various designated **sanctuaries** for nesting turtles. At these sites the eggs are dug up immediately after the turtle has laid them and reburied in sealed-off **hatcheries** on the beach. Burying the eggs in sand of the correct temperature is crucial as warm sand produces more females, while cooler sand favours males. When the hatchlings emerge, they are released at the top of the beach and their scurry to the sea is supervised to ensure their safe progress.

There are several officially sanctioned opportunities to watch nesting turtles on the east coast beaches and islands, including at Cherating, Pulau Perhentian Besar and Pulau Tioman (at Juara Beach). One excellent resource is ⊚ helpourpenyu.com, set up by a company called Ecoteer which offers opportunities to volunteer on Perhentian Besar (see p.237).

with swimming pool, tennis court and outdoor jacuzzi. Deluxe rooms make appealing use of dark wood but feel cramped, while the superior deluxe are much more spacious; some of the expensive sea-view rooms have only a glimpse of the water. Weekend rates rise drastically. RM290

Suria Cherating Beach Resort North of Cherating Lama ⊕ 09 581 9898, ⊚ suriaresorts.com. From the spacious lobby to the classy rooms, this resort ticks all the right boxes. Room prices vary with location and view, and the deluxe rooms are not always worth the slight premium. Facilities include a gym, sauna and steam bath. RM175

CHERATING BARU

Eastern Pavilion Cherating Baru ⊕ 09 581 9500, ⊚ easternpavilion.com. Twelve luxurious villas, each based on a kampung house from a different Malaysian state. All come with one or two beautifully appointed bedrooms, lounge and (screened) outdoor jacuzzi. There's also a spa, of course. Published rates are significantly higher than the typical promotional rate given here. RM710

Legend Resort Cherating Baru ⊕ 09 581 9818, ⊚ legendresort.com.my. A series of interlinked pools with a central waterfall lie at the heart of this sprawling, popular beach-side development. Plentiful activities are on offer both night and day. Basic "deluxe" rooms are comfortable if generic, higher grades are significantly more stylish; it's hard to justify the extra cost of the sea-view rooms. Rooms RM276, sea-view rooms RM463

EATING AND DRINKING

Cherating Lama has a string of inexpensive **restaurants**, many emphasizing seafood including the *lala* – a sort of clam, which turns up in various sauces – but a couple of places also offer decent Western food. *Kedai kopis* across from the *Payung Café* and the *Matahari* serve reasonable Malay cuisine, with *roti canai* in the morning and *nasi campur* later in the day.

★ **Don't Tell Mama Café** Cherating Lama. The only beach bar in Cherating Lama, open year-round, is a great place to chill out with a beer (RM10) and a burger (RM20), watching beach volleyball or enjoying the relaxed playlist. Sometimes visiting DJs from KL entertain customers well into the night. Daily 11am–2am; food until 10pm.

Duyong Cherating Lama. An old faithful, this large place overlooking the eastern end of the beach offers excellent Chinese and Thai dishes, plus a few Western standbys such as lamb chop and steak. Veggie dishes can be cooked to order. Thurs–Tues 10am–midnight, Wed 3pm–midnight.

Little Bali *Riverside* resort, Cherating Lama. It's hard to see how resort guests can get much sleep; this bar pulls in the locals with live music early on followed by pounding dance music later. Daily until late.

Matahari Seafood Restaurant Cherating Lama. Other dishes are served but it's the seafood – charged by weight – that shines here. Choose from squid, cuttlefish, crab, prawns or fish, then pick a sauce. Daily except Wed 6pm–1am.

Mimi's Café Cherating Lama ☎017 967 3810. Popular hangout, serving Western breakfasts, including French toast (RM4.50), throughout the day; the lunch menu includes Western and local dishes, and there's a barbecue on Saturday nights. Sun–Fri 8am–6pm, Sat 8am–late.

Payung Café Cherating Lama. The decor and music policy are heavy on the reggae, but it's Italian food that brings in the diners – including pizzas (RM15) and pasta (from RM7). The ambience is best after dark, when you can eat in the main pavilion or at riverside tables under dimly lit coconut palms. Wi-fi available. Daily except Tues 9am–late.

Kuantan

The state capital of **Pahang** since 1955, **KUANTAN** is an undistinguished agglomeration of concrete buildings around an older core of shophouses close to Sungai Kuantan. While there's very little by way of historical or cultural interest in the city itself, Kuantan can be a breath of fresh air after a sojourn in Kelantan or Terengganu – it's closer in feel to the west-coast cities than to Kuala Terengganu or Kota Bharu. If you're arriving from elsewhere in the country, however, Kuantan can seem mundane. With the creation of the **East Coast Highway** to Pelabuhan Kuantan, the port 40km north of the city, it's easy to bypass Kuantan altogether if you're travelling between KL and the east coast.

If Kuantan has a focus of sorts, it's the **padang**. The city's oldest streets, between there and the river, hold quite a few hotels and restaurants. The best reason to hang around for a night or two, though, is to take a day-trip to the cave temple of **Gua Charas** or the royal town of **Pekan**.

Masjid Negeri

Northeastern edge of the padang

The town's one real sight, the **Masjid Negeri**, was built in 1991, with a pastel exterior – green for Islam, blue for peace and white for purity. It's distinctly Turkish in appearance, thanks to the pencil minarets at all four corners of the sturdy square prayer hall, topped with a looming central dome. Non-Muslims can visit other than during Friday prayers: men should wear long trousers, while women will be given gowns.

The promenade

Down by the river, starting at the *Megaview Hotel*, a promenade clings to the banks of Sungai Kuantan. Early evening is a good time to take a stroll, to see fishing boats returning with the day's catch and perhaps the occasional red eagle swooping on its prey. No boat trips are currently on offer.

Teluk Chempedak

5km east of centre following Jalan Besar, which becomes Jalan Teluk Sisek and then Jalan Teluk Chempedak • Buses depart from local bus station and close to the mosque (daily 8am–6pm; 30min); taxis RM15–18

Around the corner from a wooded headland, on an east-facing stretch of coast, **Teluk Chempedak** has long been a popular evening and weekend hangout for families and young people. The sands of the bay are encouragingly white, although undertows can

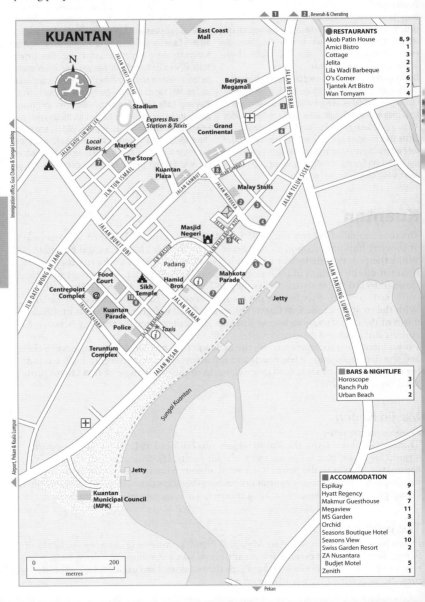

KUANTAN

RESTAURANTS	
Akob Patin House	8, 9
Amici Bistro	1
Cottage	3
Jelita	2
Lila Wadi Barbeque	5
O's Corner	6
Tjantek Art Bistro	7
Wan Tomyam	4

BARS & NIGHTLIFE	
Horoscope	3
Ranch Pub	1
Urban Beach	2

ACCOMMODATION	
Espikay	9
Hyatt Regency	4
Makmur Guesthouse	7
Megaview	11
MS Garden	3
Orchid	8
Seasons Boutique Hotel	6
Seasons View	10
Swiss Garden Resort	2
ZA Nusantara Budjet Motel	5
Zenith	1

render the sea off-limits (watch out for red flags). There is an appealing liveliness about the place, quite at variance from the langourous mood on the otherwise better sands of rural Terengganu. Bars and restaurants line the main road as you arrive, before you reach the *Hyatt*, and there are more places to eat on the promenade.

ARRIVAL AND DEPARTURE
KUANTAN

By plane Sultan Ahmad Shah airport is 15km west of town, which is a 20min, RM35 taxi ride. KL flights (3 daily; 45min) are operated by Malaysian Airlines (☎09 538 5194), while Penang (daily; 1hr 30min) and Singapore (daily; 1hr) flights are with Firefly (☎09 538 2911). Desk #21 in the express bus station sells air tickets.

By express bus The express bus station is several blocks north of the padang, close to Jalan Tun Ismail, and holds a left-luggage office (8am–12.30am; RM2/item).

Destinations Alor Star (2 daily; 10hr); Butterworth (2 daily; 9hr); Cherating (every 30min–1hr; 1hr–1hr 30min); Ipoh (2 daily; 6hr); Jerantut (7 daily; 3hr); Johor Bahru (14 daily; 5hr 30min); Kota Bharu (10 daily; 7hr); Kuala Lipis (2

daily; 5hr); Kuala Lumpur (hourly; 3hr); Kuala Terengganu (12 daily; 4–5hr); Marang (several daily; 3hr 30min); Melaka (6 daily; 4hr); Mersing (6 daily; 3hr); Seremban (2 daily; 7hr); Singapore (4 daily; 6hr 30min).

By local bus The local bus station is on Jalan Stadium, with Bee Huat bus #31 running to Pekan (at least hourly).

By taxi Local taxis can be found near the mosque; long-distance taxis arrive at the express bus station. To book a vehicle, call Station Taxis ☎095 134 478.

Car rental Avis (☎09 539 8768, ⓦavis.com), Hertz (☎09 538 4848, ⓦsimedarbycarrental.com) and Mayflower (☎09 538 4490, ⓦmayflowercarrental.com.my) are all at the airport.

INFORMATION

Tourist offices Tourism Malaysia has an office at street level in the Mahkota Square business complex, south of the padang (Mon–Thurs 8am–1pm, 2–5pm, Fri 8am–noon, 2.45–5pm; ☎09 517 7111). Pahang Tourism, the

state's tourism promotion body (Mon–Fri 9am–1pm, 2–5pm; ☎09 516 1007, ⓦpahangtourism.com.my), runs a helpful tourist office of their own on Jalan Mahkota.

4

ACCOMMODATION

There's no shortage of places to stay in Kuantan, but you can also stay **out of town** at Teluk Chempedak or the pleasant Balok Beach. For details of **homestays**, pick up the well-produced *Homestay Pahang* booklet from the state tourist office or visit ⓦgo2homestay.com.

CENTRAL KUANTAN

★ **Espikay** Jalan Mahkota ☎09 513 0655. A new addition to Kuantan's hotel scene, and something of a bargain. The decoration reflects a sense of style (albeit on a budget) and all rooms have wi-fi, a/c, flat-screen TVs and hot showers. Lone travellers should ask about the room with a single bed (RM58); though tiny, it's a great option. RM88

Makmur Guesthouse B16, first floor, Jalan Pasar Baru ☎09 514 1363. The best of the cheapies close to the bus station, although that isn't saying a lot; fan rooms with shared facilities as well as a/c en-suite rooms, all fairly simple. Fan rooms RM30, a/c en-suite rooms RM59

Megaview Jalan Besar ☎09 517 1888, ⓦmegaviewhotel.com. Business-oriented, efficient high-rise hotel on the river, with wi-fi access, a coffee house, a bar and a health centre. The more expensive rooms in particular have been decorated with retro-chic flair. Regular promotions make it good value; rates include breakfast. RM120

MS Garden Lorong Gambut, off Jalan Beserah ☎09 511 8888, ⓦwww.msgarden.com.my. Slick from its palatial lobby on up, this central hotel offers spacious rooms, several places to eat or drink, a fitness centre and a

pool complete with waterfall. Free wi-fi throughout, and breakfast is included. RM253

Orchid Jalan Merdeka ☎09 555 570. Despite the unpromising steps up to reception, the rooms in this back-street Chinese hotel – while in need of a lick of paint – are good enough for the price. RM55

Seasons Boutique Hotel 2 Jalan Beserah ☎09 516 3131, ⓔseasonsboutiquehotel@gmail.com. Good mid-range choice, with appealing and well-decorated rooms, though the cheapest have no windows. Chinese restaurant on the ground floor, plus a spa (noon–midnight) and karaoke bar upstairs. RM83

Seasons View A22 Lorong Haji Abdul Rahman 1 ☎09 516 2828, ⓔseasonsview_kuantan@ymail.com. Self-proclaimed "oasis of gracious hospitality", designed with considerable style and located in an area that has recently been extensively redeveloped. The rooms are not exactly luxurious but they're immaculate and easy to recommend for the price. Breakfast included. RM93

Zenith Jalan Putra Square 6 ☎09 565 9595, ⓦthezenithhotel.com. It's hard to miss the hulking twin buildings close to the East Coast Mall, one of which holds this 590-room business hotel. The rooms are a decent size, and finished to a high standard using slightly retro decor. With a swimming pool and spa, there's a lot to like – assuming the grand scale doesn't put you off. **RM296**

TELUK CHEMPEDAK

Hyatt Regency Teluk Chempedak ☎ 09 518 1234, ⓦ kuantan.regency.hyatt.com. A long-established beach retreat for well-heeled folk from KL and Singapore, which has two swimming pools, a gym, tennis and squash courts, childcare facilities, two restaurants and a bar in a converted ship. Rates include breakfast although internet in rooms costs an extortionate RM57/day; wi-fi is free in the restaurants. **RM383**

ZA Nusantara Budjet Motel 2A Jalan Teluk Chempedak ☎ 09 566 6885 or ☎ 017 916 7885, ✉ nusantaramotel@

yahoo.com. The best of a row of identikit concrete guesthouses, with rooms – not en suite, but a/c – decorated in tasteful shades of brown. The good-size Pelikat room is particularly recommended. Free wi-fi. **RM70**

BALOK BEACH

Balok Beach, 15km north of Kuantan, can be reached by taxi (around RM30) or on a Cherating-bound bus from the local bus station (45min).

Swiss Garden Resort Balok Beach ☎ 09 544 7333, ⓦ swissgarden.com. Balconied rooms overlooking a landscaped garden or the South China Sea, plus a free-form swimming pool and a spa with herbal and other massages. A large range of activities are available for adults and children. **RM307**

EATING AND DRINKING

Laidback *kedai kopis* dot the streets west and south of the padang, while the area around Berjaya Megamall is packed with cafés and *mamak* joints. For inexpensive Malay food, try the places on and around the northern end of Jalan Haji Abdul Aziz, the area around the Central Market or the stalls off Jalan Merdeka. Teluk Chempedak also holds plenty of eating choices, including many on the seafront, some open until as late as 2am. The **nightlife** in Teluk Chempedak is more lively than that in town, revolving around a handful of bars on the main road just before the beach.

CENTRAL KUANTAN

Akob Patin House By the river near *Megaview* hotel. The signature ingredient at this humble place under a tented canopy is *patin* (silver catfish), served at lunchtime as *asam pedas tempoyak* – with chilli, tamarind and fermented durian. Breakfast includes *mee rebung* (noodles with bamboo shoots), while you'll need to order *patin* in advance if you want it in the evening. There's also a branch on Lorong Tun Ismail. Mon–Sat 9am–midnight.

Cottage 63 Jalan Haji Abdul Aziz ☎ 09 516 1069. A touch smarter and more adventurous than most local Chinese restaurants, serving dishes such as fish-head curry (RM28). The most famous dish is *nasi petai*, fried rice with *sambal* and strong-smelling *petai* beans (RM5); if you prefer noodles then order *petai bee hoon*. Beer is served. Mon–Sat 11am–2.30pm & 5pm–12.30am, Sun 6pm–12.30am.

Horoscope Jalan Gambut. The open-air bar at the front is just the beginning; upstairs is Kuantan's liveliest nightclub – with laser lights and DJs – although it doesn't get going until well after midnight. No dress code, and while there's often an entry fee it usually includes a drink. Daily 3.30pm–3.30am.

Jelita Jalan Haji Abdul Aziz. Essentially a posh-looking metal hangar housing several food outlets, the star attraction among which is a branch of *Satay Zul* – Kuantan's best-loved satay house – offering beef, chicken, *kambing* (goat), *rusa* (venison) and even *perut* (stomach) at around 60 sen a stick. Stalls elsewhere offer rice and noodles, basic Western fare and doner kebabs. Various hours, most around 9am–midnight.

Lila Wadi Barbeque Jalan Teluk Sisek. This great spot serves barbecue that's cooked at your table; you choose a main ingredient – beef, chicken or seafood – and receive a "set" which also includes other items. The beef set, for example, also comes with some prawn, squid and chicken. The smallest set is for two people (RM33). Daily except Mon 4–11pm, food served from 6pm.

★ **O's Corner** Jalan Teluk Sisek ☎ 019 944 9433. This fantastic riverside café could hardly be more unexpected or welcome, serving Malay and western dishes plus local and imported beers. Sit inside the main building or in one of the open-sided huts, where rough wooden tables add to the charm. Live music nightly, from 8pm until closing. Sun–Fri 10am–midnight, Sat 10am–2am.

Tjantek Art Bistro 46 Jalan Besar ☎ 09 516 4144. With designer lighting and artwork plastering the walls, this is one of downtown Kuantan's most interesting places. The pasta dishes, properly al dente (from RM12), are great, and they also do sandwiches, soups and salads, plus desserts such as mango pudding and chocolate cake. Mon–Sat 6pm–late.

Wan Tomyam Jalan Teluk Sisek. Thai food seems to be particularly popular in Kuantan, and this busy restaurant – part of the small *Sara Thai Kitchen* chain – is one of several places specializing in dishes like green curry, *tom yam* and mango salad. Daily 1–11pm, closed on 14th of each month.

TELUK CHEMPEDAK

Amici Bistro Teluk Chempedak ☎ 09 551 2030. A cut above most places hereabouts, with Western dishes that attract expats and foreign tourists as well as locals, and imported beers. Food isn't cheap though: a steak burger goes for RM32 and medium pizza for RM19. Unusually they have a no-smoking policy from 7–9.30pm, when most people are eating. Tues–Fri 4pm–midnight, Sat & Sun noon–midnight.

Ranch Pub Teluk Chempedak. If you're a fan of English football you'll certainly find a talking point here – owner Jeff is a Liverpool supporter. More of a straightforward pub than some of its neighbours: there's no karaoke, a free pool table and sport on TV. Daily until late.

Urban Beach Teluk Chempedak. It may look closed from the outside, but the sound of karaoke gives the game away. One of several such bars on the road to the beach, it's aimed mostly at Malaysian Chinese and Singaporeans, and has a happy hour until 9pm. Sun–Thurs 4.30pm–1am, Fri & Sat 4.30pm–2am.

SHOPPING

Popular places to shop include the Berjaya Megamall on Jalan Tun Ismail, Kuantan Parade on Jalan Penjara, and the East Coast Mall. On Saturday evenings there's a **night market** on Jalan Gambut, close to the junction with Jalan Bukit Ubi. Hamid Bros on Jalan Haji Abdul Aziz, midway along the padang, has a limited range of English-language **books**, plus various maps of Malaysia. The Berjaya Megamall has a branch of Popular Bookstore (daily 10am–10pm).

DIRECTORY

Banks Standard Chartered Bank and Maybank are situated around the intersection of the aptly named Jalan Bank and Jalan Besar.

Cinemas Golden Screen Cinemas (ⓦ gsc.com.my) in both the Berjaya Megamall and the East Coast Mall show some English-language films, as does Lotus Five-Star cinema in the Teruntum Complex (☎ 09 515 6881).

Hospital The Hospital Tengku Ampuan Afzan (☎ 09 513 3333) is on Jalan Tanah Putih, the western continuation of

Jalan Besar; the private Kuantan Medical Centre is next to the Berjaya Megamall (☎ 09 514 2828).

Post The GPO, with poste restante, is on Jalan Haji Abdul Aziz.

Visa extensions The immigration office is 8km northwest of the centre at Kompleks KDN, Bandar Indera Mahkota (Mon–Fri 7.30am–1pm & 2–5.30pm; ☎ 09 573 2200); take a bus from the local bus station.

Gua Charas

25km northwest of Kuantan on Route C4 · RM2 donation · Local bus to Panching (30min) then 4km walk, or taxi from Kuantan

One of the great limestone outcrops close to Kuantan is home to **Gua Charas**, a **cave temple** which can be seen as a leisurely day-trip: if you charter a taxi from Kuantan (RM100 return including waiting) then you can also visit the nearby Sungai Pandan **waterfall**, where you can splash around in various pools. If you're taking the bus then you start at **Panching** village, where a sign to the cave points down a track through plantations. It's a long, hot walk, so take plenty of water with you; you may be able to hitch a lift for a few ringgit.

Once you've reached the outcrop and paid your donation, you're faced with a steep climb to the Thai Buddhist cave temple itself. Halfway up, a rudimentary path strikes off to the right, leading to the entrance of the main cave. It isn't for the faint-hearted, even though the damp mud path is dimly lit by fluorescent tubes. Inside the echoing cavern, illuminated shrines gleam from gloomy corners, guiding you to the main shrine deep in the cave. Here a 9m-long sleeping Buddha is almost dwarfed by its giant surroundings. Back through the cave, steps lead to another, lighter hollow where the rear wall opens out to give a great view of the surrounding countryside.

Pekan

Nearly 50km south of Kuantan lies the royal town of **PEKAN**, whose name literally means "small town". State capital of Pahang until 1898, Pekan still retains a measure of its charm and tranquillity, although this has been challenged in recent years with the

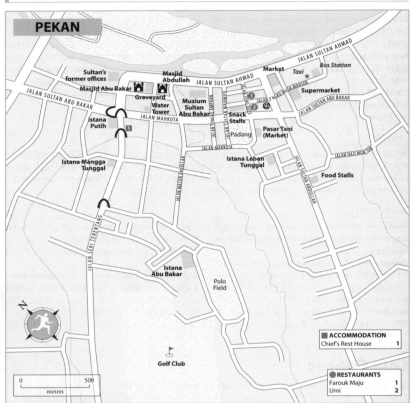

growth of its modern centre and a rather mixed makeover for its heritage buildings. This is thanks in no small part – so locals say – to the fact that the town's MP is none other than prime minister Najib Tun Razak. Still, the town is definitely a worthwhile day-trip from Kuantan: you'll find unusually spruce, almost prim **kampung houses** with pretty gardens, a couple of **museums** and a few wooden former **royal residences**.

Muzium Sultan Abu Bakar

Jalan Sultan Ahmad • Opening times to be confirmed, formerly Tues–Sun 9.30am–5pm, closed Fri 12.15–2.45pm • ☎ 09 422 1371

At the edge of the commercial sector, Jalan Sultan Ahmad faces the languid riverfront and holds the **Muzium Sultan Abu Bakar** – the State Museum of Pahang. It's housed in a well-proportioned Straits colonial building that has variously served as the sultan's istana, the centre of British administration, and the headquarters of the Japanese army during the occupation.

It became a museum in 1975, and has long been one of the main attractions for visitors to Pekan, but at the time of research it was closed for extensive renovation – the building had essentially been reduced to a shell. Along with the **Watercraft Gallery** just across the river, the museum was scheduled to reopen in 2012.

The palaces

At the intersection of Jalan Sultan Abu Bakar and Jalan Sri Terentang, an archway built to resemble elephants' tusks marks the way to the royal quarter of the town. The timber building on the corner here, once the white **Istana Putih**, is now a brightly painted centre for Koranic recitation. A few minutes' walk south, the squat **Istana Mangga Tunggal** is painted a dark blue. Continue and turn left at the archway to reach the expansive walled grounds of the **Istana Abu Bakar**, current home to the royal family and closed to the public. The other side of the road holds some attractively colourful kampung houses. Follow the walls, and after nearly ten minutes you'll come to a vast **polo field**, home to a polo club founded in 1926.

Istana Leban Tunggal

Kampung Leban Tunggal • Mon–Thurs 10am–5pm, Fri 10am–12.15pm & 2.45–5pm, Sat 9am–1pm • Free

The most impressive of Pekan's royal buildings is the **Istana Leban Tunggal**, which is also the only one open to the general public. Most easily reached from the padang, rather than via the winding lanes of the kampung in which it is located, the building is a refined wooden structure fronted by a pillared portico, flanked by two octagonal towers each topped by a yellow dome.

ARRIVAL AND DEPARTURE   PEKAN

By bus The black-and-white Bee Huat bus #31 leaves at least hourly from Kuantan's local bus station for the hour-long journey to Pekan. If your main interest is the palaces, ask to be let off the bus at the "Daulat Tuanku" arch on Jalan Sultan Abu Bakar, before the UFO-like water tower. Pekan's own bus station is in the modern centre, east of the padang.

Destinations Kuantan (frequent); Tasik Chini (4 daily); Kuala Lumpur (2 daily; 5 hr); Kota Bharu (2 daily; 7 hr) via Dungun and Kuala Terengganu; Johor Bharu (2 daily; 5hr) via Mersing.

By taxi Taxis are available from close to the bus station to Kuantan (RM60), Tasik Chini (RM70) and Kulala Rompin (RM80).

INFORMATION

Internet cafés Mostly between the padang and the bus station, including Internet Station (Mon–Sat 8am–11pm,

Sun 9.30am–11pm) on Jalan Sultan Abu Bakar.

ACCOMMODATION

Chief's Rest House Jalan Istana Permai ☎09 422 6941. Occupying a spacious timber bungalow not unlike some of the istanas, this resthouse has nine high-ceilinged rooms – some with four-poster beds and

bamboo blinds – brought up to date with a/c and TV. Showers, though, have only cold water. Booking is essential; it's a popular place, in a town with few alternatives. **RM55**

EATING AND DRINKING

The streets around the padang hold several places to **eat**, including a row of three stalls selling juice and snacks, with parasols providing a welcome break from the sun.

Restoran Farouk Maju 1 Jalan Engku Muda Mansor. This typical *mamak* restaurant serves tasty and cheap roti and curries to a fairly constant stream of locals. Daily 7am–10.30pm.

Umi Jalan Teng Quee. A small Chinese restaurant close to *Farouk Maju*, offering a *nasi campur* spread as well as dishes like *nasi goreng*. Also sells *pau* containing such fillings as chicken and beef. Daily 7am–6pm.

The south

WAITING TRISHAWS

5

The south

The south of the Malay Peninsula, below Kuala Lumpur and Kuantan, holds some of the country's most historically and culturally significant towns. Foremost among these is the west-coast city of Melaka, founded in the fifteenth century and ushering in a Malay "golden age" under the Melaka Sultanate. For all its enduring influence, though, the sultanate was short-lived and its fall to the Portuguese early in the sixteenth century marked the start of centuries of colonial involvement in Malaysia. Today Melaka fascinates visitors with its historical buildings and cultural blend, including the Peranakan community (also called Baba-Nonya), which grew from the intermarriage of early Chinese immigrant traders and Malay women.

Melaka is not, however, the only place in the region with historical resonance. Between KL and Melaka, what's now the state of Negeri Sembilan is where the intrepid **Minangkabau** tribes from Sumatra settled, making their mark with architecture which can still be seen in **Seremban** and **Sri Menanti**. Both lie just over an hour south of the capital by road. Continuing down the west coast on the train line or the North–South Expressway (NSE), travellers soon reach the tip of the Peninsula and the thriving border city of **Johor Bahru** (JB) which dates back only to 1855. Beyond it lies Singapore.

Visitors tend to avoid the mountainous interior, where the road network is poor, but Route 3 on the east coast is a good deal more varied than the NSE, and winds for 300km through oil-palm country and past pleasant beaches. The biggest attractions along the east coast are **Pulau Tioman** and the other islands of the **Seribuat Archipelago**; they are havens for divers, snorkellers and anyone else in search of white sandy beaches, clear water and a tranquil atmosphere. Back on the Peninsula, and accessible from either east or west coast, the **Endau Rompin National Park** is a more rugged and less visited alternative to Taman Negara.

Negeri Sembilan

During the fifteenth century, the **Minangkabau** tribes from Sumatra established themselves in what is now the Malay state of **Negeri Sembilan**. While the modern-day capital is **Seremban**, 67km south of Kuala Lumpur, the cultural heart of the state lies 30km east in the royal town of **Sri Menanti**. Both towns showcase traditional Minangkabau architecture, with its distinctive, saddle-shaped roofs.

Brief history
The modern state of Negeri Sembilan is based on an old confederacy of nine districts (hence its name – *sembilan* is Malay for "nine"). By the middle of the nineteenth

MINANGKABAU ARCHITECTURE, NEGERI SEMBILAN

Highlights

❶ Minangkabau architecture The spectacular and distinctive architecture of this ancient Sumatran tribe survives in Sri Menanti and Seremban. **See p.273**

❷ Melaka The UNESCO World Heritage Site of Melaka has Portuguese, Dutch and British colonial buildings as well as unique Peranakan ancestral homes and some of Malaysia's best food. **See p.274**

❸ Johor Bahru It may still be gritty by Malaysian standards, but this border city is smartening itself up with a combination of

major public projects and small-scale entrepreneurship. **See p.291**

❹ Pulau Tioman Palm-fringed, scenic and with great diving, this island is understandably popular but retains a laidback feel. **See p.299**

❺ Seribuat Archipelago Tioman attracts all the attention, but the other islands of the Seribuat Archipelago offer even better beaches. **See p.309**

❻ Endau Rompin National Park A little-visited lush tropical rainforest, rich with rare species of flora and fauna. **See p.310**

HIGHLIGHTS ARE MARKED ON THE MAP ON P.271

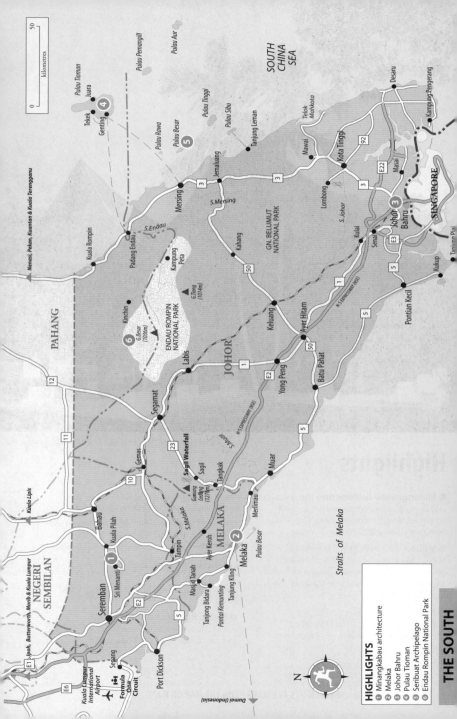

HIGHLIGHTS
1 Minangkabau architecture
2 Melaka
3 Johor Bahru
4 Pulau Tioman
5 Seribuat Archipelago
6 Endau Rompin National Park

century, the thriving **tin trade** and British control over the area were well established, with colonial authority administered from Sungai Ujong (today's Seremban). Rival Malay and Minangkabau groups fought several wars for control over the mining and transport of tin, with Chinese secret societies (triads) manipulating the situation to gain local influence, before a treaty was eventually signed in 1895.

Seremban

An hour south of the capital and just twenty minutes from KL International Airport, the bustling town of **SEREMBAN** is often overlooked by passing tourists. It is, however, the access point for **Sri Menanti** and has good examples of Minangkabau architecture at the **Taman Seni Budaya Negeri** museum complex.

Town centre

The most interesting part of the town centre is the area around the Lake Garden, which is more lake than garden. Heading north alongside it you pass the **Craft Complex** (Kompleks Kraf; daily 9am–6pm), a good place to view and buy handmade items such as ceramics and textiles. Not much further along is the white-stuccoed Neoclassical former **State Library** – built as the centre of colonial administration – with its graceful columns and portico. Past the black-and-gilt wrought-iron gates of the Istana (closed to the public), just north, a left turn leads to the current **State Secretariat**, whose architecture (such as the layered, buffalo-horn roof) reflects the Minangkabau tradition.

Taman Seni Budaya Negeri

Close to North–South Expressway, 3km northwest of the centre • Sat–Thurs 10am–6pm, Fri 10am–12.15pm & 2.45–6pm • Free • ☎ 06 763 1149 • Bus from Terminal 1; taxi from the centre RM6

Although the small museum at the centre of the **Taman Seni Budaya Negeri** (State Arts & Culture Park) is unlikely to hold your attention for long, two reconstructed buildings in the grounds provide a good introduction to the principles of Minangkabau architecture.

The first, the **Istana Ampang Tinggi**, was built as a royal residence in the mid-nineteenth century. The interior of the veranda, where male guests were entertained, displays a wealth of exuberant and intricate leaf carvings, with a pair of unusual heavy timber doors. The other building was used for formal state events and also bears elaborate carving on the exterior. Neither building has much on show inside.

ARRIVAL AND DEPARTURE

SEREMBAN

By train Seremban's train station, just south of the centre, has regular connections with Kuala Lumpur; take the Komuter train from KL Sentral or the old Kuala Lumpur station.

Destinations Batu Gajah (3 daily; 4hr); Gemas (3 daily; 2hr 30min); Ipoh (3 daily; 5hr); Johor Bahru (3 daily; 5hr); Kuala Lumpur (frequent; 1hr 30min); Singapore (3 daily; 4hr).

By bus Seremban has two bus terminals, connected by shuttle buses: Terminal 1 (used by most buses, including those from KL) is just across the river west of the town

centre, while Terminal 2 is about 1.5km further out.

Destinations Alor Star (2 daily; 8hr); Butterworth (2 daily; 6hr); Gua Musang (daily; 8hr); Ipoh (3 daily; 5hr); Johor Bahru (5 daily; 4hr); KLIA (8 daily; 1hr); Kota Bharu (2 daily; 10hr); Kuala Lumpur (every 30min; 1hr); Kuala Pilah (7 daily; 45min); Kuala Terengganu (3 daily; 8hr); Kuantan (2 daily; 4hr); Melaka (hourly; 1hr 15min); Mersing (2 daily; 5hr); Singapore (6 daily, 4hr).

By taxi A taxi from KL Sentral costs around RM90.

GETTING AROUND

Taxis wait outside Terminal 1 bus station. Call Seremban Cab (☎ 06 761 3333) if you need to be picked up.

INFORMATION

Tourist office Tourism Malaysia is in Seremban Plaza on Jalan Dato' Muda Linggi (☎ 06 762 4488).

Internet cafés Several internet cafés are located in and around the Terminal One shopping centre.

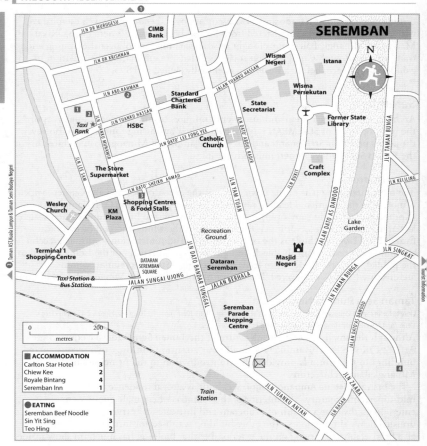

ACCOMMODATION

Seremban has a chronic shortage of decent, inexpensive **hotels** (indeed, many of the cheaper ones are brothels).

Chiew Kee 41 Jalan Tuanku Munawir ☎ 06 762 2095. Hidden away on the first floor of a building, this place has cheap, uninspiring partitioned rooms with or without private bathrooms. It's clean enough and a reassuring note above the door states "Prostitution is prohibited here". **RM35**

Royale Bintang Jalan Dato' A.S. Dawood ☎ 06 766 6666, ⓦ royalebintang-seremban.com. This four-star establishment opened as a Hilton, and the room design clearly reflects its chain-hotel past. There's live music in the lounge Mon–Sat, plus a coffee house, restaurant, gym, swimming pool and business centre. Free in-room wi-fi. **RM288**

Seremban Inn 39 Jalan Tuanku Munawir ☎ 06 761 7777. Clean and good-value mid-range hotel with helpful staff and decent rooms. Handily there's a small branch of 7-Eleven on the ground floor. If it's full, ask about the nearby *Angsana Inn*, which is under the same ownership. **RM80**

EATING, DRINKING AND NIGHTLIFE

There's no shortage of **places to eat** in the town centre; Seremban is known for its *pao* (Chinese steamed buns) and crab dishes. **Nightlife** focuses on the Taman AST area west of the centre, particularly in the new **Era Square** development, connected to the Terminal 2 bus station.

THE MINANGKABAU

The **Minangkabau people**, whose cultural heartland is in the mountainous region of western Sumatra (Indonesia), established a community in Malaysia in the early fifteenth century. As they had no written language until the arrival of Islam, knowledge of their origins is somewhat sketchy; their own oral accounts trace their ancestry to Alexander the Great, while the *Sejarah Melayu* (see p.563) talks of a mysterious leader, Nila Pahlawan, who was pronounced king of the Palembang natives by a man who was magically transformed from the spittle of an ox.

In early times the Minangkabau were ruled in Sumatra by their own overlords or rajahs, though political centralization never really rivalled the role of the strongly autonomous *nagari* (Sumatran for village). Each *nagari* consisted of numerous **matrilineal clans** (*suku*), each of which took the name of the mother and lived in the ancestral home. The household was also in control of ancestral property, which was passed down the maternal line. The *sumando* (husband) stayed in his wife's house at night but was a constituent member of his mother's house, where most of his day was spent. Although the house and clan name belonged to the woman, and women dominated the domestic sphere, political and ceremonial power was in the hands of men; it was the *mamak* (mother's brother) who took responsibility for the continued prosperity of the lineage.

When and why the Minangkabau initially emigrated to what is now **Negeri Sembilan** in Malaysia is uncertain. Their subsequent history is closely bound up with that of Melaka and Johor, with the Minangkabau frequently called upon to supplement the armies of ambitious Malay princes and sultans. Evidence of intermarriage with the region's predominant tribal group, the Sakai, suggests some acceptance by the Malays of the matrilineal system. What is certain is that the Minangkabau were a political force to be reckoned with, aided by their reputation for supernatural powers. Today, the Minangkabau are very much integrated with the Malays, and their dialect is almost indistinguishable from standard Bahasa Melayu.

★ **Seremban Beef Noodle** Stall 748, upper floor of Pasar Besar (main market). It's a little out of the way, but the fantastic (and cheap) noodles served here have been a local favourite since just after the World War II; the stall was founded by the father of current owner Mrs Goh. Wed–Mon 7.30am–3pm.

Sin Yit Sing 103 Taman AST, close to Era Square. At this busy place, you can dine inside or out in the street. Specialities include peppery fish-head noodles and crabs served various ways, including Marmite-grilled crab. Daily 5pm–midnight.

Teo Hing Jalan Datok Abdul Rahman. A long-standing local favourite, known for its Teo Chew porridge. Order a portion along with whatever side dishes take your fancy, such as pork chop (pork and fish chopped and mixed into a patty) or the renowned salted vegetables. Daily 10.30am–6.30pm, closed alternate Sats.

SHOPPING

Terminal One This handy shopping mall, connected to the Terminal 1 bus station, has a Parkson department store and Giant Hypermarket in addition to numerous smaller shops. There is also a Golden Screen Cinema. Daily 10am–10pm.

Sri Menanti

The former royal capital of Negeri Sembilan, **SRI MENANTI**, is set in a lush, mountainous landscape 30km east of Seremban. The only reason to visit is to see a jewel of Minangkabau architecture, the **Istana Lama**. As you look for it, don't be misled by the sign for the **Istana Besar**, the current royal palace, which is topped by a startling blue roof.

Istana Lama

Daily 10am–6pm · Free

A timber palace set in geometric gardens, the splendid **Istana Lama** was the seat of the Minangkabau rulers (see box above). The sacking of Sri Menanti during the Sungai

5

Ujong tin wars destroyed the original palace; today's four-storey version was designed and built in 1902 by two Malay master craftsmen, using no nails or screws.

Until 1931, the building was used as a royal residence. Its tower, which once held the treasury and royal archives, offers a lovely view and can be reached by ladder from the sultan's private rooms. At its apex is a forked projection of a type known as "open scissors", now very rarely seen.

The whole rectangular building is raised nearly 2m off the ground by 99 pillars, 26 of which have been carved in low relief with complex foliated designs. Though the main doors and windows are plain, a long external veranda is covered with a design of leaves and branches known as *awan larat*, or "driving clouds". Above the front porch is the most elaborate decoration, a pair of Chinese-style creatures with lions' heads, horses' legs and long feathery tails.

ARRIVAL AND DEPARTURE	SRI MENANTI
By bus From Seremban, take a United bus for the 45-minute journey to Kuala Pilah, then either wait for an infrequent	local bus to Sri Menanti, or take a taxi (10 min; RM14). **By taxi** A cab from Seremban costs RM35.

ACCOMMODATION

Sri Menanti Resort Next to the Istana Lama ☎ 06 497 0577, ✉ serimenantiresort@ymail.com. Rooms in Sri Menanti's only accommodation option are of a reasonable standard, and the options include double rooms and chalets. Prices rise by RM10 at the weekend; ask about discounts. Rooms RM150, chalets RM250

Melaka

When Penang was known only for its oysters and Singapore was just a fishing village, the influence of **MELAKA** (also spelled "Malacca") already extended beyond the Peninsula. Political and cultural life flourished in this trading centre under the auspices of the **Melaka Sultanate**, founded early in the fifteenth century, and helped to define what it means to be Malay.

The city subsequently suffered neglect from colonial rulers and fared little better after independence, but in some respects this added to its faded charm. Recent years, though, have seen such developments as a land reclamation project that created the Taman Melaka Raya district and, in 2008, the gaining of UNESCO World Heritage Site status jointly with Penang. The latter has helped to encourage the development of a new wave of guesthouses and restoration projects, but has also brought some less welcome tourism schemes. Melaka remains, nevertheless, an undoubted highlight of any Malaysian itinerary.

Brief history

Melaka has its roots in the fourteenth-century struggles between Java and the Thai kingdom of Ayuthaya for control of the Malay Peninsula. The *Sejarah Melayu* (Malay Annals) records that when the Sumatran prince Paramesvara could no longer tolerate subservience to Java, he fled to the island of Temasek (later renamed Singapore), where he set himself up as ruler. The Javanese subsequently forced him to flee north to Bertam, where he was welcomed by the local community. While his son, Iskandar Shah, was out hunting near modern-day Melaka Hill, a mouse deer turned on the pursuing hunting dogs, driving them into the sea. Taking this courageous act to be a good omen, Shah asked his father to build a new settlement there and named it after the *melaka* tree under which he had been sitting.

A trading centre

Melaka under its sultans rapidly became a wealthy and cosmopolitan market town, trading spices and textiles with Indonesia and India. This meteoric rise was initially

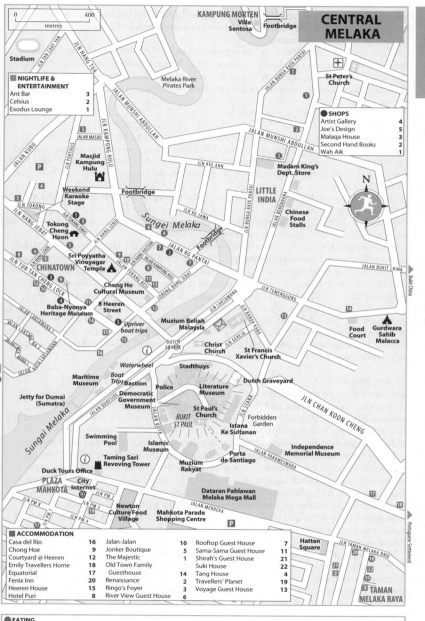

CENTRAL MELAKA

0 — 400 metres

Stadium

KAMPUNG MORTEN
Villa Sentosa
Footbridge

NIGHTLIFE & ENTERTAINMENT
Ant Bar — 3
Celsius — 2
Exodus Lounge — 1

Melaka River Pirates Park

St Peter's Church

SHOPS
Artist Gallery — 4
Joe's Design — 5
Malaqa House — 3
Second Hand Books — 2
Wah Aik — 1

N

Masjid Kampung Hulu

Madam King's Dept. Store

LITTLE INDIA

Weekend Karaoke Stage

Footbridge

Chinese Food Stalls

Tokong Cheng Hoon

Sungei Melaka

Sri Poyyatha Vinoyagar Temple

Cheng Ho Cultural Museum

8 Heeren Street

Baba-Nyonya Heritage Museum

Upriver boat trips

Muzium Beliah Malaysia

Food Court — Gurdwara Sahib Malacca

Christ Church

St Francis Xavier's Church

Maritime Museum

Boat Trips Bastion

Waterwheel

Stadthuys

Police

Democratic Government Museum

Literature Museum

Dutch Graveyard

Jetty for Dumai (Sumatra)

BUKIT ST PAUL

St Paul's Church

Istana Ke Sultanan

Forbidden Garden

Swimming Pool

Islamic Museum

Taming Sari Revolving Tower

Muzium Rakyat

Porta de Santiago

Independence Memorial Museum

Duck Tours Office

PLAZA MAHKOTA

City Internet

Newton Culture/Food Village

Mahkota Parade Shopping Centre

Dataran Pahlawan Melaka Mega Mall

Hatten Square

TAMAN MELAKA RAYA

ACCOMMODATION

Casa del Rio	16	Jalan-Jalan	10	Rooftop Guest House	7
Chong Hoe	9	Jonker Boutique	5	Sama-Sama Guest House	11
Courtyard @ Heeren	12	The Majestic	1	Shirah's Guest House	21
Emily Travellers Home	18	Old Town Family		Suki House	22
Equatorial	17	Guesthouse	14	Tang House	4
Fenix Inn	20	Renaissance	2	Travellers' Planet	19
Heeren House	15	Ringo's Foyer	3	Voyage Guest House	13
Hotel Puri	8	River View Guest House	6		

EATING

Baboon House	10	Capitol Satay	13	Little Mamma	4	Pak Putra	16
Bayonya	18	Ee Ji Ban	19	Merchant Café	14	Restoran Lee	1
Café 1511	9	Hakka Restaurant	17	Mods Café	3	Sin Yin Hoe	7
Capitol Delicious		Harper's	15	Nancy's Kitchen	6	Voyage Travellers' Lounge	12
Seafood	2	Jonker 88	5	Orang Belanda	11	Zheng He Tea House	8

5

assisted by its powerful neighbours Ayuthaya and Java, who made good use of its trading facilities, but they soon found that they had a serious rival as Melaka started a campaign of **territorial expansion**.

By the reign of its last ruler, Sultan Mahmud Shah (1488–1530), Melaka's territory included the west coast of the Peninsula as far as Perak, the whole of Pahang, Singapore and most of east-coast Sumatra. Culturally, too, Melaka was supreme – its sophisticated language, literature, hierarchical court structure and dances were all benchmarks in the Malay world.

The colonial era

It took a sea change in Europe to end Melaka's supremacy. The Portuguese were seeking to extend their influence in Asia by dominating ports in the region and, led by Alfonso de Albuquerque, conquered Melaka in 1511. They maintained their hold for the next 130 years, introducing Catholicism to the region through the efforts of St Francis Xavier.

The formation of the Vereenigde Oostindische Compagnie (VOC), or **Dutch East India Company**, in 1602 spelled the end of Portuguese rule. The primary objective was trade rather than religious conversion, but due to their high taxes the Dutch relied ever more on force to maintain their position in the Straits.

Weakened by French threats to their posts in the Indies, the Dutch handed Melaka over to the **British East India Company** on August 15, 1795. Yet the colony continued a decline that hastened when the free-trade port of Singapore was established in 1819. The British wanted Penang to be the main west-coast settlement but attempted to revitalize Melaka, introducing progressive agricultural and mining concerns. They invested in new hospitals, schools and a train line, but only when a Chinese entrepreneur, Tan Chay Yan, began to plant **rubber** were Melaka's financial problems alleviated for a time. After World War I, even this commodity faced mixed fortunes – when the **Japanese occupied** Melaka in 1942, they found a town exhausted by the interwar depression.

Modern Melaka

Whatever damage was wrought during its centuries of colonial mismanagement, nothing can take away the enduring influence of Melaka's contribution to Malay culture. Taken together with the long-standing Chinese presence – with intermarriage fostering the Peranakan community (see p.280) – and the European colonial influences, Melaka has a fascinating heritage that understandably appeals to tourists.

To the cynical eye, though, there's something about the modern centre of Melaka that smacks of slapdash "preservation", apparent in the brick-red paint wash that covers everything around **Dutch Square**. The UNESCO listing has, in some respects, not exactly helped. As landowners have scented money and rents have skyrocketed, long-established businesses have been forced out and replaced by shops aimed at the tourist dollar. Ill-fated and incongruous tourism projects have included a giant wheel called the Eye on Malaysia, and a monorail north of the centre that memorably broke down on its first day – it turned out that it couldn't operate in the rain.

Worse is yet to come: almost unbelievably, a large *Hard Rock Café* is due to open right in the centre. It's not all bad news, though, with the regeneration of the riverside particularly welcome; it is to be hoped that this kind of project may continue to breathe life into the historical core, rather than turning it into a theme-park version of itself.

The colonial centre

The heart of Melaka's colonial centre is **Dutch Square**, dominated by the **Stadthuys**; beyond that lie **St Paul's Hill** and numerous museums. The square is one of the oldest surviving parts of the city, although two of its main features date from much later

5

times: the marble fountain was built in 1904 to commemorate Queen Victoria's Diamond Jubilee, while the clock tower was erected in 1886 in honour of Tan Beng Swee, a rich Chinese merchant. Rather older are the ruins of the **Bastion of Fredrick Hendrick**, where you can see the alignment of the old Portuguese defensive wall.

Stadthuys
Daily 9am–5.30pm • RM5 • ⓦ perzim.gov.my

The sturdy red **Stadthuys**, presiding over the entire south side of Dutch Square, is not a single building but a collection of structures dating from between 1660 and 1700; one now houses the **Museum of Ethnography**. The complex was used as a town hall throughout the Dutch and British administrations and the wide, monumental interior staircases, together with the high windows, are typical of seventeenth-century Dutch municipal buildings.

It's worth visiting mostly for the buildings themselves: the Museum of Ethnography displays a fairly unengaging array of Malay and Chinese ceramics, weaponry, musical instruments and the like, plus a few dioramas and countless paintings depicting Melakan history. Several other **smaller museums** lurk behind the main buildings, although covering topics such as the Malaysian education system they are aimed mostly at domestic visitors.

Christ Church
Mon–Sat 9am–5pm; services Sun 8.30am (English), 10.30am (Mandarin) & 4.30pm (Malay) • Free

Christ Church was built in 1753 to commemorate the centenary of the Dutch occupation of Melaka. Its simple design, with neither aisles nor chancel, is typically Dutch; the porch and vestry were nineteenth-century afterthoughts. The cool, whitewashed interior has decorative fanlights high up on the walls and elaborate, 200-year-old hand-carved pews, while the roof features heavy timber beams each cut from a single tree. The plaques on the walls tell a sorry tale of early deaths in epidemics.

Dutch Graveyard
East of Christ Church, along Jalan Kota

Although the overgrown **Dutch Graveyard** was first used in the late seventeenth century, when the VOC was still in control (hence the name), British graves easily outnumber those of their predecessors. The tall column towards the centre of the tiny cemetery is a memorial to two of the many officers killed in the Naning War in 1831, a costly attempt to incorporate the nearby Naning region into Melaka's territory.

Istana Kesultanan
Daily 9am–5.30pm • RM2 • ☎ 06 282 7464, ⓦ perzim.gov.my

The **Istana Kesultanan** (Sultan's Palace) has played a central role in Malaysian history, although the current dark-timber palace is a contemporary reconstruction of the original fifteenth-century building. In the best Malay architectural tradition, its multilayered, sharply sloping roofs contain no nails. It was here that the administrative duties of the state were carried out, and also where the sultan resided when in the city (he mostly lived further upriver at Bertam, safe from attacks on Melaka). Remove your shoes to ascend the wide staircase to the ground floor, where you'll find a cultural museum housing dioramas of scenes from Malay court life.

Porta de Santiago
At the time they conquered Melaka, the Portuguese used the forced labour of fifteen hundred slaves to construct the mighty **A Famosa** fort. The Dutch East India Company later used the fort as its headquarters, but the British demolished it at the start of the nineteenth century when they relocated to Penang. All that's left today is a single gate, the crumbling **Porta de Santiago**, which was only saved thanks to last-minute intervention from Sir Stamford Raffles, the founder of Singapore (see p.487).

5

St Paul's Church

Reached by climbing the steps behind the Porta de Santiago • Free

On the summit of St Paul's Hill (**Bukit St Paul**), and now no more than a roofless shell, **St Paul's Church** was constructed in 1521 by the Portuguese as Our Lady of the Mount. The Jesuit missionary **St Francis Xavier** visited the church between 1545 and 1552, and his body was brought here for burial after his death in 1553, before being exhumed and transferred to its final resting place in Goa (India) the following year.

The Dutch Calvinists changed the denomination of the church when they took over in 1641, renaming it St Paul's Church, and it remained in use until the construction of Christ Church at the foot of the hill. The British found St Paul's more useful for military than for religious purposes, storing their gunpowder here during successive wars.

Muzium Rakyat

Jalan Kota • Sat–Thurs 9am–5.30pm, Fri 9am–12.15pm & 2.45–5.30pm • RM2 • ⑩ perzim.gov.my

The most interesting of the various museums that you pass as you skirt west around the base of St Paul's Hill from Porta de Santiago is the **Muzium Rakyat** (People's Museum). Its ground and first floors house exhibits on such topics as the construction and competitive use of spinning tops. The third floor contains the much more interesting – and at times gruesome – **Museum of Enduring Beauty**. Taking "endure" in the sense of "to suffer", the exhibits show how people around the world have sought to alter their appearance: head deformation, dental mutilations, tattooing, scarification, corsetry and foot-binding are just some of the processes on display.

Maritime Museum

Mon–Thurs 9am–5.30pm, Fri–Sun 9am–8.30pm • RM3 • ⑩ perzim.gov.my

The main part of the **Maritime Museum** (Muzeum Samudera) is housed in a towering replica of a Portuguese cargo ship, the *Flor de la Mar*, which sank in 1511 carrying treasure plundered from Melaka. Inside its hull, model ships, information boards and paintings chart the settlement's maritime history from the time of the Malay Sultanate to the arrival of the British in the eighteenth century.

It feels a little disjointed, rather than telling a single story, but there are some interesting facts in there. The same cannot be said of the drab displays across the road in the other section of the museum; the Royal Malaysian Navy patrol craft in the gardens is, however, popular with kids.

Sungai Melaka boat trips

From the jetty just southwest of Dutch Square • Daily 9am–11pm; Fri no trips 12.30–2.30pm • Return (45min) RM10, RM5 children; hop-on, hop-off RM25, RM10 children

If you feel like a rest from pavement pounding, take a **boat trip** up Sungai Melaka. A good way to see the restored riverside area, the boat takes you past the old Dutch quarter of red-roofed godowns, as far as Kampung Morten (see p.281). You can buy either a return ticket, or a hop-on, hop-off ticket which is valid all day and stops at seven points along the river.

Chinatown

Melaka owed a great deal of its nineteenth-century economic recovery to its Chinese community: it was one Tan Chay Yan who first planted rubber here, and a Chinese immigrant called Tan Kim Seng established what became the great Straits Steam Ship Company. Most of these entrepreneurs settled in what became known as **Chinatown**, across Sungai Melaka from the colonial district. For many visitors, it's the most interesting part of town.

Jalan Hang Jebat

Night market Fri–Sun 7pm–midnight

Jalan Hang Jebat – previously named Jonker Street – runs parallel to Jalan Tun Tan Cheng Lock and is Chinatown's main street. It was formerly known for its antiques, but these days most shops sell souvenirs and cheap handicrafts. Still, its bars and restaurants continue to make it a centre of tourist activity.

The street is closed to traffic on weekend evenings, for the **Jonker Walk Night Market** when the shops stay open late and the street is lined with vendors. Although very popular and often considered a must-do by visitors to the city, it's nothing special by Malaysian street market standards – in particular, anyone looking for good street food is likely to come away disappointed.

Cheng Ho Cultural Museum

51 Lorong Hang Jebat • Daily 9am–6pm • RM20 • ☎ 06 283 1135, ⓦ chengho.org/museum

Dedicated to the life of Chinese Admiral **Cheng Ho** (also spelled Zheng He), who visited Melaka several times on his epic travels across Asia, the Middle East and Africa, the **Cheng Ho Cultural Museum** provides an insight into early fifteenth-century Melaka, as well as trading and seafaring during the Ming Dynasty. Exhibits include a model of Cheng Ho's treasure ship and various navigational instruments; there's also a tea house on the premises.

Jalan Tun Tan Cheng Lock

The elegant townhouses that line **Jalan Tun Tan Cheng Lock**, formerly Heeren Street, are the ancestral homes of the Baba-Nonya community (see p.280). The wealthiest and most successful of these merchants built long, narrow-fronted houses, minimizing the "window tax" by incorporating internal courtyards designed for ventilation and the collection of rainwater.

Several of the houses are now open to the public as shops, hotels and restaurants. You can't enter the **Chee Ancestral House** at no. 117, but it's worth checking out the exterior: an imperious Dutch building of pale green stucco topped by a gold dome, it's home to one of Melaka's wealthiest families.

8 Heeren Street

8 Jalan Tun Tan Cheng Lock • Daily 11am–4pm • Free (donations welcome)

Make time for a visit to the model conservation project at **8 Heeren Street**, where you can see how the building (dating from the 1790s) has been used and modified over the years. Printed information gives background on topics such as building materials and techniques, while the knowledgeable staff are happy to answer questions. Some commercial restoration projects in Melaka introduce inauthentic elements in the name of "heritage", but here the history of the building is laid bare.

Baba-Nonya Heritage Museum

48–50 Jalan Tan Tun Cheng Lock • Daily 10am–12.30pm & 2–4.30pm • RM10 • ☎ 06 283 1273

An amalgam of three adjacent houses belonging to a single family, the **Baba-Nonya Heritage Museum** is an excellent example of the Chinese Palladian style (which blends Chinese and European influences). Connected by a common covered footway, decorated with hand-painted tiles, each front entrance has an outer swing door of elaborately carved teak, while a heavier internal door provides extra security at night. Two red lanterns, one bearing the household name, the other messages of good luck, hang either side of the doorway, framed by heavy Greco-Roman columns.

The upper level of the building is the most eye-catching: a canopy of Chinese tiles over the porch frames the shuttered windows, almost Venetian in character with their glass protected by intricate wrought-iron grilles. The eaves and fascias are covered in painted floral designs. Inside, the homes are filled with gold-leaf fittings,

5

THE BABA-NONYAS

Tales of Melaka's burgeoning success brought vast numbers of merchants and entrepreneurs to its shores, eager to benefit from the city's status and wealth. The Chinese, in particular, came to the Malay Peninsula in large numbers to escape Manchu rule. Many married Malay women, and descendants of these marriages were known as **Peranakan** or "Straits-born Chinese".

The expatriate Chinese merchants, and their descendants, became the principal wealth-generators of the thriving city. The **Babas** (male Sino-Malays) were not ashamed to flaunt their new-found prosperity, filling the lavish townhouses that they appropriated from the Dutch with Italian marble, mother-of-pearl inlay blackwood furniture, hand-painted tiles and Victorian lamps. The women, known as **Nonyas** (sometimes spelt Nyonyas), held sway in the domestic realm and were responsible for Peranakan society's most lasting legacy – its **cuisine**. Drawing on the best of Malay and Chinese styles, and traditionally eaten with hands instead of chopsticks, its dishes rely on sour sauces and coconut milk (see p.40).

blackwood furniture inlaid with mother-of-pearl, delicately carved lacquer screens and Victorian chandeliers. The guided tours, included in the entry price, add a great deal to the experience.

Jalan Tukang Emas

Jalan Tukang Emas, continuing on from Jalan Tokong, is sometimes known as "Harmony Street" in reference to its buildings from different religions. A short way east from Jalan Hang Jebat, **Cheng Hoon Teng temple** – dedicated to the goddess of mercy – is reputed to be the oldest Chinese temple in the country. A little further along, the 1748 **Masjid Kampung Kling** displays an unusual blend of styles: the minaret looks like a pagoda, there are English and Portuguese glazed tiles, and a Victorian chandelier hangs over a pulpit carved with Hindu and Chinese designs. Next door, the Hindu **Sri Poyyatha Vinayagar Temple** also has a minaret, decorated with red cows, and dates back to the 1780s.

Masjid Kampung Hulu

Jalan Kampung Hulu, north of Sri Poyyatha Vinayagar Temple • Daily 8am–6pm

Thought to be the oldest mosque in Malaysia that remains in its original location, **Masjid Kampung Hulu** was constructed around 1728 in typical Melakan style. It's a solid-looking structure, surmounted by a bell-shaped roof with red Chinese tiles and has more than a hint of pagoda in its minaret. Such architecture has its origins in Sumatra, perhaps brought over by the Minangkabau (see p.273) who settled in nearby Negeri Sembilan.

Taming Sari Revolving Tower

Jalan Merdaka • Daily 10am–11pm • RM20

You can't miss the eighty-metre-tall **Taming Sari Revolving Tower**, which offers a great (if relatively expensive) 360 degree view of the city and the sea. Its construction so close to the colonial district in 2008 was controversial, but it has nevertheless proved to be a popular attraction with big queues at the weekend. There's also a small Tourism Malaysia office, and Duck Tour tickets are sold here (see p.283).

Riverside walk

Melaka River Pirates Park: Daily 5pm–midnight • Entry free, RM5 per ride ticket

The redevelopment of Melaka's riverside has been a recent success story, encouraging the opening of guesthouses and cafés where once there were dilapidated buildings. It's possible – and pleasant – to walk from around Dutch Square to Kampung Morten (see opposite), and almost the whole stretch is illuminated at night. On the eastern side, the path goes through an area of mangrove after the Hang Tuah

5

monorail station; on the western you'll find the **Melaka River Pirates Park**. Not exactly in keeping with Melaka's heritage feel, this entertainment park – which includes a ferris wheel and a zip line – should keep children occupied for an hour or two, but closes on rainy days.

Outside the centre

Several worthwhile attractions are located just outside the centre: **St Peter's Church**, **Kampung Morten** and **Bukit China** lie within walking distance, while it's better to take a taxi or bus to the **Portuguese Settlement**.

Northeast of the centre

From Christ Church, Jalan Laksamana leads north past **St Francis Xavier's Church**, a twin-towered, nineteenth-century, neo-Gothic structure. Further up from here on Jalan Bendahara you pass through the centre of Melaka's tumbledown **Little India**, a rather desultory line of incense and saree shops interspersed with a few eating houses.

St Peter's Church

Just north of the crossroads between Jalan Bendadara and Jalan Munshi Abdullah · Free

The oldest Roman Catholic church in Malaysia, **St Peter's Church** was built by a Dutch convert in 1710 as a gift to the Portuguese Catholics, and has an unusual barrel-vaulted ceiling. The church really comes into its own at Easter as the centre of the Catholic community's celebrations.

Kampung Morten

The village of **Kampung Morten**, named after the British district officer who donated RM10,000 to buy the land, is a surprising find so close to the heart of Melaka. The wooden stilt houses here are distinctively Melakan, with their long, rectangular living rooms and kitchens, and narrow verandas approached by ornamental steps. It's easiest to explore this community on foot, and the riverside walk to get here is part of the experience. One home in the village is part of the national homestay scheme (see "Accommodation").

Villa Sentosa

Daily 9.30am–6pm · Donation expected · ☎ 06 282 3988

The **Villa Sentosa**, with its miniature kampung house and mini-lighthouse, is a seventy-year-old family home that now functions as a museum. The owner will gladly show you their artefacts and heirlooms.

Bukit China

East of the colonial heart of Melaka, **Bukit China** is the ancestral burial ground of the town's Chinese community – it's said to be the oldest and largest such graveyard outside China. Although Chinese contacts with the Malay Peninsula probably began in the first century BC, formal commercial relations were only established when the Ming Emperor Yung-Lo sent his envoy Admiral Cheng Ho here in 1409. Today, Bukit China is more an inner-city park than burial ground, where you're likely to encounter locals jogging, practising martial arts or simply admiring the view.

Sam Poh Kong Temple

At the foot of Bukit China, at the eastern end of Jalan Temenggong

The **Sam Poh Kong** temple is a working temple dedicated to Admiral Cheng Ho. Accounts are vague when it comes to the arrival of the first Chinese settlers, though it's said that on the marriage of Sultan Mansur Shah (1458–77) to the daughter of the emperor, Princess Hang Liu, the five hundred nobles who accompanied her stayed to

5

set up home on Bukit China. It was supposedly these early Chinese settlers who dug the **Sultan's Well** behind the temple.

The Portuguese Settlement
Bus #17 from Dutch Square or Jalan Merdeka; taxi RM20

The road east of Jalan Taman Melaka Raya leads, after about 3km, to Melaka's **Portuguese Settlement**; turn right into Jalan Albuquerque, clearly signposted off the main road, and you enter its heart. Today you're likely to recognize the descendants of the original Portuguese settlers only by hearing their language, **Kristao**, a blend of Malay and old Portuguese, or by seeing their surnames – Fernandez, Rodriguez and Dominguez all feature as street names.

Medan Portugis

You could almost be forgiven for thinking that the whitewashed **Medan Portugis** (Portuguese Square), at the end of the road into the Portuguese settlement, is a remnant from colonial times. In fact it dates only from 1985, but the restaurateurs in the square make an effort to conjure up a Portuguese atmosphere even if the food is Malay in character. A three-day **fiesta** – the feast of St Pedro – commences in the square on June 29 every year, with traditional Portuguese food, live music and dancing. Just beyond the square is a row of waterfront seafood restaurants.

ARRIVAL AND DEPARTURE   MELAKA

By plane Melaka's airport was upgraded in 2009, and now has a handful of services to Indonesia. Firefly (⊙ fireflyz .com.my) operates daily flights to Subang and Medan, while Sky Aviation (⊙ skyaviation.co.id) flies daily to Pekan Baru. Transnasional operates buses from Melaka to KLIA and the LCCT (4 daily; 2hr 45min), useful if you're flying to or from KL and don't want to go into the city. They arrive and depart from the Mahkota Medical Centre, close to the Mahkota Parade Shopping Centre, also passing through Melaka Sentral.

By train Tampin train station, 38km north of Melaka (⊙ 06 441 1034), is connected by regular buses with Melaka Sentral (40min); a taxi costs RM60. Note that it's quicker to take a bus to Singapore than the train.

Destinations Butterworth via Ipoh (daily); Kuala Lumpur (3 daily; 2hr); Singapore via Johor Bahru (3 daily; 4hr 45min) and Tumpat via Tanah Merah and Wakaf Bharu (daily; 11hr).

By bus Melaka's only bus station, Melaka Sentral, is 3km north of the centre, at the corner of Jalan Panglima Awang

and Jalan Tun Razak, close to a large Tesco supermarket. The #17 bus from the domestic part of the station takes you into town in 10–15 minutes; a taxi will cost RM20.

Destinations Alor Star (4 daily; 7hr); Butterworth (5 daily; 6hr); Ipoh (3 daily; 4hr); Johor Bahru (frequent 8am–8pm; 3hr); Kluang (11 daily; 2hr); Kota Bharu (2 daily; 10hr); KLIA/LCCT (4 daily; 2hr 45min); Kuala Lumpur (very frequent 5am–8pm; 2hr; RM12.20); Kuala Terengganu (daily; 8hr); Kuantan (daily; 5hr); Mersing (3 daily; 4hr); Singapore (frequent 8am–8pm; 4hr).

By ferry From the jetty on Jalan Quayside, ferries head to Dumai in Sumatra (daily; 2hr 30min; RM119 one-way). For information and tickets, best bought a day in advance, contact Tunas Rupat Follow Me Express at G29, Jalan PM10 (⊙ 06 283 2506).

By car Melaka's streets are very narrow and the one-way system is awkward, so drivers should park their cars at the first opportunity and get around the city by foot, bus, trishaw or taxi.

GETTING AROUND

By bus The town bus service has several useful routes for visitors, departing from Melaka Sentral: #17 runs through the historical centre to Taman Melaka Raya and the Portuguese Settlement (RM1); the SKA Muar-bound bus goes to Anjung Batu for Pulau Besar (RM1.20); #19 goes out to Ayer Keroh (RM1.20).

By monorail A monorail service opened to much fanfare in October 2010 but soon closed due to technical problems; having reopened at the end of 2011, it was once again quickly suspended. Even if it is eventually fixed, and a planned extension is completed, its route (to

the north of the centre) isn't particularly helpful for tourists.

By taxi or trishaw For longer journeys, taxis (⊙ 06 288 1325) or the colourful disco trishaws are the best bet. Both cost roughly the same; a sightseeing tour by trishaw, covering the major sights, should cost RM40 per hour for two people. You should be able to get a trishaw around the Dutch Square or in front of the Taming Sari Revolving Tower; there's a taxi rank by the Mahkota Parade. Note that an annoying commission system operates between Melaka's taxi drivers and some guesthouses; if you know where you want to go, don't necessarily believe a driver who tells you that the place is full.

Car rental Hawk 34 Jalan Laksamana ☎ 06 283 7878,

ⓦ hawkrentacar.com.my. Mon–Fri 8am–5pm, Sat 8am–1pm.

On foot Most places of interest lie within the compact historical centre, and so are best visited on foot.

INFORMATION AND TOURS

State tourist office Jalan Kota, just by the bridge from the colonial centre to Chinatown (daily 9am–6pm; ☎ 06 281 4803).

Tourism Malaysia A small office in the building at the base of the Taming Sari Revolving Tower (daily 10am–10pm; ☎ 06 283 6220).

Internet access There are plenty of places to get online, including the *Discovery Café*, 3 Jalan Bunga Raya;

the *Fenix Inn*, 156 Jalan Merdaka (daily 10am–11pm); and City Internet, Jalan PM 2, Plaza Mahkota (daily 11am–midnight).

Tours The Duck Tour uses an amphibious vehicle to explore Melaka on both land and water. The main ticket office is a booth at the Taming Sari Revolving Tower (daily 9am–6pm; 45min–1hr; adult RM38, child RM22; ☎ 06 292 2595, ⓦ melakaducktours.com).

ACCOMMODATION

Melaka has a huge selection of **hotels** and guesthouses, including many that are good value and well kept; book ahead for Friday and Saturday nights, as Melaka is a popular weekend break destination. The local government runs a **homestay** scheme, but the website (ⓦ homestaymelaka.gov.my) is in Malay; the sporadically updated blog is, however, in English, as is the national homestay website ⓦ go2homestay.com.

Casa del Rio 88 Jalan Kota Laksamana ☎ 06 292 1113, ⓦ casadelrio-melaka.com. A new opening in 2011, this resort-style complex is undeniably luxurious – the rooms are delightful and there's a lovely rooftop infinity pool as well as a spa – but looks as though it belongs somewhere on the Mediterranean, not in central Melaka. RM505

Chong Hoe 26 Jalan Tukang Emas ☎ 06 282 6102, ⓦ chonghoehotel.com. Not to be confused with the nearby *Cheng Ho* guesthouse, this is a well-looked-after, family-run hotel in Chinatown offering good-value rooms with a/c and shared or private showers. The location – within earshot of the temple and mosque – can be noisy at times. Free wi-fi. Rooms RM38 , en-suite rooms RM55

★ **Courtyard @ Heeren** 91 Jalan Tun Tan Cheng Lock ☎ 06 281 0088, ⓦ courtyardatheeren.com. The lobby sets the tone, with old wooden furniture, a water feature and uniformed staff. The rooms don't disappoint, with four heritage rooms offering a delightful mix of old and new: replica period tiles but also flat-screen TVs. The semi-open-air showers are a great touch too. Regular rooms are more straightforwardly modern but still comfortable. Breakfast included. RM232

★ **Emily Travellers Home** 71 Jalan Parameswara ☎ 012 301 8574 (no reservations). This peaceful and friendly backpacker gem has two chalets (with their own bathrooms) and several rooms in the heritage house with shared bathrooms; there are a few dorm beds too. The common area is a great place to hang out, with entry past a fish pond into a small garden. A cosy evening fire is lit to keep the mosquitoes away and there's even a pet rabbit. Dorms RM16, rooms RM35, chalets RM48

Equatorial Jalan Bandar Hilir ☎ 06 282 8333, ⓦ equatorial.com/mel. With 493 brightly decorated

rooms boasting huge beds, and a total of six restaurants plus poolside dining 7am–7pm, this is one of Melaka's grandest hotels. Cabled internet costs RM25/day. RM452

Heeren House 1 Jalan Tun Tan Cheng Lock ☎ 06 281 4241, ⓦ heerenhouse.com. An ideal location and tasteful rooms make this a very good choice. Rates, which include breakfast, rise by RM20 at weekends – you also pay a little more for a river view. The small café also serves lunch daily and dinner Fri–Sun, and is a great place for people-watching. Book ahead. RM129

Hotel Puri 118 Jalan Tun Tan Cheng Lock ☎ 06 282 5588, ⓦ hotelpuri.com. Set in a beautifully restored Peranakan shophouse, this place makes much of its historical appeal and even has a mini-museum. Rooms are, however, decorated in a contemporary style. Breakfast is included in the rates, while its *Galeri Café* is a good spot for dinner and there's an appealing courtyard for drinks and snacks. RM162

Jalan-Jalan 8 Jalan Tukang Emas ☎ 06 283 3937, ⓦ jalanjalanguesthouse.com. This excellent budget choice is so popular that it now occupies two non-connected buildings. The main building has the reception and the more lively common area, while the other has a/c. Free wi-fi, coffee and tea. Dorms RM14, a/c dorms RM18, fan rooms RM36, a/c rooms RM65

★ **Jonker Boutique** 82–86 Jalan Tokong ☎ 06 282 5151, ⓦ jonkerboutiquehotel.com. The three shop-houses that form this hotel are eighty years old, but the rooms are bang up to date in terms of both decor and facilities. The central location and friendly staff also contribute to making this place a winner. Free wi-fi, but room rates rise by RM40 at the weekend. RM198

★ **The Majestic** 188 Jalan Bunga Raya ☎ 06 289 8000, ⓦ www.majesticmalacca.com. Just arriving at this

5

hotel is a treat, as the lobby is housed in an impeccably restored 1920s mansion house. The bedrooms themselves are in a modern block but are delightful nevertheless, with the roll-top baths a particularly good touch. There's also an excellent spa. RM440

★ **Old Town Family Guesthouse** 119 Jalan Temenggong ☎ 06 286 0796, ⓦ melakaguesthouse.com. A friendly, family-run place with dorms and private rooms, as well as a communal kitchen and small library including some graphic novels. There are also tons of toys around, since the owners and their children live on the premises. Breakfast and wi-fi included, plus they have computers for use. Dorms RM12, fan rooms RM30, a/c rooms RM45

Renaissance Jalan Bendahara ☎ 06 284 8888, ⓦ renaissancehotels.com. Part of the Marriott group, this is one of the city's foremost high-end hotels with an imposing lobby – complete with huge chandeliers – and elegant, well-furnished rooms. RM313

Ringo's Foyer 46a Jalan Portugis ☎ 06 281 6393, ⓔ ringosfoyer@gmail.com. One of the barest-bones places in town, but also one of the friendliest. The bedrooms (which include singles at RM25) certainly aren't anything special and the shared bathrooms are shabby too, but there's a rooftop hangout with a barbecue on Saturdays, and more importantly owner Howard goes out of his way to welcome guests – he even runs food-focused trips on foot or by bike in the evenings. Dorms RM14, rooms RM35

River View Guest House 94–95 Jalan Kampung Pantai ☎ 012 327 7746 or ☎ 012 380 7211, ⓔ riverview guesthouse@yahoo.com. A 200-year-old building with seven private rooms and a three-bed mixed-sex dorm, this place has plenty of character. It overlooks the river and, in the evening, it's possible to sit out back. If the owners aren't around, try the *Rooftop Guest House*. Dorms RM20, fan rooms RM45, a/c rooms RM55

★ **Rooftop Guest House** 39 Jalan Kampung Pantai ☎ 012 327 7746 or ☎ 012 380 7211, ⓔ rooftop guesthouse@yahoo.com. The second place opened by the owners of the *River View*, this well-run guesthouse has small dorms and twin rooms; all have a/c and shared bathrooms. Book ahead for weekends (when prices rise by 20 percent). True to the name, there's a small rooftop area with chairs and a table. Dorms RM23, rooms RM45

Sama-Sama Guest House 26 Jalan Tukang Besi ☎ 06 281 5216, ⓦ voyagetogether.com. This excellent travellers' choice in a great location has rooms (including

singles for RM25) around an atmospheric skylight. The shared bathrooms have cold showers only, but there is a good communal area downstairs with wi-fi. They run daily events along with sister hostel, *Voyage*. Dorms RM12, rooms RM40

Tang House 80-1 Jalan Tokong ☎ 06 283 3969, ⓦ tanghouse.com.my. A family-run guesthouse with a small coffee shop and eight a/c rooms (including singles for RM35) with mattresses on the floor. It's no-frills but the Tang family win rave reviews and it's a great price for the location (although the Jonker St karaoke stage is noisy on weekend evenings). Free wi-fi and internet terminals, plus a small kitchen. RM55

Voyage Guest House Jalan Tukang Besi ☎ 06 281 5216, ⓦ voyagetogether.com. With the same management as *Sama Sama*, this place has a huge 14-bed dorm and a few fan rooms. It also has a common area, plus an open rooftop. The staff of the two hostels run daily events and outings. Dorms RM12, rooms RM40

TAMAN MELAKA RAYA PLAZA MAHKOTA

Fenix Inn 156 Jalan Merdaka, Taman Melaka Raya ☎ 06 281 5511, ⓦ fenixinn.com. Well-appointed rooms and friendly service. The *Fenix Inn* was already one of the most upmarket choices in Taman Melaka Raya, even before the ambitious renovations scheduled for 2012. RM115

Shirah's Guest House Second floor, 207b Jalan Melaka Raya 1 ☎ 014 644 6231. With only six rooms and a small roof terrace, this place is well looked after and has brightly coloured murals on the walls. Two a/c rooms share a lovely balcony and all have shared showers. One room (RM65) sleeps five people. Dorms RM15, rooms RM28

Suki House 271 Jalan Melaka Raya 3, Taman Melaka Raya ☎ 010 508 8995. A great choice if you're looking for a simple, cheap and friendly guesthouse. You can pay a little more for a balcony, while solo travellers can get a single room for RM30. There's free wi-fi, and bikes for rent at RM10/day. RM40

Travellers' Planet 1–19 Jalan PM 3, Plaza Mahkota ☎ 06 286 1699. Aimed at backpackers, with a big, bright common area where you can watch movies or read a book from the small library. Twelve simple rooms (including singles for RM20) with either fans or a/c; a light breakfast is included. Young owner Zharif is friendly and helpful. RM30

EATING

Melaka offers excellent dining, especially in **Chinatown**, where new and established restaurants, bars and cafés compete for the hungry tourists and locals. **Taman Melaka Raya** is fast catching up; it's also worth trying the area aound **Jalan Kota Laksamana** southwest of Chinatown. For seafood, you could try the row of near-identical restaurants on the waterfront just beyond the Medan Portugis in the **Portuguese Settlement**, where you can choose from the day's catch from around 7pm. Don't miss the chance to sample **Nonya cuisine** at some stage during your stay; the emphasis is on spicy dishes, using sour ingredients like tamarind, tempered by sweeter, creamy coconut milk. One particularly unusual ingredient is *buah keluak*, a nut which contains hydrogen cyanide (prussic acid) but which is harmless once cooked.

★ **Baboon House** 89 Jalan Tun Tan Cheng Lock. Arts and crafts shop with a lovely courtyard café inside, where a young and friendly crew serve cheap local food, soft drinks and beers. Make sure you check out the gardens at the back, but the whole place has a laidback, arty atmosphere. Mon–Thurs 10am–5pm, Fri–Sun 10am–7pm.

Café 1511 52 Jalan Tun Tan Cheng Lock. Reasonably priced snacks and mains given the location next to the Baba-Nonya Heritage Museum, with breakfasts as well as curries, Western dishes and Nonya delicacies. Try the *pai tee*, little top hats of rice flour filled with turnip, omelette and shallots and dipped in chilli sauce. Daily 9am–7.30pm.

Capitol Delicious Seafood Just off Jalan Bunga Raya. This stall has been attracting customers for more than 50 years – they're hooked on the house sauce, which includes shrimp paste, crushed peanuts, lime juice, chilli paste, sesame seeds and plum sauce. Don't go if you have qualms about dining on cockles and mussels in a grubby alleyway. Daily except Tues 6–11pm.

★ **Capitol Satay** Lorong Bukit China. Experience the Melaka version of hotpot – *satay celup* – at this lively café, where you take your pick of assorted fish, meat and vegetables skewered on sticks and cook them in a spicy peanut sauce before eating. It's cheap – RM0.80 per stick – and delicious so there are often queues; a sign out front warns customers to beware of similarly named imitators. Tues–Sun 5pm–midnight.

Harper's 2 Lorong Jang Jebat, ☎ 06 286 6592. Upmarket and with a riverside location to die for, this place does fusion cuisine, predominately Western and with a wine list to match. Most dishes – such as sea bass with pepper chutney and tomato salsa – are available in either tapas or main course size. Mon & Wed–Sat 4pm–1am, Sun 11am–1am.

Jonker 88 88 Jalan Hang Jebat. On weekend lunchtimes it can seem like half the people on Jonker Street have piled into this small restaurant, drawn in by what are often described as the best *laksa* and *cendol* in town. Expect to queue. Mon–Thurs 10.30am–5.30pm, Fri–Sat 10.30am–8pm, Sun 10.30am–6pm.

Little Mamma Jalan Kampung Pantai. A friendly little juice bar opposite *Rooftop Guest House*, where they stock whatever fruit is in season (RM5/glass). They also serve breakfast plus a few Malay and fusion dishes (the latter including curry chicken rice). Daily 9am–11pm.

Merchant Café 21 Jalan Tun Tan Cheng Lock. Next to the *Heeren Inn* and combining a bar, restaurant and deli: pick from the range of imported meats in the deli and have them cooked up, or choose one of the daily specials. Wash your selection down with imported wine or beer; there's also a beer garden where you can smoke shisha. Daily 8am–midnight.

Mods Café 14 Jalan Tokong. The young owner here loves British mod style and culture, so the decor takes its inspiration from 1960s Britain; coffees are served from a VW camper van. It's a cool place to hang out over a coffee and cake. Daily except Wed 10am–6pm.

Nancy's Kitchen 7 Jalan Hang Lekir, ☎ 06 283 6099. One of the best places to try Nonya food, such as the signature dish *candlenut chicken* (RM10 for a small portion). They also have *buah keluak* (see above). Try to sit downstairs if you can, as it has more character than the a/c rooms upstairs. Mon–Fri 11am–5.30pm, Sat & Sun 11am–9pm.

Orang Belanda 32 Jalan Tun Tan Cheng Lock ⊕ orang -belanda.com. Named after the proboscis monkey (or Dutchman as it's known by locals), this "art café" has black and white photos on the walls and serves – among other things – Dutch coffee and pancakes. Daily 9.30am–9pm.

★ **Pak Putra** 56 Jalan Kota Laksamana. Staggeringly good tandoori chicken is the main draw here and is best enjoyed with garlic or double cheese naan, although there are other Indian options such as fish fritters. Its popularity is such that it gets very busy around 7–9pm on weekend evenings. You can eat inside or in the street. Daily 6pm–1am, closed every other Mon.

Restoran Lee 155 Jalan Bendahara. It's hardly upmarket, and even verges on the grimy, but this Chinese coffee shop is renowned for its crab dishes. Check the large photos on the wall to see the different ways in which the crustaceans can be prepared – the chilli crab is a good choice. Daily 4–11pm.

Sin Yin Hoe 135 Lorong Hang Jebat. This simple Chinese place is renowned for two things. The first is the pork rib deluxe in golden yam ring (RM12), where the yam is fried and comes out like a doughnut. The second is the oyster omelette, which only appears on the Chinese-language menu (it's #67). While you're here, try the deep-fried soft-shell crab. Daily 8am–12.15am.

Voyage Travellers' Lounge 40 Lorong Hang Jebat. With the same owners as *Sama Sama* and *Voyage* guesthouses, this Bohemian-styled hangout serves tea, coffee, snacks and all-day breakfast. Check the menu for the "anatomy of backpackers in Malaysia" diagram, which includes a dig at guidebooks that encourage you to "do exactly the same as everyone else, 100 percent risk free". Daily 8am–11pm.

★ **Zheng He Tea House** 3 Jalan Kuli ☎ 016 764 0588. Formerly part of the Cheng Ho museum but now in a separate location, this is the place to come to experience a traditional Chinese tea ritual. Ms Pak, the friendly manager, is also a great source of information about Melaka. Daily 11am–8pm.

5

TAMAN MELAKA RAYA PLAZA MAHKOTA

Bayonya 164 Taman Melaka Raya ⓦbayonya
.blogspot.com. A popular Nonya restaurant, serving up
dishes like *ayam pong teh*: chicken stewed in preserved
soya bean gravy with potatoes and mushrooms (RM8.90
for a small portion). Daily except Tues 11am–10pm.

Ee Ji Ban 275 Jalan Melaka Raya. As the blown-up
newspaper cuttings testify, this simple eatery produces
some of the best chicken rice balls in town – they say that's
because they still hand-roll them. Costing RM3.80 for five

or RM6 for ten, they can be served with roasted or steamed
chicken (the former being particularly good). Daily except
Thurs 9am–8pm.

Hakka Restaurant G42 Jalan PM 6, Plaza Mahkota
☎012 331 3611. A chance to try Hakka cuisine –
developed by Chinese settlers in India – with dishes such as
pork or steamed fish served with *mui choy* (preserved
mustard cabbage). Daily 11.30am–3pm & 6–11pm,
closed every other Mon.

DRINKING AND NIGHTLIFE

Melaka's **nightlife** is no great shakes; most places tend to shut at around 1am. Cafés and bars spill into Jalan Hang Lekir,
the liveliest street in **Chinatown**; more places are also opening up along the revitalized riverfront, and **Taman Melaka
Raya** also holds some lively places for a drink, along with numerous seedy karaoke bars.

Ant Bar Jalan Melaka Raya 3. One of the biggest bars in
town, decorated all in black and with a balcony area as well
as the main a/c space. Live music at 9.30pm. Mon–Sat
11am–2am, happy hour 5–9pm.

Celsius 212–213 Jalan Melaka Raya 1 ☎06 281 0333.
Sit on stools around glass-topped barrels at the front, or
join the karaoke inside this popular bar; they also serve

Western-style snack food. Daily 11am–2am.

Exodus Lounge Jalan Hang Lekir. It's debatable whether
Melaka really needed a reggae bar, but this place has
blazed the trail as the first in town. As the evening
progresses, though, the music generally turns to more
commercial R&B fare. Usually 4pm–2am.

SHOPPING

Melaka's Chinatown was once famed for its **antiques**, but these days you'll find few bargains. If the item you're thinking
of buying is a genuine antique rather than a modern reproduction, check that it can be exported legally and fill in an official
clearance form; the dealer should provide you with this. For general shopping there are plenty of shops along Jalan Bunga
Raya and Jalan Munshi Abdullah, while the **malls** – including Dataran Pahlawan, Mahkota Parade and Hatten Square –
are concentrated in the south of the centre.

Artist Gallery 49 Jalan Tun Tan Cheng Lock ☎06 281
2112, ⓦthamsiewinn.com. This family-run gallery offers
a few different types of arts and crafts, including limited-
edition prints, hand-crafted Chinese "chops" (seals for
documents), watercolours and pencil sketches. Daily
10am–6pm, sometimes closed Wed.

Joe's Design 6 Jalan Tun Tan Cheng Lock ☎06 281
2960, ⓦjoedesignjewellery.blogspot.com. Handmade
artisan jewellery with one-of-a-kind designs, more
interesting than most of Melaka's mass-produced
handicrafts. Mon 10am–6pm, Tues–Thurs 10am–10pm,
Fri & Sat 10am–11pm, Sun 2–11pm.

Malaqa House 70 Jalan Tun Tan Cheng Lock. Describes
itself as a museum, but really it's a shop where much of
what is on sale – mostly furniture – happens to be

exquisite. Well worth a wander around even if you aren't
planning to buy. Daily 10am–6pm.

Second Hand Books Jalan Kampung Pantai ☎017 616
5884. Although there are chain bookshops in the malls,
this place is worth a look if you're after a bargain. Sells
books mostly in English, German or French, including a few
guidebooks, for around RM20; older books go for RM3–8.
They also buy books and rent out bikes (RM10/24 hr). Daily
10am–7pm.

Wah Aik 56 Jalan Toking. Moved to a new location,
this store has long been renowned for making silk shoes
for bound feet. With foot binding no longer practised,
the shoes are now lined up in the window as
slightly macabre souvenirs at RM75/pair. Daily
9am–5.30pm.

DIRECTORY

Banks and exchange In addition to ATMs in the
shopping malls, branches include Maybank at 225–227
Jalan Taman Melaka Raya, and Public Bank at 60–68 Jalan
Laksamana and also 566–568 Jalan Taman Melaka Raya.
There is a handy ATM at the Taming Sari Revolving Tower,
although it takes only Mastercard.

Cinema The Lotus Five Star in Mahkota Parade shows
English-language films, as does the Golden Screen
Cinema on the top floor of Dataran Pahlawan Melaka
Megamall.

Hospital The Hospital Besar Melaka (General Hospital) is
in the north of town on Jalan Mufti Haji Khalil (☎06 282

2344). The Putra Hospital is nearer the centre at 169 Jalan Bendahara (☎ 06 283 5888), while the well-equipped Mahkota Medical Centre is at 3 Mahkota Melaka, Jalan Merdeka (☎ 06 281 3333).

Police The police station (☎ 06 282 2222) is on Jalan Kota.

Post office The GPO (☎ 06 282 0725) is inconveniently situated on the way to Ayer Keroh on Jalan Bukit Baru – take town bus #19 from Melaka Sentral. There is also a smaller branch (☎ 06 284 8440) on Jalan Laksamana. Both are open Mon–Sat 8.30am–5pm.

Spas Several small spas cater to tourists; for traditional Malay massage try the Keyside Sanctuary, close to the ticket counter for boat trips (see p.282).

Sport There's a public swimming pool and gym on Jalan Kota.

Travel agents Atlas Travel, 5 Jalan Hang Jebat (☎ 06 282 0777) sells plane tickets.

Visa extensions The immigration office is out in Ayer Keroh, on floors 1-3 of Blok Pentadbiran, Kompleks Kementerian Dalam Negeri, Jalan Seri Negeri (Mon–Fri 8am–5pm; ☎ 06 232 2662).

Around Melaka

While there's more than enough to keep you occupied in Melaka, there are also a few popular getaways within day-trip distance. These include several opportunities to see animals: the tranquil coastal village of **Padang Kemunting** is a hatching site for hawksbill turtles, while **Ayer Keroh** has several wildlife parks as well as cultural attractions. Alternatively, the nearby island **Pulau Besar** provides an opportunity to feel some sand between your toes even if the sea is fairly polluted.

Padang Kemunting Turtle Sanctuary

24km up the coast northwest from Melaka • Daily 8am–5pm • Free • ☎ 06 384 6754 • Drive up Coastal Road 5, turn left 7km beyond Tanjung to follow Route 143 6km to the coast, then turn left again; or take Patt Hup bus #47 to Masjid Tanah, then taxi 8km (RM10–20); or taxi from Melaka Sentral (RM50)

Padang Kemunting is one of the last nesting areas of the hawksbill turtle and the painted terrapin in south Malaysia. Although open all year, it's only worth visiting the **turtle sanctuary** during hatchling season (March–Sept). It's a friendly place with lots of information, including an introductory video about the turtle population of Melaka.

ACCOMMODATION AND EATING   PADANG KEMUNTING

There are a handful of places to stay near the sanctuary, plus several Malay seafood restaurants along the shore and a couple of convenience stores.

Ismah Beach Resort Next door to Padang Kemunting Turtle Sanctuary ☎ 06 384 8141, ⊜ ismahresort.com. This resort has a restaurant and swimming pool; if the turtles appear at night, the sanctuary can contact you by prior arrangement. <u>RM110</u>

Ayer Keroh

Despite its position adjacent to the North–South Expressway, 14km north of Melaka, **AYER KEROH** is a leafy recreational area with numerous attractions and a handful of places to stay. Although it's much cheaper to visit by bus, the attractions are quite spread out across both sides of the expressway so if you plan to visit several then it's better to rent a car or charter a taxi for the duration of the trip.

In addition to the attractions listed separately below, there are several others; pick up the *Melaka Street Map* (RM5) sold by the tourist office for a small but handy map. They include the **Hutan Rekreasi** (daily 9am–6pm; free) an area of woodland set aside for walking and picnicking, the **Taman Rama–Rama & Reptilia** (Butterfly and Reptile Sanctuary; daily 9am–7pm; RM5) and the **Taman Buaya** (Crocodile Park; daily 8.30am–5.30pm; RM12).

5

Taman Mini Malaysia & ASEAN

Ayer Keroh • Daily 9am–6pm, cultural shows Tues–Sun only • RM5 • ☎ 06 232 4433, Gallop Stable ☎ 012 617 9770

Ayer Keroh's most interesting attraction, **Taman Mini Malaysia & ASEAN**, holds full-sized reconstructions of typical houses from all thirteen Malay states and the other members of the Association of Southeast Asian Nations, an economic alliance of the region's states.

Some buildings have displays inside and sell food, drink and souvenirs; cultural shows are also staged at the park's open-air arena. Note, though, that little seems to happen on weekdays. Also within the park, it's possible to ride horses or ponies at **Gallop Stable**.

Melaka Zoo

Hang Tuah Jaya, Ayer Keroh • Mon–Fri 9am–6pm; Sat, Sun and eve of holidays 9am–6pm & 8–11pm • RM7 • ☎ 06 232 4053

Malaysia's oldest and second largest zoo, the leafy 54-hectare **Melaka Zoo** holds around 200 different animal species, including the rare Sumatran rhinoceros. There's a "train" to get you around if you don't want to walk.

Melaka Wonderland

Ayer Keroh • Tues–Fri 11am–7pm, Sat–Sun 9am–7pm • Tues–Fri adults RM26, children RM20; Sat & Sun RM30/RM25 • ☎ 06 231 3333, ⓦ melakawonderland.com.my

The **Melaka Wonderland** water park can provide a welcome break on a hot day. Attractions include the Tornado Chaser (where you start in a giant bowl before passing through a darkened tunnel and into a pool) and a wide range of twisting and straight slides, as well as more sedate swimming pools. The place is quiet on weekdays outside school holidays.

ARRIVAL AND DEPARTURE AYER KEROH

By bus Town bus #19 (hourly) from Melaka Sentral.

By taxi A taxi from Melaka costs RM25; chartering the vehicle should cost RM50/hour.

ACCOMMODATION AND EATING

INB Resort Lot 3169 Sempang Padang Keladi, Lebuh Ayer Keroh ☎ 06 553 3022, ⓦ inbresort.googlepages .com. An affordable option, 15–20 min on foot from Taman Mini Malaysia & ASEAN. It's popular with local families, with comfortable rooms in pink concrete buildings arrayed around a pool. Breakfast is only served at the weekend, but there's a small eatery outside. **RM100**

Philea 2940 Jalan Ayer Keroh, off Jalan Plaza Tol ☎ 06 233 3399, ⓦ phileahotel.com. The stylish cabins at this site make great use of natural materials, built from Russian pine logs and with stone in the bathrooms, although this does mean that ground-floor rooms can be a bit noisy. There's a spa, sauna and gym; the two Royal Villas have their own swimming pools. Rooms **RM468**, Royal Villas **RM4300**

Pulau Besar

If you're looking for a beach getaway and don't have time to go further afield, then **PULAU BESAR** ("Big Island", though it covers just sixteen square kilometres) may fit the bill. The island's beaches and hilly scenery are pleasant, although the waters are fairly polluted.

Located 5km off the coast of Melaka, Pulau Besar was known as the burial ground of passing Muslim traders and missionaries; as a result locals – particularly Indian Muslims – see the island as a holy place and visitors are asked to behave accordingly.

ARRIVAL AND DEPARTURE PULAU BESAR

By ferry Two jetties southeast of Melaka have boats to the island; neither is on bus routes, and a taxi to either should cost RM30. Regular ferries run from the Anjung Batu jetty (8 daily, starting 8am, last boat back 10pm; RM14 return), while the Pengkalan Pernu jetty in Umbai has boats only on request (RM120 one-way for up to eight people).

OPPOSITE WATERFALL NEAR KOTA TINGGI >

5

D'Puteri Pulau Besar ☎ 06 295 5899, ⓦ dputeriresort pulaubesar.blogspot.com. Nothing special – simple cabins with cold water and either fan or a/c. You won't want to spend much time in your room, but the island's only resort is right on the beach. They also have a campsite. Fan rooms RM90, a/c rooms RM130, camping (own tent) RM30, camping (with tent rental) RM60

From Melaka to Johor Bahru

The journey from Melaka southeast along **Route 5** to Johor Bahru covers just over 200km. The first 45km, as far as the town of **Muar**, passes through verdant countryside dotted with neatly kept timber stilt houses in some of Malaysia's prettiest kampungs. Further south, the towns of Batu Pahat and Pontian Kecil hold scant interest (the former, slightly inland, has a reputation as a red-light resort for Singaporeans). If you want to stop anywhere else before Johor Bahru and Singapore, aim instead for **Kukup**, right at the southern end of the west coast and terrific for seafood.

To get to Johor Bahru in a hurry, skip the scenery of Route 5 and use the **North–South Expressway** instead. From Melaka, you can head north to the expressway via Ayer Keroh; it's also straightforward to join the expressway from Muar (take the Bukit Pasir road for about 20km).

Muar

Also known as Bandar Maharani, the old port town of **MUAR** is a calm and elegant place that attracts few tourists but should reward a day's exploration. Legend has it that Paramesvara, the fifteenth-century founder of Melaka, fled here from Singapore to establish his kingdom on the southern bank of Sungai Muar, before being persuaded to choose Melaka. The town later became an important port in the Johor empire (see p.567), as well as a centre for the sentimental Malay folk-pop called **ghazal music**, and its **dialect** is considered the purest Bahasa Malaysia in the Peninsula.

Today, Muar's commercial centre looks like any other, with Chinese shophouses and *kedai kopis* lining its streets. Turn right out of the **bus station**, however, following the river as the road turns into Jalan Peteri, and you'll find Muar's **Neoclassical colonial buildings**. The Custom House and Government Offices (Bangunan Sultan Abu Bakar) are on your right, and the District Police Office and Courthouse on your left; they still have an air of confidence and prosperity from the town's days as a British administrative centre. Completed in 1930, the graceful **Masjid Jamek Sultan Ibrahim** successfully combines Western and Moorish styles of architecture. Further along Jalan Petri you'll pass a jetty on your right, from where irregular **river cruises** depart.

ARRIVAL AND DEPARTURE   MUAR

By bus Muar's bus station, on Jalan Maharani, is served by local bus #2 from Melaka's Sentral station (frequent; 1hr 30min), but it's quicker to take a JB-bound express bus and hop off in Muar.

By taxi A taxi from Melaka costs RM60–80 one-way.

ACCOMMODATION

Hotel Leewa Jalan Ali ☎ 06 952 1605. A fine budget choice, the best in its price range, where the rooms have a/c and TVs. There's also a branch, with the same name but slightly nicer rooms and slightly higher prices, on Jalan Arab. RM70

Streetview Jalan Ali ☎ 06 951 3313, ⓦ riverviewhotel .com.my. The best of three hotels belonging to the same chain, all detailed on the same website, with comfortable a/c rooms in a converted shophouse. RM90

EATING

Muar has a good reputation for its coffee and its food, particularly *otak-otak* (fishcakes) and the breakfast dish *mee bandung* (see below). Another local distinction is the popularity of satay (particularly *satay perut*, made from intestines) for breakfast.

Jalan Haji Abu hawker centre Jalan Haji Abu. The stalls here – some of which have been operating for decades – serve up a range of dishes including Muar's famous colourful steamed rice cakes, dim sum, *otak-otak* and more. Daily 5.30am until late.

Wah San 9A Jalan Abdullah. The *mee bandung* (noodles, beansprouts, egg, beef and tofu served in a sauce made from prawn, chillies and beef soup) prepared here by Abu Bakar Hanipah is regarded as the best in town. Taught by his father, he's been making it for over 40 years. Daily from 8am.

Kukup

The small fishing community of **KUKUP**, 19km south of Pontian Kecil along Route 5, has opened its doors to the Singapore package-tour trade. Busloads of tourists arrive to see the old stilt houses built over the murky river and to sample Kukup's real attraction, the **seafood**: the town's single tumbledown street is packed with restaurants.

ARRIVAL AND DEPARTURE KUKUP

By bus In the absence of direct buses from either Melaka or Johor Bahru, you have to catch a bus to Pontian Kecil then take a taxi (RM20).
By ferry The jetty at Kukup is a little-known exit point

from Malaysia to Indonesia. Ferries operated by Penaga Timur (☎ 07 696 9098) run to Tanjung Balai on Karimun island (3 daily; 45min; RM65 one-way) and Sekupang on Batam island (2 daily; 1hr 20min; RM80 one-way).

ACCOMMODATION

Tanjung Piai Resort 1km north of Kucup towards Pontian Kecil ☎012 767 0699. This string of large wooden buildings stands on concrete stilts at the edge of the mangrove swamps. The resort commands a

dramatic vista of the ships coming to and from Singapore, and has a decent seafood restaurant, but is generally in need of repair. Prices rise by about half at weekends. RM140

EATING

Makanan Laut 66a Kukup Laut. This enormous place is the closest to the jetty, where you can sit on the large wooden waterfront deck and watch the fishermen and tourists floating around on the river. It serves good, mostly Chinese-style, seafood dishes. Daily 10am–10pm.

Restoran Zaiton Hussin 631 Kukup Laut. A modest establishment serving high-quality Malay seafood, although as elsewhere in Kukup the influx of visitors has pushed prices up. Daily 6am–6pm.

Johor Bahru

The southernmost Malaysian city of any size, **JOHOR BAHRU** – or simply **JB** – is the main gateway into **Singapore**, linked to the city-state by a **causeway** carrying a road, a railway, and the pipes through which Singapore imports its fresh water. More than fifty thousand vehicles each day travel across the causeway (the newer **second crossing** from Geylang Patah, 20km west of JB, is much less used because of its higher tolls), and the ensuing traffic, noise and smog affects most of downtown Johor Bahru.

The city has been moulded by its proximity to Singapore, for better or for worse – it has the air of both a border town and a boomtown. The vast majority of visitors are **day-trippers**, many drawn by the cheap shopping, and Johor Bahru's nightlife caters more than adequately to the appetite of Singaporean men for liquor, hostesses and karaoke.

That said, Johor Bahru is taking steps to broaden its appeal. An ambitious collaboration with Singapore, known as **Iskandar Malaysia**, set out to stimulate local industry but has grown to embrace property development and tourist facilities. There is also evidence of smaller-scale entrepeneurship such as a rash of new cafés and

5

THE SULTANS AND THE LAW

The antics of the British royal family are nothing compared to what some of the nine royal families in Malaysia get up to. Nepotism, meddling in state politics and flagrant breaches of their exemption from import duties are among their lesser misdemeanours, which generally go unreported in the circumspect local press. The most notorious of them was Johor's late **Sultan Mahmud Iskandar Al-Haj ibni Ismail Al-Khalidi**, usually known as Sultan Iskandar, who died in 2010. He is alleged to have beaten his golf caddy to death in the Cameron Highlands in 1987 after the unfortunate man made the mistake of laughing at a bad shot.

Such behaviour had long incensed the prime minister of the time, Dr Mahathir, who was itching to bring the lawless royals into line. He got his chance in 1993 when yet another beating incident involving Sultan Iskandar was brought up in the federal parliament along with 23 other similar assaults since 1972. Following a stand-off with Mahathir, the sultans agreed to a compromise – they would waive their immunity from prosecution on the condition that no ruler would be taken to court without the attorney-general's approval.

Despite the peccadilloes, and worse, of the various sultans being the subject of popular gossip (though little coverage in the press), the sultans are still revered by many Malays, for whom they symbolise continuing Malay dominance of a multiethnic nation.

boutiques, and already the city deserves to be seen as more than merely a hurdle to jump on the way to Singapore, Melaka or Kuala Lumpur.

Brief history

JB stands with Melaka as one of the country's most historic sites. Chased from its seat of power by the Portuguese in 1511, the Melakan court decamped to the Riau Archipelago, south of modern Singapore, before upping sticks again in the 1530s and shifting to the upper reaches of the Johor River. There they endured a century of offensives by both the Portuguese and the Acehnese of northern Sumatra.

Stability was finally achieved by courting the friendship of the Dutch in the 1640s, and the kingdom of Johor blossomed into a thriving trading entrepôt. By the end of the century, though, the rule of the tyrannical Sultan Mahmud had halted Johor's pre-eminence among the Malay kingdoms, and piracy was causing a decline in trade. In 1699, Sultan Mahmud was killed by his own nobles. With the Melaka-Johor dynasty finally over, successive power struggles crippled the kingdom.

Immigration of the Bugis peoples to Johor eventually eclipsed the power of the sultans (see p.567), and though the Bugis were finally chased out by the Dutch in 1784, the kingdom was a shadow of its former self. The Johor-Riau empire – and the Malay world – was split in two, with the Melaka Straits forming the dividing line following the Anglo-Dutch Treaty of 1824. As links with the court in Riau faded, Sultan Ibrahim assumed power, amassing a fortune based upon hefty profits culled from plantations. He established his administrative headquarters in the fishing village of Tanjung Puteri, which his son Abu Bakar – widely regarded as the father of modern Johor – later renamed Johor Bahru ("New Johor").

Downtown

JB is a sprawling city, and many of the administrative offices have been moved out of the centre to **Kota Iskandar** in the west. Most places of interest to visitors, though, are still **downtown** or close to the **waterfront** near the Singapore causeway. The downtown area blends the scruffy with the modern: the claustrophobic alleys of the sprawling market are within a few paces of thoroughly contemporary shopping malls such as City Square. Close by, the huge **CIQ** (customs, immigration and quarantine) complex – built to streamline travel between JB and Singapore – includes JB Sentral station, combining bus and train terminals.

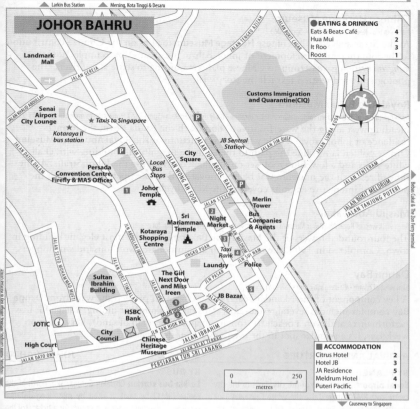

Arguably the most interesting part of the area, though, is on and around **Jalan Tan Hiok Nee** and **Jalan Dhoby**. Formerly quite seedy, these streets have been tidied up and are now at the centre of a vibrant shopping and dining scene.

Sri Mariamman Temple

Jalan Ungku Puan, south of City Square

The **Sri Mariamman Temple** lends a welcome splash of colour to JB's cityscape. Underneath its *gopuram*, and beyond the two gatekeepers on horseback who guard the temple, stand vividly depicted figures from the Hindu pantheon. Shops outside the temple sell Bollywood movies and garlands of flowers used in worship, while on the street you can have your fortune told using cowrie shells.

Around the seafront

The views across to Singapore from the **seafront**, just a short walk from Sri Mariamman Temple, are doubly impressive after the cramped streets of the city centre. Several interesting attractions lie on or around Jalan Ibrahim, while just north of here is the fortress-like **Sultan Ibrahim Building**; formerly the home of the state government, which has been moved west to Kota Iskandar, the building is eventually scheduled to become a museum.

5

Chinese Heritage Museum

Jalan Tan Hiok Nee • Tues–Sun 9am–5pm • RM3

As the name suggests, the **Chinese Heritage Museum** focuses on the Chinese contribution to the founding and development of Johor Bahru; it explains, for example, how the *kangchu* system gave permits to Chinese planters wanting to settle along rivers. The photographs and written text tell the story well.

Royal Abu Bakar Museum

Jalan Tun Dr Ismail, the western continuation of Jalan Ibrahim • Daily except Fri 9am–5pm • US$7 (converted to ringgit) • ☎ 07 223 0222

Heading west along the waterfront you soon reach the Istana Besar, the former residence of Johor's royal family which now functions as the **Royal Abu Bakar Museum**. Ornate golden lamps line the path to the Istana, a magnificent building with chalk-white walls and a low, blue roof, set on a hillock overlooking the Johor Straits. At the time of research the museum was being renovated, due to reopen in 2013 with the promise of interactive exhibits covering the local royalty.

Masjid Abu Bakar

5min walk west of Royal Abu Bakar Museum • Daily 8am–5pm, closes Fri noon–3pm for prayers

The four rounded towers of the **Masjid Abu Bakar** make it the most elegant building in town. Completed in 1900, the mosque can accommodate two thousand worshippers.

Danga Bay

5km west of centre • 🌐 dangabay.com • Taxi RM14

A key component of the Iskandar Malaysia development project, the waterfront **Danga Bay** complex includes several restaurants, stalls offering outdoor dining, a stage for live performances and even a beach bar (on an unappealing scrap of sand). Very quiet on weekdays, it's a popular spot in the evenings and at the weekend.

ARRIVAL AND DEPARTURE

BY PLANE

Senai airport 28km north of the city. Taxis to the city centre cost RM40; there's also the white Causeway Link shuttle bus to the Senai Airport City Lounge at the Kotaraya II bus terminal (11 daily, 6.10am–10.50pm; 50min; RM8), while regular buses also run to Larkin bus station (RM4).

Destinations Kota Kinabalu (2 daily; 2hr 20min); Kuala Lumpur (5–6 daily; 45min); Kuching (2 daily; 1hr 25min); Miri (3–4 weekly; 2hr); Penang (2 daily; 1hr); Sibu (3–4 weekly; 1hr 40min); Subang (KL; 2 daily; 45min).

Airline offices The MAS office is in the Persada convention centre (Mon–Fri 8.30am–5.30pm; ☎ 07 225 3509) as is the Firefly office (Mon–Fri 8.30am–5.30pm, Sat 8.30am–1pm; call centre ☎ 03 7845 4543). The AirAsia office is out in Danga Bay.

BY TRAIN

JB Sentral The train station is part of the new JB Sentral terminal.

Destinations Butterworth (1 daily; 13hr 15min); Ipoh (daily; 9hr); Gemas (7 daily; 3hr 25min); Kuala Lipis (3 daily; 8hr); Kuala Lumpur (3 daily; 6hr); Segamat (3 daily; 3hr); Seremban (3 daily; 4hr 30min); Singapore (5 daily; 40min); Tumpat (2 daily; 12hr).

BY BUS

Larkin bus station On Jalan Geruda, 5km north of the centre (RM12 by taxi), is used by most long-distance services. If you don't want to go there for a ticket, try the row of bus company offices running along the side of the Merlin Tower building in the city centre.

Destinations Alor Star (daily; 12hr); Bandar Penawar (for Desaru; 4 daily; 1hr 30min); Batu Pahat (14 daily); Butterworth (at least 4 daily; 9hr); Dungun (daily); Hap Chai (Thailand; daily; 12hr); Ipoh (4 daily; 7hr); Klang (3 daily); Kota Bharu (1 daily; 10hr); Kota Tinggi (hourly; 1hr); Kuala Lumpur (at least hourly; 4hr 30min); Kuala Perlis (1 daily; 12hr); Kuala Terengganu (4 daily; 9hr); Kuantan (8 daily; 6hr); Lumut (1 daily; 8hr); Melaka (hourly; 3hr); Mersing (3 daily; 2hr 30min); Muar (hourly; 2hr 30min); Pengkalan Kubor (for Thai border; daily); Rantau Panjang (daily); Segamat (4 daily); Seremban (10 daily; 3hr 30min); Shah Alam (3 daily); Sentosa (Singapore; 6 daily); Singapore (every 10min; 1hr); Tanah Merah (daily).

Local buses Buses heading east start from the new JB Sentral combined bus and train terminal; local buses heading west run from around City Square. The Kotaraya II bus terminal is used by buses to Singapore and Senai Airport.

5

GETTING FROM JOHOR BAHRU TO SINGAPORE

There are several ways to head into Singapore from Johor Bahru. The most obvious but least sensible would be to use the **train** from JB Sentral – the problem is that Singapore's station is only just across the causeway, at Woodlands. To reach downtown Singapore, you're better off taking either a **taxi** – which costs RM15 per person or RM60 for the whole vehicle, from the official rank at Kotaraya II bus terminal (or from touts outside JB Sentral station) – or a **bus**.

Starting from **Larkin bus station**, north of town, you can catch SBS #170X or #170 (daily 5.20am–midnight), or the faster yellow Causeway Link #CW1 and #CW2 services. The Causeway Link buses (ⓦcausewaylink.com.my; daily 5.05am–0.05pm, every 15–20min) also stop in central JB at the **Kotaraya II bus terminal**, which is a useful hub since it's connected by bus to JB's Senai airport.

All buses then proceed to the **CIQ** (Customs, Immigration and Quarantine) complex; at this point you need to get off the bus and clear customs, before getting on another to complete the journey to Singapore (take your luggage off the bus, keep your ticket and get on the same type of bus on the other side). If you're already in downtown Johor Bahru, simply board the bus at **JB Sentral**, which is part of the CIQ complex, and complete immigration formalities before you buy your ticket.

Once through customs the Causeway Link buses run nonstop to Kranji MRT (#CW1) or Queen Street (#CW2); the SBS services go to Kranji MRT, with the #170 continuing (and stopping regularly) all the way down to Little India and terminating at Queen Street, near Bugis MRT and Arab Street.

Transtar Travel also operates handy buses from Kotaraya II bus terminal: # TS1 (hourly 5am–9pm; 2hr; RM7) runs to **Changi airport** via Marsiling MRT, while #TS8 (hourly 5.45am–9.45pm; RM5) goes to **Sentosa** via Orchard Road and Outram MRT.

BY FERRY

Ferries from Tanjung Pinang (3 daily; 2hr 30min; RM86 one-way) and Pulau Batam (hourly 7.30am–6.30pm; 1hr 30min; RM69 one-way) in Indonesia arrive at The Zon, 2km east of the causeway; book tickets on ⓦzonferry.com.my.

BY TAXI

There is a taxi rank at the Kotaraya II bus terminal and another at JB Sentral.

CAR RENTAL

Rental companies in the Senai Airport City Lounge at Kotaraya II bus terminal include Avis (☏07 223 7644, ⓦavis.com), Pacific (☏019 213 9766) and Hawk (☏07 224 2854, ⓦhawkrentacar.com.my). Hertz is based in Menara Ansar on Jalan Trus (☏07 223 7520, ⓦsimedarbycarrental.com).

INFORMATION

Tourist information The Tourism Malaysia office is on level 3 of the yellow JOTIC (Johor Tourist Information Centre) building on Jalan Dato' Onn (Mon–Thurs 8am–1pm & 2–5pm, Fri 8am–12.15pm & 2.45–5pm; ☏07 222 3590). The Johor Bahru Visitor Centre is upstairs

on level 5 (Mon–Fri 8am–5pm; ☏07 224 1432, ⓦmbjb .gov.my).
Internet access Available at many places along Jalan Meldrum; the *Hanyasatu Hotel* at no.29 has 24hr internet terminals.

ACCOMMODATION

JB's manufacturing boom means the city attracts more business travellers than tourists, so **hotel** prices tend to be on the high side. Most of JB's lower-priced hotels are on or around Jalan Meldrum, in the heart of town, but some of the cheapest (not listed here) double as brothels.

Citrus Hotel 16 Jalan Stesen ☏07 222 2888, ⓦcitrushoteljb.com. Pricier than most around Jalan Meldrum, but its sense of contemporary chic makes it stand out. The *Citrus Café* is a similarly appealing place to stop for a meal, and breakfast is included (as is wi-fi). R̲M̲1̲6̲0̲
Hotel JB 80a Jalan Wong Ah Fook ☏07 224 6625. Right in the hustle and bustle of the night market – so the windowless rooms may be preferable – this place could do

with a little sprucing up but the rooms are clean enough. En-suite facilities cost RM20 extra. R̲M̲6̲0̲
JA Residence 18 Jalan Wong Ah Fook ☏07 221 3000, ⓦjaresidencehotel.com.my. Formerly known as the *Compact Hotel*. The common areas are a bit threadbare but the rooms have a little more class, and the higher floors command good views across JB and Singapore. The cheapest rooms do not include breakfast; look out for

5

discounts on deluxe rooms after midnight. RM99

Meldrum Hotel 1 Jalan Sui Nam ☎ 07 227 8988. This mid-range hotel is significantly better value than most of its rivals. All private rooms have a/c, bathrooms and TV, but for RM100 upwards you also get wi-fi and can choose a non-smoking room. There's also an eight-bed, mixed-sex dorm (but no storage lockers). Dorms RM40, rooms RM90

Puteri Pacific Jalan Abdullah Ibrahim ☎ 07 219 9999, ⊛ puteripacific.com. Downtown JB's most opulent address, with 500 sumptuous and spacious rooms plus five restaurants. Look out for promotional prices; internet access is a shocking RM75/day. RM313

EATING

There are scores of **restaurants** in JB, plus there's some good street food on offer. The most interesting little cafés and restaurants are to the west of Jalan Segget, which also has its own night market.

FOOD MARKETS AND MALLS

City Square Jalan Wong Ah Fook. Popular top-floor food court plus various Western fast-food establishments in this huge shopping centre, linked to the CIQ by a walkway. Daily 10am–10pm.

JB Bazaar Jalan Segget and around. Founded in 2010 as part of the city council's efforts to regenerate the vicinity of the old immigration centre, which was replaced by the CIQ complex further north, this Malay night market has plenty of food stalls but also clothes, toys, live music and more. Daily 6pm–midnight.

Night market Meldrum Walk. Colourful and vibrant night market with a mouthwatering array of goodies. Try the local speciality *mee rebus* – noodles in a thick sauce garnished with bean curd, sliced egg, green chillies and shallots. Daily 6pm–midnight.

RESTAURANTS AND CAFÉS

★ **Eats & Beats Café** Jalan Tan Hiok Nee. The owner is passionate about music and it shows: as well as playing his favourites in the café, he has decorated the walls with album covers. A great place to hang out with a coffee or beer while using the wi-fi, and the regulars are a friendly bunch. Mon–Sat 2–11pm.

Hua Mui 131 Jalan Trus. Western and Chinese dishes are on the menu in this two-storey restaurant, in business since 1946 and known for dishes such as *mee hailam* (noodles with chicken, prawn and vegetables). The first floor is a good place to escape the midday sun for lunch; the large windows mean a good breeze. Daily 8am–6pm.

It Roo 17–23 Jalan Dhoby. The best place in JB to try the Hainanese-Western fusion dish chicken chop – fried or grilled chicken fillet with either mushroom sauce or black pepper sauce. It's a pretty simple place, but very popular with locals. Daily noon–9.30pm.

Roost 8 Jalan Dhoby. The first of the fashionable new cafés to open in this area, *Roost* has a shabby-chic feel with vintage furniture and 70s decor. They do great beef noodles (RM8) among other dishes, and there are a couple of good boutiques upstairs. Mon–Sat noon–4pm & 6pm–midnight, Sun 6pm–midnight.

SHOPPING

Although JB has plenty of shopping malls, it's much more enjoyable to explore the boutiques around Jalan Tan Hiok Nee and Jalan Dhoby.

The Girl Next Door Above Roost Café, 8 Jalan Dhoby ☎ 07 222 4178. Typical of the boutiques in this area, with a young and enthusiastic owner selling mostly vintage clothes and shoes but also other bits and pieces which take her fancy; there's also a hairdressing section. Mon–Sat 1pm–midnight.

Miss Ireen Handmade Above Roost Café, 8 Jalan Dhoby ☎ 016 782 9215, ⊛ missireen.blogspot.com. A tiny but very cute shop, where Ireen Tan sells her vintage-style handmade jewellery plus assorted items such as plush toys. Mon–Sat 1pm–midnight.

DIRECTORY

Banks and moneychangers The main shopping centres hold ATMs and moneychangers; in JB Sentral there's a 24-hour moneychanger at the main entrance. The ground floor of City Square holds numerous banks, including a Maybank.

Up the east coast from Johor Bahru

Without the patronage of neighbouring Singapore, the area around Johor Bahru – including the seaside resort of **Desaru** – would have quietly nodded off into a peaceful slumber. Most people heading east beat a hasty path along Route 3 to **Mersing**, an attractive little town that is the departure point for boats to **Pulau Tioman**.

Desaru

As beaches in this part of Malaysia go, **DESARU** isn't bad, though there are better places up the coast. This sheltered, casuarina-fringed bay is the nearest major resort to Singapore and thus gets busy during weekends and holidays. During the monsoon months, when the current on Desaru Beach is dangerously strong, don't go in the water if the red flag is flying, and use caution at any time; fatalities have occurred even in the shallows. On nearby **Balau Beach**, which holds a couple of cheaper resorts, there's no swimming at any time; you have to walk 1km to a public beach.

ARRIVAL AND DEPARTURE
DESARU

By bus The best way is to catch a Mara liner bus from Larkin terminal to Bandar Penawar (4 daily; last bus 8pm, last bus back to JB 6pm), then a taxi (RM10) or resort transfer for the last 3km.

By ferry Most visitors from Singapore come by sea from Changi Point (see p.532), arriving at the Malaysian port of Kampung Pengerang. Shuttle buses make the 45-minute journey from the port to Desaru itself.

By taxi A taxi from Johor Bahru to Desaru costs around RM70.

ACCOMMODATION

There are a handful of **places to stay** on the main beach, plus a couple more on nearby Balau beach (RM20–30 by taxi from Desaru Beach). Be warned that room rates rise on the main beach by about half at weekends and holidays; the prices given here are the lower rates.

Chalet Tanjung Balau Balau Beach ☎ 07 822 1201. The cheapest option in this area unless you intend to camp, although unfortunately the dorms can only be booked by groups, not individual travellers. The private rooms are simple, with cold water only, but clean and well maintained. RM75

Desaru Damai Desaru Beach ☎ 07 235 0162, ⓦ desarudamai.com. Significantly more affordable than its neighbours on this beach; the rooms are less plush but still spacious enough. It also has free wi-fi, and weekend price rises are not too steep. RM110

Pelangi Balau Resort Balau Beach ☎ 07 832 2833, ⓦ pelangihotels.com. Formerly known as *Balau Bay*, this resort has 98 rooms and 10 villas; both are good value for money, with nice touches such as wooden floors and carved bedheads. The swimming pool is open to non-guests for RM10. Camping RM30, rooms RM140

Pulai Desaru Beach Resort Desaru Beach ☎ 07 822 2222, ⓦ thepulai.com.my. The most tasteful resort on this beach; most rooms are twin, so book ahead if you want a double. Activities include firefly tours, river cruises, village and farm visits, plus sea sports. RM290

EATING

All the Desaru Beach hotels have pricey **restaurants** where a very average meal costs a bare minimum of RM22. Prices are a bit more reasonable on Balau Beach, but there's still little choice.

Mersing

The industrious little fishing port of **MERSING**, 130km north of Johor Bahru, lies on the languid Sungai Mersing. It serves as the main gateway to **Pulau Tioman** and the smaller islands of the **Seribuat Archipelago**.

ARRIVAL AND DEPARTURE
MERSING

By bus While buses are supposed to stop either at the bus station or (more often) at the R&R Plaza beside the jetty, many make an unscheduled stop first outside a travel agency where the staff will be keen to sell you ferry tickets and arrange accommodation. It's better to stay on the bus and shop around at the R&R Plaza and the jetty itself.

Leaving by bus in peak season can be problematic; many are full. Buy express-bus tickets in advance, at the station or from a resort or travel agency.

Destinations Alor Star (daily); Butterworth (daily); Cherating (3 daily; 4hr 30min); Endau (every 30min); Ipoh (daily); Johor Bahru (4 daily); Kluang (12 daily); Kota Bahru

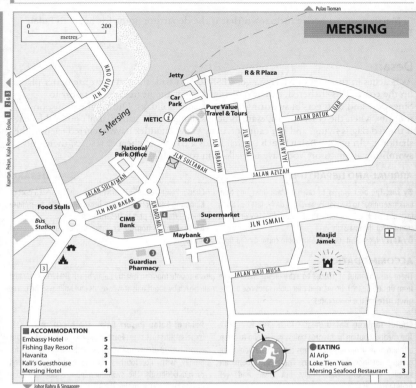

MERSING

Kuantan, Pekan, Kuala Rompin, Endau, **T.**, **2 & 3**

ACCOMMODATION

Embassy Hotel	5
Fishing Bay Resort	2
Havanita	3
Kali's Guesthouse	1
Mersing Hotel	4

EATING

Al Arip	2
Loke Tien Yuan	1
Mersing Seafood Restaurant	3

Johor Bahru & Singapore

(2 daily; 8hr); Kota Tinggi (12 daily), Kuala Lumpur (7 daily; 5hr 30min); Kuala Perlis (daily); Kuala Terengganu (3 daily, 6hr–7hr 30min); Kuantan (5 daily; 3hr 30min); Melaka (5 daily; 4hr 30min); Muar (5 daily; 4hr); Pengkalan Kubor (daily); Singapore (3–4 daily from March–Oct, otherwise daily; 2hr 30min).

By taxi Taxis can be picked up either at the main bus station or at the jetty.

GETTING TO THE ISLANDS

Mersing is the main departure point for Tioman and the other islands of the Seribuat Archipelago, although there are also departures from Tanjung Gemuk (see p.301). At the jetty there's a secure **car park** (RM7–10/day), while there and in the R&R Plaza nearby, assorted booths and offices represent various islands, boats and resorts. For impartial information, though, you're better off going to the tourist office. Change money in Mersing before you head out to the islands, where the exchange rates are lousy; the only ATM on Tioman is in Tekek, opposite the airport.

Blue Water Ferries The most established operator of express boats to Tioman (2hr; RM35 one-way; ☎07 799 4811;). Signboards at the jetty detail sailings; buy a ticket there, not from a more expensive tout or travel agent.

Tioman XL Ferry At the time of writing, this company had just started offering boats to Tekek, Air Batang and Salang (RM35; ☎07 799 7222, ⍉tiomanxlferry.weebly .com).

INFORMATION

Tourist information Mersing's tourist office is on Jalan Abu Bakar (METIC; Mon–Fri 8am–5pm; ☎07 798 1979); helpful staff can advise on differing island deals.

Travel agents Numerous agents, operators and resort offices in and around the jetty complex deal primarily with Tioman and the Seribuat Archipelago. Pure Value Travel & Tours, 7 Jalan Abu Bakar (☎07 799 6811, ⍉purevalue .com.my), also organize island-hopping trips, and trips to

Endau Rompin National Park (see p.310).

Internet Mersing is well supplied with cyber-cafés, most of which can be found along Jalan Abu Bakar, for example Blue Skynet at no. 11 (10.30am–midnight).

ACCOMMODATION

Although Mersing has many **hotels**, the cheaper end is not well represented and the only hostel is impossible to recommend. For longer stays, going a little out of town is more pleasant.

IN TOWN

Embassy Hotel 2 Jalan Ismail ☎ 07 799 3545. The best mid-range value within Mersing town; rooms have king-size beds (triple and twins also available), TVs, hot water and a/c. Wi-fi on the bottom two floors. RM60

Havanita 88 Jalan Endau ☎ 07 799 8666, ⓦ hotel havanita.com.my. Beyond its unpromising exterior, this is the most stylish option in town, just across the bridge from the centre. There's a bar and restaurant, with live music some weekends. Rates include breakfast. RM129

Mersing Hotel Jalan Dato Mohammed Ali ☎ 07 799 3613. The best of an unappealing bunch when it comes to budget hotels. Double rooms all have a/c, while solo travellers can try the RM20 single with fan. RM45

OUT OF TOWN

Fishing Bay Resort 15km north of Mersing ☎ 07 799 6753, ⓦ fishingbayresort.com. This good-value place has bungalows and rooms set around a beachside garden and small pool, and a restaurant serving excellent local and Thai food. Kayaks are available for a trip to Pulau Batu Gajah just offshore. A taxi costs RM20 one-way, or ask about transfers. Weekend rates rise by half. RM118

★ **Kali's Prada Villa (aka Kali's Guesthouse)** Kampung Sawah Air Papan, 15km north of Mersing ☎ 017 763 9274 ⓔ khalidmersing@yahoo.com. Friendly Kali welcomes guests to eight lovely Bali-inspired rooms set amid rice fields. Dinner is available, and lunch on request. Phone to be picked up from town (RM15 return); if coming by taxi make sure they don't take you to the old location in Kampung Sri Lalang. RM80

EATING

Mersing is a good place to **eat** out, with seafood topping the menu. The **market** serves the popular local breakfast dish *nasi dagang*: glutinous rice cooked in coconut milk, served with *sambal* and fish curry.

Al Arip Opposite Giant supermarket, Jalan Ismail. Now under new management, this Indian café has been serving good-quality food, including great *tosai*, for more than 40 years. Daily 6.30am–12.30am; may move to 24hr opening.

Loke Tien Yuen 55 Jalan Abu Bakar. The oldest and friendliest Chinese restaurant in town with a small, reliable

menu. The sweet and sour pork is particularly good. Averages RM6/dish, seafood around RM15. Daily 12.30–3.30pm & 6.45–8.45pm.

Mersing Seafood Restaurant 56 Jalan Ismail. Delicious seafood dishes though some can be pricey; steamed fish with delicate flavours is their speciality and the chilli crab is good. Daily around 1pm–midnight.

Pulau Tioman

Shaped like a giant apostrophe, located in the South China Sea 54km northeast of Mersing, **PULAU TIOMAN** is the largest of the 64 volcanic islands that form the **Seribuat Archipelago**. Ever since the 1970s – when *Time* magazine ranked Tioman as one of the world's ten most beautiful islands – sun worshippers and divers have been flocking to its palm-fringed shores, in search of the mythical Bali H'ai (the island in the Hollywood musical *South Pacific*, which was filmed on Tioman).

It could be argued that this popularity, and the **duty-free** status designated by Malaysian Customs, have dented the romantic isolation that once made the island so desirable. Pulau Tioman does, however, display a remarkable resilience, and you'll miss out if you fail to visit – the greater part of the island retains something of its intimate, village atmosphere, probably due to the lack of a decent road network. Anyone in search of unspoiled beaches is likely to be disappointed, though superb exceptions do exist; divers and snorkellers will find plenty to enjoy, and there are also opportunities to take jungle hikes in the largely untouched interior.

5

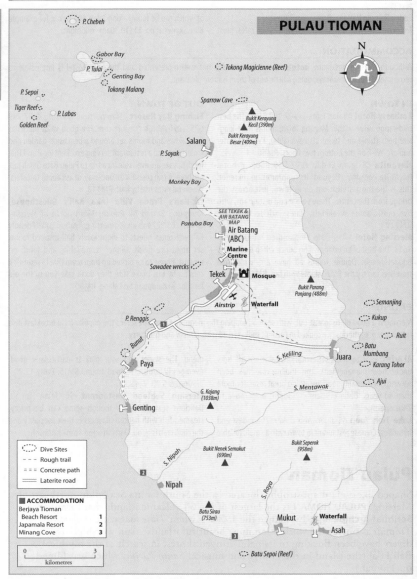

PULAU TIOMAN

P. Chebeh

Gabor Bay

P. Tulai

Genting Bay

P. Sepoi

Tokong Malang

Tiger Reef

Golden Reef

P. Labas

Tokong Magicienne (Reef)

Sparrow Cave

Bukit Kerayung Kecil (390m)

Salang

Bukit Kerayung Besar (409m)

P. Soyak

Monkey Bay

SEE TEKEK & AIR BATANG MAP

Panuba Bay

Air Batang (ABC)

Marine Centre

Sawadee wrecks

Tekek

Mosque

Bukit Parang Panjang (488m)

Airstrip

Waterfall

Semanjing

Kukup

P. Renggis

1

Bunut

Ruit

Batu Mumbang

Karang Tohor

Paya

S. Keliling

Juara

Ajui

Genting

S. Mentawak

G. Kajang (1038m)

Dive Sites

Rough trail

Concrete path

Laterite road

S. Nipah

Bukit Nenek Semukut (690m)

Bukit Seperok (958m)

2

S. Roya

ACCOMMODATION

Berjaya Tioman Beach Resort	1
Japamala Resort	2
Minang Cove	3

Nipah

Batu Sirau (753m)

3

Mukut

Waterfall

Asah

Batu Sepoi (Reef)

0 ————— 3

kilometres

Accommodation possibilities range from international-standard resorts to simple beachfront A-frames; it takes time and/or money to get from one beach to another, so choose your destination carefully. During the **monsoon**, from November to February/March, the whole island winds down dramatically; many places close until at least mid-January. July and August are the busiest months, when prices increase and accommodation is best booked in advance; visibility for divers is also at its lowest during these months.

SNORKELLING AND DIVING AROUND PULAU TIOMAN

With such abundant **marine life** in the waters around Tioman, you're unlikely to choose to be island-bound the whole time. Many nearby islets provide excellent opportunities for **snorkelling**, and most of the chalet operations offer **day-trips**; prices start at RM75, including equipment. The relatively healthy coral and huge biodiversity in these temperate waters also make for great **diving**. Dive centres on Tioman offer a full range of PADI certificates, from a four-day Open Water course (around RM1000), through to the Dive Master (RM3200) and instructor qualifications. For the already qualified, a boat dive costs around RM105 per person.

Of the many dive shops, B&J's in Air Batang is well established (☏09 419 1218, ⊛divetioman .com), and has a second shop in Salang (☏09 419 5555). Blue Heaven (☏09 419 1413, ⊛blueheavendivers.com), also in Air Batang, does a good-value Open Water package. In Tekek try Ray's Dive (☏019 330 8062, ⊛raysdive.com). To explore less-visited dive sites, contact Sunrise Dive Centre (☏09 419 3102, ⊛sunrisedivecentre.com) in Juara. The **dive sites** listed below are the most popular on the west coast, where most people dive.

Golden Reef (typical depth 10–20m). 15min off the northwestern coast; boulders provide a breeding ground for marine life, and produce many soft and hard corals. Known for nudibranchs and other macro life.

Pulau Chebeh (15–30m). In the northwestern waters, this is a massive volcanic labyrinth of caves and channels. Napoleon fish, triggerfish and turtles are present in abundance.

Pulau Labas (5–20m). South of Pulau Tulai, this island has numerous tunnels and caves that provide a home for pufferfish, stingrays and moray eels.

Tiger Reef (10–25m). Deservedly the most popular site, southwest of Pulau Tulai between Labas and Sepoi islands. Yellow-tail snappers, trevally and tuna, spectacular soft coral and gorgonian fans.

Tokong Magicienne (Magician Rock) (10–25m). Due north of Pulau Tioman, this colourful, sponge-layered coral pinnacle is a feeding station for larger fish – silver snappers, golden-striped trevally, jacks and groupers.

Sawadee wrecks (25–30m). Two wooden Thai fishing boats just offshore from Tekek airport attract scorpionfish and juvenile barracuda, as well as more common marine life.

ARRIVAL AND DEPARTURE

PULAU TIOMAN

By plane Berjaya Air (☏03 2119 6616, ⊛berjaya-air .com) fly from KL and Singapore to the airstrip in Tekek.
Arriving by boat Although most boats arrive from Mersing, there are also ferries from Tanjung Gemuk ferry terminal, just across the Sungai Endau from Padang Endau town, which is 35km north of Mersing along Route 3 (9 daily; 1hr; March–Nov; RM35; Blue Water Ferries ☏07 799 4811, Tioman XL Ferry ☏07 799 7222). Wherever you start from, decide in advance where you want to stay; express boats generally drop only at the major resorts of Genting, Paya, Tekek, Air

Batang and Salang (usually in that order). Only occasional express boats from Mersing head to Juara on the east coast. Note that there is a fee of RM5 to enter the island.
Leaving by boat Although Mersing travel agencies may try to sell you an open-return ticket to Tioman, tickets are readily available on the island. Most sailings back from Tioman are in the morning, but times change from day to day – check the schedule with your chalet-owner. If you need to catch a flight from the mainland, allow extra time as the boat services are not entirely reliable.

GETTING AROUND

On foot The best-connected stretch is on the west coast, between Tekek and Salang. A road runs from the *Berjaya* resort in the south, up through Tekek village and as far as the headland at the northern end of the bay, but it's an exposed and uninteresting walk – 30min from the village to the headland – so you're better off paying RM5 for an unlicensed taxi. Steps lead over the headland to *Sunset Corner* in Air Batang, from where a narrow concrete path runs the length of the beach, to the point where a jungle trail sets off to Penuba Bay, Monkey Beach and Salang. Other coastal trails

include one that connects Genting with Paya, while you can walk across the island from Tekek to Juara (see p.306).
By bicycle Since so much of the west coast is paved, bicycle rental is a sensible option, but remember you'll have to carry the bike over the headlands at some point. The road to Juara is only for the resilient. Outlets in Tekek and Air Batang offer dubious-quality bikes from RM5/hour, RM20/day.
By 4WD Only 4WD vehicles can safely drive the steep route between Tekek and Juara.

5

By boat Transport around the shore of the island via hired boats (known as water taxis) is very expensive by Malaysian standards, ranging from RM25 for the hop between ABC and Tekek up to RM150 between ABC and Juara. To save money you can join the Mersing ferry as it makes its scheduled stops, if there's room, for around RM10–15 per person.

Tekek

The main settlement on the island, **TEKEK**, doesn't make a great first impression. The area around the airport, marina and public jetty has been unappealingly developed, while coming from Air Batang you first pass a long stretch of deserted waterfront promenade. South of the marina, though, things start to get somewhat better. Not only are there a handful of good resorts, but the beach is also attractive and has a dive shop as well as one of the island's best bars. Further south still is the high-end *Berjaya* resort.

Marine Park Centre

North of the main jetty, at the very end of the bay • Mon–Thurs & Sat 9am–1pm & 2–5pm, Fri 9am–12.15pm & 2.45–5pm, Sun 9am–5pm • Free

The hefty concrete jetty and dazzlingly blue roofs of the government-sponsored **Marine Park Centre** make it hard to miss. Set up to protect the island's coral and marine life, and to patrol the fishing in its waters, the centre also contains an aquarium and displays about marine conservation.

ARRIVAL AND INFORMATION | TEKEK

By plane and boat Whether you fly or come by boat, you're close enough to walk to most of the resorts within Tekek, although the *Berjaya* is too far and offers a transfer. Services in and around the terminal complex next to the airstrip include an ATM, moneychangers, duty-free shops and an internet café.

Internet access Casa Rock, not far south of the airstrip (daily 9am–7pm & 8–11pm; RM8/hour).

ACCOMMODATION

Tekek holds some good **places to stay**. Backpackers should keep an eye open for the new dorms, linked to the unexceptional *Coral Reef* guesthouse, which were being built at the time of research.

Babura Seaview Resort Tekek ☎ 09 419 1139. A large and friendly complex with chalets and beachside rooms – some of the latter have hot showers, fridges and balconies. There's a good seafood restaurant overlooking the beach, plus a dive shop. Free wi-fi, though not in all rooms. Ask about discounts Nov to mid-Feb. Chalets RM60, beachfront rooms RM170

Berjaya Tioman Resort Just south of Tekek ☎ 09 419 1000, ⓦ berjayahotel.com. This village-sized complex has its own private beach, everything from double rooms to deluxe apartments, plus two pools, tennis courts, donkey riding, a large games room, watersports and a golf course. Occasional promotions offer good value. RM375

Cheers Tekek village ☎ 019 976 9285 or ☎ 013 931 1425, ⓔ cheersteo@yahoo.com. It may not be on the shore, but the surroundings are pleasant enough and the price is fair. Standard fan doubles aimed at backpackers, plus a/c rooms with hot showers. Free wi-fi, plus rental bikes. Open all year. Fan rooms RM50, a/c rooms RM120

★ **Swiss Cottage Beach Resort** Tekek ☎ 09 419 1642, ⓦ samudra-swiss-cottage.com. This family-run resort is probably the best all-round choice in Tekek, hidden away in a shady beachside spot. Well-maintained rooms include fan-cooled huts on the beach and a/c garden rooms. Rates include breakfast; no other meals are served aside from the occasional barbecue. Free wi-fi. Rooms RM85, a/c rooms RM110, huts RM130

EATING AND DRINKING

★ **Tioman Cabana** Tekek beach. On the best stretch of beach, this wooden structure is an archetypal beach bar – right down to the hammocks. It's a great place for a beer or two, and the food's pretty good too; if you like a challenge, order the mammoth Happy Eat Like Me Burger for RM35. Daily 1.30pm–midnight; food until 10.30pm.

Warong Syahirah Tekek village. The cook at this friendly and popular roadside place fires up the barbecue around 6pm, with chicken, crab, squid, stingray and barracuda all on the menu. Daily 4.30–10.30pm.

Air Batang (ABC)

Despite its ever-increasing popularity, **AIR BATANG**, 2km north of Tekek from jetty to jetty, retains a sleepy charm and rivals Juara (which admittedly has a better beach) in its appeal for budget travellers. Larger than Salang or Juara, less developed than Tekek and well connected by boat services, Air Batang (or ABC as it's often called), is a happy medium as far as many visitors are concerned. What development there is tends to be relatively low-key and there's still a definite sense of community.

A jetty divides the bay roughly in half; the beach is better at the southern end of the bay, where there are fewer rocks, though the shallow northern end is safer for children. The cement path that runs the length of the beach is interrupted by little wooden bridges over streams and overhung with greenery; stretches are unlit at night. Between the guesthouses, a few small shops sell essentials such as shorts, T-shirts, sun cream and toiletries. Like the guesthouses they also arrange snorkelling trips and boat taxis.

A fifteen-minute **trail** leads over the headland to the north. After an initial scramble, it flattens out into an easy walk and ends up at **Panuba Bay**, a secluded cove that holds just one resort and a quiet little beach, and offers some of the best snorkelling on the island. From Panuba Bay, it's an hour's walk to **Monkey Beach** and then a further 45 minutes to Salang. Heading south instead from ABC, steps lead over the headland to **Tekek**.

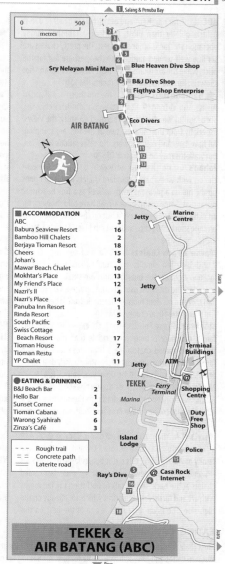

Salang & Penuba Bay

Sry Nelayan Mini Mart

Blue Heaven Dive Shop
B&J Dive Shop
Fiqthya Shop Enterprise

Eco Divers

AIR BATANG

Jetty — Marine Centre

Jetty

Juara

ACCOMMODATION	
ABC	3
Babura Seaview Resort	16
Bamboo Hill Chalets	2
Berjaya Tioman Resort	18
Cheers	15
Johan's	8
Mawar Beach Chalet	10
Mokhtar's Place	13
My Friend's Place	12
Nazri's II	4
Nazri's Place	14
Panuba Inn Resort	1
Rinda Resort	5
South Pacific	9
Swiss Cottage Beach Resort	17
Tioman House	7
Tioman Restu	6
YP Chalet	11

EATING & DRINKING	
B&J Beach Bar	2
Hello Bar	1
Sunset Corner	4
Tioman Cabana	5
Warong Syahirah	6
Zinza's Café	3

- - - Rough trail
= = Concrete path
═══ Laterite road

Jetty — ATM
Terminal Buildings

TEKEK Ferry Terminal
Marina
Shopping Centre

Duty Free Shop

Island Lodge

Police

Ray's Dive — Casa Rock Internet

TEKEK & AIR BATANG (ABC)

Paya

ACCOMMODATION

AIR BATANG

As you get off the boat, a helpful signpost indicates the numerous **places to stay** in the bay. All but the most basic A-frames have fans and their own bathrooms, and mosquito nets are usually provided. The pricier options should have hot showers. Some places charge significantly more at peak times, such as during school holidays; at the time of research several places were planning to add a/c to some of their rooms, and increase the price. **Internet** facilities are available at several guesthouses and in some of the small general stores, and a handful of places offer wi-fi. Many guesthouses rent out **bikes** (see p.301).

5

ABC At the far northern end of the bay ☎ 013 922 0263. A little quieter than most, this long-established family operation still ranks among the best. The pretty chalets are set in a well-tended garden; the cheapest are fair for the price, while the a/c rooms have great views, kettles and hot showers. Fan rooms RM50, a/c rooms RM150

★ **Bamboo Hill Chalets** On the northern headland of Air Batang ☎ 09 419 1339, ⓦ bamboohillchalets.com. Six beautiful wooden chalets perched on stilts; the views, especially from the cheapest two at the top, are stunning. All have fans and cold showers. No reservations Nov–Jan, but walk-ins are accepted. RM70

Johan's Just north of the jetty ☎ 09 419 1359. A decent choice, with well-spaced standard chalets and larger ones up the hill on a pleasant lawn, as well as a fine beachside restaurant. Some rooms have a/c, all have cold showers; for an extra RM10 you can have a hut on the waterfront. They arrange snorkelling trips and rent out bikes. Chalets RM60, a/c rooms RM90

Mawar Beach Chalets Just south of the jetty ☎ 016 732 5824. Ten simple, well-run chalets with a good location right on the beach; rooms are smallish but have verandas. The cheapest use fans. The service is very friendly and there's a resident monitor lizard; the café is decent too. Fan rooms RM40, a/c rooms RM130

Mokhtar's Place South of the jetty ☎ 09 419 1148. This family-run place is more comfortable than most, though the 14 fan-cooled chalets are a little close together and face inwards, rather than out to sea. Rooms include a single at RM25; wi-fi costs RM10/hr. Open year-round. RM30

My Friend's Place South of the jetty ☎ 019 789 0813. All the well-priced rooms packed into the site face into a straggly garden, and have fans and cold-water showers. RM30

Nazri's II At the northern end of Air Batang ☎ 09 419 1375, ✉ info@nazrisplace.com. Owned by the same family as *Nazri's Place*, this outfit boasts large a/c cottages – some with sea views – as well as some fan-cooled chalets at the back. There's talk of outfitting the fan rooms with a/c and further raising prices which are already on the high side. The *Hijau* restaurant is one of the best on this beach. Fan chalets RM100, a/c cottages RM150

★ **Nazri's Place** At the southern end of the bay ☎ 09 419 1329, ✉ info@nazrisplace.com. The nicest rooms on the beach, all a/c and located on its prime section. Even though there are quite a few, they're often booked up. Rates include breakfast. RM100

Panuba Inn Resort Panuba Bay ☎ 07 419 1424, ⓦ panubainn.com. Set on stilts, these chalets enjoy fantastic views out to sea. This is the only accommodation at Panuba Bay, so unless you scramble over the unlit headland you have to eat in the run-of-the-mill restaurant every night. They have a dive shop and internet café. A water taxi here costs RM6 during the day. RM55

Rinda Resort At the northern end of Air Batang ☎ 014 848 8751. A good spot in a neat, shaded setting; the simple en-suite huts are a good choice for long-term, cheap stays, with discounts for a month or more. You can even save a few ringgit by choosing a room without a fan. RM25

South Pacific Close to the jetty ☎ 09 419 1176. Clean chalets with attached bathrooms and mozzie nets; those right on the beach are good value. There are also a few modern chalets – among the best in Air Batang – with hot showers and a/c, plus a small café and laundry services. Strictly no alcohol. Standard chalets RM40, a/c chalets RM130

Tioman House Next door to Blue Heaven dive shop ☎ 019 704 5096. Well-maintained chalets with a/c, fridge and hot showers, plus the *Cik Yah* restaurant and internet access at RM10/hr. RM150

Tioman Restu North of the jetty ☎ 09 419 1184. Still known sometimes by its old name *Double Ace*, this friendly place offers rooms beside the main path, plus several more uphill in the Jungle View section. Some rooms have a/c and hot showers, but the RM50 weekend price hike is a little steep. Fan rooms RM80, a/c rooms RM150

YP Chalet South of the jetty ☎ 09 419 1018. Nine fan rooms and two with a/c, all simple and a little worn around the edges. Wi-fi RM10/day, computers RM10/hr. Fan rooms RM40, a/c rooms RM100

EATING, DRINKING AND NIGHTLIFE

Most chalets have their own **restaurants**, open to non-residents and generally unadventurous. The menus tend to reflect Western tastes and have fish as a staple feature. Air Batang keeps its **nightlife** fairly low-key, although there are several places to enjoy duty-free booze. Most have a happy hour, usually from around 5–7pm.

B&J Beach Bar Beside B&J dive shop. This place has beers, spirits and the occasional bottle of wine at good prices; the dive crew mostly hang out here. They give out tokens when you buy happy-hour drinks, so that you don't have to take them all at the same time. Daily from early evening–11pm.

Hello Bar At the northern end of Air Batang. A wooden shack on the shore just in front of *Nazri's II* resort, but not owned by the same people. Three beers cost RM12 during happy hour. Daily until late.

★ **Sunset Corner** At the southern end of the beach. This bar is indeed a great place to be around sunset, not least for its happy hour (three beers for RM10) or its frozen mojitos (RM13 at any time). The pizzas are surprisingly good too. Daily until late.

Zinza's Café Right by the jetty. It may be simple – and the food isn't anything out of the ordinary – but this café makes a handy place to have breakfast or a drink while you wait for the (often delayed) ferry back to the mainland. Daily 7am–4pm & 7.30–9.30pm.

Salang and Monkey Beach

Just over 4km north of Air Batang, **SALANG** is a smaller bay with a better beach at its southern end by the jetty. There has, however, been a lot of development, and every suitable inch of land has been built on. That does at least make for a vibrant atmosphere, and Salang is the only place on the island with significant **nightlife**.

The southern end of the beach is the more scenic, while swimming can be an ordeal at the northern end due to the sharp rocks and coral. Just off the southern headland a small island, Pulau Soyak, has a pretty reef for snorkelling. There are also several dive shops.

A rough trail takes you over the headland to the south for the 45-minute scramble to **Monkey Beach**. There are few monkeys around these days, but the well-hidden cove is more than adequate compensation. Walkers can carry on to **Panuba Bay** and **Air Batang**.

ACCOMMODATION   SALANG AND MONKEY BEACH

Ella's Place Northern end of the bay ☎09 419 5004. Named after the owner's daughter, this place makes a fine option; all chalets have cold showers. There's a batik classroom on the premises, and massage too (both open to non-guests). Breakfast and lunch served, but not included. Open all year. Fan doubles RM50, a/c triples RM120

Nora's Chalet Southern end of the beach ☎09 419 5003. A friendly family operation, where the simple chalets with fan and mosquito nets are good value and the two a/c rooms are a bargain. The whole place tends to book up quickly. Closed Nov–Jan. Chalets RM40, a/c rooms RM60

⭐ **Puteri Salang Inn** Set back at the southern end of the beach ☎07 799 3592 (Mersing) or ☎013 931 2953. Nice fan and a/c chalets – mostly A-frames – set in a carefully landscaped garden that's the most peaceful spot in Salang. Their water-taxi prices are very reasonable and the staff are helpful. Closed Nov–Jan. Fan rooms RM40, a/c rooms RM110

⭐ **Salang Hut** Far northern end of the bay ☎013 603 9961, ✉salanghut@gmail.com. Don't expect anything approaching luxury, but this place at the rocky end of the beach oozes character now that the site and huts alike have received an arty makeover thanks to a regular Dutch guest. No food is served. Open all year, extra RM10 at weekends. RM50

Salang Indah Towards the centre of the bay ☎09 419 5015. The largest outfit in Salang, popular with groups and tending to fill at weekends. Well-appointed chalets to suit every budget, from run-of-the-mill boxy rooms with fans to sea-facing family chalets with a/c and hot shower. Fan rooms RM50, chalets RM170

Salang Sayang Resort Southern end of the beach ☎09 419 5020, ✉salangsayang@hotmail.com. This resort has comfortable, hillside chalets and more expensive sea-facing ones. This is the best part of the beach, and you're definitely paying a premium for the location. Hillside chalets RM80, sea-facing chalets RM120

EATING, DRINKING AND NIGHTLIFE

Four-S Café North of the jetty. This bar backs up its extensive cocktail list – 60 drinks from A Day at the Beach to Zombie – with a few beers. If you just want a takeaway and surly service, try the misnamed *Ng Café* (which is a stall not a café) nearby. Daily 7pm–1am.

Salang Dreams Close to the jetty. The emphasis at this beachfront restaurant is on Malay cuisine such as *nasi goreng* (RM8) and seafood at around RM12/dish, although they also have pasta and burgers. It gets very busy, and you can sit either inside or on the beach. Daily lunch and dinner.

5

Juara

With Tioman's western shore now extensively developed, those eager for a budget hideaway often head for **JUARA**. The only east-coast settlement, it's a quiet and peaceful kampung with two excellent beaches – Juara Beach aka Barok Beach, where you arrive from Tekek, and Mentawak Beach just south. The sand is cleaner and less crowded than on the other side of the island, and Juara is altogether more laidback even than Air Batang.

The beaches here do, however, have a reputation for harbouring **sandflies** (see p.309), so take what precautions you can. The bay, facing out to the open sea, is also susceptible to bad weather. The constant sea breeze keeps the water choppy; it attracts **surfers** from November to March, with 3m-plus waves in February. The beach break is good for beginners, while more experienced surfers favour the point at the southern end of Mentawak.

A popular, clearly marked 45-minute walk leads from the south beach to a small waterfall with a big freshwater pond that's good for swimming. Someone from the *Beach Shack* will take you for RM15 per person.

Juara Turtle Project

Mentawak Beach • Tours daily at 11am & 4pm • Minimum donation RM10 • ☎017 704 8911, ⓦ juaraturtleproject.com

The southern beach is home to the **Juara Turtle Project**, whose work takes several forms. They collect eggs from the eastern beaches, then hatch and release turtles, and also campaign for greater protection, with a small visitor centre to raise awareness. Volunteers are welcome to get involved for a payment of RM120 per day, which includes accommodation and meals; they recommend a minimum of a week.

ARRIVAL AND DEPARTURE
JUARA

By road A road starting just before the *Berjaya Tioman Beach, Golf & Spa Resort* (see opposite) has given 4WD vehicles easy access to Juara, costing RM120/car or RM25–30 per person for four people for the half-hour journey (you may need to bargain hard). Regular cars will struggle with the steep roads, but it's theoretically possible by motorbike or mountain bike (don't undertake either lightly). Several guesthouses in Juara can arrange transport back to Tekek.

On foot You can also reach Juara on foot through the jungle. The steep trek from Tekek takes about 2hr 30min, not counting rest stops, and is not recommended if you have luggage. Don't walk the less appealing vehicle road, and carry plenty of water. Starting five minutes' walk from the airstrip as a concrete path, the trail soon becomes rocky, running uphill with intermittent sections of concrete steps. After an hour or so you reach the highest point, and the route then tapers off into a smooth, downhill path. Fifteen minutes on, you'll pass a waterfall where it's forbidden to bathe, since it supplies Tekek with water.

INFORMATION

Information desk An unofficial information desk by the jetty rents out bikes (RM30/day) and snorkelling equipment (RM10/day for mask and snorkel, RM7 for fins), and arranges boat tours from RM100.

ACCOMMODATION

Most of the **accommodation** is on the northern bay, within five minutes' walk of the jetty, and has attached **restaurants**. Book ahead in peak season.

★ **Beach Shack** Mentawak Beach ☎ 012 696 1093. If you're looking for a relaxed backpacker vibe, or are in Juara to surf (board rental RM60/day, lessons RM60/hr), make a beeline for this cosy family-run hangout on the southern bay. There are simple chalets on the beach, which the owners rake to keep sandflies at bay, plus some further back and a six-bed dorm. They also have a café with internet access and a book exchange; rent out kayaks; and arrange snorkelling, fishing or surfing trips. Dorms RM15, rooms RM45

Bushman's At the end of the northern bay ☎ 09 419 3109, ✉ matbushman@hotmail.com. With only five chalets (all with hot water, a couple with a/c), this is a friendly and easy-going option. There's internet access, and the restaurant serves delicious local food and great breakfast porridge. Open all year. Fan rooms RM50, a/c rooms RM80

Juara Beach Close to the jetty ☎ 09 419 3188. A good choice if you're looking for a/c and hot showers, plus activities such as snorkelling, rock climbing and a hike to a nearby waterfall. There's also an excellent Chinese restaurant. Don't pay extra for the deluxe rooms. Standard rooms RM100, deluxe rooms RM140

Mutiara Close to the jetty ☎ 09 419 3159. One of the biggest operations in Juara, with assorted rooms and prices; the a/c rooms are, though, a bit overpriced. There's a mini-market and they can arrange fishing trips. Open all year. Fan rooms RM50, a/c rooms RM130

Rainbow South of the jetty ☎ 019 912 6385, ✉ rainbow .chalets@ymail.com. Brightly painted, good-sized chalets all on the beach, with their own bathrooms and mosquito nets. They are planning upgrades but at the time of research all chalets had fans and cold showers. RM50

Riverview At the north end of the bay ☎ 09 419 3168, ⊕ riverview-tioman.com. A nice place, with a good common area, that's nevertheless a little pricey for A-frames with cold showers. The rooms back onto a river where you can spot monitor lizards and even snakes (the management insist there's no risk). No food served. RM100

Santai Bistro & Chalet Near the jetty ☎ 017 777 7200, ⊕ tiomansantaibistro.com. The first place you see when arriving by car from Tekek, this fairly new addition to the beach has a popular restaurant and eight a/c rooms (most with hot showers), decorated with more care than usual for Tioman. Rooms without sea view RM100

EATING AND DRINKING

Juara Coconuts Café North of the jetty. The café itself is upstairs in this shambolic wooden structure, making it a good place to relax and watch the sand and surf. There are also chairs and tables on the beach. Make new friends at the bar by adding to their collection of cigarette packets from around the world. Daily 5pm–1am or later.

South of Tekek

Few foreign tourists visit the western beaches south of Tekek, though they're popular with Singaporean and Malaysian holiday-makers, and tend to be busiest at the weekend and on holidays; the one exception is **Nipah**. There are also several **stand-alone resorts** south of Tekek, not connected to any village and reachable only by boat transfer.

Paya

Just 5km south of Tekek, the pristine stretch of beach in **PAYA** has been developed but still seems peaceful when compared to Genting a little further south. **Jungle walks** are worth exploring here, as the island's greenery is at its most lush. The thirty-minute trail north to Bunut ends up at a fantastic deserted beach. From here it's a hot 45-minute walk through the golf course to the *Berjaya Tioman Beach Resort* and a further half-hour to Tekek. You can also walk between Paya and Genting, a pretty thirty-minute route along a concrete **coastal path**.

Genting

Usually the first stop for boats from the mainland, **GENTING** has been very heavily developed, especially around its jetty. On the plus side there are several dive shops and the beach is usually very quiet during the week. Cheaper accommodation is concentrated at its better, southern end.

Nipah

There's no jetty, so access is by water taxi from Genting (RM25), or resort transfer from Air Batang (around RM60)

Located on the southwest coast, **NIPAH** is the closest you'll get to an idyllic yet affordable backpacker beach hideaway on the island. There is good **snorkelling** around

5

a nearby islet, and although there's no dive shop both places to stay can make arrangements (RM150 for two dives, plus RM85 equipment rental). They also offer kayak rental and jungle trekking. Don't turn up without a booking.

ACCOMMODATION   SOUTH OF TEKEK

★ **Bersatu Nipah** Nipah ☎07 797 0091, ✉bersatunipah_tioman@yahoo.com. All nine rooms in this friendly place are on the beach, in a single long building. Discounts for long-term stays, and during the monsoon. Standard rooms RM60, a/c rooms RM90

Damai Tioman Resort Genting ☎09 413 1442. Arrayed on the hillside, all rooms have a/c – the basic ones are a bit dated but good value. Open all year, rates include breakfast; there's a dive shop within the complex. Basic rooms RM80, standard rooms RM150

★ **Impiana Inn** Genting ☎09 419 7705. Popular with divers and it's easy to see why: the rooms here are the best in Genting, the common areas are well kept and there's even a small gym. Unusually there's also a dialysis machine on the premises (the owner is a doctor). In-room wi-fi, rates include breakfast. RM140

★ **Japamala Resort & Spa** On its own beach, south of Genting ☎07 419 6001, ⊛japamalaresorts.com. First-class luxury resort with impeccable service, stylish rooms and a fabulously peaceful setting. The spa treatments are of a high standard, as are meals in the two restaurants. If you can afford it, and want to treat yourself, then you're unlikely to be disappointed. RM680

Melina Beach Resort Between Paya and Genting ☎09 419 7080, ⊛tioman-melinabeach.com. On its own beach, but accessible on foot from both Paya and Genting – meaning more options for eating if you can tear yourself away from this very appealing resort. There's a good range of accommodation, from the cheapest garden-view rooms with bunks to suites overlooking the forest canopy. RM220

Minang Cove Standing alone on the southern end of the island ☎07 799 7372, ⊛minangcove.com.my. The rooms at this delightful resort are not the classiest around, but the location and service raise it well above the average. Excellent snorkelling, and they also arrange round-island trips. Half-board RM533

The Nipah Nipah ☎019 735 7853 or ☎07 797 1244, ⊛thenipah.com. Chalets facing the sea or river, plus very basic A-frames set in a garden; all are fan-cooled and built using reclaimed wood to reduce environmental impact. The resort opens only for regulars during the monsoon. A-frames RM50, chalets RM60

Paya Beach Resort The northern part of Paya bay ☎07 799 1432, ⊛payabeach.com. Paya's best accommodation, with comfortable chalets plus a restaurant, dive shop, swimming pool and spa. There's good snorkelling just in front of the resort, and staff can arrange excursions further afield. Rates include breakfast, wi-fi is available. RM100

Sun Beach Just north of the jetty, Genting ☎07 799 4918, ⊛sunbeachresort.com.my. A large enterprise with Genting's widest range of rooms and a balcony restaurant for package guests. Standard rooms are basically the same as deluxe, but without a TV. Wi-fi around reception. Fan-cooled budget rooms RM58, standard rooms RM98, deluxe rooms RM158

EATING AND DRINKING

Bar Rumah The northern end of the beach, Genting. A surprisingly good little beach bar, serving beer and cocktails from a shack on the main path. There are chairs, hammocks and even a table (with attached chairs) suspended from a palm tree. You can have food delivered from *Coral Beach Café* nearby. Daily 4pm–midnight or later.

Mukut

Lying in the shadow of granite outcrops, the ramshackle little fishing village of **MUKUT** is shrouded by dense forest. It's a peaceful and friendly spot to unwind, with a fine beach, though note that locals are unused to Western sunbathing habits and frown upon the open intake of alcohol.

One good reason to stay here is to hike up **Bukit Nenet Semukut**, whose twin peaks are known as the Dragons' Horns; guides can be arranged at *Tanjung Inn Adventure* (RM60 per person).

ACCOMMODATION   MUKUT

Tanjung Inn Adventure At the far western end of the cove ☎013 293 1619. Overlooking a small patch of beach, this place feels semi-abandoned unless a group of hikers is staying – but once you find manager Uncle Sam, you'll receive a warm welcome. The rooms are fine for the price. RM40

Tanoshi Resort Mukut ☎013 701 1919, ⍟tiomani slandresort.com. The closest thing to a fully-fledged resort in Mukut, offering full-board packages as well as B&B; they can also organize scuba diving. Closed Nov–Feb. Full-board 3D/2N RM368

The other Seribuat islands

Pulau Tioman may be the best known and most visited of the 64 volcanic islands in the **SERIBUAT ARCHIPELAGO**, but a handful of other accessible islands hold beaches and opportunities for seclusion that outstrip those of their larger rival. For archetypal azure waters and table-salt sand, three in particular stand out: **Pulau Besar**, **Pulau Sibu** and **Pulau Rawa**. There are, however, a few resorts on other islands; Pulau Aur, for example, is popular among Singapore-based scuba divers. The tourist office in Mersing can advise on the various options.

Pulau Besar

While long, narrow **PULAU BESAR**, which measures 4km by 1km, holds several resorts and sets of chalets, you're likely to have the place pretty much to yourself outside weekends and public holidays. The island is, however, a regular location for international productions of the *Expedition Robinson* TV programme – the inspiration for *Survivor* – and can therefore be booked out during filming times (usually June and July).

Pulau Rawa

The tiny island of **PULAU RAWA**, just 16km (a thirty-minute boat ride) from Mersing, holds a glorious stretch of fine, sugary-sanded beach. The only sure way to get there is by resort-owned speedboat, booked in advance, but if you're lucky then the Tioman-bound ferry might make a stop (on request).

Pulau Sibu

Closest to the mainland, **PULAU SIBU** is actually a cluster of four islands which are collectively the most popular after Tioman. Most resorts are on **Pulau Sibu Besar** which, although not as scenically interesting as some of its neighbours, does have butterflies and huge monitor lizards. The sand here is yellower and the current more turbulent than at some others; most of the coves have good offshore coral.

ARRIVAL AND DEPARTURE   THE OTHER SERIBUAT ISLANDS

Day-trips from Mersing Pure Value Travel and Tours, 7 Jalan Abu Bakar (☎07 799 6811, ⍟purevalue.com.my), charge RM80–100 per person (slow boat) or RM150 (fast boat) for a day-trip from Mersing; minimum six people.
By resort transfer Most people staying on the islands take a resort boat, included in their package, from Mersing

---

SANDFLIES

Sandflies can be a real problem on all of the Seribuat islands, including Pulau Tioman. These little pests, looking like tiny fruit flies with black bodies and white wings, suck blood and cause an extremely itchy lump, which may become a nasty blister if scratched. The effectiveness of various treatments and deterrents is much debated; the general feeling is that short of dousing yourself all over with insect repellent, covering up completely or hiding out in the sea all day long, there's not much you can do. You may find that Tiger Balm, available at any pharmacy, can reduce the maddening itch and help you sleep. If you are able to take them, antihistamines also provide some relief.

5

or a jetty nearby. Pulau Sibu, for example, is reached from Tanjung Leman, a tiny coastal village 30km south of Mersing.

By ferry Seafarest operates a ferry from Mersing to Pulau Besar (☎07 799 8990; daily at noon; RM35 each way).

ACCOMMODATION AND EATING

PULAU BESAR

At the time of research, Johor National Parks were building chalets and dorms on the island, which should prove more affordable than the resorts.

Aseania Island Resort In the middle of the bay, west-facing beach, Pulau Besar ☎07 797 0057, ⓦ saripacifica.com. Set on an appealing stretch of sand, with decent chalets, a swimming pool and notably good service – a great place to relax. All-inclusive packages also available. __RM230__

★ **Mirage Resort** Just south of the jetty, west-facing beach, Pulau Besar ☎07 799 2334, ⓦ mirage islandresort.com. This is a great choice for a combination of friendly service, well-appointed chalets and reasonable prices. Cheaper rooms are A-frames, but still clean and comfortable. Rates include breakfast; all-inclusive packages also available. __RM170__

PULAU RAWA

Rawa Safaris Island Resort West-facing beach, Pulau Rawa ☎07 799 1204, ⓦ rawasfr.com. The 70 wooden chalets at this resort are dated but equipped with a/c and hot showers, and there's kayaking, snorkelling and scuba

diving. All prices are full board including boat transfers, and decrease after the first night. __RM760__

PULAU SIBU

Except where noted, resorts operate on package deals, and the prices given are for two people for one night; subsequent nights may be cheaper. All resorts offer water-sports facilities; in some cases this includes a dive shop.

★ **Sea Gypsy Village Resort** East coast, Pulau Sibu Besar ☎019 753 4250, ⓦ siburesort.com. A well-run family resort with good diving, activities for kids, friendly staff and even a few great-value "backpacker" chalets. It's popular with Singapore-based expats, and bus transfers are available from Johor Bahru and Singapore. Backpacker chalet, room only __RM90__, regular chalet full-board __RM420__

Twin Beach Resort Straddling the small ridge in the centre of Pulau Sibu Besar ☎03 2300 2270, ⓦ twinbeach.com. This resort's name comes from its location, which allows it to have chalets on both sides of the island. The A-frames and pricier chalets are a little run-down, but it's the only place with views of both sunrise and sunset. __RM400__

Endau Rompin National Park

One of the few remaining areas of lowland tropical rainforest left in Peninsular Malaysia, the **ENDAU ROMPIN NATIONAL PARK** covers 870 square kilometres. Despite its rich **flora and fauna**, prized by conservationists, the area has only been adequately protected from logging since 1989. There's plenty on offer for nature lovers, from gentle **trekking** to more strenuous **mountain climbing** and **rafting**; for the moment, its trails remain refreshingly untrampled.

Surrounding the headwaters of the lengthy Sungai Endau, and sitting astride the Johor–Pahang state border, the region was shaped by volcanic eruptions more than 150 million years ago. The force of the explosions sent up huge clouds of ash, creating the quartz crystal ignimbrite that's still very much in evidence along the park's trails and rivers, its glassy shards glinting in the light. Endau Rompin's steeply sloped mountains level out into sandstone plateaus, and the park is watered by three **river systems** based around the main tributaries of Sungai Marong, Sungai Jasin and Sungai Endau, reaching out to the south and east.

Visiting the park

The **best time** to visit Endau Rompin is between March and October, while the paths are dry and the rivers calm. Take loose-fitting, lightweight cotton clothing that dries quickly – even in the dry season you're bound to get wet from crossing rivers – and helps to protect you from scratches and bites. Waterproofs will come in handy, and you'll need tons of insect repellent.

The park has three **entry points**: one from the west at Selai via Bekok (Johor), and two from the east, at Kuala Kinchin via Kuala Rompin (Pahang) and Kampung Peta via Kahang (Johor). The best is Kampung Peta, where more activities are available; the least interesting, Kuala Kinchin, is often used for one-night tours, not recommended as they don't give enough time to get into the jungle.

As it can be hard to arrange transport, most people come on a tour. Mersing (see p.297) is the best place to approach from the east; ask agents in KL for the western entry. Prices vary according to what you want to do, and the following prices (for the Kampung Peta entrance) are for guidance only: park entrance fee RM10, licensed guide RM180 per day, 4WD transport into the park RM350 per vehicle, chalet RM80 or dorm bed RM20.

ARRIVAL AND DEPARTURE   ENDAU ROMPIN NATIONAL PARK

Most visitors come on tours that include transport, but it is possible to visit under your own steam.

Kampung Peta Approaching from the south on the North–South Expressway, take the Ayer Hitam exit and continue straight through Kluang to Kahang (1hr from Mersing). Register and pay entry fees at the park office at Taman Kahang Baru, then continue 5km east, turn north at the park sign and follow logging tracks for 48km (2hr; passable in an ordinary car when dry, although a 4WD is better) until you reach the Visitor's Complex at Kampung Peta. From here, catch a boat (return trip RM140/boat, or RM25 per person – minimum five) to the base camp at Kuala Jasin.

Kuala Kinchin From Kuala Rompin in Pahang, a road runs through paddy fields 20km to Selandang; continue another 15km to Kuala Kinchin, on the park boundary. Although a 4WD is not required, there's no public transport; a taxi to the park entrance from Kuala Rompin costs RM120.

Selai Catch a train to Bekok from KL Sentral, then rent a 4WD to get to the park entrance. By road from the west, exit the North–South Expressway at Yong Peng and head for Chaah, Segamat (20min). After Chaah, follow signs for Bekok (15min) then Sungai Bantang (another 7km). Go past the Sungai Bantang turn-off and carry on for 20km, through an oil palm estate and past several re-settled Orang Asli villages.

INFORMATION

Kampung Peta Park office (daily 8am–5pm, registration ends 3pm; ☎07 788 2812).

Kuala Kinchin Contact Rompin Green World (gate open 9am–5pm; ☎013 707 1997).
Selai Visitor centre (daily 8am–5pm; ☎07 922 2875).

Sarawak

PROBOSCIS MONKEY, BAKO NATIONAL PARK

Sarawak

With its beguiling tribal cultures and jungled highlands, Sarawak would seem to epitomize what Borneo is all about. By far the largest state in Malaysia, it packs in a host of national parks which showcase everything from coastal swamp forest to vast cave systems, and help preserve some of the world's richest and most diverse ecosystems. There are numerous opportunities for short or extended treks both inside and outside these protected areas, and it's also possible to visit remote longhouse communities, some of which can only be reached by venturing far upriver.

Would that the reality were so blissfully perfect. For all its attractions, Sarawak encapsulates the bitter dichotomy between development and conservation more clearly than anywhere else in Malaysia. Many of its forests have been degraded by logging or cleared for oil palm, putting wildlife and the traditional lifestyles of tribal communities under severe pressure. The state government has repeatedly won electoral mandates for its policies, but critics complain it has opened up Sarawak's resources to corporate exploitation in a way that's at best not transparent and at worst mired in corruption. While much of this will have little practical impact for visitors, it's as well to be aware that the changes you will see throughout the state have a subtext in the ongoing struggle for Sarawak's soul (for more on which, see p.590).

The lie of the land is complex on many levels, not least **demographically**. Malays and Chinese each make up almost a quarter of Sarawak's two and a half million people, but indigenous tribal peoples account for nearly half that figure. They're sometimes subdivided under three broad headings, though it's nowadays much more common to refer to the tribes by name. The largest tribe by far, the **Iban**, constitute nearly thirty percent of Sarawak's population. They, along with the Muslim **Melanau** and other tribes, comprise the so-called **Sea Dyaks**, a slightly odd name given that these groups historically lived along river valleys. Then there are the **Land Dyaks**, who live up in the hills; chief among them are the **Bidayuh** of southwestern Sarawak, representing almost a tenth of the population. Finally, the **Orang Ulu** include disparate groups of the northern interior such as the **Berawan**, **Kenyah**, **Kelabit**, **Kayan** and the traditionally nomadic **Penan**. They're grouped together in that they live in the "ulu" or upriver regions of this part of the state.

While this cultural mosaic is a huge highlight of Sarawak, it would be a mistake to regard the state as some kind of ethnic menagerie full of exotically dressed peoples leading a rustic jungle lifestyle. Classic multi-doored **longhouses** do survive and can

CHILDREN IN FRONT OF AN IBAN LONGHOUSE

Highlights

❶ Kuching One of Malaysia's most endearingly chilled-out cities, with a pretty waterfront, reasonable museums and great food. **See p.321**

❷ Santubong Peninsula Lovely beaches hosting resort hotels and an impressive folk museum, all beneath the slopes of Gunung Santubong. **See p.336**

❸ Bako National Park This beautiful reserve has good trekking, sublime sea views and is home to quite a few proboscis monkeys. **See p.339**

❹ Iban longhouses at Batang Ai Traditional communities dot the rivers near the Kalimantan border in southwestern Sarawak. **See p.344**

❺ Niah National Park The superb caves here are both a natural wonder, easily explored on foot, and a workplace for men collecting edible swiftlet nests. **See p.369**

❻ Gunung Mulu National Park Simply Sarawak's top attraction, with astonishing caves and a popular three-day trek to see the shard-like Pinnacles **See p.374**

❼ The Kelabit Highlands Trek to remote communities dotted around this cool upland backwater. **See p.381**

HIGHLIGHTS ARE MARKED ON THE MAP ON PP.316–317

be superb places to visit, and some peoples still subsist semi-nomadically in the forest, but social and economic change, along with widespread conversion to **Christianity**, mean that the old ways are fast dying out. So while there's no shortage of indigenous people pursuing careers in Sarawak's cities, you'd be hard-pushed to find Orang Ulu aged under 50 still sporting, say, the once-prized distended earlobes that previous generations developed by wearing heavy earrings, and teenagers are

SOUTH CHINA SEA

P. Satang Kecil

Pandan Beach

Siar Beach
GUNUNG GADING NATIONAL PARK

Lundu

Sarawak Cultural Village

Damai Beach

Santubong

KUBAH NATIONAL PARK

Batu Kawah

Tondong

Fairy Cave/ Wind Cave

Bau

Semenggoh Orang-Utan Centre

INDONESIA

Gunung Santubong (810m)

KUCHING WETLANDS NATIONAL PARK

Buntal
Santubong River

BAKO NATIONAL PARK

Bako   Muara Tebas

Sungai Sarawak

KUCHING

Potteries

Kota Padawan

N

Kampung Benuk   Serian

Kampung Abang

Annah Rais   Tebedu

Gunung Penrissen (1325m)

Entikong

SOUTH CHINA SEA

0   10
kilometres

AROUND KUCHING

HIGHLIGHTS
1 Kuching
2 Santubong Peninsula
3 Bako National Park
4 Iban longhouses at Batang Ai
5 Niah National Park
6 Gunung Mulu National Park
7 The Kelabit Highlands

Kampung Tellian

Oya   Mukah

S. Oya   S. Mukah

Dalat

TANJUNG DATU NATIONAL PARK

Teluk Melano

Santubong Peninsula

BAKO NATIONAL PARK

Sibu

Bintangor

Sarikei   Kanowit   Batang Rajang

Sematan

Lundu

Buntal

KUCHING

Kabong   Song
Saratok
Pusa   S. Katibas

Rumah Tambi

Bau

Simunjan

Betong

BATANG AI NATIONAL PARK

G. Niut (1701m)

Serian

Kampung Sereliau
Sri Aman   S. Lupar

Nanga Serubah   Nanga Sumpa

S. Skrang   S. Engkari   Batang Ai
S. Lemanak

S.Ulu Ai   S. Kapu

SEE INSET MAP FOR DETAIL

Tebedu
Entikong

Pontianak

Lubok Antu   Batang Ai Dam

more likely to be downloading Western pop than playing folk instruments. There are fears, too, for the future of indigenous languages, as only Malay and English are used in much state-run education.

For visitors, the most popular attractions are concentrated at either end of the state. In the southwest, **Kuching**, the understated, attractive capital, makes a perfect base to explore the superb **Bako National Park**, with its wild shoreline of mangrove swamp and

hinterland of *kerangas* bush teeming with proboscis monkeys. The Kuching area also packs in lesser national parks, an **orang-utan** sanctuary and substantial **caves**. Although Sarawak is not noted for its **beaches**, there are beautiful ones in Bako and decent ones nearer Kuching at the family-friendly resorts of Santubong. A handful of longhouses are also worth visiting, notably east of Kuching at **Batang Ai**.

In terms of pulling power, Bako is exceeded only by **Gunung Mulu National Park** (just "Mulu" to locals) in the far northeast. Most tourists fly in, either making the short hop from nearby **Miri**, Sarawak's second city, or direct from Kuching, to trek to the park's limestone Pinnacles and see its extraordinary caves. Miri itself, though a bland affair that thrives on the proceeds of Sarawak's oil and gas industry, has good accommodation and is the hub for Twin Otter flights to interior settlements, most notably **Bario** and **Ba' Kelalan** in the **Kelabit Highlands**. Here, close to the Indonesian border, you can undertake extended treks through jungled and mountainous terrain, overnighting in Kelabit villages. Other Twin Otter flights head to settlements in the upper reaches of the **Baram** river system, from where it's possible to reach isolated **Penan villages** offering homestays and yet more treks. Another major draw, visitable on a day-trip from Miri, is **Niah National Park**, its extensive caves a site of major archeological significance as well as a centre for the harvesting of swiftlet nests and bat guano.

Visitors who overland between Kuching and Miri tend to breeze through central Sarawak, but the region is worth considering for the state's most accessible river journey – the popular route along the **Batang Rejang**. The boat ride, beginning at the city of **Sibu**, is its own reward for making it up to nondescript Rejang towns such as **Kapit** and **Belaga**, though it's possible to arrange longhouse trips from either. Also noteworthy in this region is **Bintulu**, a coastal oil town like Miri that's conveniently placed for the beachside forests of **Similajau National Park**.

Brief history

Cave-dwelling **hunter-gatherers** were living in Sarawak forty thousand years ago. Their isolation ended when the first trading boats arrived from Sumatra and Java around 3000 BC, exchanging cloth and pottery for jungle produce. By the thirteenth century Chinese merchants were dominant, bartering beads and porcelain with the coastal Melanau people for bezoar stones (from the gall bladders of monkeys) and birds' nests, both considered aphrodisiacs. In time, the traders were forced to deal with the rising power of the Malay sultans including the Sultan of Brunei. Meanwhile, Sarawak was attracting interest from Europe; the Dutch and English established short-lived trading posts near Kuching in the seventeenth century, to obtain pepper and other spices.

With the decline of the Brunei sultanate, civil war erupted early in the eighteenth century. Local rulers feuded, while piracy threatened to destroy what was left of the

---

SARAWAK PLACE NAMES

As you travel through Sarawak, you'll notice certain terms cropping up repeatedly in the names of places, longhouses and other features. You'll seldom encounter them elsewhere in Malaysia, so it pays to know what they mean:

Ulu From the Malay *hulu*, meaning "upriver"; when used before the name of a river, it indicates the region surrounding the headwaters of that river – for example, the Ulu Ai is the upriver part of the Ai River and its tributaries there

Batang "Trunk" or "strip"; used before a river name, it denotes that the river is the central member of a system of rivers

Long "Confluence"; used in town names in the same way as the Malay "Kuala"

Nanga "Longhouse" in Iban; many longhouses are named "Nanga" followed by the name of the river they are next to

Pa or **Pa'** In the Kelabit Highlands, denotes a village

Rumah "House" in Malay; some longhouses are named "Rumah" followed by the name of the headman (if there's a change of headman, the longhouse name follows suit)

trade in spices, animals and minerals. In addition, the indigenous groups' predilection for **head-hunting** had led to a number of deaths among the traders and the sultan's officials, and violent territorial confrontations between powerful tribes were increasing.

The White Rajahs

Just when matters were at their most explosive, the Englishman **James Brooke** took an interest in the area. A former soldier, he helped the Sultan of Brunei quell a rebellion by miners and, as a reward, demanded sovereignty over the area around Kuching. The weakened sultan had little choice but to relinquish control of the awkward territory and in 1841 James Brooke was installed as the first White Rajah of Sarawak. He had essentially created a new kingdom, not formally part of the British Empire.

Brooke built a network of small **forts** – many are now museums – to repel pirates or tribal warring parties. He also sent officials into the malarial swamps and mountainous interior to make contact with the Orang Ulu. But his administration was not without its troubles. In one incident his men killed dozens of marauding tribesmen, while in 1857 Hakka Chinese **gold miners**, based in Bau near Kuching, retaliated against his attempts to eliminate their trade in opium and suppress their secret societies. When they attacked Kuching, Brooke got away by the skin of his teeth. His nephew, **Charles Brooke**, assembled a massive force of warrior tribesmen and followed the miners; in the ensuing battle over a thousand Chinese were killed.

In 1863 Charles Brooke took over and continued to acquire territory from the Sultan of Brunei. River valleys were bought for a few thousand pounds, the local tribes either persuaded to enter into deals or crushed if they resisted. The sultan's territory had shrunk so much it was now surrounded on all three sides by Brooke's Sarawak, establishing the geographical boundaries that still define Brunei today.

Charles was succeeded by his son, **Vyner Brooke**, who consolidated his father's gains. However, the **Japanese occupation** of World War II effectively put an end to his control. Vyner escaped, but most of his officials were interned and some executed. Upon his return in 1946, he was compelled to cede Sarawak to the British government. The Brooke dynasty was effectively at an end, and a last link with its past was severed in 2011 when Vyner's nephew **Anthony Brooke**, his designated successor who had briefly run Sarawak before World War II while Vyner was in the UK, died.

To the present

With Malaysian independence in 1957, attempts were made to include Sarawak, Sabah and Brunei, but Brunei declined at the last minute to join the present-day **Federation of Malaysia**, inaugurated in 1963. Sarawak's inclusion was opposed by Indonesia, and the **Konfrontasi** broke out, with Indonesia arming communist guerrillas inside Sarawak. The insurgency continued for three years until Malaysian troops, aided by the British, put it down. To this day, many inhabitants of the interior remain displaced.

Since then, Sarawak has developed apace with the rest of Malaysia, though at some cost to the environment. Politically, the state today is closely identified with the policies of its veteran chief minister, **Taib Mahmud**, a Melanau, who has been in power for thirty years. The support of his PBB party and allied parties has helped prop up the ruling coalition in general elections, and the PBB is often viewed as a proxy for UMNO (Sarawak is the only state where Malaysia's main Malay party has no presence). There are signs of a backlash, however, brought on perhaps by the rising cost of living, economic disparity and allegations, from international environmental groups as well as Taib's opponents, that Sarawak's administration is tainted by corruption. The 2011 local elections saw an unprecedented swing to the opposition in the cities, though the PBB and allies still won through comfortably with the help of rural voters – despite their supposedly being at the sharp end of the government's liberal attitude to exploiting the state's natural resources.

6

GETTING TO SARAWAK

By plane It's easy enough to fly into Kuching, Miri, Bintulu or Sibu from the Peninsula, and there are also decent connections with Sabah, Brunei and Singapore; Malaysia Airlines, AirAsia, Firefly, MASwings and SilkAir provide a comprehensive service between them. There are also flights from Pontianak in Indonesian Kalimantan to Kuching, operated by MASwings. Note that Sarawak has its own immigration controls (see p.54), so you will be stamped in and out even if flying between here and the other states of Malaysia.

By boat There's a boat from Labuan island, off the Sabah coast, to Lawas.

By bus A handful of buses connect Bandar Seri Begawan and Miri, and Kota Kinabalu and Miri via Lawas. The only official border crossing between Kalimantan and Sarawak is at Entikong/Tebedu (daily roughly 6am–6pm), 100km south of Kuching by road; it's used by frequent buses plying between Pontianak and Kuching and all the way to Miri.

GETTING AROUND

Sarawak covers pretty much the same area as England or the state of Mississippi, but with much of the state wild and thinly populated, there's not that much ground to cover unless you wish to visit remote communities or the interior's national parks, such as Mulu. The key thing to bear in mind with public transport is that, as ever, it's essential to book at least a week in advance to travel around the time of a major festival, notably the two-day *gawai* harvest festival at the start of June, when huge numbers of indigenous people return to their original longhouses.

By plane Flying is a useful timesaver between Kuching and Miri, and to reach Mulu from either Kuching or Miri. However, the most memorable flights are on the tiny Twin Otter planes, serving the interior (see p.374).

By bus Numerous buses ply the trunk road between Kuching and Miri, though thanks to slow-moving trucks journeys take a little longer than distances might suggest. Buses operated by MTC (ⓦ www.mtcmiri.com), Biaramas/Bus Asia (no relation of AirAsia; ⓦ www.busasia.net) and Asia Star (Biaramas's luxury brand; ⓦ www.asiastar.my) are a cut above the rest in terms of comfort. Fares are reasonable – Kuching to Sibu, for example, costs RM50 one-way (7hr). Local bus services also radiate from the main cities, in daylight hours only.

By boat The only scheduled boat services you're likely to catch are those between Kuching and Sibu, and express boats along the Rejang River.

By taxi On some routes, buses are supplemented by *kereta sapu* (see p.31); any "taxis" mentioned in small towns here will usually be of this type). Useful in rural areas, such share taxi services are generally reliable though, of course, their operators are neither licensed nor insured. Prices are comparable to bus fares, except with 4WDs (see below).

By car Sarawak's road network is simplicity itself. Given that signage is adequate and drivers' behaviour a little less manic than in the Peninsula, renting a car is seriously worth considering. The state's one and only trunk road, part of the so-called Pan-Borneo Highway, runs between Kuching and Miri, via Sibu and Bintulu, and on into Brunei. It's a dual carriageway only as far east as the turning for Sri Aman, a 3hr drive from Kuching; beyond that it becomes little more than a two-lane country road. The coastal highway between Bintulu and Miri is also mostly a two-lane affair. Unlike its counterpart, it holds few facilities or settlements; if you intend to use it, fill up beforehand and set off in plenty of time to arrive before nightfall.

By longboat or 4WD Finally, in remote areas, you might need to charter a longboat for a river trip or a 4WD to gain access to the network of rough logging roads that have begun to supplant boat travel. As always in Malaysia, getting off the beaten track isn't cheap unless you're travelling in a small group. Chartering a longboat for a two-hour trip might cost RM200–250 for three passengers, assuming you can get hold of a boatman at all, while four passengers might pay the driver around RM200 to go 100km in a 4WD. Details are given in the text where relevant, but it's often more worthwhile to pay a tour operator to arrange things where possible.

Southwestern Sarawak

Visitors flying in from Peninsular Malaysia or Singapore are treated to a spellbinding view of muddy rivers snaking their way through the jungle beneath lush peaks. It not only just about sums up Borneo, but also sets the tone for what the southwest of Sarawak has in store. The area is home to several of Sarawak's national parks, notably **Bako**, with its proboscis monkeys and excellent trekking. It's also a good place to get a grounding in Borneo's tribal cultures, which you can do at the museums in the likeable state capital **Kuching**. Among other top draws are the orang-utans of the **Semenggoh Wildlife Rehabilitation Centre** and the **Sarawak Cultural Village**, a brilliant collection of tribal houses near the beaches of Damai. To see proper longhouses, though, head east to the edges of **Batang Ai National Park**, home to many Iban communities.

Kuching

KUCHING is the perfect gateway to Sarawak – and not just because it's the state's oldest, largest city. This is simply one of Malaysia's most charming and laidback cities, revelling in a picturesque setting on the Sarawak River, with Mount Santubong looming on the western horizon. Despite central high-rises, much of the recent development has been confined to the bland but burgeoning suburbs, and the historical core remains appealingly sleepy and human in scale, its colonial architecture redolent of a bygone era. Kuching's blend of contradictions – of commerce alongside a sedate pace of life, of fashionable cafés rubbing shoulders with old-fangled *kedai kopi*s – makes it an appealing place to chill out for several days while exploring such museums as the **Sarawak Museum**, showcasing the state's ethnological heritage, and making excursions out to the numerous national parks and other sights in the vicinity.

Most of Kuching lies on the south bank of the river, its core an easily walkable warren of crowded lanes. The area sandwiched between Jalan Courthouse to the west, Jalan Wayang to the east and Reservoir Park to the south, usually referred to as **old Kuching**, includes several colonial churches and administrative buildings. **Chinatown** occupies the same general area, incorporating what were once the main shopping streets of Main Bazaar, facing the river, and Carpenter Street, and Chinese businesses and restaurants also dominate Jalan Padungan to the east. The traditional **Malay district** is dominated by the domes of the **Masjid Negeri**, with several Malay kampungs north of the river too. The Chinese and Malays together make up nearly two-thirds of Kuching's population of just over 600,000, though there are also substantial communities of Bidayuh and Iban.

Brief history

When James Brooke came up the river in 1841, he arrived at a village known as Sarawak, on a small stream called Sungai Mata Kuching ("Cat's Eye"), adjoining the main river; he probably shortened the stream's name, which came to refer to the fast-expanding settlement. However, a much-repeated tale has it that the first rajah pointed to the village and asked its name. The locals, thinking Brooke was pointing to a cat, replied – reasonably enough – "kucing" ("cat"). Either way, only in 1872 did Charles Brooke officially change the settlement's name from Sarawak to Kuching.

Until the 1920s, the capital was largely confined to the south bank of the Sarawak River, stretching only from the Chinese heartland around Jalan Temple east of today's centre, to the Malay kampung around the mosque to the west. On the north bank, activity revolved around the fort and a few dozen houses reserved for British officials. It was the prewar **rubber boom** that financed the town's expansion, with tree-lined Jalan Padungan, running east from Chinatown, becoming one of its smartest streets. During World War II Kuching escaped relatively lightly, since Japanese bombing raids largely focused on destroying the oil wells in northern Sarawak.

In recent decades the city has sprawled south, but perhaps the most significant transformation in the centre has been the closure of port facilities and warehouses as new shipping terminals and industrial estates have been created downriver, to the northeast. Robbed of waterborne traffic, downtown's riverside was reinvented in the 1990s with partial success as a leafy, pedestrianized recreation area, its quaint panoramas spoiled only by the bizarre oversized hulk of the State Assembly building, completed in 2009 on the north bank.

The waterfront

Beginning along Jalan Gambier and continuing for just over a kilometre until it peters out close to the *Grand Margherita* hotel, Kuching's central **waterfront** is where most

6

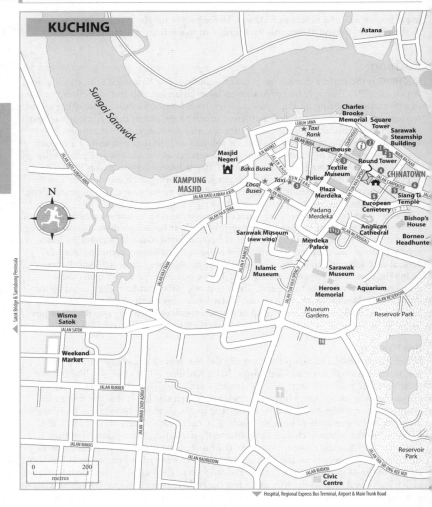

visitors begin exploring the city – almost everything of interest is within five hundred metres of this esplanade. Sporting the odd fountain and several dull food kiosks, it has a somewhat sanitized feel, but a sprinkling of whitewashed colonial buildings, tranquil river views and the shophouses of Main Bazaar and Jalan Gambier make for a worthwhile wander.

For views alone, the best time to turn up is around 6pm on a fine day, when you'll be treated within an hour to a fiery **sunset** behind Gunung Serapi (one of the peaks of Kubah National Park), casting an orange glow over city and river. To get an aerial view, head up to the cinema on the top floor of the nearby Medan Pelita building on Lebuh Temple, where a large balcony offers a fine vista over old Kuching. It's possible to do an expensive sunset river trip, marketed as the **Sarawak River Cruise** (daily at 5.30pm, from the jetty near the Sarawak Steamship Company building; 1hr 30min; RM60, children up to 12 RM30), but the views are little better than those seen from on dry land.

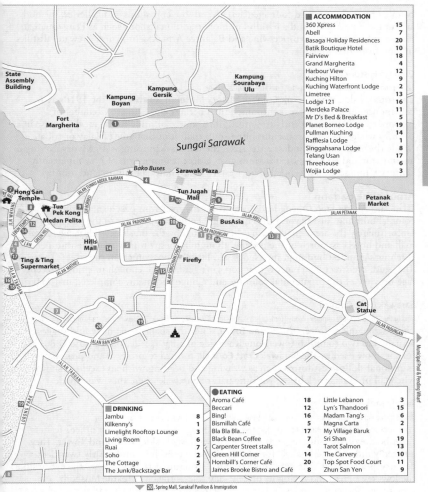

■ ACCOMMODATION	
360 Xpress	15
Abell	7
Basaga Holiday Residences	20
Batik Boutique Hotel	10
Fairview	18
Grand Margherita	4
Harbour View	12
Kuching Hilton	9
Kuching Waterfront Lodge	2
Limetree	13
Lodge 121	16
Merdeka Palace	11
Mr D's Bed & Breakfast	5
Planet Borneo Lodge	19
Pullman Kuching	14
Rafflesia Lodge	1
Singgahsana Lodge	8
Telang Usan	17
Threehouse	6
Wojia Lodge	3

■ DRINKING	
Jambu	8
Kilkenny's	1
Limelight Rooftop Lounge	3
Living Room	6
Ruai	7
Soho	2
The Cottage	5
The Junk/Backstage Bar	4

● EATING			
Aroma Café	18	Little Lebanon	3
Beccari	12	Lyn's Thandoori	15
Bing!	16	Madam Tang's	6
Bismillah Café	5	Magna Carta	2
Bla Bla Bla…	17	My Village Baruk	1
Black Bean Coffee	7	Sri Shan	19
Carpenter Street stalls	4	Tarot Salmon	13
Green Hill Corner	14	The Carvery	10
Hornbill's Corner Café	20	Top Spot Food Court	11
James Brooke Bistro and Café	8	Zhun San Yen	9

▼ 20, Spring Mall, Sarakraf Pavilion & Immigration

Along Main Bazaar

At the junction of Main Bazaar and Jalan Tun Haji Openg, the renovated **Old Courthouse** complex is the natural place to begin a wander, as it houses the helpful tourist office and a national parks booking office (see p.328). Built in 1874, and sporting impressive Romanesque columns, the complex is fronted by the **Charles Brooke Memorial**, a six-metre-high granite obelisk erected in 1924. Stone figures at its base represent the state's Chinese, Malay, Dayak and Orang Ulu communities.

Diagonally across, on the waterfront itself, the single-turreted **Square Tower** is all that's left of a fortress built in 1879. An earlier wooden construction burned during the 1857 gold-miners' rebellion. The trio of compact 1930s buildings next door, once belonging to the **Sarawak Steamship Company**, now house the so-called waterfront bazaar, a disappointing collection of souvenir outlets; you're better off checking out the touristy shophouses opposite on the fast-gentrifying **Main Bazaar**, now home to a couple of guesthouses and tour agencies, several souvenir shops and galleries, the odd attempt at a posh café, and a handful of more traditional shops such as Peng Guan at no. 90, which sells its own rice wine and Balantee Arrack, a brownish firewater distilled in Sibu from rice wine.

Chinese History Museum

Eastern end of Main Bazaar • Daily 9am–4.30pm • Free • ☎ 082 231520

6

The squat, pale orangey-pink **Chinese History Museum** was built in the 1910s as a courthouse for the Chinese community, then became the Chinese Chamber of Commerce. Slick and recently revamped, it's a source of pride to the local Chinese in a country where state-run museums often snub traditions that aren't Malay or tribal. While the artefacts are modest apart from the initial, depressingly large ivory carving of an emperor and empress, the museum gives a decent impression of how nineteenth-century Chinese migrants opened up western Sarawak to agriculture and mining.

Around the padang

Jalan Tun Abang Haji Openg leads away from the riverfront past a smattering of colonial buildings just beyond the courthouse complex and close to the padang. Unfortunately the area's character has been diluted by the brash new Plaza Merdeka mall and hotel just north of the padang, though it doesn't totally steal the thunder of Kuching's grandest building, the Neoclassical central **post office** on the street's east side. That said, the street is so narrow that you can't get far back enough to enjoy a decent face-on view of the ornamental columns and a huge pediment, completed in 1931.

Sarawak Craft Council

Next to the Old Courthouse complex • Mon–Fri roughly 8.30am–1pm & 2–4.30pm • Free • ⓦ sarawakhandicraft.com.my

Unlike the Square Tower, the **Round Tower** is not the shape its name would suggest – it actually has two roundish towers on either side of a flat facade. Built in the 1880s as a fort, it's now used by the **Sarawak Craft Council**, formed to preserve and promote traditional skills in art forms such as weaving and beading, with an excellent showroom where all products are labelled with the part of Sarawak where they were made.

Textile Museum

Beside the Round Tower, Jalan Tun Haji Openg • Daily 9am–4.30pm • Free • ⓦ www.museum.sarawak.gov.my

"A piece of New Orleans transplanted to Kuching" is how the tourist office's leaflets describe the ornate building with shuttered windows beside the Round Tower. They advisedly didn't say "literally", for it was originally built here in the early twentieth century as a hospital. The handsome restored structure certainly catches the eye, unlike the low-key signs announcing its present-day role as the city's **Textile Museum**, presenting Borneo costumes and artefacts across the centuries – headdresses, belts, traditional woven fabrics known as *pua kumbu*, alongside models of traditional Iban and Malay weddings. Worthwhile though the collection is, it's less well presented than the Iban weaving at the gallery of the Tun Jugah Foundation (see p.327).

St Thomas's Cathedral and the Bishop's House

On a hillock off the east side of Jalan Tun Haji Openg, the Anglican **St Thomas's Cathedral** is a tidy if plain 1950s edifice, one of a cluster of colonial churches and mission schools hereabouts. Only the vaguely mock-Tudor **Bishop's House**, built in 1849 and the oldest surviving building in the city, is worth a look; reach it by turning left off Jalan McDougall and walking uphill for a couple of minutes.

Chinatown

East of the Old Courthouse complex, a gaudy Chinese archway marks the entrance to the historical Chinese quarter via Carpenter Street (the name is still used rather than the Malay "Jalan Carpenter"), which becomes Jalan Ewe Hai at its eastern end. Truth be told, the district's Chinese flavour is somewhat diluted these days, but a few old-fashioned *kopitiams*, herbalists and snack shops still dot the shophouses of Carpenter Street and the tiny lanes running off it, and a handful of well-maintained temples merit a peek, the largest being **Tua Pek Kong** on Jalan Temple, at the district's eastern end. Tua Pek Kong, one explanation has it, is a sort of patron saint of Chinese communities in Southeast Asia; temples throughout Malaysia and Singapore bear his name. Raised behind a gaudy retaining wall, Kuching's version was built in the mid-eighteenth century, though a rather plastic restoration has left it slightly charmless; you may find the Siang Ti (Northern Deity) temple on Carpenter Street and the Hong San (Phoenix Hill) temple on Jalan Ewe Hai more atmospheric. Any of these temples may play host to theatrical or musical performances during festivals, especially Chinese New Year.

6

Sarawak Museum

Jalan Tun Abang Haji Openg, a little way southeast of the padang • Daily 9am–4.30pm, 1hr guided tour Fri 9.30am • Free • ☎ 082 244232, ⓦ www.museum.sarawak.gov.my

Set in lush grounds, the **Sarawak Museum** used to be regarded locally as one of the country's finest museums, thanks largely to its former curator, **Tom Harrisson** (1911–76). Best remembered for discovering a 39,000-year-old skull at Niah in 1957, which led to a reappraisal of the origins of early man in Southeast Asia, he also frequently visited tribal peoples to collect the artefacts that comprise the museum's biggest attraction. Sadly the museum has been resting on its laurels for too long, and funding for various ideas to rid it of its fusty, static feel has yet to materialize; the unexciting new wing southwest of the padang, linked to the original building by a long footbridge over Jalan Tun Abang Haji Openg, has not helped either.

Still, the museum certainly rewards at least an hour of exploration, and you can also take in a couple of minor attractions, notably the **Islamic Museum** and the **Art Museum**. There's also a tiny **aquarium** in the gardens behind the museum, and beyond it the **Heroes' Memorial**, commemorating the dead of World War II and the Konfrontasi.

The old wing

It was Charles Brooke who conceived the idea of a museum in Kuching, prompted by the nineteenth-century naturalist Alfred Russel Wallace, who spent two years in Sarawak in the 1850s. Wallace's specimens now dominate the fairly pedestrian displays on the ground floor of the old wing, which also houses even duller displays on Sarawak's oil industry, but the English Baroque building itself remains impressive: the largest colonial edifice in Kuching, it was built in the 1890s.

Most visitors linger in the **ethnographic** section upstairs, containing a huge model of a wooden Iban longhouse. You can climb up into the rafters of the *sadau* (loft), traditionally used to store bamboo fish baskets, ironwork and sleeping mats. There's also a Penan hut of bamboo and rattan, containing blowpipes and *parang*s (machetes), animal hides and coconut husks used as drinking vessels. Other exhibits include intricately glazed, sturdy Chinese ceramic jars, fearsome Iban war totems, and woodcarvings from the Kayan and Kenyah ethnic groups who live in the headwaters of the Rejang, Baram and Balui rivers. Wall cabinets showcase **musical instruments** used by various tribes, such as the Bidayuh's heavy gongs and the Kayan *sape*, a lute-like instrument.

The new wing

The modern and spacious new wing packs in a miscellany that ranges from unexciting Neolithic shards to the Brunei sultanate and World War II. The best exhibition shows how Chinese ceramics arrived through trade and wormed their way into the culture of the local Malays and tribal peoples, and includes some fine *celadon* jars.

6

SARAWAK'S CERAMIC JARS

The status and wealth of members of Sarawak's indigenous tribes depended on how many **ceramic jars** they possessed, and you can still see impressive models in longhouses as well as in the Sarawak Museum. Ranging from tiny, elegantly detailed bowls to much larger vessels, over a metre in height, the jars were used for such purposes as storage, brewing rice wine and making payments – dowries and fines for adultery and divorce settlements. The most valuable jars were only used for ceremonies like the Gawai Kenyalang (the rite of passage for a mature man of means, involving the recitation of stories by the longhouse bard), or for funerary purposes. When a member of the Kelabit people died, the corpse was packed into a jar in a foetal position to await rebirth from the jar, its "womb". The Berawan did the same, and as decomposition took place, the liquid from the body was drained through a bamboo pipe, leaving the individual's bones or clothing to be placed in a canister and hoisted onto an ossuary above the riverbank. It's said that the jars can also be used to foretell the future, and can summon spirits through the sounds they emit when struck.

Nearby museums

Just southwest of the Sarawak Museum's new wing, a former Malay college and religious school houses the **Islamic Museum** (daily 9am–4.30pm; free; ☎082 244232, ⓦwww.museum.sarawk.gov.my). Seven galleries in its cool, tiled interior hold unexpectedly fine examples of Islamic art and displays on architecture, coinage and textiles. Downhill from the old wing are the much smaller **Art Museum** (same hours and contact details), displaying modern work by local artists, and a building already labelled the **History Museum**, though whether it will officially assume this role is unclear; at the time of writing it housed a privately funded, ticketed exhibition of Chinese artefacts.

West of the centre

The pocket of town immediately west of the padang has a noticeably Islamic feel, with the golden-domed **Kuching Mosque** (Masjid Negeri; daily except Fri 9am–3pm) atop a hillock at its heart and nearby streets packed with Malay and Indian Muslim *kedai kopis*. The most colourful approach to the area is via **Jalan India**, named for the Indian coolies who arrived in the early twentieth century to work at Kuching's port; today it's a pedestrianized street packed with market stalls selling cheap shoes, clothing and household items. The mosque aside, the only specific sight is a popular **weekend market**, further southwest.

Weekend market

Off Jalan Satok, in backstreets south of Wisma Satok mall • Sat mid-afternoon until late, Sun early morning until noon • City Public Link buses #K5 and #K7 from Jalan Masjid bus park, or walk from the tourist office – head to the bus park (10min), then down Jalan Haji Taha and under the flyover at Jalan Kulas, turning right into Jalan Satok at the second flyover (15min)

Variously known as the **Sunday market** or night market, the market off Jalan Satok is not quite the spectacle it used to be – but for once, that's no bad thing. The bush meat trade of years gone by has been halted by better environmental enforcement; these days the most exotic thing you might see on sale are edible sago grubs, which live on thorny sago palms in the jungle. Otherwise, the market is certainly frenetic and features a good range of snacks as well as local vegetables such as the ubiquitous fern tops.

East of the centre

Downtown Kuching's commercial district, east of Chinatown, is home to most of the city's modern hotels, a handful of very ordinary shopping malls and several banks. The easiest way to get there is to follow Jalan Tunku Abdul Rahman, the continuation of Main Bazaar, east until it swings away from the river at the *Grand Margherita* hotel to join the area's other main thoroughfare, **Jalan Padungan**, which feels like a natural extension of Chinatown, its shophouses still home to several largely Chinese restaurants and *kopitiams*, though Western-style cafés and bars have made their presence felt too.

The archway by the major gyratory further east on Jalan Padungan's has a certain notoriety as the site of Kuching's original **cat statue**, a tacky 1.5-metre-high white-plaster effigy, paw raised in welcome. Though the location isn't at all prepossessing, the statue was regarded as a city icon for many years, so much so that more cat statues have since appeared elsewhere on Jalan Padugan and in other parts of town.

Tun Jugah Foundation gallery

Level 4, Tun Jugah mall, 18 Jalan Tunku Abdul Rahman • Mon–Fri 9am–noon & 1–4.30pm • ☎ 082 239 672, ⓦ www.tunjugahfoundation.org.my

The Tun Jugah Foundation is a charity set up to honour a long-serving Iban politician who died in 1981. Its excellent modern **gallery** showcases fine Iban weaving – three dozen examples of **pua kumbu** cloth, wall-mounted or framed in sliding panels. The geometrical patterns are fascinating but bafflingly abstract to the untrained eye, though once you read the labelling you might be able to make out the animal and other motifs. Most are in shades of reddish brown and black, the colour applied through *ikat* (tie-dying) with a base brown pigment traditionally made from the bark of the *engkudu* tree (*Morinda citrifolia*); vegetable indigos are added on top, yielding black in areas already dyed brown. The depth of colour depends on the type of yarn and the number of times it's dipped in the dyes.

In a large **teaching room**, the arts of weaving are passed on to a new generation of local women, not just Iban; you may be able to sit in on some classes or talk to the instructors or participants. An additional side gallery is devoted to **beads**, as used in the jewellery of the Iban and other tribes, and featuring examples in semiprecious stone and snazzy multicoloured glass.

The north bank

The leafy far side of the Sarawak River, views of which are the major part of the waterfront's appeal, is underwhelming once you get there – one of the two important colonial buildings here is largely closed to the public, and the shoreline is essentially dominated by the outlandish **State Assembly Building** (also called the DUN Building), a sort of giant espresso maker crossed with a spaceship that locals disdain as a huge waste of taxpayers' money. Still, it is worth crossing the water to look back at downtown Kuching and perhaps to wander through the Malay kampungs, though there's nothing specific to see. **Sampans** shuttle across the river all day and into the evening, leaving when full from various small jetties along the waterfront (RM1); ideally you should depart from the jetty more or less opposite where you want to go.

The Astana

Built by Charles Brooke in 1869, the **Astana** is still the official home of Sarawak's governor, a figurehead appointed by the supreme sultan. Set within grassy grounds on a low hill by the river, it affords good views of the courthouse on the opposite bank. Unfortunately you can only visit the Astana on the first day of the two-day Hari Raya Puasa holiday at the end of Ramadan.

Fort Margherita and the orchid garden

600m east of the Astana • Orchid Garden Tues–Sun 10am–6pm • Free

Dwarfed by the nearby State Assembly Building, **Fort Margherita** is one of the best examples of the Brookes' system of fortifications. Unfortunately, though, protracted talk of restoring it has come to nothing. You may be able to take a quick peek inside if you find an obliging caretaker, but otherwise it's better to take a rest in the nearby **orchid garden**, home to around one hundred orchid species.

6

The Malay kampungs

While quite a few Malay kampungs are visible on the north bank from downtown Kuching, those generally visited form a cluster of three villages east of Fort Margherita. The obvious target is **Kampung Boyan**, marked out by its new waterside food court with its twin-humped roof, though the mixture of traditional clapboard dwellings and more modern houses is not particularly atmospheric. Look out for the local cottage industry, the manufacture of multicoloured *kek lapis* (layer cake); street traders all along Main Bazaar hawk examples. If you come in the evening, consider dining at a fine Malay restaurant, *My Village Baruk* (see p.332).

ARRIVAL AND DEPARTURE   KUCHING

BY PLANE

KUCHING INTERNATIONAL AIRPORT

The airport (☎082 457373) is 12km south of the city. AirAsia, Malaysia Airlines and Firefly have ticket offices in the departure terminal. Firefly also has a downtown office on Jalan Song Thian Cheok, opposite the former Malaysia Airlines building.

Facilities There's a small Tourism Malaysia desk (generally daily 9am–10pm) in the baggage hall, though the tourist office in the courthouse complex is much better. The arrivals hall also holds car rental agencies, ATMs and a foreign exchange counter, while at least one booth sells coupons for the taxi ride into town (RM26).

Getting into town City Public Link's #K13 service heads infrequently to the town centre from the main road beyond the car park (approximately 7am, 10am, 1pm & 4pm; RM3), ending up at the Kuching mosque area, where most local buses terminate. The same service returns from here at 8am, 11am, 2pm & 5pm.

Destinations Bandar Seri Begawan (3 weekly; 1hr 15min); Bintulu (4 daily; 55min); Johor Bahru (3 daily; 1hr 20min); Kota Kinabalu (6 daily; 1hr 25min); Kuala Lumpur (frequent; 1hr 30min); Miri (at least 8 daily; 1hr); Mukah (3 daily; 1hr); Mulu (3 weekly; 1hr 30min); Sibu (7 daily; 40min); Singapore (3–4 daily; 1hr 20min).

BY BUS

If you're leaving by bus, and want to avoid trekking out to the bus station to buy a ticket in advance – advisable around the time of a festival – it's useful to travel with Biaramas/BusAsia, which has a ticket office just off Jalan Padungan.

REGIONAL EXPRESS BUS TERMINAL

Kuching's long-distance bus station is 6km from the centre, just off the main road south out of town; Biaramas/Bus Asia uses a separate bus park close to the main terminal.

Getting into town Taxi drivers may attempt to charge RM25 to take you to the city centre, and are unlikely to be bargained below RM20. To catch a bus, cross the main road and walk 5min west along any side road to reach the road taking northbound traffic into town, where you can flag down any bus.

Destinations Bintulu (1–3 hourly; 11hr); Miri (1–3 hourly; 15hr); Mukah (at least 2 daily; 9hr); Pontianak (Indonesia; 6 daily; 8hr); Sarikei (2–3 hourly; 5hr 30min); Sibu (2–3 hourly; 7hr); Sri Aman (4–5 daily; 3hr).

KUCHING SENTRAL

A vast new bus station, probably to be named Kuching Sentral, is under construction on Jalan Penrissen just west of the airport, and may be open by the time you read this; it should be served by local as well as intercity services.

BY BOAT

Ferries Express Bahagia (☎082 410076 or ☎016 8966235) operate passenger ferries to and from Sibu (1 daily at 8.30am via Sarikei; 4hr 30min; RM50), via Sarikei on the coast, using the Pending terminal 6km east of the centre. From here it's a half-hour walk out to the main road, where you can pick up City Public Link's #K1 bus to town (2 hourly).

INFORMATION

Visitors' Information Centre Excellent service operated by the state's tourism authority, in the Old Courthouse complex at the western edge of the waterfront (Mon–Fri 8am–5pm; ☎082 410944, ⓦ www.sarawaktourism.com).

Sarawak Forestry Corporation Next door to the information centre in the courthouse complex; takes bookings for accommodation at many national parks, though not Mulu (Mon–Fri 8am–5pm; ☎082 248088, ⓦ www.sarawakforestry.com).

Newspapers English-language newspapers such as the

Borneo Post, *New Sarawak Tribune* and *The Star* (which has a separate Sarawak edition) detail cultural and other happenings in town and around the state.

Guides Kuching is the ideal place to engage the services of a licensed guide through the Sarawak Tourist Guides Association (☎082 415 027). Guides are experienced, speak good English and have expert knowledge of such subjects as tribal customs or nature; they can also arrange visits – sometimes more cheaply than a tour agency – to longhouses, parks or other points of interest that are otherwise hard to reach or have few amenities. Prices, open of course to discussion, depend upon factors like whether overnight stays are required and whether the guide drives or arranges transport.

TOUR OPERATORS

Sarawak's tour operators come into their own for **longhouse stays**, typically around the Batang Ai area, and other trips off the beaten track – which could mean the less touristed national parks or a foray into an *ulu* area where local contacts are needed to ensure transport and accommodation. Don't expect packages to be cheap, though you won't pay through the nose either; many firms require a minimum number of people for bookings, and will not allow one or two travellers to join an existing party. A fair cross section of agencies are listed below, but the tourist office can suggest plenty more.

Borneo Adventure 55 Main Bazaar ☎082 245175, ⓦborneoadventure.com. Award-winning, pioneering operation, particularly good on longhouse stays – its jungle lodge at Nanga Sumpa (see p.347) is a fine example of best practice when it comes to Malaysian ecotourism. They also have a lodge at Mulu.

CPH Travel 70 Jalan Padungan ☎082 243708, ⓦcphtravel.com.my. Especially good on boat trips, for example to the mouth of the Santubong River to spot Irrawaddy dolphins (see p.337), though they also do longhouse tours.

Diethelm Travel Jalan Chan Chin Ann ☎082 412778, ⓦdiethelmtravel.com. A major chain offering tours all over Sarawak and indeed the whole country.

Kuching Caving ⓦkuchingcaving.com. Led by the knowledgeable and ebullient James Handfield-Jones, they will take you to explore little-visited limestone cave systems near Serian, southeast of Kuching. All you need is a reasonable level of fitness; gloves, helmets and helmet-mounted lamps are provided, while boots and other gear can be rented if they're not included. Two-day trips may feature accommodation in Bidayuh villages.

Planet Borneo Old Courthouse complex ☎082 241300, ⓦplanetborneotours.com. The Kuching branch of this established Miri adventure travel/diving specialist offers the usual longhouse stays at Batang Ai and further afield, plus Mulu packages and many off-the-beaten-track options in the north of Sarawak.

Rainforest Kayaking ☎082 240571, ⓦrainforest kayaking.com. Superb kayaking day-trips down a tributary of the Sarawak River, taking in a couple of Bidayuh villages and bizarrely shaped limestone hills. Packages start at RM200 including a riverside picnic and transfers; pricier trips can include a side visit, for example, to the Annah Rais longhouse.

GETTING AROUND

By city bus and minivan You're unlikely to use Kuching's city buses in the easily walkable downtown area, where bus stops offer practically no information or labelling. Also, while some services run two or three times per hour, many only go a few times a day, and local buses have in any case been in flux for years; ask at the tourist office for the latest schedules. All buses operate dawn–dusk only, and most start out from the area just east of the Kuching mosque, where cramped shared minivans – avoid if you value comfort – also shadow many bus routes.

By local bus Most bus services that start and end inside Kuching are run by Rapid Kuching (whose red vehicles bear logos like those of the London Underground) or City Public Link (largely green vehicles). Both firms, along with the Sarawak Transport Company (green and cream buses) and some minor operators, also provide handy services out into Kuching's hinterland; details are given in the relevant accounts. Journeys within town generally cost RM1–2.

By taxi There are taxi ranks near the mosque and in front of hotels along Jalan Tunku Abdul Rahman; alternatively, try Kuching Taxi (☎082 480000) or T&T (☎082 343343). Downtown journeys cost at least RM12.

By bike Borneo Bicycle Hire, on the ground floor of Tun Jugah Mall on Jalan Padungan, has bikes for RM33/day on weekdays (plus RM100 deposit), rising by RM5 at weekends and RM11 on public holidays.

By car Kuching Holidays (☎016 8828222 or ☎082 422955) has desks at the airport and at the Old Courthouse Complex; also at the airport are Khong Teck (☎082 574787), Flexi (☎082 452200), Hornbill (☎082 613369) and Hertz (☎082 450740).

ACCOMMODATION

Kuching's range of accommodation has got even broader thanks to a slew of new openings, so there's ample choice. **Guesthouses** are clustered in Chinatown and the area to the south, while most **hotels** are in the commercial district to the east. To stay at or near the beach, consider the Santubong Peninsula, half an hour's bus ride west (see p.338). As ever, book ahead to stay during a major festival; if you intend to be here over the weekend of July's Rainforest festival (see p.338), try to book a month ahead.

6

GUESTHOUSES AND B&BS

Fairview 6 Jalan Taman Budaya ☎082 240017, ⓦ thefairview.com.my. This family-run guesthouse – a rare thing in Kuching – is fraying slightly at the edges but hospitable and set amid the lushest of gardens. On the downside, traffic can be noisy and Jalan Reservoir, the shortest route to Chinatown, is badly lit and eerie at night. Assorted a/c, en-suite rooms, plus a fan dorm; prices fall by a third Sept–May. Dorms RM35, doubles RM90

Kuching Waterfront Lodge 15 Main Bazaar ☎082 231111, ⓦ kuchingwaterfrontlodge.com. They call themselves a "licensed hostel", but it's really a cosy B&B housed in a refurbished shophouse done out like a Chinese mansion. Rooms are less slick and occasionally a bit tatty, but all are en suite, with a/c and TV. RM115

★ **Lodge 121** Jalan Tabuan, near *Aroma Café* ☎082 428121, ⓦ lodge121.com. A touch slicker than most backpacker places, with a/c throughout and friendly staff. Rooms include doubles, triples and a ten-bed attic dorm. Dorms RM24, doubles RM38, en suite RM70

Mr D's Bed & Breakfast 26 Carpenter St ☎082 248852, ⓦ misterdbnb.com. The "D" is apparently short for drowsy, which you might often be at this competently run but unexciting place, with simple decor and plain wooden floors. Some rooms have a/c and/or a private shower, unusually. Fan dorms RM18, doubles RM55

Planet Borneo Lodge 10 Lorong Park ☎082 412100, ⓦ planetborneolodge.com. A 1960s luxury home, now a high-end lodge run by the eponymous tour operator. Three a/c dorms of various sizes plus two a/c en-suite family rooms, though no doubles. The best feature is the pleasant courtyard area with loungers and a paddling pool – a converted fishpond. Bike rental available, worthwhile as it's a 20min walk from Chinatown. Dorms RM60, 3-bed room RM210

Rafflesia Lodge 12 Main Bazaar ☎082 238541, ⓦ rafflesialodge.com. Functional sort of place squeezed into a long, narrow shophouse, with ten-bed fan dorms, a/c doubles and a family room. Dorms RM20, doubles RM50

★ **Singgahsana Lodge** 3 Lorong Temple ☎082 429277, ⓦ singgahsana.com. Behind the unprepossessing orange and yellow facade is a warren of rooms, all in bright colours, with a spacious central lounge featuring rattan lamps. Impeccably run and deservedly popular. Single or mixed 10-person dorms, plus doubles with and without bathrooms. Dorms RM300, doubles RM90, en suite RM100

Threehouse Lebuh China ☎082 423499, ⓦ threehousebnb.com. Run by noted Iban tattoo artist Ernesto Kalum and his Swedish partner, *Threehouse* impresses with well-maintained, cosy six-bed fan dorms and a/c doubles. Dorms RM17, doubles RM60

Wojia Lodge 17 Main Bazaar ☎082 251776, ⓦ wojialodge.com. The name means "my house" in Mandarin and the place does try to be homely, its spacious lounge featuring floor matting and a large sofa, though nothing is terribly fancy. An a/c dorm, plus single as well as double rooms, some with a/c. Dorms RM20, doubles RM45

HOTELS

360 Xpress Wisma Phoenix, Jalan Song Thian Cheok (lobby at the back of the building) ☎082 236060, ⓦ 360xpress.com.my. Part of a budget hotel chain, with bland, functional, keenly priced rooms – singles (which must be booked online) are half-price. Rates exclude breakfast. RM100

Abell 22 Jalan Tunku Abdul Rahman ☎082 239449, ⓦ abellhotel.com. Every floor is themed around a different colour at this business-oriented, modern hotel – and that would be its most exciting aspect, except that it's non-smoking throughout and they have a popular restaurant to delight hungry carnivores (see p.332). Most rooms are doubles of various kinds, though there are a handful of singles. RM160

Basaga Holiday Residences Jalan Tabuan, nearly 2km from the centre ☎082 417069, ⓦ basaga.com. Take one disused school built around a colonial mansion, apply a large dose of design expertise, and the result is the *Basaga* – a charming complex where you can only just tell the sleek rooms were once classrooms and dorms. Choose from rooms in the old house, or facing the swimming pool or the back garden (the latter have outdoor showers). The distance from town is a drag, but they have a convivial restaurant and bar with a central open-air dining area shaded by a great old tree. Rates include breakfast. Doubles RM170

★ **Batik Boutique Hotel** 38 Jalan Padungan ☎082 422845, ⓦ batikboutiquehotel.com. Kuching's only true boutique hotel has some of the classiest and cosiest rooms in town. Though not eye-poppingly stunning, all rooms boast silk bedding, an iPod dock and a terrazzo bath or overhead rain shower, and there's also a decent Japanese restaurant (see p.332), a small lobby bar and a courtyard jacuzzi. Rates include breakfast. RM250

Grand Margherita Jalan Tunku Abdul Rahman ☎082 423111, ⓦ grandmargherita.com. Swanky top-end affair, with Cantonese restaurant, river-facing pool and, unusually for this grade of hotel, free Internet in all rooms. Rates on Fri & Sat can fall by RM50 or so. RM320

Harbour View Lebuh Temple ☎082 274666, ⓦ harbourview.com.my. Popular with locals for its location and decent rates, but the rooms are often smallish and nothing to write home about. RM160

Kuching Hilton Jalan Tunku Abdul Rahman ☎082 223888, ⓦ kuching.hilton.com. As well organized as you'd expect a *Hilton* to be, with many newly refurbished rooms, a pool, mini-gym and plenty of restaurants. RM330

The Limetree Jalan Abell ☎082 414600, ⓦlimetreehotel.com.my. Occupying what was a failed office development, the *Limetree* boasts modern rooms, including some jumbo-sized executive suites, and a pleasant rooftop bar. As befits a hotel whose owners made a pile from citrus agriculture, it also features lime-based toiletries and lime-green fittings. Non-smoking throughout. Rates include breakfast. RM170

Merdeka Palace Jalan Tun Abang Haji Openg ☎082 258000, ⓦmerdekapalace.com. This pricey hotel overlooking the Padang boasts a pool, mini-gym and sauna, but it's the apartments, occupying the topmost floors and eminently suited to families, that offer the best value. Both rooms and apartments aren't much to look at, unlike the over-the-top marbled lobby, but great deals are often available if you book early online. Doubles RM220, two-bedroom apartments RM360

Pullman Kuching 1a Jalan Mathies ☎082 222888, ⓦpullmankuching.com. The interior of this huge new hotel, atop the hill behind Jalan Padungan, can't match the dazzling-white facade; the minimalist atrium looks more like a corporate headquarters than warm and welcoming. Still, there are great views from some rooms plus the usual top-end amenities, including swimming pool and restaurants, plus an hour's free internet use per day. Look for these bargain rates online. RM230

Telang Usan Off Jalan Ban Hock ☎082 415588, ⓦtelangusan.com. Now in its third decade, this pioneering hotel is Kayan-owned, hence the swirly Orang Ulu motifs in its decor. The rooms are dated but comfortable enough; on the downside, reaching the waterfront requires you to head south to Jalan Ban Hock and double back. Rates include breakfast. RM120

EATING AND DRINKING

Kuching's lively and dynamic **eating** scene offers opportunities to sample indigenous dishes as well as international cuisine. Popular local dishes include *manok pansoh* (or *ayam pansoh*), a Bidayuh/Iban dish of chicken and tapioca leaves stewed in bamboo tubes; *umai*, Sarawak's answer to sashimi, raw fish or prawn shreds mixed with chilli and lime juice; *ambal*, delicious rubbery little clams, usually curried; and, as greens, the ubiquitous fern tops *paku* and *midin*. And of course Sarawak has its own variants of common Malaysian dishes, notably *laksa* – the Sarawakian variety uses rice vermicelli and is usually served in the morning – and *kuay teow*, here often prepared in a tangy tomato gravy whereas elsewhere people add a little vinegar to get the same sourness. Many top-end restaurants close for several days over the gawai festival, when staff return to their "hometown" longhouses or jungle villages.

HAWKERS, FOOD COURTS AND KEDAI KOPIS

Bismillah Café Jalan Khoo Hung Yeang. This little Malay place does a good range of rice and noodle dishes, plus roti and curries – just the place to fill up before catching a bus from nearby to the many attractions in the Kuching area. Daily roughly 7.30am–7pm.

Carpenter Street stalls Opposite Siang Ti temple. A tiny, venerable clutch of stalls selling Sarawak *laksa* (from RM4) plus other popular favourites such as chicken rice and *kuey chap* (pork and pig offal in broth). As ever stalls keep their own time; don't expect to find *laksa* in the afternoon. Open early until at least 9.30pm.

Green Hill Corner Jalan Green Hill. This atmospheric old-fashioned *kopitiam* sells an excellent range of food – rojak, satay and curry rice, though they're most famous for their *mee sapi* (beef noodle) at RM4 a bowl. The most likely time to get beef noodles is in the evening but the seller is doing so well he keeps hours as he pleases. Open early to late.

★ **Top Spot Food Court** Jalan Padungan. Forget the unpromising location, atop a multistorey car park; this is a great place, featuring a dozen large stalls focusing on seafood. Sit near a stall you like the look of, and they'll present you with their menu; try *ambal*, or crab and prawns done with garlic or chilli, or *oh jian* – the Sarawak version of this oyster omelette is like an enormous bowl-shaped

crêpe. No pork served. Not super-pricey – one seafood dish plus veg and other things to share should cost RM30 per head, excluding alcohol. Generally 11am–2pm & 6–10pm; all stalls open in the evening.

CAFÉS

Bing! 84 Jalan Padungan. Kuching's plushest, slickest independent café chain, with prices to match – you'll pay at least RM16 for coffee and, say, a brownie. Free wi-fi. Mon–Thurs 10am–midnight & Fri–Sun 10am–1am.

Black Bean Coffee 87 Jalan Ewe Hai. This tiny café and shop serves locally grown coffee from the Bau area and parts of Indonesia, made using *robusta* and the little-known *liberica* beans – certainly worth a try, though some people find it sourish or even "burnt". A takeaway cappuccino blended from both types of bean costs around RM4. Daily except Sun 9am–6pm.

Magna Carta Old Courthouse complex. It's a tourist trap, the service can be lackadaisical and the food and drink merely so-so – but the airiness of the building, the antique fittings, the location and faintly colonial ambience largely compensate. Quench your thirst with coffees and teas (from RM7), smoothies (RM13), plus a limited range of alcoholic drinks, including *tuak*. A food menu includes light meals such as pasta and burgers (around RM15). Free wi-fi. Daily except Mon 11am–11pm.

6

RESTAURANTS

★ **Aroma Café** Jalan Tabuan ☎082 417163. This simple Bidayuh-run restaurant, on the ground floor of a dreary commercial block, is a fine place to sample tribal dishes such as *umai*, *ayam pansoh* and *midin* with garlic. Best value is the popular lunchtime *campur*-style spread (Mon–Fri 11.30am–1.30), but going à la carte is unlikely to cost more than RM15 per person with soft drinks. Daily 7am–11pm.

Beccari Merdeka Palace Hotel, Jalan Tun Abang Haji Openg ☎082 258000, ⑩merdekapalace.com. Smart, convivial and one of the few places in east Malaysia to get a decent – thin-crust – pizza straight from the wood oven and reasonably priced at around RM25. There's a salad bar at lunchtime, too. Daily noon–10.30pm.

Bla Bla Bla… 27 Jalan Tabuan ☎082 233944. Designer touches such as oriental water features set the tone at this fusion restaurant where you can savour Chinese-style renditions of un-Chinese ingredients such as salmon and lamb, and round off your meal with cheesecake. Their speciality is a tangy *midin* salad (RM12), but many main courses will set you back double that. Daily except Tues 6–11.30pm.

The Carvery Abell Hotel, 22 Jalan Tunku Abdul Rahman ☎082 239449, ⑩abellhotel.com. Much of the hotel's ground floor is taken up by this busy restaurant majoring on the Brazilian meatfest *churrasco*. Indulge in a protein-heavy buffet of nine (lunch; RM40) or fourteen (dinner; RM60) different grilled meats and steaks, plus salads and desserts, or simply order a steak – it'll be much cheaper and they'll cook it how you like it (the buffet is mostly medium to well done). Daily 11.30am–2pm & 6.30–10.30pm.

Hornbill's Corner Café Close to the Telang Usan hotel, off Jalan Ban Hock. Among the best-known places in town for steamboat – for RM18 per head you get unlimited helpings from their spread of seafood and other morsels, to be cooked by yourself at the table. Daily 5–11.30pm.

★ **Jambu** 32 Jalan Crookshank ☎082 235292. Housed in a sumptuously refurbished colonial house, half an hour's walk from the centre, *Jambu* combines Western and Malaysian elements and much else into "modern Borneo cuisine". Quite expensive – main courses start at RM30, though cheaper pasta and wrap options are available, and there are to-die-for desserts like Moroccan date tart. Daily except Mon 6–11pm.

James Brooke Bistro and Café Waterfront, near the Hilton. The biggest tourist trap in town, this open-sided building surrounded by greenery offers some nice views, even if the food – a mixture of Western and local standards such as Sarawak *laksa* – is nothing special and the prices on the high side (mains from RM20). Unusually for this class of restaurant, they don't take plastic. Daily 10.30am–11pm.

The Junk 80 Jalan Wayang ☎082 259450. You'll either love the junk-shop look of this bar-restaurant, serving Western cuisine, or find it just a tad too clever to be convincing, but it's hard not to be impressed with the generous portions of lamb shank, steak and other standards. Around RM30 for mains. Daily except Tues 6–11pm.

Little Lebanon Under the arches at the Old Courthouse complex (Jalan India end) ☎082 233523. The food can be ersatz, just like their Tutankhamun face-mask replica and curry-with-pitta options, optimistically intended to pull in the punters, but they do offer a good range of Levantine dishes, such as a falafel sandwich platter (RM12) and chicken kebab (RM16). There's also lots of shisha tobaccos to savour, and you can eat in an a/c dining room or (like the local youths) while lounging on divans outdoors. Mon–Fri 4pm–midnight, Sat & Sun 9am–midnight.

Lyn's Thandoori Jalan Song Thian Cheok ☎082 234934. This informal restaurant offers largely North Indian food with a few South Indian items thrown in for good measure. Tandoori chicken is the speciality (RM17). Otherwise, there's a wide choice of curries (from RM10) and *biriyanis* (from RM6) and, in the morning, roti and noodles. Mon–Sat 9am–10pm, Sun 5–10pm.

Madam Tang's Carpenter St. Smack in the middle of Chinatown, and part of a chain serving *kopitiam* food in unfussy modern surroundings, with no a/c. Enjoy Sarawak laksa (RM6) into the afternoon, plus *nasi lemak* and beef noodle, and that Chinese breakfast favourite, toast with *kaya* or soft-boiled eggs. Daily 8am–3.30pm.

★ **My Village Baruk** Kampung Boyan, down the lane from the jetty and then to the right. Here's that rare thing, an excellent Malay restaurant and in interesting surroundings too – a two-storey wooden building decorated with drapes and lanterns and meant to recall a *baruk*, or Bidayuh roundhouse. *Ayam penyet* – chicken tenderized by pummelling and then grilled – is the speciality, but they also grill mussels and fish, plus (off-menu) *ayam pansoh*, emptied gloopily from bamboo tubes, and *nasi goreng dabai*, rice fried with the locally grown olive-like *dabai* fruit, when available. Dance or music performances some Sundays, around 7pm & 9pm. Daily 5.30–11pm or so.

Sri Shan Jalan Ban Hock. Simple, dirt-cheap South Indian diner with *dosais* from just RM3. As usual, there's *nasi campur* featuring the likes of chicken korma or *rendang*, plus à la carte options such as chicken *biriyani* for RM10. Sun & Mon 7am–3pm, Wed–Sat 7am–10pm.

Tarot Salmon Batik Boutique Hotel, 38 Jalan Padungan ☎082 424837, ⑩batikboutiquehotel.com. This intimate little restaurant offers a sort of greatest hits of Japanese food – sashimi and sushi, *katsudon* (with chicken rather than pork), *okonomiyaki* (pancake) with salmon, and so forth, and does them more than passably. Wash down your meal with strength of tarot, their delicious non-alcoholic lime juice and mint concoction. Reckon on RM30 per head. Daily 11.30am–2.30pm & 6–10pm.

Zhun San Yen Jalan Chan Chin Ann. The best of a handful of Chinese vegetarian places in the area, with a plain glass frontage concealing cafeteria-like premises where you can choose from a spread of two dozen stir fries and soups (noodles dominate at breakfast). A meal with soft drinks seldom comes to more than RM10 per person. Mon–Sat 8am–2.30pm & 5–8.30pm.

DRINKING AND ENTERTAINMENT

Kuching's **drinking** scene is distinctly lacklustre and is dominated, with some welcome exceptions, by tacky karaoke bars. While most places serve the usual Western beers, wines and spirits, a handful, such as *Magna Carta* (see p.331) and a couple of venues below, have *tuak*. For a city with a sizeable middle class, the **entertainment** on offer is surprisingly meagre too. The Rainforest Festival is the highlight of the cultural year (see p.338), but otherwise a lack of performance venues means there's not that much on apart from the occasional *wayang* (Chinese opera) on or close to Carpenter Street during Chinese festivals, and some free events involving local performers on a riverside stage by the Square Tower, again at festival time – though there are a few cinemas (see p.334).

BARS

The Cottage Jalan Bukit Mata Kuching. Passable bar with Tiger, Kilkenny and Guinness on draft and, sometimes, local bands from 9pm at the weekend. Sun–Thurs 4pm–1am, Fri & Sat 4pm–2am.

Jambu 32 Jalan Crookshank ☎ 082 235292. If you don't come here to dine, it's worth making the trek out from the centre to enjoy the lovely garden bar and terrace. There's Tiger on draught plus Strongbow cider, *tuak* and even a *tuak mojito*. Tues–Fri & Sun 6pm–midnight, Sat 6pm–2am.

Junk/Backstage Bar 80 Jalan Wayang. The tiny *Junk* bar feels like an extension of the restaurant, whereas *Backstage* – right at the bar – has its own look, festooned with Chinese lanterns. Both draw in a suave clientele. There's draught Heineken and Hoegaarden, among other beers, but no happy hour. Sun–Fri 6pm–midnight, Sat 6pm–2am.

Kilkenny's Jalan Padungan. Probably the best bar on Jalan Padungan, with a relaxed pub-like atmosphere at its best and bottled Leffe and Hoegaarden as well as the usual draft Tiger and (of course) Kilkenny. Mon–Fri 5pm–late, Sat 5pm–1am.

Limelight Rooftop Lounge Limetree Hotel, Jalan Abell ☎ 082 414600, ⊛ limetreehotel.com.my. Relaxed, spacious bar frequented by business types, yuppies and a few tourists, with a large balcony offering views over Jalan Padungan and soccer on TV. Tiger and Heineken on draught, plus a range of bottled beers. Daily 5pm–midnight (Sat until 1am), happy hour until 9pm.

Living Room 84 Jalan Wayang. A chilled, ultramodern drinking haunt. Patrons can order food, too, from *Junk* or *Bla Bla Bla* on either side – all three venues are commercially linked. Daily except Tues 7pm–midnight.

★ **Ruai** Off Jalan Ban Hock. A simple but excellent Iban-run community chill-out joint featuring tribal decor, Iban, Bidayuh and Orang Ulu sounds (with a couple of live music sessions a month at weekends) and home-made *tuak* – not just regular rice wine but also varieties they've concocted from apple or dragonfruit. Daily 4pm–2am, with happy hour until 9pm.

Soho Jalan Padungan. Just across a lane from (and sharing ownership with) *Kilkenny's*, this two-storey bar has a DJ playing house and other sounds and tries its best to be a happening nightspot, with occasional success. Mon–Fri 5pm–late, Sat 5pm–1am.

SHOPPING

Although Kuching offers the best **shopping** in Sarawak, that's not always obvious from a stroll around downtown, which remains refreshingly devoid of huge modern malls – though the Plaza Merdeka development by the padang may prove to be an exception. There are certainly more souvenir shops than anywhere else in Sarawak; numerous interchangeable outlets along Main Bazaar sell tribal textiles, pottery, rattan mats, locally grown pepper and so forth. As ever, however, their handicrafts may well have been made abroad – especially in Indonesian Kalimantan. The listing here concentrates on places selling domestically made items, with the Sarawak Craft Council being the obvious place to start. If you're heading out to longhouses, you may prefer to defer buying crafts until you get there, though what you'll be offered will probably vary considerably in quality.

ARTS AND CRAFTS

Artrageously Ramsay Ong 94 Main Bazaar. This unusual shop sells paintings by two artists – Ramsey Ong himself, whose work tends to be abstract, and more naturalist art by Narong Duan. You'll also find examples of their craftwork – necklaces, cat statuettes, even phenomenally expensive beaded dresses. Mon–Sat 8.30am–5.30pm.

Ngee Tai Pottery Factory Eighth mile, Jalan Penrissen (the airport road). Kuching has a cottage industry producing

Chinese ceramics with tribal influences, and this is probably the best of the potteries, on the road out of town. Watch the potters in action at the wheel and firing kilns, and buy wares ranging from huge pots to small souvenir items such as coffee mugs and flower vases. Rapid Kuching bus #3a or #6, or STC bus #K3 or #K6. Daily 8am–6pm.

Sarawak Craft Council Round Tower, Jalan Tun Abang Haji Openg. Their shop showcases some of the best crafts made in the state, labelled by area of origin. Here you'll find the likes of beaded necklaces, hats made from breadfruit-tree bark and bags woven from *bemban* reeds, all costing several tens of ringgit, and the sun hats of the Orang Ulu, shaped like giant mushroom caps and sold for several hundred ringgit. Mon–Fri 8.30am–1pm & 2–4.30pm.

Sarakraf Pavilion 78 Jalan Tabuan. Locally produced crafts, a half-hour walk south of the centre, with a decent stock of baskets, woodcarvings, ceramics and other items, some made to their own designs. Mon–Sat 8am–5pm.

BOOKS

Mohamad Yahia & Sons Basement of the Sarawak Plaza, Jalan Tunku Abdul Rahman. A small range of specialist books about Borneo, plus maps; they also have a small branch at the *Grand Margherita Hotel*. Daily 10am–9pm.

Times The Bookshop Hills Mall, Jalan Bukit Mata Kuching. Easily the best bookshop downtown, this branch

of the well-established chain offers the usual wide range of English fiction and nonfiction, plus magazines. Daily 10am–10pm.

CAMPING GEAR

Greek's Outgear Discovery Second floor, Sarawak Plaza, Jalan Tunku Abdul Rahman. This oddly named store sells a range of high-end rucksacks, waterproofs, tents and so forth. Daily 10am–9pm.

MALLS AND SUPERMARKETS

Hills Mall Jalan Bukit Mata Kuching. Next to the *Pullman Hotel*, this was the one major new shopping development downtown at the time of writing, but is seriously punching under its weight despite a couple of designer outlets.

Riverside Shopping Complex Jalan Tunku Abdul Razak. Apart from a branch of the Parkson department store, there's little to recommend about this mall.

Spring Mall 3km from centre on Jalan Simpang Tiga (the extension of Jalan Tabuan). Kuching's biggest, busiest mall holds a Parkson department store plus plenty of outlets selling electronic gadgets, clothes, household items and so forth. Sarawak Transport Company bus #8G comes here every 45min during daylight hours.

Ting & Ting Jalan Tabuan. This well-established supermarket is a convenient place to buy bottled *tuak*. Closed Sun.

DIRECTORY

Banks and exchange There are numerous banks downtown, especially in the commercial area east of Chinatown, and you'll also find moneychangers in a few malls, such as Mohamad Yahia & Sons, the bookshop in the basement of the Sarawak Plaza.

Cinemas Mainstream English flicks are screened at the Star Cineplex, on the top floor of Medan Pelita, the multicoloured tower on Lebuh Temple; and at the Lotus Five Star Cineplex on the fourth floor of the Riverside Shopping Complex (next to the *Riverside Majestic Hotel* on Jalan Tunku Abdul Rahman).

IBAN TATTOOS

For the Iban, **tattooing** is not just a form of ornamentation, but also an indication of personal wealth and other achievements. Many designs are used, from a simple circular outline for the shoulder, chest or outer side of the wrists, to more elaborate motifs (highly stylized dogs, scorpions or crabs) for the inner and outer thigh. The two most important places for tattoos are the hand and the throat. The tattooing process starts with a carved design on a block of wood that's smeared with ink and pressed to the skin; the resulting outline is then punctured with needles dipped in dark ink, made from sugar-cane juice, water and soot. For the actual tattooing a hammer-like instrument with two or three needles protruding from its head is used. These are dipped in ink and the hammer is then placed against the skin and tapped repeatedly with a wooden block.

Kuching has become a magnet for people wanting to have a Bornean tattoo, and guesthouses may be able to introduce you to practitioners. The leading light of the scene, however, is the Iban artist and musician Ernesto Kalum, whose studio, Borneo Headhunter, is upstairs at 47 Jalan Wayang (make appointments two weeks in advance; ☎ 082 237062, ⓦ borneoheadhunter.com). He offers traditional motifs done either the traditional way or by machine (as in any Western tattoo parlour), and can also do modern designs (always by machine). Prices depend on size and complexity.

OPPOSITE BAKO NATIONAL PARK (P.339) >

Consulates Australia ☎082 233350; Indonesia ☎082 241734; UK ☎082 250950.

Cookery classes If you like Borneo food, consider doing the Bumbu cookery class at 57 Carpenter St (☎019 879 1050). They'll teach you how to do a few local indigenous dishes – for example one using chicken and another based on veg – and you get to eat the results afterwards. It costs RM120 per person (minimum class size is two), or RM150 if you opt for the additional market tour-cum-shopping trip.

Hospitals The main state-run hospital is the Sarawak General Hospital, 2km south of the centre off Jalan Tun Abang Haji Openg (☎082 276666). You can also try the private clinics at the Timberland Medical Centre on Jalan Rock (☎082 234466), not far from the long-distance bus station.

Internet All guesthouses and many cafés offer free wi-fi, which probably explains why Kuching is unique among Malaysian cities in having no downtown internet cafés.

Massage The Blind Health Massage Centre in the Timberland Medical Centre (see above) offers excellent massage from blind people at very reasonable prices (RM40 for 1hr; 10am–7pm).

Pharmacy Watson's, first floor, Sarawak Plaza; Guardian, basement of the Riverside Shopping Complex, Jalan Tunku Abdul Rahman.

Police At the start of Jalan Khoo Hun Yeang, by the padang (☎082 241222).

Post office The main post office is on Jalan Tun Haji Openg (Mon–Sat 8am–4.30pm); poste restante/general delivery can be collected here.

Swimming There's a municipal pool located where Jalan Padungan becomes Jalan Pending, 600m east of the original cat statue (Mon–Fri 2.30–9pm, Sat 6.45–8.45pm, Sun 9.30am–9pm but closed public holidays; ☎082 426915; RM3).

Visa extensions Immigration Office, first floor, Bangunan Sultan Iskandar, Jalan Simpang Tiga (Mon–Fri 8am–noon & 2–4.30pm; ☎082 245661). Get there by 3pm to have your application processed on the day; City Public Link bus #K8 heads here every 20min during the day.

Around Kuching

One joy of visiting Kuching is the sheer number of potential excursions within the vicinity, including several worthy of an overnight stay. Within an hour's bus ride north are the beaches and resorts of the **Santubong Peninsula**, also known as **Damai** after the beach area at its tip. Nearby is the **Sarawak Cultural Village**, a showpiece community where model longhouses are staffed by guides from each ethnic group. **Bako** is the essential national park to visit nearby, but there's also decent trekking at **Kubah National Park**.

South of Kuching, the main attractions are the orang-utans at the **Semenggoh Wildlife Rehabilitation Centre** and the Bidayuh longhouse at **Annah Rais**. Sarawak's remote western edge draws a trickle of visitors who mainly head to the **Gunung Gading National Park** to see *Rafflesia* blooms, though the beaches at **Sematan** and near **Lundu**, and the stunning **Tanjung Datu National Park**, further west, are also worthwhile.

Unless otherwise stated, all **buses** mentioned below are local services leaving from the area east of Kuching mosque.

The Santubong Peninsula and Damai

Privately operated shuttles leave from the *Grand Margherita* hotel for Damai and the Cultural Village (every 1–2hr; RM20 return), and some Kuching guesthouses can arrange transport for the same price; otherwise City Public Link bus #K15 (8 daily; 45min; RM4) goes to Buntal and Santubong villages, 4km short of Damai

Cut off from Kuching by the Santubong River to the south, the **Santubong Peninsula** has been inhabited since prehistoric times. Excavation in the 1960s and 1970s found tens of thousands of artefacts, including digging implements, across six neighbouring sites; they dated back to 3000 BC, when the Indian/Javanese Empire extended here, though little of any ancient civilization can be seen today.

Dominated by the 810-metre **Gunung Santubong**, the area is dotted with oddly shaped geological formations amid patches of thick forest. The mountain is actually a **national park** (though there are no facilities and no entrance fee to pay) and makes for a moderately taxing trek. It takes around four hours to reach the summit, with rope ladders to help where things get steep; one trail up is clearly signed next to the *Green Paradise Café* on the main road. However, most visitors prefer to venture out to the **beaches** of **Damai**, 35km from Kuching at the Peninsula's northwest tip, or the excellent if pricey

6

SPOTTING SANTUBONG WILDLIFE

The mouth of the Santubong River is a promising spot to see the rare **Irrawaddy dolphin**. With a rounded snout rather than a beak, these marine mammals live in brackish coastal waters and river deltas, as well as in fresh water further upriver – for example, along the Mekong in Indochina, where the population is dwindling. In fact the dolphin is considered vulnerable in many habitats due to human activity – they may get snared in nets or see their range whittled away by barrages, for example.

Several tour operators can take you on dolphin-spotting cruises (see p.329), though the specialist is CPH Travel, which has its own launch; their trips leave in the morning (3hr; RM140) with pick-up from your accommodation. CPH's related evening tour takes you along the Santubong River in search of proboscis monkeys and fireflies as well as dolphins (4hr; RM160). The odds of spotting dolphins aren't great during the rainy season if seas are rough; the rest of the time you have a fair chance of seeing them though not necessarily close up.

folk museum nearby, the **Sarawak Cultural Village**. Since the 1980s, stretches of the river and coastline have been developed as retreats for tourists and city-weary locals, though thankfully the resorts have left the tranquil, almost lonesome, nature of the area largely undisturbed. There are also two low-key villages, **Buntal** and **Kampung Santubong**.

Buntal

Travelling by public bus, you come to the first of two low-key villages, **BUNTAL**, half an hour out from Kuching's centre, having first crossed the impressive modern **bridge** over the Santubong River. A quiet riverside kampung, it's rated by locals for its **seafood**.

Kampung Santubong

Beyond Buntal, the bus returns to the main road, which runs north, then west and north again, curling around the peninsula's mountainous spine. The bus soon leaves the main road, continuing west down a side road for 1km to **KAMPUNG SANTUBONG**, a quiet village that's noteworthy for its one excellent place to stay, *Village House*.

Sarawak Cultural Village

3km north of Kampung Santubong • Daily 9am–5pm (cultural shows 11.30am & 4pm) • RM60 (children under 12 RM30) • ☎ 082 846411, Ⓦ scv.com.my

From the Kampung Santubong turning, the main road continues 4km north past several resorts, ending at the *Damai Puri Resort*. Not far from the end, the **Sarawak Cultural Village** features five authentically styled if rather too perfect tribal dwellings of timber and thatch, close to a central lake, with the jungle escarpment of Gunung Santubong looming dramatically behind. As folk museums go, it's worth the steep price of admission and doesn't feel forced; in fact many of the staff you see kitted out in traditional finery live on site, and the place has become a community in itself.

Arguably the most impressive dwelling is the massive **Orang Ulu longhouse**, raised almost impossibly high off the ground, though the Melanau "tall house" also grabs the eye, with windows on two levels. You'll also see Iban and Bidayuh longhouses, a refreshingly simple Penan lean-to shelter, and – mundane by comparison – a Chinese kampung house and a formal Malay house in a style that only someone of status could have afforded to build.

The twice-daily cultural shows are worth catching, striking the right balance between entertainment and education, and worthwhile demonstrations of activities such as weaving, sago-processing and blowpipe-making are staged throughout the day.

Damai beach

While the pleasant stretches of beige sand at **Damai** have individual names, such as Teluk Bandung and Teluk Penyuk, most people simply refer to the area as Damai

6

beach. The beaches don't belong to the resorts, though resort staff may levy a small fee if you try to access them via their compounds. One way to avoid this is to head to **Damai Central**, the new shopping development opposite the Cultural Village, from where a path leads down to the beach.

ACCOMMODATION   SANTUBONG PENINSULA

★ **Damai Beach Resort** Teluk Bandung beach, Damai, 3km beyond Santubong village ☎ 082 846200, ⓦ damaibeachresort.com. The rooms are mostly modern and not all that special, but the lovely freeform pool set back from the beach sets the tone beautifully at this huge complex, all the more homely for being one of the area's oldest resorts. Rooms near the reception and in the blocks stacked up on the lush hillside behind are cheaper, though you might feel like splashing out on a *baruk* suite, built to look like a Bidayuh roundhouse with a conical roof. There's also the obligatory spa plus a couple of restaurants and bars, and staff can organize guided jungle walks and other activities. Rates include breakfast . Rooms $\overline{RM250}$, suites $\overline{RM450}$

Damai Puri Resort Teluk Penyuk beach, Damai, 4km from Santubong village ☎ 082 846900, ⓦ damaipuriresort-kuching.com. Secluded at the end of the road, this newish place has a nice beach, along with a pool, gym and tennis courts, but can be overpriced unless you find a good deal online. Rates include breakfast. $\overline{RM270}$

Nanga Damai 2km from Santubong village, right of the road as you head north ☎ 019 887 1017, ⓦ nangadamai.com. Not a longhouse, as *nanga* might suggest, but a swish six-room B&B in a substantial, beautifully decorated modern house. Good value, with rates including breakfast. No under-14s. $\overline{RM100}$

Permai Rainforest Resort ☎ 082 846487, ⓦ permairainforest.com. The *Permai* is hard to find; cross the car park by the *Damai Puri Resort*'s front gate, then follow a boardwalk into the forest. You could come here to laze by the beach, but the emphasis is on being active – they offer kayaking, Santubong climbs and even an obstacle course. Guests stay in individual en-suite timber units, mostly sleeping up to six and good value if you're in a group of three or more. Only the two-person treehouse and some of the so-called cabins have a/c. Rates include breakfast but activities cost extra. $\overline{RM240}$, treehouse $\overline{RM270}$

★ **The Village House** Kampung Santubong, 30m down the track to the beach from Santubong crossroads ☎ 082 846166, ⓦ villagehouse.com.my. With the same owners as Kuching's *Singgahsana Lodge*, this gorgeous timber-built development features en-suite rooms set around a long, narrow swimming pool. Many rooms have four-poster beds, but otherwise the decor is elegant without being over the top. They also have two of the slickest six-bed dorms you'll ever see, each with its own bathroom. The restaurant serves Western, local and fusion food. No under-12s. Rates include breakfast. Dorms $\overline{RM88}$, doubles $\overline{RM250}$

EATING

If you don't want to eat where you're staying, your best bet is one of Buntal's celebrated **seafood restaurants**, mostly rustic affairs though all are reliable; your accommodation may be able to arrange transport. Stalls at Damai Central's food court are nothing out of the ordinary.

THE RAINFOREST MUSIC FESTIVAL

Since 1998, the Sarawak Culture Village has been home to the annual **Rainforest Music Festival** (day tickets RM110, three-day pass RM300; ⓦ rwmf.net), now usually held during the second weekend of July. It would be hard to find a more appropriate and evocative setting for a major world music event, with the Village's beautiful tribal homes not far from the stages and Gunung Santubong the perfect backdrop.

While the event attracts performers from across the globe, it's especially worthwhile for the opportunity to watch indigenous Bornean musicians – some of whom can seem decidedly exotic even to city-dwelling Sarawakian youth, never mind audiences from further afield. With some noted performers having died since the festival was first staged, the sense that many traditions are living on borrowed time makes the chance to glimpse *sape* players (pronounced *sup-ay*, the *sape* is the Orang Ulu lute, shaped like a longboat), gong ensembles, and the like that much more valuable (especially if you catch them in the intimate confines of a workshop). Favourites have included Tuku Kame, led by the flautist (and head of the Village's Heritage Resource Centre), Narawi Rashidi, and featuring charismatic electric *sape* player Jerry Kamit. Beds are hard to come by in Damai and Kuching over the period, so book accommodation early.

VISITING SARAWAK'S NATIONAL PARKS

Sarawak's two dozen or so **national parks** vary enormously, not just in terms of terrain and habitats – some boast accommodation for various budgets, well-marked trails and other amenities, while many others have nothing more than a ranger post and require a minor expedition to reach. All are managed by the state-owned Sarawak Forestry Corporation (ⓦ sarawakforestry.com) with the notable exception of Mulu, where tourist facilities have been privatized. You can pick up information about park conditions and accommodation at Sarawak Forestry's downtown offices in Kuching (see p.328) and Miri (see p.366). Informal accommodation bookings can be made by calling the park concerned, while the Kuching office can confirm reservations – with payment up front.

A park **permit** costs RM10, and an RM40 **pass** valid for five visits (or one visit by a group of five) is also available. Those park offices that exist are open between 8am and 5pm (sometimes with a 1–2pm lunch break), so aim to arrive during these times. **Guides** can be engaged at just a few parks for around RM80 per day, though they may well not speak good English. Contact knowledgeable, licensed guides for parks in the Kuching area through the Tourist Guide Association (see p.328).

Bako National Park

RM10 • ☎ 082 478011, ⓦ sarawakforestry.com

East of the Santubong Peninsula, and no further away from Kuching, a second peninsula is occupied by the fabulous **BAKO NATIONAL PARK**, named for its location at the mouth of the Bako River. Sarawak's oldest national park (once a timber reserve, it attained its present, fully protected status in 1957), it's also among its most memorable. Its steep coastal cliffs, offering huge vistas over the South China Sea, are thrillingly different from the rest of the predominantly flat and muddy Sarawak coastline, and there are opportunities to spot proboscis monkeys, swim in jungle streams or at isolated sandy coves, and hike through terrain that takes in rainforest, mangrove and *kerangas* (see below), with pitcher plants easily visible on some trails.

Bako is such a gem that trying to pack it all into one day is not ideal, though you can make a go of it if you set out early from Kuching and pay a boatman at the park to take you out to a remote beach, then walk back to the park headquarters; this gives you a good taste of the park without having to do a trek in both directions. A stay of at least one night is still preferable, though, and there's a range of accommodation to choose from, some newly built.

Inside the park

First impressions of Bako, of coastal forest and craggy outcrops visible from out at sea as you head there by boat, don't begin to do justice to its riches. The park boasts a multitude of different types of **vegetation**, including peat bog, scrub and mangrove; most trails run through a mixture of primary dipterocarp forest and *kerangas*, an Iban term referring to soil too poor to support rice, and now used to mean a type of woodland on poor soil characterized by fairly sparse, small trees and scrub, plus insect-eating plants such as pitcher plants. The *kerangas* stems from the unusual, largely infertile **sandstone** geology of the peninsula, eroded down to produce striking honeycomb weathering on some trails, and contorted rock arches rising from the sea. As for fauna, proboscis monkeys are obviously top of most visitors' lists; there's a good chance of seeing them not far from the park headquarters itself, though silverleaf monkeys tend to be harder to spot. Less exotically, monitor lizards and assorted snakes are sometimes seen, along with bearded pigs (a group have even made themselves at home close to the park cafeteria) and the usual assortment of creepy-crawlies, best spotted on a guided night walk.

No special equipment is needed, but pay particular attention to sun protection – it's amazing how you can be walking through a jungle glade one minute and in baking hot *kerangas* the next.

6

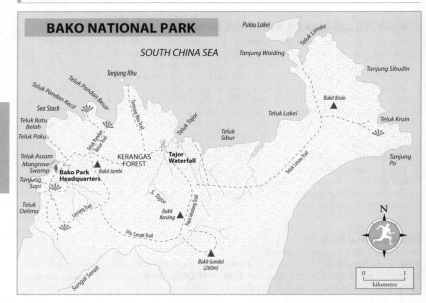

The trails

A free map from the park headquarters shows the **trails**, colour-coded and waymarked with splashes of paint on trees and rocks. Park staff can advise on what you can expect to complete in the time you have available, or whether to take a boat ride as a short cut (see opposite).

Most trails start from a spot north of the park headquarters, back towards the jetty and reached by a series of boardwalks through mangrove. You then ascend through steepish jungle, with the option of branching off left early on to **Teluk Paku**, a small, not particularly attractive cove where proboscis monkeys are often seen. Most people carry on, to reach the **Padang** about 45 minutes from the start – here not a grassy colonial town square, but a rocky plateau of *kerangas* that's another hangout for proboscis monkeys.

At the Padang you're on the park's most popular trail, the looping **Lintang** trail that leads alternately through jungled slopes and *kerangas* via occasional stretches of boardwalk, and returns to the park headquarters from the south. Taking around four hours to complete if you don't pause frequently to rest or take photos, it can get monotonous after a while.

You may find it more interesting to branch off the Lintang trail at a clearly marked point only a few minutes' walk along the Padang. This two-hour side trail heads east to the **Tajor Waterfall**; a couple of low cascades in a jungled stream, the waterfall itself is no great shakes, but the pool just down from it is good for a swim. From here you can return to the headquarters the way you came, or continue east and south along a much bigger loop, the **Ulu Serait trail**, and returning along the southern part of the Lintang trail; allow at least six hours to do this.

Even more worthwhile may be to branch off the Tajor trail at another signed side trail, less than a quarter of the way towards the falls, which leads north towards two beautiful **beaches**, Teluk Pandan Kecil and Teluk Pandan Besar. Curiously, semi-dry stream beds seem to serve as the trail in some sections, eventually bringing you to viewpoints with superb views of the beaches and the South China Sea. The Pandan

Kecil viewpoint also features bizarre hexagonal sandstone formations in the ground, where iron-rich rock has eroded less than the surrounding material. The steep descent to Pandan Kecil (15min) is rewarded with a swim at a secluded cove with whitish sand; unfortunately no path leads down to Pandan Besar.

Other possible treks include heading to the remote Teluk Limau or Teluk Kruin beaches at the park's eastern end, taking at least eight hours (you'll probably want to travel one-way by boat), or hikes off the main trails up to hills such as Bukit Gondol (260m) for great views.

6

ARRIVAL AND DEPARTURE
BAKO NATIONAL PARK

By bus and boat Reaching the park is straightforward: Rapid Kuching's bus #1 heads east to Bako village roughly hourly from Jalan Khoo Hun Yeang, close to the Kuching mosque (1hr; RM3.50). It stops en route at the Old Courthouse complex and along Jalan Tunku Abdul Rahman, though given the lack of signage at bus stops, be sure to ask other commuters if the bus will call where you hope to flag it down. At the Bako boat terminal, where the bus terminates, you can buy your national park permit (RM10) and board a park-bound boat (25min; RM47 for five passengers). They leave when full; individuals and smaller groups can travel together to make up the numbers.

INFORMATION

Park HQ Just a few minutes' walk from the jetty, where you can pick up a simple park map, hire a guide (RM80/day for up to eight people) or book to go on a guided night walk (at 8pm; 1hr 30min; RM20), which takes you south along the Lintang trail to spot insects, spiders and, with luck, nocturnal mammals and birds.

Information Centre Close to the Park HQ, the excellent information centre holds displays on the park's geology and history, and plenty of photographs to help you get a handle on the plants and animals you may see on the trails.

GETTING AROUND

By boat Saving time by using a boat to reach one of Bako's beaches is well worth considering; park staff can give an idea of the going rate, though you'll still have to negotiate with the boatmen at the jetty once you've signed in at the headquarters. The longest journey possible, out to Teluk Kruin, costs around RM250 one-way for a group of five, but you're more likely to make the short hop to a popular beach such as Teluk Paku (RM18) or Teluk Pandan Kecil (RM36).

ACCOMMODATION

Bako National Park accommodation ☎ 082 478011, ⓦ sarawakforestry.com. The park's accommodations include a campsite; a slightly scruffy hostel with four-bed dorms; forest lodges, also a little worn, where the three-bedded rooms share facilities; and en-suite doubles. Best of all are the gleaming new chalets, with two bedrooms that sleep up to seven. As at Malaysian hotels, the park office may not allow you to check in until 2pm. If you arrive earlier, carry whatever you need for the trails (including drinking water and swimming gear) in a day pack, and leave your luggage at the park office. Camping RM5, dorms RM16, lodge rooms RM105, en-suite doubles RM53, chalets RM225

EATING

Park cafeteria In one of the park's breezy new buildings. This self-service **cafeteria** is the only place to eat in the park; it's much cheaper to buy provisions in town before you arrive. It does *nasi campur* and a limited range of other dishes and breakfasts at inflated prices (RM15–20 for a main meal), plus bottled water and snacks for the trails. Note that the outdoor tables at the front can be the target of intrepid macaques, who snatch food and drink off plates at lightning speed. Daily 7.30am–10pm.

Kubah National Park
☎ 082 845033, ⓦ sarawakforestry.com • City Public Link bus #21 (every 3hr – check timetable with the tourist office; 30min; RM3.50)

Some 20km west of Kuching, **Kubah National Park** is a rainforest reserve considered one of the world's richest sites for **palm** species: of the 95 types found, including coconut, sago and many rattans, eighteen are endemic to the region.

Three modest peaks, **Selang**, **Sendok** and **Serapi**, emerge out of the lush forest; they're crisscrossed by trails, waterfalls and streams. Marked hikes include the three-hour **Ulu Raya Trail**, a good walk to catch sight of the palms, and the **Waterfall Trail**, a

6

ninety-minute uphill hike to impressive, split-level falls. Kubah's best views, however, come on the three-hour **Gunung Serapi (Summit) Trail** – from the top of the peak, you can take in Kuching and much of southwestern Sarawak.

ACCOMMODATION AND EATING   KUBAH NATIONAL PARK

Kubah National Park accommodation ☎082 845033, ⓦsarawakforestry.com. The park offers accommodation in either a hostel or a two-bedroom lodge.

There's no canteen, or anywhere to eat nearby, but guests cook their own supplies. Dorms RM15, standard lodge RM150, en-suite lodge RM250

Semenggoh Wildlife Rehabilitation Centre

Off Sarawak's main trunk road, 25km south of Kuching • Feeding times daily 9am & 3pm • RM3 • ☎082 442180 • City Public Link bus #K6 and Sarawak Transport Company bus #6 (6 daily combined; 45min; RM3) will drop you close by on the main road, a 1.5km walk from the centre along an undulating access road

The first forest reserve in the state, the **Semenggoh Wildlife Rehabilitation Centre** was set aside by Vyner Brooke in 1920. Today it's a sort of open zoo in a surviving pocket of forest, where tourists flock to watch orang-utans being fed fruit by rangers, who have names for all of them. How many you're likely to see will depend on the time of year – when wild fruits are in season, fewer orang-utans emerge from the forest to seek out the rangers.

Most of the action takes place at a clearing, with seating close by, reached by a short jungle trail from the car park. Don't be surprised if you see the critters roaming around the car park itself – and give them a wide berth if you do. Look out also for orang-utan nests, which they build in the treetops using clumps of leaves and branches, for sleeping.

Annah Rais

55km south of Kuching • RM8, payable at the information booth in front of the longhouse • City Public Link bus #K6 and Sarawak Transport Company bus #6, which also serve Semenggoh, head to the small town of Kota Padawan (at least 4 daily; 30min; RM3) from whose market you can catch a minivan (1hr; RM6) to Annah Rais; or catch STC bus #3A or #3 and ask to get off on the main road at the Kota Padawan turning, a few minutes' walk from the town centre

Near the mountains that straddle the border with Kalimantan, the Bidayuh longhouse settlement of **ANNAH RAIS**, while touristy, makes a decent day-trip from Kuching, particularly if you don't have time to see longhouses elsewhere in Sarawak. It's easy to combine a visit with a trip to Semenggoh if you're driving, and not too hard by bus, though confirm bus times with the tourist office.

The settlement feels like a hybrid of longhouse and village – assorted differently styled wooden "houses" are joined together in two long parallel rows and raised off the ground, with platforms of bamboo slats on planks serving as "streets". Behind the facades, individual family quarters open off vast corridors, just as in a regular longhouse, and as ever there's a river nearby for bathing (a bridge across it brings you to a third longhouse). You'll probably be offered a small glass of *tuak* upon arrival, while depending on the season, you may see the rice harvest or longhouse-made latex sheets

---

GUNUNG PENRISSEN

The most accessible mountain on the Sarawak/Kalimantan border, the spectacular 1300-metre-high **GUNUNG PENRISSEN** stands 5km west of Annah Rais. The Penrissen hike involves tough walking along narrow paths and crossing fast-flowing streams that descend from the source of the Sarawak River; vertical ladders help on the last section. As the trails aren't easy to follow, you must hire a guide. Some hikers opt to come with a Kuching-based tour operator (most don't advertise Penrissen but can arrange trips); some contact the Tourist Guide Association (see p.328); and others try to find guides in Annah Rais. The last is a good option if you have your own car (there's no public transport), but don't just drive up and expect a guide to be available; contact Edward (☎016 871 1957), one of the residents, in advance for help.

being dried. Be sure to pop into the *panggah* or skull house, where skulls hark back to a martial tradition that only ceased a few generations ago.

ACCOMMODATION ANNAH RAIS

Borneo Highlands Resort Gunung Penrissen ☎ 082 577930, ⊛ borneohighlands.com.my. A plush affair, high up Gunung Penrissen, complete with golf course and spa. Various good-value packages are available, including tours or golf or guided hikes. Rates include breakfast. <u>RM450</u>

6

The caves of Bau

Daily 8.30am–5pm • Each cave RM3 • Sarawak Transport Company bus #2 goes to Bau (3 daily; RM4.50), from where the Bau Transport Company's #3 bus (2 hourly) runs to the caves; each cave has its own bus stop on the main road, at least 15min walk from its entrance, while a taxi charter for the round trip, including waits at the caves, costs around RM80

Nineteenth-century prospectors were drawn to **BAU**, half an hour's drive southwest of Kuching, by the gold that veined the surrounding countryside, but the modern-day market town is mundane in the extreme, though it does have a picturesque mining lake, **Blue Lake**, on its southwestern edge. Pretty though the lake is, it contains arsenic and is unsafe to swim in; the main reason to come to Bau is to visit the two nearby caves, around 4km apart to the west. If you have to pick one of the two – which you may well have to do if relying on public transport – go to the larger, **Fairy Cave**. Steps inside enable you to wander through the gloom towards a gaping maw at one end of the system, which lets in refreshing breezes and enough light for the cave floor to be blanketed in ferns and moss. **Wind Cave** meanders through a rocky outcrop on the banks of one branch of the Sarawak river system, and again steps and planks make it possible to wander from one side of the outcrop to the other.

ACCOMMODATION BAU

Lan e Tuyang 14km short of Bau and 23km out from Kuching on the Batu Kawa road, which runs parallel to and north of the main Bau road ☎ 013 820 3365. This excellent homestay is run by the Kayan *sape* exponent and artist Mathew Ngau Jau, a mainstay of the Rainforest Festival. He has created a sort of mini-longhouse decorated with swirly Orang Ulu motifs and *sapes* built in his workshop below, and can teach you the rudiments of the instrument and how to build one, or you can try your hand at woodcarving. Several simple guest rooms have fans and mosquito netting, and a separate block holds toilets and showers; take meals in the house or at simple restaurants in the Chinese hamlet of Tondong a few minutes' walk away. The Bau Transport Company #8A bus heads this way en route between Kuching and Bau (4–5 daily; RM4), or arrange for Mathew to pick you up from town or the airport. RM50 per person B&B.

Gunung Gading National Park

RM10 • ☎ 082 735144 • Catch Sarawak Transport Company bus #EP07 from Kuching's regional express bus terminal to the town of Lundu (departs 8am, 11am, 2pm & 4pm; 1hr 15min; RM10), then either walk 2km north along the main road, or catch a shared minivan or taxi (RM15)

The main claim to fame of **Gunung Gading National Park**, 75km by road west of Kuching, is that it's home to the parasitic **Rafflesia** plant (see p.596), with its stinky blooms. However, when the buds are maturing the park can go for months without a single *Rafflesia* in flower; if you're coming specifically to see the plants, check with the park in advance.

The park can be visited as a day-trip from Kuching. With an early start, you can tackle the **Waterfall Trail**, on which it takes ninety minutes to reach the end at waterfall 7 – it really is the seventh waterfall en route – where you can have a good, refreshing swim. With more time, you can also climb two of the park's hills, Gading and Perigi. Both are full-on hikes: the first is a six-hour round trip, the second, eight hours.

ACCOMMODATION GUNUNG GADING NATIONAL PARK

Gunung Gading National Park Accommodation ☎ 082 735144. Gunung Gading has a campsite; a hostel where four rooms offer dorm beds, or can be let as four-bed rooms; and a lodge holding six-bed chalets. There's no canteen, but you can cook at the park's kitchens. Camping <u>RM5</u>, dorms <u>RM15</u>, rooms <u>RM40</u>, chalets <u>RM150</u>

Pandan and Siar beaches

8km north of the entrance to Gunung Gading National Park, on the road from Lundu • Take a bus to Lundu (see p.343), then a taxi (RM30, or a few ringgit if you can find a share one)

Considered by many locals to be the best in the area, **Pandan Beach** is a half-kilometre-long stretch of white sand near a beachfront kampung. Two kilometres beyond Pandan, the smaller **Siar Beach** is another pleasing spot with a good place to stay.

ACCOMMODATION AND EATING   PANDAN AND SIAR

Siar Beach Resort Jalan Siar ☎082 412898, ⓦwww .siarbeachresort. It's not much of a resort, more a simple collection of buildings with newly built rooms as well as family bungalows holding two, three or four rooms. They don't serve food, though they do have kitchens and barbecue facilities. Rooms RM150, bungalows RM250

Sematan

Catch a bus to Lundu, then a taxi (from around RM40)

Some 40km west of **Lundu town**, and at the end of the road from Kuching, lies the seaside town of **SEMATAN**, whose long, picturesque **beach** and reasonably clean yellow sands lure visitors in.

ACCOMMODATION SEMATAN

Holiday Chalet Sematan Sematan ☎082 256012 or ☎082 712476, ⓦsematan.com. The chalets are pleasant enough, if bland, and there's a great little swimming pool though the beach is just metres away. However, the place is a tad overpriced; rates include breakfast, but rise fifteen percent at weekends. The café serves predictable rice and noodle dishes. RM210

Sematan Palm Beach Resort 3km west of Sematan

☎082 712388, ⓦspbresort.com. This modern development offers one- and two-room chalets (sleeping four), plus larger options. Best of all, they have a swimming pool, bike rental and can arrange snorkelling and diving trips. Prices include half-board (they have their own restaurant) and rise by a quarter at weekends. One-room chalet RM170 , two-room chalet RM320

Tanjung Datu National Park

Visits not advised in the rainy season (Nov–Feb) because of rough seas; boats seldom go in those months • RM10 • ⓦsarawakforestry. com • Only access is by boat from Sematan (1hr; RM450 for four people, RM600 overnight; contact Nazit, ☎014 880 9696); Kuching tour operators including CPH Travel (see p.329) can arrange trips

At the very western tip of Sarawak, tiny **Tanjung Datu National Park** covers a mountainous region around a coastal spur close to the Kalimantan border. Although it offers splendid rainforest, swift, clean rivers and isolated bays, the main draws are its dazzling **beaches**, with shallow, unspoilt **coral reefs** perfect for snorkelling only a short distance from the shore. The park is also among the few destinations in Sarawak where green **turtles** come to lay eggs. It holds four marked **trails**, too; the longest, the Belian trail, takes just two hours, leading to the summit of Gunung Melano (542m).

ACCOMMODATION   TANJUNG DATU NATIONAL PARK

Tanjung Datu Campsite ⓦsarawakforestry.com. The park's basic campsite also rents out tents for a nominal extra fee. Bring all equipment and provisions. RM5

Batang Ai and the Iban longhouses

The **Iban longhouses** of the Ai headwaters, both 150km due east of Kuching beyond the lake of the Batang Ai hydroelectric dam, and also to the north along the **Lemanak** river system, are the best excuse for anyone travelling between western and central Sarawak not to catch the fast Kuching–Sibu ferry. Despite being on the tourist trail, the longhouses continue to offer a glimpse of a semi-traditional lifestyle in a remote corner of the state, much of which is protected as a **national park** and wildlife sanctuary.

THE IBAN

Easily the most numerous of Sarawak's indigenous peoples, the **Iban** make up nearly thirty percent of the state's population. Their language is from the same family as Malay, and any Malay speakers will notice considerable overlap in vocabulary as well as predictable changes in word endings – *datang* (come) and *makan* (eat) in Malay, for example, become *datai* and *makai* in Iban.

ORIGINS AND CONFLICTS

Having outgrown their original home in the Kapuas river basin of west Kalimantan, the Iban migrated to the Lupar River in southwest Sarawak in the sixteenth century, and came into conflict with the Melanau and Malays. With the Brunei sultanate at its height, the Malays pushed the Iban back inland up rivers such as the Rejang, into interior areas dominated by the Kayan. Great battles were waged between the two groups; one source recorded seeing "a mass of boats drifting along the stream, [the combatants] spearing and stabbing each other; decapitated trunks and heads without bodies, scattered about in ghastly profusion". Although such inter-ethnic conflict stopped as migration itself slowed, the Iban were still taking heads as recently as the 1960s during the Konfrontasi, when the Indonesian army came up against Iban who had thrown their lot in with Malaysia.

SOCIETY

The Iban figure prominently in the minds of visitors, thanks to their traditional communal dwelling, the **longhouse**. Each has its own *tuai* (headman), who leads more by consensus than by barking orders. For details of longhouse architecture, see p.346.

Traditionally, young men left the longhouse to go on **bejalai**, the act of joining a warring party – essentially a rite of passage for a youth to establish his independence and social position before marriage. Nowadays, to the extent that *bejalai* has meaning, it may translate into going to university or earning a good wage on offshore oil rigs or in a hotel or factory in Singapore.

Further complicating the *bejalai* tradition, of course, is that women are now much more socially mobile, and can pursue education and their own careers. Traditionally, however, women had distinct duties. They never went hunting, but were great weavers; indeed, an Iban woman's weaving prowess used to determine her status in the community. The women are most renowned for their **pua kumbu** (blanket or coverlet) work, a cloth of intricate design and colour. The *pua kumbu* once played an integral part in Iban rituals, hung up prominently during harvest festivals and weddings, or used to cover structures containing charms and offerings to the gods.

DEVELOPMENT AND URBANIZATION

More than half of Sarawak's Iban have moved permanently to the cities and towns in the west of the state, or may spend the working week there and weekends back in their longhouse. Most rural Iban no longer live purely off the land but also undertake seasonal work in the rubber and oil industries. By no small irony, logging – the business that most devastated their traditional lands – also long supplied plentiful and lucrative work; these days oil-palm cultivation and production provide more employment.

Batang Ai dam and lake

Around three and a half hours' drive from Kuching, a couple of kilometres beyond the village of **Jelukong**, a signed 38km turning branches southeast off the main trunk road, passing a few modernish longhouses en route to the small border town of **Lubok Antu**. Some 12km short of that, another small road branches east (left) towards the **Batang Ai dam**, a necessary though impressive way station en route to the upper Ai. Built in the 1980s as Sarawak's first hydroelectric venture, the Ai dam created a lake covering 90 square kilometres. Though now dwarfed in scale, generating capacity and controversy by the much-delayed Bakun dam (see p.358), it's an impressive sight and the road up gives good views of the narrow valley downriver that must have made the site seem ideal to the dam's planners. No parts of the dam are open to tourists, though, and once you get there you'll head to one of the jetties to continue east by boat to an Ai longhouse or the *Hilton Batang Ai*.

Batang Ai National Park
Organized day-trips required • RM10 • ⓦ sarawakforestry.com

East of the lakeshore, an hour by boat from the dam, the little-visited **Batang Ai National Park** preserves an important area of rainforest that merges with the Lanjak Entimau Wildlife Sanctuary (LEWS; off-limits to visitors), which itself merges with another protected area across the border in Kalimantan. **Orang-utans** are occasionally spotted on various trails in the national park; it holds no residential or other facilities, and all visitors must be accompanied by guides. You therefore have to pay a tour operator for a day-trip to be added onto a longhouse package.

The Ai river system
An hour east from the dam, longhouse-bound boats leave the lake and head up the Ai. As is clear from the tall trees that come right to the water's edge, the initial stretch is still a drowned portion of the river. Further up you'll observe a transition to the true riverbanks, the vegetation more open and compact. Also visible sporadically to either side are the odd school and clinic in simple metal-roofed timber buildings, and areas of hillslope cleared for traditional rice cultivation. The Iban leave paddies to the jungle once the soil is exhausted and move on to clear new areas. As the river narrows, you also begin to see the occasional longhouse lurking in the vegetation. Among those that take tourists are **Nanga Delok** (also called Rumah Ipang, on the Delok, a tributary of the Ai) and the more distant **Nanga Sumpa** (the Sumpa being a tributary of the Delok). Wherever you stay, will offer opportunities for additional longboat trips to areas where you can make short treks or local beauty spots such as waterfalls.

The Lemanak River
The **Lemanak River** is, like the dam, reached by the Lubok Antu road, though you turn off earlier to head to the jetties. Again, several longhouses here regularly host travellers, notably **Ngemah Ulu**. Guests here are put up in the longhouse itself, which has been adopted by Diethelm Travel in Kuching (see p.329), though they can take advantage of separate washing facilities. You can do a worthwhile trek if you come on a two-night package.

ARRIVAL AND DEPARTURE   BATANG AI

By longboat and bus Roads have reached some longhouses north of the Ai, but having your own car is little advantage unless you have local friends who can arrange for you to stay and give accurate directions (since many longhouses aren't signed). In practice, most visitors book a Kuching or Miri package from a tour operator, which usually includes the traditional journey in and out by longboat, plus all meals. When the time comes to leave, there's no need to backtrack all the way to Kuching; to head on to Sibu and beyond, flag down a

---

LONGHOUSE ARCHITECTURE

Longhouses can be thought of as indoor villages, housing entire communities under one roof. Although several indigenous peoples build dwellings that are sometimes called longhouses, the definitive article is the **Iban** longhouse. This has a long veranda or *tanju* at the front where rice, rubber and other produce can be laid out to dry; it's accessed by steps or sometimes a log into which notches are cut. Behind the front wall, running the entire length of the building, a corridor or *ruai* serves as a sort of main street where the community can socialize. Multiple doors (*pintu*) open on to the *ruai*, behind which lie each family's quarters (*bilik*); locals describe a longhouse not in terms of its length or the number of inhabitants, but by how many *bilik* or *pintu* it has. Above the living quarters, a loft space (*sadau*) is used for storage.

Traditionally longhouses were built of hardwood timber and bamboo, perhaps with ironwood shingles on the roof. Even though recent longhouses may feature plenty of unsightly concrete, they still retain their characteristic *ruai* inside, and most continue to be sited close to rivers or streams, where people enjoy bathing even when piped water supplies exist.

passing bus on the main road. There are at least a couple of buses an hour and tickets can be bought on board or from a ticket booth at the rest stops along the way, if the tour operator can set you down there.

ACCOMMODATION

Hilton Batang Ai On southeastern shore of Batang Ai lake, 40min from the dam ☎ 082 584388, ⓦ hilton.com. A *Hilton* is definitely a misfit in this isolated area, but then, so is the dam – so you might as well just enjoy the lake vistas from the hotel terrace. Each block is a timber building with rooms on one side of a long corridor, just as in a longhouse; built in the 1990s, the rooms now look a tad dated. Either drive up and be collected at the dam, or pay extra for shuttle transport from the *Kuching Hilton*, who can also tell you about packages and add-on longhouse visits. **RM250**

Nanga Sumpa Ai river, 1hr 30min boat ride from the dam; only bookable as part of a package from a tour operator. This longhouse deserves special mention as the site of an excellent purpose-built tourist lodge, sited at a discreet distance from the longhouse itself across a creek. Run in partnership with tour operator Borneo Adventure (see p.329), it has played host to Michael Palin and his BBC film crew, but don't expect anything plush – rooms have wooden platforms that hold a simple mattress and a mosquito net, but little else, though there's a pleasant open communal sitting/dining area and modern shared bathrooms. If you book with Borneo Adventure (other tour operators use the lodge too), ask about their jungle lodge *Lubok Kasai*, a half-hour boat journey away. This is where to stay for more serious trekking, with the small possibility of sighting orang-utans, and packages are available that feature stays in both lodges. Prices vary; only bookable through tour operators.

Central Sarawak

For travellers, central Sarawak offers rather slim pickings compared to Kuching's hinterland and the north of the state. Those visitors who venture here tend to be drawn by the prospect of travelling into the interior along the **Rejang** (also spelled **Rajang**), Malaysia's longest river. All such trips start from the bustling city of **Sibu**, some 50km inland near where another major river, the **Igan**, splits away from the Rejang. Express boats depart daily to zip up the Rejang to **Kapit**, beyond which, through the **Pelagus Rapids** and on to the sleepy town of **Belaga**, eight hours from Sibu, the Rejang becomes wild and unpredictable and the scenery spectacular. There's not much to do in either Kapit or Belaga though, and while there are longhouse communities near both, as well as east of Kapit along the Balui River, public transport is thin on the ground, so it's best to regard the Rejang journey as an end in itself or else fork out for (pricey) local guides to arrange trips for you.

With Sibu being so far from the sea, and the coast here dominated by mangrove swamp, the main trunk road runs deep inland until it finally hits the coast again at Bintulu. Halfway along, a side road leads off through a chink in the vegetation to the coastal town of **Mukah**, which has an appealing museum-cum-guesthouse nearby. **Bintulu** itself is a nondescript but (thanks to oil and gas) prosperous town, whose main attraction is as a base for **Similajau National Park**, easily reached yet appealingly quiet.

Sibu

From its humble 1850s origins as a tiny Melanau encampment, **SIBU** has grown into Sarawak's third largest city and its biggest port. Nearly half its quarter-million population are ethnic Chinese. Unusually for Malaysia, many are Foochow, descended from migrants from what's now Fuzhou in southeast China. Their diligence is often credited with helping the city become the commercial centre it is today. Its Foochow flavour aside, Sibu is also identified with Sarawak's controversial **logging** industry, which helped the city recover from the Japanese occupation, when many Chinese were forced into slave labour. Sibu subsequently became, for a time, the centre for timber processing in Sarawak. Investors, many drawn from long-established Chinese families, made large fortunes as a result.

Today the city retains one glaringly obviously link with the timber industry – its tallest building, a downtown office and shopping development, is the headquarters of

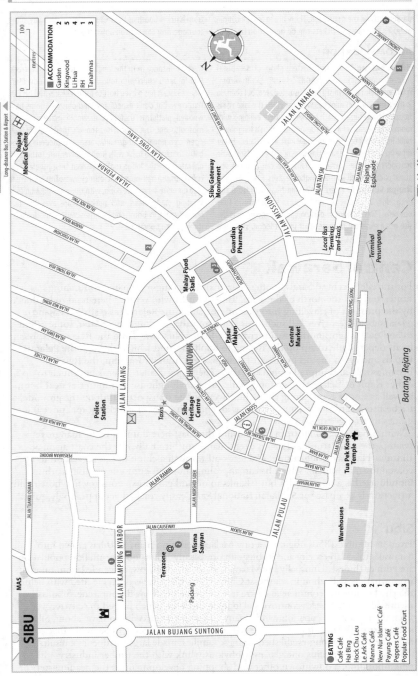

SIBU

MAS

■ ACCOMMODATION
Garden	2
Kingwood	5
Li Hua	4
RH	1
Tanahmas	3

Rejang Medical Centre

Jalan Tong Sang
Jalan Pedada
Jalan Hoe Ping
Hardin Walk
Jalan Lockwood
Jalan Tong Hua
Jalan Mui Wong
Jalan Empsam
Jalan Lai Chee
Jalan Hua Kiew
Persiaran Brooke
Jalan Tuanku Osman
Jalan Kampung Nyabor

Police Station

Sibu Gateway Monument

Jalan Bridge East

Guardian Pharmacy

Malay Food Stalls

Chinatown

Sibu Heritage Centre

Taxis

Jalan Mong Hak Song
Jalan Ramin
Jalan Central
Jalan Morshidi Sidek
Jalan Causeway
Jalan Sukan

Pasar Malam

Jalan Chambers
Jalan Mission
Jalan Tan Sri
Jalan Maju
Jalan Maju
Jalan Lanang

Central Market

Jalan Khoo Ping Loong
Jalan Market
Jalan Channel
Jalan Cross
Jalan Tukang Besi
Jalan Bank
Jalan Bank
Jalan Temple
Jalan Chew Geok Lin
Jalan Wharf
Jalan Pulau

Terazone @
Wisma Sanyan
Padang

Tua Pek Kong Temple

Warehouses

Local Bus Terminus and Taxis

Rejang Esplanade

Terminal Penumpang

Batang Rejang

JALAN BUJANG SUNTONG

● EATING
Café Café	6
Hai Bing	7
Hock Chu Leu	5
Le Ark Café	8
Manna Café	2
New Nur Islamic Café	1
Payung Café	9
Peppers Café	4
Popular Food Court	3

N

metres
0   100

6

the major logging concern, Sanyan. More interesting for visitors are an excellent though small history museum and the city's **waterfront**, with its Chinese temple nearby. Boasting a huge central market, too, Sibu has enough to keep you occupied for half a day, which is just as well as most travellers en route to or from the upper Rejang spend at least a night here.

The waterfront

If you arrive on the boat from Kuching, you'll find yourself on the waterfront on the Rejang's right bank, facing rows of dull modern shophouses and commercial buildings. Having experienced devastating fires in 1889 and 1928, plus serious damage during World War II, Sibu is characterized more by energy than visual appeal. Efforts have been made to landscape and beautify the **Rejang Esplanade** – the tiny riverside recreation area by the ferry terminal – but it's still a fairly humdrum spot. Look out, however, for a riverside marker indicating the Rejang's level during historic floods. Sibu's commercial lifeline is also a scourge, and it's scary to realize that every few years the river overtops this area and thus inundates the city centre. Efforts are ongoing to tame the Rejang by dredging away sediment, some of which no doubt results from forest clearance.

Central Market

Northern end of the riverside Jalan Khoo Peng Loong • Daily dawn to dusk, hawker stalls upstairs stay open into the evening

Sibu's modern and entertaining **Central Market** complex is housed in a long, curved-roofed building. It's best to turn up on a Saturday, when the market is at its busiest and the entire ground floor is taken up with vendors selling items such as bamboo tubes for stewing *ayam pansoh*, live roosters tied up in newspaper, slabs of what look like mummified bats but are in fact smoked fish, and, in the run-up to tribal festivals, gongs – which prospective buyers have no qualms about trying out. Stalls at the edge offer a tasty Sibu speciality, *kongbian*, sometimes called Chinese bagels but more like dainty versions of the sesame-seed breads sold in Turkey and Lebanon. An upstairs **food court** offers a few vantage points overlooking the colourful goings-on below.

Tua Pek Kong temple

A small wooden temple stood on the site of Sibu's **Tua Pek Kong temple**, at the northern end of the riverfront, as early as 1870. Soon afterwards it was rebuilt on a much grander scale, with a tiled roof, stone block floor and decorative fixtures imported from China. Two large concrete lions guard the entrance. The **statue** of Tua Pek Kong, the temple's most important image, survived both the fire of 1928 and Japanese bombardment.

Ask the caretaker for a key to the seven-storey **pagoda** at the back, added in the 1980s, for 360-degree views over the vast brown Rejang to the west, and Sibu's jumble of buildings stretching east.

Chinatown

Back from the Tua Pek Kong temple, the network of streets around Jalan Market constitutes Sibu's historic **Chinatown**. It doesn't have a noticeably stronger Chinese character than elsewhere, but in the evening there's a lively **pasar malam** on and around Jalan Market, with the usual stalls selling anything from snacks to mobile-phone chargers, including at least one vendor who sells Buddhist, Christian, Hindu and Muslim religious paraphernalia – a great example of Malaysian multiculturalism in practice, albeit driven only by commercial pragmatism. Note that some of the nearby streets around the tourist office can be decidedly seedy at night.

Sibu Heritage Centre

Jalan Central • Daily except Mon 9am–5pm • Free

The large circular building on Jalan Central is a former library that's been sleekly modernized to house the **Sibu Heritage Centre**, a fine museum that puts the city's history and cultural diversity centre stage. There's a good discussion of how Chinese pioneers, with the support of Brooke officials, founded the settlement and got it off the ground with crops such as rubber – logging didn't arrive until the 1930s – and of Foochow immigration, which only began in earnest at the start of the twentieth century. Among the artefacts, look out for a striking nineteenth-century Kayan burial hut or *salong* atop a metre-high totem pole, plus less spectacular examples of basketware, beadwork and so forth.

ARRIVAL AND DEPARTURE   SIBU

By plane Sibu's airport (☎084 307770) is 25km east of the centre. While you could walk 10min to the nearest major road junction and flag down a passing bus or yellow-topped van into town (roughly hourly; RM3), it's a lot easier to pay for a taxi (RM32). Heading out to the airport, any bus from the local bus station bound for Sibujaya or Kanowit can drop you at the same junction. Unusually, MAS still has a downtown office on 61 Jalan Tunku Osman (☎084 323717); both AirAsia and Firefly are at the airport.

Destinations Bintulu (3 daily; 35min); Johor Bahru (4 weekly; 1hr 30min); Kota Kinabalu (2 daily; 1hr 35min); Kuala Lumpur (4 daily; 1hr 45min); Kuching (7 daily; 40min); Miri (3 daily; 1hr).

By boat Sibu's express-boat terminal on the esplanade, **Terminal Penumpang**, is used by fast boats between here and Kuching via Sarikei downriver (1 daily, 11.30am; 4hr; operated by Bahagia, ☎084 319228; RM50), and upriver to Kanowit (1–2 daily; 30min); Kapit (18 daily; 3hr); and Belaga (1 daily at 5.45am; 8hr). For more on upriver travel, see p.352.

By long-distance bus All express buses use the long-distance bus station, 5km northeast of the centre off Jalan Pahlawan. A taxi to the centre costs around RM15.

Destinations Bintulu (2–3 hourly; 4hr); Kuching (2–3 hourly; 7hr); Miri (2–3 hourly; 8hr); Mukah (at least 3 daily; 3hr 30min); Pontianak (Indonesia; at least 2 daily; 18hr).

By local bus Hourly Lanang Bus Company services #20 & #21 go to the **local bus station** in front of the express-boat terminal.

INFORMATION AND TOURS

Tourist Information Staff at Sibu's central Visitors' Information Centre, 16 Jalan Tukang Besi (Mon–Fri 8am–5pm; ☎084 340980) field questions on Sibu, and also cover the Rejang river towns plus Bintulu and Mukah, which don't have tourist offices.

pepper being cultivated and stay in a wooden Iban longhouse. Even more unusually, they can take you north down the Igan River to Mukah (see p.359). Book a few days in advance.

Great Holiday ☎084 348196. This agency may with advance notice be able to arrange longhouse visits and stays up the Rejang, though it's not something they do regularly.

TOUR OPERATORS

Greatown Travel ☎084 211243. Unusual trips downriver to Sarikei, where you can do some trekking, see

GETTING AROUND

By taxi Downtown taxi ranks include those by the local bus station and on Jalan Wong Nai Siong; otherwise, call

Sibu Taxis (☎084 320773).

ACCOMMODATION

Sibu hasn't enough backpackers to keep any backpacker lodges going, though there are a couple of decent inexpensive hotels, plus loads of choice once you get to mid-range and above.

Garden Jalan Hoe Ping ☎084 317888, ⓦgardenhotelsibu.com.my. A decent fallback if the *Li Hua* is full – rooms cost quite a bit more, but you get a breakfast buffet, plus free wi-fi. For a slightly classier experience, get one of the recently refurbished executive rooms on the upper floors, for around RM30 extra. RM100

Kingwood 12 Lorong Lanang ☎084 335888, ⓔkingwood.sibu@yahoo.com.my. Incredibly this huge hotel, with a gleaming new extension back from the river, has never seen fit to have a website despite boasting a

pool, gym, sauna and other amenities. Rooms in the old wing are unexceptional; the new wing costs RM30 or so extra, and features unfussy, more contemporary decor. Prices can be slashed when things are quiet, making the place an absolute steal. Rates include breakfast. RM150

★ **Li Hua** By the river at the junction of Lorong Lanang 2 and Jalan Maju ☎084 324000. It's not the place to come for little refinements, and the sound of guests' raucous chatter echoes round the small lobby, but this is a terrific budget hotel, efficiently run, with dated and plain but well-kept en-suite rooms and free wi-fi on quite a few floors. The coffee house does passable Western breakfasts, not included in rates. Reserve ahead. RM75

RH Jalan Kampung Nyabor ☎084 365888, ⓦrhhotels .com.my. New, business-oriented hotel, sleek in a minimalist kind of way, with spacious rooms that come with bathtub

and safe. Facilities include a pool and steam bath. RM200

★ **Tanahmas** Off the eastern end of Jalan Chambers ☎084 333188, ⓦtanahmas.com.my. This slick mid-range hotel boasts some of the nicest rooms in its class, with elegant modern furnishings, and there's wi-fi throughout, a swimming pool and a popular restaurant. RM160

EATING AND DRINKING

While a few moderately upmarket restaurants are scattered downtown, the eating scene is otherwise dominated by the usual *kopitiams* – particularly in the streets back from the Esplanade and in Chinatown – and food courts, such as at the central market. Local specialities include **Foochow noodles** – steamed and then served in a soy and oyster sauce with spring onions, chilli, garlic and dried fish; and *kang puan mee*, which literally translates as "dry-plate noodles" though it is in fact *mee* fried in lard and garnished with pork slices. Worthwhile **bars** are thin on the ground, but not for lack of trying; a few venues are beautifully done out but lack a certain finesse and descend rather predictably into karaoke at the slightest opportunity – even in the fancier hotels.

Café Café 10 Jalan Chew Geok Lin ☎084 328101. While not as swish as *Le Ark*, *Café Café* is for many middle-class locals the place for a smart night out. The food is mostly a mix of Chinese, Malay and Indian dishes, served in different portion sizes with rice. Mains from RM15. Daily except Mon noon–4pm & 6–11pm.

Hai Bing 31 Jalan Maju ☎084 321491. This well-established and often busy Chinese restaurant is known for its seafood dishes such as ginger crab, and has separate open-air and a/c sections. Daily 11.30–1.30pm & 5.30–11.30pm.

Hock Chu Leu Upstairs at 28 Jalan Tukang Besi ☎084 330254. *Kopitiams* aside, you'd expect Sibu to have a more formal downtown place offering Foochow cuisine – and this is it, though it's a fusty old restaurant and not much to look at. Come here for classics such as Foochow noodles and *ang chow kai*, chicken that's red from being cooked with the sediment from a certain type of Chinese wine. Around RM20 per head, excluding drinks. Daily 11am–1.30pm & 5–8pm; sometimes closed Tues.

Le Ark Café Rejang Esplanade ☎084 313445. It may look like a designer home that wandered in error onto the riverfront, but *Le Ark* is actually a Thai restaurant that also serves a few Western and Malaysian dishes. The best that can be said of the food is that it's not bad, but the contemporary decor compensates, and prices are reasonable at around RM25 per person without alcohol. Several outdoor tables, set around a courtyard that's nicely lit at night, have river views by day. There's also a small karaoke-free bar. Daily 11am–11pm.

Manna Café Fifth floor, Wisma Sanyan mall. A large but still cosy Chinese-run place with good views over the padang and a variety of local dishes, including Sarawak

laksa, plus some Western offerings, including attempts at posh cakes. Daily 11am–9pm.

New Nur Islamic Café Jalan Kampung Nyabor, near the RH Hotel. A *kedai kopi* with reasonable if unexciting Indian curries, roti, rice and noodles and so forth. Daily 7am–8pm.

★ **Payung Café** Jalan Lanang. This simple restaurant, smartened up with a few tribal artefacts and a thatched awning, is one of the quirkiest anywhere in Sarawak, with a fusion menu that reflects enthusiasm rather than fancy culinary training. Their cooking often uses local herbs and could feature anything from Indochinese pomelo salad to prawns with starfruit and spaghetti. You can wash down your meal with, say, roselle tea – better known as the Egyptian hibiscus drink *karkaday* – or their brilliant home-made pineapple ginger soda, or even fresh durian milk shake, if the pongy fruits are in season. Around RM30 per person including soft drinks. Daily 11am–3pm & 6–11pm.

Popular Food Court Corner of Jalan Ramin and Jalan Morshidi Sidek. Despite the name, it's really a large, unusually airy *kedai kopi* with Chinese and Malay *nasi campur*, plus stalls offering Malay standards like *nasi lemak* and *sup tulang*, and another stall selling cheap Western breads and pastries. Daily 7am–8pm or so.

Peppers Café Tanahmas Hotel, off eastern end of Jalan Chambers ☎084 333188, ⓦtanahmas.com.my. The usual hotel restaurant menu ranging from Western staples – including lamb chop and rump steak – to Chinese noodles, in plush surroundings and at somewhat elevated prices. Not a bad option for a slap-up buffet breakfast either, at RM30. Daily 6am–1.30am.

SHOPPING

Wisma Sanyan near the padang has a Parkson Ria department store and a Giant supermarket. Sibu is not a great place to look for handicrafts; downtown, a drab hole-in-the-wall shop at the western end of Jalan Market is about all there is, though if you're interested in ceramics with Bornean motifs, try heading out to Toh Brothers Pottery on Jalan Oya some 12km out of town (catch a blue Sibujaya bus or a Lanang bus #2A or #2C; every 1–2hr).

DIRECTORY

Banks Quite a few banks downtown, including a convenient branch of Standard Chartered just up the road from the tourist office where Jalan Tukang Besi splits off from Jalan Cross.

Cinema The Star Cineplex on Jalan Ramin shows a few Hollywood flicks.

Hospitals and clinics The hospital is on Jalan Ulu Oya (☎ 084 343333); alternatively, try the Rejang Medical Centre, 29 Jalan Pedada (☎ 084 330733).

Internet access Terazone, fifth floor, Wisma Sanyan (10am–10pm; RM4/hr).

Pharmacies A branch of Guardian on Jalan Chambers, near the *Tanahmas* hotel, and a small pharmacy called KKMP at the Wisma Sanyan mall.

Police Jalan Kampung Nyabor ☎ 084 336144.

Post office Jalan Kampung Nyabor (Mon–Fri 8am–5pm; every other Sat 8am–noon).

Up the Batang Rejang

Even though it's a much diminished experience compared to even ten or fifteen years ago, a journey to the upper reaches of the Rejang should still engender a little frisson of excitement. This area was, after all, once synonymous with remoteness and with mysterious warring tribes. Even a century ago, conflict persisted between the Iban and the Orang Ulu, particularly the Kayan. Things had been much worse before the arrival of the Brookes, who wanted to develop – and therefore subjugate – the interior. To that end, James Brooke bought a section of the Rejang from the Sultan of Brunei in 1853, while his successor, Charles, asserted his authority over the Iban and Kayan tribes and encouraged the Chinese to open up the interior to agriculture and trade.

Thus began the gradual pacification of the Rejang. Even today, despite development and modern communications, it's still possible to glimpse something of that pioneer spirit in these upriver towns, while forts at **Kanowit** and **Kapit** hint at the lengths taken by the Brookes to get the region under their thumb. The furthest boats go upriver is the nondescript town of **Belaga**, reached by a thrilling ride through the **Pelagus Rapids**. There is, however, another exciting route into or out of Belaga – by **4WD**, the road

---

REJANG BOATS

One explanation for the nickname "flying coffins" – formerly attached jokingly to the **Rejang express boats** – is that they are indeed long and narrow, and feature aircraft-like seating. Otherwise they are serviceable, if not massively comfortable or user-friendly: boarding means stepping off the jetty onto the boat's rim or gunwale and walking around until you reach the entrance hatch. You may also have to fling your luggage atop the roof yourself, although sometimes staff are on hand to help load and unload.

Several companies operate the boats, but look out for people selling **Bahagia** and **Husqvarna** tickets at the boat terminal; both stand out for having more comfortable boats that are also more likely to leave on time and to have windows through which you can see clearly – though the jungle views get monotonous after a while. Otherwise you'll have to be entertained by the onboard DVDs of Hong Kong soaps or gory Hollywood action flicks.

SCHEDULES AND FARES

Boats **depart** Sibu at least twice an hour from the crack of dawn until 11am, then every 45 minutes until 3pm. All go to Kapit (around 3hr), just a couple to Kanowit (45min; many more serve Song, the stop before Kapit). Downriver boats from Kapit operate to a similar schedule. Only one a day, leaving Sibu at 5.45 am, sails all the way to Belaga, with a half-hour stop at Kapit at 8.30am. The Belaga leg takes around five hours, with frequent stops. Note that during the dry season, if the river level is low, Belaga boats are cancelled – ask at the jetty or tourist office in Sibu for the latest. Note also that there is a piece of red tape involving permits to weigh up if you want to go to Belaga (see p.356).

The **fare** from Sibu to Kapit is RM20 (RM5 extra for first class, which when available offers a bit more legroom and slightly better air conditioning). A Sibu–Belaga ticket costs RM60, Kapit–Belaga RM25. At busy times, say during the run-up to a festival, buy tickets a day or two before.

CLOCKWISE FROM TOP LEFT TREKKING AND BOAT RIDES IN GUNUNG MULU NATIONAL PARK (P.374); IBAN LONGHOUSE, KAPIT (P.354) >

connecting up with the main trunk road near Bintulu (see p.362). Unfortunately **longhouse visits** can be difficult to pull off – notable exceptions are a family-friendly longhouse near Kanowit and possible excursions from Belaga – unless you are willing to pay often steep sums for guides to make the arrangements.

Kanowit

Two boats daily from Sibu (RM10) and Kapit (RM20); also Lanang Company buses every 2hr from Sibu's express bus station (1hr 45min) via the local bus station downtown (1hr 30min; RM7)

At the confluence of the Kanowit River and the Rejang, 65km by road from Sibu, **KANOWIT** amounts to little more than a couple of commercial streets leading away from the waterfront, the dull concrete shophouses packed with simple stores and *kedai kopis*, and with a bank on the waterfront itself. There's no reason to venture here, unless you've arranged to stay at the fine Iban **longhouse** nearby, in which case they'll probably pick you up from the tiny bus station or jetty.

Fort Emma

Close to the waterfront, a few minutes' walk downriver from the jetty • Mon–Fri 9am–5pm • Free

Kanowit's one sight, if sight it be, is **Fort Emma**, one of James Brooke's outposts to quell the restive Rejang. It's a surprisingly sturdy-looking two-storey timber structure, built in the 1850s, though the modern red-tiled roof does it no favours. It now holds a mini-museum retelling the history of Kanowit, from its foundation through to wartime Japanese occupation. A little hut to the left of the building holds a crocodile effigy of the sort that the Iban worshipped in the days before they accepted Christianity.

ACCOMMODATION   KANOWIT

Rumah Benjamin Angki Rantau Kemiding, 4km southwest of Kanowit ☎084 753576, ✉ben_8845 @yahoo.com. Painted bright yellow, this venerable longhouse with more than 50 doors and a correspondingly vast *ruai* dates back to the 1930s. Being set in an agricultural area just uphill from the Kanowit River, it isn't some kind of full-on outback experience, which is precisely why it's so good for families with young children. Guests can stay in a purpose-built modern block with two a/c rooms, or in the longhouse itself, where some of the Iban speak good English. Call Benjamin in advance to discuss prices and some kind of programme; potential activities, all costing extra, include guided walks through the woods, fishing trips and so forth. Per person, full board in modern block RM65, longhouse without meals RM75

Kapit

KAPIT is the main commercial centre upriver from Sibu, and it looks it too, trapped in an architectural no-man's-land between the modern town it could become and the rustic backwater it was a generation ago. New municipal buildings and even a small shopping complex springing up right on the riverbank are pulling focus from the nondescript concrete blocks of earlier decades, and the place feels like an utter jumble, despite a certain appealing energy. If you do end up in Kapit, you may well stay the night – either because you can't face the journey to Belaga in one go or because this is as far as you intend to get – so it's just as well that it holds a couple of minor sights, notably the old fort. Although the town holds several banks and a couple of internet cafés, there's not much else to do beyond wandering the riverbank or having a look around the town's market.

Fort Sylvia

Tues–Sun 10am–noon & 2–5pm (you may need to wait for the caretaker to show up with the keys) • Free

The white, low-slung building a couple of minutes' walk upriver from the boat terminal is **Fort Sylvia**, built in 1880 of tough *belian* (ironwood) timber. It makes quite a grand first impression, though its almost total lack of windows gives away that it was not intended as a homely haven in the middle of nowhere. Instead it was an attempt to prevent the marauding Iban attacking smaller and more peaceable tribes, and to limit Iban migration

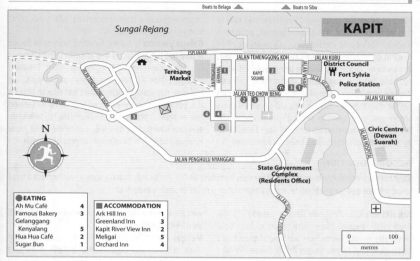

along the nearby Sungai Baleh, confining them to the Rejang below Kapit; diamond-shaped holes all along the facade were, as you might guess, intended to stick guns out of.

The fort is now a small **museum** and conference venue, managed by the people behind Kuching's Tun Jugah Gallery. Evocative photographs depict great moments in the history of the Ulu Rejang, including the 1924 peacemaking ceremony in Kapit between Brooke officials and the warring Iban and Kayan tribal representatives. In addition, ceramic jars, *pua kumba* textiles and small cannon are on display.

Civic Centre and Museum
Jalan Hospital • Mon–Fri 9am–5pm • Free

Also known by its Malay name, **Dewan Suarah**, Kapi's **Civic Centre and Museum** holds interesting exhibits on the tribes in the Rejang region, including a well-constructed longhouse and a mural painted by local Iban. Sketches and watercolours of Kapit, Belaga and Song portray a life that is slowly disappearing. The museum also describes the lives of the Hokkien traders who helped put towns like Kapit on the map.

ARRIVAL AND DEPARTURE   KAPIT

By boat Kapit's large boat terminal is used by all boats except Belaga services, which use a pier just a couple of minutes' walk downriver.
Destinations Belaga (1 daily; 5hr); Kanowit (1–2 daily; 2hr); Sibu (18 daily; 2hr 30min).
By minivan Shared minivans serving longhouses in the

area circulate around the market and town square, but the system is chaotic; if you want to chance using one of these, staff at your hotel may be able to advise. A ride shouldn't cost more than RM5 one-way, but tourists are sometimes charged much higher prices.

INFORMATION AND TOURS

Alice and Christina Chua ☏019 8593126 or ☏013 8466133, ☏084 799778. Licensed guides based near Kapit, this mother-and-daughter team arrange trips to longhouses on the nearby Baleh and Gaat rivers. Prices vary considerably depending on the size of the group and your requirements, but a one-night stay at Rumah Bundong – a substantial old timber longhouse – might cost around

RM550 for two people, including land transport, meals and a guide. Day-trips and longer stays are possible, so call the Chuas (several days in advance) to discuss your needs and negotiate a price.
Local guides If you prefer to ask around at your hotel about local guides, be cautious as there have been problems – for example, people may pay a couple of

6

hundred ringgit for a one-night longhouse stay only to find when they arrive that no arrangements have been made for their board and lodging. Such issues are often more to do with bad communication than petty crime, but try to be sure of what you're being promised when you hand cash over. You can also chance doing your own day-trip by minivan – Bundong and Jandok longhouses are the main targets – though here old-fashioned codes apply: you may have to present yourselves to the headman, and should watch for small flags being flown as this indicates there has been a death and the community is in a state of mourning, which will affect how you should behave.

Belaga permits In theory, travellers heading to Belaga require free permits, issued free at the Resident's Office in the State Government Complex off Jalan Penghulu Nyanggau (Mon–Fri 8am–5pm; show your passport). The half-hour stop made by Belaga boats isn't enough time for this, but luckily the whole system, once useful for keeping tabs on activists protesting the Bakun dam, has fallen into abeyance now that the dam is up and running, and you're extremely unlikely to be asked about permits anymore.

ACCOMMODATION

Kapit has a few reasonable budget hotels (if the ones listed here are full, you'll easily stumble upon a handful more around town) and one mid-range option, though accommodation tends to be slightly overpriced.

Ark Hill Inn Jalan Penghulu Gerinang ☎084 796168. Good-value budget place with spartan but quite serviceable en-suite rooms. Note that "single" rooms hold a bed large enough for two. Singles RM50, doubles RM80

Greenland Inn Jalan Teo Chow Beng ☎084 796388. Kapit's second-best hotel has snug, clean and very plain en-suite rooms, all with a/c and TV, though they're not really worth the tariff. It can be noisy at reception, so try to get a room on an upper floor. No breakfast. RM90

Kapit River View Inn 10 Jalan Sit Leong ☎084 796310, ✉krvinn@tm.net.my. Plain en-suite doubles

with a/c, at reasonable prices – and what's more, the staff are friendly. RM85.

Meligai Jalan Airport ☎084 796611, ⊕hotelmeligai .com. In theory this large concrete complex is the best hotel in town; in reality it's past its prime and can be rather gloomy, though at least it's generally quieter than the other hotels. RM90

Orchard Inn Diagonally across from Kapit's food court ☎084 796325. As drab as its fellow budget hotels, with uninspiring en-suite rooms, though the a/c is unusually effective. RM80

EATING

Not surprisingly, eating in Kapit is largely a matter of picking from the numerous *kedai kopis* and ordering from a fairly predictable palette of dishes. If you want to stick your neck out a bit, ask if they can cook fish or even wild boar (*babi hutan*) to order – though of course don't try ordering the latter in a Muslim place.

Ah Mu Café Across from the Orchard Inn. This unremarkable-looking *kopitiam* is one of the livelier examples of its kind in town, serving *nasi campur* by day plus the usual noodle options and the odd dessert. Best of all, they can also whip up stir fries and other Chinese dishes to order using ingredients to hand – anything from a whole steamed fish to fried chicken. Daily 7am until 9pm or so.

Famous Bakery 18 Jalan Teo Chow Beng. In usual Malaysian small-time-bakery fashion, the cakes and pastries here are not quite right, but what distinguishes it from its brethren is the cafeteria-like setup – there are plenty of tables and it's a friendly sort of place to hang around for an hour. Mostly self-service except for the beverages, including a good range of bubble teas, and some fancier cream cakes. Daily 9am–6pm.

Gelanggang Kenyalang One block back from Jalan

Teo Cheow Beng. This large hangar of a building is what passes for the town's food court, particularly good for Malay food, though with quite a few Chinese stalls too (and no stand-outs). Some hawkers are territorial, and won't serve you if your table is even slightly outside their patch. Daily 7am–8pm.

Hua Hua Café Jalan Teo Chow Beng. The slickest *kopitiam* in town, with gleaming white floors and walls thanks to its location in a newish block. It does a good range of noodle dishes throughout the day, including *kampua mee*, but winds down at dusk. Daily 7am–7.30pm.

Sugar Bun Jalan Teo Chow Beng. This ghastly fast-food franchise is one of the few places to serve burgers, chips and so forth – and a good spot to watch Kapit's youth congregate. Daily 11am–9.30pm or so.

Belaga

Belaga-bound boats make frequent stops upriver from Kapit, and some passengers decamp to the roof for views of longhouses as the Rejang narrows. Forty minutes from

Kapit, the **Pelagus Rapids** is an 800m-long, deceptively shallow stretch of the river where large, submerged stones make the through passage treacherous. According to local belief, the rapids' seven sections represent the seven segments of an enormous serpent that was chopped up and floated downriver by villagers to the north. Further upriver, the population shifts from being largely Iban to featuring a mix of other tribes, including the Kayan and Kenyah.

Five hours on from Kapit, the boat finally reaches tiny **BELAGA**, 40km west of the confluence of the Rejang and the Balui. The town started life as a small bazaar, and by 1900 pioneering Chinese *towkays* were supplying the tribespeople – both the Kayan and the then-nomadic Punan and Penan – with kerosene, cooking oil and cartridges, in exchange for beadwork and mats, beeswax, ebony and tree gums. The British presence in this region was nominal; Belaga has no crumbling fort to serve as a museum, as no fort was built this far upriver.

The first sight that confronts new arrivals climbing the steps from the riverbank is the town's slightly shabby tennis and basketball court. Next door a small garden serves as the town square, containing a hornbill statue atop a traditional-style round pillar bearing tribal motifs. There are only half a dozen streets and alleys in the centre, and while quite a few shops sell provisions, there's no market, though Orang Ulu traders may arrive at weekends to sell jungle produce in the streets.

Having made it all the way here, the best thing you can do is luxuriate in Belaga's tranquillity, a welcome contrast from Kapit. Short walks lead through the **Malay kampung** just downriver or along the start of the logging road at the back of town (head away from the river till you hit the street with the town's bank, turn left – south – and keep going), head out this way and you'll spot quite a few surprisingly smart modern houses. In the morning, picturesque mists settle on the Rejang, while in the evening you can play pool with the local youths (there's a small venue on the main street, Jalan Teo Tia Kheng, facing the square).

THE KAYAN AND KENYAH

The **Kayan** and the **Kenyah** are the most populous and powerful of the Orang Ulu groups who have lived for centuries in the upper Rejang and, in the northern interior, along the Batang Baram. The Kayan are more numerous, at around forty thousand, while the Kenyah population is around ten thousand (with substantially more Kenyah over the mountains in Kalimantan). Both groups migrated from East Kalimantan into Sarawak roughly six hundred years ago; they were pushed back to the lands they occupy today during the nineteenth century, when Iban migration led to clashes between the groups.

The Kayan and the Kenyah have a fair amount in common: their language, though of the same family as the other Bornean tongues and Malay, has a singsong quality that sounds like Chinese, and they have a well-defined social hierarchy, unlike the Iban or Penan. Traditionally, the **social order** was topped by the **tuai rumah** (chief) of the longhouse, followed by a group of three or four lesser aristocrats or **payin**, lay families and slaves (slavery no longer exists). Both groups take pride in their **longhouses**, which can be massive.

KAYAN ART

Artistic expression plays an important role in longhouse culture. The Kayan especially maintain a wide range of **musical traditions** including the lute-like **sape**, used to accompany long voice epics. **Textiles** are woven by traditional techniques in the upriver longhouses, and Kayan and Kenyah **woodcarvings**, among the most spectacular in Southeast Asia, are produced both for sale and for ceremonial uses. One artist, Tusau Padan, originally from Kalimantan, became much revered. He used mixed media of vibrant colours to create the flowing motifs he applied to painting and textiles – adorning burial poles, longboats and the walls of many Ulu Sarawak chiefs' homes. Some Kayan still drink potent **rice wine**, although now that nearly all the communities have converted to Christianity, alcohol is harder to come by.

ARRIVAL AND DEPARTURE

By bus The one daily boat to Kapit, and on to Sibu, leaves around 7.30am. Boats terminate at a large sandbank below the town.

By 4WD Most days a couple of 4WD vehicles leave for **Bintulu** from the town square at 7.30am (3hr 30min;

RM50 per person). It costs RM40 to reach the main trunk road, where you can flag down a long-distance bus. Any hotel can book a seat for you, or contact Mr Hamdani (see p.362).

INFORMATION AND TOURS

Banks The town has a Bank Simpanan Nasional, with ATM, three streets back from the river.

Longhouse trips Mr Hamdani offers day-trips that

include longboat charter and a little jungle trekking (RM95 per person, RM75 in groups of four or more; ☎019 886 5770). For an overnight stay, add RM30 per person.

ACCOMMODATION AND EATING

The town's *kedai kopis* include a desultory Malay place on the main street, while across from the bank is a simple wooden building housing an unnamed Chinese place that does stir fries to order and draws the odd local with its bottled beer.

Belaga On the main street ☎086 461244. The oldest of the town's three all-but-identical hotels and it looks it too, with dated fittings. Simple en-suite rooms with a/c, and there's also a drab café below. **RM35**

Sing Soon Hing On the main street ☎086 461257 or ☎086 461307. Slightly smarter than the *Belaga*, opposite

across a lane, albeit with similarly basic en-suite, a/c rooms. **RM35**

Sing Soon Huat At the end of a lane, just back from the Sing Soon Hing ☎086 461346. Sharing management with the *Sing Soon Hing*, and the en-suite, a/c rooms are little different. **RM35**

The coast from Sibu to Bintulu

The drive from Sibu to Bintulu is mundane, the roadscape lacking the grandeur of southwest Sarawak's mountains, with occasional glimpses of (usually modern) longhouses by the highway to perk up your spirits. The chief point of interest on this coastal stretch is **Similajau National Park**, a strip of forest with isolated beaches half an hour's drive beyond the industrial town of **Bintulu**. With plenty of time, you could also get a dose of the culture of the largely Muslim Melanau people by diverting off the trunk road to the small coastal town of **Mukah**. While not of huge interest in itself, it's

---

THE BAKUN DAM

The massive **Bakun hydroelectric dam** (🌐 sarawak-hidro.com), 37km east of Belaga on the Balui tributary of the Rejang, has been dogged by controversy since the project got the go-ahead in the 1990s. The 200-metre-high dam was designed to generate 2400 megawatts – much more power than Sarawak could use – but construction would flood an area of rainforest the size of Singapore, displacing ten thousand Orang Ulu and destroying many thriving longhouses.

Furious environmentalists and human-rights campaigners asked what was the point, and for years their concerns seemed vindicated as the dam was beset by delays. First, the Asian economic crisis of 1997 put the project on hold, but even so the government continued to resettle local communities to Asap, two hours' drive along the logging road connecting Belaga with the coast. When construction resumed it lumbered on until, in mid-2011, the dam finally began operation. However, it will not run at anything near capacity, since there is still no obvious market for the surplus power (one idea, to lay a submarine cable to Peninsular Malaysia, would be technically challenging and prohibitively expensive). Despite this, yet another dam is already being built just upriver at Long Murum, and there's talk of building yet more dams on the Rejang and Baram rivers.

Attempts have already begun to create tourist facilities at the dam lake, as has been tried with limited success at Batang Ai and Tasik Kenyir in Terengganu. Sibu's tourist office has details of a Kenyah longhouse that accepts guests, and whose inhabitants have a fishing lodge on the lake itself.

a potential base for the Melanau village of **Kampung Tellian**, which has an interesting heritage centre, **Lamin Dana**, that you can also stay at.

Mukah

MUKAH consists of a congested but atmospheric **old town** – a simple grid of streets along the south bank of the Mukah River – plus a newer section to the west. Old Mukah's casuarina-lined waterfront, its defining image, holds both new shophouses and more charismatic wooden versions. The two modest sights are the **sago furnace**, a simple, unobtrusive brick construction that commemorates the region's role in the collection and processing of the vitamin-rich sago palm, and, close by, the **Tua Pek Kong temple**, from whose veranda you can view the river's stilt houses and boats.

ARRIVAL AND DEPARTURE   MUKAH

By plane No buses run between Mukah's airport, 4km northwest, and the town itself; a taxi costs around RM15.
Destinations Kuching (3 daily; 1hr) and Miri (6 weekly; 1hr 10min), both on MASwings.

By bus The **bus station** lies off Jalan Sedia Raja, on the southern edge of the old town.
Destinations Bintulu (3 daily; 3hr); Miri (1–2 daily; 7hr); Sibu (3 daily; 3hr 30min).

INFORMATION

Tourist information Sibu's tourist office provides information on Mukah (see p.350). You can also talk to Diana Rose of *Lamin Dana* (see below) or the Mukah

Resident's Office (☏ 084 872596), a government department that has some responsibility for local tourism.

ACCOMMODATION

There's no reason to stay in Mukah rather than at *Lamin Dana*, but either of the two places below will do at a pinch.

Sri Umpang Hotel 29 Jalan Lintang ☏ 084 872415. Mukah's best choice, in the old town, not far from the bus station, with a bright and appealing foyer and clean, a/c rooms with sizeable bathrooms. RM40

Weiming Hotel 19 Main Bazaar, close to the Umpang ☏ 084 872278. Newish en-suite rooms with TV; in the heart of the old town and handy for buses, it's not a bad choice at all. RM35

EATING

Nibong House Jalan Orang Kaya Setia Raja, a 5min walk from the old town ☏ 084 871 935. The only Mukah restaurant worth making a beeline for, thanks to its marvellous Melanau and Chinese cuisine. The house speciality is sago grubs – they look unappetizingly like plump caterpillars, though some diners find them

reminiscent of prawn – grilled or stir-fried with garlic and ginger. Also popular are the raw-fish salad *umai*, plus seafood including crab and squid. Just don't turn up late in the evening when the place becomes karaoke city. Daily 10am–midnight.

Kampung Tellian

3km east of Mukah • Taxi from Mukah's bus terminus RM6

The Melanau water village of **KAMPUNG TELLIAN** is a veritable spaghetti junction of winding paths, precarious crisscrossing boardwalks and bridges. Some of the Melanau residents of its many stilt houses still process sago the traditional way – by pulverizing the pith in large troughs and squeezing the pulp through a sieve, then leaving it to dry.

Lamin Dana

Daily 9am–5pm for non-residents; closed public hols • RM3 entry fee • ☏ 019 849 5962, ✉ genistarose@gmail.com

Aside from its picturesque appeal, Tellian's main attraction is its beautiful heritage centre and guesthouse, **Lamin Dana**, built in 1999 in the style of a traditional Melanau tall house, though not quite on the scale of the one you may have seen at the Sarawak Cultural Village in Santubong. Exhibits include a collection of betel-nut jars, once used to store heirlooms, finely woven textiles for ceremonial occasions, musical instruments – including the obligatory gongs – and handicrafts such as handwoven rattan baskets

6

for which the Melanau are well known. A short walk along the plankway to the front of the tall house reveals a Melanau burial ground, or *bakut*, amid a clump of bare, ancient trees.

ACCOMMODATION AND EATING   **KAMPUNG TELLIAN**

Lamin Dana Kampung Tellian ☏019 849 5962, ✉genistarose@gmail.com. This recreated tall house makes an atmospheric place to stay, with eight variously sized, airy doubles and a couple of family rooms. Bathrooms are shared and there's no a/c. If you come on a package, you'll be taken

on a boat trip through the mangroves, do a guided village walk, and see a sago-processing demonstration; contact proprietor Diana Rose for details and to customize an itinerary. Doubles with breakfast RM75, three-day, two-night full-board package for two RM300

Bintulu

Forty years ago, **BINTULU** was little more than a resting point en route between Sibu (220km to the southwest) and Miri (210km northeast). Since large **natural gas** reserves were discovered offshore in the 1960s, however, speedy expansion has seen Bintulu follow in Miri's footsteps as a primary resources boom town. Today some quite prosperous neighbourhoods can be seen on the outskirts, though the old centre remains as unassuming as ever. In some ways it's reminiscent of Sibu – lacking Sibu's few sights, but with somewhat better eating. There are only two reasons why you might want to stop over: to use Bintulu as a base for the excellent **Similajau National Park** or, if you're heading south from Miri, as a springboard for **Belaga** and the Batang Rejang (see p.352). You can also reach **Niah National Park** (see p.369) from Bintulu, though it's easier from Miri as backpacker lodges there organize trips, while any express bus headed to Miri can drop you at **Lambir Hills National Park** (see p.369).

The old centre

You could spend a couple of hours strolling around Bintulu's centre, a grid of streets squashed between the defunct airfield to the east and the wide Kemena River to the west. This is why the town feels so low-key: the centre simply hasn't been able to grow. It looks as though developers and road builders may soon finally be allowed to chip away at the unaccountably abandoned airfield, however, so the heart of Bintulu may soon look very different.

The obvious place to start is on Main Bazaar in front of **Tian En Ting**, a grand Chinese temple that's really in too good a state of repair to impress. Recent beautification of the **riverfront has created** the open square here, as well as an esplanade and parkland area leading north towards the South China Sea – only 3km away, concealed beyond the Kemena's final bend.

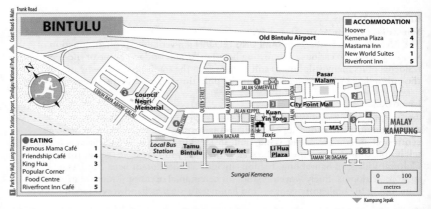

Just downriver are the modern **day market** (*pasar utama*) and the more informal **Tamu Bintulu**, where locals still bring in small quantities of goods and lay them on rough tables to sell. The jetties behind are a good place to observe life on the river: fishing boats bring their catch in every morning, barges laden with timber or building materials lumber past, while the opposite bank is dotted with rustic kampung houses.

Five minutes' walk from the *tamu*, amid a bunch of restaurants and shops, is an unattractive minaret-like clock tower built over one of Bintulu's few monuments, the **Council Negeri Memorial**. It's a sort of granite slab with a sign commemorating a meeting of Brooke officials with local chieftains in 1867, which inaugurated Sarawak's state legislature.

ARRIVAL AND DEPARTURE

BINTULU

By plane Bintulu's airport, 8km southwest of town (☎ 086 331073), holds an AirAsia ticket office. It can only be reached by a circuitous road route, detouring east and then south of town. A taxi into the centre costs RM35.

Destinations Kota Kinabalu (3 daily; 1hr 15min); Kuala Lumpur (3 daily; 2hr); Kuching (4 daily; 55min); Miri (2 daily; 30min); Sibu (3 daily; 55min).

By bus Bintulu's long-distance bus station is 5km northeast of town in the lively suburb of Medan Jaya. You might be able to find an infrequent local bus into the centre, but otherwise you'll have to pay around RM15 for a taxi.

Destinations Kuching (1–3 hourly; 11hr); Miri (2–3 hourly; 4hr); Mukah (3 daily; 3hr); Pontianak (Indonesia; at least 3 daily; 19hr); Sibu (2–3 hourly; 4hr).

GETTING AROUND

By taxi The main taxi rank (☎ 086 332009) is next to the Tian En Ting temple.

By car For car rental, try Kong Teck, near the Park City mall (☎ 086 336 197) and at the airport (☎ 086337767).

ACCOMMODATION

Central Bintulu holds a number of unexciting budget hotels, all with a/c, en-suite rooms; if those reviewed below are full, you will have no trouble stumbling upon others. Several business-oriented hotels, including some north of the centre towards the seafront, cater especially to visiting oil-industry executives.

Hoover 92 Jalan Keppel ☎ 086 337166. Brightly lit at night, this concrete block has slightly more comfortable rooms than others in its class, as reflected in the prices. RM80

Kemena Plaza Jalan Abang Galau ☎ 086 335111. A business-oriented hotel with an opulent lobby and a rooftop swimming pool, though the atmosphere can be predictably sterile. The unusually keen rates include breakfast. RM120

Mastama Inn Off Jalan Keppel ☎ 086 317203. This nondescript squat building holds a reasonable budget hotel, often quite full thanks to keen rates. RM55

New World Suites Above Park City mall, 1500m north of the centre off Jalan Tun Zaidi ☎ 086 331122, ⓦ newworldsuites.net. This slick new development pitches for business travellers and boasts contemporary decor, flat-screen TV and minibar in all rooms, plus sea views, though there's no pool. Rates drop by around RM40 at weekends. RM230

★ **Riverfront Inn** 256 Taman Sri Dagang ☎ 086 333111, ⓔ riverfrontinn@hotmail.com. Both smart (for Bintulu) and homely, and thus deservedly popular even though it lacks the facilities of the *Kemena Plaza*. Rooms are comfortable and done out in muted colours, and a busy restaurant is open all hours. Doubles vary in size, but discounts for single occupancy are trifling. RM85

EATING

Buoyed by oil and gas money and a small expat population, Bintulu boasts several decent restaurants, though many – along with a handful of bars – are in the suburbs. Still, quite a few central eating places are worth trying, and for evening snacks you can always try the *pasar malam* in the open space close to the airfield.

Famous Mama Café Jalan Somerville. The closest thing you'll find to a West Malaysian *mamak*-style joint, this Indian *kedai kopi* draws in people of all colours and faiths to socialize and stuff their faces from the great *nasi campur* spread (eaten with plain or *biriyani* rice) or various roti plates. Daily 7.30am– midnight.

Friendship Café Jalan Court. A bright and airy *kedai kopi* in a modern block offering a mix of Chinese (wonton soup, noodles etc) and Malay (great *nasi campur* plus *nasi lemak* and yet more noodles) food, though sadly they close once offices have shut. Daily 7am–6pm.

★ **King Hua** Between Jalan Keppel and Jalan Masjid.

6

The most popular venue on a lane turned over to open-air restaurants, the *King Hua* packs them in with its yummy seafood – black pepper crab, steamed pomfret, even prawns cooked in Guinness – plus more usual Chinese dishes such as lemon chicken and vegetable stir fries. While not in any way salubrious, it's hugely atmospheric. The menu is devoid of prices, partly because seafood is sold by weight, but they don't overcharge; reckon on RM25 per person, excluding drinks. Daily 8am–midnight.

★ **Popular Corner Food Centre** Lebuhraya Abang Galau. The size of four or five *kedai kopis* put together, this brilliant food court could hold its own in downtown KL. An endless range of stalls sell the likes of duck noodles, *yong tau foo*, even dim sum, plus a pastry stall doing custard tarts and local savouries such as sweet potato or yam fritters. Daily 7am–10pm.

Riverfront Inn Café Riverfront Inn, 256 Taman Sri Dagang ☎ 086 333111. A mere hotel coffee house it may be, but in Bintulu's centre it counts as posh. Come for the slap-up "Borneo breakfast" (sausage, beans and eggs, plus toast and coffee or tea for RM10) or a late meal if you arrive at an ungodly hour. Western fare includes fish and chips and spaghetti. Daily 24hr.

DIRECTORY

Hospital Lebuhraya Abang Galau ☎ 086 331455.
Internet Even down-at-heel hotels have wi-fi; otherwise try King's internet café on Jalan Masjid (daily 9am–11pm).
Pharmacies The Park City Mall has branches of Guardian and Watsons.

Police Branch on Jalan Somerville ☎ 086 332113.
Post office There's a branch post office on the unnamed road behind Jalan Somervile.
Visa extensions Immigration Department, 3km north of the centre on Jalan Tun Razak (☎ 086 312211).

Similajau National Park

28km northeast of Bintulu by road, the last 9km an access road off the coastal road to Miri • RM10 • ☎ 086 327284, ⓦ sarawakforestry.com • No buses; taxis from Bintulu cost at least RM40 one-way, the driver can collect you for the same price

With its sandy beaches broken only by rocky headlands and freshwater streams, the seventy-square-kilometre **Similajau National Park** has something of the appeal of the highly popular Bako, near Kuching. Enjoyable trekking makes for a great day-trip, and there's even good accommodation – if only the place were served by public transport, it would figure much more in visitors' itineraries. Though wildlife is not a major highlight, the park is well known for its population of saltwater **crocodiles** (signs along the creeks pointedly warn against swimming), with a few dolphins also sighted each year off the coast outside the rainy season. Birdlife includes black hornbills and, in the mangroves, kingfishers.

The main trail

The first stretch of the 10km **main trail** – which runs northeast, mostly just inland, from the park office – has you crossing a bridge over the mouth of the Likau, more of a

---

BINTULU TO BELAGA BY ROAD

When the water level in the Batang Rejang is too low for boats to reach Belaga, the one sure way to get there – and an interesting drive through remote terrain – is by **4WD** from Bintulu. The journey involves turning south off the main trunk road, 50km out of Bintulu, onto the road for the Bakun dam (see p.358), 125km southeast. After 80km, another right turn puts you on a logging road which, while not a classic bone-shaker, is roughish much of the way. The road undulates at first through jungled areas, then climbs steadily, snaking past isolated communities and through areas either already under oil palm or being cleared for it. Eventually there are gorgeous views of lushly forested peaks in the distance; the highest, **Bukit Lumut** at nearly 1000m, is 25km west of Belaga. If you do the return leg in the morning you'll probably see whole valleys blanketed in mist, too. Just as bumping along begins to pall, the road descends quite steeply, and you pull into Belaga four hours after leaving Bintulu.

One or two 4WDs leave Bintulu daily at 1.30pm for Belaga, with pick-up from hotels or other central locations by arrangement; a seat costs RM50. You can book the service with, among others, Mr Hasbie (☎ 013 842 9767) or Mr Hamdani (☎ 019 886 5770). Note that in future it may be possible to do the journey in an ordinary car – the government has announced plans to build a road from Bakun to Belaga.

large brown creek than a river, and heading into the jungle. Around 1km in, a short side branch leads west to a **viewpoint** – a wooden pavilion perched over a rocky beach, from where you can just spot Bintulu's oil and gas installations at Tanjung Kidurong, 15km north of town. Return to the trail and you come eventually to **Turtle Beach I** (6km along; allow 3hr to reach it), then **Turtle Beach II** (total 7.5km along) and finally **Golden Beach** (10km; 4hr). You can overnight at any of them in the hope of spotting **turtles**, who nest here from March to September, though there are no facilities and you should inform park staff of your intentions. Sadly, **swimming** at these beaches is not advised, because the sea is deep even close to shore and there's a strong undertow, though other smaller stretches of sand en route are okay for a dip.

Minor trails

A few short trails branch inland off the main trail within its first kilometre. The best leads to **Batu Anchau**, a curious flat rock formation in a stream bed, close to a small waterfall. It's a good site for a picnic and for spotting pitcher plants; allow ninety minutes to reach it from the park headquarters. You don't need to return the way you came – continue north along the trail, and you soon rejoin the main trail near the 3km marker.

INFORMATION

SIMILAJAU NATIONAL PARK

Park HQ Staff at the park HQ can provide a schematic trail map; find you a guide (RM30/hr); book you on a night walk on which you just might see pangolins or wild boar (RM40 for a group of five); and arrange boat trips.

GETTING AROUND

By boat As at Bako, boats are a useful timesaver – instead of trekking in two directions, you can pay RM150/boat (up to five passengers) to head out to Golden Beach, or RM100 to either of the Turtle beaches, then trek back. You can also use boats to reach Batu Mandi ("bath rock" in Malay), a rock formation out at sea with large depressions that regularly fill with sea water (RM100), or do a so-called night cruise along the Likau to spot kingfishers and those notorious crocodiles (RM100).

ACCOMMODATION AND EATING

Similajau National Park Accommodation 086 391284. The park's generally under-utilized accommodation makes it a relaxing place to spend a night or two. There's quite a range on offer, from two hostels that have rooms rather than dorms, each with one bunk bed and some with a bathroom too, to quite fancy new a/c accommodation; check for the latest pricing. A simple canteen serves the usual rice and noodle dishes. RM42

The northern coast

North of Bintulu, the scenery along the main trunk road is increasingly dominated by oil-palm estates; if you're driving, the quiet coastal highway is a more scenic option for the 210km drive to **Miri**, Sarawak's second largest city. Though boasting no important sights, Miri is nearly as important a gateway to Sarawak as Kuching, thanks to good flight connections and its location amid the riches of northern Sarawak, mostly deep inland and requiring days to explore properly. A couple of national parks lie close to the coast south of Miri: **Niah** is noted for its formidable **limestone caves**, while **Lambir Hills** offers more predictable jungle trekking.

Sarawak's northern coastal strip is also home to **Lawas**, near the Sabah state boundary. It has an air connection to Ba Kelalan that's useful if you want to see the Kelabit Highlands immediately after or before visiting Sabah.

Miri

Before oil was discovered in 1882, **MIRI** was a tiny, unimportant settlement. While production has now shifted offshore, the petroleum industry largely accounts for the

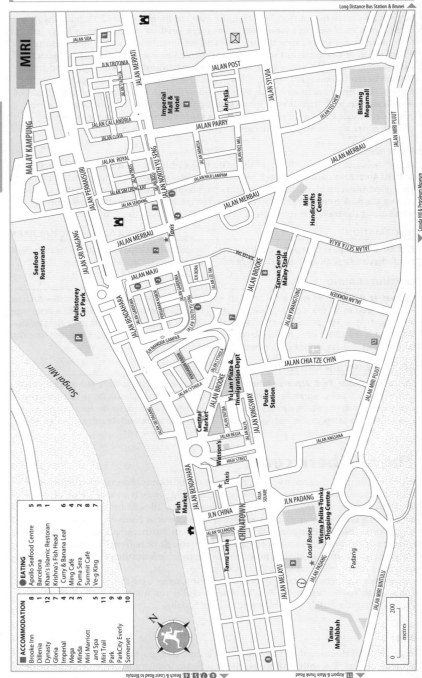

Long Distance Bus Station & Brunei

MIRI

MALAY KAMPUNG

JALAN SIDA

JLN TRITONIA

JALAN MERPATI

JALAN POST

Imperial
Mall &
Hotel

Air-Asia

JALAN SYLVIA

Bintang
Megamall

JALAN PARRY

JALAN CALLANDRIA

JALAN CLIVIA

JALAN ROYAL

JALAN MIMOSA

JALAN RICE MILL

JALAN PERMAISURI

JALAN NORTH YU SENG

JALAN HAJI LAMPAM

JALAN MERBAU

JALAN MERBAU

JALAN SIM CHENG KAY

JALAN SERDANG

Miri
Handicrafts
Centre

Seafood
Restaurants

JALAN SRI DAGANG

JALAN MERBAU

Taxis

JALAN SETIA RAJA

JALAN MAJU

Multistorey
Car Park

JALAN BENDAHARA

JALAN GARDENIA

PERSIARAN MIOR

JALAN SOUTH YU SENG

JALAN LEE TAK

JALAN NAKHODA GAMPAR

JALAN BROOKE

Taman Seroja
Malay Stalls

JALAN KWANGTUNG

JALAN HOKKIEN

Sungai Miri

JALAN CYTHIA

JALAN BROOKE

JALAN SRI DAGANG

PERSIARAN KABOR

JALAN ENTIRA

Yu Lan Plaza &
Immigration Dept

JALAN CHIA TZE CHIN

JALAN MIRI PUJUT

JALAN KINGSWAY

Police
Station

Central
Market

JALAN RAJA

JALAN BEGIA

Watson's

JALAN ANGSANA

HIGH STREET

Fish
Market

JALAN BENDAHARA

Taxis

RAJA SQUARE

JLN CHINA

JLN PADANG

Wisma Pelita Tunku
Shopping Centre

JALAN OLEANDER

CHINATOWN

Tamu Lama

Local Buses

JALAN PADANG

Padang

JALAN MELAYU

JALAN MIRI BINTULU

Tamu
Muhibbah

N

0   200
   metres

Canada Hill & Petroleum Museum

Airport & Main Trunk Road

Beach & Coast Road to Bintulu

ACCOMMODATION

Brooke Inn	8
Dillenia	1
Dynasty	12
Gloria	7
Imperial	4
Mega	2
Minda	3
Miri Marriott	
and Spa	5
Miri Trail	11
Park	9
ParkCity Everly	6
Somerset	10

● EATING

Apollo Seafood Centre	5
Barcelona	3
Khan's Islamic Restoran	1
Krishna's Fish Head	
Curry & Banana Leaf	6
Ming Café	4
Puma Sera	2
Summit Café	8
Ve-g King	7

thriving city of today, with a population of 300,000. Some of Miri's earliest inhabitants were pioneering **Chinese** merchants who set up shops to trade with the Kayan longhouses southeast along the Batang Baram, and the city retains a strong Chinese flavour, though the Iban and Malays are also well represented, along with a significant number of Orang Ulu.

Now blandly modern for the most part, Miri makes a surprisingly pleasant base from which to see northern Sarawak; visitors generally wind up staying longer than expected, sometimes in several stints interspersed with trips into the interior. In terms of sights, it holds one museum focusing on – guess – the oil industry, plus a few markets and an okay stretch of beach – in short, nothing compelling. Where Miri shines is in its great restaurants, accommodation and air connections. The hub for MASwings' services to the tiny settlements of the interior (see p.374), Miri also has flights to Kuching, KK, KL and Singapore.

The markets

Mostly open daily during daylight hours

Miri is unusually placed within a hairpin bend of the Miri River, with its centre on the east bank close to the river mouth; beyond the west "bank", a mere sliver of land seldom more than 500m wide, lies the South China Sea. Though eminently walkable and easy to navigate, the centre lacks any obvious focus, but it makes sense to start exploring at the clutch of **markets** close to Jalan China and the padang. The most interesting, the **Tamu Muhibbah** on Jalan Padang, is across from the tourist office. Nothing very unusual is sold in its main building, but the little building at the back is used by indigenous traders selling produce such as *akar bakawali*, spiny twigs boiled up as a high blood pressure cure, and "Bario rice" in various colours (it may in fact be varieties from Bario and grown elsewhere, rather than the genuine article for which the Kelabit Highlands are known). Less positively, you may also spot items that it's no longer legal to sell, such as porcupine quills and other animal-derived products.

A few minutes' walk north, in the **Tamu Lama** (also signed **Tamu Kedayan**) on Jalan Oleander, Malay traders sell foodstuffs and dried-leaf strips woven into square parcels for cooking *ketupat*, the rice cakes eaten with satay. Just beyond on Jalan Bendahara, next to the Chinese temple, is a lively **fish market**. Most prominent but least interesting of all is the large **Central Market** a couple of minutes' walk east on Jalan Brooke, known to Malays as the *pasar babi* or "pig market", as it's where Chinese meat traders operate. If you're around at the weekend, look out for more jungle produce being sold at a **Sunday market** in the streets to the south of the Tamu Lama (until around 1pm).

Petroleum Museum

Canada Hill (aka Bukit Tenaga); turn off Jalan Miri Pujut opposite Jalan Setia Raja • Daily except Mon 9am–4.30pm, closed some public hols • Free • Taxis up cost at least RM15, or it's a stiff 20min climb

From certain points in downtown Miri, for example along Jalan Kingsway, you can catch glimpses of what appears to be a tapering tower on the wooded ridge east of the centre. The tower is the **Grand Old Lady**, Miri's first oil well, drilled in 1910 and now marking Miri's one purpose-built sight, the **Petroleum Museum**. Unfortunately the displays are – pardon the pun – boring, concentrating on the technical aspects of drilling and refining, with some historical context but no tales of the human impact the nascent industry must surely have had.

The beach

Just over 3km southwest of the padang • buses #11 and #13 head out here from the local bus station; taxi fare at least RM15

The coast road out of town (the extension of Jalan Kubu) holds a stretch of public beach around 500m long. The sands are fairly narrow, but it's a relaxed enough spot and a fine place to watch the sun go down. The beach's proper name is **Tanjung Lobang**, though many locals (and bus timetables) call it **Taman Selera** as Malay stalls

6

sell seafood at a simple evenings-only food court. Buses stop around 6pm, so hanging around for the sunset means either trudging back into town or hoping that a taxi is available at the *ParkCity Everly* hotel 800m in towards the centre.

ARRIVAL AND DEPARTURE   MIRI

By plane Miri International Airport is 10km south of town (☎085 417315); AirAsia and MAS/MASwings have ticket offices in the departure lounge. To get a taxi into town, buy a RM25 voucher from the taxi counter.

Destinations Ba Kelalan (4 weekly, 3 of them via Lawas; 55min–1hr 30min); Bario (2 daily, some via Marudi; 50min–1hr 15min); Bintulu (4 daily; 35min); Johor Bahru (3 weekly; 2hr); Kota Kinabalu (at least 5 daily, including 2 via Labuan; 1hr–1hr 40min); Kuala Lumpur (at least 6 daily; 2hr 15min); Kuching (at least 8 daily; 1hr); Labuan (2 daily; 40min); Lawas (at least 2 daily; 45min); Limbang (2–3 daily; 35min); Long Akah (2 weekly, 1 via Marudi; 40min–1hr); Long Banga (2 weekly via Marudi; 1hr 20min); Long Lellang (2 weekly, 1 via Marudi; 45min–1hr 15min); Long Seridan (2 weekly, 1 via Marudi; 40min–1hr); Marudi (2–3 daily; 20min); Mukah (6 weekly; 1hr); Mulu (2 daily; 40min); Sibu (3 daily; 1hr); Singapore (4 weekly; 2hr).

By bus The long-distance bus station is at Pujut Corner, 4km northeast of the centre off Jalan Miri Pujut. Services to Bandar Seri Begawan in Brunei, via Kuala Belait and Seria, are run by PHLS (☎085 407175; daily 8.15am & 3.15pm; 4hr; RM40); it's seldom necessary to book tickets in advance, but you must show up half an hour before departure, as the conductor gathers passport details for the border crossing. Borneo Express runs a bus to Kota Kinabalu (☎085 430420; 3 weekly 8am; 11hr, RM90), which passes through Brunei but does not call at the capital. Heading all the way to KK entails four border crossings and thus eight new stamps in your passport.

Destinations Bintulu (2–3 hourly; 4hr); Kuching (1–3 hourly; 15hr); Lawas (2–3 daily; 6hr 30min); Limbang (2–3 daily; 5hr); Mukah (1–2 daily; 7hr); Pontianak (Indonesia; at least 3 daily; 24hr); Sibu (2–3 hourly; 8hr).

By kereta sapu Miri is one part of Sarawak where you might want to make use of informal taxis to head into the northern interior – most places can be reached by logging roads, although it will be a long and expensive slog. Some vehicles leave regularly from the streets close to the tourist office; others will need to be arranged in advance. One English-speaking driver to try for Marudi and points beyond in the Ulu Baram is Willykent (☎012 8794428); the tourist office should be able to give you details of other routes and drivers. Some drivers, including Mr Chin (☎019 814 2325; RM50), also head regularly into Bandar Seri Begawan (either the airport or downtown).

Car rental To rent a car, contact Transworld, second floor, Wisma Pelita Tunku ☎085 422227, or Kong Teck, at the airport ☎085 617767.

INFORMATION

Tourist office Miri's Visitors' Information Centre, on Jalan Padang at the southern end of the centre (Mon–Fri 8am–5pm, Sat & Sun 9am–3pm; ☎085 434181), covers all of northern Sarawak as well as Bintulu, and has good maps and leaflets. A Sarawak Forestry desk here (Mon–Fri) has up-to-date information on nearby national parks.

TOUR OPERATORS

A small number of tour operators offer Mulu and Kelabit Highlands packages, as well, more usefully, as genuinely imaginative trips to help you get off the beaten track in the upriver Baram and other parts of the interior. A couple of firms offer **dive trips** at the reefs off Miri's coast, which offer a few wreck dives; practically all sites are within an hour's boat ride.

Borneo Mainland Lot 1081 Jalan Merpati ☎085 433511, ⊛borneomainland.com. Trips to little-visited Loagan Bunut National Park, as well as packages to the usual Sarawak destinations.

Planet Borneo/Tropical Dives Brighton Centre, Jalan Temenggong Datuk Oyong Lawai, on road out to the beach ☎085 415582, ⊛planetborneotours.com. A veteran company with a good range of trips throughout Borneo. Northern Sarawak offerings include the Headhunters' Trail into Mulu starting from Limbang, plus an ambitious nine-day affair that begins in Loagan Bunut, then goes via 4WD to Long San in the Ulu Baram, where you spend a couple of nights in a longhouse, followed by a trip to the Tenyok Rimba reserve near Long Lama, followed by another 4WD ride to Long Terawan and a boat ride to Mulu. They also have a dive operation.

Red Monkey Divers Off Jalan Dato Abang Indeh, a few minutes' walk south of tourist office ☎085 416445, ⊛redmonkeydivers.com. PADI courses plus guided and unguided dives.

Tropical Adventure Across the road from Puma Sera restaurant on Jalan Maju ☎085 419337, ⊛borneotropicaladventure.com. Well-thought-through packages available from this excellent outfit include a grand trip that combines Mulu with skirting across Brunei to Lawas, then a 4WD drive up to Ba Kelalan in the Kelabit Highlands for a trek to Bario. They're also good for excursions on the Headhunters' Trail.

GETTING AROUND

By local bus As Miri's centre is easily walkable, you're only likely to catch a bus from the tiny local bus station, across the padang next to the tourist office, to get to the beach, airport (#22 & #28; hourly at best), or long-distance bus terminal (#33a; hourly).

By taxi Miri Taxi Association (☎085 432277) and Koperasi Teksi Miri (☎085 431000) are both 24hr.

ACCOMMODATION

GUESTHOUSES

★ **Dillenia** Jalan Sida ☎085 434204, ⓦsites .google.com/site/dilleniaguesthouse. Named after a shrub found all over Malaysia, the *Dillenia* has a cosy lounge painted green, plus dorms and rooms on two floors, including a family room that sleeps four. All well and good, and the place is very relaxed – but what really sets it apart is that it's impeccably managed by the super-efficient Mrs Lee, who can organize transport to the two nearby national parks and other local destinations (open to non-guests). Dorms RM30, doubles RM80, family room RM110

Minda North Yu Seng Road ☎085 411422, ⓦminda guesthouse.com. Somewhat haphazardly run, though it partly makes amends through informality: thus residents and staff just might get together and, say, cook a meal. While located on a busy street for bars and restaurants, near several malls, it's relatively quiet. It's also big, with a rooftop area where you can take in the nightlife below. Dorms RM20, doubles RM50

Miri Trail Across the road from the airport, behind the MASWings office ☎017 8503666, ⓦmiritrail guesthouse.com. This useful transit point saves air passengers the taxi fare into town, but also means you miss out on Miri's restaurants and shops. Discounts if you stay just a few hours. Dorms RM25, doubles RM55

HOTELS

Brooke Inn 14 Brooke Inn ☎085 412881, ⓔbrookeinn@hotmail.com. One of the oldest hotels in town and a bit of a museum piece, too – the rooms are plain and worn, and don't seem to have been altered much in fifty years. Still, they do have a/c and TV, and rates are low. RM50

★ **Dynasty** Jalan Miri Pujut ☎085 421111, ⓦwww .dynastyhotelmiri.com.my. The good impression given by the sizeable marbled lobby is reinforced by the spacious, comfortable rooms; some have bathtubs and sea views, too. Facilities include a mini-gym and sauna, though no pool, and this is among the best-value places in its class. Rates include breakfast. RM160

Gloria 27 Jalan Brooke ☎085 416699. Rooms in two wings, of which the newer has modernish decor and is generally in better condition than the similarly priced Park – though rates don't include breakfast. Old wing RM90, new wing RM105

Imperial Jalan North Yu Seng ☎085 431133, ⓦimperialhotel.com.my. A good top-end choice – rooms feature contemporary decor, the buffet breakfasts (included) are sumptuous and there's a lovely freeform pool and a mini-gym. It's also conveniently placed for the admittedly unexciting Imperial Mall, next door. RM200

Mega 907 Jalan Merbau ☎085 432432, ⓦmegahotel .com.my. Slightly dull, slightly neglected but still acceptable upper-end hotel, with a pool offering sea views, plus various restaurants and a gym. Look for weekend discounts. Rates include breakfast. RM200

Miri Marriott and Spa Jalan Temenggong Datuk Oyong Lawai, nearly 2km south of the padang ☎085 421121, ⓦmarriotthotels.com/myymc. One of Miri's two seaside hotels, this has had to smother its beach with boulders after the new marina nearby raised the risk of flooding; if you stay, it will be for the five-star amenities, giant freeform swimming pool and the spa offering Balinese massage. Packages offering spa discounts usually available. RM370

Park Jalan Raja, by the tourist office ☎085 414555. This large 1970s hotel, one of the oldest in town, could do with a little refurbishment though rooms aren't a bad size. Good value – rates include breakfast. RM90

ParkCity Everly Jalan Temenggong Datuk Oyong Lawai, 2.5km southwest of padang ☎085 440288, ⓦvhhotels.com. Unlike the *Marriott*, this seaside hotel has kept its beach and boasts reasonable rates, too. Some of the spacious rooms have great views over the lush garden with its pool, and the sands just beyond; sea views cost RM25 extra. RM190

Somerset 12 Jalan Kwangtung ☎085 422777, ⓔsomerhot@streamyx.com. Cosier and simpler than the *Dynasty* nearby, with unremarkable rooms and nicer, quite spacious one-bedroom apartments, which sleep two. Doubles RM115, apartments RM150

EATING, DRINKING AND ENTERTAINMENT

Miri's eating scene rivals Kuching's for quality, if not variety. Many visitors delight in being able to stuff their faces with genuinely delicious and interesting food after days spent hiking in the northern interior. North and South Yu Seng roads hold a particular concentration of restaurants, while along the riverfront you'll find a bunch of okay seafood places though no great sea views (more interesting are occasional sightings of crocodiles in the inky-black Miri River). For inexpensive

6

stalls, try the Chinese options at the Central Market (also good for cheap beer) or the Malay outlets on Jalan North Yu Seng and at Taman Seroja, up the road from the *Brooke Inn*.

Unfortunately the city's **bars** aren't up to much. Apart from a couple of so-so establishments near the *Dillenia* guesthouse and right below *Highlands*, not geared towards backpackers as such, venues on Jalan North Yu Seng are your best bet for a drink in generally karaoke-free surroundings. Miri does have one annual cultural event of note, however – the **Borneo Jazz Festival**, held in May at the *ParkCity Everly* hotel.

Apollo Seafood Centre 4 Jalan South Yu Seng ☎085 420813. Not much to look at, this old-fashioned Chinese place serves well-regarded standards such as fish-head curry. Around RM25 per head without drinks. Daily 10.30am–11pm.

★ **Barcelona** Jalan North Yu Seng ☎085 413388. Only one page of the menu at this so-called tapas bar features the stuff, followed by vast lists of pizzas, pasta dishes and sandwiches. The good news is that everything is pretty tasty – the pizzas especially – and the venue itself features an outdoor bar under a thatched roof, a pool table and chilled-out R&B/jazzy sounds. Reckon on RM25 per head with a soft drink. Daily 4pm–1am; happy hour until 9pm.

Khan's Islamic Restoran 233 Jalan Maju. Though a little dreary, this Is a well-established *kedai kopi* where the cheap-and-cheerful description really does apply. Offerings are predictable: *nasi campur*, a range of *biriyani* dishes, vindaloo curries and tandoori chicken, plus various roti and *murtabak* options. Daily 7am–9pm or so.

★ **Krishna's Fish Head Curry & Banana Leaf** Jalan Kubu. A modern, airy open-air restaurant serving enormous portions of classic South Indian food: order a plain or *biriyani* set plate and you'll be presented with a mound of rice, four curries, four dhal curries and soups, and poppadoms – enough to feed two. Around RM15 per head with a soft drink. Daily 11am–10pm.

Ming Café Corner of Jalan North Yu Seng and Jalan Merbau. Locals struggle to understand why foreigners love this place, essentially a food court that's been partitioned into a regular section and a prominent "restaurant" with powerful ceiling fans. Separate menus feature Chinese stir fries, Indian curries and some Western offerings such as fish and chips, all okay though a little overpriced. Still, it's not a bad place for a drink – they do Corona and Paulaner bottled

beers, among others, and there's a separate glassed-off bar area too. Daily 9am–midnight; later on Fri & Sat.

★ **Puma Sera** Corner of Jalan Maju and Persiaran Kabor. A tiptop Malay/Indonesian *kedai kopi* with a fantastic *nasi campur* spread that might feature *ikan patin* (catfish) curry or *umai* or chilli-fried aubergine. It's also a good place to try the Indonesian dish that's become a fad in Miri, *lalapan*: *lapan* means "eight" in Malay, so chicken *lalapan*, for example, is a plate of fried chicken, rice, Malay *ulam* (herbal salad) and some condiments – eight items in all. Reckon on RM10–15 per head with a soft drink. Daily 24hr.

★ **Summit Café** Off Jalan Melayu; head up the lane with Maybank on the corner and you'll see it on the left. One of Sarawak's most interesting restaurants: run by a friendly Kenyah woman whose husband is Kelabit, it serves Kelabit food of a sort you may struggle to turn up in Bario. Specialities include *labo senutuk*, smoked shredded pork or wild boar, and *kasam*, a sour/salty fermented combination of wild boar and rice. The latter is sold in plastic tubs, but you order most dishes from a *nasi campur* spread to be eaten with rice or *nuba laya*, made by pounding cooked rice till smooth and then steaming it wrapped in leaves. RM10–15 per head; don't confuse it with a Chinese place of the same name on Jalan South Yu Seng. Daily except Sun 7am–4pm; closed 2 wks at Christmas/New Year.

Ve-g King A minute's walk south beyond *Krishna's* on Jalan Kubu ☎085 435217. Slicker than most Chinese vegetarian places and, unusually, not vegan – they do use egg. There's a popular lunchtime-only *nasi campur* spread and, the rest of the day, a good range of rice and noodle options plus dishes such as vegetarian satay. Around RM20 per person with soft drinks if you order à la carte. Daily 7.30am–3pm & 5–9pm.

SHOPPING

Miri's shopping isn't especially distinguished and it's disappointing when it comes to handicrafts, though at least the malls are lively. The best downtown mall by some way is the **Bintang Megamall** at the corner of Jalan Miri Pujut and Jalan Merbau. With two wings – the newer extension is at the back – it houses a branch of the Parkson department store, a Giant supermarket and outlets of several Western fast-food chains. Numerous small shops sell phone chargers, memory cards and the like , while if you're looking for **camping equipment**, Chinese discount shops here and in the Imperial Mall stock endless paraphernalia and are worth checking out for cooking equipment and assorted gear. Rubber shoes are on sale in the small shops of Chinatown, and some may also sell mosquito nets, though you'll need to ask around.

Outdoor Life 2nd floor, new wing, Bintang Megamall ☎085 425303. Expensive torches, sleeping bags, tents and so forth. Daily 10am–9.30pm.

Popular Book Store 2nd floor, Bintang Megamall. As good a bookshop as Miri can muster; a couple of newsagents in the same mall stock small selections of

English-language books and magazines. Daily 10am–10pm.

Crafts The Miri Handicraft Centre on the corner of Jalan Brooke and Jalan Merbau is meant to be a showcase, but the shops here are a little desultory, and many of their wares are from Kalimantan. Borneo Arts on Jalan South Yu Seng is worth a look, with some woodcarving and Kenyah shields on show.

DIRECTORY

Banks and exchange As well as banks all over downtown, there's a moneychanger on the ground floor of the Imperial Mall on Jalan North Yu Seng.

Cinema MBO, Bintang Megamall.

Hospital Miri General Hospital, Jalan Lopeng (☎085 420033).

Internet access Cyber Corner.biz and Cyberworld, first floor, Wisma Pelita Tunku (by the *Park Hotel*); Fast Net Cyber Station, ground floor, Imperial Mall.

Laundry Two excellent laundries stand practically side by side a couple of doors along from the *Minda Guesthouse*.

Pharmacy Guardian and Watsons are both at Bintang Megamall.

Police HQ Jalan Kingsway (☎085 433677).

Post office Jalan Post.

Visa extensions First floor of the Yu Lan Plaza, the tallest building in town, unmissable on Jalan Kingsway (☎085 432209).

Lambir Hills National Park

35km out of Miri, beside the main trunk road to Bintulu • RM10 • ☎085 471630, ⓦ sarawakforestry.com • Any long-distance bus en route between Miri and Bintulu can drop you here; a taxi from Miri will cost RM60 and can collect you for the same price

If you haven't had your fill of classic rainforest elsewhere in Malaysia, then **Lambir Hills**, the closest national park to Miri, is especially worth considering. Popular with day-trippers at weekends, it holds some pleasant trails – though leeches can be annoying – and also good accommodation. Mixed dipterocarp forest makes up over half the park, with giant hardwood trees such as *meranti*, *kapur* and *keruing* creating deep shadows on the forest floor; there's also *kerangas* forest, with its peat soils and scrubby vegetation.

The trails

The park's most popular trail, the short **Latak trail** passes three **waterfalls**. The furthest – Latak itself, 1.5km or 30min from the park office – is the nicest, its 25m cascade feeding an alluring pool, but is inevitably busy at the weekends.

The **Inoue trail** from the park office joins the **Lepoh–Ridan trail** half an hour along, which leads after an hour to three more falls, **Dinding**, **Tengkorong** and **Pancur**; swimming isn't allowed at the last two as their pools are deep. The end of the Lepoh–Ridan trail marks the start of the trek to the top of **Bukit Lambir** (2hr 30min one-way from here; set off by 10am from the park office to be back by sunset). It's a tough but rewarding climb with a wonderful view across the park.

ACCOMMODATION	LAMBIR HILLS NATIONAL PARK
Lambir Hills National Park Accommodation ☎085 471630, ⓦ sarawakforestry.com. Though accommodation in the park is limited, more rooms have recently been built, and as few people stay you shouldn't have trouble	overnighting. Choose either a two-bedroom lodge, or take a room within a lodge, sharing facilities. There's also a campsite. Camping RM5, standard rooms RM40, a/c rooms RM100, standard lodges RM75, a/c lodges RM150

EATING	
Lambir Hills National Park Canteen ☎085 471630, ⓦ sarawakforestry.com. A small menu of simple Malay and	Chinese dishes; if you're overnighting, tell them in advance and they will stay open into the evening. Daily 7am–5pm.

Niah National Park

110km from Miri and 130km from Bintulu, off the main trunk road • RM10 • ☎085 737454, ⓦ sarawakforestry.com • For transport details, see p.372

NIAH NATIONAL PARK, ninety minutes' drive south of Miri, is practically a compulsory visit even if you're already caved out from visiting Mulu. Yes, its main attractions are massive **limestone caves**, but there any similarity with Mulu ends. Whereas almost all excursions at Mulu are regimented and chaperoned, visitors at Niah simply wander the caves at will, in places stumbling along tunnels – lightless but for your own torch – like questers from *The Lord of the Rings*. Elsewhere the caves are alive, with not just bats but people, who harvest bat guano and swiftlet nests for much of the year. This potent combination of vast caverns, communities at work, the rainforest and Niah's archeological significance – it's famous for prehistoric cave paintings and early human settlement – makes even a day-trip to Niah a wonderful experience. It is indeed possible to see much of Niah in a day: allow two to three hours to get from the park offices to the most distant caves, with breaks along the way.

Park museum

Daily except Mon 9.30am–4.30pm • Free • No photography

Before becoming a national park in 1974, Niah was made a National Historic Monument in 1958, after Tom Harrisson discovered that early man had been using it as a cemetery. Fragments of human skull, nearly 40,000 years old, were the earliest examples of *homo sapiens* found in Southeast Asia. For a sense of the park's history and archeological importance, spend half an hour at the simple but worthwhile **museum** across the stream beyond the park headquarters. Fascinating photos, from a mere half-century ago, but seeming much older, show Harrisson at work, and Iban and other indigenous people engaged in traditional dances or sporting activities.

The caves

The nearest cave to the museum is nearly 3km along a concrete path that soon becomes a jungle boardwalk. En route, you may stumble upon monkeys (including silverleafs and even gibbons), butterflies, skinks and odd scarlet millipedes. Twenty minutes' walk from the museum, a few traders sell refreshments and souvenirs at the start of a clearly marked path on the left that leads in ten minutes to a small, not all that enthralling, longhouse/village, **Rumah Patrick Ribau** (often still signed Rumah Chang).

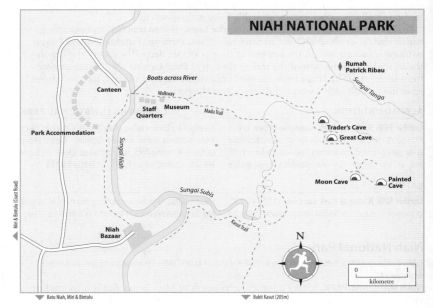

NIAH NATIONAL PARK

Trader's Cave

About 45 minutes from the museum, a great metal grille crosses the entire boardwalk, with a small gate below marking the entrance to the cave area. Within a few minutes you reach the **Trader's Cave**, not so much a cave as a long, wedge-shaped gash in the rock, open to the jungle along the entire right-hand side. The wooden platforms here were used as shelters by nest-gatherers, who until the 1970s used to barter their harvests here for goods brought by the townsfolk.

The Great Cave and Gan Kira (Moon Cave)

The huge, 250m-wide west mouth of the **Great Cave** is not far beyond Trader's Cave (labelled "Niah Cave" on some maps). A fenced-off stretch to the left marks the site of Tom Harrisson's groundbreaking archeological **digs** in 1957. The dark, gradually ascending area of cave floor beyond is known thanks to its breadth and flatness as the **Padang**; bear left to begin a path that leads down into the depths of the cave, where you will certainly need your torch. The smell of bat **guano** is pervasive, though it has a curiously inoffensive earthy quality. People you may see wandering off-path with sacks on their backs are harvesting the guano to sell as fertilizer. Between September and March you'll also see **bird's-nest collectors** shinning up ropes dangling from the ceiling in search of the edible swiftlet nests so prized by the Chinese. At around 6pm, visitors can see the swiftlets fly in and vast numbers of bats stream out for the night, and from much closer up than at Mulu – arrange this with a boatman in advance (see p.372).

The path curls round and then branches, the right-hand track taking you back up and out towards the padang. Head more or less straight on, past several cave mouths with jungle views on the left, to reach the pitch-black, stuffy tunnel out to Gan Kira at the southern end of the Great Cave system. It takes ten minutes to traverse, though it feels like years.

At the mouth of **Gan Kira**, a delightful spot nearly 4km from the park offices, the boardwalk ends at a shelter bathed in fabulous breezes. A blessed relief after the stuffiness of the preceding tunnel, it offers views of lushly forested hillside beyond.

The Painted Cave

A ten-minute walk through the jungle from Gan Kira, and then up some steep stairs, brings you to the mouth of the **Painted Cave**. Early Sarawak communities buried their dead in **boat-shaped coffins**, or "death ships", perched around the cave walls. When Harrisson first entered, the cave had partially collapsed, and the contents were spilled all around. Subsequent dating proved that the caves had been used as a cemetery for tens of thousands of years.

Although the reason visitors plod here is to view the cave's **wall paintings**, they're fenced off and so faded as to be almost impossible to make out – quite at odds with park photos showing bright red boats on a journey, ridden by figures that look to be jumping or dancing. A second painting site at the back of the cave was off-limits for excavation at the time of writing, with no word as to when and if it will be visitable.

The trails

It would be a tough ask to squeeze in the park's two trails plus the caves on a day-trip. Splitting off very near the start of the walkway to the caves, the **Jalan Madu** trail cuts south, across a peat swamp forest, where you see sword-leaved pandanus plants. It crosses the Subis River to end after an hour at the start of the **Bukit Kasut trail**. It's nearly another hour's walk to the hilltop, which has a fine view of both of the forest canopy and the plains beyond. Park staff may advise against the Bukit Kasut trail if it has recently rained, as it can be slippery when muddy.

ARRIVAL AND INFORMATION

By road The park is accessible from both the main trunk road and the coastal highway. All Miri guesthouses organize trips (RM60 per person), or catch any express bus between Miri and Bintulu and get off at the Batu Niah junction (RM12 from Miri, slightly more from Bintulu), where buses use the food court as a rest stop. Catch a *kereta sapu* for the 11km drive to the park entrance (RM25–30/ car one-way); park staff can summon a vehicle for the return trip. Driving, following signs from either main road for Batu Niah, Niah Bazaar or the park; after a few minutes take a signed turning east for Niah Bazaar, and then another turning north (left) for the park itself.

NIAH NATIONAL PARK

Ferry crossings To cross the stream just beyond the park headquarters to the museum and trails, you have to take a RM1 ferry ride (RM1.50 after 5.30pm). To see the bats flying out at the Great Cave, arrange with a boatman to be at the stream at 7.30pm, and leave the cave by 6.45pm – unless you have your own transport out, you will have to stay the night at the park.

Equipment Other than items you might bring to trek at any national park, the only thing that is essential for Niah is a reliable torch (flashlight) with fresh batteries. Some locals insist on bringing gloves as the walkway railings in the Great Cave aren't spared from guano, but this is overkill.

ACCOMMODATION AND EATING

Niah National Park Accommodation ☎ 085 737454, ⓦ sarawakforestry.com. Though ageing, Niah's accommodation is in reasonable condition as it's little used – there are no park guides and thus no night walks, so there's little reason to stay except to see the dusk exodus of the bats and to enjoy a little quiet. Options include four-room lodges and fancier rooms with bathroom and a/c, plus a campsite. A simple canteen serves a limited menu. Camping RM5, lodge rooms RM45, en-suite a/c rooms RM160

Lawas

One of the eleven administrative **divisions** into which Sarawak is parcelled is a horseshoe-shaped territory named **Limbang**, whose western arm splits Brunei into two and whose eastern arm slots between Brunei and Sabah. This eastern prong was bought by Charles Brooke from the Sultan of Brunei in 1905 and is home to **LAWAS**, a bustling bazaar town on the Lawas River, with a **tamu** above the river. The only reason to visit is because Lawas has flights to Ba Kelalan in the Kelabit Highlands, making it possible to reach the Highlands en route to or from Sabah.

ARRIVAL AND DEPARTURE

By plane Lawas's airport is 2km south of town; a taxi into town costs RM8.
Destinations Ba Kalalan (3 weekly; 35min); Kota Kinabalu (2 weekly; 45min); Miri (at least 2 daily; 45min).
By bus Destinations Bandar Seri Begawan (Brunei; 1 daily; 3hr); Kota Kinabalu (2 daily; 4hr 30min); Limbang (2 daily;

LAWAS

1hr 30min); Miri (1 daily; 6hr 30min).
By boat The jetty is beside the old mosque, 300m east of town.
Destinations Labuan (daily at 7.30am; 2hr 30min; RM30); Limbang (daily at 9am; 2hr; RM25).

ACCOMMODATION

Seri Malaysia Jalan Trusan ☎ 085 283200. This enormous new hotel is the plushest place to stay, which isn't saying much, and has no amenities other than a coffee house. Rates include breakfast. RM150

Shangsan Jalan Trusan ☎ 085 285522. In a drab concrete box, this used to be the best place to stay in town, though its en-suite, a/c rooms are arguably still better value than its nearby rival. RM75

The northern interior

For visitors who take the time and trouble to explore it, Sarawak's **northern interior** often ends up being the most memorable part of their stay. Some of the wildest, most untouched parts of Sarawak are interspersed, sometimes in close proximity, with badly degraded patches, thus putting everything you may have read about the state's environmental problems into sharp relief. The timber industry has been systematically

FROM TOP ROCK FORMATION, BAKO NATIONAL PARK (P.339); DEER CAVE, GUNUNG MULU NATIONAL PARK (P.376) >

6

logging here since the 1960s, with tracts of land already under oil palm or being cleared to grow it, yet the rugged terrain still offers fabulous **trekking** – something most visitors only experience at **Gunung Mulu National Park**, with its limestone Pinnacles and extensive caves.

As central Sarawak has the Rejang, so the north has its major river system, the **Batang Baram**. There the resemblance ends, for only the lowest part of the Baram – from **Marudi**, 50km southeast of Miri, to the river mouth at **Kuala Baram** near the Brunei border – has anything like a proper boat service, and that stretch is any case devoid of sights. Further upriver, the days of being able to just turn up and find a longboat and someone who can pilot it have long since gone. Much travel is therefore by small **aircraft** (see below) or **4WD**, using the spider's web of logging roads, which adds to the outback feel. Anyone wanting to get off the beaten track will most likely have to talk to the Miri tour operators (see p.366), who have contacts with boatmen and drivers and can arrange accommodation in towns with hardly any formal places to stay. That said, it is possible to visit remote **Penan settlements** in the upper Baram using a homestay programme, though this doesn't come cheap.

Mulu aside, the highlight is the lush **Kelabit Highlands**, accessible by air, where the pleasant climate is ideal for long treks in the rainforest. Of much lesser significance unless you're an avid birdwatcher is **Loagan Bunut National Park**, some distance off the Miri–Bintulu road and difficult to visit independently.

Gunung Mulu National Park

RM10 · ☎ 085 792300, ⦿ mulupark.com

GUNUNG MULU, Sarawak's premier national park and a UNESCO World Heritage Site, is named after the 2376m mountain at its heart. Modern explorers have been coming here since Spenser St John in the 1850s, who didn't reach the summit of Gunung Mulu but wrote inspiringly about the region in *Life in the Forests of the Far East*. A more successful bid in 1932 saw Edward Shackleton, son of the Antarctic explorer, get to the top during a research trip organized by Tom Harrisson.

The park's best-known feature, however, is atop another mountain, Gunung Api – the dozens of fifty-metre-high razor-sharp limestone spikes known as the **Pinnacles**. It is to catch sight of them – a three-day trek, there and back, from the park offices – and of

---

TWIN OTTERS

One entertaining aspect of travel in the northern interior is the chance to fly on **Twin Otters**, 19-seater propeller planes. More formally known as the de Havilland DHC-6, the Twin Otter can turn on the proverbial dime and take off from a standing start in around ten seconds, making it ideally suited to the tiny airfields hereabouts. As such, the plane forms the backbone of the Rural Air Services operated by Malaysia Airlines subsidiary **MASwings**, mostly out of Miri (though it's not used for Mulu, where the airport can take larger aircraft).

As the Twin Otter isn't pressurized – you can see daylight around the door rim – it doesn't fly above 3000m, and affords great views of the north's mountain ranges. That MASwings' Twin Otters are 30 years old and slightly shabby (though perfectly serviceable) only adds to the experience; the cabin will be fan-cooled and the cockpit door may well be open, letting you see what the pilots are up to.

On a practical note, passengers sit where they like, and luggage is limited to ten kilos per person (you may well have to weigh yourself at check-in so staff know the laden weight of the plane). At some airfields, departing passengers are slapped with a "service fee" of RM10–15 atop the taxes included in ticket prices. Levied by the small private concerns that run the airfields, these fees appear to be condoned by the authorities. Finally, while flights are seldom cancelled except in very gusty or stormy weather, note that the planes get booked solid during public and school holidays and over Christmas and New Year, when you may have to reserve weeks in advance.

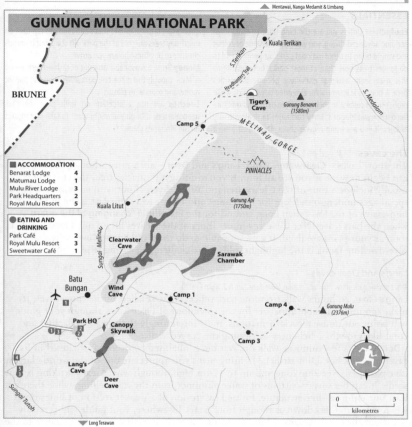

GUNUNG MULU NATIONAL PARK

the park's incredible network of **caves**, that visitors stream into Mulu (as the park is generally known) year-round. The park contains the largest limestone cave system in the world, formed when surface water eroded vast amounts of material, dividing the limestone belt that runs southwest–northeast across the middle of the park into separate mountains as well as carving cave passages within. Most people see some or all four of the dramatic **show caves**, though other caves are accessible on adventure packages and yet more are still being explored (see ⓦmulucaves.org).

Attractions aside, Mulu is a national park like no other in Sarawak, for the simple reason that it has been **privatized**. While the Sarawak Forestry Corporation remains in overall charge, most things to do with tourism, including the accommodation, is now run by Borsarmulu, the firm that owns the *Royal Mulu Resort* a few kilometres away. Now Mulu feels more Singapore than Sarawak: **tours** are timetabled and formatted, and you can explore few parts of the park unaccompanied. The tours are certainly well run, the guides are better communicators than at any other Sarawak park, and close supervision has helped prevent the poaching of valuable plants – but if it were possible to make the jungle somehow corporate, this is it. The only way to avoid taking the tours is by having your own registered guide, which enables you to book boat charter and accommodation on the trails separately, though this only makes sense if you are in a group.

6

ESSENTIALS

Equipment Unless you are climbing Gunung Mulu itself or doing advanced caving, you will need the same gear that you would bring to other national parks. As people tend to do longer treks here than at most parks, however, items that may seem optional elsewhere become necessities here. A poncho is essential for extended downpours, while rubber shoes come into their own when paths and trails are flooded or waterlogged; carry bandages to deal with any blisters. If you are using regular shoes, they must have a good grip. Ponchos, rubber shoes and food you can cook on multi-day treks are sold at the park gift shop, but it's much cheaper to buy these before you arrive.

Money Bring a reasonable amount of cash – there are no ATMs – though this is the one park where you can pay for rooms and tours with plastic.

Leeches are not a problem on trails near the park headquarters, though you might want to take precautions on the Pinnacles climb.

The caves

The show caves – **Clearwater, Wind, Lang's** and **Deer** – are a must, though the interest can begin to wane if you see all four. If you're doing a Pinnacles trek, the cost will usually include a tour of the Clearwater and Wind caves. If not, and you don't want to spend ages underground, opt for the Lang's and Deer caves – the last is the most impressive of the lot – then hang around for the incredible **"changing of the guard"**, when the bats leave Deer Cave at sunset. Tours of these caves fill up quickly, so book as soon as your plans are fixed. It's also possible to do tours of **Lagang Cave**, where obscure cave-dwelling fauna is the highlight, plus more challenging caving trips.

Lang's and Deer caves

3km from the park office, from where tours leave daily 2pm & 2.30pm • RM20

Lang's Cave, an hour's walk from the park office, is the smallest of the show caves. It makes an unremarkable appetizer for the splendour of Deer Cave, though your guide will point out unusual rock formations, most interestingly the curtain stalactites and coral-like growths – helictites – gripping the curved walls.

Deer Cave, a few minutes' walk on, was once inhabited by deer that sheltered in its cavernous reaches. Dim artificial lighting helps you appreciate one of the world's largest cave passages, over 2km long and up to 174m high, though what's really striking is how scenic it can be: silvery curtains of water plummet from the cave ceiling, while there's at least one chimney-like structure, formed by erosion of a weaker section of limestone, where rainwater jets down as though from a tap. Elsewhere, your guide will certainly point out the cave's Abraham Lincoln-in-profile rock formation and the entrance to the Garden of Eden (see below).

Once the tour is over, walk back to the park offices unaccompanied or linger with the guide at a viewpoint – the so-called Bat Observatory, with snacks on sale and toilets – near the caves. As it approaches 6pm, swiflets fly into the caves for the night, which isn't necessarily easy to make out, but what you can't fail to notice is the **bats**. They emerge from various holes in the roof in their hundreds of thousands, at first in little cloud-like bursts, then in continuous streams that can last for minutes at a time.

The Garden of Eden

Pools tour daily 1pm, Valley Walk tour daily 10am; both tours (minimum three people) include Lang's Cave and Deer Cave • Pools tour RM75, Valley RM105 including lunch

A hole at one point in Deer Cave offers a glimpse of lush ferns in the so-called **Garden of Eden**, a veritable "lost world" penned in by the steep cliffs of Mulu's limestone formations. It was discovered by a Royal Geographical Society expedition in 1976 whose leader, Robin Hanbury-Tenison, noted that "even the fish were tame and gathered in shoals around a hand dipped in the water". Today the park offers two trips to the area, reached by walking along a river that flows through a dark passage at Deer Cave. The Pools tour ends at a pool where you can swim, while the Valley Walk tour continues to small waterfalls and yet more pools, and ends with lunch in the wilds.

Wind and Clearwater caves

Daily 8.45am & 9.15am from the park offices • RM20 if on foot, RM50 including boat transport and a stop at Batu Bungan

As Wind and Clearwater lie upriver of the starting point for the Pinnacles trek, almost everyone heading to the Pinnacles sees these two caves as well. Most park trips include boat transport and a not-very-interesting stop en route at the Penan settlement of Batu Bungan (see p.377); you can, however, pay just for the cave tour, in which case you have to report earlier, and then set off on your own along the path that leads first to the Moonmilk Cave (see below), then Wind Cave, where you rendezvous with your guide and group.

Wind Cave feels rather closed-in compared to its much larger siblings, and is home to a great array of golden, contorted rock shapes and pillars, best seen from extended metal stairways. It's five minutes on to the base of **Clearwater Cave**, either by boat along the Melinau River or using a cliffside walkway that passes some "mini-Pinnacles", waist-high limestone shards embedded in the cliff face. Two hundred steps lead up to the cave mouth itself, adorned with curious glossy one-leafed plants unique to Mulu. Inside, the cave certainly impresses with its size – the entire system, probing 150km through Mulu's substratum, is thought to be the longest in Southeast Asia – though it's not all that visually interesting other than for its subterranean river, which joins the Melinau, and for its **notch**, a great horizontal groove in the cave wall running alongside the river. Half an hour is set aside for a dip in the chilly Melinau after the tour (there are changing facilities at the open area below).

Moonmilk and Lagang caves

Moonmilk is free to visit and walkable from the park office • Lagang "Fast Lane" tours leave daily 1.30pm from the park office (RM55 including boat rides); bring a torch (flashlight) for both caves

The small **Moonmilk Cave**, an hour's walk from the park office towards Wind Cave, isn't the only cave at Mulu to feature deposits of moonmilk – a derivative of limestone, produced by bacterial action and looking like dried-up cottage cheese. More significantly, it's the only cave in the park that can be visited without a guide; just be prepared to climb more than 400 steps to reach the cave mouth.

In the **Lagang Cave**, beyond Moonmilk, animals rather than geology are the highlight. The tour proceeds at a relaxed pace, the guide pausing all along the cave boardwalk to locate bats sleeping in little round holes in the ceiling, blind cave crabs, mossy-nest swiflet nests (made of a mixture of moss and saliva), cave crickets and the like. It may be possible to call at Moonmilk afterwards, though you will have to trek back to the park office as the boat probably won't wait for you.

ADVENTURE CAVING

Several of Mulu's caves are open for so-called **adventure caving** activities, though only a few count as hard-core, with caving experience compulsory; all require a group of at least three for the trip to go ahead. One advanced trip, the **Clearwater Connection** (RM170 per person), takes you through a chamber linking the Clearwater and Wind caves, wading or swimming through the Clearwater River en route. Another, the visit to the **Sarawak Chamber** (RM225), one of the world's largest caves, starts at the crack of dawn and lasts an entire day though there's no descent into the chamber itself.

If you just want to try something that isn't a regular trek or cave walk, **Racer Cave** (RM95) is probably best; you spend two hours ascending and descending through tunnels, with guide ropes to help you pull yourself along. More simply, **Lagang Cave** can be visited on a trip in which, as on the Fast Lane tour, you search for wildlife, but now in a separate, "off-piste" section (RM95), an escapade that's suitable for families. For details of other caving opportunities and what equipment to bring, speak to the park office.

Batu Bungan

A stop on boat tours to Wind/Clearwater caves, or a signed 30min walk from the airport in the opposite direction from the park

Just outside the park boundary, a couple of kilometres northwest of the park entrance, is a somewhat desultory collection of timber houses called **Batu Bungan** which, a worthwhile information display notes, is "probably the most-visited Penan settlement in Sarawak". Tourists indeed visit every morning en route to the caves, and the locals sell souvenirs, but the whole experience is rather artificial.

Canopy skywalk and Tree Top Tower

Six skywalk tours daily; 2hr • RM35, Tree Top Tower free (get key from the park office; RM50 deposit; no guide needed)

Mulu's **canopy skywalk**, 480m long and 20m up in the air, is reached by a side trail off the Deer Cave trail. The skywalk laces around six broad hardwood *kasai*, *betang*, *meranti*, *peran* and *segera* trees and takes around half an hour to complete. Though it's not that different to the canopy walkways at Taman Negara or at Temburong in Brunei, the tours are often full, so book promptly or try spotting birdlife from the elevated hide called the **Tree Top Tower**, just fifteen minutes from the park office.

Paku waterfall

3km from the park office • Free, but notify the Sarawak Forestry office (close to the park office)

As somewhere you can walk to on your own, the **Paku waterfall** is useful for whiling away a spare half-day. The signed track to the falls (actually the start of the multi-day 24km trek to Gunung Mulu) branches off the Deer Cave path 1.5km from the park headquarters, eventually arriving at a stream where a couple of minor cascades empty out of low gashes in the limestone cliff face. It's a pleasant, shady spot for a swim, though there are no facilities.

The Pinnacles

Five million years ago, the splatter of raindrops gradually dissolved Gunung Api's limestone and carved out the **Pinnacles** – fifty-metre-high shards, as sharp as samurai swords – from a solid block of rock. Erosion is still continuing and the entire region is pockmarked with deep shafts penetrating far into the heart of the mountain: one third of Gunung Api has already been washed away, and in another ten million years it might all be gone.

The chance to view the Pinnacles draws many visitors to Mulu, and the trek offers exactly that, by heading not to the Pinnacles but to a **ridge** across the way from where you can take everything in. It's a three-day, two-night hike, but only the ascent of the steep final ridge and the awkward descent are genuinely demanding; you will ache afterwards in places that may never have ached before. That said, if you're reasonably fit and suitably equipped, you should cope fine, and the guides put safety first and make allowances as appropriate for the slower members of their group. With whomever you arrange the trek, book or make enquiries at least a week in advance; base camp, **Camp 5**, sleeps fifty people, so there's a firm ceiling on the number of climbers per day. The park itself charges RM325 for the trek, including accommodation but no food; tour operators offer similar packages, as well as the Headhunters' Trail north of the Pinnacles; see opposite.

The hike

The itinerary is simple. **Day 1** usually sees trekkers visiting the Wind and Clearwater caves after which the boat takes them down the Melinau to **Kuala Litut**, the start of the 8km trek to Camp 5. Following a rough track of coarse stones embedded in the ground, it's mostly flat and perfectly straightforward, and you can expect to arrive well before sunset.

Camp 5 itself is spruce and homely; all accommodation is dorm-style, and there's a large, reasonably well-equipped kitchen and communal eating area. If you book through the park office, you'll have to bring your own provisions (see p.381). It's close to the **Melinau Gorge**, across which nearby **Gunung Api** (1750m) and **Gunung Benarat** (1580m) cast long shadows in the fading afternoon light. A bridge straddles the river here, with a path disappearing into the jungle on the far side – the first stage of the Headhunters' Trail. It's possible to explore the gorge instead of tackling the Pinnacles; ask at the park office for details.

Day 2 is the only time you are accompanied by a guide, setting off around 7.30am for the ascent. Departure may be delayed in heavy rain; if the weather fails to let up, and the climb has to be called off, you'll get half your money back if you booked through the park office. After two hours, a striking vista opens up: the rainforest stretches below as far as the eye can see, and wispy clouds drift along your line of vision. Eventually the trail reaches **moss forest**, where pitcher plants feed on insects, and ants and squirrels dart in and out among the roots of trees. The last thirty minutes of the climb is especially steep, with ladders and ropes to assist.

Parties usually arrive at the top of the **ridge** that overlooks the Pinnacles in late morning. The ridge is itself a pinnacle, sited across a ravine from the main cluster, and if you tap the rocks around you, they reverberate because of the large holes in the limestone underneath. After an hour it's time for the return slog, which can be more awkward on the legs and nerves, and takes longer, especially when the route is slippery. You'll probably arrive back at Camp 5 around 4pm.

On **day 3** trekkers retrace their steps to Kuala Litut for the boat ride back to the park office, usually arriving in plenty of time to catch an afternoon flight out.

Gunung Mulu

The route to the summit of **Gunung Mulu** (2376m) was first discovered in the 1920s by Tama Nilong, a Berawan rhinoceros-hunter. Earlier explorers had failed to find a way around the huge surrounding cliffs, but Nilong followed rhinoceros tracks along the southwest ridge trail, and thus enabled Lord Shackleton to become the first mountaineer to reach the summit in 1932. It's still an arduous climb, a 48km round trip that usually takes four days. Few visitors attempt it, but with enough notice, the park office can usually arrange it for groups of three or more. Expect to pay around RM400 per person, including accommodation and a guide, though you'll have to bring provisions and sleeping bags; a porter costs around RM100 extra.

THE HEADHUNTERS' TRAIL

A wonderful way to start or end a Pinnacles trek, the **Headhunters' Trail** adds just one day to the total duration, but when you consider the itinerary it's clearly all but impossible to make the necessary arrangements independently. The 11km trail – which corresponds to a route once taken by Kenyah and Kayan warring parties – leads north from Camp 5 to **Kuala Terikan**, at the confluence of the Terikan and Medalam rivers on the park's northern boundary. From here it's necessary to find a longboat down the Terikan to reach **Mentawai**, also on the park's edge, where you sign out of the park at a **ranger post** (or sign in if doing the route in reverse). The boat then continues to a longhouse near **Nanga Medamit** where tour operators put visitors up for the night. From here you can drive to the coastal town of **Limbang**, in between the two lumps of Brunei, and pick up a flight to Miri or bus to Kota Kinabalu, Bandar Seri Begawan or Miri.

As a trek, the trail is similar to the path from Kuala Litut to Camp 5, but less well maintained and 3km longer. Some say it's therefore better for exiting the park than entering it, as there's a lot of ground to cover to reach Camp 5 from Nanga Medamit before dark. In practice, people continue to trek in both directions.

To tackle the route, contact a tour operator in Miri or Kuching (the park itself is not currently offering this service). As an example, Tropical Adventure (see p.366) has a five-day excursion at RM1400 per person, covering the flight from Miri to Mulu, a night's accommodation at their own lodge near the park, meals, the Pinnacles trek (including the two show caves), and the exit to Limbang via Nanga Medamit.

6

Day 1, for most groups, is usually spent heading to **Camp 3** roughly midway along the route, passing Camp 1 en route (there is no Camp 2). The trek takes you from the limestone belt that most tourists associate with Mulu into sandstone terrain that dominates the southeast of the park. On **day 2** you spend the night 1800m up at **Camp 4**. Most climbers set off well before dawn on **day 3** for the hard ninety-minute trek to the **summit**, if possible arriving there at sunrise. Big clumps of pitcher plants dot the final stretch, though it's easy to miss them as by this point you are hauling yourself up by ropes onto the cold, windswept, craggy peak. From here, the view is exhilarating, looking down on Gunung Api and, on a clear day, far across the forest to Brunei Bay. Once again you spend the night at Camp 4. **Day 4** is a very full day as the aim is to get right back to the park HQ by nightfall.

ARRIVAL AND DEPARTURE   GUNUNG MULU NATIONAL PARK

By plane MASwings flies from Mulu's airport, 1500m from the park entrance, to Kota Kinabalu (1 daily, sometimes via Miri; 50min–2hr) and Miri (2 daily; 40min). They're not

Twin Otter services, but demand is high, so book a week or two in advance.

INFORMATION

Park office The office stocks good listings of treks, cave tours and activities, as well as browseable reference books on the park and Borneo.
Discovery Centre The informative displays on cave formation and Mulu's topography and ecology in the

excellent Discovery Centre, a small free museum alongside the park office, are worth at least half an hour of your time. The gift shop offers internet access at RM5/half-hour (RM10 for non-guests).

GETTING AROUND

By private taxi For transport around the Mulu area – for example, to eat somewhere other than where you are staying

– contact Edward at the *Sweetwater Café* (see opposite), who drives people around for a few ringgit per trip.

ACCOMMODATION

Accommodation within the park is limited to a hostel – basically a 21-bed dorm – and much more expensive private rooms; the dorm fills up, so enquire at least a week in advance to use it. Other places to stay nearby range from a hostel-type place to the *Royal Mulu Resort*; anyone residing outside the park is technically liable to pay the RM10 park fee each day that they enter, though it's not always enforced.

Benarat Lodge Nearly 2km southeast of park gates ☎085 419337 or ☎012 8703541, ⓦborneotropical adventure.com. Though Miri tour operator Tropical Adventure manages this place and puts up its customers here, independent visitors can book a room in advance. They have doubles plus some larger rooms, all with bathroom and fan; rates include breakfast, and lunch or dinner cost little extra. **RM120**
Matumau Lodge On the main road close to the airport ☎082 245175, ⓦborneoadventure.com. Run by the well-established Kuching operator Borneo Adventure, this resembles a large family home, with six en-suite rooms, a lounge and a dining room (rates include half-board). **RM350**
Mulu River Lodge Right outside the park entrance ☎012 8527471 or ☎012 8504431. Friendly guesthouse in a large timber building backing onto the Melinau River, containing a 22-bed dorm and clean bathrooms. When things are quiet they may give you a private room at the back of the *Sweetwater Café* next door, which they also run,

at no extra cost. With advance warning they may be able to provide an independent guide for Mulu. The good-value rates include a simple cooked breakfast. Dorms **RM35**
Park Headquarters ☎085 792300, ⓦmulupark.com. Clustered around the park office are various chalets, some recently built and all with a/c and bathroom, plus its hostel; the cheapest doubles are a leap up in price. All rates include breakfast. Dorms **RM40**, doubles **RM180**
Royal Mulu Resort 2km from the park entrance ☎085 792388, ⓦroyalmuluresort.com. The only moderately upmarket place to stay at Mulu, the *Resort* is well known for its swimming pool, which sticks out amid the jungle when viewed from the air, and its sprawling collection of longhouse-like blocks, raised on stilts. Rooms are spacious if slightly worn at the edges, and there's a vaguely smart restaurant and bar too. Rates include breakfast and the fancy buffet dinner. Note that the resort was being refurbished at the time of writing to be rebranded as a *Marriott*, so rates may have altered by the time you read this. **RM385**

EATING

Most people simply eat where they're staying, but it can be worth moving around a bit for variety. For the Pinnacles and other long treks, the park gift shop sells sachets of instant pasta, canned beans and curries, biscuits, chocolate and so forth.

Park Café Next to park office. An airy modern affair, overlooking the Melinau River and serving pretty decent food. Their highly spicy and creamy Sarawak *laksa* is their strongest suit, and they also do omelettes, French fries, a limited range of stir fries to be eaten with rice, and the odd dessert such as chocolate cake. At breakfast they offer Western and Asian options and fruit. Beer and wine available too. Around RM15 per person with a soft drink. Daily 7.30am–9pm.

Royal Mulu Resort 2km from park entrance ☎ 085 792388. The hotel restaurant's buffet dinner – a grand spread of rice and pasta, salads and stir fries, and *kuih* for dessert, plus a half-hour tribal dance show at 8pm – will set you back RM78 per head. *Tuak* is available, too, at a

shocking RM50 a bottle. There's also a bar, which serves reasonably priced light bites at night. Daily 7am–9.30pm, bar late afternoon till 11pm.

Sweetwater Café Next to Mulu River Lodge, right outside park entrance. This is endearingly like a roadside *kedai kopi* though the food is nothing special – simple stir fry plates, say, chicken curry or sweet and sour fish with rice and vegetables, are the mainstay at RM15. They also serve Western cooked breakfasts (RM10) and can prepare a limited range of dishes to order. Beer and home-made *tuak* served, too. Daily 7am–9.30pm or so, though they may effectively shut down between mealtimes.

Loagan Bunut National Park

80km south of Miri as the crow flies • RM10 • ☎ 085 775119, ⓦ sarawakforestry.com

Loagan Bunut National Park, best visited on an overnight trip, is a good spot for the dedicated birdwatcher, boasting stork-billed kingfishers and hornbills among many other species. Many live around the park's lake, **Tasik Bunut**, tucked away on the upper reaches of the **Teru River**, a tributary of the Tinjar, which in turn flows into the Baram. During prolonged dry spells, when the lake level drops drastically, a peculiar form of fishing, which the local **Berawan** people call *selambau*, is carried out. Just before the lake dries out, fishermen use giant spoon-shaped wooden frames to scoop up any fish that haven't escaped down the lake's two watercourses.

For birds, these dry times are a perfect time to feed too, and in May and June the surrounding peat-swamp forest supports breeding colonies of such species as darters, egrets and bitterns. Initially the lake can appear huge, its edges hard to detect as the sunlight is often hazy; however, it's only around 500m wide and 1km long. Small cabins built on rafts house Berawan fishermen, while around them lies an intricate network of fishing plots, with underwater nets and lines tied to stakes pushed into the lake bed. The best times to drift by boat across the lake are early morning and dusk, when the birds are at their most active.

ARRIVAL AND DEPARTURE   LOAGAN BUNUT NATIONAL PARK

By 4WD There's no public transport to the park, but *kereta sapu* 4WDs may head here in the morning from near Miri's tourist office; ask staff there where to wait (3hr; RM40–50 per person if you can fill the car). When you want to head back, park staff can usually arrange a vehicle.

By private taxi One Miri driver who tends to head to the area is Wilfred (☎ 019 8857471).

Tours Miri tour operators such as Borneo Mainland (see p.366) offer trips to the park.

ACCOMMODATION AND EATING

If you're here on a trip with Borneo Mainland you have the option to stay at a nearby farm with which the company has links.

Loagan Bunut National Park Accommodation ☎ 085 775119, ⓦ sarawakforestry.com. Located near the lake, the in-park accommodation is limited to a hostel

and a so-called VIP chalet with two bedrooms, a/c and its own bathroom; a small canteen serves basic meals and snacks. Dorms RM15, chalet RM225

6

The Kelabit Highlands

Right up against the Kalimantan border, 100km southeast of Gunung Mulu, the long, high plateau of the **Kelabit Highlands** has been home to the Kelabit people for hundreds of years. Western explorers had no idea this self-sufficient mountain community existed until the early twentieth century, and the Highlands were literally not put on the map until World War II, when British and Australian commandos, led by Major Tom Harrisson, used Kelabit settlements as bases during a guerrilla war against the occupying Japanese. Before Harrisson's men built an airstrip at Bario, trekking over inhospitable terrain was the only way to get here – it took two weeks from the nearest large town, Marudi, on the opposite side of Mulu. When missionaries arrived and converted the animist Kelabit to Christianity after the war, many traditions, like burial rituals and wild parties called *irau*s (where Chinese jars full of rice wine were consumed) disappeared. Many of the magnificent Kelabit **megaliths** associated with these traditions have been swallowed up by the jungle, but some dolmens, urns, rock carvings and ossuaries used in funeral processes can still be found, so the region draws archeologists and anthropologists from far and wide. The Kelabit are not the only inhabitants of this part of the state, however; there are also populations of **Penan** and **Lun Bawang** (formerly called the Murut).

Despite logging in the Bario area, the Highlands remain generally unspoiled, with occasional wildlife sightings and a refreshing climate – temperatures are only a few degrees lower than in Miri by day, but at night they can drop to an untropical 15°C (60°F). As such the region is a great target for walkers, and it is easily accessible by air, with three villages served by MASwings. Most visitors head to **Bario** or **Ba' Kelalan** as they have formal accommodation, but the real point of being here is to get out into the countryside, doing day-walks or longer treks through the jungle, on which you can be hosted in little settlements or longhouses en route. It's also possible to do more challenging treks up to the peaks of the **Pulong Tau**

Map: Kelabit Highlands. Labels include: Lawas, Ba'Kelalan, Gunung Murud Trail, G. Murud (2423m), Long Medang, Batu Lawi (2044m), Pa Rupai, Long Rapung, Pa'Lungan, Lembudud, Megalith, Bario Asal, Padang Pasir, Pa Ukat, Ullong Pallang, Pa Umor, BARIO, KALIMANTAN, Kampung Baru, INDONESIA, Pa' Berang, Pa'Main, PULONG TAU NATIONAL PARK, Pa'Mada, Pa'Dali, Ramudu, Batu Patung, G. Apad Runan (2100m), G. Murud Kecil (2112m), S. Kelapang, Harrison Trail, S. Selungo, Long Kerong, Long Lellang, Lio Matoh, Long Banga, Batang Baram, S. Puak, S. Baiong, Marudi, ABU RANGE, TAMA, **KELABIT HIGHLANDS**. Scale: 0–10 kilometres.

National Park (which has no facilities and no one to collect the entrance fee), notably **Gunung Murud**. There are **no banks**, so bring enough cash to cover board and lodging plus guiding/trekking fees.

Bario

The short flight from Miri makes a thrilling introduction to this corner of Sarawak, the Twin Otter giving passengers amazing **views** (sit on the left on the way in, on the right on the way back) of serried ranks of blue limestone ridges at Gunung Mulu National Park and then of the double-humped **Batu Lawi** (see p.387) before landing at **BARIO**. From the air, it's a sprawling jumble of little paths and houses, as well as fields planted with the **rice** for which the village is well known. There is a centre of sorts, a grassy space 2km northwest of the airfield, ringed by a few modern buildings housing a few shops, including one selling Penan baskets, and uninteresting *kedai kopis*, but much of the village is scattered around the fields 2km further northwest, along the main road and a couple of minor tracks off or parallel to it.

Situated on a plateau, with very little shade thanks to agriculture, Bario is visually dull in places but scenic in others, with vistas of rice fields and water buffalo against the lush mountains of the **Tama Abu Range** to the north and west. Extended treks aside, half-day and full-day walking opportunities lie in all directions, and there are a couple of things to look at in the village itself. Bring a **torch** if you might be returning at dusk.

Bario Asal

While not the sole longhouse in the vicinity, **Bario Asal** is the oldest and the only one in the village proper, close to the northern end of the main street. The unassuming timber building is unusual for effectively having two *ruais* – the second one, at the back, houses a communal kitchen with a long row of individual fireplaces for cooking. As a social venue, it's as important as the main *ruai* at the front. The longhouse also has a special area where travellers can stay (see p.384), and sells some Kelabit beadwork, jackets and hats.

The Tom Harrisson memorial

Beyond the longhouse the road soon curls round to the left, passing a hillock atop which stands a **memorial to Tom Harrisson** in the shape of a *sape*, the Orang Ulu lute. Despite the enormous contribution Harrisson made to our understanding of Sarawak's history, as curator of the Sarawak Museum in Kuching and as a roving anthropologist and archeologist (notably at Niah), it was only in 2010 that this memorial was erected. The inscription, besides paying tribute to the military work of Harrisson and his British and Australian comrades, also cites the "sacrifice of the tribal warriors of the Baram and Rejang basins" in helping liberate Sarawak from Japanese occupation.

SMK Bario

The village's secondary school, **SMK Bario**, near the longhouse along the track parallel to the main road, is a source of some pride locally. With beautifully kept gardens and a small orchid collection, it's well run, and a good proportion of its students go on to university. A hill at the back offers a view over the whole village.

ARRIVAL AND DEPARTURE   BARIO

By plane Passengers arriving by air are met by Bario's guesthouse owners every morning, so you should be collected if you've booked to stay, and be able to arrange a room if not.

Destinations Marudi (2 weekly; 40min); Miri (2 daily, sometimes via Marudi; 50min–1hr 15min).

INFORMATION

Maps Most guesthouse owners can provide sketch maps of Bario's trekking options and talk you through them, though they may emphasize areas for which they specialize in making arrangements.

6

Internet Internet access in Bario, where there's no phone cabling and mobile phone coverage arrived only recently, used to be synonymous with the village's pioneering eBario project. It works by beaming signals from the Telecentre in the middle of the village to reflectors all over the area, and eventually to the subscriber's receiver. Unfortunately, power-supply problems at the Telecentre mean the system is down more often than not. When it works, you can use the Telecentre as an internet café, but for some time villagers (as well as travellers) have been popping into Bario's airfield to get on the staff wi-fi network (no password needed), which sits atop a satellite internet connection.

ACCOMMODATION AND EATING

Travellers can **stay** in several simple places in and around Bario, and there is even unconfirmed talk of a small hotel being put up in the village centre. Most places have some solar-powered lighting at night (there's no mains electricity), though hot water is a bit of a luxury, and the tap water can be icy cold. Prices tend to include meals, so people eat where they stay. You may have trouble finding a place to stay over Christmas and New Year – when guesthouses may shut for lack of incoming tourists – and during the annual **Bario Food Festival** in July (ⓦ nukenen.com), when the village centre is transformed into a mini-fair. Not spicy by Malaysian standards, Bario cuisine features ingredients such as wild boar and locally farmed fish such as carp, though guesthouses may not serve traditional staples unless you request them. Mounds of rice are de rigueur; nearly as common an ingredient is pineapple, the village's second most important crop. Don't be surprised if you're served pineapple curry, pineapple cake and so on; it's even possible to buy weak home-made pineapple "cider" in the village. If you're out for the day, you can request a packed lunch. The Y2K shop on the main road, nearly ten minutes' walk north of the centre, sells drinks and snacks at steepish prices.

★ **Bariew Lodge (aka Reddish's Place)** 500m north of the centre, on the main road ☎014 8923431, ✉ bariewlodge@yahoo.com. Reddish has a spacious lodge with seven nicely decorated little rooms, three sitting rooms and an outhouse for meals, and is a good person to talk to about local treks, whether easy or involving a couple of days in the mountains. B&B per person R̄M̄3̄5̄, full-board per person R̄M̄7̄0̄

Bario Asal 4km northwest of the airport ☎019 8259505. The longhouse has a nicely set up guest area with two bedrooms, each containing a double bed, and there's a reasonable bathroom, a huge lounge area plus a space where spare beds can be set up. Per-person rate R̄M̄4̄0̄

De Plateau Lodge 3km east of Bario centre, towards Pa Umor ☎019 8559458, ✉ deplateau@gmail.com. Douglas Munney Bala's tranquil and well-equipped compound comprises seven comfortable rooms, and a sitting and dining area. Bala specializes in birdwatching trips nearby, and is a fount of knowledge on Kelabit culture and lands. Full-board per person R̄M̄7̄0̄

Gem's Lodge Pa Umor, 6km northeast of Bario, backing onto the Dapur River ☎013 8280507,

---

HIGHLANDS TREKS

Guesthouse owners can either find **guides** for longer treks or say in which villages guides can be found. Some owners, like Reddish of the *Bariew Backpacker Lodge* and Jaman Riboh at *Gem's Lodge* in Pa Umor, may even take you themselves if their schedules permit. Guides can be in short supply, during the June–August peak season, and you can't arrange one weeks in advance, so make enquiries a couple of days before you plan to set out. Guides estimate the **fitness** of the group and set the pace accordingly. Trips may involve gathering wild vegetables, catching fish and cooking, Kelabit-style, on the campfire, as well as locating dolmens and visiting longhouses.

The usual **rate** to hire a guide in the Bario area is RM80 per day, or RM100 if overnighting (prices in Ba'Kelalan may be slightly higher). For a challenging mountain trek, you may be charged an extra RM20 per day; a **porter** costs around RM100 a day. These fees generally do not include provisions, which cost around RM15 per person per day. Where you overnight in villages, expect to pay RM50–60 per person for board and lodging.

As regards **equipment**, travel light bearing in mind the strict baggage limits on Twin Otters. On top of what you'd normally bring for a day-trek at a national park, it makes sense to have a sleeping bag and poncho, plus warm clothing if you want to overnight outdoors or do any mountain trekking. A tent can be useful though it obviously weighs down luggage; some guesthouses (eg *Bariew Lodge*) may have tents and other gear for rent, and guides may have canvas sheets that will suffice for shelter.

e gems_lodge@yahoo.com. This large timber building, run by the knowledgeable and friendly Jaman Riboh on behalf of owners in Kuching, is one of the area's oldest lodgings, and has a suitably rustic feel. Bedrooms simply have mattresses on the floor, though the place is more than habitable. Jaman seldom meets guests at the airport, though; to get to the lodge, follow the directions for Pa' Lungan (see p.386), but take the right fork on the road and look out for the turning, 1km on. Per-person rate RM70

Hill View Lodge (aka Nancy & Harriss) A couple of minutes' walk off the main road, reached by a signed track **☎** 013 8505850, **e** nancyharriss@yahoo.com. This blue-roofed house contains a multitude of pleasant rooms with shared facilities, and Nancy may have dorms ready by

the time you read this. Prices vary through the year; veggies get a small discount. Per-person rate RM60

★ **Junglebluesdream** 3km from centre, reached by a signed path northeast off main road **☎** 019 8901797, **e** junglebluesdream@gmail.com. Local artist Stephen and his Danish partner Tine offer nice accommodation, with four simple, cosy rooms in their section of a longhouse. Stephen's artwork decorates a lot of the building and his cooking is a treat; everyone eats together on a spacious terrace. Per-person rate RM70

Keludai On the main road more or less opposite the Y2K shop. Not a guesthouse, this timber building is what passes for a tavern — it's even packed with men in cowboy hats (a local affectation) and country music is sometimes spun too. Open by day and night; no fixed hours.

Short walks from Bario

Little walks that you can do without a guide around Bario are numerous and varied. Besides the destinations mentioned here, it's possible to head to a "microhydro" power plant on a stream north of the village, and a couple of hills around town offer views; your accommodation will have details.

Millennium Gap

By far the best short walk from Bario is the four-hour round trip to the hilltop gap in the forest northwest of the village, as obvious as missing front teeth. Local custom dictates that trees can be felled to create a visible dent in the jungle to celebrate major events, so it's not hard to guess when this example, the **Millennium Gap**, was created.

To reach it, head out of the village using the track parallel to the main road, which passes the secondary school and the far end of the Bario Asal longhouse. It soon takes a left turn around paddy fields and then swings to the right, bringing you after ten minutes to a hamlet called **Arul Daran**, with a few longhouse-style buildings. The **wind turbines** up against the hill on the left, meant to provide power to the residents, were a government prestige project and might have seemed a sound choice in an area known for its breezes (*bariew* means "wind" in Kelabit), but they're screened from the air currents and hardly turn.

Beyond, through another rice field or two and then over a stile, is a slightly scruffy **Penan settlement** comprising a few wooden houses; the inhabitants only arrived a few years ago. After this the track simply heads uphill into the jungle, eventually reaching the gap, with magnificent views over the Bario plateau.

Kampung Baru

The short trek to the longhouse settlement of **Kampung Baru**, an hour from Bario, starts by crossing the former Bario airfield (west of the present one), and continues for the rest of the way along a wide, streamside track. En route you will experience the slightly odd spectacle of sheep being farmed, and may also spot pitcher plants and wild orchids.

The Kelapang River trail

Tracing the **Kelapang River** south of Bario used to be a popular option, though logging in the area has reduced its allure (and truncated what was once a much larger route). The idea is to head to Pa' Mada on the first night, then to Pa' Ramudu via Pa' Dali. Thereafter people either retrace the route or elect to be driven back to Bario by 4WD (around RM200 for up to four people; best arranged in Bario or Pa' Dali).

6

Pa' Mada

The eight-hour slog from Bario to Pa' Mada begins by heading to Kampung Baru, 1km beyond which you follow a path to the left over a wobbly steel-and-bamboo bridge and onto a narrow, undulating buffalo path. Four or five hours out, you pass through the area where the longhouse of **Pa' Main** used to stand, until its residents relocated closer to Bario during the Konfrontasi. Another three hours' walk brings you to the longhouse community of **Pa' Mada**, nestling amid tended fields beside a small brook. A room in the longhouse is usually reserved for walkers to sleep.

Pa' Dali

The track from Pa' Mada to the scattered settlement of **Pa' Dali** is quite easy, taking just two hours. It's tempting to push on to Pa' Ramudu, but since this next leg is arguably the most exacting of the loop, you might want to rest briefly before the tough four-hour hike ahead, or even overnight in Pa' Dali. Comprising two longhouses, Pa' Dali is also a springboard to several highland adventures, among them the half-day hike to see the village's huge stone drums, once used as caskets.

Pa' Ramudu

The journey from Pa' Dali to **Pa' Ramudu** kicks off by skirting paddy fields. Shortly afterwards you emerge into buffalo pasture, where on the left is a large rock in whose carved niches the remains of the village's dead were once left in jars. Three or four hours of steep rises and drops follow, before you reach the compact Pa' Ramudu longhouse, set behind fields of pineapple and sugar cane. The community is famed for producing skilfully woven rattan baskets, worn on the back, and may have some for sale.

Pa' Lungan

The five-hour hike from Bario to **Pa' Lungan** is popular enough that some villagers offer homestays. In all honesty the trek, though not hard – the trail is fairly clear and a guide not needed – is not that interesting either, passing mainly through woodland. However, the village itself is a base for day-treks into dense forest, with the possibility of camping overnight in the jungle, as well much more challenging treks; guides can be found in the village itself.

The first stretch of the journey involves heading past the airport and northeast out of town along the main road. About 3km from the centre the road forks; take the left-hand branch to reach, 1km on, the settlement of **Pa' Ukat**. Three or four hours on you finally arrive at Pa' Lungan, with detached houses around a large rectangular field for pigs and buffalo. The best-known homestay is run by Supang and informally called the *Batu Ritung Lodge* (☎019 805 2119; RM80 per person full board); if Supang has no room, she can point you to several decent alternatives.

To save time, some trekkers opt to be taken part of the way to Pa' Lungan (or back) by **boat** (1–2hr; RM250 for four passengers), which Bario guesthouses can usually arrange. To meet the boatman, take the right-hand fork on the main road heading towards another settlement, **Pa' Umor**, then another track on the right down to the Dapur River; your guesthouse will tell you where to rendezvous. The boatman takes you to a point on the river called **Long Palungan**, and can point out the trail to follow uphill from the bank; from the right spot on the hilltop, a clear wide trail takes you on to Pa' Lungan (1hr 30min).

Bario to Ba' Kelalan

It's possible to head to Ba' Kelalan from Bario, either via Indonesia (3 days one-way) or Gunung Murud, which takes six days and is of course much tougher. The first night has you staying in **Pa' Lungan**, while on the second day you must reach **Long Rapung** as

GUNUNG MURUD

Barring the way between Bario to the south and Ba'Kelalan to the northeast, **Gunung Murud** is the highest peak in Sarawak at 2423m, and is part of the Pulong Tau National Park. It presents a challenging but rewarding trek, with spectacular views across the Highlands to Batu Lawi and even Mulu. From Ba'Kelalan, it takes six days there and back; from Bario, allow one day extra.

Leaving Ba'Kelalan, trekkers generally head to Lepo Bunga (8hr) on the first night, traversing some steep hills. In the past, people saved a day by using a 4WD on this leg, but the logging road has fallen into disrepair; check whether it's once again usable. On day 2 the target is **Church Camp** (4–5hr) – a wooden shelter built by local Lun Bawang evangelical groups for a three-day Christian meeting held once a year, and otherwise deserted. The next morning sees the haul up to the summit (3hr) via the **Rock Garden**, an exposed area of stunted trees and sharpish boulders. After another night back at Church Camp, you retrace your steps back to Ba'Kelalan.

If you're starting from Bario, the first day is spent reaching **Pa' Lungan**, where you stay the night. The next day brings a trek to a simple wooden shelter at **Long Rapung** (7hr), with about half an hour's worth of climbing en route. On day 3 some guides head to Church Camp (7hr), others to the slightly nearer Camp 2 at **Long Belaban**, with hammocks to sleep in (5–6hr), though you have to ford a few streams en route and climb for a couple of hours at the end of the day. If you start from Camp 2, day 4 is gruelling, the climb up to the summit beginning at dawn (6hr); the descent usually means heading to the Rock Garden and Church Camp (4hr). On day 5 you head back to Camp 2 for the night; it's then possible, with some effort, to get all the way back to Pa'Lungan on day 6.

for the Murud trek (see box above). On the third day you head initially to **Pa Rupai** (4hr). You're now in Kalimantan, though you're unlikely to be asked for your passport and there's no border post. Two hours further on is the village of **Long Medang** from where the re-entry point into Sarawak is up a steep hill. A couple of hours from here and you should be safely in Ba' Kelalan.

Batu Lawi

The most challenging local trek, apart from Murud, is the climb up **Batu Lawi** (2044m), the strange double-horned peak that you may have seen on the flight out. The trek is an attractive prospect as it's less arduous and time-consuming than tackling Gunung Murud, though as ever logging roads blight the landscape here and there, making it look as though the forest has been gnawed by rats.

The first night out from Bario is spent camping at **Bila Bigan**, reached via Pa' Ukat, which is home to an excellent Batu Lawi guide, Richard Luang. On the second day you scramble to the lower and much blunter of the peak's two "horns" for an amazing view of the other, looking like a huge upright stone pillar, though ruder interpretations are possible. The descent has trekkers camping at the base of the mountain, from where it should be possible to head back to Bario on the third day. It's also possible to do the trek from Ba' Kelalan; contact Borneo Jungle Safari (see p.388) or village guides for details.

Ba' Kelalan

Ba' Kelalan is known locally for its apples, which tend to be smallish, green and crisp, with quite a sharp flavour; passionfruit and citrus are also grown, though not in such quantities. Otherwise, the place amounts to a mere smattering of houses, a handful of coffee shops and places selling basic provisions, and an airfield. The chief reason to come here is to trek – as in Bario, you can head to Gunung Murud and Batu Lawi, or less ambitiously do short walks, say, into Kalimantan and then back within a day.

| **ARRIVAL AND DEPARTURE** | **BA' KELALAN** |

By plane The airfield, right next to the village, has flights to Miri (3 weekly; 1hr 15min) and Lawas (3 weekly; 35min).

By 4WD A logging road from Ba' Kelalan to Lawas makes it possible to arrange a 4WD (6hr; RM1200 for up to four people).

INFORMATION

Borneo Jungle Safari ☎085 422595, ⓦborneo junglesafari.com. Until such time as Ba' Kelalan has mobile-phone coverage, this Miri tour operator is the best source for updates on the village and trekking. Staffed by Lun Bawang with links to the Highlands, they offer a three-day package with a tour of the area including some use of a 4WD (around RM800/person with accommodation and meals, but not flights), and can organize treks to Murud and Batu Lawi.

ACCOMMODATION

Apple Lodge Book through either its sister establishment in Miri, ☎085 419696, or Borneo Jungle Safari, ☎085 422595, ⓦborneojjunglesafari .com. This surprisingly large and well-maintained place has a total of twenty single and double rooms and the option of en-suite facilities. En-suite facilities cost RM10 extra, breakfast is RM8 per person, and lunch and dinner around RM15 each. In the (unlikely) event that it's full, there are a couple of other options. **RM50**

The Ulu Baram

The Baram river system so dominates northern Sarawak that you could consider virtually all the interior here, excepting Limbang division, to be the **Ulu Baram** – practically every river, including the Melinau and Tutoh at Mulu, the Tinjar at Loagan Bunut and the Dapur and Kelapang at Bario, ends up flowing into the Baram. The Batang Baram itself, however, wends its way more or less constantly southeast from the town of **Marudi**, 80km from Miri, occasionally passing little confluence towns such as **Long Lama** and **Long San**, before approaching the border with Kalimantan. Here it swings east to peter out beyond **Lio Matoh**, 200km southeast of Miri. This Ulu Baram, due south of Mulu and southwest of the Kelabit Highlands, is definitely outback territory, rugged and lushly forested, though not spared the attention of the logging companies, whose roads penetrate even here. There are, of course, no specific sights; the reason you might venture here is to trek through virgin rainforest and stay in remote settlements as part of a **homestay** programme.

THE PENAN

For some travellers, the **Penan** have a mystique beyond that of any of Sarawak's many Orang Ulu groups, as a kind of poster child for the ongoing struggle for native peoples' rights. That status is largely thanks to the high-profile campaign waged on their behalf by the Swiss activist **Bruno Manser** in the 1980s and 1990s. Manser lived with the Penan for many years and became a thorn in the side of the Sarawak government, successfully drawing the world's attention to the destruction of their traditional forest habitat, though his PR successes had little impact on the juggernaut that is Sarawak's logging industry. The Penan lost their champion when Manser disappeared in 2000, having trekked alone from Bario to meet the Penan in the jungle; he was never seen again, but the campaign he founded soldiers on (ⓦbmf.ch).

Most of Sarawak's twelve thousand Penan live in the upper reaches of the Baram and Belaga rivers. Their language is of the same family as Iban and Malay. Traditionally they were nomadic hunter-gatherers, but these days the vast majority live in tiny villages – thanks not simply to habitat loss but also to the inescapable embrace of the outside world and the cash economy. Their old staple of sago has often been supplanted by rice, which the Penan grow like the Iban, in jungle clearings using shifting cultivation. Many Penan still struggle to make ends meet, both in towns where they may be in poorly paid work, and in their villages, where food is in reasonable supply but cash hard to come by. Another perennial problem is the lack of formal identity documents, without which many Penan cannot access services, education and jobs.

6

PICNIC WITH THE PENAN PRICES

Approximate costs for travellers participating in the **Picnic with the Penan** scheme are listed below. Make sure the programme organizers tell you the precise cost for your specific itinerary: the unfamiliar geography may lead you to underestimate the need for boat rides, and a guide may show up whether you think you need one or not. In addition, all participants pay a RM100 fee towards a community project – at the time of writing, a Penan training centre in Miri. For full details, visit ⓦ picnicwiththepenan.org.

COSTS

4WD from Long Akah to Long Siut (a Kenyah settlement where you pick up longboats to the Selungo River)	2hr; RM300 one-way
Boat from Long Siut to Long Kerong	1hr 30min; RM250 one-way
Guide	RM90 50 per day/half-day
Porter	RM40 per day
Crafts courses	RM15 per person per hour
Board and lodging (not payable if you overnight in the jungle, in which case you may have to discuss small extra charges for food)	RM50 per person per night

---

Penan homestays

It's possible to visit Penan settlements near **Lio Matoh** (see map, p.382), such as **Long Kerong** close to the Selungo River, and **Long Lamai** on the Balong, as part of a scheme calling itself **Picnic with the Penan** (ⓦ picnicwiththepenan.org). The experience is similar to visiting tiny villages in the Kelabit Highlands, but much more cut off from the wider world. Unfortunately, it doesn't come cheap. As this area has, to an extent, resisted the blandishments of the logging industry, logging roads and bridges are fewer and further between, and expensive boat charter is required to reach the villages. Furthermore, while MASwings flies to Long Banga near Lio Matoh, until (and if) the logging roads there are repaired, you will have to fly into **Long Akah** or **Long Lellang**, 50km away, and then head in by 4WD – another major expense (flights are detailed on p.366). For these reasons a group of three is ideal, the most the longboats can carry with luggage.

When you finally arrive, however, the rewards can be considerable. There are ample chances to **trek** through dense, unspoiled jungle, using "trails" hacked out by your guide with a machete, spending the night perhaps in a simple hut of the type the Penan erect near their fields, or in a makeshift shelter that your guide might build using branches and leaves. From the Selungo River it's also possible to climb **Gunung Murud Kecil** ("Little Murud"; 2112m), at the opposite end of the Tama Abu Range from its larger and more famous sibling. Bring similar gear to what you'd need in the Kelabit Highlands (see p.384).

Village life can itself be a highlight. Local people can teach crafts such as basket-making, and then there's the simple pleasure of bathing in the river with the villagers, or the spectacle of being at the simple village church on Sunday (many Penan belong to the evangelical Sidang Injil Borneo or SIB movement, which has churches throughout Sarawak); it's great to witness hymns sung in Penan with the village youths showing off their self-taught skills on guitar, keyboards and drums. After the rice is planted (June) or harvested (February), you can even accompany the men as they **hunt** wild pig, aided by dogs, blowpipes and the odd antique rifle.

On the downside, the usual **caveats** about Malaysia homestays are especially valid here. One key point is that villagers take turns to put up guests, so quite how adept your hosts will be is a matter of luck. You may have your own room or space, or sleep alongside everyone and their screaming babies; meals can be meagre and there may be little to drink other than tepid, weak and sickly sweet coffee. Communication is another problem as few villagers speak good English.

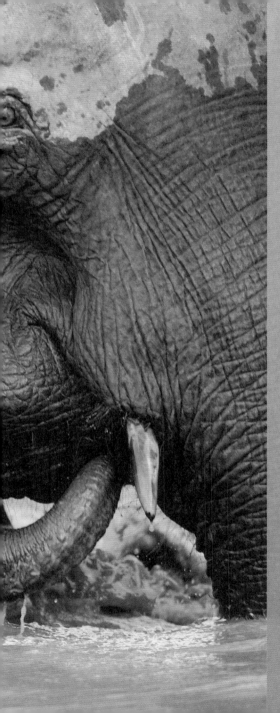

Sabah

ELEPHANTS BATHING IN THE KINABATANGAN RIVER

Sabah

Until European powers gained a foothold at the northern tip of Borneo in the nineteenth century, the tribal peoples of Sabah had only minimal contact with the outside world. Since then – and particularly since joining the Malaysian Federation in 1963 – these groups have largely exchanged traditional ways for a collective Malaysian identity. As Sabah's cultural landscape has changed, so has its environment: the logging industry has been allowed to exploit huge swathes of the rainforests, with cleared regions used to plant oil palm – a monoculture that makes a poor habitat for wildlife. On the other hand, many locals would argue, this agro-industry provides work for thousands, and generates much-needed income into the state coffers.

7

While arguments rage between campaigners, corporations and politicians, tourists continue to enjoy the remaining natural riches of "the land below the wind" (so called because Sabah's 72,500 square kilometres lie just south of the typhoon belt). The **terrain** ranges from wild, swampy, mangrove-tangled coastal areas, through the dazzling greens of paddy fields and pristine rainforests, to the dizzy heights of the Crocker mountain range – home to the highest peak between the Himalayas and New Guinea, **Gunung Kinabalu** (Mount Kinabalu). Although habitats for Sabah's indigenous animals have shrunk dramatically, the remaining forests still offer some of the best **wildlife-watching** opportunities in Malaysia. Offshore, damaging fishing practices have as elsewhere in the region taken their toll, but marine parks protect areas of magnificent coral – most famously around **Sipadan** – and the attendant sea life.

Sabah's **urban centres** are not especially attractive or historically rich, thanks to World War II bombs and hurried urban redevelopment. While places like **KK** (**Kota Kinabalu**) and **Sandakan** lack notable buildings, however, they abound in atmosphere and energy, plus good places to eat and sleep. That said, Sabah's remarkable natural attractions are the major draw for most visitors.

The **Klias Peninsula** south of KK offers activity-based day-trips such as whitewater rafting or firefly cruises, while with more time you could visit the island of **Pulau Tiga**; you may also need to transit through duty-free **Labuan** on the way to Brunei. North of KK lie the beaches and coconut groves of the **Kudat Peninsula**, where it's possible to visit longhouses belonging to the Rungus tribe; the northernmost point, the **Tip of Borneo**, features windy shorelines and splendid isolation.

Heading east from KK, things get truly exciting. Dominating the landscape are the huge granite shelves of the awesome **Gunung Kinabalu**, a major attraction as getting up and down involves spending just one night on the mountain. Further east is Sandakan, a rapidly modernizing town with offshore attractions including the **Turtle Islands National Park**. Back on the mainland, at the nearby **Sepilok Orang-utan Rehabilitation**

Highlights

❶ Pulau Tiga With the TV crews long gone, "Survivor Island" remains largely undeveloped with attractive beaches, jungle walks and a natural mud bath for good measure. **See p.413**

❷ Gunung Kinabalu The arduous climb to see dawn over the South China Sea is well worth the effort. **See p.422**

❸ Sepilok Orang-Utan Rehabilitation Centre Orphaned and injured orang-utans are nursed back to health in this popular rainforest reserve; visitors can observe feeding sessions. **See p.436**

❹ Labuk Bay Proboscis Monkey Sanctuary With their distinctive noses and round bellies, proboscis monkeys are among Borneo's most sought-after endemic species. **See p.438**

❺ The Kinabatangan River Home to a great diversity of bird and animal life including orang-utans, proboscis monkeys and the occasional pygmy elephant herd. **See p.439**

❻ Danum Valley Stunning stretches of untouched rainforest with treks and wildlife galore. **See p.443**

❼ Tabin Wildlife Reserve More animal-spotting possibilities in a well-run jungle camp. **See p.444**

❽ Sipadan and Mabul Spectacular marine life makes these two islands a must for scuba divers; reefs off other nearby islands are also worth exploring. **See p.446**

HIGHLIGHTS ARE MARKED ON THE MAP ON P.394

SABAH

HIGHLIGHTS
1. Palau Tiga
2. Gunung Kinabalu
3. Sepilok Orang-Utan Rehabilitation Centre
4. Labuk Bay Proboscis Monkey Sanctuary
5. The Kinabatangan River
6. Danum Valley
7. Tabin Wildlife Reserve
8. Sipadan and Mabul

Zamboanga (Philippines)

SULAWESI SEA

CELEBES SEA

Cagayan Sulu (Philippines)

Sibutu (Philippines)

TURTLE ISLANDS NATIONAL PARK

Pulau Lankayan

Pulau Banggi

Tip of Borneo

KINABALU NATIONAL PARK

Gunung Kinabalu 4095m

Kinabalu Park HQ

Labuk Bay Proboscis Monkey Sanctuary

Sandakan

Sepilok

Gomantong Caves

Batu Putih

LOWER KINABATANGAN WILDLIFE SANCTUARY

Abai

Sukau

Bilit

S. Segama

TABIN WILDLIFE RESERVE

Bandar Sahabat

Tungku

TUN SAKARAN MARINE PARK

Pulau Pom Pom

Pulau Maataking

Pulau Mabul

Pulau Kapalai

Lahad Datu

Kunak

Semporna

Tawau

DANUM VALLEY CONSERVATION AREA

MALIAU BASIN CONSERVATION AREA

TAWAU HILLS STATE PARK

Sungai Kinabatangan

Telupid

S. Sugut

Kudat

Teluk Marudu

Pitas

Kanibongan

Kota Marudu

Kota Belud

Poring

Ranau

Kundasang

Kampung Patau

Tambunan

Gunung Trus Madi 2642m

Kampung Tulid

Keningau

Kg. Sook

Kampung Dalit

Sapulut

Pensiangan

Sikuati

Matunggong

Kampung Bawanggazo

Pulau Balambangan

Pulau Mantanani

Pulau Mantanani Kecil

Penambawan

Tuaran

Kinarut

KOTA KINABALU

CROCKER RANGE

Papar

Kuala Penyu

Membakut

Beaufort

Padas Gorge

Tenom

Sipitang

Sindumin

Merapok

Pulau Layang Layang

TUNKU ABDUL RAHMAN NATIONAL PARK

PULAU TIGA

Klias Peninsula

Menumbok

Pulau Labuan

S. Padas

Lawas

Bangar

BRUNEI

Murara (Brunei) & Limbang (Sarawak)

SARAWAK

KALIMANTAN

N

0   50

Centre and **Labuk Bay Proboscis Monkey Sanctuary**, you can get a ringside view of animals at feeding times.

Deeper into the oil-palm plantations of east Sabah lies the protected **Kinabatangan River**, where visitors can take boat trips to see wild proboscis monkeys, elephants and orang-utans. Further south, the **Danum Valley Conservation Area** offers a spectacular canopy walkway, with the choice of staying at a luxury lodge or a humbler research centre. Alternatively try the more affordable **Tabin Wildlife Reserve**, with a mud volcano and an elephant colony. In the deep south, accessible via the boom town of Tawau, nestles the untouched forest sector of the **Maliau Basin**, now open for challenging trekking.

For divers, the offshore islands near the southern town of **Semporna** are the jewel in Sabah's crown. **Sipadan** offers world-class diving off coral walls, while its neighbour **Mabul** is known for its fabulous macro (small-scale) marine life. These two are simply the best known, and the area can keep divers and snorkellers enchanted for days.

Brief history

Little is known of Sabah's **early history**, though archeological finds in limestone caves indicate that the northern tip of Borneo has been inhabited for well over ten thousand years. **Chinese merchants** were trading with local settlements by 700 AD, and by the fourteenth century the area was under the sway of the sultans of **Brunei** and **Sulu**.

Colonialism

Europe's superpowers first arrived in 1521, when the ships of **Portuguese** navigator Ferdinand Magellan stopped off at Brunei before sailing northwards. Almost 250 years later, in 1763, colonial settlement began when one Captain Cowley established a short-lived trading post on Pulau Balambangan, an island north of Kudat, on behalf of the **British East India Company**. Further colonial involvement came in 1846, when Pulau Labuan (at the mouth of Brunei Bay) was ceded to the British by the Sultan of Brunei. By 1881 the **British North Borneo Chartered Company** had full sovereignty over northern Borneo.

First steps were then taken towards making the territory pay its way: rubber, tobacco and, after 1885, timber were commercially harvested. By 1905 a **rail line** linked the coastal town of **Jesselton** (later Kota Kinabalu) with the resource-rich interior. When the company introduced taxes, the locals were understandably displeased and some resisted; **Mat Salleh**, the son of a Bajau chief, and his followers sacked the company's settlement on Pulau Gaya in 1897. Another uprising, in **Rundum** in 1915, resulted in the slaughter of hundreds of Murut tribespeople by British forces.

World War II

On New Year's Day 1942, Japanese imperial forces invaded Pulau Labuan; Sandakan fell less than three weeks later. By the time the Japanese surrendered on September 9, 1945, almost nothing of Jesselton and Sandakan remained standing (although the worst structural damage was inflicted by Allied bombing). Even worse were the hardships endured by civilians and captured Allied troops, the most notorious of which were the Death Marches of 1945 (see p.433).

Towards independence

Unable to finance the postwar rebuilding of North Borneo, the Chartered Company sold the territory to the British Crown in 1946, and Jesselton was declared the new capital of the **Crown Colony of North Borneo**. Within fifteen years, however, plans had been laid for an independent federation consisting of Malaya, Singapore, Sarawak, North Borneo and (it was intended) Brunei. The **Federation** was proclaimed at midnight on September 15, 1963, with North Borneo renamed Sabah.

Modern politics

Relations with federal Kuala Lumpur have seldom been smooth, but differences had seemed to narrow until, in 1985, the opposition **Parti Bersatu Sabah** (PBS), led by the Christian Joseph Pairin Kitingan, was returned to office in the state elections. This was the first time a non-Muslim had attained power in a Malaysian state. Anti-federal feelings were worsened by much of the profits from Sabah's flourishing **crude oil** exports being siphoned off to KL.

Nowadays, with PBS having joined the country's ruling BN coalition, central government is following a policy of patching up long-running, cross-state disunity to realize a vision of a multi-ethnic – but Muslim-dominated – nation.

The people

Although many traditions have died out, Sabah's three-million-plus population includes more than a dozen recognized ethnic groups, and numerous dialects are still in use. The peoples of the **Kadazan/Dusun** tribes constitute the largest indigenous group; then there are the **Murut** of the southwest, and Sabah's so-called "sea gypsies", the **Bajau**. In recent years, Sabah has also seen an influx of **Filipino** and **Indonesian** immigrants, particularly on its east coast.

Town and village **tamus** (markets), usually held weekly, are a wonderful opportunity for visitors to take in the colourful mixture of cultures. Large *tamus* include those held on Sundays in the state capital **Kota Kinabalu** (KK) and in the small town of **Kota Belud**, two hours north by bus. The biggest annual **festival** is the **Pesta Kaamatan**, a harvest festival celebrated in May by the Kadazan/Dusun.

GETTING TO SABAH

By plane Kota Kinabalu airport, the major international gateway, is also served domestically by AirAsia, Firefly, Malaysian Airlines and MASwings. Domestic airports in Labuan, Lahad Datu, Sandakan and Tawau are served by flights from the Peninsula as well as within Borneo.

Overland The only overland route into Sabah is from Lawas in Sarawak, which is a short bus ride from the border at Merapok, close to Sipitang (see p.412). Express buses follow this route all the way to KK from Bandar Seri Begawan in Brunei and also from Miri in Sarawak.

By boat Ferries run from Sarawak and Brunei to Labuan, and from there to Sipitang Menumbok or KK. Ferries also sail from Kalimantan (Indonesian Borneo) to Tawau, and from the Philippines to Sandakan.

GETTING AROUND

By plane Internal flights are inexpensive and can save a lot of time. Thus flying from KK to Lahad Datu – for onward travel to Semporna and Sipidan – costs around RM180 and takes just fifty minutes, compared to around eight hours by bus.

By bus and minivan Travel in the morning if at all possible: minivans leave throughout the day once full, but other passengers can be in short supply by the afternoon, while buses are usually more frequent in the mornings. For travel on rough upcountry roads, say for the Tawau–Keningau loop (see p.450), you may have to charter or take a seat in a 4WD.

Kota Kinabalu

While first impressions of **KOTA KINABALU**, which everyone calls KK, may be of a rather utilitarian concrete sprawl, many visitors end up charmed by its lively buzz and the friendliness of its citizens. As well as good places to eat, it also has excellent transport links and is the headquarters of most of the main tour operators.

The best of the city's few specific sights are its **markets**, the **Sabah Museum** and the **Mari Mari Cultural Village**. A further highlight lies offshore in the **Tunku Abdul Rahman Park**, whose popular islands are just a short trip away by boat.

Brief history

Modern-day KK can trace its history back to 1882, when the British North Borneo Chartered Company established an outpost on nearby **Pulau Gaya**. After followers of

KOTA KINABALU

0 — 200 metres

Jesselton Point Hawkers, Jesselton Point Ferry Terminal, Likas Bay & Inanam

ACCOMMODATION			
Akinabalu	12	Manja	22
Best Western		Masada Backpacker	18
Kinabalu Daya	7	Myne	2
Borneo Backpackers	15	Sarangnova	11
Horizon	5	Sensi Backpackers Hostel	14
Hyatt Regency	4	Shangri-La Rasa Ria Resort	8
Imperial International	3	Shangri-La Tanjung	
Jesselton	13	Aru Resort	19
Langkah Syabas	21	Summer Lodge	9
Lavender Lodge	10	Sutera Harbour Resort	20
Le Meridien	1	Travellers' Light	17
Lucy's Homestay	16	Wah May	6

EATING		
First Beach Seafood Restaurant		Little Italy	5
Borneo 1945	1	Rasa Nonya	6
El Centro	4	Suang Tain (Twin Sky)	7
First Beach Café	2	Seafood Restaurant	10
Jarrod & Rawlins	5	Tam Nak Thai	1
Jothy's Banana Leaf	3,4	Tambayan	2

BARS & CLUBS	
BED	
Shenanigan's	1
Sully's	5
Upperstar Café and Bar	3,4

Waterfront Food & Bar Court

Port View Seafood Village

Central Market

Filipino Handicrafts & Night Food Markets

Food Stalls

Segama Complex

Wisma Merdeka

Wisma Yakim

Taxi Stand

Maybank

Gaya Centre

Wisma Sabah

Suria Sabah

Tong Hing Supermarket

Signal Hill Observatory

Sabah Tourism

HSBC

K.K. LAMA

Sunday Market

Alliance Bank

RHB

Guardian

Police Station

Atkinson Clock Tower

Merdeka Field

AUSTRALIA PLACE

KK Plaza

Bank Negara

High Court

City Park Bus Terminal

Bus and Share Taxi Stand

Sabah Parks Office

Sinsuran Complex

JLN SEMBILANBELAS

JLN DATUK SALLEH SULONG

JALAN LIMABELAS

JALAN HAJI SAMAN

BEACH STREET

JALAN PANTAI

JALAN GAYA

JALAN TUNKU ABDUL RAHMAN

JALAN TUN RAZAK

JALAN TUGU

JALAN TUN FUAD STEPHENS

JALAN PASAR BARU

JALAN DUABELAS

JALAN SAPULUH

JLN KAMPUNG AIR

KAMPUNG AIR

JALAN HAJI YACOB

JALAN ISTANA

JALAN PADANG

Centrepoint

Warisan Square

Tourism Malaysia

Marina Court Condominiums

Promenade Hotel

Api-Api Centre

Public Bank

Asia City

Seri Selera Kampung Air

Cathay Cineplex

Bandaran Berjaya

Wisma Budaya

Wawasan Plaza

7

the Bajau rebel, Mat Salleh, burned that down in 1897, the Company chose a mainland site – a fishing village called **Api-Api** – to develop as a new town. Renamed **Jesselton** after Sir Charles Jessel, the vice-chairman of the Chartered Company, the town prospered. By 1905 the Trans-Borneo Railway reached from Jesselton to Beaufort, allowing rubber to be transported efficiently from the interior to the coast.

The Japanese invasion of North Borneo in 1942 marked the start of three and a half years of **military occupation**; little of old Jesselton survived the resultant Allied bombing. In 1968 the name was changed to **Kota Kinabalu** and city planners set about expanding outwards into the sea. Interconnecting concrete buildings have been constructed on the reclaimed land – the Sinsuran and Segama complexes and Asia City in particular have developed their own identities. Progress has been startling, and today, with a population of over a quarter of a million, KK is a beehive of activity once again.

The historical centre

Only a handful of notable buildings survived World War II, but you can find a few remnants of the past in the east of the city.

Signal Hill

The historical centre lies between the South China Sea and **Signal Hill**, the highest point in KK. In the lower reaches of the hill, the robust wooden **Atkinson's Clock Tower** was built in 1903 to commemorate the first district official of Jesselton, Francis George Atkinson, who died of malaria at 28. The city's oldest surviving structure, it occupies a lovely vantage point overlooking the padang.

Further up the hill on Jalan Bukit Bandera, the more modern **Signal Hill Observatory Platform** is best visited at sunset when the views are particularly dramatic.

Jalan Gaya

One block northwest of Australia Place, so named because the Australian army made camp here in 1945, lies **Jalan Gaya**. Known under the British as Bond Street, it's KK's most elegant stretch and includes the city's oldest and most attractive hotel, the *Jesselton* (built in 1954). A few metres away is the wood-boarded, belian-tiled old **General Post Office** which now houses the Sarawak Tourism Board.

The markets

Jalan Gaya street market Sun 6am–1pm • **Central Market** Daily 6am–6pm, fish market from 5am • **Handicraft Market** Daily 7am–8pm • **Night food market** Daily 5–10pm

A lively **street market** is held along Jalan Gaya every Sunday morning, with stalls selling items as disparate as herbal teas, handicrafts, orchids and rabbits. In addition, a huddle of **markets** on the waterfront are open daily, and together form one of the city's highlights. Approaching from the northeast, you first reach the labyrinthine **Central Market**, which includes a **fish market** that's at its best very early in the morning. Next comes the **Handicraft Market**, also known as the Filipino Market thanks to the ethnicity of many of its stallholders. Around sundown, the area west of here becomes a gargantuan **night food market**; further west still is the waterfront parade of bars and restaurants.

Sabah State Museum

Daily 9am–5pm • RM15 • ☎ 088 253199, ⓦ museum.sabah.gov.my • Bus #13 from City Hall or Wawasan Plaza, or taxi (RM20)

Styled after Murut and Rungus longhouses, the buildings of the **Sabah State Museum** are set in grounds that also hold several splendid steam engines. The **botanical garden** in front of the museum is bordered by finely crafted traditional houses, representing all Sabah's major tribes and known as the **Heritage Village** (Kampung Warisan).

The other highlight of the complex, the **ethnographic collection** in the main building, includes human skulls dating from Sabah's head-hunting days, and a *sininggazanak*, a totemic wooden figurine placed in the field of a Kadazan man who died without heirs. Photographs in the **history gallery** depict the city when Jalan Gaya still constituted the waterfront, lined with lean-tos thatched with nipah-palm leaves.

Exhibits on oil drilling in the **Science and Technology Centre** next door are less than gripping; head instead to the **Art Gallery** upstairs, where the centrepiece is a giant string of Rungus beads, created by Chee Sing Teck, hanging from the ceiling.

Kota Kinabalu Wetland Centre Park

3km north of city centre in Likas Bay • Tues–Sun 8am–6pm • RM10 • ☎ 088 247 955, ✉ likaswetlands@hotmail.com • Bus #1 from Wawasan Plaza – walk for 20min from the turn-off before Likas – or RM25 by taxi

The 24 hectares of mangrove forest at **Kota Kinabalu Wetland Centre Park** is the only remaining patch of an extensive system that once covered the coastline. Designated as a bird sanctuary in 1996, it's an important refuge and feeding ground for many species.

From marked trails on **boardwalks**, you may catch sight of herons, egrets, sandpipers, pigeons and doves; come early in the morning or late in the afternoon for optimum viewing conditions. Other mangrove wildlife includes fiddler crabs, mudskippers, monitor lizards, weaver ants, water snakes and mud lobsters.

ARRIVAL AND DEPARTURE   KOTA KINABALU

BY PLANE

KK International Airport (KKIA) The two terminals are a few kilometres from each other – check which you need before setting out. Terminal 1, 7km south of the centre in the Kepayan district, covers international destinations and many domestic flights; the older Terminal 2, 5km from the centre in Tanjung Aru, is used by AirAsia, Cebu Pacific and Eastar Jet. City buses run from the terminals to Wawasan bus terminal in the centre (every 30min; daily 7am–7pm), or you can take a coupon taxi (RM30). AirAsia has an office in Wisma Sabah (no direct phone; Mon–Fri 8.30am–5.30pm, Sat 8.30am–3pm).

Destinations Bandar Seri Bagawan (2 daily); Bintulu (2 daily); Johor Bahru (3 daily); KL (21 daily); Kuching (3 daily); Kudat (2 weekly); Labuan (5 daily); Lahad Datu (4 daily); Miri (4 daily); Mulu (2 daily); Penang (1 daily); Perth (1 daily); Sandakan (6 daily); Sibu (3 daily); Singapore (2 daily); Tawau (5 daily); Tokyo (4 weekly).

BY TRAIN

Tanjung Aru Sabah State Railway (☎ 088 254 611) provides a limited service from Tanjung Aru station, 5km southwest of central KK (bus #16 from Wawasan Plaza, taxi RM15). Trains stop at Kinarut and Papar before terminating in Beaufort (daily; 2hr 15min; RM5), where you can change for Tenom (daily; 1hr; RM3).

BY BUS

City Bus Terminal North (CBTN) Better known as Inanam after the suburb where it's located, 8km east of

the centre, this is used by buses to Sandakan and other places north or east of KK. Bus #3 (6am–8pm; every 20 min) runs between Inanam and Wawasan local bus terminal in the city centre. Arriving at Inanam outside these hours requires a taxi (RM25) from directly outside the terminal.

Destinations Lahad Datu (4 daily; 8hr); Sandakan (17 daily, most before 2pm; 6hr); Semporna (3 daily; 9hr); Tawau (7 daily; 10hr).

Merdeka Field This more central bus stand on Jalan Tunku Abdul Rahman is served mostly by buses and minivans from southern Sabah.

Destinations Beaufort (5 daily; 2hr); Keningau (5 daily; 2hr 30min); Kota Belud (hourly 7am–5pm; 1hr); Kudat (hourly 7am–4pm; 3hr); Ranau (hourly 7am–5pm; 2hr); Tambunan (hourly 7am–5pm; 1hr 30min); Tenom (3 daily; 3hr); Tuaran (hourly 7am–5pm; 30min).

City Park Bus Terminal A few useful buses depart from in front of the City Hall, including services to Sarawak and Brunei.

Destinations Brunei (daily at 8am; 7hr); Kuala Penyu (for Pulau Tiga; hourly; 2hr); Lawas (2–3 daily; 4hr); Menumbok (6 daily; 2hr 30min); Miri (3 weekly; 11hr).

BY FERRY

Jesselton Point Ferry Terminal On Jalan Haji Saman. Services to Labuan are operated by Double Power (☎ 088 236 834; 3hr; daily 8am & 1.30pm; RM31); Labuan has connections to Muara in Brunei (take the 8am ferry from KK, combined ticket RM53). Book at least a day ahead for weekend or holiday travel. Speedboats go regularly from the same terminal to the Tunku Abdul Rahman Park islands a few kilometres offshore.

BY TAXI

Merdeka Field Shared taxis are available at Merdeka Field, with bays indicated for different destinations. Many are served both by ordinary taxis (seating four passengers) and by larger Toyota Unsers (seating seven). Unser prices can be a little cheaper but vehicles take longer to fill up, and chartering the whole vehicle is more costly.

Destinations Beaufort (RM15); Keningau (RM20); Kudat (RM35); Menumbok (RM30); Mount Kinabalu (RM15–20); Papar (RM10); Ranau (RM20); Sipitang (RM25); Tenom (RM25).

GETTING AROUND

On foot The city centre is compact enough to cover on foot inside an hour.

By taxi Drivers rarely turn the meter on, but taxis are inexpensive – it costs no more than RM10 to travel across the city centre. Ranks outside the *Hyatt* hotel, at the post office on Jalan Tun Razak, along Jalan Perpaduan in Kampung Air and at Centre Point Mall.

By bus or minivan Local buses and minivans leave from the Wawasan bus terminal, 600m southwest of the Waterfront complex along Jalan Tun Fuad Stephens.

Car rental Companies include: Kinabalu Rent-A-Car, Ground Floor, Wisma Sabah (☎ 088 232 602, ⊛ kinabalurac .com.my); Hertz, Arrival Level, Terminal 1, KK International Airport (☎ 088 413 326, ⊛ hertz.com); Hawk, Ground Floor, Wisma Sabah (☎ 016 886 7745 or ☎ 088 235 900, ⊛ hawkrentacar.com.my). Rent a 4WD if you plan to get far off the beaten track.

INFORMATION

Tourist information The Sabah Tourism Board is in the old GPO at 51 Jalan Gaya (Mon–Fri 8am–5pm, Sat & Sun 9am–4pm; ☎ 088 212121, ⊛ sabahtourism.com). The friendly and well-organized staff can help with just about anything. Be sure to pick up the excellent free tourist map of KK.

Tourism Malaysia 107 Api-Api Centre, Jalan Pasar Barul (Mon–Fri 8.30am–4.30pm, Sat 8.30am–noon; ☎ 088 248698, ⊛ tourism.gov.my). They also stock leaflets on Sabah but are better at answering questions about Peninsular Malaysia or Sarawak.

National parks For information about the environment and ecology of Sabah's national parks, visit the Sabah Parks office, 45 & 46, Block H, KK Times Square (Mon–Fri 8am–5pm; ☎ 088 523 500, ⊛ sabahparks.org.my).

Internet Most accommodation has wi-fi, while many hostels also have computers with internet access. Otherwise, The Internet Studio at 88 Jalan Gaya (Mon–Sat 9am–2am, Sun 10.30am–2am) is refreshingly free of kids playing online games.

Magazines The monthly *Sabah Malaysian Borneo* magazine lists upcoming events.

TOURS

KK has plenty of handy **tour operators**, many based in the Wisma Sabah building, offering trekking, rafting, diving and wildlife-watching packages, for example to see proboscis monkeys on the Garama River near Beaufort. Most of these things can be arranged independently, including trips on the **Kinabatangan River**, but going through a tour operator can save time and effort. The companies are also useful for arranging day-trips from KK such as wildlife cruises or firefly-watching on the **Klias Peninsula**. See also the list of operators in Sandakan (p.431).

Borneo Divers 9th floor, Menara Jubili, 53 Jalan Gaya ☎ 088 222 226, ⊛ borneodivers.info. Diving specialists with many years' experience in Sabah and with a resort on Mabul. They can also arrange dives off the Tunku Abdul Rahman islands.

★ **Borneo Eco Tours** Lot 1, Pusat Perindustrian, Kolombong Jaya, Jalan Kolombong, Mile 5.5 ☎ 088 438 300, ⊛ borneoecotours.com. Ecotourism pioneer running *Borneo Backpackers* in town and the superb *Sukau Rainforest Lodge* on the Kinabatangan River, as well as offering a wide array of tours.

Borneo Fullforce Lot 21c, 2nd Floor, Likas Plaza, Mile 4.5, Jalan Tuaran ☎ 088 386 380, ⊛ borneofullforce .com. Takes tourists to the Sunday market at Kota Belud or to the Tambunan Rafflesia Forest Centre, in addition to more usual trips such as to Gunung Kinabalu.

Borneo Icons Ground floor, Wismah Sabah ☎ 088 255 513, ⊛ borneoicons.com. This outfit arranges tours ranging from Klias river cruises to trips to the Tip of Borneo.

★ **Borneo Nature Tours** Ground floor, Lot 10, Sadong Jaya Complex ☎ 088 267 637, ⊛ borneonaturetours.com. BNT runs the luxurious *Borneo Rainforest Lodge* in Danum Valley; it's also the only operator with a licence to take groups into the inaccessible Maliau Basin, Sabah's "lost world".

Borneo Ultimate Ground floor, Wisma Sabah ☎ 088 225 188, ⊛ borneoultimate.com.my. Adventurous options

7

including kayaking, mountain biking and whitewater rafting.

Field Skills Second floor, Block C, City Mall, Jalan Lintas ☏ 088 484 734, ⍟ fieldskills.com.my. This unusual outfit offers rock-climbing and mountain biking, among other trips.

Nasalis Larvatus Second floor, Wisma Sabah ☏ 088 230 534, ⍟ nasalislarvatustours.com. Named after the scientific name for proboscis monkeys, this operator runs *Nature Lodge Kinabatangan* in Bilit plus a full range of nature tours.

Only in Borneo Tours Ground floor, Wisma Sabah ☏ 088 260 506, ⍟ oibtours.com. Along with trips to Mantanani island, Gunung Kinabalu and elsewhere, this operator runs an 80ft wooden houseboat on the Klias River for firefly-watching.

River Junkie Tours Ground floor, Wisma Sabah ☏ 019 6012145, ⍟ river-junkie.com. Part of Semporna-based Scuba Junkie, offering whitewater rafting on the Padas and Kiulu rivers and a proboscis monkey river cruise.

Sabah Divers Ground floor, Wisma Sabah ☏ 088 256 483, ⍟ sabahdivers.com. Diving outfit offering both PADI and SSI courses, plus fun dives around Semporna and off the Tunku Abdul Rahman islands.

Sipadan Dive Centre 11th floor, A1103, Wisma Merdeka ☏ 088 240584, ⍟ sipadandivers.com. Offers diving trips around Semporna and also runs the *Pulau Tiga Resort*.

Traverse Tours 227–229, 2nd floor, Wisma Sabah ☏ 019 088 260 501, ⍟ traversetours.com. Provides the full range of tours, including trips to Mantanani island, and operates Mari-Mari Cultural Village. Their whitewater rafting arm is known as Riverbug.

7

ACCOMMODATION

KK is king when it comes to **accommodation** in east Malaysia, with good deals to be had in all price ranges. Note that most hostels are set above shopfronts, while for the resorts, you need to head out of the city.

HOSTELS

Akinabalu Floors 1–4, 133 Jalan Gaya ☏ 088 272 188, ✉ akinabaluyh@yahoo.com. Inexpensive backpackers' place with clean, fairly spacious five-bed dorms, compact double rooms and an airy communal area with TV. All rooms have shared bathrooms with hot showers. Breakfast included. Fan dorms RM20, a/c dorms RM25, fan rooms RM56, a/c rooms RM66

Borneo Backpackers 24 Lorong Dewan ☏ 088 234 009, ⍟ borneobackpackers.com. An excellent hostel above *Borneo 1945* café in Australia Place. As well as four double rooms and a number of four- to ten-bed dorms, there's a communal area with TV and internet. Dorms RM25, rooms RM50

★ **Lavender Lodge** 6 Jalan Laiman Diki, Kampung Air ☏ 088 217 119, ⍟ lavenderlodge.com.my. Immaculately clean private rooms and single-sex a/c dorms, plus a helpful manager, make this a great backpacker choice. You can pay a little extra for an en-suite room or dorm. The communal areas have a TV, pool table and internet terminals, plus there's wi-fi in rooms. Breakfast included. Dorms RM30, rooms RM70

Lucy's Homestay (aka Backpacker Lodge) Lot 25, Lorong Dewan, Australia Place ☏ 088 261 495, ⍟ welcome.to/backpackerkk. This homely, cluttered place with small four- and six-bed dorms, TV, library and washing facilities is a KK institution – as is knowledgeable owner Lucy. Wi-fi and breakfast are included. Dorms RM23, rooms RM58

★ **Masada Backpacker** No. 9, 1st Floor, Jalan Masjid Lama ☏ 088 238 494, ⍟ masadabackpacker.com. Winning rave reviews from travellers, this was the hostel to beat at the time of research. Rooms are clean and comfortable, breakfasts are good, staff go the extra mile to help and – although central enough – it's an oasis of calm. Free wi-fi and use of their computer. Dorms RM35, rooms RM80

Sensi Backpackers Hostel 103 Jalan Gaya ☏ 088 272 796, ⍟ sensihostel.com. A decent budget choice, with a bit more attention paid to decor than in some places. There's a shared kitchen with dining table, microwave, toaster and fridge. Dorms RM30, rooms RM70

Summer Lodge 120 Jalan Gaya ☏ 088 244 499, ⍟ summerlodge.com. This hostel has prime position above the Beach St action. A magnet for young travellers, it has small, functional doubles, compact dorms and free internet. Dorms RM20, rooms RM55

Travellers' Light 19 Lorong Dewan, Australia Place ☏ 088 250 141, ⍟ travellerslight.com. A small and very quiet place tucked up against the KK hill, with cosy doubles and decent six-bed dorms. There's a small terrace at the back where you can talk, smoke or just relax. Dorms RM22, rooms RM65

HOTELS

Best Western Kinabalu Daya Lot 3 & 4, 9 Jalan Pantai ☏ 088 240 000, ⍟ kkdayahotel.com. Very good mid-range establishment, perfectly placed in the busy northern section of town opposite Wisma Merdeka. Rooms are snug and en suite, and there's a ground-floor café and an alfresco bar. Free wi-fi. RM128

Horizon Jalan Tun Tun Razak ☏ 088 518 000, ⍟ horizonhotelsabah.com. It's hard to miss this bold new arrival, thanks to its size and prominent location. At the time of research it was not fully open and therefore was too soon to judge it, but the chic contemporary design makes it one to watch – and look out for discounts. RM452

7

★ **Hyatt Regency** Jalan Dutuk Salleh Sulong ☎088 221 234, ⓦkinabalu.regency.hyatt.com. The elegant, four-star *Hyatt* ranks among Southeast Asia's best city-centre hotels. From its sprawling dining area to the wonderful swimming pool and the perfectly appointed rooms with sea views, the *Hyatt* ticks all the boxes. RM382

Imperial International Warisan Square, Jalan Tun Fuad Stephens ☎088 522 888, ⓦimperialkk.com. The rooms in this mid-range hotel have more character than most, with furnishings such as big red designer chairs. Super-deluxe rooms have sea views and bathrooms with huge windows (and blinds) so you can watch the sun set. There's also a rooftop restaurant. Free internet access. Rooms RM200, super deluxe RM275

Jesselton 69 Jalan Gaya ☎088 223 333, ⓦjesselton hotel.com. Lady Mountbatten and Muhammad Ali are just two of this KK's institution's most famous guests. A combination of colonial-era charm and a central location make this hard to beat and, as elsewhere in KK, promotional prices are often on offer. RM191

Le Meridien Jalan Tun Fuad Stephens ☎088 322 222, ⓦkotakinabalu.lemeridien.com. A convenient location and sumptuous facilties, including high-spec rooms, bars, restaurants, pool and a gym. Although many guests will be more interested in higher-end dining, it's right opposite the lively Filipino night market. RM441

Manja 26, Block E, KK Times Square ☎088 486 601, ⓦmanjahotel.com. If you fancy staying in KK Times Square, an entertainment development south of the centre, then this is your best bet. Rooms are a good size, wi-fi equipped, comfortable and well furnished. RM88

Myne Lot 21, First Floor, Block A Warisan Square; Jalan Tun Fuad Stephens ☎088 448 787, ⓦmyne.com.my. The entrance is inside the Warisan Square mall, but don't let that put you off – this stylish hotel has good-sized rooms, equipped with flat-screen TVs. Promotional rates, as indicated here, are much lower than published tariffs. RM148

★ **Sarangnova** 98 Jalan Gaya ☎088 233 750, ⓦsarangnova.com. A popular choice, and understandably so – rooms are good value for money (including single rooms for RM25 less), the location is central and the staff are helpful. A striking lobby and decor themed around the bird life of Sabah also add a touch of character. RM130

Wah May 36 Jalan Haji Saman ☎088 266 118, ⓦwahmayhotel.com. This friendly, central place has well-maintained rooms and neat bathrooms. Most rooms face the front; the standard ones are rather cramped, but the deluxe twins at the back are not only larger but quieter. RM75 deluxe twins RM108

RESORTS

Langkah Syabas Kinarut Laut, 20km south of KK ☎088 752 000, ⓦlangkahsyabas.com.my. Appealing, small-scale beachfront resort, managed by an Australian/Malaysian couple and attracting plenty of Antipodean guests. The older chalets are set in a garden and encircle a small swimming pool, while the newer ones facing the sea cost almost double. The surprisingly good Kinarut Beach Cheese is made on the premises. RM200

Shangri-La Rasa Ria Resort Pantai Dalit, Tuaran, 30km north of KK ☎088 792 888, ⓦshangri-la.com. This massive yet laidback resort is set on a gorgeous bay. The grounds include a large forest nature reserve where monkeys can be spotted and there are even a few resident orang-utans. Prices are high, but good-value promotional rates are often available. RM1624

Shangri-La Tanjung Aru Resort Tanjung Aru Beach, 4km southwest of central KK ☎088 327 888, ⓦshangri-la.com. Set in rolling, landscaped grounds, this luxury resort boasts two pools, watersports and fitness centres, plus several food outlets. Hourly shuttle buses to the city and speedboats to Manukan Island (see p.406). RM963

Sutera Harbour Resort 1 Sutera Harbour Blvd, Sutera Harbour, 1.5km south of central KK ☎088 318 888, ⓦsuteraharbour.com. Spectacular shore-side development, divided into two separate hotels: *Pacific* is designed with business needs to the fore, whereas *Magellan* goes for luxury. From the marina squeezed between the two, boats run to the islands of the Tunku Abdul Rahman marine park; there's also a massive golf course. RM487

EATING

In recent years KK has become one of Malaysia's best cities for **dining**; the only real disappointment is that Sabahan cuisine is poorly represented compared to Malay, Chinese and international cuisines. There are plenty of restaurants and food courts within the centre, but if you're after seafood then join the locals at the beach in **Tanjung Aru** (bus #16 from Wawasan Plaza).

HAWKER STALLS & FOOD COURTS

Central Market Jalan Tun Fuad Stephens. The *nasi campur* stalls on the upper floor of the market provide filling, good-value meals during the day. Daily 7am–5pm.

First Beach Food Centre Tanjung Aru First Beach. This popular collection of around sixty stalls unsurprisingly specializes in seafood, but you can also get other Malay favourites such as satay. There's a great atmosphere in the evening – particularly at weekends – when families arrive to dine and socialize. Daily 11am–11pm.

OPPOSITE NIGHT MARKET, KOTA KINABALU (P.404) >

Jesselton Point Hawker Centre These stalls roar to life in the evenings selling satay, fried fish and other popular dishes. There's even an Aussie steak house and the seating is pleasantly alfresco, looking out over the harbour toward the islands. Daily 8am–11pm.

★ **Night market** Jalan Tun Fuad Stephens. West of the Central Market, the narrow stretch between the road and the South China Sea is transformed at sunset by dozens of stalls selling vegetables, fruit, juices and fish as well as spicy barbecued meats, noodles, and rice. Daily 5–10pm.

Seri Selera Kampung Air Jalan Sepuluh ⓦ seriselera .com. Cavernous indoor food court, still widely known as Sedco Square. It holds half a dozen seafood outlets as well as more than twenty other food stalls – serving satay, chicken rice, noodles and more – and hundreds of tables. Considered a little expensive, it's nevertheless popular with local families and tour groups. Daily 3pm–2am.

★ **Waterfront** Jalan Tun Fuad Stephens. A boardwalk in the western corner of the city where more than a dozen restaurants, bars and cafés compete for business, including the *Cock and Bull Bistro* (Western), *The Aussie* (barbecue), *Kohinoor* (Indian) and *Oregano Café* (Asian and Mediterranean). One cheap option is satay and *ketupat* (small parcels of rice) at *Aesha Corner*. Opening times vary, most 6pm–late.

CAFÉS AND RESTAURANTS

Borneo 1945 24 Lorong Dewan, Australia Place. This welcoming coffee shop doubles as a tiny World War II museum, serving *kaya* (coconut jam) toast for breakfast as well as dishes such as *pandan* chicken rice and a spicy *sup kambing* (lamb soup). Bicycles can be rented for RM20/day. Mon–Sat 7.30am–midnight.

★ **El Centro** 32 Jalan Haji Saman. A welcome addition to the city's hangouts, great for lunch, dinner or a few beers in the evening. Portions can be pretty large – the tacos (RM20), for example, are too big for one person. If you're on a tight budget try the set lunch at RM12. No smoking indoors. Daily 10am–11pm.

First Beach Café Aru Drive, Tanjung Aru First Beach. The main draw at this large open-fronted café, which serves drinks and Malay meals, is its prime beachfront position for KK's famous sunset. Grab a table on the beach itself if you can. Sun–Thurs 10am–1am, Fri & Sat 10am–2am.

First Beach Seafood Restaurant Food Court B, Jalan Tanjung Aru, Tanjung Aru First Beach, ⓣ 088 318 332. This seafront place is something of a KK institution, popular

with locals and tour groups alike despite being a little on the pricey side. Specialities include mantis shrimp fried with chilli and salt. Daily 8am–2pm & 5–10.30pm.

★ **Jarrod & Rawlins** KK Times Square ⓣ 088 231 890, ⓦ jarrod-rawlins.com. What sets this pub apart is the attached deli, which stocks many of the things that Western visitors may be missing from home, including sausages, cheese, serrano ham and steaks. You can buy to take away, but they'll also whip up dishes such as sausage and mash to eat on the premises. Daily 10am–1am.

★ **Jothy's Banana Leaf** 1/G9, Api-Api Centre. Excellent South Indian establishment serving satisfying *dosai* and a variety of delicious curries. Foreign diners rate the "chicken 65" (small, boneless fried pieces), while the locals' favourite is the fish-head curry (RM25) – significantly tastier than it may sound. Daily 11am–10pm.

Little Italy Ground floor of Capitol Hotel, Jalan Haji Saman ⓣ 088 232 231. While the mains will set you back around RM80 for two, the pizzas are a bit more affordable (RM18–23) and are widely considered to be the best in town. The set lunch, at RM20, is also reasonably affordable. Daily 10am–11pm.

Rasa Nyonya 50 Jalan Gaya. A/c restaurant serving very good versions of nyonya (fusion Chinese and Malay) cuisine. Specialities include *ayam limanu purut* (RM14, chicken cooked with lime leaves in coconut milk) and oxtail *asam pedas* (RM24, in a spicy and sour broth). Mon–Fri 11.30am–2.15pm & 6–9.45pm, Sat–Sun 6–9.45pm.

Suang Tain (Twin Sky) Seafood Restaurant No 12, Block A, Seri Selera Kampung Air ⓣ 088 223 080, ⓦ sungtain-seafood.com. Tucked away behind the Seri Selera Kampung Air food court, this has been a local favourite since 1983. It's particularly known for its crab dishes, as well as its keen prices. Daily 3pm–1.30am.

Tam Nak Thai Unit 5/G5, Api-Api Centre ⓣ 088 258 328. Fine Thai cuisine and a pleasing ambience make this place popular: it's best to book, especially if you intend to eat after 8pm. Mon–Sat 11.30am–2.30pm & 6–10.15pm, Sun 6–10.15pm.

Tambayan Block 3/G8, Api-Api Centre. Standing out due to the kitsch bamboo and palm-hut decor, this is a favourite for KK's sizeable Filipino population. Classic dishes include chicken *adobo* (cooked with soy sauce and vinegar), *sinigang baboy* (pork and vegetables in a sour tamarind broth) and breakfasts such as *longsilog* (sweet sausage with rice and egg). They have cheap Filipino San Miguel and you can even try *balut* – fertilized duck egg. Daily 24hr.

DRINKING AND NIGHTLIFE

Although there are a few good **bars**, KK is not generally noted for its **nightlife**. Within the centre there's a backpacker scene on Beach St but the bars are nothing special and the karaoke may not appeal; the **Waterfront** complex is generally a better place to hang out. One up-and-coming area is **Times Square KK**, 1km southwest of the centre, although it only really gets going around 11pm.

BED Waterfront. The name stands for Best Entertainment Destination, apparently, and it does indeed host some of the liveliest nights out in the city. Sun–Thurs 6 or 7pm–1.30am, Fri–Sat until 2 or 3am.

Shenanigan's Hyatt Regency (entrance on Jalan Datuk Salleh Sulong). A stalwart on the nightlife scene, this is still one of KK's top town-centre bars despite frighteningly inflated prices. No trainers, shorts or T-shirts, although foreigners seem to get away with it. Daily 5pm–midnight.

Sully's Lot 12, Block B, KK Times Square ⓦ sullys.com .my. Opened by English expats, this bar is trying to do something a little different to the KK norm: it has a resident jazz and blues band, plus an emphasis on cocktails, wines and single malt whisky designed to appeal to the thirty-plus crowd. Daily 5pm–2am.

Upperstar Café & Bar Segama Complex. Youthful bar spread across two buildings and on two floors, including a balcony. Expect an eclectic soundtrack, friendly service, competitively priced beers and tasty tapas-style dishes. There are also internet-connected PCs on the ground floor. Mon–Thurs & Sun 4.30pm–1.30am, Fri–Sat 4.30pm–2am.

SHOPPING

The newest and shiniest shopping mall in the centre is **Suria Sabah**, built on recealaimed land and with plenty of big-brand stores plus good sea views from the wi-fi-equipped food court on the third floor. Older shopping centres include **Wisma Merdeka** and **Centre Point**, both of which have mostly small local stores rather than international brands. The biggest mall is **1Borneo**, 7km north of the centre – a free shuttle bus runs from Warisan Square.

Bookshops For a wide range of English-language books, including Rough Guides to other Asian countries, try the branches of Times bookshop in Warisan Square and Suria Sabah. For books on Southeast Asia, plus a few secondhand novels, head for Borneo Books (ground floor, Wisma Merdeka, ☎ 088 241 050, ⓦ borneobooks .com). There's also a branch of Popular Book Store in Centrepoint. Tong Hing supermarket – which specializes in imported food – stocks a range of international newspapers and magazines.

Handicrafts In addition to the Handicraft Market, try the tourist board subsidiary Sri Pelancongan (ground floor, Lot 4, Block L, Sinsuran Complex, ☎ 088 232 121) for a small but high-quality selection of baskets, artwork and textiles.

Outdoor equipment Out Door Gear (☎ 088 448 806) on the first floor of the Star City conference and event centre, which you'll find in the western portion of Asia City, has a small range of clothing and accessories. There are also a couple of places selling basic camping gear on the ground floor of the Centrepoint mall, and a shop called Tech City at Jesselton Point.

DIRECTORY

Banks and exchange Banks include HSBC, Alliance and RHB on Jalan Gaya and Maybank on Jalan Haji Saman. There's a Maybank foreign exchange booth on the ground floor of Wisma Merdeka, along with several other independent moneychangers.

Cinemas Places showing some films in English include Cathay Cineplex on Jalan Haji Yaacob, the Growball Cinemax in Centrepoint mall and Golden Screen Cinemas in Suria Sabah.

Consulates Konsulat Jenderal Indonesia, Jalan Kemajuan ☎ 088 218 600, issues visas for Kalimantan. There is also an office in Tawau (see p.450).

Hospital Queen Elizabeth Hospital is beyond the Sabah State Museum, on Jalan Penampang (☎ 088 218 166).

Laundry The Laundry Shop, Asia City (Mon–Sat 7.30am–5pm, Sun 7.30am–noon).

Pharmacies In addition to the pharmacies in many malls, there's a handy branch of Guardian on Jalan Gaya.

Police The main police station, Balai Polis KK ☎ 088 247111, is below Atkinson's Clock Tower on Jalan Padang.

Post office The GPO (Mon–Sat 8am–5pm, Sun 10am–1pm) lies between the Sinsuran and Segama complexes, on Jalan Tun Razak.

Visa extensions Immigration Department, Block B, Federal Administration Complex, Jalan Sulaman (☎ 088 488 700; Mon–Fri 8am–5pm). Bus #5A from Wawasan.

Day-trips from KK

Good day-trip options from KK include **Mari Mari Cultural Village** and **Monsopiad Cultural Village** for anyone interested in local culture, or taking a ride south on the **North Borneo Railway** if you fancy a taste of colonial Sabah. Also south of KK is the **Tambunan Rafflesia Reserve**, where you may be able to see the world's largest flowering plant. The most popular attraction of all, however, are the beaches of **Tunku Abdul Rahman Park** just offshore.

Tunku Abdul Rahman Park

Named after Malaysia's first prime minister, and just a short boat trip away from KK, the five islands of **Tunku Abdul Rahman Park** (TAR Park) represent the most westerly ripples of the Crocker mountain range. The islands' forests, beaches and coral reefs lie within 8km of the city, with park territory as close as 3km off the mainland. The three most often visited are **Manukan**, **Mamutik** and **Sapi**, and it's easy to book a day's island hopping. Try to avoid weekends and public holidays when facilities are often overstretched; don't expect desert island solitude at any time.

Snorkelling is popular around the islands. Although careless tourists have damaged much of the coral, there's enough marine life around to make it worthwhile. **Scuba divers** will find the best conditions from January to March, although visibility is still typically just 5m.

Pulau Gaya

The site of the British North Borneo Chartered Company's first outpost in the region, **Pulau Gaya** is the closest of the islands to KK and also the largest. It doesn't feature on standard island-hopping routes; tourists can only visit by chartering a boat, staying at one of the island's resorts, or booking a tour with an operator such as Tanjung Aru Tours & Travel (☎088 225 302, ⓦgo2borneo.com).

If you do make it over, you'll find idyllic stretches of sand such as **Polis Beach** as well as lovely hiking trails; Downbelow (☎012 866 1935, ⓦdivedownbelow.com) runs a dive shop. The eastern end is taken up by a stilt village inhabited by Filipino immigrants.

Pulau Sapi

Though far smaller than its neighbour Gaya, **Pulau Sapi** also has trails and is home to macaques and hornbills; with the best **beaches** of any of the islands, it's popular with swimmers, snorkellers and picnickers. Sapi has simple facilities including toilets, a small café (daily 8am–4pm) and changing rooms. There's also a dive shop, 50 Bar (daily 9am–1pm; ☎013 854 5567), charging a steep RM250 per dive.

Pulau Manukan

The park HQ is situated on crescent-shaped **Pulau Manukan**, site of a former stone quarry and now the most developed island. Indeed Manukan has become something of a victim of its own success, drawing hundreds of visitors on a busy day. That said, the beach is attractive, watersports are good and there's a café serving a buffet (RM95) or à la carte meals – *nasi lemak* or curry *laksa* cost RM18. To escape the crowds, take the thirty-minute walk to Sunset Point.

Pulau Mamutik

Across a narrow channel from Manukan, tiny **Pulau Mamutik** is a snorkeller's delight. The island is surrounded by coral gardens with the best stretch off the beach at the southwest, towards the back of where the boat drops you, but it's necessary either to clamber over rocks or to swim right round.

Borneo Divers (☎088 222 226, ⓦborneodivers.info) have a small dive shop, offering better prices to walk-in customers than you'll get by booking ahead. Head out on the first boats of the day if that's your plan; it's much more cost-effective to do two or three dives than just one.

Pulau Sulug

The last island of the group, **Pulau Sulug**, is the most remote and consequently the quietest, though its lovely coral makes it popular with divers. It has no facilities, and few boats visit.

ARRIVAL AND DEPARTURE

TUNKU ABDUL RAHMAN PARK

By boat Frequent boats to Manukan, Mamutik and Sapi leave from the Jesselton Point Ferry Terminal (departures from around 7.30am, last boat back leaves around 5pm). Boat company desks at the terminal compete for business; prices vary slightly but are officially RM23/18 (adult/child) for one island, RM33/28 for two or RM43/38 for all three. If you find an operator that includes Sulug, the official price

for four islands is RM53/48. The operator should give you a timetable and explain the arrangements for moving from one island to another. There's also an RM10/6 park fee and RM7.20/3.60 terminal fee. The same companies also arrange activities such as parasailing, jet skiing and wakeboarding. Rent your snorkelling gear (RM15) at the terminal if you plan to go to more than one island.

ACCOMMODATION

In addition to the resorts listed here, all owned by the same company, it's possible to **camp** on the three main islands for just RM5; tents can be rented for RM30, but don't rely too much on availability.

Bunga Raya Resort Pulau Gaya ☎ 088 271 000, ⓦ bungarayaresort.com. A delightful luxury resort with villas hidden away within the forest and access to a secluded white-sand beach. Free transfers to sister property *Gayana Eco Resort* if you want a change of scene or to try the excellent seafood restaurant. RM1486

Gayana Eco Resort Pulau Gaya ☎ 088 245 158, ⓦ gayana-resort.com. This resort has attractive chalets on either side of a boardwalk jutting out from the beach over the sea, plus two fantastic restaurants in the same rustic complex. At one end of the plankway, a marine

conservation centre holds various tanks containing eels, lobsters and strange-looking flora and fauna. RM1130

Manukan Island Resort Pulau Manukan ☎ 088 318 888, ⓦ suterasanctuarylodges.com.my. The only accommodation on Manukan, with around twenty well-appointed units; if you're splashing out anyway, it's worth paying a little extra for a more luxurious hillside villa. Manukan is at its best at night, as the crowds depart by 5pm. Prices include boat transfers and breakfast. RM1200, hillside villa RM1340

7

Monsopiad Cultural Village

Penampang, 13km south of KK • Daily 9am–5pm; guided tours 10am, noon, 3pm & 5pm; cultural show 11am, 2pm & 4pm • Adult RM75, child free • ☎ 088 761 336, ⓦ monsopiad.com • Bus or minivan to Kampung Kandazon then walk 3km or take a share taxi; or private taxi from KK (20 min; RM20)

Based around the tale of a legendary head-hunter, **Monsopiad Cultural Village** provides an introduction to the history and traditions of the Kadazan people. Tours are led by knowledgeable guides who take visitors to a hut where Monsopiad's grisly harvest of 42 skulls is displayed, and then explain traditions such as the rituals practised by the *bobohizan* (priestess). Next comes the chance to taste *lihing* (rice wine) and test your accuracy with a blowpipe and sling. Finally there's a dance show with scope for a little audience participation.

Although the exhibits and activities are interesting, the entrance price is high and the slightly dated approach has stiff competition from the newer Mari Mari Cultural Village. That said, it has an advantage in that it deals with people from a single tribe – and in the place where they lived – rather than taking a scattergun approach to tribal culture.

Mari Mari Cultural Village

Near Inanam, 18km east of KK • Tours daily 10am–noon, 2–4pm, 6–8pm • Adults RM150, children RM130, including lunch and transport from KK; RM75/RM65 without transport (in which case a return taxi will cost RM100–120, including waiting time) • Operated by Traverse Tours, Lot 227 – 229, 2nd Floor, Wisma Sabah ☎ 088 260 501, ⓦ riverbug.asia

A newer alternative to the similar Monsopiad Cultural Village, with rather more of a theme park feel but also more interaction right from the start: groups have to assign a leader who will introduce them to the costumed "tribal leader" at the village entrance. Inside, visitors are taken on a whistle-stop tour through the longhouses and customs of Sabah's various tribes.

Activities and demonstrations include rice wine tasting, beekeeping for honey and glue production, starting a fire using bamboo, bouncing on a trampoline, making sweets and using a blowpipe. Towards the end there's a dance show, followed by a buffet meal. It may all feel a little phoney but, taken in the right spirit, it is also great fun and you come away both entertained and educated.

Lok Kawi Wildlife Park

South of Penampang, 25km from KK • Daily 9.30am–5.30pm (last ticket 4.30pm); Animal show daily (except Fri) 11.15–11.45am & 3.30–4pm; Public feedings daily (except Fri) 10.20am & 2–2.30pm • RM20 adult, RM10 child • ☎ 088 765 793, ⓦ lokkawiwildlifepark .com • 19B bus from Wawasan; taxi RM40 (one-way) or RM100–120 (return including waiting)

If you don't like zoos, the rather old-fashioned **Lok Kawi Wildlife Park** – covering 280 acres on the old road between Penampang and Papar – is unlikely to change your mind. While its enclosures generally seem pretty good, in a few cases the animals look quite miserable. The star exhibits are indigenous species such as orang-utans, sun bears, pygmy elephants and tigers, but other attractions include ankole (African cattle with huge horns), as well as a botanical garden and *Rafflesia* trail.

North Borneo Railway

Departures Wed & Sat 9.30am; 4hr • Round-trip RM250 adults, RM150 children; prices include breakfast and lunch, advance booking essential • ☎ 088 263 933, ⓦ suteraharbour.com

You don't have to be a railway buff to appreciate the romance of taking a steam train along the 36km of the colonial-era **North Borneo Railway** from Tanjung Aru station (see p.399) to the small town of Papar. The locomotive is a wood-burning British Vulcan, while the five carriages were built to a 1900s-style design in the 1970s.

Tambunan Rafflesia Reserve

On the main highway, 61km southeast of KK and 20km north of Tambunan • Daily 8am–3pm • Entry RM5, guide RM100 (for up to 6 people) • ☎ 088 898 500 • Bus towards Tambunan, or taxi (RM100–120 return including waiting)

If you feel you really must see a *Rafflesia* (see p.596) in flower while you are in Sabah, then the prospects at the **Tambunan Rafflesia Reserve**, often visited as a day-trip from KK, are good. As each bloom lasts for only a few days, however, it's essential to check ahead. Assuming that one is flowering, expect a walk of up to two hours in total.

The interior

The highway southeast out of KK claws its way up onto the ridges of the **Crocker mountain range**, passing Gunung Alab (1964m). The mountains separate the state's west coast and the swampy Klias Peninsula from the area christened the **interior** in the days of the Chartered Company. The former isolation of this sparsely populated region ended at the start of the twentieth century, when a rail line was built between Jesselton

---

EXPLORING THE INTERIOR

Travelling by bus or car, it's possible to circumnavigate the interior from KK, starting with a drive southeast over the mountains to the Kadazan/Dusun town of **Tambunan**, which sits on a plain chequered with paddy fields. From Tambunan, the road continues further south to **Keningau** and **Tenom**, which marks the start of Murut territory stretching down to the Brunei–Kalimantan **border**. Although this is one route to the **Maliau Basin** – only negotiable by 4WD vehicles – most trekkers arrive from the other direction, via Tawau in eastern Sabah (see p.448).

From Tenom, the road west makes for **Beaufort**, once a favourite outpost for colonial officials, arriving back at the coast at **Kuala Penyu**, from where boats travel to the tiny **Pulau Tiga National Park**.

(modern-day KK) and Tenom to transport the raw materials being produced by the region's thriving **rubber** industry.

Today, **oil-palm** cultivation takes precedence, though the Kadazan/Dusun and Murut peoples still cultivate rice, maize and cocoa.

Tambunan

The drive from KK starts with teasing glimpses of valleys until, far beyond the Tambunan Rafflesia Reserve (see opposite), a kink in the road reveals the paddy fields of **Tambunan Plain** below. **Gunung Trus Madi**, Sabah's second highest mountain (2642m), towers above the plain's eastern flank; climbing it is an exciting – if rather less easily arranged – alternative to ascending Gunung Kinabalu.

After such a riveting approach, bustling little **TAMBUNAN**, centred on an ugly square of modern shophouses, is bound to disappoint. The best thing about the town itself is its lively *tamu*, held on Thursday in town and Saturday mornings nearby in Kampung Toboh.

Gunung Trus Madi

4WD from Tambunan to Taman Kitangan (1 hr)

The second tallest mountain in Sabah, **Gunung Trus Madi** is renowned as a good place to catch sight of rare insectivorous pitcher plants, including one endemic species (*Nepenthes x trusmadiensis*). Climbing it can be arranged through either the Borneo Heritage Village or tour operators in KK, but it's essential to plan ahead; getting a permit takes around a month, and you'll also need a guide and transport. Reckon on a total cost of around RM1600 for two people – and you'll need your own tent and sleeping bags.

The summit trail from **Taman Kitangan** takes five hours up and three hours down on rough, often steep paths with occasional rest shelters. You can do it as a strenuous day-trip or stay overnight on the mountain. The latter is preferred not just because it means less of a rush, but also because the dawn views of Gunung Kinabalu are stunning.

ARRIVAL AND DEPARTURE | TAMBUNAN

By bus and minivan Buses and vans to and from KK, Ranau and Keningau (RM9) stop in Tambunan's main square, surrounded by unremarkable cafés.

ACCOMMODATION

Borneo Heritage Village (aka Tambunan Village Resort Centre or TVRC) 2km north of Tambunan ☏ 087 774 076. Although there's accommodation in Tambunan, this lodge just north of town is your best bet. A large site with a holiday camp feel, it's set around a lake and has a riverside café. Accommodation ranges from backpacker rooms – reached via 127 steps – to family chalets with kitchens. Staff can organize activities such as kayaking, hiking (including up Trus Madi) or buffalo-riding, and there's wi-fi and an internet terminal. Transport from KK should be able to drop you at the turning (or even take you to the door if you're in a taxi or van). Rooms RM66, chalets RM176

Keningau

A fifty-kilometre journey south from Tambunan brings you to the town of **KENINGAU**. A hectic, noisy place, it holds some decent hotels if you want to break a journey. If you're here on a Thursday morning, check out the *tamu* (**market**) a short walk up the main Keningau–Tambunan road; on Sundays a *tamu* is held in the town centre.

Taipaek-gung Temple

Keningau's single attraction is its **Chinese temple**, right beside the bus terminus. The brightly painted murals that cover its walls and ceilings are more reminiscent of those in a Hindu temple, while the altars are packed with figurines.

THE MURUT HEARTLAND

Rather than moving on from Keningau to either Tenom or Tambunan, a more exciting alternative is to head for **Sapulut** to explore Sabah's Murut heartland; a boat trip from Sapulut will take you to the limestone outcrop of **Batu Punggul**, which has magnificent views. After that you can either backtrack to Keningau or take a 4WD and strike east along the logging roads that connect the interior with Tawau, southern Sabah's largest town.

ARRIVAL AND INFORMATION
KENINGAU

By road Minivans run to Keningau from Tambunan (90min; RM9), Tenom (1hr; RM6) and KK (2hr 30min). Most terminate around the central square (close to the *Juta* hotel) or near BSN Bank (near *Honey Sweet* restaurant). Ask in the main square if you need a 4WD to Tawau (RM100–150 depending on number of passengers); you'll need to turn up early (around 6.30am) and have a little luck, as some days there aren't enough passengers to make the trip viable. For Sapulut (RM25), drivers hang out near Taipaek-gung temple.

Internet access Central internet cafes include BJ Nethouse, Lot 1, Block A3, Juta Commercial Centre (Mon–Fri 8.30am–8.30pm, Sat 8.30am–7pm, Sun 10.30am–8.30pm).

ACCOMMODATION

Juta Jalan Milimewa Lama ☎087 337 888, ⓦsabah .com.my/juta. The classiest accommodation in town, close to the padang, with stylish rooms with crisp white bed linen and (in the larger, more expensive rooms) art on the walls. The building has a business centre and gym, plus you can arrange a massage. There's a non-smoking floor and free wi-fi in all rooms. <u>RM175</u>

Kristal Above Hiap Lee Shopping Centre ☎087 338 888. The best budget option, holding no-frills a/c rooms that are clean and reasonably priced. There's no restaurant but plenty of restaurants close by. <u>RM75</u>

Sabindo Lots 45–46 Yee Shing Commercial Centre ☎087 337 130, ⓦsabindohotel.blogspot.com. Decorative touches include glass-topped tables in the bedrooms and coloured tiles in the bathrooms; some of the cheapest rooms do not have windows, while more expensive ones have balconies. <u>RM88</u>

EATING AND DRINKING

For the most economical food, try the cluster of **food stalls** that set up in the main square (close to the *Juta* hotel) daily from 4–11pm. Keep an eye open for yellow dragonfruit, a Keningau speciality.

Honey Sweet Ground floor, Pengalan Shopping Centre. Although they serve other dishes such as fish ball soup, the speciality is chicken rice (RM5.50) with the meat either fried or steamed. There's seating inside and outside. Daily 9am–9.30pm.

Tenom

After Keningau, the small town of **TENOM**, 42km southwest, comes as some relief. Once the bustling headquarters of the Interior District of British North Borneo, Tenom is now a peaceful backwater with simple hotels and good cafés. Lying within a mantle of forested hills, the town also boasts tasteful wooden shophouses and a blue-domed mosque.

The surroundings are extremely fertile, supporting maize, cocoa and soybean – predominantly cultivated by the indigenous Murut people. Within Malaysia, though, Tenom is best known for **coffee**; there are opportunities to taste the local product or to stay in a small plantation. The town's *tamu* (**market**) takes place 6am–12.30pm on Sunday.

Sabah Agricultural Park

15km northeast of Tenom • Tues–Sun 9am–4.30pm • RM25 • ☎087 737 952, ⓦsabah.net.my/agripark • Taxi (RM60 including 2hr wait) or minivan (RM20) from Tenom (ask to be dropped at Lagud Seberang, then walk 1km)

The **Sabah Agricultural Park** (Taman Pertanian), where the state's Agricultural Department carries out studies on a wide range of crops, is a pleasant enough spot to spend an hour or two. The research station is renowned for its **Orchid Centre**, which has 400 species, plus there's a **Living Crop Museum** with groves of exotic fruit trees and tropical plants. Other attractions include the **Bee Centre**, planned gardens, a mini zoo and a couple of lakes. Stay overnight if you want to explore the park's three trekking routes.

ARRIVAL AND DEPARTURE

TENOM

By train The train station is on the eastern side of the padang.

Destinations Beaufort (2 daily; 2hr 45min), where you can change for Papar, Kinarut or Tanjung Aru (for KK).

By bus Buses stop at the padang – there's a Nai Lok Express (☎ 087 735 325) ticket office on the eastern side.

Destinations Beaufort (hourly; 50min); Keningau (hourly; 1hr); KK (hourly; 1hr 30min).

By minivan Minivans congregate on Tenom's main street, Jalan Padas, which runs along the north side of the padang; minivans north to Keningau (RM6) circle around Tenom all day, looking for passengers.

By taxi Share taxis wait at the southern edge of the padang.

Destinations Beaufort (2hr 30min; RM35); Keningau (30min; RM8/person); Sipitang (2hr; RM30).

ACCOMMODATION

Sabah Agriculture Park 15km northeast of Tenom ☎ 087 737 952. The park has simple accommodation, with dorm rooms and also camping spaces. The main reason to stay the night is that it's a requirement if you want to go jungle trekking (for which it's best to contact them in advance). Camping RM10, dorms RM25

Sri Perdana, Jalan Tun Mustapha ☎ 087 734 001. A reliable choice, just off the padang; although a bit grubby in places, the floors and bedding are clean enough. Only one room has a queen-size bed, the rest are all twin or

bigger. Double RM36, twins RM46

Teak Wood Cabin Fatt Choi coffee plantation ☎ 087 735 230, ⓦfccoffee.com. The four- or six-person cabins at this site, in the hills just behind Tenom, come with a/c and hot water. No meals are provided, although you can bring your own food to barbecue. Ask about transfers from the owner's café, and about activities such as an early morning Tai Chi lesson or a hike to see a *Rafflesia*. RM80

EATING

Places to eat are plentiful, with a clutch of coffee shops and restaurants in a pedestrian plaza set one street back from *Asia Rasa* hotel and the large statue of Ontoros Antanom, a Murut warrior who gave his name to Tenom.

Asia Rasa 3 Lot 12, Tenom Commercial Centre. Located near the *Asia Rasa* hotel, which is not recommended, this place serves fried rice, roti etc for breakfast and has *nasi campur* for lunch. The dark wood tables and chairs make it feel slightly classier than most. Daily 6.30am–5pm.

Tenom Fatt Choi Coffee Jalan Tun Mustapha. There may be no such thing as a free meal, but here you can

partake of a free coffee. An outlet for one of Tenom's best-known coffee brands, it sells beans, ground coffee and instant powders and also provides gratis drinks as tasters – and there's no pressure to buy. Enquire here about the owners' *Teak Wood Cabin*. Mon–Sat 8.30am–noon & 1.30–5pm.

Southwest of KK

Following the coast southwest of KK, the highway passes through Kinarut and Papar before reaching **Beaufort**, the main access point for the **Klias Peninsula**. This is prime country for **day-trips** organized by tour operators in KK, whether for whitewater rafting, proboscis-monkey watching or firefly tours. Offshore is **Pulau Tiga**, the setting for the first series of the TV show *Survivor*.

Beaufort

Named after Leicester P. Beaufort, an early governor of British North Borneo, **BEAUFORT** is a quiet, uneventful town whose commercial significance has declined since the sealed road from KK into the interior lessened the importance of its rail link with Tenom. The town's position on the banks of the Padas leaves it prone to flooding, which explains why its shophouses are raised on steps.

It's also the river that attracts most of the tourists who visit the town – Beaufort is the starting point for many whitewater rafting trips. Otherwise, once you've poked around in the market, inspected angular **St Paul's Church** at the top of town and taken a walk past the stilt houses on the riverbank, you've exhausted its sights.

ARRIVAL AND DEPARTURE   BEAUFORT

By train Beaufort is the main hub on the railway line. Trains run in one direction to Tenom (twice daily; 2hr 45min), and in the other to Papar, Kinarut and Tanjung Aru (for KK).
By bus The bus rank is at the southern end of Jalan Masjid.

If you're heading for Lawas in Sarawak, the sole daily bus from KK arrives around 3pm (1hr 45min; RM13).
Destinations KK (4 daily; 90min); Kuala Penyu (8 daily; 1hr); Menumbok (8 daily; 1hr 30min); Sipitang (4 daily; 1hr 30min); Tenom (hourly; 50min).

ACCOMMODATION

MelDe 19 & 20, Taman Lo Chung ☎087 222 266, ✉ meldehotel.bfort2007@hotmail.com. Nothing special, but the small rooms are clean even if the carpets

are a bit worn. Rooms are en suite, with hot water. Reception is above the *Restoran Kim Wah*, which serves decent Chinese food. RM60

Sipitang

Reached by a newly surfaced road southwest of Beaufort, the seafront town of **SIPITANG** is notable only as a departure point for **boats to Labuan**. As you approach from the north, a bridge marks the start of town – look out for the pretty stilt houses to your left as you cross. The jetty is just beyond the bridge, next to the Shell petrol station.

ARRIVAL AND DEPARTURE   SIPITANG

By bus Two daily buses running each way between KK and Lawas in Sarawak stop in the town centre; Sairah Express (☎089 757 357 or ☎019 581 4274) runs daily buses to Tawau.

By boat Speedboats run by Kaka Express leave the jetty twice daily for Labuan (7.30am & 1pm; RM30).
By taxi From the share taxi stand, next to the bus stop, you can join a vehicle to Beaufort (RM6) or Tenom.

ACCOMMODATION

Dhiya Esplanad Upper floors, Bangunan TBB ☎016 813 6397. The first hotel you come to heading along the main road from the jetty, with simple but clean rooms. Some of the more spacious deluxe rooms have sea views.

Rooms RM60, deluxe rooms RM100
Lian Hin Lot 5, Kedai Pekan. The rooms here are small but at least they are clean and have a/c, plus drawings on the walls to help make them more cheerful. RM60

EATING AND DRINKING

By far the best **places to eat** are the satay and fried-chicken stalls that open on the waterfront around dusk.

Azmia Curry House Lot 16, Sabaran Lega. The most inviting of a row of similar Indian restaurants. It serves rice

and noodle dishes, plus a *nasi campur* buffet. Daily 6.30am–midnight.

CROSSING INTO SARAWAK

Buses from KK to Lawas – or continuing on to Brunei – stop in Sipitang, but if you're already in town it's easier to get a seat in a taxi. Heading west from Sipitang, buses stop first at Kampung Sindumin on the Sabah side, where you show your passport. They then cross the border and stop 200m further on at Merapok. This is where your passport is stamped, entitling you to remain in Sarawak for thirty days.

Official **taxis** from Sipitang cannot cross into Sarawak, so you'll need to pay RM10 per person to the border then take another RM10 taxi on the other side. The other option is to take an unlicensed taxi all the way from Sipitang to Lawas for RM20 per person.

The Klias Peninsula

Thirty kilometres west of Beaufort, and served by regular minivans from the centre of town, the **Klias Peninsula** is an area of flat marshland that's popular with KK-based tour operators for proboscis monkey or firefly tours (see p.400).

Menumbok

The most westerly settlement on the Klias Peninsula, tiny **MENUMBOK** has no accommodation. It's notable only for the jetty that links it to Labuan; a couple of cafés here may be useful when waiting for a boat.

ARRIVAL AND DEPARTURE   MENUMBOK

By bus Buses are scheduled to take arriving ferry passengers to KK, and share taxis to KK (2hr 30min; RM30) wait for the arrival of speedboats. You may have to hang around a while for enough passengers for smaller destinations, such as Beaufort (1hr; RM10) or Kuala Penyu (45min). An alternative route to Kuala Penyu is to take a KK-bound vehicle as far as Kayul, where there are plenty of onward minibuses.

By boat Regular speedboats and two larger ferries travel daily between Menumbok and Pulau Labuan (see p.414).

Kuala Penyu

Around an hour northeast of Beaufort, or 45 minutes from Menumbok, at the northern point of the peninsula, **KUALA PENYU** is the departure point for **Pulau Tiga National Park**. It's a simple grid of streets with little more than a few stores, filled with basic supplies, and a couple of *kedai kopis*.

ARRIVAL AND DEPARTURE   KUALA PENYU

By bus or minivan Leaving Kuala Penyu, it takes just over two hours to travel by minivan to KK's Merdeka Field bus stand, or you can get a minivan to Beaufort (RM5). These vehicles leave from one block back from the jetty.

By boat Boats run to the Pulau Tiga Resort (see p.414) twice daily, usually at 10am and 3pm.

ACCOMMODATION

★**Tempurung Seaside Lodge** 13km west of Kuala Penyu ☎088 773 066, ✉info@borneo-authentic.com. Charming chalets connected by wooden walkways on a hillside overlooking the South China Sea. The lodge has a private beach, where sandflies can sometimes be a problem. If you're feeling more active then they have mountain bikes for rent (RM15/hr), or you can arrange a day-trip to Pulau Tiga for RM185 per person (minimum of four people). **RM300**

Pulau Tiga National Park

In the South China Sea, 12km north of Kuala Penyu, **Pulau Tiga National Park** once consisted of three islands, but wave erosion has reduced one to a mere sand bar. Of the remaining two, Tiga and Kalampunian Damit, only the former holds any accommodation. It acquired a degree of fame in 2001 as the location of the first series of the American reality-TV show *Survivor*.

Most visitors today content themselves with relaxing on the sandy beaches and **snorkelling** or **diving** in the azure sea, but it's possible to hike right around the island in

---

DIVING AROUND PULAU TIGA

Pulau Tiga's prime dive site is probably **Asmara Point**, close to the Sabah Parks jetty. With a maximum depth of 10m it's a nice easy dive, albeit sometimes with a slight current, with good coral attracting lionfish, Moorish idols and groupers, plus sometimes sea turtles. Other good sites include Phukat Point (where they very occasionally see white-tip sharks), Larai Point (notable for its excellent coral) and Dunlop Point.

Expect to pay RM180 per person for two dives (minimum two people), plus RM120 per day for equipment rental. Discover Scuba Diving classes (RM200) get non-divers underwater straight away.

six hours. An easy twenty-minute walk to the centre of Pulau Tiga leads to a couple of (lukewarm) **mud volcanoes**. Slip and slide around there, then walk 1.2km further to clean up at lovely **Pagong-Pagong** beach. Be warned, though, that walking can be hard going if your feet and flip-flops are muddy.

Pulau Kalampunian Damit
Just 1km northeast of Pulau Tiga, **Kalampunian Damit** is also known locally as Pulau Ular (Snake Island), because it attracts a species of venomous sea snake called the yellow-lipped sea krait. The island is normally visited as part of a morning trip from Pulau Tiga Resort, combined with some snorkelling (RM70 per person). It used to be possible to see dozens of snakes on a good day, but now they seem to be much more scarce and some visitors come away disappointed.

ARRIVAL AND DEPARTURE   **PULAU TIGA NATIONAL PARK**

By boat No public boats run to Pulau Tiga; most visitors come on tour packages that include transport. If you're staying at the Sabah Parks accommodation, check whether there's room on a resort boat – expect to pay RM60 each way (departures around 10am & 3pm daily; 30min). Otherwise you may be able to charter a boat (30min; RM500 return), which can hold 12 people; talk to the Sabah Parks office at the Kuala Penyu jetty, and if that doesn't help try the *Pulau Tiga Resort* office. Boats back to Kuala Penyu leave the island at 9am and 2pm. There's a RM15 conservation fee for the island.

ACCOMMODATION

At the time of research only two **accommodation** options were open on Pulau Tiga, although the *Borneo Survivor Resort* was expected to reopen at some point (most likely with a new name).

Pulau Tiga Resort ☎ 088 240584, ⓦ pulautiga.com.my. This well-run beach resort has dozens of twin-bed chalets and two cheaper (but significantly less appealing) longhouses, with triples shared as small dorms. Activities include kayaking and snorkelling, plus there's a dive shop. Rates include full board and ferry. Dorms <u>RM210</u>, rooms <u>RM610</u>

Sabah Parks ☎ 088 211 881, ⓦ sabahparks.org.my /eng/pulau_tiga_park. The park authorities offer two simple dormitories and a chalet with two twin-bed rooms; you can also camp (with your own tent). There is no restaurant but you can use the kitchens or go to *Pulau Tiga Resort*. Camping <u>RM5</u>, dorms <u>RM30</u>, rooms <u>RM120</u>

Pulau Labuan

A short distance west of the Klias Peninsula, **PULAU LABUAN** is not strictly part of Sabah, being Federal Territory governed directly from KL. Labuan town holds few tourist attractions, but its centre has decent eating, good mid-range accommodation and a lively nightlife. Some worthwhile sights lie beyond the town, while scuba divers are attracted by the chance to dive four **wrecks**. You might also want to take advantage of the island's **duty-free** prices while passing through.

Labuan Town
The centre of Labuan, previously known as Victoria but now simply **LABUAN TOWN**, lies on the island's southeastern side. Along with the international airport, the gleaming ferry terminal on Jalan Merdeka attests to the island's prosperity and geographic importance.

General Market
Market Daily 6am–6pm • **Bazaar** Mon–Sat 7am–5pm, Sun 7am–1pm
The upper floor of the busy *gerai* (**general market**), at the western end of Labuan Town, affords good views of Kampung Patau Patau – the modest **water village** northwest of town. To reach the *gerai* itself you pass through **Labuan Bazar**, which sells clothes, handicrafts and souvenirs.

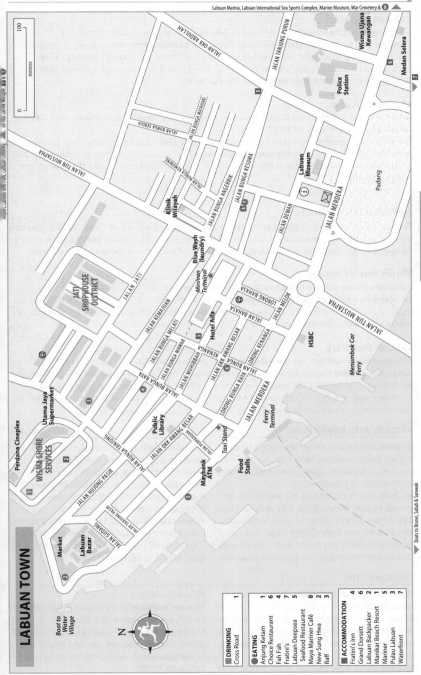

Labuan Marina, Labuan International Sea Sports Complex, Marine Museum, War Cemetery & ⑧

LABUAN TOWN

100 metres

Boat to Water Village

JATI SHOPHOUSE DISTRICT

Perdana Cineplex

WISMA SHORE SERVICES

Utama Jaya Supermarket

JALAN TUN MUSTAPHA

JALAN OKK ABDULLAH

JALAN TANJUNG PURUN

Wisma Ujana Kewangan

Medan Selera

Police Station

Labuan Museum

JALAN MERDEKA

Padang

JALAN DEWAN

JALAN BUNGA KESUMA

JALAN BUNGA ANGGRIK

JALAN BUNGA MAWAR

JALAN BUNGA SEROJA

JALAN BUNGA KEBUNG

JALAN BUNGA MELATI

JALAN BUNGA MAHAHH

Klinik Wilayah

Blue Wash (laundry)

JALAN JATI

JALAN KEMAJUAN

JALAN MUHIBBAH

JALAN OKK AWANG BESAR

JALAN BUNGA RAYA

JALAN BUNGA TANJUNG

Minivan Terminal

Hotel Aita

LORONG BAHASA

JALAN BAHASA

JALAN MELOK

LORONG KENANGA

KENANGA

Menumbok Car Ferry

HSBC

JALAN TUN MUSTAPHA

LORONG BUNGA RAYA

JALAN MERDEKA

JALAN PERDANA

Public Library

Taxi Stand

Maybank ATM

Food Stalls

Ferry Terminal

Boats to Brunei, Sabah & Sarawak

Labuan Bazar

Market

JALAN GUDANG

JALAN TANJUNG PASIR

JALAN HUJUNG PASIR

N

DRINKING
Cross Road 1

EATING
Anjung Ketam 1
Choice Restaurant 6
Fah Fah 4
Fratini's 5
Labuan Deepsea
Seafood Restaurant 8
Maya Mariner Café 2
New Sung Hwa 3

Raff

ACCOMMODATION
Fratini's Inn 4
Grand Dorsett 6
Labuan Backpacker 2
Manikar Beach Resort 1
Mariner 5
Pulau Labuan 3
Waterfront 7

7

Labuan Museum

Behind the padang on Jalan Dewan · ☎ 087 414 135 · Daily 8.30am–5pm · Free · Wheelchair available for visitors

Housed in a yellow concrete building, the small **Labuan Museum** contains a maze of rooms where photo- and caption-led exhibits document the island's history. Most notable were the dramatic events of World War II, as it was through Labuan that the Japanese forces penetrated British North Borneo.

Marine Museum

Labuan International Sea Sports Complex (Kompleks Sukan Laut), Jalan Tanjun Purun, 1km east of Labuan Museum · Daily 8.30am–5pm, fish feeding Sat 10am · Free · ☎ 087 425 927 · RM8 by taxi

Set within a complex that also houses a food court and businesses including Borneo Star Dive (see below), the **Marine Museum** mostly features conventional tanks with fish and other sea creatures, but starts with a pool of small black-tip sharks that guests are allowed to touch.

7

Around the island

A couple of sites outside town are worth visiting if you have a little time to kill; you can reach them by bus, or charter a taxi for RM45 per hour. The lovely **beaches** from Batu Manikar Beach to Sungai Miri Beach are devoid of both development and facilities.

World War II Cemetery

3km northeast of centre, along Jalan Tanjung Batu · 45min walk, #1 bus or taxi (RM10–15)

In Malaysia's largest **World War II Cemetery**, over 3900 war graves are neatly laid out on perfectly manicured lawns. It's a serene, reflective spot, with a memorial to one side where the soldiers' names are listed.

Labuan Bird Park

Jalan Tanjung Kubong · Daily 10am–5pm · RM3 · ☎ 087 463 544 · Bus #6 (30 min); taxi RM25–30

Arranged around three aviaries in geodesic domes, the **Labuan Bird Park** holds tropical birds from throughout the region, such as hornbills, kingfishers, sharmas, herons, ostriches and peacocks. Perhaps the biggest hits are the mynah birds that say "hello" as you approach; there are printed lists of words to which they will respond.

ARRIVAL AND DEPARTURE
PULAU LABUAN

By plane From Labuan's airport, 5km north of town, the only way into the centre is by taxi (RM10).

Destinations KK (6 daily; 30min); Kuala Lumpur (3 daily; 2hr 20min); Miri (4 daily; 40min).

By boat Most ferries dock at the international ferry terminal on Jalan Merdeka (ticket office ☎ 087 581 006; daily 7.10am–5.30pm). Passenger ferries to Menumbok leave from the main terminal, while vehicle ferries use a separate jetty close by. They connect on the mainland to bus services for KK (see p.413); buy bus tickets from the booth in

Labuan's international ferry terminal. In addition, smaller speedboats run hourly to Menumbok (30min; RM15).

Destinations KK (2 daily; 3hr 15min); Lawas (daily if there are enough passengers; 2hr 15min); Limbang (daily; 2hr); Menumbok (passenger 2 daily; 50 min; vehicle 2 daily; 50min); Muara, Brunei (5 daily; 1hr 15min).

Vehicle rental There are a few rental counters at the ferry terminal, where you can arrange both cars and motorcycles. They include GG Rent a Motorbike (Mon–Sat 9am–6pm; ☎ 087 429 792, ⊕ gogosabah.com).

INFORMATION

Tourist information centre Jalan Merdeka, close to the Labuan museum (Mon–Thurs 8am–5pm, Fri 8–11.30am & 2–5pm, Sat 9am–3pm; ☎ 087 423 445). Helpful staff have plenty of material, including some very good maps, and can inform you about the island's highly recommended homestay programme.

Internet There's an internet café in the ferry terminal

(daily 8am–midnight).

Tours and activities The only company arranging diving on Labuan's wrecks is Borneo Star Dive, based at Labuan International Sea Sports Complex (☎ 087 429 278, ⊕ stardivers2005@yahoo.com). For island-hopping trips in the nearby marine park, enquire at the tourist office or try Seri Ganti (☎ 016 840 006).

ACCOMMODATION

As a business centre, Labuan Town holds plenty of **hotels**, almost all mid-range or higher up the scale; at the time of research there was just one backpacker hostel (plus an excellent **homestay** programme). Whatever you're looking for, it pays to book ahead.

LABUAN TOWN

Fratini's Inn Jalan Bunga Kesuma ☎ 087 424 545. Upstairs from *Fratini's Restaurant*, this place goes some way towards living up to its billing of "boutique hotel" with small but well-furnished rooms in a modern style. RM140

Grand Dorsett Jalan Merdeka ☎ 087 422 000, ⓦ granddorsett.com. Great rooms, some with sea views, plus a swimming pool, restaurant and pub to keep you busy at Labuan's only five-star hotel. Since most guests are visiting on business, the best deals (such as the price indicated here) are from Fri–Sun. RM346

Labuan Backpacker Above Olympic Pool & Snooker Centre, Shore Services Centre ☎ 016 803 0868, ⓦ labuanbackpacker.blogg.se. Also known as *Uncle Jack's* – named after the friendly owner – the only hostel in town, located in a prime nightlife district, has four private rooms and two dorms. Dorms RM20, rooms RM28

★ **Labuan Homestay Programme** Contact tourist information centre or Ministry of Tourism office at the Sea Sports Complex, ☎ 087 422 622. The participants in this well-organized scheme include homes in a water village as well as on land, and hosts can also arrange affordable activities such as night fishing or making traditional food. Meals cost RM5–10. RM50

Mariner Jalan Tanjung Purun ☎ 087 418 822, ⓔ mhlabuan@tm.net.my. A very good deal, the *Mariner's* rooms are small but a cut above most of the other mid-range places. This does, however, mean that you'll need to reserve ahead. RM110

Pulau Labuan 27–28 Jalan Muhibbah ☎ 087 416 288. Comfortable and large a/c, en-suite rooms; rather oddly, each VIP room has a car CD player mounted into a bedside table. There are a few sister hotels, including *Pulau Labuan 2* close by on Jalan Kemajuan which has very similar rooms. RM128, VIP rooms RM138

Waterfront Jalan Wawasan ☎ 087 418 111. Stylish foyer, perfectly appointed rooms and prompt service. All rooms are basically the same; prices vary according to location and view. Facilities include a pool, fitness centre, restaurant and – perhaps best of all – the poolside *Sunset Bar*. Promotional rates often available. RM288

AROUND THE ISLAND

Manikar Beach Resort Northern tip of island ☎ 087 418 700. Reached by bus #6 or by taxi (RM35), this resort has a lovely little pool and a good if slightly neglected stretch of beach. At the time of research only 100 of the 250 rooms were available, with the rest in need of repair. RM207

EATING AND DRINKING

Jalan Merdeka and Jalan OKK Awang Besar hold lots of adequate, no-frills, Chinese and Indian **restaurants**; more notable places are listed below. Labuan is particularly known for its seafood; to try something distinctively Brunei-Malay, look out for *ambuyat* – a gluey white substance made from sago and water, it's almost flavourless and served instead of rice. If you're stuck late at night then seek out the Malay, Thai and even vegetarian dishes at the 24-hour outdoor **food court** (Medan Selera) close to the *Grand Dorsett*. Labuan is somewhat notorious when it comes to **nightlife**. You're unlikely to see anything particularly sleazy out in the open, but single men may be approached in the karaoke bars. The main bar districts are the Jati Shophouses, the area north of Jalan Bunga Angerrik, and the Shore Services Centre (behind the Utama Jaya supermarket).

Anjung Ketam Kampung Tanjung Aru ☎ 013 896 1180. Locals flock to this collection of four stalls in the northeast of the island for crabs (*ketam*) and other seafood. Book ahead or aim to arrive early for dinner – it tends to have sold out by around 7pm. A taxi from town should cost RM15. Daily 4–10pm.

★ **Choice Restaurant** Jalan Okk Awang Besar. Spacious café with a long à la carte menu, as well as the lunchtime *nasi campur* buffet with a wide range of meat and fish curries. The roti and *dosai* are excellent – try the *ghee masala dosa* for breakfast. Daily 8am–10.30pm.

Cross Road Shore Services Centre. Unapologetically loud, this place has live music out front in the evenings, while inside there's a bar where they turn the music all the way up to eleven. Daily 6pm–3am.

Fah Fah Jalan Bunga Mawar. With most of its seating outdoors on a street corner, this café serves *bak kut teh* and a few other dishes, but mostly it's popular with both expats and locals as a place to enjoy a few beers. In fact, the drinking starts pretty early in the afternoon. Daily 6am–1am.

Fratini's Jalan Bunga Kesuma ⓦ fratinis-restaurant .com. This chain, based in Brunei, offers a pretty good simulation of an Italian restaurant in terms of both food and ambience. Prices are high though, with pizzas (eat in or take away) costing RM25–30 and pasta at RM20–45. At lunch there's an RM25 express menu. Daily 10am–10pm.

Labuan Deepsea Seafood Restaurant Jalan Merdeka ☎ 019 266 9239. The menu at this popular

7

waterfront restaurant, formerly known as Port View, is firmly focused on seafood; some has to be ordered in advance. Other options include *nasi campur*, from 9am–4pm. Daily 8am–midnight.

Maya Mariner Café Labuan Marina, Jalan Wawasan. This small café at the back of the main marina building serves up authentic Punjabi cuisine including chicken *biriyani* on Saturdays (RM12). More unusual dishes include deer meat curry (RM14), while for breakfast they serve *paratha* bread. Daily except Tues 9.30am–9pm.

New Sung Hwa Ujong Pasir, PCK Building ☎ 087 411 008. It may not look especially promising from outside, but this Chinese seafood restaurant on the edge of the market is incredibly popular. Book ahead if possible, particularly at the weekend. Daily 10am–2pm & 6–10.30pm.

Raff 240C Jalan Kemajuan. This restaurant specializes in home-style Malay cooking, such as a popular *nasi ayam penyek* (chicken rice). They also do a good *laksa*, based on a Kuching recipe. Daily 7.30am–3pm.

SHOPPING

All the shops are duty-free, including places selling alcohol in the ferry terminal; there are lots more outlets on Jalan Merdeka and Jalan Tun Mustapha. For general shopping, try the mall at Ujama Kewangan (Financial Park), which has a Parkson department store, food court, internet café and CIMB Bank.

DIRECTORY

Banks and exchange The bureau de change (8.45am–3.30pm) at the ferry terminal has a 24-hour ATM; there's also a Maybank ATM close to Labuan Deepsea Seafood Centre on Jalan Merdeka.

Laundry Blue Wash 7am–10pm has coin-operated machines, a rarity in Malaysia, as well as offering service washes, plus wi-fi to pass the time.

Medical Klinik Wiliyah, 391 Jalan Bunga Rampai (Mon–Thurs & Sat 8am–9pm, Fri 8am–noon & 2–9pm, Sun 8am–1pm & 6–9pm; ☎ 087 413 140).

North of KK

Sabah's trunk highway hurries through the northern suburbs of KK to the more pastoral environs of **Tuaran**. From here, the *atap* houses of the Bajau water villages, Mengkabong and **Penimbawan**, are only a stone's throw away. Just outside Tuaran, the main road forks, with the eastern branch heading towards Gunung Kinabalu National Park and Ranau, then onwards to Sandakan.

Continuing north instead, the main road arrives at bustling **Kota Belud**, where a weekly *tamu* attracts tribespeople from all over the region. Beyond, the landscape becomes more colourful: jewel-bright paddy fields and stilted wooden houses line the road for much of the way up to the **Kudat Peninsula**, with Gunung Kinabalu dominating the far distance.

On the way to **Kudat**, the first administrative capital of the East India Company, it's possible to stay at a Rungus longhouse in **Kampung Bavanggazo**. North of town the area known as the **Tip of Borneo** has quiet beaches and a few guesthouses. Remote islands reached from the peninsula include **Pulau Banggi** and **Pulau Mantanani**.

Tuaran

It takes just under an hour to travel the 34km from Kota Kinabalu to **TUARAN**. There's little of interest in the town itself, but it's a useful base for visiting the water village of **Penimbawan**; avoid Mengkabong water village as, although easier to reach and sometimes promoted by tour companies, it has little charm. There's a *tamu* in Tuaran on Sundays.

Penimbawan water village

From the road west of Tuaran's brown clock tower, take a minivan (10 min) to the tiny settlement of Kampung Serusup, then ask at the jetty for a boat (15min; RM40 return including waiting)

The Bajau homes in the **Penimbawan water village** are made of *atap*, bamboo and wood interconnected by labyrinthine boardwalks – called *jambatan* ("bridge") – along which fish are laid out to dry. There isn't much to do as a visitor, but if you come with a Malay speaker it's easier to get an insight into village life. KK tour companies charge around RM200 for a trip.

ARRIVAL AND DEPARTURE

TUARAN

By bus and minibus Vehicles from KK arrive in Tuaran a block from the main road, Jalan Teo Teck Ong. Minibuses to Kota Belud (RM10) run from close to the clock on Jalan Teo Teck Ong until around 3–4pm.

ACCOMMODATION

Bear in mind that the *Shangri-La Rasa Ria Resort* (see p.402) is 5km west of Tuaran on Dalit Bay.

★ **Tang Dynasty** Jalan Tuaran, Kampung Panjut ☎088 788 555, ⓦhoteltangdynasty.com. Although it's just outside the centre, on the road to KK, if you have to stay in Tuaran this is by far the best bet. In fact it's significantly better than you might expect in a small town. RM58

EATING AND DRINKING

Berungis Café Behind Tang Dynasty hotel, Jalan Tuaran, Kampung Panjut. It's on the edge of a car park, hidden behind a hotel, but this coffee shop is still a pleasant place to hang out. Free wi-fi. Daily 8am–9.30pm.

Medan Selera Tuaran Jalan Tuaran. Holding half a dozen stalls, mostly selling *nasi campur*, this food court is by some way the most appealing place in town to eat. One stall, the Monalisa Café, serves a good range of drinks and ABC (shaved ice). Daily 9am–midnight.

Kota Belud

For six days of the week, **KOTA BELUD**, 75km northeast of KK, is a busy but undistinguished town; arriving tourists usually head straight to the jetty for **Pulau Mantanani**. Early on Sunday, however, the town springs to life as hordes of villagers congregate at Sabah's largest weekly **tamu**. Fulfilling a social as well as commercial role, the market draws Rungus, Kadazan/Dusun and Bajau indigenous groups.

Though the market's popularity among KK's tour operators means there are always a few tourists, you won't see many souvenirs for sale: instead you're far more likely to come across dried fish, chains of yeast beads (used to make rice wine), buffalo, betel nut and *tudung saji* (colourful food covers used to keep flies at bay). Arrive early – if you're coming from KK, set off by 8am at the latest.

Kota Belud's annual *tamu besar*, or "big market", usually held in October, sees cultural performances, traditional horseback games and handicraft demonstrations in addition to the more typical stalls.

ARRIVAL AND DEPARTURE

KOTA BELUD

By bus Regular buses from KK's Merdeka Field bus stand (1hr 30min; RM5) drop passengers at the district office in the centre, a 20min walk from the *tamu*; minivans ply the stretch on market days. Vehicles heading from KK to Kudat often don't enter Kota Belud itself; if you're continuing north, try in town first, but you may need to flag one down by the main roundabout on the edge of town.

By boat Regular boats (1hr; RM50) run to Pulau Mantanani from Kuala Abai jetty.

ACCOMMODATION

Kota Belud Travelers Lodge 6 Plaza Kong Guan, 200m southwest of the mosque ☎088 977 228, ⓦmykbtl.com. Although the rooms here hold seemingly random jumbles of furniture, some of it in a bad way, they're clean and cheerful; the cheapest share bathrooms. The building also holds the Plaza Café restaurant. RM65

EATING AND DRINKING

Kota Raya Lot 1, Block E, Kompleks Centenary. Malay and Chinese dishes served in a pleasant environment, between the market and the *Travelers Lodge*. Popular dishes include *nasi goreng liking* (fried rice with dried fish) and *nasi goreng lalap* (fried rice with sliced chicken). Daily 7.30am–1am.

7

Pulau Mantanani

Popular with KK tour operators as a day-trip destination, **Pulau Mantanani** is actually a collection of three tiny islands 40km off the coast from Kota Belud (from where you can take a boat) that also holds a few resorts. It's a lot of travel for a single day, but a lovely place to stay for a night or two; snorkelling, kayaking and scuba diving are available by arrangement.

ACCOMMODATION

Mari Mari Mantanani Backpacker Lodge Pulau Mantanani c/o Traverse Tours ☎088 260 501, ⓦ traversetours.com. A collection of simple *sulaps* (huts) on stilts, with a hammock and chairs under each one, plus more expensive chalets which are en suite but otherwise very similar. RM150

Kampung Bavanggazo

Although the shift to modern housing means that few traditional **Rungus longhouses** survive, a couple have been constructed in **KAMPUNG BAVANGGAZO**, 98km north of KK, to give tourists a chance to spend the night. In addition to room-only prices, it's possible to book a package (RM75) including dinner, breakfast and a **tribal dance** performance – call a couple of days ahead, to make sure that a performance is scheduled. Other activities include an early-morning jungle trek (RM50/group).

ARRIVAL AND DEPARTURE   KAMPUNG BAVANGGAZO

By bus or taxi Kampung Bavanggazo is 41km south of Kudat, 2.5km off the main highway. Public transport will only go as far as the junction on the highway; alternatively, you can take a share taxi from Kudat (RM8 per person) or KK (RM18 per person).

ACCOMMODATION

Maranjak Longhouse Lodge Kampung Bavangazzo ☎088 622 524, ✉maranjaklonghouse@gmail.com. Made from traditional materials, the two longhouses offer mattresses, each with their own mosquito net, on low sleeping platforms. You can also camp – they provide the tent. Mattress per person RM25, camping for two people RM45

Kudat

Overlooking Marudu Bay, **Kudat** is a friendly town centred on the intersection of Jalan Ibrahim Arshad and Jalan Lo Thien Chock. The latter, the main street, holds some of Sabah's oldest wooden shophouses and a Standard Chartered Bank. During a visit, leave time to peek at the central, orange-hued **Chinese temple** close to the *Ria Hotel*, plus the **stilt village** and the **harbour**, now significantly quieter than in the days when Kudat had an active fishing industry.

ARRIVAL AND DEPARTURE   KUDAT

By plane Kudat's airport, for MASwings flights from KK and Sandakan, is 9km northwest of town (minivan RM2; taxi RM10).

By boat Ferries to Pulau Banggi (daily 9am & 3pm;

THE RUNGUS

The Kudat Peninsula is home to the **Rungus people**, members of the wider Kadazan/Dusun ethnic group. Like most, the Rungus have gradually modernized, but many still hold their traditions dear. Older people in the kampungs still dress in black, and only two generations ago some Rungus wore coils of brass and copper on their bodies.

The architectural style of the traditional longhouse is distinctive too, built with outwards leaning walls and decorated with motifs and imagery from farming and nature. Today though, most dwellings are made from sheets of corrugated zinc, whose durability makes it preferable to the traditional materials like timber, tree bark, rattan and nipah leaves.

1hr; RM18) leave from the jetty at the southern end of Jalan Lo Thien Chock.

By taxi Share taxis to and from Kota Belud and KK stop around the corner from the *Hotel Sunrise*. Ask there or around the market for a taxi to the Tip of Borneo (20–30min); an entire car costs around RM35 one-way or RM80 return, including a 2hr wait.

ACCOMMODATION

Kudat Golf & Marina Resort 4km north of town ☎088 611 211, ⓦkudatgolfmarinaresort.com. Airy, pleasant rooms, many overlooking the large pool and the sea. The golf course is close by; ask about packages or promotions if you plan to play. RM130

Ria Hotel 3 Jalan Marudu ☎088 622 794. The nicest place to stay in Kudat. Beyond the scrupulously clean foyer lie 24 small and neat rooms, with en-suite bathrooms. The cheapest (superior) rooms have twin beds, while they are king size in the deluxe rooms. RM118

Sunrise Jalan Kecil, Sedco Building ☎088 611 517. Typical of the hotels in the Sedco Building area, east of the *Upper Deck Hotel*, but better value than some of its neighbours – book ahead as it tends to fill up. The cheapest rooms share bathrooms. Fan rooms RM20, a/c rooms RM28, en-suite rooms RM40

Upper Deck Hotel Jalan Lintas ☎088 622 272. Located 5min south of the *Ria Hotel*, this place commands a fine view over Marudu Bay. The rooms are reasonably sized, and comfortable enough despite some peeling paint. RM80

EATING

For a choice of places to eat, head to the Esplanade seafront area east of the Sedco Building complex; at the nearest end there's a small food court, while further along you'll find a series of "floating" restaurants on stilts. The Sedco Building area itself is also reasonably lively in the evening.

Sungai Wang Lot 7 & 8, Block F, Sedco Building. While it looks a bit grubby, this restaurant has some of the best food in town, with dishes such as butter tiger prawn and steamed fish. Daily 10am–2pm & 6pm–midnight.

Terminal Tom Yam Block D, Sedco Building. A popular place serving Thai food, with most of the seating outdoors and walls painted with underwater scenes. Evening showings of Malay movies bring in a crowd. Tues–Sun 11am–11pm.

The Tip of Borneo

Promoted as a tourist attraction in recent years, the thin promontory known as the **Tip of Borneo** (Tanjung Simpang Mengayau) has seen limited development but retains a great deal of charm. It's easy to see what keeps visitors coming: cliffs drop away to steep, forested hills and waves crash onto the golden sandy beaches. While it's well worth a visit – or, better, a night or two – if you're in the vicinity, whether it's worth a special journey all the way from KK is more debatable.

At the tip itself, Sabah Tourism has built a car park where steps lead down to a viewing area and a monumental globe. It's busiest at the weekend, when local families visit; no buses or minivans come this way, so you'll need to use your own transport, or a taxi.

ACCOMMODATION   THE TIP OF BORNEO

Bay View Chalet Tanjung Simpang Mengayau ☎013 868 2112. A collection of nine chalets on the cliffs beside the car park and café right at the tip, with seven of them boasting sea views. They get busy at the weekends so book ahead. Fan RM100, a/c RM150

Borneo Tip Beach Lodge On the approach to the tip from Kudat ☎016 817 0163, ✉borneotip@yahoo.com. Next door to the *Tip of Borneo Resort*, with a row of sea-facing a/c chalets linked by wooden walkways plus a traditional longhouse. The latter is very basic, inevitably, with semi-open sides. Longhouse RM28, room RM150

Tip of Borneo Resort On the approach to the tip from Kudat ☎088 493 468. The last accommodation option on the seafront road, also known as *Tommy's Place*, is before you reach the car park and the tip itself. There are just eight rooms, each with a veranda, or you can rent a tent. The place also has a simple restaurant and rents out kayaks. Prices include breakfast. Tents RM55, rooms RM130

Pulau Banggi

The island of **Pulau Banggi**, 40km north of Kudat and accessible by daily ferry, is the largest in Sabah. It's mostly flat but has lovely beaches, including one close to the jetty at the main settlement Karakit, and is worth a visit just for the boat ride and an amble on the beach. There are few tourist facilities; to dive the reefs here, for example, you'd need to make arrangements with a tour company in KK.

ARRIVAL AND DEPARTURE   PULAU BANGGI

By boat The Kudat Express ferry leaves town at 9am & 3pm, and departs from Karakit at 8am & 2pm (1hr; RM18).

ACCOMMODATION

Bonggi Resort Karakit ☎088 671 495. This no-frills place offers fan or a/c accommodation in a long wooden building, and has cooking facilities for guests to use. Fan chalets RM60, a/c chalets RM75

Kinabalu National Park

Sabah holds no more impressive sight than **Gunung Kinabalu** (Mount Kinabalu), 85km northeast of KK and plainly visible from the west coast. Revered as "aki nabalu" (home of the spirits of the dead) by the Kadazan/Dusun, it's 4095m high and dominates the 750 square kilometres of **KINABALU NATIONAL PARK**, a World Heritage Site renowned for its ecology, flora and geology. Although there are other hikes within the park, the prospect of reaching the summit fires the imagination of Malaysian and foreign tourists alike.

Preparing to climb Gunung Kinabulu

Climbing the mountain has become a must-do in Borneo itineraries. For the thousands of people who come here annually to haul themselves up, the process is made easier by a well-defined, 8.5-kilometre-long path that weaves up through jungle on the southern side to the bare granite of the summit.

Despite its popularity, it's a very **tough trek** and not to be undertaken lightly. Even given perfect weather conditions, there's a remorseless, freezing, final **pre-dawn ascent** to contend with and it's quite possible to suffer from altitude sickness and not get to the top. Bad weather can also scupper an ascent, or at least make it a pretty miserable experience.

Don't undertake the challenge unless you are fully prepared with **suitable clothing** and in **good general health**. If you suffer from **vertigo** then you shouldn't have a problem on the route up to Laban Rata (where there's foliage to hide any drops), or even for the summit ascent (since it's in the dark), but the way down from the summit may cause you problems.

Booking ahead

If you want to do the climb in just **one day** – an option only available from tour operators based in KK (see p.400) – then you can substantially cut costs. This does, however, mean an exceptionally long and tiring day on the mountain, while the view from the top will almost certainly be obscured by clouds by the time you get there. Getting a permit for a day-trip can also be difficult. All in all, it isn't really worth it.

For the vast majority of visitors, therefore, ascending and descending Gunung Kinabalu takes **two days**. The standard route begins at the park HQ, two hours from KK and 1588m up. It's possible to arrive on the morning of the climb, but spending the previous night in the area is a good idea; it gives time to acclimatize and means you can make an **earlier start** in the morning. Climbers then have to spend a night two-thirds of the way up the mountain in huts at Laban Rata, allowing for a final **dawn ascent**.

The accommodation on the mountain is often booked up long in advance, although tour operators in KK may be able to offer a package at short notice for an additional fee; you can also call direct in the hope of a cancellation. Avoid booking packages with overseas tour operators, which can work out a lot more expensive.

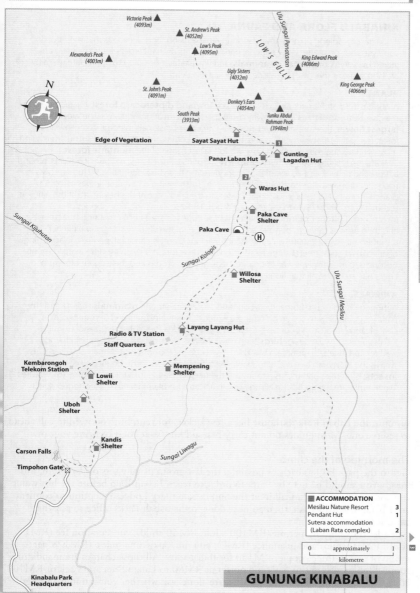

N

Victoria Peak
(4093m)

St. Andrew's Peak
(4052m)

Low's Peak
(4095m)

Alexandra's Peak
(4003m)

King Edward Peak
(4086m)

Ugly Sisters
(4032m)

St. John's Peak
(4091m)

King George Peak
(4066m)

Donkey's Ears
(4054m)

South Peak
(3933m)

Tunku Abdul
Rahman Peak
(3948m)

LOW'S GULLY

Ulu Sungai Penataran

Edge of Vegetation

Sayat Sayat Hut

Panar Laban Hut

Gunting
Lagadan Hut

Waras Hut

Paka Cave
Shelter

Paka Cave

(H)

Sungai Kijuhutan

Sungai Kolopis

Willosa
Shelter

Ulu Sungai Mesilau

Radio & TV Station

Staff Quarters

Layang Layang Hut

Kembarongoh
Telekom Station

Mempening
Shelter

Lowii
Shelter

Uboh
Shelter

Kandis
Shelter

Carson Falls

Timpohon Gate

Sungai Liwagu

■ ACCOMMODATION	
Mesilau Nature Resort	3
Pendant Hut	1
Sutera accommodation (Laban Rata complex)	2

0   approximately   1
kilometre

GUNUNG KINABALU

Kinabalu Park
Headquarters

7

What to bring

Essential items to carry with you include a torch (preferably a headlamp), headache tablets, suntan lotion, energy boosters (such as nuts, fruit and muesli bars), and a water bottle (there's unfiltered but drinkable water along the trail). Wear waterproof shoes or hiking boots with a good tread, and bring a few layers of warm clothing for the

KINABALU FLORA AND FAUNA

If you dash headlong up and down Gunung Kinabalu and then depart, as many visitors do, you'll miss out on many of the national park's riches. Its diverse terrains have spawned an incredible variety of **plants** and **animals**, and you are far more likely to appreciate them by walking some of the lower trails (see p.426) at a leisurely pace.

PLANTS

Around a third of the park's area is covered by **lowland dipterocarp forest**, characterized by massive, buttressed trees and allowing only sparse growth at ground level. The **world's largest flower**, the parasitic – and elusive – *Rafflesia*, occasionally blooms in the lowland forest (see p.596). Between 900m and 1800m, you'll come across the oaks, chestnuts, ferns and mosses (including the *Dawsonia* – the world's tallest moss) of the **montane forest**.

Higher up (1800–2600m), the **cloudforest** supports a huge range of flowering plants: around a thousand orchids and 26 varieties of rhododendron have been identified, including Low's rhododendron with its enormous yellow flowers. The hanging lichen that drapes across branches of stunted trees lends a magical feel to the landscape at this height. It's at this altitude, too, that you're most likely to see the park's most famous plants – its nine species of insectivorous **pitcher plants** (*Nepenthes*) whose cups secrete a nectar that first attracts insects and then drowns them, as they are unable to escape up the slippery sides of the pitcher.

Higher still, above 2600m, only the most tenacious plantlife can survive – like the agonizingly gnarled sayat-sayat tree, and the heath rhododendron found only on Mount Kinabalu – while beyond 3300m, soil gives way to granite. Here, grasses, sedges and the elegant blooms of Low's buttercup are all that flourish.

ANIMALS

Although orang-utans, Bornean gibbons and tarsiers are among **mammals** that dwell in the park, you're unlikely to see anything more exotic than squirrels, rats and tree shrews, or conceivably a mouse deer or a bearded pig if you're lucky. The higher reaches of Gunung Kinabalu boast two types of **birds** seen nowhere else in the world – the Kinabalu friendly warbler and Kinabalu mountain blackbird. Lower down, look out for hornbills and eagles, as well as the Malaysian tree pie, identifiable by its foot-long tail. You're bound to see plenty of **insects**: butterflies and moths flit through the trees, while the forest floor is home to creatures like the trilobite beetle, whose orange-and-black armour-plating lends it a fearsome aspect.

summit; the Laban Rata resthouse has a few jackets for rent, but you need to call ahead to reserve one. Most guides do not carry first-aid kits, so it's best to bring your own.

The morning of the climb

Get to the park HQ as early as possible: the last group usually sets off by 11am, but ideally you should be here by 9am, in order to reach Laban Rata before the hot water runs out in the showers. Call in at the Sutera Sanctuary Lodges reception to confirm your place at Laban Rata, then go next door to the Sabah Parks office to pay the various **fees**.

Besides the climbing permit (RM100 adult, RM40 child), conservation fee (RM15 adult, RM10 child) and insurance (RM7), you must pay for a **guide** (RM128 per group of one to three people; RM150 for four to six). All those charges are mandatory; some climbers also opt to pay for a **porter** at RM80 to Laban Rata and back or RM102 all the way (maximum load 10kg). If you're alone, ask whether you can join another group for company and to save on the guide fee. Lockers and a safe room are available at the HQ to deposit valuables or even your pack.

Gunung Kinabulu: the climb

Conquering Gunung Kinabalu today is far easier than it was in 1858, when Spenser St John, British consul-general to the native states of Borneo, found his progress blocked by Kadazan "shaking their spears and giving us other hostile signs". Hugh Low, then British colonial secretary on Pulau Labuan, had made the first recorded ascent of the mountain seven years earlier, though he baulked at climbing its highest peak, considering it "inaccessible to any but winged animals". The peak – subsequently named after Low – was finally conquered in 1888 by John Whitehead.

Here we detail the **Timpohon trail** to the top as it is by far the most popular, although a longer and quieter route up, the **Mesilau trail**, starts 17km east of the park HQ, and offers a greater chance of spotting wildlife.

The first day

The summit route begins with an optional but time-saving minibus ride (25min; RM16.50/vehicle) to the start of the **Timpohon trail**. The day's climb to the mountain huts at Laban Rata takes between five and seven hours, depending on your fitness and trail conditions. Roots and stones along the trail serve as steps, with wooden "ladders" laid up the muddier stretches. There are regular rest shelters with toilets along the path.

To Layang Layang

The air gets progressively cooler as you climb, but the walk is still hard and sweaty, and you'll be glad of the water tanks and rest point at **Layang Layang** (2621m), three hours into the climb. Around this point, if the weather is kind, incredible views of the hills, sea and clouds start to unfold below you.

To Laban Rata

At just above 3000m, a detour to the left brings hikers to **Pondok Paka**, a large overhanging rock that was the site of overnight camps on early expeditions. It's a further 6km to **Laban Rata**, which lies at 3272m. The final 2km, dominated by large boulders and steep slippery rock surfaces, are demanding even for the fittest, particularly considering the lower oxygen levels. The rewards are the view of the mighty granite slopes of the **Panar Laban rock face**, plus the promise of reaching your accommodation.

The second day

Most climbers get up at 2.30am for the final ascent, although those who are particularly fit might leave slightly later to avoid getting to the summit too long before sunrise.

To the summit

The trail crosses the sheer **Panar Laban** rock face, past the **Sayat Sayat** hut and onwards to the summit at **Low's Peak**. Although ropes, handrails and wooden steps help in places, it's a stiff climb at the very least. You'll also be doing it in pitch darkness so headlamps are an advantage and a powerful torch a must. Climbers should also be aware of the symptoms of altitude sickness (see p.44).

After the final push, the beautiful spectacle of sunrise at **Low's Peak** will rob you of any remaining breath. Remember that it'll be bitingly cold, so bring very warm clothing for that brief photo stop at the summit.

Descending from the mountain

After all that toil, it's back to Laban Rata for a hearty breakfast – prepare to be shocked when you see the sharp drops along the trail, which were not visible in the dark. Then it's time to head back down to park HQ, which usually takes three to five hours. As your leg muscles ache from the relentless downhill trudge – which is likely to get worse the next day – take a moment to reflect on the fact that the record time for the annual **Kinabalu Climbathon** is just over two and a half hours. That's up and down.

Around the park headquarters

Twenty kilometres of **trails** loop the montane forest around the park HQ, much quieter than the route to the top. Walkers don't have to take a guide on the lower slopes, although there is a daily guided two-hour walk along the Liwagu trail (daily 11am; RM3).

ARRIVAL AND INFORMATION

KINABALU NATIONAL PARK

By bus, minivan or taxi Hourly buses (RM15) leave KK's Inanam bus terminal from 7am onwards for Sandakan and Ranau, taking two hours to reach the park entrance. A better option is to catch a Ranau minivan (roughly hourly; RM20), or split a share **taxi** (RM80); both leave from the Merdeka Field bus stand from 7am.

Park HQ A cluster of lodgings, restaurants and offices directly inside the gates includes the park HQ (daily 7am–7pm), where you pay the RM15 entrance fee and pick up information at the Sabah Parks office, and confirm your accommodation with Sutera Sanctuary Lodges.

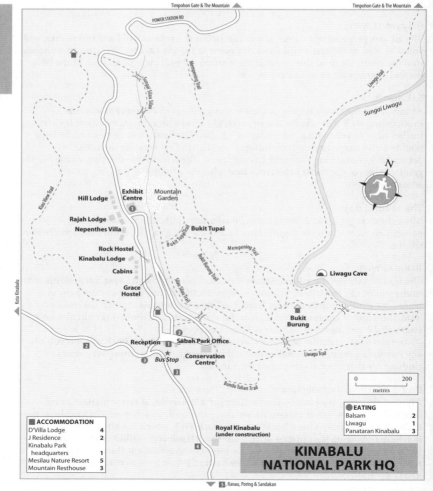

Timpohon Gate & The Mountain

Timpohon Gate & The Mountain

POWER STATION RD

Mempening Trail

Sungai Silau Silau

Liwagu Trail

Sungai Liwagu

N

Bus View Trail

Hill Lodge

Exhibit Centre ❶

Mountain Garden

Rajah Lodge

Nepenthes Villa

Bukit Topih Trail

Bukit Tupai

Mempening Trail

Rock Hostel

Kinabalu Lodge

Silau Silau Trail

Bukit Burung Trail

Cabins

Grace Hostel

Liwagu Cave

Kota Kinabalu

❷

Bukit Burung

Reception ❶

Sabah Park Office

❷

❸ **Bus Stop**

★

Conservation Centre

Liwagu Trail

❸

Bundu Tuhan Trail

0	200
	metres

● EATING
Balsam	2
Liwagu	1
Panataran Kinabalu	3

■ ACCOMMODATION
D'Villa Lodge	4
J Residence	2
Kinabalu Park headquarters	1
Mesilau Nature Resort	5
Mountain Resthouse	3

Royal Kinabalu
(under construction)

❹

KINABALU NATIONAL PARK HQ

5 Ranau, Poring & Sandakan

7

MOUNTAIN TORQ

Mountain Torq office: 3–36, 3rd Floor, Asia City, KK, ☎ 088 268 126, ⓦ mountaintorq.com • Via ferrata from RM420 (activity only)

If merely walking up to the summit isn't enough of a challenge, then Asia's first **via ferrata** – pathways of rungs, ropes, rails and planks running along sheer cliffsides – may provide the adrenaline rush you are looking for. It's exhilarating stuff with some incredible views, yet it's safe because you're always clipped onto something. Of the two routes, one is suitable for anyone over ten years old, the other has a minimum age of seventeen.

Located close to Laban Rata, the Mountain Torq centre also runs **climbing** and **abseiling** courses. Participants can arrange to stay at the *Pendant Hut* (see below) instead of at Laban Rata.

ACCOMMODATION

Within the park itself, **accommodation** is run almost solely by **Sutera Sanctuary Lodges** (SSL), who take full advantage by charging outrageous prices. If you're taking the main route then you can save money by staying just outside the park before the climb, but once on the mountain most people are stuck with SSL accommodation (though see also *Pendant Hut* below).

INSIDE THE PARK

Kinabalu Park headquarters c/o Sutera Sanctuary Lodges ☎ 088 243 629, ⓦ suterasanctuarylodges.com. The overpriced official accommodation at the HQ has a range of options from dorms with cooking facilities, through more comfortable private rooms, to the Rajah Lodge which sleeps six provided with full board (others include only breakfast). Dorms RM160, rooms RM450, Rajah Lodge RM8000

Mesilau Nature Resort 17km east of park HQ, c/o Sutera Sanctuary Lodges ☎ 088 243 629, ⓦ sutera sanctuarylodges.com. Reached by minivan shuttle from park HQ (RM85), this resort has a special atmosphere with a gushing river running through it and abundant birdlife; accommodation consists of simple dorms as well as spacious chalets and lodges. Dorms RM155, rooms RM400

OUTSIDE THE PARK

D'Villa Lodge 10min walk east from the park entrance ☎ 088 889 282, ⓦ dvillalodge.com.my. A twelve-bed dorm, plus pricey standard rooms with balconies offering lovely views over the Kinabalu valley. The restaurant benefits from the same great scenery, and there are also a couple of cheap eateries opposite; breakfast is included. Dorms RM30, rooms RM120

★ **J Residence** Just west of the park entrance ☎ 012 869 6969, ⓦ jresidence.com. A great choice close to the

HQ. There are only ten rooms, including three in a villa with a kitchen (you can rent the whole place or just one room). The design and furnishings are much more modern than most places around here. Book ahead as it fills up; prices rise by more than half at the weekend. RM80

Mountain Resthouse 200m east of the park entrance ☎ 016 837 4060. Very basic, ramshackle place with a few rooms including single-sex dorms; only a couple are en suite. It can be hard to work out who is a member of staff and who is just hanging out. Dorms RM30, rooms RM60

ON THE MOUNTAIN

Laban Rata complex On Gunung Kinabalu, c/o Sutera Sanctuary Lodges ☎ 088 243629, ⓦ sutera sanctuarylodges.com. A complex of several separate guesthouses, some of them unheated, at an altitude of 3000m. Prices are calculated per person, including three buffet meals (it may be possible to bring your own food and get a discount), and can hardly be regarded as good value for money, but there's no choice unless you qualify to stay at the *Pendant Hut*. Non-heated dorms RM415, heated dorms RM475, rooms RM990

Pendant Hut On Gunung Kinabalu ☎ 088 268 126. Exclusively for customers of Mountain Torq (see box above), this no-frills place lacks heating but has sleeping bags available. No price is listed because accommodation is included in via ferrata packages.

EATING

Balsam Within the park HQ. A restaurant offering predictably expensive, but wholesome, buffets with Chinese, Malay, Indian and Western dishes. Most people eat here at the end of their hike, as part of the package. Daily 7am–10pm, Sat & Sun until 11pm.

Liwagu Inside the Exhibit Centre. The à la carte option if you want to eat within the park HQ, but as it's pricey it's likely to be of interest only if you stay at the official

accommodation overnight. Daily 11am–11pm.

Panataran Kinabalu At the turning for the park HQ. There's nothing special about the food here, but the views from the car park are certainly impressive and even with inflated prices it's a lot cheaper than the places inside the park. They also do a packed lunch for RM13.50, which may be useful if you're hiking around the HQ. Daily 6.30am–8pm.

7

Around Mount Kinabalu

The most popular attraction close to the national park is the **Poring Hot Springs**, but those interested in World War II may also want to visit the memorial at **Kundasang**. The town of **Ranau** is mostly just a transport hub, but a nearby **tea plantation** serves as a relaxing place to hang out.

Poring Hot Springs

43km from park HQ, on the southeastern side of Kinabalu National Park • Daily 7am–6pm • RM15 (adult) or RM10 (child), including use of outdoor tubs; RM15–20 per hour for enclosed tubs

The **Poring Hot Springs** were developed during World War II by the Japanese, who installed wooden tubs that have been replaced by tiled versions. Don't come expecting natural pools, luxury or solitude, but it can be a good place to relax aching muscles after descending from Mount Kinabalu.

There are also a few other attractions within the site, including an orchid garden, a butterfly farm, a **canopy walkway** and a few walking trails. Outside the gates you'll see signs advertising places to see **Rafflesia flowers** but these are best avoided: the plants have often been dug up and brought to Poring from more remote areas.

ARRIVAL AND DEPARTURE   PORING HOT SPRINGS

By bus or minivan Official shuttle buses run from park HQ (1hr; RM18 per person) and *Mesilau Nature Resort* (RM60), although it's cheaper to flag down a share taxi. From Poring it's impossible to get direct public transport to Sandakan or back to KK; instead take a minivan (RM10) from outside the park gates to **Ranau**, where buses stop on trips across the state.

ACCOMMODATION

The official **accommodation** within the hot springs area is run by Sutera Sanctuary Lodges and is very expensive. Luckily a handful of more affordable (if unexceptional) lodges lie just outside the entrance, with a great option in the jungle nearby.

Ernah Lodge On the main road. The lino-covered floors are pretty uneven, but the rooms are clean enough and there's a common area where you can watch TV. They also do laundry (8am–8pm) at RM7/kilo. **RM55**

★ **Lupa Masa** 20min walk from the park entrance ☎019 581 3863 or ☎019 802 0549, ✉lupamasaborneo @gmail.com. Set in a glorious patch of jungle, this place (whose name means "forget time") has everything you could want in a jungle lodge – so long as your wish list doesn't include creature comforts. Food and accommodation are both very basic, but the experience earns plaudits from visitors. Call ahead to be guided into the camp. **RM85**

Sutera Sanctuary Lodges Within the park ☎088 243 629, ⌨suterasanctuarylodges.com. The official accommodation includes everything from a dorm – nice enough but beyond the budget of most backpackers – to the very expensive Palm Villa which sleeps six. Dorms **RM145**, rooms **RM300**, Palm Villa **RM4150**

EATING

Rainforest Restaurant Within the park. The surroundings are pleasant , and the location within the site itself is convenient, but the prices here are hard to stomach. The buffets have plenty of choice, but at RM50 (lunch) or RM55 (dinner) they don't feel like good value; à la carte dishes include hot and sour mackerel (RM17) and spaghetti (RM22). Quality is variable, too. Daily 7am–10pm.

Round Inn On the main road close to the entrance. This place stands out among the options on the main road, not least for its circular entrance and large drum which customers are allowed to beat. It serves up decent Chinese dishes.

Kundasang

Ten kilometres along the road from Poring to Ranau, **KUNDASANG** is little more than a junction where simple stalls sell fruit and vegetables. It is, however, worth a stop for those interested in the World War II history of Borneo.

Kundasang War Memorial

Just off the Poring–Ranau road, Kundasang • Daily 8.30am–5.30pm • RM10

The **Kundasang war memorial** commemorates the victims of the Sandakan Death Marches of 1945, when Japanese troops force-marched POWs from Sandakan to Ranau (see p.453). No soldiers are buried here.

The site has been extensively renovated, and now includes an information centre that shows an Australian documentary about the death marches, plus three peaceful and well-tended memorial gardens (Australian, British and Bornean).

ARRIVAL AND DEPARTURE   KUNDASANG

By bus or minivan These stop close to the main junction on the highway, though you may need to flag them down.

ACCOMMODATION

Cottage Hotel ☎ 088 888 882, ⓦ thecottagehotel .com.my. The wi-fi-equipped rooms here are small but clean with crisp white linen; the views of hills and vegetable farms are appealing. A Chinese restaurant on the ground floor specializes in steamboat (hot pot). Weekday RM115, weekend RM135

Kinabalu Pine Resort Kundasang–Ranau Highway ☎ 088 889 388 ⓦ kinabalupineresort.com. Kundasang's best hotel has appealing rooms in a white building on stilts – some have mountain views. RM160

Ranau

While there's little reason to spend time in the undistinguished town of **Ranau**, it's the main hub for travelling between Kinabalu National Park and eastern Sabah. The first day of each month sees a large and lively *tamu* (market), 1km out of town towards Sandakan; there's also a smaller *tamu* every Saturday.

Sabah Tea Garden

Kampung Nalapak, 17km east of Ranau • Take a bus in the direction of Sandakan from KK, or taxi from Ranau

The **Sabah Tea Garden** is a well-run organic tea plantation that makes a great place to stay for a night or two, but may also be worth a daytime visit if you're passing through. Contact them in advance to arrange **hikes** and **factory tours**, as it's very popular with groups and gets busy. Ask also about visiting the **fish massage** place nearby, where surprisingly large river fish nibble at customers' dead skin.

ARRIVAL AND DEPARTURE   RANAU

By bus or minivan Long-distance buses (Sandakan RM30; KK RM15) stop on the trunk road beside the turning into town, while minivans arrive at the eastern edge of town.

ACCOMMODATION

Orchid 1st floor, Tokogaya Building ☎ 088 876 533. The plain rooms in this hotel, in the same block as the Milimewa supermarket, are just about good enough for a night. Fan rooms RM40, a/c rooms RM60

Sabah Baru Block D, Jalan Persiaran. A decent option where some of the simple rooms have a/c, and others fan only. The cheapest rooms are not en suite, but the shared bathrooms are fine. Fan rooms RM30, a/c rooms RM50

⭐ **Sabah Tea Garden** Kampung Nalapak, 17km from Ranau on the road to Sandakan ☎ 088 440 882, ⓦ sabahtea.net. This plantation has a campsite and longhouses popular with student groups, as well as cosy cottages equipped with flat-screen TVs. The food in the restaurant is excellent. Call about transfers from Ranau. Camping (own tent) RM10, camping (their tent) RM30, longhouse rooms RM120, cottages RM240

EATING

Medan Selera Jalan Lintas. On the eastern side of town, this food court overlooking a pink mosque is as good a place to eat as any in Ranau. At least there's plenty of choice. Daily 6.30am–6pm.

Restoran Islamic No 2 Lorong Taman. A standard *mamak* restaurant, serving curries and above average *roti canai*. Its corner location makes it a decent place to sit and watch the world go by. Daily 7am–10pm.

East Sabah

While the west may have majestic Gunung Kinabalu, East Sabah is the destination of choice for animal encounters. Around former capital **Sandakan** alone, visitors can see orang-utans in **Sepilok**, proboscis monkeys at **Labuk Bay** – and there are no prizes for guessing the attraction at the **Turtle Islands National Park**.

Next stop on the itinerary is the **Kinabatangan River**, where lodges arrange longboat journeys to see pygmy elephants, orang-utans and more in the wild. Further into the interior, there is the option of visiting **Danum Valley**, a primary rainforest area with a majestic canopy walkway, or the equally appealing **Tabin Wildlife Reserve**.

Back on the coast, divers especially are pulled to **Semporna**, the jumping-off point for the myriad flora and fauna hidden in the waters surrounding **Palau Sipadan**, **Palau Mabul** and numerous other islands. Serious trekkers keen to explore the **Maliau Basin**, referred to by some as "Sabah's Lost World", set off by 4WD from the frontier boom town **Tawau**.

Sandakan

7

Situated at the neck of Sandakan Bay, facing the Sulu Sea and towards the Philippines, the commandingly positioned town of **SANDAKAN** was all but destroyed during World War II. Postwar reconstruction on reclaimed land, worked around an unimaginative grid system of indistinguishable concrete blocks but without the sense of space you find in KK. Today, though, there's a bracing sense of regeneration focused on the **waterfront**.

Sandakan's main visitor attractions, beyond its excellent accommodation and eating options, are away from the centre. The **Sandakan Memorial Park**, commemorating the horrors of the Sandakan POW camp is 11km northwest of town, whereas Sandakan's **colonial heritage** is mostly concentrated immediately north of the centre on Trig Hill.

Brief history

Although eighteenth-century accounts mention a trading outpost called Sandakan within the Sultanate of Sulu, whose centre was in what's now the Philippines, the town's modern history began in the late 1870s.

The area of northeast Borneo between Brunei Bay and Sungai Kinabatangan had been leased by the Sultan of Brunei to the American Trading Company in 1865 but its attempt to establish a settlement here failed, and in 1879 an Anglo-American partnership took up the lease, naming Englishman **William Pryer** as the first Resident of the east coast. By 1884 Sandakan was the **capital** of British North Borneo, its natural harbour and proximity to sources of timber, beeswax, rattan and edible birds' nests transforming it into a thriving commercial centre.

In 1942 the Japanese army took control, establishing the POW camp from which the infamous Death Marches to Ranau commenced (see p.433). What little of the town was left standing after intensive Allied bombing was burned down by the Japanese, and the end of the war saw administration Sabah's shift to KK. Nevertheless, by the 1950s a rebuilt Sandakan profited from the **timber** boom and by the 1970s had generated such wealth that the town was reputed to have the world's greatest concentration of millionaires.

Once the region's decent timber had been exhausted in the early 1980s, Sandakan looked to **oil palm** and cocoa, crops that now dominate the surrounding landscape.

The waterfront

Sandakan's central grid of streets is hemmed in by Bukit Berenda (Trig Hill) to the north and Sandakan Bay to the south. The massive three-storey **Central Market** (daily 6am–8pm) dominates the eastern end of the waterfront, while the esplanade known as **Sandakan Harbour Square** lies to the southwest of it. The streets around the esplanade form a major tourist district, with cafés, hostels and hotels; the area is set to change further once the new *Four Points by Sheraton* hotel and attached Harbour Mall finally open.

Goddess of Mercy Temple & · Mile 4, Labuk Road, Airport,

SANDAKAN

EATING

1 Malaysia Steamboat and Seafood	1
Ba Lin	11
English Tea House	2
Harbour Garden Café	10
H84	7
Imperial Bayview	9
Masarap	3
Nam Choon	8
Sim Sim Seafood Restaurant	6
Taste Restaurant	5
Wojamama	4

Recreation Club

Sam Sing Kung Temple

St Michael's & All Angels

JALAN PADANG

JALAN SINGAPORA

JALAN PUNCAK

St Mary Catholic Church

JALAN SEKOLAH

LORONG SEKOLAH

N

JALAN CHENG MING

Long-distance bus station & Karamunting Jetty

JALAN LEILA

JALAN LEILA

JALAN LEILA

JALAN LEILA

JALAN ELOPURA

Footbridge

Hokkien Association

Sandakan Regional Library

Night Food Market

Tun Abdul Razak Memorial Park

Sandakan Community Hall

Halal Food Court

JALAN COASTAL 1

JALAN COASTAL 1

SULU SEA

0 · 200 metres

Around the padang

Close to the padang, now rarely used, are a couple of the oldest buildings in Sandakan. On the northern side, the Taoist **Sam Sing Kung Temple** (daily 7am–4pm), completed in 1887, is dedicated to three deities – Lui Bei, Guan Gong and Zhang Fei – who were the heroes of the fourteenth-century *Romance of the Three Kingdoms*. Northwest of the padang, **St Michael's and All Angels Church** (daily 9.30am–4.30pm, English service Sun 7.15am; RM10, except for service) is a quintessentially English stone building dating back to 1893.

Trig Hill

Most of the colonial relics of Sandakan can be found in the hills north of the centre. The easiest way up is to use the so-called **hundred steps** (there are rather more) leading up from the tourist office, which bring you out on **Jalan Istana**. From here head left to the **Agnes Keith House** or right to the **town cemetery**.

Agnes Keith House

Jalan Istana · Daily 9am–5pm · RM15

The **Agnes Keith House** is a museum based on the life and achievements of the American writer whose works (see p.597) introduced many in the West to the history and culture of Borneo. Downstairs, reproductions of colonial furniture and period photographs

Agnes Keith House, Town Cemetery & Sepilok — 2, Agnes Keith House & Town Cemetery

Jetty to Turtle Island, Sim Sim, Water Village

ACCOMMODATION

The Mark's Lodge	2
May Fair	6
Nak	9
Rose Guesthouse	4
Sabah	1
Sandakan	3
Sandakan Backpackers	8
Seaview Sandakan Budget Hotel	5
Swiss-Inn Waterfront	7

DRINKING & NIGHTLIFE

520 Café	1

decorate the rooms while the staircase landing is adorned with artefacts including Murut blowpipes; upstairs the highlight is a small cinema showing a documentary called *Sandakan 1950*, a vivid home-movie testimony to the era that's well worth watching.

The town cemetery

Heading down Jalan Istana, past the half-Tudor, half-kampung-like **Istana** (a government building) you'll reach a modest Chinese World War II memorial. From here you'll be able to see part of the huge **town cemetery**, with horseshoe-shaped Chinese graves arranged for good feng shui on the hillside. Continue round to come across simple Christian grave markers by the side of the path and, further along, a collection of Japanese graves reached through an entrance arch.

Sandakan Memorial Park

Mile 7, 10km west of Sandakan, • Daily 9am–5pm • Free • Bus #4 from Jalan Pryer bus station 1, get off at Taman Rimba, walk 10min along Jalan Rimba; RM25 taxi from central Sandakan

Sandakan Memorial Park marks the site of the World War II POW camp where the infamous **death marches** began. In 1942, around 2700 British and Australian soldiers were transported from Singapore to Sandakan and set to work building an airstrip. They were kept in appalling conditions and around 300 had already died by early 1945, when the decision was made to re-locate them to Ranau (260km away through mud and jungle). Around five hundred prisoners died on three forced marches, while many more either perished after they arrived in Ranau or – if ill or injured – were left behind to die in Sandakan. In the end only six soldiers, all Australian, survived.

Signboards explain the few scattered remnants of the camp, while a small but informative and moving museum covers the harsh conditions in the camp and the actual death marches. If you are interested in walking or cycling part of the death march route, contact the highly regarded TYK Adventure Tours (☎ 088 232 821, ⓦ sandakan-deathmarch.com).

ARRIVAL AND DEPARTURE   SANDAKAN

By plane Sandakan's airport, 11km north of town, welcomes daily flights on AirAsia and MAS from KL (3 daily; 2hr 45min) and KK (7 daily; 50min); MASwings also flies from KK and Tawau (1 daily; 30min). For buses into town walk to the main road; otherwise catch a minivan from arrivals, or a RM22 taxi. MAS has its main branch at the airport (☎ 089 674 813), and an office in the Sabah Building, Jalan Pelabuhan ☎ 089 273 966 (Mon–Fri 8am–4.30pm, Sat 8am–3pm, Sun 8am–noon).

By bus The long-distance bus station is 5km northwest of town; local buses and minivans pass along the main road in front, as do taxis (RM10 to the centre), which also congregate in the station.

Destinations KK (several daily, but none 2–6pm; 6hr; these reach Ranau after 4hr and Gunung Kinabalu park after 4hr 30min); Lahad Datu (3 daily; 3hr); Semporna (2 daily; 5hr 30min); Tawau (5 daily; 5hr 30min).

By minivan Minivans head from the long-distance bus station to destinations including Lahad Datu and Sukau (for the Kinabatangan River).

By ferry Aleson Lines, whose agent is Timarine (☎ 089 212 063), run ferries from the Karamunting Jetty, 4km west of town via Pasir Putih bus, minivan or taxi (RM15).

Destinations Zamboanga in the Philippines (departures Tues & Fri; 20hr; RM280 economy, RM300 a/c, RM320 cabin).

GETTING AROUND

By bus Local buses vie for space on Jalan Pryer, although only the blue-and-white ones (for Sepilok Junction) are likely to be of use. To go straight to the Orang-utan Rehabilitation Sanctuary, take a minibus from beside the Millimewa supermarket.

By taxi It's not hard to find a taxi on the main streets or outside large hotels.

By car Cars can be rented from Borneo Express (☎ 016 886 0789, ⓦ borneocar.com), Lot 8, Ground Level, Terminal Building, Sandakan Airport.

INFORMATION

Tourist information Sandakan's excellent tourist office is easily reached via the steps on Lebuh Tiga (Mon–Fri 8am–4pm; ☎ 089 229 751). The centre's indefatigable coordinator, Elvina Ong, is highly knowledgeable and has good local contacts. Ask for the self-guided *Sandakan Heritage Trail* leaflet.

Addresses Sandakan addresses rely on numbers rather than street names – Jalan Tiga, for example, literally

means "Road Three". Similarly, addresses outside the centre are described according to the distance from downtown: "Mile 4" (also called "Batu 4") is the entertainment district four miles out of town.

Internet Cyberjazz.net & Komputer Jazz, Lot 7, Centre Point mall; Internet Cybercafé, second floor, room 219, Wisma Sandakan.

TOURS

Pulau Sipadan Resort and Tours Block C, Ground Floor, Lot 38 & 39, Mile 6, Bandar Tyng ☎ 089 673 999, ⓦ dive-malaysia.com. For Sepilok Nature Resort and accommodation at *Lankayan Island Dive Resort*.

Red Ape Encounters Office not open to visitors ☎ 089 230 268, ⓦ redapeencounters.com. A community-based ecotourism project operated by Sabah Wildlife Department in collaboration with villagers in Sukau. Tours combine a visit to an orang-utan study site with the usual boat trips and a hike to an oxbow lake, plus optional side trips; accommodation is in homestays.

Sepilok Tropical Wildlife Adventure Lot 3a, Block 13,

Lebuh Tiga ☎ 089 271 077, ⓦ stwadventure.com. Well-established operator which runs *Bilit Adventure Lodge* on the Kinabatangan River, plus *Sepilok Jungle Resort*.

SI Tours Block HS-5, Lot 59, Sandakan Harbour Square ☎ 089 213 502, ⓦ sitoursborneo.com. Runs *Kinabatangan Riverside Lodge* plus the remote Abai Lodge on the Kinabatangan River, as well as offering many other tours.

Wildlife Expeditions 9th floor, Wisma Khoo Siak Chew ☎ 089 219 616, ⓦ wildlife-expeditions.com.my. For Sukau, Sepilok, Turtle Islands and Labuk Bay Proboscis Monkey Sanctuary.

ACCOMMODATION

Sandakan holds a wide range of accommodation, but many visitors head straight for the lodges close to Sepilok Orang-utan Rehabilitation Centre, 20km west. The opening of the *Four Points by Sheraton*, after several years in the making, will mark a major change for visitors with a large budget.

The Mark's Lodge 1–7 Jalan Cecily, Mile 4 ☏ 089 210 055, ✇ markslodge.com. A modern, tastefully decorated hotel located on the edge of the dining and nightlife district at Mile 4 – look out for the old photos of Sandakan on the main staircase. Rooms are not large, but the beds have crisp white linen and deluxe rooms are equipped with Bose Wave sound systems. RM170

⭐ **May Fair** 1st floor, 24 Jalan Pryer ☏ 089 219 855. A great find: a well-located, clean and tidy guesthouse that's the pride and joy of owner Mr Lum. All rooms are equipped with flat-screen TVs and DVD players, and guests can borrow DVDs for free from the owner's massive collection. Free wi-fi, plus computers for use at RM4/hour. RM45

Nak Jalan Pelahuban ☏ 089 272 988, ✇ nakhotel.com. Thanks to a much-needed renovation in 2010, the *Nak* – a landmark since the 1970s – is well worth considering. Rooms are simply decorated but have a few nice design features such as bowl-shaped sinks and (in the suites) roll-top baths. The *Ba Lin* roof garden café is excellent, too. Free wi-fi. RM85

Rose Guesthouse Jalan Tiga ☏ 089 676 442. A new addition to the backpacker scene, with walls painted jolly colours and clean rooms and dorms – overall a good budget choice. Fan dorms RM18, a/c dorms RM22, fan rooms RM38, a/c rooms RM45

Sabah 1km north of town on Jalan Utara ☏ 089 213 299, ✇ sabahhotel.com.my. Sandakan's five-star finest, with a restful lobby, two swish restaurants, business centre, swimming pool and sports facilities. The place has two wings, and recent renovations mean that the older (and cheaper) Borneo wing is in many ways preferable. RM140

Sandakan Jalan Empat ☏ 089 221 122, ✇ hotelsandakan .com.my. Popular with business folk and families alike, this is quite good value, given the fine service and large rooms, but it has seen better days and remains old-fashioned despite recent renovation. Ask about discounts, particularly at weekends. Rates include breakfast and wi-fi. RM197

Sandakan Backpackers Sandakan Harbour Square ☏ 089 221 104 ✇ sandakanbackpackers.com. A budget favourite right on the waterfront – take a look at the graffiti in the stairwell, added by satisfied customers. There are both mixed and single-sex dorms as well as single rooms; all are clean and quiet. Rates include breakfast, a/c and wi-fi. Dorms RM30, doubles RM70

⭐ **Seaview Sandakan Budget Hotel** 126 Jalan Dua, Harbour Square ☏ 089 221 221, ✇ sandakanbudget hotel.com. Now under new management, this backpacker place (formerly called *Sunset Harbour*) has distinctly average rooms but its friendly and helpful owner Nafisah helps to make it stand out. She even offers Indian cookery lessons for RM30 per person. Rates for all but the fan-cooled dorm include breakfast, which is either roti or pancakes with curry. There's free wi-fi too. Fan dorms RM18, a/c dorms RM28, fan rooms RM50, a/c rooms RM65

Swiss-Inn Waterfront Sandakan Harbour Square ☏ 089 240 888, ✇ swissgarden.com. Formerly the *@ease Hotel*, and a fine mid-range choice right on the waterfront – which means it's close to places to eat, but also that it can get a little noisy at night. Breakfast is included. RM140

EATING, DRINKING AND NIGHTLIFE

Sandakan may not be able to match KK's range of **restaurants**, but it still has enough choice to suit most people, with Malay, Chinese, Indian and Western food all well represented. The set of cafés in Sandakan Harbour Square are a good starting point, while many of the best **seafood** places are outside the centre. You're best off taking a taxi, for example, to reach **Sim Sim water village**. For **hawker stalls**, head for the Central Market (especially for breakfast) or the small night market on Jalan Leila. Beer is widely available in Chinese restaurants and coffee shops but the centre holds few dedicated **bars**. There's significantly more **nightlife**, as well as numerous restaurants, in the **Mile 4** district (aka Bandar Indah) west of town. A taxi should cost RM20 each way.

1 Malaysia Steamboat and Seafood Trig Hill ☏ 089 238 878. The most popular of several similar places on the hill. Either take your pick of the seafood – a kilo of crab costs RM18 – or help yourself to the steamboat (hotpot buffet) at RM25. Just don't take more than you can eat, as there's a fine for wastage. Daily 6–10.30pm.

520 Café Lot 68, Block HS–6, Sandakan Harbour Square. One of the few bars close to the waterfront and popular with backpackers, who are drawn in by the flashing lights and open sides as much as by the pricey beer

and shisha (RM15). Daily 9am–12.30am.

⭐ **Ba Lin** Nak Hotel, Jalan Pelahuban, ☏ 089 272 988. A real surprise: a seriously stylish rooftop bar and restaurant which, while not cheap, is a great place to hang out. The menu, designed to look like a newspaper, includes pizza (starting at RM22), pasta (from RM14) and the signature dish of sticky New Zealand lamb with greens and mash (RM30). They also do a great brunch. Daily 7am–1am.

⭐ **English Tea House** Jalan Istana ☏ 089 222 544, ✇ englishteahouse.org. A genteel hillside spot close to

Agnes Keith House (see p.431), with a colonial theme including a small croquet lawn. Waitresses dressed in black and white serve English favourites including shepherd's pie (RM32), as well as local dishes. You can also get afternoon tea (RM21) with scones, jam and cream. Daily 10am–midnight.

H84 Between bridges 7 and 8, Sim Sim water village. Simply known by its address, *H84* is a family home that serves fish balls and wonton, as well as dishes such as *wan tan hor* (rice noodles with seafood) but is renowned for its century egg dumplings (for which the eggs have been preserved for several weeks). Daily 6am–3pm & 5–10pm.

Harbour Garden Café Lot 109, Block HS-11, Sandakan Harbour Square. One of several good cafés on the waterfront strip, serving set meals (main, rice, soup and water) for RM6.50–10 as well as an à la carte menu. It's particularly known for its *pau* (steamed buns). Daily 11am–midnight.

Imperial Bayview Central market, ☏ 089 246 888. In a circular building connected to the main market, right where fishermen bring in the day's catch. As well as the freshest of seafood, they also do dim sum in the mornings. Mon–Fri 9.30am–2pm & 6.30–10pm, Sat & Sun 8am–2pm & 6.30–10pm.

★ **Nam Choon** Block A, Lot 2a, Old Slipway. You could easily walk past this local favourite restaurant without realizing that it's special. It only serves four dishes: *nasi ayam* (chicken rice, RM4), *nasi paha-paha atas* (the same, with chicken on the bone RM4.50), nasi fish ball (RM4) and *nasi ikan* (fried fish, RM4–10). Each dish is brilliant, and to make it even more of a bargain you get free hot or cold Chinese tea. You may have to share a table at busy times. Mon–Sat 6am–3pm.

★ **Sim Sim Seafood Restaurant** Bridge 8, Sim Sim Water Village. The most highly regarded of the various eateries in the Sim Sim water village, known for having the freshest, tastiest and best-value seafood around. It's out on stilts over the water, on the left-hand side of the bridge. A meal here is a great local experience, whether it's breakfast, lunch or dinner. Daily except Wed 8am–10pm.

MILE 4

Masarap Lot A4, Block 33, Bandar Indah, Mile 4. The name means "delicious" in Tagalog, and this restaurant dishes up Filipino favourites such as *lumpia* (spring rolls), *lechon kawali* (pork which has been boiled then deep-fried) and *sinigang baboy* (pork and vegetables in a sour broth). Mon–Fri 10.30am–3pm & 5–11pm, Sat & Sun 10.30am–midnight.

Taste Restaurant 8 Jalan Utara, Mile 4. Specializing in Hakka cuisine, with a particular emphasis on pig-based dishes such as herbal pork leg or pineapple with pork intestine. Portions are big enough to share, although they also do set meals (main, rice, veg and drink) for RM9.90. Tues–Sun 8.30am–10pm.

Wojamama Lot 1, Block 4, Jalan Bandar Indah, Mile 4. A Japanese restaurant with a grocery store attached, boasting a miniature train that carries sushi past seated diners. The menu also includes bento boxes and hot dishes. Daily 11am–10pm.

DIRECTORY

Banks There are several banks at the intersection of Jalan Pelabuhan and Lebuh Tiga, including HSBC, Standard Chartered and CIMB. There's a Public Bank nearby on Lebuh Tiga.

Hospital Duchess of Kent, Jalan Utara, 2km north of the centre (☏ 089 212 111).

Laundry New Laundry Service, 1 Jalan Elopura (☏ 012 816 3384)

Pharmacy Several branches of Borneo Dispensary including one at 11b Jalan Dua, as well as the usual Guardian and Watsons.

Police The main police station is on Jalan Utara, 1.5 km from town (☏ 089 211 222).

Post office Sandakan's GPO is 5min walk west of town, on Jalan Leila.

Spas Lynn Beauty, 112 Sandakan Harbour Square (☏ 089 246 002).

Visa extensions Immigration Office, Mile 7, Ranau Rd ☏ 089 668 308.

Sepilok

The town of Sepilok, 25km west of Sandakan, is best known for its **Orang-utan Rehabilitation Centre**. That's not the only attraction, though, as the **Rainforest Discovery Centre** is worth visiting for its canopy walkway. There are also plans to open a conservation centre for Malayan sun bears, the world's smallest bear species. See ⓦsunbears.wildlifedirect.org for the latest news.

Sepilok Orang-utan Rehabilitation Centre

3km south of Sepilok Junction, a turning at Mile 14 on the highway to KK, 23km west of Sandakan • Daily 9am–noon & 2–4pm, feeding times 10am & 3pm • RM30, photo pass RM10 • ☏ 089 531 180, ✉ sorc64@gmail.com • Served by Sepilok Batu #14 minibus from beside

> ## ORANG-UTANS AT SEPILOK
>
> **Orang-utans** – tail-less, red-haired apes (their name means "man of the forest" in Malay) – can reach a height of around 1.65m, and can live to over thirty years old. Solitary but not aggressively territorial, these primates live a largely arboreal existence, eating fruit, leaves, bark and the occasional insect.
>
> Most of the orang-utans at the Sepilok centre are victims of forest clearance; many have been orphaned, injured and traumatized in the process. Some have also been kept as pets, something now prohibited by law, which means that their survival instincts remain undeveloped. Orang-utans are trained at Sepilok to fend for themselves in the wild. Although not always successful, the training process has seen many animals reintroduced to their natural habitat.

Sandakan's Millimewa supermarket (5 daily; 40min); 9am & 2pm buses arrive in good time for feeding sessions; last bus back at 4pm; RM35 by taxi from Sandakan

Set up in 1964 and occupying a 43-square-kilometre patch of lowland rainforest, the **Sepilok Orang-utan Rehabilitation Centre** is one of only a few such sanctuaries. It's also among Sabah's most popular tourist sites, with over two hundred people crowding onto the viewing platform during feeding hours on most days. In general it's best to go for the afternoon session, as most tour buses come in the morning.

Leave valuables in the free lockers, along with food, drink and insect repellent (which can be harmful to the orang-utans if they ingest it). There's little shade on the viewing platform, so bring a hat. You'll find a café near the information centre.

The **feeding station** is a ten-minute walk from the entrance, so arrive with plenty of time. There are usually at least a couple of orang-utans waiting for their meal, often the very young ones, and they immediately cluster round the warden as he sets out the fruit. Others may soon come along, swinging, shimmying and strolling towards their breakfast or lunch, jealously watched by gangs of macaques that loiter around for scraps.

If you have time, stick around after feeding time and take one of several **trails** through the forest; you'll need to register at reception. Besides the pleasure of the walk, there's a chance you may see one or more orang-utans.

Rainforest Discovery Centre

2km from the Orang-utan Rehabilitation Centre: heading towards Sepilok Junction, turn left onto Jalan Fabiar at the government Forest Research Centre • Daily 8am–5pm • RM10 • ☎ 089 533 780, Ⓦ forest.sabah.gov.my/rdc

For most visitors (vertigo sufferers aside) the highlight of the **Rainforest Discovery Centre** is the 150m-long series of walkways through the forest canopy. Other attractions include boating on the lake at the weekend; forest trails that take in more than 250 species of orchid and cross a suspension bridge; and an exhibition hall with displays on Borneo's flaura and fauna.

ARRIVAL AND DEPARTURE   SEPILOK

By bus or minibus To reach Sepilok Junction from Sandakan, catch any blue and white local bus from Jalan Pryer. From the junction unlicensed taxis head to accommodation (from RM3) or the Orang-utan Rehabilitation Centre (RM10).

ACCOMMODATION

Many visitors stay in Sepilok rather than Sandakan, for its high-standard, good-value **accommodation**, and handy location for onward bus travel to Lahud Datu or Semporna.

★ **Paganakan Dii Tropical Retreat** 2km northwest of Sepilok Junction ☎ 089 532 005, ✉ info@paganakandii.com. The furthest lodge from the orang-utan centre, in the opposite direction from all the rest. Spacious landscaped grounds and relaxed atmosphere, plus neat little touches that would normally be found in more expensive accommodation. The newer cabins have particularly good rainforest views, as does the wi-fi-equipped restaurant. Breakfast is included, along with shuttles to the sanctuary and Rainforest Discovery Centre. Dorms RM30, rooms RM130, cabins RM150

Sepilok B&B Jalan Arboretum ☏089 534 050, ⓦ sepilokbednbreakfast.com. This friendly place, close to the Rainforest Discovery Centre, has small, pleasant rooms and just-about-acceptable dorms; the new a/c Hornbill rooms are the most appealing. You can also camp here with your own tent. Rates include breakfast. Camping per person RM12, dorms RM26, fan rooms RM68, a/c rooms RM88, Hornbill rooms RM98

Sepilok Hostel and Breakfast Jalan Arboretum ☏012 817 5132. A small blue and white building on the road to the Rainforest Discovery Centre, with only three rooms (more are planned) and space for camping. The rooms are clean and bright, with wooden floors and fans. Breakfast is included and there's a free shuttle to the orang-utan sanctuary. Camping RM15, rooms RM50

★ **Sepilok Forest Edge Resort and Labuk B&B** Jalan Rambutan, 1km from orang-utan centre ☏089 533 190, ⓦ sepilokforestedge.com. This charming place has a "longhouse" with small dorms and simple rooms plus a series of appealing chalets. All are dotted around a multi-level landscaped garden complete with a jacuzzi. Dorms RM30, rooms RM70, chalets RM180

Sepilok Jungle Resort Jalan Rambutan, close to the orang-utan centre ☏089 533 031, ⓦ sepilokjungleresort.com. A large complex with dorms and private rooms; the latter have interesting touches such as labels for the different types of wood used. You can also camp with your own tent. There's a pool with a jacuzzi and sauna, although even guests have to pay RM5 to use it (RM35 for outsiders). Dorms RM28, fan rooms RM69, a/c rooms RM105

Sepilok Nature Resort Jalan Sepilok, close to the orang-utan centre ☏089 673 999, ⓦ sepilok.com. Twenty-three plush, spacious and eco-aware chalets nestling in lush jungle; the in-house restaurant serves the best food in Sepilok although like the accommodation it's quite pricey (around RM25 for a main course). Wi-fi costs RM15/half-hour. RM250

Uncle Tan's B&B Jalan Sepilok, 100m south of Sepilok Junction ☏016 824 4749, ⓦ uncletan.com. A Sabah institution, enormously popular with backpackers. Prices include all meals, making it quite a bargain even if the dorms and a/c rooms are nothing fancy. They also offer packages at *Uncle Tan's Wildlife Camp* on the Kinabatangan River. Free shuttle to the orang-utan sanctuary. Dorms RM38, rooms RM90

Labuk Bay Proboscis Monkey Sanctuary

Near Kampung Samawang • Daily 9am–5.30pm; feeding times: platform A 9.30am & 2.30pm, platform B 11.30am & 4.30pm • RM60, RM30 child, RM10 camera • ☏089 674 133, ⓦ proboscis.cc • Minibus tours (RM90, excluding lunch) leave Sandakan 9.30am, Sepilok 10.30am; or take a taxi (RM200 return from Sandakan, RM150 from Sepilok)

Set amid mangrove forest and reached via a track through an oil-palm plantation, **Labuk Bay Proboscis Monkey Sanctuary** functions as a companion to the more famous orang-utan sanctuary at Sepilok. Most visitors come on a **day-trip** from Sandakan or Sepilok, which is significantly closer, but it's also possible to stay **overnight**.

Two large observation platforms, each with two feeding times, offer perfect vantage points from which to view the long-nosed proboscis monkeys; at the same time you can also see silverleaf monkeys scavenge fruit left behind, and there's some fantastic birdlife including hornbills. On a day-trip you could see all four feedings if you like, or even leave after just one, but it's more usual to see one from each platform.

Other activities

If you make arrangements in advance then it's possible to combine watching the monkey feeding with other activities. These include a short jungle trek or a bird-watching walk (each 1hr; RM30) or a boat trip (2hr; RM250/boat) to a fishing village. If you're staying the night then you can also sign up for a firefly walk (45min; RM20) and a morning birdwatching walk (1hr; RM30).

ACCOMMODATION LABUK BAY

★ **Nipah Lodge** Labuk Bay ☏089 230 708, ✉ labukbay@proboscis.cc. As well as a large communal area and café, Labuk Bay's only option offers a few dozen lovely chalets – including a 3-bedroom family house – amid the mangroves, and a couple of longer buildings with small dorms. The latter have mosquito screens but no nets; insect spray is available. Rates include breakfast. Dorms RM28, rooms RM180

Pulau Lankayan

Ninety minutes' boat ride north of Sandakan in the Sulu Sea lies the **Sugud Islands Marine Conservation Area**, managed by a nonprofit organization called Reef Guardian (wreef-guardian.com), and consisting of three islands: Lankayan, Billiean and Tegaipil. Only **PULAU LANKAYAN** is open and has a single resort.

Although the island itself is beautiful and has an active turtle-hatching programme, diving and snorkelling is the real pull, thanks to a marine environment protected by a ban on fishing. The island is surrounded by hard and soft corals that are in very good condition, and the macro life in particular is excellent. Divers may see whale sharks in April and May.

ACCOMMODATION   PULAU LANKAYAN

Lankayan Island Dive Resort C/o Pulau Sipadan Resort and Tours, Ground floor, Block C, Lot 38 & 39, Mile 6, Bandar Tyng, Sandakan ☎089 673 999, wlankayan-island.com. A delightful resort with large, comfortable chalets and helpful staff. The dive shop is also excellent, well equipped and with good guides. It's normal to book multi-day packages including transport. 3D/2N package, non-diving RM3000, diving RM3700

7

Turtle Islands National Park

Peeping out of the Sulu Sea 40km north of Sandakan, three tiny islands comprise the **TURTLE ISLANDS NATIONAL PARK**. They are favoured egg-laying sites of green and hawksbill turtles, which haul themselves laboriously above the high-tide mark to bury their clutches of eggs almost every night of the year. Although all three islands – Pulau Selingan, Pulau Bakungan Kecil and Pulau Gulisan – hold hatcheries, tourists can only visit **Selingan**.

All the action is at night. As well as seeing a mother turtle laying her eggs, you can watch as the park wardens release newly hatched turtles that waddle, Chaplin-like, into the sea to face an uncertain future. Before dark there's plenty of time – arguably too much time, given the lack of facilities – for **swimming**, **snorkelling** (equipment rental RM25) and **sunbathing**. Take precautions against sandflies, which can be voracious especially when it rains.

ARRIVAL AND DEPARTURE   TURTLE ISLANDS NATIONAL PARK

Tours You can only visit the park as part of an overnight tour that includes transfer and accommodation. Book with a travel agent or, more cheaply, direct with Crystal Quest (☎089 212 711, ⓔcquest@tm.net.my). Boats leave the Crystal Quest jetty, 500m east of Sandakan town centre, around 9.30am and arrive at the island an hour later. The return trip is at 7am the next morning.

ACCOMMODATION

Selingan Island Resort Book through Crystal Quest ☎089 212 711, ⓔcquest@tm.net.my. The park's only accommodation has beds for fifty visitors a night. Despite the significant costs, the chalets offer nothing in the way of luxury. The rather average buffet spreads are included in the package, as are transport and park fees. RM690

Sungai Kinabatangan

Southeast of Sandakan Bay, Sabah's longest river – the 560km **Sungai Kinabatangan** – ends its journey to the Sulu Sea. Whereas logging has had an adverse impact on the river's ecology upstream, the creation of the **Lower Kinabatangan Wildlife Sanctuary** has kept its lower reaches largely free of development. This is the largest forested flood plain in Malaysia, laden with oxbow lakes, mangrove and grass swamps, and distinctive vegetation including massive fig trees overhanging the water's edge.

The sanctuary offers some of Sabah's best opportunities for seeing wildlife. Although some tour operators offer day-trips from Sandakan, it's much better to stay overnight

7

LOWER KINABATANGAN WILDLIFE SANCTUARY

Despite Sabah's rather haphazard approach to making the most of its superb natural resources, the designation of the Lower Kinabatangan as a **wildlife sanctuary** in 2005 was a commendable move. That said, sanctuary status is one level below that of a national park, so villages and agricultural development have been allowed to crisscross the protected sections. Furthermore, only the area immediately alongside the river is protected; as animals have lost their habitats when the surrounding areas have been converted into palm-oil plantations, they have effectively been pushed into the narrow protected corridor.

This means that it is highly likely that, over a number of boat rides and short treks, you will see elephants (if they are in the area), orang-utans, proboscis monkeys, macaques and gibbons. The resident **birdlife** is equally impressive. With luck, visitors get glimpses of hornbills, brahminy kites, crested serpent eagles, egrets, exquisite blue-banded and stork-billed kingfishers, and oriental darters, which dive underwater to find food and then sit on the shore, their wings stretched out to dry. The river itself holds freshwater sharks, crocodiles and rays, and a great variety of fish species.

---

given the travel time; the ideal is a two-night stay (see "Accommodation"). Although there are a few exceptions, most lodges are located either in or around the villages of **Sukau** or **Bilit**. From November to April, the rainy season can lead to flooding at some lodges – at its worst in January – and even force their closure.

Sukau and Bilit

The first tourist lodges on the Sungai Kinabatangan opened around the kampung of **Sukau**, 134km from Sandakan by road or 87km by boat. Still the easiest place to reach, it's particularly popular with independent travellers as it's possible to stay in the village itself on a B&B basis then charter boats as needed. Most of the all-inclusive lodges are on the riverbanks close to the village.

Many would argue, however, that Sukau is a victim of over-development. In July and August in particular, dozens of boats converge along the same narrow tributaries at the same times and shatter any sense of peace. Although many boats now use quieter electric motors when the current allows, some still do not.

Once tourism became well established in Sukau, a few operators decided to open lodges further upriver around the kampung of **Bilit**. Although not the undeveloped spot it once was, Bilit remains quieter than Sukau partly because there's no public transport to the village – it's upstream of Sukau and reached via a lower-quality road.

ARRIVAL AND DEPARTURE   SUKAU AND BILIT

Although tour operators arrange transport to their lodges and camps – go by **boat** (2hr 30min to Sukau; not possible to Bilit) if you have the choice – it's relatively easy to get all the way to **Sukau** by public transport. There are two reasons to do this: if you're staying on a B&B basis, or if you want to arrange a discount on a tour package by removing transfers from the equation.

By bus From Sandakan, take any southbound bus 89km to Sukau Junction (3hr; RM15), then wait for a Sukau minivan to depart when full (45min; RM20). From KK, catch a bus bound for Tawau or Lahad Datu, and get off at Sukau Junction (around RM30); from Lahad Datu take any northbound vehicle. No public transport goes to Bilit; arrange a pick-up from Sukau Junction.

ACCOMMODATION

Most people visit on a **tour**, typically including all meals plus boat trips; prices given here are for two people (unless dorms are involved). While tour operators normally quote prices for two-day/one-night itineraries, as indicated below, it's far preferable (and more common) to stay for at least two nights. A single night may only allow time for a single boat trip, whereas two-night itineraries generally include three, plus a short jungle hike and optional night walk. Furthermore, the second and subsequent nights are usually significantly cheaper than the first (expect to pay about 40 percent of the first-night price). If you really are pushed for time consider a **day-trip**. New lodges open regularly; get the latest information from the tourist office in Sandakan. Although booking a package is often a good idea, **independent** travellers can save money by staying at a B&B, then paying for any boat trips.

KAMPUNG SUKAU

Balai Kito Homestay Various locations ☎013 869 9026 or ☎089 568 472, ⍟sukauhomestay.com. This homestay programme arranges B&B accommodation, to which you can add other meals (RM15 each) and boat trips (RM100 for up to six people). B&B **RM40**

Barefoot Lodge Eastern side of Kampung Sukau ☎089 235 525, ⍟barefootsukau.com. Owned by prominent local nature photographer Cede Prudente (⍟cedeprudente.com), who sometimes runs specialist tours. A two-night package (RM480 per person) includes three cruises, one jungle walk and food; transport from Sandakan is RM80 each way. Otherwise lunch and dinner cost RM15–20 each and cruises are RM55–65. Look out for promotions March–June. B&B **RM100**

Sukau B&B Eastern side of Kampung Sukau ☎013 553 2619 or ☎019 583 5580, ✉sukaubandb_shu@yahoo .com. The 13 rooms here – either twin or triple, with fans and shared bathrooms – are nothing special, but fine if you're on a budget. Breakfast is included, other meals are RM10 and boat trips cost RM30 per person. **RM50**

Sukau Greenview Eastern side of Kampung Sukau ☎013 869 6922, ✉sukau_greenview@yahoo.com. This popular place is located beside the site of the Sunday market. The en-suite bathrooms are tiny, other than in rooms 10 and 11, and the facilities are generally basic. Cruises cost RM50 and meals are RM20, but a package may be cheaper. Rooms **RM60**, 2D/1N package **RM370**, 2D/1N package with transport **RM530**

Sukau River Homestay Just west of Kampung Sukau ☎012 812 0678, ✉marinamait@ymail.com. Also known as *Manati's* this place was becoming more guesthouse-like at the time of research, with the addition of a restaurant and three new rooms. Morning boat trips are combined with a hike, and cost RM150/boat; afternoon boat trips cost RM100. Breakfast and dinner included. **RM50**

AROUND SUKAU

★ **Borneo Nature Lodge** ☎089 210 718, ⍟borneonaturelodge.com.my. A more interesting site than most, with comfortable cabins linked by wooden walkways to the only a/c restaurant in Sukau. The owners have taken steps to make the place environmentally friendly, using excess heat from the a/c to heat water in the showers. 2D/1N package **RM980**

Bukit Melapi (aka Proboscis Lodge) Run by Sipadan Dive Centre ☎088 240 584, ⍟proboscislodge.com. Thirty large a/c en-suite doubles, close to the Sukau jetty. The restaurant and bar are quite grand, with wine available

by the bottle, barbecues on request and a pool table upstairs. 2D/1N package, excluding transport **RM660**

Kinabatangan Riverside Lodge Run by S.I. Tours ☎089 213 503, ⍟www.sitoursborneo.com. A large site with good accommodation and a room for massage and reflexology. The same company also runs the *Abai Lodge*, an hour away, and can organize trips combining the two. Other tours include the Gomantong Caves (RM150 per person). 2D/1N package **RM760**, additional nights **RM900**

Sukau Rainforest Lodge Run by Borneo Eco Tours ☎088 438 300, ⍟sukau.com. Twenty appealing but very overpriced rooms in longhouses, just 200m upstream from the kampung; expansion was underway at the time of research. The lodge is a fine example of ecotourism, heating water with solar power, recycling, harvesting rainwater and employing locals if possible. The meals (included) are better than average, as are the boat tours. 2D/1N package, including transport **RM2800**

Usman Homestay ☎019 841 5259. The only place offering B&B accommodation on the river around Sukau, rather than in the village itself. It's very much a family-run affair, and a very popular one with backpackers – reports describe them being a little overstretched at times. They charge RM50 per person for each cruise (maximum 8 people), with the morning cruise including a jungle trek. Full-board **RM100**

AROUND BILIT

Bilit Adventure Lodge ☎089 271 077. The first lodge to open in Bilit, and currently extending its restaurant. Associated with the *Sepilok Jungle Resort*, it's a deservedly popular place with appealing a/c and fan rooms. Someone has a sense of humour: if you get bitten by a leech, you'll be awarded a blood donor certificate. 2D/1N package **RM900**

Bilit Homestay Programme Various locations ☎013 553 6712, ⍟bilithomestay.wordpress.com. Twelve houses in the village, offer two-night packages that include food, transport from Sandakan, accommodation, three boat trips and a night walk. 2D/1N package **RM620** 3D/2N package **RM720**

★ **Bilit Kinabatangan Heritage B&B** ☎016 552 5709, ⍟bilitkinabatangan.com. The nearest thing to a budget option in the Bilit area, with two no-frills private rooms and a ten-bed dorm. The latter is handy if for solo travellers as most other places charge a single supplement. Packages include return transport from Sandakan. 2D/1N package: dorms **RM270**, rooms **RM720**; 3D/2N package: dorms **RM330**, rooms **RM800**

Bilit Rainforest Lodge ☎089 202 388. Chalets on stilts, linked by wooden walkways. Rooms are spacious and

7

comfortable, particularly the four split-level VIP bungalows, and even the normal rooms have interesting features – the bathroom doors, for example, are hidden by screens made from branches. There's free wi-fi plus three internet terminals. 2D/1N package RM1530

★ **Kinabatangan Jungle Camp (KJC)** ☎089 533 190 or ☎019 804 7756, ⊛kinabatangan-jungle-camp.com. While the rooms are simpler than most along this stretch, what draws visitors is the wealth of experience of no-nonsense owner Robert Chong. He tailors trips to meet the needs of guests, making it popular with birdwatchers, photographers and naturalists; the listed price is therefore for comparison only. Groups are kept small and smaller engines are used; for birdwatching the staff use paddles to keep it quiet. Wi-fi available. 2D/1N package including transport RM960

★ **Last Frontier** ☎016 676 5922, ⊛thelast frontierresort.com. Located up a jungled hill, and only accessible via 600 steps; the reward for the effort is a wonderfully isolated lodge with only four guest rooms and some great food. Don't worry, the packages still include river trips. Ask about porters if you need help getting your luggage up the steps. 2D/1N package RM700

Myne ☎089 278 288, ⊛myne.com.my. Located on a bend in the river, giving it great views which can be admired from chairs and loungers, this lodge has well-appointed rooms with balconies. Morning, evening and night cruises, plus a 3hr jungle trek, and they're planning to build a trail for a 4WD night safari. 2D/1N package, not including transport RM810

OTHER LOCATIONS

Abai Homestay Kampung Abai ☎013 550 5349. This community-run homestay project offers simple accommodation in a quiet village with only one tourist lodge. River cruises cost RM50 per person, while a boat transfer (1hr 30min) one-way from Sandakan is RM100 per person. Room and meals RM160

Abai Jungle Lodge Kampung Abai run by S.I. Tours ☎089 213 503, ⊛sitoursborneo.com. A spacious base 47km from Sandakan, with easy access to quiet tributaries – there are no other lodges in the area, only a homestay programme. The lodge has eighteen en-suite doubles, and is run along environmentally friendly lines. In addition to boat trips, it's possible to walk short trails. 2D/1N package RM1300

★ **Miso Walai Homestay** Kampung Mengaris ☎089 551 064, ⊛misowalaihomestay.com. Also known as *Mescot*, the name of the overall community initiative, this very well-organized scheme places tourists in village homes. Boat tours can be arranged as well as trips to burial caves at the Batu Putih limestone outcrop, plus *Mescot* has a rainforest camp and runs volunteer projects. Public transport can stop at the office, under the bridge where the Sandakan–Lahad Datu highway crosses the Sungai Kinabatangan. Room and meals RM130, 2D/1N package RM700

Nature Lodge Kinabatangan Downstream from Sukau ☎013 863 6263, ⊛naturelodgekinabatangan .com. This budget option, located on its own stretch of riverbank, has the added advantage of trails in the surrounding forest. Unusually, one-night itineraries include both an afternoon and a morning boat trip; transfers from Sandakan or Sepilok cost RM30 per person. 2D/1N package: dorms RM320, double rooms RM710; 3D/2N package: dorms RM370, double rooms RM880

Uncle Tan's Wildlife Camp Close to the Lokan River ☎089 531 639 or ☎016 824 4749, ⊛uncletan.com. Relocated upriver from Bilit, this long-standing budget favourite continues to attract backpackers. As their printed information points out "the camp is not exactly the Hilton", but intrepid travellers consistently come away recommending the place. Twinned with *Uncle Tan's B&B* in Sepilok. Dorm with meals RM38, room with meals RM100, 2D/1N package RM320

Gomantong Caves

South of a turning halfway between Kampung Sukau and Sukau Junction • Daily 7.30am–6pm, but occasional closures; check before you set out • RM30, RM30 camera permit • ☎019 883 5271, ⊛sabah.gov.my/jhl • Best visited as a tour from Sungai Kinabatangan lodges; or take a Sukau-bound minivan from Sandakan and get off at the Gomantong junction; from Lahad Datu, get off at the turning for Sukau and catch a minivan or motorbike taxi (either RM10) to the Gomantong junction; either way you'll probably need to walk the last 4.5km

The **Gomantong Caves** are vast limestone cavities inhabited by swiftlets whose nests are harvested twice a year (normally Feb–April and July–Sept) for the bird's-nest-soup trade (see p.371). The caves are also home to a huge number of bats, and the enormous piles of guano (droppings) give them a distinctive acrid smell.

There are two main caves. The black cave, smaller but only a ten-minute walk from the ticket office, mostly contains black nests, a combination of twigs and bird saliva. The white cave is rarely visited by tourists as it's another hour away, but nest collectors go there for the more valuable white nests, made from pure saliva. Note that the guano attracts a huge number of cockroaches, so don't wear flip-flops or sandals.

There's nowhere to stay or eat in and around Gomantong, so plan to leave the caves well before dark if you are not on a tour.

From Lahad Datu to the Maliau Basin

Sabah's main trunk road continues southeast from Sandakan and the Sungai Kinabatangan to **Lahad Datu**. This unenthralling town offers access to two excellent rainforest areas: **Danum Valley Conservation Area** and **Tabin Wildlife Reserve**. Further south, **Semporna** draws scuba divers headed for the world-renowned **Pulau Sipadan**. It's possible to stay in town or in an island resort; the latter range from backpacker shacks to luxurious retreats.

The main road around Sabah stops at the busy, noisy town of **Tawau**, from which ferries depart for Indonesian Kalimantan. Also from Tawau, 4WDs head daily for Keningau along rough routes that complete a **ring road** of sorts. This is also the way to the **Maliau Basin**, a magnet for trekkers although only accessible within expensive tour packages.

Lahad Datu

LAHAD DATU, 175km south of Sandakan, has something of a frontier feel. Once a centre for cocoa production, it could not compete with South American rivals and turned to palm oil instead. During its 1990s boom, it became a magnet for immigrants, mostly Indonesian and Filipino, many of whom have found gainful (if often illegal) employment on the plantations and in the construction industry.

Most visitors simply use Lahad Datu as a jumping-off point for the outstanding natural attractions of **Danum Valley Conservation Area** and **Tabin Wildife Reserve**. Within the town, almost everything of interest is on or just off the main road Jalan Teratai.

ARRIVAL AND DEPARTURE
LAHAD DATU

By air The airport north of town, used by MASwings daily flights to KK (4 daily; 55min) is only a short taxi ride (RM5) from the centre; no buses serve the route.

By bus Buses from Sandakan, Semporna and Tawau stop at the bus terminus on Jalan Bunga Raya, a couple of minutes' walk east of Jalan Teratai.

ACCOMMODATION

Hotel De Leon Block L, Lot 1-6, Darvel Bay Commercial Centre ☎ 089 881 222, ☻ hoteldeleon.com.my. Set back from Jalan Teratai, this business hotel stands out for its rather mixed decor. On the one hand the lobby has a zen-like water feature; on the other it has a tacky glittering dolphin sculpture. The rooms have a little pizzazz, including deep-pile rugs in the executive rooms (RM30 extra). Breakfast included. RM148

Ocean 1 Jalan Cempaka ☎ 089 888 851. If you can't handle the *Tabin Lodge*, and nowhere else will do a decent discount, this is probably your best budget bet. Some rooms are a bit musty, but they have a/c and are fine for a night or two. RM60

Tabin Lodge Jalan Urusetia Kecil, ☎ 089 889 552. One of the few budget options in town, conveniently located opposite the bus and minivan terminus and with singles for just RM25, The rooms are just about OK, as long as you can ignore the fact that all those tiled walls are distinctly creepy. Fan rooms RM35, a/c rooms RM45

EATING AND DRINKING

Lahad Datu Food Centre Jalan Anggrek. A pretty average Chinese food court, but significantly better than most of the other options. In addition to the usual dishes, they serve beer (including Filipino San Miguel for RM4) making this a lively spot in the evening. Daily 10am–10pm.

★ **Tain Yen Liew** Corner of Jalan Dahlia and Jalan Kenaga. While nothing fancy to look at, this small coffee shop has fabulous fried *mee* (noodles), served in a broth with pork and great for breakfast. Also popular is *sui kow* (wonton soup, where the dumplings contain prawn, pork and fish paste). Daily 6.30am–noon.

Danum Valley Conservation Area

65km west of Lahad Datu; owned by nonprofit Sabah Foundation ☎ 088 422 211, ☻ ysnet.org.my

Spanning 438 square kilometres, over ninety percent of it primary dipterocarp rainforest, the **Danum Valley Conservation Area** (DVCA) is contained within a sprawling logging concession. Wildlife includes bearded pigs, orang-utans, proboscis monkeys, clouded leopards and elephants, as well as reptiles, fish, insects and more than 320 bird species. Short hiking **trails** are limited to the eastern side, where the tourist accommodation is located. The remainder is pristine forest, out of bounds to all but researchers.

Activities

Your experience of Danum Valley will depend greatly on which accommodation option you choose. The more expensive, the *Borneo Rainforest Lodge* offers highly skilled guides to take you on walks. The standard itinerary includes a walk on a 27-metre-high canopy walkway, night safaris and a visit to a burial hill with a coffin belonging to a tribal chief.

Staying at the much cheaper *Danum Valley Field Centre*, your options are more limited. The centre is primarily set up for researchers, so although rangers will accompany you on the well-marked trails (RM20/hr), they're not employed to spot wildlife on your behalf. If you're a nature enthusiast and know what you're looking for, that may suit you; otherwise you may come away disappointed.

ACCOMMODATION   **DANUM VALLEY**

Borneo Rainforest Lodge 9km into the conservation area, on a bend on the Danum River; c/o Borneo Nature Tours office: Lot 20, Block 3, Fajar Lorong 9, Fajar Centre, Lahad Datu ☎089 880 207, ⓦborneonaturetours.com. A luxurious network of hardwood chalets, each with an outdoor deck. It's all very stylish considering that it's within the primary forest; prices include excellent buffet meals and a range of activities. A single night would be too much of a rush. 3D/2N package **RM4400**

Danum Valley Field Centre On the eastern edge of the conservation area; office: Block 3, Fajar Lorong 9, Fajar Centre, Lahad Datu ☎089 880 441, ✉danum_valley @yahoo.com. Travellers report receiving conflicting information about the booking policy here, but the official line is that you must either have student ID or get special approval. Give at least three weeks' notice; transport (RM65 each way) runs Mon, Wed and Fri. The simple accommodation is mostly in 48-bed dorms, plus there's a café (three meals a day cost RM111). Camping **RM78**, dorms **RM91**, rooms **RM286**

Tabin Wildlife Reserve

Tabin Wildlife Reserve, a government-owned tract of land twice the size of Singapore, holds a single resort managed by a private company. It's around 44km northeast of Lahad Datu airport, where the reserve office is based, of which the last 25km is unsurfaced. Although just eleven percent primary dipterocarp forest, Tabin offers excellent opportunities to see wildlife. Indeed, charismatic manager Fernando argues that Tabin's strength as a habitat is in its combination of primary forest, secondary forest and plantation (which is rich in fruit for animals to eat).

Both **hiking** and **night drives** offer opportunities to come across pygmy elephants, macaques or wild boar as they cross the tracks from the forest to the plantations in search of food; orang-utans can also be spotted, and even the rare clouded leopard. Birdwatchers can look out for such endemic species as the Bornean bristlehead, blue-headed pitta and all eight local species of hornbills.

A visit to Tabin will typically include a walk to a **mud volcano**, used by animals as a mineral lick; a nearby tower allows guests to observe the scene and you can even sleep there by arrangement. Serious trekkers can explore the virgin forest of the Core Area, although this is not part of the normal schedule.

ARRIVAL AND DEPARTURE   **TABIN WILDLIFE RESERVE**

By minivan The resort runs a daily minivan (1hr 15min) from central Lahad Datu.

ACCOMMODATION

★**Tabin Wildlife Resort** ☎088 267 266, ⓦtabinwildlife.com.my. The reserve came under new management in 2008, and has seen a notable upturn in quality. There are rooms beside the river and others on a

hillside; all are comfortable and spacious. The food is excellent, with buffets including a wide range of Western, Malaysian and Asian dishes. 2D/1N package **RM1920**, 3D/2N package **RM2720**

Semporna

Travellers usually only visit the chaotic, traffic-clogged town of **SEMPORNA** because they plan to **scuba dive** and **snorkel** off nearby islands such as **Sipadan**, **Mabul** and **Kapalai**. While some divers base themselves on the islands, particularly Mabul, a **backpacker** scene has developed in Semporna since staying inexpensively can release funds for an extra dive or two. It also gives access to the more northerly islands, not usually visited from Mabul (see p.446).

Semporna broadly consists of three sections: **downtown**, the commercial centre where buses and minivans stop; **Semporna Seafront**, home to dive operators (there are yet more out in the resorts themselves) and most tourist accommodation (plus an ATM in front of the Giant supermarket); and the jetty-lined **Jalan Kastam**, which holds more dive kiosks, a few cafés and the business-oriented *Seafest Hotel*.

ARRIVAL AND DEPARTURE
SEMPORNA

By plane Tawau airport is located between Semporna and Tawau, with buses running direct to Semporna so you don't need to go into Tawau at all.

By bus The main bus terminal is on the same road as the mosque, northwest of the Seafront. Buses operated by Dyana Express (☏ 089 784 494) leave further back from the sea in the downtown area.

Destinations KK (2 daily; 10hr); Lahad Datu (2 daily; 2 hr); Sandakan (2 daily; 5hr); Tawau (5 daily; 1hr 30min).

By minivan Most minivans leave from just beside the main bus terminal, though Tawau services set off from close to KFC, downtown.

Destinations Lahad Datu (daily 7am–5pm; RM29); Tawau (RM15; RM20 to airport).

ACTIVITIES

★ **Scuba Junkie** Block B, Lot 36, Semporna Seafront ☏ 089 785372, ⊚ scuba-junkie.com. This highly regarded outfit runs courses all the way from Discover Scuba Diving to Instructor. They use their excellent Mabul resort as a base for Sipadan trips, while from Semporna you can visit the more northerly islands. Dedicated to environmental protection, the company is staffed by enthusiastic instructors and divemasters. Open Water course RM900, three fun dives RM300, snorkelling trip RM100.

Sipidan Scuba Semporna Seafront ☏ 089 919 128, ⊚ sipidanscuba.com. This well-established and popular dive shop was due to move into a (much needed) new location within the seafront area at the time of research.

ACCOMMODATION

Borneo Global Sipadan Backpackers Jalan Causeway, close to the Seafest Hotel ☏ 089 785 088, ⊚ bgbackpackers.com. A no-nonsense (but none too exciting) backpacker place, 10min walk from the main Seafront area, with private rooms (the cheapest of which have a bunk bed) and eight-bed dorms. They also arrange scuba diving and snorkelling. Dorms **RM20**, rooms **RM50**

Scuba Junkie 36 Semporna Seafront ☏ 089 785 372, ⊚ scuba-junkie.com. This hectic, super-friendly place is a focal point for budget travellers, with a recommended dive shop next door (see above). The rooms are overpriced at the standard rate, but prices are halved for divers, who thus get great value. Dorms **RM40**, rooms **RM110**

Seafest Hotel Jalan Kastam ☏ 089 782 333, ⊚ seafesthotel.com. This imposing concrete block, 10min walk from the main tourist area, is the smartest hotel in town. It's also the only one with a swimming pool; other facilities include a gym and sauna, plus (unreliable) in-room wi-fi. **RM100**

THE SEA GYPSIES

Generations of Muslim Bajau and Suluk peoples have farmed the Celebes and Sulu seas for fish, sea cucumbers, shells and other marine products. Often dubbed **sea gypsies**, these people were originally nomads who lived aboard intricately carved wooden boats called *lepa-lepa*. Most are now settled in Semporna or on the islands around it, but their love of (and dependence upon) the sea remains strong, and the traditional red and yellow sails of the Bajau boats can sometimes still be seen billowing in the breeze. Every April, the Regatta Lepa Semporna (⊚ etawau.com/Semporna/LEPA/LEPA.htm) sees the boats converge on the town for two days. Amid traditional singing and dancing, as well as sea sports and competitions, awards are given for the best *lepa-lepa*.

Sipadan Inn ☎089 781 766, ⓦsipadaninn-hotel
.com. Central mid-range option. Surprisingly classy
common areas lead to small, boxy but clean rooms with
TVs, desks and a/c. Free internet terminals for guests' use
in the reception. RM85

EATING

Anjung Lepa Jalan Kastam ☎089 782 333,
ⓦseafesthotel.com. The outdoor restaurant attached to
the *Seafest Hotel* may be a short walk from the main
Seafront area, but it's worth seeking out. Take a table on
the waterfront terrace, strung with coloured lights, and
pick from an admittedly limited menu while boats drift
past. Daily 4pm–midnight.

Mabul Café and Seafood Restaurant Semporna
Seafront. Popular with foreign visitors partly for its
first-floor location, where you can watch the world go by.
The food is decent enough, but service can be erratic. Daily
11am–11pm.

★ **Scuba Junkie** Semporna Seafront. Now benefiting
from the skills of Kiwi chef Rory, this bar-restaurant is the
number one social hub in town. In keeping with the
company's emphasis on conservation, the restaurant does
not serve fish since local fishing practices are not
sustainable. Live music Friday nights. Daily 4pm–late.

7

Islands around Semporna

Visitors come to Semporna not to hang out in town, but to explore the magnificent
islands offshore. The prime destination for divers is **Pulau Sipadan**, but nearby **Pulau
Mabul** and **Pulau Kapalai** are also renowned for marine life, and the latter in particular
offers great snorkelling.

These well-known islands are, however, just the beginning. **Sibuan**, for example, on
the edge of the chain and just over 45 minutes by boat from Semporna, has a
breathtaking beach and shallow coral reefs. On **Mantubuan** there's amazing pristine
coral and very good visibility – a popular dive is to a section of very rare black coral
(actually white), where you swim through a forest of what resemble underwater
Christmas trees.

Pulau Sipadan

Acclaimed by Jacques Cousteau as "an untouched piece of art", Sipadan is a cornucopia
of marine life, its waters teeming with turtles, moray eels, sharks, barracuda, vast
schools of colourful tropical fish, and a diversity of coral comparable to that at
Australia's Great Barrier Reef.

There is no accommodation on the island and thanks to Sipadan's popularity, a **permit
system** limits the number of divers each day. As a result, dive shops and resorts will
typically require you to dive with them at other islands for three or four days before you
get a day at Sipadan; you should also book **well in advance**. Dive shops regularly take
less experienced divers, but you are likely to enjoy your time here more if you have some
experience and preferably Advanced Open Water certification – there can be fairly
strong drifts and some of the best dives go below 20m. At the very least you should be
sure that you have enough buoyancy control to avoid damaging the coral.

You can also use the same permit to **snorkel** in Sipadan, but it's hard to justify the
huge premium over snorkelling trips to the other islands.

Dive sites

Most of the dozen-plus commonly visited **dive sites** around Sipadan offer the
chance to see abundant turtles and white-tip sharks. The most popular, **Barracuda
Point**, is a drift dive where divers hold onto rocks while shoals of barracuda pass by.
Another great site is the **Drop-off**, close to the jetty, where you often find large
schools of barracuda, bump-head parrot fish and Napoleon wrasse. Close to here is
the entrance to **Turtle Cave**, a watery grave for the skeletal remains of turtles that
have strayed in and become lost; fatal accidents have occurred when divers have
gone in without proper guidance.

Pulau Mabul

Mabul, the chain's largest island, holds the lion's share of **accommodation**. It's evenly split between posh resorts and affordable guesthouses; many of the latter are on the western side of the island, also home to a lively stilt-village inhabited by **Bajau** fisherfolk. Although there's a beach on the eastern side, development means that this is not a very picturesque island and non-divers are not likely to find much to do (other than, perhaps, laze around the more upmarket resorts). Litter is also a major problem on the western side.

Visibility in the water can be 20m or more but it's much less reliable than at Sipadan, particularly from July to September. Actually, though, the **muck diving** – seeking out creatures in the sediment – is famous here. Divemasters tend to prefer Mabul to Sipadan: while the latter has the big-ticket attractions like sharks and turtles, Mabul rewards patience. Among the marine life close to the island are seahorses – including the rare pygmy seahorse – frog fish, cuttlefish, mimic octopus, lion fish, stone fish, ribbon eels, mandarin fish and crocodile fish.

Pulau Kapalai

Little more than a sand bar, tiny **Kapalai** is exquisite and other-wordly. It has room only for one resort and an expensive one at that, although its reef is enjoyed by many visitors who are staying on Mabul. Again, the main attractions are the macro life: divers go looking for pygmy seahorses, harlequin ghost pipefish, frog fish and mandarin fish.

Pulau Pom Pom

The diving at **Pom Pom Island** itself is not the best in the area, but the island is lovely and a real desert-island escape which even has a relatively affordable resort. You also have access to plenty of other islands if diving is your passion.

Pulau Mataking

This great little island had only a single resort at the time of research, though another was under construction. Dive boats come here sometimes, as **Mataking** is renowned for turtles and magnificent rays, as well as interesting hammerhead nudibranchs.

7

ACCOMMODATION   ISLANDS AROUND SEMPORNA

Whether at a posh resort or cheap guesthouse, most accommodation on the islands is on a **package** basis including transport to the island and all meals. Pricing is often quoted per person; other than for dorms the prices listed here are for two people for one night, unless otherwise noted, but single supplements mean that solo travellers pay more than half that price. In many of the more expensive resorts, the nightly price drops significantly after the first night. Very short stays do not, therefore, make financial sense. Almost all accommodation offers **diving for an extra fee**, though less reputable places employ uncertified "dive masters"; ask for proof of qualifications.

MABUL RESORTS

Borneo Divers Mabul Pulau Mabul ☏ 088 222 226, ⓦ borneodivers.info. A very good mid-range choice: fifteen lovely two-room chalets, a small pool, a good wi-fi-equipped restaurant and a fine stretch of beach. *Borneo Divers* is also a very well-established dive operator; you have to stay for four nights to receive a Sipadan permit. Diving package RM1060

★ **Mabul Beach Resort** Pulau Mabul ☏ 089 785 372, ⓦ scuba-junkie.com. Run by Scuba Junkie in Semporna, this is a perfect middle ground between the resorts and the village guesthouses, with its own stretch of public beach but without the price tags of its neighbours. There are

private rooms (both a/c and fan) and dorms, fine buffet food and a bar for post-dive socializing. Discounts are available for divers. Dorms RM80, rooms RM198

Mabul Water Bungalows Pulau Mabul ☏ 088 486 389, ⓦ mabulwaterbungalows.com. The posh sibling of the *Sipidan-Mabul Resort*, with chalets perched on stilts over the sea. The spa is open to the sea, while VIP rooms have their own jacuzzis plus glass-floored living rooms. Check when booking that your balcony faces the sea, not the restaurant. Diver RM5900, non-diver RM3500

Seaventure Just off the coast of Pulau Mabul ☏ 088 261 669, ⓦ seaventuresdive.com. They may have painted this place bright colours, but that doesn't disguise the fact that it's an oil rig and a bit of an eyesore. It is, nevertheless, popular with divers. Three-day two night package prices do not include equipment rental. Diver RM2900, non-diver RM2300

Sipadan Water Village Pulau Mabul ☎ 089 752 996, ⊕ swvresort.com. While marginally less plush than the rival *Mabul Water Bungalows*, it's a good deal cheaper and is still a lovely kampung-style resort. Chalets are built to Bajau design, and the big verandas are particularly good. Massage is available from 2–10pm at RM120/hr. Diver RM1550, non-diver RM1320

Sipadan-Mabul Resort (aka SMART) Pulau Mabul ☎ 088 486 389, ⊕ sipadan-mabul.com.my. This well-run resort boasts more than forty wooden en-suite chalets, a swimming pool and a very good restaurant. They have a good dive shop with some unusual offerings such as photography tuition and trips into Turtle Cave (see p.446). Diver RM3892, non-diver RM2584

MABUL GUESTHOUSES

★ **Arung Hayat Resort** Kampung Bajau, Pulau Mabul ☎ 012 822 9984, ⊕ sipadanadventures.com. This longhouse on stilts has 13 compact, neat rooms and a dive shop; at time of research they were building two eight-bed dorms. They were also planning to operate a budget live-aboard dive boat. There are discounts on the accommodation for divers. Dorm package RM60, room package RM160

Lai's Homestay Kampung Bajau, Pulau Mabul ☎ 089 685 399 or ☎ 014 284 2723. A very basic guesthouse close to *Uncle Chang's*. The bedrooms aren't anything special, and neither are the shared bathrooms, but the food is tasty and Big John's dive shop is popular. They also have free wi-fi. Fan room package RM160, a/c room package RM220

Seahorse Sipadan Scuba Kampung Bajau, Pulau Mabul ☎ 089 782 289, ⊕ seahorsesipadanscuba.com. While not flashy, the rooms at this new place are decent enough for the price. They have a dive shop. Fan room package RM160

Uncle Chang's Backpacker Lodge Kampung Bajau, Pulau Mabul ☎ 017 895 002, ⊕ ucsipadan.com. Always-busy backpacker favourite, perched on stilts over the sea,

with shabby dorms and basic private rooms. The shared bathrooms are not so clean. The diving is cheap, but there are varying reports as to the quality of the rental equipment and of the experience overall. Dorm package RM60, room package RM160

KAPALAI

Sipadan-Kapalai Resort Pulau Kapulai; run by Pulau Sipadan Resort and Tours, 484 Bandar Sabindo, Tawau ☎ 089 765 200, ⊕ sipadan-kapalai.com. Spectacular chalets built on stilts, and shallow azure water that's perfect for snorkelling. Boats take divers to nearby Sipadan and Mabul, although there is also good diving on the artificial house reef. 3D/2N package divers RM4000, non-divers RM3200

POM POM

★ **Celebes Beach Resort** Pulau Pom Pom ☎ 089 782 828, ⊕ celebesscuba.com. This down-to-earth (and relatively affordable) resort was the second to open on Pom Pom. The ten a/c rooms are simple white concrete boxes, but surprisingly well furnished (ask for one with a sea view). Dive packages include unlimited shore dives as well as three boat dives/day. Diving package RM1280, non-diving package RM940

Pom Pom Island Resort Pulau Pom Pom; Office: Block B, Seafest Fishery Complex, Jalan Causeway ☎ 089 781 918, ⊕ pompomisland.com. Arriving at the jetty here on a sunny day – with clear blue sea to both sides, pale sands ahead and chalets both on stilts and on the beach – is a truly memorable experience. It's a delightful resort, with some environmental credentials. There's also a spa and a dive shop (from RM117/dive plus RM105 equipment rental/day). RM2100

MATAKING

Reef Dive Resort Pulau Mataking ☎ 089 782 080, ⊕ mataking.com. Attractive and spacious luxury development, with appealing rooms, friendly staff and facilties including a spa and jacuzzi. The dive shop is consistently praised by guests and the snorkelling is great. Note that it's much cheaper to arrange diving in advance rather than once you arrive. RM1200

Tawau

The only town of any size in southeast Sabah, **TAWAU** is growing quickly and losing its previous Chinese character. While most travellers don't even give the town a nod, as they head straight from the airport to Semporna, it does see a steady trickle of foreign visitors as the only gateway into **Kalimantan** from Sabah. Central Tawau is a heady mixture of polluting vehicles and sprawling, chaotic **markets**; of these the most interesting are the clothes and trinket stalls beside the *Soon Yee Hotel* and the markets around the wharf.

7

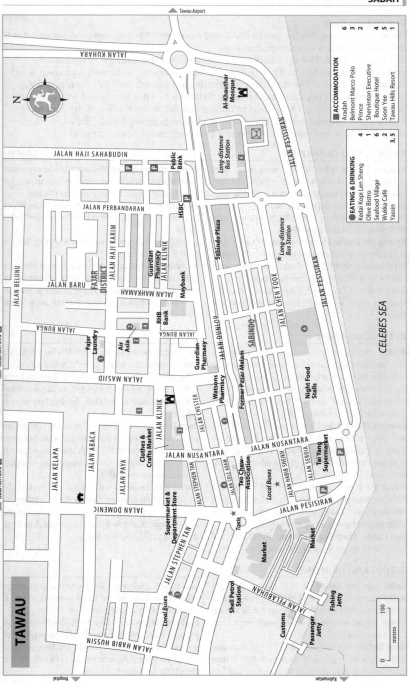

TAWAU

0 — 100 metres

▲ Tawau Airport

CELEBES SEA

◄ Kalimantan

◄ Hospital

■ ACCOMMODATION	
Aradah	6
Belmont Marco Polo	3
Prince	2
Shervinton Executive Boutique Hotel	4
Soon Yee	5
Tawau Hills Resort	1

● EATING & DRINKING	
Kedai Kopi Len Sheng	4
Olive Bistro	1
Seafood Village	6
Wukka Café	2
Yassin	3, 5

JALAN KUHARA

JALAN HAJI SAHABUDIN

JALAN PERBANDARAN

JALAN BARU

FAJAR DISTRICT

JALAN BELUNU

JALAN BUNGA

JALAN HAJI KARIM

JALAN MAKAMAHA

JALAN MASJID

JALAN KELAPA

JALAN ABACA

JALAN PAYA

JALAN DOMENIC

JALAN NUSANTARA

JALAN KLINIK

JALAN CHESTER

JALAN STEPHEN TAN

JALAN COLE ADAM

JALAN HABIB SHEIKH

JALAN SEROIA

JALAN NUSANTARA

JALAN CHEN FOOK

JALAN DUNLOP

JALAN PESISIRAN

JALAN PESISIRAN

JALAN HABIB HUSSIN

JALAN STEPHEN TAN

JALAN PELABUHAN

Al-Khauthar Mosque

Long-distance Bus Station

Public Bank

HSBC

Guardian Pharmacy

Maybank

RHB Bank

Guardian Pharmacy

Air Asia

Fajar Laundry

Watsons Pharmacy

Former Pasar Malam

Night Food Stalls

Sabindo Plaza

SABINDO

Long-distance Bus Station

Clothes & Crafts Market

Teo Chew Association

Local Buses

Tai Yang Supermarket

Supermarket & Department Store

Taxis

Local Buses

Shell Petrol Station

Market

Market

Customs

Passenger Jetty

Fishing Jetty

Tawau Hills Park

An hour's drive north of town • Daily 7am–6pm • Entry RM10, guide RM30 • ☎ 089 925 719 • No bus; taxi RM30 one-way; vehicles back to Tawau can be scarce, so ask for a return price including waiting

The hard-to-reach 270-square-kilometre **Tawau Hills Park**, a stretch of lowland rainforest with the Tawau River cutting through its centre, is the only attraction worth visiting near Tawau. The thirty-minute **Bombalai** trail leads up a hill from park HQ, but the main trail is a three-hour hike up **Gelas Hill** to a hot spring and waterfall that's perfect for swimming. Open close to the start, as the lower reaches of the park have been logged, the trail continues through thick, damp, mossy forest. The park authorities have built shelters, toilets and changing rooms at the waterfall.

ARRIVAL AND DEPARTURE   TAWAU

By plane MAS and AirAsia fly from Tawau's airport, 30km east of the centre. AirAsia has an office on the first floor. Small buses run to Tawau (6 daily), taxis cost RM38; buses and minivans also run east to Semporna.
Destinations KK (4 daily; 50min); Kuala Lumpur (5 daily; 2hr 40min); Sandakan (2 daily; 40min).

By long-distance bus Some long-distance buses (and the airport buses) use the bus station in a square at the eastern end of Tawau's main street, Jalan Dunlop, while others depart from the ticket offices on Jalan Chen Hock nearby.
Destinations KK (daily; 9hr); Lahad Datu (hourly; 2hr); Sandakan (daily; 5hr 30min); Semporna (frequent; 1hr 30min).

By minivan or local bus Minivans to Semporna run from Sabindo Square; local buses stopped on Jalan Stephen Tan at the time of research but were due to be relocated.

By ferry Ferries from Indonesia arrive at Customs Wharf, Jalan Pelabuhan, 150m south of Jalan Dunlop's Shell petrol station.
Destinations Nunakan (3 weekly; 1hr 30min); Tarakan (Mon-Sat daily; 3hr 30min).

By 4WD While uncomfortable and not cheap, the route from Tawau to Keningau by 4WD (departure by arrangement; 8hr; RM100–150 per person) is quite an experience. The main reason to venture this way is to visit the Maliau Basin (5hr).

ACCOMMODATION

Aradah 50 Sabindo Square (outer edge) ☎089 775 222. Small hotel, tucked away close to the mosque and the post office, that's also convenient for the bus stations. The fourteen rooms are sparsely furnished with dark wood furniture but have flat-screen TVs, and are certainly better than most at their price point. RM60

Belmont Marco Polo Jalan Stephen Tan ☎089 777 988. Classy address, with large and well-furnished a/c rooms, a friendly bar and a fitness centre. The more expensive rooms are higher up, to take advantage of the views. Free wi-fi. RM175

Prince 208 Jalan Bunga ☎089 778 989. Formerly the First Hotel, renovated and reopened in 2010, this is a good mid-range choice. Bedrooms have mood lighting and bold wallpaper, and there's a spa. Free wi-fi. RM88

Shervinton Executive Boutique Hotel 224–227 Jalan Bunga ☎089 770 000, ⓦshervintonhotel.com.

The standard rooms here are windowless but still packed with features such as purple "velvet" desk chairs and glass coffee tables. The laquer sinks in the bathrooms are pretty cool too; the junior suite has a spa bath with a window into the bedroom (and Venetian blinds). Ask about promotions. RM200

Soon Yee 1362 Jalan Stephan Tan ☎089 772447. The best budget spot; most rooms share bathrooms but a few are en suite. It might be a bit rough around the edges but owner Joseph makes up for it by being happy to impart advice and information. RM28

Tawau Hills Resort Park HQ, Tawau Hills Park ☎019 581 2600. A large block contains basic dorms, but there are also more comfortable four-bed chalets. An on-site canteen serves up simple dishes, charging RM30 for three meals. Dorms RM20, chalets RM70

EATING AND DRINKING

Kedai Kopi Len Sheng 92 Jalan Chester. The signs declare that it sells Mongolian Chicken Rice, though there's nothing particularly Mongolian about the dish. That aside, it's very popular with locals and well worth seeking out. Daily 8am–3.30pm.

Olive Bistro Jalan Masjid ☎089 770 093. Appealing restaurant, with a quiet jazz soundtrack and Western dishes including pizza and pasta plus twists on local fare

such as garlic chicken rice. The *kerabu mango* (a mango salad with peanuts and Thai sauce) makes for a tasty, if sour, starter. Daily noon–9pm.

Seafood Village Jalan Chen Hock. Considered a little pricey by locals, this food court is still very popular. The stalls on the main road are Chinese, and therefore serve alcohol, while the Malay eateries such as *Restoran 101* are closer to the sea. Daily 4.30–11pm.

★ **Wukka Café** 8 Bangunan MAA, Fajar Complex ⓦ wukkacafe.com. Cute little café with gingham drapes and a focus on Korean dishes including a tasty *bibimbap* (rice, veg, meat, chilli and an egg served in a hot bowl). To complete the Korean experience, you can sit on a cushion at a low table if you like. The menu also includes pasta and other Western food, and there are cake and ice-cream counters. Daily noon–10pm.

Yassin Branches on Jalan Dunlop and Jalan Chester. Indian café with curries, rotis and *murtabak*. The Jalan Chester branch has the more extensive menu, but most popular in both is the *nasi biriyani*, rice served with chicken, beef or mutton. The fish-head curry is another speciality. Daily 6.30am–10pm.

Maliau Basin

Sabah's last true wilderness, and one of the world's oldest rainforests, the **MALIAU BASIN CONSERVATION AREA** (ⓦ borneoforestheritage.org.my) remains barely explored; most visitors are scientists or researchers. Featuring various types of forest including lower montane, heath and dipterocarp, the basin is home to an impressive range of large mammals, notably the Borneo pygmy elephant, clouded leopard, Malayan sun bear and banteng (wild cattle), while birds include rare species found otherwise only at Gunung Kinabalu and Gunung Trus Madi.

To visit you must be on a **tour**, for which Borneo Nature Tours (five-day tours RM4575 per person, or RM3969 in larger groups; ☎ 088 267 637, ⓦ borneonaturetours.com) are the sole providers. The standard five-day itinerary starts at Tawau, a five-hour drive from the park, and includes long and strenuous hikes suitable only for the fit. You'll need a doctor's certificate to prove this, plus insurance that covers helicopter evacuation. The itinerary follows a circular route, spending the first and last night in dorms at the spartan *Agathis Camp* close to the park entrance, and the rest at the similarly basic *Nepenthes* (aka *Camel Trophy*) *Camp*, six hours' walk deeper. Also included are night drives and a side-trip to the Maliau Falls.

Brunei

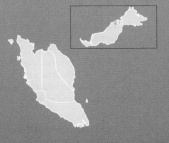

OMAR ALI SAIFUDDIEN MOSQUE

Brunei

A tiny oil-rich monarchy that seems, superficially, more Middle Eastern than Southeast Asian, the enigmatic country of BRUNEI intrigues visitors. Its official title is Negara Brunei Darussalam, Darussalam meaning "Abode of Peace" – and tranquil it certainly is, with little crime and a sense of calm, bordering on ennui, thanks to the income generated by massive offshore oil and gas deposits. The 400,000 inhabitants – two-thirds Malay, a tenth Chinese, nearly a fifth expatriates and foreign workers, and just a few percent indigenous peoples – enjoy a cosseted existence. While the genuinely wealthy elite form a select few, there's a large middle class; education and healthcare are free; and houses, cars and even pilgrimages to Mecca are subsidized.

Brunei's sultan, **Hassanal Bolkiah** (see p.458), is famously one of the world's richest men. Ruling as an absolute monarch, he is prime minister, defence minister and finance minister rolled into one, and his extended family, the Bolkiahs, control virtually all government departments and the vast majority of the nation's wealth; it's said that nothing of any real importance is decided without the thumbs-up from a family member.

This is, however, no glitzy Gulf sheikhdom. Brunei is basically low-rise and low-key, feeling not unlike Malaysia's oil-rich state of Terengganu, only more relaxed and with more discernible signs of wealth. Primary and secondary tropical forest still cover seventy percent of the land area; indeed the country's boundaries are easily discerned from the air, as Sarawak's logging roads and oil-palm plantations halt as if by magic at the border. Most of Brunei is less than 150m above sea level, its rainforest, peat swamp and heath forest running down to sandy beaches and mangrove swamps. The country is divided into four districts: **Muara**, which contains the capital, **Bandar Seri Begawan**; agricultural **Tutong**; oil-rich **Belait**; and **Temburong**, a sparsely populated enclave severed from the rest of Brunei by Sarawak's Limbang district.

For most travellers, Brunei is simply a transit zone on the long bus ride between Miri and Kota Kinabalu. Those who stay seldom do so for more than two or three nights, long enough to glimpse the main sights and the way of life without the cost of living – much higher than in Malaysia – creating too much of a dent in their bank account. Conveniently, the capital is home to many of the key attractions, notably the fascinating **Kampung Ayer**, a rambling collection of houses built over the wide Brunei River, and offers one of the best chances to see **proboscis monkeys** in all of Borneo. The other big attraction is the pristine rainforest in **Ulu Temburong National Park** in Temburong, though this is a much more sanitized experience than any Malaysian national park, with few trails to explore. Otherwise, the sultanate holds some interesting Islamic architecture; a clutch of moderately interesting museums, beaches, small nature parks and modern longhouses; and one solitary nod to Dubai-style excess – a hotel/country club, the *Empire*, that's worth seeing for its ludicrous grandiosity.

ULU TEMBURONG NATIONAL PARK

Highlights

❶ Kampung Ayer This scenic collection of wooden houses, built out over the Brunei River, offers a glimpse of traditional life. **See p.461**

❷ The Royal Regalia Building One of Brunei's most entertaining museums, housing processional chariots, ceremonial paraphernalia and offbeat official gifts. **See p.461**

❸ Proboscis monkeys Just minutes from downtown by boat, a group of these curious-looking creatures can usually be seen foraging by the river. **See p.465**

❹ The Empire Hotel Come to witness how a royal folly with a cavernous marble atrium now functions as a successful hotel, then hang around for a bite. **See p.470**

❺ Ulu Temburong National Park Brunei's premier nature reserve holds a heart-stopping canopy walkway and opportunities for river rafting and tubing. **See p.471**

HIGHLIGHTS ARE MARKED ON THE MAP ON P.456

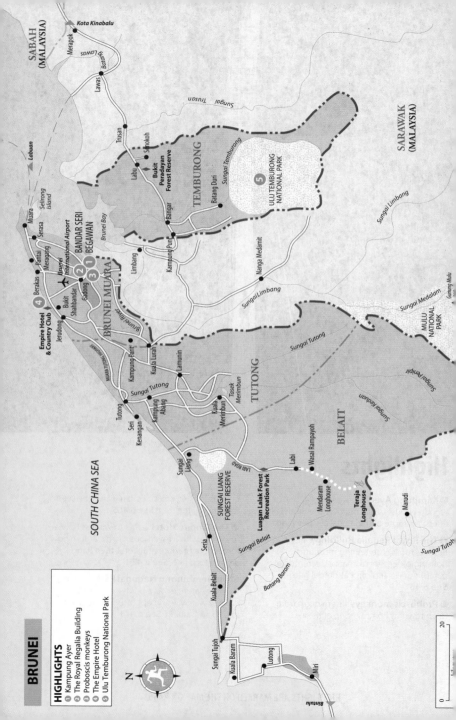

GETTING TO BRUNEI

By plane Bandar's airport has flights from Kota Kinabalu, Kuala Lumpur, Kuching and Singapore, and reasonable connections with cities elsewhere in the region and further afield. Royal Brunei's long-standing Kuching flight had been dropped at the time of writing, though another airline may step in to fill the gap.

By bus Reaching Brunei by bus is easy. A couple of daily services run to Bandar from Miri in Sarawak, via the coastal towns of Kuala Belait and Seria, and from Kota Kinabalu in Sabah. Daily buses also run all the way from Pontianak in western Kalimantan.

By boat Muara, Bandar's port, is served by boats from Labuan and from Lawas in Sarawak.

GETTING AROUND

By car Brunei is small enough to visit most towns as day-trips from the capital. However, the bus system is indifferent, so renting a car is the ideal way to explore. It's not overly expensive, starting at B$80 a day and with fuel cheap.

ESSENTIALS

Money The Brunei dollar (also called the ringgit in Malay) has the same value as the Singapore dollar, widely used in Brunei.

Opening hours Brunei has a split weekend as far as government bodies are concerned: Fridays and Sundays are days off. Some private businesses follow government hours, while others work Monday to Friday with a half-day on Saturday.

Alcohol Brunei is famously dry, though tourists are permitted to bring two bottles of liquor and twelve cans of beer for private consumption – ie not in a public place. That said, those Chinese restaurants that serve pork just might have a stash of beer or wine discreetly available to diners, perhaps unceremoniously poured out of a teapot.

Brief history

The Brunei of today is just the rump of a vast, powerful sultanate that was gradually gobbled up by the Brookes' regime in Sarawak in the nineteenth century. Trade was the powerhouse behind its growth. Tang and Sung dynasty coins and ceramics, found a few kilometres from Bandar Seri Begawan suggest that China was trading with Brunei as early as the seventh century. Brunei subsequently benefited from its strategic position on the trade route between India, Melaka and China, and exercised a lucrative control over merchant traffic in the South China Sea. As well as being a staging post, where traders could stock up on supplies and offload cargo, Brunei was by the fourteenth century commercially active in its own right; the *nakhoda*, or Bruneian sea traders, traded local produce such as camphor, rattan and brassware for ceramics, spices, woods and fabrics.

The Brunei Sultanate

Islam had begun to make inroads into Bruneian society by the mid-fifteenth century, a process accelerated when wealthy Muslim merchant families decamped to Brunei after Melaka fell to the Portuguese in 1511. Brunei was certainly an Islamic sultanate by the time its first **European visitors** arrived from Spain in 1521. Commonly acknowledged as the sultanate's golden age, this period saw its territory and influence stretch as far as the modern-day Philippines.

However, things turned sour towards the close of the sixteenth century. Following a sea battle in 1578, Spain took the capital, only to reliquish it days later due to a cholera epidemic. The threat of piracy caused more problems, scaring off passing trade. Worse still, factional struggles loosened the sultan's control at home.

With the arrival of **James Brooke** (see p.319) in 1839, the sultanate was to shrink steadily as he siphoned off its territory to neighbouring Sarawak. This trend culminated when Charles Brooke's capture of the Limbang region split Brunei in two. By 1888, the British had declared Brunei a **protected state**, meaning responsibility for its foreign affairs lay with London.

The twentieth century and beyond

The start of the twentieth century was marked by the **discovery of oil**, which drove the British to set up a Residency in 1906. By 1931 the **Seria oil field** was on stream, but the

THE SULTAN OF BRUNEI

Brunei's head of state, **Sultan Hassanal Bolkiah** (whose full title is 31 words long), is the 29th in a line stretching back six hundred years. Educated in Malaysia and Britain, he has been sultan since 1967, following the voluntary abdication of his father Omar.

Hassanal Bolkiah was once deemed the world's richest man, though today a conservative estimate of his net worth, at a mere US$20 billion, would put him only in the top 30 of *Forbes'* list of billionaires, behind the king of Thailand. Tales of his extravagance are legion – of private jets festooned with palatial touches such as gold bathroom fittings, for example. However the sultan takes pains to live down that persona by cultivating an image of accessibility. Brunei's highly compliant press is full of stories of his majesty's presence at community events – the launching of a new school, say – and for two days a year, at Hari Raya Aidilfitri, the sultan throws open the Istana Nurul Iman to the public, with tens of thousands standing in line for hours to meet him and other members of the royal family.

The sultan defined the philosophy underlying his rule when, in the 1990s, he introduced an ideology called Melayu Islam Beraja, essentially that the monarchy is founded on the twin pillars of Islam and Malayness. There are few signs of participatory democracy, however. In 2004 the sultan reconvened Brunei's **legislative assembly**, two decades after it was suspended, using appointed members. They voted to enlarge the assembly to include up to fifteen elected members, but no elections have so far taken place.

Japanese invasion of 1941 temporarily halted Brunei's path to prosperity. As in Sabah, Allied bombing during the occupation that followed left much rebuilding to be done.

While Sabah, Sarawak and Labuan became Crown Colonies in the early postwar years, Brunei remained a British protectorate. The British Residency was finally withdrawn in 1959, and a new constitution established, with provisions for a democratically elected legislative council. At the same time, Sultan Omar Ali Saifuddien (the present sultan's father) was careful to retain British involvement in defence and foreign affairs – a move whose sagacity was made apparent when, in 1962, an attempted coup led by Sheik Azahari's pro-democratic **Brunei People's Party** was crushed by British Army Gurkhas. Ever since the failed coup, which stemmed from Omar's refusal to convene the first sitting of the legislative council, the sultan has ruled by decree in his role as an unelected prime minister, and emergency powers have been in place. Despite showing interest in joining the new Malaysian Federation in 1963, Brunei chose to opt out rather than risk losing its oil wealth and compromising the pre-eminence of its monarchy; not until 1984 did it cease to be a British protectorate and become fully independent.

Little scrutinized by the outside world, modern Brunei charts an unruffled course, though there's no clear sense how the country plans to cope when its oil runs out in a couple of decades, and even fairly well-educated young people find it hard to find jobs. The sultanate retains close ties with the UK and, regionally, especially with Singapore. Relations with Malaysia, by no means poor, look set to become yet warmer following a 2009 pact. Details remain sketchy, but Brunei is said to have given up its claims to the **Limbang** district of Sarawak, while Malaysia conceded its claim to certain offshore oil fields, and offered to help Brunei exploit them. The fruits of the agreement are already being seen elsewhere: the two countries are jointly working on yet another Sarawakian **dam**, in Limbang, apparently to supply power to Brunei, and a new bridge is being created over the **Pandaruan River** to link Limbang and Temburong, eliminating the present ferry crossing.

Bandar Seri Begawan

BANDAR SERI BEGAWAN (known locally as **Bandar** or **BSB**) feels more like a provincial town than a capital. It is also a newish, largely postwar city, dominated by drab concrete – until comparatively recently, the seat of power and main settlement was

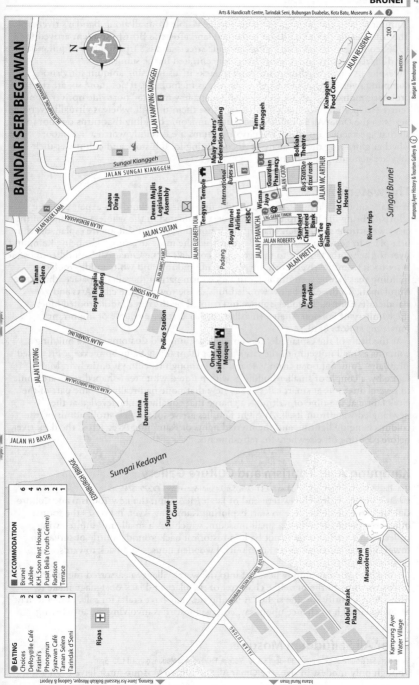

BANDAR SERI BEGAWAN

Arts & Handicraft Centre, Tarindak Seni, Bubungan Duabelas, Kota Batu, Museums & ⑦

N

0   100   200
metres

Bangar & Temburong ▶

Kampung Ayer History & Tourism Gallery & ①

EATING
Choices	3
DeRoy@lle Café	2
Fratini's	6
Phongmun	5
Syazwan Café	4
Taman Selera	1
Tarindak d'Seni	7

ACCOMMODATION
Brunei	3
Jubilee	2
K.H. Soon Rest House	6
Pusat Belia (Youth Centre)	5
Radisson	4
Terrace	1

JALAN KAMPUNG KIANGGEH

JALAN KAMPUNG BATU

JALAN TASEK LAMA

JALAN BENDAHARA

Sungai Kianggeh

JALAN SUNGAI KIANGGEH

Lapau
Diraja

Dewan Majlis
Legislative Assembly

Malay Teachers'
Federation Building

Tamu
Kianggeh

JALAN SULTAN

Tengyun Temple

International
Buses

Bolkiah
Theatre

Guardian
Pharmacy

Kianggeh
Food Court

JALAN RESIDENCY

JALAN ELIZABETH DUA

Royal Brunei
Airlines

Padang

JALAN PEMANCHA

Wisma
Jaya

JALAN CATOR

Bus Station
& taxi rank

JALAN MC ARTHUR

LRG GERAI TIMOR

HSBC

Standard
Chartered
Bank

JALAN ROBERTS

Glok Tee
Building

JALAN PRETTY

Old Custom
House

River trips

Sungai Brunei

JALAN JAMES PEARCE

Royal Regalia
Building

JALAN STONEY

Taman
Selera

JALAN TUTONG

JALAN SUMBILING

Police Station

JALAN ISTANA DARUSSALAM

Omar Ali
Saifuddien
Mosque

Yayasan
Complex

Istana
Darussalem

JALAN HJ BASIR

EDINBURGH BRIDGE

Sungai Kedayan

Supreme
Court

Ripas

Abdul Razak
Plaza

Royal
Mausoleum

Kampung Ayer
Water Village

LEBUHRAYA SULTAN HASSANIL BOLKIAH

JALAN TUTONG

Istana Nurul Iman ▼

Kiarong, Jame Asr Hassanil Boitkiah Mosque, Gadong & Airport ▼

8

Kampung Ayer, the picturesque water village visible from all along Bandar's riverbank. The commercial centre, built on reclaimed land after the British Resident arrived in 1906, comprises a mere handful of riverside streets and is surprisingly tranquil, not to say dull; recent development has been concentrated in the suburbs.

Despite its underwhelming air, Bandar packs in a surprising amount for visitors. **Kampung Ayer** is the obvious sight, but just as memorable, if not more so, are the **proboscis monkeys** that live in woodland just a few minutes' boat ride upriver from the centre (see p.464). Not many tourists glimpse them though, whereas virtually everyone heads to the **Omar Ali Saifuddien mosque** – an iconic building that turns out not to be all that spectacular up close. The city's **museums** are certainly worth a look, too; whether glorifying the sultanate or documenting local history and culture, at their best they are genuinely enlightening.

The waterfront

Bandar's suburbs having long grabbed the limelight at downtown's expense, recent efforts to bring life back to the centre have culminated in the wholesale revamp of the city's **waterfront** along Jalan Macarthur. It now boasts a half-kilometre esplanade, the best place to get your bearings in Bandar, with the most arresting sight being **Kampung Ayer** to the south. Upriver to the west, but concealed, the Omar Ali Saifuddien mosque is set back from the river; both the golden onion dome and white saddle-roofed building that can be seen in the far distance form part of the sultan's palace, the **Istana Nurul Iman**. To the east, below wooded hills, is the tower of the city's **Arts and Handicrafts Centre**, the foliage above interrupted by the three saddle-roofed blocks of the Ministry of Foreign Affairs. Invisible further east are a couple of important museums at **Kota Batu**.

At the heart of the esplanade, the simple low-slung old **Customs House** building contains a small museum of the city's development (daily 9am–5pm except Fri closed 11.30am–2pm, Sat open from 9.45am; free), though labelling is entirely in Malay. Close by, a couple of smaller buildings with pointed white tent-shaped roofs are home to several attempts at smart cafés, all so new that none had really become part of the city's fabric at the time of writing – a charge that equally can be levelled at the newfangled waterfront itself. At night families arrive for a quick stroll, admiring the colour-changing lighting and the myriad lights of Kampung Ayer across the dark river, before scooting off elsewhere for refreshments.

Kampung Ayer Tourism and Culture Gallery

Mon–Thurs & Sun 9am–5pm, Fri 9–11.30am & 2.30–5pm, Sat 9.45am–5pm • Free • ☎ 220 0874

Clearly visible facing the eastern end of Jalan McArthur, the new **Tourism and Culture Gallery** is the obvious place to start exploring Kampung Ayer. It houses the **tourist office** (see p.464) as well as a small museum, which has a small and uninteresting collection of artefacts but is not bad on historical background. A little **observation tower** offers good views over the colourful wooden houses and back towards downtown.

From here you can simply head off into the water village via assorted meandering walkways, though the mazelike character of the place and lack of signage make it difficult to identify specific sights. A few homes may have crafts for sale, and you may be lucky enough to chance upon, say, cottage industries involving rattan-weaving.

Omar Ali Saifuddien Mosque

Mon–Wed, Sat & Sun 8.30am–noon, 1.30–3pm & 4.30–5.30pm, Thurs open to Muslims only, Fri 4.30–5pm

Though only modest in size, the **Omar Ali Saifuddien Mosque** must have been a

KAMPUNG AYER

While neighbouring Malaysia still holds a few water villages, notably in Kota Kinabalu, none can match Bandar's **Kampung Ayer** for size. Practically a small town by itself, it snakes downriver for 2km beyond the city centre and upriver for another 1km or so, as well as up the Kedayan tributary of the river to the Edinburgh Bridge. Timber houses built on stilts and piles have occupied this stretch of the Brunei River for hundreds of years, and Kampung Ayer's historical significance cannot be underestimated. A census in 1911 showed that nearly half Brunei's population lived here, including the sultan, whose long-vanished palace was a suitably souped-up wooden affair.

Today the area comprises several villages with their own shops, clinics, mosques, schools and fire services, minus fire engines, of course. They also have electricity and mains water, but many houses remain unconnected to the sewerage system, which seems not to deter the boys who swim in the river. While residents are content with their lot, insofar as they have stayed put rather than move to dry land, the authorities are intent on tinkering with Kampung Ayer. They have recently embarked on a project to build several dozen non-timber homes in the area, boasting solar panels and billed as eco-friendly, and they continue to extend sanitation to the villages. There's also talk of action to arrest the decline in village traditions, notably crafts; one plan is to market Kampung Ayer as an "artisanal village" to showcase what trades linger, for example silversmithing and boat-building, though it's not clear when this might be put into effect. See p.464 for details of *boat trips* around the water villages.

marvellous sight when completed in 1958. Topped by a 52m-high dome, it would have dominated what was then very much a small town, and is beautifully located on the edge of a circular lagoon. The decision to plonk the modern Yayasan Complex of shops just southeast has done it no favours, however, and the mosque is now at that awkward in-between age where it looks neither gleaming new nor venerable, merely a bit grimy in places. Still, the mosque, commissioned by and named after the father of the present sultan, makes tasteful use of opulent fittings – Italian marble, granite from Shanghai, Arabian and Belgian carpets, and English chandeliers and stained glass. The lagoon holds a replica of a sixteenth-century royal barge, or *mahligai*, used on special religious occasions.

Royal Regalia Building

Jalan Sultan • Mon–Thurs, Sat & Sun 9am–4.30pm, Fri 9–11.30am & 2.30–4.30pm • Free • ☎ 222 8358

In addition to a handful of dispensable museums, downtown Bandar holds one that is simply essential – the **Royal Regalia Building**, easy to pick out as its roof is shaped like a strange domed helmet. While the name might lead you to expect a dry costume collection, it's a simply hilarious collection of regal paraphernalia whose subtext is to serve as a massive paean to the sultan. Perhaps the most significant objects are those used during his coronation, including the *tongkat aja* – a model of a human arm in gold, used to support the royal chin during the ceremony, which took place just across the road in the grand-looking Lapau Diraja building. Most visitors get an even bigger kick out of two massive **chariots**, one used for the coronation, the other for his highness's silver jubilee in 1992, the throng on the day recreated by dozens of mannequins in aristocratic Malay dress. Elsewhere there's an eccentric display of gifts the Brunei royals have been lumbered with, courtesy of blue-blooded intimates and world statesmen – replica temples made of crystal and the like.

Tamu Kianggeh

Jalan Sungai Kianggeh • Daily dawn to dusk

Half a century ago, Bandar still had *padian* – women traders who would hawk their produce from boats in and around Kampung Ayer, rather as women still do in Thailand's floating markets. Their role was gradually usurped by the central produce market, **Tamu Kianggeh**, alongside the canalized Kianggeh creek. The *tamu* sells everything from machetes to *midin* – nothing you can't see in markets in Sarawak or Sabah, but entertaining all the same. Friday morning is the busiest, and thus the best, time to turn up.

Arts and Handicrafts Centre

Jalan Residency, just over five minutes' walk east of Tamu Kianggeh • Mon–Thurs, Sat & Sun 9am–4.30pm, Fri 9–11.30am & 2.30–4.30pm • Free • ☎ 224 0676

Bandar's **Arts and Handicrafts Centre** is a substantial complex where young Bruneians are taught traditional skills such as weaving, brass-casting and the crafting of the *kris*, the traditional Malay dagger. Unfortunately classes are not generally open to public view without prior arrangement, so you'll have to make do with browsing the pricey **gift shop**. The other reason to visit is to enjoy classic Bruneian food at their restaurant, *Tarindak d'Seni* (see p.468).

Bubongan Duabelas

On Jalan Residency, 1.5km southeast of Tamu Kianggeh • Mon–Thurs, Sat & Sun 9am–4.30pm, Fri 9–11.30am & 2.30–4.30pm • Free • ☎ 222 6937 • Bus #39 or a water taxi; if the boatman doesn't know the house, ask to be let off at Bukit Subok nearby

Brunei's lingering ties with the UK are enshrined at the **Bubongan Duabelas**. Up a signed turning on a leafy hillside, it was built in 1907 as the bungalow home of the British Resident, who arrived the year before, then housed the High Commissioner until independence in 1984. The two-layered, multi-eaved roof gives the house its name – "twelve roofs", in the local Malay dialect – but there's no obvious connection with the number twelve. Stripped of original furnishings, and thus any colonial atmosphere, when it became a museum, the building is most memorable for the numerous photos of the sultan hanging out with British royals over the years. That rapport feeds through in unexpected ways in Brunei, where you'll see highway posters exhorting people to use Malay' more – many locals, not just the Chinese, are far more comfortable with English.

The museums at Kota Batu

It's fitting that Brunei's main **museums** should be a little way east of the centre at **Kota Batu**, the site of the capital when the Brunei sultanate was at its height. The area was excavated in the early 1950s by Tom Harrisson, who was instrumental in uncovering so many aspects of Sarawak's history and culture. A few old walls aside, however, this largely wooded area, close to the river, holds scant signs of former habitation.

Brunei Museum

Jalan Kota Batu, 4km east of the centre • Sun–Thurs 9am–5pm, Fri 9–11.30am & 2.30–5pm, Sat 9.45am–5pm; Ramadan daily 9am–3pm (Fri until noon); closed religious holidays • Free • ☎ 224 4545 • Bus #11 or #39

An old-school non-interactive affair occupying a charmless hunk of 1970s concrete, the **Brunei Museum** has a few worthwhile sections where you could happily while away an hour or two. Skip the mediocre petroleum and natural history galleries on the ground floor in favour of the **Islamic art gallery**. While sadly this makes no attempt to put its contents into historical context, the selection of Levantine, Persian and Mughal artefacts such as kilims, illuminated Korans and inlaid boxes is exquisite at times. Most of the collection belongs to the sultan and his relations; indeed a special display highlights a handwritten manuscript of the Koran's opening surah by the sultana herself, though the illumination around it is rather finer than the calligraphy. Upstairs, the **traditional culture gallery** is the highlight, with its dioramas of village life and some great examples of *bedil* and *meriam* – carved cannon bearing crocodile and dragon-like naga heads, their jaws forming the muzzle. The **archeology and history gallery** rewards a quick look too, offering a neat recap of Brunei's glory days at Kota Batu and its near-obliteration in the nineteenth century.

Malay Technology Museum

Jalan Kota Batu, 4km east of the centre • Sun–Thurs 9am–5pm, Fri 9–11.30am & 2.30–5pm, Sat 9.45am–5pm; Ramadan daily 9am–3pm (Fri until noon); closed religious holidays • Free • ☎ 224 4545 • Bus #11 or #39

Right by the Brunei River, the endearingly misnamed but surprisingly good **Malay Technology Museum** focuses not on kampung-built MP3 players but on traditional lifestyles and architecture, with – despite Brunei's tiny population of indigenous tribes – some creditable ethnographic exhibits that are sorely lacking in northern Sarawak. The first hall has a thought-provoking display on different styles of kampung house and their bewildering roof shapes; next along, a hall is devoted to activities such as fishing using traditional traps. Best of all is the third hall, with scaled-down replicas of a Lun Bawang longhouse, a Penan shelter and a hut for trampling sago pith to make flour, among other tribal structures. Such themes will continue at a proposed **Maritime Museum** nearby, showcasing local boat-building and so forth; it may well be open by the time you read this.

Istana Nurul Iman

By the Brunei River 4km west of the centre, off Jalan Tutong • Open two days a year during the Hari Raya Aidilfitri festival marking the end of Ramadan • Bus #42, #44, #46, #48 or #56

Unless you are in town at the right time of year, the closest you're likely to get to the sultan's palace, the **Istana Nurul Iman**, is on a river trip to spot Bandar's proboscis monkeys. Even viewed from afar, the palace impresses with its scale: it's bigger than London's Buckingham Palace, the main buildings stretching for nearly half a kilometre. Needless to say, it's also a monument to sheer self-indulgence, with nearly 1800 rooms – including 257 toilets – and at least 500 chandeliers. The design, by Filipino architect Leandro Locsin, incorporates Islamic motifs such as arches and domes, plus a traditional saddle-shaped roof. There's even said to be a secret passage connecting the palace with the sultan's former home, the considerably more modest Istana Darul Hana, also by the river nearly 1km closer to the centre.

Jame 'Asr Hassanal Bolkiah Mosque

3km northwest of the centre, on the northern edge of Kiarong suburb • Mon–Wed, Sat & Sun 8am–noon, 2–3pm & 5–6pm; Thurs & Fri open to Muslims only • Free • Bus #1 or #22

With sky-blue roofs, six golden domes and pleasant grounds with fountains, the **Jame 'Asr Hassanal Bolkiah mosque** is a grander sibling to the Omar Ali Saifuddien mosque downtown. Built in the 1990s to mark the sultan's silver jubilee, it's also the largest mosque in Brunei, though some of the neat mosaic decoration has a slightly plastic appearance. The mosque is conveniently close to the malls and restaurants of the suburb of Gadong, 1km north, but getting there on foot means traversing some fearsome highways. If you happen to pass this way at night, look out for the evocative lighting which gives the building an air of serenity despite the fast-moving traffic.

Gadong

5km northwest of the centre • Bus #1 or #22 run along the main drag, right past the Abdul Razak Complex; a taxi from downtown costs B$12–15

If you spend much time outside the centre while in Bandar, it's likely to be in the most thriving suburb of **Gadong**. The place isn't much to look at, a collection of mundane concrete blocks and traffic-clogged streets surrounding the multiple blocks of the **Abdul Razak Complex**, which includes two hotels and the **Gadong Mall**, where despite the

8

grandiose exterior the shopping is unmemorable. Gadong is, however, a good spot for **eating**, with decent restaurants and a terrific **pasar malam** where they sell all manner of Bruneian Malay goodies; see p.468.

ARRIVAL AND DEPARTURE
BANDAR SERI BEGAWAN

By plane Brunei International Airport (☎ 233 1747) is 8km north of the city. A taxi into town costs around B$30, while during daylight hours buses #11, #23, #24, #36, #38 and #57 (B$1) run to the bus station. Royal Brunei Airlines is on Jalan Sultan (☎ 221 2222); Bangunan Haji Ahmad, the building that holds the *DeRoy@alle Café*, houses Malaysia Airlines (☎ 222 3074), Philippine Airlines (☎ 222 6971) and Singapore Airlines (☎ 224 4902).

Destinations Kota Kinabalu (3–4 daily; 40min); Kuala Lumpur (2–3 daily; 2hr 30min); Kuching (3 weekly; 1hr 15min); Singapore (1–2 daily; 2hr).

By bus All domestic buses use the bus station on Jalan Cator, while international services park on Jalan Sungai Kianggeh by a conspicuous modern glass tower. Buses to Malaysia, operated by PHLS (☎ 277 1668 or ☎ 718 3838), comprise the Jesselton Express, which heads daily at 8am to Kota Kinabalu (7hr 30min; B$45) via Limbang (1hr 30min), Lawas (3hr), Sipitang (4hr 30min and

Beaufort (5hr 30min), and a Miri bus at 7am and 1pm (4hr; B$18). You seldom need to buy tickets in advance, but can do so either from bus conductors before departure, or from the *DeRoy@alle Café* (see p.468). Indonesian buses run by Damri and SJS make the massive haul to Pontianak daily at 2.30pm and 4pm respectively (24–28hr; B$80). Both pass through Sarawak's main cities, but can't set passengers down in Malaysia, for which you will have to catch a bus to Miri and change if you want to continue west. Ticket agents can be found on the floor above the bus station and, across the elevated concrete link, on the same level in the building on the north side of Jalan Cator.

By boat The only boats that serve Bandar itself, to and from Bangar in the Temburong district, use a jetty on Jalan Residency close to the Kianggeh food court (every 30min from around 7am until 4pm; 50min; B$8). All international ferries use the terminal in Muara (see p.470).

INFORMATION

Tourist offices Brunei Tourism (ⓦ bruneitourism.travel) run offices at the airport (Mon–Thurs & Sat 7.45am–12.15pm & 1.30–4.30pm), and the Kampung Ayer Cultural and Tourism Gallery (Mon–Thurs & Sat 9am–5pm; ☎ 220 0874). Both supply maps and brochures. Tourism Malaysia is on the first floor of the *Rigan* noted (see p.466; ☎ 238 1575).

Internet access SFFNB, next to the Guardian Pharmacy on Jalan Sultan, charges B$1/hr. The *DeRoy@alle Café* and adjacent rivals have free wi-fi.

Newspapers Local English newspapers such as the *Borneo Bulletin* and *Brunei Times*, inevitably filled with news about the royal family, offer useful leads on events and new venues.

BRUNEI RIVER TRIPS

Most Bandar tour operators (see opposite) offer guided half-day trips on the Brunei River that take in **Kampung Ayer**. Unfortunately the tours tend to be a little pricey, starting at $85 per person, and at least in Kampung Ayer they show you little that you can't see on your own, though most include tea and cakes at one of the houses. Where such trips come in handy is in combining Kampung Ayer with the chance to see **proboscis monkeys**. If you were in Kuching or Kota Kinabalu, the nearest groups of the monkeys would be a long excursion away in Bako or the Garama River, so it's incredible that here in Bandar they can be found a mere twenty minutes' boat ride upriver from the centre, past the royal palace in a sliver of woodland and mangrove hemmed in between a residential neighbourhood and the river. The best time of day to see them is around 8am or 5pm, say, when it's cooler and the monkeys come out to forage. It's perfectly possible to arrange a river trip **independently**: village boatmen hang around at the jetty area at the western end of Jalan McArthur, close to the *Fratini's* restaurant, which is also where the tour operators' boats leave from. The boatmen won't proffer life jackets or slick commentary (and may not speak that much English), but they charge much less than a tour company: with some bargaining, reckon on around B$25 per hour (and note that it will take at least ninety minutes to have a reasonable go at spotting the monkeys and enjoy a quick spin around Kampung Ayer). Another advantage of arranging your own trip is that you can ask to be let off elsewhere along the river later – after monkey-spotting first thing in the morning, possible places to visit include Bubongan Duabelas and the Handicraft Centre (see p.462).

PROBOSCIS MONKEYS

For many visitors, a trip to Borneo would not be complete without an encounter with a **proboscis monkey**, found only in riverine forests and coastal mangrove swamps. The reddish-brown monkey derives its name from the adult male's enlarged, drooping nose; females and young animals are snub-nosed. The role of the male's oversized member, which seems to straighten out when the animal is issuing its curious honking call, is likely to do with establishing dominance within a group and, so, in attracting a mate.

The monkeys specialize in eating hard-to-digest mangrove leaves, an adaptation that has enlarged their stomachs and left them with distinctive pot-bellies – and limited their distribution. Entirely arboreal, they're capable of making spectacular leaps across the river channels that cut through mangrove forests, arms thrown wide to catch foliage on the far side – though, in case they miss, they're also proficient swimmers, with webbed toes.

As well as the Brunei River near Bandar Seri Begawan, good places to spot proboscis monkeys include the Kinabatangan (see p.439) and Labuk Bay (see p.438) sanctuaries of Sabah, and Bako National Park (see p.339) in Sarawak.

TOUR OPERATORS

Although Bandar's tour operators major on rather predictable city tours, Ulu Temburong trips and river excursions, they also offer a few destinations that are awkward to visit independently, notably Selirong Island in Brunei Bay – a great spot for birding – and the Bukit Peradayan Forest Reserve on the eastern edge of Temburong.

Borneo Guide Unit 5, second floor, Plaza Al-Abrar, Simpang 424a, Gadong ☏ 242 6923, ⓦ borneoguide .com. Fairly standard offerings, with two notable exceptions: one is their day-trip out to Berambang Island in the Brunei river estuary (B$100 per person) for an unexpected slice of rural Brunei, including a short jungle trek to a hilltop for great views, and a visit to a water village. The other is a two-day package with a proper forest trek just outside the Ulu Temburong National Park, plus a night's stay at their Sumbiling Eco Village near Batang Duri.

Freme Travel 403b Wisma Jaya, Jalan Pemancha ☏ 223 4280, ⓦ freme.com. The usual destinations, plus trips to Selirong Island and out to the Seria oil field (see p.473).

Intrepid Tours First floor, Brunei Malay Teachers' Federation Building, Jalan Sungai Kianggeh ☏ 222 1687, ⓦ bruneibay.net. The chance to overnight on the islands of Brunei Bay is one of their more unusual trips.

Mona Florafauna Tours First floor of the same building as *K.H. Soon Resthouse*, 140 Jalan Pemancha ☏ 884 9410, ⓦ jungle-dave.blogspot.com. Run by "Jungle" Dave, who specializes in nature tours, particularly involving camping and trekking in little visited reserves. By the time you read this they may well have shifted their office. It's also best to get in touch early – they can be out of contact for days at a time if in the forest.

Sunshine Borneo 2 Simpang 146, Jalan Kiarong ☏ 244 1791, ⓦ exploreborneo.com. Veteran company with a comprehensive portfolio of packages, featuring such destinations as the Mendaram longhouse in the southwest of Brunei for B$110 (see p.473), and the Bukit Peradayan Forest Reserve, which they combine with nearby longhouses for B$115.

GETTING AROUND

Nowhere in Bandar's compact centre is more than a 20min walk from anywhere else, but you'll probably use the city's modest public transport system to reach outlying attractions and the suburbs. Note that the distinction between city transport and out-of-town routes can be hazy.

BY BUS

Bus station On the ground floor of Kompleks Darussalam on Jalan Cator.

Routes Most domestic buses are compact, purple 22-seater vehicles, and operate only between 6am and 6.30pm. A painted "line" – the Circle line, the Central line and so forth – gives a general idea where each bus might be heading, but you must note the route number for your destination. On average there are two buses an hour on each route

(popular services such as #1 to Gadong and #39 to Muara via the Kota Batu museums might run every 15–20min).

Fares and stops A standard fare of B$1 covers any journey within and even quite far out of Bandar. Outside the city centre, designated stops may be thin on the ground, but drivers halt anywhere convenient.

Inter-town buses Painted in colours other than purple, a handful of buses serve Tutong (1hr) and Seria (1hr 30min), generally leaving the bus station every 1–2hr until 4pm or so.

For Kuala Belait, change at Seria. While many buses head out beyond the city limits, no services run to Temburong. Driving to the enclave requires traversing Limbang in Sarawak.

BY TAXI

Ranks and companies Taxis come into their own at night, when the bus network has shut down, but are relatively rare – many people can afford cars. While there are a couple of taxi cooperatives (☎ 222 2214 or ☎ 222 6853), most drivers work independently and can only be summoned by mobile phone; hotels keep lists of favourites. In downtown Bandar, there's a taxi rank outside the Jalan Cator bus station. Taxis show up sporadically at suburban malls too, though they can be so scarce in Gadong that you may have to ask a hotel there to book one.

Fares Taxis aren't metered, so get an idea of current fares from your hotel; reckon on B$10–15 between the centre and nearby suburbs.

BY WATER TAXI

Routes and access Little speedboats plying the Brunei River, known as water taxis, are fun for whizzing around the river, but of limited use since most of the few waterside attractions are perfectly walkable. You can attract the attention of a boatman at numerous little jetties and steps leading down to the river and Kianggeh canal (by Tamu Kianggeh).

Fares The fare for any journey along the central stretch of the river is B$1, though for the hop from Jalan McArthur to the Kampung Ayer Tourism Gallery you may be charged just 50 cents.

BY CAR

Car rental Avis is at the airport (☎ 233 3298) and the *Radisson* hotel (☎ 222 7100); other companies include Budget U-Drive (☎ 234 5573) and Qawi (☎ 265 5550).

ACCOMMODATION

Brunei not being backpacker territory, Bandar holds no great budget options, though the city has an adequate array of hotels. Some visitors prefer to stay outside Bandar, commuting in for the sights – certainly feasible, though it won't save you any money and you'll have to head out well before sunset if you're using public transport. The obvious out-of-town place to stay is the lavish *Empire* (see p.470), though it's possible to base yourself in Seria or even Bangar in Temburong.

DOWNTOWN

★ **Brunei** 95 Jalan Pemancha ☎ 224 4828, ⓦ thebruneihotel.com. The nicest and best-value place in the centre, transformed from a dowdy lump of 1960s concrete into a well-run business-oriented hotel. All rooms have beautiful timber flooring and stylish modern fittings, though there's no discount for singles. Free shuttle transport to and from Gadong for the shops and night market. Rates include breakfast. **B$120**

Jubilee Jalan Kampung Kianggeh ☎ 222 8070, ⓦ jubileehotelbrunei.com. A dull concrete tower with somewhat cramped rooms and dated, slightly worn furniture. Weirdly, many of the supposedly en-suite bathrooms are actually just outside the rooms they belong to. Still, with rates including breakfast, it is inexpensive. **B$85**

K.H. Soon Rest House Third floor, 140 Jalan Pemanacha ☎ 222 2052. Archetypal Chinese-run flophouse, of a kind that's vanishing elsewhere. Rooms are large and have a/c, but are a bit tatty and bare, with rough cement floors; some rooms have a bathroom enclosure within, but these may leak water into the rest of the room. Soundproofing isn't great either and cleanliness could be better. At least the prices shouldn't trouble you. Doubles **B$39**, en- suite doubles **B$45**

Pusat Belia (Youth Centre) Jalan Sultan Kianggeh ☎ 222 2900. Used for student conferences, Bandar's youth centre features various dorms – single-sex in line with local values – that take travellers. Facilities include a small pool (B$1) and internet café. Awkwardly, reception keeps to standard office hours (Mon–Thurs & Sat 7.45am–4.30pm); at any other time, call the manager using the number on display or hope to bump into a staff member. Dorms **B$10**

Radisson Jalan Tasek Lama ☎ 224 4272, ⓦ radisson .com. Despite being Brunei's first top-notch hotel, with a pool, fitness centre and other amenities, this place is a little nondescript and showing its age. That said, renovations as part of its takeover by Radisson may have given it a new gloss – and raised prices – by the time you read this. **B$190**

Terrace Jalan Tasek Lama ☎ 224 3554, ⓦ terrace brunei.com. Ageing, like the *Jubilee* but a slightly better deal, with larger rooms and a pool, though maintenance could be better. **B$65**

GADONG

Centrepoint Northwestern end of Abdul Razak Complex ☎ 243 0430, ⓦ thecentrepointhotel.com. Decent mid-range hotel with pool, tennis court and gym, though the place isn't anything special for the prices, which do at least include breakfast. **B$145**

Rizqun Southeastern end of Abdul Razak Complex ☎ 242 3000, ⓦ rizquninternational.com. The priciest hotel in town, adjoining the Gadong Mall, with an ostentatious lobby featuring lots of marble and gaudy stained glass. Facilities include a pool and spa, and there are sometimes weekend discounts. Not a bad deal if you get one of the regular promotional rates, which include breakfast. **B$225**

OPPOSITE EMPIRE HOTEL & COUNTRY CLUB >

EATING

In a country where eating and shopping count as the main pastimes, Bandar has a good sprinkling of venues catering to both. There are inexpensive stalls downtown at **Tamu Kianggeh** and a stone's throw away at the so-called **Kianggeh food** court on Jalan Residency, the latter good for river views at dusk, but both pale in comparison to those at Taman Selera and at **Gadong's pasar malam**, reviewed below. If Brunei has a national dish, it's **nasi katok**. Widely sold for as little as B$1 at stalls and in a few cheap diners, it's a more substantial answer to *nasi lemak* – featuring plain rather than coconut rice, topped with a large joint of chicken or sometimes a helping of beef. Various tales explain the name (meaning "knock rice"), the most common being that hawkers devised it as a breakfast for people working night shifts, and used to knock on workplace doors in the morning to announce its arrival. Malay food doesn't dominate the culinary scene – there are plenty of Chinese and a few Indian options as well, plus a smattering serving Japanese and other international cuisines. A good **website** covering Brunei's restaurant scene is ⓦ lovefoodhatewaste.org.

DOWNTOWN

Choices Brunei Hotel, 95 Jalan Pemancha ☎ 224 4828. The *Brunei Hotel's* coffee house is great for a Western-style breakfast – B$10 buys a buffet of sausage, beans, hash browns, cereals and so forth, with eggs and pancakes cooked to order, plus the usual local rice or noodle options. The rest of the day they serve up a mixture of Western and Malaysian food. Daily 6–10.30am, 11.30am–2.30pm & 7–11pm.

DeRoy@lle C@fe Jalan Sultan ☎ 223 2519. This stands out among several cafés in the area as Bandar's most established hangout, with an extensive menu of so-so food: sub-style sandwiches, burgers etc, free wi-fi and newspapers to read, plus two screens with BBC news and international sport. Not a bad place for breakfast – egg on French bread plus juice and coffee or tea, for example, only costs B$6. Daily 24hr.

★ **Fratini's** In a riverside block at the Yayasan Complex on Jalan McArthur ☎ 223 2555. Highly popular, *Fratini's* is an upmarket Italian chain with branches around the country. The food tends to be not bad rather than great, but the breadth of the menu compensates: a wide range of pizzas in three sizes (from B$12), plus pasta options (B$15) and more expensive mains such as sea bass with ratatouille (B$30). This riverside branch has a few tables outside with good views, and they'll deliver at no extra charge. Daily 10am–11pm.

Phongmun Second floor (only accessible by elevator), Teck Guan Plaza, Jalan Sultan ☎ 222 9561. Downtown's best Chinese restaurant, predictably done out with temple-style red arches and dragons. Cantonese food is the order of the day, including dim sum in the mornings; otherwise the house specialities are braised pork leg, eaten with buns (from B$15), and claypot chicken. The full menu runs to several pages but you'll probably be given a cut-down version with no dish costing more than B$10. Daily 7am–10pm.

Syazwan Café 30a Jalan Sultan. A cut above the area's other Indian Muslim *kedai kopis*, frying a full range of rice or noodle dish to order (RM3 buys an ample portion), plus a good *nasi campur* spread, *thosai* and *murtabak* and, unusually, several sandwich options and even Chinese-style stir fries. Daily 7.30am–9pm or so.

★ **Taman Selera** Off Jalan Tutong, close to the Terrace hotel. The most atmospheric downtown place for dinner, bar none, is this open-air food court, where dozens of stalls sell Malay food. *Ayam penyet* – barbecued chicken pounded to tenderize it – is especially popular (try stall #7) and a couple of vendors sell satay and *nasi katok* too. For something a little pricier, head to the Mizu Seafood Village amid the throng, where they have live lobster in tubs and other seafood, all sold by weight and cooked to order. Sit close to the stall you're ordering from. Daily 4.30–11pm.

★ **Tarindak d'Seni** Eastern end of the Arts and Handicrafts Centre complex, Jalan Residency ☎ 224 0422. Despite the bland modern decor, this buffet restaurant serves one of Borneo's most impressive Malay spreads; lunch costs B$15, dinner B$22; on Sundays, breakfast is B$8 and high tea B$12. Tables groan with dishes such as beef *rendang*, stir-fried *keladi* (yam greens), *ikan kicap* (fish stewed in soy sauce), eaten with plain or *biriyani* rice. They also serve a classic Bruneian staple, *ambuyat* – sago starch, looking and smelling like congealed glue; tease it out of the bowl with chopsticks and eat it with sauces such as *tempoyak* (fermented durian). More palatably, they have Western salads and oodles of local and European cakes. Mon–Sat noon–2.30pm & 7–10pm; Sun 8–11am & 3–5pm.

GADONG

Excapade Sushi On the first floor of Block C of the Abdul Razak Complex, north of the main drag ☎ 244 3012. Highly popular sushi chain, thanks to reasonable prices and a menu that also includes a range of Japanese staples, such as *teppenyaki*. Daily 11am–2.30pm & 6–10.30pm.

★ **Fratini's** In the same block as the Centrepoint Hotel ☎ 245 1300. The usual range of pizza and pasta dishes for which the chain is known. Mon–Wed & Sun 10am–10.30pm, Thurs–Sat 10am–11.30pm.

Gadong Pasar Malam Just east across the canal from the Rizqun hotel. Many tourists trek out to Gadong for this entertaining night market. Besides a section selling fruit and vegetables, it has a few dozen stalls selling all manner of local snacks, including grilled chicken and fish, *kelupis* (glutinous rice, often stuffed with minced beef or prawn and steamed in the leaves of the *irik* plant) and the sweet crêpe *apam balik*. As ever with night markets, though, there's nowhere to sit. Daily 4.30–11pm.

★ **Thiam Hock** 5 Yong Siong Hai Building ☎ 244 1679. Nothing much to look at, but then the best Chinese restaurants are often like that. Revered by locals for its excellent fish head – curried, cooked in a spicy tamarind sauce, or chopped up with noodles. There's also a wide range of other seafood, plus the usual pork, veg and tofu; mornings are dominated by noodles. Most non-seafood dishes start at B$8. To find the building, head south out of the Gadong Mall, for example using the exit by the Guardian pharmacy. Daily 8.30am–10.30pm.

TT Blues Café 12 Yong Siong Hai Building. This informal café-restaurant has big-screen soccer and is good for inexpensive steaks (B$12) and Western snacks, though they also have Malay options ranging from *rojak* to *cendol*. Especially busy at lunch and weekends. Daily 7.30am–midnight.

SHOPPING

Despite the population's healthy disposable incomes and attachment to shopping, Brunei's malls are disappointingly devoid of glitz – plenty of people drive across the border to Miri to shop, while the genuinely rich jet off to Singapore or Kuala Lumpur on a regular basis.

Arts and Handicrafts Centre Jalan Residency. The gift shop here is a great place to browse a wide selection of crafts, though anything really worth having – notably silverware and brocade – is priced in the hundreds of Brunei dollars. Mon–Thurs, Sat & Sun 9am–4.30pm, Fri 9–11.30am & 2.30–4.30pm.

Best Eastern Times Square mall, Jalan Berakas, near the airport. The biggest selection of English books in town. Even here, though, any foreign titles about Brunei and its royal house – the book you are holding included – are likely to be impossible to find. Bus #23, #24, #36 or #38. Daily 9.45am–9.45pm.

Gadong Mall Abdul Razak development. While the sheer size of the Gadong Mall is impressive, its shops, mostly selling trinkets, phone accessories, cheap clothes and so on, are nothing special; the big name, such as it is, is the Utama Grand department store. Otherwise, it's more of a place where young people turn out to see and be seen. The paltry selection of English-language books in the ground-floor magazine shop is the best you can get anywhere close to central Bandar.

Yayasan Complex South of Omar Ali Saifuddien mosque. A much earlier attempt to revive downtown Bandar than the revamped waterfront, this multi-building mall is rapidly losing ground to its out-of-town rivals. The only outlet worth much of a look is the Hua Ho supermarket and department store.

8

DIRECTORY

Banks and exchange There are several banks downtown, notably HSBC at the corner of Jalan Sultan and Jalan Pemancha, plus Standard Chartered on Jalan Sultan. Banking hours are Mon–Fri 9am–4pm, Sat 9–11am.

Cinemas The 1950s Bolkiah Theatre on Jalan Sungai Kianggeh looks attractively antiquated, but has recently shut. Your best bet is the multiplex cinema at Gadong Mall (☎ 242 2455, ⓦ simpur.net.bn/atthemovies).

Embassies and consulates Australia, Dar Takaful IBB Utama, Jalan Pemancha ☎ 222 9435; Canada, fifth floor, McArthur Building, Jalan McArthur ☎ 222 0043; Indonesia, Lot 4498, Simpang 528, Sungai Hanching Baru, Jalan Muara ☎ 233 0180; Malaysia, 61 Simpang 336, Kampong Sungai Akar, Jalan Kebangsaan ☎ 238 1095; Philippines, 17 Simpang 126, Mile 2, Jalan Tutong ☎ 224 3465; Singapore, 8 Simpang 74, Jalan Subok ☎ 226 2741;

Thailand, 2 Simpang 682, Kampung Bunut, Jalan Tutong ☎ 265 3108; UK, Unit 2.01, Block D, Complex Yayasan Sultan Hassanil Bolkiah ☎ 222 2231; US, Simpang 336-52-16-9, Jalan Kebangsaan ☎ 238 4616.

Hospital The RIPAS Hospital is close to the centre on Jalan Tutong (☎ 224 2424). For an ambulance, call ☎ 991.

Pharmacies Guardian Pharmacy has outlets on Jalan Sultan and on the ground floor of Gadong Mall.

Police Central Police Station, Jalan Stoney ☎ 222 2333, or call ☎ 999.

Post office The GPO (Mon–Thurs & Sat 7.45am–12.15pm & 1.30–4.30pm) is at the intersection of Jalan Elizabeth Dua and Jalan Sultan.

Visa extensions The Immigration Office is out towards the airport on Jalan Menteri Besar (Mon–Thurs & Sat 7.45am–12.15pm & 1.30–4.30pm; ☎ 238 3106; bus #1 or #24).

Muara District

As most of Brunei's nature attractions are in Temburong and Tutong there's little to detain you in the capital's district, **Muara**. However, no visit to Brunei would be complete without checking out two eccentric attractions in Jerudong, the **Empire Hotel & Country Club** and the **Jerudong Park Playground**. Also worth a visit is **Muara Beach** and the **Bukit Shahbandar Forest Recreation Park**, a medium-sized nature reserve with only the most basic facilities for visitors.

Muara town

MUARA, Brunei's main port 25km northeast of Bandar, has nothing else to recommend it apart from **Muara Beach** 2km north, which boasts an adequate stretch of sand.

ARRIVAL AND DEPARTURE   MUARA TOWN

By ferry Brunei's international ferry terminal, a couple of kilometres south of what passes for the town centre, is served by the erratic bus #33 (every 1hr–1hr 30min; 1hr). To reach Bandar, you can instead catch any bus from Muara's centre, but it's a tedious, hot walk away: head out to the main road (5min), then go right till you reach a roundabout (5min) and go right again, past the container port, to another roundabout (10min); from here the bus park is just a couple of minutes away on the right. The latest boat departure schedules appear daily

in the local English press.
Destinations Labuan (daily at 7.30am, 8.45am, 9.30am, 3.30pm & 4.40pm; 1hr 30min; standard class B$13–17 depending on the vessel, cars B$50); Lawas (daily at 10am; 2hr; B$22).
By bus From Bandar, the most reliable buses for Muara are #38, which heads north to the airport and then east to Muara, and #39, which goes east to the Kota Batu museums and then north to Muara. The only bus to the beach is #33.

Empire Hotel & Country Club

Close to Jerudong, 15km northwest of Bandar, off the Muara–Tutong Highway • ☎ 241 8888, ⓦ theempirehotel.com • Bus #57 may on request call at the hotel itself; if the driver refuses, get off on the highway and walk in (around 10min); a taxi from Bandar costs B$30

It might seem odd to traipse out of Bandar just to see a hotel, but then the **Empire Hotel & Country Club** is no ordinary hotel. A personal project in the 1990s of Prince Jefri, the wayward and discredited former finance minister, the complex cost US$1 billion to build and put such a drain on the state's coffers that the government had to take a stake in what had been intended as a private development.

The result, benefiting from the skills of thousands of craftsmen from assorted artistic traditions, is jaw-dropping. Just to stroll through the lofty central atrium with its 25-metre-high marble columns, is striking enough. Then there's the gold-plated balusters of the lobby staircase, laden with 370 tiger's eye gemstones, and the handrails coated with mother-of-pearl. Royal influence, of course, extends here; renovations can only go ahead once the designs are approved very high up. While the hotel doesn't really throw open its doors as a tourist attraction, it's vast enough that no one minds neatly dressed visitors who come to gawp and then, more often than not, eat at one of the restaurants.

ACCOMMODATION   EMPIRE HOTEL

Empire Hotel & Country Club Near Jerudong, 15km northwest of Bandar ☎ 241 8888, ⓦ theempirehotel .com. The great thing about staying here is that while the rooms, unlike the public areas, aren't exceptional for a five-star-type resort, rates can be very reasonable. A dive shop

offers PADI courses, snorkelling and diving trips and watersports such as kitesurfing (☎ 261 2551, ⓦ thebananahutbrunei.com); other amenities include a golf course, spa, cinema, swimming pools and a private lagoon. **B$220**

EATING

Li Gong Empire Hotel & Country Club, near Jerudong, 15km northwest of Bandar. Housed in a separate building – look for the red lanterns outside – this is the best known of the *Empire*'s restaurants, serving halal Cantonese food, with dim sum available at lunchtime

over the weekend. The crispy chicken is particularly well regarded. Tues–Thurs 6.30–10.30pm, Fri & Sat 11am–3pm & 6.30–10.30pm, Sun 10.30am–2.30pm & 6.30–10.30pm.

Bukit Shahbandar Park

Along the Muara–Tutong highway, directly south of the *Empire Hotel* • Free • Bus #57

The **Bukit Shahbandar Forest Recreation Park**, a compact area of acacia, pine and heath forest equipped with trails, carpets a hilly area with lookout points over the *Empire Hotel* complex, Bandar and the South China Sea. Marking the entrance to the park is an information centre with displays on the surrounding terrain. The trails are well signposted and popular with joggers, and there are a few rest huts for shade and shelter.

Jerudong Park Playground

Jerudong, south off the Muara–Tutong highway, 4km southwest of the *Empire Hotel* • Various ticket prices valid for different ride combinations • Wed–Fri & Sun 5–10.30pm, Sat 5pm–midnight • ⓦ jerudongparkcountryclub.com • Bus #57

In its 1990s heyday, the **Jerudong Park Playground** was the wonder of Brunei, almost like the country's answer to the Tivoli Gardens in Copenhagen. Built by the government as an amusement park for the sultan's subjects, it was an essential stopover for visitors, the rides all totally free; famously, Michael Jackson and Whitney Houston even played the park's theatre. Like all extravagances the place inevitably became uneconomic to maintain, even with Brunei's oil revenues, and it slowly descended into moribundity. Relaunched in 2011, albeit on a much diminished scale, the park is once again worth a visit if you're in the area. It's at its most atmospheric in the evening; if using public transport, be sure to arrange a taxi in advance to collect you after the buses stop.

Temburong district

8

With a population of only ten thousand, including some Iban and Lun Bawang (Murut), **Temburong district** is the wilds of Brunei. Forested and hilly, it contains Brunei's best-known attraction, the 500-square-kilometre **Ulu Temburong National Park**, with its entrancing canopy walkway. The park has limited possibilities for walks, though, so some people visit on a short day-trip from Bandar, while most opt for two-day packages.

Bangar

The starting point for all Ulu Temburong trips is the district's only town, **BANGAR**, normally reached by speedboat from Bandar (see p.464). The boats head downriver through narrow mangrove estuaries before shooting off into the open expanse of Brunei Bay and then curling back south to head up the Temburong River. It's also possible to drive here via Limbang in Sarawak, or catch the Kota Kinabalu bus from Bandar, which passes through at about 10am. The town itself is nothing to write home about; its main street, running east from the jetty to the town mosque, holds a handful of *kedai kopi*s and general stores.

ACCOMMODATION	BANGAR
Bangar Government Resthouse Bangar ☎ 522 1239. A pretty, well-laid-out place two blocks behind the harbour across the main road, the *Resthouse* has just a handful of	en-suite singles and doubles; they give priority to bookings by public-sector staff. B$30

Ulu Temburong National Park

Park HQ daily 8am–6.30pm • Prebooked tours compulsory, park fees included in package price

Contained within the Batu Apoi Forest Reserve, which constitutes a tenth of the area of Brunei, the **Ulu Temburong National Park** undoubtedly impresses as a pristine nature area. Unfortunately there isn't that much to do – the only trails are simple and short – though the park is great for peace and quiet.

On a standard two-day package, the first day is spent reaching your accommodation from Bandar, and much of the second day given over to the park before you zip back to Bandar in the late afternoon. You may pay slightly less if you make your own way to Bangar and join a tour there, though you must still book in advance. Tour operators also offer somewhat rushed day-trips at around B$150 per person.

From Bangar, van transport is laid on to the jetty at **Batang Duri**, 15km south. The final leg is via longboat, with dense jungle cloaking the hills on either side and birds and monkeys bustling around in the trees; though lasting less than an hour, the journey sets the tone for the park itself. Besides the climb up to the canopy walkway, activities in and around the park include **night walks**, **rafting** or **tubing** down the river and treks to a nearby waterfall, each costing B$10–30 per person.

Canopy walkway

The park's main attraction, the **canopy walkway**, is reached by an hour-long trek taking in two hanging bridges and a plankway, followed by a giddying climb up the stairs around a near-vertical, sixty-metre-high aluminium structure. The view from the top, of Brunei Bay to the north and Sarawak's Gunung Mulu National Park to the south, is quite breathtaking. At this height (on a good day) you can see hornbills and gibbons in the trees, as well as numerous squirrels and small birds. Fifty species of birds have been sighted on the netting around the walkway, while flying lizards, frogs and snakes feed regularly at ground level.

ACCOMMODATION · ULU TEMBURONG NATIONAL PARK

Freme Lodge Just outside Ulu Temburong National Park ☏ 223 4277, ⊛ freme.com. A substantial comfortable place with a/c rooms and dorms, and a large open-air communal dining area. The price here is per person, for a two-day package including one night's stay, meals and transfers B$220

Sumbiling Eco Village Sumbiling Lama, the penultimate village before Batang Duri ☏ 242 6923, ⊛ borneoguide.com/ecovillage. Run as a joint venture with local Iban, this is a fairly simple jungle encampment with accommodation in tents and three basic huts, though proper toilets are provided. In keeping with the eco theme,

meals are eaten off leaves rather than plastic plates. Packages include a night walk in the vicinity. Per person on a two-day package, including one night's stay, meals and transfers B$185

Ulu-Ulu Resort Beside Ulu Temburong National Park HQ ⊛ uluuluresort.com. Run by tour operator Sunshine Borneo (see p.465), the only accommodation within the park is quite an upmarket affair, with 17 en-suite rooms featuring sleek modern decor. The advantage of staying here, comfort aside, is that only resort guests can get to the canopy walkway at sunrise. Per person on a two-day package, including one night's stay, meals and transfers B$300

Belait District

West of Muara, beyond the noticeably agricultural Tutong district, is **Belait district**, whose coastal section is oil and gas country, and has been the economic heart of the sultanate ever since the Seria oil field was established in 1931. The oil boom led directly to the rise of the region's two main towns, **Seria** and **Kuala Belait**, both still fairly sleepy, with generally ugly concrete centres that contrast with suburbs that have quite a rural feel. Inland, though, it's a much more rural story: down the fifty-kilometre-long road to **Labi** are a few modern Iban **longhouses** and forest reserves to visit.

The Labi road

No public transport, though Bandar tour operators such as Sunshine Borneo offer trips here

More or less midway between Tutong and Seria, a turning south off the highway marks the start of the Labi road. Just 500m on, the thick lowland forest of the **Sungai Liang Forest Reserve** can be explored by following various walking trails from the lakes. Twenty kilometres further along, at the **Luagan Lalak Forestry Recreation Park**, a freshwater swamp swells into a lake with the onset of the monsoon rains. A little further on and you reach **LABI** itself, a small agricultural settlement where durian and rambutan are cultivated.

The road beyond turns into a laterite track; around 300m along, a trail off to the east leads, after two hours' walk, to **Wasai Rampayoh**, a large waterfall. Continue south on the track to reach **Mendaram Longhouse**, the first of several Iban communities here, and home to a few dozen people. Like most Iban architecture in Brunei, it's a modern structure, with electricity and running water. The people here can guide you to **Wasai Mendaram**, a small waterfall twenty minutes' walk away with a rock pool perfect for swimming.

Seria

SERIA, 65km west of Bandar, stands at the epicentre of Brunei's oil and gas wealth. Before oil was discovered here at the start of the twentieth century, this was nothing more than a malarial swamp, known locally as Padang Berawa, or "Wild Pigeon's Field". Once S1, the sultanate's first oil well, began to deliver commercially in 1931, Seria expanded rapidly, with offshore drilling following in the 1950s. As you approach from Tutong, you may see small oil wells called "nodding donkeys" because of their rocking motion. Around the town are numerous bungalows, constructed by petroleum companies for their employees, while on the seafront nearly 2km west of the centre the interlocking arches of the **Billionth Barrel Monument** celebrate the huge productivity of the first well. Bandar's tour operators can organize trips to oil-related sights, including the Oil and Gas Discovery Centre.

Oil and Gas Discovery Centre

A 10min walk northwest from the bus station – head 500m north up Jalan Sultan Omar Ali, the road running west of the Plaza Seria mall, then 250m west • Tues–Thurs & Sat 9am–5pm, Fri 9am–noon & 2–5pm, Sun 10am–6pm • $5 • ⊕ bsp.com.bn/ogdc

Seria's only specific sight is the **Oil and Gas Discovery Centre**, a museum created by Brunei Shell to bolster understanding of technology in general and the petroleum industry in particular. With its interactive exhibits, it's a lot more entertaining than the similar museum not far away in Miri, though you still need more than a passing interest in oil extraction to get much out of it.

ARRIVAL AND INFORMATION   SERIA

By bus Seria's bus terminus is diagonally across from the bank, to the south of the mall.
Destinations Bandar (every 1–2hr until 4pm; 1hr 45min); Kuala Belait (1–2 hourly; 45min); Miri (daily at 9am & 3pm; 2hr).

Services There's a bank, HSBC, at the southern end of the drab Plaza Seria shopping mall, which dominates Seria's small centre.

ACCOMMODATION

Hotel Koperasi Jalan Sherif Ali ☎322 7589, ✉hotel_seria@brunet.bn. A dark green building just a minute's walk up Jalan Bunga Kemantin from the bus terminal, the *Koperasi* is dated in a somehow restful way, its simple rooms equipped with TV, fridge and bathroom. <u>B$85</u>

EATING

Fratini's 46 Jalan Bunga Melor, one block north and two blocks west of the Koperasi ☎322 1055. Excellent thick- and thin-crust pizzas, plus pasta dishes and fancier mains. Daily 10am–10pm.

Muwaffaq Below the *Koperasi* hotel, Jalan Sherif Ali. This new café bids to be Seria's community hangout by offering something for everyone – noodles, *murtabak*, *roti canai*, plus Western cakes, buns and milk shakes. Daily 6am–late.

8

Singapore

THE SINGAPORE FLYER AND FINANCIAL DISTRICT

9

Singapore

Singapore is certainly the handiest city I ever saw, as well planned and carefully executed as though built entirely by one man. It is like a big desk, full of drawers and pigeon-holes, where everything has its place, and can always be found in it.

William Hornaday, 1885

Despite the immense changes the past century has wrought upon the tiny island of Singapore, natural historian William Hornaday's succinct appraisal is as valid today as it was in 1885. This absorbing city-state, just 1 degree north of the Equator and only 700 square kilometres in size – if all the outlying islands are included – has evolved from a mere colonial port, albeit one of strategic importance, into a slick shrine to wealth and consumerism.

Lacking any noteworthy natural resources, Singapore began its rise in 1819 when Sir Stamford Raffles took advantage of the island's superb natural harbour and strategic position on the maritime route between China and India to set up a British trading post here. The port thrived from the word go, and remains among the busiest in the world. The country's coffers were also boosted by **industrialization**, and when Singapore grew too successful to remain a cheap sweatshop for multinationals, it maintained its competitive edge and kept the money flowing in by developing a super-efficient infrastructure and work ethic, and diversifying into technology and finance.

With its dynamism and lack of a welfare system, Singapore appears to be a paragon of capitalism, and enjoys a standard of living on a par with western Europe. Yet a huge slice of the economy is dominated by conglomerates that were set up by the state, in which it retains a controlling interest. At the core of the success story is **paternalism**, in which some personal freedoms have been sacrificed so that the government can manipulate the economy and society to deliver affluence. It's this unwritten pact that has allowed kampungs and slums to be cleared and the historic parts of the city remodelled, with much of the population resettled in bland though well-planned new towns. Such is the rate of churn even today that Singapore is dogged by a feeling of impermanence, its modern complexes scarcely bedding down in the public consciousness before being replaced by something even grander. If prosperity has been the carrot, there have also been sticks: there are regulations governing everything from flushing public toilets after use to jaywalking, and, less benignly, a low tolerance of **dissent**. Consequently, Singaporeans have acquired a reputation, partly deserved, for unquestioning subservience.

While Singapore lacks the personality of some Asian cities, and many travellers view it simply as a pricey stopover en route to Malaysia or some other part of Southeast Asia, to dismiss it as sterile is unfair. As with Malaysia, much of Singapore's fascination springs from its **multicultural population**, the main groups being the Chinese (75.6 percent), Malays (13.6 percent) and Indians (8.7 percent). This diversity can turn a ten-minute walk across town into what seems like a hop from one country to another.

Getting a decent taste of the island – and there's plenty to see – requires at least three days. Each of the original ethnic enclaves boasts a fair amount of period architecture in

THIAN HOCK KENG TEMPLE, CHINATOWN

Highlights

❶ The National Museum A slick showpiece celebrating Singapore's history, culture and food. **See p.490**

❷ Little India Old Singapore's most atmospheric district is a sensory overload of Tamil temples, colourful sarees and aromatic spice-grinding shops. **See p.495**

❸ Chinatown Heritage Centre The colour and the slums of the Chinatown of old are brilliantly recreated at this museum. **See p.504**

❹ The Buddha Tooth Relic Temple One of Singapore's newest temples is also one of its grandest, housing thousands of Buddha figurines, a sacred tooth and even its own Buddhist art museum and roof garden. **See p.506**

❺ The Baba House At long last, Singapore boasts a showcase Peranakan residence comparable to those in Melaka and Penang. **See p.510**

❻ The Botanic Gardens A relaxed and distinguished park with an immaculate orchid collection and forest walks. **See p.515**

❼ Bukit Timah Reserve This pocket of primary rainforest offers a decent taste of the jungle, without the leeches. **See p.518**

❽ Food Not for nothing does Singapore market itself as a foodie paradise – hundreds of restaurants serve up every style of Chinese cuisine, sophisticated fusion fare and more. **See p.541**

HIGHLIGHTS ARE MARKED ON THE MAP ON P.478

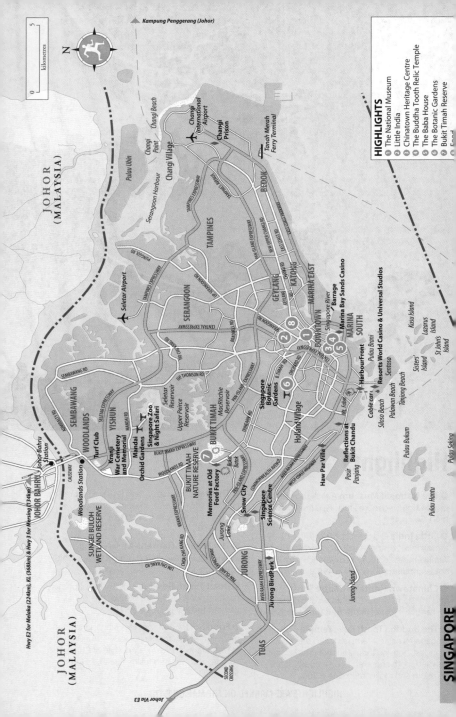

Kampung Penggerang (Johor)

N

5
kilometres
0

JOHOR
(MALAYSIA)

JOHOR
(MALAYSIA)

Hwy E3 for Melaka (224km), KL (368km) & Hwy 3 for Mersing (134km)

Johor via E3

Johor Bahru
Station

JOHOR BAHRU

Woodlands Station

CAUSEWAY

SECOND
CROSSING

SUNGEI BULOH
WETLAND RESERVE

WOODLANDS

SEMBAWANG

YISHUN

Turf Club

Kranji
War Cemetery
and Memorial

Mandai
Orchid Gardens

Singapore Zoo
& Night Safari

Seletar Airport

SELETAR EXPRESSWAY

SEMBAWANG RD

MANDAI RD

ADMIRALTY RD

KRANJI EXPRESSWAY

BUKIT TIMAH
NATURE RESERVE

Memories at Old
Ford Factory

Snow City

Singapore
Science Centre

Jurong
Lake

TUAS

JURONG

Jurong BirdPark

AYER RAJAH EXPRESSWAY

LIM CHU KANG RD

TENGAH AIR BASE

PAN-ISLAND EXPRESSWAY

BUKIT
TIMAH

Upper Peirce
Reservoir

Seletar
Reservoir

MacRitchie
Reservoir

UP THOMSON RD

CENTRAL EXPRESSWAY

SERANGOON

PUNGGOL

TAMPINES

Changi Village

Changi Beach

Changi Point

Changi
International
Airport

Changi
Prison

Pulau Ubin

Serangoon Harbour

PASIR RIS RD

TAMPINES EXPRESSWAY

PAN-ISLAND EXPRESSWAY

EAST COAST PARKWAY

BEDOK

KATONG

GEYLANG

MARINA EAST

Tanah Merah
Ferry Terminal

Singapore River

Barrage

Marina Bay Sands Casino

DOWNTOWN

MARINA
SOUTH

②
⑧

①
③ ④
⑤

⑥

Singapore
Botanic
Gardens

Holland Village

Haw Par Villa

Reflections at
Bukit Chandu

Pasir
Panjang

WEST COAST HIGHWAY

Mt John

Cable car

Siloso Beach
Palawan Beach
Tanjong Beach

Sentosa

HarbourFront

Resorts World Casino & Universal Studios

Pulau Brani

Pulau Bukum

Pulau Hantu

Pulau Sebing

Jurong Island

Sisters'
Island

St John's
Island

Lazarus
Island

Kusu Island

the form of neatly restored shophouses, and retains its own distinct flavour: **Little India** has its garland-sellers and curry houses, **Chinatown** its calligraphers and fortune-tellers, while **Arab Street** is home to cluttered stores selling fine cloths and curios. Right at the core of downtown Singapore are historic public buildings and the lofty cathedral of the **Colonial District**. Old Singapore is looking better than ever thanks to belated conservation work, and that historical emphasis carries over into a clutch of fine **museums** – including the **National Museum**, recounting Singapore's story from the fourteenth century onwards; the **Chinatown Heritage Centre**, evoking the harsh conditions endured by Chinatown's earlier inhabitants; and the **Peranakan Museum** and **Baba House**, which celebrate Singapore's Baba-Nonya heritage, just as important as that of Melaka and Penang.

There's much to enjoy by way of modern and, perhaps surprisingly, nature-oriented attractions too. The wings of reclaimed land around the mouth of the Singapore River, together forming **Marina Bay**, are the site of the striking new **Marina Bay Sands** hotel and casino, and the bug-eyed **Theatres on the Bay**. The latter is at the heart of a huge programme of investment in the **arts**; even on a short visit, you may well catch world-renowned performers in town. North of the city, there's primary rainforest to explore at **Bukit Timah Nature Reserve**, and the splendid **Singapore zoo**, which you can even tour at night. Should you want to venture away from the main island, the best offshore day-trip is south to **Sentosa**, the island amusement arcade that features Singapore's other casino resort.

Brief history

Little is known of Singapore's ancient history. Third-century Chinese sailors could have been referring to Singapore in their account of a place called Pu-Luo-Chung, or "island at the end of a peninsula". In the late thirteenth century, Marco Polo reported seeing a place called Chiamassie, which could also have been Singapore: by then the island was known locally as Temasek and was a minor trading outpost of the Sumatran Srivijaya Empire. The island's present name is derived from one first recorded in the sixteenth century, when a legend recounted in the *Sejarah Melayu* (*Malay Annals*) told how a Sumatran prince saw what he thought was a lion while sheltering on the island from a storm. He then founded a city here and named it **Singapura**, "Lion City" in Sanskrit.

Throughout the fourteenth century, Singapura felt the squeeze as the Ayuthaya and Majapahit empires of Thailand and Java struggled for control of the Malay Peninsula. Around 1390, a Sumatran prince called **Paramesvara** threw off his allegiance to Majapahit and fled from Palembang to present-day Singapore. There he murdered his host and ruled the island until a Javanese offensive forced him to flee up the Peninsula, where he and his son, **Iskandar Shah**, subsequently founded the Melaka Sultanate; meanwhile, Singapore faded away into an inconsequential fishing settlement.

The British colony takes shape

By the late eighteenth century, with China opening up for trade with the West, the British East India Company felt the need to establish outposts along the Straits of Melaka. Enter **Thomas Stamford Raffles** (see p.487), lieutenant-governor of Bencoolen in Sumatra. In 1819, he stepped ashore on the north bank of the Singapore River accompanied by Colonel William Farquhar, former Resident of Melaka and fluent in Malay. At the time, inhospitable swampland and tiger-infested jungle covered Singapore, and its population is thought to have been under a thousand. Raffles recognized the island's potential for providing a deep-water harbour, and immediately struck a treaty with **Abdul Rahman**, the *temenggong* (chieftain) of Singapore and a subordinate of the Sultan of Johor, to establish a British trading station.

The Dutch were furious at this British incursion into what they considered their territory. Raffles, realizing that the sultan's loyalties to the Dutch would make implementation of his deal impossible, recognized the sultan's brother, **Hussein**, as His

Highness the Sultan Hussein Mohammed Shah, and concluded a second treaty with both him and the *temenggong*. The Union Jack was raised, and Singapore's future as a trading post was set.

In 1822, Raffles set about drawing up the demarcation lines whose effects can still be seen in the layout of modern Singapore. The area south of the Singapore River was earmarked for Chinese migrants; a swamp at the mouth of the river was filled and the commercial district established there; while Muslims were settled around the sultan's palace in today's Arab Street area. In 1824, Hussein and the *temenggong* were bought out, and Singapore was ceded outright to the British. Three years later, the new trading post was united with Penang and Melaka to form the **Straits Settlements**, which became a British Crown Colony in 1867.

Singapore consolidates

With its duty-free stance and **strategic position** at the gateway to the South China Sea, Singapore experienced a meteoric expansion. By 1860 the population had reached eighty thousand; Arabs, Indians, Javanese and Bugis all came, but most numerous of all were southern Chinese. The opening of the Suez Canal and advent of the steamship had consolidated Singapore's position as the hub of the region's international trade by the end of the nineteenth century. This status was further enhanced by the steady drawing of all of the Malay Peninsula into British clutches, allowing Singapore to gain further from its hinterland's tin- and rubber-based economy.

By the 1920s, Singapore's communities were finding their voices; in 1926, the Singapore Malay Union was established, and four years later, the Malayan Communist Party, backed by local Chinese. But rumblings concerning independence were barely audible when an altogether more immediate problem reared its head.

World War II

In December 1941, the **Japanese** bombed Pearl Harbour and invaded the Malay Peninsula; less than two months later they were at the Causeway between Johor and Singapore. "Fortress Singapore" had not been prepared for an attack from the north – Singapore's artillery were pointed south from what is now Sentosa Island. On February 15, 1942, the **fall of Singapore** was complete. Winston Churchill called the surrender "the worst disaster and the largest capitulation in British history"; ironically, it later transpired that the supply lines of the Japanese forces had been hopelessly stretched prior to the surrender. Three and a half years of brutal Japanese rule ensued, during which Europeans were either herded into **Changi Prison** or marched up the Peninsula to work on Thailand's infamous "Death Railway". Less well known is the vicious **Operation Sook Ching**, during which upwards of 25,000 Chinese men were shot dead at Punggol and Changi beaches as enemies of the Japanese.

Independence

After the war, Singaporeans demanded a say in the island's administration, and in 1957 the British agreed to the establishment of an elected legislative assembly. Full internal self-government was achieved in 1959, when the **People's Action Party** (PAP) emerged on top in elections. Cambridge law graduate **Lee Kuan Yew**, Singapore's first prime minister, quickly looked for the security of a natural-looking merger with Malaya (now Peninsular Malaysia). In 1963 Singapore joined with Malaya, Sarawak and British North Borneo (now Sabah) to form the **Federation of Malaysia**, but within two years Singapore was asked to leave (see p.575).

Things looked bleak for the tiny, newly independent island, but Lee's personal vision and drive transformed Singapore into an Asian economic heavyweight and enabled his party to utterly dominate Singapore politics to this day, albeit at a price. The media has been treated in a heavy-handed fashion, and even more disturbing was the government's attitude towards **political opposition**. When the Workers' Party won a by-election in 1981, the new MP, the late J.B. Jeyaretnam, found himself charged with several criminal offences, and chased through the Singapore courts for the next decade. In more recent times the few successful opposition candidates have found themselves similarly in court over apparent affronts to the government's probity.

New leaders

Upon Lee's retirement in 1990, **Goh Chok Tong** became prime minister, though many felt that Lee still called the shots in his new role as senior minister. In 2004, Goh was succeeded by **Lee Hsien Loong**, Lee Kuan Yew's son, and on the same day the elder Lee was named "minister mentor", a new cabinet position that gave him an official high horse from which to influence affairs. While the younger Lee has a sternness reminiscent of his father, Singapore was already becoming less uptight before his tenure, and that trend has continued. The new climate may be linked to the government loosening the reins to try to foster enterprise and creativity, and lure back the many Singaporeans who have emigrated. One spin-off has been a more relaxed attitude to artistic expression and gay life, but the most startling expression of the city-state's evolving character was to come in the 2011 polls.

The 2011 polls

On the face of it, the government's schemes had been going swimmingly in the run-up to the elections. A massive project to build a barrage and turn Marina Bay into a freshwater **reservoir** (to reduce dependence on Malaysian water) was completed, as was the contentious venture to build two casinos, or so-called "**integrated resorts**", in the face of much public hand-wringing over the introduction of large-scale **gambling**.

Yet the government did not have everything its own way. In 2008, the island, with its major reliance on banking, suffered its worst-ever recession in the wake of the global financial crisis. Though it soon bounced back, losses by the state's investment arms caused some to re-examine the government's record. This came against a backdrop of ongoing challenges for ordinary people, with inflation outstripping the derisory interest offered by Singapore banks and healthcare costs rising. The government's fairly open stance on **immigration** – part of a strategy to keep Singapore in the spotlight for global business – was a talking point too, though not out of racism, as many of the new arrivals hail from China and India as Singapore's own citizens once did. Instead, people saw migrants as taking jobs from them at all levels, and there was some resentment over the building of luxury apartments to tempt the super-rich. Even the government's much-vaunted water-management schemes came under scrutiny in the wake of more than one **flash flood** on Orchard Road, Singapore's prime shopping street.

When the island went to the polls in May 2011, the opposition took 6 out of the 87 parliamentary seats, with the foreign minister among government casualties. In a country where the opposition had been reduced to a measly one or two seats over decades, this was a minor political earthquake, and Lee Kuan Yew gave up his minister mentor post in the aftermath. While the status quo is unlikely to change any time soon, it seems that for many Singaporeans, activism is no longer a dirty word, and that ordinary citizens will be demanding a greater say in the island's economic and social affairs in the years to come.

Downtown Singapore

Downtown Singapore, occupying the southern part of the diamond-shaped main island, is a convenient place to tour given its compactness and the excellent transport network, though individual districts are best explored on foot. You need at least two days to do justice to the main areas, namely the **Colonial District**, **Chinatown**, **Little India** and the **Arab Quarter**, though three days would be more sensible, especially if you want to have a quick look around the **Financial District** or **Marina Bay Sands**, or shop in **Orchard Road**.

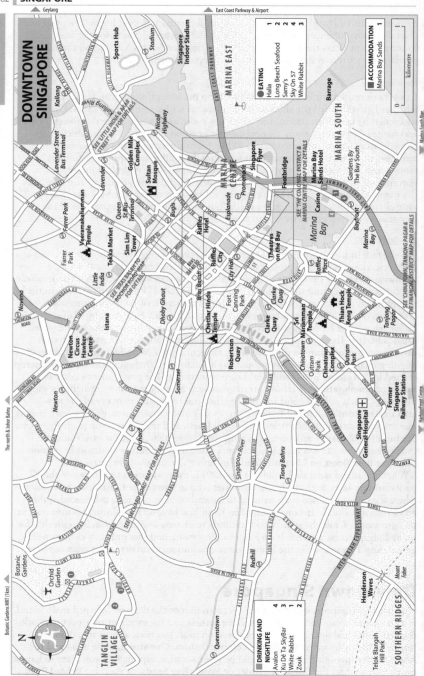

DOWNTOWN SINGAPORE

● EATING
Halia	1
Long Beach Seafood	2
Samy's	4
Sky On 57	4
White Rabbit	3

■ ACCOMMODATION
Marina Bay Sands	1

■ DRINKING AND NIGHTLIFE
Avalon	4
Ku Dé Ta SkyBar	3
White Rabbit	1
Zouk	2

N

0   kilometre   1

SEE LITTLE INDIA & ARAB STREET MAP FOR DETAILS

SEE BRAS BASAH TO ROCHOR MAP FOR DETAILS

SEE THE COLONIAL DISTRICT & MARINA CENTRE MAP FOR DETAILS

SEE CHINATOWN, TANJONG PAGAR & THE FINANCIAL DISTRICT MAP FOR DETAILS

SEE ORCHARD ROAD MAP FOR DETAILS

MARINA EAST

MARINA SOUTH

MARINA CENTRE

MARINA BAY

SOUTHERN RIDGES

TANGLIN VILLAGE

Sports Hub
Stadium
Singapore Indoor Stadium
Singapore Stadium
Singapore Flyer
Footbridge
Promenade
Esplanade
Theatres on the Bay
Gardens By The Bay South
Marina Bay Sands Hotel
Casino
Bayfront
Marina Bay
Barrage

Golden Mile Complex
Sultan Mosque
Lavender Street Bus Terminal
Nicoll Highway
Bugis
Raffles Hotel
Raffles City
City Hall
Raffles Place
Veeramakaliamman Temple
Tekka Market
Sim Lim Tower
Queen St Bus Terminal
Little India
Farrer Park
Dhoby Ghaut
Istana
Fort Canning Park
Chettiar Hindu Temple
Clarke Quay
Sri Thian Hock Keng Temple
Sri Mariamman Temple
Chinatown Complex
Outram Park
Robertson Quay
Somerset
Newton Circus Hawker Centre
Newton
Orchard
Tiong Bahru
Redhill
Singapore General Hospital
Former Singapore Railway Station
Tanjong Pagar
Botanic Gardens
Orchid Garden
Henderson Waves
Mount Faber
Telok Blangah Hill Park
Kallang
Kallang River
Singapore River

Geylang
East Coast Parkway & Airport
Botanic Gardens MRT (1km)
The north & Johor Bahru
Holland Village
Jurong & Johor
Queenstown
HarbourFront Centre
Marina South Pier

The Colonial District

9

North of the Singapore River, the Padang is the nexus of the **Colonial District**, flanked by dignified reminders of British rule. The view from here defines Singapore's past and present. On the Padang's southern edge, the Singapore Cricket Club epitomizes colonial man's stubborn refusal to adapt to his surroundings. Behind that cluster yet more colonial edifices, including the former Parliament House and what's now the Asian Civilizations Museum, and behind them is the river, snaking inland past the last few godowns from Singapore's original trade boom, all converted into trendy nightspots. West of the Padang are City Hall and the former Supreme Court, screening **Fort Canning Hill** from view, while to the north are the grand old *Raffles Hotel* and a string of nineteenth- and early twentieth-century churches. This being Singapore, modernity is hardly absent amid all these echoes of the past: to the north is the towering *Swissôtel* on Stamford Road; the southern sky is dominated by the arresting *Marina Bay Sands* and the spires of the **Financial District** (see p.511); while to the east in the **Marina Centre** area (see p.513) sit the ultramodern Theatres on the Bay arts complex and the glorified Ferris wheel that is the Singapore Flyer. Come in September, and you'll see crash barriers and fences sprouting in both the Colonial District and Marina Centre, whose main roads form the racetrack of Singapore's night-time Formula One Grand Prix.

Cavenagh Bridge

Cavenagh Bridge, with its elegant suspension struts, is a good place to start a tour of Singapore's colonial centre. It's easily reached from the Raffles Place MRT station, the walk taking you past the former GPO on the south bank, now the beautiful *Fullerton* hotel (see p.540). Named after Major General Orfeur Cavenagh, governor of the Straits Settlements from 1859 to 1867, the bridge was constructed in 1869 by Indian convict labourers using imported Glasgow steel. Times change, but not necessarily on the bridge, where a police sign still maintains: "The use of this bridge is prohibited to any vehicle of which the laden weight exceeds 3cwt and to all cattle and horses." The bridge takes only pedestrians nowadays. From its north side you can take in a quintet of towers on the south bank: from left to right, the grey-and-blue metallic sliver of the Maybank Tower, the clean, white Bank of China, 6 Battery Rd and finally the two UOB Plaza towers.

Asian Civilizations Museum

1 Empress Place, north side of Cavenagh Bridge • Mon 1–7pm; Tues–Thurs, Sat & Sun 9am–7pm; Fri 9am–9pm • S$5, or S$10 for joint ticket with Peranakan Museum • ☏ 6332 2982, ⓦ www.acm.org.sg

A robust Neoclassical structure, the **Empress Place Building** was named after Queen Victoria and completed in 1865. It served for ten years as a courthouse before the Registry of Births and Deaths and the Immigration Department moved in. Today it houses the fine **Asian Civilizations Museum**, tracing the origins and growth of Asia's many cultures, from the Middle East through to China. In the small Malay World section, look out for a spectacular Kelantan *makara*, a huge goggle-eyed mongrel creature once used in rituals, while elsewhere there are Dayak masks from Borneo, *kerises* from Indonesia, Hmong garments from Laos and so forth.

A bit of a misfit here – though apt, given the museum's location – is the excellent **Singapore River gallery**. There are displays of sampans and other river craft, and a diorama of a timber dwelling for coolies that recalls the grim lodging houses that once featured in London's docklands, but best of all are fascinating oral history clips featuring people who once worked on and lived by the river. The museum is frank about the side effects of the successful Clean River Project launched in 1977, which saw commercial traffic on the river moved west to Pasir Panjang within the space of a few years: "[the project] also washed away…[the river's] thriving vibrant history as a trade waterway. Its newly cleaned waters now appeared characterless and sterile." At

9

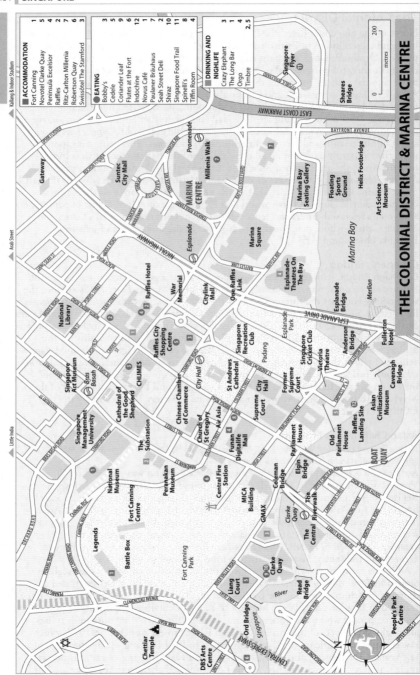

THE COLONIAL DISTRICT & MARINA CENTRE

ACCOMMODATION
Fort Canning	1
Novotel Clarke Quay	5
Peninsula Excelsior	4
Raffles	2
Ritz-Carlton Millenia	7
Robertson Quay	6
Swissôtel The Stamford	3

EATING
Bobby's	3
Cedele	9
Coriander Leaf	6
Flutes at the Fort	12
Indochine	1
Novus Café	7
Paulaner Bräuhaus	2
Seah Street Deli	10
Shiraz	11
Singapore Food Trail	8
Spinelli's	4
Tiffin Room	

DRINKING AND NIGHTLIFE
Crazy Elephant	3
The Long Bar	1
Orgo	4
Timbre	2, 5

least the river is now enjoying a renaissance as a major area for wining and dining
– several slick riverside restaurants are housed in the same building as the museum.

Victoria Concert Hall and Victoria Theatre

Two fine examples of colonial architecture, the **Victoria Concert Hall** and adjoining
Victoria Theatre, stand next door to the Empress Place Building; both are shut until
2013 for major renovations. The theatre was completed in 1862 as Singapore's town
hall, the concert hall added in 1905. During the Japanese occupation, the statue of
Raffles that once stood in front of the tower only narrowly escaped being melted down.
The newly installed Japanese curator of the National Museum (where the statue was
sent) valued it sufficiently to hide it and report it destroyed. A copy of the statue nearby
marks the **landing site** where, in January 1819, the great man apparently took his first
steps on Singaporean soil. Sir Stamford now stares contemplatively across the river
towards the business district.

The parliament buildings

A dignified white Victorian building, the **Old Parliament House** was originally the
private dwelling of a rich merchant. It was designed by Singapore's pre-eminent colonial
architect, the Irishman George Drumgould Coleman. Relieved of its legislative role in
1999, the building now holds a contemporary arts centre called **The Arts House** (ⓦwww
.theartshouse.com.sg), including a shop stocking literature, DVDs and so forth by
home-grown talent. The bronze elephant in front was a gift to Singapore from King
Rama V of Thailand (upon whose father *The King and I* was based) after a visit in 1871.

Just across the road is the back of the rather soulless new **Parliament House**, whose
front facade can be viewed from North Bridge Road and across the river. The public is
allowed to view parliamentary sessions; for details, see ⓦwww.parliament.gov.sg.

The Padang

The **Padang**, earmarked by Raffles as a recreation ground shortly after his arrival, is
the very essence of colonial Singapore. Its borders have never been encroached upon
by speculators and so it remains much as it was in 1907, when G.M. Reith wrote in

---

THE SINGAPORE RIVER

Nothing more than a creek, in the nineteenth century the **Singapore River** became the main
artery of Singapore's growing trade, and was clogged with **bumboats** – traditional cargo
boats, the size of houseboats, with eyes painted on their prows as if looking where they are
going. The boat pilots ferried coffee, sugar and rice to warehouses called **godowns**, where
coolies loaded and unloaded sacks. In the 1880s the river itself was so busy it was practically
possible to walk from one side to the other without getting your feet wet. Of course **bridges**
were built across it as well, mostly endearingly compact and old-fangled, apart from the
massive new Esplanade Bridge at the mouth of the river.

Walk beside the river today, all sanitized and packed with trendy restaurants and bars, some
occupying the few surviving godowns, and it's hard to imagine that in the 1970s this was still a
working river. It was also filthy, and the river's current status as one of *the* leading nightlife
centres of Singapore ultimately originates in a massive clean-up campaign launched back
then. Several of Singapore's museums explore the commercial role played by the river and the
pros and cons of its transformation; there's a particularly good discussion at the Asian
Civilizations Museum (see p.483).

You can get a view of the city from river level on trips in tarted-up versions of bumboats
(daily 9am–10.30pm; 3–4 hourly; ☎6336 6111, ⓦwww.rivercruise.com.sg): the **Singapore
River Experience** (40min; S$17), which takes in Clarke Quay, Boat Quay and Marina Bay, and
the **New River Experience** (1hr; S$22; until 5pm), which adds Robertson Quay. You can
board the boats at several ticket booths along the final stretch of the river. It's also possible to
buy a day pass for unlimited river rides (S$23) with the Duck Tours company (see p.536).

9

his *Handbook to Singapore*, "Cricket, tennis, hockey, football and bowls are played on the plain… beyond the carriage drive on the other side, is a strip of green along the sea-wall, with a foot-path, which affords a cool and pleasant walk in the early morning and afternoon." Once the last over of the day had been bowled, the Padang assumed a more social role: the image of Singapore's European community hastening to the corner once known as Scandal Point to catch up on the latest gossip is pure Somerset Maugham.

The brown-tiled roof, whitewashed walls and green blinds of the **Singapore Cricket Club**, at the southwestern end of the Padang, have a nostalgic charm. Founded in the 1850s, the club was the hub of colonial British society and still operates a "members only" rule. Eurasians, formerly ineligible for membership, founded their own establishment instead in 1883: the **Singapore Recreation Club**, at the opposite end of the Padang. The current grandiose, colonnaded clubhouse dates back to an overhaul, completed in 1997.

Old Supreme Court

West of the Padang, identifiable by its domed roof of green lead, Singapore's erstwhile **Supreme Court** was built in Neoclassical style between 1937 and 1939. Occupying a site once home to the exclusive *Hotel de L'Europe*, whose drawing rooms allegedly provided Somerset Maugham with inspiration for many of his Southeast Asian short stories, the building was itself usurped early in the new millennium by the Sir Norman Foster-designed **New Supreme Court**, behind it on North Bridge Road – and unmistakable with its flying-saucer-like upper tier.

City Hall

Like the former Supreme Court, its younger next-door neighbour on St Andrew's Road, the **City Hall** now stands vacant. Its grandiose Corinthian columns lend it the austere air of a mausoleum and reflect its role in recent Singaporean history: it was on the steps of this building that Lord Louis Mountbatten (then supreme allied commander in Southeast Asia) announced Japan's surrender to the British in 1945. Fourteen years later, Lee Kuan Yew chose the same spot from which to address his electorate at a victory rally celebrating self-government for Singapore. For now, newlyweds line up to have their big day captured in front of one of Singapore's most imposing buildings, but both City Hall and the old Supreme Court are being renovated as they will jointly comprise the prestigious new **National Art Gallery of Singapore** (www.nationalartgallery.sg), to be launched in 2013.

St Andrew's Cathedral

In its own expansive grounds next to Coleman St, west of the Padang, with a small visitor centre on North Bridge Rd • Mon–Sat 9am–5pm; free volunteer-led 20min tours Mon, Tues, Thurs & Fri 10.30am–noon & 2.30–4pm, Wed 2.30–4pm, Sat 10.30am–noon • ☎ 6337 6104

St Andrew's Cathedral, the third church to stand on the same site, was built in high-vaulted Neo-Gothic style, using Indian convict labour, and consecrated by Bishop Cotton of Calcutta on January 25, 1862. The exterior walls were plastered using Madras *chunam* – an unlikely composite of eggs, lime, sugar and shredded coconut husks which shines brightly when smoothed – while the small cross behind the pulpit was crafted from two fourteenth-century nails salvaged from the ruins of England's Coventry Cathedral after it was razed to the ground during World War II. Closed-circuit TVs allow the whole congregation to view proceedings at the altar – a reflection of the Asian fascination with things hi-tech, since the cathedral's size hardly requires it.

Raffles City

Raffles City, a huge development that sits beside the intersection of Bras Basah and North Bridge roads, north of the cathedral and Padang, comprises two hotels – one of

SIR STAMFORD RAFFLES

Let it still be the boast of Britain
to write her name in characters of light;
let her not be remembered as the tempest
whose course was desolation,
but as the gale of spring reviving
the slumbering seeds of mind and
calling them to life
from the winter of ignorance and oppression.
If the time shall come
when her empire shall have passed away,
these monuments will endure when her triumphs
shall have become an empty name.

This verse, written by **Sir Stamford Raffles** himself, speaks volumes about the man whom history remembers as the founder of modern Singapore. Despite living and working in a period of imperial arrogance and land-grabbing, Raffles maintained an unfailing concern for the welfare of the people under his governorship, and a conviction that his country was, as Jan Morris says in her introduction to Maurice Collis's biography, *Raffles*, "the chief agent of human progress… the example of fair Government."

Fittingly for a man who was to spend his life roaming the globe, Thomas Stamford Raffles was born at sea on July 6, 1781, aboard the *Ann*, whose master was his father Captain Benjamin Raffles. By his fourteenth birthday, the young Raffles was working as a clerk for the **East India Company** in London, his schooling curtailed because of his father's debts. Even then, Raffles' ambition and self-motivation were evident as he studied through the night. His hunger for knowledge would later spur him to learn Malay, amass a treasure-trove of natural history artefacts and write his two-volume *History of Java*.

Raffles' diligence showed through in 1805, when he was chosen to join a team going out to Penang, then being developed as a British entrepôt. Once in Southeast Asia, he enjoyed a meteoric rise: by 1807 he was named chief secretary to Penang's governor. Upon meeting Lord Minto, the Governor-General of the East India Company in India, in 1810, Raffles was appointed secretary to the Governor-General in Malaya; this was quickly followed by his appointment as **governor of Java** in 1811. Raffles' rule of Java was libertarian and compassionate, his economic, judicial and social reforms transforming an island bowed by Dutch rule.

Post-Waterloo European rebuilding saw Java handed back to the Dutch in 1816 – to Raffles' chagrin. He was transferred to the governorship of **Bencoolen** in Sumatra, but not before he had returned home for a break. While there he met his second wife, Sophia Hull (his first, Olivia, died in 1814), and was knighted.

Raffles and Sophia sailed to Bencoolen in 1818. There, he found time to study its flora and fauna, discovering the incredible *Rafflesia arnoldii* (see box, p.596) on a jungle trip. By now, Raffles strongly believed that Britain should establish a base in the Straits of Melaka. Meeting Hastings – Minto's successor – in late 1818, he was given leave to pursue this possibility and in 1819 duly sailed to the southern tip of the Malay Peninsula, where his securing of Singapore early that year was a daring masterstroke of diplomacy.

For a man inextricably linked with Singapore, Raffles spent remarkably little time there. His last visit was in 1822; by August 1824, he was back in England. Awaiting a possible pension from the East India Company, he busied himself founding **London Zoo** and setting up a farm in Hendon, now in northwest London. But the new life he had planned for Sophia and himself never materialized. Days after he heard that a Calcutta bank holding £16,000 of his capital had folded, his pension application was refused; worse still, the company was demanding £22,000 for overpayment. Three months later, on July 4, 1826, the brain tumour that had caused him headaches for several years took his life. He was buried in Hendon with no memorial tablet – the vicar had investments in West Indian slave plantations and was unimpressed by Raffles' friendship with the abolitionist William Wilberforce. Only in 1832 was Raffles commemorated, by a statue in Westminster Abbey.

9

which is the 73-storey **Swissôtel** – as well as floor upon floor of offices and shops. Completed in 1985, the complex was designed by Chinese-American architect I.M. Pei – the man behind the glass pyramid that fronts the Louvre in Paris – and required the controversial demolition of the Raffles Institution, a school established by Raffles himself and built in 1835 by George Drumgould Coleman. Once a year, athletes compete to run all the way up to the top floor (ⓦwww.swissotelverticalmarathon.com); the current record stands at under seven minutes.

The War Memorial

The open plot east of Raffles City is home to four seventy-metre-high white columns, nicknamed "the chopsticks" but actually the **Civilian War Memorial**, commemorating those who died during the Japanese occupation. Beneath it are remains reinterred from unmarked wartime graves around the island.

Raffles Hotel

1 Beach Rd • ☏ 6337 1886, ⓦ www.raffleshotel.com

Across the way from what was, for a time, the world's tallest hotel is one of the world's most famous. The lofty halls and peaceful gardens of the legendary **Raffles Hotel**, almost a byword for colonialism, prompted Somerset Maugham to remark that it "stood for all the fables of the exotic East". Oddly, this inherently British hotel started life as a modest seafront bungalow belonging to an Arab trader, Mohamed Alsagoff. After a spell as a tiffin house run by an Englishman, one Captain Dare, the property was bought in 1886 by the Sarkies brothers, enterprising Armenians who eventually controlled a triumvirate of quintessentially colonial lodgings: the *Raffles* in Singapore, the *Eastern & Oriental* in Penang (see p.150), and the *Strand* in Rangoon.

History of the hotel

Raffles Hotel opened for business on December 1, 1887. Despite a guest list heavy with politicians and film stars over the years, the hotel is proudest of its **literary connections**. Hermann Hesse, Somerset Maugham, Rudyard Kipling, Noël Coward and Günter Grass all stayed here, and Maugham is said to have written many of his Asian tales under a frangipani tree in the garden.

The hotel's heyday was during the first three decades of the twentieth century, when it established its reputation for luxury and elegance – it was the first building in Singapore with electric lights and fans. In 1902, a little piece of Singaporean history was made at the hotel, according to an apocryphal tale, when the last tiger to be killed on the island was shot inside the building. Thirteen years later, bartender Ngiam Tong Boon created another *Raffles* legend, the **Singapore Sling** cocktail (which you can partake of in the hotel's *Long Bar* for the princely sum of S$31).

In 1942, British expatriates who had gathered in *Raffles* as the Japanese swept through the island were quickly made POWs, and the hotel became a Japanese officers' quarters. After the Japanese surrender in 1945, *Raffles* became a transit camp for liberated Allied prisoners. Postwar deterioration earned it the affectionate but melancholy soubriquet, "grand old lady of the East", and the hotel was little more than a shabby tourist diversion when the government finally declared it a national monument in 1987. An expensive and contentious facelift and extension followed, lasting four years.

The museum

Daily 10am–7pm • Free

Though much of the revamped hotel still oozes colonial grace, the modern arcade on North Bridge Road is relatively mundane. The only part of the hotel open to people not staying or eating here, it includes a memorabilia-crammed **museum** upstairs on Level 3.

Hill Street

A couple of blocks west of the Padang, **Hill Street** leads south along the eastern side of Fort Canning Park to the river. The brash building at no. 47 with a striking pagoda roof is the **Singapore Chinese Chamber of Commerce**, dating from 1964 though remodelled since. Along its facade are two large panels, each depicting intricately crafted porcelain dragons flying from the sea up to the sky.

Church of St Gregory the Illuminator

60 Hill St • Daily 9am–6pm • ⓦ armeniansinasia.org

One of the most appealingly intimate buildings in downtown Singapore, the Armenian **Church of St Gregory the Illuminator** was designed by George Drumgould Coleman, and completed in 1835, which ranks it among the country's oldest buildings. The white circular interior, fronted by a marble altar and a painting of the Last Supper, includes a framed photo of the few dozen Armenians who lived in Singapore in 1917, for whom the tiny church would have been room enough. Among the handful of graves in the tranquil garden is the tombstone of Agnes Joaquim, a nineteenth-century Armenian resident of Singapore, after whom the national flower, the delicate, purple *Vanda Miss Joaquim* orchid is named; she discovered it in her garden and had it registered at the Botanic Gardens.

Central Fire Station

Junction of Coleman and Hill sts • Galleries Tues–Sun 10am–5pm • Free

Part of the splendid red-and-whitestriped **Central Fire Station** is now taken up by the **Civil Defence Heritage Galleries**, tracing the history of firefighting in Singapore from the formation of the first Voluntary Fire Brigade in 1869. Of more interests than the displays – restored vintage fire engines and the like – are the accounts of historic fires in Singapore, notably the Bukit Ho Swee fire of 1961, which ripped through a district of *atap*-thatched huts and timber yards, destroying sixteen thousand homes. The disaster led directly to a public housing scheme that would ultimately spawn Singapore's many new towns.

Freemasons' Hall

Coleman St, directly behind the Central Fire Station

Built in the 1870s, Singapore's compact **Freemasons' Hall** remains in use and features a proud Palladian facade bearing the masonic compass-and-square motif. It's worth noting that Raffles himself was apparently a mason.

Peranakan Museum

39 Armenian St, just west of Hill St • Mon 1–7pm, Tues–Thurs, Sat & Sun 9.30am–7pm, Fri 9.30am–9pm • S$6, or S$10 joint ticket with the Asian Civilizations Museum (see p.483) • ☎ 6332 7591, ⓦ www.peranakanmuseum.sg

A beautifully ornamented three-storey building that began life in 1910 as the Tao Nan School – Singapore's first school to cater for new arrivals from China's Fujian province – now houses the **Peranakan Museum**. It honours a culture which, in its own way, is to Singapore, Malaysia and Indonesia what Creole culture is to Louisiana. But while the museum boasts that the island's Peranakans are "fully integrated into Singapore's globalized society", in reality they are at best keeping a low profile, and in a country where ethnicity is stated on everyone's ID, "Peranakan" isn't recognized as a valid category – meaning they are inevitably lumped together with the wider Chinese community. At least the launch of the museum and the Baba House (see p.510) indicates recognition that the culture represents a distinctive tourist draw for Singapore (and one which Malaysia, with its ethnic fault lines, has not fully exploited). Such considerations aside, the museum should whet your appetite for not only the Baba House but also the Peranakan heritage of the Katong area (see p.522).

9

MUSEUM PASSES

For S$20 (or S$50 for a group of five), you can buy a three-day pass valid for, and available from, the National Museum, the Asian Civilizations Museum, the Peranakan Museum, the Singapore Art Museum and two wartime museums, Memories at Old Ford Factory and Reflections at Bukit Chandu.

The diversity of the Peranakans in the widest sense of the term comes through in the first gallery, which includes video interviews with members of Melaka's small **Chitty** community, a blend of Tamil, Chinese and Malay. Thereafter the galleries concentrate on the **Baba-Nonyas** who comprise Singapore's Peranakans, and on their customs (in particular the traditional twelve-day **wedding**, which gets four galleries to itself) and possessions (theirs was always largely a material culture). Memorable displays show the classic entrance into a Peranakan home, overhung with lanterns and with a pair of *pintu pagar* – tall swing doors – across the doorway; plus artefacts such as beautiful repoussé silverware, including "pillow ends", coaster-like objects used for some reason as end-caps for bolsters.

National Museum

93 Stamford Rd • Daily 10am–8pm, History Gallery 10am–6pm • S$10, free after 6pm • ☎ 6332 3659, ⓦ www.nationalmuseum.sg

An eye-catching dome, seemingly coated with silvery fish scales, on Stamford Road marks the **National Museum of Singapore**, to give it its full title. Its original Neoclassical building is now home to the **Living Galleries**, focusing on Singapore culture and society, while the substantial, hangar-like rear extension houses the **History Gallery**.

History Gallery

All textual descriptions in the History Gallery, plus audio clips of extended commentaries or oral history, are stored on the **Companion**, a device like a jumbo iPod. While the sound clips enliven a collection of artefacts that can be mundane, they take a frustrating amount of time to get through.

The first gallery focuses on **Temasek** (as the Malays called Singapore) before the colonial era. Pride of place goes to the mysterious Singapore Stone, all that survives of an inscribed monolith that stood near where the *Fullerton* hotel is today, though more memorable is beautiful gold jewellery excavated at Fort Canning in 1926 and thought to date from the fourteenth century.

From here onwards the displays are split into a chronological **Events Path** and a human-interest-driven **Personal Path**, covering the same developments in parallel; switch from one to the other as you please. The Personal Path is often more entertaining, featuring, for example, a video reminiscence by a revue performer from Shanghai who arrived to perform in postwar Singapore and ended up staying. Keep an eye out for the few items the museum designates **national treasures**; those truly worthy of the label include some gorgeous **Chinese watercolours** depicting hornbills and tropical fruit, acquired by William Farquhar.

Two aspects of the twentieth-century coverage deserve special attention: the dimly lit, claustrophobic area dealing with the **Japanese occupation** and the horrors of Operation Sook Ching (see p.519), and the sections on **postwar politics** in Singapore – including interviews with figures who took a different line from the ruling PAP in the days, before the 1970s, when many questions as to how Singapore should be run were still up for grabs.

Living Galleries

The most accessible of the four **Living Galleries** focuses on **street food**, covering the history of local favourites such as *laksa* and *char kuay teow*, displaying soft drinks and kitchenware that generations of Singaporeans remember from their childhood, and explaining why Singapore uses the term *roti prata* for what everyone in Malaysia calls *roti canai*. Also appealing is the **photography** gallery that, under the banner of "Framing the Family", displays many Singapore family portraits made over the past hundred years, enriched with yet more oral history clips. It includes some interesting commentary on the prevalence of polygamy – not as you might assume in Muslim families but among the Chinese. The most edifying gallery tackles **film and wayang** and includes memorabilia of the Malay-language film industry that took off in Singapore in the middle of the last century; it's a sign of how the times have changed since the divorce from Malaysia that this cinematic flowering is news to many non-Malay Singaporeans today. Finally, the **fashion** gallery uses trends in women's clothing over the years as an indicator of the changing status of Singapore women.

Fort Canning Park

No formal hours; information point Mon–Sat 9am–12.30pm & 1.30–5.30pm • ⓦ www.nparks.gov.sg

When Raffles first caught sight of Singapore, **Fort Canning Park** was known locally as Bukit Larangan (Forbidden Hill). Malay annals tell of the five ancient kings of Singapura who ruled the island from here six hundred years ago, and unearthed artefacts prove it was inhabited as early as the fourteenth century. The last of the kings, Sultan Iskandar Shah, reputedly lies here, and it was out of respect for – and fear of – his spirit that the Malays decreed the hill forbidden. Singapore's first Resident, William Farquhar, displayed typical colonial tact by promptly having what the British called Government Hill cleared and erecting a bungalow, Government House, on the summit; the fateful Anglo-Dutch treaty of 1824 was probably signed here. The building was replaced in 1859 by a fort named after Viscount George Canning, Governor-General of India, but only a gateway, guardhouse and adjoining wall remain today.

Its jumble of colonial relics aside, Fort Canning Park offers a welcome respite from Singapore's crowded streets and is packed with shady, mature trees (which also tend to put paid to panoramas over the Singapore River). The most obvious route up the hill starts by the National Museum, while a popular alternative climbs a long flight of steps beside the MICA Building on Hill Street. If you use the museum route, you enter the park down the slope from the grandiose and slightly incongruous **Fort Canning Centre**, a former British barracks now home to a dance company and other organizations; an information point here stocks **maps** of the park.

The Battle Box

To the right of Fort Canning Centre, Fort Canning Park • Daily 10am–6pm, last admission 5pm • S$8

Now restored and called the **Battle Box**, the 1939 underground operations bunkers from which the Allied war effort in Singapore was masterminded hold an animatronics-based exhibition that brings to life the events leading up to the British surrender of Singapore in February 1942.

Raffles Terrace

To the left of Fort Canning Centre, Fort Canning Park

A *keramat* (auspicious place) just left of the Fort Canning Centre, on the supposed site of Iskandar Shah's grave, attracts a trickle of local Muslims. Continue round the hill and you meet the staircase from Hill Street at **Raffles Terrace**, where there are replicas of a colonial flagstaff and a lighthouse – the hill was the site of an actual lighthouse that functioned up until the middle of the last century.

Along River Valley Road

At the eastern end of **River Valley Road**, which defines the southwest boundary of Fort Canning Park, the **MICA Building**, formerly the Hill Street Police Station, is now home to the Ministry of Information, Communications and the Arts, with shuttered windows in bright colours; its central atrium houses several galleries majoring in Asian artworks.

9

GMAX

Eastern end of River Valley Rd • Mon–Thurs 2pm–1am, Fri 2pm–3am, Sat 1pm–3am, Sun 1pm–1am • S$45 • ☎ 6338 1146,
ⓦ www.gmax.com.sg

Hill Street meets the Coleman Bridge over the Singapore River, next to which is a
bizarre structure, looking like an alien war machine, called **GMAX**. Billed as a "reverse
bungy", it's more like a metal pod suspended from cables, allowing it – and screaming
customers within – to be tossed around in the air for several minutes at a time. If you
are tempted to try it, it's probably better to do so before rather than after you settle into
a bar or restaurant at nearby Clarke Quay.

Clarke Quay

3 River Valley Rd • ⓦ clarkequay.com.sg

Painted in gaudy colours and housing flashy eating and nightlife venues, the
nineteenth-century godowns of **Clarke Quay** feel about as authentic as the translucent
plasticky canopy that shelters them; nearby Boat Quay (see p.510) feels homelier even
when at its busiest. Further up the road, the quieter **Robertson Quay** boasts a few
entertainment venues of its own.

Chettiar Temple

Northeast of Robertson Quay; turn right into Tank Rd off River Valley Rd • Daily roughly 8.30am–12.30pm & 5.30–8.30pm • Free •
ⓦ www.sttemple.com • Bus #143 from Orchard Road or Chinatown

Officially the Sri Thendayuthapani Temple, the shrine that many still refer to as the
Chettiar Temple boasts a large, attractive *gopuram*. *B*uilt in 1984 to replace a
nineteenth-century temple constructed by *chettiars* (Indian moneylenders), it's the
destination of every participant in Singapore's annual Thaipusam festival (see p.498).

Bras Basah Road to Rochor Road

The zone between **Bras Basah Road** – the main thoroughfare between Orchard Road
and what would have been the seafront – and **Rochor Road** at the edge of Little India
has a transitional sort of feel, sitting as it does between the Colonial District and what
were intended to be "ethnic" enclaves to the northeast. The aptly named Middle Road,
running smack through the centre of the grid, was originally meant to be the boundary
between the two. Despite modernization, the area still boasts some long-established
places of worship and has been transforming into a nexus for the visual and performing
arts. City planners have turned many distinguished old properties on and around
Waterloo Street over to arts organizations, including the **Singapore Art Museum**, and
lured the country's leading institutes in the field here, among them the Nanyang
Academy of Fine Arts (**NAFA**) on Bencoolen Street; the **Lasalle College of the Arts**,
whose futuristic glass buildings under a translucent canopy between McNally Street
and Albert Street deserve a look; and the **School of the Arts**, in an imposing new
building next to the Cathay cinema.

CHIJMES

Just up Bras Basah Rd from the *Raffles* hotel • ⓦ www.chijmes.com.sg

CHIJMES (pronounced "chimes"), a complex of shops, bars and restaurants, is based in
the restored Neo-Gothic husk of the former Convent of the Holy Infant Jesus – from
which name the acronym for the complex is derived. Its lawns, courtyards, waterfalls,
fountains and sunken forecourt give a sense of spatial dynamics that is rare in
Singapore. For some locals, however, it sticks in the craw that planners allowed what
had been one of several historic schools in the area to assume its present role; if the
arts-district idea had matured earlier, chances are it might have evaded that fate. A relic
from CHIJMES' original role survives on its Victoria Street flank, where local families
left unwanted babies at the **Gate of Hope**, to be taken in by the convent.

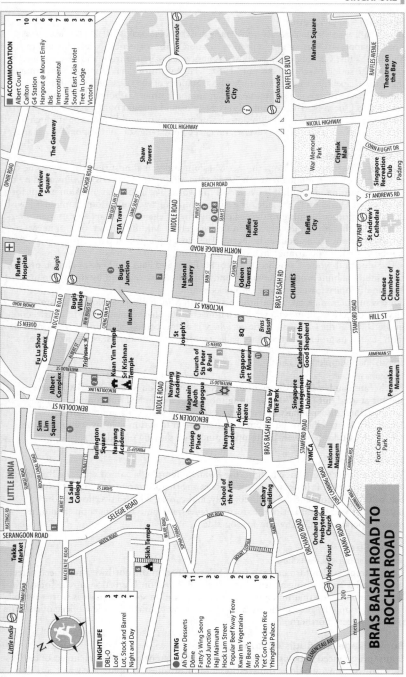

BRAS BASAH ROAD TO ROCHOR ROAD

■ ACCOMMODATION
Albert Court	1
Carlton	10
G4 Station	2
Hangout @ Mount Emily	6
Ibis	4
Intercontinental	7
Naumi	8
South East Asia Hotel	3
Tree In Lodge	5
Victoria	9

■ NIGHTLIFE
DBL-O	3
Loof	4
Lot, Stock and Barrel	2
Night and Day	1

● EATING
Ah Chew Desserts	4
Dôme	11
Fatty's Wing Seong	1
Food Junction	3
Haji Maimunah	6
Hock Lam Street	
Popular Beef Kway Teow	9
Kwan Im Vegetarian	2
Mr Bean's	5
Soup	10
Yet Con Chicken Rice	8
Yhingthai Palace	7

9 **Singapore Art Museum**

71 Bras Basah Rd, at Queen St • Sat–Thurs 10am–7pm, Fri 10am–9pm • S$10, free Fri 6–9pm • ☎ 6332 3222, ⓦ www.singart.com

The **Singapore Art Museum** has a peerless location in the former St Joseph's Institution, Singapore's first Catholic school, whose impressive semicircular front and silvery dome rang to the sound of school bells until 1987. Many of the original rooms survive, among them the chapel (now an auditorium), whose Stations of the Cross and mosaic floor remain intact. There's also an annexe, **8Q**, in another former Catholic school round the corner at 8 Queen St. The museum showcases a certain amount of international work, including occasional visiting exhibitions featuring artists of world renown, but much greater emphasis is placed on a diverse and challenging range of contemporary local art.

Waterloo Street

Head up Waterloo Street from the Art Museum and you almost immediately come to the peach-coloured **Maghain Aboth Synagogue**, dating from the 1870s. Dwarfed by the modern buildings around, it looks for all the world like a colonial mansion except for the Stars of David on the facade. The surrounding area was once something of a Jewish enclave – another building midway along nearby Selegie Road bears a prominent Star of David – though the Jewish community, largely of Middle Eastern origin, never numbered more than about a thousand. The synagogue, which dates from the 1870s, can be visited, if you arrange in advance by calling ☎ 6337 2189.

The blue-and-white Catholic **Church of Sts Peter and Paul** (ⓦ www.sppchurch.org.sg), opposite, was built around the same time and is likewise dwarfed by the hyper-modern National Library tower a couple of blocks behind.

A few minutes' walk on, at the intersection with Middle Road, **Sculpture Square** (ⓦ www.sculpturesq.com.sg) resembles a little church. That's explained by its construction in the 1870s as the Christian Institute, where residents could debate and read about their faith. Today, its grounds and interior gallery space feature modernist works by local artists.

Sri Krishnan Temple

152 Waterloo St

Just before you hit the pedestrianized stretch of Waterloo Street, the **Sri Krishnan Temple** started out in 1870 as nothing more than a thatched hut containing a statue of Lord Krishna under a banyan tree. The present-day shrine is a good example of Southeast Asian religious harmony and syncretism in action, with worshippers from the nearby Buddhist Kwan Im Temple sometimes praying outside.

Kwan Im Temple

Waterloo Street's best-known sight, the **Kwan Im Temple**, is named after the Buddhist goddess of mercy. It looks too classy for comfort thanks to renovations over the years, but still draws thousands of devotees daily, and can be filled to overflowing during festivals. As you might anticipate, fortune-tellers, religious artefact shops and other traders operate in a little swarm just outside.

Albert Street

Northern end of Waterloo St, close to Rochor Rd

Albert Street, which formerly ran from Selegie Road in the northwest to Queen Street, used to offer street eating approaching that still found on Jalan Alor in KL. Today it's been so remodelled that much of it isn't even shown on some maps; it is worth a stroll, however, if only to gaze at the zigzagging glass facades of the Lasalle College of the Arts near the street's northern end.

Bugis Village and Bugis Junction

Bugis (pronounced "boogis") **Street**, the southern extension of Albert Street, once crawled with rowdy sailors, transvestites and prostitutes by night. The street was duly cleared, partly because it was anathema to the government and partly to build the Bugis MRT station. In its place today is **Bugis Village**, a bunch of stalls and snack vendors lining two covered alleyways. It's hardly the Bugis Street of old, though it does recapture something of the bazaar feel that some Singapore markets once had. Amid the T-shirt sellers, at least one outlet sells sex toys – unthinkable in Singapore until recently, and about the only obvious link to the area's seedy past.

Across Victoria Street from here, is another throwback to the past, the **Bugis Junction** development, in which whole streets of shophouses have been gutted, scrubbed clean and then encased under glass roofs as part of a modern shopping mall and hotel, the *Intercontinental*. The mall itself has some good places to eat, particularly *Food Junction* on level 3 (see p.547).

Little India

Of all the quarters of old Singapore, the most charismatic has to be **Little India**, just fifteen minutes' walk from the Colonial District. The area retains more cultural integrity than Chinatown: Indian pop music blares out from speakers outside cassette shops; the air is perfumed with incense, curry powder and jasmine garlands; Hindu women parade in bright sarees; and a wealth of restaurants (see p.548) serve up excellent, inexpensive curries. Though the remaining shophouses are fast being touched up from the same pastel paintbox that has "restored" Chinatown to its present doll's-house cuteness, the results seem to work better in an Indian context.

The original occupants of this downtown niche were Europeans and Eurasians who established country houses here, and for whom a racecourse was built (on the site of modern-day Farrer Park) in the 1840s. Only when Indian-run brick kilns began to operate here did an Indian community start to take shape. Since then Indians have featured prominently in the development of Singapore, though not always out of choice: from 1825 onwards, **convicts** were transported from the subcontinent and by the 1840s over a thousand Indian prisoners were slaving away on buildings such as St Andrew's Cathedral and the Istana. Today migrant Tamil and Bangladeshi men labour on the island republic's MRT stations, shopping malls and private villas, and on Sundays they descend on Little India in their tens of thousands, making the place look like downtown Calcutta or Chennai after a major cricket match, and helping it retain its identity in the face of encroaching development.

The district's backbone is **Serangoon Road**, one of the island's oldest roadways, dating from 1822. It's a kaleidoscopic whirl of Indian life, its shops selling everything from nose studs to *kum kum* powder (used to make the red dot Hindus wear on their foreheads). As with Chinatown, there is no ideal route through the area, so exploring means doing some backtracking, which is no ordeal as there are always interesting pickings to be had. The account below starts from Tekka Market, conveniently next to Little India MRT, and then covers the side roads off Serangoon Road in stretches. The best time of year to visit is in the run-up to **Deepavali** (Oct or Nov) when much of Serangoon Road is festooned with festive lighting and special markets are set up in the open space beyond the Angullia Mosque (opposite Syed Alwi Road) and on Campbell Lane, selling decorations, garlands and Indian sweets.

Tekka Market

At the southwestern end of Serangoon Road, **Tekka Market** is a must-see, combining many of Little India's commercial elements under one roof. It's best to arrive in the morning when the wet market is at its busiest. Made more sanitary by recent renovations, the market is nevertheless hardly sanitized – at seafood stalls live crabs, their claws tied together, shuffle in buckets. Look out also for a couple of stalls selling nothing but banana leaves, used to serve up delicious curry meals all over Singapore. Talking of food, the hawker centre here is excellent, and though the same can't be said

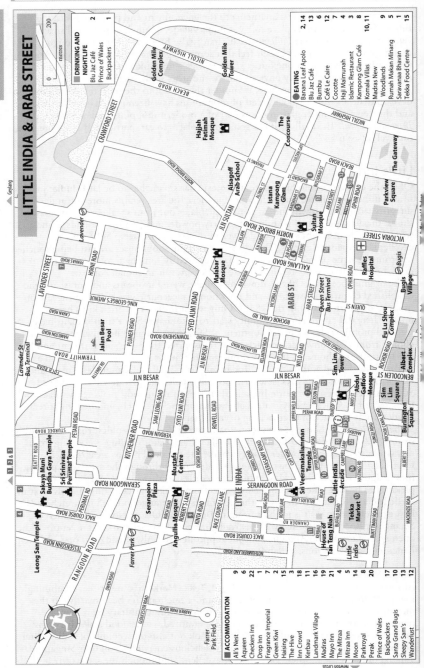

of the mundane outlets upstairs selling Indian fabrics and household items, there are great views over the wet market to be had from above.

Buffalo Road

Buffalo Road, along the northern side of Tekka Market, sports a few provisions stores with sacks of spices and fresh coconut, ground using primitive machines. Its name, and that of neighbouring Kerbau ("buffalo" in Malay) Road, recall the latter half of the nineteenth century when **cattle and buffalo yards** opened in the area, causing the enclave to grow as more Indians were lured here in search of work.

Kerbau Road

Kerbau Road is notable for its meticulously renovated shophouses and for being, like Waterloo Street 1km south, a designated "arts belt", home to several creative organizations. Curiously, the road itself has been split into two parts with a pedestrianized bit of greenery in the middle. Here, at no. 37, you can't miss the restored **Chinese villa**, its window shutters and fretwork eave ornamentations painted in garish colours. Now used as commercial premises, the shophouse-style property was built by a confectionery magnate, Tan Teng Niah, in 1900. Look out also for the traditional picture framer's at no. 57, packed with images of Hindu deities.

Sri Veeramakaliamman Temple

141 Serangoon Rd, 100m short of Klang Rd · Free · ☎ 6295 4538, ⓦ www.sriveeramakaliamman.com

The eye-catching *gopuram* of the **Sri Veeramakaliamman Temple** is dedicated to the Hindu goddess, Kali. Worshippers ring the bells hanging on the temple doors as they enter, in the hope that their prayers will be answered. Inside, the *mandapam*, or worship hall, holds a ferocious image of Kali, the goddess of power and incarnation of Lord Shiva's wife. Flanking her are her sons, Ganesh (left) and Murugan (right).

Hastings Road to Cuff Road

Across Serangoon Road from the Tekka Market, the **Little India Arcade** is a lovingly restored block of shophouses bounded by Hastings Road and Campbell Lane. It's a sort of Little India in microcosm: behind pastel-coloured walls and green shutters you can purchase textiles and tapestries, bangles, religious statuary, Indian sweets, tapes and CDs, and even traditional Ayurvedic herbal medicines. Exiting the arcade onto **Campbell Lane** brings you opposite the riot of colours of the Jothi flower shop, where staff thread jasmine, roses and marigolds into garlands for prayer offerings. A new **Indian Heritage Centre** museum at the corner with Clive Street is due to open in 2013.

Dunlop Street

Dunlop Street is defined by beautiful **Abdul Gaffoor Mosque** at no. 41 (daily 8.30am–noon & 2.30–4pm), whose green dome and bristling minarets have enjoyed a comprehensive and sympathetic renovation in the last few years. Set amid gardens of palms and bougainvillea and within cream walls decorated with stars and crescent moons, the mosque features an unusual sundial whose face is ringed by elaborate Arabic script denoting the names of 25 Islamic prophets. One more street along are **Dickson Road** and, back towards Serangoon Road, **Upper Dickson Road** where a shop at no. 15 sells pricey *kulfi*, Indian ice cream. Next along is **Cuff Road**, where a traditional spice grinder can still be seen at no. 2, though it's mainly open at weekends.

Rowell and Desker roads

It might seem odd to spend any time on two roads long synonymous in Singapore with **vice**, but something about the openness of goings-on on Rowell and Desker roads seems almost radical on this straitlaced island. Between the two, running along the backs of two rows of shophouses, is an alleyway punctuated by open doorways that are illuminated at

9

night by pink-tinted fluorescent lighting. Here gaggles of bored-looking prostitutes sitting around inside watching TV, seemingly oblivious to the men – usually poor migrant labourers – gathered outside, often not so much to gawp as simply to observe as though it's all a kind of free entertainment. This being Singapore, there's nothing edgy about any of this, though women visitors will probably want to give it a wide berth. Even if you do, it's hard not to notice the massage parlours that have sprung up all over Little India.

Syed Alwi Road to Petain Road

Syed Alwi Road, the next side street along from Desker Road, is notable for being the hub of the shopping phenomenon that is **Mustafa**, an agglomeration of department store, moneychanger, travel agent, jeweller and supermarket, much of it open 24/7. Having started modestly, the business somehow carried on growing to become a behemoth, occupying two interlinked buildings of its own as well as part of the Serangoon Plaza at the junction of Serangoon and Syed Alwi roads. You'll probably find it more appealing than most places on Orchard Road as you rub shoulders with Indian families seeking air-flown confectionery from Delhi, and Chinese and Malay shoppers wanting durians, luggage or pots and pans.

Sam Leong Road is home to some surviving **Peranakan shophouses** decorated with stags, lotuses and egrets. There's more Peranakan architecture a few blocks north on **Petain Road**, where the shophouses have elegant ceramic tiles reminiscent of Portuguese *azulejos*, and on **Jalan Besar** – turn left into it near the southern end of Petain Road.

Sri Srinivasa Perumal Temple

397 Serangoon Rd • Daily 6.30am–noon & 6–9pm, though it may be possible to look around at other times • Free • ☎ 6298 5771

Little India more or less comes to an end at Rangoon and Kitchener roads, but it's worth continuing up Serangoon Road to see two very different temples. Dating from the late nineteenth century, though rebuilt in the 1960s, the **Sri Srinivasa Perumal Temple** has an attractive five-tiered *gopuram* with sculptures of the various manifestations of Lord Vishnu the preserver. On the wall to the right of the front gate, a sculpted elephant, its leg caught in a crocodile's mouth, trumpets silently. But the temple's main claim to fame is as the starting point for the annual **Thaipusam** festival in late January, when its courtyard witnesses a gruesome melee. Hindu devotees don huge metal frames (*kavadi*), fastened to their flesh with hooks and prongs. The devotees leave the temple in procession, pausing only while a coconut is smashed at their feet for good luck, and parade all the way to the Chettiar Temple on Tank Road (see p.492).

Sakaya Muni Buddha Gaya Temple

366 Race Course Rd • Daily 8am–4.45pm • Free

Just beyond the Sri Srinivasa Temple complex, a small path leads northwest to Race Course Road, where the slightly kitsch **Sakaya Muni Buddha Gaya Temple** (also called the Temple of the Thousand Lights) betrays a strong Thai influence – which isn't surprising as it was built by a Thai monk, Vutthisasala. On the left as you enter is a massive replica of Buddha's footprint, inlaid with mother-of-pearl; beyond sits a huge Buddha ringed by the thousand electric lights from which the temple takes its alternative name, while 25 scenes from the Buddha's life decorate the pedestal on which he sits. The left wall of the temple features a sort of wheel of fortune – to discover your fortune, spin it (for a small donation) and take the sheet of paper bearing the number at which the wheel stops.

Arab Street and around

Bugis or Nicoll Highway MRT

Before the arrival of Raffles, the area of Singapore south of the Rochor River housed a Malay village known as Kampong Glam, after the Gelam tribe of sea gypsies who lived

OPPOSITE CHINATOWN'S THIAN HOCK KENG TEMPLE (P.509) >

9

there. After signing the dubious treaty with the newly installed "Sultan" Hussein Mohammed Shah (see p.479), Raffles allotted the area to him and designated the land around it as a Muslim settlement. Soon the zone was attracting Malays, Sumatrans and Javanese, as well as Hadhrami Arab traders from what's now eastern Yemen, as such modern road names as **Arab Street**, Baghdad Street, and Bali Lane suggest. Today Singapore's Arab community, descended from those Yemeni traders, is thought to number around 15,000, though they don't stand out visually or geographically, having intermarried with the rest of Singapore society and being resident in no particular area.

Like Little India, the Arab Street district (see map, p.496) remains one of the most atmospheric pockets of old Singapore, its lanes home to the golden-domed **Sultan Mosque** and the **Istana Kampong Glam**, now a Malay heritage museum. Most of all, though, it's the mixed identity of the place that appeals: rubbing shoulders with the mosque, traditional fabric stores and old-style curry houses are brash Middle Eastern restaurants and a peppering of alternative boutiques.

Arab Street

While Little India is memorable for its fragrances, it's the vibrant colours of the shops of **Arab Street** and its environs that stick in the memory. Textile and carpet stores are most prominent, but you'll also see leather, basketware, gold, gemstones and jewellery for sale; the pavements of Arab Street in particular are an obstacle course of merchandise. Most of the shops here have been modernized, though one or two (like Bamadhaj Brothers at no. 97 and Aik Bee at no. 69) still retain their original dark wood and glass cabinets, and wide wooden benches where the shopkeepers sit. There's also a good range of basketware and rattan work – fans, hats and walking sticks – at Rishi Handicrafts, at no. 58. It's easy to spend a couple of hours weaving in and out of the stores, but some traders are masters of persuasion and will have you loaded with sarongs and whatnot before you know it.

Haji Lane and Bali Lane

South of Arab Street, **Haji Lane** and tiny **Bali Lane** are Singapore's answer to London's Brick Lane, sporting both an Islamic feel and a distinctly left-field vibe. The restored shophouses are home to several trendy clothes shops, and youths chill out on the pavement puffing on hubble-bubbles in the evening. Bali Lane also boasts the excellent *Blu Jaz Café* (see p.548).

Sultan Mosque

3 Muscat St • Sat–Thurs 9am–noon & 2–4pm, Fri 2.30–4pm • Free • ☎ 6293 4405, ⓦ www.sultanmosque.org.sg

Along the eastern side of North Bridge Road (though the best views of its golden domes are from the pedestrianized Bussorah Street to the east), the **Sultan Mosque** or Masjid Sultan is the beating heart of the Muslim faith in Singapore. An earlier mosque stood on this site, finished in 1825 and constructed with the help of a donation from the East India Company. The present building was completed a century later to a design by colonial architects Swan and MacLaren. The wide lobby has a digital display listing prayer times. Beyond, and out of bounds to non-Muslims, is the main prayer hall, a large, bare chamber fronted by two more digital clocks that enable the faithful to time their prayers to the exact second.

During the Muslim fasting month of **Ramadan**, neighbouring **Kandahar Street** is awash with stalls of the Ramadan bazaar from 2pm onwards, selling *biriyani*, *murtabak*, dates and cakes for consumption by the faithful after dusk. South of the mosque, **Bussorah Street** is home to some smart restaurants and worthwhile souvenir outlets.

Istana Kampong Glam

Sultan Gate, between Kandahar and Aliwal sts • Mon 1–6.30pm, Tues–Sun 10am–6.30pm • S$4; times and prices may alter following a recent revamp • ☎ 6391 0450, ⓦ www.malayheritage.org.sg

Possibly the handiwork of George Drumgould Coleman, the **Istana Kampong Glam** was built as the royal palace of Sultan Ali Iskandar Shah, son of Sultan Hussein who negotiated with Raffles to hand over Singapore to the British. The sultan's descendants lived here until a few years ago, when it was compulsorily acquired by the state and transformed from a tumbledown building into an over-smart museum, the **Malay Heritage Centre**, featuring exhibits on traditional Malay life. Incidentally, the similarly styled though much smaller yellow house in the same grounds, Gedung Kuning, once belonged to the descendants of a wealthy Malay merchant but now houses an upmarket restaurant, *Tepak Sireh*.

North of Sultan Mosque

The stretch of **North Bridge Road** around the Sultan Mosque has, not entirely surprisingly, a conservative feel. Here, men sport Abe Lincoln beards, and the women fantastically colourful shawls and robes, while some shops are geared more towards locals than tourists: Kazura Aromatics at no. 705, for instance, sells alcohol-free perfumes, while neighbouring stores stock prayer beads, the fez-like *songkok* hats worn by Malay men, *miswak* sticks – twigs the width of a finger used to clean teeth – and even swimwear for Muslim women.

A little way east of the mosque, Jalan Kubor (Grave Street) leads north off North Bridge Road and across Victoria Street to an unkempt Muslim **cemetery** where, it is said, Malay royalty are buried. A block northeast of here, at the junction of Kallang Road and Jalan Sultan, stands the attractive blue **Malabar Mosque** topped with golden domes – a little cousin of the Sultan Mosque.

Hajjah Fatimah mosque

Beach Road's ships' chandlers and fishing-gear shops betray its former proximity to the sea. The one attraction here, a stone's throw east from Arab Street, is the **Hajjah Fatimah Mosque**, named after a wealthy businesswoman from Melaka who amassed a fortune through her mercantile vessels, and whose family home formerly stood here. She moved elsewhere after two break-ins and an arson attack on her home, then underwrote the construction of a mosque on the site, finished in 1846. Looking strangely like a church steeple (perhaps because its architect was European), the minaret has a six-degree slant – locals call it Singapore's Leaning Tower of Pisa.

The Gateway

Beach Rd, just south of Arab St

Designed by I.M. Pei, the two logic-defying office buildings that comprise **The Gateway** rise magnificently into the air like vast razor blades, appearing two-dimensional from certain angles. When the huge, Gotham-esque tower of **Parkview Square** was built across on North Bridge Road, much care was taken to site it dead between The Gateway's sharp points for feng shui considerations. To be on the safe side its developers placed four giant figures carrying good-luck pearls along the top of the tower.

Chinatown

Chinatown or Tanjong Pagar MRT; buses run southwest along North and South Bridge rds and New Bridge Rd, and northeast along Eu Tong Sen St

Bounded roughly by Eu Tong Sen Street to the northwest, Neil and Maxwell roads to the south, Cecil Street to the southeast and the Singapore River to the north, the two square kilometres of **Chinatown** once constituted the focal point of Chinese life and culture in Singapore. The area was first earmarked for Chinese settlement by Sir Stamford Raffles, who decided in 1819 that Singapore's communities should be segregated. As immigrants poured in, the land southwest of the river took shape as a place where new arrivals from China, mostly from Fujian (Hokkien) and Guangdong (Canton) provinces and to a lesser extent Hainan island, would have found temples,

9

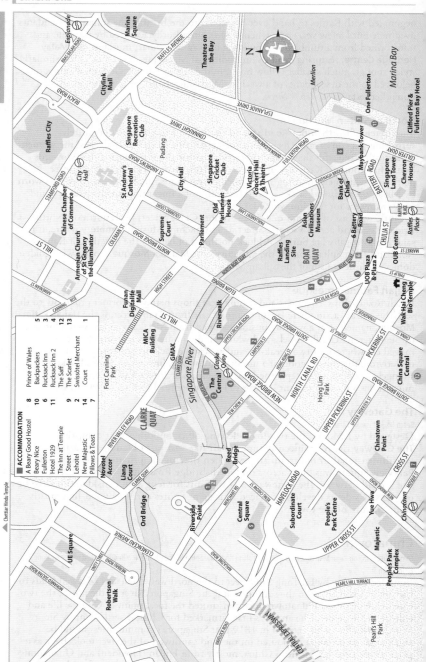

◀ Chettiar Hindu Temple

■ ACCOMMODATION

A Beary Good Hostel	8
Beary Nice	10
Fullerton	6
Hotel 1929	11
The Inn at Temple Street	4
Lehotel	9
New Majestic	2
Pillows & Toast	14
Prince of Wales	7
Backpackers	5
Rucksack Inn	3
Rucksack Inn 2	4
The Saff	12
The Scarlet	13
SwissÔtel Merchant Court	1

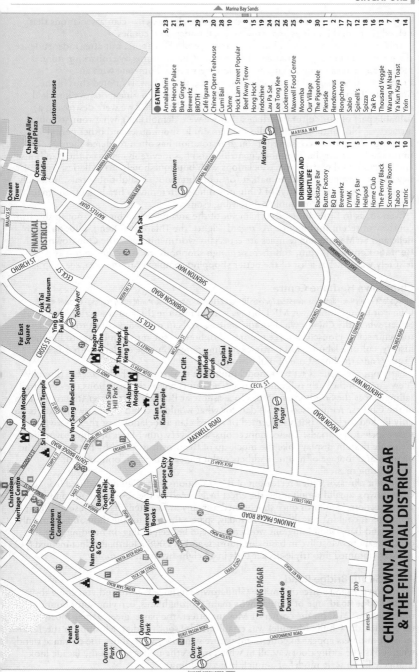

CHINATOWN, TANJONG PAGAR & THE FINANCIAL DISTRICT

▲ Marina Bay Sands

● EATING

Annalakshmi	5, 23
Bee Heong Palace	21
Blue Ginger	31
Brewerkz	1
BROTH	29
Café Iguana	3
Chinese Opera Teahouse	20
Cumi Bali	28
Dôme	10
Hock Lam Street Popular Beef Kway Teow	8
Hong Hock	15
Indochine	19
Lau Pa Sat	24
Lee Tong Kee	22
Lockerroom	26
Maxwell Food Centre	25
Moomba	9
Our Village	6
The Pigeonhole	30
Pierside	11
Rendezvous	2
Rongcheng	17
Sabio	27
Spinelli's	12
Spizza	18
Tak Po	16
Thousand Veggie	13
Warung M Nasir	7
Ya Kun Kaya Toast	4
Yixin	14

■ DRINKING AND NIGHTLIFE

Backstage Bar	8
Butter Factory	7
BQ Bar	4
Brewerkz	2
DYMK	11
Harry's Bar	5
Helipad	3
Home Club	1
The Penny Black	6
Screening Room	9
Taboo	12
Tantric	10

9

shops with familiar products and, most importantly, *kongsis* – clan associations that helped them find lodgings and work as small traders and coolies.

This was one of the most colourful districts of old Singapore, but after independence the government chose to grapple with its tumbledown slums by embarking upon a **redevelopment** campaign that saw whole streets razed. Someone with an unimpeachable insight into those times, one Lee Kuan Yew, is quoted thus in the Singapore City Gallery (see p.508): "In our rush to rebuild Singapore, we knocked down many old and quaint buildings. Then we realized that we were destroying a valuable part of our cultural heritage, that we were demolishing what tourists found attractive." Not until the 1980s did the remaining shophouses and other period buildings begin to be conserved, though restoration has often rendered them improbably perfect. Furthermore, gentrification has inevitably replaced the clan houses and religious and martial arts associations with boutique hotels, art galleries, new-media companies and upmarket (or sometimes not so salubrious) bars. Ironically, getting a taste of the old ways of Chinatown now often means heading off the main streets into the concrete municipal housing estates.

Even so, as in Little India, the character of the area has had a bit of a shot in the arm courtesy of recent immigrants. As regards sights, the **Thian Hock Keng**, **Buddha Tooth Relic** and **Sri Mariamman** temples are especially worthwhile, as is the **Chinatown Heritage Centre** museum, and there's enough shophouse architecture to justify a leisurely wander. For a list of the better **shopping complexes** in the area, see p.559.

Chinatown Heritage Centre

48 Pagoda St · Daily 9am–8pm, last admission 7pm · S$10 · ☎ 6221 9556, ⓦ www.chinatownheritage.com.sg · Chinatown MRT

One exit from Chinatown MRT brings you up into the thick of the action on Pagoda Street, where the **Chinatown Heritage Centre** stands in marked contrast to the tacky souvenir stalls. Housed in three restored shophouses, the museum brings to life the history, culture, labours and pastimes of Singapore's Chinese settlers, with evocative displays and the liberal use of oral history clips.

Early on, the scene is set by a model junk, like those on which the *singkeh* (literally "new guests"), the early migrants, arrived; accounts tell of the privations they endured sailing across the South China Sea. Once ashore at Bullock Cart Water (the translation of the Chinese name, used to this day, for what would become Chinatown), settlers not only looked for work but also formed or joined clan associations, or the less savoury secret societies or triads. These connections, and every other facet of Chinatown life, are made flesh in displays like the mock-up of the prostitute's shabby boudoir and the pictures and footage of haunted addicts seeking escape through opium, their "devastating master".

The tour climaxes with a recreation of the conditions that migrants endured in Chinatown's squalid shophouses, the effect heightened by the absence of air conditioning in this section. Landlords once shoehorned as many as forty tenants into a single floor; if you think it couldn't possibly happen today, spare a thought for the thousands of mainly Indian and Bangladeshi migrant workers who can be seen toiling on building sites all over Singapore. Most live in basic dormitories, and in 2008 a journalist documented 54 workers crammed into triple-decker beds in an eight-by-six-metre room.

Along South Bridge Road

Head down Pagoda Street from the Chinatown Heritage Centre and you come to **South Bridge Road**, one of Chinatown's main thoroughfares, carrying southbound traffic. At no. 218, on the corner of Mosque Street, the pastel green **Jamae Mosque** (also called the Chulia Mosque) was established by south Indian Muslims in the 1820s. Its twin minarets appear to contain miniature windows while above the entrance stands what looks like a tiny doorway, all of which makes the upper part of the facade look strangely like a scale model of a much larger building.

One street northeast, at the junction with **Upper Cross Street**, roadblocks were set up during the Japanese occupation, and Singaporeans vetted for signs of anti-Japanese sentiment in the infamous **Sook Ching** campaign (see p.519). That tragic episode is commemorated by a simple, signposted monument in the **Hong Lim Complex**, a housing estate that also happens to boast walkways lined with medical halls, makers of *chops* (rubber stamps), stores selling dried foodstuffs and so forth – much more representative of the area's original character than more recent arrivals.

To top up your blood-sugar level while wandering the area, pop into the **Tong Heng pastry shop** (daily 9am–10pm) at no. 285, which sells custard tarts, lotus seed paste biscuits and other Chinese sweet treats.

Sri Mariamman Temple

244 South Bridge Rd, a few doors down from the Jamae Mosque, • Daily 7am–noon & 6–9pm, though it may be possible to look around at other times • Free • ☎ 6223 4064

Singapore's oldest Hindu shrine, the **Sri Mariamman Temple**, boasts a superb entrance *gopuram* bristling with brightly coloured deities. A wood and *atap* hut was first erected here in 1827 on land belonging to Naraina Pillay, a government clerk who arrived on the same ship as Stamford Raffles when he first came ashore at Singapore; the present temple was completed around 1843. Inside, look up at the roof to see splendid friezes depicting a host of Hindu deities, including the three manifestations of the supreme being: Brahma the creator (with three of his four heads showing), Vishnu the preserver, and Shiva the destroyer (holding one of his sons). The main sanctum is devoted to Mariamman, a goddess worshipped for her healing powers. Smaller sanctums dotted about the walkway circumnavigating the temple honour other deities. In the one dedicated to the goddess Periachi Amman, a sculpture portrays her with a queen lying on her lap, whose evil child she has ripped from her womb; it's odd, then, that Periachi Amman is the protector of children, to whom babies are brought when one month old.

Once a year, during the festival of **Thimithi** (Oct or Nov), an unassuming patch of sand to the left of the main sanctum is covered in red-hot coals that male Hindus run across to prove the strength of their faith. The participants, who line up all the way along South Bridge Road waiting for their turn, are supposedly protected from the heat of the coals by the power of prayer.

Eu Yan Sang Medical Hall

269 South Bridge Rd • Mon–Sat 8.30am–6pm • ☎ 6223 6333

The beautifully renovated **Eu Yan Sang Medical Hall** stands across the road from the Hindu temple. The smell in the hall is the first thing you'll notice (a little like a compost heap on a hot day); the second, the weird assortment of ingredients on the shelves, which to the uninitiated look more likely to kill than cure. Besides the usual herbs and roots favoured by the Chinese, there are various dubious remedies derived from exotic and endangered species. Blood circulation problems and wounds are eased with centipedes and insects, crushed into a "rubbing liquor"; the ground-up gall bladders of snakes or bears apparently work wonders on pimples; while deer penis is supposed to provide a lift to any sexual problem.

Upstairs, the small but engaging **Birds' Nest Gallery** casts light on this most famous of Chinese delicacies. Produced by swiftlets, the edible nests are a mixture of saliva, moss and grass, and emerged as a prized supplement among China's royal and noble classes during the Ming Dynasty. Today they are still valued for their supposed efficacy in boosting the immune system and curing bronchial ailments. The birds live high up in the caves of Southeast Asia, and if you've been to Niah in Sarawak you may well have seen their nests being harvested – arduous and sometimes dangerous work. With the nests commanding high prices, some Malaysians are employing the dubious practice of rearing the swiftlets in bricked-up town-centre shophouses, around which swiftlets can be seen wheeling at dawn and dusk.

9

Buddha Tooth Relic Temple

288 South Bridge Rd, just after Sago St • Daily 7am–7pm • Free • ☎ 6220 0220, ⊛ www.btrts.org.sg • no shorts, vests or non-vegetarian food

The imposing **Buddha Tooth Relic Temple** is the most startling addition to Chinatown's shrines in many a year. The place simply clobbers you with its opulence – even the elevators have brocaded walls – and the thousands upon thousands of Buddhist figurines plastered up and down various interior surfaces. It also boasts its own museum and a gallery of Buddhist art.

The temple has its origins in the discovery, in 1980, of what was thought to be a tooth of Buddha inside a collapsed stupa at a Burmese monastery. The monastery's chief abbot visited Singapore in 2002 and decided the island would make a suitable sanctuary for the relic, to be housed in its own temple if there were a chance of building one. A prime site in Chinatown was duly secured, and the temple opened in 2007.

The main hall

The focus of the main hall is **Maitreya**, a Buddha who is yet to appear on Earth. Carved from juniper wood said to be 1000 years old, his statue has a yellow flame-like halo around it. But what really captures the attention are the Buddhas covering the entire side walls. There are a hundred main statuettes, individually crafted, interspersed with thousands more tiny figurines embedded in a vast array of shelving, each with its own serial number displayed. Signage soon makes you aware that many things in the temple are up for "**adoption**" – figurines and fittings can be the object of sponsorship, presumably winning donors good karma while recouping the S$62 million construction bill and helping the temple keep up with its outgoings. Behind the main hall, another large hall centres on the **Avalokitesvara** bodhisattva.

The **mezzanine** affords great views over proceedings and chanting ceremonies in the main hall, while **level 2** contains the temple's own **teahouse**.

Buddhist Culture Museum

Daily 8am–6pm

On **level 3** are some seriously impressive examples of Buddhist **statuary** in brass, wood and stone, plus other artworks. They're all part of the **Buddhist Culture Museum**, with panels telling the story of Gautama Buddha in the first person. At the back, the relic chamber displays what are said to be the cremated remains of Buddha's nose, brain, liver etc, all looking like fish roe in different colours.

Sacred Buddha Tooth Relic Stupa

Daily 9am–noon & 3–6pm

On **level 4** you finally encounter what all the fuss is ultimately about – the **Sacred Buddha Tooth Relic Stupa**. Some 3m in diameter, it sits in its own chamber behind glass panels and can't be inspected close up, though there is an accurate scale model at the front. The Maitreya Buddha is depicted at the front of the stupa, guarded by four lions, with a ring of 35 more Buddhas below; floor tiles around the stupa – a S$5000 adoption – are "made of pure gold".

The roof garden

Above is the temple's lovely **roof garden**, its walls lined with twelve thousand 5cm figurines of the Amitayus Buddha. But the centrepiece is "the largest cloisonné **prayer wheel** in the world", around 5m tall. Each rotation (clockwise, in case you have a go) dings a bell and represents the recitation of one sutra.

Sago Street

Today, the tight knot of streets west of South Bridge Road between Sago Street and Pagoda Street is Chinatown at its most touristy, packed with souvenir sellers and foreigner-friendly restaurants. But in bygone days these streets formed Chinatown's nucleus, teeming with trishaws and food hawkers, while opium dens and brothels lurked within the shophouses. Until as recently as the 1950s, **Sago Street** was home to several death houses – rudimentary hospices where skeletal citizens saw out their final hours on rattan camp beds. Trishaw riders collecting the dead would, as one interviewee recounts at the Chinatown Heritage Centre, "put a hat on the corpse, put it onto the trishaw, and cycle all the way back to the coffin shop". Sago, Smith, Temple and Pagoda streets recapture something of the best of their original atmosphere around Chinese New Year, when they're crammed with stalls selling festive branches of blossom, oranges, sausages and waxed chickens – which look as if they have melted to reveal a handful of bones inside. The ugly concrete **Chinatown Complex** at the end of the street is a workaday place housing outlets selling silk, kimonos and household goods.

Trengganu Street

To the right of the Chinatown Complex, Sago Street becomes **Trengganu Street**. Despite the hordes of tourists, there are occasional glimpses of Chinatown's **old trades** and industries, such as Nam's Supplies at 22 Smith St, producing shirts, watches, mobile phones and laptops – all made out of paper so that they can be burned at Chinese funerals to ensure the deceased don't lack creature comforts in the next life.

Keong Saik Road and Bukit Pasoh Road

In the southernmost corner of Chinatown, west of Kreta Ayer Road and accessible from Outram Park MRT, a pocket of streets are lined with **restored shophouses**, worth a look not only for their beautifully painted facades, shuttered windows and tilework but also because the area is the evolving new Chinatown in microcosm. Already *in situ* are several boutique hotels; the Gan Clan Association at 18/20 Bukit Pasoh Rd now shares space with karaoke bars. Glimpses of the old Chinatown survive, for example, at 13 Keong Saik Rd, where you'll find a shrine that looks slightly too pristine for its own good; and even in modern residential towers like Block 334, Keong Saik Road, where in unit #01-04 Nam Cheong & Co produces houses and near-life-size safes, servants and Mercedes cars out of paper for funerary use.

New Bridge Road and Eu Tong Sen Street

Chinatown's main shopping drag comprises southbound **New Bridge Road** and northbound **Eu Tong Sen Street**, along which are a handful of shopping malls. Try to pop into one of the barbecued-pork vendors around the intersection of Smith, Temple and Pagoda streets with New Bridge Road – as they're cooked, the thin, flat, red squares of *bak kwa*, coated with a sweet marinade, produce a rich, smoky odour that is pure Chinatown. As you chew on your *bak kwa*, check out two striking buildings across the road. Nearest is the flat-fronted **Majestic Opera House**, which no longer hosts performances but still boasts five images of Chinese opera stars over its doors. Just beside it, the Yue Hwa Chinese Products Emporium occupies the former **Great Southern Hotel**, built in 1927 by the son of Eu Yan Sang, Eu Tong Sen. In its fifth-floor nightclub, wealthy locals would drink liquor, smoke opium and pay to dance with so-called local "taxi girls".

Ann Siang Hill

Ann Siang Hill is both the name of a little mound and of a lane that leads off South Bridge Road up a slope, where it forks into Club Street on the left and Ann Siang Road, which veers gently right. Despite being only a few paces removed from the hubbub of the main road, the hill is somehow a different realm, a little collection of gentrified shophouses with a distinct villagey feel. Packed with swanky restaurants, cafés and bars, plus the odd boutique, the area typifies the new Chinatown. At the southern end of the road, a short flight of steps leads up to **Ann Siang Hill Park**, a sliver of generic greenery whose only attraction is that it offers a **short cut** to Amoy Street.

Club Street

The temple-carving shops on **Club Street** have long since gone, and just a handful of the **clan associations** and **guilds** whose presence gave the street its name now remain. They're easy to spot: black-and-white photos of old members cover the walls, and old men sit and chat behind the screens that almost invariably span the doorway. Most notable of all is the **Chinese Weekly Entertainment Club** at no. 76, on a side street also called Club Street. Flanked by roaring lion heads, it's an imposing mansion that was built by a Peranakan millionaire in 1891.

Singapore City Gallery

URA Centre, 45 Maxwell Rd • Mon–Sat 9am–5pm • Free • ☎ 6321 8321, ⓦ www.ura.gov.sg/gallery

Town planning may not sound the most fascinating premise for a gallery, but then again, no nation remodels with such ambition as Singapore, whose planners are constantly erasing roads here and replacing one ultramodern complex with an even more souped-up development there. The latest grand designs for the island are exhibited west of Ann Siang Hill at the surprisingly absorbing **Singapore City Gallery**, within the government Urban Redevelopment Authority's headquarters.

The URA has rightly been criticized in the past for slighting Singapore's architectural heritage, so it is heartening that displays on the first and second floors make reassuring noises about the value of the venerable shophouses and colonial villas that remain. But the gallery's emphasis is more upon the future than the past, amply illustrated by the vast and incredibly intricate **scale model** of downtown Singapore on the ground floor, every row of shophouses, every roof of every building – including some not yet built – fashioned out of plywood. This and other scale models are turned out by a dedicated team whose first-floor workshop is sadly not open to the public, though you might catch a glimpse of them at work through the glass.

Amoy Street

Amoy Street, together with Telok Ayer Street, was designated a Hokkien enclave in the colony's early days (Amoy being the old name of Xiamen city in China's Fujian province). Long terraces of smartly refurbished shophouses flank the street, all featuring characteristic **five-foot ways**, or covered verandas, so called because they jut five feet out from the house. If you descend here from Ann Siang Hill Park, you'll emerge by the small **Sian Chai Kang Temple** at no. 66. With the customary dragons on the roof, it's dominated by huge urns, full to the brim with ash from untold numbers of burned incense sticks. Two carved stone lions guard the temple; their fancy red neck ribbons are said to attract good fortune and prosperity.

Telok Ayer Street

One street removed from Amoy Street is **Telok Ayer Street**, whose southern end starts near Tanjong Pagar MRT. The name, meaning "Watery Bay" in Malay, recalls the mid-nineteenth century when the street would have run along the shoreline. Nowadays, thanks to land reclamation, it's no closer to a beach than is Beach Road, but some of Singapore's oldest buildings cling on between the modern towers – temples and mosques where newly arrived immigrants and sailors thanked their god(s) for their safe passage.

The first building of note you come to if you walk up from the station is the square 1889 **Chinese Methodist Church**, whose design – portholes and windows adorned with white crosses and capped by a Chinese pagoda-style roof – is a pleasing blend of East and West. Just beyond McCallum Street, the blue-and-white **Al-Abrar Mosque** is built on the spot where Chulia worshippers set up a thatched *kuchu palli* (in Tamil, small mosque), in 1827.

Thian Hock Keng Temple

158 Telok Ayer St • Daily 7.30am–5.30pm • Free • ☎ 6423 4616, ⓦ www.thianhockkeng.com.sg

The immaculately restored **Thian Hock Keng Temple** stands in marked contrast to the gleaming glass building opposite, belonging to the Hokkien clan association, which manages it. From across the street, the temple looks spectacular: dragons stalk its broad roofs, while the entrance to the compound bristles with ceramic flowers, foliage and figures. Construction began in 1839 using materials imported from China, on the site of a small joss house where immigrants made offerings to Ma Zu, the queen of heaven. A statue of the goddess, shipped in from southern China in time for the temple's completion in 1842, stands in the centre of the main hall, flanked by the martial figure of Guan Yu on the right and physician Bao Sheng on the left. Against the left wall, look out for an altar containing the curious figures of General Fan and General Xie. The two are said to have arranged to meet by a river bridge, but Xie was delayed; Fan waited doggedly in the appointed spot and drowned in a flash flood, which supposedly accounts for his black skin and the grimace on his face. When Xie finally arrived, he was filled with guilt and hanged himself – hence his depiction, with tongue hanging down to his chest.

Nagore Durgha Shrine

140 Telok Ayer St • Museum daily 10am–6pm • Free

It's a testament to Singapore's multicultural nature that Thian Hock Keng's next-door neighbour is the charming brown-and-white **Nagore Durgha Shrine** to the Muslim ascetic, Shahul Hamid of Nagore. It was built in the 1820s by Chulias from southern India, as was the Jamae Mosque (see p.504), so it's not surprising that the buildings appear cut from the same cloth, so to speak. Part of the shrine now houses an excellent small **museum** of the history of Telok Ayer Street, and how earth from nearby hillocks was used to push the coastline south. The few simple artefacts and photographs do a good job of unpacking the nuances of Muslim Indian identity in Singapore, a place (along with Malaysia) where Hindu members of the Indian community are referred to by the part of India they emigrated from, whereas their Muslim counterparts have been carelessly lumped together under the banner of their faith.

Ying Fo Fui Kun

98 Telok Ayer St, beyond the junction with Cross St • Daily 10am–10pm • Free

Among the smartest of Chinatown's surviving clan houses, the **Ying Fo Fui Kun** was established in 1822 by Hakkas from Guangdong province. It has narrowly avoided being swallowed up by the adjacent Far East Square complex, but in its present orderly state, with an immaculate altar boasting gilt calligraphy and carvings, it's hard to imagine it having been the social hub of an entire community. The clan association that runs it has been undertaking membership drives to stop itself decaying into a senior citizens' club, a real danger in a country where provincial dialects – traditionally used as a marker of identity among the Chinese – have been on the decline since the 1970s after a sometimes aggressive state campaign to standardize on Mandarin.

Far East Square

Far East Square is a sort of heritage development that incorporates the northernmost section of Amoy Street into what is otherwise a rather mundane collection of shops, restaurants and offices on Cross Street. Also co-opted into the complex is the **Fuk Tak Chi Street Museum**, 76 Telok Ayer St (daily 10am–10pm; free). This was once Singapore's oldest surviving temple, having been established by the Hakka and Cantonese communities in 1824; today it's a mere "street museum", its altar holding a model junk crewed by sailors in blue shorts. A diorama depicts Telok Ayer Street in its waterfront heyday, with pigtailed labourers taking part in a procession to the temple, depicted with a stage set up in front where opera performers are getting ready to strut their stuff.

9

Boat Quay

Close to the old mouth of the Singapore River, the pedestrianized row of waterfront shophouses known as **Boat Quay** is one of Singapore's most successful bids at urban regeneration. Derelict in the early 1990s, it's since become a thriving hangout, sporting a huge collection of restaurants and bars. The area's historical significance may be easier to appreciate through its street names – Synagogue Street nearby, for example, was the site of the island's first synagogue.

The Wak Hai Cheng Bio Temple

Philip St, south of Boat Quay

The **Wak Hai Cheng Bio Temple** (also called the Yueh Hai Ching Temple) completes Chinatown's string of former waterfront temples. Its name, "Temple of the Calm Sea", made it a logical choice for early worshippers who had arrived safely in Singapore; an effigy of Tian Hou, the queen of heaven and protector of seafarers, is housed in the temple's right-hand chamber. The incredibly ornate roof is crammed with tiny depictions of Chinese village scenes.

Tanjong Pagar

The district of **Tanjong Pagar**, south of Chinatown between Neil and Tanjong Pagar roads, was once a veritable sewer of brothels and opium dens. Then it became earmarked for regeneration as a conservation area, following which many dozens of shophouses were painstakingly restored and converted into bars, restaurants and shops, notably on Neil Road and Duxton Hill. The main attraction here is the **Baba House**, though as an architectural attention-grabber it's rivalled by the seven interlinked towers of **Pinnacle@Duxton**, a showpiece municipal housing development on Cantonment Road, dominating the southern skyline of Chinatown.

Baba House

157 Neil Rd • Book compulsory tours (2 weekly) in advance • S$10 • ☎ 6227 5731 or ⊛ edu.nus.sg/museum/baba • Use the Cantonment Road exit from Outram Park MRT, or ride bus #174 from Orchard Rd or Bras Basah Rd to its terminus

The **Baba House** is one of Singapore's most impressive museums, because it is and isn't a museum: what you see is a late nineteenth or early twentieth-century Peranakan house, meticulously restored to its appearance in the late 1920s, a particularly prosperous time in its history.

Like the Cheong Fatt Tze Mansion in Penang, the place is easily spotted as it's painted a vivid blue. Note the **phoenixes** and **peonies** on the eaves above the entrance, signifying longevity and wealth and, together, marital bliss. Even more eye-catching is the **pintu pagar**, the pair of swing doors with beautiful gilt and mother-of-pearl inlays.

TAKING CHINESE TEA

Two Tanjong Pagar **teahouses** enable visitors to glean something of the intricacies of the deep Chinese connection with tea by taking part in a tea workshop lasting up to an hour. Participants are introduced to different varieties of tea and talked through the history of tea cultivation and the rituals of brewing and appreciating the drink. The water, for example, has to reach an optimum temperature that depends on which type of tea is being prepared; experts can tell its heat by the size of the rising bubbles, described variously as "sand eyes", "prawn eyes", "fish eyes", etc. Both venues also stock an extensive range of tea-related accoutrements such as tall "sniffer" cups used to savour the aroma of the brew before it is poured into squat teacups for drinking.

Tea Chapter 9–11 Neil Rd; ☎ 6226 1175. Tea workshops for S$20–30 per head, or around $10 per person for a quick tea-making demonstration and sampling session.

Yixing Yuan Teahouse 30–32 Tanjong Pagar Rd; ☎ 6224 6961. Workshops from per head for a group of at least five.

The ground floor

Beyond the *pintu pagar*, yet more exquisite inlay work is in evidence on the antique chairs in the **main hall**, used for entertaining guests. The altar here, among the last of its kind in Singapore, is backed by an exquisitely carved wood screen behind which the women of the household could eavesdrop on proceedings. Behind is the **family hall**, with an air well, open to the sky, in its midst. Note the original tilework depicting roses and tulips, indicating a European influence, and the gilt bats on the walls; the Mandarin term for bats is *bianfu*, and the *fu* in question is a homonym for the Chinese character meaning "good fortune".

The upper floors

Upstairs at the front end of the house, the centrepiece of the **main bedroom** is an ornate wooden four-poster bed with gilt and red lacquer decorations, and bearing carved motifs such as musical instruments and yet more bats. Your guide will almost certainly open up the **peephole** in the floor, exposing a small shaft down to the main hall. The **third storey**, a later addition, is used for temporary exhibitions.

The Financial District

The area south of the mouth of the Singapore River was swamp until land reclamation in the mid-1820s rendered it fit for building. Within just a few years, Commercial Square here had become the colony's busiest business address, boasting the banks, ships' chandlers and warehouses of a burgeoning trading port. The square was later Singapore's main shopping area until superseded by Orchard Road in the late 1960s; today the square, now called Raffles Place, forms the nucleus of Singapore's **Financial District** (see map, pp.502–503). Until recently, if the area figured in the popular imagination at all, it would have been because of the rogue trader Nick Leeson, whose antics here brought about the **Barings Bank collapse** of 1995, though it seems like small beer when set against the global financial improprieties of recent years. East of here, the southern jaw of Marina Bay, **Marina South**, is home to yet more banks and features risk-taking in a different vein as the site of the striking **Marina Bay Sands** hotel and casino.

Raffles Place

Raffles Place makes a good prelude to a stroll along the south bank of the river to Boat Quay (see opposite) or across Cavenagh Bridge to the Colonial District (see p.483), but the main reason to visit the Financial District itself is to feel like an ant in a canyon of skyscrapers. Surfacing from Raffles Place MRT, follow the signs for Raffles Place itself to be confronted by a veritable grove of gleaming towers. To the left is the soaring metallic triangle of the **OUB Centre** (home to the Overseas Union Bank), and to its right, the twin towers of the rocket-shaped **UOB Plaza** and the slightly older **UOB Plaza 2** (United Overseas Bank); in front of you are the rich-brown walls of **6 Battery Rd**; and to the right rise sturdy **Singapore Land Tower** and the almost Art Deco **Chevron House**. The three roads that run southwest from Raffles Place – Cecil Street, Robinson Road and Shenton Way – are all chock-a-block with more high-rise banks and financial houses.

Battery Road

Heading towards the river from Raffles Place, you come to **Battery Road**, whose name recalls the days when Fort Fullerton (named after Robert Fullerton, first governor of the Straits Settlements) and its attendant battery of guns used to stand to the east on the site of the *Fullerton* hotel. From here Bonham Street, to the right of the UOB Plaza, leads to the riverside promenade, with Cavenagh Bridge (see p.483) a short distance away to the right.

The main attraction here, Boat Quay aside, is the elegant **Fullerton Building**, worth viewing from Collyer Quay to the east for its facade fronted by sturdy pillars. In

9

keeping with the rest of the area, this was one of Singapore's tallest buildings when it was constructed in 1928 as the headquarters for the General Post Office (a role it fulfilled until the mid-1990s). These days, the building is the luxury *Fullerton* hotel, whose atrium is worth a peek if only to admire the enormous columns within; the lighthouse that used to flash up on the roof is now a swanky Italian restaurant.

Collyer Quay

Collyer Quay runs south along the western shore of Marina Bay from what was the mouth of the Singapore River, linking the Colonial District with Raffles Quay and Shenton Way further south, both of which mark the former line of the seafront. Just east of Collyer Quay, the Merlion Park is home to the **One Fullerton** development, whose bars and restaurants and nightclub look out over the bay, and to a cement statue of Singapore's national symbol, the **Merlion**. Half-lion, half-fish and wholly ugly, the creature reflects the island's maritime connections and the old tale concerning the derivation of its present name, derived from the Sanskrit "Singapura", meaning "Lion City".

South of the park, the Art Deco **Clifford Pier** building, long the departure point for boat trips out to Singapore's southern islands, was rendered defunct by the barrage that seals Marina Bay off from the sea. Mirroring the development at Marina South, the building, along with the **Customs House** building a minute's walk on, have been transformed into restaurant and leisure complexes, run by the company that owns the *Fullerton* hotel; part of Clifford Pier forms the entrance to the hotel's pricier new sibling, the *Fullerton Bay*.

Lau Pa Sat

A short walk along Raffles Quay, the southern continuation of Collyer Quay, a simple octagonal cast-iron structure houses the atmospheric **Lau Pa Sat**, literally "old market". Built in 1894 and also called **Telok Ayer Market**, it's a great place for refreshments as it is home to a 24-hour food court (see p.544).

Marina Bay Sands

10 Bayfront Ave, Marina South • ☎ 6688 8868, ⓦ www.marinabaysands.com • Bayfront MRT, or bus #106 from Orchard Rd/Bras Basah Rd or #133 from Victoria St

Rarely does a building become an icon quite as instantly as the **Marina Bay Sands** hotel and casino, its three 55-floor towers topped and connected by a vast, curved-surfboard-like deck, the **SkyPark**. The most ambitious undertaking yet by its owners, Las Vegas Sands, it opened in April 2010 and quickly replaced the Merlion as the Singapore image of choice in the travel brochures, summing up the country's glitzy fascination with mammon. Even if you have no interest in the casino – open, naturally, 24/7 – the complex, which includes a convention centre, a shopping mall, two concert venues and numerous restaurants, is well worth exploring. The hotel atrium, often so busy with people come to gawp that it feels like a busy train station concourse, is especially striking, the sides of the building sloping into each other overhead to give the impression of being inside a narrow glassy pyramid.

In the evening, a free laser show, **Wonder Full** (Sun–Thurs 8pm & 9.30pm; Fri & Sat 8pm, 9.30pm & 11pm; 15min), splays multicoloured beams from atop the hotel's towers onto Marina Bay, with fountains shooting up from below. Visible from all around the area, the display only looks at all interesting if you're at the hotel itself.

SkyPark

Marina Bay Sands; tickets and access from box office on basement 1 of tower 3, at the northern end of the complex • Observation deck Mon–Thurs 9.30am–10pm, Fri–Sun 9.30am–11pm • S$20

From what would have been an impossible vantage point, high above the sea before the creation of Marina Bay, the SkyPark's observation deck affords superb views over

Singapore's Colonial District on one side and the conservatories of the new **Gardens by the Bay** project on the other (see below). Unfortunately tickets are overpriced, and you only get close up to one of the SkyPark's iconic features, its 150m **infinity pool**, if you buy a ticket to coincide with a guided tour (daily at 10am, 2pm & 9pm; 15min). There's no charge to access the area if you dine or drink at any SkyPark venue.

ArtScience Museum

At the northern end of the Marina Bay Sands complex, close to the helix footbridge that links the area with the Singapore Flyer and Theatres On The Bay • Daily 10am–10pm, last admission 9pm • Prices vary, generally S$15 for one exhibition or S$28 for all areas

The casino resort's **ArtScience Museum**, perhaps meant to temper the relentless obsession with consumption everywhere else in the complex, is easily spotted: its shape is meant to represent a stylized lotus blossom, though from certain angles it looks more like a stubby-fingered hand in concrete. The museum's remit is to decode the connections between art and science, but its permanent gallery is so tiny and full of waffle as to be almost laughable. In practice it majors on world-class travelling exhibitions, sometimes only tenuously linked to the museum's supposed theme – highlights have included artefacts salvaged from the *Titanic* and a collection of works by Salvador Dalí.

Gardens By The Bay South

18 Marina Gardens Drive • See website for times and prices • Gardens free, though fees payable to access conservatories • Ⓦ www.gardensbythebay.org.sg • Bayfront MRT or bus #400 from Marina Bay MRT

Two vast conservatories, roofs arched like the backs of foraging dinosaurs, are the most eye-catching feature of the southern section of **Gardens By The Bay** (see map, p.482). Intended to be a brand new botanic garden for Singapore, the gardens are split into three chunks around Marina Bay; the southern area, next to *Marina Bay Sands*, is the first to open and the largest. The conservatories, one housing Mediterranean and African flora including baobab and olive trees, the other cloud forest of the kind found on Malaysia's highest peaks, are the big draw, but it's also worth checking out the **Supertree Grove** – a collection of towers shaped like giant golf tees and swathed in creepers and climbers.

Marina Centre

Promenade or Esplanade MRT, or City Hall MRT via the subterranean CityLink Mall

Marina Centre (see map, p.484) is the name generally applied to the large tract of reclaimed land east of the Padang and the *Raffles* hotel, forming the northern arc of Marina Bay and robbing Beach Road of its beach. The area still has a somewhat artificial feel, boasting no residential districts or traditional places of worship, and dominated by malls, conference centres and expensive offices and hotels. Visitors come here mostly to enjoy views of the Singapore cityscape from either the southern end of Marina Centre or the Singapore Flyer – or both.

Esplanade – Theatres on the Bay

1 Esplanade Drive • Daily 10am–late, self-guided tours daily 10am–6pm • S$10 • ☎ 6828 8377, Ⓦ www.esplanade.com

Opinion is split as to whether the two huge, spiked shells that roof the **Esplanade – Theatres on the Bay** project, just east of the Padang, are peerless modernistic architecture or indulgent kitsch. They have variously been compared to kitchen sieves, hedgehogs, even durians (the preferred description among locals), though two giant insect eyes is perhaps the best comparison.

Opened in 2002, Esplanade boasts a concert hall, theatres, gallery space and, on the third floor, **library@esplanade**, with a wide range of arts-related books and other resources. It's possible to take a self-guided **iTour** of the building based around audiovisual content stored on a hand-held gizmo, but what lures most casual visitors

9

are the **views**, particularly fine at dusk, across the bay to the Financial District and *Marina Bay Sands*.

Singapore Flyer

30 Raffles Ave, 10min east of Theatres on the Bay • Daily 8.30am–10pm, every 30min • S$29.50 • ☎ 6333 3311, ⓦ www.singaporeflyer.com

Standing a lofty 165m tall – the same elevation as the summit of Bukit Timah, the island's highest point, and about 30m taller than the London Eye – the **Singapore Flyer** falls slightly flat as an attraction because it's simply not in the right place. From here the most atmospheric areas of old Singapore, including the remaining rows of shophouses in Chinatown and Little India, are largely obscured by a forest of somewhat interchangeable towers; better views can be had from various high-rise hotels.

The flight

The dollar-a-minute ride – billed as a **flight** – initially has you looking east over the **Kallang** district, where the grand new Sports Hub stadium complex is due to be completed in 2014. Also visible is the narrow **barrage** allowing Marina Bay to be used as a freshwater reservoir. In the distance beyond the shipping lanes, Indonesia's **Riau archipelago** is so close yet much less connected to Singapore than Malaysia, thanks to the 1824 Anglo-Dutch treaty under which the British let the islands south of Singapore slip into the Dutch sphere of influence. Looking north, it's much more exciting to pick out the golden domes of the Sultan Mosque and the shophouses of **Arab Street** beyond the twin **Gateway** buildings on Beach Road. As your capsule reaches maximum height, you might just make out the low hump of **Bukit Timah**, topped with a couple of radio masts, on the horizon beyond Theatres on the Bay.

The descent affords good views of **Marina Bay Sands** and the **Financial District**. Originally the latter could be seen on the ascent, but feng shui concerns meant the wheel's direction had to be reversed (apparently having the capsules ascend pointing towards the banks' towers was channelling good luck up and away from the area).

Orchard Road and around

It would be hard to conjure an image more at odds with the present reality of **Orchard Road** than the late May Turnbull's depiction, during early colonial times, of "a country lane lined with bamboo hedges and shrubbery, with trees meeting overhead". In the early part of the last century, merchants here for constitutionals would have strolled past rows of nutmeg trees, followed at a discreet distance by their manservants. Today, Orchard Road is synonymous with **shopping** – huge, often glitzy malls selling everything you can imagine line the road (see p.558). But with malls all over downtown and in every new town on the island, Orchard Road has not been totally untouched by the malaise afflicting other city-centre shopping areas the world over. Perhaps with this in mind, Singapore's planners have put Orchard Road through a costly makeover in recent years, revamping walkways and adding three new malls. The most striking, **Ion Orchard**, right above Orchard MRT, vaguely resembles a smaller version of Theatres on the Bay.

Orchard Road begins as the continuation of Tanglin Road and channels traffic east for nearly 3km to Bras Basah and Selegie roads, near the Colonial District. The bucolic allure of the Orchard Road of old survives 1500m west of the start, where you'll find Singapore's excellent **Botanic Gardens**.

Dhoby Ghaut

In the **Dhoby Ghaut** area, at the eastern end of Orchard Road, Indian *dhobies* (laundrymen) used to wash clothes in the Stamford Canal, which once ran along Orchard and Stamford roads. Those days are long gone, though something of the past survives in the **Cathay building** (ⓦ www.cathay.org.sg), home to the company behind one of Singapore's and Malaysia's oldest cinema chains. The building houses a multiplex cinema and boasts a 1939 Art Deco facade that looks better than ever after a recent remodelling which saw the tower behind demolished and, unusually, replaced by a smaller construction.

Cathay Gallery

Level 2, the Cathay building, Dhoby Ghaut • Mon–Sat 11am–7pm • Free • ☎ 6732 7332, ⓦ www.thecathaygallery.com.sg

The **Cathay Gallery** offers a window into the past by displaying memorabilia of the Cathay Organization's eight decades in the movie business, including its heyday in the 1950s and 1960s, when the company made its own Chinese- and Malay-language films.

The Istana

Istana and grounds open five days a year (see website for details) • S$1 • ⓦ www.istana.gov.sg

A three-minute walk west along Orchard Road from Dhoby Ghaut MRT takes you past the **Plaza Singapura** mall, beyond which stern-looking soldiers guard the main gate of Singapore's **Istana**, built in 1869. With ornate cornices, elegant louvred shutters and a high mansard roof, the building was originally the official residence of Singapore's British governors; now it's home to Singapore's president, a ceremonial role for which elections are nonetheless contested. The first Sunday of the month sees a **changing of the guard** ceremony at the main gate at 5.45pm.

Emerald Hill

Not ten minutes' walk west of the Istana, a number of architecturally notable houses have survived the bulldozers at **Emerald Hill**, behind the Centrepoint mall. Granted to Englishman William Cuppage in 1845, the hill was for some years afterwards the site of a large nutmeg plantation. After his death in 1872, the land was subdivided and sold off, much of it to members of the Peranakan community. Walk up Emerald Hill Road today and you'll see exquisite houses from the era, in the so-called Chinese Baroque style, typified by the use of coloured ceramic tiles, carved swing doors, shuttered windows and pastel-shaded walls with fine plaster mouldings. Unsurprisingly, quite a few now host trendy restaurants and bars, with a few more in a less distinguished row of restored shophouses called **Cuppage Terrace**, east of the Centrepoint mall.

Goodwood Park Hotel

A few minutes' walk north up Scotts Road from Orchard MRT, the impressive **Goodwood Park Hotel** has gleaming walls and a distinctive squat, steeple-like tower. Having started life in 1900 as the Teutonia Club for German expats, it was commandeered by the British Custodian of Enemy Property with the outbreak of war across Europe in 1914, and didn't open again until 1918, after which it served for several years as a function hall. In 1929, it became a hotel, though by 1942 it and the *Raffles*, designed incidentally by the same architect, were lodging Japanese officers; fittingly, the *Goodwood Park* was later used for war-crimes trials. Today the hotel remains one of the classiest in town and is a well-regarded venue for a British-style tea.

Botanic Gardens

1 Cluny Rd • Daily 5am–midnight • Free, with free weekend tours of some sections plus free concerts • ☎ 6471 7138, ⓦ www.sbg.org. sg • Tanglin gate: bus #7 from Arab St area or #174 from Chinatown, both via Somerset Rd, next to Orchard Rd; Bukit Timah Rd entrance: Botanic Gardens MRT or bus #66 or #170 from Little India, or #171 from Somerset Rd

Singapore has long made green space an integral part of the island's landscape, but none of its parks comes close to matching the refinement of the **Singapore Botanic Gardens**. Founded in 1859, the gardens were where the Brazilian seeds that gave rise to the great **rubber plantations** of Malaya were first nurtured in 1877. Henry Ridley, named the gardens' director the following year, recognized the financial potential of rubber and spent the next twenty years persuading Malayan plantation-owners to convert to this new crop, an obsession that earned him the nickname "Mad" Ridley. In later years the gardens

9

■ ACCOMMODATION	
Goodwood Park	2
Grand Central	4
Innotel	8
Lloyd's Inn	9
Marriott	3
Mandarin Orchard	6
Regent	7
Shangri-La	1
Supreme	5

● EATING					
Akashi	4	Crystal Jade La Mian Xiao Long Bao	8	Marché	9
Café l'Espresso	1	Lao Beijing	6	Min Jiang	1
Cedele	8	Maharajah	3	PS Café	2, 5

became a centre for the breeding of new **orchid** hybrids. Recent additions have extended the park all the way north to Bukit Timah Road, where the Botanic Gardens MRT station (a long journey from downtown on the Circle Line) offers a route to the least interesting part of the gardens; the itinerary that follows assumes the classic approach up Tanglin and Napier roads to the **Tanglin gate** at the start of Cluny Road.

Into the gardens

Once through the Tanglin gate, you can take a sharp right up the slope to the **Botany Centre** just ahead, a large building containing an information desk with free garden **maps**. Alternatively, continue straight down the path from the gate, lined with frangipanis, casuarinas and the odd majestic banyan tree, for five minutes to reach the tranquil main **lake**, nearly as old as the gardens themselves. At the lake's far end, paths run through a small tract of surviving **rainforest** to the **ginger garden**, packed with flowering gingers as exotic and gaudy as anything you could hope to see in the tropics, and home to the fine *Halia* (Malay for "ginger") restaurant.

National Orchid Garden

Daily 8.30am–7pm, last admission 6pm • S$5

A feast of blooms of almost every hue are on show at the **National Orchid Garden**. Most orchids anchor themselves on trees in the wild, so it's initially odd to see them thriving here at ground level in specially adapted beds. There's an entire section of orchids named after visiting dignitaries and celebrities; *Dendrobium Margaret Thatcher* turns out to be a severe pink with two of its petals looking like twisted ribbons, while *Vandaenopsis Nelson Mandela* is a reassuring warm yellowy-brown. In the attached gift shop you can buy orchids encased in glass paperweights or plated with 24-carat gold (or even silvery rhodium for extra snob value).

Back to Tanglin gate

By now you've seen the best of what the gardens have to offer, and there's not that much to be gained by continuing north. An alternative route back from the orchid

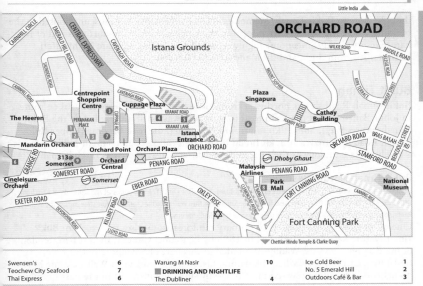

Swensen's	6	Warung M Nasir	10	Ice Cold Beer	1
Teochew City Seafood	7	■ **DRINKING AND NIGHTLIFE**		No. 5 Emerald Hill	2
Thai Express	6	The Dubliner	4	Outdoors Café & Bar	3

garden involves proceeding up the Maranta Avenue path to one of the park's most stunning trees, a 47-metre *jelawai*; this and several other exceptionally tall trees are fitted with lightning conductors. Close by, to the right, is a lovely grassy area with a gazebo-like 1930s **bandstand** in the middle, encircled by eighteen rain trees for shade. From here you can either go straight on to arrive eventually at the Botany Centre, or head downhill through the **sundial garden** to end up back at the lake.

North to Bukit Timah Road

Exiting the orchid garden, head up the boardwalk to enter a second patch of **rainforest** with a trail past numbered highlights, including a spectacular banyan tree (#8) that's a mass of aerial roots. The trail and forest end above **Symphony Lake**, to one side of which is an impressive colonial-era house with more than a hint of mock Tudor; the gardens' assistant director once lived here. Nearby, marooned in the middle of the gardens, the **Visitor Centre** has its own gift shop and café. Next comes the dreary **Evolution Garden**, where fake petrified trees help to illustrate how plant life has evolved over millennia. From here, it's several minutes' walk, skirting the back of the National University of Singapore's Bukit Timah campus, to the mundane **Eco Garden** dominating the northern end of the park, with the MRT station to the left. To reach the main road, head generally right (northeast) past the enclosed **Jacob Ballas Children's Garden** (daily 8am–7pm) containing a water play area (kids will need swimming gear and buckets), treehouse and maze; beyond is Bukit Timah Road, where you can cross to **Dunearn Road** on the far side of the canal to catch a bus back into town.

Central Catchment Nature Reserve

For a taste of Singapore's wilder side, head to the **Central Catchment Nature Reserve** (informally known as the "central nature reserve"). The lush heart of the island is dominated by **rainforest** and several large **reservoirs**, and there are opportunities for **hikes** up **Bukit Timah**, the island's tallest hill. The interest isn't limited to the jungle

9

though: close to Bukit Timah, **Memories at Old Ford Factory** is a museum housed in the building where the British surrendered to the Japanese, while the northern end of the nature reserve holds Singapore's highly regarded **zoo**, with a separate **Night Safari** section open from dusk, and the **Mandai Orchid Gardens**.

Bukit Timah

Bukit Timah Road shoots northwest from Little India, passing leafy suburbs en route to Johor Bahru (it was the main road to the Causeway until superseded by the Bukit Timah Expressway). Some 9km on from Little India, the road becomes Upper Bukit Timah Road and arrives at **Bukit Timah** itself, often called "Bukit Timah Hill" by locals – a deliberate tautology as the surrounding district is also known as Bukit Timah.

Bukit Timah Nature Reserve

Hindhede Drive • Daily 6am–7pm, Visitor Centre exhibition 8.30am–5pm • Free • Bus #171 from Somerset and Scotts rds, or #170 from Little India MRT; ask to be let off opposite Bukit Timah Shopping Centre, then walk on to the Courts furniture store and use the overhead footbridge; buses back to town use the stop on the left as you leave Hindhede Drive

One of Singapore's last pockets of primary rainforest comprises the excellent **Bukit Timah Nature Reserve**, established in 1883 by Nathaniel Cantley, then superintendent of the Botanic Gardens. **Wildlife** abounded in this part of Singapore in the mid-nineteenth century, when the natural historian Alfred Russel Wallace came here to do fieldwork; he later observed that "in all my subsequent travels in the East I rarely if ever met with so productive a spot". Wallace also noted the presence of tiger traps, but by the 1930s Singapore's tigers had met their end (the Visitor Centre displays a photo of the last specimen to be shot on the island). **Long-tailed macaques** haven't dwindled though – you'll see numerous groups, some even wandering around the houses at the base of the hill peeking in bins for discarded food. Otherwise, what really impresses is the dipterocarp forest itself, with its towering **emergents** – trees that have reached the top of the jungle canopy as a result of a lucky break, a fallen tree allowing enough light through to the forest floor to nurture saplings to maturity.

Exploring the reserve

Four colour-coded **trails** head uphill from the Visitor Centre (the information counter has **maps**, also downloadable from the "nature reserves" section of ⑩ www.nparks.gov.sg). All require only a moderate level of fitness, though three share a very steep start up a sealed road (the exception, the green trail, meanders along the side of the hill before rejoining the others). Most people tackle the red trail (30min), which is the road up to the summit at a paltry 164m; a flight of narrow steps halfway along – the Summit Path – offers a short cut to the top.

A great place for **refreshments** after your exertions is *Al-Ameen*, serving *murtabak*, *roti prata* and other local favourites; if you arrived by bus, you'll spot it in the row of shophouses where the bus dropped you.

Memories at Old Ford Factory

351 Upper Bukit Timah Rd • Mon–Sat 9am–5.30pm, Sun 9am–noon • S$3 • ⑩ www.s1942.org.sg • Bus #171 from Somerset and Scotts rds, or #170 from Little India MRT; get off just beyond the Hillside apartment complex

The old Ford car factory was the first plant of its type in Southeast Asia when it opened in October 1941. But by February 1942 the Japanese had shown up, and on February 15 Lieutenant General Percival, head of the Allied forces in Singapore, surrendered to Japan's General Yamashita in the factory's board room. Today the Art Deco building houses a little wartime museum, **Memories at Old Ford Factory**, making good use of military artefacts, period newspapers and oral history recordings.

While the surrenders that bookended the Japanese occupation obviously get some attention, as does the life of British POWs, it's with its coverage of the **civilian experience** of the war that the museum really scores. Predictably, the occupiers mounted cultural indoctrination campaigns, and displays recall how locals were urged to celebrate Japanese imperial birthdays, and how Japanese shows were put on at Victoria Memorial Hall. This was not a benign intellectual sort of occupation, however. Stung by local Chinese efforts to raise funds for China's defence against Japan, the Japanese launched **Sook Ching**, a brutal purge of thousands (the exact number is unknown) of Singapore Chinese thought to hold anti-Japanese sentiments. These violent events are illustrated by, among other items, some moving sketches by Chia Chew Soo, who witnessed members of his own family being killed in 1942. Not least among the privations of occupation were **food shortages**, as recalled by displays on wartime crops – speak to any Singaporean above a certain age today, and chances are they can tell you of having to survive on stuff like tapioca during those dark years.

Singapore Zoo

80 Mandai Lake Rd · ☎ 6269 3411, ⊚ www.zoo.com.sg · Bus: #138 from Ang Mo Kio MRT, #927 from Choa Chu Kang MRT or Woodlands Rd, or privately run service from BusHub (S$4.50; ☎ 6753 0506, ⊚ www.bushub.com.sg), with useful return departures from the Night Safari (every 30min 9.30–11.30pm), plus two morning and one evening service from downtown

Both the **Singapore Zoo** and its **Night Safari** offshoot, on a promontory jutting into peaceful Seletar Reservoir, off the Bukit Timah Expressway, have an "open" philosophy, preferring to confine animals in naturalistic enclosures behind moats, though creatures such as big cats still have to be caged. By the time you read this another spin-off may be ready – the **River Safari**, presenting the animals (including pandas) and fish of rivers as diverse as the Mekong and the Mississippi.

The zoo

Daily 8.30am–6pm · S$20, or S$42 with Night Safari or $32 with BirdPark (see p.526), or S$58 with both

The zoo could easily occupy you for half a day if not longer. A **tram** (S$5) does a one-way circuit of the grounds, but as it won't always be going your way, be prepared for a lot of legwork. Highlights include the **Fragile Forest** biodome, a magical zone where you can actually walk among ring-tailed lemurs, sloths and fruit bats, and the **white tigers**, which aren't white but resemble Siamese cats in the colour of their hair and eyes. **Animal shows** and **feeding shows** run throughout the day, including the excellent Splash Safari, featuring penguins, manatees and sea lions. There are also elephant (S$8) and pony (S$6) rides, plus a popular water play area called **Rainforest Kidzwalk** (bring your children's swimming gear).

The Night Safari

Daily 7.30pm–midnight, with shops/restaurants from 6pm and last admission at 11pm · S$32, or S$42 with zoo or BirdPark, or S$58 with both

Many animals are nocturnal, so why not run a night-time zoo? The Night Safari section of the zoo addresses this question so convincingly that you wonder why similar establishments aren't more common. The Borneo-style tribal show at the entrance is admittedly somewhat tacky, and there can be lengthy queues for the tram rides around the whole complex, but these are just niggles. It's enjoyable to forgo the tram rides altogether and simply walk around the leafy grounds, an atmospheric experience in the muted lighting, but that way you miss out on half the enclosures, notably those for large mammals such as elephants and hippos. Areas you can visit on foot include the **Fishing Cat Trail**, featuring the Indian *gharial* – a kind of crocodile, disarmingly log-like in the water, and the *binturong*, sometimes called the bearcat (you'll understand why when you see it); and the **Leopard Trail**, where your eyes will strain to spot the clouded leopard and slow loris.

9

Mandai Orchid Garden

Mandai Lake Rd · Mon 8am–6pm, Tues–Sun 8am–7pm · S$3.50 · ⓦ www.mandai.com.sg · Bus #138 from Ang Mo Kio MRT, or #927 from Choa Chu Kang MRT or Woodlands Rd

It's only a ten-minute walk from the zoo back up Mandai Lake Road to the **Mandai Orchid Garden**. A colourful diversion, the site boasts several gardens packed with not only orchids but also other tropical plants and fruit trees, plus areas where you can view orchids being grown commercially; the shop sells orchid bouquets and sprays.

Kranji and Sungai Buloh

While land reclamation has radically altered the east coast and industrialization the west, the **northern** expanses of the island up to the Straits of Johor still retain pockets of the **rainforest** and mangrove swamp that blanketed Singapore on Raffles' arrival in 1819. Though thickets of state housing blocks are never far away, something of rural Singapore's agricultural past also clings on tenaciously by way of the odd prawn or poultry farm or vegetable garden. For visitors, two attractions make it worth considering coming this far from town: the **Kranji War Cemetery and Memorial**, in the **Kranji** area, dominated by a reservoir, and the wetland reserve at **Sungai Buloh**, on the opposite, western side of the reservoir.

Kranji War Cemetery

Next to the Turf Club, Woodlands Rd · Daily 7am–6pm · Free · Kranji MRT, then 10min walk west and south, or bus #170 from Little India, or #927 from the zoo

Kranji War Cemetery and Memorial is the resting place of the many Allied troops who died in the defence of Singapore. Row upon row of graves slope up the landscaped hill, some identified only as "known unto God". Beyond the simple stone cross that stands over the cemetery is the **memorial**, around which are recorded the names of more than twenty thousand soldiers (including personnel from Britain, Canada, Australia, New Zealand, Malaya and South Asia) who died in this region during World War II. Two unassuming **tombs** stand on the wide lawns below the cemetery, belonging to Yusof bin Ishak and Dr B.H. Sheares, independent Singapore's first two presidents.

Sungai Buloh Wetland Reserve

301 Neo Tiew Crescent · Mon–Sat 7.30am–7pm, Sun 7am–7pm; guided tours Sat 9.30am, video shows Mon–Sat 9am, 11am, 1pm, 3pm & 5pm, Sun hourly 9am–5pm · Sat & Sun S$1, otherwise free · ☎ 6794 1401, ⓦ www.sbwr.org.sg · Bus #925 from Kranji MRT to the Kranji reservoir car park, then 15min walk; bus heads directly to the reserve on Sun

The **Sungai Buloh Wetland Reserve**, the island's only wetland nature park, stands on the coast 4km northwest of the Kranji War Cemetery. Beyond its Visitor Centre, café and video theatre, trails and walkways lead through and over an expanse of mangrove, mud flats and grassland, home to kingfishers, herons, sandpipers, kites and sea eagles and, in the waters, archerfish – which squirt water into the air to knock insects into devouring range. Between September and March, you may catch sight of migratory birds from around Asia roosting and feeding, especially in the early morning.

The five-hundred-metre **mangrove boardwalk** offers an easy way to get a sense of the shoreline environment, and tortoises, crabs and mudskippers can often be seen. From here you can graduate to walks of several kilometres into the guts of the reserve. Time your visit right on a Saturday and you can join a free **guided tour** of the mangrove boardwalk or one of the trails.

Geylang and Katong

Malay culture has held sway in and around the eastern suburbs of Geylang and Katong since the mid-nineteenth century, when Malays and Indonesians arrived to work first in the local *copra* (dried coconut kernel) processing factory and later on its *serai* (lemon grass) farms. **Geylang** retains quite a strong Malay feel today, and the shops, markets and restaurants are worth checking out for Malay fare or merchandise, though there are no specific sights. **Katong**, on the other hand, has been through more of a transformation. In prewar times, the wealthy, including many of Peranakan ancestry, built their villas here in what was then a beachfront district. Thankfully, the area's **Peranakan heritage** lives on to some degree, and provides the main lure for visitors. You can sample what both districts have to offer by heading south from the **Geylang Serai** area, in the east of Geylang, to Katong via **Joo Chiat Road**, as described below.

Geylang Serai

Paya Lebar MRT, then a short walk south and east, or bus #2 or #51 (from Chinatown) and #7 (from the Botanic Gardens and Orchard Rd) and #51, all of which pass through Victoria St, and will drop you on Sims Ave, the main eastbound drag

Geylang has acquired a certain notoriety as something of a red-light district. Arrive by bus, and you'll spot numerous numbered *lorong*s (lanes) on the way, mainly to the right of Sims Avenue; brothels along them are recognizable by the coloured lights outside. But Geylang's main attraction is the newly rebuilt Geylang Serai **market** on the left of Sims Avenue, its sloping roofs reminiscent of certain styles of kampung house. The stalls are predominantly Malay, selling textiles, *kuih* and snacks such as *rempeyek*, fried flour rounds containing spices and peanuts. Just west, a collection of incongruous kampung houses, genuine in style but not substance, comprise the so-called **Malay Village**, set up years ago as a sort of right-on heritage showcase, and now practically defunct. Some are being converted into retail space, a sad fate for the few examples of kampung architecture left on Singapore's main island.

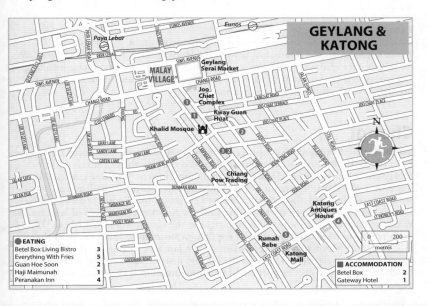

GEYLANG & KATONG

EATING
Betel Box Living Bistro	3
Everything With Fries	5
Guan Hoe Soon	2
Haji Maimunah	1
Peranakan Inn	4

ACCOMMODATION
Betel Box	2
Gateway Hotel	1

9

Joo Chiat Road

At the northern end of **Joo Chiat Road**, opposite the Geylang Serai market, the **Joo Chiat Complex** looks like a drab suburban mall but feels more like market inside. There's a notable Malay/Islamic feel, the shops selling batik, rugs and silk; you'll also find outlets selling Malay music CDs and *jamu* – herbal remedies.

After the bustle of Singapore's downtown streets, Joo Chiat Road can seem almost languid, and this laidback air, along with several distractions en route, makes walking the 1500m southeast to East Coast Road in Katong hardly a chore. At no. 95, look out for Kway Guan Huat, one of several cottage-industry setups along the road, making spring-roll wrappers; by the time you read this they should have an associated restaurant nearby serving up spring rolls in the local style, where the wraps are steamed rather than fried (☎9677 3441). A little further on, Fatimah Trading at no. 140 sells more Malay medicines. At no. 252, Chiang Pow Joss Paper Trading produces funerary paraphernalia in one of several nicely restored shophouses on the road, while an outlet at no. 267 makes mackerel *otah-otah* being a kind of dumpling. Just beyond, the immaculate **Peranakan shophouses** on Koon Seng Road (on the left) are the architectural highlight of the area, with their restored multicoloured facades, French windows, eaves and mouldings. Finally, at no. 320, peek in at the workaday Ann Tin Tong Medical Hall, with its 1960s louvred windows, a world away from Chinatown's slick herbalists.

Katong

Bus #12 from Chinatown, Victoria St and Lavender MRT, or #14 from Orchard Rd; both call at Mountbatten MRT en route

From the Koon Seng Road intersection, Joo Chiat Road runs 600m on to **East Coast Road**. The beach hinted at by that name has long since gone – pushed further south by the creation of the East Coast Park, with its leisure facilities and restaurants, on several kilometres of reclaimed land. However, the area is worth visiting thanks to a pocket of outlets celebrating its Peranakan traditions. Highlights among the cosy shops include Rumah Bebe, selling clothing and jewellery at 113 East Coast Rd (see p.560).

Katong Antiques House

208 East Coast Rd · Daily except Mon 11am–5pm · Optional tours S$15 per person · ☎6345 8544

In the **Katong Antiques House**, just beyond the Holy Family Church, owner Peter Wee has amassed a treasure-trove of artefacts from wedding costumes to vintage furniture. A veteran spokesman for the Peranakan community, he leads tours of the traditionally decorated shophouse by prior arrangement.

Changi

Tanah Merah MRT, then bus #2; alternatively, and much slower, pick up the bus from Chinatown or elsewhere downtown

Even in the 1970s, eastern Singapore still looked the way the outskirts of some Malaysian towns do today, dotted with kampungs, low-rise housing estates and tracts of wooded land or stands of coconut palms. It's hard to visualize that landscape as you head out through areas of new towns like Bedok (a quiet seaside suburb until the arrival of state housing projects and the reclamation of land for the East Coast Park) on the way to **Changi**, right at the eastern tip of the island. The main reason to head this far east is to see **Changi Museum**, commemorating the internment of Allied troops and civilians by the Japanese during World War II. In Singaporean popular consciousness, the Changi district has long embodied a beachside idyll; just a bit further afield from the museum is the **beach**, for a dip and bask on a hot day.

Changi Museum

1000 Upper Changi Rd North • Daily 9.30am–5pm • Free, audio guides or guided tours S$8 • ☎ 6214 2451, ⓦ www.changimuseum.com • Tanah Merah MRT, then 20min by bus

The infamous Changi Prison was the site of a World War II POW camp in which Japanese jailers subjected Allied prisoners, both military and civilian, to the harshest of treatment. Those brutalities are movingly remembered in the **Changi Museum**. Formerly housed within the prison itself, which is still in use – drug offenders are periodically executed here – the museum moved just up the road during an expansion of the prison a few years ago.

Novelist **James Clavell** drew on his experience of Changi in writing *King Rat*, never forgetting that in the cells "the stench was nauseating…stench from a generation of confined human bodies." No museum could possibly bring home the horrors of internment, though this one does a reasonable job of picking over the facts of the Japanese occupation and the conditions prisoners endured. Memorable exhibits include artworks by internees, with pride of place given to reproductions of Stanley Warren's so-called Changi Murals, depicting New Testament scenes (the originals are housed within an army camp nearby where Warren was interned). A final section features a recreation of an improvised **theatre** where internees put on entertainments to amuse fellow inmates, though here there's only a TV screen showing wartime footage.

In the museum courtyard is a simple wooden **chapel**, typical of those erected in Singapore's wartime camps; the brass cross on its altar was crafted from spent ammunition casings. The messages on its board of remembrance are often touching and worth a read (ask staff for pen and notepaper to add your own).

Changi Village and the beach

Beyond Changi Prison, the tower blocks thin out and the landscape becomes a patchwork of fields, often a relic of colonial-era military bases still used by Singapore's forces. Ten minutes on via the #2 bus is **Changi Village**, a cluster of eating places and shops mainly serving the beachgoing public. To reach the **beach** from the bus terminus, head on past the market and food court and bear left to the *Ubin First Stop* seafood restaurant, where you'll see a canalized inlet from the sea. The footbridge here leads to a stretch of manicured grass and trees, the prelude to a narrow strip of brownish sand fronting greenish-blue water – actually not uninviting (unless you were expecting something out of coastal Terengganu), and the sight of aircraft rumbling in low every few minutes on the Changi flight path soon ceases to be a distraction. Facilities, including showers and a camping area, are shown on a map of the so-called Changi Beach Park available from ⓦ www.nparks.gov.sg, while for **food** there's ample choice in Changi Village itself – the food court isn't at all bad and the restaurants on the main road offer everything from pizzas to *murtabak*.

The Southern Ridges and Pasir Panjang

While no less endowed with new towns and industrial estates than the east of the island, western Singapore has retained a leafier, more open feel to this day. An unusually verdant example of this is at the **Southern Ridges**, an umbrella term recently dreamed up for the coastal ridge that begins at the southern tip of the island and continues 9km northwest, under various names, to a site just beyond the main campus of the National University of Singapore. The ridge is lined by a chain of parks and general greenery, and it's now possible to do an extended walk along it using a series of ingenious footbridges and elevated walkways. The main attractions en route are **Reflections at Bukit Chandu**, a museum commemorating the wartime defence of that hill by Singapore's Malay Regiment; and **Mount Faber**, with views over downtown

9

Singapore and cable-car rides across to Sentosa island (see p.528). In between the Southern Ridges and the sea, **Pasir Panjang**, once a sleepy district of kampungs and still a relatively quiet residential area, is home to just one sight, the tacky but amusing Buddhist theme park of **Haw Par Villa**.

The account below takes the Southern Ridges walk in an easterly direction, ending at Harbourfront MRT beneath Mount Faber – a sensible choice as this avoids a steep climb up the hill and allows you to finish at the massive VivoCity mall, where you can assuage any appetite and thirst worked up along the way. Haw Par Villa, the furthest site west covered here, is really an optional extra as far as the walk is concerned. One more practical point: the links between parks on the walk often offer little shade, so be assiduous about **sun protection** and bring a reasonable supply of water.

Haw Par Villa

262 Pasir Panjang Rd • Daily 9am–7pm • Free • ☏ 6872 2780 • Haw Par Villa MRT or bus #200 from Buona Vista MRT or #51 from Chinatown

As an entertaining exercise in bad taste, **Haw Par Villa** has few equals. Featuring a gaudy parade of over a thousand statues of people and creatures from Chinese myth and legend, it was once a zoo owned by the Aw brothers, Boon Haw and Boon Par, who made a fortune early last century selling Tiger Balm – a cure-all ointment created by their father. When the British began licensing the ownership of large animals, the brothers closed their zoo and replaced it with statuary; subsequently the park acquired a new appellation, a mishmash of the brothers' names.

The best, and most gruesome, statues lie in the **Ten Courts of Hell** section (closes 6pm), whose portrayal of the Buddhist belief in karma and reincarnation is not for the faint-hearted. Accessed through the gaping mouth of a huge dragon, the displays depict deceased sinners being tortured by leering demons: prostitutes are drowned in pools of blood, thieves and gamblers frozen into blocks of ice, and loan sharks thrown onto a hill of knives. Finally, the dead have their memories wiped in the Pavilion of Forgetfulness before being returned to Earth to have another stab at virtue.

Reflections at Bukit Chandu

31K Pepys Rd • Tues–Sun 9am–5pm • S$3, or S$4 with Memories at Old Ford Factory • ⓦ www.1942.org.sg • Pasir Panjang MRT, then a 10min walk north uphill

The defence of Pasir Panjang against the Japanese by the 1st and 2nd Battalion of the Malay Regiment is remembered at the tiny **Reflections at Bukit Chandu** museum. It's housed in a lone colonial building that once served as officer accommodation, though it became a food and munitions store during the war. Here "C" company of the Malay Regiment's second battalion made a brave stand against the Japanese on February 13, 1942 – two days before the British capitulation – and sustained heavy casualties.

There's nothing special about the small collection of artefacts focusing on this event, though the displays do get across the human toll of the conflict, as well as highlighting British ambivalence about working with the Malays: the Malay Regiment was only begun as an experiment in Negeri Sembilan to see "how the Malays would react to military discipline", and only when they proved themselves was it taken seriously, with members sent to Singapore for training. This type of apparent slighting of the Malay community is still cited in Malaysia today as one reason for maintaining the controversial "bumiputra policy" (see p.576).

The canopy walk

Bear left along the ridge from the Reflections at Bukit Chandu for your first taste of the Southern Ridges trail – and a wonderful introduction it is too, for this is where the

canopy walk begins. Soaring above the actual trail, the walkway takes you east through the treetops, with signage pointing out common Singapore trees such as cinnamon and *tembusu*, and views north across rolling grassy landscapes, the odd mansion poking out from within clumps of mature trees. After just a few minutes, the walkway rejoins the trail leading downhill to some mundane nurseries and the west gate of the desultory **Hort Park** on Alexandra Road.

From Alexandra Arch to Mount Faber

The Alexandra Road end of Hort Park is very close to one of the huge, purpose-built footbridges on the Southern Ridges trail, the white **Alexandra Arch**, meant to resemble a leaf but looking more like North Bridge Road's Elgin Bridge on steroids. On the east side of the bridge, a long, elevated metal walkway zigzags off into the distance; it's called the **forest walk** though it passes through nothing denser than mature woodland on its kilometre-long journey east. The walkway zigzags even more severely as it rises steeply to the top of **Telok Blangah Hill**, whose park offers good views of the usual residential tower blocks to the north and east, and of Mount Faber and Sentosa to the southeast.

Proceed downhill, following signage for **Henderson Waves**, and after 700m or so you come to a vast footbridge of wooden slats over metal. High up in the air over broad Henderson Road, the bridge has undulating parapets – Henderson Waves indeed – boasting built-in shelters against the sun or rain.

Mount Faber
On the east side of Henderson Waves • Free • ⓦ mountfaber.com.sg • A stiff walk up from Harbourfront MRT

In bygone years, leafy **Mount Faber**, named in 1845 after government engineer Captain Charles Edward Faber, was a favourite recreation spot for its superb **views** over downtown. These days, you'll have to look out for breaks in the dense foliage for vistas over Bukit Merah new town to Chinatown and the Financial District, or head to the **Jewel Box**, a smart bar and restaurant complex at the very summit. The *Jewel Box* is also the departure point for the slick **cable car** to the HarbourFront Centre and on to Sentosa island (daily 8.30am–10pm; S$24 one-way, S$26 return).

To descend, follow signs for the **Marang trail**, which eventually leads down a steep flight of steps on the south side of the hill to VivoCity, with the HarbourFront Centre next door.

HarbourFront Centre and VivoCity
Harbourfront MRT

On Telok Blangah Road, the **HarbourFront Centre** is nothing more than a glorified ferry terminal from where boats set off for Indonesia's Riau archipelago (see p.532), as well as the departure point for **cable cars** heading to Mount Faber and Sentosa island. Much more interesting is the **VivoCity** mall, with a curious fretted white facade that looks like it was cut out of a set of giant false teeth, and housing three good food courts (in particular *Food Republic* on level 3), a slew of restaurants, a cinema and other amenities; from here Sentosa is just ten minutes' walk away (see p.528). The red-brick box of a building with the huge chimney east of the mall, and connected to it by an elevated walkway, is **St James Power Station**, a clubbing mecca housed in, surprise surprise, a converted power plant.

Jurong

Occupying a sizeable slab of southwestern Singapore, sprawling **Jurong** was notoriously dubbed "Goh's folly" in the 1960s when, with the island on the road to independence, Goh Keng Swee, then Singapore's finance minister, decided it was vital to create a

9

major industrial town here on unpromising swampy terrain. To the surprise of not just the avowed sceptics, the new town took off, and today Jurong boasts a diverse portfolio of industries, including pharmaceuticals and oil refining – in which Singapore is a world leader despite having nary a drop of black gold of its own. Jurong also has sizeable residential quarters and various leisure attractions, though only two constitute a serious temptation to make a trip here: the extensive avian zoo that is the **Jurong BirdPark**, and the **Singapore Science Centre**, genuinely ahead of the curve as such museums go, with an entertaining emphasis on interactivity.

Jurong BirdPark

2 Jurong Hill • Daily 8.30am–6pm • S$18, S$32 with zoo, S$42 with Night Safari, S$58 all three • ☏ 6265 0022, ⓦ www.birdpark.com.sg • Boon Lay MRT, then bus #194 or #251

Lining Jalan Ahmad Ibrahim, the **Jurong BirdPark** is home to one of the world's biggest bird collections, with nearly four hundred species. You'll need at least a couple of hours to have a good look around the grounds, which are spacious enough to have a circular **Panorail** (S$5), like an airport transit train, with commentary describing the main attractions.

Besides the four huge walk-in aviaries, described below, the park also has a number of worthwhile smaller enclosures, such as the hugely popular **Penguin Coast** (feeding times 10.30am & 3.30pm). Just inside the entrance, it juxtaposes half a dozen penguin species against the backdrop of a mock Portuguese galleon, meant to evoke the sighting of penguins by explorers such as Vasco da Gama. Utterly different is **World of Darkness**, a fascinating owl showcase that uses special lighting to swap day for night. The best of various **bird shows** throughout the day involve feeding birds of prey such as vultures and brahminy kites; check the website for details.

The walk-in aviaries

While not the most impressive of the major aviaries, the **Southeast Asian Birds** section makes seeing local birdlife far easier than overnighting in a hide in Taman Negara; you find fairy bluebirds and other small but delightful creatures feasting on papaya slices, with a simulated thunderstorm at midday. Close by are **Jungle Jewels**, featuring South American birdlife in "forest" surroundings, and the **Lory Loft**, a giant aviary under netting, its foliage meant to simulate the Australian bush. Its denizens are dozens of multicoloured lories and lorikeets, which have no qualms about perching at the viewing balcony or perhaps even on your arm, hoping for a bit of food (suitable feed is on sale).

At the far end of the park from the main entrance is the **African Waterfall Aviary**, long the park's pride and boasting a thirty-metre-high waterfall. Its design not only allows visitors to enter on foot but also lets the Panorail chug in without providing an escape route for the 1500 winged inhabitants – including carmine bee-eaters and South African crowned cranes.

Singapore Science Centre

15 Science Centre Rd • Daily 10am–6pm • S$9 • ☏ 6425 2500, ⓦ www.science.edu.sg • Jurong East MRT, then a 10min walk or bus #66 or #335, or ride the #66 all the way from Little India

Interactivity is the watchword at the **Singapore Science Centre**, on the eastern edge of the parkland around the artificial Jurong Lake. Galleries here hold hundreds of hands-on displays focusing on genetics, space science, marine ecology and other disciplines, allowing you to calculate your carbon footprint, test your ability to hear high-pitched sounds and be befuddled by weird optical illusions. The material goes down well with the seemingly hyperactive schoolkids who sweep around the place in deafening waves.

FROM TOP UNIVERSAL STUDIOS, SENTOSA (P.529); SRI SRINIVASA PERUMAL TEMPLE, LITTLE INDIA (P.498) >

9

Omni-Theatre

Singapore Science Centre • Mon–Fri 10am–6pm, Sat & Sun 10am–8pm; Observatory Fri 7.50–10pm • S$10 or S$16 joint ticket with Science Centre; Observatory free • W www.omnitheatre.com.sg

At the northern end of the site, the **Omni-Theatre** shows hourly IMAX movies about the natural world. It also houses an **observatory** that does free stargazing sessions on Fridays.

Snow City

15 Jurong Town Hall Rd • Daily 9.45am–5.15pm • 1hr costs S$14 including loan of jackets and boots; S$16 for joint ticket with the Science Centre, S$24 with Science Centre and Omni-Theatre • T 6560 2306, W www.snowcity.com.sg

If you're at the Singapore Science Centre with kids in tow, you might want to extend your visit to check out the winter-themed **Snow City** next to the Omni-Theatre, featuring tobogganing and opportunities to explore an igloo or build snowmen.

Sentosa

Thirty years of rampant development have transformed **Sentosa** into the most built-up of Singapore's southern islands (with the possible exception of one or two that are home to petrochemical installations), so it's ironic that its name means "tranquil" in Malay. The island has certainly come a long way since World War II, when it was a British military base known as Pulau Blakang Mati ("Island of Death Behind"). Contrived but enjoyable in parts, Sentosa today is a hybrid of so-so resort island and out-of-town theme park, promoted for its rides, passable beaches and the massive new casino resort on its northern shore, which also features a Universal Studios theme park, a maritime museum and six hotels.

If you want to visit, avoid the weekends and the school holidays unless you don't mind the place being positively overrun. Sentosa's restaurants and bars are covered on p.552.

ARRIVAL AND INFORMATION   SENTOSA

Though it's easy enough to **walk** to Sentosa – Harbourfront MRT, then a 10min walk using the Sentosa Boardwalk footbridge from VivoCity mall – most visitors prefer to get there using the **Sentosa Express**. You can, of course, get a **taxi** as well, though journeys to and from the island incur a surcharge of several dollars depending on the time of day.

By monorail The Sentosa Express operates every 5min from level 3 of the VivoCity mall (S$3). Once on the island it stops at Waterfront station on the northern shore (for Resorts World), Imbiah station a little further south, and terminates at Beach station on the southern shore, for the three beaches. Note that you do not need a ticket for the monorail ride back to the mainland.

By bus The orange Sentosa Rider bus serves certain parts of Orchard Road, Chinatown, the Colonial District and Marina Centre, heading in to Resorts World and then following the monorail route down to Beach Station (hourly 9am–10pm; S$5, one-way pass S$8; W www.sentosarider.com).

By cable car The most stylish way to arrive is via the newly revamped cable-car system from Mount Faber via tower 2 of the HarbourFront Centre (daily 8.45am–10pm; S$24, or S$26 return), though the harbour and city views and plush cabins don't quite live up to the outlay.

Information T 1800 736 8672 W www.sentosa.com.sg.

GETTING AROUND

By shuttle bus Sentosa is just large enough that you might want to use its shuttle buses (all free), including the so-called beach trams that serve the island's beaches, plus red, yellow and blue line buses that head to destinations such as Fort Siloso at the western tip. Routes are given in the text where appropriate, and are shown on the widely available free maps as well as W www.sentosa.com.sg.

By monorail The three Sentosa Express stops are the Waterfront station on the northern shore (for Resorts World), Imbiah station a little further south, and Beach station on the southern shore, for the three beaches. You do not need a ticket to ride the monorail train within the island.

Resorts World Sentosa

Close to Waterfront station on the island's north shore

The Resorts World development is visually plastic, like something out of a Silicon Valley corporate headquarters, but it does boast some of Sentosa's biggest attractions, soon to be joined by their Marine Life Park (which may be open by the time you read this).

Universal Studios Singapore

Resorts World Sentosa • Daily 10am–7pm • S$66/S$48, plus a S$6/S$4 surcharge at weekends; many rides have minimum height requirements and may not be suitable for young children • ☎ 6577 8888, ⓦ www.rwsentosa.com

The ersatz character of Resorts World becomes rather entertaining at the **Universal Studios theme park**, where fairy-tale castles and American cityscapes rear bizarrely into view in the sultry heat. The park is divided into seven themed zones, encompassing everything from ancient Egypt – the least convincing of the lot – to DreamWorks' animated hit *Madagascar*. Standard tickets offer unlimited rides (though be prepared for long queues in the sun), but there's much more to do than get flung around on cutting-edge roller coasters: museum-type exhibits unwrap the world of film production, and you can watch musical spectaculars in a recreation of Hollywood's Pantages theatre.

Early booking on the Resorts World website is recommended; tickets can sell out days or weeks in advance.

Maritime Experiential Museum

To the right of Sentosa Boardwalk as you reach the island • Mon–Thurs 10am–7pm, Fri–Sun 10am–9pm • S$5

A touch more intellectual than most sights on the island, the resort's **Maritime Museum** highlights the historical sea trade between China and India and the Middle East. Its centrepiece is a massive replica of the bow of a ship used by the Ming-dynasty emissary Cheng Ho (also called Zheng He), though rather more impressive is the eighteen-metre *Jewel of Muscat*, an immaculate evocation of a ninth-century Arab dhow. Built according to techniques of the time, using coconut fibre rather than nails to bind the timbers together, it was a gift to Singapore from the Omani government and was delivered in 2010 by the obvious method – sailing it across the Indian Ocean, a journey that took 68 days. The museum will soon have its own aquarium, too.

Other Sentosa attractions

Just about every patch of Sentosa that isn't a beach, hotel or golf course is packed with rides or other diversions, ranging from a Merlion replica whose inside you can walk around to a vertical wind tunnel that replicates the sensation of skydiving by keeping a person aloft on a continuous upward blast of air. The selection here covers a few of the more interesting and sensibly priced offerings.

Images of Singapore

Imbiah Lookout, west of Imbiah station • Daily 9am–7pm, free guided tours Fri–Sun 11am & 2pm • S$10

Images of Singapore uses life-sized dioramas to present Singapore's history and heritage from the fourteenth century through to 1945. Iconic images from Singapore's past – Raffles forging a treaty with the island's Malay rulers, rubber tappers at the Botanic Gardens, coolies at the Singapore River – spring to life, and actors dressed as labourers and kampung dwellers are on hand to provide further insight.

Luge and Skyride

Daily 10am–9.30pm • S$12.50 • ☎ 6274 0472, ⓦ www.hg.sg/sentosa/luge • Beach station for Skyride, Imbiah station for Luge

Unexpectedly fun, the **Skyride**, akin to a ski lift, takes you up a leafy slope at the start of Siloso beach, after which you ride your Luge – like a small unmotorized go-kart – and coast down either of two long, curving tracks back to your starting point.

9

Megazip Adventure Park

Daily 11am–7pm · S$29 · ☎ 6884 5602, ⓦ www.megazip.com.sg · 5min walk west of Imbiah station

Megazip is a flying-fox setup where you slide, suspended from a steel cable, from a hilltop down to an islet beyond Siloso Beach. Additional possibilities here include a mini-bungee jump (S$12), an obstacle course that's all ropes and netting (S$39) and a climbing wall (S$20).

WaveHouse

Siloso Beach · Daily 11am–11pm · First hour S$30 or S$40 depending on "ride", S$5 more at weekends · ☎ 6377 3133, ⓦ www.wavehousesentosa.com

WaveHouse does for surfing what Universal Studios does for ancient Egypt, conjuring up a semblance of the real thing using torrents of water sent along two contoured blue slopes. One generates a continuous two-metre curling wave; the other is flat and suitable for beginners.

Fort Siloso

At the northwest tip of the island, beyond Siloso Beach · Daily 10am–6pm, free tours Fri–Sun 12.40 & 3.40pm · S$8

Fort Siloso, a cluster of buildings and gun emplacements above a series of tunnels bored into the island, guarded Singapore's western approaches from the 1880s until 1956, but its obsolescence was revealed when the Japanese marched in from Malaya. Today, the recorded voice of one Battery Sergeant Major Cooper talks you through a mock-up of a nineteenth-century barracks, complete with living quarters, guardroom, laundry and assault course. Be sure to check out the Surrender Chambers, where life-sized figures re-enact the British and Japanese surrenders of 1942 and 1945, respectively. After that you can explore the complex's hefty gun emplacements and tunnels.

Underwater World

Next to Fort Siloso · Daily 9am–9pm, "Meet the Dolphins" 11am, 2pm, 4pm & 5.45pm · S$26 · ☎ 6275 0030, ⓦ www.underwaterworld.com.sg

It remains to be seen if **Underwater World** can hold its own after the Marine Life Park at Resorts World opens, but the site does excite kids with its moving walkway inside a hundred-metre tunnel, taking visitors through two large tanks of sharks, stingrays and shoals of gaily coloured fish. Another highlight is the dolphin lagoon, where the marine acrobatics of Indo-Pacific humpback dolphins (and some seals) can be seen during the "Meet the Dolphins" sessions.

Songs of the Sea

Close to Beach station · Daily 7.40pm & 8.40pm · S$10

Many visitors leave Sentosa by dusk; those who hang around into the evening are either heading to one of the beach bars (see p.552) or to **Songs of the Sea**, a lavish, 25-minute sound-and-light show whose canvas is not ancient monuments but screens of water; seating is right at the seafront just off Beach station.

Crane Dance

Close to the Maritime Museum and Waterfront station · Daily except Tues 9pm · Free

A worthwhile (and free) alternative to Songs of the Sea, **Crane Dance** is another hi-tech installation metres from the shore, featuring two enormous mechanical birds. They conduct a ten-minute computer-manipulated courtship accompanied by dazzling lighting and water effects.

The beaches

The best that can be said about Sentosa's three **beaches**, created with vast quantities of imported beige sand, is that they're decent enough, with bluey-green waters, the odd lagoon and facilities for renting canoes, surfboards and aqua bikes. For tranquillity, however, you'd probably do better at Changi Beach (see p.523), because at Sentosa you have to deal with not only crowds but also the view of one of the world's busiest shipping lanes – expect a parade of container ships and other vessels all day.

Siloso Beach, which extends 1500m northwest of Beach Station, is the busiest of the three, with well-established resorts and facilities, including good restaurants. **Palawan Beach**, just southeast of Beach Station, is nearly as popular and, unusually, features a suspension bridge leading out to an islet billed as the "Southernmost Point of Continental Asia" – though a sign concedes that this is so only by virtue of three man-made links, namely the suspension bridge itself, the bridge from HarbourFront to Sentosa, and the Causeway. Beyond Palawan, **Tanjong Beach** tends to be slightly quieter than the other two as it starts a full kilometre from Beach Station.

ARRIVAL AND DEPARTURE   SINGAPORE

Most visitors fly into **Changi Airport**, in the east of the island, or arrive by bus or train via the 1km **Causeway** that links Johor Bahru to the island (although some luxury buses use the **Second Crossing** bridge to Tuas in the west). Wherever you arrive, the well-oiled public transport system, including MRT metro **trains** and an elaborate **bus** network, means that you'll have no problem getting into the city centre.

BY PLANE
CHANGI INTERNATIONAL AIRPORT
Singapore's airport (ⓦ www.changiairport.com), at the eastern tip of the island, 16km from downtown, is Singapore in microcosm, well laid out and organized. As well as three main terminals, connected by free Skytrains and shuttle buses, there's a separate budget terminal some 1500m southwest (at the time of writing, used mainly by Tiger Airways, Berjaya Air and Firefly), with a free shuttle bus to terminal 2. The main terminals have every facility you could wish for, including tourist offices (daily 6am–midnight, or 2am in terminal 3), and accommodation counters taking bookings for members of the Singapore Hotel Association, which don't include many of the cheaper hotels and guesthouses.

Destinations Bandar Seri Begawan (1–2 daily; 2hr); Ipoh (daily; 1hr 30min); Kota Kinabalu (2 daily; 2hr 15min); Kuala Lumpur (hourly; 55min); Kuantan (4 weekly; 50min); Kuching (3–4 daily; 1hr 20min); Langkawi (daily; 1hr 30min); Miri (4 weekly; 2hr); Penang (6 daily; 1hr 15min); Pulau Redang (March–Oct at least 4 weekly; 1hr 30min); Pulau Tioman (at least 3 weekly; 35min).

Airlines AirAsia, ground floor, Peninsula Plaza, 111 North Bridge Rd ☎ 6307 7688; Berjaya Air, 67 Tanjong Pagar Rd ☎ 6227 3688; Firefly, #16-92 The Central, 6 Eu Tong Sen St (above Clarke Quay MRT) ☎ 6227 3883; Malaysia Airlines, #02-09, Singapore Shopping Centre, just off Orchard Rd ☎ 6336 6777; Royal Brunei #03-11 UE Shopping Mall, 81 Clemenceau Ave ☎ 6235 4672; Singapore Airlines, #04-05, ION Orchard (above Orchard MRT) ☎ 6223 8888 (helpline is 24hr). For the numerous other airline offices, see ⓦ yellowpages.com.sg.

Transport connections The easiest way to get into the city centre from the airport is on an MRT metro train (Mon–Sat 5.30am–11.15pm, Sun 6am–11.15pm; 30min; S\$2).

Alternatively, bus #36 (daily 6am–11pm, roughly every 10min; S\$1.80, no change given) heads to the Orchard Road area via Marina Centre and the Colonial District. A taxi to downtown costs at least S\$20 and takes up to half an hour; there's an airport surcharge of S\$3–5, and a fifty percent surcharge midnight–6am. Finally, the Beesybus shuttle serves backpacker lodges and budget hotels in Katong, the Arab St area and Little India (☎ 6396 6694, ⓦ www.beesybus.com; S\$8).

BY TRAIN
After eighty years, trains from Malaysia abruptly ceased to serve downtown Singapore in mid-2011 when the two countries finally resolved a long-standing dispute over the status of the railway within Singapore. The deal meant that Malaysia relinquished ownership of the KTM railway line in Singapore, likely to be dismantled for redevelopment, plus the impressive Art Deco train station in Tanjong Pagar, now a gazetted Singapore monument, in return for pieces of prime land elsewhere on the island. As a result, trains now terminate just inside Singapore at Woodlands station by the Causeway checkpoint.

WOODLANDS STATION
KTM revises its schedules often; check the latest timetables on ⓦ www.ktmb.com.my. At the time of writing there were three daily services to KL, one of them a sleeper, and three trains daily to the interior, two of which continue to Kelantan on the east coast, again with one sleeper. It's also possible to ride the sumptuous Eastern & Oriental Express (ⓦ www.orient-express.com) all the way to Bangkok, with around 15 journeys each year; bookings can be made in Singapore with E&O Services (☎ 6395 0678).

Destinations Gua Musang (2 daily; 12hr); Jerantut (for Taman Negara; 3 daily; 7hr 30min); Johor Bahru (7 daily;

9

5min); Kuala Lipis (3 daily; 9–10hr); Kuala Lumpur (3 daily; 6hr 30min); Seremban (3 daily; 5hr 30min); Wakaf Bharu (for Kota Bharu; 2 daily; 14hr).

Transport connections To reach the centre, catch bus #170 or #170X to Kranji MRT (daily 6am–midnight); #170 continues all the way down to Little India and terminates at Queen St near Bugis MRT and Arab St. As KTM charges a premium for journeys ending or starting in Singapore, it's cheaper to buy a ticket to Johor Bahru and continue by bus (see below).

BY BUS

Lavender Street Terminal Long-distance buses to the rest of Malaysia from the Lavender Street Terminal – a mere bus park, around five minutes' walk from Lavender MRT – are run by Transnasional (KL and the east coast; ☎ 6294 7034), Hasry Express (KL and the west coast; ☎ 6294 9306, ⓦ www .hasryexpress.com), and Malacca–Singapore Express (Melaka; ☎ 6292 2436). Bus #145 passes the Lavender Street Terminal on its way into Chinatown down North Bridge Rd and South Bridge Rd, while nearby on Jalan Besar, bus #65 heads to the Orchard Rd area via Bencoolen St.

Destinations Kota Bharu (1 daily; 12hr); Kuala Lumpur (at least 6 daily; 6hr); Kuala Terengganu (2 daily; 10hr); Kuantan (3 daily; 6hr 30min); Melaka (10 daily; 3hr 30min); Mersing (3 daily; 4hr); Seremban (2 daily; 5hr).

Golden Mile Complex For west-coast destinations beyond KL and also Hat Yai in Thailand, try the companies at the Golden Mile Complex on Beach Rd, such as Transtar (luxury buses; ☎ 6299 9099, ⓦ www.transtar.com.sg); Konsortium (☎ 6392 3911, ⓦ www.konsortium.com.sg) and Grassland Express (Hat Yai; ☎ 6293 1166, ⓦ www .grassland.com.sg). Any westbound bus from outside the complex will take you to the City Hall MRT station, while Nicoll Highway station is a 10min walk away.

Destinations Alor Star (daily; 12hr 30min); Butterworth (daily; 10hr); Cameron Highlands (daily; 10hr); Hat Yai (at least 2 daily; 14hr); Ipoh (7 daily; 6hr 30min); Kuala Kangsar (3 daily; 7hr); Kuala Lumpur (at least 10 daily; 6hr); Melaka (at least 2 daily; 3hr 30min); Penang (at least 5 daily; 11hr); Kuala Terengganu (1 daily; 10hr 30min).

Queen St terminal Bus SBS #170, to and from Johor Bahru, departs frequently from Queen St downtown, near Bugis MRT (daily 5.30am–midnight, every 15min; 1hr–1hr 30min; S$1.90). Alternatively, there are two nonstop services, the Singapore–Johor Express (every 10min; 6am–10.30pm; S$2.40) and the Causeway Link CW2 service (same fare). If you're on the #170 bus, hang onto your ticket at immigration so you can use it to resume your journey (not necessarily on the same vehicle) once you're through. These buses terminate at JB's Larkin bus station; if you want to reach the town centre, leave the bus at the Causeway. Queen St also holds a rank for share taxis (☎ 6296 7054); the trip to JB costs S$10 per person.

BY FERRY

Ferries to Batam, Bintan and Karimun in Indonesia's Riau archipelago (all around S$25 one-way, with weekend surcharges) use two Singapore terminals. Services are summarized on ⓦ www.singaporecruise.com.sg. For tickets and schedules, contact the operators: BatamFast (☎ 6270 0311, ⓦ www.batamfast.com), Bintan Resort Ferries (☎ 6542 4369, ⓦ www.brf.com.sg), Indofalcon (☎ 6270 6778, ⓦ www.indofalcon.com.sg), and Sindoferry (☎ 6271 4886, ⓦ sindoferry.com.sg).

HarbourFront Centre The southern terminus of the MRT's North East line, off Telok Blangah Rd at the southern tip of Singapore.

Destinations Batam (hourly; 40min); Karimun (at least 6 daily; 40min).

Tanah Merah ferry terminal In the east of the island, linked by bus #35 to Tanah Merah and Bedok MRT stations.

Destinations Batam (several daily; 40min); Bintan (several daily; 45min).

Changi Point ferry terminal From the Changi Point terminal near Changi Beach, humble bumboats sail, when full, to Kampung Pengerang in Malaysia, just east of Singapore in the Straits of Johor (daily 7am–7pm; 45min; S$10; ☎ 6542 7944). Most passengers get a taxi from there to the unexciting resort of Desaru (see p.297). In the unlikely event you arrive via this route, catch bus #2 to Tanah Merah MRT station or on to Geylang, Victoria St and Chinatown.

GETTING AROUND

All parts of Singapore are accessible by bus or **MRT** (Mass Rapid Transit). Fares are eminently reasonable (ⓦ publictransport .sg lists the fare for any journey), though overcrowding is rife during rush hour (7.30–9.30am & 5–7pm). The MRT metro system is a marvel of engineering – the island's soft subsoil made drilling train tunnels a real challenge – as well as cleanliness, efficiency and value for money. The public transport network is operated by two companies, **SBS Transit** (☎ 1800 225 5663, ⓦ www.sbstransit.com.sg) – historically a bus company, but now responsible for one MRT metro line – and **SMRT** (☎ 1800 336 8900, ⓦ www.smrt.com.sg), set up to run the MRT system, but now also running quite a few bus services of its own. Taxis are also affordable and usually easy to find.

TICKETS

ez-link card Most Singaporeans avoid the rigmarole of buying tickets for each bus or MRT ride by purchasing an ez-link card (ⓦ www.ezlink.com.sg) available at MRT stations and bus interchanges. Besides offering convenience, the card shaves at least ten percent off the cost of each trip.

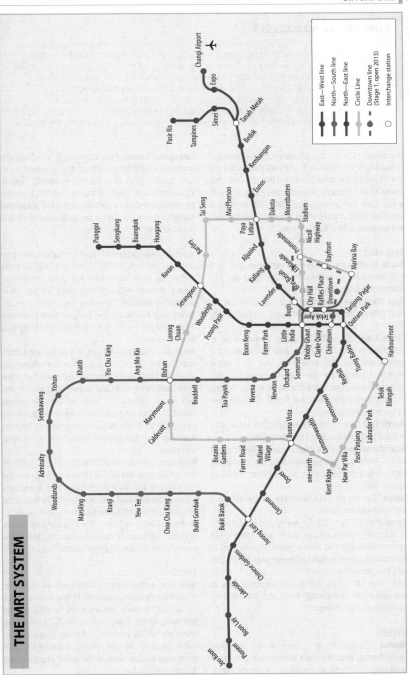

THE MRT SYSTEM

Legend:
- East—West line
- North—South line
- North—East line
- Circle Line
- Downtown line (Stage 1, open 2013)
- ○ Interchange station

Stations shown on map:

Changi Airport, Expo, Tanah Merah, Simei, Tampines, Pasir Ris, Bedok, Kembangan, Eunos, Dakota, Mountbatten, MacPherson, Tai Seng, Paya Lebar, Aljunied, Stadium, Nicoll Highway, Promenade, Bayfront, Marina Bay, Kallang, Esplanade, Lavender, Bras Basah, Bugis, City Hall, Raffles Place, Downtown, Telok Ayer, Tanjong Pagar, Outram Park, Harbourfront, Punggol, Sengkang, Buangkok, Hougang, Bartley, Serangoon, Lorong Chuan, Kovan, Woodleigh, Potong Pasir, Boon Keng, Farrer Park, Little India, Dhoby Ghaut, Clarke Quay, Chinatown, Tiong Bahru, Redhill, Telok Blangah, Labrador Park, Pasir Panjang, Haw Par Villa, Kent Ridge, one-north, Buona Vista, Commonwealth, Queenstown, Dover, Clementi, Jurong East, Chinese Gardens, Lakeside, Boon Lay, Pioneer, Joo Koon, Bukit Batok, Bukit Gombak, Choa Chu Kang, Yew Tee, Kranji, Marsiling, Woodlands, Admiralty, Sembawang, Yishun, Khatib, Yio Chu Kang, Ang Mo Kio, Bishan, Braddell, Toa Payoh, Novena, Newton, Orchard, Somerset, Marymount, Caldecott, Botanic Gardens, Farrer Road, Holland Village, Bishan

9

SINGAPORE ADDRESSES

Addresses pertaining to high-rise towers, shopping complexes and other buildings are generally written using two numbers preceded by #, as in #xx-yy. Here xx refers to the floor (ground level is 01, the next floor up 02, and so on) while yy refers to the unit number – thus a restaurant whose address includes #04-08 can be found in unit 8 on the building's fourth storey. All buildings within municipal housing estates have a **block number**, displayed prominently on the side, rather than a number relating to their position on the street.

If you want to look up an address on a map, entering the street, building name or six-digit postal code into ⓦ www.streetdirectory.com will usually give a fairly precise fix on the location.

The cards cost S$5 with no credit loaded, and can be bought at post offices, 7-11 stores and some MRT stations. The cost of each journey you make is deducted from the card when you hold it over a reader as you exit an MRT barrier or step off a bus. Cards can be topped up with S$10 or more of additional credit at ticket offices or using ticket machines, and remain valid for at least five years.

THE MRT

North South Line A vaguely horseshoe-shaped route from Marina Bay up to the north of the island and then southwest to Jurong, operated by SMRT.

East West Line Connecting Boon Lay in the west to Pasir Ris and Changi airport in the east, and operated by SMRT.

Circle Line This SMRT line passes through little of downtown as it runs from the Colonial District out to the eastern suburbs, then curls north and west before heading south to the Harbourfront Centre. A short extension, from Promenade station to Marina Bay via Bayfront station (for *Marina Bay Sands*) should be open by the time you read this.

North East Line Linking the HarbourFront Centre with Punggol in the northeast, and operated by SBS Transit.

Downtown Line The first stage of this new line, operated by SBS Transit and running from Chinatown to Bugis via Bayfront, was scheduled when this book went to press to open in 2013.

Hours Trains run every five minutes on average from 6am until midnight downtown.

Fares From S$1.20 to S$2.40/journey (S$0.80–2.20 with ez-link card). You can use your mobile in the tunnels, but you're not allowed to eat, drink or smoke on trains. Signs in the stations appear to ban hedgehogs from the MRT; in fact, they signify "no durians".

LRT Three LRT (Light Rail Transit) networks connect suburban estates with the MRT. As a tourist, you're unlikely to make use of any of them.

BUSES

Routes Singapore's bus network is incredibly comprehensive and can initially be confusing, as so many routes seem to be available downtown. Thankfully, central

Singapore Tourist Pass Alternatively, the Singapore Tourist Pass, valid for up to three days unlimited travel, costs S$8/day (plus S$10 refundable deposit). Sold at Visitor Centres and a few MRT stations (including the one at the airport), the cards can be topped up at MRT stations for additional days' travel, though any credit added this way is not refundable.

bus stops display detailed lists of destinations served by each bus, and both the SBS Transit and SMRT websites contain full route information and rather complicated journey planners – though they don't tell you about potential connections involving each other's buses. Pocket-sized bus guides are available from bookshops (S$4), while the free SBS app, Iris, is handy for looking up their bus routes.

Hours Buses start running around 6am and wind down from 11.30pm. The very last regular buses leave downtown around 12.30am, but between midnight and 2am a few Night-Rider (run by SMRT, and prefixed "NR") and Nite Owl (SBS Transit, suffixed "N") buses are available; costing around S$4, they can be useful for travel within the city centre, but then operate as express services between downtown and their ultimate destinations, the outlying new towns.

Fares Cash fares range from S$1 to S$2.20 (S$0.75–S$1.95 with ez-link card, and slightly cheaper again on the few buses with no a/c). Some buses charge a flat fare while a few don't take cash at all – check signage at the front of the bus. Paying cash, drop the fare into the metal chute next to the driver; change isn't given. If you have an ez-link card, you must tap the card on the card reader upon entering the bus *and* at the exit door when you get off.

TAXIS

Taxis Thousands of taxis roam the streets of Singapore, so you'll hardly ever have trouble hailing a cab – except late at night or when demand soars during a tropical downpour. All are clearly marked "TAXI". On the whole, drivers are friendly, but their English isn't always good; if you're heading off the beaten track, have your destination written down, or be aware of a landmark that they can aim for.

Fares Unlike in KL, all drivers use their meters, the fare starting at S$2.80 for the first kilometre, then rising 20¢ for every third of a kilometre or so (classier limousine taxis are only slightly more expensive). A surcharge of one third is payable Mon–Fri 7–9.30am & 5–8pm, Sat 5–8pm, and of fifty percent between midnight and 6am nightly. Journeys involving Changi airport or the casinos incur a surcharge of several dollars, and there's a fee of S$3.50–5 if you book a taxi over the phone. Tolls levied on journeys along expressways and within the CBD are also factored into fares.

Taxi companies Comfort/CityCab ☎ 6552 1111, ⓦ www .cdgtaxi.com.sg; Silvercab ☎ 6363 6888, ⓦ www .premiertaxi.com; SMRT Taxis ☎ 6555 8888, ⓦ www.smrt .com.sg.

DRIVING

Driving in Singapore Given the efficiency of public transport, there's hardly any reason to rent a car in Singapore, especially when it's a pricey business. Major disincentives to driving are in place in order to combat traffic congestion: a permit just to own a car costs more than many makes of car.

Tolls Drivers have to pay tolls to enter a restricted zone encompassing Chinatown, Orchard Rd and the Financial District, and to use many of the island's expressways. This being Singapore, it's all done in the most hi-tech way using Electronic Road Pricing (ERP): all Singapore cars have a gizmo that reads a stored-value CashCard from which the toll is deducted as you drive past an ERP gantry.

Parking Generally expensive, though at least many car parks offer the convenience of taking the fee off your CashCard, failing which you have to purchase coupons from a licence booth, post office or shop.

Car rental The only sensible reason to rent a car in Singapore is to travel up into Malaysia – and even then it's far cheaper to rent in JB. If you are still keen to rent in Singapore itself, contact Avis (ⓦ www.avis.com.sg) or Hertz (ⓦ www.hertz.com); both have offices at Changi airport.

Driving from Malaysia To drive a Malaysian car into Singapore, you need to buy a stored-value Autopass card at the Causeway or Second Crossing. The card magically records any ERP tolls you incur without requiring a card reader on board; the total charge is deducted from the card when you return to Johor. For more details on this and other matters to do with driving in Singapore, see ⓦ www.lta.gov.sg.

CYCLING

Cycling in Singapore Though largely flat, Singapore is hardly ideal cycling country. There are few bike lanes along main roads, where you'll have to brave furious traffic, though this doesn't put off the few dedicated locals and expats whom you'll see pedalling equally furiously along suburban thoroughfares such as Bukit Timah Rd. Cycling downtown isn't such a great idea though, and bicycles aren't allowed on expressways.

Cycling outside the city Where bikes come into their own is in out-of-town recreational areas and nature parks, which are linked by a park connector network; see ⓦ www.nparks.gov.sg. The East Coast Park, on the southeast shore of the island, has a popular cycle track with rental outlets along the way (expect to pay S$5–8/hr for a mountain bike, and have some form of ID). It's also possible to cycle at Bukit Timah Nature Reserve (see p.518). Wherever you cycle, you'll need a high tolerance for getting very hot and sweaty – or drenched if you're caught in a downpour.

USEFUL BUS ROUTES

Handy **bus routes** are listed below. One-way systems downtown mean that services that use Orchard Road and Bras Basah Road in one direction return via Stamford Road, Penang Road, Somerset Road and Orchard Boulevard; buses up Selegie and Serangoon roads return via Jalan Besar and Bencoolen Street; and services along North and South Bridge roads and New Bridge Road return via Eu Tong Sen Street, Hill Street and Victoria Street.

#2 From Eu Tong Sen Street in Chinatown all the way to Changi Prison and Changi Beach, via the Arab Quarter and Geylang Serai.

#7 From the restaurants of Holland Village to the Botanic Gardens and on to Orchard Road, Bras Basah Road and Victoria Street (for the Arab Quarter), then on to Geylang Serai.

#36 A loop service between Orchard Road and Changi airport via Suntec City and the Singapore Flyer.

#65 Orchard Road to Little India and on up Serangoon Road.

#170 From the Ban San Terminal at the northern end of Queen Street to JB in Malaysia, passing Little India, the Newton Circus food court, the northern end of the Botanic Gardens, Bukit Timah Nature Reserve and Kranji War Cemetery on the way.

#174 Runs between the Botanic Gardens and the Baba House in Neil Road, via Orchard Road, the Colonial District, Boat Quay and Chinatown.

9

ORGANIZED TOURS

Sightseeing tours range from guided walks to Singapore River trips (see p.485). It's also possible to take a ride in a **trishaw**, a three-wheeled cycle rickshaw; once these functioned like taxis, but they now exist only to give tourists a spin on certain routes (and aren't allowed on some major roads). In Chinatown, freelance trishaw men congregate near the Buddha Tooth Relic Temple, though you'll have to bargain with them to arrange a ride; alternatively you can book a trip with the operator listed below.

To engage a specialist guide for a more personalized look at, say, Singapore's architecture or historical districts, try the directory at ⓦ guides-online.yoursingapore.com.

DuckTours ☏ 6338 6877, ⓦ www.ducktours.com. sg. Tour the Colonial District and Marina Bay on an amphibious vehicle; fun for families. Hourly 10am–6pm; $33.

Harbour cruises ☏ 6533 9811, ⓦ www.watertours .com.sg. These offer views of the Financial District and the Singapore Flyer, and supposedly evoke the spirit of journeys made by the fifteenth-century Chinese mariner Cheng Ho, though the boats used look not so much like a traditional junk as a mini palace stuck on top of a floating platform. Boats depart daily from the Marina South Pier, 1500m southeast of Marina Bay MRT station, with prices starting at S$27 including light refreshments and free pick-up from the station or a few downtown hotels.

The Original Singapore Walks ☏ 6325 1631, ⓦ www.singaporewalks.com. Guided walks of downtown and Changi, generally lasting 2hr 30min; around $30.

Trishaw Uncle Booth on Queen St, close to Bugis MRT ☏ 9012 1233, ⓦ www.trishawuncle.com.sg. The only trishaw cooperative at the time of writing, charging S$39 for a half-hour ride around the immediate vicinity and Little India, or S$49 with Clarke Quay included. Daily 11am–10pm.

INFORMATION

Visitors Centres Tourist offices run by the Singapore Tourism Board (STB; helpline daily 8am–7pm ☏ 1800 736 2000, ⓦ www.yoursingapore.com) are billed as Visitors Centres. Their main downtown location is in the middle of Orchard Rd, at Cairnhill Rd (daily 9.30am–10.30pm; Somerset MRT); they also have a much smaller office on Cheng Yan Place (daily 11am–11pm; Bugis MRT), and a counter in the ION Orchard mall (daily 10am–10pm; above Orchard MRT).

Heritage trails Booklets providing historical background on downtown districts ere available from the Singapore City Gallery (see p.508), and can be downloaded from ⓦ www.singaporecitygallery.sg.

Internet access Little India is the best place to look for internet cafés, fairly numerous here and cheap, charging as little as S$2/hr. Orchard Rd and Chinatown have internet cafés too, though Orchard Rd rates are high at S$5/hr.

Listings Listings of entertainment events, restaurant reviews and so forth can be found in the weeklies *I-S* (free) and *8 Days* (S$1.50) and the monthly *Time Out* (S$4; ⓦ www.timeoutsingapore.com). The "Life!" section of the *Straits Times* also has a decent listings section. Both *The Finder*, a free monthly available at downtown bars and restaurants, and ⓦ www.expatsingapore.com, are geared towards the large expat community but hold information of interest to visitors.

Maps The only street map that keeps pace with Singapore's incessant changes is the *Singapore Street Directory* (S$12; online at ⓦ www.streetdirectory.com).

ACCOMMODATION

Room rates in Singapore having soared in recent years, mid-range hotel rooms seldom come cheaper than S$100 a night. Most accommodation is well run, wi-fi access is widely available (though the priciest hotels tend to charge for it) and, as in Malaysia, **promotional rates** are available most of the year, except perhaps during the Formula One race in the third week of September. Budget travellers can choose from a plethora of **hostels** and **guesthouses**, mostly situated in Little India and the surrounding area, though Chinatown holds a few as well. Most hotels are blandly modern, but there has also been a new wave of **boutique hotels**, usually characterful or quirky affairs in refurbished shophouses, especially in Chinatown. Those **budget hotels** that offer hourly or "transit" rates tend to be used by locals for illicit liaisons; some, notably in Little India, have an obvious seedy underside, though even members of the ubiquitous and well-run chains *Hotel 81* and *Fragrance* have been known to quote hourly rates. The establishments reviewed here are largely untainted by this. At the other end of the scale, **five-star** and some four-star hotels continuously adjust their rates depending on demand. The reviews here reflect what are meant to be typical starting prices (including taxes). Besides contacting places directly, you can also book and find discounts through sites such as ⓦ www.agoda.com or, if you're after a guesthouse, ⓦ www.hostelworld.com.

LITTLE INDIA, ARAB STREET AND LAVENDER STREET

Little India is very much the centre for budget accommodation in Singapore, and easily accessible thanks to the Little India station. The area around Arab St also has a few good places to stay and is convenient for Bugis MRT station. Both districts are atmospheric and packed with inexpensive restaurants. There are also quite a few decent budget and mid-range places to stay beyond Little India proper, in the zone extending up to Lavender St, reachable via Farrer Park or Lavender stations, and with an excellent public swimming pool close by (see p.561).

HOSTELS AND GUESTHOUSES

Ali's Nest 23 Roberts Lane ☎9245 2376, ⊕alisnest .com; map p.496. Probably the cheapest place to stay in Singapore, a bit spartan but the more appealing for that. All rooms have a/c; amenities are limited to a kitchen, small sitting area and internet access. If you have difficulty finding this old shophouse, look out for the "Shanghai Kotat Trading" sign above. Dorms **S$14**, rooms **S$25**

★ **Checkers Inn** 46–50 Campbell Lane ☎6392 0693, ⊕ www.checkersinn.com.sg; map p.496. This slick place bills itself as a "boutique backpackers", and for once the hype isn't misplaced: the kitchen looks like something out of a posh furnishings store, while dangling from the ceiling of the swanky lounge are dozens of little toys, spray-painted white. No private rooms. Dorms **S$30**

Drop Inn 253 Lavender St ☎6299 3817, ⊕www .dropinnhostel.com; map p.496. Not the most exciting place to stay, but the lounge has a wide central platform for lolling about on, and there's a range of doubles in addition to the dorms. A decent option. Dorms **S$22**, doubles **S$50**

Green Kiwi 280a Lavender St (no phone), ⊕www .greenkiwi.com.sg; map p.496. The pleasant 24hr roof garden is the standout feature at this maze at this hostel in a large building opposite the start of Jalan Besar. The place also boasts bathrooms with slick fittings, and there are cosier two- and four-bed rooms in addition to larger mixed and female-only dorms. Dorm beds **S$16**, double room **S$80**

The Hive 624 Serangoon Rd (corner of Lavender St) ☎6341 5041, ⊕www.thehivebackpackers.com; map p.496. A large hostel where every room is named after a flower and the exterior is done out in black and yellow. Putting the bee metaphors aside, the place is well managed, with a/c in all rooms and dorms. Dorms **S$20**, doubles **S$50**

★ **Inn Crowd** 73 Dunlop St (reception) & 35 Campbell Lane ☎6296 9169, ⊕www.the-inncrowd.com; map p.496. Endearing, recently renovated hostel with dorms plus a range of rooms with TV and a/c. Shared showers and toilets are kept spotless, and there's a comfy lounge, cheap beer and free internet access. Dorms **S$20**, rooms **S$60**

★ **The Mitraa** 427 Race Course Rd ☎6396 3925, ⊕www.mitraa.com.sg; map p.496. It bills itself as "the

friendliest backpacker hostel", and friendly it certainly is, plus well organized. If they're full they may be able to put you up at their *Mitraa Inn* offshoot (531 Serangoon Rd, ☎6396 3317), where many dorms have an en-suite bathroom, though you pay a bit extra to stay here. Dorms **S$25–35**, five-bed family room at *Mitraa Inn* **S$150**

Prince of Wales Backpackers 101 Dunlop St ☎6299 0130, ⊕pow.com.sg; map p.496. An established favourite done out in primary colours, with a/c six-bed dorms, a couple of double rooms and a popular 24hr bar/ beer garden. Dorms **S$22**, doubles **S$60–70**

★ **Sleepy Sam's** 55 Bussorah St (no phone) ⊕www .sleepysams.com; map p.496. Brilliantly placed in the heart of the Arab St area, with a few private rooms plus mixed and women-only dorms; amenities include a kitchen and a laundry service. Dorms **S$28**, doubles **S$90**

HOTELS

Aqueen 139 Lavender St ☎6395 7788, ⊕www .aqueenhotels.com; map p.496. The bizarre name is of greater interest than the modern, functional fittings at this nondescript but good-value hotel. Rates include breakfast. **S$150**

Fragrance Imperial 28 Penhas Rd ☎6297 9888, ⊕www.fragrancehotel.com; map p.496. Despite the drab yellow exterior, this a cut above its fellow members of the budget chain, with slick if smallish rooms, a café, and rooftop swimming pool. Rates include breakfast. **S$150**

Haising 37 Jalan Besar ☎6298 1223, ⊕www.haising .com.sg; map p.496. Friendly, secure Chinese-run cheapie offering simple, a/c en-suite rooms, rather boxy but not bad for the price. **S$60**

Kerbau 54–62 Kerbau Rd ☎6297 6668, ⊕kerbauinn @pacific.net.sg; map p.496. Well located in a row of shophouses near Tekka Market and Little India MRT, the *Kerbau* is a compact place with plain en-suite rooms. **S$70**

Landmark Village 390 Victoria St (entrance on Arab St) ☎6297 2828, ⊕www.stayvillage.com/landmark; map p.496. Beyond the dated shopping centre downstairs is this modern hotel, recently given a partial facelift, with a pool and various restaurants. **S$240**

Madras 28–32 Madras St ☎6392 7889, ⊕www .madrassingapore.com; map p.496. Smallish, slightly tatty rooms with the standard mod cons and the bonus of a DVD player in each room, just in case the usual TV channels don't thrill you. **S$140**

★ **Mayo Inn** 9 Jalan Besar ☎6295 6631, ⊕www .mayoinn.com; map p.496. A partial refurbishment has given a new lease of life to the two dozen rooms at this simple, good-value hotel, which now feature modern bathrooms and, in some cases, a neat Japanese-style "bed" – a wooden dais with a mattress on top. **S$110**

★ **Moon** 23 Dickson Rd ☎6827 6666, ⊕www.moon .com.sg; map p.496. Aiming to offer a boutique-hotel

9

experience without straining your wallet, the *Moon* has stylishly kitted-out rooms with snazzy wallpaper, iPod docks and strategically placed drapes – to help take your mind off the fact that many are actually windowless. Rates include breakfast. S$150

Parkroyal 181 Kitchener Rd ☎6428 3000, ⓦwww .parkroyalhotels.com; map p.496. Little India's classiest place to stay boasts a recently redesigned marbled lobby, spacious and tasteful rooms, a pool and a couple of restaurants. If you're heading here by taxi, mention the address as there's a sister hotel of the same name on Beach Rd. S$270

Perak 12 Perak Rd ☎6299 7733, ⓦwww.peraklodge .net; map p.496. Set within a nicely restored shophouse and somewhat sedate – probably not a bad thing given the hullaballoo of Little India. Rooms are comfy but otherwise unremarkable. Rates include breakfast. S$150

Santa Grand Bugis 8 Jalan Kubor ☎6298 8638, ⓦwww.santagrand.com.sg; map p.496. This functional, modern hotel has decent rooms and a pool, but what really edges it ahead of the competition are the family and deluxe rooms in a nicely restored old house next door. Rates include breakfast. S$170

Wanderlust 2 Dickson Rd ☎6396 3622, ⓦwww .wanderlusthotels.com; map p.496. As at its more established boutique sibling, Chinatown's *New Majestic*, there's a touch of modern-art wackiness at *Wanderlust*: the "industrial glam" lobby includes barber's chairs and many rooms are colour-themed, some even equipped with multicoloured lighting whose hues you can control. Facilities include a jacuzzi and French restaurant. Rates include breakfast. S$240

BRAS BASAH ROAD TO ROCHOR ROAD

The grid of streets between Bras Basah Rd and Rochor Rd, also boxed in by Beach Rd to the east and Selegie Rd and the Istana grounds to the west, has been rendered a bit sterile by redevelopment – though a sprinkling of shophouses, temples and churches still lend character. The area has some modern mid-range places to stay, though even these generally charge around S$200 a night or more. Given its colonial connections, the *Raffles*, on the southern edge of the area, is reviewed on opposite page.

HOSTELS AND GUESTHOUSES

G4 Station 11 Mackenzie Rd ☎6334 5644, ⓦg4station.com; map p.493. Short on atmosphere but impeccably run, with dorms of various sizes plus double rooms, all with a/c, plenty of modern fittings (including chunky lockers). There's a communal Wii, too. Dorms S$28, rooms S$80

★ **Hangout @ Mount Emily** 10a Upper Wilkie Rd ☎6438 5588, ⓦwww.hangouthotels.com; map p.493. Owned by the company behind the historic Cathay cinema at the foot of Mount Emily, the *Hangout* is an impressive designer guesthouse with a breezy rooftop terrace that's great for chilling out in the evening. The only drawback is that it's 10min walk uphill from Selegie Rd. Book online; the place is popular, and so you can get much lower rates than if you simply turn up. All rates include a buffet breakfast. Dorms S$40, rooms S$120

★ **Tree In Lodge** Top floor, 2 Tan Quee Lan St ☎6844 5512, ⓦwww.treeinlodge.com; map p.493. This guesthouse puts its green credentials in the spotlight – they recycle, use eco cleaning products and avoid plastic – but just as importantly it's well kept, the dorms (of six to twelve beds) complemented by plenty of toilets and showers. The friendly management are full of suggestions for visits to unusual nooks and crannies of the island, and sometimes organize trips. Dorms S$28

HOTELS

Albert Court 180 Albert St ☎6339 3939, ⓦwww .albertcourt.com.sg; map p.493. This self-styled boutique hotel benefits from preserved shophouse facades and amenities such as a gym, jacuzzi and sauna. The superior and deluxe rooms boast old-fashioned ceiling fans – which you're unlikely to use as there's a/c – while the pricier executive rooms are ultramodern. S$230

★ **Carlton** 76 Bras Basah Rd ☎6338 8333, ⓦwww .carltonhotel.sg; map p.493. Boasting a grand new extension and a redesigned lobby dominated by a spidery glass artwork suspended from the ceiling, this multistorey tower of a four-star hotel has elegant rooms, a pool and gym – and excellent rates for what's on offer. S$270

★ **Ibis** 170 Bencoolen St ☎6593 2888, ⓦwww .ibishotel.com; map p.493. If you've stayed in other hotels run by this no-frills chain, you'd probably describe them as functional, modern and a little dull – a perfect match for Singapore, then. The 7-11 shop in the lobby feels totally apt, though on a more positive note the place is well insulated from traffic noise. S$200

Intercontinental 80 Middle Rd ☎6338 7600, ⓦwww .intercontinental.com; map p.493. Like the adjoining Bugis Junction mall, the *Intercontinental* incorporates some original shophouses, here converted into so-called "shophouse rooms" with supposedly Peranakan decor, which merely amounts to oriental-looking vases. Regular rooms, S$50 cheaper, attempt to evoke a "Victorian" flavour. Still, the hotel is luxurious and has all the amenities you could want, and rates can fall by a quarter at weekends. Regular rooms S$350

Naumi 41 Seah St ☎6403 6000, ⓦwww.naumihotel .com; map p.493. The slate-grey exterior, on which what look like vines crawling up behind netting, doesn't inspire, but inside is a stunning boutique hotel where every room is kitted out like a luxury apartment and boasts an iPod dock and a kitchenette. There's also a rooftop pool, while rooms on one floor are reserved for women only. Breakfast sometimes included. **S$400**

★ **South East Asia Hotel** 190 Waterloo St ☎6338 2394, ⓦwww.seahotel.com.sg; map p.493. Behind the yellow and white 1950s facade is a reasonable hotel with functional but unexciting doubles, all featuring the usual mod cons. Right next door is the lively Kwan Im temple. Substantially cheaper than anything else in the area. **S$100**

Victoria 87 Victoria St ☎6622 0909, ⓦwww.santa grandhotels.com; map p.493. This compact hotel is dwarfed by the new buildings around, but punches above its weight with modern en-suite rooms equipped with flat-screen TV and fridge. No breakfast though. **S$150**

THE COLONIAL DISTRICT AND MARINA CENTRE

Between the north bank of the Singapore River and Bras Basah Rd (including the area around Fort Canning Park) are a handful of mid-range and pricey hotels, though most owe little to the area's colonial heritage. The rather soulless triangle of reclaimed land called Marina Centre, forming the northern jaw of Marina Bay, has a few swanky hotels of its own.

Fort Canning 11 Canning Walk, northern side of Fort Canning Hill ☎6559 6770, ⓦwww.hfcsingapore.com; map p.484. Hotel facades don't come much more imposing than that of the former British military HQ that houses this plush boutique hotel, though little colonial atmosphere survives inside, and it's a bit of a trek down flights of steps to Dhoby Ghaut MRT and Orchard Rd. Rooms are spacious, immaculately decorated, and boast a bathtub that's curiously often either smack in the middle of the room or out towards the window, with blinds for privacy. Pools on two levels and lush gardens, too. **S$380**

Novotel Clarke Quay 177a River Valley Rd ☎6338 3333, ⓦwww.novotel.com; map p.484. This dull tower block might appear just another bland business-oriented hotel, but the elegant wood-panelled lobby and tasteful contemporary furnishings make clear this is all about giving the boutique hotels a run for their money. Comes with the usual four-star amenities, including pool and jacuzzi. **S$250**

Peninsula Excelsior 5 Coleman St ☎6337 8080, ⓦwww.ytchotels.com.sg/peninsulaexcelsior; map p.484. Really two hotels merged together – as hinted at by the presence of swimming pools at either end, one of which abuts the lobby – and nicely modernized, unlike the 1970s shopping arcade below. **S$225**

Raffles 1 Beach Rd ☎6337 1886, ⓦwww.raffleshotel .com; map p.484. The modern extension is a mixed bag, but the *Raffles* remains refreshingly low-rise and still has colonial-era charm in spades, especially evident in the opulent lobby and the courtyards fringed by frangipani

trees and palms. Amenities include a dozen restaurants and bars, a rooftop pool and a spa. You'll need deep pockets to stay, of course, even though online discounts knock a third off the rack rate. **S$750**

Ritz-Carlton Millenia 7 Raffles Ave ☎6337 8888, ⓦwww.ritz-carlton.com; map p.484. Arguably king of the pricey hotels in Marina Centre, with magnificent views across to the towers of the Financial District – even from the bathrooms, where butlers will fill the bath for you. **S$500**

Robertson Quay 15 Merbau Rd ☎6735 3333, ⓦwww.robertsonquayhotel.com.sg; map p.484. A circular riverside tower with great views of the river, a cute round pool and a gym. Rooms are on the small side and the place can be a little disorganized, but with these rates, which include breakfast, you can probably put up with all that. **S$160**

Swissôtel The Stamford 2 Stamford Rd ☎6338 8585, ⓦwww.singapore-stamford.swissotel.com; map p.484. Upper-floor rooms – and the restaurants and bars on the 70th to 72nd floors – aren't for those with vertigo, though the views are as splendid as you'd expect from one of the tallest hotels in the world, with over a thousand rooms. **S$460**

CHINATOWN AND MARINA SOUTH

Accommodation south of the Singapore River is largely upmarket, though Chinatown holds decent backpacker options as well as chic designer establishments. East of Chinatown and the Financial Distrct, the area south of Marina Bay holds just one option, the iconic *Marina Bay Sands*.

HOSTELS AND GUESTHOUSES

A Beary Good Hostel 66a & 66b Pagoda St ☎6222 495, ⓦwww.abearygoodhostel.com; map on pp.502–503. A spick-and-span hostel with ten- to fifteen-bed mixed dorms and Wii consoles, plus an all-but-identical offshoot, *Beary Nice* (46b Smith St; ☎6222 4951). Dorms **S$26**

Pillows & Toast 40 Mosque St ☎6220 4653, ⓦwww .pillowsntoast.com; map on pp.502–503. A friendly place with a chilled-out loft lounge and a variety of female or mixed dorms, all with at least eight beds. Dorms **S$26**

Prince of Wales Backpackers 51 Boat Quay ☎6536 9697, ⓦwww.pow.com.sg; map on pp.502–503. Just like the Little India original, this hostel has a downstairs bar – and that's where the similarity ends; things are a lot less laidback here given the location in the thick of the Singapore River's nightlife. There's a 20-bed mixed dorm and a 16-bed women's dorm, each with its own facilities and great river views, plus a couple of private rooms. Dorms **S$25**, rooms **S$90**

9

Rucksack Inn 33b Hong Kong St ☎ 6438 5146, ⓦ www.rucksackinn.com; map on pp.502–503. A well-run hostel with a massive 28-bed dorm and several private rooms, plus an all-day self-service breakfast and free walking tours of Chinatown to boot. It also has a nearby branch, *Rucksack Inn 2* (38a Hong Kong St; ☎ 6532 4990), with ten-bed mixed and women's dorms plus more rooms. Dorms S$30, rooms S$95

HOTELS

Fullerton 1 Fullerton Square ☎ 6733 8388, ⓦ www.fullertonhotel.com; map on pp.502–503. As impressive as the *Raffles*, its stunning atrium propped up on massive columns like an Egyptian temple. Rooms and bathrooms are spacious, with contemporary rather than Art Deco stylings; amenities include a gym, spa and pool. Book some way ahead to get the best rates. S$450

Hotel 1929 50 Keong Saik Rd ☎ 6222 3377, ⓦ www.hotel1929.com; map on pp.502–503. Less pricey than its sister hotel, the *New Majestic*, this shophouse building looks genuinely 1929 on the outside, but the interior has been renovated to look like a twenty-first-century version of the early 1960s, all very retro chic. Rates include breakfast. S$210

The Inn at Temple Street 36 Temple St ☎ 6221 5333, ⓦ www.theinn.com.sg; map on pp.502–503. It's packed with old-fangled furniture for that period feel, but the rooms are boxy; still, you can't argue with the rates. S$110

Lehotel 16 Carpenter St ☎ 6534 4859, ⓦ www.lehotel.com.sg; map on pp.502–503. A worthwhile budget offering in the heart of Chinatown, with decent but sterile modern rooms. S$100

Marina Bay Sands 10 Bayfront Ave, Marina South ☎ 6688 8868, ⓦ www.marinabaysands.com; map pp.502–503. At a stroke *Marina Bay Sands* has become the largest hotel in Singapore, with an astonishing 2500 rooms. Frankly they're no better than most of the other five-star hotels, unless you shell out for, say, one of the Straits suites, with two en-suite bedrooms, a baby grand piano and butler service – for at least S$5000 a night. Otherwise, stay here for the architecture and that infinity pool. S$540

★ **New Majestic** 31–37 Bukit Pasoh Rd ☎ 6511 4700, ⓦ www.newmajestichotel.com; map on pp.502–503. If money is no object, this is the boutique hotel to make a beeline for. In a country whose buildings aspire to arctic levels of a/c, its open-air lobby and shabby ceiling (highlighting the vintage status of the building) offer the first of many surprises. Every room has been eccentrically decorated by local designers – one has arty seaweed simulations growing out of the wall, for example. Other quirks include a pool with floor portholes that allow you to look down into the restaurant – just as diners can look up at you swimming by. Rates include breakfast. S$320

★ **The Saff** 55 Keong Saik Rd ☎ 6221 8388, ⓦ www.thesaffhotel.com; map on pp.502–503. Spread over several adjacent shophouses, this Arabian Nights fantasy of a boutique hotel might have been better sited in Arab St, but *The Saff* impresses anyway with its gaudy colours and decor wth tinges of Morocco or Moghul India. Standard rooms have no windows, which actually makes them feel all the more cosy. Rates include breakfast. S$150

The Scarlet 33 Erskine Rd ☎ 6511 3333, ⓦ www.thescarlethotel.com; map on pp.502–503. Housed in an impressive shophouse refurbishment, this boutique hotel has an exceptionally extravagant lobby, though here and in the rooms the opulence of the decor seems to lack a unifying theme. Amenities include a gym and an outdoor jacuzzi. S$225

Swissôtel Merchant Court 20 Merchant Rd ☎ 6337 2288, ⓦ www.singapore-merchantcourt.swissotel.com; map on pp.502–503. One of downtown's best located hotels, well placed for Clarke and Boat quays and with part of its *Ellenborough Market Café* encroaching on the riverside promenade itself. Discounts can shave a third off rates. S$260

ORCHARD ROAD

You generally pay a premium to stay in the Orchard Rd shopping area, though it's hardly the most interesting part of downtown, and now that many stores have branches across town, only the sheer modernity of the district gives it any edge.

Goodwood Park 22 Scotts Rd ☎ 6737 7411, ⓦ www.goodwoodparkhotel.com; map on pp.516–517. Set on a leafy hillock, designed by the architect responsible for the *Raffles*, and likewise a genuine landmark in a cityscape characterized by transience. It still oozes the refinements of a bygone era, too, and boasts a variety of rooms and suites, plus several highly rated restaurants and two pools. Not as pricey as you might think. S$330

Grand Central 22 Cavenagh Rd ☎ 6737 9944, ⓦ ghihotels.com; map on pp.516–517. This ugly 1970s relic has somehow resisted redevelopment despite its prime location, and being somewhat dated, it has rates from yesteryear – sometimes as low as S$150 for a double. The swimming pool is the only noteworthy feature. S$200

Innotel 11 Penang Lane ☎ 6327 2727, ⓦ innotel.com.sg; map on pp.516–517. Styling itself the "jewel of Penang Lane", this new business-oriented hotel is hardly a gem but does offer stripped-down, cosy modern rooms. S$240

Lloyd's Inn 2 Lloyd Rd ☎ 6737 7309, ⓦ www.lloydinn.com; map on pp.516–517. Less than 10min walk from Orchard Rd, this motel-like building has large if rather bland and dated accommodation; rates are a steal. S$90

★ **Mandarin Orchard** 333 Orchard Rd ☎ 6737 4411, ⓦ www.meritushotels.com; map on pp.516–517. Female staff at this old favourite wear kitsch scarlet quasi-oriental uniforms, but don't let that put you off; the hotel is still at the top of its game, luxurious to a fault, well placed right in the middle of Orchard Rd, and has its own high-end mini-mall, too. **S$400**

Marriott 320 Orchard Rd ☎6735 5800, ⓦwww .marriott.com. One of the plushest hotels on Orchard Rd, occupying a pagoda-style tower rising above Tangs department store, and featuring a hot tub in every room plus the obligatory pool, spa and gym and plenty of restaurants. **S$540**

Regent 1 Cuscaden Rd ☎6733 8888 ⓦwww .regenthotels.com; map on pp.516–517. Top-flight hotel with an impressive pyramidal atrium above the lobby and beautifully styled rooms, plus a pool, gym and spa. **S$420**

Shangri-La 22 Orange Grove Rd ☎6737 3644, ⓦwww .shangri-la.com; map on pp.516–517. This old faithful still epitomizes elegance, with seven-hundred-plus rooms set in oodles of landscaped greenery. Facilities include pitch-and-putt golf, tennis courts and a spa. It's 10min walk from Orchard Rd, with free shuttle buses laid on. Recommended, if you can afford the rates. **S$500**

Supreme 15 Kramat Rd ☎6737 8333, ⓦwww .supremeh.com.sg; map on pp.516–517. Next to the *Grand Central* and likewise a 1970s concrete box. The rooms are very tired though not too poky, and rates include breakfast. **S$150**

GEYLANG (JOO CHIAT ROAD)

With such a huge range of accommodation available downtown, there are few compelling reasons to stay in the suburbs except to save a little money. Joo Chiat Rd, which runs 2km between Geylang and the adjacent Katong district, holds a great backpacker place and a couple of inexpensive hotels.

★ **Betel Box** 200 Joo Chiat Rd ☎6247 7340, ⓦbetelbox.com; map on p.521. Singapore's socially committed hostel, *Betel Box* tries to highlight the island's cultural heritage by taking guests on trips to interesting districts, has its own little resource library and even runs a retro-themed restaurant below (see p.552). Accommodation comprises mixed and female-only dorms of various sizes, some with facilities inside, plus some private rooms. 15min walk from Paya Lebar MRT, or bus #33 from Bedok or Kallang MRT. Dorms **S$20**, rooms **S$60**

Gateway Hotel 60 Joo Chiat Rd ☎6342 0988, ⓦwww .gatewayhotel.com.sg; map on p.521. They dare to call themselves a boutique hotel, but this is really a rather stodgy place with bland modern rooms, most with a bathtub, at keen prices. 10min walk from Paya Lebar MRT. **S$110**

SENTOSA

Improved transport connections mean Sentosa no longer feels cut off from the mainland, though returning to your hotel for a short break from sightseeing downtown is still time-consuming unless you catch a cab.

Hotel Michael ☎6577 8899, ⓦwww.rwsentosa.com. The only hotel at Resorts World that's memorable, thanks to fittings and artwork by American architect and designer Michael Graves. Look out for packages that include Universal Studios, if you're so inclined. **S$350**

Mövenpick Sentosa 23 Beach View, near Imbiah station ☎6818 3388, ⓦwww.moevenpick-hotels .com. Splendid new hotel, split into an elegant modern wing and a heritage wing housed in former British barracks dating from 1940. All rooms feature elegant contemporary fittings, but the most impressive are the pricey onsen suites with their own large outdoor Japanese hot tub. **S$320**

Rasa Sentosa Resort Western end of Siloso Beach ☎6275 0100, ⓦwww.shangri-la.com. One of the best pre-casino-era hotels, in leafy grounds at the far end of Siloso Beach. Recently refurbished and family-friendly, it boasts a large freeform pool with water slides, a "kids' club" where staff take under-12s on activities such as treasure hunts and beach walks, plus a spa. **S$400**

Sentosa Resort and Spa ☎6275 0331, ⓦwww .thesentosa.com. Swanky affair, in secluded grounds above Tanjong Beach, with a spa featuring outdoor pools and imported mud from New Zealand. Other spa resorts on the island are fancier and fiendishly expensive. **S$320**

Siloso Beach Resort Middle of Siloso Beach ☎6722 3333, ⓦwww.shangri-la.com. The central swimming pool is a stunner, its curvy fringes planted with lush vegetation and featuring a waterfall and slides; it far outshines the slightly dated rooms. Still, the resort is tranquil enough (the music from the nearby beach bars stops around 10pm) and rooms include breakfast. **S$220**

EATING

Along with shopping, **eating** ranks as Singapore's national pastime. Walk along any street downtown and just about every other building seems to be overflowing with food outlets, from proper restaurants to corner kiosks serving snacks, all kept afloat by the island's incredible population density. As in Malaysia, food is both a widespread passion and a unifier across ethnic divides. Certain foods are largely or uniquely Singaporean: chilli crab, a sweet-spicy dish pioneered at long-gone rural seaside restaurants and now served all over the island; and *mee rebus*, a Malay dish of egg noodles served in a thick, spicy gravy based on yellow-bean sauce, with tofu, boiled egg and beansprouts as accompaniments – to name but two. By far the cheapest and most fun places to eat are the ubiquitous **hawker centres,** also called **food courts**, particularly those housed within shopping malls. Old-fangled **kopitiams** (the same as *kedai kopi* in Malaysia) are also inexpensive, though not that common

9

downtown; the best concentrations are in Little India and the Arab St area. Prices aside, Chinese *kopitiam*s and simpler restaurants often make a big thing of being *zichar* places – essentially being able to offer cooked-to-order dishes that don't necessarily correspond to what's on the menu; take advantage where possible, as having things fried up how you like them won't cost any extra. Naturally, food stalls and *kopitiam*s mainly serve up local cuisines. For the full range of Asian and international food, there are numerous **restaurants**, some specialist, others with menus that are a patchwork of cuisines.

Costs Prices at restaurants can be steep: while you can eat well for S$15 a head at plenty of no-frills, open-fronted establishments, there are just as many sophisticated places with a/c where you'll pay three or four times that. As with hotel bills, there's also the matter of the ten percent service charge and seven percent tax, levied by all but the cheapest restaurants and cafés (price indications here include these surcharges).

Singapore Food Festival Events around the annual Singapore Food Festival in July (ⓦwww.singapore foodfestival.com) include everything from cookery classes to food-themed guided walks and appearances by international celebrity chefs.

CAFÉS AND HIGH-TEA VENUES

Western-style café chains, including *Starbucks*, are easy to find in downtown Singapore, though they're thin on the ground in Little India. The places reviewed here have only a limited selection of food, typically pastries, muffins, sandwiches and so forth, but make inexpensive spots for a Western breakfast nonetheless. Also reviewed are a couple of hotel venues renowned for that most colonial of traditions, high tea. It doesn't come cheap but it's a good excuse for a blowout – you get a lot more than just tea and scones for your money.

Café l'Espresso *Goodwood Park Hotel*, 22 Scotts Rd ☏ 6730 1743, see map pp.516–517. A legendary array of English cakes, scones and speciality coffees, not to mention chocolate fondue, for high tea – so successful they've extended it to lunchtimes at weekends. S$45 weekdays, S$50 weekends. Daily 10am–midnight; high tea Mon–Thurs 2–5.30pm, Fri–Sun noon–2.30 & 3–5.30pm.

Dôme *Singapore Art Museum*, Bras Basah Rd, see map, p.493. Slick Australian café with an impressive list of coffees and teas. Daily 8.30am–10.30pm.

Dôme at Raffles Place #01-02 UOB Plaza 1, 80 Raffles Place, see map pp.502–503. Enjoying river views by Boat Quay, this appealing Australian café offers a tremendous selection of hot beverages. Mon–Fri 8am–8pm, Sat 8am–3pm.

Novus Café National Museum, 93 Stamford Rd ☏ 6337 1397, ⓦnovus.sg, see map, p.484. A refined, cosy café, slightly pricier than elsewhere but perfect for an intimate tête-à-tête or a catch-up with old friends. Besides coffees, muffins and so forth, the menu includes light bites such as croque monsieur or risotto. Daily 10am–6pm.

★ **The Pigeonhole** 52 Duxton Rd ☏ 6226 2880, ⓦwww.thepigeonhole.com.sg; map pp.502–503. So unlike its upmarket Tanjong Pagar neighbours, this unpretentious café-bar is, to quote the management, "like visiting a cool Singaporean friend's home" – the place is filled with preloved furniture and totally chilled out. They do good coffee, sweet treats like bread-and-butter pudding and some light meals, but even more appealing is the rolling programme of art exhibits, acoustic nights and socially aware talks – their website has details. Tues–Thurs 10am–11pm, Fri 10am–1am, Sat 11.30am–1am, Sun 11.30am–8pm.

Spinelli's Ground floor, *Peninsula Excelsior Hotel*, 3 Coleman St, see map p.484. Part of a chain that's generally a safe bet for a good coffee, with croissants, muffins, and a few sandwiches available too. Daily at least 9am–8pm.

Tiffin Room *Raffles Hotel*, 1 Beach Rd ☏ 6412 1190; map, p.484. High tea at this Anglo-Indian-themed restaurant is a splendid buffet of, oddly, dim sum plus servings of English scones, pastries, cakes and sandwiches – a real treat at S$65. High tea daily 3.30–5.30pm.

Ya Kun Kaya Toast #01-31 The Central, 6 Eu Tong Sen St, see map pp.502–503. Now a ubiquitous chain, *Ya Kun* started out in the prewar years as a Chinatown stall offering classic *kopitiam* breakfast fare – *kaya* toast (the same as *roti kahwin* in Malaysia) plus optional soft-boiled eggs eaten with white pepper and soy sauce. Of course there's strong local coffee too, normally drunk with condensed or evaporated milk. Branches at the Level B1 Food Court, Bugis Junction, and #01-32 313@Somerset, 313 Orchard Rd. Daily 7.30am–10.30pm.

RESTAURANTS, HAWKER CENTRES AND FOOD COURTS

While all Singapore's top hotels have reliable restaurants, it's usually more interesting to check out the many great independent establishments, some of which have evolved into chains. If you're after an unhurried meal in tranquil surroundings, cuisine is no guide to ambience: some Western restaurants emphasize bustle and chatter just as would any self-respecting Chinese restaurant. Food courts, having started out as hygienic but faceless markets to organize the stalls that once lined the island's streets, are moving up in the world these days, not just in terms of having a/c. Singapore now boasts several food-court chains, including *Food Junction*, *Food Republic* and *Kopitiam*, all featuring snazzy decor and, in some cases,

MARKETS AND SUPERMARKETS

The most entertaining places to buy fresh food are **wet markets**, so called because puddles often cover the floor, which is hosed down to keep it clean. Market traders are usually helpful even if you don't know a mango from a mangosteen. Downtown's best wet market is the Tekka Centre in Little India (see p.495).

Plenty of malls have a **supermarket** carrying familiar brands, including foreign beers, and with a deli counter. For more obscure imported fare, try **Market Place** (Level B1, Tanglin Mall, 163 Tanglin Rd; Level B1, Paragon, 290 Orchard Rd, near Orchard MRT), which is popular with expats for its specialist Western and Japanese fare, including organic produce.

even a "curated" selection of stalls, with every tenant chosen for their culinary pedigree rather than their ability to keep up with the rent.

CHINATOWN

Chinatown in Singapore is, of course, no Chinese ghetto. Its eating places are thus pretty diverse, though Chinese food retains a high profile in the heart of the area, on and around South Bridge Rd. A few touts on touristy Sago, Smith, Terengganu and Pagoda sts will try to lure you into the clutch of foreigner-friendly restaurants here, all decent enough though not the best in their class. For places on the south bank of the river, including Boat Quay, see p.544 .

Annalakshmi #01-04 Central Square, 20 Havelock Rd ☎6339 9993, ⓦwww.annalakshmi.com.sg; map on pp.502–503. Come here for excellent Indian vegetarian dishes served up by volunteers, with no prices specified; you pay what you feel the meal was worth. Profits go to Kala Mandhir, an association promoting South Indian culture. It's best to turn up for their superb buffets (at lunchtime plus dinner Fri–Sun), though note that they take a dim view of people helping themselves to more than they can finish. A branch at 104 Amoy St (☎6223 0809; Mon–Sat 11am–3pm) serves buffets only. Daily 11am–3pm & 6–9.30pm.

Bee Heong Palace 132–134 Telok Ayer St ☎6222 9074; map on pp.502–503. Less crowded than more famous rivals for Hokkien cuisine, this nondescript modern place nevertheless serves up creditable *hae cho*, minced pork and prawn fried up like little rissoles, plus *kong bak*, pork stewed in soy sauce and eaten stuffed into semicircular buns. Portions are quite large and prices reasonable – reckon on S$40 for two, without alcohol. Mon & Wed 11.30am–3pm, Tues & Thurs–Sun 11.30am–3pm & 6–10.30pm.

Hong Hock Eating House South Bridge Rd opposite the Jamae Mosque; map on pp.502–503. Somewhere between a *kopitiam* and a small food court, this excellent place takes a multicultural approach: Chinese fare includes claypot curry fish and oyster omelette, while an Indian Muslim stall serves *nasi campur* and *tissue prata* – a sweet roti artfully folded up like a napkin. A good place to head after partying into the small hours. Daily 11.30am–7am.

Indochine Upstairs at 47 Club St ☎6323 7347,

ⓦwww.indochine.com.sg; map on pp.502–503. Classy Vietnamese, Lao and Cambodian cuisine in chic surroundings sums up this chain, and their Club St venue is no exception. The Vietnamese *chao tom* (minced prawn wrapped round sugar cane) and deep-fried Vietnamese spring rolls (in veggie and non-veggie versions) are mouthwatering starters, while the Lao *larb kai* (spicy chicken salad) is one of many excellent main courses. Mon–Fri noon–3pm & 6.30–11pm, Sat 6.30–11pm.

★ **Lee Tong Kee** 278 South Bridge Rd ☎6226 0417, ⓦwww.ipohhorfun.com; map on pp.502–503. For years the speciality of this retro-styled restaurant, with old-fashioned fans and marble tables, has been Ipoh-style *hor fun*, supposedly smoother than regular tagliatelle-type rice noodles. Though you may have trouble discerning that difference, their many *hor fun* offerings are undeniably good whether served dryish or in soup (all around S$6). Also available are assorted dumplings plus their signature lime juice, usually served with a pinch of salt. Get there early for lunch, when it gets packed out. Daily except Tues 10am–9pm.

Maxwell Food Centre Corner of South Bridge & Maxwell rds; map on pp.502–503. One of Singapore's first hawker centres and home to a clutch of popular Chinese stalls, including *Tian Tian* for Hainanese chicken rice, plus others that are good for satay or *rojak*. Daily roughly 7am–midnight.

Rongcheng 271 New Bridge Rd ☎6536 4415; map on pp.502–503. One of several Sichuan hotpot places here, though not signed in English – look out for the Chinese name in black on a big orange sign and for the cafeteria-style metal display of meats, seafood and vegetables. Hotpots are akin to the steamboats you may encounter elsewhere in Singapore and Malaysia: help yourself to the raw ingredients, then cook them in your choice of stock, which will be boiling away on the stove at your table. You mix your own dips too, choosing from different chilli sauces, minced garlic and even tahini. Eat as much as you want for S$20 per head. Things only really get going in the evening. Daily 11.30am until the small hours.

Spizza 29 Club St ☎6224 2525, ⓦwww.spizza.sg; map on pp.502–503. Modern, unpretentious pizzeria with a tempting A to Z of thin-crust offerings cooked in a

9

traditional wood oven (from S$20). They deliver all over the island, too (order on ☏ 6377 7773). Mon–Fri noon–3pm & 6–11pm, Sat & Sun noon–11pm.

Swensen's #01-02/03/04 Chinatown Point, 133 New Bridge Rd ⓦ www.swensens.com.sg; map on pp.502–503. An ice-cream parlour with a range of simple meals including burgers and sandwiches. Mon–Fri 10.30am–10.30pm, Sat & Sun 8am–10.30pm.

Tak Po 42 Smith St ☏ 6225 0302; map on pp.502–503. Compact, competent and inexpensive Cantonese restaurant, refreshingly untouristy considering the location, with a/c inside and some tables out on the street. All the usual dim sum favourites, including *siu mai* dumplings, yam cake and excellent pork ribs with black beans, plus a wide range of *congees* (savoury rice porridges). For afters, try the baked egg tarts, which are spot on, the pastry not too flaky and the custard filling not oversweet. Daily 7am–10.30pm.

Thousand Veggie 200 South Bridge Rd ⓦ www .delivege.com.sg; map on pp.502–503. Inexpensive but surprisingly slick vegetarian restaurant, whose menu advises that "chewing between 25 and 100 times" is needed for good digestion. Thankfully their own food – tasty local favourites such as *laksa* or (mock) duck rice, plus Western and Japanese options – goes down with no such bother. Daily 11am–11pm.

Yixin 39 Temple St, no phone; map on pp.502–503. Workaday vegetarian *kopitiam* that turns out *zichar* dishes such as mock Peking duck (S$8), plus rice and noodle standards like *lor mee* (noodles in a tangy, gloopy sauce). A picture menu makes ordering easy. Barely signed in English, but easy to spot by the *Santa Grand Chinatown* hotel. Daily 7.30am–9.30pm.

Yum Cha #02-01 20 Trengganu St (entry via Temple St) ☏ 6372 1717, ⓦ www.yumcha.com.sg; map on pp.502–503. Grand dim sum restaurant, with several dining rooms and a wide-ranging menu. They call their house speciality pomfret "tapino" – it's a fish hotpot for around S$50. Mon–Fri 11am–11pm, Sat & Sun 9am–11pm.

TANJONG PAGAR, THE FINANCIAL DISTRICT AND MARINA SOUTH

You're unlikely to head to these areas bordering Chinatown for the food alone but they do boast some excellent, if often pricey, independent restaurants.

Blue Ginger 97 Tanjong Pagar Rd ☏ 6222 3928, ⓦ www.theblueginger.com; map on pp.502–503. In a smartly renovated shophouse, this trendy Nonya restaurant has become a firm favourite thanks to such dishes as *ikan masal asam gulai* (mackerel in a tamarind and lemon-grass gravy), and that benchmark of Nonya cuisine, *ayam buah keluak* – chicken braised in soy sauce together with savoury Indonesian black nuts. Daily noon–2.30pm & 6.30–10.30pm.

BROTH 21 Duxton Hill ☏ 6323 3353, ⓦ www.broth .com.sg; map on pp.502–503. The "Bar Restaurant On The Hill" serves beautifully presented Aussie-influenced fusion cuisine, including an exquisite spinach and portobello mushroom salad, and their trademark lamb loin in a "green coat" – a marinade of herbs, including mint. Not cheap though, with main courses at S$35. Mon–Fri noon–2.30pm & 6.30–10.30pm, Sat 6.30–10.30pm.

Cumi Bali 66 Tanjong Pagar Rd ☏ 6220 6619, ⓦ www .cumibali.com; map on pp.502–503. Bamboo sieves and flutes line the walls at this tiny, inexpensive *nasi padang* joint. Both the beef *rendang* and satay Madura, marinated in sweet soy sauce, hit the spot, and they have generous S$7 set lunches too. Mon–Sat 11.30am–3pm & 6–9.30pm.

★ **Lau Pa Sat** 18 Raffles Quay ⓦ www.laupasat.biz; map on pp.502–503. This historic market building is home to an excellent *Kopitiam*-franchised food court. Foods to try include Hokkien *mee* (stall #81), *yong tau foo* (#17) and satay – satay sellers set up just outside on Boon Tat St in the evenings. Pricier outlets offer cooked-to-order seafood such as chilli crab. Open 24hr.

Pierside #01-01 One Fullerton, 1 Fullerton Rd ☏ 6438 0400, ⓦ www.pierside.com.sg; map on pp.502–503. Well-established restaurant serving modern European cooking with fusion influences: expect the likes of hazelnut-encrusted king prawns in a lemongrass and oyster sauce. There's a good view of *Marina Bay Sands*, too. Mains from S$30. Mon–Fri 11.30am–2.30pm & 5–11pm, Sat 5–11pm.

★ **Sabio** 5 Duxton Hill ☏ 6223 4645 (no reservations), ⓦ www.sabio.sg; map on pp.502–503. Spanish-owned and -run, this elegant but tiny restaurant serves delicious tapas, including excellent pan-fried calamari, tender grilled lamb cutlets and aged ham from acorn-fed pigs, these last sold by weight (most tapas S$10–15). Wash it down with sangria or Estrella Damm beer from Barcelona. Often packed. Mon–Fri noon–late, Sat 6pm–late.

★ **Sky on 57** SkyPark at *Marina Bay Sands* ☏ 6688 8857; map on p.482. Here's how to circumvent that huge SkyPark admission charge – by eating at this fine restaurant featuring a harmonious marriage of Far Eastern and French cooking. Fiendishly expensive at dinner, when mains start at S$50, but reasonable value at lunchtime when their superb king prawn *laksa* costs S$30, or a three-course set menu is S$60. Head up via tower 1. Daily 7.30–10am, noon–2.30pm, 6–10.30pm.

BOAT QUAY TO RIVERSIDE POINT

The south bank of the Singapore River is packed with busy restaurants and bars, at their most atmospheric in the restored shophouses of boisterous Boat Quay, though even

9

the modern complexes can be a more enticing prospect than overpriced Clarke Quay on the north bank. All places reviewed here are in riverside buildings or no more than a couple of streets back from the river.

Brewerkz #01-05/06 Riverside Point, 30 Merchant Rd ☎6438 7438, ⊛brewerkz.com; map on pp.502–503. This buzzing restaurant is popular for its highly rated beers, brewed on site, and American fare, including excellent burgers and sandwiches, plus barbecued ribs, pizzas, nachos, grilled potato skins and the like. It's on the pricey side though, with burgers starting at S$25. Busy at weekends. Sun–Thurs noon–midnight, Fri & Sat noon–1am.

★ **Café Iguana** #01-03 Riverside Point, 30 Merchant Rd ☎6236 1275, ⊛cafeiguana.com; map on pp.502–503. This open-fronted restaurant features a huge mural of Frida Kahlo, plus assorted other Mexicana. Fajitas, tacos, burritos and all the other standards, with plenty for veggies; mains cost around S$20. The avocado ice cream makes a great dessert. Great as a drinking venue too, and can get very crowded in the evenings. Mon–Thurs 4pm–1am, Fri 4pm–3am, Sat noon–3am, Sun noon–1am.

Hock Lam Street Popular Beef Kway Teow 6 North Canal Rd ☎6535 0084; map on pp.502–503. For decades this was a highly regarded stall on the now-vanished Hock Lam St, through the site of the present Funan DigitaLife Mall. The stall survives, albeit as a little shophouse restaurant, serving the same *kuay teow* noodles with beef slices or beefball dumplings, dry or with soup; servings cost around S$6. Mon–Fri 11am–8pm, Sat & Sun 11am–4.30pm.

Moomba 52 Circular Rd ☎6438 0141, ⊛themoomba .com; map on pp.502–503. With snazzy Aboriginal-influenced murals, this place has a great reputation for Australian fusion cuisine, including a dish or two of kangaroo and more conventional steaks. Most menu items have wine recommendations drawn from their on-site wine shop. Mains start at S$30. Mon–Fri 11am–2.30pm & 6.30–10pm, Sat 6.30–10pm.

Our Village Entrance on fifth floor, 46 Boat Quay ☎6538 3092; map on pp.502–503. A hidden gem, with fine North Indian and Sri Lankan food, and peachy views of the river and Colonial District from its lamplit sixth-floor terrace. Mon–Fri noon–1.45pm & 6–11pm, Sat & Sun 6–11pm.

Rendezvous #02-72 The Central, 6 Eu Tong Sen St ☎6339 7508, ⊛rendezvous-hlk.com.sg; map on pp.502–503. For decades *Rendezvous* has been serving up revered *nasi padang*, first as the *Rendezvous kopitiam* at the start of Bras Basah Rd, then in the hotel of that name that replaced it. Its new location in a mediocre mall doesn't suit at all, but thankfully the curries have stayed the course, in particular the superb chicken korma, here a curried stew of

just the right degree of richness, derived from coconut milk rather than cream or yogurt. A couple of curries with rice and side dishes are unlikely to cost more than S$25 a head. Daily 11am–9pm.

Warung M Nasir 61 Circular Rd ☎6536 7998; map on pp.502–503. Tiny Indonesian *nasi padang* standards such as fried chicken *balado*, beef and chicken *rendang* and tofu or beans fried with *sambal*. Mon–Fri 11am–8pm.

THE COLONIAL DISTRICT AND MARINA CENTRE

While shopping malls house most Colonial District restaurants, some of the more interesting places have found a home within beautifully refurbished heritage buildings. Marina Centre, nothing but malls and hotels, is not the most atmospheric place for a meal, but compensates with some good offerings.

Bobby's #B1-03, CHIJMES, 30 Victoria St ☎6337 5477, ⊛www.bobbys.com.sg; map on p.484. With an atmospheric setting around the basement fountain courtyard, *Bobby's* specializes in barbecued beef rib and other meaty delights, including steaks and burgers, though veggie burgers, pizzas and pasta dishes are also available. Mains from S$25. Sun–Thurs 3pm–1am, Fri & Sat 3pm–2am.

★ **Cedele** #03-28A Raffles City Shopping Centre ☎6337 8017, ⊛cedeledepot.com; map on p.484. Brilliant sandwiches plus light meals, at reasonable prices; see p.549 for more. Daily 11am–10.30pm.

Coriander Leaf Block A, Clarke Quay #02-03 ☎6732 3354, ⊛corianderleaf.com; map on p.484. Pan-Asian and Mediterranean food in elegant upstairs premises, encompassing everything from Lebanese meze to Vietnamese spring rolls. Main courses start at S$30, or you can order a good-value sampler platter for S$20. Mon–Fri noon–2pm & 6.30–10pm, Sat 6.30–10.30pm.

★ **Flutes at the Fort** 23B Coleman St ☎6338 8770, ⊛www.flutes.com.sg; map on p.484. If you think Singapore's colonial architecture is all about grand Palladian buildings, you'll be pleasantly put right at this restaurant, in a beautiful black-and-white wooden colonial house on the leafy slopes of Fort Canning Hill. You can sit indoors or out on the veranda to enjoy set lunches (two courses for around S$40), or a full menu of modern European and fusion dishes. To get there, take the little path through the car park by the Freemasons' Hall. Mon–Fri noon–2pm & 6.30–10pm, Sat 11.30am–2.30pm (brunch) & 6.30–10pm.

Indochine Asian Civilizations Museum, Empress Place ☎6339 1720 (café ☎6338 7596), ⊛www.indochine .com.sg; map on p.484. *Indochine* just about monopolizes the museum's river frontage with a restaurant, café and bar (see p.552). The restaurant has great views of Boat Quay and the Financial District, and both it and the café have somewhat different menus from the original Club St premises, with the café's *pho bo* (beef noodle soup) particularly highly rated. Restaurant open for lunch Mon–Fri noon–3pm, dinner Mon–Fri & Sun 6.30–11.30pm, Fri & Sat 6.30pm–12.30am; *Siem Reap II* café daily 11am–11pm.

Paulaner Bräuhaus #01-01 Millennia Walk, 9 Raffles Blvd ☎6883 2572, ⓦwww.paulaner.com.sg; map on p.484. The cavernous ceiling with a maypole sticking up into it is impressive, as is the menu of Bavarian delights such as the bitty *spätzle* pasta, but the best reason to come is the terrific Sunday brunch spread, including superb pork knuckle, sausages and salads, and desserts like strudel and cheesecake. It's good value at S$55 with unlimited soft drinks, or S$65 with unlimited beer from their own microbrewery. Mon–Fri noon–2.30pm & 6.30–10.30pm, Sat 6.30–10.30pm, Sun 11.30am–2.30pm & 6.30–10.30pm.

Seah Street Deli *Raffles Hotel*, 1 Beach Rd (entrance on North Bridge Rd) ☎6412 1816; map on p.484. The soda and root beer signs and jukebox make this the most un-colonial establishment in *Raffles Hotel*. A great place for burgers, pizzas, mountainous sandwiches and barbecued ribs; most mains cost S$20–30. Sun–Thurs 11am–10pm, Fri & Sat 11am–11pm.

★ **Shiraz** Block A, Clarke Quay #01-06 ☎6334 2282; map on p.484. The best Iranian restaurant in town, not that there's much competition, but the many Iranians among the clientele can't be misguided. Massive portions of tender kebabs and stews, all served with mounds of fluffy, aromatic saffron rice. Not cheap – main courses from S$30 – but still better value than most places in overpriced Clarke Quay. Belly-dancing some evenings, too. Mon 6.30–11pm, Tues–Thurs & Sun noon–2.30pm & 6.30–11pm, Fri & Sat noon–2.30pm & 6.30pm–12.30am.

★ **Singapore Food Trail** Beneath the Singapore Flyer; map on p.484. Arguably more interesting than the Flyer itself, this retro-style food court evokes Singapore's street food scene of half a century ago, its stalls mocked up as pushcarts. The food can be retro too – for example satay *bee hoon*, rice vermicelli drenched in the peanut sauce normally eaten with satay, and popular in the 1970s – though it also features lots of evergreens, including oyster omelette and *popiah* (steamed spring rolls). Nothing costs more than S$10. Mon–Thurs 10.30am–10.30pm, Fri–Sun 10.30am–11.30pm.

BRAS BASAH ROAD TO ROCHOR ROAD

Sandwiched between the Colonial District and Little India, this part of town features plenty of well-established restaurants, including a good cluster close to *Raffles Hotel*. Three great food courts are also worth checking out, two of them in the Bugis Junction mall near Bugis MRT. On level 3 here, the plush *Food Junction* features an excellent range of local fare, including beef noodles and *yong tau foo*, while

level B1 is dominated by Japanese food outlets, complete with plastic models of *yakitori* and even ice cream. Elsewhere, there's a *Kopitiam* food court at Plaza On The Park, 51 Bras Basah Rd, open round-the-clock and popular with revellers wanting late-night munchies.

Ah Chew Desserts #01-11, 1 Liang Seah St ☎6339 8198; map on p.493. Taking up two restored shophouses, *Ah Chew* confronts you with nothing but strange local sweets containing beans or other unexpected ingredients. The cashew-nut paste is not bad if you like the sound of a broth made of nut butter; also available are the likes of *pulot hitam*, made with black sticky rice and better warm than with the optional ice cream. Cautiously sample a few items by ordering the small servings; most bowls cost S$4 or so. Mon–Thurs 12.30–11.30pm, Fri 12.30pm–12.30am, Sat 1.30pm–12.30am, Sun 1.30–11.30pm.

Fatty's Wing Seong #01-31 Burlington Square, 175 Bencoolen St ☎6338 1087; map on p.493. Run by an avuncular chubby cook in bygone decades, *Fatty's* was an institution on the now-vanished foodie paradise that was Albert St. Today this restaurant maintains the original's no-frills *zichar* approach, and also does standards such as chicken rice. Around S$20 a head. Daily noon–2.30pm & 5.15–10.15pm.

★ **Haji Maimunah** 51 Bencoolen St ☎6338 5684, ⓦwww.hjmaimunah.com; map on p.493. Part of the Bencoolen Mosque, this Malay diner serves great *nasi campur* plus a range of dishes to order. Daily 11am–9pm.

Hock Lam Street Popular Beef Kway Teow 38 Seah St ☎6339 9641. Once a street stall, now a simple diner serving noodles with beef or beef dumplings, either stir-fried or in soup. Tues–Sat 10.30am–8pm.

Kwan Im Vegetarian Restaurant South East Asia Hotel, 190 Waterloo St ☎6338 2394; map on p.493. More formal than the other Chinese veggie places clustered near the Kwan Im temple, this restaurant serves meatless versions of classic Chinese dishes (as opposed to street food). It's pricier too, though most dishes still cost under S$10, and there's a good range of takeaway Chinese pastries. Daily 8.30am–8.30pm.

Mr Bean's 30 Selegie Rd ☎6333 3100; map on p.493. Not to be confused with the *Mr Bean* chain of soya-milk outlets, this café-restaurant offers okay steaks and pizzas, plus good-value two-course lunches (S$13) and dinners (S$19) daily except Sun. Breakfasts also available for S$10. Service may not be great but is still slicker than Mr Bean, whose visage is stuck over the *Mona Lisa* above the cake counter, would have managed. Daily 24hr.

★ **Soup** 39 Seah St ☎6333 9388; map on p.493. So-called *samsui* women once sailed from China's Canton province in droves, incredibly, to work on Singapore building sites. This fine little restaurant celebrates the cuisine of these redoubtable women, most famously their

9

ginger chicken; similar to the steamed chicken in chicken rice, it comes with a gingery dip and iceberg-lettuce leaves to roll it up in. Reckon on S$20 per head. Daily 11.30am–10.30pm.

Yet Con Chicken Rice Restaurant 25 Purvis St ☎ 6337 6819; map on p.493. Cheap and cheerful old-time restaurant known not just for chicken rice but also for its roast pork with pickled cabbage and radish. Around S$15 for two people. Daily 11.30am–8.30pm.

Yhingthai Palace #01-04, 36 Purvis St ☎ 6337 1161, ⊛ www.yhingthai.com; map on p.493. A smartly turned-out Chinese-influenced Thai restaurant, where you can't go wrong with the deep-fried pomfret with mango sauce, Thai fishcakes or deboned chicken wings stuffed with asparagus and mushroom. Around S$40 per head, excluding drinks. Daily 11.30am–2pm & 6–10pm.

LITTLE INDIA

Little India is paradise if you're after maximum flavour for minimum outlay; the first part of Serangoon Rd and its side streets, as well as Race Course Rd, are packed with inexpensive, excellent curry houses specializing in South Indian food, often dished out onto banana leaves and with plenty of vegetarian options; some places offer North Indian and Nepali dishes too. The only drawback to eating here is that there isn't a lot that isn't Indian.

★ **Banana Leaf Apolo** 54 Race Course Rd ☎ 6293 8682, ⊛ www.thebananaleafapolo.com; map on p.496. Pioneering banana-leaf-type restaurant with a wide selection of Indian dishes, including fish-head curry (S$22–30 depending on size) plus chicken, mutton and prawn curries (S$12). The "South Indian vegetarian meal" is a steal, a huge *thali* of rice, poppadoms, two main curries and several side ones, plus a dessert, for just S$8. There's another branch tucked away in the Little India Arcade. Daily 10am–10pm.

Cocotte *Wanderlust Hotel*, 2 Dickson Rd ☎ 6298 1188, ⊛ restaurantcocotte.com; map on p.496. It's an obvious misfit in the area, but one that impresses with its eccentric decor and modern French cuisine using prime ingredients. The three-course executive lunch is best for value (S$35), though it's a shame that its top main-course option, the superb duck leg confit, costs S$11 extra. Mains from S$40; reservations essential. Mon–Thurs noon–2.30pm & 6.30–10.30pm, Fri & Sat 6.30–11pm, Sun noon–3pm.

Komala Villas 76–78 Serangoon Rd ☎ 6293 6980; map on p.496. A veteran, rather cramped vegetarian establishment with more than a dozen variations of *dosai* at just a few dollars each, plus fresh coconut to wash it down. They also do more substantial rice-based meals upstairs from 11am to 4pm. Branch at 12–14 Buffalo Rd (☎ 6293 366, map on p.496; open from 8am). Daily 7am–10.30pm.

Madras New Woodlands 12–14 Upper Dickson Rd ☎ 6297 1594; map on p.496. Canteen-style place serving up decent vegetarian food at bargain prices. House specialities are the *thali* set meals (around S$8), and there's a good-value daily special (S$8) too. Daily 7.30am–11.30pm.

Saravanaa Bhavan 84 Syed Alwi Rd ☎ 6297 7755, ⊛ www.saravanabhavan.com; map on p.496. This South Indian vegetarian franchise, gone global out of Chennai, has a modern Singapore venue that offers all the staples, from *vada* (dhal-flour doughnuts) to *dosai*, plus their popular Indian take on Chinese food – the Gobi Manchurian is a classic, stir-fried battered cauliflower with a spicy, tangy sauce. Daily 9am–midnight.

★ **Tekka Food Centre** Alongside Tekka market, at start of Serangoon Rd; map on p.496. One of the best old-school hawkers' centres on the island, generally steamy hot and busy. A couple of the worthwhile Indian and Malay stalls offer exceptional Indian *rojak* – assorted fritters with sweet dips. Daily 7am–late.

ARAB STREET AND AROUND

It seems natural that Arab St (see map, p.496) should boast several Middle Eastern and North African restaurants with meze to nibble at and shishas to puff on, but in fact these places have only been around for a few years; the mainstay of the area's dining has long been Malay and Indonesian food. Whatever you end up eating, the atmosphere won't be lacking, as many restaurants are housed in cosy refurbished shophouses.

★ **Blu Jaz Café** 11 Bali Lane ☎ 6292 3800, ⊛ www .blujaz.net; map on p.496. Chilled-out café-restaurant stretching between Bali and Haji lanes, and easily spotted with its gaudy decor. Reliable local and Western food – everything from chicken kebab to fish and chips – at affordable prices; a steak will set you back around S$18. Live jazz Mon, Fri & Sat evenings. Mon–Thurs noon– midnight, Fri noon–1am, Sat 4pm–1am.

Bumbu 44 Kandahar St ☎ 6392 8628, ⊛ bumbu.com .sg; map on p.496. Boasting fine Peranakan artefacts amassed by owner, Robert Tan, *Bumbu* is as much a social history document as a restaurant. Happily, the furnishings don't outshine the fine Thai cuisine, with a few Indonesian offerings too. Around S$25 per person. Tues–Sun 11am–3pm & 6–10pm.

★ **Café Le Caire** 33, 37 & 39 Arab St ☎ 6292 0979, ⊛ www.cafelecaire.com; map on p.496. This relaxed diner spearheaded the advent of Arab cuisine in the area and is a good inexpensive bet for Lebanese and Egyptian kebabs, dips and wraps, plus Yemeni harissa, a spicy stew of minced lamb and cracked wheat. For those into hubble-bubbles, they do over a dozen tobaccos. Sun–Thurs 10am–3.30am, Fri & Sat 10am–5.30am.

Haji Maimunah 11 & 15 Jalan Pisang ⊛ www .hjmaimunah.com; map on p.496. A cosy restaurant

9

STREET ICE CREAM

A couple of generations ago, **ice cream** in Singapore (and Malaysia) often meant stuff sold by hawkers from pushcarts, in exotic flavours like sweetcorn, red (aduki) bean and yam. This was so-called *potong* ("cut" in Malay) ice cream because it came in bricks and the seller would use a cleaver to slice it into slabs, to be served either between wafers or, oddly, rolled up in white bread.

The general elimination of street stalls put paid to that trade to Singapore, but in recent years the ice-cream vendors have made a comeback. They're often to be seen at Cavenagh Bridge (see p.483), on Orchard Road near Somerset MRT and outside Bugis MRT. The bread option complements the ice cream surprisingly well, serving as a sort of neutral sponge cake. As for the weird flavours, they're all more than palatable; you can also find red-bean ice cream on a stick in supermarkets and convenience stores, sold under the name "Potong".

that's great for inexpensive Malay food. Mon–Sat 7am–8pm (closed during Ramadan).

Islamic Restaurant 745 North Bridge Rd ☎ 6298 7563; map on p.496. The bland, modernized premises of today don't hint at this restaurant's impeccable pedigree, for which check out the photos of functions they catered for in the 1920s. *Biriyanis* are their trademark offering (S\$7) though they also do a huge range of North Indian chicken, mutton, prawn, squid and veg curries, with good-value set meals at around S\$8. Daily 10am–10pm; closed Fri 1–2pm.

★ **Kampong Glam Café** 17 Bussorah St; map on p.496. Fantastic roadside *kopitiam* serving inexpensive rice and noodle dishes, cooked to order, plus curries. Come not just for the food but for a good chinwag with friends over *teh tarik* late into the evening. Daily 8am–1am.

★ **Rumah Makan Minang** 18a Kandahar St; map on p.496. A street-corner place serving superb *nasi padang*, including the mildly spiced chicken *balado* and more unusual curries made with *tempeh* (fermented soybean cakes) or offal. For dessert there are freshly made sweet pancakes stuffed with peanuts and corn – much better than they sound. Just S\$6 per head for a good feed. Daily 8am–8pm.

ORCHARD ROAD AND AROUND

Eating in the heart of Singapore's shopping nexus – Orchard Rd, Tanglin Rd and Scotts Rd – is almost completely about restaurants in malls and hotels, though a few venues are housed in two rows of refurbished shophouses on Emerald Hill Rd and at Cuppage Terrace next to the Centrepoint mall; both are near Somerset MRT. Most malls have food courts, and indeed two of the island's slickest are to be found here: *Food Republic* inside Wisma Atria and 313@Somerset, and *Food Opera* in the basement of ION Orchard.

Akashi #B1-09 Tanglin Shopping Centre, 19 Tanglin Rd ☎ 6732 8662; map on pp.516–517. An understated, classical Japanese restaurant, where the *sake teriyaki* and the *tempura* are both good and there's a decent range of sakes, sushi and sashimi. Daily noon–3pm & 6.30–10.30pm.

★ **Cedele** #B1-37, Ngee Ann City, 391 Orchard Rd ☎ 6235 2380, ⓦ www.cedeledepot.com; map on pp.516–517. A café-bakery combo, *Cedele* serves up some of the very best sandwiches in Singapore (S\$6–8) – think, say, honey dijon chicken on rosemary focaccia – and sells a vast variety of specialist breads. Some branches, like this one, also have a restaurant with soups, pies and inventive light meals such as the beetroot burger, which even non-veggies love. Daily 10am–10pm.

★ **Crystal Jade La Mian Xiao Long Bao** #04-27, Ngee Ann City ☎ 6238 1661, ⓦ www.crystaljade.com; map on pp.516–517. *Crystal Jade* is an umbrella for several linked Chinese restaurant chains, each with a different emphasis. Their mid-priced *La Mian Xiao Long Bao* outlets focus on Shanghai and northern Chinese cuisine, as exemplified by *xiao long bao*, succulent Shanghai pork dumplings, and the northwestern speciality *la mian*, literally "pulled noodles", the strands of dough being stretched and worked by hand. Not fantastic for veggies though. Daily 11am–10pm.

★ **Lao Beijing** #03-01 Plaza Singapura, 68 Orchard Rd ☎ 6738 7207, ⓦ www.laobeijing.com.sg; map on pp.516–517. Styled like a classy, old-fangled Chinese teahouse, this restaurant specializes in northern Chinese fare, including Peking duck and "Chairman Mao's Favourite Braised Pork" – suitably red in colour – plus dishes from elsewhere in China. There's also a high-tea buffet featuring not scones and cream but plenty more Chinese specialities (3–5pm; S\$15 weekdays, S\$20 weekends). Daily 11.30am–5pm & 6–10pm.

Maharajah 39 Cuppage Terrace ☎ 6732 6331, ⓦ www.maharajah.com.sg; map on pp.516–517. This splendid North Indian restaurant has a large terrace and a tempting menu that includes several tandoori options plus the sublime fish *mumtaz* – fillet of fish stuffed with minced mutton, almonds, eggs, cashews and raisins. Around S\$35 per person without alcohol. Daily 11am–11pm.

★ **Marché** Ground floor and basement, 313@Somerset, 313 Orchard Rd ☎ 6834 4041; map on pp.516–517. Never mind that Mövenpick's Marché restaurants are formulaic: what a formula, when you can have rösti, sausages or crêpes cooked to order in front of

9

you, or help yourself to the superb salad bar. Daily lunch specials offer a meal and drink for S$10, while the bakery counter does takeaway sandwiches (from S$5), bread sticks and Berliners, doughnuts with a range of fillings. Daily 11am–11pm; bakery from 7.30am.

Min Jiang *Goodwood Park Hotel*, 22 Scotts Rd ☎6730 1704; map on pp.516–517. This stylish affair serves some Cantonese food and lunchtime dim sum, though their spicy Sichuan specialities are the most interesting. Good choices include the prawn fried with dried chillies, Sichuan smoked duck and long beans fried with minced pork. Reasonably priced for a top hotel. Daily 11am–2.30pm & 6–10.30pm, plus dim sum buffet Sat & Sun 3.30–5.30pm.

Newton Circus Hawker Centre Corner of Clemenceau Ave North and Bukit Timah Rd, near Newton MRT; map p.482. A venerable open-air place with a wide range of food. It's noted for its seafood, for which you can end up paying through the nose; prices are on the high side for stalls anyway, as the place is very much on the tourist trail. Mostly gets going in the late afternoon and stays open till the small hours.

★ **PS Café** Level 2, Palais Renaissance, 390 Orchard Rd ☎9834 8232; ⓦwww.pscafe.sg; map on pp.516–517. Marvellous if pricey restaurant set in something resembling a glasshouse and offering an inventive, constantly revised menu of fusion fare and great desserts; (mains from S$30). Another branch – actually the original *PS Café* – in the Project Shop home-furnishings store (Level 3, The Paragon, 290 Orchard Rd ☎9297 7008), serves lighter meals (daily 9.30am–10.30pm, with breakfast served until 11.30am). Mon–Fri 11.30am–midnight, Sat & Sun 9.30am–midnight.

Swensen's #03-23 Plaza Singapura, 68 Orchard Rd ⓦwww.swensens.com.sg; map on pp.516–517. Wins no prizes for trendiness, but for what is essentially a chain of ice-cream parlours, the food menu is extensive – salads, pasta dishes, jumbo-sausage subs, etc. Prices are reasonable, with soups and many of the huge range of ice-cream concoctions weighing in at around S$8. Breakfasts served at weekends. Mon–Fri 11.30am–10.30pm, Sat & Sun 8am–10.30pm.

Teochew City Seafood Restaurant #05-16 Centrepoint, 176 Orchard Rd ☎6733 3338, ⓦwww.pfs .com.sg; map on pp.516–517. Despite the name, seafood isn't the only focus at this reasonably priced restaurant; it's also known for its classic Teochew-style goose, braised in soy sauce and served on a bed of tofu that soaks up the juices. They also do a mean cold crab with lemon sauce. Daily 10.30am–3pm & 6–10.30pm.

Thai Express #03-24 Plaza Singapura, 68 Orchard Rd ☎6339 5442, ⓦwww.thaiexpress.com.sg; map on pp.516–517. A modern chain with plenty of wood and chrome fittings and where everything is chop-chop. The menu is packed with Thai rice and noodle standards (from

S$12) plus lots of desserts. Sun–Thurs 11.30am–10.30pm, Fri & Sat 11.30am–11.30pm.

Warung M Nasir 69 Killiney Rd ☎6734 6228; map on pp.516–517. Respected *nasi padang* joint. Daily 10am–10pm.

TANGLIN VILLAGE (DEMPSEY) AND THE BOTANIC GARDENS

The so-called Tanglin Village (sometimes called Dempsey; ⓦwww.tanglinvillage.com.sg), off Holland Rd and a couple of kilometres west of the start of Orchard Rd, is a sprawling collection of fields dotted with bungalows. If it feels like something out of rural England, that's because it was originally a British military camp; later it housed Singapore's Ministry of Defence, and nowadays it's home to a jumble of posh restaurants and bars, plus health spas, antique shops and so forth. The venues reviewed here are not too far from the main road, and can be reached on foot. Opposite the village, the Botanic Gardens is itself home to one upmarket place to eat. Buses #7, #77 and #174 head along this stretch of Holland Rd from Orchard Blvd.

Halia Botanic Gardens, near the ginger garden and Burkill gate on Tyersall Ave ☎6476 6711, ⓦhalia.com .sg; map on p.482. A sophisticated menu of modern fusion cooking, some dishes seasoned with – surprise – ginger. Lunch specials are sensibly priced at around S$35 for two courses; otherwise expect to pay upwards of S$40 for mains. Arriving by taxi, ask the driver to drop you on Tyersall Ave rather than at Tanglin gate. Daily noon–4pm & 6.30–10.30pm, Sat & Sun 10am–5pm (brunch until 4pm, high tea 3–5pm) & 6.30–10pm.

Long Beach Seafood Block 25, Dempsey Rd ☎6323 2222, ⓦwww.longbeachseafood.com.sg; map on p.482. Once you had to trek to the beaches to find Singapore's best Chinese-style seafood, but no longer, now that this beachside stalwart has set up here. The best dishes really are magic, including treacly crisp baby squid, chunky Alaska crab in a white pepper sauce, steamed *soon hock* (goby) and, of course, chilli crab. An expensive but worthwhile blowout. Dempsey Rd is a 10min walk west of the Botanic Gardens' Tanglin gate. Daily 11am–3pm & 5.30pm–1.30am.

★ **Samy's** Block 25, Dempsey Rd ☎6472 2080, ⓦwww.samyscurry.com; map on p.482. Housed in a colonial-era hall with ceiling fans whirring overhead, *Samy's* is an institution that's been serving superb banana-leaf meals for decades. Choose from curries of jumbo prawn, fish head, crab or mutton, and either plain rice or the delicate, fluffy *biriyani*. There's excellent freshly squeezed lemonade or *teh tarik* – made the old-fashioned way with much ostentatious pouring of fluid – to wash it all down. You'll eat well for S$15–20 a head excluding drinks. Daily 11am–3pm & 6–10pm.

The White Rabbit 39c Harding Rd ☎6473 9965, ⓦwww.thewhiterabbit.com.sg; map on p.482.

A beautifully refurbished church with a high ceiling and stained-glass windows is the setting for this restaurant serving fine modern European cuisine. Main courses start at S$35; weekday set lunches are good value (three courses S$45). It's a 10min walk from Holland Rd: head up Minden Rd, then take a right into Harding Rd. Tues–Fri noon–2.30pm & 6.30–10.30pm, Sat & Sun 10.30am–3pm & 6.30–10.30pm.

HOLLAND VILLAGE

A couple of kilometres west of the Botanic Gardens, the residential Holland Village suburb is nothing like Tanglin Village – proximity aside, the tenuous link between the two is that some British soldiers based in Singapore once had homes in Holland Village. To this day it remains an expat stronghold, with a plethora of Western restaurants and shops. Get here on bus #7 from the Botanic Gardens, Orchard Blvd and the Colonial District, or using the Circle Line's Holland Village MRT, which is only a few stops from HarbourFront.

2am Dessert Bar 21a Lorong Liput ☏ 6291 9727, ⊛ 2amdessertbar.com; map below. Hidden down a side street, this slick upstairs venue features a slew of sinful puddings (from S$18), plus simpler delights such as Spanish churros dunked in hot chocolate. There's a full range of wines and cocktails, too. Daily except Sun 6pm–2am.

Bistro Petit Salut 44 Jalan Merah Saga #01-54 ☏ 6474 9788, ⊛ aupetitsalut.com; map below. Classic French fare and wines, in a nutshell. Most people take advantage of the two-course set lunches (S$33) or three-course

dinners (S$55), featuring Provençale-style braised pork shoulder, baked *escargots* and so on. Daily except Sun 11.30am–2.30pm & 6.30–10.30pm.

Café 211 #04-01 Holland Road Shopping Centre ☏ 6462 6194, ⊛ www.cafe211.com.sg; map below. The "hidden gem" cliché does apply to this rooftop café-restaurant, serving decent pizza and pasta dishes, snacks and cakes. In the cool of evening you can sit out in their terrace garden area for surreal views of residential tower blocks all around. Cooked breakfasts are available too. Cheaper than similar places downtown, with mains from S$15. Daily 9am–10.45pm.

Cha Cha Cha 32 Lorong Mambong, Holland Village ☏ 6462 1650; map below. Classic Mexican dishes in this vibrantly coloured restaurant start at S$15. Book ahead for the few open-air patio tables outside, ideal for posing with a bottle of Dos Equis beer. Sun–Thurs 11am–11pm, Fri & Sat 11am–midnight.

★ **Crystal Jade La Mian Xiao Long Bao** 241 Holland Ave ☏ 6463 0968, ⊛ www.crystaljade.com; map below. This chain is best known for its Shanghai and northern Chinese dumplings and noodles, though in the evenngs they also do a Sichuan-style hotpot, where you cook raw ingredients in boiling stock at the table. Daily 11.30am–3pm & 6.30–11pm.

★ **Everything With Fries** 40 Lorong Mambong ☏ 6463 3741, ⊛ www.everythingwithfries.com; map below. As the name suggests, all mains come with shoestring or straight-cut fries, featuring such seasonings as garlic and herbs. Have, say, a burger or grilled pork

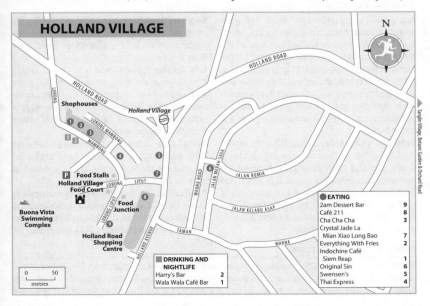

HOLLAND VILLAGE

EATING
2am Dessert Bar	9
Café 211	8
Cha Cha Cha	3
Crystal Jade La Mian Xiao Long Bao	7
Everything With Fries	2
Indochine Café Siem Reap	1
Original Sin	6
Swensen's	5
Thai Express	4

DRINKING AND NIGHTLIFE
Harry's Bar	2
Wala Wala Café Bar	1

9

chop, then mess up your blood-sugar level with a sickly cupcake or their flan that uses a well-known chocolate spread to good advantage. Small wonder it's popular with 20-somethings when mains are reasonably priced at S$10–15; takeaway fries S$5. Sun–Thurs noon–11pm, Fri & Sat noon–1am.

Indochine Café Siem Reap 44 Lorong Mambong ☎6468 5798, ⊚www.indochine.com.sg; map on p.551. Swanky representative of the *Indochine* empire, with a slightly different menu from its other venues. The rice vermicelli with beef and the Lao *laksa* are among dishes that hit the spot. Daily except Sun noon–2.30pm & 6–11.30pm.

Original Sin #01-62 Block 43, Jalan Merah Saga ☎6475 5605, ⊚www.originalsin.com.sg; map on p.551. Quality vegetarian Mediterranean and Asian fare, everything from Thai green curry to mushroom and asparagus polenta with truffle oil. Pricey for what it is though, with mains from S$25, yet often full. Daily 11.30am–2.30pm & 6–10.30pm.

Swensen's 251/253 Holland Ave ☎6467 1825, ⊚www.swensens.com.sg; map on p.551. Ice cream desserts plus sandwiches, soups and other light meals, round the clock. Daily 24hr.

Thai Express 16 Lorong Mambong ☎6466 6766, ⊚thaiexpress.com.sg; map on p.551. No-nonsense chain offering reliable Thai food. Sun–Thurs 11.30am–10.30pm, Fri & Sat 11.30am–11.30pm.

GEYLANG AND KATONG

In line with their heritage, the suburbs of Geylang and Katong hold several inexpensive Nonya and Malay restaurants, though there's no reason to come especially for the food. Besides the places reviewed here, there are also Malay stalls in and around Geylang Serai market, and two *kopitiams* offering Katong *laksa* at 49 and 51 East Coast Rd (either side of Ceylon Rd and just west of the Rumah Bebe shop). The dish is like regular *laksa* except that the noodles are in short strips, and isn't hard to find elsewhere in Singapore, though there's a certain cachet in eating it in Katong itself.

Betel Box Living Bistro 200 Joo Chiat Rd ☎6440 5440, ⊚betelbox.com/bistro; map on p.521. Run by the socially committed hostel upstairs, this restaurant and community space serves up a mixture of Peranakan food (including *roti babi*) and colonial-era favourites such as roast beef (weekends only) and mulligatawny soup. Western fry-up breakfasts available too. Most mains are around S$10. Daily 7.30am–10pm.

★ **Everything With Fries** 458 Joo Chiat Rd ☎6345 5034, ⊚everythingwithfries.com; map on p.521. Main courses built around their fries with a range of seasonings, plus suitably sickly desserts; see p.521 for more. Daily noon–11pm (Fri & Sat until 1am).

Guan Hoe Soon 38/40 Joo Chiat Place ☎6344 2761, ⊚guanhoesoon.com. Open in one form or another for more than half a century, this restaurant turns out fine Nonya cuisine in home-cooked style, including *ngoh hiang*, a yummy sausage-like item in which minced prawn is rolled up in a wrapper made from bean curd, and *satay babi* – not as in Malay satay, but a sweetish red pork curry. Around S$40 for two. Daily 11am–3pm & 6–9.30pm.

★ **Haji Maimunah** 20 Joo Chiat Rd #01-02 ⊚www.hjmaimunah.com; map on p.521. Inexpensive Malay diner serving good breakfasts (*nasi lemak*, *lontong* etc) and a fine *nasi campur spread*, featuring the likes of *ayam bakar sunda* (Sundanese-style barbecued chicken), with cooked-to-order choices such as *siput lemak sedut* (snails with coconut milk) and assorted *kuih* for afters. Daily except Mon 8am–9pm (buffet in Ramadan noon–10pm).

Peranakan Inn 210 East Coast Rd ☎6440 6195; map on p.521. As much effort goes into the food as went into the renovation of this immaculate, bright green shophouse restaurant, which offers a great range of authentic Nonya favourites including a delectable *bakwan kepiting*, a pork meatball soup. Reckon on S$30 for two, without alcohol. Daily 11am–3pm & 6–9.30pm.

SENTOSA

Bora-Bora Beach Bar Palawan Beach ☎6278 0838. This cheery bar has a huge menu featuring everything from vegetarian platters to banana-and-Kahlua freezes. Sun–Thurs 10.30am–9pm, Fri & Sat 10.30am–10pm.

Café del Mar Opposite Siloso Beach Resort ☎6235 1296, ⊚www.cafedelmar.com.sg. An offshoot of the Ibiza original, with a poolside bar, Mediterranean-influenced cuisine, diverse sounds ranging from reggae to electronica, and occasional beach parties – check website for details. Daily noon–9pm.

Koufu Palawan Beach. The cheapest place to eat on the island, this food court offers standard such as chicken rice and other rice and noodle dishes, plus a good range of juices and desserts. Daily 9am–9pm.

Trapizza Siloso Beach ☎6376 2662. Of the eating places on Siloso Beach, *Trapizza* stands out for its excellent pizzas and pasta dishes starting at S$20, with drinks served after the kitchen closes for the evening. Daily noon–9pm.

DRINKING AND NIGHTLIFE

With its affluence and large expat community, Singapore supports a huge range of drinking holes, from elegant colonial chambers through hip rooftop venues with skyline views to slightly tacky joints featuring karaoke or middling covers bands; the best **bars** cluster mainly in the Colonial District, along the Singapore River and on Orchard Rd. There's also a bunch of glitzy and vibrant **clubs** that spin cutting-edge sounds, and one or two regularly manage to lure the world's leading DJs to play. European and American dance music dominates in the best Western-style clubs, though some venues feature bands playing cover versions of current hits and pop classics. There are also more Asian-oriented places playing Chinese pop; some can be seedy, with hostesses trying to hassle you into buying them a drink. Fortunately, venues of this sort are easy to spot: even if you manage to get beyond the heavy wooden front door flanked by brandy adverts, the pitch darkness inside gives the game away.

Bar essentials Bars tend to open in the late afternoon, closing anywhere between midnight and 3am, an hour or two later on Friday and Saturday, and may be shut on Sunday; a few places are also open at lunchtime. A pint of Tiger beer starts at around S$12, but prices can be much higher in fancier venues or for imported brews. A glass of house wine usually costs much the same as a beer, and spirits a dollar or two more. During happy hour, which can last half the evening, you'll either get a considerable discount off drinks or a "one-for-one" deal (meaning two drinks for the price of one), and some bars also have a "house pour" – basically a discounted cocktail on offer all night. For venues with a strong emphasis on live music, see p.557.

Club essentials Most clubs have a cover charge, if not all week then at least on Friday and Saturday; the charge almost always includes your first drink or two, and varies between S$15 and S$30 (weekends are pricier, and men pay slightly more than women). Where women get in free on ladies' night, they have to pay for their first drink but may get unlimited refills of the "house pour" cocktail at certain times.

BARS

BOAT QUAY TO RIVERSIDE POINT, AND CHINATOWN

BQ Bar 39 Boat Quay ☎6536 9722, ⓦwww.bqbar .com; map on pp.502–503. One of Boat Quay's cooler venues, thanks to the friendly staff, memorable views of the river from upstairs and diverse sounds, anything from dance to rock. Kebabs available too from a nearby outlet run by the same management. Mon & Tues 11am–1am, Wed–Fri 11am–3am, Sat 5pm–4am; happy hour until 8pm.

Brewerkz/Café Iguana #01-05/06 Riverside Point, 30 Merchant Rd ☎6438 7438, ⓦbrewerkz.com; map on pp.502–503. Owned by the same company, *Brewerkz* serves up beers from its own microbrewery, while *Café Iguana* offers a huge selection of tequilas and margaritas, plus the same beers. *Brewerkz* has discounts on drinks for much of the day; special deals at *Café Iguana* are available until 8pm and after 11pm. Sun–Thurs noon–midnight, Fri & Sat noon–1am.

Harry's Bar 28 Boat Quay ☎6538 3029, ⓦwww .harrys.com.sg; map on pp.502–503. A well-established joint with branches all over downtown. There's a range of light meals and snacks; happy hour is until 8pm. Mon–Thurs 11am–1am, Fri 11am–2am, Sat 6pm–midnight.

★ **Helipad** #05-22 The Central, 6 Eu Tong Sen St ☎6327 8118, ⓦhelipad.com.sg; map on pp.502–503. It's not encouraging that the entrance is via the fifth-floor car park, but you're immediately into a tunnel like something in a spaceship, leading into a circular bar with a terrace offering good views over the river. A staircase gives access to an actual helipad, where you can sit out on the "H" symbol while your drinks are brought up to a collection point. Sun–Thurs 6pm–2am, Fri & Sat 6pm–3am; happy hour until 9pm (Sat 8–9pm only).

The Penny Black 26 & 27 Boat Quay ☎6538 2300, ⓦwww.pennyblack.com.sg; map on pp.502–503. Not a convincing evocation of a "Victorian London pub", but pleasant enough, with one table built around a red pillar box, Strongbow cider and Old Speckled Hen on draught, plenty of pub grub – cottage pie, ploughman's lunches, etc – and live UK football matches on TV. Mon–Thurs 11.30am–1am, Fri & Sat 11.30am–2am, Sun 11.30am–midnight.

Screening Room 12 Ann Siang Hill ☎6221 1694, ⓦwww.screeningroom.com.sg; map on pp.502–503. The unpretentious rooftop bar here (officially *La Terraza*, though few people know it as that) is a convivial spot for an evening drink, with the bonus of views of Chinatown's shophouses and modern towers, plus plenty of snacks available from the restaurant below. Mon–Thurs 6pm–1am, Fri & Sat 6pm–3am.

THE COLONIAL DISTRICT AND MARINA CENTRE

★ **Bar Opiume** Asian Civilizations Museum, Empress Place ☎6339 2876; map on p.484. Cool-as-ice venue, graced by chandeliers, modish leather furniture and lordly Buddha statues, with a vast range of cocktails and plenty of Indochinese snacks, courtesy of its sibling restaurant and café next door. The views across to Boat Quay are splendid at night. Mon–Thurs 5pm–2am, Fri & Sat 5pm–3am, Sun 5pm–1am.

Ku Dé Ta SkyBar SkyPark at *Marina Bay Sands* ☎6688 7688, ⓦkudeta.com.sg; map p.482. The bar at the SkyPark's fanciest venue is one of the best ways to bypass the SkyPark's admission fee and enjoy fabulous views over downtown Singapore. Stella and Hoegaarden on draft; no happy hour, though. Daily noon–late.

The Long Bar *Raffles Hotel*, 1 Beach Rd ☎6412 1816; map on p.484. It's still just about mandatory to have a

9

Singapore Sling amid the old-fashioned elegance of the bar where Ngiam Tong Boon invented it in 1915. Daily 11am–12.30am.

Orgo #04-01 (rooftop) Esplanade – Theatres On The Bay ☎6336 9366, ⓦwww.orgo.sg; map on p.484. They make a big thing of their huge range of cocktails, which emphasize fresh fruit and herbs, but the views of the spires of the Financial District sell themselves. Daily 5pm–2am; happy hour 5–8pm.

BRAS BASAH ROAD TO LITTLE INDIA AND ARAB STREET

Loof Top of the Odeon Towers Extension, 391 North Bridge Rd #03-07; map on p.493. A rooftop chill-out joint with views into the back of the *Raffles* hotel opposite, lots of low sofas, "buffalo" chicken wings and other snacks, and DJs spinning varied sounds through the week. Sun–Thurs 5pm–1am, Fri & Sat 5pm–3am; happy hour daily 5–8pm.

★ **Lot, Stock and Barrel Pub** 30 Seah St; map on p.493. Cheerful, unpretentious venue frequented by a post-work crowd in the early evening, with some backpackers making their presence felt later on, drawn partly by a jukebox featuring everyone from Sinatra to Beyonce. Daily 4pm–3am; happy hour 4–8pm.

Night and Day 139a/c Selegie Rd ⓦwww .nightandday.sg; map on p.493. Though funky cartoons on the walls hint that this is not just a bar but also a gallery space, it's a down-to-earth place with nothing self-important about it. Tucked away upstairs in a restored 1950s building, but it's not hard to spot, as there's a touch of Art Deco about the facade. Sun–Thurs 5pm–1am, Fri & Sat 5pm–3am; happy hour daily 5–9pm.

Prince of Wales Backpackers Hostel 101 Dunlop St ⓦwww.pow.com.sg; map on p.496. Below the hostel is a buzzing travellers' bar with live acoustic music or bands most nights, plus an Australian Pilsner-style microbrewery beer and pale ale on tap at keen prices. Sun–Thurs 9am–1am, Fri & Sat 9am–2am.

ORCHARD ROAD AND AROUND

Quite a few of Orchard Rd's most interesting drinking venues occupy restored Peranakan shophouses at the start of Emerald Hill Rd, close to Somerset MRT.

★ **The Dubliner** 165 Penang Rd ☎6735 2220, ⓦwww.dublinersingapore.com; map on pp.516–517. Set in a colonial-era mansion, this is hardly your typical ersatz Irish pub. The grub – fish and chips, Irish stew and burgers – is a notch above as well, and there's a live band every Fri. Daily 11.30am–late, happy hour until 9pm.

Ice Cold Beer 9 Emerald Hill Rd ⓦwww.emerald-hill .com; map on pp.516–517. Noisy, happening place where the beers are kept in ice tanks under the glass-topped bar. Shares a kitchen with *No. 5 Emerald Hill*. Sun–Thurs

5pm–2am, Fri & Sat 5pm–3am; happy hour daily 5–9pm.

★ **No. 5 Emerald Hill** 5 Emerald Hill Rd ⓦwww .emerald-hill.com; map on pp.516–517. Set in one of Emerald Hill Rd's restored houses, *No. 5* is not only an opulent feast for the eyes but also offers speciality cocktails plus great chicken wings and thin-crust pizzas. Tetley's on tap, some outdoor seating and a pool table upstairs. Mon–Thurs noon–2am, Fri & Sat noon–3am, Sun 5pm–3am; happy hour until 9pm.

Outdoors Café & Bar Peranakan Place, corner of Orchard rds and Emerald Hill Rd ☎6732 6966; map on pp.516–517. Pleasant alfresco place with a canopy for shade, a great spot to watch the passing trade on Orchard Rd. Erdinger on draught, plus other beers and a range of cocktails, and an extensive menu of Western and Asian mains and light meals. Sun–Thurs 11am–2am, Fri & Sat 11am–3am; happy hour till 7pm.

TANGLIN VILLAGE AND HOLLAND VILLAGE

Harry's Bar @ Holland Village 27 Lorong Mambong, Holland Village ☎6467 4222, ⓦwww.harrys.com.sg; map on p.551. A relaxing venue to retire to after a meal elsewhere in the area. Mon–Fri 4pm–1am, Sat & Sun noon–1am.

Wala Wala Café Bar 31 Lorong Mambong, Holland Village ☎6462 4288; map on p.551. This rocking joint has Tetley's, Kronenbourg and other beers on draught, and acoustic and electric acts nightly upstairs. Sun–Thurs 4pm–1am, Fri & Sat 4pm–2am; happy hour until 9pm.

The White Rabbit 39c Harding Rd, Tanglin Village ☎6473 9965, ⓦwww.thewhiterabbit.com.sg; map on p.482. This restaurant housed in a restored church has a marvellous open-air bar at the back that buzzes after 10pm at weekends. There's Erdinger on draught, though no happy hour, and loungey sounds. A great spot for a drink away from the bustle of downtown. Sun–Thurs 6.30pm–midnight, Fri & Sat 6.30pm–2am.

CLUBS

Avalon South Crystal Pavilion, *Marina Bay Sands* ☎6597 8333, ⓦavalon.sg; map p.482. An outpost of the Hollywood original, *Avalon* is entombed within a squat glass islet, reached by a walkway out over the water. The music extends from trance through house to general electronica, and the see-through architecture ensures all-round views of the Financial District and Singapore Flyer. Cover charges S$25–35.Thurs–Sun 10pm–late.

★ **Butter Factory** Level 2, One Fullerton, 1 Fullerton Rd ⓦwww.thebutterfactory.com; map pp.502–503. This fun, glossy venue has two spaces: *Bump*, where it's all hip-hop and R&B, and the trance-dominated *Fash*. Men pay S$28 for *Bump*, slightly less for *Fash*; women pay slightly less than men; and anyone who gets into *Bump* can also access *Fash*, but the converse doesn't hold true. More straightforwardly, Wednesday is ladies' night, when women get in free and have free drinks after 10pm. Wed, Fri & Sat 10pm–4am.

DBL-0 222 Queen St ☎6735 2008, ⓦwww.dblo.com .sg; map p.493. Even veteran outfits take a while to find their feet sometimes. *DBL-O* is a case in point, its street cred benefiting no end from new premises festooned with funky art by local designers, and from a much improved mix of house and R&B. Their website details the complex cover charges. Wed–Fri 8pm–3am, Sat 8pm–4am.

Home Club #B01-06 The Riverwalk, 20 Upper Circular Rd ☎6538 2928, ⓦwww.homeclub.com.sg; map. pp.502–503. This cosy venue makes the best of its riverside location with a chilled-out patio area outside; inside DJs spin cutting-edge sounds, from trance to grime. Friday nights see a switch to indie, however, as local bands play original material that wouldn't sound out of place on US college radio. Cover charge of around S$12–15. Tues–Thurs 9pm–3am, Fri & Sat 10pm–6am.

Powerhouse St James Power Station, next to VivoCity and Harbourfront MRT ☎6270 7676, ⓦwww .stjamespowerstation.com. Arguably the best of the venues at this renovated power station, the cavernous *Powerhouse* spins R&B on Wed & Sat and house on Fri. Only men pay the S$20 cover charge. Wed, Fri & Sat 9pm–4am; happy hour until 10pm.

Zouk/Phuture/Velvet Underground 17 Jiak Kim St ☎6738 2988, ⓦwww.zoukclub.com; map p.482. Launched in the 1990s, *Zouk* is one of Singapore's most successful clubs and still the best for many, though for others it's getting a little mainstream. House remains the mainstay, with guest sets from world-renowned DJs from time to time. *Zouk* also houses two smaller clubs, *Phuture*, majoring in hip-hop and R&B, and *Velvet Underground*, with a more relaxed mix of everything from Afrobeat to jazz. The cover charge depends on the venue and the night, but typically starts at S$25. Bus #16 from Somerset/ Orchard MRT; ask to be let off close to the *Grand Copthorne Waterfront* hotel, next door. Zouk Wed, Fri & Sat 10pm till late; Phuture Wed, Fri & Sat 9pm till late; Velvet Underground Wed–Sat 9pm till late.

GAY VENUES

Singapore's more liberal climate these days means that gay venues thrive largely unhindered. In return, they keep a lowish profile, barely using the word "gay" in promotional material, for example. Most of the handful of gay bars and clubs are located in Tanjong Pagar and Chinatown, while there's a small gay library project, the Pelangi Pride Centre, in Geylang (ⓦwww .pelangipridecentre.org); new venues are often listed by Singapore's gay lifestyle website ⓦwww.fridae.asia. Note that the bars only really get busy at weekends, and even then only after 10pm. For more on the social backdrop to local gay life, see p.55.

Backstage Bar 13a Trengganu St ☎6227 1712, ⓦwww.backstagebar.moonfruit.com; map on pp.502–503. Entered through a side door in Temple St (look for the discreetly placed rainbow flag), this tiny bar offers a view over the souvenir stalls of Trengganu St. Sun–Thurs 7pm–2am, Fri & Sat 7pm–3am.

DYMK 41 Neil Rd ⓦdymk.sg; map on pp.502–503. Probably the friendliest gay bar in town. They tend to keep the music a tad quieter than elsewhere, making it a good place for a relaxed chat. Most of the crowd are 20- and 30-somethings. Mon–Thurs & Sun 7pm–midnight, Fri 7pm–1am, Sat 8pm–2am.

Lockerroom 43 Neil Rd ☎6221 7988, ⓦwww .lockerroom.com.sg; map on pp.502–503. All very droll – staff strut around in baggy workout shorts and the place is strewn with gym lockers. The place draws quite a mixed clientele, including more than a smattering of expats. Daily 7pm–late.

Taboo 65/67 Neil Rd ⓦwww.taboo97.com; map on pp.502–503. Small club spinning the usual mix of house, trance and other pulsating sounds. Wed & Thurs 10pm–2am, Fri 10pm–3am, Sat 10pm–4am.

Tantric 78 Neil Rd ☎6423 9232, ⓦwww.backstagebar .moonfruit.com; map on pp.502–503. Pleasant enough shophouse bar with a clientele that's slightly more reflective of Singapore's multi-ethnic make-up than the largely Chinese crowd you find elsewhere. Sun–Fri 8pm–3am, Sat 8pm–4am.

ENTERTAINMENT

Even on a brief visit, it's hard not to notice how much money has been poured into developing an **arts** community and infrastructure: prime downtown property has been turned over to arts organizations in areas like the Waterloo St and Little India "arts belts", and prestige venues like Theatres on the Bay attract a stream of world-class performers. Cynics might say this cultural push is mainly about keeping Singapore attractive to skilled expats, while others say a more important issue is whether world-class art can bloom where **censorship** still lingers, if not as overtly as in the 1970s and 1980s, then in terms of few daring to cross well-established red lines concerning party politics, ethnicity and religion. Even if pushing the boundaries is now tolerated provided projects make money, as some claim, it's hard to see how this can happen reliably when the Singapore audience is relatively small. Whatever the truth, it would be a shame not to catch a performance of some kind if you are visiting for a few days, whether one drawing on Asian artistic traditions or a gig by a big-name Western band.

9

Tickets You can usually buy tickets for concerts, plays and dance performances at the venues themselves, though it can be easier to use ticketing agencies such as SISTIC (the largest; ☎6348 5555, ⓦwww.sistic.com.sg) and Gatecrash (☎6100 2005, ⓦwww.gatecrash.com.sg). Cinema tickets cost around S$10.

Festivals There are two major international arts festivals: the Singapore Arts Festival (over four weeks in May & June; ⓦwww.singaporeartsfest.com), running the gamut from theatre through dance and film to concerts; and the Singapore Fringe Festival (February; ⓦwww.singaporefringe.com), concentrating on theatre, dance and the visual arts. September's annual Singapore International Film Festival (ⓦsiff.sg) screens dozens of films and shorts over two weeks, while the best music festival, Mosaic (March; ⓦwww.mosaicmusicfestival.com), showcases an excellent range of jazz and rock acts at Theatres on the Bay.

ARTS CENTRES AND GENERAL-PURPOSE THEATRES

The Arts House 1 Old Parliament Lane ☎6332 6919 (tickets), ⓦwww.theartshouse.com.sg. Plays, concerts, films and art exhibitions.

DBS Arts Centre 20 Merbau Rd, Robertson Quay ☎6221 5585, ⓦwww.srt.com.sg. Plays and concerts.

Drama Centre Level 3, National Library, 100 Victoria St ☎6837 8400. Mainly plays by local companies.

Esplanade – Theatres on the Bay 1 Esplanade Drive ☎6828 8222, ⓦwww.esplanade.com.sg. Sucks up all the biggest events to hit Singapore's shores.

Singapore Indoor Stadium 2 Stadium Walk, Kallang ⓦwww.sportshub.com.sg. The usual venue for big-name bands in town. The Circle Line's Stadium MRT is close by. Tickets through SISTIC.

Substation 45 Armenian St ☎6337 7800, ⓦwww.substation.org. Self-styled "home for the arts" with a multipurpose hall for performances, as well as art, sculpture and photography exhibitions in its gallery.

Victoria Concert Hall and Theatre 11 Empress Place ☎6338 8283, ⓦwww.vch.org.sg. Distinguished colonial-era venue staging concerts and plays; due to reopen in 2013 after major refurbishment.

FILM

As well as the latest Hollywood blockbusters, Singapore's cinemas show a wide range of Chinese, Malay and Indian movies, all with English subtitles. Western movies in languages other than English also pop up occasionally, as do features by a small but competent group of local directors. Cinema-going is popular in Singapore, and it's worth turning up early or booking in advance if the film is a hot new release. Be prepared, also, for noise during shows: Singaporeans are great ones for chattering through the movie. If you intend to be in Singapore for a while, you might want to sign up to the Singapore Film Society (ⓦsfs.org.sg), which puts on monthly members-only screenings and occasional mini-festivals, with discounts for members.

MULTIPLEX CHAINS

Cathay Cinemas include: Cineleisure Orchard, 8 Grange Rd (near Somerset MRT); Cathay Cineplex, 2 Handy Rd (near Dhoby Ghaut MRT); ⓦwww.cathaycineplexes.com.sg.

Golden Village Cinemas include: Level 7, Plaza Singapura, 68 Orchard Rd; Levels 2 & 3, Vivocity, Harbourfront; #03/04-01 Marina Leisureplex, 5a Raffles Ave, Marina Centre; ⓦwww.gv.com.sg.

Shaw Cinemas include: Lido 8 Cineplex, Shaw House, 350 Orchard Rd (IMAX-equipped); Bugis Cineplex, Bugis Junction, 200 Victoria St; ⓦshaw.sg.

INDEPENDENT VENUES

Alliance Française 1 Sarkies Rd ⓦwww.alliancefrancaise.org.sg/cineclub.html. Weekly French-language films with English subtitles; tickets through SISTIC. A 10min walk from Newton MRT.

National Museum Cinematheque National Museum, 93 Stamford Rd ⓦwww.nationalmuseum.sg. The museum mounts its own laudable programme of films from around the world, including some vintage classics.

Omni-Theatre See p.528. One of Singapore's two IMAX cinemas.

The Picturehouse Cathay Building, 2 Handy Rd ⓦwww.thepicturehouse.com.sg. Not strictly an indie but, unlike Cathay's multiplexes, devoted to art-house films from Asia and the rest of the world.

The Screening Room 12 Ann Siang Hill ☎6221 1694, ⓦwww.screeningroom.com.sg. "Where art meets film" is the motto of this complex, incorporating a basement lounge, restaurant, gallery space, rooftop bar and a cinema screening the relatively intellectual end of Hollywood's output, plus the odd Asian flick.

THEATRE, DANCE AND CLASSICAL MUSIC

Singapore's arts scene is probably at its best when it comes to drama: a surprising number of small theatre companies have sprung up over the years, performing works by local playwrights that dare to include a certain amount of social commentary. Themes that have been tackled range from gay issues to the notorious "en bloc" craze, fuelled by Singapore's regular property-market frenzies, when developers buy up whole apartment blocks just so they can tear them down and build something grander in their place. Foreign theatre companies tour regularly too, and lavish Western musicals are staged from time to time. The island has a lively Western classical music scene, with the Singapore Symphony Orchestra at its heart. Dance is

STREET THEATRE

If you walk around Singapore long enough, you're likely to stumble upon some sort of streetside cultural event, most usually a *wayang*, a Malay word used in Singapore to denote **Chinese opera**. Played out on outdoor stages that spring up next to temples and markets, or in open spaces in the new towns, *wayangs* are highly dramatic and stylized affairs, in which garishly made-up and costumed characters enact popular Chinese legends to the accompaniment of crashing gongs and cymbals. They're staged throughout the year, but the best time to catch one is during the Festival of the Hungry Ghosts, when they are held to entertain passing spooks (late Aug). Another fascinating traditional performance, **lion dancing**, takes to the streets during Chinese New Year, when **puppet theatres** also appear. The Singapore Tourism Board may be able to help you track down examples, though one good bet is the area around the Kwan Im temple on Waterloo Street.

another active area, with several local troupes and regular visits by international companies.

COMPANIES AND ORCHESTRAS

Action Theatre 42 Waterloo St ☎ 6837 0842, ⓦ www .action.org.sg. Stages work by Singaporean playwrights as well as the standard repetoire, with its own hundred-seater venue on site.

Chinese Opera Teahouse 5 Smith St ☎ 6323 4862, ⓦ www.opera.com.sg. For an interesting culinary and musical experience, come here for the Sights and Sounds of Chinese Opera Show (7pm), a meal followed by performances of excerpts from Chinese operas. The package costs S$35, though you can watch the opera selections alone for S$20 (includes tea and snacks; admission at 7.50pm).

City Chinese Orchestra ⓦ www.cityco.com.sg. Chinese classical and folk music recitals, at various venues.

Singapore Chinese Orchestra Singapore Conference Hall, 7 Shenton Way, Financial District ☎ 6440 3839, ⓦ www.sco.com.sg. Performances of traditional Chinese music through the year, plus occasional free concerts.

Singapore Dance Theatre ☎ 6338 0611, ⓦ www .singaporedancetheatre.com. Contemporary and classical works at various venues, sometimes by moonlight at Fort Canning Park.

Singapore Lyric Opera ⓦ www.singaporeopera .com.sg. Western opera and operetta, at various venues.

Singapore Repertory Theatre DBS Arts Centre (see opposite). English-language theatre, and not just the most obvious British and American plays.

Singapore Symphony Orchestra ⓦ www.sso.org.sg. Performances throughout the year at Esplanade – Theatres on the Bay and other venues, including some chamber-music recitals and with many stellar international guests. Occasional free concerts at the Botanic Gardens and hour-long daytime shows for children.

Temple of Fine Arts ☎ 6535 0509, ⓦ www .templeoffinearts.org. This Indian cultural organization is dedicated to perpetuating traditional music and dance, and puts on occasional concerts and exhibitions.

POP, ROCK, BLUES AND JAZZ

Singapore's thriving live music scene attracts Western stadium-rock outfits as well as indie bands, though some gigs can be marred by a rather staid atmosphere as locals can be uncomfortable about letting their hair down. Rivalling Western music in terms of popularity in Singapore is **Canto-pop**, a bland hybrid of Cantonese lyrics and Western disco beats; Hong Kong Canto-pop superstars visit periodically, to rapturous welcomes that make their shows quite an experience.

SMALL VENUES

Blu Jaz Café 11 Bali Lane ☎ 6292 3800, ⓦ www .blujaz.net; map on p.496. Bar restaurant with live jazz Mon, Fri & Sat eves. Mon–Thurs noon–midnight, Fri noon–1am, Sat 4pm–1am.

Crazy Elephant #01-03 Block E, Clarke Quay ☎ 6337 7859, ⓦ www.crazyelephant.com; map, p.484. Of the hotchpotch of brash venues along Clarke Quay, this bar has more street cred than most, with live music – blues and rock – practically every night and an open-mike jam session on Sun. Some tables are by the water's edge. Sun–Thurs 5pm–2am, Fri & Sat 5pm–3am; happy hour until 9pm.

Home Club #B01-06 The Riverwalk, 20 Upper Circular Rd ☎ 6538 2928, ⓦ www.homeclub.com.sg; map. pp.502–503. Local indie bands play original material here on Fridays (9–11pm). Cover S$12–15. Tues–Thurs 9pm–3am, Fri & Sat 10pm–6am.

Timbre Substation, 45 Armenian St, ⓦ www.timbre .com.sg; map, p.484. Open-air bar-restaurant with local bands and singer-songwriters serving up original material, though it can be a little derivative; you'll find the place tucked away by the car park behind Armenian St. Daily from 6pm.

Timbre The Arts House, 1 Old Parliament Lane; ⓦ www.timbre.com.sg; map, p.484. More sets by local musicians, though with a slightly brasher feel than at the Substation in view of the high-visibility riverside location. Mon–Sat from 6pm.

9

SHOPPING

Choice and convenience make **shopping** in Singapore a rewarding experience. While the scores of malls and department stores may appear uniform at first sight, housing local and international chains, they all feature a fair number of independent retailers too. Prices are often on a par with Western cities, however; Kuala Lumpur or Penang can be better hunting grounds for bargains, though Singapore boasts the best range. If you're around during the **Great Singapore Sale** (late May to late July; ⊕ www.greatsingaporesale.com.sg), you'll find prices seriously marked down in many stores. **Orchard Rd** offers the biggest cluster of malls, plenty of them high-end affairs bulging with designer names. Between them they stock more or less anything you could want: clothes, sports equipment, electronic goods, antiques, and so on. Malls elsewhere tend to be smaller and slightly more informal; the most interesting in **Chinatown** are like multistorey markets, home to a few more traditional outlets stocking Chinese foodstuffs, medicines, instruments and porcelain. Chinatown also has a few antique and curio shops along South Bridge Rd, and more knick-knacks are on sale around **Arab St**, where you'll also find textiles and batiks, robust basketware and some good deals on jewellery. **Little India** has silk stores and goldsmiths as well as **Mustafa**, a department store that's known all over the island for being open 24/7. South of Little India, the grid of streets between **Rochor Rd** and the Singapore River is home to a few malls specializing in electrical and computer products. Elsewhere downtown, there are more malls at **Marina Centre** and **HarbourFront**, and **Marina Bay Sands** has its own mall; just outside downtown, **Holland Village** is another place to head for if you want to buy Asian art, crafts or textiles.

Complaints In the unlikely event you have a complaint against a particular store that can't be resolved, you can report it to the Singapore Tourism Board on ☎ 1800 736 2000 or even go to the Small Claims Tribunal at the Subordinate Courts at 1 Havelock Square (on Upper Cross St near Chinatown MRT; ☎ 6435 5946, ⊕ www.smallclaims .gov.sg), which has a fast-track system for tourists; it costs S$10 to have your case heard.

SHOPPING COMPLEXES AND DEPARTMENT STORES
ORCHARD ROAD AND AROUND

313@Somerset 313 Orchard Rd (above Somerset MRT) ⊕ 313somerset.com.sg; map pp.516–517. Home to Uniqlo and ZARA, plus various small designer outlets, an HMV store for music and a *Food Republic* food court. Daily 10am–9pm.

Centrepoint 176 Orchard Rd (close to Somerset MRT) ⊕ www.fraserscentrepointmalls.com; map pp.516–517. Dependable all-round complex, whose seven floors of shops include Robinsons, Singapore's oldest department store. Daily 10am–10pm.

Forum the Shopping Mall 583 Orchard Rd (near *Orchard Parade* hotel) ⊕ www.forumtheshoppingmall .com. Plenty of items to please the pampered brat – upmarket kids' clothes, toys and so forth. Daily 10am–9pm.

ION Orchard 2 Orchard Turn (above Orchard MRT) ⊕ ionorchard.com; map pp.516–517. Despite the impressive hyper-modern facade and a sprinkling of designer names, Armani included, by far the most popular section of this cavernous mall is *Food Opera*, its excellent food court on basement 4. Daily 10am–9pm.

Ngee Ann City 391a Orchard Rd ⊕ www.ngeeanncity .com.sg; map pp.516–517. A brooding twin-towered complex, home to the Japanese Takashimaya department store and the excellent Kinokuniya bookstore, plus several jewellery outlets. Daily 10am–10pm.

Palais Renaissance 390 Orchard Rd; map pp.516–517. A classy complex housing Prada, DKNY and other heavyweights. Daily 10am–9pm.

Paragon Opposite Ngee Ann City ⊕ www.paragon.sg; map pp.516–517. Calvin Klein, Hugo Boss, Versace and many more at this swanky mall. Daily 10am–10pm.

Plaza Singapura 68 Orchard Rd ⊕ www .plazasingapura.com.sg; map pp.516–517. Veteran mall with a bit of everything: Marks & Spencer, the Singapore department store chain John Little, sportswear and sports equipment, musical instruments, audio, video and general electrical equipment. Daily 10am–10pm.

Tanglin Shopping Centre 19 Tanglin Rd (next to *Orchard Parade* hotel) ⊕ www.tanglinsc.com; map pp.516–517. Good for art, antiques and curios. Daily 10am–9pm.

Tangs Corner of Orchard and Scotts rds ⊕ www.tangs .com. One of Singapore's most famous department stores,

TAX REFUNDS

Tourists flying out of Singapore can claim a refund of the island's goods and services tax (**GST**; 7.7 percent at the time of writing) on purchases over a certain amount (at least S$100 from any one retailer, though some firms require a larger outlay) at stores displaying a **Premier Tax Free** or **Tax Free Shopping** or **eTRS** sticker. It's a fairly complicated process, and some stores deduct an administration fee; for detailed information, see the "For consumers" section of ⊕ iras.gov.sg or pick up the relevant leaflet from a tourist office.

its pagoda-style construction among Orchard Rd's most recognizable landmarks. Daily 10am–10pm.

Wisma Atria 435 Orchard Rd (opposite Tangs) ⓦwww.wismaonline.com; map pp.516–517. A good range of middle-market local and international fashion shops, plus the Japanese department store Isetan. Daily 10am–9pm.

CHINATOWN

Hong Lim Complex 531–531a Upper Cross St; map pp.502–503. Several Chinese provisions stores, fronted by sackfuls of dried mushrooms, cuttlefish, chillies, garlic cloves, onions, fritters and crackers. Other shops sell products ranging from acupuncture accessories to birds' nests. Daily 10am–9pm.

Pearl's Centre 100 Eu Tong Sen St; map pp.502–503. Home to some Chinese medicine clinics and a few shops selling Buddhist paraphernalia. Daily 10am–9pm.

People's Park Centre 101 Upper Cross St; map pp.502–503. Stall-like shop units selling Chinese handicrafts, CDs, electronics, silk, jade and gold. Daily 10am–9pm.

People's Park Complex 1 Park Rd; map pp.502–503. A venerable shopping centre that, like the Hong Lim Complex and adjacent People's Park Centre, is among the most entertaining places to browse in Chinatown because it's so workaday, a place for ordinary folk to buy day-to-day needs. Also here is the Overseas Emporium on level 4, selling Chinese musical instruments, calligraphy pens, lacquerwork and jade. Daily 10am–10pm.

THE COLONIAL DISTRICT AND MARINA CENTRE

Funan DigitaLife Mall 109 North Bridge Rd ⓦwww .funan.com.sg; map p.484. A variety of stores here sell computer and electronics equipment. Daily 10am–9pm.

Marina Square 6 Raffles Blvd ⓦwww.marinasquare .com.sg; map p.493. Nowhere near as large as its sprawling neighbour, Suntec City, but better laid out and with a very diverse range of outlets. If you've time for just one Marina Centre mall, this is probably it. Daily 10am–9pm.

Raffles City 252 North Bridge Rd (above City Hall MRT) ⓦwww.rafflescity.com; map p.484. Home to a branch of Robinsons department store with a Marks & Spencer within it, plus numerous fashion chains. Daily 10am–10pm.

BRAS BASAH ROAD TO ROCHOR ROAD

Bugis Junction Victoria St, above Bugis MRT ⓦwww .bugisjunction-mall.com.sg; map p.493 . Mall encasing several streets of restored shophouses, and featuring the Japanese/Chinese department store BHG and a number of fashion outlets. Daily 10am–10pm.

Sim Lim Square 1 Rochor Canal Rd ⓦwww .simlimsquare.com.sg; map p.493. Cameras and electronic goods. Daily 10am–9pm.

LITTLE INDIA

Mustafa Syed Alwi Rd ⓦwww.mustafa.com.sg; map, p.496. Totally different in feel to the malls of Orchard Rd, Mustafa is a phenomenon, selling electronics, fresh food, luggage, you name it – and it never closes. Daily 24hr.

ELSEWHERE IN SINGAPORE

Holland Road Shopping Centre 211 Holland Ave, Holland Village; map p.551. The shops above the supermarket are good places for curios. Daily 10am–9pm.

Marina Bay Sands 10 Bayfront Ave; map p.482. A hotchpotch of swish designer outlets and some quite humdrum stores. Daily 10am–9pm.

VivoCity Next to HarbourFront Centre and above HarbourFront MRT ⓦwww.vivocity.com.sg; map p.522. A humdinger of a mall, containing a branch of Tangs department store, the Page One bookstore, a cinema, a *National Geographic* outlet, three food courts (*Food Republic* is exceptional) and many restaurants. Daily 10am–10pm.

THINGS TO BUY

ART, ANTIQUES, CURIOS AND SOUVENIRS

Antiques of the Orient #02-40 Tanglin Shopping Centre ☎6734 9351. Antiquarian books, maps and prints. Mon–Sat 10am–6pm, Sun 11am–4pm.

Elliott's Antiques #02-13 Raffles Hotel Arcade ☎6337 1008. Chinese antique furniture and art. Daily 10.30am–7.30pm.

Eng Tiang Huat 284 River Valley Rd ☎6734 3738. Oriental musical instruments plus *wayang* costumes and props. Mon–Sat 11am–6pm.

Jasmine Fine Arts #03-01 Mandarin Gallery (in front of the *Mandarin Orchard* hotel) ☎6734 5688. Appealing artwork from all over the world. Daily 11am–9pm.

Katong Antiques House 208 East Coast Rd, Katong ☎6345 8544. Peranakan artefacts and Chinese porcelain (see p.522). Daily except Mon 11am–5pm.

Kwok Gallery #03-01 Far East Shopping Centre, 545 Orchard Rd (opposite the Thai embassy) ☎6235 2516. An impressive inventory of antique Chinese artwork. Mon–Sat 11am–6pm.

Lim's Arts & Living #02-01 Holland Rd Shopping Centre ☎6467 1300; #02-154 Vivocity ☎6376 9468. A sort of Asian Conran Shop, packed with bamboo pipes, dainty teapots, cherrywood furniture and lamps crafted from old tea jars. Daily: Holland Rd 10am–8.30pm, Vivocity 10.30am–10pm.

Little Shophouse 43 Bussorah St, near Sultan Mosque ☎6295 2328. Well named, this small outlet boasts some fine but pricey examples of Peranakan beaded slippers (from S$300), plus replica Peranakan crockery. Daily 10am–6pm.

9

Malay Art Gallery 31 Bussorah St ☎ 6294 8051. Stocks *songket* and *kerises* from Malaysia and Indonesia. Mon–Sat 10am–6pm, Sun 11am–5pm.

MICA Building 140 Hill St ⊛ www.artriumatmica.com. The glass-ceiling atrium here – artfully named the ARTrium – is home to half a dozen galleries selling work from around Southeast Asia. Typically daily 11am–7pm.

Melor's Curios 39 Bussorah St ☎ 6292 3934. Aladdin's cave probably had fewer treasures than this shop, which sells Javanese and other Asian furniture, hangers made of bamboo for displaying fabrics, plus an assortment of batik, silk and *congkak* (mancala) sets. Daily 10am–5.30pm.

Rishi Handicrafts 5 Baghdad St, close to Arab St ☎ 6298 2408. Leather sandals, necklaces and knick-knacks. Daily 10am–5.30pm (Sun from 11am).

Rumah Bebe 113 East Coast Rd, Katong ☎ 6247 8781 ⊛ www.rumahbebe.com. Peranakan products such as beaded bags and the traditional *garb* – kebaya and *sarongs* – worn by women. Daily except Mon 9.30am–6.30pm.

Teajoy #01-05 North Bridge Centre, 420 North Bridge Rd ☎ 6339 3739. Close to the National Library, this sells Chinese tea sets with special attention paid to oolong accoutrements. Daily noon–8pm.

Tong Mern Sern 51 Craig Rd, Tanjong Pagar ☎ 6223 1037, ⊛ tmsantiques.com. "We buy junk and sell antiques", proclaims the banner outside this great little establishment. The owner is quite a character and can tell you all about the collection of crockery, old furniture and other bric-a-brac he has amassed. Mon–Sat 9am–6pm, Sun 1–6pm.

Zhen Lacquer Gallery 1 Trengganu St, Chinatown ☎ 6222 2718. Specializes in lacquerware boxes and bowls. Daily 10.30am–9pm.

FABRICS, SILK AND JEWELLERY

C.T. Hoo #01-22 Tanglin Shopping Centre ☎ 6737 5447. Specializes in pearls. Mon–Sat 9.30am–6.30pm.

Dakshaini Silks 65 Serangoon Rd, Little India ☎ 6291 9969. Premier Indian embroidered silks. Mon–Sat 10am–9pm, Sun 10am–7pm.

Flower Diamond #03-02 Ngee Ann City ☎ 6734 1221. Contemporary designs as well as more traditionally styled bling, at sensible prices. Daily 10am–9pm.

Risis National Orchid Garden, Singapore Botanic Gardens ☎ 6471 7138. Gold-plated orchids, either a classic Singapore souvenir or an utter cliché, depending on your viewpoint, are available here as well as at a few malls and at Changi airport. Daily 8.30am–7pm.

Rumah Bebe 113 East Coast Rd, Katong ☎ 6247 8781, ⊛ www.rumahbebe.com. This delightful place sells beaded shoes and handbags, costume jewellery and the traditional garb – *kebaya* and sarong – of Nonya women. They also offer courses in beading and Nonya cookery. Daily except Mon 9.30am–6.30pm.

Toko Aljunied 95 Arab St ☎ 6294 6897. Batik cloth and *kebaya* – the blouse/sarong combinations traditionally worn by Nonyas. Mon–Sat 10.30am–7pm, Sun 11am–5pm.

Wong's Jewellery 62 Temple St, Chinatown ☎ 6323 0236. Chinese-style outlet, good for jade, gold and pearls. Daily 10am–7.30pm.

BOOKS

Singapore bookshops are as well stocked as many in the West; all the larger ones carry a good selection of Western and local fiction, plus books on Singapore, Malaysia and the rest of East Asia, and a range of magazines.

Kinokuniya Level 3, Ngee Ann City; ⊛ kinokuniya.com.sg. One of Singapore's best bookshops, with titles on every conceivable subject and some foreign-language literature too, plus loads of magazines. There's another branch at #03-09 Bugis Junction. Daily 10am–9.30pm.

Littered With Books 20 Duxton Rd ☎ 6220 6824. Despite its name, this indie outlet has a neatly laid out, though somewhat random, collection of literary fiction, thrillers and travel writing. Daily at least noon–8pm, slightly longer hours Fri–Sun.

MPH #B1-24, Raffles City ⊛ www.mph.com.sg. Veteran of the local book trade, though not as comprehensive as it once was. Daily 10am–10pm.

Page One #02-41 Vivocity ⊛ www.pageonegroup.com. Similar in feel to Kinokuniya, Page One started out as a publisher of art and architecture books and stocks plenty of titles on these areas, along with books on most other subjects. Daily 10am–10pm.

Select Books #03-15 Tanglin Shopping Centre ☎ 6732 1515, ⊛ www.selectbooks.com.sg. The very best bookshop in town for specialist titles on Singapore, Malaysia and the rest of Southeast Asia, with a mail order service. Mon–Sat 9.30am–6.30pm, Sun 10am–4pm.

Times Bookstores #04-08 Centrepoint; #04-18 Plaza Singapura; ⊛ www.timesbookstores.com.sg. A well-stocked local chain. Daily 10.30am–9.30pm.

CDS AND DVDS

Western CDs and DVDs are widely available in Singapore. If you want to buy Asian material, you'll find Chinese music and DVDs widely available; for Indian releases, there are quite a few outlets in Little India; and for Malay music, head to the Joo Chiat Complex, Geylang (see p.522).

Earshot Arts House, 1 Old Parliament Lane ☎ 6334 0130. Nothing but CDs, DVDs and books by Singaporean creatives. Daily 11am–9pm.

Gramophone Cathay Building, 2 Handy Rd (where Orchard Rd becomes Bras Basah Rd) ☎ 6235 4105. Largely mainstream CD releases. Sun–Thurs noon–10pm, Fri & Sat noon–11pm.

HMV Level 4, 313@Somerset ☎6733 1822. This substantial store is your best bet for mainstream releases and with dedicated jazz and classical music sections. Sun–Thurs 10am–10pm, Fri & Sat 10am–11pm.

Roxy Records #02-15 Excelsior Shopping Centre (at the Hill St end of the *Peninsula Excelsior* hotel) ☎6337 7783. A range of imported indie and other hard-to-find releases, plus some secondhand vinyl. Mon–Sat noon–9.30pm.

Straits Records 24 Bali Lane ☎9681 6341. Stocking CDs and vinyl by obscure US metal/thrash bands and better-known 1970s punk and reggae acts, plus a little Malay music, this minuscule shop epitomizes the strange mix of sensibilities at play in and around Arab St. Daily 3–10pm.

DIRECTORY

Banks and exchange The banks with the most branches include DBS, HSBC, Standard Chartered, UOB and OUB, though as an international financial centre, Singapore is home to offices of many other major international banks. Normal banking hours are Mon–Fri 9.30am–3pm & Sat 9.30am–12.30pm. Licensed moneychangers, offering slightly more favourable exchange rates than the bank, aren't hard to find – particularly in Little India (eg at Mustafa, see p.559) and on Orchard Rd.

Embassies and consulates Australia, 25 Napier Rd ☎6737 7465; Brunei, 325 Tanglin Rd ☎6733 9055; Cambodia, #10-03 Orchard Towers, 400 Orchard Rd ☎6341 9785; Canada, #11-01 One George St, 95 South Bridge Rd ☎6854 5900; China, 150 Tanglin Rd ☎6418 0328; India, 31 Grange Rd ☎6737 6777; Indonesia, 7 Chatsworth Rd ☎6737 7422; Ireland, #08-02 Liat Towers, 541 Orchard Rd ☎6238 7616; Japan, 16 Nassim Rd ☎6235 8855; Laos, #13-04 Goldhill Plaza, 51 Newton Rd ☎6250 6044; Malaysia, 301 Jervois Rd ☎6235 0111; The Netherlands, #13-01 Liat Towers, 541 Orchard Rd ☎6737 1155; New Zealand, #15-06/10 Ngee Ann City, 391a Orchard Rd ☎6235 9966; Philippines, 20 Nassim Rd ☎6737 3977; South Africa, #15-01 Odeon Towers, 331 North Bridge Rd ☎6339 3319; Thailand, 370 Orchard Rd ☎6737 2158; UK, 100 Tanglin Rd ☎6424 4218; US, 27 Napier Rd ☎6476 9100; Vietnam 10 Leedon Park ☎6462 5938. The Ministry of Foreign Affairs website ⓦwww.mfa.gov.sg carries a full list.

Emergencies See p.54.

Gyms California Fitness (ⓦcaliforniafitness.com), True Fitness (ⓦtruefitness.com.sg) and Fitness First (ⓦwww.fitnessfirst.com.sg) all operate downtown gyms, though you will need to take out membership to use them.

Hospitals The state-run Singapore General Hospital, Outram Rd (SGH; ☎6222 3322, ⓦwww.sgh.com.sg), is near Outram Park MRT and has a 24hr casualty/emergency department, as do the privately run Raffles Hospital, 585 North Bridge Rd (☎6311 1111, ⓦrafflesmedicalgroup.com); and Mount Elizabeth Hospital off Orchard Rd (☎6737 2666, ⓦparkwayhealth.com).

Pharmacies Both Guardian and Watson's are ubiquitous downtown, with branches in shopping malls and even in a few MRT stations, though only the largest outlets handle prescriptions.

Phones For details of mobile phone providers, see p.59.

Police In an emergency, dial ☎999; otherwise call the police hotline ☎1800 225 0000.

Post offices The island has dozens of post offices (typically Mon–Fri 8.30am–5pm & Sat 8.30am–1pm), with the one at 1 Killiney Rd (near Somerset MRT) keeping extended hours (Mon–Fri until 9pm, Sat until 4pm, plus Sun 10am–4pm). Poste restante/general delivery (bring proof of ID) is at the Singapore Post Centre, 10 Eunos Rd (near Paya Lebar MRT; Mon–Fri 8am–6pm, Sat 8am–2pm). For more on the mail system, contact SingPost (☎1605, ⓦwww.singpost.com).

Swimming Singapore has some of the world's best state-run swimming pools; just about every new town has a well-maintained 50m open-air pool, open from the early morning until well into the evening. Convenient venues include the Jalan Besar Swimming Complex on Tyrwhitt Rd, near Lavender and Farrer Park MRT stations and Buona Vista Swimming Complex in Holland Village. Charges are a mere S$1–1.50; have coins available for the ticket gates and lockers.

Travel agents The following are good for discounted airfares and packages: STA Travel, 534a North Bridge Rd ☎67377188, ⓦwww.statravel.com.sg; Sunny Holidays, #01-220 Marina Square, Marina Centre ☎6767 6868, ⓦwww.sunnyholidays.com.sg; and Zuji ⓦwww.zuji.com.sg.

Vaccinations Tan Tock Seng Hospital, across the road from Novena MRT, has a Travellers' Health & Vaccination Centre (☎6357 2222, ⓦttsh.com.sg).

Women's helpline AWARE ☎1-800/774 5935, ⓦwww.aware.org.sg.

ORANG-UTAN

Contexts

History

The modern-day nations of Malaysia, Singapore and Brunei only became independent in 1963, 1965 and 1984 respectively. Before that, their history was inextricably linked with events in the larger Malay archipelago, from Sumatra across Borneo to the Philippines.

Unfortunately, little hard archeological evidence in the region pertains to the prehistoric period, while events prior to the foundation of Melaka are known only from unreliable accounts written by Chinese and Arab traders. For an understanding of the formative fourteenth and fifteenth centuries, there are two vital sources: the **Suma Oriental** (Treatise of the Orient), by Tomé Pires, a Portuguese emissary who came to Melaka in 1512 and used his observations to write a history of the region, and the seventeenth-century **Sejarah Melayu**, the "Malay Annals", which recount oral historical tales in a poetic style. Portuguese and Dutch **colonists** who arrived in the sixteenth and seventeenth centuries supplied written records, though these tended to concern commercial rather than political or social matters. At least there's a wealth of information from **British colonial** times that, despite an imperialistic bias, gives detailed insights into Malay affairs.

Beginnings

The oldest remains of *Homo sapiens* in the region, discovered in the Niah Caves in Sarawak, are thought to be those of hunter-gatherers, dating back some 40,000 years; other finds in the Peninsular state of Kedah are only 10,000 years old. The variety of **ethnic groups** now found in both east and west Malaysia – from small, dark-skinned Negritos through to paler Austronesian Malays – has led to the theory of a slow filtration of peoples through the Malay archipelago from southern Indochina. That theory is backed by an almost universal belief in animism, celebration of fertility and ancestor worship among the various peoples.

The Malay archipelago acquired a strategic significance thanks largely to the **shipping trade**, which flourished as early as the first century AD. This was engendered by the two major markets of the early world – India and China – and by the richness of its own resources. From the dense jungle of the Peninsula and northern Borneo came aromatic woods, timber and nipah palm thatch, traded by the forest-dwelling Orang Asli with the coastal Malays, who then bartered or sold it on to Arab and Chinese merchants. The region was also rumoured to be rich in **gold**, leading to its being described by contemporary Greek writers as "The Golden Chersonese" (*chersonese* meaning "peninsula"). Although gold was never found in the supposed quantities, ornaments made of the metal helped to develop decorative traditions among craftsmen, and survive today. More significant, however, were the **tin fields** of the Malay Peninsula, mined in early times to provide an alloy used for temple sculptures. Chinese traders were also attracted by the medicinal properties of various sea products, such as sea slugs, collected by the Orang Laut (sea people), as well as by pearls and tortoise shells.

c.35,000 BC	200 AD	7th c.
Human settlement at Niah in what is now northern Sarawak	Malay Peninsula comes under Indian cultural and religious influence	The Sumatran Sriviyajan empire, encompassing the Malay Peninsula, rises to prominence

For their part, the indigenous peoples acquired cloth, pottery, glass and absorbed the beliefs of those with whom they traded. From as early as 200 AD, **Indian traders** brought their Hindu and Buddhist practices, and archeological evidence from later periods, such as the tenth-century temples at Lembah Bujang (p.170), suggests that the local population not only tolerated these new belief systems, but adapted them to suit their own experiences. Perhaps the most striking contemporary example of such cultural interchange is the traditional entertainment of *wayang kulit* (shadow plays), whose plots are drawn from the Hindu *Ramayana*.

While trade with India developed very early, contact with **China** was initially less pronounced due to the pre-eminence of the Silk Road, further north. Only in the eighth and ninth centuries did Chinese ships first venture into the archipelago. By the time Srivijaya appeared on the scene, a number of states – particularly in the Kelantan and Terengganu areas of the Peninsula – were sending envoys to China.

Srivijaya

The inhabitants of the western Peninsula and eastern Sumatra were quick to realize the geographical advantage afforded by the Melaka Straits, which provided a refuge where ships could wait for several months for a change in the monsoon winds. From the fifth century onwards, a succession of **entrepôts** (storage ports) were created to cater for the needs of passing vessels. One such entrepôt eventually became the mighty empire of **Srivijaya**, eminent from the start of the seventh century until the end of the thirteenth, and encompassing all the shores and islands surrounding the Straits of Melaka. Its exact location is still a matter for debate, although most sources point to **Palembang** in southern Sumatra. Srivijaya's stable administration attracted commerce when insurrection elsewhere frightened traders away, while its wealth was boosted by extracting tolls and taxes from passing ships. Srivijaya also became an important centre for **Mahayana Buddhism** and learning. When the respected Chinese monk I Ching arrived in 671 AD, he found more than a thousand monks studying the Buddhist scriptures.

Political concepts developed during Srivijayan rule were to form the basis of Malay government in future centuries. Unquestioning **loyalty** among subjects was underpinned by the notion of *daulat*, the divine force of the ruler (called the Maharajah), which would strike down anyone guilty of *derhaka* (treason) – a powerful means of control over a deeply superstitious people.

The decision made around 1080 to shift the capital, for reasons unknown, north from Palembang to a place called **Melayu** seems to have marked the start of Srivijaya's decline. Piracy became almost uncontrollable, and even the Orang Laut, who had previously helped keep it in check, turned against the Srivijayan rulers. Soon both local and foreign traders began to seek safer ports, and the area that's now Kedah was a principal beneficiary. Other regions were soon able to compete by replicating the peaceable conditions and efficient administration that had allowed Srivijaya to thrive.

Srivijaya's fate was sealed when it attracted the eye of foreign rivals. In 1275, the Majapahit empire of Java invaded Melayu and made inroads into many of Srivijaya's peninsular territories. Sumatra and Kedah were raided by the Cholas of India, while the Thai kingdom of Ligor was able to extract **tributes** of gold from Malay vassals, a practice

c.14th c.	Early 15th c.	15th c.	1511
Srivijaya is challenged by the Majapahit empire of Java and declines	Paramesevara, a Srivijayan prince, establishes a kingdom at Melaka, which soon flourishes as a Muslim sultanate	The Brunei Sultanate rises to prominence, exercising power over most of northern Borneo	The Portuguese capture Melaka

that continued until the nineteenth century. Moreover, trading restrictions in China were relaxed from the late twelfth century onwards, making it more lucrative for traders to bypass the once mighty entrepôt and go directly to the source of their desired products. Around the early fourteenth century Srivijaya's name disappears from the records.

The Melaka Sultanate

With the collapse of Srivijaya came the establishment of the **Melaka Sultanate**, the Malay Peninsula's most significant historical period. Both the *Sejarah Melayu* and the *Suma Oriental* document the tale of a Palembang prince named **Paramesvara**, who fled the collapsing empire of Srivijaya to set up his own kingdom, finally settling on the site of present-day Melaka.

As well placed as its Sumatran predecessor, with a deep, sheltered harbour and good riverine access to lucrative jungle produce, Melaka set about establishing itself as an international marketplace. The securing of a special agreement in 1405 with the new Chinese emperor, Yung-lo, guaranteed trade to Melaka and protected it from its main rivals. To further ensure its prosperity, Melaka's second ruler, Paramesvara's son **Iskandar Shah** (1414–24), took the precaution of acknowledging the neighbouring kingdoms of Ayuthaya and Majapahit as overlords. In return Melaka received vital supplies and much-needed immigrants, which bolstered the expansion of the settlement.

Port taxes and market regulations were managed by four **shahbandars** (harbour masters), each in charge of trade with certain territories. Hand in hand with the commodities trade went the exchange of ideas. By the thirteenth century, Arab merchants had begun to frequent Melaka's shores, bringing with them **Islam**, which their Muslim Indian counterparts helped to propagate among the Malays. Melaka's prestige was enhanced both by its conversion to Islam, making it part of a worldwide community with profitable trade links, and by territorial expansion which, by the reign of its last ruler **Sultan Mahmud Shah** (1488–1528), included the west coast of the Peninsula as far as Perak, Pahang, Singapore, and most of east-coast Sumatra.

The legacy of **Melaka's golden age** reaches far beyond its material wealth. One significant development, the establishment of a hierarchical **court structure**, was to lay the foundations for a system of government lasting until the nineteenth century. According to Malay royal tradition, the ruler, as head of state, traced his ancestry back through Paramesvara to the maharajahs of ancient Srivijaya; in turn Paramesvara was believed to be descended from Alexander the Great. The ruler also claimed divinity, a belief strengthened by the kingdom's conversion to Islam, which held sultans to be Allah's representatives on earth. To further secure his power, always under threat from the overzealous nobility, the Melaka sultan embarked on a series of measures to emphasize his "otherness": no one but he could wear gold unless it was a royal gift, and yellow garments were forbidden among the general population.

The Melaka Sultanate also allowed the **arts** to flourish; the principal features of the courtly dances and music of this period can still be distinguished in traditional entertainments today. Much more significant, however, was the refinement of **language**, adapting the primitive Malay that had been used in the kingdom of Srivijaya into a language of the elite. Such was Melaka's prestige that all who passed through the entrepôt sought to imitate it, and by the sixteenth century, Malay was the most widely

c.1530	**1641**	**1786**
Alauddin Riayat Shah, son of the deposed Melaka sultan, establishes the Johor Sultanate	The Dutch East India Company seizes Melaka from the Portuguese	Francis Light establishes a port at Penang – the first British settlement in the Malay Peninsula

used language in the archipelago. Tellingly, the word *bahasa*, although literally meaning "language", came to signify Malay culture in general.

The Portuguese conquest of Melaka

It wasn't long before Europe set its sights on the prosperous sultanate. At the start of the sixteenth century, the **Portuguese** began to take issue with Venetian control of the Eastern market. They planned instead to establish direct contacts with the commodity brokers of the East by gaining control of crucial regional ports. The key player in the subsequent conquest of Melaka was Portuguese viceroy **Alfonso de Albuquerque**, who led the assault on the entrepôt in 1511, forcing its surrender after less than a month's siege. Aloof and somewhat effete in their high-necked ruffs and stockings, the Portuguese were not well liked, but despite the almost constant attacks from upriver Malays, they controlled Melaka for the next 130 years.

There are few physical reminders of the Portuguese in Melaka, apart from the gateway to their fort, A Famosa, and the small **Eurasian** community, descendants of intermarriage between the Portuguese and local Malay women. The colonizers had more success with religion, however, converting large numbers of locals to **Catholicism**; their churches still dominate the city.

The Dutch in Melaka

Portuguese control over Melaka lasted for well over a century, until it was challenged by the Vereenigde Oostindische Compagnie (VOC), or **Dutch East India Company**, who were already the masters of Indonesia's valuable spice trade. Melaka was the VOC's most potent rival, and the company's bid to seize the colony succeeded in 1641 when, after a five-month siege, the Dutch flag was hoisted over Melaka.

Instead of trying, like the Portuguese, to rule from above, the Dutch cleverly wove their subjects into the fabric of government. Each racial group was represented by a *kapitan*, a respected figure from the community who mediated between his own people and the new administrators – often becoming wealthy and powerful in his own right. The Dutch were also responsible for the rebuilding of Melaka, much of which had turned to rubble during the protracted takeover of the city; many of these structures, in their distinctive Northern European style, still survive today.

By the mid-eighteenth century, conditions for Melaka's trade with China were at their peak: the relaxation of maritime restrictions in China itself had opened up the Straits for their merchants, while Europeans were eager to satisfy the growing demand for tea. The Chinese came to Melaka in droves and soon established themselves as the city's foremost entrepreneurs. Chinese settlement in the area and, in some cases, intermarriage with local Malay women, created a new cultural blend, known as **Peranakan** or Baba-Nonya – the legacies of which are the opulent mansions and unique cuisine of Melaka, Penang and Singapore.

A number of factors prevented Dutch Melaka from fulfilling its potential, however. Since their VOC salary was hardly bountiful, Dutch administrators found it more lucrative to trade on the black market, taking backhanders from grateful merchants, a situation that severely damaged Melaka's commercial standing. High taxes forced traders to more economical locations such as the newly established British port of

1795	1819	1824
The British East India company captures Dutch possessions in Southeast Asia, including Melaka	Exploiting a succession dispute in Johor, Stamford Raffles negotiates the creation of a British settlement in Singapore	The Anglo-Dutch treaty leaves the British firmly in control of the Malay Peninsula and Singapore

Penang, whose foundation in 1786 heralded the awakening of British interest in the Straits. In the end, Melaka never stood a chance: the company's attention was distracted by other centres such as Batavia (modern-day Jakarta), the VOC "capital", and by the kingdom of Johor.

Johor and Brunei

When Melaka fell to the Portuguese, the deposed sultan, Mahmud Shah, made for Bintan island in the Riau archipelago, just south of Singapore, where he established the first **court of Johor**. When, in 1526, the Portuguese attacked and razed the settlement, Mahmud fled once again, this time to Sumatra, where he died in 1528. It was left to his son, Alauddin Riayat Shah, to found a new court on the upper reaches of the Johor River, though the kingdom's capital was to shift repeatedly during a century of assaults on Johor territory by Portugal and the Sumatran Sultanate of Aceh.

The **arrival of the Dutch** in Southeast Asia marked a distinct upturn in Johor's fortunes. Hoping for protection from its local enemies, the court aligned itself firmly with the Dutch, and was instrumental in their successful siege of Portuguese Melaka. That loyalty was rewarded with trading privileges and assistance in securing a treaty with Aceh, which at last gave Johor the breathing space to develop. Johor was the supreme Malay kingdom for much of the seventeenth century, but by the 1690s its empire was fraying under the despotic rule of another Sultan Mahmud. Lacking strong leadership, Johor's Orang Laut turned to piracy, scaring off trade, while wars with the Sumatran kingdom of Jambi, one of which resulted in the total destruction of Johor's capital, weakened it still further. No longer able to tolerate his cruel regime, Mahmud's nobles stabbed him to death in 1699. Not only did this change the nature of power in

---

THE BUGIS AND MINANGKABAU

Through the second half of the seventeenth century, a new ethnic group, the **Bugis** – renowned for their martial and commercial skills – trickled into the Peninsula, seeking refuge from the civil wars that wracked their homeland of Sulawesi (in the mid-eastern Indonesian archipelago). By the start of the eighteenth century, they were numerous enough to constitute a powerful court lobby, and in 1721 they took advantage of factional struggles to capture the kingdom of Johor, now based in Riau. Installing a Malay puppet sultan, the Bugis ruled for over sixty years, making Riau an essential port of call on the eastern trade route; they even almost succeeded in capturing Melaka in 1756. But when Riau-Johor made another bid for Melaka in 1784, the Dutch held on with renewed vigour and finally forced a treaty placing all Bugis territory in Dutch hands.

In spiritual terms, the **Minangkabau** (see box, p.273), hailing from western Sumatra, had what the Bugis lacked, being able to claim cultural affinity with ancient Srivijaya. Although this migrant group had been present in the Negeri Sembilan region since the fifteenth century, it was in the second half of the seventeenth century that they arrived in the Malay Peninsula in larger numbers. Despite professing allegiance to their Sumatran ruler, the Minangkabau were prepared to accept Malay overlordship, which in practice gave them a great deal of autonomy. Although the warrior Minangkabau were not natural allies of the Bugis or the Malays, they did occasionally join forces to defeat a common enemy. In fact, over time the distinction between various migrant groups became less obvious as intermarriage blurred clan demarcations, and Malay influence, such as the adoption of Malay titles, became more pronounced.

1826	1841	1846	1851
Singapore joined administratively with Penang and Melaka to form the Straits Settlements	With the Brunei Sultanate in decline, James Brooke is installed as the first rajah of Sarawak	Brunei cedes Labuan island to the British	Hugh Low makes the first documented ascent of Gunung

Malay government – previously, law deemed that the sultan could only be punished by Allah – but it also marked the end of the Melaka dynasty.

During Melaka's meteoric rise, **Brunei** had been busily establishing itself as a trading port of some renown. The Brunei Sultanate's conversion to **Islam**, no doubt precipitated by the arrival of wealthy Muslim merchants fleeing from the Portuguese in Melaka, also helped to increase its international prestige. When geographer **Antonio Pigafetta** visited Brunei with **Ferdinand Magellan**'s expedition of 1521, he found the court brimming with visitors from all over the world. This, indeed, was Brunei's "golden age", with its borders embracing land as far south as present-day Kuching in Sarawak, and as far north as the lower islands of the modern-day Philippines. Brunei's efforts, however, were soon curtailed by Spanish colonization in 1578, which, although lasting only a matter of weeks, enabled the Philippine kingdom of Sulu to gain a hold in the area – and thus put paid to Brunei's early expansionist aims.

The arrival of the British

At the end of the eighteenth century, Dutch control in Southeast Asia was more widespread than ever, and the VOC empire should have been at its height. Instead, it had somehow become **bankrupt**. Defeat in the Fourth Anglo-Dutch War (1781–83) lowered Dutch morale still further, and when the British, in the form of the **East India Company** (EIC), moved in on Melaka and the rest of the Dutch Asian domain in 1795, the VOC barely demurred; it was dissolved five years later.

Initially, the British agreed to a caretaker administration whereby they would assume sovereignty over the entrepôt to prevent it falling under French control, now that Napoleon had conquered Holland. By the time the end of the Napoleonic Wars in Europe put the Dutch in a position to retake Melaka, between 1818 and 1825, the EIC had established the stable port of **Penang** and – under the supervision of **Sir Thomas Stamford Raffles** – founded the new settlement of **Singapore**. The strategic position and free-trade policy of Singapore – backed by the impressive industrial developments of the British at home – threatened the viability of both Melaka and Penang, forcing the Dutch finally to relinquish their hold on Melaka to the British, and leaving Penang to dwindle to a backwater. In the face of such stiff competition, smaller Malay rivals inevitably linked their fortunes to the British.

The British assumption of power was sealed by the **Anglo–Dutch Treaty of 1824**, which apportioned territories between the two powers using the Straits of Melaka and the equator as the dividing lines, thereby splitting the Riau-Johor kingdom as well as putting the brakes on centuries of cultural interchange with Sumatra. This was followed in 1826 when Melaka, Penang and Singapore were unified into one administration, known as the **Straits Settlements**. Singapore replaced Penang as its capital in 1832.

Raffles had at first hoped that **Singapore** would act as a market to sell British goods to traders from all over Southeast Asia, but it soon became clear that **Chinese** merchants, the linchpin of Singapore's trade, were interested only in Malay products such as birds' nests, seaweed and camphor. But passing traders were not the only Chinese to come to the Straits. Although settlers had trickled into the Peninsula

1874	1881	1887
Perak becomes the first Malay state to take a British adviser or Resident after the signing of the Pangkor Treaty	The British North Borneo Company takes control over all of what is now Sabah	Having launched Penang's *Eastern and Oriental* hotel two years earlier, the Sarkies brothers create Singapore's *Raffles*

since the early days of Melaka, new **plantations** of pepper and gambier (an astringent used in tanning and dyeing), and the rapidly expanding **tin mines**, attracted floods of workers eager to escape a life of poverty in China. By 1845, half of Singapore's population was Chinese, and likewise principal towns along the Peninsula's west coast (site of the world's largest tin field) and, for that matter, Kuching, became predominantly Chinese.

The Pangkor Treaty

Allowed a large degree of commercial independence by both the British and the Malay chiefs, the Chinese formed **kongsis** (clan associations) and triads (secret societies). The **Malays**, too, were hardly immune from factional conflicts, which frequently became intertwined with Chinese squabbles, causing a string of **civil conflicts**: in Penang in 1867, for example, the triads allied themselves with Malay groups in a bloody street battle that lasted several days.

Such lawlessness was detrimental to commerce, giving the British an excuse to increase their involvement in local affairs. A meeting involving the chiefs of the Perak Malays was arranged by the new Straits Governor, Andrew Clarke, on Pulau Pangkor, just off the west coast of the Peninsula. In the meantime, Rajah Abdullah, the man most likely to succeed to the Perak throne, had written to Clarke asking for his position as sultan to be guaranteed; in return, he offered the British the chance to appoint a **Resident**, a senior British civil servant whose main function would be to act as adviser to the local sultan, and who would also oversee the collecting of local taxes. On January 20, 1874, the **Pangkor Treaty** (see p.134) was signed, formalizing British intervention in Malay political affairs.

Perak's first Resident, J.W.W. Birch, was not sympathetic to the ways of the Malays; his centralizing tendencies were opposed by Abdullah when he became sultan. Fearful of a Malay rebellion, senior British officials announced that judicial decisions would from now on be in the hands of the British. This went against the Pangkor Treaty, and furious Malays soon found a vent for their frustration: on November 2, 1875, Birch was killed on an upriver visit. Only with the appointment of the third Resident of Perak, the respected Hugh Low, did the system start to work more smoothly.

Other states soon saw the arrival of a Resident, and agreements along the lines of the Pangkor Treaty were drawn up with Selangor, Negeri Sembilan and Pahang during the 1880s. In 1896, these three and Perak became bracketed together under the title of the **Federated Malay States**, with the increasingly important town of **Kuala Lumpur** as the capital.

British Malaya

By 1888 the name **British Malaya** had come into use – a term that reflected the intention to extend British control over the whole Peninsula. Over subsequent decades, the economic and administrative powers of the Malay sultans were eroded, while the introduction of rubber estates in the first half of the twentieth century made British Malaya one of the world's most productive colonies. The rapidity and extent of the British takeover in the Peninsula was unprecedented, aided by advances in communications.

1890	1890s	1896
Charles Brooke, second rajah of Sarawak, captures Limbang from Brunei, splitting the sultanate in two	Henry Ridley, director of Singapore's Botanic Gardens, works out how to tap rubber commercially	The Federated Malay States are created, encompassing the four states that have a British Resident, with Kuala Lumpur as capital

The extension of British power brought further unrest, particularly in the east-coast states, where the Malays proved just as resentful of British control as in Perak. A set of skirmishes took place in Pahang in the early 1890s, when Malay chiefs protested about the reduction of their privileges. After one powerful chief, Dato' Bahaman, was stripped of his title by Pahang's Resident, Hugh Clifford, the Dato' led a small rebellion that soon became the stuff of legends. One fighter, **Mat Kilau**, earned a place in folklore as a hero who stood up to the British. From this time, Malays would interpret the uprisings as a valiant attempt to safeguard their traditions and autonomy.

By 1909, the northern Malay states of Kedah and Perlis had been brought into the colonial fold. In 1910, Johor accepted a British general-adviser; a 1914 treaty between Britain and Johor made his powers equal to those of Residents elsewhere. Terengganu, which was under Thai control, was the last state to accept a British adviser, in 1919. These four states, together with Kelantan, were sometimes collectively referred to as the **Unfederated Malay States**, though they shared no common administration.

By the outbreak of World War I, British political control was more or less complete. The Peninsula was subdivided into groups of states and regions with the seat of power split between Singapore and Kuala Lumpur.

The expansion of British interests in Borneo

The Anglo-Dutch Treaty did not include **Borneo**, where official expansion was discouraged by the EIC, which preferred to concentrate on expanding its trading contacts rather than territorial control. The benefits of Borneo did not, however, elude the sights of one British explorer, **James Brooke** (1803–68). Finding lawlessness throughout the island, Brooke persuaded the Sultan of Brunei to award him his own area – **Sarawak** – in 1841, becoming the first of a line of "**White Rajahs**" who ruled the state until World War II. Brooke quickly asserted his authority by involving formerly rebellious Malay chiefs in government, although the interior's tribes proved more of a problem. Subsequently Brooke and his successors proved adept at siphoning more land into the familial fiefdom.

Though the association between the British and James Brooke was informal (Brooke was careful not to encourage European contacts that might compromise his hold), trade between Singapore and Sarawak flourished. By the mid-nineteenth century, however, the British attitude had altered; they chose Brooke as their agent in Brunei, and found him a useful deterrent against French and Dutch aspirations towards the valuable trade routes. Eventually, in 1888, Sarawak, North Borneo (Sabah) and Brunei were transformed into **protectorates**, a status that entailed responsibility for their foreign policy being handed over to the British.

The legacy of James Brooke was furthered by his nephew **Charles Brooke** in the second half of the nineteenth century. Like his uncle, Charles ruled Sarawak in paternalistic fashion, recruiting soldiers, lowly officials and boatmen from the ranks of the tribal groups and leaving the Chinese to get on with running commercial enterprises and opening up the interior. **Vyner Brooke**, Charles's eldest son, became rajah in 1917; his reign saw no new territorial acquisitions, though there was a steady development in rubber, pepper and palm-oil production. The tribal peoples mostly continued living a traditional lifestyle in longhouses along the river, while the end of their practice of head-hunting was followed by some degree of integration among the area's varied racial groups.

1917	1933	Dec 1941	Feb 1942
Vyner Brooke becomes the third and, as it turns out, last rajah of Sarawak	The first Malay-language feature film, *Laila Majnun*, is made in Singapore	Japan lands forces in Kelantan and captures Miri in Sarawak	Singapore falls to the Japanese

By way of contrast, the **British North Borneo Chartered Company**'s writ in what became Sabah encountered some early obstacles. The company's plans for economic expansion involved clearing the rainforest, planting **rubber** and **tobacco** over large areas, and levying taxes on the tribes. Resistance ensued, with the most vigorous action, in 1897, led by a Bajau chief, **Mat Salleh**, whose men rampaged through the company's outstation on Pulau Gaya. Another rebellion by **Murut** tribespeople in 1915 resulted in a heavy-handed response from British forces, who killed hundreds.

By the start of the twentieth century, the majority of the lands of the once-powerful **Sultanate of Brunei** had been dismembered – the sultanate was now surrounded by Sarawak. But the sultan's fortunes had not completely disappeared and with the discovery of oil, the British thought it prudent to appoint a Resident. Exploitation of the small state's oil fields gathered pace in the 1930s following investment from British companies.

Development and ethnic rivalries

In the first quarter of the twentieth century, the British encouraged hundreds of thousands of **immigrants** from China and India to come to Peninsular Malaysia, Sarawak, North Borneo and Singapore. They arrived to work as tin miners or plantation labourers, and Malaya's population in this period doubled to four million. This bred increasing resentment among the Malays, who believed that they were being denied the economic opportunities advanced to others.

A further deterioration in Malay–Chinese relations followed the success of mainland Chinese revolutionary groups in Malaya. Malayan Chinese joined the **Malayan Communist Party** (MCP) from 1930 onwards and also formed the backbone of postwar Chinese movements that demanded an end to British rule and what they perceived as special privileges extended to the Malays. At the same time, Malay nationalism was gathering its own head of steam. The **Singapore Malay Union**, which held its first conference in 1939, advocated a Malay supremacist line. A year earlier, the first All-Malaya Malays Conference, organized by the Selangor Malays Association, had been held in KL.

The Japanese occupation

Landing in Kelantan in December 1941, Japanese forces took barely two months to sweep down the Peninsula and reach Singapore. The **surrender** of the British forces there in February 1942 ushered in a Japanese regime that brutalized the Chinese, largely because of Japan's history of conflict with China; at least 25,000 people were tortured and killed in the two weeks immediately after the surrender of the island by the British military command. Allied POWs were rounded up into prison camps; many of the troops were subsequently sent to build the infamous "Death Railway" in Burma.

In **Malaya**, towns and buildings were destroyed as the Allies attempted to bomb strategic targets. But with the Japanese firmly in control, the occupiers ingratiated themselves with some of the Malay elite by suggesting that after the war the country would be given independence. Predictably, it was the Chinese activists in the MCP, more than the Malays, who organized resistance during wartime.

December 1941 also saw the Japanese invade **Sarawak**, beginning with the capture of the Miri oil field. Although the Japanese never penetrated the interior, they quickly

September 1945	1946	1946
Japanese forces in Southeast Asia formally surrender in Singapore	Britain introduces the Malayan Union, turning Malaya into a full colony rather than a protectorate	Despite local protests, Vyner Brooke cedes Sarawak to the British government, bringing the White Rajahs' dynasty to an end

established control over the populated towns along the coast. The Chinese in Miri, Sibu and Kuching were the main targets: the Japanese put down rebellions brutally, and there was no organized guerrilla activity until late in the occupation. What resistance there was arose from "Z Force", namely Major **Tom Harrisson** and a team of British and Australian commandos, who in 1945 parachuted into the remote Kelabit Highlands to build a resistance movement.

In **North Borneo**, the Japanese invaded Pulau Labuan on New Year's Day, 1942. Over the next three years the main suburban areas were bombed by the Allies, destroying most of Jesselton (modern-day KK) and Sandakan. Captured troops and civilians suffered enormously – the worst single outrage being the "Death March" in September 1944, when 2400 POWs were forced to walk from Sandakan to Ranau (see p.433).

In September 1945, just prior to a planned Allied invasion to retake Singapore, the **Japanese surrendered** following the dropping of atom bombs on Nagasaki and Hiroshima. The surrender led to a power vacuum in the region, with the British initially having to work with the MCP's armed wing, the **Malayan People's Anti-Japanese Army** (MPAJA), to maintain order in many areas. Violence occurred between the MPAJA and Malays, particularly against those accused of collaborating with the Japanese.

Postwar upheaval

Immediately after the war, the British introduced the **Malayan Union**, in effect turning the Malay States from a protectorate into a colony and removing the sovereignty of the sultans. Another effect was to give the Chinese and Indian inhabitants citizenship and equal rights with the Malays. This quickly aroused opposition from the Malays, the nationalists among whom formed the **United Malays National Organization** (UMNO) in 1946. Its main tenet was that Malays should retain special privileges, largely because they were the first inhabitants, and that the uniquely powerful position of the sultans should not be tampered with.

UMNO's resistance led to the Malayan Union idea being replaced by the **Federation of Malaya**. Established in 1948, this upheld the sultans' power and privileges and brought all the Peninsula's territories together under one government, apart from Chinese-dominated Singapore, whose inclusion would have led to the Malays being in a minority overall. Protests erupted in Singapore at its exclusion, with the **Malayan Democratic Union** (MDU), a multiracial party, calling for integration with Malaya – a position that commanded little support among the Chinese population.

After the Japanese surrender in **Borneo**, the Colonial Office in London made Sarawak and North Borneo **Crown Colonies**, with Vyner Brooke offering no objection. Sarawakians were torn over the change in arrangements, however: while the ruling assembly, the Council Negeri (composed of Malays, Chinese, Iban and British), had voted to transfer power to Britain, some Malays and prominent Iban in Kuching opposed the move. Protests reached a peak with the assassination in Sibu in 1949 of the senior official in the new administration, Governor Duncan Stewart. But on the whole, resentment at the passing of the Brooke era was short-lived as the economy expanded and infrastructure improved. Britain also signed a Treaty of Protection with the Sultan of Brunei, who remained the chief power in the state while Sarawak's high commissioner took on the purely decorative role of governor of Brunei.

1946	1948	1948
The British North Borneo Company cedes Sabah to the British government	Malay opposition to the Malayan Union leads to its replacement by the Federation of Malaya, which respects the status of the sultans	The Malayan Community Party launches an insurgency from the jungle, which comes to be called The Emergency

The Emergency

Many Chinese in the Peninsula were angered when the country changed status from a colony to a federation, effectively making them second-class citizens. According to the new laws, non-Malays could only qualify as citizens if they had lived in the country for fifteen out of the last twenty-five years, and they also had to prove they spoke Malay or English.

Following the communist takeover in China in 1949, most Malayan Chinese ceased to look to China; the more political among them founded a new political party, the **Malayan Chinese Association** (MCA). Some local Chinese, however, identified with the MCP, which under its new leader, **Chin Peng**, declared its intention of setting up a Malayan republic. Peng fused the MCP with the remains of the MPAJA, and, using arms supplies that the latter had dumped in the forests, from June 1948 he launched sporadic attacks on rubber estates, killing planters and employees as well as spreading fear among rural communities. This civil conflict, which lasted until 1960, was euphemistically called **the Emergency** for insurance purposes; planters would have had their policies cancelled if war had been officially declared. At its peak, around ten thousand of Chin Peng's guerrillas were hiding out in jungle camps, using a support network of Chinese-dominated towns and villages in the interior. In many cases inhabitants were cowed into submission by means of public executions, though many poor rural workers identified with the insurgents' struggle.

Although the Emergency was never fully felt in the main urban areas, British rubber-estate owners would arrive at the *Coliseum Hotel* in KL with harrowing stories of how "communist terrorists" had hacked off the arms of rural Chinese workers who refused to support the cause, and of armed attacks on plantations.

The British were slow to respond to the threat, but once Lieutenant-General Sir Harold Briggs was put in command of police and army forces, Malaya was on a war footing. Briggs' most controversial policy was the **resettlement** of 400,000

THE EMERGENCY AND THE ORANG ASLI

The impact of the Emergency on the **Orang Asli** of the interior was dramatic. All but the most remote tribes were subject to intimidation and brutality, from guerrillas on one side and government forces on the other. In effect, the Orang Asli's centuries-old invisibility had ended; the population of Malaysia was now aware of their presence, and the government of their strategic importance.

The Orang Asli had no choice but to grow food and act as porters for the guerrillas, as well as – most important of all – provide intelligence, warning them of the approach of the enemy. In response, the government implemented a disastrous policy of removing thousands of Orang Asli from the jungle and relocating them in new model villages in the interior, which were no more than dressed-up prison camps. Hundreds died in captivity before the government dismantled these settlements. By then, not surprisingly, active support for the insurgents among the Orang Asli had risen – though allegiances switched to the security forces when it became clear the guerrillas were heading for defeat. Government attempts to control the Orang Asli during the Emergency turned out to be the precursor to initiatives that persist to the present day, drawing the Orang Asli away from their traditional lifestyle and into the embrace of the Malaysian nation-state.

---

rural Chinese – mostly squatters who had moved to the jungle fringes to avoid the Japanese during the war – as well as thousands of Orang Asli. Although these forced migrations were successful in breaking down many of the guerrillas' supply networks, they alienated many Chinese and Orang Asli who had previously been sympathetic to the British.

The violence peaked in 1950 with ambushes and attacks near Ipoh, Kuala Kangsar, Kuala Lipis and Raub. The most notorious incident occurred in 1951 on the road to Fraser's Hill, when the British high commissioner to Malaya, **Sir Henry Gurney**, was assassinated. Under his replacement, Sir Gerald Templer, a new policy was introduced to win hearts and minds. "White Areas", perceived as free of guerrilla activity, were established; communities in these regions had food restrictions and curfews lifted, a policy that began to dissipate guerrilla activity over the next three years. The leaders were offered an amnesty in 1956, which was refused, and Chin Peng and most of the remaining cell members fled over the border to Thailand where they received sanctuary.

Towards independence

The Emergency had the effect of speeding up political change prior to independence. UMNO stuck to its "Malays first" policy, though its president, **Tunku Abdul Rahman** (also the chief minister of Malaya), won the 1955 election by cooperating with the MCA and the Malayan Indian Association. The resulting bloc, the **UMNO Alliance**, swept into power under the rallying cry of **Merdeka** (Freedom). The hope was that ethnic divisions would no longer be a major factor if **independence** was granted.

With British backing, *merdeka* was proclaimed on August 31, 1957 in a ceremony in Kuala Lumpur's padang – promptly renamed Merdeka Square. The British high commissioner signed a treaty that decreed that the **Federation of Malaya** was now independent of the Crown, with Tunku Abdul Rahman the first prime minister. The new **constitution** allowed for the nine Malay sultans to alternate as king, and established a two-tier **parliament**, comprising a house of elected representatives and a senate with delegates from each state. Under Rahman, the country was fully committed to economic expansion, with foreign investment actively encouraged – a stance that has survived to the present.

Similarly, in **Singapore** the process of gaining independence acquired momentum throughout the 1950s. In 1957, the British gave the go-ahead for the setting up of an elected 51-member assembly, and full **self-government** was attained in 1959, when the People's Action Party (PAP) under **Lee Kuan Yew** won most of the seats. Lee immediately entered into talks with Tunku Abdul Rahman over the notion that Singapore and Malaya should be joined administratively. Tunku initially agreed, although he feared the influence of the far left in the PAP.

In 1961, Tunku Abdul Rahman proposed that Sarawak and North Borneo should join Malaya and Singapore in an enlarged federation. Many in Borneo would have preferred the idea of a separate Borneo Federation, although the Konfrontasi (see opposite) was to make clear how vulnerable such a federation would be to attack from Indonesia. Rahman's suggestion was, however, not fuelled by security concerns but by **demographics**: if Singapore were to join the federation, the country would acquire a Chinese majority. This made the two Borneo colonies useful as a counterweight to Singapore's Chinese.

September 1963	**August 1965**	**May 1969**
The Federation of Malaya becomes the Federation of Malaysia, augmented by Singapore, Sarawak and Sabah; Brunei opts out	Singapore leaves the Federation and goes it alone as an independent country	Deadly race riots scar Kuala Lumpur

Although Abdul Rahman had wanted **Brunei** to join the Malaysian Federation, Sultan Omar refused when he realized Rahman's price – a substantial proportion of Brunei's oil and gas revenues. Brunei remained under nominal British jurisdiction until its **independence** on January 1, 1984.

Federation and the Konfrontasi

In September 1963, North Borneo (quickly renamed Sabah), Sarawak and Singapore joined Malaya in the **Federation of Malaysia** – "Malaysia" being a term coined by the British in the 1950s when the notion of a Greater Malaya had been propounded. Both Indonesia, which laid claim to Sarawak, and the Philippines, which claimed jurisdiction over Sabah as it had originally been part of the Sulu Sultanate, reacted angrily. Border skirmishes with Indonesia known as the **Konfrontasi** ensued, and a wider war was only just averted when Indonesian President Sukarno backed down from taking on British and Gurkha troops brought in to bolster Sarawak's small armed forces.

Within the federation, further differences surfaced in Singapore during this period between Lee Kuan Yew and the Malay-dominated Alliance over the lack of egalitarian policies; many Chinese were concerned that UMNO's overall influence in the federation was too great. Tensions rose on the island and racial incidents developed into full-scale **riots** in 1964, in which several people were killed.

These developments were viewed with great concern by Tunku Abdul Rahman in Kuala Lumpur, and when the PAP subsequently attempted to enter Peninsular politics, he decided it would be best if Singapore left the federation. This was emphatically not in Singapore's best interests, since it was an island without any obvious natural resources; Lee cried on TV when the expulsion was announced and Singapore acquired full **independence** on August 9, 1965. The severing of the bond between Malaysia and Singapore has led to a kind of sibling rivalry between the two nations ever since (see p.578).

Racial issues and riots

Singapore's exit from the Malaysian Federation was not enough to quell ethnic tensions. Resentment grew among the Malaysian Chinese over the principle that Malay be the main language taught in schools and over the privileged employment opportunities offered to Malays. After the Alliance lost ground in elections in May 1969, Malays in major cities reacted angrily to a perceived increase in power of the Chinese, who had commemorated their breakthrough with festivities in the streets. Hundreds of people, mostly Chinese, were killed and injured in the **riots** that followed; KL in particular became a war zone with large crowds of youths on the rampage. Rahman kept the country under a state of emergency for nearly two years, during which the draconian **Internal Security Act** (ISA) was used to arrest and imprison activists, as well as many writers and artists, setting a sombre precedent for authoritarian practices still followed today.

Rahman never recovered full political command and resigned in 1970. That September, the new prime minister, **Tun Abdul Razak**, initiated a form of state-orchestrated positive discrimination called the **New Economic Policy** (NEP), which

1971	**1981**	**1984**
The Malaysian government introduces its New Economic Policy, including positive discrimination in favour of Malays	Mahathir Mohamad, to become Malaysia's long-serving prime minister, takes office	Brunei becomes independent

gives ethnic Malays and members of Borneo's tribes favoured positions in business and other professions. Also under Razak, a crucial step was taken towards Malaysia's current political map with the formation in 1974 of the **Barisan Nasional** ("National Front", usually abbreviated to **BN**), comprising UMNO plus the main Chinese and Indian parties and – since the 1990s – parties representing indigenous groups in Sabah and Sarawak. This multi-ethnic coalition has governed the country ever since.

The Mahathir era

The dominant figure in Malaysian politics since independence has been **Dr Mahathir Mohamad**, prime minister from 1981 until 2003. Even Malaysians not generally favourably disposed towards the BN credit him with helping the country attain economic lift-off; under Mahathir, industrialization changed the landscape of regions like the Klang Valley and Johor, manufacturing output eclipsed agriculture in importance, and huge **prestige projects** like the Petronas Towers and KLIA were completed. Mahathir meanwhile kept his supporters happy with a raft of populist pronouncements, including railing against the West for criticizing Malaysia's human-rights record (he claimed that by what he termed "Asian values", prosperity was valued

---

THE BUMIPUTRA POLICY

Provisions in the New Economic Policy (NEP), introduced in the wake of the 1969 race riots, became known as the **bumiputra policy** as they were intended to provide a more level economic playing field for Malays, Orang Asli and the indigenous peoples of east Malaysia (*bumiputra* means something like "sons of the soil" in Malay). In terms of wealth, these communities (as well the Indians) were lagging far behind the Chinese. This was partly the result of colonial policy: the immigrant Chinese made strides as businesspeople in the towns, while the Malays were either employed as administrators or left to get on with farming and fishing in rural areas, while the Indians toiled on the railways and the plantations.

The policy has been moderated over the years, but basically awards *bumiputras*, in particular the Malays, privileges such as subsidized housing and easier access to higher education and civil-service jobs. The *bumiputra* policy has undoubtedly achieved a reasonable degree of **wealth redistribution**, though a less laudable consequence has been the creation of a super-rich Malay elite. What's more, the policy is deeply resented by the non-beneficiaries. The Indians are especially aggrieved, having never been wealthy; the Chinese have continued to rely on their own devices in business while shunning the public sector, where they feel the odds have been stacked against them.

Despite the policy's undoubted popularity among Malays, Mahathir and his successors have questioned the wisdom of allowing the system to continue indefinitely, fearing that it has fostered complacency in the very communities it is meant to help. The difficulty for all UMNO leaders is that any meaningful retreat from the policy requires political daring. Only the opposition, which generally wants to reform Malaysian politics in a nonracial mould, has attempted to make progress in this regard, though it is just as risky an enterprise for them. In 2008, when a leading opposition figure suggested that the publicly funded MARA Technology University should at last be open to non-Malay students, Malays in the opposition's own grassroots were unsettled. They had not quite realized that they, too, would be called upon to make sacrifices in the cause of a more transparent and equitable country.

1987	1997	1998
The Malaysia government launches Operation Lalang, a major crackdown against its critics and sectors of the press	The Asian economic crisis envelopes the region	Anwar Ibrahim, Malaysia's deputy prime minister and finance minister, is sacked by Mahathir and subsequently convicted of corruption and sodomy

more highly than civil liberties). Less well remembered is the fact that Mahathir's tenure also saw the extensive use of the ISA in what became known as **Operation Lalang** when, in 1987, more than a hundred politicians and activists were detained following tensions between UMNO and Chinese political parties over matters to do with Chinese-language education. These arrests were bad enough, but more durable in its effects was state action to curb press freedom. Especially notable was the government's closure of the pro-MCA English-language *Star* newspaper for several months; when it reopened, many of its senior managers had been replaced.

In 1997, the economy suffered a major setback when Malaysia was sucked into the **Asian economic crisis**, which began in Thailand and Korea. Mahathir took personal charge of getting the economy back on track, sacking his deputy and finance minister **Anwar Ibrahim** in 1998. A former student leader and once an espouser of progressive Islamic policies, Anwar had enjoyed a meteoric rise upon joining UMNO and had been groomed to succeed Mahathir, though relations between the two subsequently soured. The nation was stunned when, within a week of his dismissal, Anwar was arrested on corruption and sexual misconduct charges; a succession of mass demonstrations in his support ensued. Anwar's treatment in detention became the subject of much concern when he appeared in court on the corruption charge sporting a black eye. He was eventually found guilty – leading many observers to question the independence of the judiciary – and sentenced to six years in jail. In 2000, he was also found guilty of sodomizing his driver and sentenced to nine years in prison.

Meanwhile, Anwar's wife, Wan Azizah Wan Ismail, formed a new party, **Keadilan** ("Justice", sometimes also called **PKR**), which has contested subsequent elections in alliance with other opposition parties, including the Chinese-dominated Democratic Action Party (**DAP**) and the Islamist **PAS**.

Malaysia under Abdullah Badawi

Momentously, in 2003, Mahathir resigned and handed power to Anwar's replacement as deputy prime minister, **Abdullah Badawi**. Hailing from Penang, Abdullah (often referred to as Pak Lah) is a genial man, in marked contrast to his abrasive predecessor, and he asserted himself effectively, winning a landslide general election victory in 2004. Soon after, Anwar's sodomy conviction was overturned and he was released, though he remained barred from standing for parliament until 2008 as his corruption conviction was not quashed.

As a relatively new broom, Abdullah enjoyed much goodwill early on; it was hoped he would make good on his promises to sweep cronyism and corruption out of Malaysian politics. But as time wore on, authority seemed to ebb away from his government in the face of crises and scandals.

The first and most sensational of these was the affair of **Altantuya Shaariibuu**, a Mongolian woman who went missing in the KL area in 2006. Her remains, which had been blown to bits with explosives, were soon discovered, and it transpired that she was an associate of a defence analyst with links to **Najib Tun Razak**, Abdullah's deputy. The case created a stink around the government, but potentially more damaging was the brief flowering of **HINDRAF**, the Hindu Rights Action Force, in 2007. Representing Malaysia's Hindu Indian community, HINDRAF was aggrieved over dubious

2003	2004	2004
Abdullah Badawi succeeds Mahathir as Malaysian prime minister	Anwar Ibrahim is freed from jail having had only his sodomy conviction overturned	Lee Hsien Loong, Lee Kuan Yew's son, becomes prime minister of Singapore

NEIGHBOURLY SPATS: THE CASE OF MALAYSIA AND SINGAPORE

Ever since 1965, when Singapore left the Federation of Malaysia after just two bitter years of membership, relations between the governments of the two countries have been characterized by constant **bickering**. Early on, tiny Singapore attempted to bolster its security by establishing close ties with Indonesia and military links with Israel, moves that could only annoy Malaysia. Subsequent decades have seen a series of issues souring relations, ranging from rows over the price at which Malaysia supplies Singapore with water to recriminations over unguarded remarks made by various politicians. These included a notorious episode when Singapore's ex-prime minister, Lee Kuan Yew, appeared to intimate that Johor Bahru was a hotbed of crime. There have also been tensions over Malaysia's creation of a port at **Tanjung Pelepas** in southern Johor, which Singapore sees as a threat to its historic *raison d'être* in shipping. Furthermore, Malaysia for a time threatened to build a bizarre "**crooked bridge**" replacing the portion of the causeway within its waters, in order, so it argued, to improve access to ports on its side. Diplomatic tensions aside, some Malaysians view Singaporeans as being brash and uptight, while Singaporeans occasionally look down on Malaysians as poor relations.

Ironically, all this belies the fact that the two countries are like a pair of twins who squabble despite having a vast amount in common. Each also has significant **investments** on the opposite side of the causeway: for example, the Malaysian company behind the Genting Highlands casino near KL runs Singapore's casino at Sentosa. Furthermore, many Malaysians head to Singapore for work or to attend university courses. At least relations have thawed in recent years, with new prime ministers at the helm in both countries. In 2011 the two states unexpectedly resolved a long-standing quarrel over the KTM railway line in Singapore, allowing Singapore to take possession of the line and shut it down for redevelopment; meanwhile Malaysia is encouraging Singapore to extend its considerable investments in Johor, with new transport links among grand projects in the pipeline.

conversions of Hindus to Islam, the demolitions of several Hindu shrines said by the government to have been built without proper approval, and the fact that Hindu Indians continue to languish near the bottom of the economic pile in Malaysia, without the benefits that Muslim Indians can claim. That November, the group tried to deliver a petition to the British High Commission in KL asking for reparations for the transport of Tamil indentured labourers to Malaysia by the British. During a nasty stand-off between police and thousands of marchers nearby in KLCC, tear gas and water cannon were used to disperse demonstrators. What could not be so readily dispelled was the damage to the BN's reputation for protecting the rights and livelihoods of all of Malaysia's ethnic groups.

The 2008 elections

In February 2008, Abdullah called a **snap general election** for the following month – when Anwar Ibrahim was still barred from standing. If the timing was maximally convenient for Abdullah, the result was anything but: the BN was duly returned to power, but on its **worst showing** since its formation in 1974. This time, the BN failed to win more than two-thirds of seats in parliament, which had hitherto afforded it the right to tinker with the constitution. To make matters worse, the opposition alliance unseated the BN in an unprecedented number of **state assemblies**, not just in largely

Dec 2004	March 2008	August 2008
Penang and Kedah in Malaysia are struck by the Indian Ocean tsunami, though with only modest loss of life	Malaysia's opposition enjoys its best general election showing since independence	A ban on his standing for election having elapsed, Anwar Ibrahim wins a by-election and returns to parliament

Malay Kedah, where voters had previously flirted with PAS, but also in cosmopolitan, prosperous Selangor, Penang and Perak.

In the wake of the election, amid euphoria and recrimination, everything in Malaysian politics seemed to be up for grabs. A more clinical assessment would be that a large number of voters, not necessarily comprehending the opposition's platform but galvanized by such issues as cronyism, social and racial inequalities, rising crime and the soaring cost of fuel, were intent on firing a warning shot across the BN's bows. Perhaps the worst news for Abdullah was how badly the BN fared in the Peninsula, home to three-quarters of the population: its majority there was wafer-thin, and it took just one out of eleven seats in KL. Only victories by the BN-allied parties of Sabah and Sarawak had secured the coalition a working majority.

Testing times

Unfortunately for Abdullah, things got no better for the BN in the aftermath of the polls, as the various affairs that had come to light beforehand played themselves out like a tragicomic drama. Against this turbulent backdrop, **Anwar Ibrahim** made a triumphant return to parliament in August 2008, his wife resigning her seat so that he could stand in a by-election. Just prior to all this, however, Anwar was sensationally arrested once again on a charge of sodomy, this time involving a young aide of his. Allowed bail, Anwar took up his new role as leader of the opposition coalition, **Pakatan Rakyat**, while having to make appearances in court. Then in 2009 Abdullah Badawi stepped down, to be replaced by his deputy **Najib Tun Razak**. The son of Malaysia's second prime minister, he perhaps lacks the common touch but has performed creditably enough thus far, though any intentions he may have of introducing meaningful reforms are constrained by the presence of conservatives within his own ranks.

As this book went to press, prospects for the ruling coalition to hold its ground at the next election (due in or before 2013) were not assured, as demonstrated by its relatively poor performance in the 2011 local elections in Sarawak, hitherto one of its key strongholds. While Anwar was cleared of the second sodomy charge at the start of 2012, he and other opposition leaders will need to articulate their vision more clearly if they are to make significant headway.

If there is a ray of hope amid the murk, it is that Malaysian democracy is enjoying a little renaissance. Now that there are so many more elected opposition politicians, the press is less cowed about reporting their activities, and civil rights organizations are campaigning more vocally, as borne out by the **Bersih 2** rally to clean up electoral fraud, which brought parts of downtown KL to a standstill in July 2011. All this means that thorny issues around corruption, race and religion, long swept under the carpet of economic progress, are being debated with some rancour, but also more thoroughly and purposefully.

2009	May 2011	2012
Najib Tun Razak becomes Malaysian prime minister	The Singapore opposition enjoys its best election showing since independence	Anwar Ibrahim is cleared of his second sodomy charge

Religion

Islam is a significant force in Malaysia, given that virtually all Malays, who comprise just over half the population, are Muslim; in Singapore, where three-quarters of the population are Chinese, Buddhism is the main religion. There's a smaller, but no less significant, Hindu Indian presence in both countries, while the other chief belief system is animism, adhered to by many of the indigenous peoples of Malaysia. While the colonial period drew Christian missionaries to the region, the British, in a bid to avoid unrest among the Malays, were restrained in their evangelical efforts. Christian missionaries had more success in Borneo than on the Peninsula; indeed, the main tribal group in Sabah, the Kadazan, is Christian, as are many or most Kelabit and Iban in Sarawak. That said, Christianity is a significant minority religion in Peninsular Malaysia and Singapore, with a notable following among middle-class Chinese and Indians.

One striking feature of religion here is that it can be a **syncretic** blend of beliefs and influences. In a region where fusion is visible in everything from food to language, it's not hard to come across individuals who profess one faith, yet pray or make offerings to deities of another, in the warm-hearted belief that all religions contain some truth and that it therefore makes sense not to put all your spiritual eggs in one devotional basket.

Animism

Although many of Malaysia's indigenous groups are now nominally Christian or Muslim, many of their old animist beliefs and rites still survive. In the animist world-view, everything in nature – mountains, trees, rocks and lakes – has a controlling soul or spirit (**semangat** in Malay) that has to be mollified. For the Orang Asli groups in the interior of the Peninsula, remaining animist beliefs often centre on healing and funeral ceremonies. A sick person, particularly a child, is believed to be invaded by a bad spirit, and drums are played and incantations performed to persuade the spirit to depart. The death of a member of the family is followed by a complex process of burial and reburial – a procedure that, it is hoped, ensures an easy passage for the person's spirit.

In Sarawak, **birds**, especially the **hornbill**, are of particular significance to the Iban and Kelabit peoples. Many Kelabit depend upon the arrival of migrating flocks to decide when to plant their rice crop, while Iban augury interprets sightings of the hornbill and other birds as good or bad omens. In some accounts of Iban beliefs, two bird spirits are involved in the creation of the Earth and sky, and the Iban themselves are descended from a bird spirit named Sengalang Burong.

Hinduism

Hinduism arrived in Malaysia long before Islam, brought by Indian traders more than a thousand years ago. While almost all of Malaysia's ancient Hindu past has been obliterated, elements live on in the popular arts like *wayang kulit* (shadow plays), the plots of which are drawn from the sacred *Ramayana*.

The central tenet of Hinduism is the belief that life is a series of rebirths and reincarnations that eventually lead to spiritual release. A whole variety of deities are worshipped, which on the surface makes Hinduism appear complex; however, a loose understanding of the *Vedas* – the religion's holy books – is enough for the characters and roles of the main gods to become apparent. The deities you'll come across most often are the three manifestations of the faith's supreme divine being: **Brahma** the creator, **Vishnu** the preserver and **Shiva** the destroyer.

Hinduism returned to the Peninsula in the late nineteenth century when immigrants from southern India arrived to work on the Malayan rubber and oil-palm plantations. The Hindu celebration of Rama's victory – the central theme of the *Ramayana* – in time became the national holiday of **Deepavali** (or Diwali; the festival of lights), while another Hindu festival, **Thaipusam**, when Lord Subramaniam and elephant-headed Ganesh, the sons of Shiva, are worshipped, is marked by some of the region's most prominent religious gatherings.

Step over the threshold of a **Hindu temple** in Malaysia or Singapore and you enter a kaleidoscope world of gods and fanciful creatures. The style is typically Dravidian (South Indian), as befits the largely Tamil population, with a soaring **gopuram**, or entrance tower, teeming with sculptures and a central courtyard leading to an inner sanctum housing the presiding deity. In the temple precinct, you'll invariably witness incense being burned, the application of sandalwood paste to the forehead, and *puja* (ritualistic acts of worship).

Islam

Islam gained its first firm foothold in the Malay Peninsula with the conversion of Paramesvara, the ruler of **Melaka**, in the early fifteenth century. The commercial success of Melaka accelerated the spread of Islam; one after another the powerful Malay court rulers took to the religion, adopting the Arabic title "sultan", either because of sincere conversion or because they took a shrewd view of the advantages to be gained by embracing this international faith. On a cultural level, too, Islam had its attractions – its concepts of equality before Allah freed people from the Hindu caste system that had dominated parts of the region. Even after the Melaka Sultanate fell in 1511, the hold of Islam was strengthened by the migration of Muslim merchants to Brunei.

The first wave of Islamic missionaries were mostly **Sufis**, representing the mystical and generally more liberal wing of Islam. In the region Sufism absorbed some animist and Hindu beliefs, including the tradition of pluralist deity worship. However, Sufism's influence declined in the early nineteenth century when the puritanical **Wahhabi** sect of mainstream **Sunni** Islam captured Mecca. The return to the Koran's basic teachings became identified with a more militant approach, leading to jihads in Kedah, Kelantan and Terengganu against the Malay rulers' Siamese overlords and, subsequently, the British.

Islam in Malaysia and Singapore today is a mixture of Sunni and Sufi elements, and its adherents are still largely comprised of Malays, though a minority of the Indian community is Muslim, too. While Islam as practised locally is relatively liberal, the trend away from tacit secularism that has swept the Muslim world in the last two or three decades, has not left the two countries untouched. There's now a better understanding of Islam's tenets – and thus better compliance with them – among Muslims in both countries.

Of course, this drift has its social and political dimensions. In Malaysia, with its history of sometimes awkward race relations, Islam is something of a badge of identity for the Malays; it's significant that the Malaysian **constitution** practically regards being Malay as equivalent to being Muslim. Thus Malaysia has seen an increase in religious programming on TV and in state spending on often ostentatious new mosques, while even in consumerist Singapore, the Malay minority is becoming more actively engaged in religion. Malaysia's religious establishment has also become more vocal, making proclamations to discourage Muslims from practising yoga (because of its supposed Hindu origins) and Muslim women from wearing short hair and trousers (because this would apparently encourage lesbianism), though such decrees have no legal weight unless states of the federation adopt them into their law. All of this said, for most Muslims in Malaysia and Singapore, Islam remains a matter not of dogma but of blending a personal interpretation of the religion with living in a multi-faith community and exploiting the opportunities for personal development brought by economic growth.

Islam and the law

One striking way in which Islam influences day-to-day affairs is that in certain areas, Muslim and non-Muslim citizens are subject to different **laws**. In Malaysia, for example, a Muslim man may avail himself of the Islamic provision for a man to take up to four wives, if certain criteria are met, but non-Muslim men are subject to the usual injunctions against bigamy and polygamy. Likewise, while it would be acceptable for an unmarried couple to share a hotel room if neither person is Muslim, it would be illegal (an act known as **khalwat**) if both were Muslim; if only one of them were Muslim, only that person would be committing an illegal act. This legal divide is reflected in the judicial systems of both Malaysia and Singapore, in which **syariah** (sharia) courts interpreting Islamic law exist alongside courts and laws derived from the British legal system.

Both Malaysia and Singapore limit Islamic jurisprudence to matters concerning the family and certain types of behaviour deemed transgressions against Islam, such as *khalwat*, or for a Muslim to consume alcohol in public. In this regard, the *syariah* courts are in many ways subservient to the secular legal framework. This also means the harsher aspects of Islamic justice, such as stoning or the cutting off of a thief's hand, are not deemed permissible; an attempt in the 1990s by the state government of Kelantan, run by the Islamist opposition PAS party, to introduce them within the state was thwarted by Malaysia's federal government. The Islamic standard of proof in a case concerning rape – requiring the victim to be able to produce four witnesses – also does not apply, since rape cases are tried within the secular system.

However, the two juridical systems are experiencing a sort of territorial dispute in the important area of **religious conversion**. It's very difficult for Malaysian Muslims to convert out of Islam as the secular courts are unwilling to uphold their choice without the involvement of the *syariah* court, which might refuse permission or, worse, wish to punish them as apostates. In this Catch-22 situation, any Muslims who take up a new faith or no faith at all can never make their choice official, and for the most part simply keep mum. Controversy has also arisen when one person in a marriage converts to Islam and then wants to use Islamic law to divorce the spouse or change the registered religion of their children, for example. The roles of the two legal systems in these situations ought to be clarified as a matter of urgency, but this looks a distant prospect. When, in 2008, the Malaysian Bar Council held a meeting in KL on these matters, the event had to be called off after an angry crowd of Muslim demonstrators accused them of trying to undermine the status of Islam, and few Malay politicians were willing to back the idea of resolving the legal impasse through rational debate.

THE BOMOH

An important link between animism and the Islam of today is provided by the Malay **bomoh**, a kind of shaman. While *bomohs* keep a low profile in these times of greater Islamic orthodoxy – no *bomoh* operates out of an office, and there are no college courses to train *bomohs* or listings of practitioners in the telephone directory – the fact is that every Malay community can still summon a *bomoh* when it's felt one is needed to cure disease, bring rain during droughts, exorcize spirits from a newly cleared plot before building work starts, or rein in the behaviour of a wayward spouse. A central part of the *bomoh's* trade is recitation, often of sections of the Koran, while – like his Orang Asli counterparts – he uses techniques such as burning herbs to cure or ease pain and disease.

Mosques

In Malaysia, every town, village and hamlet has its mosque, while the capital city of each state hosts a grandiose **Masjid Negeri** (state mosque). You'll rarely see contemporary mosques varying from the standard square building topped by onion domes and minarets, though the oldest mosques reveal unusual Sumatran or other Southeast Asian influences. Two additional standard features can be found inside the prayer hall, namely the **mihrab**, a niche indicating the direction of Mecca, towards which believers face during prayers (the green *kiblat* arrow on the ceiling of most Malaysian hotel rooms fulfils the same function), and the **mimbar** (pulpit), used by the imam.

One of the five **pillars of Islam** is that the faithful should pray five times a day – at dawn (called the *subuh* prayer in Malay), midday (*zuhur*, or *jumaat* on a Friday), mid-afternoon (*asar*), dusk (*maghrib*) and mid-evening (*isyak*). Travellers soon become familiar with the sound, sometimes recorded, of the **muezzin** calling the faithful to prayer at these times; loudspeakers strapped to the minaret amplify his summons, though a few mosques have their own distinctive methods for summoning the faithful, such as at the Masjid Langgar in Kota Bharu, where traditionally a giant **drum** is banged before prayer time. On **Friday**, the day of the communal *jumaat* prayer, Muslims converge on their nearest mosque around noon to hear the imam deliver a *khutbah* (sermon); all employers allow Muslim staff a three-hour break for the purpose.

Chinese beliefs

The three different strands in Chinese belief ostensibly point in very different directions. **Confucianism** is a philosophy based on piety, loyalty, humanitarianism and familial devotion, a set of principles that permeate every aspect of Chinese life; **Buddhism** is a religion primarily concerned with the attainment of a state of personal enlightenment, nirvana; and **Taoism** propounds unity with nature as its chief tenet. When Chinese pioneers opened up the rivers of Sarawak to trade, they could identify with many of the animist practices of the Iban and Melenau tribesmen they dealt with, thanks to the Taoist emphasis on harmony with nature.

Malaysian and Singaporean Chinese who consider themselves Buddhist, Taoist or Confucianist may in practice be a mixture of all three. This blend is first and foremost pragmatic: the Chinese use their religion to ease their passage through life, whether in the spheres of work or family, while temples double as social centres for people to meet and exchange views.

Chinese temples

The rules of **feng shui** are rigorously applied to the construction of Chinese temples, so that each building has a layout and orientation rendering it free from evil influences. Visitors wishing to cross the threshold of a temple have to step over a kerb intended to trip up evil spirits, and walk through doors flanked by fearsome door gods; fronting the doors may be two stone lions, providing yet another defence.

Temples are normally constructed around a framework of huge, lacquered timber beams, adorned with intricately carved warriors, animals and flowers. More figures are moulded onto outer walls, which are dotted with octagonal, hexagonal or round grille-worked windows. Larger temples typically consist of a front entrance hall opening onto a walled-in courtyard, beyond which is the hall of worship, where joss sticks are burned below images of the deities. The most striking element of a Chinese temple is often its **roof** – a grand, multi-tiered affair with low, overhanging eaves, the ridges alive with auspicious creatures such as dragons and phoenixes and, less often, with miniature scenes from traditional Chinese life and legend. In the temple grounds you'll see sizeable ovens, stuffed constantly with paper money, prayer books and other offerings; and possibly a **pagoda** – the presence of which is, once again, a defence against evil spirits.

Peoples

Largely because of their pivotal position on maritime trade routes between the Middle East, India and China, the present-day countries of Malaysia, Singapore and Brunei have always been a cultural melting pot. During the first millennium AD, Malays arrived from Sumatra and Indians from India and Sri Lanka, while later the Chinese migrated from mainland China and Hainan Island. All these traders and settlers arrived to find that the region already held a gamut of indigenous tribes, thought to have migrated around 50,000 years ago from the Philippines, then connected by a land bridge to Borneo and Southeast Asia. The indigenous tribes who still live on the Peninsula are known as the Orang Asli, Malay for "the original people".

Original people they may have been, but their descendants now form a minority of the overall populations of the three countries. Over the last 150 years a massive influx of Chinese and Indian immigrants, escaping poverty, war and revolution, has swelled the population of **Malaysia**, which now stands at over 25 million. Just over half are Malays, while the Chinese make up nearly a quarter of the population, the Indians eight percent, and the various indigenous groups just over a tenth.

Brunei's population of around 380,000 is heavily dominated by Malays, with minorities of Chinese, Indians and indigenous peoples. In **Singapore**, only tiny numbers of indigenes were left on the island when Raffles arrived. They have no modern-day presence in the state, where around three quarters of the 4.6-million-strong population are of Chinese extraction, around fourteen percent are Malay, and nearly nine percent Indian.

The Malays

The **Malays** are believed to have originated from the meeting of Mainland Southeast Asian, Taiwanese and even Papuan groups over the last 5000 years. Also known as Orang Laut (sea people), they sustained an economy built around fishing, boat-building and, in some communities, piracy. The growth in power of the Malay sultanates from the fifteenth century onwards – coinciding with the arrival of Islam – established Malays as a force to be reckoned with in the Malay Peninsula and Borneo. They developed an aristocratic tradition, courtly rituals and a social hierarchy that have a continued influence today. The rulers of Malaysia's states still wield great influence, reflected in the fact that they elect one of their number to hold the post of Yang di-Pertuan Agong, a pre-eminent sultan who holds the title for a five-year term. Although a purely ceremonial position, the *agong* is seen as the ultimate guardian of Malay Muslim culture and, despite recent legislation to reduce his powers, is still considered to be above the law. The situation is even more pronounced in **Brunei**, to which many Muslim Malay traders fled after the fall of Melaka to the Portuguese in 1511. There, the sultan remains the supreme ruler (as his descendants have been, on and off, for over five hundred years).

Even though Malays have been Muslims since the fifteenth century, the region as a whole is not fundamentalist in character. Only in Brunei is alcohol banned, for instance. Perhaps the most significant recent development affecting Malays in Malaysia has been the introduction of the **bumiputra** policy (see box, p.576).

The Chinese and Straits Chinese

Although **Chinese traders** began visiting the region in the seventh century, the first significant community established itself in Melaka in the fifteenth century. However, the ancestors of most of the Chinese now living in Peninsular Malaysia – ethnic Hakka, and migrants from Teochew (Chaozhou) and Hokkien (Fujian) – emigrated from southeastern China during the nineteenth century to work in the burgeoning tin-mining industry and, later, rubber and oil plantations.

A large number of Chinese in the Peninsula came as labourers, but they swiftly graduated to shopkeeping and business ventures, both in established towns like Melaka and fast-expanding centres like KL, Penang and Kuching. Chinatowns developed throughout the region, even in Malay strongholds like Kota Bharu and Kuala Terengganu, while **Chinese traditions**, religious festivities, theatre and music became an integral part of a wider multiracial culture. On the political level, the Malaysian Chinese are well represented in parliament and occupy around a quarter of current ministerial positions. By way of contrast, **Chinese Bruneians** are not automatically classed as citizens and suffer significant discrimination at the hands of the majority Malay population.

Singapore's nineteenth-century trade boom drew many Cantonese, Teochew, Hokkien and Hakka Chinese traders and labourers, who established a Chinatown on the south bank of the Singapore River. Today, the Chinese are the most economically successful racial group in Singapore.

One of the few examples of regional intermarrying is displayed in the **Peranakan** or "Straits Chinese" heritage of Melaka, Singapore and, to a lesser extent, Penang. Male Chinese immigrants who settled in these places from the sixteenth century onwards, to work as miners or commercial entrepreneurs, often married local Malay women; the male offspring of such unions were termed "Baba" and the females "Nonya". **Baba-Nonya** society, as it became known, adapted elements from both cultures to create its own unique culinary and architectural style (see pp.279–280), and even had its own dialect of, for example, Malay. During the colonial era, many Baba-Nonyas acquired an excellent command of English and so prospered, but after the British departed they came under pressure to assimilate into the mainstream Chinese community. That helps to explain why many of their traditions have since gone into serious decline.

The Indians

The second largest non-*bumiputra* group in Malaysia, the **Indians**, first arrived as traders more than two thousand years ago, although few settled only in the early fifteenth century did a small community of Indians (from present-day Tamil Nadu and Sri Lanka) become based in Melaka. Like the majority of Chinese, however, the first large wave of Indians – Tamil labourers – arrived as indentured workers in the nineteenth century, to build the roads and rail lines and work on the European-run rubber estates. An embryonic entrepreneurial class from North India soon followed, and set up businesses in Penang and Singapore; mostly Muslim, these merchants and traders found it easier to assimilate themselves within the existing Malay community than did the Hindu Tamils.

Although Indians comprise under a tenth of the populations of Malaysia and Singapore, their impact is widely felt. The Hindu festival of Thaipusam is celebrated annually at KL's Batu Caves by upwards of a million people (with a smaller but still significant celebration in Singapore); the festival of Deepavali is a national holiday; and Indians dominate certain professional areas like medicine and law. And then, of course, there's the food – very few Malaysians these days could do without a daily dose of *roti canai*, so much so that this Indian snack has been virtually appropriated by Malay and Chinese cafés and hawkers.

The Orang Asli

Most of the **Orang Asli** – the indigenous peoples of Peninsular Malaysia – belong to three distinct groups, within which various tribes are related by geography, language or physiological features. It's difficult to witness much of Orang Asli life as they largely live off the beaten track, though touristed communities at Taman Negara and the Cameron Highlands can be visited. To learn more about the disappearing Asli culture, the best stop is KL's Orang Asli Museum (see p.110).

Senoi

The largest group, the **Senoi** (the Asli word for "person"), number about forty thousand. They live in the large, still predominantly forested interior, within the states of Perak, Pahang and Kelantan, and divide into two main tribes, the Semiar and the Temiar. These still adhere to a traditional lifestyle, following animist customs in marriage ceremonies and burial rites. On the whole they follow the practice of shifting cultivation (a regular rotation of jungle clearance and crop planting), although government resettlement drives have persuaded many to settle and farm just one area.

Semang

The two thousand or so **Semang** live in the northern areas of the Peninsula. They comprise six distinct, if small, tribes, related to each other in appearance – most are dark-skinned and curly-haired – and traditionally shared a nomadic, hunter-gatherer lifestyle. However, most Semang nowadays live in settled communities and work within the cash economy, either as labourers or selling jungle produce in markets. Perhaps the most frequently seen Semang tribe are the Batek, who live in and around Taman Negara.

Aboriginals

The third group, the so-called **Aboriginal Malays**, live in an area roughly south of the Kuala Lumpur–Kuantan road. Some tribes in this category, like the Jakun and the Semelais who live around the lakes of the southern interior, vigorously retain their animist religion and artistic traditions despite living in permanent villages near Malay communities, and working within the regular economy.

Others

One of Malaysia's other Orang Asli tribes, the Lanoh in Perak are sometimes regarded as Semang, their language is closer to that of the Temiar. Another group, the semi-nomadic Che Wong, of whom just a few hundred survive on the slopes of Gunung Benom in central Pahang, still depend on foraging to survive, and live in temporary huts made from bamboo and rattan. Two more groups, the Jah Hut of Pahang and the Mah Meri of Selangor, are particularly fine carvers, and it's possible to buy their sculptures at regional craft shops.

Indigenous Sarawak: the Dayak

In direct contrast to the Peninsula, indigenous groups make up a larger chunk of the population in **Sarawak**, which currently stands at two million. Although the Chinese comprise 29 percent of the state's population and the Malays and Indians around 24 percent together, the remaining 47 percent are made up of various indigenous **Dyak** groups – a word derived from the Malay for "upcountry". Certain general aspects of their culture – for instance, the importance of bronze drums and reburial ceremonies – might indicate that the Dyak arrived in the region from mainland Southeast Asia around 2000 years ago.

The largest Dyak groups are the Iban, Bidayuh, Melenau, Kayan, Kenyah, Kelabit and Penan tribes. They have very distinct cultures as well as a few commonalities. Many live in **longhouses** along the rivers or on hillsides in the mountainous interior, and maintain a proud cultural legacy that draws on animist religion, arts and crafts production and jungle skills.

The Iban

The **Iban** (see p.345) make up nearly thirty percent of Sarawak's population. Originating hundreds of miles south of present-day Sarawak, in the Kapuas Valley in Kalimantan, the Iban migrated north in the sixteenth century, and came into conflict over the next two hundred years with the Kayan and Kenyah tribes and, later, the British. Nowadays, Iban longhouse communities are found in the Batang Ai river system in the southwest and along Batang Rajang and tributaries. These communities are quite accessible, their inhabitants always hospitable and keen to demonstrate such aspects of their culture as traditional dance and textile weaving. In their time, the Iban were infamous head-hunters – some longhouses are still decorated with heads taken in battle long ago.

The Bidayuh

Unlike most Dyak groups, the **Bidayuh** traditionally lived away from the rivers, building their longhouse on the sides of hills. Culturally, the most southerly of Sarawak's indigenous groups are similar to the Iban, although in temperament they are much milder and less gregarious, keeping themselves to themselves in their inaccessible homes on Sarawak's mountainous southern border with Kalimantan.

The Melanau and Kelabit

The **Melanau** are a coastal people, living north of Kuching in a region dominated by mangrove swamps. Many Melanau, however, now live in towns, preferring the kampung-style houses of the Malays to the elegant longhouses of the past. They are expert fishermen and cultivate sago as an alternative to rice. The **Kelabit** people live on the highland plateau separating north Sarawak from Kalimantan. Like the Iban, they live in longhouses and maintain a traditional lifestyle, but differ from some other groups in being Christian.

The Penan

The semi-nomadic **Penan** traditionally live in temporary lean-tos or small huts in the upper Rajang and Limbang areas of Sarawak. They rely, like some Orang Asli groups in the Peninsula, on hunting and gathering and collecting jungle produce for sale in local markets. In recent years, however, the state government has tried to resettle the Penan in small villages – a controversial policy not entirely unconnected with the advance of logging in traditional Penan land. For more, see p.388.

The Kenyah and Kayan

Most of the other groups in Sarawak fall into the all-embracing ethnic classification of **Orang Ulu** (people of the interior), who inhabit remote inland areas, further north than the Iban, along the upper Rajang, Balui and Linau rivers. The most numerous, the **Kayan** and the **Kenyah**, are closely related and in the past often teamed up to defend their lands from the invading Iban. But they also have much in common with their traditional enemy, since they are longhouse-dwellers, animists and shifting cultivators.

Indigenous Sabah

Sabah has a population of around 2.6 million, made up of more than thirty distinct racial groups, between them speaking over eighty different dialects. The **Dusun** account for around a third of the population. Traditionally agriculturists (the word *Dusun* means "orchard"), various Dusun subgroups inhabit the western coastal plains and the interior. These days they are known generically as **Kadazan/Dusun**, although strictly speaking "Kadazan" refers only to the Dusun of Penampang. Other Dusun branches include the **Lotud** of Tuaran and the **Rungus** of the Kudat Peninsula, whose convex longhouses are all that remain of the Dusun's longhouse tradition. Although most Dusun are now Christians, remnants of their animist past are still evident, most obviously in the harvest festival, or *pesta kaamatan*, when their *bobohizans*, or priestesses, perform rituals to honour the *bambaazon*, or rice spirit.

The mainly Muslim **Bajau** tribe, who drifted over from the southern Philippines some two hundred years ago, now constitute Sabah's second largest ethnic group, accounting for around ten percent of the population. Their penchant for piracy quickly earned them the sobriquet "sea gypsies", though nowadays they are agriculturalists and fishermen, noted for their horsemanship and buffalo rearing. The Bajau live in the northwest of Sabah and annually appear on horseback at Kota Belud's market (see p.419).

Sabah's third sizeable tribe, the **Murut**, inhabit the area between Keningau and the Sarawak border, in the southwest. Their name means "hill people", though they prefer to be known by their individual tribal names, such as Timugon, Tagal and Nabai. The Murut farm rice and cassava by a system of shifting cultivation; their head-hunting days are over, but they retain other cultural traditions, such as constructing brightly adorned grave huts to house the graves and belongings of the dead.

Development and the environment

Malaysia is gradually becoming more environmentally friendly, largely as a result of well-organized and scientifically persuasive organizations within the country, rather than pressures from outside, but the pace of change is slow and huge problems remain. Logging and large-scale development projects, like dams, hog the spotlight, and remain a prime focus for NGOs, but just as pressing are concerns over oil-palm cultivation and wetlands erosion, as well as the impact of environmental degradation on the lifestyles of indigenous groups.

As a small, highly built-up island, **Singapore** has few wild areas left to spoil. Nevertheless, the country maintains an area of rainforest around its central reservoirs as well as other nature reserves, such the wetland area at Sungai Buloh. Singapore's very compactness dictates that it has to be vigilant on matters of pollution, and thus the island has strict laws on waste emissions and even an island, Pulau Semakau, created entirely out of ash from incinerated refuse.

The tiny kingdom of **Brunei** is perhaps the most enlightened of all. With a small, wealthy population, there's no rampant commercial exploitation of natural resources as in Malaysia. Forest protection is successfully applied and the state's small percentage of indigenous peoples treated respectfully.

Logging and deforestation

The **sustainable exploitation** of forest products by the indigenous population has always played a vital part in the domestic and export economy of the region – for almost two thousand years, ethnic tribes have bartered products like rattan, wild rubber and forest plants with foreign traders.

Although blamed for much of the deforestation in Sarawak and Sabah, the bulk of indigenous agricultural activity occurs in secondary rather than primary (untouched) forest. Indeed, environmental groups believe that only around one hundred square kilometres of primary forest – a tiny proportion compared to the haul by commercial timber companies – is cleared by the indigenous groups annually. **Logging**, despite having slowed, is still a cause of huge grievances among the indigenous peoples of east Malaysia.

The Peninsula

Peninsular Malaysia's pre-independence economy was not as reliant on timber revenues as those of Sabah and Sarawak. Although one sixth of the region's 120,000 square kilometres of forest, predominantly in Johor, Perak and Negeri Sembilan states, had been cut down by 1957, most of the logging had been done gradually and on a small, localized scale. As in Sabah, it was the demand for rail sleepers during the 1920s' expansion of the Malayan train network that first attracted the commercial logging companies. Wide-scale clearing and conversion to rubber and oil-palm plantations in the more remote areas of Pahang, Perlis, Kedah and Terengganu intensified in the 1960s. By the end of the 1970s, more efficient extraction methods, coupled with a massive increase in foreign investment in the logging industry, had led to over forty percent of the Peninsula's remaining forests being either cleared for plantation purposes or partially logged.

Logging in west Malaysia has, however, slowed significantly in the last few decades, with environmental impact assessments being carried out before logging is allowed to proceed. One positive piece of legislation is the creation, more than a century ago, of

Permanent Forest Reserves, though it doesn't involve a watertight system: even if a parcel of land is labelled a reserve, it can still be partially logged. But at least now the work must be carried out in a sustainable manner integrating checks and impact assessments.

Sabah

Commercial logging began in **Sabah** in the late nineteenth century, when the British Borneo Trading and Planting Company started to extract timber for use as railway sleepers in China. By World War II, the larger **British Borneo Timber Company** (BBTC) was primarily responsible for the extraction of five million cubic metres of rainforest timber, and Sandakan became one of the world's main timber ports. Areas were logged indiscriminately, and the indigenous tribal groups who lived there were brought into the economic system to work on the rubber and tobacco plantations that replaced the forests.

By the early 1960s, timber had accelerated past rubber as the region's main produce; by 1970, nearly thirty percent of Sabah's forests had been logged, accounting for over seventy percent of exports. Nowadays much of the logged land is used for oil-palm cultivation (see opposite), while powerful companies continue to pressure the state government for access to the remaining forests to expand this lucrative, but ecologically suffocating monoculture.

Sarawak

In many ways **Sarawak** seems to exemplify Malaysia's environmental policies at their worst. It's here that all the problems come into sharp focus – the forest is either being degraded by commercial logging or felled altogether for oil-palm cultivation, in the process ruining the ancestral lands of native peoples.

Having accelerated in northern Sarawak under Vyner Brooke during the 1930s, timber extraction became a major revenue earner for the state during its short postwar period as a Crown Colony and after independence as part of Malaysia. Accurate figures as to the current state of Sarawak's rainforest are notoriously hard to come by, though perhaps less than thirty percent of the primary forest cover remains, and even that can be so fragmented that it's practically useless from a wildlife conservation point of view.

In principle the indigenous peoples have so-called **native customary rights** over their ancestral forest, and can use them in court to block the government granting logging or other concessions. However, the system is fraught with difficulty, partly because such rights are based on incomplete colonial-era data as to where the various groups once lived. Besides, even where the tribes can establish their rights, they may not wish to exercise them – they may instead be more interested in what the logging companies can offer, such as new roads and schools, plus jobs in the cash economy.

Of course, logging, unlike clearing land for oil palm, does not mean the wholesale destruction of the forest: the logging companies are after hardwood trees, which they should try to remove as cleanly as possible. In practice felling may involve collateral damage to other trees, and it's notable that none of the Sarawak timber concerns has Forest Stewardship Council certification to indicate that they manage forests responsibly.

Meanwhile the state continues to trumpet its target of gazetting 10,000 square kilometres (eight percent of Sarawak's land area) as national parks or wildlife reserves that are off-limits to the public, plus a further 60,000 square kilometres as permanent forest reserve. Impressive though these figures may sound, it's notable that many of the newer national parks scarcely function as such, since they are sited in inaccessible areas and have barely any facilities. This haphazard creation of parks might be thought to augment their effectiveness as conservation areas, but there is no such fringe benefit as policing to stop logging or poaching is minimal. It could be argued that the parks are, in fact, a smokescreen for what's happening elsewhere in Sarawak – for example, the intensive logging of the Baram River basin in the north, in areas around the Kelabit Highlands and

OIL-PALM CULTIVATION IN MALAYSIA

Malaysia is the world's biggest producer of **oil palm**, a valuable economic crop that's used as a biofuel and in food products. The industry has been a massive stimulus for employment – over half a million people are now involved in its production, and many more in various subsidiary industries. Sabah, Malaysia's poorest state, is benefiting in particular. Furthermore, land surrounding the cultivation areas has been subject to improved infrastructure: public services such as schools and hospitals have been developed, while roads are built and telecommunication networks established.

Yet the industry's speedy proliferation has had a harmful impact on the environment: critics say the land cleared for the agro-crop contributes significantly to global warming, notably greenhouse gas emissions. Palm trees are increasingly replacing native tropical rainforest and thus threatening the survival of many animal species, including the orang-utan. Communities may also have their food and water supplies cut off or contaminated, while their cash-crop farms – fruit trees and rubber plantations – are wiped out. Meanwhile, social conflict is triggered between the planters and local residents who are forced off their land.

And the industry keeps on growing: the oil's use as an alternative, "clean" biofuel has meant that demand is kept stable. While the negative impacts are ongoing, at least on some level there's increased awareness, fuelled by organizations like Friends of the Earth, of the substantial environmental impact. The recognition is growing that a stronger sustainability policy is needed to safeguard Malaysia's rainforests and all who depend on them.

Gunung Mulu National Park. Meanwhile land also continues to be cleared for oil palm, with a target of having 20,000 square kilometres under cultivation by 2015.

Dam-building is another big issue on the Sarawak environmental agenda. The prime example is the massive Bakun dam project, which will generate electricity for no obvious market – and is only the first in a series of dams scheduled to be built in the coming years.

While the picture in Sarawak may appear bleak, there are a few reasons for optimism: some logging companies are beginning to have their practices assessed as a first step towards gaining FSC certification, and there is genuine commitment among some government biodiversity managers to try to reform the state's policies.

Air pollution

For the inhabitants of Peninsular Malaysia and Singapore, the environmental issue that has affected them most has not been forest depletion or land rights, but **air pollution**, particularly dust and smoke caused by forest fires – dubbed "the haze" by the local media. During a severe, prolonged episode in 1997–98, the haze was so bad that motorists were warned to keep their distance from one another, and respiratory illnesses rose alarmingly. Visibility in the Straits of Melaka, one of the world's busiest shipping routes, also dropped dramatically.

The Malaysian government originally suggested that the agricultural methods of the indigenous peoples – which involve the burning of excess vegetation at the end of growing cycles – were to blame. However, further research indicated that small longhouse communities could not have caused such extensive fires. It's now thought that the haze is caused by Indonesian plantation companies using fire to clear large areas of forest to facilitate the planting of crops such as oil palm and acacia. The Indonesian government does not appear to have been able to change the habits of its forest developers, given that the 1997 catastrophe was repeated, albeit to a lesser extent, in 2000, 2002 and 2005. The 2005 event – caused by forest fires in Sumatra – prompted a state of emergency to be declared and crisis talks with Indonesia. Thankfully, at the time of writing there had been no recurrence of the haze, but it must be regarded as a problem waiting to recur unless Indonesia markedly improves the way it polices the plantation owners.

The threat to traditional lifestyles

Although large-scale projects such as the Bakun Dam are the most prevalent threat to indigenous tribes' way of life, **logging**, whether licensed or illicit, represents a constant challenge. The effect on wildlife has an obvious impact on communities' ability to hunt, but the failure to respect native customary rights has also led to the desecration of burial places and sections of rivers used for fishing – notably in the forests around Bintulu, Belaga and Limbang. In southwest Sarawak, the Iban have had some success in challenging logging, however: a historic court case in 2001, Rumah Norv. Borneo Pulp and Paper, led to a ruling in favour of the longhouse community, after the community's map was accepted as court evidence for ownership of land. Emboldened by this ruling, several communities have filed petitions, but in many cases the courts have not revoked the state-awarded logging concessions.

The **Penan** have arguably been the worst hit by logging, as their traditionally semi-nomadic lifestyle makes it hard for their land rights to be defined and recognized. In addition, the Sarawak state government's avowed policy since the mid-1980s has been to bring the Penan into what it views as the development process (as applied to the more settled Dyak and Orang Ulu groups for many decades), urging them to move to permanent longhouses, work in the cash economy and send their children to school. Very often, the Penan receive no notice that their land has been earmarked for logging until extraction actually begins – examples in remote areas around Belaga have been documented by the environmental group **Sahabat Alam Malaysia** (SAM). Reports from one of the remaining semi-nomadic Penan communities situated in Sarawak's Ulu Baram area reveals that loggers continue to penetrate their last reserves illegally.

Wildlife

Set well inside the tropics and comprising everything from pristine ocean to coastal mangroves, lowland rainforest and mountain moorland, the range of habitats on the Malay Peninsula and Borneo is only matched by the diversity of its fauna – over 700 species of birds and more than 200 kinds of mammals. You don't have to be an ardent nature-spotter to appreciate this: even a brief visit to any of the region's national parks – or just the FRIM forestry reserve on Kuala Lumpur's outskirts – will put you face to face with clouds of butterflies, troops of monkeys, and an incessant background orchestra of insect noise.

Despite being separated by the South China Sea, the wildlife and plant communities of the Peninsula and east Malaysia are similar, since the two were joined by a land bridge until after the last Ice Age – though the various regional wildlife reserves offer a range of experiences. On Peninsular Malaysia, **Taman Negara** provides full-on tropical jungle, a good place to see large mammals; **Fraser's Hill**, on the other hand, is better known for its birdlife. Sabah's **Sungai Kinabatangan** and **Bako National Park** in Sarawak are good for estuarine and river forest creatures, while shallow lakes at Sarawak's **Loagan Bunut National Park** are home to many different bird species, as is Brunei's **Ulu Temburong National Park**.

Even though it's now predominantly urban, with little plant or animal life, **Singapore** still holds several remnants of its verdant tropical past, particularly at **Bukit Timah Nature Reserve**, the splendidly manicured Botanic Gardens, and the **Sungai Buloh Nature Wetland Reserve** in the far north of the island. Day-trippers to Pulau Ubin, just off Singapore and easily accessible by boat from the Changi Point ferry terminal, can also see the mangrove flats of **Chek Jawa**.

Poaching and habitation loss due to deforestation mean that the future of the region's wildlife is far from assured. Fortunately, many **not-for-profit organizations**, such as WWF Malaysia (ⓦwwfmalaysia.org), are campaigning to preserve the species and terrains most under threat.

FORESTS

Coastal mud flats are usually protected by **mangroves**, a diverse family of trees that thrive in brackish water and tend to support themselves on a platform of elevated roots that form an impenetrable barrier to exploration – and refuge for small creatures such as mudskippers, crabs and young fish.

Moving inland, the region's lowland forests are thick with **dipterocarps** (meaning "two-winged fruit"), a diverse group of trees often prized for timber. Other forest species include several palm trees (one of which, the spiky, vine-like rattan palm, is used to make cane furniture and the like); liana vines; massive fig trees (many of which support their huge trunks with buttress roots); 50m-tall *tualang*, Southeast Asia's tallest tree; and wild **fruit trees**, such as durian, mango, guava and rambutan. You'll seldom see flowers though (except fallen petals); so little light reaches the forest floor that trees and climbing plants only flower high up in the canopy. To get around this, a whole group of small plants have become epiphytes – using the trees as perches to get nearer the sunlight – including orchids and a wide range of small ferns, which sometimes cover the upper surface of larger branches.

Montane forest predominates above 1000m, comprising mainly oak and evergreen native conifers with a shrub layer of bamboo and dwarf palm. Above 1500m is **cloud forest**, where trees are often cloaked by swirling mist, and the stunted, damp boughs bear thick growths of mosses and ferns; at elevations of over 1700m, you'll find miniature montane forest of rhododendrons, the boughs heavily laden with dripping mosses, pitcher plants and colourful orchids.

HOW TO FIND WILDLIFE

Tropical wildlife is most active at dawn and dusk, though some larger mammals forage through the night. It's surprising how even large animals can be fairly invisible, especially in forest, where low light and random vegetation can break up their otherwise recognizable outlines. Here are some tips for finding creatures, without doing anything dangerous – such as turning over logs to look for snakes:

Listen – aside from calls, many creatures make distinctive noises as they move, from the raucous crashing of active monkey troops, to staccato rustlings of mice and lizards in leaf litter.

Look – many smaller creatures spend the day hidden under leaves and in hollows and crevices in tree trunks. At night, insects – and insect-eating animals – are attracted to lights; check ranger offices, chalets and huts around national park headquarters.

Signs – footprints, scarred bark, mud wallows and flowers, fruit and torn twigs strewn along paths are all signs of animals, some of which might be feeding in the canopy above you.

Eyeshine – at night, use a torch held at or above eye level to reflect eyeshine, either from invertebrates such as crickets and spiders, or nocturnal mammals – anything from tapir to deer, mice and civets.

Mammals

Big mammals are exciting to encounter in the wild, and several are unique to the region. Asian **elephant** are found both in Peninsular Malaysia and Borneo, though probably the best chance to see them is at Taman Negara, which is also good for **tapir** – a pony-sized relative of the rhino, with a black-and-white body and vestigial trunk.

Other mammals you might encounter include **clouded leopards** – a beautifully marked cat species with a pattern of cloud-like markings on the sides of the body – spotted **leopard cat** (around the size of a large domestic cat), and nocturnal **civet**, tree-dwelling creatures that look like a cross between a cat and a weasel. Don't get your hopes up about seeing **tigers**, now thought to number no more than 500 in the Peninsula, or reclusive **sun bears**, marked with a white crescent across their chest – though you do occasionally see their deep claw grooves in tree bark.

Another possibility in undisturbed forest on the Peninsula are *seladang* or *gaur*, a giant type of wild cattle with white leg patches, which look like ankle socks. There are also several species of **deer**: the larger *sambar*; the *kijang* or barking deer, the size of a roe deer; and the lesser and greater mouse deer.

Primates (monkeys and gibbons) are found throughout the Peninsula and Borneo. Most common are the long-tailed and pig-tailed **macaques**, which come to the ground to feed, the latter identified by its shorter tail, brown fur and pinkish-brown face. There are dusky and spectacled **langurs** too, elegant grey monkeys with white patterns that spend most of their time up in the trees – they're also known as leaf-monkeys, after their diet. The region's several gibbon species are entirely arboreal, with specially elongated forearms that allow them to swing athletically through the canopy – they tend to have very loud, wailing calls too, easily recognized. Big-nosed, pot-bellied proboscis monkeys – and Southeast Asia's sole ape, the **orang-utan** (see box, p.437) – are found only in Borneo.

One of the most unusual smaller mammals to keep eyes peeled for is the **colugo**, a bizarre forest creature that looks like a cross between a fruit bat and a squirrel. It spends the day sleeping in tree hollows, and the night gliding through the forest looking for flowers and fruits.

Birds

One fairly common bird that epitomizes the entire Malay region – and is even a totem to some Dyak tribes – is the **hornbill**. Its huge size, bold black-and-white markings, large curved beak and noisy, swooshing flight make it easily identifiable, even in thick jungle. Other forest birds include **trogons** (brightly coloured, mid-storey birds); green **fruit pigeons** – strongly coloured but strangely hard to see; **bulbuls**, vocal, fruit-eating birds that often flock to feed; **minivets**, slender birds with long, graduated tails and white, yellow or red bands in the wings; and round-winged **babblers**.

Plump and brilliantly coloured, **pitas** are notoriously shy and difficult to approach, though sometimes easily found thanks to their noisy progress through leaf litter on the forest floor. Other ground-dwelling birds to look for include the shy **Malaysian peacock pheasant**, with a blue-green crest and distinctive "eye spots" along its back and long tail; the similar **fireback**; and the 1.7m-long **great argus pheasant**.

The most common birds of prey are kites, buzzards and, along the coast, fish eagles, very large white and grey birds with a wedge-shaped tail. In forest, you might encounter the **crested serpent eagle** and the **changeable hawk eagle**, often spotted soaring over gaps in the forest canopy.

Other species confined to tropical forests are **trogons**, of which five species are present at Taman Negara, and several species of **hornbill** – large, broad-winged, long-tailed forest birds, some of which have huge, almost outlandish bills.

A feature of montane forest bird flocks is the **mixed feeding flock**, which may contain many different species. These pass rapidly through an area of forest searching for insects as they go, and different observers are likely to register entirely different species in the same flock. Look for **racket-tailed drongo**, a black bird with long tail streamers; the **speckled piculet**, a small spotted woodpecker; and the **blue nuthatch**, a small species – blue-black in colour with a white throat and pale eye ring – which runs up and down tree trunks. Several species of brightly coloured **laughing thrushes**, thrush-sized birds that spend time foraging on the ground or in the understorey, also occur in these flocks.

Reptiles

Small lizards – mostly skinks – are probably the commonest **reptiles** in the region; you'll often hear their frantic scuffling among forest-floor leaf litter. Nocturnal geckos have sucker-like pads on their toes that enable them to run up walls (and even glass); they're often seen around lights, stalking any insects that settle nearby. On forest fringes, look for flying lizards, which at rest are small, bony, grey and unimpressive – until they unfold wings and glide between trees like paper darts. Fairly common, even in semi-rural parks, they're easily missed. Around water – and especially near popular picnic spots, where they can pick up scraps – you'll see heavily built **monitor lizards**, the largest of which can approach 2m.

Snakes – Malaysia and Borneo hold over 200 species, including poisonous cobras, kraits and pit vipers – are another common but seldom-seen creature; they tend to

---

HORNBILLS

You should have little difficulty in identifying **hornbills**: they are large, black-and-white birds with disproportionately huge bills (often bent downwards), topped with an ornamental **casque** – a generally hollow structure attached to the upper mandible. The function of the casque is unknown; it may play a role in attracting a mate and courtship ceremonies. Ten of the world's 46 species of hornbill are found in Malaysia, many of them endangered or present only in small, isolated populations.

One of the smallest and most commonly seen species, the **pied hornbill**, can be identified by its white abdomen and tail, and white wingtips in flight. Reaching only 75cm in length, it may even be spotted in leafy suburban areas. Also widely seen, the **black hornbill** is only slightly larger and black, save for the white tips of the outer tail feathers (some individuals also show a white patch behind the eye).

Larger species include the **helmeted hornbill** and the **rhinoceros hornbill**, both over 120cm in length, mainly black, but with white tails and bellies. Although it's the symbol of Sarawak, the rhinoceros hornbill is rarely seen there or elsewhere; it has a bright orange rhino-horn-shaped casque, whereas the helmeted hornbill has a bright red head, neck and helmet-shaped casque. The call of the helmeted hornbill is notable for being a remarkable series of "took" notes that start slowly and accelerate to a cackling crescendo.

RAFFLESIAS

The *Rafflesia* is a strange plant that parasitises tree roots, and whose presence can only be detected when its rubbery flowers, up to a metre across, burst into bloom. Its full name, *Rafflesia arnoldii*, recalls its discovery in Sumatra in 1818 by Sir Stamford Raffles (see p.487) and his physician, the naturalist Dr Joseph Arnold, who collected a 7kg specimen and sent a description of it to the Royal Society in London. The blooms, which are the world's largest and stink of rotting meat, are pollinated by carrion flies. Each flower's central "bowl" holds around 7 litres of nectar, while the petals, as Raffles recorded, "are of a brick-red with numerous pustular spots of a lighter colour. The whole substance of the flower is not less than half an inch thick, and of a firm fleshy consistence". The flower buds have been very much in demand by *bomohs* (Malay shamen) and their Chinese *sinseh* counterparts for use in medicine, particularly as an aid to accelerate the shrinking of a woman's womb after she has given birth. There's no specific flowering season, though in any one locality the plants seem to bloom at particular times of the year. As each flower lasts only a few days, however, there's a lot of luck involved in actually seeing one; national park rangers might be able to give likely times.

move off as soon as they detect your footfalls. The largest, the reticulated python, is capable of growing 8m long, though you're much more likely to see either harmless **whip snakes** (which eat insects and lizards) and green **tree snakes**.

Saltwater **crocodiles** – the world's largest, heaviest reptile – are now virtually extinct throughout Peninsular Malaysia, though numbers are increasing in Borneo. Scuba divers might encounter several species of marine **turtle**, all of whose populations are declining (see p.258); certain beaches are also famous as turtle rookeries, where you might see adults coming ashore to lay eggs above the high tide line, or young turtles hatching, digging themselves out of the sand and heading for the sea en masse.

Books

Although in the past, most books about Malaysia, Singapore and Brunei tended to be penned by Western visitors to the region, local writing and publishing in English has gathered momentum in the last couple of decades. Independent publishers include Select Books (ⓦselectbooks.com.sg), Editions Didier Millet (ⓦedmbooks.com), Pelanduk (ⓦpelanduk.com), Media Masters (ⓦmediamasters.com.sg), Silverfish Books (ⓦsilverfishbooks.com) and Natural History Publications, Borneo (ⓦnhpborneo.com). It's obviously easiest to buy locally published material while you're travelling around the countries concerned, though a few titles are available internationally, while Select Books and MPH (ⓦmph.com.my) have online mail-order services.

In the reviews that follow, publishers are only listed for books published outside the UK and US. Books marked ★ are especially recommended, while o/p signifies that a book is out of print. As per Chinese custom, surnames are given first for those Chinese authors who don't have Christian names.

TRAVEL AND GENERAL INTEREST

★ *Encyclopedia of Malaysia* (Editions Didier Millet). A brilliantly produced series of tomes on different aspects of Malaysia, all beautifully illustrated and – not always the case with locally published material – competently edited. The volumes on the performing arts and architecture are particularly recommended. Available as individual volumes or as a set.

Isabella Bird *The Golden Chersonese*. Delightful epistolary romp through old Southeast Asia, penned by the intrepid Bird, whose adventures in the Malay states in 1879 ranged from strolls through Singapore's streets to elephant-back rides. A free download from various online libraries.

Harry Foster *A Beachcomber in the Orient*. Recently reissued, this is a hilarious first-person account of a proto-backpacker who travelled through Malaya and other parts of Southeast Asia in the 1920s.

Tom Harrisson *Borneo Jungle* and *World Within*. Tough, eccentric British anthropologist Tom Harrisson spent much of his professional life studying Sarawak's Dyak groups, especially the Kayan, Kenyah and Punan, whom he greatly admired. *Borneo Jungle* is a lively account of his first trip during the 1930s; *World Within* the story of how he parachuted into the highlands during World War II to organize Dyak resistance against the Japanese.

★ **Agnes Keith** *Land Below the Wind*. Bornean memories galore, in this charming account of expat life in pre-war Sabah; Keith's true eye and assured voice produce a heartwarming picture of a way of life now long gone. Her naive sketches perfectly complement the childlike wonder of the prose.

Redmond O'Hanlon *Into The Heart of Borneo*. A hugely entertaining yarn recounting O'Hanlon's refreshingly amateurish romp through the jungle to a remote summit on the Sarawak/Kalimantan border, partnered by the English poet James Fenton.

HISTORY AND POLITICS

★ **Munshi Abdullah** *The Hikayat Abdullah*. Raffles' one-time clerk, Melaka-born Abdullah became diarist of some of the most formative years of Southeast Asian history; his firsthand account is crammed with illuminating vignettes and character portraits.

★ **Charles Allen** *Tales from the South China Seas*. Mosaic of the final colonial decades in Malaysia, Singapore and Brunei, formed from the personal reminiscences of former estate managers, teachers, nurses, engineers, soldiers, police chiefs and District Officers. Not nearly as pro-Raj as you might expect, and the drama of everyday lives, often in inhospitable conditions, is evinced with considerable pathos.

★ **Barbara Watson Andaya and Leonard Andaya** *The History of Malaysia*. Unlike more paternalistic histories penned by former colonists, this standard text on the region takes a more even-handed view of Malaysia, and finds time for cultural coverage, too.

Maurice Collis *Raffles* (o/p). The most accessible and enjoyable biography of Sir Stamford Raffles.

Roy Follows *The Jungle Beat*. The Malaysian jungle proved as unforgiving an enemy as the Malayan communist insurgents when Follows joined the Malay police in the 1950s. His story engages from beginning to end.

Images of Asia series Maya Jayapal's *Old Singapore* and Sarnia Hayes Hoyt's *Old Malacca* and *Old Penang* chart the growth of three of the region's most important outposts, drawing to engrossing effect on contemporary maps, sketches and photographs.

★ **Patrick Keith** *Ousted* (Media Masters). Most of the largely young population of Malaysia and Singapore know little of the events that saw Singapore leaving the federation in 1965. And yet, as this excellent memoir by a former Malaysian government adviser demonstrates, many of the issues that led to the rift continue to shape both countries and their mutual ties today – Malaysia is still laden with ethnically based politics, while Singapore remains the fiefdom of the PAP.

Wendy Khadijah-Moore *Malaysia: A Pictorial History 1400–2003* (Editions Didier Millet). If you're going to produce coffee-table books on Malaysia's history, you could do a lot worse than this well-illustrated portable museum. Don't come to it expecting trenchant commentary, though: Anwar's arrest in the late 1990s, for instance, gets a mere couple of lines.

James Minchin *No Man Is An Island* (o/p). This well-researched, and at times critical, study of Lee Kuan Yew refuses to kowtow to Singapore's ex-prime minister and is hence unavailable in Singapore itself.

★ **Amir Muhammad** *Malaysian Politicians Say the Darndest* (sic) *Things Vols 1 & 2* (Matahari). Incredibly crass utterances from the mouths of top public figures, ranging from the thought that only unattractive women should get state-sector jobs (as the pretty ones can find rich husbands) to the strange contention that Singapore, being small, lacks opportunities for corruption, "unlike in our country". Read them and weep.

Farish Noor *What Your Teacher Didn't Tell You* (Matahari). An enjoyable series of lectures on subjects that remain awkward in Malaysia, from ethnicity to sexual attitudes.

Bob Reece *The White Rajahs of Sarawak* (Editions Didier Millet). A handsome coffee-table book about the extraordinary Brooke dynasty.

Carl A. Trocki *Singapore: Wealth, Power and the Culture of Control*. Highly readable dissection of how the PAP, after co-opting and marginalizing Singapore's Left in the 1960s and then allying "with international capital to create a workers' paradise", acquired its present grip on all aspects of life in Singapore.

★ **C.M. Turnbull** *A History of Modern Singapore 1819–2005* (NUS Press). Mary Turnbull had barely completed a major update of this standard work when she died in 2008, and what a fine legacy: the new edition is lucid, thorough, nearly always spot-on in its analysis and utterly readable.

WORLD WAR II

★ **Russell Braddon** *The Naked Island*. Southeast Asia under the Japanese: Braddon's disturbing yet moving first-hand account of the POW camps of Malaya, Singapore and Siam salutes courage in the face of appalling conditions and treatment; worth scouring secondhand stores for.

★ **Spencer Chapman** *The Jungle is Neutral*. This riveting first-hand account of being lost, and surviving, in the Malay jungle during World War II reads like a breathless novel.

★ **Agnes Keith** *Three Came Home*. Pieced together from scraps of paper secreted in latrines and teddy bears, this is a remarkable story of survival in the face of Japanese attempts to eradicate the "proudery and arrogance" of the West in the World War II prison camps of Borneo.

Eric Lomax *The Railway Man*. Such is the power of Lomax's artless, redemptive and moving story of capture during the fall of Singapore, torture by the Japanese and reconciliation with his tormentor after fifty years, that many reviewers were moved to tears.

★ **Lucy Lum** *The Thorn of Lion City*. You might expect a memoir of a wartime childhood in Singapore to be dominated by the savagery of Japanese, but that's nothing compared to the torment inflicted on the author at the hands of her manipulative and violent mother and grandmother. That it's all told with zero artifice only makes it more compelling.

CULTURE AND SOCIETY

James Harding and Ahmad Sarji *P. Ramlee: The Bright Star* (Pelanduk). An uncritical but enjoyable biography of the Malay singer, actor and director sometimes likened to Malaysia's Harry Belafonte. More importantly, it's a window onto what seems like a different era – though only half a century ago – when Singapore was the centre of the Malay entertainment universe, and when Malay life was, frankly, more carefree than today.

Michael Heppell *Iban Art: Sexual Selection and Severed Heads* This excellent illustrated volume provides a deeper coverage of Iban art than the pretty pictures might lead you to assume, detailing the motifs and symbolism of traditional clothes, tattoos and carvings.

★ **Erik Jensen** *Where Hornbills Fly*. In the 1950s, before he became a British diplomat, the author arrived in Sarawak as a callow young man with idealistic notions of learning about the Iban. He soon wound up living in longhouses in the Undup area (near Sri Aman), helping the Iban make the change to a settled existence without imposing upon them as a "superior" foreigner. His memoir is so intricately and tenderly observed you can only wonder why he waited half a century to write up his experiences.

Lat *Kampung Boy* and *Town Boy*. Two comic-strip albums by the country's foremost cartoonist about growing up in Malaysia during the 1950s and 60s; gentle and fun, though without any sentimentality.

Andro Linklater *Wild People* (o/p). As telling a glimpse into the lifestyle of the Iban as you could find, depicting the survival of their age-old traditions amid the T-shirts, baseball caps and rock posters of Western influence.

Heidi Munan *Music Without Borders: The Rainforest World Music Festival in Sarawak*. This coffee-table book makes a great festival memento, with informative text by ethnomusicologist Munan.

Colin Nicholas *The Orang Asli and the Contest for Resources* (International Workgroup for Indigenous Affairs). Puts into context the way in which the Orang Asli have been both drawn into mainstream society and yet marginalized over the years.

James Ritchie *Penan on the Move*. You might approach a book by a former public relations officer for the Sarawak government with some scepticism, but Ritchie is also a veteran journalist who has been covering the Penan for many years. This self-published work, despite its amateurish layout and numerous typos, gives a reasonable overview of the Penan and the awkwardness of their transition to a settled new lifestyle, including the social problems this has brought about.

Bernard Sellato *Innermost Borneo: Studies in Dayak Cultures* (Seven Orients). Anthropologist Sellato spent much of the 1990s with the indigenous Borneo tribes of Kalimantan, who are related to the Sea Dyaks of Sarawak. This excellent ethnographic work contains ravishing images of a traditional, isolated world that will eventually be subsumed into greater Indonesia.

Tan Kok Seng *Son Of Singapore*. Tan Kok Seng's candid and sobering autobiography on the underside of the Singaporean success story, telling of hard times spent as a coolie.

★ **Dina Zaman** *I Am Muslim* (Silverfish). A well-observed set of wry essays, with more candour than would have been appropriate in this guidebook, on Islam as practised in Malaysia; form without enough substance is, sadly, often the verdict. The section on sexual attitudes is particularly recommended.

COOKBOOKS

Aziza Ali *Aziza's Creative Malay Cuisine* (PEN). A posh take on Malay food, by the woman who, for years, ran one of Singapore's best Malay restaurants. You won't find northern fare like *nasi kerabu* or *laksam* in here, but then, many of the recipes are intended more to impress at dinner parties than to reflect what's served on the street.

★ **Betty Saw** *Rasa Malaysia* (Marshall Cavendish). A nicely illustrated cookbook that covers dozens of the standard dishes you'll find served at food courts and in homes around the country, including various Chinese and Nonya recipes, though very little South Indian fare. It's all organized by state, which helps give a feel for regional cuisine, though annoyingly there's no index.

Seashore Books publish a range of bilingual cookbooks on Malay food: *Truly Nonya Penang*; *Authentic Homestyle Cuisines*, *Sino-Malaysia Flavours*, *Kampung Curry* and more. All recipes are easy to follow and produce good results; they're available in most Malaysian bookshops.

NATURAL HISTORY AND ECOLOGY

G.W.H. Davison and Chew Yen Fook *A Photographic Guide to Birds of Borneo*; **M. Strange and A. Jeyarajasingam** *A Photographic Guide to Birds of Peninsular Malaysia and Singapore*; **Charles M. Francis** *A Photographic Guide to the Mammals of Southeast Asia*. Well keyed and user-friendly, these slender volumes carry oodles of glossy plates that make positive identifying a breeze.

Jeffrey McNeely and Paul Spencer Sochaczewski *Soul of the Tiger*. Insights into the wide-ranging importance of wildlife for Southeast Asia's indigenous peoples. The particularly fascinating chapter on Borneo suggests that birds are viewed as "messengers from the gods" in local culture.

Junaida Payne *Wild Malaysia: The Wildlife and Landscapes of Peninsular Malaysia, Sarawak and Sabah*. Coffee-table book, recently reissued, capturing forest and beach vistas of the kind that linger in the mind long after you've left Malaysia.

Ivan Polunin *Plants and Flowers of Malaysia* (Times Editions). A single volume simply can't do justice to the vast quantity of flora packed into tropical rainforest, and this doesn't attempt to try, instead providing a handy illustrated survey of plants in environments ranging from sandy beach to upland forest.

★ **Alfred Russel Wallace** *The Malay Archipelago*. The immensely readable journal of Wallace's 1854–62 expedition to collect natural history specimens in Borneo and Indonesia, during which he independently formulated the theory of evolution by natural selection – prompting Charles Darwin to publish his landmark *Origin of Species*. Though little of the book is set in Malaysia, it's essential reading for anyone interested in natural history.

ART AND ARCHITECTURE

Julian Davison and Luca Invernizzi Tettoni *Black & White: The Singapore House* (Talisman); **Peter and Waveney Jenkins** *The Planter's Bungalow* (Editions Didier Millet). Two tomes dealing with colonial "Anglo-Malay" residences, often strange hybrids of mock-Tudor and Southeast Asian elements, and sometimes raised off the ground on posts like a kampung house. Both volumes also examine the lives of those who occupied these houses, not always as wealthy as you might assume.

Peter Lee and Jennifer Chen *The Straits Chinese House* (Editions Didier Millet). A beautifully illustrated volume exploring Peranakan domestic artefacts and their now largely vanished traditions; an excellent memento of a visit to the Baba-Nonya museums of Penang, Melaka and Singapore.

★ **Lim Huck Chin and Fernando Jorge** *Malacca: Voices From the Street* (self-published; ⊕ malaccavoices.com). By the architects responsible for the restoration of 8 Heeren Street (see p.279), this labour of love chronicles the evolution of Melaka, street by street, the decline of traditional trades and pastimes, and the degeneration of some areas into a crass modernity. Printed on heavy-duty paper and illustrated with the authors' own colour photographs.

★ **Farish A. Noor and Eddin Khoo** *The Spirit of Wood: The Art of Malay Woodcarving* (Periplus). Much weightier in tone than your average coffee-table book, this deals not only with the superb woodcarving produced on the east coast of the Peninsula and in southern Thailand, but also with the whole pre-Islamic consciousness that subtly imbues the woodcarver's art. Packed with great photos, too, of gorgeous timber mosques, incredibly detailed *kris* hilts and the like.

Anthony Ratos and H. Berber *Orang Asli and their Wood Art*. One of few accessible explorations of Orang Asli lifestyles and cultures, though note that only a third of this picture-heavy volume is devoted to their fantastical carvings; the rest of the photos are of Asli settlements and generic, if pretty, jungle scenes.

★ **Robert Winzeler** *The Architecture of Life and Death in Borneo*. Highly readable, illustrated study of the traditional architecture of Borneo, looking at the evolution of longhouses over the years and symbolism in building design.

FICTION

★ **Anthony Burgess** *The Long Day Wanes* (o/p). Burgess's Malayan trilogy (*Time for a Tiger*, *The Enemy in the Blanket* and *Beds in the East*), published in one volume, provides a witty and acutely observed vision of 1950s Malaya, underscoring the racial prejudices of the period.

James Clavell *King Rat*. Set in Japanese-occupied Singapore, a gripping tale of survival in the notorious Changi Prison.

★ **Joseph Conrad** *Lord Jim*. Southeast Asia provides the backdrop to the story of Jim's desertion of an apparently sinking ship and subsequent efforts to redeem himself; modelled upon the sailor A.P. Williams, Jim's character also yields echoes of Rajah Brooke of Sarawak.

★ **J.G. Farrell** *The Singapore Grip*. Lengthy novel – Farrell's last – of World War II Singapore in which real and fictitious characters flit from tennis to dinner party as the countdown to the Japanese occupation begins.

Henri Fauconnier *The Soul of Malaya*. Fauconnier's semi-autobiographical novel is a lyrical, sensory tour of the plantations, jungle and beaches of early twentieth-century Malaya, and pierces deeply into the underside of the country.

K.S. Maniam *In A Far Country*; *Haunting the Tiger*. The purgative writings of this Tamil-descended Malaysian author are strong, highly descriptive and humorous – essential reading.

Preeta Samarasan *Evening Is The Whole Day*. Set mostly in 1950s Ipoh, this debut novel ruthlessly dissects the lives of a dysfunctional upper-middle-class Indian family, with precious few laughs to be had in a tale of infidelity, class disparities and violence behind closed doors.

★ **W. Somerset Maugham** *Short Stories Volume 4*. Peopled by hoary sailors, bored plantation-dwellers and colonials wearing mutton-chop whiskers and topees, Maugham's short stories resuscitate Malaya c.1900; quintessential colonial literature graced by an easy style and a steady eye for a story.

Tan Tuan Eng *The Gift of Rain* and *The Garden of Evening Mists*. By a South Africa-based Malaysian, both these novels are deliberately paced and infused with the author's passion for Japanese culture. The first, set in Penang, focuses on the curious relationship between a Eurasian boy and his family's Japanese tenant as war breaks out, while the second follows a Chinese wartime internee during the subsequent Emergency, when she returns to the Cameron Highlands to confront her ghosts and an old Japanese acquaintance.

Language

Malay, officially referred to as Bahasa Melayu (literally "Malay language"), is the national language of Malaysia, Singapore and Brunei. Part of the Austronesian language family, it's an old tongue that became a regional lingua franca through its use in the ancient kingdom of Srivijaya and during the fifteenth-century Melaka Sultanate. Native speakers of the language are found not just in Peninsular Malaysia and northern Borneo but also in pockets of Indonesia, where a version of Malay has been adopted as the official language.

Malay is only one of many languages used in the three countries covered in this book. In Singapore, English, Mandarin and Tamil are also official tongues, with English pre-eminent as the language of government and business, while Hokkien is the most used regional Chinese dialect. In Malaysia itself, English retains an important position in business, law and government, Tamil is widely spoken among the Indian community, while Mandarin is much used by the Chinese, as are Chinese dialects such as Cantonese (especially in KL and Ipoh) and Hokkien (in Penang and on the east coast).

In practice, **English** is fairly widely understood except in rural areas and in the Malay-dominated east coast and the north of the Peninsula, where it really does pay to pick up a few words of Malay, especially since the basics are simple enough to learn. Besides, it's entertaining to get to grips with a tongue that, like English, is a ready absorber of loan words. The influence of English on modern Malay is apparent to most travellers, and with an awareness of Asian languages, it's not hard to discern the infusion of words from Sanskrit (stemming from the ancient impact of Hinduism on Southeast Asia), such as *jaya* ("success") and *negara* ("country"), as well as from Arabic, which has contributed words like *maaf* ("sorry") and many terms to do with Islam.

To pick up the language, it's best to buy a coursebook that focuses on **vernacular** Malay, as our vocabulary section does, rather than the formal language used in print and broadcasting. A good choice is *A Course in Conversational Malay* by Malcolm W. Mintz (SNP Publishing, Singapore).

Pronunciation

Malay was once written in Arabic script, but over the years this has been almost completely supplanted by a Romanized form. However, the Romanized **spellings** are prone to inconsistencies: for example, *baru*, "new", crops up in variant forms in place names like Johor Bahru and Kota Bharu, while new and old spellings of certain common words still coexist, for example *sungai/sungei, kampung/kampong*, and so forth.

Spelling quirks aside, Bahasa Malaysia is one of the more straightforward languages to pronounce, once you get your head round a few rules. One basic point to remember is that the consonants **k, p, t** have slightly less force in Malay than in English (to be precise, they aren't aspirated in Malay); if you emulate the sounds at the start of the Spanish words *cuatro, pero* and *toro*, you'd be in the right ball park. Other points of difference are listed below.

Syllable stress isn't complicated in Malay, though it can seem unnatural to English speakers. As a general rule, the stress lands on the **penultimate syllable** of a word (or, with words of two syllables, on the first syllable), hence SaRAwak, TerengGAnu. The chief exception concerns two-syllable words whose first syllable contains a short vowel (usually denoted by an "e"); in such cases, the stress sometimes falls on the second syllable – as in *beSAR* (big), *leKAS* (fast), and so forth; unfortunately, this isn't predictable.

MANGLISH AND SINGLISH

Manglish and **Singlish**, the distinctive forms of English widely spoken in Malaysia and Singapore respectively, can be as confusing to the uninitiated as Jamaican patois. They're really two sides of the same coin: in both, conventional English syntax gives way to a word order that's more akin to Malay or Chinese, and tenses and pronouns are discarded. Ask someone if they've ever been abroad, and you might be answered "I ever", while enquiring whether they've just been shopping might yield "Go, come back already". Responses are almost invariably distilled down to single-word replies, often repeated for stress. Request something in a shop and you'll hear "have, have", or "got, got". Other stock manglings of English include:

aidontch-main	"I don't mind"
betayudon(lah)	"You'd better not do that!"
debladigarmen	A contraction of "the bloody government"
is it?	(pronounced *eezeet*?) "Really?"
tingwat	"What do you think?"
watudu	"What can we do?", a rhetorical question
yusobadwan	"You're such a bad one!" meaning "that's not very nice!"

Suffixes and **exclamations** drawn from Malay and Hokkien complete this patois, the most notable being the Malay intensifier "lah", which seems to finish off just about every other utterance. In Malaysia you may hear the Malay question marker "kah" at the ends of queries, while Chinese on both sides of the Causeway might apply the suffix "ah", as in "so cheap one ah", which translates as "is it really that cheap?" or "wow, that's cheap" depending on the intonation; "ah" on its own can also mean "yes", especially if accompanied by a nod of the head. If Manglish and Singlish have you baffled, you might try raising your eyes to the heavens and crying either "ayoh" (with a drop of tone on the second syllable) or "alamak", both expressions denoting exasperation or dismay.

While these linguistic quirks often amuse foreigners and locals alike, both countries are worried that an apparent decline in **English standards** could affect their ability to do business globally. During the colonial era, the minority who could speak English tended to have a decent facility for the language. Now all students learn some English in school (in Singapore, English is actually the official language of education), but often they emerge with a weak grasp of the language. In Malaysia, there is an ongoing debate over English, with Malay nationalists wanting to emphasize Malay and other communities wanting English to get more prominence in the school curriculum. For its part, Singapore, a country with a history of preachy state campaigns, has seen the creation of a government-backed Speak Good English movement (Ⓦ www.goodenglish.org.sg).

VOWELS AND DIPHTHONGS

a somewhere in between the vowels of c**a**rp and c**u**p, but changes to a short indeterminate vowel if at the end of a word, as in banan**a**

aa like two "a" vowels separated by the merest pause; thus *maaf* (forgiveness) is rendered ma + af

ai as in f**i**ne (written "ei" in older spellings)

au as in h**ow**

e as in h**er**, though in many instances (not predictable) it is like the é of saut**é**, as in *kereta* (car), pronounced *keréta;* in yet others it denotes a short indeterminate vowel

i somewhere between the **i** of t**i**n and the **ee** of t**ee**n

o as in st**o**ne, though shorter and not as rounded as in English

u sometimes short as in p**u**ll, sometimes long (eg, if at the end of a word) as in p**oo**l

ua as in d**oer**

CONSONANTS

c as in **ch**ip (and written "ch" in older spellings), though slightly gentler than in English

d becomes **t** when at the end of a word

g hard, as in **g**irl

h can drop out when flanked by vowels; thus *tahu*, "know", is usually pronounced as though spelt **tau**

k drops out if at the end of the word or if followed by another consonant, becoming a glottal stop (a brief pause); thus *rakyat* (people) is pronounced ra + yat

kh as in the Scottish lo**ch**; found in loan words from Arabic

l unlike in English, l is not swallowed if it occurs at the end of a word

ng as in ta**ng** (the "g" is never hard – thus *telinga*, "ear", is te-ling-a and not te-lin-ga); can occur at the start of a word

ngg as in ta**ng**o
ny as in ca**ny**on; can occur at the start of a word
r is lightly trilled (though in some accents it can be

rendered like the French r of Paris); drops out at the ends of words when preceded by a vowel
sy as in **sh**ut

Grammar

Word order in Malay is similar to that in English, though note that adjectives usually follow nouns. **Nouns** have no genders and don't require an article, while the **plural** form is constructed either by saying the word twice, if the number of objects is unspecified (thus "book" is *buku*, "books" *buku-buku*, sometimes written *buku2*), or by specifying the number of objects before the singular noun ("three books" is thus *tiga buku*). **Verbs** have no tenses either, the time of the action being indicated either by the context, or by the use of words such as *akan* (functioning like "will") and *sudah* ("already") for the future and past. The verb "to be" seldom appears explicitly, so, for example, *saya lapar* literally means "I [am] hungry". There are two words for **negation**: *bukan*, used before nouns (for example *saya bukan doktor*, "I'm not a doctor"), and *tak* (formally *tidak*), used before verbs and adjectives (as in *saya tak lapar*, "I'm not hungry"; *saya tak makan*, "I've not eaten"). Possessive constructions are achieved simply by putting the "owner" after the thing that's "owned"; thus *kampung saya*, literally "village [of] I", is "my village".

Malay words and phrases

One point to note regarding **pronouns** is that Malay lacks a convenient word for "you", all the options being either too formal or informal. In fact, the normal way to address someone is to use their name to their face, which can seem strange to English-speakers. If you don't know someone's name, then you can use *abang* (brother) or *kak* (sister) to address a person of roughly the same age as you, or *adik* to a child, or *pak cik* or *mak cik* to a much older man or woman respectively.

You'll often see the word Dato' (or Datuk) or Tun placed before the name of a government official or some other worthy. Both are honorific titles of distinction roughly equivalent to the British "Sir". Royalty are always addressed as Tuanku.

PERSONAL PRONOUNS

I/my	saya	**he/she**	dia
we (excludes the person being spoken to) or **kita** (includes the person being spoken to)	kami	**they**	mereka
		Mr	Encik *or* Tuan
		Mrs	Puan
		Miss	Cik
you (formal) or **awak** (informal)	anda		

GREETINGS AND OTHER BASICS

"Selamat" is the all-purpose greeting derived from Arabic, which communicates a general goodwill.

good morning	selamat pagi	**safe journey**	selamat jalan
good afternoon	selamat petang	**welcome**	selamat datang
good midday (used around noon)	selamat tengah hari	**bon appetit**	selamat makan
		how are you?	apa khabar?
good evening	selamat malam	**fine**	baik *or* bagus
good night (literally "peaceful sleep")	selamat tidur	**see you again**	jumpa lagi
		please	tolong
goodbye (literally "peaceful stay"; used by someone leaving)	selamat tinggal	**thank you**	terima kasih
		you're welcome	sama-sama
		sorry/excuse me	maaf

never mind, no matter	tak apalah	**husband**	suami
yes	ya (sometimes pronounced a bit like "year")	**wife**	isteri
		friend	kawan
no	tidak	**person**	orang
this/that	ini/itu	**do you speak English?**	boleh cakap bahasa inggeris?
here	sini		
there (very nearby),	situ	**I (don't) understand**	saya (tak) faham
(further away)	sana	**that's fine/allowed**	boleh
what is your name?	siapa nama awak?	**can you help me?**	boleh tolong saya?
my name is…	nama saya…	**can I…?**	boleh saya…?
where are you from?	dari mana?	**to have, there is/are**	ada
I come from…	saya dari…	**what?**	apa?
…England	…England	**what is this/that?**	apa ini/itu?
…America	…Amerika	**when?**	bila?
…Australia	…Australia	**where?**	di mana?
…Canada	…Kanada	**who?**	siapa?
…New Zealand	…Zealandia Baru (or just "New Zeelan")	**why?**	mengapa? or kenapa?
		how?	bagaimana?
…Ireland	…Irlandia	**how much/many?**	berapa?
…Scotland	…Skotlandia		

USEFUL ADJECTIVES

good	bagus	**enough**	cukup
a lot	banyak	**open/closed**	buka/tutup
a little	sikit or sedikit	**hungry**	lapar
cheap/expensive	murah/mahal	**thirsty**	haus
hot/cold	panas/sejuk	**tired**	letih
big/small	besar/kecil	**ill**	sakit

USEFUL VERBS

come/go	datang/pergi	**know (someone)**	kenal
do	buat	**like**	suka
eat/drink	makan/minum	**push/pull**	tolak/tarik
enter, go in	masuk	**see**	tengok
give/take	beri/ambil	**sit**	duduk
have, possess	punya or ada	**sleep**	tidur
hear	dengar	**want**	mahu
help	tolong	**wish to, intend to**	nak
know (something)	tahu		

GETTING AROUND AND DIRECTIONS

where is…?	di mana…?	**wait**	tunggu
I want to go to…	saya mahu pergi ke…	**turn**	belok
how do I get there?	bagaimanakah saya boleh ke sana?	**left**	kiri
		right	kanan
how far?	berapa jauh?	**straight on**	terus
how long will it take?	berapa lama?	**in front**	di depan or di hadapan
when will the bus leave?	bila bas berangkat?	**behind**	di belakang
what time does the train arrive?	jam berapa keretapi sampai?	**north**	utara
		south	selatan
go up, ride	naik	**east**	timur
get down, disembark	turun	**west**	barat
nearby/far away	dekat/jauh	**street**	jalan
stop	berhenti	**airport**	lapangan terbang

bus station	stesen bas *or sometimes* hentian bas	**ticket**	tiket
		fare (adults/children)	tambang (dewasa/kanak-kanak)
train station	stesen keretapi		
jetty	jeti *or* pangkalan	**house**	rumah
bicycle	baisikal	**post office**	pejabat pos
boat	bot *or* bot penambang (the latter is used of small passenger-carrying craft)	**restaurant**	restoran
		church	gereja
		mosque	masjid
longboat	perahu *or* bot panjang	**Chinese temple**	tokong
car	kereta	**museum**	muzium
motorcycle	motosikal	**park, reserve**	taman
plane	kapal terbang	**toilet (men/women)**	tandas (lelaki/perempuan)
taxi	teksi	**entrance**	masuk
trishaw	beca	**exit**	keluar

ACCOMMODATION

hotel	hotel	**bath, shower**	mandi
guesthouse	rumah tumpangan *or* rumah rehat	**I need a room**	saya perlu satu bilik
		I'm staying for... nights	saya mahu tinggal...malam
dorm	asrama	**please clean my room**	tolong bersih-kan bilik saya
room (double/single)	bilik (untuk dua/satu)	**can I store my luggage here?**	boleh titip barang?
bed (double/single)	katil (kelamin/bujang)		
fan	kipas	**I want to pay**	saya nak bayar
air-conditioned	berhawa dingin		

BANKING AND SHOPPING

how much is...?	berapa harga...?	**market**	pasar
I want to buy...	saya mahu beli...	**night market**	pasar malam
can you reduce the price?	boleh kurang?	**supermarket**	pasaraya
I'll give you no more than...	saya bayar tidak lebih dari...	**bank**	bank
I'm just looking	saya hanya lihat-lihat	**money**	wang *or* duit
shop	kedai	**moneychanger**	pengurup wang

NUMBERS

0	kosong	**10**	sepuluh
1	satu (sometimes shortened to the prefix "se-" when used with a noun)	**11**	sebelas
		12	duabelas
		20	duapuluh
2	dua	**21**	duapuluh satu
3	tiga	**100**	seratus
4	empat	**121**	seratus duapuluh satu
5	lima	**200**	duaratus
6	enam	**1000**	seribu
7	tujuh	**2000**	duaribu
8	lapan	**1 million**	sejuta
9	sembilan	**a half**	setengah

TIME AND DAYS OF THE WEEK

what time is it?	pukul jam berapa?	**quarter to six ("five three-quarters")**	lima tiga suku
time is...	pukul...		
three o'clock	tiga	**six-thirty ("six half")**	enam setengah
ten past four	empat sepuluh	**7am**	tujuh pagi
quarter past five	lima suku	**8pm**	lapan malam

hour	jam	**later**	nanti
minute	minit	**next...**	...depan
second	detik	**last...**	....yang lalu, ...lepas
day	hari	**not yet**	belum lagi
week	minggu	**never**	tak pernah
month	bulan	**Monday**	hari Isnin
year	tahun	**Tuesday**	hari Selasa
today	hari ini	**Wednesday**	hari Rabu
tomorrow	esok or besok	**Thursday**	hari Kamis
yesterday	semalam or on the east coast kelmarin	**Friday**	hari Jumaat
		Saturday	hari Sabtu
now	sekarang	**Sunday**	hari Ahad or Minggu

Food and drink glossary

The list below concentrates on Malay terminology, though a few Chinese and Indian terms appear (unfortunately, transliteration of these varies widely), as well as definitions of some culinary words used in local English.

BASICS, INCLUDING COOKING METHODS

Deciphering menus and ordering is sometimes a matter of matching ingredients and cooking methods – for example, to get an approximation of chips or French fries, you'd ask for *kentang goreng*, literally "fried potatoes". If you don't want your food spicy, say *jangan taruh cili* ("don't add chilli") or *saya tak suka pedas* ("I don't like spicy [food]").

bakar baked
bubur porridge
garpu fork
goreng fried
istimewa special (as in "today's special")
kari curry
kedai kek bakery ("cake shop")
kedai kopi a diner ("coffee shop") concentrating on inexpensive rice spreads, noodles and other dishes, while serving some beverages
kering dried
kopitiam Hokkien Chinese term for a *kedai kopi*; commonly used in Singapore
kuah gravy
kukus steamed
layan diri self-service
lemak "fatty"; often denotes use of coconut milk

makanan/minuman food/drink
mangkuk bowl
manis sweet
masam sour
masin salty
medan selera food court
panggang grilled
pedas spicy
pinggan plate
pisau knife
rebus boiled
restoran restaurant
sedap tasty
sudu spoon
sup/sop soup
tumis stir-fried, sautéed
warung stall

MEAT (DAGING) AND POULTRY

ayam chicken
babi pork
burong puyuh quail
char siew Cantonese honey roast pork

daging lembu (**sapi** in Borneo) beef
itek duck
kambing mutton
lap cheong sweetish, fatty pork sausage (Cantonese)

FISH (IKAN) AND OTHER SEAFOOD

ambal bamboo clams, a Sarawak delicacy
fishball spherical fish dumpling, rubbery in texture, often added to noodles and soups
fishcake fish dumpling in slices, often added to noodles
ikan bawal pomfret

lian bilis anchovy
ikan keli catfish
ikan kembong mackerel
ikan kerapu grouper
ikan kurau threadfin

ikan merah red snapper
ikan pari skate
ikan siakap sea bass
ikan tongkol tuna
ikan yu or **jerung** shark
kepiting or **ketam** crab

kerang cockles
keropok lekor tubular fish dumplings (an east-coast
speciality)
sotong squid, cuttlefish
udang prawn
udang galah lobster

VEGETABLES (SAYUR)

bangkwang a radish-like root (also called *jicama*), used
in Chinese *rojak* and in *popiah* fillings
bawang onion
bawang putih garlic
bayam spinach or spinach-like greens
bendi okra, ladies' fingers
bunga kobis cauliflower
bendawan mushroom
chye sim or **choy sum** brassica greens, similar to *pak choy*
cili chilli
halia ginger
jagung corn
kacang beans, pulses or nuts
kangkung convolvulus greens with narrow leaves and
hollow stems; aka water spinach or morning glory
keladi yam

keledek sweet potato
kentang potatoes
kobis cabbage
lada chilli
lobak radish
lobak merah carrot
midin jungle fern, much served in Sarawak
pak choy or **pek chye** soft-leaved brassica greens with
broad stalks
petai beans in large pods from a tree, often sold in bunches
pucuk paku fern tips, eaten as greens
rebung bamboo shoots
tauge beansprouts
terung aubergine
timun cucumber
ubi kayu tapioca

OTHER INGREDIENTS

asam tamarind; also used to indicate a dish flavoured
with tamarind
belacan pungent fermented shrimp paste
daun pandan pandanus (screwpine) leaf, imparting a
sweet bouquet to foods with which it's cooked; used
not only in desserts but also in some rice dishes
garam salt
gula sugar
gula Melaka palm-sugar molasses, used to sweeten
cendol and other desserts

kaya orange or green curd jam made with egg and
coconut; delicious on toast
kicap soy sauce
kicap manis sweet dark soy sauce
mentega butter
minyak oil
tahu tofu (beancurd)
telur egg
tempeh fermented soybean cakes, nutty and slightly
sour

NOODLES AND NOODLE DISHES

The three most common types of noodle are *mee* (or *mi*), yellow egg noodles made from wheat flour; *bee hoon* (or *bihun* or *mee hoon*), like vermicelli; and *kuay teow* (or *hor fun*), like tagliatelle.

char kuay teow Chinese fried *kuay teow*, often seasoned
with *kicap manis*, and featuring any combination of
prawns, Chinese sausage, fishcake, egg, vegetables
and chilli
Foochow noodles steamed and served in soy and oyster
sauce with spring onions and dried fish
Hokkien fried mee *mee* and *bee hoon* fried with pieces
of pork, prawn and vegetables; a variant in KL has the
noodles cooked in soy sauce with *tempeh*
kang puan (or **kampua**) **mee** a rich Sibu speciality –
noodles cooked in lard
kolok mee *mee* served dryish, accompanied by *char
siew* slices

laksa basically noodles in a curried soup featuring
some seafood and flavoured with the *laksa*-leaf
herb (*daun kesom*); variations include Nonya *laksa*
(featuring coconut milk), *asam laksa* (Penang-
style, with tamarind) and *laksa Johor* (made with
spaghetti)
laksam *kuay teow* rice noodles in a fish sauce made
with coconut milk and served with *ulam* (salad); an
east-coast speciality
mee bandung *mee* served in thickish gravy flavoured
with beef and prawn (both of which garnish the dish)
mee goreng Indian or Malay fried noodles; Indian
versions are particularly spicy

mee hailam *mee* in an oyster-sauce-based gravy

mee kari noodles in a curried soup

mee pok Teochew dish using ribbon-like yellow noodles, served with fishballs and a chilli dressing

mee rebus boiled *mee*; varies regionally, but one of the best is that sold in Singapore, featuring *mee* in a sweetish sauce made with yellow bean paste, and garnished with boiled egg and tofu

mee siam *bee hoon* cooked in tangy-sweet soup

flavoured with tamarind, and garnished with slices of hard-boiled egg and beancurd

mee suah like *bee hoon* but even more threadlike and soft; can be made crispy if fried

sar hor fun flat rice noodles served in a chicken-stock soup, to which prawns, fried shallots and beansprouts are added; a speciality in Ipoh

wan ton mee roast pork, noodles and vegetables, accompanied by pork dumplings

RICE (NASI) DISHES AND SPREADS

char siew fan common one-plate meal, featuring *char siew* and gravy on a bed of steamed rice

claypot rice Chinese dish of rice topped with meat (such as *lap cheong*), cooked in an earthenware pot over a fire to create a smoky taste

daun pisang Malay term for banana-leaf curry, a Southern Indian meal with chutneys and curries, served on a mound of rice, and presented on a banana leaf with poppadums

Hainanese chicken rice Singapore's unofficial national rice dish: steamed or boiled chicken slices served on rice cooked in chicken stock, and accompanied by chicken broth, and a chilli and ginger dip

lemang glutinous rice stuffed into lengths of bamboo

nasi ayam Malay version of Hainanese chicken rice

nasi berlauk simply "rice with dishes"

nasi biryani saffron-flavoured rice cooked with chicken, beef or fish; a North Indian speciality

nasi campur standard term for a rice spread, served with an array of meat, fish and vegetable dishes to choose from

nasi dagang east-coast speciality; a slightly glutinous rice steamed with coconut milk, and often brownish in appearance, usually served with fish curry

nasi goreng rice fried with diced meat and vegetables and sometimes a little spice

nasi kandar a spread of rice and curries originating with Indian Muslim caterers in Penang; the rice is often stored in a container made of wood, which is said to give it a distinctive flavour

nasi kerabu blue or green rice traditionally coloured with flower pigments, though these days food colourings may be used; found particularly in Kelantan, it's usually served with a fish curry

nasi kunyit rice given a bright yellow colour by turmeric

nasi lemak a Malay classic, rice cooked with a little coconut milk and served with *ikan bilis*, cucumber, fried peanuts, fried or hard-boiled egg slices and *sambal*

nasi Minang rice spread featuring dishes cooked in the style of the Minang Highlands of western Sumatra; similar to **nasi Padang**

nasi minyak rice cooked with *ghee*

nasi Padang rice spread with the dishes cooked in the style of Padang, Sumatra

nasi putih plain boiled rice

nasi ulam rice containing blanched herbs and greens

pulut glutinous rice

ROTI (BREAD) DISHES

The word roti refers both to griddle breads and to Western bread, depending on the context.

murtabak thick griddle bread, usually savoury stuffed with onion, egg and chicken or mutton

murtabak pisang a sweet version of *murtabak*, stuffed with banana.

roti bakar toast, usually served with butter and *kaya*

roti bom an especially greasy *roti canai*, containing a cheesy-tasting margarine

roti canai light, layered griddle bread served with a thin curry sauce

roti John simple Indian dish, a French loaf split and stuffed with an egg, onion and sweet chilli sauce mixture; versions containing meat are occasionally seen

roti kahwin toast spread with butter and *kaya*

roti prata Singapore name for *roti canai*

roti telur *roti canai* with an egg mixed into the dough

roti telur bawang *roti canai* with an egg and chopped onion mixed into the dough

OTHER SPECIALITIES

ayam goreng Malay-style fried chicken

ayam percik barbecued chicken with a creamy coconut sauce; a Kota Bharu speciality

bak kut teh literally "meat bone tea", a Chinese soup made by boiling up pork ribs with soy sauce, ginger,

herbs and spices

chap chye a Nonya stew of mixed vegetables, fungi and sometimes also glass noodles (aka *tang hoon*, a rather elastic vermicelli)

chee cheong fun Cantonese speciality, vaguely like

ravioli, featuring minced shrimp rolled up in rice-flour sheets, steamed and dredged in a sweet-salty red sauce

chye tow kuay also known as "carrot cake", comprising a rice flour/white radish mixture formed into cubes and fried with egg and garlic; a savoury-sweet version with added *kicap manis* is also worth trying

congee watery rice gruel eaten with slices of meat or fish or omelette; sometimes listed on menus as "porridge"

dim sum Chinese meal of titbits – dumplings, pork ribs, etc – steamed or fried and served in bamboo baskets

dosa/dosai/thosai Southern Indian pancake, made from ground rice and lentils, and served with dhal (lentils); *masala dosa* features a potato stuffing, while *rava dosa* has grated carrot in the batter

fish-head curry the head of a red snapper (usually), cooked in a spicy curry sauce with tomatoes and okra

gado-gado Malay/Indonesian salad of lightly cooked vegetables, boiled egg, slices of rice cake and a crunchy peanut sauce

idli South Indian rice-and-lentil cakes, steamed

kari kepala ikan *see* fish-head curry

kongbian Chinese-style bagels, found only in Sibu

kuih pai tee Nonya dish vaguely resembling fried spring rolls, except that the *pai tee* are shaped like cup cakes; filling is like that for *popiah*

lontong a pairing of a *sayur lodeh*-like curry with rice cakes similar to *ketupat*

oothapam rice-and-lentil pancakes; South Indian

otak-otak mashed fish mixed with coconut milk and chilli paste, then steamed in strips wrapped in banana leaf; a Nonya dish

popiah spring rolls, consisting of a steamed dough wrapper filled with peanuts, egg, bean shoots, vegetables and a sweet sauce; sometimes known as *lumpia*

rendang dry, highly spiced coconut curry with beef, chicken or mutton

rojak The Chinese version is a salad of greens, beansprouts, pineapple and cucumber in a peanut and prawn-paste sauce; quite different is Indian *rojak*, a variety of fritters with sweet chilli dips

satar similar to *otak-otak* but made in triangular shapes; found on the east coast

satay marinated pieces of meat, skewered on small sticks and cooked over charcoal; served with peanut sauce, cucumber, raw onion and *ketupat* (rice cake)

sayur lodeh mixed vegetables stewed in a curry sauce containing coconut milk

sop ekor Malay oxtail soup

sop kambing spicy Malay mutton soup

sop tulang Malay beef-bone soup

steamboat Chinese fondue: raw meat, fish, veggies and other titbits dunked into a steaming broth until cooked

umai raw fish salad, mixed with shallots and lime, found in east Malaysia and Brunei

umbut kelapa masak lemak young coconut shoots, cooked in coconut milk

vadai South Indian fried lentil patty

yam basket Sarawak speciality: meat, vegetables and soya bean curd in a fried yam crust

yong tau foo bean curd, fishballs and assorted vegetables, poached and served with broth and sweet dipping sauces

SNACKS AND ACCOMPANIMENTS

acar pickle, often sweet and spicy

bak kwa Chinese-style sweet barbecued pork slices, eaten as a snack

budu fermented fish sauce

cempedak goreng *cempedak*, similar to jackfruit, fried in batter, allowing not just the flesh but also the floury stones to be eaten

curry puff also called *karipap* in Malay; a semicircular pastry parcel stuffed with curried meat and vegetables

kerabu not to be confused with *nasi kerabu*, this is a salad of grated unripe fruit, mixed with chilli, grated coconut, cucumber and other ingredients

keropok (goreng) deep-fried prawn or fish crackers, derived from a dough like that used to make *keropok lekor* (see p.248)

ketupat unseasoned rice cubes boiled in packets of woven coconut-leaf strips, served as an accompaniment to satay

pau or **pow** Chinese stuffed bun made with a sweetish dough and steamed; *char siew pau* contains Cantonese honey-roast pork, *kai pau* chicken and egg, while there are also *pau* with sweet fillings include bean paste, dried coconut or *kaya*

rasam sour-spicy South Indian soup flavoured with tamarind and tomato

sambal dip made with pounded or ground chilli; *sambal belacan* is augmented with a little *belacan* for extra depth of flavour

sambar watery South Indian curry served with *dosa*

tempoyak fermented durian paste, a Malay condiment

ulam Malay salad of raw vegetables and herbs

yew char kuay Chinese fried dough sticks, good dunked in coffee; not unlike Spanish *churros* in flavour and texture

DRINKS

When ordering beverages in a *kedai kopi*, there are various standard terms to bear in mind. *Kosong* ("zero") after the name of the drink means you want it black and unsugared; the suffix *-o* (pronounced "oh") means black with sugar, *susu* means with milk (invariably of the sweetened condensed variety), *ais* or *peng* means iced, *tarik* ("pulled") denotes the popular practice of frothing a drink by pouring it repeatedly from one mug to another and back, and *kurang manis* ("lacking sweetness") means to go easy on the sugar or condensed milk. A few places also allow you to order your drink *see* or *si*, meaning with unsweetened evaporated milk. It's quite possible to combine these terms, so in theory you could order *kopi susu tarik kurang manis peng*, which would be a frothy milky coffee, iced and not too sweet. Note that condensed milk is often assumed to be wanted even if you don't say *susu*.

air botol a bottled drink (usually refers to soft drinks)

air kelapa coconut water

air laici tinned lychee juice, very sweet, usually with a couple of lychees in the glass

air minum drinking water

air tebu sugar-cane juice

bandung or **air sirap bandung** a sweet drink, bright pink in colour, made with rose essence and a little milk

bir beer

chrysanthemum tea delicately fragrant tea made from chrysanthemum blossom, and served slightly sweet, either hot or cold

cincau or **chinchow** sweet drink, the colour of cola or stout, made with strips of jelly-like seaweed

jus juice (the word *jus* is usually followed by the name of the fruit in question)

kopi coffee; some *kedai kopis* offer it freshly brewed, others serve instant

kopi jantan coffee that's claimed to be a male tonic, often advertised with posters showing avuncular Malay men apparently endorsing the drink

kopi tongkat Ali similar to *kopi jantan* (*tongkat Ali* is a herb that Malays believe has aphrodisiac qualities for men)

lassi Indian sweet or salty yoghurt drink

susu milk

teh tea

teh bunga kekwa chrysanthemum

teh limau ais iced lemon tea

tuak rice wine (Borneo)

FRUIT (BUAH)

belimbing starfruit

betik papaya

cempedak similar to jackfruit

duku, duku langsat small round fruits containing bittersweet segments

durian famously stinky large fruit containing rows of seeds coated in sweet creamy flesh

durian belanda soursop

epal apple

jambu batu guava

kelapa coconut

laici lychee

limau lime or lemon

limau bali pomelo

mangga mango

manggis mangosteen

nanas pineapple

nangka jackfruit

nyiur alternative term for coconut

oren orange

pisang banana

rambutan hairy-skinned stone fruit with sweet white flesh

salak teardrop-shaped fruit with scaly brown skin and bitter flesh

tembikai watermelon

DESSERTS

agar-agar seaweed-derived jelly served in squares or diamonds, and often with coconut milk for richness

air batu campur ("ABC") another name for *ais kacang*

ais kacang ice flakes with red beans, cubes of jelly, sweetcorn, rose syrup and evaporated milk

bubur cha cha sweetened coconut milk with pieces of sweet potato, yam and tapioca

cendol coconut milk, palm sugar syrup and pea-flour noodles poured over shaved ice

cheng tng clear, sweet Chinese broth containing fungi and dried fruit

kuih or **kuih-muih** Malay/Nonya sweetmeats, ranging from something like a Western cake to fudge-like morsels made of mung bean or rice flour

kuih lapis layer cake; either a simple rice-flour confection, or an elaborate wheat-flour sponge comprising numerous very thin layers and unusually rich in egg

pisang goreng bananas or plantains coated in a thin batter and fried

Glossary

adat customary or traditional law

air water

air panas hot springs

air terjun waterfall

atap/attap palm thatch

Baba Straits-born Chinese (male)

bandar town

bandaraya city

bangunan building

banjaran mountain range

batang river system

batik wax and dye technique of cloth decoration

batu rock/stone

bejalai period in an Iban youth's life when he ventures out from the longhouse to experience life in the towns

belian a hardwood traditionally used to construct Sarawak longhouses

belukar secondary rainforest, essentially woodland that regrows in areas where primary forest has been disturbed or cut down

bomoh traditional spiritualist healer

bukit hill

bumbun hide

bumiputra person deemed indigenous to Malaysia ("son of the soil")

bungalow in local English, any detached house

candi temple

Cantonese pertaining to the Guangdong province of southeast China

daerah an administrative district

daulat divine force possessed by a ruler that commands unquestioning loyalty

Dayak/Dyak a now largely obsolete umbrella term once used to denote the tribal peoples of Borneo

dipterocarp the predominant family of trees in the rainforest, comprising many types of exceptionally tall trees reaching up to the top of the forest canopy

ekspres express (used of boats and buses)

empangan dam

Foochow pertaining to Fuzhou, a city in Fujian province, southeast China

gasing spinning top

gawai annual festivals celebrated by indigenous groups in Sarawak

gelanggang seni cultural centre

gereja church

godown warehouse

gongsi Chinese clan-house

gopuram sculpted deities over the entrance to a Hindu temple

gua cave

gunung mountain

Hainanese pertaining to Hainan Island, southeast China

halal something permissible in Islam

hill station a settlement or resort at relatively high altitude usually founded in colonial times as an escape from the heat of the lowlands

Hokkien pertaining to the Fujian province of southeast China, the main dialect of which is more formally called **minnan**

hutan forest

ikat woven fabric

istana palace

jalan road, street

jambatan bridge

kampung village

kelong a kind of fishing platform that extends out to sea from some beaches; it comprises two rows of vertical poles in the sea bed with a net at the far end, to which the fish are lured by a light hung over the water

kerangas sparse forest ("poor soil")

khalwat an offence under Islamic law, typically involving an unmarried Muslim couple being together in private

kongsi Chinese clan-house/temple; has entered Malay as a word meaning "share"

kota fort

kris wavy-bladed Malay dagger

kuala river confluence or estuary

labu gourd; also used of the gourd-like ceramic bottles made as souvenirs in some parts of the Peninsula

lata waterfall

laut sea

lebuh avenue

lebuhraya highway/expressway

lorong lane

mak yong courtly dance-drama

makam grave or tomb

Malaya old name for the area now called Peninsular Malaysia

Mamak Indian Muslim; used particularly of restaurants run by Indian Muslims

mandi Asian method of showering by dousing with water from a tank using a small bucket or dipper

masjid mosque

Mat Salleh Malaysian colloquial term for a foreigner, usually a white person

Melayu Malay

menara minaret or tower

merdeka freedom, in general; can specifically refer to Malaysian independence

Minangkabau matriarchal people from Sumatra
negara national
nipah a type of palm tree
Nonya Straits-born Chinese (female)
Orang Asli Peninsular Malaysia aborigines ("original people"); also Orang Ulu (upriver people) and Orang Laut (sea people)
padang field/square; usually the main town square
pangkalan jetty or port (literally "base")
pantai beach
parang machete
pasar market
pasar malam night market
pasir sand
pejabat Daerah district office
pejabat Pos post office
pekan town
pelabuhan port/harbour
penghulu chieftain, leader
Peranakan Straits-born Chinese
perigi well
persekutuan federal
pintu arch/gate/door
pondok hut or shelter
pulau island
rajah prince
Ramadan Muslim fasting month
rebana drum
rotan rattan; used in the infliction of corporal punishment
rumah persinggahan lodging house
rumah rehat older guesthouse (literally "rest house"), now mainly privately run, though once state-owned
rumah tumpangan boarding house
samping songket worn by a man as a short sarong over loose trousers
saree traditional Indian woman's garment, worn in conjunction with a **choli** (short-sleeved blouse)

sarung/sarong cloth worn as a wrap around the lower body
sekolah school
semenanjung Peninsula
seni art or skill
shophouse a two-storey terraced building found mainly in town centres, and often featuring a facade that is recessed at street level, providing a shaded walkway that serves as a pavement
silat Malay art of self-defence
songket brocade
songkok Malay male headgear, a little like a flattish fez, made of black velvet over cardboard
storm corridor an exterior pathway with an overhead shelter throughout its length
sultan ruler
sungai/sungei river
t'ai chi Chinese martial art; commonly performed as an early-morning exercise
taman park
tamu market/fair
tanjung/tanjong cape, headland
tasik/tasek lake
telaga freshwater spring or well
teluk/telok bay or inlet
Teochew pertaining to Chaozhou, a city in Fujian province, southeast China
tokong Chinese temple
towkay Chinese merchant
tuai tribal headman (Sarawak)
Wasai Waterfall or an area with a pool (Brunei)
wau kite
wayang show, ranging from a film screening to Chinese opera
wayang kulit shadow-puppet play (literally "skin show", after the fact that the puppets are made of hide)
wisma house (used of commercial buildings rather than residences)

ACRONYMS

ASEAN Association of Southeast Asian Nations, an economic and political grouping of ten regional states, including Malaysia, Singapore and Brunei
BN Barisan Nasional or National Front – the coalition, dominated by UMNO, which has governed Malaysia since 1974
KTM Keretapi Tanah Melayu, the Malaysian national railway company
MAS Malaysia Airlines
MCA Malaysian Chinese Association, the Chinese wing of the governing BN

MCP Malayan Communist Party
MRT Singapore's Mass Rapid Transit system
PAP Singaporean People's Action Party
PAS Parti Islam SeMalaysia, the Pan-Malaysian Islamic Party
PKR Parti Keadilan Rakyat, the Malaysian opposition People's Justice Party (usually called simply Keadilan)
SIA Singapore Airlines
UMNO United Malays National Organization

Small print and index

A ROUGH GUIDE TO ROUGH GUIDES

Published in 1982, the first Rough Guide – to Greece – was a student scheme that became a publishing phenomenon. Mark Ellingham, a recent graduate in English from Bristol University, had been travelling in Greece the previous summer and couldn't find the right guidebook. With a small group of friends he wrote his own guide, combining a highly contemporary, journalistic style with a thoroughly practical approach to travellers' needs.

The immediate success of the book spawned a series that rapidly covered dozens of destinations. And, in addition to impecunious backpackers, Rough Guides soon acquired a much broader readership that relished the guides' wit and inquisitiveness as much as their enthusiastic, critical approach and value-for-money ethos.

These days, Rough Guides include recommendations from budget to luxury and cover more than 200 destinations around the globe, as well as producing an ever-growing range of eBooks and apps.

Visit **roughguides.com** to see our latest publications.

Rough Guide credits

Editor: Greg Ward
Layout: Sachin Tanwar, Pradeep Thapliyal
Cartography: Ashutosh Bharti
Picture editor: Sarah Ross
Proofreader: Karen Parker
Managing editor: Keith Drew
Assistant editor: Dipika Dasgupta
Production: Rebecca Short
Cover design: Nicole Newman, Chloë Roberts, Pradeep Thapliyal

Editorial assistant: Eleanor Aldridge
Senior pre-press designer: Dan May
Design director: Scott Stickland
Travel publisher: Joanna Kirby
Digital travel publisher: Peter Buckley
Reference director: Andrew Lockett
Operations coordinator: Becky Doyle
Publishing director (Travel): Clare Currie
Commercial manager: Gino Magnotta
Managing director: John Duhigg

Publishing information

This seventh edition published July 2012 by
Rough Guides Ltd,
80 Strand, London WC2R 0RL
11, Community Centre, Panchsheel Park,
New Delhi 110017, India
Distributed by the Penguin Group
Penguin Books Ltd,
80 Strand, London WC2R 0RL
Penguin Group (USA)
375 Hudson Street, NY 10014, USA
Penguin Group (Australia)
250 Camberwell Road, Camberwell,
Victoria 3124, Australia
Penguin Group (NZ)
67 Apollo Drive, Mairangi Bay, Auckland 1310,
New Zealand
Penguin Group (South Africa)
Block D, Rosebank Office Park, 181 Jan Smuts Avenue,
Parktown North, Gauteng, South Africa 2193
Rough Guides is represented in Canada by Tourmaline
Editions Inc. 662 King Street West, Suite 304, Toronto,
Ontario M5V 1M7
Printed in Singapore by Toppan Security Printing Pte. Ltd.

© David Leffman & Richard Lim 2012
Maps © Rough Guides
No part of this book may be reproduced in any form
without permission from the publisher except for the
quotation of brief passages in reviews.
632pp includes index
A catalogue record for this book is available from the
British Library
ISBN: 978-1-40539-034-7
The publishers and authors have done their best to
ensure the accuracy and currency of all the information in
The Rough Guide to Malaysia, Singapore and Brunei,
however, they can accept no responsibility for any loss,
injury, or inconvenience
sustained by any traveller as a result of information or
advice contained in the guide.
1 3 5 7 9 8 6 4 2

MIX
Paper from
responsible sources
FSC™ C018179

Help us update

We've gone to a lot of effort to ensure that the seventh
edition of **The Rough Guide to Malaysia, Singapore and
Brunei** is accurate and up-to-date. However, things change
– places get "discovered", opening hours are notoriously
fickle, restaurants and rooms raise prices or lower standards.
If you feel we've got it wrong or left something out, we'd like
to know, and if you can remember the address, the price,
the hours, the phone number, so much the better.

Please send your comments with the subject line
**"Rough Guide Malaysia, Singapore and Brunei
Update"** to ✉ mail@uk.roughguides.com. We'll credit all
contributions and send a copy of the next edition (or any
other Rough Guide if you prefer) for the very best emails.
Find more travel information, connect with fellow
travellers and book your trip on ⓦ roughguides.com

ABOUT THE AUTHORS

David Leffman has been travelling around and writing about Southeast Asia since 1988. His guidebooks include the *Rough Guide to Indonesia, Rough Guide to Hong Kong* and *Rough Guide to Southwest China*.

Not to be confused with his Singapore journalist namesake, **Richard Lim** (goo.gl/2jY9c) spent many years working in book publishing, including a stint as a Rough Guides editor. Nowadays, he edits articles for magazines while taking regular time out to wander around Southeast Asia and the Middle East. He lives in London.

Acknowledgements

David: Thanks to Susanna Goho-Quek, Salma Khoo, Kim Sifu, Richard Lim, Fong Sutton.

Richard would like to thank the Sarawak Tourism Board, particularly Maurice Balang for advice and friendship over the years, plus Rose, Deckson, Amirul, JC, Rudy, Amirul and 'Soff. Thanks also to Elaine and Roselan at the Sarawak Forestry Corporation; Wayne and Emong at Borneo Adventure; James Jinyong; James and Jonathan at Planet Borneo; Mathew Ngau-Jau; Benjamin Angki; James Handfield-Jones; Enang; Tom Hewitt; Reddish; Mohd Fazil at KTM; and Tan Teck Guan. In Brunei, special thanks to Chris and Salinah at Brunei Tourism, plus Hoe Guan Hui. Over in Singapore, thanks are due to Susanah at the Singapore Tourism Board, and to Tony Tan, Joe Ng and Case. Special gratitude to Neil Morsley for sharing his experiences of Kelabit Highlands treks, to Surin and Cynthia for their perennially sound advice on background matters, and to David for being a great co-author and the all-too-infrequent Sichuan meal. Biggest thanks of all to my family in Singapore for their support and their help with reviews; and to Ooi Kee Beng, John Gee and Rabih Yazbeck.

The authors would also like to thank Greg for thorough editing, the cartographers in London and Delhi for preparing excellent maps, John for such detailed updating of the East Coast, South and Sabah chapters, plus of course Keith for pulling the whole book together.

John: On the east coast, thanks to Nur Azmina Ahmad; Pawi Bin Jafar; Ain Nadia Kamarudin; Kang at Ideal Travellers' House; Lee Khing Kit; Alex Lee and his staff at Ping Anchorage (particularly Maslina Mansor); Wan Halimi Wan Muhammad; Daniel Quilter from Ecoteer; Amran Abdul Rahman; the ladies of Pewanis; and the crew from Turtle Bay Divers and Steffen Sea Sports. In the south, thanks to Musalmah Mohd Akil; Zainal Hamid; Rohanna Ibrahim; Noraini Jalikin; Zarina Johari; Mani and Raymond at Rooftop Guest House; Kevin Soh (and friends) at Eats & Beats; and Louis van Wermeskerken at Salang Hut. In Sabah, special thanks to Robin Chin, Sharon Kenny and Elvina Ong, each of whom went out their way to make my job easier. Thanks also to Tom Hewitt; George Hong and his staff in both KK and Danum Valley; Kattie Hoo; Bernadette Jiliu; Martin Kong; Johnny Lim; David Michael; Linn Ngui; KL Tan; Fernando Rulloda; the friendly staff at Scuba Junkie; and the taxi driver (whose name I have forgotten) who waited for ages with me at a roundabout in Kota Belud. Back in London, thanks to Laurence Logan Lechumanan. Finally, Sheryll Sulit deserves credit for her support both on and off the road.

Readers' letters

Thanks to all the readers who have taken the time to write in with comments and suggestions (and apologies if we've inadvertently omitted or misspelt anyone's name):

John Adams; Geraldine Barton; Coen Brouwer; Victor Brumby; Tristran Cooper; Elgon Corner; Aja Dailey; Fabio Datri; Valerie Ferguson; Wouter Karsten; Monica Mackaness and John Garratt; Emily Mackie; Neil McWhinnie; Emma Ramsdale; Syahrul Razlan; Carla Alexandra Ferreira Rodrigues; Chris Sinclair; Jeroen van Marle

Photo credits

All photos © Rough Guides except the following:
(Key: t-top; c-centre; b-bottom; l-left; r-right)

p.1 Ocean/Corbis
p.2 ADS/Alamy
p.4 Atlantide Phototravel/Corbis (l); Rod Porteous/Robert Harding World Imagery/Corbis (c); Getty Images (r)
p.5 MacDuff Everton/Corbis
p.9 Peter Horree/Alamy (t); Carlos Munoz/Getty (b)
p.11 Robert Harding/Alamy
p.12 BAZUKI MUHAMMAD/Corbis
p.13 Victor Paul Borg/Alamy
p.14 Macduff Everton/CORBIS
p.15 Paul Seheult/Eye Ubiquitous/Corbis (t); Cockrem/Alamy (b)
p.16 Crystite licenced/Alamy (t); Getty (c); Scubazoo/Alamy (b)
p.17 James Davis Photography/Alamy (t); Victor Paul Borg/Alamy (b)
p.18 Thomas Cockrem/Alamy (t); Robert Francis/Robert Harding World Imagery/Corbis (b)
p.19 David Poole/Robert Harding World Imagery/Corbis (t); Felix Hug/Corbis (b)
p.20 Morris, Steven/the food passionates/Corbis (t); Andrew Watson/Getty (b)
p.21 Adrian Lyon/Alamy (tl); ULTRA.F/Getty (tr); Then Chih Wey/Xinhua Press/Corbis (bl); Inmagine Asia/Corbis (br)
p.22 Chris Hellier/Corbis (t); Rainforest World Music Festival (b)
p.23 Fiona Rogers/Corbis (t); David Kirkland/Getty (c); Sergio Pitamitz Collection/Alamy (b)
p.24 Thomas Cockrem/Alamy (l); Bruno Morandi/Hemis/Corbis (r)
p.26 Moon Yin Lam/Alamy
pp.62–63 Atlantide Phototravel/Corbis
p.65 Simon Reddy/Alamy
p.81 Jose Fuste Raga/Corbis (t); Peter Guttman/Corbis (bl); Jon Hicks/Corbis (br)
p.109 Tibor Bognar/Corbis
pp.116–117 Gavin Hellier/JAI/Corbis
p.119 Angelo Cavalli/Robert Harding World Imagery/Corbis

p.147 John Oates (t); Peter Adams/Corbis (b)
p.165 Rob Walls/Alamy
pp.186–188 Getty Images/Dorling Kindersley
p.190 Crystite licenced/Alamy
p.203 ADS/Alamy (t); Marc Anderson/Alamy (b)
pp.216–217 Hugh Sitton/Corbis
p.219 Aqua Image/Alamy
p.239 Mike Sivyer/Alamy
pp.266–267 Peter Adams/Corbis
p.269 Beaconstox/Alamy
p.289 © LOOK Die Bildagentur der Fotografen GmbH/Alamy
pp.312–313 Fiona Rogers/Corbis
p.315 Jay Sturdevant / Alamy
p.335 Richard Lim
p.353 David Poole/Robert Harding World Imagery/Corbis (tl); Asia Images Group Pte Ltd/Alamy (tr); dbimages/Alamy (b)
p.373 Joel W. Rogers/CORBIS (t); Tony Waltham/Robert Harding World Imagery/Corbis (b)
pp.390–391 Clownfishphoto/Alamy
p.393 Paul Kingsley/Alamy
p.403 Ozimages/Alamy
p.429 Stephanie Rabemiafara/Art in All of Us/Corbis (t); Lawson Wood/CORBIS (b)
pp.452–453 Stefano Paterna/Alamy
p.455 MJ Photography/Alamy
p.467 Iain Dainty/Alamy
pp.474–475 Allan Symon Gerry/Alamy
p.476 Travelscape Images/Alamy
p.499 Gavin Hellier/JAI/Corbis
p.527 Kumar Sriskandan/Alamy (t); GoPlaces/Alamy (b)
p.545 Andrew Woodley/Alamy (t); Travelscape Images/Alamy (b)
p.562 Ben Queenborough/Getty

Front cover Corbis
Back cover DK Limited/Corbis (t); Chris Hellier/Corbis (l); Louise Murray/Robert Harding World Imagery/Corbis (r)

Index

Maps are marked in grey

In this index, geographical features are mainly indexed under their Malay prefixes, for example "Tasik" for lakes – the exceptions being mountains, hills, islands and rivers, which are indexed by name (so to find Gunung Tahan, look under T).

Map symbols

The symbols below are used on maps throughout the book

- ✈ Airport
- ✈ Airport (regional)
- Ⓗ Helipad
- ⊖ MRT station (Singapore)
- ★ Transport stop
- Ⓟ Parking
- ⧫ Point of interest
- @ Internet access
- ⓘ Tourist office
- ✉ Post office
- ✚ Hospital
- Ⓒ Telephone
- Ⓗ Helipad

- ⊤ Public gardens
- ⏦ Golf course
- ∩ Arch
- ⚔ Castle/fort
- ♛ Museum
- 🏛 Monument
- ⚲ Swimming pool
- ⊠ Gate
- ▲ Peak
- ☄ Rock
- ☀ Hill shading
- ⌒ Cave
- ∴ Ruins

- ⛰ Marshland
- ⏀ Waterfall
- ⛰ Gorge
- ⛰ Viewpoint
- ⛩ Lighthouse
- ⛺ Campsite
- ⌂ Hut/hide
- 🕌 Mosque
- ☸ Buddhist temple
- 🕉 Hindu/Sikh temple
- 🏯 Chinese temple
- ✡ Synagogue
- 🐟 Snorkelling

- ⛪ Church (regional maps)
- ⛪ Church (town maps)
- ▭ Market
- ⬭ Stadium
- ▬ Building
- ▦ Park
- ▭ Beach
- ⊞ Christian cemetery
- ⊡ Muslim cemetery
- ━━ Wall
- – – – Ferry route
- ┅┅┅ Funicular

Listings key

- ■ Accommodation
- ● Eating
- ■ Drinking/nightlife
- ● Shop

ROUGH GUIDES

SO NOW WE'VE TOLD YOU
HOW TO MAKE THE MOST
OF YOUR TIME, WE WANT
YOU TO STAY SAFE AND
COVERED WITH OUR
FAVOURITE TRAVEL INSURER

WorldNomads.com
keep travelling safely

GET AN ONLINE QUOTE
roughguides.com/insurance

RECOMMENDED BY
ROUGH GUIDES

MAKE THE MOST OF YOUR TIME ON EARTH™

ROUGH GUIDES

MAKE THE MOST OF YOUR TIME IN BRITAIN

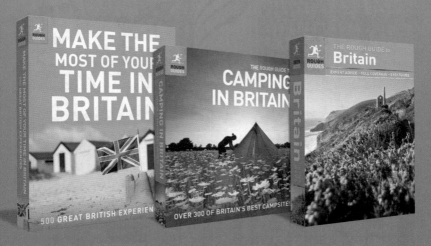

WITH OVER 700 **BOOKS, EBOOKS, MAPS**
AND **APPS** YOU'RE SURE TO BE INSPIRED

Start your journey at **roughguides.com**
MAKE THE MOST OF YOUR TIME ON EARTH™

MAKE THE MOST OF YOUR CITY BREAK

BARCELONA

LONDON

NEW YORK CITY

PARIS

ROME

FREE PULL OUT MAP WITH EVERY SIGHT AND LISTING FROM THE GUIDE

ESSENTIAL ITINERARIES AND RELIABLE RECOMMENDATION

ROUGH GUIDES

MAKE THE MOST OF YOUR GADGETS

roughguides.com/downloads

FROM **ANDROID** TO **iPADS** TO **WINDOWS 7**

BOOKS | EBOOKS | APPS

MAKE THE MOST OF YOUR TIME ON EARTH™

GET LOST

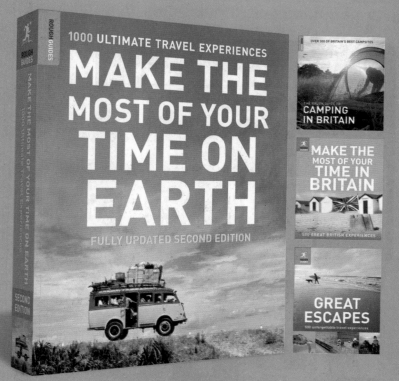

ESCAPE THE EVERYDAY
WITH OVER 700 **BOOKS**, **EBOOKS** AND **APPS**
YOU'RE SURE TO BE INSPIRED

Start your journey at **roughguides.com**
MAKE THE MOST OF YOUR TIME ON EARTH™